THE
SOURCE BOOK
OF
FRANCHISE
OPPORTUNITIES
1990–1991 EDITION

ROBERT E. BOND
CHRISTOPHER E. BOND

DOW JONES-IRWIN
HOMEWOOD, ILLINOIS 60430

DISCLAIMER

The information provided in the listings that follow has been submitted by the franchisors themselves. Although the author and Dow Jones-Irwin feel confident that the information provided is accurate and reliable, we have not attempted to independently verify or corroborate the data submitted. Therefore, we cannot guarantee the accuracy of the information displayed, nor do we in any way endorse any of the franchisors listed. Any subsequent agreements that might be made as a result of information provided herein shall be the sole responsibility of the reader.

While every effort has been made to ensure that the listing of franchisors is both current and complete, some active franchisors may not be included. Others who have been included may have subsequently decided to terminate franchising operations.

The inherent advantage of having an annual publication is that new franchisors can be added and those no longer franchising can be deleted. Accordingly, we would encourage franchisors to keep us apprised of any change in their status or address (those included in the *1990 - 1991 Source Book of Franchise Opportunities* will be contacted again in November, 1990 to update the data currently presented). Please write to:

SOURCE BOOK
P. O. Box 12488
Oakland, California 94604

This publication is designed to provide accurate and authoritative information in regard to the subject matter covered. It is sold with the understanding that the publisher is not engaged in rendering legal, accounting, or other professional service. If legal advice or other expert assistance is required, the services of a competent professional person should be sought.

From a Declaration of Principles jointly adopted by a Committee of the American Bar Association and a Committee of Publishers.

Sponsoring editor: James Childs
Production manager: Irene H. Sotiroff
Printer: Malloy Lithographing, Inc.

ISBN 1-55623-331-0

Library of Congress Catalog Card No. 88-649161 (annual paperback)

Printed in the United States of America.

1 2 3 4 5 6 7 8 9 0 ML 7 6 5 4 3 2 1 0

This book is dedicated to the hundreds of thousands who willingly and unselfishly served in the Vietnam War. Most especially, it is dedicated to those whose names are now memorialized on a simple slab of black granite in Washington, D.C. and to those still living who are unable to enjoy the full life taken for granted by the rest of us.

PREFACE

The seed for this book began in 1979 as I was writing business plans for two companies I was trying to develop. Although I had no direct experience in franchising, I felt each would be logical franchising type of business. In researching the industry and how other franchisors developed their products and services, I found that the available literature fell into one of two categories:

1. The first group was made up of publications written in a sophomoric manner and intended for the potential franchisee who had only a modest business background. Basically, these were "how-to" books that started with the premise that the reader had no applied business experience and which, accordingly, provided little insight into the intricacies of what is a very unique and demanding industry.

2. The second group was made up of "knock-offs" of the U.S. Department of Commerce publication

Franchise Opportunities Handbook. Without exaggerating, there were at least four publications that copied word for word the information in this publication. Most clearly left the impression that it was original research on the part of the author(s).

While the Government data was very informational, it was nevertheless incomplete in terms of providing data on a number of key areas of critical importance in the initial evaluation process, as well as being unwieldy in comparing similar franchising opportunities. In addition, it provided data on less than half of the firms in the franchising universe (including no listing of Canadian franchises).

Realizing that there was a market need for a value-added publication that acted as a source book for the sophisticated potential franchisee, I initiated the due diligence phase of this book. Like most "reinvent-the-wheel" efforts, there were numerous false starts and several faulty assumptions about 1) what information was most helpful and 2) what information the franchisors themselves were actually willing to provide. Ultimately, the book assumed its current form, and, while there is less instructional material than originally intended, the end result is a great deal of in-depth information on both domestic and Canadian franchisors. Most importantly, the data is directly comparable, thus allowing the reader to evaluate numerous franchising opportunities in the same industry and to feel comfortable that he has enough data to go to the next logical step. Basically, the book allows the potential franchisee to narrow down his options - to concentrate on those franchising opportunities that most closely meet his needs, experience and financial position.

For those who have read earlier editions of the book, you will notice several changes in format and content. Of real significance, however, is a change in emphasis from "more (franchisor listings) is better" to "accuracy is of greater importance than sheer volume." In previous editions, I mistakenly felt it was important to list all companies purported to franchise - even though I couldn't get any direct confirmation or acknowledgement that they were still (or ever) franchising. This edition has eliminated some 1,000 companies that I couldn't confirm as active franchisors, as well as various distributors that had listed themselves as franchisors in my annual franchisor survey. My hope is that this reduction in the number of listings will save you much unnecessary time and effort in trying to correspond with firms that won't respond to your inquiry.

The book is admittedly only the first step in the long and tedious process of selecting a franchise that combines operating independence on the part of the franchisee with a marketing and management system that has already proven itself in the field. To those who follow the process to its final conclusion, I can only hope that I have been of value in introducing you to an industry that has

an incredibly successful track record, and in helping you to efficiently evaluate the vast number of franchising opportunities that are open to you. If you are rigorous in your analysis and evaluation, realistic about your capabilities and shortcomings, willing to take full advantage of the franchising formula that you have chosen, and have the fortitude to "put in the hours," you will find the franchise that is right for you. I wish you every success in this time-consuming and sometimes frustrating process.

Be advised at the outset, however, that your ultimate success is a function of two key variables: first, the thoroughness with which you evaluate the industry and ultimately select a single franchisor; second, the hard work and dedication you are willing to devote to making the system work as designed. Because this book is not intended to be inspirational or motivational, we can be of no help in the latter area. We can, however, expedite the evaluation process - ensuring that the potential franchisee is exposed to the full universe of options open to him and that he goes about the selection process in a logical and thorough manner.

Some 2,650 franchising opportunities are listed on the following pages. A detailed franchisor format is available on roughly 1,020 franchising opportunities. The names, addresses and industry segment are available on some 1,600 additional active franchisors. No doubt you will have either heard of or be familiar with a large number of the listings. Pick out the ones that interest you. Request additional information on each of these. Carefully analyze the information that is sent. Develop a thorough knowledge of the business/services that you are considering. Seek the advice of professionals even if you are experienced in various areas of the evaluation process. **DO YOUR HOME-WORK!** Remember, the hours that you spend in the short-term can save you from long-term embarrassment at best and financial loss at worst.

TABLE OF CONTENTS

RENT OUR CUSTOM FRANCHISOR MAILING LIST

- **GUARANTEED ACCURACY** - $.50 REBATE FOR ANY INCORRECT ADDRESS

- CONTINUOUSLY UPDATED FOR ADDRESS CHANGES / NEW ADDITIONS

- SORTED BY ZIP / POSTAL CODE / BUSINESS CATEGORY / MARKET AREAS

- ALSO **CUSTOM SORTING** AND CUSTOM LABELS

- **QUICK TURN-AROUND TIME**

	U.S. ONLY	*CANADIAN ONLY*	*COMBINED LISTING*
APPROXIMATE LISTINGS:	~1,800	~750	~2,550

STANDARD PRICING SCHEDULE:

Standard Size:	$135	$60	$175
3 7/8" x 2 7/8" with Return Address:	$185	$100	$240

Director of Franchising
World Class Athlete
1814 Franklin Street, # 700
Oakland, CA 94612

RETURN TO:
Your Company Name
Return Address
Your City, State, Zip

OR

Director of Franchising
Cottman Transmission Services
240 New York Drive, # 2014
Fort Washington, NY 19034

President
World Class Athlete
1814 Franklin Street # 700
Oakland, CA 94612

Standard Pressure Sensitive Label   Larger 3 7/8" by 2 7/8" Presddure Sensitive Label

FOR INFORMATION, PLEASE CONTACT: **SOURCE BOOK**
P.O. BOX 12488
OAKLAND, CA 94604
415/547-3245

CHAPTER 1

30 MINUTE OVERVIEW

The reason for writing this book was and is to provide the maximum amount of in-depth data on the maximum number of companies currently franchising. In short, the intent was to be a *source book* for the sophisticated reader seriously interested in franchising. Three basic assumptions have been made. The first is that the reader is interested in the data provided, not in what I might say about how he should go about his selection process. The second is that the reader has a basic understanding of business and franchising. Little space, therefore, will be devoted to detailing the advantages, disadvantages, pitfalls, etc., associated with franchising. As with any investment, it goes without saying that the reader must vigorously evaluate and investigate the various companies under consideration, their promises vs. their historical performance, the industry, the proposed territory and the franchise agreement. The third assumption presupposes that the potential franchisee knows himself - his strengths and weaknesses, whether he has the drive to make the system work and whether he is willing, over

the long-term, to work within the system, without trying to modify or improve on it. To the extent that the reader requires background data on the franchising industry, he should pursue some of the books noted in Chapter 3 - Bibliography. While many of these sources might be helpful in the evaluation process, good business sense, access to trusted professional guidance and dedication to hard work are essential.

Having dispensed with these critical assumptions in a very cavalier manner, let me provide a brief overview of the industry and how to initiate the selection process.

FRANCHISING DEFINED

In its most basic form, shown below, franchising is a marketing technique, or method of doing business, whereby a parent company (the franchisor) grants (via a franchise agreement) an individual outlet owner (the

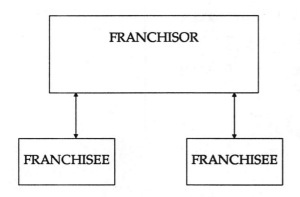

CLASSIC BUSINESS FORMAT MODEL

franchisee) the right to market its products and services while using the parent's proven name, reputation and marketing techniques. This is known as business format franchising. Following a lengthy and mutually rigorous selection process, the franchisor assists the new franchisee in selecting a site, negotiating a lease (if necessary), hiring and training staff, outfitting the site, establishing supply lines and generally setting the franchisee up in business. In return for this, the franchisee pays the franchisor a front-end franchise fee, generally in the neighborhood of $15,000 - $35,000. In addition to this initial hand-holding, business format franchising is characterized by an on-going relationship that includes not only the product, service and trade-mark, but also the entire business format itself - a market-ing strategy and plan, operating manuals and standards, quality control and continuing two-way communica-tions. In return, the franchisee is obligated to pay an on-going royalty fee to the franchisor. Although the formula varies considerably among industries and franchisors, the standard royalty fee is usually 4 - 8 % of gross sales. In order to effectively mount a national or regional advertising campaign, the franchisor generally requires the franchisee to pay for his pro rata share of the costs incurred. This takes the form an advertising fee.

The end result is a pre-packaged, or "paint by the num-bers," business that allows 1) the franchisor to expand his distribution more rapidly than he could on his own and 2) the franchisee to substantially reduce his risk and

exposure by riding on the coattails of the franchisor's success. To work, the relationship must be continuing and symbiotic - both parties must be better off together than apart. Generally speaking, what is good for one is good for the other.

FRANCHISING IN THE ECONOMY

The size and importance of the franchising industry should be put into perspective. For an industry that didn't exist thirty years ago, franchising has certainly come of age. It has grown at a rate substantially higher than the GNP and this trend is expected to continue into the foreseeable future. When one includes automotive and truck dealers, soft drink bottlers and gasoline ser-vice stations in the statistics, franchising accounts for over $600 billion of retail sales per annum, or ap-proximately <u>one third of all retail sales</u>. Backing out automotive and truck dealers, soft drink bottlers and gasoline service stations, which are not considered as true business format franchisors for the purposes of this book, franchise sales of goods and services are expected to total over $200 billion for 1990. Put into context, this means that for every $100 the average consumer spends at the retail level, over $10 is spent in franchised estab-lishments. Employment in franchising, both at the part-time and full-time level, totals 7 million.

Exhibit 1 on the following page breaks these gross numbers down into meaningful industry groupings by type of service/product provided. The reader should spend a few minutes trying to digest this general data then go to the chapter that relates to his specific level of interest(s) for a detailed analysis of the trends and relationships within that area of the franchising industry. An analysis of these exhibits may be helpful in determin-ing which areas of the franchising industry can be ex-pected to grow the most rapidly and where there may already be some overcapacity. To the extent that you wish to approach the selection process from a market need standpoint, you should purchase a copy of *Franchising In The Economy, 1988 - 1990,* published by the International Franchise Association and the account-ing firm of Horwath International.

SURVIVAL RATE

In terms of risk reduction and the basic survival of your business, the facts are persuasive. According to the U.S. Department of Commerce statistics noted below, a stag-gering 38% of new, independent businesses fail within

EXHIBIT 1

FRANCHISING IN THE ECONOMY – 1990

(BUSINESS FORMAT FRANCHISING ONLY)

	# of Establish- ments	% Company Owned	Total Sales ($000)	% Company Owned	Average Sales /Yr./Unit
Automotive Products/Services	38,561	13.3%	13,632,245	33.6%	353,524
Auto/Truck/Trailer Rental	10,613	22.8%	7,577,830	54.0%	714,014
Construction/Home Improvement	28,270	2.2%	6,751,382	23.9%	238,818
Business Aids & Services:					
Accounting/Credit/Collection	1,859	1.5%	214,440	4.4%	115,352
Printing/Copying Services	7,366	2.3%	1,890,294	2.9%	256,624
Tax Preparation	8,460	40.4%	708,330	54.0%	83,727
Misc. Business Systems	25,079	3.3%	4,144,953	11.9%	165,276
Convenience Stores	17,467	62.3%	14,418,459	66.4%	825,469
Educational Products/Services	13,265	5.0%	2,322,445	26.6%	175,081
Employment Services	7,552	38.9%	5,785,325	49.2%	766,065
Retailing–Food (Non–Convenience)	25,374	17.0%	11,889,718	21.2%	468,579
Restaurants – All Types	102,135	28.7%	76,516,121	33.6%	749,167
Laundry/Dry Cleaning Services	2,629	5.4%	334,855	12.0%	127,370
Hotels/Motels/Campgrounds	11,103	11.6%	23,864,231	28.6%	2,149,350
Real Estate	16,955	0.7%	6,750,425	1.1%	398,138
Recreation/Entertainment/Travel	10,344	4.2%	4,721,110	16.1%	456,410
Rental Services – Equipment	3,358	26.7%	811,045	32.7%	241,526
Retailing – Non–Food	54,062	24.3%	28,642,588	30.2%	529,810
Miscellaneous	8,402	6.0%	2,178,673	21.1%	259,304
Total	392,854	19.7%	213,154,469	32.6%	542,579

Source: Franchising In The Economy, 1988 – 1990, IFA Education Foundation & Horwath International, Published January, 1990.

  1) 1990 data was estimated by respondents.

COMPARATIVE SUCCESS RATE
FRANCHISED BUSINESSES vs. INDEPENDENT BUSINESSES

	FRANCHISED BUSINESSES	INDEPENDENT BUSINESSES
AFTER 1ST YEAR IN BUSINESS	97%	62%
AFTER 5TH YEAR IN BUSINESS	92%	23%
AFTER 10TH YEAR IN BUSINESS	90%	18%

the first year of operation and 77% fail within the first 5 years. Conversely, only 3% of franchised businesses fail in the first year and only 8% fail by the fifth year. Unless you are either exceptionally talented and/or well-heeled, logic would suggest that franchising is the desired avenue for most businessmen to follow. Doesn't it make sense to be in the group that has a 92% chance of survival at the end of year 5 rather than in the 23% group?

(**Note:** While the Department of Commerce can no doubt substantiate these persuasive figures (which I continue to quote in all my presentations and lectures on franchising), I have increasing difficulty in accepting their accuracy. This hesitancy is based on the feedback I get each year as a result of my on-going correspondence with the franchising community. Not only is a significant amount of mail returned as undeliverable (suggesting that the franchisor is no longer in business), but a surprising number of franchisors report sizable reductions in the number of total operating units from year to year. My sense is that the failure rate for franchisors is greater that the failure rates noted above, but that the failure rate for franchisees may be in line with the figures quoted. To the extent that this assumption is correct, it is incumbent on you to make sure you have left no stone unturned before settling on a single franchisor).

THE 4 R'S

As in school, where we learned that the 3 R's of reading, 'riting, and 'rithmatic were critical to scholastic success, franchising success is also largely dependent on what I will refer to as the 4 R's. In this case, however, the 4 R's refer to 1) **realism** about your personal strengths and weaknesses, 2) **research** into the industry and careful selection of a specific franchisor and 3) **resources** to ensure that you have the financial wherewithal to survive the initial stages of developing your business. A fourth

R that should not be overlooked is **resolve** - the willingness to continue to work within the system as it has been designed *after you have achieved personal success.* Each of these attributes will be discussed very briefly below.

REALISM

Realism is essential for one to maximize his happiness in life in general. It is possible to avoid reality in one's day-to-day life, however, and still survive. This is equally true when you work for someone else. It clearly is not true when you are in business for yourself. In this case, the realities of the marketplace are swift and unforgiving. To the extent that this interpretation is true, you, as a potential franchisee, should be realistic about all variables affecting your choice and operation of a franchise business.

This should start with a clear understanding of your personal strengths and weaknesses. Do you have the ability to deal with financial insecurity? Know at the outset that there will be plenty of this, at least during the initial start-up period. Do you have the strong support of your spouse? This is absolutely essential if there is any significant deviation from your business plan! Can you manage people effectively? Can you smile when you know that the customer is wrong? There are literally hundreds of similar introspective questions that should be addressed truthfully and in a straightforward manner. Some of the books noted in the bibliography are especially helpful in this regard, as are various books that specialize in personal growth and career path choices. I would strongly recommend that anyone wishing to invest his life's savings in a franchise take the time necessary to do a personal audit of his personal strengths and weaknesses - possibly with the help of outside professionals.

Having passed muster in your personal audit, then be equally realistic about the advantages and disadvantages of the products/services offered by the franchisor, the unique demographics of your particular market area, the trends in the marketplace, pro forma financials, etc. Although these latter points will be determined in large part by exhaustive research, be objective and open-minded in interpreting the results.

RESEARCH

The sole lasting value of this book is to assist the reader in researching the franchising industry and in narrowing down the myriad of choices that are open to him. Over 1,000 franchises are listed below in a great deal of detail. The addresses of another 1,600+ are listed by type of business. This effectively represents the universe that is out there for you to investigate. Given the universe, request information from all those that may potentially be of interest to you. Don't necessarily limit yourself to a particular type of service or product. Explore the options. Even if you think that you already know what the best franchise would be through personal experience, it is still important that you evaluate other firms that provide a similar product and/or service to convince yourself that you have made the optimal choice. Don't find out after the fact that there is a competing franchise with a nearly identical product/service, but which charges a royalty fee of 5% vs. the 7% of gross sales that you are locked into. Put into perspective, a 2% differential in royalty payments for a business grossing $600,000 per year amounts to $120,000 (not present valued) over 10 years. The incremental cost of fully researching all of the franchisors within a chosen industry is negligible compared to the cost of making a sub-optimal choice.

Once you have been able to narrow the field of potential franchisors down to a manageable size, say 5 to 9 companies, be equally aggressive in the manner in which you research each firm. I have found that the most meaningful and persuasive research results from talking with actual franchisees, preferably at their sites. For the most part, they tend to be completely open in discussing their level of satisfaction with the franchisor and the industry they have chosen. Before making a final commitment, I would make every effort to talk with as many franchisees as I could. Within reason, I would disregard the minor costs of visiting actual franchisee sites and the amount of time off from my current employment.

RESOURCES

Lack of adequate working capital is the single most common reason for business failure. Make sure that you have adequate financial resources before committing to a business that has an uncertain source of cash inflows, but which has required fixed operating costs that must be paid regardless of profitability. Whether these resources are obtained from savings, relatives, bank loans, etc., make sure that they are available when and if you need them. Again, be realistic about the potential need for additional funds. Don't underestimate the period needed before you achieve break-even and find out that you have run out of cash 6 months before revenues cover costs. There will be great temptation to assume, because of your raw talents, drive, dedication, etc., that you can achieve a break-even operating position faster than the period recommended by the franchisor. Don't bet the ranch on it. Literally! If anything, the franchisor will have an incentive to underestimate the break-even period himself. To be safe, assume that you will need an additional 3 - 6 months of working capital on top of the period recommended by the franchisor.

RESOLVE

After you have gotten to the point of a positive cash flow, you now need resolve to ensure that you are going to succeed in franchising over the long-term. Recall the compelling reasons why you chose franchising in the first place - to take advantage of someone else's proven formula for success, the desire to beat the odds of business failure, etc. Keep in mind the symbiotic basis upon which franchising is built - franchisor and all franchisees working within the system for the common good. Unfortunately, two problems invariably come up.

The first is the difficulty in writing a monthly royalty check to the franchisor. It is easy to forget the fact that they brought you into "their business" in the first place, that they taught you everything you now know about the business, that they provide on-going product improvements and refinements, an 800-telephone number to resolve problems as they come up, and the entire panorama of services that good franchisors provide on a continuing basis. Conversely, it is hard not to notice the check that goes out monthly in increasing amounts, and that is expected to increase over the length of the franchise relationship. Although this is a difficult intellectual process, keep in mind that royalty fees are simply another cost of doing business. It is also a legal obligation that you incurred when you entered franchising and a cost you knowingly agreed to pay in return for being part of a successful team. Now that you have achieved that objective, don't begrudge the franchisor the chance to share in that success. Keep in mind that, if the franchisor isn't successful and profitable, your franchise will flounder and you will no longer receive the centralized support that you have come to count on.

Similarly, you need resolve in your willingness to live within the system. The franchise is successful in large part because of the establishment of a common format for doing business, consistent quality control, routinized operating procedures, rigorous market research on new products and services, etc. Now is not the time to become an entrepreneur and unilaterally test the market with modifications you feel will streamline the business or increase profits in your particular market. These ideas should instead be submitted as recommendations to the franchisor for evaluation. You will have to trust his wisdom in what he does with the idea from that point on. If you find that you cannot accept the role of a good and loyal soldier in the field over the long-term, you will probably not make a good franchisee.

THE CHOICE IS YOURS

Choosing the optimal franchise for your personal needs requires many times the hard work and energy that goes into buying a home. The prudent man would not buy into a new area without first considering all the important variables (schools, taxes, condition of the house, zoning, etc.) before making his offer. Unlike homebuying, however, where the penalty for poor research is a maximum 10-20% loss in original investment, a flawed choice of franchisors can result in a 100% loss of your savings, the equity in your house, your marriage (to the extent that your spouse was not equally committed to franchising and the inherent risks involved), and, possibly most importantly, your self-esteem. The risks are high. There are no guarantees. To think that you can automatically pay a franchise fee and step into a guaranteed money machine is naive at best and calamitous to your financial well-being at worst. There is no substitute for the attributes noted above. The burden is on you to do your homework and to ensure that the choice is researched to the fullest extent possible. Only then can you maximize the chances of success and minimize the chances of failure or unfulfilled expectations.

My recommendation is that you plan on taking 8 - 12 months before deciding on a specific franchising company. Establish an orderly and well-thought-out business plan for going through the evaluation process (including a realistic self-appraisal and lining up the necessary financial resources). Although there will be a great deal of pressure on you to speed up the process, especially if you are working with an aggressive marketing or brokerage firm, don't be browbeaten into making a premature decision. Try to stick with your business plan. You will most likely spend the majority of your business life working with the company you ultimately choose. Another few months spent in ensuring you have made the right choice is indeed a small price to pay.

Enough narrative! You are now on your own to select those franchises that best meet your needs and experience. Without being tedious, I can only repeat the recommendation of every writer on franchising. That recommendation - Investigate! Investigate! Investigate!

CHAPTER 2

HOW TO USE THE DATA

The 41 questions noted on the 3-page questionnaire in Appendix A have been condensed into the format shown on the following pages. Each piece of data provided is felt to be of value in helping the reader in his decision-making process. In addition to consolidating a great deal of information into a small space, the consistent layout of the data results in direct comparability and efficient evaluation of alternative franchising opportunities. Rather than bypass this section, you should take 30 minutes to familiarize yourself with the format and what the data provided really means. Where relevant, I have attempted to add any observations I felt would be helpful in interpreting the franchisor's response.

Again, I would like to emphasize that neither Dow Jones-Irwin nor the author assume any responsibility for the accuracy of the information provided. All of the data displayed has been submitted by the franchisors themselves (including numerous follow-up phone calls) and no effort has been made to independently corroborate or verify their accuracy or completeness. You should feel comfortable, however, in knowing that any intentionally misleading information submitted by the franchisor would be self-defeating from the franchisor's standpoint. Any half-truths or "puffery" would undoubtedly be uncovered by the potential franchisee upon any subsequent rigorous examination of the franchisor. To the extent that the deception were of a serious nature, it would most likely terminate the relationship, resulting in an unnecessary loss of time and effort on everyone's part. Given this, there is no incentive for the franchisor to play games or to intentionally mislead the reader.

WORLD CLASS ATHLETE, a San Francisco Bay Area franchising company that has enjoyed considerable success over the past few years, has been chosen as a sample company for illustrative purposes. Please refer to the sample format when reading the description that follows.

WORLD CLASS ATHLETE

1814 Franklin St., # 700
Oakland, CA 94612
TEL: (800) SURF-RAT (415) 547-1596 C
FAX: (415) 835-3779 C
Mr. Jeff McKee, President

WORLD CLASS ATHLETE offers a unique, specialty sporting goods concept. Product mix concentrates on athletic footwear, running, tennis and swimwear. Emphasis on race sponsorship, training programs and custom fitting. All major lines of footwear, accessories, warm-up suits and bags. Custom re-soling at Company-owned distribution centers.

HISTORY: . . . . IFA/WIF	FINANCIAL: OTC-WCA	FRANCHISOR TRAINING/SUPPORT:
Established in 1976; . . 1st Franchised in 1977	Cash Investment: $75K	Financial Assistance Provided: . . .Yes(D)
Company-Owned Units (As of 12/1/1989): . 15	Total Investment: $120-225K	Site Selection Assistance: . . . . .Yes
Franchised Units (12/1/1989): 66	Fees: Franchise - $18K	Lease Negotiation Assistance: . . . . .Yes
Total Units (12/1/1989): 81	Royalty: 6%, Advert: 2%	Co-operative Advertising: . . . . .Yes
Distribution: US-74;Can-7;Overseas-0	Contract Periods (Yrs.): 15/15	Training: . . . . 3 Wks. Headquarters,
North America: . . . . 15 States, 2 Provinces	Area Development Agreement: Yes/15	. . . . .2 Wks. Site, On-going
Concentration: . . 25 in CA, 8 in WA, 5 in KY	Sub-Franchise Contract: . . . . . Yes	On-Going Support: . . . a,B,C,D,E,f,G,H,I
Registered: . . . CA,FL,HI,IL,MN,MI,NY,OR	Expand in Territory: . . . . . . .No	Full-Time Franchisor Support Staff: . . 24
. . . . WA,WI,AB	Passive Ownership: . . . Not Allowed	EXPANSION PLANS:
Average # of Employees: . . . . . . 2 FT, 4 PT	Encourage Conversions: . . . . . Yes	US: . . . . All US
Prior Industry Experience: . . . . Helpful	Franchisee Purchase(s) Required: Yes	Canada - Yes, ... Overseas - No

GENERAL INFORMATION

1. The name and address are self-explanatory.

2. **(800) SURF-RAT (415) 547-2144 C.**

A "C" following the telephone number listed means that the company will accept a collect call, usually from in-state callers. Initial calls should be made using the (800) number. Where in-state (800) numbers are available, the abbreviation for the state is noted in parentheses.

Observation: Keep in mind that maintaining an (800) telephone number is a significant additional expense. It is, nevertheless, an indication of management priorities - in this case the need to attract potential franchisees as efficiently as possible, as well as to respond to problems encountered by existing franchisees. My sense is that it is a very positive indication. Those companies that require the caller to foot the bill are unnecessarily restricting the number of potential franchisees. More importantly, the lack of an (800) number may mean that the franchisor is failing to provide the proper service to his franchisees. (Keep in mind, however, that the franchisor may have an (800) number reserved for his franchisees and not available to potential franchisees).

3. Whether calling or writing, all initial correspondence should be directed to the individual noted.

Observation: Although it is unfair in many cases, one could draw some general conclusions from the position of the company contact. Where the contact is identified as the Vice President or Director of Franchising (or the equivalent), the Company is obviously large enough and successful enough to delegate marketing and franchisee selection responsibilities to a second-tier manager. Where all incoming correspondence is directed to the attention of the Chairman or President, however, it may be that there is only a very modest staff. One has to assume that there is an upper limit on the number of franchised units and the ability of the President/CEO to continue to effectively respond directly with potential franchisees. To the extent that he is answering the phone on a routine basis, he is not attending to other, possibly more pressing, business.

DESCRIPTION OF BUSINESS

4. Franchisors were given complete latitude and discretion in describing their business. The only constraint was that they had to limit their comments to 6 lines of text. To the extent that they over-indulged or gave a boiler-plate description from another write-up of the business, some editing may have been required.

Observation: In a surprising number of cases, the franchisors merely noted that they were in the "fast food - chicken" business (or some equally unimaginative description). While it may be premature to judge a company on the basis of the answer provided by a single employee, a disinterested response may be indicative of the enthusiasm, involvement and attention to detail on the part of the company's management. I personally find it hard to believe that a respondent would not take the minimal time required to distinguish his company from the competition. Basically, the description of the company provides free exposure to the 25,000 - 40,000 potential franchisees who will ultimately purchase and/or read this book. And yet, these same companies may be willing to spend thousands of dollars and hours of time to develop a short ad in the *Wall Street Journal* that may be read by only 1,000 potential franchisees.

HISTORY

5. **IFA/WIF/CFA.** This means that the franchisor is an active member in either the International Franchise Association, Women in Franchising or the Canadian Franchise Association.

The **International Franchise Association (IFA)** is a non-profit trade association representing some 650 franchising companies in the U.S. and around the world and is recognized as one of the leading spokespersons for responsible franchising. The IFA has historically supported the principle of full disclosure of all pertinent information to potential franchisees, as well as being a strong advocate of reasonable legislation to assure greater protection of potential investors. The IFA was founded in 1960 by a group of franchising executives who saw the need for an organization that would 1) speak on behalf of franchising, 2) provide services to member companies as well as those interested in franchising, 3) set standards of business practice, 4) serve as a medium for the exchange of experience and expertise and 5) offer educational programs for top industry executives and managers. Although I have serious doubts in many cases, membership is purported to be selective and must be approved by the Association's Executive Committee. A *Full* Member must 1) have a satisfactory financial statement, 2) have been in business for at least 2 years, 3) have complied with all applicable state and federal full disclosure requirements and 4) have satisfactory business and personal references. *Associate* Membership is reserved for those companies who are either new in franchising, considering franchising or who cannot meet all of the requirements of Full Membership. Further information on the IFA's array of services and

membership requirements may be obtained from the Association's offices at 1350 New York Avenue, NW, Suite 900, Washington, DC 20005 or (202) 628-8000.

Women In Franchising (WIF) is a relatively new organization supported by Corporate Members who find that women or female-male partnerships are successful as franchisees. The program is unique because it positions member companies as the leader in their respective industry when it comes to selling businesses to two of today's hottest target markets - women and minorities. The stated primary goal is to put enterprising women together with credible companies. Probably the single greatest benefit received by Corporate Members in WIF is a consistent flow of inquiries received by WIF from women interested in business ownership. WIF members automatically receive these leads on a monthly basis - in fact, WIF guarantees member companies a minimum of 1,200 leads per year. In addition, WIF conducts "Franchising For Women," "Franchising For Women and Minorities" and a "Marketing to Women and Minorities" conference once each month in various locations around the country. Lastly, the group was originally founded with the specific intent of forming a national networking organization for the women involved in franchising: franchise company executives, franchisees and potential franchisees. A newsletter specifically written for women in franchising is available on a subscription basis.

The group has done an exceptional job in promoting the involvement of women and minorities in franchising and provides member companies with a real value-added service in attracting potential franchisees. For further information, write 175 North Harbor Drive, Suite 405, Chicago, IL 60601. (312) 819-0600. FAX (312) 917-1707.

The **Canadian Franchise Association (CFA)** is similar in function to the IFA, but specifically focused on franchising in Canada. It is a trade association of franchisors and companies providing products and services to franchisors. As a condition of membership, all members must agree to adhere to the CFA Code of Ethics. Founded in 1967 as the Association of Canadian Franchisors, the CFA currently has some 250+ members. There are three types of membership: 1) a Regular Member - who has been in business in Canada at least 2 years, has a minimum of 4 units in operation and has the right to sell franchises, 2) an Associate Member, who is engaged in the business of franchising or can demonstrate the intent to become a franchisor and 3) an Affiliate Member, who provides products and/or services to franchisors. Their address is 88 University Ave., Suite 607, Toronto, ON M5J 1T6 CAN. (416) 595-5005. FAX (416) 595-9519.

6. Established in 1976 represents the year the Company was founded. To the extent the Company has been around for 5 or more years, this lends some credibility to its ability to be around for 5 more.

7. 1st Franchised in 1977 represents the year the Company first became a franchisor of franchised unit(s). Again, the longer the Company has been around, the better staying power it has to weather times of uncertainty in the future.

> **Observation:** From the perspective of the franchisee, it is important that the franchisor have actual franchising experience in house, and that he not be forced to rely on outside consultants to make the system work. This is a form of business that requires specific skills and experience - skills and experience that are markedly different from those required to manage a non-franchised business. To the extent that you are thinking about establishing a long-term relationship with a firm just starting out in franchising, I would not feel remotely awkward about insisting that the franchisor prove that he has the team on board and in place that will ensure its and, more importantly, your success.

8. Company-Owned Units: . . . . 15 are basically franchised units that, as of 12/1/1989, are owned by the franchisor, rather than by franchisees.

> **Observation:** The mix of Company-owned units vs. franchised units is indicative of the willingness of the franchisor to "put his money where his mouth is" to some extent. One important thing to find out from the franchisor, however, is the trend in Company-owned units, i.e. is the Company increasing its ownership of outlets or not, and why? My own feeling is that the acquisition of existing units or opening of new units would generally be a favorable trend, as the franchisor is obviously convinced of the long-term profitability of the business and of its ability to successfully compete. (Hopefully, the franchisor is not buying units from franchisees to preclude litigation from unhappy franchisees. To the extent that the franchisor is buying out existing

units, I would most certainly call each franchisee that is selling his unit and determine the real reason).

9. Franchised Units: . . . . 66 are outlets owned and operated by franchisees as of 12/1/1989.

> **Observation:** In your discussions with franchisors, most franchisors will be extremely optimistic about Company growth in the near-term. It should be noted that an extremely ambitious growth program is very expensive to achieve and maintain. Unless the franchisor has direct access to adequate working capital required both to support its projected growth and to provide the necessary on-going support for its existing franchisees, it is possible that neither of these objectives can be satisfactorily maintained. I would want some strong assurances from the franchisor that I would receive the start-up training and assistance and on-going support I had been promised. Without this required corporate support (especially if your success is largely tied to a national advertising campaign), you will be left largely to your own devices. A second problem associated with rapid growth is that talented and experienced management can only cover so many bases before it becomes ineffective. It will take sufficient time and on-the-job experience before new management can perform as well as the original management team. To the extent that the original management is devoting its limited time and energies to expansion and opening new franchised outlets, the new franchisee may well be forced to work with a less experienced staff that doesn't yet fully understand the system. Again, I would want to know that any transition to new personnel would be smooth and well thought out.

To reiterate, this is an extremely important area to cover with the franchisor before you commit yourself to his program. Other things being equal, controlled growth is preferred to rampant growth. The fact that management is convinced that its franchise is the hottest franchise in the country in terms of growth may sound very attractive to the new franchisee who has the opportunity to "get in on the ground floor." Keep in mind, however, that someone has to make it all work as designed, and this takes the same people who have made the system what it is today. Management can only do so many things well before the system gets overloaded.

10. Distribution: .... US : 74; Can : 7; Overseas : 0 means that, of the 81 units operating as of 12/1/1989, 74 were in the US, 7 were in Canada and none (0) were Overseas.

11. Distribution: North America .... 15 States, 2 Provinces means that the Company had units in 15 States and 2 Provinces in Canada.

> **Observation:** If the Company has wide geographic representation and has been able to maintain it for several years, this is an exceptionally strong indication of its ability to develop, market and support a sustainable national or regional program. It has been able to overcome one of the most serious obstacles to franchise success - the ability to grow on its own merits without the overriding influence of its developers.

12. Concentration: .... 25 in CA, 8 in WA, 5 in KY means that the franchisor has 25 units in California, 8 in Washington and 5 in Kentucky. (The franchisor was asked to note which 3 states and/or provinces had the highest concentration of operating units, whether Company-owned or franchisee-owned).

> **Observation:** Unless there were offsetting benefits in terms of a "special deal" or guaranteed support, I would be hesitant to be the pioneer in a new area. For instance, if the franchisor has 25 units operating on the West Coast, and none east of the Rockies, and I were considering opening a unit in Florida, I would tend to be very skeptical about verbal assurances of "don't worry, we'll support you." On the other hand, if the franchisor has a successful franchised operation and has the financial wherewithal to initiate and support an expansion 3,000 miles away, it may be a great opportunity to get in on the ground floor. This is especially true if you have an option to open new outlets within your territory after you have proven yourself. Keep in mind the incremental risk associated with being a missionary in a new area.

13. Registered refers to specific states that require registration by the franchisor before the franchisor may offer his franchises in that state. Disclosure to the Federal Trade Commission and State registration are separate issues and are discussed briefly below:

Federal Trade Commission Rule 436

After 7 years of effort, Federal Trade Commission Rule 436 was enacted in 1979, thereby requiring the submission of certain specific information and disclosure requirements about companies wishing to franchise. Franchises may not be sold without this disclosure.

Basically, the Rule requires the following information:

1. Identifying Information As To Franchisor.

2. Business Experience Of Franchisor's Directors And Executive Officers.

3. Business Experience Of The Franchisor.

4. Litigation History.

5. Bankruptcy History.

6. Description Of Franchise.

7. Initial Funds Required To Be Paid By A Franchisee.

8. Recurring Funds Required To Be Paid By A Franchisee.

9. Affiliated Persons The Franchisee Is Required To Do Business With By The Franchisor.

10. Obligations To Purchase.

11. Revenues Received By The Franchisor In Consideration Of Purchases By A Franchisee.

12. Financing Arrangements.

13. Restriction Of Sales.

14. Personal Participation Required Of The Franchisee In The Operation Of The Franchise.

15. Termination, Cancellation, and Renewal Of The Franchise.

16. Statistical Information Concerning The Number Of Franchises (And Company-Owned Outlets).

17. Site Selection.

18. Training Programs.

19. Public Figure(s) Involvement In The Franchise.

20. Financial Information Concerning The Franchisor.

As a potential franchisee, it is imperative that you review and fully understand the disclosure statement before making any commitment. As noted earlier, this should be thoroughly reviewed by a lawyer who is familiar with the intricacies of franchising. You should also be aware of the requirements placed on the franchisor by the FTC to provide you with this information on a timely basis. It must be made available to you upon your first face-to-face meeting with the franchisor and at least 10 days *before* either 1) any money changes hands or 2) a franchise agreement is signed. The end result of these disclosure regulations is that you are infinitely better protected and informed than you would have been before the legislation was enacted. It is up to you to take full advantage of all of the information at your disposal.

State Registration

Whereas FTC Rule 436 is a national disclosure statement, several states have taken it upon themselves to add a further element of protection for their residents. Before a franchise may be offered in these states, additional information (not necessarily the same as that required by the FTC) must be submitted and approved by the relevant state regulatory agencies. The states requiring this additional registration are: California, Florida, Hawaii, Illinois, Indiana, Maryland, Michigan, Minnesota, New York, North Dakota, Oregon, Rhode Island, South Dakota, Virginia, Washington and Wisconsin. The province of Alberta also requires separate registration. Some states, such as California and Illinois, have especially demanding requirements for registration. The more states in which the franchisor has "passed muster," the more confidence you should have that every rock has already been overturned in evaluating past and current operations.

Unfortunately, separate registration in multiple states is expensive, time-consuming and generally an unnecessary duplication of effort of the part of franchisors. It would appear to be much more efficient if the FTC or some other national body could act on behalf of the states in protecting the franchisees, and maybe this will come about in the near-term. In the interim, however, if you happen to live in a state that requires separate registration, you cannot become a franchisee until the franchisor has gone through the registration process. Keeping in

mind that this process may serve to weed out some potentially fraudulent franchisors, it may also mean that you cannot take advantage of a particular franchising opportunity until the franchisor can afford the time and funds to register in your state.

States that do not require a separate registration allow the franchisor to supply the potential franchisee with a Uniform Franchise Offering Circular (U.F.O.C.). This is a standardized, uniform disclosure document that details information about the Company similar to that required by the FTC.

14. **Average # of Employees : ....2 FT, 4 PT** means that the *average* franchised unit is recommended to have 2 full-time employees and 4 part-time employees. Where relevant, these totals *include* the services of the owner/operator.

> **Observation:** As a franchisee, once the number of employees reaches a certain level, the bulk of your time will be spent in managing them and their daily problems, and not in managing the business. Be sure that you feel comfortable with being a people manager and that you have the temperament to do it well. Working with part-time, minimum wage employees can be particularly vexing for many. If you are not people-oriented, and this requires some close introspection, you should opt for a franchise that draws on other strengths that you possess.

15. **Prior Industry Experience: .... Helpful.** The questionnaire gave franchisors only two choices in responding to the importance of prior industry experience in determining success as a franchisee - either 1) *Necessary* or 2) Unnecessary, But *Helpful*. Many franchisors, based upon their experience, feel that prior industry experience is essential to the success of franchised units. Unless there are over-riding circumstances, I would tend to accept this constraint as a fact of life rather than fighting it. If you don't have the required in-depth experience, find a franchise where your background is an asset or where specific industry experience is not required.

FINANCIAL

16. **OTC - WCA** notes that World Class Athlete is a publicly-traded company on the Over The Counter Exchange and that its stock symbol is WCA. Many franchisors failed to note their symbol and, accordingly,

only the Exchange is noted. To the extent that a firm is publicly traded, this is an indication that it has passed the early stages as an "infant" company. Be aware, however, that there is a quantum leap in requirements for listing on either the New York or American Exchanges and being listed on the OTC Exchange. Regardless, it is a positive step that only a few franchisors have been able to achieve.

17. Cash Investment: . . . . $75K means that, *on average*, the franchisee will be required to make a *cash investment of approximately* $75,000 by the time he opens his franchise.

> **Observation:** Although franchisors may interpret the question differently (i.e. does it include X months working capital until the outlet reaches break-even, etc.), it nevertheless suggests the level of financial commitment expected of the franchisee. If you can't raise this amount of cash without unnecessarily stretching yourself, you would probably do better finding a franchise that is less financially demanding. The last thing that any new franchisee needs is the additional stress created by unforeseen financial requirements. Accordingly, be completely candid with the franchisor in discussing your current financial position. Bluffing on your part could ultimately be disastrous. If you are prepared to trust the franchisor in every other facet of your business, don't let financial counseling be the sole exception. Remember that the franchisor has no motive to disqualify you on financial grounds other than to protect both himself and you from potential future problems.

18. Total Investment: . . . . $120 - 225K means that, *on average*, your *total investment, including both cash and debt, will total approximately* $120,000 - 225,000.

> **Observation:** Again, there may be room for interpreting this question, especially if the building/facilities/equipment may be purchased or leased. What is important, however, is the relative magnitude of the investment, and your understanding that you may well be liable for paying this amount off if things don't work out as planned. Keep in mind that a single-purpose building in a sub-optimal location or highly specialized equipment on the auction block may be worth only 35 - 50% of its original value. In your discussions with the franchisor, ensure that these totals include adequate working capital for the initial start-up period,

which in most cases is in excess of 6 months.

19. Fees: Franchise . . . . $18K means that the franchisor will require a front-end payment (generally cash) of $18,000 before you can become a franchisee. This amount is considered a franchise fee and is a non-recurring expense to reimburse the franchisor for his costs in locating, selecting, qualifying and training new franchisees.

> **Observation:** Keep in mind that the franchise fee is generally considered a break-even proposition as far as the franchisor is concerned. When one considers the expense of running ads in the *Wall Street Journal*, of registering the franchise in multiple states, of meeting with and selecting potential franchisees (only some small percentage of whom actually become franchisees), of the initial training and hand-holding, etc., the fees may not be unreasonable at all. Most franchisors try to keep the franchise fee in the $15,000 - 35,000 range. It would be a good idea to determine what that average franchise fee is within a given industry and compare that with the fee charged by the firms you are interested in joining. If their fees are significantly above the average, there should be some reasonable explanation.

20. Fees: Royalty . . . . 6% means that 6% of gross sales (or other measure as defined in the Franchise Agreement) is paid directly to the franchisor in the form of royalties. These payments represent your on-going cost of doing business as a part of the franchise organization - i.e. of funding your share of the costs of running a centralized national organization that is working on your behalf. In some cases the Royalty Fee is fixed at a certain amount per period.

> **Observation:** A basic tenet of franchising is that the franchisor should make no profit on the franchise fee. His rewards instead come in future years as the franchisee's sales and profits grow and the royalty proceeds grow. As the system grows from 6 units to 80 units, and as sales per outlet increase from $250,000 to $400,000, royalty fees (at 6%) would increase from $90,000 to $1,920,000 per year. While this may seen like a lot of money, consider the franchisor's overhead in supporting 80 separate businesses before you condemn his "excessive profits."

What you, as a potential franchisee, have to resolve

before you commit to franchising is whether the support you get in setting up and managing the business is worth the annual royalty fee, both in the short-term and long-term. If you make the decision that it is, keep in mind that the royalty fee is going to grow as you grow. Begrudging the franchisor his profits in the future, after he has helped make your business a success, is counter-productive and useless.

By the same token, however, a 1% difference in royalty fees charged by two otherwise equal franchisors can amount to a great deal of money over the 15 - 20 years of a relationship. It pays to choose carefully, but never make the royalty % the over-riding consideration in your decision.

21. Fees: Advert.....2% means that 2% of gross sales (or other measure as defined in the Franchise Agreement) will go toward corporate advertising. In most cases, the % is given and is a function of sales volume. In some cases, the fee is fixed.

> **Observation:** Since the percentage for advertising varies significantly throughout this book, there are no hard and fast rules. To the extent that your business is dependent upon name association by the general public, expenditures for advertising, if well done, should be justified. Rigorous market research, both before and after any major advertising campaign, should be able to determine the effectiveness of the campaign. Of all the functions provided by the franchisor, advertising has the greatest economy of scale. Consider the time, effort and expense it would take each franchisee to independently advertise his products and/or services. It is doubtful that a single franchisee could do this at twice the cost of the advertising fee paid to the franchisor.

22. Contract Period(s) : .... 15 / 15 refers to the term of the original franchise agreement and to the term of the first renewal period. In most cases, the longer the term of the contract, the better. At a very minimum, the Contract Term should exceed the term of any property that is leased.

> **Observation:** It is critical to fully understand and to document in writing under what circumstances the Franchise Contract cannot be renewed and/or may be cancelled. You would hate to spend years developing a business, only to find out that a poorly

worded Franchise Agreement allows the franchisor the unilateral right to cancel the relationship. This requires specific legal expertise that few franchisees possess.

MULTI-LEVEL FRANCHISING

In recent years, the classic business format model shown in Chapter 1 has been modified to provide the franchisor with additional options to grow more rapidly and at less cost than might otherwise be the case. Generically, these options are known as multi-level franchising. Although there are numerous variations on the classic franchising theme, there are three primary methods that are generally employed. These are: 1) Master (or regional) Franchising, 2) Sub-franchising and 3) Area Development Franchising. In each case, the franchisee still receives all of the benefits normally associated with franchising - the full use of the franchisor's trademarks and logos, the use of the business format system, initial training, site selection, on-going support, etc. The primary difference lies in 1) the on-going relationship between the franchisee and the franchisor, 2) to whom the franchisee should look for this support and 3) to whom he pays the required fees. Each of these methods is described briefly.

With **Master Franchising**, the franchisor chooses to

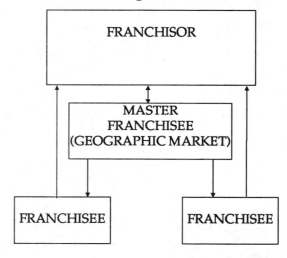

MASTER FRANCHISING MODEL

expand in a particular geographic area, which may be metropolitan, state, or national in scope. Realizing that he may not have the financial wherewithal or staff to expand on his own as rapidly as he might wish, he enlists the support of a Master Franchisee. The Master

Franchisee has the responsibility to not only sign up new franchisees within his geographic area, but also to provide these new franchisees with the initial training and support that are normally provided directly by the franchisor. Once established, on-going support of the franchisee is generally provided directly and totally by the franchisor. The Master Franchisee is nevertheless involved in the on-going sharing of future royalty fees (and frequently the advertising fees). Again, the franchisee still receives all the benefits normally associated with franchising, for which he pays an on-going percentage royalty fee and (usually) advertising fee directly to the franchisor. The contract between the franchisor and the Master Franchisee clearly spells out what is expected of each party and sets a specific period within which the Master Franchisee must meet certain stated objectives. In return for the front-end fee paid to the franchisor for his exclusive geographic market, the Master Franchisee receives a future stream of royalty payments from the franchisor, based strictly on the performance (usually gross sales) of the franchisees that he brings into the system. Unlike other methods of subcontracting out the development of new franchisees, this method is successful for all parties concerned because the Master Franchisor has to be selective at the outset and supportive throughout the relationship in order to personally profit.

In **Sub-franchising**, the Sub-franchisor also develops a specific territory and provides the initial training, site

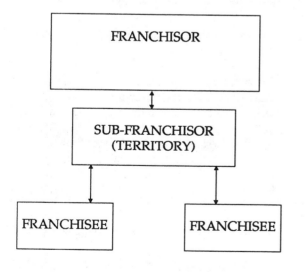

SUB-FRANCHISING MODEL

selection, etc., noted above to those franchisees he signs

up. What differs, however, is that the franchisee deals directly with the Sub-franchisor on an on-going basis and has only limited direct involvement with the franchisor. He pays the royalty and advertising fees directly to the Sub-franchisor, who in turn pays a portion to the franchisor. Basically, the Sub-franchisor becomes the franchisor for his territory, and the franchisee is dependent upon him for his on-going support. To the extent that the Sub-franchisor lacks the necessary financial, managerial or marketing skills normally expected of the franchisor, the franchisee will suffer. Accordingly, the potential franchisee should be doubly careful in selecting a Sub-franchise relationship, as he is dependent on the follow-through and business acumen of both the franchisor and the sub-franchisor if he is to be ultimately successful.

In an **Area Development Agreement**, the franchisor grants exclusive development rights to a group of inves-

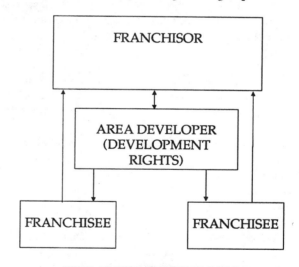

AREA DEVELOPMENT MODEL

tors for a particular geographic area. The investors in turn either develop individual franchise units within their territory which they own directly or find franchisees to develop units within their territory. In the latter case, the Area Developer has a residual ownership position. In return for the rights to develop this exclusive territory, the Area Developer pays the franchisor a front-end fee and is required to develop a certain number of units within a specified time period. Once established, the individual franchisees within the territory pay all royalty and advertising fees directly to the franchisor. The Area Developer shares in neither the franchise fee nor in on-going royalties or advertising fees. Instead, he shares only in the net profitability of the individual franchises that he has established.

Note: For a more detailed explanation of multi-level franchising, and the benefits see "Multi-Level Franchising: How Far? How Fast?" by John Campbell in *Franchising World*, February, 1988, pp. 36 - 39 published by the IFA.

23. Area Development Agreement: . . . . Yes/15 indicates that the franchisor permits Area Development Agreements and that the term of the agreement is 15 years.

> **Observation:** This may be an attractive option for an investor who has considerable experience with franchising and who has the financial backing to commit to opening multiple units over a specified period. If you are convinced that the franchisor has come up with a unique service and can provide the necessary continuing support, you may want to tie up an entire geographic area in order to preserve future growth potential for yourself. It most certainly is not an option that should be explored by an individual who has limited or no previous franchising experience and/or limited financial strength.

24. Sub-Franchise Contract: . . . . Yes means that the franchisor will consider using a Sub-Franchising Agreement in order to expand more rapidly than he could otherwise.

> **Observation:** Reiterating the point made above, it is imperative that the Sub-franchisor have the strength to support the franchisee throughout the long-term relationship of the franchise agreement. If he should be unable to follow through as expected, your ability to work directly with the franchisor may be severely constrained because of the terms of the Sub-franchise Agreement. Be sure that you know everything about the Sub-franchisor that you should know about the franchisor. Also, be fully versed about the conditions spelled out in the Sub-franchising Agreement.

25. Expand In Territory: . . . .No refers to the right of the franchisee to establish additional units within his franchised territory or area. This right is frequently granted to an individual franchisee in place of the Area Development Agreement noted above. If the franchise

should prove successful and the franchisee is convinced that he could effectively manage additional units, it would certainly be desirable to have the right to expand. Usually this right would be granted without the requirement to pay a full additional franchise fee.

26. Passive Ownership: . . . . Not Allowed means that the franchisor will not allow the franchisee/investor to hire an on-site manager to manage the business on a day-to-day basis. Instead, the franchisee himself must be the owner/operator. Other franchisors either discourage or allow the practice within certain guidelines.

> **Observation:** My own feeling is that active, "hands-on" management of the unit is necessary in most cases, at least until the franchisee has built up the experience and know-how to properly monitor the management of others.

27. Encourage Conversions: . . . . Yes means that the franchisor actively encourages existing businesses that are operating independently to become a member of the franchise team, enjoy the benefits of franchising and prosper to a greater extent than by continuing to run as a "mom and pop" operation. Other franchisors may feel that it is preferable to start afresh with a franchisee who has no preconceived notions as to how the business ought to be run and who will follow the dictates of the franchisor to the letter.

28. Franchisee Purchase(s) Required: . . . . Yes means that some portion of the supplies you need to run your business will have to be purchased directly from the franchisor or from franchisor-selected suppliers.

> **Observation:** To the extent that the franchisor has established a clearly superior product, such as a gourmet ice cream or a proprietary line of hair care products, this should present no problem. If, however, you, as the franchisee, are required to purchase more generic products that could be obtained elsewhere at equivalent or less cost and with no degradation of quality or image, then you should question the requirement.

FRANCHISOR TRAINING / SUPPORT

29. Financial Assistance Provided: . . . . Yes(D) means that the franchisor is *directly* involved in helping the franchisee secure the investment necessary to start and finance a franchise. Generally this would be in the form of leases or loans made by the franchisor. Other franchisors are *indirectly* involved, meaning that they may assist by introducing the franchisee to their financial contacts and standing behind him, possibly as a co-guarantor of a loan or lease.

> **Observation:** There is an increasing trend within the industry to let potential franchisees secure their own financing without any assistance from the franchisor. The objective, presumably, is to let the franchisee stand on his own two feet - to see if he is enough of a businessman to deal directly with lending institutions. It may turn out that the prospect is unable to secure the necessary funding. If so, the franchisor's attitude would be that he may not have been a strong team member in the long-run and the franchisor is better off having learned this at the outset.

30. Site Selection Assistance: . . . . Yes means that the franchisor will assist in determining the site location for the franchise. Site selection is an especially critical variable in the long-term profitability of many types of franchises, especially those with a strong retail orientation. Determining the optimal location within a franchised territory requires a thorough knowledge of the area and the type of business and should be left to experienced professionals.

> **Observation:** Assuming that site selection were essential, I would be very reluctant to involve myself with a company that was not actively involved in the site selection process, either directly or through a consulting firm. No amount of hard work or business savvy can overcome a poor choice of location. In many cases, the franchise agreement will not allow the franchisee to move from one location to another - so make certain that your first choice is your best shot.

31. Lease Negotiation Assistance: . . . . Yes means that the franchisor will assist in negotiating the original lease on the franchise site. Again, negotiating a lease is not something that someone inexperienced in real estate can jump into. There are a number of trade-offs that must be considered and negotiated before signing a contract. This also is an area best left to the professionals - hopefully with the active involvement of the franchisor.

32. Co-op Advertising: . . . Yes refers to the franchisor's willingness to pick up part of the

franchisee's costs incurred in promoting (usually on a local level) the products and/or services each has a vested interest in selling. The most common media include direct mail, newspaper, radio, billboards, etc. Even where the franchisor will not pick up at least a portion of the out-of-pocket expenses, it should at least provide samples of effective advertising and promotional campaigns to the franchisee. Co-op advertising is especially important during the pre-opening and grand-opening period when the franchisee is making his debut.

33. Training is absolutely critical to the success of the franchise. To the extent that the franchisor cannot successfully impart to the franchisee his knowledge, formulae, short-cuts and methods of doing business (those reasons why he has been successful where others have failed), then the franchisee is only marginally better off than the entrepreneur starting from scratch. Consequently, the duration and depth of initial training is of paramount importance in most cases. Although space limitations preclude any elaboration of the training provided, one should nevertheless be able to derive an overall impression about the franchisor's emphasis on training.

34. On-Going Support. Like initial training, the ongoing support services provided by the franchisor are of the highest importance. Having a solid and responsive team behind you can certainly make your life much easier and allow you to concentrate your energies on other areas. As is noted below, franchisors were asked

SERVICE PROVIDED	Incl. In Fees	At Add'l Cost	NA
Central Data Processing	A	a	NA
Central Purchasing	B	b	NA
Field Operations Evaluation	C	c	NA
Field Training	D	d	NA
Initial Store Opening	E	e	NA
Inventory Control	F	f	NA
Newsletter	G	g	NA
Regional/National Meetings	H	h	NA
Telephone Hotline	I	i	NA

to indicate their support for 9 separate on-going services:

If the franchisor provides the service (as indicated by letters A-I) at no additional cost to the franchisee, a capital letter was used to indicate this. If the service is provided, but only at an additional cost, then a lower case letter was used. If the franchisor responded N. A. or failed to note an answer for a particular service, the corresponding letter was omitted from the data sheet.

35. Full-Time Support Staff: . . . .24 means that the franchisor has 24 full-time employees on his staff.

> **Observation:** The intent was to establish the level of on-going support a franchisee could expect from the franchisor. For example, a staff of 3 to service 47 units would not provide a very high comfort level for the franchisee who needs questions answered right away or who needs on-site support to resolve a major problem. Even though there is ample room for the franchisor to be very creative in answering the question, it is assumed that the franchisee will find out about the actual support capability before signing on. While the question could be improved, one nevertheless gets an impression of relative support potential.

EXPANSION PLANS

36. US: . . . .All US tells you that the franchisor is actively seeking to franchise his business throughout the entire United States.

37. Canada . . . . Yes, ...Overseas . . . . No indicates that the franchisor is interested in adding units in Canada, but is not interested at this point in expanding overseas.

> **Observation:** As noted above, rapid expansion of a franchise, or any business for that matter, is fine at the conceptual level. Unfortunately, it is extremely difficult to put into practice where it counts - in the market. My sense is that it is unrealistic to think that a fledgling franchise with less than 10 or so operating units in a specific geographic area can concurrently expand throughout the US, Canada and Overseas. You will note, however, that many of the firms listed suggest that this is their objective. Be properly skeptical. Make them prove to your satisfaction that they have the necessary management and financial wherewithal to make it work.

Note: Keep in mind that the questionnaires were answered by one employee of the company and may not have been reviewed by the president or senior management. If the information supplied by a particular company is of interest to you, but you are concerned about a few answers, give the franchisor the benefit of the doubt and assume that the answer may have been mistakenly answered or interpreted.

STATISTICAL DATA

In many cases, I have included the most current statistical data on various segments of the franchising industry. This data is extracted from *Franchising In The Economy, 1988 - 1990* published by the IFA Education Foundation and Horwath International. A careful review of the data is particularly useful in determining expected average sales per unit within a particular segment of the industry. The data is also helpful in arriving at a better understanding of the dynamics of a segment of franchising - average employees per outlet, the split between company-owned units and franchised units, recent and expected trends, etc. Keep in mind that the respondents estimated data for 1990. Unfortunately, the industries broken out by the study do not coincide in all cases with the segments outlined in this book. Therefore, extrapolation of the statistical data to the industry groupings outlined below may not be appropriate.

SUPPLEMENTAL LISTING OF FRANCHISORS

In addition to an on-going correspondence with franchising industry, I have used various sources to assist in updating the addresses of franchisors noted throughout the book.

1) **Canadian Franchise Association (CFA) National Membership Directory, 1989.** 88 University Ave., # 607, Toronto, ON M5J 1T6 CAN. 88 pp. $10.00.

2) **Entrepreneur Magazine,** "Annual Franchise 500," January, 1990 and "223 New Franchises Across America," April, 1990.

3) **The Franchise Handbook,** Enterprise Magazine, 1020 North Broadway, Suite 111, Mil-

waukee, WI 53202. 212 pp. Published quarterly. $4.95.

4) **Franchising Opportunities**, International Franchise Association, 1350 New York Avenue, N.W., Suite 900, Washington, D.C. 20005. $14.00 per year.

5) **The 1990 Franchise Annual**, Info Franchise News, 728 Center Street, P.O. Box 550, Lewiston, NY 14092, 278 pp. $34.95 + Postage.

6) **The IFA Membership Guide, 1989.** IFA. $4.95.

7) **Opportunities Canada**, 2550 Golden Ridge Rd., # 44, Mississauga, ON L4X 2S3 CAN. 128 pp. $9.95.

8) **Wall Street Journal**, Thursday Section on "New Business Offerings."

Note: Having been through the process of sending questionnaires and mailings to all known franchisors on several occasions, my experience is that, over a 12 month period, roughly 20% of the mailings are returned as "undeliverable" for various reasons. As all of the addresses noted below were felt to be current as of January, 1990, the return rate should be well under 15%. If, however, you wish to get in touch with a franchisor and you cannot find his current address, please send us the name of the company in question, enclose a self-addressed, stamped envelope and we will let you know the most recent address we have in our files. Similarly, if you are a new franchisor, or an existing franchisor who has inadvertently been left out of this publication, please let us know. You will be sent a questionnaire in November, 1990 for the 1991 - 1992 update. Our mailing address is:

Source Book

P.O. Box 12488

Oakland, CA 94604

CHAPTER 3

BIBLIOGRAPHY

For an industry that has such a dramatic impact on the national economy, and which presents a vast and ready market for true value-added publications, the paucity of sophisticated current literature on franchising is disconcerting. There are, however, several books that provide an adequate starting point for the potential franchisee's due diligence process.

Of these, there are four publications that I would heartily recommend to any serious potential franchisee before he commits to franchising or a particular franchising company. These are:

1) **THE CONTINENTAL FRANCHISE REVIEW**, published 26 times annually by Trend Communications, Inc., 5000 S. Quebec, Suite 450, Denver, CO 80237 (303) 740-7031. A six-month trial subscription is available for $77.50. The annual subscription is $155.00. This is an 8-page analytical newsletter that discusses current topics of interest to both franchisees and franchisors alike. The newsletter is well written, accurate and highly informative. Given the constantly changing registration and disclosure requirements of franchising, it is especially helpful in keeping the reader abreast of this tricky aspect of the industry. The format is broken down into: Bulletins, Trends, Finance, Legal and Editorial. All subjects covered are indexed annually. Although the subject matter may be too specific for the newcomer, it nevertheless provides insights that are well worth the $77.50 investment.

2) **THE FRANCHISE OPTION, EXPANDING YOUR BUSINESS THROUGH FRANCHISING**, DeBanks M. Henward, III and William Ginalski, Franchise Group Publishers, 3644 E. McDowell, Suite 214, Phoenix, AZ 85008, 1985. $25.95.

Although the revised edition of this classic is written primarily for potential franchisors, it is nevertheless an excellent overview of the interworkings of the industry from the franchisee's standpoint. Basically, the book offers a do-it-yourself approach to successful franchise development and in so doing discusses what franchising is, how it works, what it takes to be a successful franchisor and how to undertake the development of a franchise system. There is an in-depth discussion of planning for a franchise system, test-marketing the franchise concept, system implementation, prohibitions and liabilities and when and how to terminate a franchise relationship. The Appendix contains the Federal Trade Commission's Franchising Rule 436 and a useful glossary of franchising terms. Unlike most other books available on franchising, this book is addressed to the sophisticated potential franchisee/franchisor.

3) FRANCHISE LAW BIBLIOGRAPHY, Section of Antitrust Law, American Bar Association, 750 North Lake Shore Drive, Chicago, IL 60611 (312) 988-6064. 1984. $20.00.

This is undoubtedly the most complete (if dated) bibliography of books, periodicals and articles about the subject of franchising. Although the thrust is toward a legal-orientation, the bibliography nevertheless covers all areas of franchising. It is my understanding that the ABA is in the process of updating the Bibliography.

4) FRANCHISING OPPORTUNITIES, International Franchise Association (IFA), 1350 New York Avenue, NW, Suite 900, Washington, D.C. 20005. $14.00 per year.

This glossy magazine is published 6 times per year by the International Franchising Association and gives the most current news on what's happening in franchising in a news magazine format. As with all things done by the IFA, it is extremely self-serving in that it only includes articles about its membership, thus severely limiting the scope for potential franchisees who would like information on the universe of franchisors. To the extent that one approaches the IFA's representation as a "spokesman for the industry" with skepticism, however, it is a useful source of information about the industry.

Although there are well in excess of 200 books, periodicals, directories, etc. that relate to the franchising industry, I have attempted to use some discretion in listing those that I feel best cover the industry. The following listing is alphabetic:

BLUEPRINT FOR FRANCHISING A BUSINESS, Steven S. Raab with Gregory Matusky, John Wiley & Sons, New York, NY. 1987. 244 pp. $24.95.

One of the few books on franchising written by someone who actually has years of industry experience. Raab discusses how franchising works, its advantages and disadvantages (including legal, business, marketing and sales issues) and the crucial steps required to launch a successful franchise program. The book is interspersed with "nuggets" - insightful summaries of the author's experience in various facets of franchising. The appeal is for potential and actual franchisors rather than franchisees. Understanding the mechanics, however, better prepares the franchisee for a knowledgeable investment decision.

THE COMPLETE HANDBOOK OF FRANCHISING, David D. Seltz, Addison-Wesley, Reading, MA 01867. 1981. $49.95.

For both franchisors and franchisees, this definitive handbook takes a step-by-step approach through the entire process - from planning and feasibility determination through set-up and daily operation.

THE FRANCHISE ADVANTAGE, Donald and Patrick Boroian, Francorp, 20200 Governors Dr., Olympia Fields, IL 60461. 1987. 235 pp. $30.00.

Although clearly a marketing effort to solicit potential clients for their consulting business, the authors nevertheless do a good job of explaining the steps from franchise concept to successful franchisor, as well as a look at the costs of getting there. Don't conclude, however, that any reasonable idea has franchise potential or that the average person can convert a great idea into a successful franchise operation. Both the concept and the entrepreneur have to be exceptional to successfully launch a new franchise.

A FRANCHISE CONTRACT, Jerrold G. Van Cise, IFA. $4.95.

A legal examination of the proper elements of a contract to protect both franchisor and franchisee.

THE FRANCHISE ENCYCLOPEDIA, Dr. Alfred J.

Modica, ADA Publishing, 28 Sandrock Avenue, Dobbs Ferry, NY 10522. 1986. 300 pp. $75.00

Includes articles on franchising and articles relevant to franchising as a means for economic growth. Various charts and graphs put the industry in proper perspective.

THE FRANCHISE GAME, (RULES AND PLAYERS), Harold Nedell, Olempco, Dept. C, P.O. Box 27963, Houston, TX 77027. $8.00

Deals with the potential emotional, physical and mental traumas experienced by franchisees and provides insight from the point of view of both franchisors and franchisees.

THE FRANCHISE MANUAL, Dr. Alfred J. Modica and Dr. Anthony F. Libertella, National/International Institute for Franchise Research and Development, 3 Barker Avenue, White Plains, NY 10601. 1986. 2 volumes, 450 pp. $85.00.

This weighty manual provides step-by-step direction on how to franchise your business from concept to design, proving out your program before selling a franchise, making the go or no-go decision, testing pro forma cash flow, legal ramifications and marketing techniques. Examples of case studies, legal franchise agreements and how to capitalize your franchise program from blueprint to opening your pilot operation.

FRANCHISE RESTAURANTS, The National Restaurant Association, 311 1st Street, NW, Washington, D.C. 20001. 1987. $5.00

Statistical appendix highlighting franchise restaurant growth between 1973 and 1986. Includes sales and establishment data, employment, international franchising and minority ownership.

FRANCHISE RIGHTS - A SELF-DEFENSE MANUAL FOR THE FRANCHISEE, Alex Hammond, Hammond & Morton, 1185 Ave. of the Americas, New York, NY 10036. 1980. $29.95 plus $1.50 postage.

Contains some perceptive insight into the franchisor/franchisee relationship, and, in advising franchisees, highlights some of the pitfalls which can ensnare the unwary franchisor.

FRANCHISE SELECTION: SEPARATING FACT FROM FICTION, Raymond Munna, Granite Publishers, 80 Granada Dr., Kenner, LA 70065. 1986. 215 pp. $19.95.

A valuable source of checklists for the franchisee who is unaware of the potential pitfalls that clearly exist. Especially helpful are the sections on analyzing the franchise contract, laws affecting franchising and the critical but hard to find information on a franchisor and how to get it.

FRANCHISING, Dr. Alfred J. Modica, ADA Publishing, 28 Sandrock Avenue, Dobbs Ferry, NY 10522. 1981. 159 pp. $12.95.

Provides the practical advice necessary to succeed in franchising. Geared to special situation, service-related franchises. How to get into your own franchise business for less than $5,000.

FRANCHISING, Small Business Reporter, Bank of America, Department 3120, PO Box 37000, San Francisco, CA 94137. 16 pp. $2.00.

This short publication gives a good overview of franchising, including various franchise systems, the franchisor/franchisee relationship, the franchise agreement, finding and evaluating a franchise, franchising and its critics, legislation and arbitration, etc.

FRANCHISING, P.F. Zeidman, Federal Publications, Inc., Washington, D.C. 1982.

Course manual with extensive sites, covering virtually all facets of franchising.

FRANCHISING: A PLANNING AND SALES COMPLIANCE GUIDE, Norman D. Axelrod and Lewis G. Rudnick, IFA. $35.00

A realistic discussion of the industry and the legal and procedural considerations of a franchise program. Divided into two sections, this guide addresses the major business decisions and typical management problems, as well as state and federal regulations of franchise and business opportunity sales.

FRANCHISING FOR FREE, OWNING YOUR

OWN BUSINESS WITHOUT INVESTING YOUR OWN CASH, Dennis L. Foster, John Wiley & Sons, New York, NY. 1988. 229 pp. $12.95.

This book concentrates on the two primary reasons that businesses, including franchises, fail - inadequate financing and poor planning. In addition to a methodology for financing a franchise investment with little or no cash, the book also covers tips on packaging and circulating a loan application, names and addresses of financial sources, comparative advantages and disadvantages of various sources and a partial listing of those franchisors that offer financial assistance.

FRANCHISING: REGULATION OF BUYING AND SELLING A FRANCHISE, Philip F. Zeidman, Perry C. Ausbrook and H. Bret Lowell, Bureau of National Affairs, 9435 Key WBest Avenue, Rockville, MD 20850. $50.00.

Provides a "how to" guide to franchise registration and disclosure and an in-depth analysis of the legal requirements for determining when a franchise exists.

FRANCHISING - 1987: BUSINESS STRATEGIES AND LEGAL COMPLIANCE, IFA. 920 pp. $45.00.

An overview of current federal and state regulation of franchising: registration, disclosure and franchisee/ franchisor relationships, as well as formats, techniques and procedures structuring the franchise relationship. An excellent reference manual for attorneys and franchise professionals.

FRANCHISING: ITS NATURE, SCOPE, ADVANTAGES AND DEVELOPMENT, Charles L. Vaughn, D.C. Heath and Company, 125 Spring St., Lexington, MA 02173. 1979. 304 pp. $21.95.

A comprehensive overview of the nature, scope and history of franchising, including practical advice and information to students of marketing, potential franchisors and franchisees, lawyers, bankers and large companies contemplating entering the industry.

FRANCHISING: THE HOW-TO BOOK, Lloyd T. Tarbutton, Prentice Hall, Englewood Cliffs, NJ. 1986. 226 pp. $17.95.

A practical guide presented by an acknowledged industry expert, providing a soup-to-nuts action plan for building and expanding a successful franchising operation. In addition to valuable check lists, the book answers critical questions on franchise marketing and sales, fee structures, franchise agreements, franchisee training programs and various assistance programs. Worthwhile reading for franchisor and franchisee alike.

FRANCHISING: THE INSIDE STORY, John Kinch, Trimark Publishing, P.O. Box 10530, Wilmington, DE 19850. $17.95.

This book will lead you through the basic and essential steps in exploring the opportunities in franchising. A comprehensive overview of the hows and whys of buying a franchise.

FRANCHISING IN THE ECONOMY, 1988 -1990, IFA Education Foundation, Inc. and Horwath International, IFA. 110 pp. $25.00.

For the past 16 years, this detailed and highly reliable statistical analysis of franchising in the US has been published by the US Department of Commerce. With the Government's decision to discontinue its publication, the IFA and Horwath International have very capably filled the void and come out with a slicker, more readable, version. In so doing, they provide the industry with a very valuable service. This statistical analysis covers virtually all facets of the industry and documents the growth and success that the industry has enjoyed over the past 2 decades. Not only is the industry as a whole covered, but key product/service categories within the industry are covered in great detail. An excellent source book for potential franchisees, who can ask prospective franchisors hard questions as to how their franchise compares with other franchisors in terms of average sales per unit, average employees per unit, averages sales of company-owned vs. franchised units, etc. This is clearly the most authoritative source of any statistics regarding the industry.

FRANCHISING REALITIES & REMEDIES, Harold Brown, Law Journal Seminar Press, 111 Eighth Avenue, New York, NY 10011. 1986. $70.00.

Outlines sound courses of action that potential franchisees may consider as well as sound principles against which franchisors must examine their operations if their enterprises are to avoid destruction through legal attacks.

FTC FRANCHISING RULE: THE IFA COMPLIANCE KIT, IFA. $100.00.

A newly revised edition contains a comprehensive overview of the Federal Trade Commission rule on franchising. It also includes an analysis of the rule, an outline of compliance steps and requirements, considerations in selecting a format, comparisons with state laws, bibliographies and more.

HANDBOOK OF SUCCESSFUL FRANCHISING, M.P. Friedlander, Jr., Van Nostrand Reinhold Company, New York, NY. 1981.

A factual, non-legal reference guide for prospective franchisees, providing specific information regarding over 40 types of franchisors. Final chapters summarize current state and federal law and regulation, set out a sample franchise agreement with comments, and provide a sample real estate lease with comments.

HOW TO BE A FRANCHISOR, Robert E. Kushell and Carl E. Zwisler, III, IFA. $5.00.

This booklet describes step-by-step details about how to launch a franchise program. Written from both the operational and legal perspectives, this is necessary reading for all potential franchisors.

HOW TO GET STARTED IN YOUR OWN FRANCHISED BUSINESS, David Seltz, Farnsworth Publishing Company, 78 Randall Ave., Rockville Center, NY 11578. Revised 1980. 320 pp. $19.95.

Provides a step-by-step direction for judging a franchise, choosing a location, evaluating an agreement, obtaining financing, promoting your business and understanding franchising laws.

HOW TO SELECT A FRANCHISE, Robert McIntosh, IFA. $10.00.

A workbook and cassette tape, designed to help individuals decide whether and how to become a franchisee.

THE HOW-TO'S OF RETAIL FRANCHISING, A.

Smart, Vol. 6, Retailing for Profit Series, Lebhar-Friedman Books, Chain Store Publishing Corp., New York, NY. 1982.

A practical, succinct, businessman's guide to franchising, including a chapter on the franchise agreeement and one on state and Federal regulation.

INTERNATIONAL FRANCHISING: AN OVERVIEW, Science Publishing Company, P.O. Box 1663, Grand Central Station, New York, NY 10163. $61.50.

A volume containing papers presented by the International Franchising Law Committee on the International Bar Association's section on business law. Includes a survey of more than 20 countries and an introduction to franchising and its legal implications in those territories.

INVESTIGATE BEFORE INVESTING: A GUIDE FOR PROSPECTIVE FRANCHISEES, Jerome L. Fels and Lewis G. Rudnick, IFA. 1974. 32 pp. $4.00.

A 34-page handbook designed to help prospective franchisees evaluate a franchise offer. Tells what questions to ask, what to expect in the way of costs and training programs, as well as an explanation of the laws and regulations that apply.

IS FRANCHISING FOR YOU?, Robert K. McIntosh, IFA. $3.95.

Basic primer for prospective franchisees with emphasis on self-evaluation to determine whether the opportunities and challenges offered by a franchise system meet the ambitions and abilities of a prospective franchisee.

OWN YOUR OWN FRANCHISE: EVERYTHING YOU NEED TO KNOW ABOUT THE BEST FRANCHISE OPPORTUNITIES IN AMERICA. Ray Bard and Sheila Henderson, Addison-Wesley, Reading, MA 01867. 1987. 455 pp. $14.95.

Detailed data on 160 top franchises. Each franchise profile includes relevant statistics, the business, what it takes, getting started, making it work and getting more information.

THE RATING GUIDE TO FRANCHISES, Dennis L. Foster, Facts On File Publications, New York. 1988.

298 pp. $ 29.95.

A fairly detailed, readable rating guide to some 100+ individual franchise opportunities. Included in the indivudual analyses are the franchisor's range of services, advertising effectiveness, training program, past franchise disputes, litigation record and the satisfaction level of current franchises. Although much of the information has no doubt changed since the publication first came out, this is an excellent overview of what is available. It is especially valuable in providing some basic information on various segments of the industry for comparison with those companies listed in this publication.

ROADSIDE EMPIRES - HOW THE CHAINS FRANCHISED AMERICA, Stan Luxenberg, Viking Penguin Press, New York, NY. 1985. $17.95.

A readable history of how franchising has transformed the American landscape, diet and economy. Includes folklore on advertising and marketing techniques, the fanatic attention to detail displayed by certain franchisors and profiles on franchising legends Ray Kroc, Colonel Sanders, Howard Johnson and others. Most informative, however, is the critical look that Luxenberg takes at the real effect of franchising on the economy. This includes the diversion of capital from real factories to fast-food factories, mass standardization, get-rich-quick schemes, and, sadly, the transition of the American workforce from skill-intensive jobs to often dead-end, stultifying, minimum wage jobs.

U.F.O.C. GUIDELINES, IFA. $30.

Instructions for completing the Uniform Franchise Offering Circular. Prepared by the Midwest Securities Commissioners Association for use by franchisors in meeting state and Federal disclosure requirements.

YOUR FORTUNE IN FRANCHISING, Richard P. Finn, Contemporary Books, 180 North Michigan Ave., Chicago, IL 60601. 1979. 202 pp. $9.95.

A fairly basic, as well as dated, analysis of franchising - how it works, the proper steps to take prior to signing a contract, franchisee and franchisor rights, etc. Roughly half the book is devoted to a listing of names and addresses of franchisors, using 1978 data.

220 BEST FRANCHISES TO BUY, Constance Jones, The Philip Lief Group, 319 East 52nd Street, New York, NY 10022. 1987. 459 pp. $10.95.

An in-depth description of 220 franchises from 12 major franchising industries. The book provides a good overview of the mechanics by industry and represents an excellent starting point for potential franchisees initiating the exploration process.

Note: FOR AUTHORS WHOSE BOOKS ARE NOT NOTED ABOVE, I WOULD ENCOURAGE YOU TO SEND COPIES FOR EVALUATION TO **SOURCE BOOK,** P.O. BOX 12488, OAKLAND, CA 94604.

CHAPTER 4

AUTOMOTIVE PRODUCTS AND SERVICES

**60 MINUTE TUNE /
10 MINUTE LUBE**
11811 NE 1st St., # 208
Bellevue, WA 98005
TEL: (206) 453-8078 C
FAX:
Mr. Thomas Reid, VP Saes/Mktg.

Computerized major tune-up, plus 14-point lube, oil, filter, valve adjustment, fuel adjustment, fuel injection, radiator, transmission and air conditioning service. Computer diagnosis, used vehicle inspection, brake inspection. Miscellaneous parts replacement (water pumps, fuel pumps, alternators, carburetor, etc.).

HISTORY: . . . .
Established in 1979; . . 1st Franchised in 1980
Company-Owned Units (As of 12/1/1989): . .2
Franchised Units (12/1/1989): 94
Total Units (12/1/1989): 96
Distribution: US-96;Can-0;Overseas-0
North America: . . . . 4 States
Concentration: . .41 in WA, 11 in CA, 8 in OR
Registered: . . . . CA,FL,OR,WA
. . . .
Average # of Employees: . . . . . . 6 FT, 1 PT
Prior Industry Experience: . . . . . . Necessary

FINANCIAL:
Cash Investment: $50-70K
Total Investment: $120-150K
Fees: Franchise - $30K
   Royalty: 7%, Advert: 7%
Contract Periods (Yrs.): 10/10
Area Development Agreement: Yes/10
Sub-Franchise Contract: . . . . . Yes
Expand in Territory: . . . . Yes
Passive Ownership: . . . Discouraged
Encourage Conversions: . . . . . Yes
Franchisee Purchase(s) Required: .No

FRANCHISOR TRAINING/SUPPORT:
Financial Assistance Provided: . . . Yes(I)
Site Selection Assistance: . . . . . . .Yes
Lease Negotiation Assistance: . . . . .Yes
Co-operative Advertising: . . . . .Yes
Training: . . . 1 Wk. New Store Ops,1 Wk.
   . . .New Store Tech., 130 Hours Courses
On-Going Support: . . . . . . .C,D,E,G,H
Full-Time Franchisor Support Staff: . . 18
EXPANSION PLANS:
US: . . . . FL, CA, OR, WA
Canada - No, ... Overseas - No

AUTOMOTIVE PRODUCTS & SERVICES

	1988	1989	1990	Percentage Change 1988-1989	Percentage Change 1989-1990
Number of Establishments:					
Company–Owned	4,621	4,776	5,119	3.4%	7.2%
Franchisee–Owned	30,017	31,059	33,442	3.5%	7.7%
Total	34,638	35,835	38,561	3.5%	7.6%
% of Total Establishments:					
Company–Owned	13.3%	13.3%	13.3%		
Franchisee–Owned	86.7%	86.7%	86.7%		
Total	100.0%	100.0%	100.0%		
Annual Sales ($000):					
Company–Owned	$3,842,145	$4,151,206	$4,585,980	8.0%	10.5%
Franchisee–Owned	7,520,550	8,089,692	9,046,265	7.6%	11.8%
Total	11,362,695	12,240,898	13,632,245	7.7%	11.4%
% of Total Sales:					
Company–Owned	33.8%	33.9%	33.6%		
Franchisee–Owned	66.2%	66.1%	66.4%		
Total	100.0%	100.0%	100.0%		
Average Sales Per Unit ($000):					
Company–Owned	$831	$869	$896	4.5%	3.1%
Franchisee–Owned	251	260	271	4.0%	3.9%
Total	328	342	354	4.1%	3.5%
Sales Ratio	331.9%	333.7%	331.2%		

	1st Quartile	Median	4th Quartile
Average 1988 Total Investment:			
Company–Owned	$71,250	$100,000	$318,750
Franchisee–Owned	75,000	100,000	150,000
Single Unit Franchise Fee	$15,000	$20,000	$25,000
Multiple Unit Franchise Fee	17,500	22,500	29,500
Franchisee Start–up Cost	25,000	40,000	73,750

	1988	Employees/Unit	Sales/Employee
Employment:			
Company–Owned	38,000	8.2	101,109
Franchisee–Owned	129,583	4.3	58,037
Total	167,583	4.8	67,803
Employee Performance Ratios		190.5%	174.2%

Source: Franchising In The Economy, 1988 – 1990, IFA Education Foundation & Horwath International, Published January, 1990.

1) 1989 and 1990 data were estimated by respondents.

AAMCO TRANSMISSIONS

1 Presidential Blvd.
Bala Cynwyd, PA 19004
TEL: (800) 523-0402 (215) 668-2900 C
FAX: (215) 664-4570
Mr. Don Limbert, Dir. Fran. Sales

AAMCO, the world's largest chain of transmission specialists, makes in-house resources available to help you build a customer-satisfying, successful business. Among these: extensive training programs, effective advertising and marketing, and solid operational assistance. AAMCO Centers' warranties are honored throughout the United States and Canada.

HISTORY: . . . . IFA	FINANCIAL:	FRANCHISOR TRAINING/SUPPORT:
Established in 1963; . . 1st Franchised in 1964	Cash Investment: . . . . $~48K	Financial Assistance Provided: . . . Yes(I)
Company-Owned Units (As of 12/1/1989): . .0	Total Investment: . . . .$~115K	Site Selection Assistance: . . . . . . .Yes
Franchised Units (12/1/1989): 714	Fees: Franchise - . . . . $~48K	Lease Negotiation Assistance: . . . . .Yes
Total Units (12/1/1989): 714	Royalty: 7%, Advert: . . . . Var%	Co-operative Advertising: . . . . No
Distribution: US-691;Can-23;Overseas-0	Contract Periods (Yrs.): 15/15	Training: . . . . 5 Wks. Headquarters
North America: . . . . 48 States, 3 Provinces	Area Development Agreement: . .No	. . . .
Concentration:	Sub-Franchise Contract: . . . . .No	On-Going Support: . . . . .G,I
Registered: . . . . .All	Expand in Territory: . . . . .No	Full-Time Franchisor Support Staff: . .175
. . . .	Passive Ownership: . . . Not Allowed	EXPANSION PLANS:
Average # of Employees: . . . . .5 FT	Encourage Conversions: . . . . .No	US: . . . . .All US
Prior Industry Experience: . . . . . . Helpful	Franchisee Purchase(s) Required: .No	Canada - Yes, ...Overseas - No

ACC-U-TUNE & BRAKE

2510 Old Middlefield Way
Mountain View, CA 94043
TEL: (415) 968-8863
FAX:
Mr. Jack W. Fox, Franchise Director

We have successfully packaged the most profitable auto services: drive-thru oil change, tune-up, state inspections, coupled with While-U-Wait brake and manufacturer's 15/30,000 mile service packages. A one-stop, well-lighted, modern, clean place, where customers can take care of all their vehicle preventative maintenance needs.

HISTORY:	FINANCIAL:	FRANCHISOR TRAINING/SUPPORT:
Established in 1975; . . 1st Franchised in 1979	Cash Investment: $80K	Financial Assistance Provided: . . . Yes(I)
Company-Owned Units (As of 12/1/1989): . .6	Total Investment: $70-140K	Site Selection Assistance: . . . . . . .Yes
Franchised Units (12/1/1989): 10	Fees: Franchise - $25K	Lease Negotiation Assistance: . . . . .Yes
Total Units (12/1/1989): 16	Royalty: 7.5%, Advert: 7.5%	Co-operative Advertising: . . . . . . .Yes
Distribution: US-16;Can-0;Overseas-0	Contract Periods (Yrs.): . . 10/10/10	Training: . . . . 3 Wks. Headquarters,
North America: . . . . .1 State	Area Development Agreement: . .No	. . . . .2 Wks. On-site
Concentration: . . . . 16 in CA	Sub-Franchise Contract: . . . . .No	On-Going Support: . . . . C,D,E
Registered: . . . . CA	Expand in Territory: . . . . . . Yes	Full-Time Franchisor Support Staff: . . 10
. . . .	Passive Ownership: . . . Not Allowed	EXPANSION PLANS:
Average # of Employees: . . . . . . 5 FT, 2 PT	Encourage Conversions: . . . . . Yes	US: . . . . CA and OR
Prior Industry Experience: . . . . Helpful	Franchisee Purchase(s) Required: .No	Canada - No, ...Overseas - No

ACTION AUTO STORES

2128 S. Dort Hwy.
Flint, MI 48507
TEL: (800) 733-2323 (313) 235-5600
FAX: (313) 235-8444
Mr. Wayne Girard, Franchise Director

ACTION AUTO has taken four related markets - parts, service, tires and gas - and put them under one roof. Our concept allows more cross-selling opportunities with every customer. More ways to make money, attract new customers and to keep them coming back.

HISTORY: . . . . .IFA	FINANCIAL: NASD-AAST	FRANCHISOR TRAINING/SUPPORT:
Established in 1976; . . . 1st Franchised in 19	Cash Investment: $150K	Financial Assistance Provided: . . . Yes(I)
Company-Owned Units (As of 12/1/1989): . 67	Total Investment: $400K	Site Selection Assistance: . . . . . . .Yes
Franchised Units (12/1/1989): 4	Fees: Franchise - $35K	Lease Negotiation Assistance: . . . . .Yes
Total Units (12/1/1989): 71	Royalty: 1-7% Var, Advert: . . 0%	Co-operative Advertising: . . . . . . .Yes
Distribution: US-71;Can-0;Overseas-0	Contract Periods (Yrs.): 10/5	Training: . . . . 12 Wks. Headquarters
North America: . . . . .1 State	Area Development Agreement: . .No	. . . .
Concentration: . . . . .71 in MI	Sub-Franchise Contract: . . . . .No	On-Going Support: . . .A,B,C,E,D,f,G,H,I
Registered: . . . . IL,IN,MI, WI	Expand in Territory: . . . . . . Yes	Full-Time Franchisor Support Staff: . . . 5
. . . .	Passive Ownership: . . . Not Allowed	EXPANSION PLANS:
Average # of Employees: . . . . . . 4 FT, 3 PT	Encourage Conversions: . . . . . NA	US: . . . . Midwest Only
Prior Industry Experience: . . . . Helpful	Franchisee Purchase(s) Required: .No	Canada - No, ...Overseas - No

AID AUTO STORES

475 Doughty Blvd., P.O. Box 1100
Inwood, NY 11696
TEL: (516) 371-4330
FAX:
Mr. Philip Stephen, President

Retail sales of automotive parts, accessories, tools, chemicals and equipment.

HISTORY: . . . .
Established in 1954; . . 1st Franchised in 1966
Company-Owned Units (As of 12/1/1989): . .2
Franchised Units (12/1/1989): 86
Total Units (12/1/1989): 88
Distribution: US-88;Can-0;Overseas-0
North America: . . . . 2 States
Concentration: . . . . 79 in NY, 9 in NJ
Registered: . . . .
. . . .
Average # of Employees: . . . . . . 3 FT, 3 PT
Prior Industry Experience: . . . . . . Helpful

FINANCIAL:
Cash Investment: $135-175K
Total Investment: $135-175K
Fees: Franchise - $15K
  Royalty: $400, Advert: $675
Contract Periods (Yrs.): 10/10
Area Development Agreement: . .No
Sub-Franchise Contract: . . . . .No
Expand in Territory: . . . . Yes
Passive Ownership: . . . Discouraged
Encourage Conversions: . . . . . Yes
Franchisee Purchase(s) Required: .No

FRANCHISOR TRAINING/SUPPORT:
Financial Assistance Provided: . . . . .No
Site Selection Assistance: . . . . . . .Yes
Lease Negotiation Assistance: . . . . .Yes
Co-operative Advertising: . . . . . . .Yes
Training: . . . . .Min. 30 Days Train-
. . . . .ing at HQ/Stores
On-Going Support: . . A,B,C,D,E,F,G,H,I
Full-Time Franchisor Support Staff: . . 35
EXPANSION PLANS:
  US: . . . . NY, NJ, NE
  Canada - No, ...Overseas - No

AUTO ONE ACCESSORIES & GLASS

580 Ajax Dr.
Madison Heights, MI 48071
TEL: (313) 583-7290
FAX: (313) 583-9050
Mr. John Harper, Franchise Director

AUTO ONE franchises automotive accessories and glass centers in Michigan, Indiana, Ohio and Florida. AUTO ONE Centers sell and install cellular phones, auto security systems, sunroofs, running boards, auto glass, rustproofing and detailing.

HISTORY: . . . .
Established in 1963; . . 1st Franchised in 1973
Company-Owned Units (As of 12/1/1989): . .4
Franchised Units (12/1/1989): 29
Total Units (12/1/1989): 33
Distribution: US-33;Can-0;Overseas-0
North America: . . . . 3 States
Concentration: . . . .22 in MI, 7 in IN, 4 in FL
Registered: . . . . FL,IN,MI
. . . .
Average # of Employees: . . . . . . 5 FT, 1 PT
Prior Industry Experience: . . . . . . Helpful

FINANCIAL:
Cash Investment: $40-70K
Total Investment: $100-150K
Fees: Franchise - $18K
  Royalty: 6%, Advert: 2.5%
Contract Periods (Yrs.): 10/10
Area Development Agreement: . .No
Sub-Franchise Contract: . . . . . Yes
Expand in Territory: . . . . .No
Passive Ownership: . . . Discouraged
Encourage Conversions: . . . . . Yes
Franchisee Purchase(s) Required: .No

FRANCHISOR TRAINING/SUPPORT:
Financial Assistance Provided: . . . . .No
Site Selection Assistance: . . . . . . .Yes
Lease Negotiation Assistance: . . . . .Yes
Co-operative Advertising: . . . . . . .Yes
Training: . . . . .60 Days Headquarters
. . . .
On-Going Support: . . . .B,C,D,E,F,G,H,I
Full-Time Franchisor Support Staff: . . 11
EXPANSION PLANS:
  US: . . . . .Midwest, Southeast,Northeast
  Canada - No, ...Overseas - No

AUTOPRO

7025 Ontario St. E.
Montreal, PQ H1N2B3 CAN
TEL: (514) 256-5031
FAX:
Mr. Andre Hardy, Natl. Coord.

AUTOPRO is the perfect add-on program for a regular station or independent repair shop wishing to compete with the market's big names. AUTOPRO offers marketing and advertising assistance, along with lifetime warranties in 5 specialties: brakes, mufflers, suspensions, front-end and FWD parts.

HISTORY: . . . .
Established in 1926; . . 1st Franchised in 1983
Company-Owned Units (As of 12/1/1989): . .0
Franchised Units (12/1/1989): 550
Total Units (12/1/1989): 550
Distribution: US-0;Can-550;Overseas-0
North America: . . . . 7 Provinces
Concentration: . 332 in PQ,132 in ON,47 in BC
Registered: . . . .
. . . .
Average # of Employees: . . . . .5 FT
Prior Industry Experience: . . . . . .Necessary

FINANCIAL: TSE - UAP
Cash Investment: . . . .$
Total Investment: . . . .$
Fees: Franchise - $4K
  Royalty: 0%, Advert: 3%
Contract Periods (Yrs.): 1/1
Area Development Agreement: . .No
Sub-Franchise Contract: . . . . . .No
Expand in Territory: . . . . Yes
Passive Ownership: . . . . . .Allowed
Encourage Conversions: . . . . . Yes
Franchisee Purchase(s) Required: Yes

FRANCHISOR TRAINING/SUPPORT:
Financial Assistance Provided: . . . . .No
Site Selection Assistance: . . . . No
Lease Negotiation Assistance: . . . . .No
Co-operative Advertising: . . . . . . .Yes
Training: . . . . .On-going Manu-
. . . . .facturers Training
On-Going Support: . . . . .A,D,G,H
Full-Time Franchisor Support Staff: . . .5
EXPANSION PLANS:
  US: . . . . .No
  Canada - Yes, ...Overseas - No

AVIS LUBE

900 Old Country Rd.
Garden City, NY 11530
TEL: (800) AVIS-LUBE (516) 222-3400
FAX:
Mr. Jay Sanderson, Dir. Bus. Dev.

AVIS LUBE FAST OIL CHANGE CENTER will provide basic preventive maintenance for automobiles and light trucks. Service will include oil change, oil filter change, lubrication of chassis, checking and bringing up to proper level transmission, brake, differential, battery and windshield washer fluids. Net worth of $250,000 and $100,000 in liquid assets required.

HISTORY: . . . . IFA
Established in 1986; . . 1st Franchised in 1987
Company-Owned Units (As of 12/1/1989): . .3
Franchised Units (12/1/1989): 57
Total Units (12/1/1989): 60
Distribution: US-60;Can-0;Overseas-0
North America: . . . . 20 States
Concentration: . . 20 in TX, 12 in NY, 8 in FL
Registered: . . . . All States
. . . .
Average # of Employees: . . . . . .2 FT, 10 PT
Prior Industry Experience: . . . . . . Helpful

FINANCIAL:
Cash Investment: $100-160K
Total Investment: $160K
Fees: Franchise - $35K
  Royalty: 5-6%, Advert: 1%
Contract Periods (Yrs.): 20
Area Development Agreement: Yes/20
Sub-Franchise Contract: . . . . . .No
Expand in Territory: . . . . Yes
Passive Ownership: . . . . . .Allowed
Encourage Conversions: . . . . . Yes
Franchisee Purchase(s) Required: .No

FRANCHISOR TRAINING/SUPPORT:
Financial Assistance Provided: . . . Yes(I)
Site Selection Assistance: . . . . . . .Yes
Lease Negotiation Assistance: . . . . .Yes
Co-operative Advertising: . . . . . . .Yes
Training: . . . . 2 Wks. Headquarters
. . . .
On-Going Support: . . A,B,C,D,E,F,G,H,I
Full-Time Franchisor Support Staff: . . 25
EXPANSION PLANS:
US: . . . . .All US
Canada - No, ...Overseas - No

BIG O TIRES

11755 E. Parkview Ave.
Englewood, CO 80111
TEL: (800) 622-2446 (303) 790-2800
FAX: (303) 790-0225
Mr. Mike Manning, Dir. Fran. Devel.

Franchised retail tire stores, offering a complete line of private brand BIG O passenger and light truck tires, and other automotive related services.

HISTORY: . . . . IFA
Established in 1962; . . 1st Franchised in 1962
Company-Owned Units (As of 12/1/1989): . .8
Franchised Units (12/1/1989): 325
Total Units (12/1/1989): 333
Distribution: US-333;Can-0;Overseas-0
North America: . . . . 16 States
Concentration: . 37 in CA, 32 in UT, 31 in AZ
Registered: . . . . CA,IN,WA
. . . .
Average # of Employees: . . . . . 2 FT, 4-6 PT
Prior Industry Experience: . . . . . . Helpful

FINANCIAL: OTC-BIGOTR
Cash Investment: $75-100K
Total Investment: $150-250K
Fees: Franchise - $15K
  Royalty: 2%, Advert: 4%
Contract Periods (Yrs.): 10/10
Area Development Agreement: Yes/5
Sub-Franchise Contract: . . . .
Expand in Territory: . . . . Yes
Passive Ownership: . . . Discouraged
Encourage Conversions: . . . . . Yes
Franchisee Purchase(s) Required: Yes

FRANCHISOR TRAINING/SUPPORT:
Financial Assistance Provided: . . . Yes(I)
Site Selection Assistance: . . . . . . .Yes
Lease Negotiation Assistance: . . . .Yes
Co-operative Advertising: . . . . . . .Yes
Training: . . . . 2 Wks. Headquarters
. . . . .2 Wks. At Designated Store
On-Going Support: . . . a,B,C,D,E,F,G,H
Full-Time Franchisor Support Staff: . .200
EXPANSION PLANS:
US: . . . . .All US
Canada - No, ...Overseas - No

BOB'S CAR WASH

119 N. Main St.
Elmira, NY 14901
TEL: (816) 421-1855
FAX:
Mr. Larry Childers, Fran. Sales Rep.

Our years of experience and expertise will guide you through the entire process of becoming a BOB'S CAR WASH operator. From site selection to on-site assistance on grand opening day, and every step along the way, we will be with you. Our proven system will allow you to tap into an industry with dynamic growth potential right away.

HISTORY: . . . .
Established in 1981; . . 1st Franchised in 1986
Company-Owned Units (As of 12/1/1989): . .6
Franchised Units (12/1/1989): 0
Total Units (12/1/1989): 6
Distribution: US-6;Can-0;Overseas-0
North America: . . . . .1 State
Concentration: . . . . 6 in NY
Registered: . . . . NY
. . . .
Average # of Employees: . . . . . . 3 FT, 3 PT
Prior Industry Experience: . . . . . . Helpful

FINANCIAL:
Cash Investment: $35-100K
Total Investment: $500-800K
Fees: Franchise - $18.5K
  Royalty: 5.5%, Advert: 1%
Contract Periods (Yrs.): 15/5
Area Development Agreement: Yes/15
Sub-Franchise Contract: . . . . . .No
Expand in Territory: . . . . Yes
Passive Ownership: . . . . . .Allowed
Encourage Conversions: . . . . . Yes
Franchisee Purchase(s) Required: .No

FRANCHISOR TRAINING/SUPPORT:
Financial Assistance Provided: . . . . .No
Site Selection Assistance: . . . . . . .Yes
Lease Negotiation Assistance: . . . .Yes
Co-operative Advertising: . . . .
Training: . . . .
. . . . 5 Days Headquarters
On-Going Support: . . . . . . C,D,E,G,h,I
Full-Time Franchisor Support Staff: . . .
EXPANSION PLANS:
US: . . . . .All US
Canada - Yes, . . . Overseas - Yes

BUDGET BRAKE & MUFFLER

422 - 4940 Canada Way
Burnaby, BC V5G4K7 CAN
TEL: (604) 294-6114
FAX: (604) 294-1648
Mr. Warren Swanson, President

Retail brake and muffler specialists. Fast service with a package price.

HISTORY: . . . . .CFA	FINANCIAL:	FRANCHISOR TRAINING/SUPPORT:
Established in 1969; . . 1st Franchised in 1972	Cash Investment: $65-75K	Financial Assistance Provided: . . . Yes(I)
Company-Owned Units (As of 12/1/1989): . .2	Total Investment: $170-185K	Site Selection Assistance: . . . . . . .Yes
Franchised Units (12/1/1989): 21	Fees: Franchise - $25K	Lease Negotiation Assistance: . . . . .Yes
Total Units (12/1/1989): 23	Royalty: 4%, Advert: 3%	Co-operative Advertising: . . . . . . .Yes
Distribution: US-0;Can-23;Overseas-0	Contract Periods (Yrs.): 10/10	Training: . . . . . . 2-3 Wks. Headquarters
North America: . . . . .1 Province	Area Development Agreement: . .No	. . . .
Concentration: . . . . 23 in BC	Sub-Franchise Contract: . . . . .No	On-Going Support: . . . . B,C,D,E,F,G,H
Registered:	Expand in Territory: . . . . Yes	Full-Time Franchisor Support Staff: . . .6
. . . .	Passive Ownership: . . . Not Allowed	EXPANSION PLANS:
Average # of Employees: . . . . .4 FT	Encourage Conversions: . . . . . Yes	US: . . . . .No
Prior Industry Experience: . . . . Helpful	Franchisee Purchase(s) Required: .No	Canada - Yes, ...Overseas - No

CAR-X MUFFLER & BRAKE

8430 W. Bryn Mawr, # 400
Chicago, IL 60631
TEL: (800) 736-6733 (312) 693-1000
FAX: (312) 693-0309
Director of Fran. Development

CAR-X MUFFLER & BRAKE is a retail automotive service chain, specializing in the undercar services including: exhaust systems, brakes, ride control and front-end repair. The market for these services is large and growing, with an estimated service market of 9 billion dollars.

HISTORY: . . . . .IFA	FINANCIAL:	FRANCHISOR TRAINING/SUPPORT:
Established in 1971; . . 1st Franchised in 1973	Cash Investment: $70-90K	Financial Assistance Provided: . . . Yes(I)
Company-Owned Units (As of 12/1/1989): . 51	Total Investment: $180-200K	Site Selection Assistance: . . . . . . .Yes
Franchised Units (12/1/1989): 81	Fees: Franchise - $18.5K	Lease Negotiation Assistance: . . . . .Yes
Total Units (12/1/1989): 132	Royalty: 5%, Advert: 5-10%	Co-operative Advertising: . . . . .No
Distribution: . . . US-132;Can-0;Overseas-0	Contract Periods (Yrs.): 10/5	Training: . . . . . 3 Wks. Ann Arbor, MI, 1
North America: . . . . 10 States	Area Development Agreement: . .No	. Wk OJT, 1 Wk. HQ, 1 Wk. Shop Open.
Concentration: . .50 in IL, 16 in WI, 16 in MO	Sub-Franchise Contract: . . . . .No	On-Going Support: . . . .B,C,D,E,F,G,H,I
Registered: . . . . IL,IN,MN,ND,SD,WI	Expand in Territory: . . . . Yes	Full-Time Franchisor Support Staff: . . 23
. . . .	Passive Ownership: . . . Discouraged	EXPANSION PLANS:
Average # of Employees: . . . . .4 FT	Encourage Conversions: . . . . . Yes	US: . . . . Midwest and Northeast
Prior Industry Experience: . . . . Helpful	Franchisee Purchase(s) Required: .No	Canada - No, ...Overseas - No

CARLINE MUFFLER

500 Conestoga Blvd.
Cambridge, ON N1R5T7 CAN
TEL: (519) 621-3360
FAX: (519) 740-4422
Mr. Greg Paleczny, Account Executive

Retail automotive under-car specialists, emphasizing exhaust, shocks, brakes and front-end. Supported by a leading maunfacturer in the exhaust business with total support through training and a professional coast-to-coast sales staff.

HISTORY:	FINANCIAL:	FRANCHISOR TRAINING/SUPPORT:
Established in 1981; . . 1st Franchised in 1981	Cash Investment: $70-80K	Financial Assistance Provided: . . . . .No
Company-Owned Units (As of 12/1/1989): . .0	Total Investment: $70-80K	Site Selection Assistance: . . . . . . .Yes
Franchised Units (12/1/1989): 123	Fees: Franchise - $0	Lease Negotiation Assistance: . . . . .Yes
Total Units (12/1/1989): 123	Royalty: 0%, Advert: 0%	Co-operative Advertising: . . . . .Yes
Distribution: . . . US-0;Can-93;Overseas-30	Contract Periods (Yrs.): . . . . Infin.	Training: . . . . As Required On-site,
North America: . . . . 8 Provinces	Area Development Agreement: . .No	. . . . 1 Week Training Facility
Concentration: . 30 in BC, 21 in ON, 14 in AB	Sub-Franchise Contract: . . . . .No	On-Going Support: . . .a,B,C,D,E,F,G,H,I
Registered: . . . . AB	Expand in Territory: . . . . Yes	Full-Time Franchisor Support Staff: . . .2
. . . .	Passive Ownership: . . . Discouraged	EXPANSION PLANS:
Average # of Employees: . . . . . . 3 FT, 1 PT	Encourage Conversions: . . . . . Yes	US: .No
Prior Industry Experience: . . . . Helpful	Franchisee Purchase(s) Required: Yes	Canada - Yes, . . . Overseas - Yes

CARRIAGE TRADE PERSONAL AUTO-MOTIVE LIAISON SERVICES
2242 E. 45th Ave.
Vancouver, BC V5P1N8 CAN
TEL: (604) 321-5058
FAX:
Mr. Neal R. McRae, President

A unique and innovative opportunity, requiring low initial investment. Ideal opportunity for automotive service managers who wish to own their own business and work in a positive environment. The business is a personal automotive liaison service that, for a low monthly fee, provides a car with a personal time and money-saving service.

HISTORY: . . . .
Established in 1989; . . 1st Franchised in 1989
Company-Owned Units (As of 12/1/1989): . .1
Franchised Units (12/1/1989): 1
Total Units (12/1/1989): 2
Distribution: US-0;Can-2;Overseas-0
North America: . . . . .1 Province
Concentration: . . . . 2 in BC
Registered: . . . .
. . . .
Average # of Employees: . . . . .2 FT
Prior Industry Experience: . . . . . .Necessary

FINANCIAL:
Cash Investment: $20-40K
Total Investment: $20-40K
Fees: Franchise - $10-20K
Royalty: 5%, Advert: 2%
Contract Periods (Yrs.): 5/5
Area Development Agreement: . .No
Sub-Franchise Contract: . . . . .No
Expand in Territory: . . . . . . Yes
Passive Ownership: . . . Discouraged
Encourage Conversions: . . . . . NA
Franchisee Purchase(s) Required: .No

FRANCHISOR TRAINING/SUPPORT:
Financial Assistance Provided: . . . Yes(I)
Site Selection Assistance: . . . . .Yes
Lease Negotiation Assistance: . . . . .NA
Co-operative Advertising: . . . . .Yes
Training: . . . . 7 Days Headquarters
. . . .
On-Going Support: . . . . . . B,C,D,H,I
Full-Time Franchisor Support Staff: . . .2
EXPANSION PLANS:
US: . . . . .Northwest, Southwest
Canada - Yes, ...Overseas - No

CERTIGARD / PETRO-CANADA

111 - 5th Ave. SW
Calgary, AB T2P3E3 CAN
TEL: (403) 296-7440 C
FAX: (403) 296-3030
Mr. B. C. Carruthers, Manager

CERTIGARD is a one-stop convenience automotive service concept, built on the belief that financial success results from Trust and Professionalism. CERTIGARD is supported by a unique computer system that makes the business proactive, a tool that sets CERTIGARD apart from all the rest.

HISTORY: . . . . .CFA
Established in 1973; . . 1st Franchised in 1987
Company-Owned Units (As of 12/1/1989): . 19
Franchised Units (12/1/1989): 106
Total Units (12/1/1989): 125
Distribution: . . . US-0;Can-125;Overseas-0
North America: . . . . 7 Provinces
Concentration: . 34 in ON, 21 in BC, 16 in AB
Registered: . . . . AB
. . . .
Average # of Employees: . . . . . . 6 FT, 1 PT
Prior Industry Experience: . . . . Helpful

FINANCIAL:
Cash Investment: $80K
Total Investment: $250K
Fees: Franchise - $13K
Royalty: 5%, Advert: 2%
Contract Periods (Yrs.): 5/5
Area Development Agreement: . .No
Sub-Franchise Contract: . . . . .No
Expand in Territory: . . . . . . Yes
Passive Ownership: . . . Not Allowed
Encourage Conversions: . . . . . Yes
Franchisee Purchase(s) Required: Yes

FRANCHISOR TRAINING/SUPPORT:
Financial Assistance Provided: . . . Yes(I)
Site Selection Assistance: . . . . .Yes
Lease Negotiation Assistance: . . . . .Yes
Co-operative Advertising: . . . . .Yes
Training: . . . . . . 5-10 Days Headquarters,
. . . On-going At Site Toronto/Montreal
On-Going Support: . . . . . .C,D,E,F,G,H
Full-Time Franchisor Support Staff: . . 40
EXPANSION PLANS:
US: . . . . .No
Canada - Yes, ...Overseas - No

CHAMPION AUTO STORES

5520 N. Highway 169
New Hope, MN 55428
TEL: (800) 444-3055
FAX:
Ms. Susan Kerber, Fran. Sales Rep.

CHAMPION AUTO STORES offers the qualified entrepreneur the opportunity to own his own business in the automotive retail after-market. CHAMPION stores sell a wide variety of automotive parts, accessories, performance products and tires. Complete assistance provided in the areas of: training, inventory control, accounting, site selection, etc. No franchise fee.

HISTORY: . . . . .IFA
Established in 1956; . . 1st Franchised in 1961
Company-Owned Units (As of 12/1/1989): . 16
Franchised Units (12/1/1989): 122
Total Units (12/1/1989): 138
Distribution: . . . US-138;Can-0;Overseas-0
North America: . . . . 9 States
Concentration: . 52 in MN, 16 in NE, 14 in MT
Registered: . . . . .MN,ND,SD,WI
. . . .
Average # of Employees: . . . . . . 2 FT, 3 PT
Prior Industry Experience: . . . . Helpful

FINANCIAL:
Cash Investment: $65-100K
Total Investment: $130-200K
Fees: Franchise - $0
Royalty: 0%, Advert: 0%
Contract Periods (Yrs.): 1/1
Area Development Agreement: . .No
Sub-Franchise Contract: . . . . .No
Expand in Territory: . . . . . . Yes
Passive Ownership: . . . Discouraged
Encourage Conversions: . . . . . No
Franchisee Purchase(s) Required: .No

FRANCHISOR TRAINING/SUPPORT:
Financial Assistance Provided: . . . Yes(I)
Site Selection Assistance: . . . . .Yes
Lease Negotiation Assistance: . . . . .Yes
Co-operative Advertising: . . . . .Yes
Training: . . . .1 Wk. Headquarters, 2 Wks
. . . . Store Training, 1 Wk. Site
On-Going Support: . . . A,B,C,d,e,f,G,H,I
Full-Time Franchisor Support Staff: . .130
EXPANSION PLANS:
US: . . . . . . West, Midwest (Denver)
Canada - No, ...Overseas - No

CO-CO CAR CARE CENTRES

450 Mulock Dr.
Newmarket, ON L3Y4W1 CAN
TEL: (416) 836-0202
FAX: (416) 853-6598
Mr. George Moore, President

CO-CO SHINE offers a complete turn-key operation. We service the dealer, commercial and retail markets with our own brands of rust-proofing, shine and general care products. We also sell and service cellular telephones, window tinting, radios, mountings, etc.

HISTORY:	FINANCIAL:	FRANCHISOR TRAINING/SUPPORT:
Established in 1977; . . 1st Franchised in 1986	Cash Investment: $20-50K	Financial Assistance Provided: . . .Yes(D)
Company-Owned Units (As of 12/1/1989): . .2	Total Investment: $50K	Site Selection Assistance: . . . . .Yes
Franchised Units (12/1/1989): 5	Fees: Franchise - $20K	Lease Negotiation Assistance: . . . . .Yes
Total Units (12/1/1989): 7	Royalty: 8%, Advert: 2%	Co-operative Advertising: . . . . .Yes
Distribution: US-0;Can-7;Overseas-0	Contract Periods (Yrs.): 10/10	Training: . . . . 2 Days Headquarters,
North America: . . . . .1 Province	Area Development Agreement: Yes/10	. . . . 1 Wk. Franchisee Location
Concentration: . . . . 7 in ON	Sub-Franchise Contract: . . . . .No	On-Going Support: . . . . . B,C,D,e,F,H,I
Registered:	Expand in Territory: . . . . Yes	Full-Time Franchisor Support Staff: . . .5
. . . .	Passive Ownership: . . . Discouraged	EXPANSION PLANS:
Average # of Employees: . . . . .4 FT	Encourage Conversions: . . . . . Yes	US: . . . . Northeast
Prior Industry Experience: . . . . . . Helpful	Franchisee Purchase(s) Required: Yes	Canada - Yes, . . . Overseas - Yes

COBRA CAR PROTECTION CENTRES

2576 Haines Rd., # 4
Mississauga, ON L4Y1Y6 CAN
TEL: (416) 273-3061
FAX:
Mr. Sven Sverdrup, President

COBRA CAR PROTECTION CENTRES targets the rapidly-growing appearance and accessory market. Anchored by the PROTECTOIL rust protection system, COBRA provides professional cleaning, polishing and rust proofing services for both the wholesale and retail markets. A full line of light truck accessories is available for this explosive market.

HISTORY:	FINANCIAL:	FRANCHISOR TRAINING/SUPPORT:
Established in 1988; . . 1st Franchised in 1989	Cash Investment: $35K	Financial Assistance Provided: . . . . .No
Company-Owned Units (As of 12/1/1989): . .1	Total Investment: $60K	Site Selection Assistance: . . . . . . .Yes
Franchised Units (12/1/1989): 2	Fees: Franchise - . . . .$	Lease Negotiation Assistance: . . . . .Yes
Total Units (12/1/1989): 3	Royalty: 5%, Advert: 3%	Co-operative Advertising: . . . . . . .Yes
Distribution: US-0;Can-3;Overseas-0	Contract Periods (Yrs.): 10/10	Training: . . . . . . 7-10 Days Franchisee's
North America: . . . . .1 Province	Area Development Agreement: . .No	. . . . .Shop
Concentration: . . . . 3 in ON	Sub-Franchise Contract: . . . . .No	On-Going Support: . . . . a,B,C,D,E,F,H,I
Registered:	Expand in Territory: . . . . Yes	Full-Time Franchisor Support Staff: . . .2
. . . .	Passive Ownership: . . . Discouraged	EXPANSION PLANS:
Average # of Employees: . . . . . . 3 FT, 1 PT	Encourage Conversions: . . . . . NA	US: . . . . Northeast
Prior Industry Experience: . . . . . . Helpful	Franchisee Purchase(s) Required: Yes	Canada - Yes, ...Overseas - No

COTTMAN TRANSMISSION SYSTEMS

240 New York Dr.
Fort Washington, PA 19034
TEL: (800) 233-5515 (215) 643-5885 C
FAX:
Mr. Gregory A. Mowry, Natl. Sales

COTTMAN TRANSMISSIONS began franchising 26 years ago and continues to build a solid foundation. Presently, there are 127 Centers making COTTMAN the 2nd largest transmission repair organization. COTTMAN franchisees are provided with training, location assistance, financial consulting, center preparation and recruitment, advertising and promotions.

HISTORY: . . . . IFA	FINANCIAL:	FRANCHISOR TRAINING/SUPPORT:
Established in 1962; . . 1st Franchised in 1964	Cash Investment: $35-40k	Financial Assistance Provided: . . . Yes(I)
Company-Owned Units (As of 12/1/1989): . .2	Total Investment: $97.5K	Site Selection Assistance: . . . . . . .Yes
Franchised Units (12/1/1989): 125	Fees: Franchise - $22.5K	Lease Negotiation Assistance: . . . . .Yes
Total Units (12/1/1989): 127	Royalty: 7.5%, Advert: . . . . . Varies	Co-operative Advertising: . . . . . . .Yes
Distribution: US-125;Can-2;Overseas-0	Contract Periods (Yrs.): 15/15	Training: . . . . 3 Wks. Headquarters,
North America: . . . . 20 States, 2 Provinces	Area Development Agreement: . .No	. . . . 1 Wk. On-site
Concentration: . . 29 in PA, 18 in NJ, 15 in FL	Sub-Franchise Contract: . . . . .No	On-Going Support: . . . .B,C,D,E,F,G,H,I
Registered: . . .CA,IL,IN,MD,MI,MN,NY,ND	Expand in Territory: . . . . Yes	Full-Time Franchisor Support Staff: . . 35
. . . . .RI,SD,VA,WI	Passive Ownership: . . . Discouraged	EXPANSION PLANS:
Average # of Employees: . . . . .4 FT	Encourage Conversions: . . . . . Yes	US: . . . . .All US
Prior Industry Experience: . . . . . . Helpful	Franchisee Purchase(s) Required: .No	Canada - Yes, ...Overseas - No

DETAIL PLUS CAR APPEARANCE CENTERS
P.O. Box 14276
Portland, OR 97214
TEL: (800) 284-0123 (503) 231-4810 C
FAX: (503) 231-7512
Mr. R.L. Abraham, President

DETAIL PLUS CAR APPEARANCE CENTERS offers a high-tech, professional facility that provides a wide selection of auto detail services, including washing, engine cleaning, interior shampoo, buff and wax, etc. The Company provides everything - equipment, accessories, chemicals, training, management systems.

HISTORY: . . . .
Established in 1982; . . 1st Franchised in 1982
Company-Owned Units (As of 12/1/1989): . .2
Franchised Units (12/1/1989): 98
Total Units (12/1/1989): 100
Distribution: . . . US-77;Can-5;Overseas-18
North America: . . . . . 15 States, 1 Province
Concentration: . . . .
Registered: . . . . AB
. . . .
Average # of Employees: . . . . . . 3 FT, 3 PT
Prior Industry Experience: . . . . Helpful

FINANCIAL:
Cash Investment: $25-50K
Total Investment: $50-150K
Fees: Franchise - . . . . $10K+
　Royalty: 0%, Advert: 0%
Contract Periods (Yrs.): . . . .Varies
Area Development Agreement: Yes/Var
Sub-Franchise Contract: . . . . . Yes
Expand in Territory: . . . . Yes
Passive Ownership: . . . Discouraged
Encourage Conversions: . . . . . Yes
Franchisee Purchase(s) Required: .No

FRANCHISOR TRAINING/SUPPORT:
Financial Assistance Provided: . . . Yes(I)
Site Selection Assistance: . . . . .Yes
Lease Negotiation Assistance: . . . . .NA
Co-operative Advertising: . . . . .NA
Training: . . . . .1-2 Wks. on Site
. . . .
On-Going Support: . . . . . b,C,D,E,F,h,I
Full-Time Franchisor Support Staff: . . 15
EXPANSION PLANS:
US: . . . . .All US
Canada - No, ... Overseas - Yes

DR. NICK'S TRANSMISSIONS

150 Broadhollow Rd.
Melville, NY 11747
TEL: (516) 385-0330 C
FAX:
Mr. Nick Costa, Sales Director

Transmission service centers, providing quality repairs to all types of auto and light-duty commercial vehicles in both the retail and wholesale trade.

HISTORY: . . . .
Established in 1971; . . 1st Franchised in 1977
Company-Owned Units (As of 12/1/1989): . .0
Franchised Units (12/1/1989): 34
Total Units (12/1/1989): 34
Distribution: US-34;Can-0;Overseas-0
North America: . . . . 5 States
Concentration: . . .18 in NY, 5 in MA, 4 in NJ
Registered: . . . . .FL,NY,RI
. . . .
Average # of Employees: . . . . .4 FT
Prior Industry Experience: . . . . Helpful

FINANCIAL:
Cash Investment: $35-45K
Total Investment: $75-85K
Fees: Franchise - $21.5K
　Royalty: 7%, Advert: . . . . . Flat
Contract Periods (Yrs.): 15/15
Area Development Agreement: . .No
Sub-Franchise Contract: . . . . .No
Expand in Territory: . . . . Yes
Passive Ownership: . . . Not Allowed
Encourage Conversions: . . . . . Yes
Franchisee Purchase(s) Required: .No

FRANCHISOR TRAINING/SUPPORT:
Financial Assistance Provided: . . . Yes(I)
Site Selection Assistance: . . . . .Yes
Lease Negotiation Assistance: . . . . .Yes
Co-operative Advertising: . . . . .Yes
Training: . . . . 2 Wks. Headquarters,
. . . . .2 Wks. Site, On-going
On-Going Support: . . . A,C,D,E,F,G,H,I
Full-Time Franchisor Support Staff: . . . 6
EXPANSION PLANS:
US: . . . . Northeast & Southeast
Canada - No, ...Overseas - No

EAGLESPEED OIL & LUBE

20 Brace Rd.
Cherry Hill, NJ 08034
TEL: (609) 428-4315
FAX:
Mr. Boyce Overstreet

EAGLESPEED provides franchise owners with a total turn-key package, including real estate, equipment leasing and financing, training, advertising and continuous assistance from the auto service industry. List of all franchise locations is available.

HISTORY: . . . .
Established in 1986; . . 1st Franchised in 1986
Company-Owned Units (As of 12/1/1989): . .2
Franchised Units (12/1/1989): . . . . . .,. . 21
Total Units (12/1/1989): 23
Distribution: US-23;Can-0;Overseas-0
North America: . . . . 7 States
Concentration: . . . 13 in NJ, 6 in PA, 1 in CT
Registered: . . . . NY
. . . .
Average # of Employees: . . . . . . 2 FT, 1 PT
Prior Industry Experience: . . . . Helpful

FINANCIAL:
Cash Investment: $25-100K
Total Investment: $80-100K
Fees: Franchise - $16K
　Royalty: 6%, Advert: 6%
Contract Periods (Yrs.): 10/5
Area Development Agreement: Yes/10
Sub-Franchise Contract: . . . . . Yes
Expand in Territory: . . . . Yes
Passive Ownership: . . . . . .Allowed
Encourage Conversions: . . . . . Yes
Franchisee Purchase(s) Required: .No

FRANCHISOR TRAINING/SUPPORT:
Financial Assistance Provided: . . .Yes(D)
Site Selection Assistance: . . . . .Yes
Lease Negotiation Assistance: . . . . .Yes
Co-operative Advertising: . . . . .Yes
Training: . . . . .1 Wk. Headquarters,
. . . . 1 Wk. Site
On-Going Support: . . . . . B,C,D,E,G,H
Full-Time Franchisor Support Staff: . . 14
EXPANSION PLANS:
US: . . . . Northeast
Canada - No, ...Overseas - No

ECONO LUBE N' TUNE

4911 Birch St.
Newport Beach, CA 92660
TEL: (800)327-4802 (800)542-2003(CA)
FAX:
Franchise Development Dept.

Turn-key franchise opportunity, specializing in Automotive Aftermarket Services. We feature Multi-Service menu including: Lube/oil, tune-up, brakes, shocks, transmission, emission control and minor repairs. Custom, free-standing 5- or 6-bay buildings in high-traffic/growth areas.

HISTORY: . . . .
Established in 1973; . . 1st Franchised in 1978
Company-Owned Units (As of 12/1/1989): . 29
Franchised Units (12/1/1989): 137
Total Units (12/1/1989): 156
Distribution: US-156;Can-0;Overseas-0
North America: . . . . 11 States
Concentration: . . 107 in CA, 15 in AZ, 13 TX
Registered: . . . . CA,MD,VA,WA
. . . .
Average # of Employees: . . . . 5-6 FT, 1-2 PT
Prior Industry Experience: . . . . Helpful

FINANCIAL:
Cash Investment: $85-115K
Total Investment: $190-210K
Fees: Franchise - $79.5K
Royalty: 6%, Advert: 8%
Contract Periods (Yrs.): 15/5
Area Development Agreement: . .No
Sub-Franchise Contract: . . . . .No
Expand in Territory: . . . . . . Yes
Passive Ownership: . . . Not Allowed
Encourage Conversions: . . . . .No
Franchisee Purchase(s) Required: .No

FRANCHISOR TRAINING/SUPPORT:
Financial Assistance Provided: . . .Yes(D)
Site Selection Assistance: . . . . . . .Yes
Lease Negotiation Assistance: . . . . .NA
Co-operative Advertising: . . . . . . .Yes
Training: . . . . .2 Wks. in Class, 1-2
. . . . Wks. in Store
On-Going Support: . . . . . A,B,C,D,E,H
Full-Time Franchisor Support Staff: . . 35
EXPANSION PLANS:
US: . . . . .All US
Canada - No, ...Overseas - No

ENDRUST AUTO APPEARANCE CENTERS

1725 Washington Rd., # 205
Pittsburgh, PA 15241
TEL: (412) 831-1255
FAX:
Mr. Gary Griser, VP Mktg.

Engaged in establishing dealerships for ENDRUST AUTO APPEARANCE CENTERS. Services include exterior paint sealants, fabric protection, clean-ups, waxing, detailing, reconditioning, sun roofs, rustproofing, sound deadening, undercoating. All appearance protection services. ENDRUST products supplied to the dealer are the finest quality products.

HISTORY: . . . .
Established in 1969; . . 1st Franchised in 1969
Company-Owned Units (As of 12/1/1989): . .1
Franchised Units (12/1/1989): 80
Total Units (12/1/1989): 81
Distribution: US-81;Can-0;Overseas-0
North America: . . . . 8 States
Concentration: . . . .
Registered: . . . . All States
. . . .
Average # of Employees: . . . . .Varies
Prior Industry Experience: . . . . Helpful

FINANCIAL:
Cash Investment: $30K
Total Investment: $30K
Fees: Franchise - $0
Royalty: 0%, Advert: 0%
Contract Periods (Yrs.): . . . .
Area Development Agreement: . Yes
Sub-Franchise Contract: . . . .
Expand in Territory: . . . . . . Yes
Passive Ownership: . . . . . .Allowed
Encourage Conversions: . . . . Yes
Franchisee Purchase(s) Required: Yes

FRANCHISOR TRAINING/SUPPORT:
Financial Assistance Provided: . . . . .No
Site Selection Assistance: . . . . . . .Yes
Lease Negotiation Assistance: . . . . .Yes
Co-operative Advertising: . . . . .No
Training: . . . . Varies at Site
. . . .
On-Going Support: . . . . . . .B,C,D,E,G
Full-Time Franchisor Support Staff: . . .
EXPANSION PLANS:
US: . . . . .All US
Canada - Yes, . . . Overseas - Yes

EXPRESS 10 MINUTE LUBE CENTER

66 Rte. 125, Unit 5
Kingston, NH 03848
TEL: (603) 642-8893 C
FAX: (603) 642-7723
Mr. Gary Krause, Dir. Fran. Ops.

EXPRESS 10 MINUTE LUBE is a strong competitor in the fastest-growing segment of the automotive after-market industry, commonly called "fast lube," "quick lube," "quick tune-up," etc. The history-making growth rate is high due to an ever-increasing market and the proven track record of strong return on investment.

HISTORY: . . . . .IFA
Established in 1985; . . 1st Franchised in 1988
Company-Owned Units (As of 12/1/1989): . .5
Franchised Units (12/1/1989): 5
Total Units (12/1/1989): 10
Distribution: US-10;Can-0;Overseas-0
North America: . . . . 2 States
Concentration: . . . . 6 in NH, 4 in MA
Registered: . . . .
. . . .
Average # of Employees: . . . . . . 4' FT, 4 PT
Prior Industry Experience: . . . . Helpful

FINANCIAL:
Cash Investment: $25-50K
Total Investment: $85-125K
Fees: Franchise - $25K
Royalty: 5%, Advert: 8%
Contract Periods (Yrs.): 5/5/5
Area Development Agreement: Yes/5
Sub-Franchise Contract: . . . . .No
Expand in Territory: . . . . Yes
Passive Ownership: . . . Discouraged
Encourage Conversions: . . . . .No
Franchisee Purchase(s) Required: .No

FRANCHISOR TRAINING/SUPPORT:
Financial Assistance Provided: . . . Yes(I)
Site Selection Assistance: . . . . . . .Yes
Lease Negotiation Assistance: . . . . .Yes
Co-operative Advertising: . . . . . . .Yes
Training: . . . . 2 Wks. Headquarters,
. . . . .1 Wk. Massachusetts Site
On-Going Support: . . . . .B,C,D,E,G,H,I
Full-Time Franchisor Support Staff: . . .6
EXPANSION PLANS:
US: . . . . New England Only
Canada - No, ... Overseas - No

EXPRESS OIL CHANGE

1725 27th Court S.
Birmingham, AL 35209
TEL: (205) 870-1771
FAX:
Mr. Robert Daniel, Mktg. Dir.

A fast automobile maintenance store, designed to provide 4 quality services: 1) Ten Minute Express Oil Change; 2) Twenty Minute Express Transmission Service; 3) Thirty Minute Express Tune-Up; 4) Sixty Minute Express Brake Service.

HISTORY:	FINANCIAL:	FRANCHISOR TRAINING/SUPPORT:
Established in 1979; . . 1st Franchised in 1983	Cash Investment: $62-105K	Financial Assistance Provided: . . . . .No
Company-Owned Units (As of 12/1/1989): . .7	Total Investment: $100-250K	Site Selection Assistance: . . . . .No
Franchised Units (12/1/1989): 18	Fees: Franchise - $10K	Lease Negotiation Assistance: . . . . .No
Total Units (12/1/1989): 25	Royalty: 5%, Advert: 3%	Co-operative Advertising: . . . . .Yes
Distribution: US-25;Can-0;Overseas-0	Contract Periods (Yrs.): 10/10	Training: . . . . 2 Wks. Headquarters,
North America: . . . . 2 States	Area Development Agreement: . Yes	. . . . 1 Wk Site
Concentration: . . . . .23 in AL, 2 in SC	Sub-Franchise Contract: . . . . . Yes	On-Going Support: . . . . . . .B,C,D,E,G
Registered:	Expand in Territory: . . . . Yes	Full-Time Franchisor Support Staff: . .100
. . . .	Passive Ownership: . . . Discouraged	EXPANSION PLANS:
Average # of Employees: . . . . .6 FT	Encourage Conversions: . . . . . Yes	US: . . . . Southeast
Prior Industry Experience: . . . . . . Helpful	Franchisee Purchase(s) Required: .No	Canada - No, ...Overseas - No

FANTASY COACHWORKS

6034 S. Lindbergh Blvd.
St. Louis, MO 63123
TEL: (314) 487-0054
FAX:
Mr. James Smoot, President

A new concept in automotive retailing - the world's first "Auto Boutique," featuring motoring accessories for all cars, vans, imports and pickups, plus designer wearables for the driving enthusiast. Sheepskin seat covers, sunroofs, louvers, window tint, front bras, driving gloves, automotive jewelry and exotic art works. Installation available.

HISTORY: . . . . .IFA	FINANCIAL:	FRANCHISOR TRAINING/SUPPORT:
Established in 1975; . . 1st Franchised in 1982	Cash Investment: $20-30K	Financial Assistance Provided: . . . Yes(I)
Company-Owned Units (As of 12/1/1989): . .3	Total Investment: $65-85K	Site Selection Assistance: . . . . .Yes
Franchised Units (12/1/1989): 24	Fees: Franchise - $19K	Lease Negotiation Assistance: . . . . .Yes
Total Units (12/1/1989): 27	Royalty: 6%, Advert: 2%	Co-operative Advertising: . . . . .Yes
Distribution: US-27;Can-0;Overseas-0	Contract Periods (Yrs.): . . . 10/10	Training: . . . . 2 Wks. Headquarters
North America: . . . . 6 States	Area Development Agreement: Yes/10	. . . .
Concentration:	Sub-Franchise Contract: . . . . Yes	On-Going Support: . . . . C,d,E,f,G,H,i
Registered: . . . . FL,IL,IN	Expand in Territory: . . . . .No	Full-Time Franchisor Support Staff: . . . 6
. . . .	Passive Ownership: . . . Discouraged	EXPANSION PLANS:
Average # of Employees: . . . . . . 3 FT, 1 PT	Encourage Conversions: . . . . . .No	US: . . . . .All US
Prior Industry Experience: . . . . Helpful	Franchisee Purchase(s) Required: .No	Canada - No, ...Overseas - No

FLY-N-HI OFFROAD CENTER

701 S. 7th St.
Phoenix, AZ 85034
TEL: (602) 263-1225
FAX:
Mr. Ken Hollowell, Mktg. Dir.

FLY-N-HI offers a specialty outlet for the selling of truck parts and accessories, as well as service to its customers.

HISTORY:	FINANCIAL:	FRANCHISOR TRAINING/SUPPORT:
Established in 1982; . . 1st Franchised in 1989	Cash Investment: $150-200K	Financial Assistance Provided: . . . . .No
Company-Owned Units (As of 12/1/1989): . .0	Total Investment: $150-200K	Site Selection Assistance: . . . . .Yes
Franchised Units (12/1/1989): 4	Fees: Franchise - $15K	Lease Negotiation Assistance: . . . . .Yes
Total Units (12/1/1989): 4	Royalty: 5%, Advert: 2%	Co-operative Advertising: . . . . .Yes
Distribution: US-4;Can-0;Overseas-0	Contract Periods (Yrs.): 10/10	Training: . . . . 2 Wks. Headquarters
North America: . . . . .1 State	Area Development Agreement: . .No	. . . .
Concentration: . . . . 4 in AZ	Sub-Franchise Contract: . . . . . .No	On-Going Support: . . . .B,C,D,E,F,G,h,I
Registered: . . . . CA	Expand in Territory: . . . . .No	Full-Time Franchisor Support Staff: . . . 4
. . . .	Passive Ownership: . . . . . .Allowed	EXPANSION PLANS:
Average # of Employees: . . . . . 4-8 FT, 2 PT	Encourage Conversions: . . . . . Yes	US: . . . . Southwest Only
Prior Industry Experience: . . . . Helpful	Franchisee Purchase(s) Required: .No	Canada - No, ...Overseas - No

GIBRALTAR TRANSMISSION

5 Delaware Dr.
Lake Success, NY 11042
TEL: (516) 358-5500
FAX:
Mr. William Grimm, VP Sales/Mktg.

GIBRALTAR TRANSMISSIONS offers its franchisees an exclusive territory, a computerized software program that aids in all phases of management and sales, personalized field operations support and regional offices in local areas. Additionally, we provide technical support and a hot line for technical questions.

HISTORY: . . . . IFA
Established in 1977; . . 1st Franchised in 1978
Company-Owned Units (As of 12/1/1989): . .8
Franchised Units (12/1/1989): 70
Total Units (12/1/1989): 78
Distribution: US-78;Can-0;Overseas-0
North America: . . . . 11 States
Concentration: . .43 in CA, 28 in NY, 28 in NJ
Registered: . . . . CA,FL,NY
. . . .
Average # of Employees: . . . . .4 FT
Prior Industry Experience: . . . . . . Helpful

FINANCIAL:
Cash Investment: $45-100K
Total Investment: $120K
Fees: Franchise - $30K
Royalty: 8%, Advert: 0%
Contract Periods (Yrs.): 15/15
Area Development Agreement: Yes/1
Sub-Franchise Contract: . . . . .No
Expand in Territory: . . . . . . .No
Passive Ownership: . . . Discouraged
Encourage Conversions: . . . . .No
Franchisee Purchase(s) Required: Yes

FRANCHISOR TRAINING/SUPPORT:
Financial Assistance Provided: . . . Yes(I)
Site Selection Assistance: . . . . . . .Yes
Lease Negotiation Assistance: . . . . .Yes
Co-operative Advertising: . . . . No
Training: . . . . 3 Wks. Headquarters,
. . . . On-going Schools at Headquarters
On-Going Support: . . . . . .C,D,E,G,H,I
Full-Time Franchisor Support Staff: . . 25
EXPANSION PLANS:
US: . . . . .All US
Canada - No, ...Overseas - No

GOODYEAR CERTIFIED AUTO SERVICE

10 Four Seasons Place
Etobicoke, ON M9B6G2 CAN
TEL: (416) 626-4611
FAX:
Mr. Mario Ricci, Mgr. of Finance

More people in N. America ride on GOODYEAR tires than any other brand. GOODYEAR CERTIFIED AUTO SERVICE offers consumers complete and reliable automobile servicing. World-wide consumer confidence in our products lets us know, when people want tires, they think GOODYEAR and that means profit for you.

HISTORY: . . . .
Established in 1914; . . 1st Franchised in 1973
Company-Owned Units (As of 12/1/1989): . 94
Franchised Units (12/1/1989): 46
Total Units (12/1/1989): 140
Distribution: . . . US-0;Can-140;Overseas-0
North America: . . . . 9 Provinces
Concentration: . 63 in ON, 28 in PQ, 19 in AB
Registered: . . . . AB
. . . .
Average # of Employees: . . . . . . 8 FT, 2 PT
Prior Industry Experience: . . . . . . Helpful

FINANCIAL: TSE-GDYR
Cash Investment: $125K
Total Investment: $150K
Fees: Franchise - $0
Royalty: 3%, Advert: . . . Varies
Contract Periods (Yrs.): 5/5
Area Development Agreement: . .No
Sub-Franchise Contract: . . . . .No
Expand in Territory: . . . . . . Yes
Passive Ownership: . . . Discouraged
Encourage Conversions: . . . . . Yes
Franchisee Purchase(s) Required: Yes

FRANCHISOR TRAINING/SUPPORT:
Financial Assistance Provided: . . . Yes(I)
Site Selection Assistance: . . . . . . .Yes
Lease Negotiation Assistance: . . . . .Yes
Co-operative Advertising: . . . . .Yes
Training: . . . . Varies According To
. . . . Individual Experience
On-Going Support: . . A,B,C,D,E,F,G,H,I
Full-Time Franchisor Support Staff: . . . .
EXPANSION PLANS:
US: . . . . .No
Canada - Yes, ...Overseas - No

GREASE 'N GO

526 E. Juanita, # 6
Mesa, AZ 85204
TEL: (602) 497-4710
FAX:
Mr. Richard Lindstrom

GREASE 'N GO is an operations-based company. Our roots come from the actual day-to-day operations of quick-lube centers. We know what it takes to make it in the quick-lube business!

HISTORY: . . . .
Established in 1984; . . 1st Franchised in 1985
Company-Owned Units (As of 12/1/1989): . .0
Franchised Units (12/1/1989): 24
Total Units (12/1/1989): 24
Distribution: US-24;Can-0;Overseas-0
North America: . . . . 18 States
Concentration: . . . . 15 in AZ
Registered: . . . . FL,HI,OR,RI
. . . .
Average # of Employees: . . . . . . 4 FT, 1 PT
Prior Industry Experience: . . . . . . Helpful

FINANCIAL:
Cash Investment: $25-50K
Total Investment: $75-125K
Fees: Franchise - $27.5K
Royalty: 5%, Advert: 8%
Contract Periods (Yrs.): . . . 20/10
Area Development Agreement: Yes/Var
Sub-Franchise Contract: . . . . .No
Expand in Territory: . . . . . . Yes
Passive Ownership: . . . . . .Allowed
Encourage Conversions: . . . . . Yes
Franchisee Purchase(s) Required: .No

FRANCHISOR TRAINING/SUPPORT:
Financial Assistance Provided: . . . Yes(I)
Site Selection Assistance: . . . . . . .Yes
Lease Negotiation Assistance: . . . . .Yes
Co-operative Advertising: . . . . No
Training: . . . . 2 Wks. Headquarters,
. . . . 1 Wk. Franchisee Location
On-Going Support: . . . . .A,C,D,E,F,G
Full-Time Franchisor Support Staff: . . .5
EXPANSION PLANS:
US: . . . . .All US
Canada - Yes, . . . Overseas - Yes

GREASE MONKEY

1660 Wynkoop St., # 1160
Denver, CO 80202
TEL: (800) 822-7706 (303) 534-1660
FAX: (303) 534-2906
Mr. Kurt R. Kempfer, Fran. Dev. Mgr.

Ten-minute oil change and vehicle lubrication business. Complete training school, followed by full operations field support. Site approval, building design, marketing and accounting procedures supplied.

HISTORY: . . . . IFA
Established in 1978; . . 1st Franchised in 1978
Company-Owned Units (As of 12/1/1989): . 12
Franchised Units (12/1/1989): 384
Total Units (12/1/1989): 396
Distribution: . . . US-396;Can-0;Overseas-0
North America: . . . . 35 States
Concentration: . .39 in CO, 10 in OH, 7 in VA
Registered: . . . . .All
. . . .
Average # of Employees: . . . . .5 FT
Prior Industry Experience: . . . . . . Helpful

FINANCIAL: NASD-GMHC
Cash Investment: $75-135K
Total Investment: . . . . $250-300K+
Fees: Franchise - $25K
Royalty: 5%, Advert: 6%
Contract Periods (Yrs.): 15/15
Area Development Agreement: . .No
Sub-Franchise Contract: . . . . .No
Expand in Territory: . . . . Yes
Passive Ownership: . . . . . .Allowed
Encourage Conversions: . . . . . Yes
Franchisee Purchase(s) Required: .No

FRANCHISOR TRAINING/SUPPORT:
Financial Assistance Provided: . . . Yes(I)
Site Selection Assistance: . . . . . . .Yes
Lease Negotiation Assistance: . . . . .Yes
Co-operative Advertising: . . . . . . .Yes
Training: . . . . .1 Wk. Headquarters,
. . . . 1 Wk. Field Training
On-Going Support: . . . . B,C,D,E,F,G,H
Full-Time Franchisor Support Staff: . . 30
EXPANSION PLANS:
US: . . . . .All US
Canada - No, ...Overseas - No

GREAT BEAR AUTOMOTIVE CENTERS

100 Merrick Rd., # 206W
Rockville Centre, NY 11570
TEL: (800) US-BEARS (516) 764-6700
FAX: (516) 764-6972
Mr. Ken Loderhose, EVP

GREAT BEAR AUTO CENTERS are old-fashioned neighborhood repair centers, featuring brakes, tune-ups, front-end, exhaust, oil changes, state inspections, shocks, struts, coils and springs.

HISTORY: . . . .
Established in 1933; . . 1st Franchised in 1965
Company-Owned Units (As of 12/1/1989): . .8
Franchised Units (12/1/1989): 52
Total Units (12/1/1989): 60
Distribution: . . . US-60;Can-0;Overseas-0
North America: . . . . 5 States
Concentration: . . . 38 in NY, 7 in FL, 3 in NJ
Registered: . . . . FL,NY
. . . .
Average # of Employees: . . . . . . 4 FT, 2 PT
Prior Industry Experience: . . . . Helpful

FINANCIAL: OTC
Cash Investment: $75-100K
Total Investment: $175-250K
Fees: Franchise - $20K
Royalty: 7%, Advert: 5%
Contract Periods (Yrs.): 15/15
Area Development Agreement: Yes/15
Sub-Franchise Contract: . . . . .No
Expand in Territory: . . . . Yes
Passive Ownership: . . . Discouraged
Encourage Conversions: . . . . . Yes
Franchisee Purchase(s) Required: .No

FRANCHISOR TRAINING/SUPPORT:
Financial Assistance Provided: . . . Yes(I)
Site Selection Assistance: . . . . . . .Yes
Lease Negotiation Assistance: . . . . .Yes
Co-operative Advertising: . . . . . . .Yes
Training: . . . . 2 Wks. Headquarters,
. . . . .2 Wks. in FL
On-Going Support: . . . . D,E
Full-Time Franchisor Support Staff: . . . 6
EXPANSION PLANS:
US: . . . . .New York Metro, FL and GA
Canada - No, ...Overseas - No

GUARANTEED TUNE UP

101 Eisenhower Pkwy.
Roseland, NJ 07068
TEL: (800) 543-5829 (201) 403-1996 C
FAX: (201) 226-3096
Mr. William Okita, President

Although we specialize in automotive tune-ups for $59.88, with a 6 month/6,000 mile guarantee, we allow our franchisees to perform all automotive repairs, such as brakes, engine repairs, etc., thereby increasing their cash flow and sales volume.

HISTORY: . . . .
Established in 1983; . . 1st Franchised in 1984
Company-Owned Units (As of 12/1/1989): . .1
Franchised Units (12/1/1989): 18
Total Units (12/1/1989): 19
Distribution: US-19;Can-0;Overseas-0
North America: . . . . 6 States
Concentration: . . . 10 in NJ, 2 in NC, 1 in NY
Registered: . . . . FL,MN,NY,RI,VA
. . . .
Average # of Employees: . . . . .4 FT
Prior Industry Experience: . . . . Helpful

FINANCIAL: OTC-Gtui
Cash Investment: $25K
Total Investment: $85-115K
Fees: Franchise - $15K
Royalty: 6%, Advert: 4%
Contract Periods (Yrs.): 10/10
Area Development Agreement: Yes/10
Sub-Franchise Contract: . . . . . Yes
Expand in Territory: . . . . Yes
Passive Ownership: . . . . . .Allowed
Encourage Conversions: . . . . . Yes
Franchisee Purchase(s) Required: .No

FRANCHISOR TRAINING/SUPPORT:
Financial Assistance Provided: . . . Yes(I)
Site Selection Assistance: . . . . . . .Yes
Lease Negotiation Assistance: . . . . .Yes
Co-operative Advertising: . . . . . . .Yes
Training: . . . . 1 Wk. New Jersey,
. . . . 1 Wk. Local Franchisor
On-Going Support: . . . . .B,C,D,E,F,H
Full-Time Franchisor Support Staff: . . . 5
EXPANSION PLANS:
US: . . . . .All US
Canada - Yes, . . . Overseas - Yes

JIFFY LUBE

6000 Metro Dr.
Baltimore, MD 21215
TEL: (800) 327-9532 (301) 764-3555
FAX:
Mr. Fred J. Gibson

Automobile fluid specialists, providing preventive maintenance for your car's vital fluids. We offer the consumer quality and convenience at a competitive price.

HISTORY: . . . . IFA	FINANCIAL: OTC-JLUB	FRANCHISOR TRAINING/SUPPORT:
Established in 1979; . . 1st Franchised in 1979	Cash Investment: $35K	Financial Assistance Provided: . . . Yes(I)
Company-Owned Units (As of 12/1/1989): . 70	Total Investment: $130K	Site Selection Assistance: . . . . .Yes
Franchised Units (12/1/1989): 1052	Fees: Franchise - $35K	Lease Negotiation Assistance: . . . . .Yes
Total Units (12/1/1989): 1122	Royalty: 6%, Advert: 8%	Co-operative Advertising: . . . . .Yes
Distribution: . . . US-1095;Can-20;Overseas-7	Contract Periods (Yrs.): 20/0	Training: . . . . 2 Wks. Headquarters
North America: . . . . 40 States, 3 Provinces	Area Development Agreement: Yes/Var	. . . .
Concentration:	Sub-Franchise Contract: . . . . .No	On-Going Support: . . . . a,B,C,D,E,G,H,I
Registered: . . . . .All	Expand in Territory: . . . . Yes	Full-Time Franchisor Support Staff: . .226
. . . .	Passive Ownership: . . . Not Allowed	EXPANSION PLANS:
Average # of Employees: . . . . . . 6 FT, 2 PT	Encourage Conversions: . . . . . Yes	US: . . . . .All US
Prior Industry Experience: . . . . Helpful	Franchisee Purchase(s) Required: .No	Canada - No, ... Overseas - Yes

K & N MOBILE DISTRIBUTION

4909 Rondo Dr.
Fort Worth, TX 76106
TEL: (817) 626-2885
FAX: (817) 624-3721
Mr. Curtis L. Nelson, VP

When manufacturing and service businesses need electrical connectors, fasteners, wire and cable fast, your custom Mobile Warehouse delivers. Easy-to-use, on-board computer and electronic communications equipment make record keeping a snap, leaving you more time to service customers.

HISTORY: . . . . IFA	FINANCIAL:	FRANCHISOR TRAINING/SUPPORT:
Established in 1972; . . 1st Franchised in 1987	Cash Investment: $45-55K	Financial Assistance Provided: . . . Yes(I)
Company-Owned Units (As of 12/1/1989): . 16	Total Investment: $75-120K	Site Selection Assistance: . . . . .Yes
Franchised Units (12/1/1989): 19	Fees: Franchise - $23.5K	Lease Negotiation Assistance: . . . . .NA
Total Units (12/1/1989): 35	Royalty: 13%, Advert: 1%	Co-operative Advertising: . . . . .NA
Distribution: US-35;Can-0;Overseas-0	Contract Periods (Yrs.): 5/5	Training: . . . . . . 15 Days, Headquarters,
North America: . . . . 14 States	Area Development Agreement: Yes/5	. . . . .3 Days On-site, On-going On-site
Concentration: . . .21 in TX, 2 in OK, 2 in LA	Sub-Franchise Contract: . . . . .No	On-Going Support: . . . . .A,B,C,D,G,h,I
Registered: . . . CA,FL,HI,IL,MD,MN,OR,RI	Expand in Territory: . . . . Yes	Full-Time Franchisor Support Staff: . . 40
. . . . VA,WA,WI	Passive Ownership: . . . Discouraged	EXPANSION PLANS:
Average # of Employees: . . . . . . 1 FT, 1 PT	Encourage Conversions: . . . . . Yes	US: . . . . .All US
Prior Industry Experience: . . . . Helpful	Franchisee Purchase(s) Required: .No	Canada - Yes, . . . Overseas - Yes

KENNEDY TRANSMISSION

9345 Penn Ave. S.
Bloomington, MN 55431
TEL: (612) 884-3688 C
FAX:
Mr. Dennis Bain, President

Service and repair of automobile transmissions and related drive line components, including light trucks, motor homes and foreign cars.

HISTORY:	FINANCIAL:	FRANCHISOR TRAINING/SUPPORT:
Established in 1962; . . 1st Franchised in 1975	Cash Investment: $30-45K	Financial Assistance Provided: . . . Yes(I)
Company-Owned Units (As of 12/1/1989): . .0	Total Investment: $75-125K	Site Selection Assistance: . . . . .Yes
Franchised Units (12/1/1989): 13	Fees: Franchise - $15K	Lease Negotiation Assistance: . . . . .Yes
Total Units (12/1/1989): 13	Royalty: 6%, Advert: 6%	Co-operative Advertising: . . . . .Yes
Distribution: US-13;Can-0;Overseas-0	Contract Periods (Yrs.): 15/10	Training: . . . . 2 Wks. Headquarters
North America: . . . . .1 State	Area Development Agreement: . Yes	. . . .
Concentration: . . . . 13 in MN	Sub-Franchise Contract: . . . . .No	On-Going Support: . . . . . . B,C,D,E,H,I
Registered: . . . . MN	Expand in Territory: . . . . Yes	Full-Time Franchisor Support Staff: . . . 4
. . . .	Passive Ownership: . . . Discouraged	EXPANSION PLANS:
Average # of Employees: . . . . .4 FT	Encourage Conversions: . . . . . Yes	US: . . . . MW, SE, SW
Prior Industry Experience: . . . . Helpful	Franchisee Purchase(s) Required: .No	Canada - No, ...Overseas - No

KING BEAR AUTO SERVICE CENTERS
1390 Jerusalem Ave.
North Merrick, NY 11566
TEL: (516) 483-3500
FAX: (516) 483-0615
Mr. Frank J. Garton, Fran. Dir.

KING BEAR AUTO SERVICE CENTERS, specializing in automotive repairs and sales, general auto repairs. All work performed by our specially-trained mechanics. Franchisees are not required to have any automotive backgrounds, but must have some sales or managerial experience.

HISTORY: . . . . IFA	FINANCIAL:	FRANCHISOR TRAINING/SUPPORT:
Established in 1973; . . 1st Franchised in 1974	Cash Investment: $95-126K	Financial Assistance Provided: . . . Yes(I)
Company-Owned Units (As of 12/1/1989): . .0	Total Investment: . . . .$	Site Selection Assistance: . . . . . . .Yes
Franchised Units (12/1/1989): 61	Fees: Franchise - $19.9K	Lease Negotiation Assistance: . . . . .Yes
Total Units (12/1/1989): 61	Royalty: 5%, Advert: 7%	Co-operative Advertising: . . . . . . .Yes
Distribution: US-61;Can-0;Overseas-0	Contract Periods (Yrs.): . . . 15/10	Training: . . . . 2 Wks. Headquarters,
North America: . . . . 2 States	Area Development Agreement: . Yes	. . . . . . On-going Franchisee Location
Concentration: . . . . . . .38 in NY, 23 in CA	Sub-Franchise Contract: . . . . . Yes	On-Going Support: . . A,B,C,D,E,F,G,H,I
Registered: . . . . CA,NY	Expand in Territory: . . . . .No	Full-Time Franchisor Support Staff: . . 21
. . . .	Passive Ownership: . . . Not Allowed	EXPANSION PLANS:
Average # of Employees: . . . . . . 4 FT, 1 PT	Encourage Conversions: . . . . . Yes	US: . . . . . Northeast, Southeast, S-west
Prior Industry Experience: . . . . Helpful	Franchisee Purchase(s) Required: .No	Canada - No, ...Overseas - No

LEE MYLES TRANSMISSIONS

25 E. Spring Valley Ave.
Maywood, NJ 07607
TEL: (800) LEE-MYLE (201) 843-3200
FAX:
Mr. Bert Stadtman, Fran. Sales

LEE MYLES automotive transmission service and repair. Operational, administrative and sales support systems. Lowest weekly franchise fees - 6%. Amongst the lowest license fee - $20,000. Business format franchisor. Automotive after-market repair business.

HISTORY: . . . . IFA	FINANCIAL:	FRANCHISOR TRAINING/SUPPORT:
Established in 1947; . . 1st Franchised in 1964	Cash Investment: $106K	Financial Assistance Provided: . . . Yes(I)
Company-Owned Units (As of 12/1/1989): . .1	Total Investment: $106K	Site Selection Assistance: . . . . . . .Yes
Franchised Units (12/1/1989): 101	Fees: Franchise - $20K	Lease Negotiation Assistance: . . . . .Yes
Total Units (12/1/1989): 102	Royalty: 6%, Advert: . . . . Varies	Co-operative Advertising: . . . . . . .Yes
Distribution: . . . US-102;Can-0;Overseas-0	Contract Periods (Yrs.): . . . 15/15	Training: . . . . 2 Wks. Headquarters
North America: . . . . 5 States	Area Development Agreement: Yes/15	. . . .
Concentration: . . 48 in NY, 28 in NE, 7 in AZ	Sub-Franchise Contract: . . . . . Yes	On-Going Support: . . . A,C,D,E,F,G,H,I
Registered: . . . . FL,NY,RI	Expand in Territory: . . . . Yes	Full-Time Franchisor Support Staff: . . 28
. . . .	Passive Ownership: . . . Discouraged	EXPANSION PLANS:
Average # of Employees: . . . . . . 1 FT, 3 PT	Encourage Conversions: . . . . . Yes	US: . . . . .All US
Prior Industry Experience: . . . . Helpful	Franchisee Purchase(s) Required: .No	Canada - No, ...Overseas - No

LENTZ U.S.A. SERVICE CENTER

1001 Riverview Dr.
Kalamazoo, MI 49001
TEL: (616) 342-2200
FAX:
Mr. Gordon Lentz, President

Automotive services - specializing in exhaust systems, braking systems, suspension systems and front-end work.

HISTORY: . . . . IFA	FINANCIAL:	FRANCHISOR TRAINING/SUPPORT:
Established in 1983; . . 1st Franchised in 1986	Cash Investment: $35-50K	Financial Assistance Provided: . . . Yes(I)
Company-Owned Units (As of 12/1/1989): . .9	Total Investment: . . . $60-80K+RE	Site Selection Assistance: . . . . . . .Yes
Franchised Units (12/1/1989): 1	Fees: Franchise - $18.5K	Lease Negotiation Assistance: . . . . .Yes
Total Units (12/1/1989): 10	Royalty: 7%, Advert: 5%	Co-operative Advertising: . . . . .No
Distribution: US-10;Can-0;Overseas-0	Contract Periods (Yrs.): . . . 15/15	Training: . . . . 4 Wks. Headquarters
North America: . . . . .1 State	Area Development Agreement: . .No	. . . .
Concentration: . . . . .10 in MI	Sub-Franchise Contract: . . . . . .No	On-Going Support: . . . . . . C,D,E,F,H,I
Registered: . . . . .MI	Expand in Territory: . . . . Yes	Full-Time Franchisor Support Staff: . . 53
. . . .	Passive Ownership: . . . Discouraged	EXPANSION PLANS:
Average # of Employees: . . . . . . 4 FT, 1 PT	Encourage Conversions: . . . . . Yes	US: . . . . Midwest
Prior Industry Experience: . . . . Helpful	Franchisee Purchase(s) Required: .No	Canada - No, ...Overseas - No

LUBE PRO'S INTERNATIONAL

1900 N. Roselle Rd., # 403
Schaumburg, IL 60195
TEL: (800) 654-5823 (312) 882-3500 C
FAX:
Mr. David Beebe, Fran. Dir.

Automotive quick-oil change and lubrication service. Extensive site evaluation, 17 days of training (incl. franchisee's center) and a pool of pre-trained managers available for employment by franchisee. Growth is anticipated in the Eastern 2/3rds of the US. Area Development available.

HISTORY: . . . . IFA	FINANCIAL:	FRANCHISOR TRAINING/SUPPORT:
Established in 1978; . . 1st Franchised in 1985	Cash Investment: $45-150K	Financial Assistance Provided: . . . Yes(I)
Company-Owned Units (As of 12/1/1989): . .5	Total Investment: $160-500K	Site Selection Assistance: . . . . . . .Yes
Franchised Units (12/1/1989): 15	Fees: Franchise - $25K	Lease Negotiation Assistance: . . . . .Yes
Total Units (12/1/1989): 20	Royalty: 5%, Advert: 5%	Co-operative Advertising: . . . . No
Distribution: US-20;Can-0;Overseas-0	Contract Periods (Yrs.): . . . 20/10	Training: . . . . . . 10 Days Headquarters,
North America: . . . . 2 States	Area Development Agreement: Yes/20	. . . . 7 Days Site
Concentration: . . . . 8 in IL, 5 in WI	Sub-Franchise Contract: . . . . .No	On-Going Support: . . . . . . B,C,D,E,G,I
Registered: . . . . IL,IN,MI	Expand in Territory: . . . . Yes	Full-Time Franchisor Support Staff: . . .7
. . . .	Passive Ownership: . . . . . .Allowed	EXPANSION PLANS:
Average # of Employees: . . . . .5 FT	Encourage Conversions: . . . . . Yes	US: . . . . NE, SE and Midwest
Prior Industry Experience: . . . . Helpful	Franchisee Purchase(s) Required: .No	Canada - No, ...Overseas - No

LUBE WAGON, THE

9430 Mission Blvd.
Riverside, CA 92509
TEL: (714) 685-8570
FAX:
Mr. Ray Teagarden, President

Portable quick lube service business on wheels. Low overhead lube service that goes to the customer's home or business. Can be operated from your home phone. You furnish the pick-up truck or van and we supply the tilt trailer, equipment and tools.

HISTORY:	FINANCIAL:	FRANCHISOR TRAINING/SUPPORT:
Established in 1974; . . 1st Franchised in 1977	Cash Investment: $12K	Financial Assistance Provided: . . . . . No
Company-Owned Units (As of 12/1/1989): . .0	Total Investment: $12K	Site Selection Assistance: . . . . .NA
Franchised Units (12/1/1989): 33	Fees: Franchise - $0	Lease Negotiation Assistance: . . . . .NA
Total Units (12/1/1989): 33	Royalty: 0%, Advert: 0%	Co-operative Advertising: . . . . No
Distribution: US-33;Can-0;Overseas-0	Contract Periods (Yrs.): . . . . . Inf.	Training: . . . . Not Required
North America: . . . . 29 States	Area Development Agreement: .No	. . . .
Concentration: . . . . 4 in CA	Sub-Franchise Contract: . . . . .No	On-Going Support: . . . .
Registered:	Expand in Territory: . . . . Yes	Full-Time Franchisor Support Staff: . . .2
. . . .	Passive Ownership: . . . . . .Allowed	EXPANSION PLANS:
Average # of Employees: . . . . .1 FT	Encourage Conversions: . . . . . Yes	US: . . . . .All US
Prior Industry Experience: . . . . Helpful	Franchisee Purchase(s) Required: .No	Canada - Yes, ...Overseas - No

MAD HATTER MUFFLER AND BRAKE CENTER

3493 Tyrone Blvd. N.
St. Petersburg, FL 33710
TEL: (800) 443-9764 (813) 347-4144 C
FAX: (813) 343-7829
Mr. Joe Kotow, President

Complete undercar specialist, offering fast, professional automotive services, such as exhaust repair, brakes, struts, shock absorbers, front-end alignment, air condition repair and lubrication. Computerized inventory control and billing procedures in an updated, clean, sales-inducing atmosphere.

HISTORY: . . . . IFA	FINANCIAL:	FRANCHISOR TRAINING/SUPPORT:
Established in 1986; . . 1st Franchised in 1986	Cash Investment: $25-35K	Financial Assistance Provided: . . . Yes(I)
Company-Owned Units (As of 12/1/1989): . .1	Total Investment: $102-130K	Site Selection Assistance: . . . . . . .Yes
Franchised Units (12/1/1989): 73	Fees: Franchise - $17.5K	Lease Negotiation Assistance: . . . . .Yes
Total Units (12/1/1989): 74	Royalty: 8%, Advert: 4%	Co-operative Advertising: . . . . No
Distribution: US-74;Can-0;Overseas-0	Contract Periods (Yrs.): . . . 15/5/5	Training: . . . . . 1 Wk. Chicago, 1 Wk. St.
North America: . . . . 16 States	Area Development Agreement: Yes/5	. . . . . . Louis, 1 Wk. HQ, 1 Wk. Site
Concentration: . . . 27 n FL, 5 in NJ, 5 in CT	Sub-Franchise Contract: . . . . .No	On-Going Support: . . .B,C,D,E,F,G,H,I
Registered: . . . . CA,FL,IL,MD,MI,NY	Expand in Territory: . . . . Yes	Full-Time Franchisor Support Staff: . . 12
. . . .	Passive Ownership: . . . . . .Allowed	EXPANSION PLANS:
Average # of Employees: . . . . . . 3 FT, 1 PT	Encourage Conversions: . . . . . Yes	US: . . . . .All US
Prior Industry Experience: . . . . Helpful	Franchisee Purchase(s) Required: .No	Canada - No, ...Overseas - No

MEINEKE DISCOUNT MUFFLER SHOPS

128 S. Tryon St., # 900
Charlotte, NC 28202
TEL: (800) 634-6353 (704) 377-8855
FAX: (704) 377-1490
Mr. Gene Zhiss, VP Dealer Services

MEINEKE DISCOUNT MUFFLER SHOPS offer fast, courteous service in the merchandising of automotive exhaust systems, shock absorbers, struts and brakes. Unique inventory control and group purchasing power enable MEINEKE dealers to support a "Discount Concept" and deliver quality service. No mechanical skills required.

HISTORY: . . . . IFA
Established in 1971; . . 1st Franchised in 1972
Company-Owned Units (As of 12/1/1989): . . 1
Franchised Units (12/1/1989): 938
Total Units (12/1/1989): 939
Distribution: US-925;Can-14;Overseas-0
 North America: . . . . . 45 States, 1 Province
 Concentration: . . 68 in NY, 64 in TX, 62 in IL
Registered: . . . . .All
. . . .
Average # of Employees: . . . . . . 3 FT, 1 PT
Prior Industry Experience: . . . . . . Helpful

FINANCIAL: LONDON-GKN
Cash Investment: $70-107K
Total Investment: $107K
Fees: Franchise - $22.5K
 Royalty: 7%, Advert: 10%
Contract Periods (Yrs.): 15/15
Area Development Agreement: . .No
Sub-Franchise Contract: . . . . . .No
Expand in Territory: . . . . Yes
Passive Ownership: . . . Discouraged
Encourage Conversions: . . . . . Yes
Franchisee Purchase(s) Required: .No

FRANCHISOR TRAINING/SUPPORT:
Financial Assistance Provided: . . . Yes(I)
Site Selection Assistance: . . . . .Yes
Lease Negotiation Assistance: . . . . . No
Co-operative Advertising: . . . . .No
Training: . . . . 4 Wks. Headquarters
. . . .
On-Going Support: . . . .B,C,D,E,F,G,H,I
Full-Time Franchisor Support Staff: . . 81
EXPANSION PLANS:
 US: . . . . .All US
 Canada - Yes, ...Overseas - No

MERLIN'S MUFFLER & BRAKE

33 W. Higgins, # 2050
South Barrington, IL 60010
TEL: (800) 652-9900 (312) 428-5000
FAX:
Mr. Mark Hemeister, Man. Fran. Dev.

Central to MERLIN'S retail concept is an up-scale, 6-bay building, designed and developed as an important result of MERLIN'S complete real estate program. MERLIN'S typical franchise business plan and working cash requirement facilitates first year cash flows appropriate to owner operation, as well as semi-absentee management.

HISTORY: . . . .
Established in 1975; . . 1st Franchised in 1975
Company-Owned Units (As of 12/1/1989): . .7
Franchised Units (12/1/1989): 35
Total Units (12/1/1989): 42
Distribution: US-42;Can-0;Overseas-0
 North America: . . . . 5 States
 Concentration: . . . 36 in IL, 2 in TX, 2 in MI
Registered: . . . . IL,IN,MI,WI
. . . .
Average # of Employees: . . . . . . 2 FT, 1 PT
Prior Industry Experience: . . . . . . Helpful

FINANCIAL: NYSE-ABM
Cash Investment: $45-50K
Total Investment: $155-170K
Fees: Franchise - $26-30k
 Royalty: 4.9%, Advert: 5%
Contract Periods (Yrs.): 20/20
Area Development Agreement: . .No
Sub-Franchise Contract: . . . . . .No
Expand in Territory: . . . . .No
Passive Ownership: . . . . . .Allowed
Encourage Conversions: . . . . . Yes
Franchisee Purchase(s) Required: .No

FRANCHISOR TRAINING/SUPPORT:
Financial Assistance Provided: . . . Yes(I)
Site Selection Assistance: . . . . .Yes
Lease Negotiation Assistance: . . . . .Yes
Co-operative Advertising: . . . . .Yes
Training: . . . . 4 Wks. Headquarters/Shop,
. . . . .1 Wk. Technical School
On-Going Support: . . . . . . B,C,D,E,H,I
Full-Time Franchisor Support Staff: . . 11
EXPANSION PLANS:
 US: . . . . . . .Midwest, Southeast & TX
 Canada - No, ...Overseas - No

MERMAID CAR WASH

526 Grand Canyon Dr.
Madison, WI 53719
TEL: (608) 833-9273
FAX:
Mr. Peter Aspinwall, President

Own a MERMAID franchise. MERMAID CAR WASH was designed with the feeling that our customers have a love affair with their vehicle. It is our desire to have customers visit an enjoyable, attractive business run by friendly, helpful, well-groomed, well-trained employees and leave MERMAID with a pleasant experience and a professionally-cleaned vehicle.

HISTORY: . . . .
Established in 1984; . . 1st Franchised in 1986
Company-Owned Units (As of 12/1/1989): . .2
Franchised Units (12/1/1989): 3
Total Units (12/1/1989): 5
Distribution: US-5;Can-0;Overseas-0
 North America: . . . . 3 States
 Concentration: . . . .2 in WI, 2 in MN, 1 in IL
Registered: . . . .
. . . .
Average # of Employees: . . . . 30-60 FT
Prior Industry Experience: . . . . . . Helpful

FINANCIAL:
Cash Investment: $50-300K
Total Investment: $1.6-1.8MM
Fees: Franchise - $50K
 Royalty: 2%, Advert: 0%
Contract Periods (Yrs.): 20/20
Area Development Agreement: . .No
Sub-Franchise Contract: . . . . . .No
Expand in Territory: . . . . Yes
Passive Ownership: . . . . . .Allowed
Encourage Conversions: . . . . . Yes
Franchisee Purchase(s) Required: .No

FRANCHISOR TRAINING/SUPPORT:
Financial Assistance Provided: . . . . .No
Site Selection Assistance: . . . . .Yes
Lease Negotiation Assistance: . . . . .Yes
Co-operative Advertising: . . . . .No
Training: . . . . 3 Wks. Minimum at Head-
. . . . quarters, As Needed Site Location
On-Going Support: . . . . . . C,D,E,F,h,I
Full-Time Franchisor Support Staff: . . . 4
EXPANSION PLANS:
 US: . . . . .All US
 Canada - No, ...Overseas - No

MIDAS

225 N. Michigan Ave.
Chicago, IL 60601
TEL: (800) 621-0144 (312) 565-7625
FAX: (312) 565-7881
Mr. Richard Pope, Natl. Dir. Fran.

MIDAS MUFFLER AND BRAKE SHOPS engage in the retail sale and installation of automotive exhaust systems, brake components, suspension and alignment and other related automotive parts and services.

HISTORY: . . . . IFA
Established in 1956; . . 1st Franchised in 1956
Company-Owned Units (As of 12/1/1989):   218
Franchised Units (12/1/1989): 2073
Total Units (12/1/1989): 2291
Distribution: . US-1704;Can-228;Overseas-354
North America: . . . .
Concentration: . . . . CA, NY, OH
Registered: . . . . .All
. . . .
Average # of Employees: . . . . . . 6 FT, 4 PT
Prior Industry Experience: . . . . Helpful

FINANCIAL: NY-WHIT
Cash Investment: $60-80k
Total Investment: $175-250k
Fees: Franchise - $10K
  Royalty: 10%, Advert: 0%
Contract Periods (Yrs.): 20/20
Area Development Agreement: . .No
Sub-Franchise Contract: . . . . .No
Expand in Territory: . . . . Yes
Passive Ownership: . . . Discouraged
Encourage Conversions: . . . . . Yes
Franchisee Purchase(s) Required: Yes

FRANCHISOR TRAINING/SUPPORT:
Financial Assistance Provided: . . . Yes(I)
Site Selection Assistance: . . . . . . .Yes
Lease Negotiation Assistance: . . . . .Yes
Co-operative Advertising: . . . . . . .Yes
Training: . . . . 4 Wks. Palatine, IL
. . . .
On-Going Support: . . A,B,C,D,E,F,G,H,I
Full-Time Franchisor Support Staff: . . . .
EXPANSION PLANS:
US: . . . . .All US
Canada - Yes, . . . Overseas - Yes

MIGHTY DISTRIBUTING SYSTEM

50 Technology Park/Atlanta
Norcross, GA 30092
TEL: (404) 448-3900
FAX: (404) 446-8627
Mr. Timothy Galfas, Dir. Fran. Ops.

Sales and distribution of automotive equipment and supplies to service stations and other repair facilities in the automotive aftermarket. Services to franchisees and their customers include inventory control and technical assistance programs.

HISTORY: . . . .
Established in 1963; . . 1st Franchised in 1970
Company-Owned Units (As of 12/1/1989): . 10
Franchised Units (12/1/1989): 183
Total Units (12/1/1989): 193
Distribution: US-193;Can-0;Overseas-0
North America: . . . . 43 States
Concentration: . .18 in FL, 15 in TX, 13 in PA
Registered: . . . . All Except AB
. . . .
Average # of Employees: . . . . . . 2 FT, 1 PT
Prior Industry Experience: . . . . Helpful

FINANCIAL:
Cash Investment: $75-250K
Total Investment: $75-250K
Fees: Franchise - . . . . $15K+
  Royalty: 5%, Advert: 05%
Contract Periods (Yrs.): 5/5/5
Area Development Agreement: . .No
Sub-Franchise Contract: . . . . .No
Expand in Territory: . . . . Yes
Passive Ownership: . . . Discouraged
Encourage Conversions: . . . . . NA
Franchisee Purchase(s) Required: .No

FRANCHISOR TRAINING/SUPPORT:
Financial Assistance Provided: . . . . .No
Site Selection Assistance: . . . . . . .Yes
Lease Negotiation Assistance: . . . .NA
Co-operative Advertising: . . . . . . .Yes
Training: . . . . . . 5-10 Days Headquarters,
. . . . .3-6 Days On-site, 3 Days On-site
On-Going Support: . . . . . a,B,C,D,G,H,I
Full-Time Franchisor Support Staff: . . 39
EXPANSION PLANS:
US: . . . . .All US
Canada - No, ...Overseas - No

MINIT-TUNE AUTO CENTRES

497 W. 5th Ave.
Vancouver, BC V5Y1J9 CAN
TEL: (604) 873-5551
FAX:
Mr. Roy Shand, Officer

We utilize computerized scopes to provide tune-ups and diagnostic service for our customers. We also provide oil changes and brake service and other minor repairs.

HISTORY: . . . .
Established in 1976; . . 1st Franchised in 1976
Company-Owned Units (As of 12/1/1989): . .0
Franchised Units (12/1/1989): 50
Total Units (12/1/1989): 50
Distribution: US-0;Can-50;Overseas-0
North America: . . . .
Concentration: . . . .
Registered: . . . . AB
. . . .
Average # of Employees: . . . . .4-5 FT
Prior Industry Experience: . . . . Helpful

FINANCIAL:
Cash Investment: $50-60K
Total Investment: $95-125K
Fees: Franchise - $20K
  Royalty: 5%, Advert: 5%
Contract Periods (Yrs.): . . 10/10/10
Area Development Agreement: Yes/10
Sub-Franchise Contract: . . . . Yes
Expand in Territory: . . . . Yes
Passive Ownership: . . . Not Allowed
Encourage Conversions: . . . . . Yes
Franchisee Purchase(s) Required: .No

FRANCHISOR TRAINING/SUPPORT:
Financial Assistance Provided: . . . Yes(I)
Site Selection Assistance: . . . . . . .Yes
Lease Negotiation Assistance: . . . .Yes
Co-operative Advertising: . . . . . . .Yes
Training: . . . . 2 Wks. Field and Site
. . . .
On-Going Support: . . . . C,D,E,H,I
Full-Time Franchisor Support Staff: . . . 3
EXPANSION PLANS:
US: . . . . No
Canada - Yes, ...Overseas - No

MINUTE MUFFLER

1600 - 3rd Ave. S.
Lethbridge, AB T1J0L2 CAN
TEL: (403) 329-1020
FAX: (403) 328-9030
Mr. Robb Sloan, VP Sales/Mktg.

Retail exhaust after-market specialist, non-factory owned, i.e. the interests of the franchisee are our first and foremost concern. Discount structures and long-term support unmatched in the industry. Leading industry in heavy duty as well.

HISTORY: . . . .
Established in 1968; . . 1st Franchised in 1976
Company-Owned Units (As of 12/1/1989): . .1
Franchised Units (12/1/1989): 112
Total Units (12/1/1989): 113
Distribution: US-2;Can-109;Overseas-2
  North America: . . . . . 2 States, 9 Provinces
  Concentration: . 24 in AB, 15 in SK, 14 in BC
Registered: . . . . WA,AB
. . . .
Average # of Employees: . . . . . 4 FT, 1-2 PT
Prior Industry Experience: . . . . Helpful

FINANCIAL:
Cash Investment: $50-100K
Total Investment: $100-350K
Fees: Franchise - $0
  Royalty: 0%, Advert: 4%
Contract Periods (Yrs.): . . . .
Area Development Agreement: . .No
Sub-Franchise Contract: . . . . . Yes
Expand in Territory: . . . . Yes
Passive Ownership: . . . . . .Allowed
Encourage Conversions: . . . . . Yes
Franchisee Purchase(s) Required: Yes

FRANCHISOR TRAINING/SUPPORT:
Financial Assistance Provided: . . . Yes(I)
Site Selection Assistance: . . . . . . .Yes
Lease Negotiation Assistance: . . . . .Yes
Co-operative Advertising: . . . . . . .Yes
Training: . . . . . .4-10 Wks. Headquarters
. . . .
On-Going Support: . . .A,B,C,d,E,F,G,H,i
Full-Time Franchisor Support Staff: . . 15
EXPANSION PLANS:
US: . . . . .All US Except Pacific N'west
Canada - Yes, . . . Overseas - Yes

MISTER TRANSMISSION

30 Wertheim Ct., # 5
Richmond Hill, ON L4B1B9 CAN
TEL: (416) 886-1511
FAX: (416) 886-1545
Mr. Kevin Brillinger

MISTER TRANSMISSION is Canada's largest automatic transmission repair specialist, serving Canadian motorists since 1963. MISTER TRANSMISSION offers first-rate advertising support, a nationwide warranty program and a national network of dealers.

HISTORY: . . . . .CFA
Established in 1963; . . 1st Franchised in 1969
Company-Owned Units (As of 12/1/1989): . .0
Franchised Units (12/1/1989): 97
Total Units (12/1/1989): 97
Distribution: US-0;Can-97;Overseas-0
  North America: . . . . 8 Provinces
  Concentration: . . .74 in ON, 7 in PQ, 5 in BC
Registered: . . . . AB
. . . .
Average # of Employees: . . . . . . 4 FT, 1 PT
Prior Industry Experience: . . . . Helpful

FINANCIAL:
Cash Investment: $30-60K
Total Investment: $60-90K
Fees: Franchise - $20K
  Royalty: 7%, Advert: 4-7%
Contract Periods (Yrs.): 10/10
Area Development Agreement: . .No
Sub-Franchise Contract: . . . . .No
Expand in Territory: . . . . Yes
Passive Ownership: . . . Not Allowed
Encourage Conversions: . . . . . NA
Franchisee Purchase(s) Required: .No

FRANCHISOR TRAINING/SUPPORT:
Financial Assistance Provided: . . . Yes(I)
Site Selection Assistance: . . . . . . .Yes
Lease Negotiation Assistance: . . . . .Yes
Co-operative Advertising: . . . . No
Training: . . . . .1 Wk. Headquarters,
. . . . 1 Wk. In Shop
On-Going Support: . . . . . A,C,D,E,G,H
Full-Time Franchisor Support Staff: . . 10
EXPANSION PLANS:
US: . . . . No
Canada - Yes, ...Overseas - No

MOBICARE

115 Airport Dr., # 100
Westminster, MD 21157
TEL: (301) 875-5823
FAX:
Mr. Terry Smith, Dir. Sales

MOBICARE is a quick oil change, lube center and car wash on wheels, bringing total car care to the customer's fleet vehicles, clusters of cars at office buildings, parking lots and garages, and to individual residences.

HISTORY: . . . . .IFA
Established in 1987; . . 1st Franchised in 1987
Company-Owned Units (As of 12/1/1989): . .0
Franchised Units (12/1/1989): 28
Total Units (12/1/1989): 28
Distribution: US-28;Can-0;Overseas-0
  North America: . . . . 15 States
  Concentration: . . . 5 in MD, 4 in FL, 3 in PA
Registered: . . . CA,HI,IL,IN,MD,MI,MN,NY
. . . . .RI,VA,WI
Average # of Employees: . . . . . . 2 FT, 3 PT
Prior Industry Experience: . . . . Helpful

FINANCIAL:
Cash Investment: $25K
Total Investment: $70K
Fees: Franchise - . . . . . . $15K+
  Royalty: 8%, Advert: 2%
Contract Periods (Yrs.): 10/5
Area Development Agreement: Yes/10
Sub-Franchise Contract: . . . . Yes
Expand in Territory: . . . . . . Yes
Passive Ownership: . . . Discouraged
Encourage Conversions: . . . . Yes
Franchisee Purchase(s) Required: .No

FRANCHISOR TRAINING/SUPPORT:
Financial Assistance Provided: . . .Yes(D)
Site Selection Assistance: . . . . . . .NA
Lease Negotiation Assistance: . . . .NA
Co-operative Advertising: . . . . . . .Yes
Training: . . . . .1 Wk. Headquarters,
. . . . .2 Wks. Field Training
On-Going Support: . . . . . b,C,D,E,G,H,I
Full-Time Franchisor Support Staff: . . 16
EXPANSION PLANS:
US: . . . . .All US
Canada - No, ... Overseas - No

MORALL BRAKE CENTERS

160 Larrabee Rd.
Westbrook, ME 04092
TEL: (800) 272-5375 (207) 856-6738
FAX: (207) 856-6090
Mr. Robert Tortoriello, Dir. Fran.

Automotive brake service specialists. Brake service is the fastest-growing segment of the automotive aftermarket. MORALL BRAKE CENTERS carry full parts inventories and are equipped to service all vehicles weighing up to 1- ton. Services are competitively priced, completed in 1 hour or less and carry a lifetime guarantee.

HISTORY: . . . . IFA
Established in 1974; . . 1st Franchised in 1984
Company-Owned Units (As of 12/1/1989): . .2
Franchised Units (12/1/1989): 12
Total Units (12/1/1989): 14
Distribution: US-14;Can-0;Overseas-0
North America: . . . . 4 States
Concentration: . . .7 in MA, 4 in NH, 3 in ME
Registered: . . . . FL,MD,NY,RI,VA
. . . .
Average # of Employees: . . . . 3-5 FT, 1-3 PT
Prior Industry Experience: . . . . Helpful

FINANCIAL:
Cash Investment: . . . . $Varies
Total Investment: $87-128K
Fees: Franchise - $24K
  Royalty: 5%, Advert: 6%
Contract Periods (Yrs.): 15/15
Area Development Agreement: Yes/Var
Sub-Franchise Contract: . . . . . Yes
Expand in Territory: . . . . Yes
Passive Ownership: . . . . . .Allowed
Encourage Conversions: . . . . . Yes
Franchisee Purchase(s) Required: .No

FRANCHISOR TRAINING/SUPPORT:
Financial Assistance Provided: . . . Yes(I)
Site Selection Assistance: . . . . . . .Yes
Lease Negotiation Assistance: . . . . .Yes
Co-operative Advertising: . . . . . . .Yes
Training: . . . . 2 Wks. Headquarters,
. . . . 2 Wks. Franchise Location
On-Going Support: . . .a,B,C,D,E,F,G,H,I
Full-Time Franchisor Support Staff: . . 30
EXPANSION PLANS:
US: . . . . .All US
Canada - Yes, . . . Overseas - Yes

MOTORWORKS

4210 Salem St.
Philadelphia, PA 19124
TEL: (800) 327-9905 (215) 533-4112 C
FAX: (215) 533-7801
Mr. Terrance Corkery, Dir. Sales

MOTORWORKS is the nation's only automotive service franchise to specialize in motor replacement and installation. Franchisees receive comprehensive training in the management and marketing of their businesses. No experience necessary. Skilled technicians install and replace factory-remanufactured motors. Motor replacement in a high-demand, high-profit service. Wholesale, retail, car, truck and marine accounts served.

HISTORY: . . . . IFA
Established in 1987; . . 1st Franchised in 1987
Company-Owned Units (As of 12/1/1989): . .1
Franchised Units (12/1/1989): 21
Total Units (12/1/1989): 22
Distribution: US-22;Can-0;Overseas-0
North America: . . . . 7 States
Concentration: . . . . 12 in PA, 3 in NJ
Registered: . . . . .All
. . . .
Average # of Employees: . . . . . . 2 FT, 2 PT
Prior Industry Experience: . . . . Helpful

FINANCIAL:
Cash Investment: $20-30K
Total Investment: $80-100K
Fees: Franchise - $17.5K
  Royalty: 4%, Advert: 1%
Contract Periods (Yrs.): 10/5
Area Development Agreement: . .No
Sub-Franchise Contract: . . . . .No
Expand in Territory: . . . . .No
Passive Ownership: . . . Discouraged
Encourage Conversions: . . . . . Yes
Franchisee Purchase(s) Required: Yes

FRANCHISOR TRAINING/SUPPORT:
Financial Assistance Provided: . . . Yes(I)
Site Selection Assistance: . . . . . . .Yes
Lease Negotiation Assistance: . . . . .Yes
Co-operative Advertising: . . . . . . .Yes
Training: . . . . .1 Wk. Headquarters,
. . . . 1 Wk. Site
On-Going Support: . . A,B,C,D,E,F,G,H,I
Full-Time Franchisor Support Staff: . . 10
EXPANSION PLANS:
US: . . . . .All US
Canada - No, ...Overseas - No

MULTISTATE TRANSMISSIONS

29200 Vassar Ave., # 501
Livonia, MI 48152
TEL: (313) 478-9206 c
FAX:
Mr. Aaron Reavis, VP

MULTISTATE TRANSMISSION CENTERS service, repair and replace foreign and domestic, standard and automatic transmissions for automobiles, small trucks, vans and RV's, usually in a building large enough to service 5 vehicles with outside parking for up to 20 cars.

HISTORY: . . . .
Established in 1973; . . 1st Franchised in 1974
Company-Owned Units (As of 12/1/1989): . .0
Franchised Units (12/1/1989): 74
Total Units (12/1/1989): 74
Distribution: US-74;Can-0;Overseas-0
North America: . . . . 12 States
Concentration: . . 20 in IL, 10 in MI, 13 in CA
Registered: . . . .
. . . .
Average # of Employees: . . . . 6 Ft, 1 PT
Prior Industry Experience: . . . . Helpful

FINANCIAL:
Cash Investment: $35-45K
Total Investment: $85-100K
Fees: Franchise - $20K
  Royalty: 6%, Advert: 0%
Contract Periods (Yrs.): 15/15
Area Development Agreement: . .No
Sub-Franchise Contract: . . . . .No
Expand in Territory: . . . . Yes
Passive Ownership: . . . Discouraged
Encourage Conversions: . . . . . Yes
Franchisee Purchase(s) Required: .No

FRANCHISOR TRAINING/SUPPORT:
Financial Assistance Provided: . . . Yes(I)
Site Selection Assistance: . . . . . . .Yes
Lease Negotiation Assistance: . . . . .Yes
Co-operative Advertising: . . . . No
Training: . . . . 2 Wks. Headquarters,
. . . 1 Wk. Site, On-going Site As Req'd.
On-Going Support: . . . . .C,D,E,F,G,H,I
Full-Time Franchisor Support Staff: . . 10
EXPANSION PLANS:
US: . . . . .All US
Canada - No, ...Overseas - No

NATIONAL CAR CARE CENTERS

2470 Windy Hill Rd.
Marietta, GA 30067
TEL: (404) 955-4506
FAX:
Mr. H. B. Rust, Fran. Devel.

Specialty automotive service, with emphasis on brakes, mufflers, shock absorbers, MacPherson struts, trailer hitches, oil/lube and air conditioning. No mechanical experience required.

HISTORY:	FINANCIAL:	FRANCHISOR TRAINING/SUPPORT:
Established in 1977; . . 1st Franchised in 1986	Cash Investment: $45K	Financial Assistance Provided: . . . Yes(I)
Company-Owned Units (As of 12/1/1989): . .2	Total Investment: $119K	Site Selection Assistance: . . . . . . .Yes
Franchised Units (12/1/1989): 6	Fees: Franchise - $20K	Lease Negotiation Assistance: . . . . .Yes
Total Units (12/1/1989): 8	Royalty: 6%, Advert: 4%	Co-operative Advertising: . . . . . . .Yes
Distribution: US-8;Can-0;Overseas-0	Contract Periods (Yrs.): 20/20	Training: . . . . 2 Wks. Headquarters
North America:	Area Development Agreement: . .No	
Concentration:	Sub-Franchise Contract: . . . . .No	On-Going Support: . . . . .B,C,D,E,G,H,I
Registered:	Expand in Territory: . . . . Yes	Full-Time Franchisor Support Staff: . . . .
	Passive Ownership: . . . Discouraged	EXPANSION PLANS:
Average # of Employees: . . . . .3 FT	Encourage Conversions:	US: . . . . .All US
Prior Industry Experience: . . . . . . Helpful	Franchisee Purchase(s) Required: .No	Canada - No, ...Overseas - No

NOVUS WINDSHIELD REPAIR

10425 Hampshire Ave. S.
Minneapolis, MN 55438
TEL: (800) 328-1117 (612) 944-8000 C
FAX: (612) 944-2542
Mr. David Schuh, Mgr. Sales/Mktg.

NOVUS WINDSHIELD REPAIR franchisees repair stone-damaged windshields at 20-25% of the cost of replacement. NOVUS has also established national accounts with major fleet companies and works closely with insurance companies nationwide. Emphasis on R & D and on-going training perpetuates NOVUS as industry leader.

HISTORY: . . . . .IFA	FINANCIAL:	FRANCHISOR TRAINING/SUPPORT:
Established in 1972; . . 1st Franchised in 1985	Cash Investment: $6-7K	Financial Assistance Provided: . . . . .No
Company-Owned Units (As of 12/1/1989): . .0	Total Investment: $8-10K	Site Selection Assistance: . . . . . . .NA
Franchised Units (12/1/1989): 943	Fees: Franchise - $3K	Lease Negotiation Assistance: . . . . .NA
Total Units (12/1/1989): 943	Royalty: 6%, Advert: 2%	Co-operative Advertising: . . . . . . .NA
Distribution: . . . US-789;Can-87;Overseas-67	Contract Periods (Yrs.): 5/5	Training: . . . . 5 Days Headquarters
North America: . . . . 50 States,10 Provinces	Area Development Agreement: . .No	
Concentration: . 63 in CA, 46 in WA, 31 in TX	Sub-Franchise Contract: . . . . .No	On-Going Support: . . . . .d,G,h,I
Registered: . . . . .All	Expand in Territory: . . . . Yes	Full-Time Franchisor Support Staff: . . 48
	Passive Ownership: . . . Discouraged	EXPANSION PLANS:
Average # of Employees: . . . . . . 1 FT, 1 PT	Encourage Conversions: . . . . . Yes	US: . . . . .All US
Prior Industry Experience: . . . . . . Helpful	Franchisee Purchase(s) Required: Yes	Canada - Yes, . . . Overseas - Yes

OIL EXPRESS FAST LUBE SYSTEMS

15 Spinning Wheel Rd., # 428
Hinsdale, IL 60521
TEL: (312) 325-8666
FAX:
Mr. Daniel R. Barnas, EVP

OIL EXPRESS began in 1980. 38 centralized locations and growing. All brand new buildings, with drive-thrus and full basements. Extensive management development school (classroom) and on-the-job training. No failures and very high average store volume. All owner-operated franchises.

HISTORY:	FINANCIAL:	FRANCHISOR TRAINING/SUPPORT:
Established in 1980; . . 1st Franchised in 1981	Cash Investment: $75-100K	Financial Assistance Provided: . . . Yes(I)
Company-Owned Units (As of 12/1/1989): . 10	Total Investment: $425-500K	Site Selection Assistance: . . . . . . .Yes
Franchised Units (12/1/1989): 28	Fees: Franchise - $25K	Lease Negotiation Assistance: . . . . .Yes
Total Units (12/1/1989): 38	Royalty: 6%, Advert: 4.5%	Co-operative Advertising: . . . . . . .Yes
Distribution: US-38;Can-0;Overseas-0	Contract Periods (Yrs.): 20	Training: . . . . . . 9 Wk. (27 Hr, Total) at
North America: . . . . 3 States	Area Development Agreement: Yes/Var	. . Headquarters, Min. 10 Days OJT Site
Concentration: . . . .34 in IL, 3 in IN, 1 in TN	Sub-Franchise Contract: . . . . . Yes	On-Going Support: . . . . .B,C,D,E,G,H,I
Registered: . . . . .IL,IN	Expand in Territory: . . . . Yes	Full-Time Franchisor Support Staff: . . 55
	Passive Ownership: . . . Not Allowed	EXPANSION PLANS:
Average # of Employees: . . . . .6-9 FT	Encourage Conversions: . . . . .No	US: . . . . . .All US, Especially Midwest
Prior Industry Experience: . . . . . . Helpful	Franchisee Purchase(s) Required: .No	Canada - No, ...Overseas - No

PERFORMANCE TRANSMISSION

6458 W. Commercial Blvd.
Lauderhill, FL 33319
TEL: (305) 572-4131 C
FAX:
Mr. Benny Muran, President

Sales, service, repair of transmission. Great opportunity!

HISTORY: . . . .
Established in 1988; . . 1st Franchised in 1989
Company-Owned Units (As of 12/1/1989): . .3
Franchised Units (12/1/1989): 0
Total Units (12/1/1989): 3
Distribution: US-3;Can-0;Overseas-0
North America: . . . . .1 State
Concentration: . . . . 3 in FL
Registered: . . . . .FL

. . . .
Average # of Employees: . . . . . . 3 FT, 1 PT
Prior Industry Experience: . . . . . . Helpful

FINANCIAL:
Cash Investment: $40K
Total Investment: $100K
Fees: Franchise - . . . .$Varies
Royalty: 1%, Advert: 4%
Contract Periods (Yrs.): 10/10
Area Development Agreement: . .No
Sub-Franchise Contract: . . . . .No
Expand in Territory: . . . . . . Yes
Passive Ownership: . . . . . .Allowed
Encourage Conversions: . . . . NA
Franchisee Purchase(s) Required: .No

FRANCHISOR TRAINING/SUPPORT:
Financial Assistance Provided: . . .Yes(D)
Site Selection Assistance: . . . . . . .Yes
Lease Negotiation Assistance: . . . .Yes
Co-operative Advertising: . . . . . . .Yes
Training: . . . . Conducted at Headquarters
. . . .
On-Going Support: . . . . B,D,E,I
Full-Time Franchisor Support Staff: . . . 6
EXPANSION PLANS:
US: . . . . .Florida Only
Canada - No, ...Overseas - No

PRESTIGE LUBE & CLEAN

1979 Tellepsen St.
Houston, TX 77023
TEL: (800) 833-5823 (713) 921-6100
FAX: (713) 921-6150
Mr. Jack Herthneck, President

Totally new concept - lube, detail, window tint, pin striping, windshield repair, battery, windshield wipers and other services for auto, boat or airplane.

HISTORY: . . . .
Established in 1972; . . 1st Franchised in 1985
Company-Owned Units (As of 12/1/1989): . .0
Franchised Units (12/1/1989): 67
Total Units (12/1/1989): 67
Distribution: US-67;Can-0;Overseas-0
North America: . . . . 6 States
Concentration: . . . 36 in TX, 9 in FL, 4 in LA
Registered: . . . . .CA,FL

. . . .
Average # of Employees: . . . . .4 PT
Prior Industry Experience: . . . . . . Helpful

FINANCIAL:
Cash Investment: $29.9K
Total Investment: $43-51K
Fees: Franchise - $29.9K
Royalty: 7.5%, Advert: 0%
Contract Periods (Yrs.): . . . . Infin.
Area Development Agreement: . Yes
Sub-Franchise Contract: . . . . Yes
Expand in Territory: . . . . . . Yes
Passive Ownership: . . . Discouraged
Encourage Conversions: . . . . .No
Franchisee Purchase(s) Required: Yes

FRANCHISOR TRAINING/SUPPORT:
Financial Assistance Provided: . . .Yes(D)
Site Selection Assistance: . . . . . . .Yes
Lease Negotiation Assistance: . . . .Yes
Co-operative Advertising: . . . . . . .Yes
Training: . . . . .1 Wk. Headquarters,
. . . . .2 Wks.+ Franchisee Location
On-Going Support: . . . .A,B,C,D,E,F,G,I
Full-Time Franchisor Support Staff: . . 52
EXPANSION PLANS:
US: . . . . .All US
Canada - Yes, . . . Overseas - Yes

PREVENT-A-CRACK

3116 E. Shea Blvd., # 247
Phoenix, AZ 85028
TEL: (602) 996-4450
FAX:
Mr. Gerd D. Linke, President

A company which sells franchises for the operation of windshield and glass repairs known as PREVENT-A-CRACK mobile services. Vehicles which experience cracks to their windshields can be repaired. The repair will permanently stop crack extension and restore visibility to rock-damaged areas.

HISTORY: . . . .
Established in 1987; . . 1st Franchised in 1987
Company-Owned Units (As of 12/1/1989): . .3
Franchised Units (12/1/1989): 6
Total Units (12/1/1989): 9
Distribution: US-9;Can-0;Overseas-0
North America: . . . . 3 States
Concentration: . . . .5 in AZ, 2 in CA, 1 in MI
Registered: . . . .

. . . .
Average # of Employees: . . . . . . 2 FT, 1 PT
Prior Industry Experience: . . . . . . Helpful

FINANCIAL:
Cash Investment: $10K
Total Investment: $10K
Fees: Franchise - $5K
Royalty: 6%, Advert: 2%
Contract Periods (Yrs.): 10/10
Area Development Agreement: . .No
Sub-Franchise Contract: . . . . .No
Expand in Territory: . . . . . . Yes
Passive Ownership: . . . Discouraged
Encourage Conversions: . . . . .No
Franchisee Purchase(s) Required: Yes

FRANCHISOR TRAINING/SUPPORT:
Financial Assistance Provided: . . . . .Yes
Site Selection Assistance: . . . . . . .Yes
Lease Negotiation Assistance: . . . .Yes
Co-operative Advertising: . . . . . . .Yes
Training: . . . . All Training at Head-
. . . . quarters
On-Going Support: . . . . . B,C,D,E,F,h,I
Full-Time Franchisor Support Staff: . . . 1
EXPANSION PLANS:
US: . . . . .All US
Canada - Yes, . . . Overseas - Yes

PROLUBE

625 E. Merritt Ave.
Merritt Island, FL 32953
TEL: (407) 452-7893
FAX:
Mr. Joe Haggard, Fran. Sales

Drive-thru lubrication, fluid and inspection service. 34 items performed. Marketing emphasis on convenience, confidence and ego gratification. Solid state fluid dispensing system with no pumps or reels. Unique percentage control system and compensation system. Precise, methodical, sequenced method of performance service.

HISTORY: . . . .
Established in 1975; . . 1st Franchised in 1986
Company-Owned Units (As of 12/1/1989): . .4
Franchised Units (12/1/1989): 3
Total Units (12/1/1989): 7
Distribution: US-7;Can-0;Overseas-0
North America: . . . . .1 State
Concentration: . . . . 7 in FL
Registered: . . . . .FL
. . . .
Average # of Employees: . . . . .6 FT
Prior Industry Experience: . . . . . . Helpful

FINANCIAL:
Cash Investment: $90-140K
Total Investment: $240-350K
Fees: Franchise - $10K
Royalty: 6%, Advert: 0%
Contract Periods (Yrs.): 5/5
Area Development Agreement: Yes/5
Sub-Franchise Contract: . . . . .No
Expand in Territory: . . . . . Yes
Passive Ownership: . . . . . .Allowed
Encourage Conversions: . . . . Yes
Franchisee Purchase(s) Required: .No

FRANCHISOR TRAINING/SUPPORT:
Financial Assistance Provided: . . . . .No
Site Selection Assistance: . . . . . . .Yes
Lease Negotiation Assistance: . . . .Yes
Co-operative Advertising: . . . . . . .Yes
Training: . . . . 2 Wks. Headquarters
On-Going Support: . . . . E,F,G,H,I
Full-Time Franchisor Support Staff: . . . 6
EXPANSION PLANS:
US: . . . . All Except California
Canada - No, ...Overseas - No

QUAL-TECH IMPORT CENTER

4000 Atlanta Rd.
Smyrna, GA 30080
TEL: (404) 432-8411
FAX:
Mr. Barry Rosenberg, President

Import repair - brakes, tune-ups, transmissions, engines, etc. In-house parts and a full-service facility for import car owners. Complete computer software included that will do 80% of office work and parts management.

HISTORY: . . . .
Established in 1985; . . 1st Franchised in 1986
Company-Owned Units (As of 12/1/1989): . .2
Franchised Units (12/1/1989): 0
Total Units (12/1/1989): 2
Distribution: US-2;Can-0;Overseas-0
North America: . . . . .1 State
Concentration: . . . . 2 in GA
Registered: . . . .
. . . .
Average # of Employees: . . . . . . 6 FT, 2 PT
Prior Industry Experience: . . . . . .Necessary

FINANCIAL:
Cash Investment: $80-150K
Total Investment: $250K
Fees: Franchise - $22.5K
Royalty: 4-6%, Advert: 2%
Contract Periods (Yrs.): 20/10
Area Development Agreement: . .No
Sub-Franchise Contract: . . . . .No
Expand in Territory: . . . . . . .No
Passive Ownership: . . . Discouraged
Encourage Conversions: . . . . Yes
Franchisee Purchase(s) Required: .No

FRANCHISOR TRAINING/SUPPORT:
Financial Assistance Provided: . . . . .No
Site Selection Assistance: . . . . . . .Yes
Lease Negotiation Assistance: . . . .Yes
Co-operative Advertising: . . . . . . .Yes
Training: . . . . 2 Wks. Headquarters,
. . . . .2 Wks. Franchisee Location
On-Going Support: . . . . . B,C,D,E,F,G,H
Full-Time Franchisor Support Staff: . . . 8
EXPANSION PLANS:
US: . . . . Southeast
Canada - No, ...Overseas - No

RADIATOR WORKS

2611 West Ave., # 310
San Antonio, TX 78201
TEL: (512) 735-1919 C
FAX: (512) 734-0112
Mr. Al Heizer, VP Fran. Devel.

A complete, professional automotive cooling system service center, specializing in the sale, service and installation of radiators, air conditioners and related products, such as water pumps, heater cores, thermostats, air conditioning compressors, condensors, dryers and assorted belts, hoses and clamps.

HISTORY: . . . .
Established in 1985; . . 1st Franchised in 1986
Company-Owned Units (As of 12/1/1989): . .1
Franchised Units (12/1/1989): 10
Total Units (12/1/1989): 10
Distribution: US-10;Can-0;Overseas-0
North America: . . . . 2 States
Concentration: . . . . 5 in TX, 5 in GA
Registered: . . . . FL,IN
. . . .
Average # of Employees: . . . . .2 FT
Prior Industry Experience: . . . . . . Helpful

FINANCIAL:
Cash Investment: $25-35K
Total Investment: $85-90K
Fees: Franchise - $20K
Royalty: 7%, Advert: 10%
Contract Periods (Yrs.): . . . 10/10
Area Development Agreement: . .No
Sub-Franchise Contract: . . . . .No
Expand in Territory: . . . . . . Yes
Passive Ownership: . . . Discouraged
Encourage Conversions: . . . . Yes
Franchisee Purchase(s) Required: Yes

FRANCHISOR TRAINING/SUPPORT:
Financial Assistance Provided: . . . . .No
Site Selection Assistance: . . . . . . .Yes
Lease Negotiation Assistance: . . . .Yes
Co-operative Advertising: . . . . No
Training: . . . . 2 Wks. Headquarters
. . . .
On-Going Support: . . . . . C,D,E,F,G,h,I
Full-Time Franchisor Support Staff: . . . 5
EXPANSION PLANS:
US: . . . . . South, Southwest, Southeast
Canada - No, ...Overseas - No

RUST CHECK

1285 Britannia Rd., E.
Mississauga, ON L4W1C7 CAN
TEL: (800) 387-6743 (416) 670-7878
FAX: (416) 564-7077
Mr. Dave Worrall, GM

Canada's largest automotive rust prevention franchise. Unique annual treatment is guaranteed forever on new and qualified used cars. Over 1,000,000 applications in 17 years and we've never had a product failure claim. Appearance/detailing services and accessories available at selected dealers.

HISTORY: . . . . .CFA
Established in 1978; . . 1st Franchised in 1982
Company-Owned Units (As of 12/1/1989): . .3
Franchised Units (12/1/1989): 245
Total Units (12/1/1989): 248
Distribution: US-11;Can-236;Overseas-1
North America: . . . . 4 States, 10 Provinces
Concentration: . 72 in ON, 42 in PQ, 27 in NS
Registered: . . . .
. . . .
Average # of Employees: . . . . . . 2 FT, 2 PT
Prior Industry Experience: . . . . Helpful

FINANCIAL:
Cash Investment: $30K
Total Investment: . . . .$
Fees: Franchise - . . . . $Varies
Royalty: 0%, Advert: 5%
Contract Periods (Yrs.): . . . . Open
Area Development Agreement: . .No
Sub-Franchise Contract: . . . . .No
Expand in Territory: . . . . . . .No
Passive Ownership: . . . Discouraged
Encourage Conversions: . . . . . NA
Franchisee Purchase(s) Required: Yes

FRANCHISOR TRAINING/SUPPORT:
Financial Assistance Provided: . . . . .No
Site Selection Assistance: . . . . . . .Yes
Lease Negotiation Assistance: . . . . .No
Co-operative Advertising: . . . . .No
Training: . . . . .1 Wk. Headquarters,
. . . . 1 Wk. Franchisee's Location
On-Going Support: . . . A,B,C,D,E,G,H,I
Full-Time Franchisor Support Staff: . . 24
EXPANSION PLANS:
US: . . . . Northwest
Canada - Yes, ...Overseas - No

SAF-T AUTO CENTERS

209 Forbes Ave.
New Haven, CT 06512
TEL: (203) 468-8935 C
FAX:
Mr. Richard Bilodeau, President

SAF-T AUTO CENTERS is an owner-operated auto repair shop, offering steering, suspension, brake, muffler, lubrication and minor repair. Our main effort is to put good mechanics in a business opportunity where they can capitalize on their trade.

HISTORY: . . . .
Established in 1978; . . 1st Franchised in 1985
Company-Owned Units (As of 12/1/1989): . .1
Franchised Units (12/1/1989): 9
Total Units (12/1/1989): 10
Distribution: US-10;Can-0;Overseas-0
North America: . . . . 2 States
Concentration: . . . . .9 in CT, 1 in FL
Registered: . . . . .FL
. . . .
Average # of Employees: . . . . .1 FT
Prior Industry Experience: . . . . . .Necessary

FINANCIAL:
Cash Investment: $32.5-65K
Total Investment: $32.5-65K
Fees: Franchise - $15K
Royalty: $400/Mo., Advert: . . 1%
Contract Periods (Yrs.): 5/5
Area Development Agreement: Yes/50
Sub-Franchise Contract: . . . . . Yes
Expand in Territory: . . . . . . Yes
Passive Ownership: . . . Not Allowed
Encourage Conversions: . . . . Yes
Franchisee Purchase(s) Required: .No

FRANCHISOR TRAINING/SUPPORT:
Financial Assistance Provided: . . . Yes(I)
Site Selection Assistance: . . . . . . .Yes
Lease Negotiation Assistance: . . . .Yes
Co-operative Advertising: . . . . . . .Yes
Training: . . . . .1 Wk. Headquarters,
. . . . 1 Wk. Site
On-Going Support: . . . .A,C,D,E,G,H,I
Full-Time Franchisor Support Staff: . . . 4
EXPANSION PLANS:
US: . . . . .CT and FL Only
Canada - No, ...Overseas - No

SHINE FACTORY, THE

116 Monument Pl. SE
Calgary, AB T2A1X3 CAN
TEL: (403) 273-3525
FAX:
Mr. Bruce Cousens, President

THE SHINE FACTORY offers a proven program and system to establish a franchisee in the automotive polishing and detail business. We offer exclusive products with insured warranties, a complete turn-key package and 10 years of experience and steady growth.

HISTORY: . . . .
Established in 1979; . . 1st Franchised in 1979
Company-Owned Units (As of 12/1/1989): . .0
Franchised Units (12/1/1989): 25
Total Units (12/1/1989): 25
Distribution: US-0;Can-25;Overseas-0
North America: . . . . 6 Provinces
Concentration: . . .11 in NS, 9 in AB, 2 in BC
Registered: . . . . .AB
. . . .
Average # of Employees: . . . . . . 5 FT, 2 PT
Prior Industry Experience: . . . . Helpful

FINANCIAL:
Cash Investment: . . . .$
Total Investment: $70-85K
Fees: Franchise - $10-50K
Royalty: 8%, Advert: 5%
Contract Periods (Yrs.): 5/5
Area Development Agreement: Yes/5
Sub-Franchise Contract: . . . . . Yes
Expand in Territory: . . . . . . Yes
Passive Ownership: . . . Discouraged
Encourage Conversions: . . . . Yes
Franchisee Purchase(s) Required: Yes

FRANCHISOR TRAINING/SUPPORT:
Financial Assistance Provided: . . . . .No
Site Selection Assistance: . . . . . . .Yes
Lease Negotiation Assistance: . . . . .Yes
Co-operative Advertising: . . . . .No
Training: . . . . 2 Wks. Training Plus
. . . 1 Wk. On-site in Calgary or Halifax
On-Going Support: . . . . B,C,D,E,F,G,H
Full-Time Franchisor Support Staff: . . .5
EXPANSION PLANS:
US: . . . . . .Seeking Partner to Fran. US
Canada - Yes, ...Overseas - No

SPARKS TUNE UP CENTERS

1400 Opus Pl., # 800, Opus West III
Downers Grove, IL 60515
TEL: (800) 458-9289 (312) 515-5100
FAX:
Mr. Ralph Loberger, Dir. Fran. Sales

A national retail tune-up chain of 129 locations that specializes in not only tune-ups, but also the following under-the-hood repairs: carburetors, air conditioning servicing, radiator flush and fills, fuel injector cleaning/servicing, belts and hose replacement and quick-lube services. Owned by GKN and a part of the same automotive division that developed and owns Meineke Discount Mufflers.

HISTORY: . . . . IFA	FINANCIAL: BRIT-GKN	FRANCHISOR TRAINING/SUPPORT:
Established in 1980; . . 1st Franchised in 1980	Cash Investment: $50K	Financial Assistance Provided: . . . Yes(I)
Company-Owned Units (As of 12/1/1989): . .3	Total Investment: $105-135K	Site Selection Assistance: . . . . .Yes
Franchised Units (12/1/1989): 126	Fees: Franchise - $20K	Lease Negotiation Assistance: . . . . .Yes
Total Units (12/1/1989): 129	Royalty: 7%, Advert: . . $400/Mo.	Co-operative Advertising: . . . . . . .Yes
Distribution: US-129;Can-0;Overseas-0	Contract Periods (Yrs.): 15/15	Training: . . . . 4 Wks. Chicago Area
North America: . . . . 29 States	Area Development Agreement: Yes/10	. . . .
Concentration: . . 22 in OH, 16 in PA, 15 in IL	Sub-Franchise Contract: . . . . .No	On-Going Support: . . . a,B,C,D,E,F,G,H,i
Registered: . . . . All States	Expand in Territory: . . . . Yes	Full-Time Franchisor Support Staff: . . 72
. . . .	Passive Ownership: . . . Discouraged	EXPANSION PLANS:
Average # of Employees: . . . . . . 2 FT, 1 PT	Encourage Conversions: . . . . . Yes	US: . . . . All US
Prior Industry Experience: . . . . . . Helpful	Franchisee Purchase(s) Required: .No	Canada - No, ...Overseas - No

SPEEDEE OIL CHANGE & TUNE-UP

6660 Riverside Dr., # 101
Metairie, LA 70003
TEL: (800) 451-7461 (504) 454-3783
FAX: (504) 454-3890
Mr. Kevin Bennett, EVP

Specializes in 9-minute oil change and diagnostic tune-ups. All services are performed while the customer waits and no appointment is necessary. Also performed are fuel injector cleanings, air conditioning recharges, radiator flushes, transmission services and differential service.

HISTORY: . . . . IFA	FINANCIAL:	FRANCHISOR TRAINING/SUPPORT:
Established in 1980; . . 1st Franchised in 1982	Cash Investment: $75-135K	Financial Assistance Provided: . . . . .No
Company-Owned Units (As of 12/1/1989): . .5	Total Investment: $75-700K	Site Selection Assistance: . . . . . . .Yes
Franchised Units (12/1/1989): 270	Fees: Franchise - $25-35K	Lease Negotiation Assistance: . . . .Yes
Total Units (12/1/1989): 275	Royalty: 5-6%, Advert: 10%	Co-operative Advertising: . . . . . . .Yes
Distribution: US-275;Can-0;Overseas-0	Contract Periods (Yrs.): 15/5/5	Training: . . . . 3-Day Orientation HQ,
North America: . . . . 12 States	Area Development Agreement: Yes/15	. . . 2 Wks. Local Office, As Necc. Shop
Concentration: . . 24 in LA, 11 in FL, 8 in MA	Sub-Franchise Contract: . . . . . Yes	On-Going Support: . . . . B,C,D,E,F,G,H
Registered: . . . . CA,FL,HI,RI,VA	Expand in Territory: . . . . Yes	Full-Time Franchisor Support Staff: . . 15
. . . .	Passive Ownership: . . . Discouraged	EXPANSION PLANS:
Average # of Employees: . . . . . 3-8 FT, 2 PT	Encourage Conversions: . . . . . Yes	US: . . . . All US
Prior Industry Experience: . . . . . . Helpful	Franchisee Purchase(s) Required: .No	Canada - Yes, ...Overseas - No

SPEEDY MUFFLER KING

8430 W. Bryn Mawr, # 400
Chicago, IL 60631
TEL: (800) 736-6733 (312) 693-1000
FAX: (312) 693-0309
Director of Fran. Development

SPEEDY MUFFLER KING is a retail automotive chain, specializing in the undercar services of: exhaust systems, brakes, ride control and front-end repair. The market for these services is large and growing.

HISTORY: . . . . IFA	FINANCIAL:	FRANCHISOR TRAINING/SUPPORT:
Established in 1956; . . 1st Franchised in 1986	Cash Investment: $70-90K	Financial Assistance Provided: . . . Yes(I)
Company-Owned Units (As of 12/1/1989): 582	Total Investment: $180-200K	Site Selection Assistance: . . . . . . .Yes
Franchised Units (12/1/1989): 12	Fees: Franchise - $18.5K	Lease Negotiation Assistance: . . . .Yes
Total Units (12/1/1989): 594	Royalty: 5%, Advert: 5-10%	Co-operative Advertising: . . . . .No
Distribution: . . US-222;Can-141;Overseas-231	Contract Periods (Yrs.): 10/5	Training: . . . . . . 3 Wks. Ann Arbor, MI,
North America: . . . . 13 States,10 Provinces	Area Development Agreement: .No	. .1 Wk. OJT, 1 Wk. HQ, 1 Wk. Opening
Concentration: . 38 in OH, 35 in PA, 33 in MA	Sub-Franchise Contract: . . . . .No	On-Going Support: . . .B,C,D,E,F,G,H,I
Registered: . . . . MD,MI,NY,RI,VA	Expand in Territory: . . . . Yes	Full-Time Franchisor Support Staff: . . 23
. . . .	Passive Ownership: . . . Discouraged	EXPANSION PLANS:
Average # of Employees: . . . . .4 FT	Encourage Conversions: . . . . . Yes	US: . . . . All US
Prior Industry Experience: . . . . . . Helpful	Franchisee Purchase(s) Required: .No	Canada - Yes, ...Overseas - No

SPEEDY TRANSMISSION CENTERS

1239 E. Newport Center Dr., # 115
Deerfield Beach, FL 33442
TEL: (800) 326-0310 (305) 428-0077 C
FAX:
Mr. D'Arcy J. Williams, President

Automotive and truck transmission repair. Program geared to quality service at a lower price with reduced break-even point. Training, nationwide warranty, technical hot line, on-going communication, advertising, fleet programs, product purchase discounts, customer relations program and insurance programs.

HISTORY: . . . . IFA
Established in 1983; . . 1st Franchised in 1983
Company-Owned Units (As of 12/1/1989): . .0
Franchised Units (12/1/1989): 24
Total Units (12/1/1989): 24
Distribution: US-24;Can-0;Overseas-0
North America: . . . . 4 States
Concentration: . . . 20 in FL, 2 in CA, 1 in NC
Registered: . . . . FL,NY
. . . .
Average # of Employees: . . . . . . 4 FT, 1 PT
Prior Industry Experience: . . . . Helpful

FINANCIAL:
Cash Investment: $30-35K
Total Investment: $65-70K
Fees: Franchise - $12.5K
Royalty: 7%, Advert: 0%
Contract Periods (Yrs.): 20/10
Area Development Agreement: . .No
Sub-Franchise Contract: . . . . . .No
Expand in Territory: . . . . Yes
Passive Ownership: . . . Discouraged
Encourage Conversions: . . . . . Yes
Franchisee Purchase(s) Required: .No

FRANCHISOR TRAINING/SUPPORT:
Financial Assistance Provided: . . . Yes(I)
Site Selection Assistance: . . . . . . .Yes
Lease Negotiation Assistance: . . . . .Yes
Co-operative Advertising: . . . . No
Training: . . . . 3 Wks. Headquarters
. . . .
On-Going Support: . . . . . .C,D,E,G,H,I
Full-Time Franchisor Support Staff: . . . 3
EXPANSION PLANS:
US: . . . . East Coast, NE and SE
Canada - No, ...Overseas - No

SPOT-NOT CAR WASHES

2011 W. 4th St.
Joplin, MO 64801
TEL: (417) 781-2140
FAX:
Mr. Forrest Uppendahl, Dir. Fran.

Coin-operated self-service and brushless automatic car wash. Equipment, including the No-Spot Rinse feature, is exclusively available to SPOT-NOT franchisees. Parent company is the oldest continuous manufacturer of high-pressure, no-touch systems. Business is simple to operate with few employees; low inventory; no receivables; little direct competition in a stable industry.

HISTORY: . . . . IFA
Established in 1967; . . 1st Franchised in 1985
Company-Owned Units (As of 12/1/1989): . .1
Franchised Units (12/1/1989): 37
Total Units (12/1/1989): 38
Distribution: US-38;Can-0;Overseas-0
North America: . . . . 6 States
Concentration: . . . .16 in IL, 8 in IN, 8 in OH
Registered: . . . . IL,IN,MI,MN,WI
. . . .
Average # of Employees: . . . . . . 2 FT, 2 PT
Prior Industry Experience: . . . . Helpful

FINANCIAL:
Cash Investment: $430-825K
Total Investment: $430-825K
Fees: Franchise - $25K
Royalty: 5%, Advert: 1%
Contract Periods (Yrs.): 10/5
Area Development Agreement: Yes/Var
Sub-Franchise Contract: . . . . .No
Expand in Territory: . . . . Yes
Passive Ownership: . . . . .Allowed
Encourage Conversions: . . . . . Yes
Franchisee Purchase(s) Required: Yes

FRANCHISOR TRAINING/SUPPORT:
Financial Assistance Provided: . . . Yes(I)
Site Selection Assistance: . . . . . . .Yes
Lease Negotiation Assistance: . . . .Yes
Co-operative Advertising: . . . . . . .Yes
Training: . . . . 4 Days Headquarters,
. . . . .5 Days On-site
On-Going Support: . . . .B,C,D,E,F,G,H,I
Full-Time Franchisor Support Staff: . . . 6
EXPANSION PLANS:
US: . . . . Midwest & Southeast
Canada - No, ...Overseas - No

STAR TECHNOLOGY WINDSHIELD REPAIR

P. O. Box 724766
Atlanta, GA 30339
TEL: (404) 499-STAR
FAX:
Mr. David A. Casey, President

Mobile repair of rock-damaged windshields. Emphasis on servicing major fleets, rental car agencies, new and used car auto dealers, insurance companies and the motoring public. Complete turn-key package. Account base provided. Most comprehensive training and follow-up in industry. Continuous corporate support. Regional seminars, annual convention, newsletters and hotline. Oldest, most experienced franchisor in windshield repair industry.

HISTORY: . . . .
Established in 1983; . . 1st Franchised in 1984
Company-Owned Units (As of 12/1/1989): . .1
Franchised Units (12/1/1989): 137
Total Units (12/1/1989): 138
Distribution: US-133;Can-0;Overseas-5
North America: . . . . 34 States
Concentration: . . .25 in CO, 9 in AR, 6 in PA
Registered: . . . . FL,OR,SD
. . . .
Average # of Employees: . . . . .1 FT
Prior Industry Experience: . . . . Helpful

FINANCIAL:
Cash Investment: $10K
Total Investment: $10K
Fees: Franchise - $5.5K
Royalty: 3%, Advert: 0%
Contract Periods (Yrs.): 10/10
Area Development Agreement: Yes/10
Sub-Franchise Contract: . . . . . Yes
Expand in Territory: . . . . Yes
Passive Ownership: . . . . . .Allowed
Encourage Conversions: . . . . . Yes
Franchisee Purchase(s) Required: Yes

FRANCHISOR TRAINING/SUPPORT:
Financial Assistance Provided: . . . . .No
Site Selection Assistance: . . . . . . .NA
Lease Negotiation Assistance: . . . .NA
Co-operative Advertising: . . . . . . .Yes
Training: . . . . .1 Wk. Headquarters,
. . . . .1 Wk. Fran. Territory, Varies HQ
On-Going Support: . . A,B,C,D,E,F,G,H,I
Full-Time Franchisor Support Staff: . . . 6
EXPANSION PLANS:
US: . . . . . . .SE, SW, Midwest and NE
Canada - Yes, . . . Overseas - Yes

STOP BRAKE SHOPS

579 N. Citrus Ave.
Covina, Ca 91723
TEL: (800) 223-4727 (818) 967-0832
FAX:
Mr. Don L. St. Ours, President

STOP BRAKE SHOPS offers a unique specialty of repairing auto and truck brakes with emphasis on "brakes while you wait." We use only the latest in equipment and on-going service bulletins. With our high volume and low overhead, we maintain the highest in gross profit margins.

HISTORY: . . . . IFA	FINANCIAL:	FRANCHISOR TRAINING/SUPPORT:
Established in 1980; . . 1st Franchised in 1981	Cash Investment: $20K	Financial Assistance Provided: . . . Yes(I)
Company-Owned Units (As of 12/1/1989): . .2	Total Investment: $125K	Site Selection Assistance: . . . . . . .Yes
Franchised Units (12/1/1989): 11	Fees: Franchise - $20K	Lease Negotiation Assistance: . . . . .Yes
Total Units (12/1/1989): 13	Royalty: 6%, Advert.: 5%	Co-operative Advertising: . . . . .Yes
Distribution: US-13;Can-0;Overseas-0	Contract Periods (Yrs.): 10/10	Training: . . . . 2 Wks.+ Headquarters,
North America: . . . . .1 State	Area Development Agreement: Yes/10	. . . . .1 Wk.+ New Location
Concentration: . . . . 13 in CA	Sub-Franchise Contract: . . . . . Yes	On-Going Support: . . . .B,C,D,E,F,G,H,I
Registered: . . . . CA	Expand in Territory: . . . . Yes	Full-Time Franchisor Support Staff: . . . 5
. . . .	Passive Ownership: . . . Discouraged	EXPANSION PLANS:
Average # of Employees: . . . . .2 FT	Encourage Conversions: . . . . . Yes	US: . . . . .All US
Prior Industry Experience: . . . . Helpful	Franchisee Purchase(s) Required: .No	Canada - No, ...Overseas - No

SUN COUNTRY AUTO CENTERS

2005 E. Michigan Ave.
Jackson, MI 49202
TEL: (800) 333-7177 (517) 789-7177
FAX:
Mr. Hank Weber, President

SUN COUNTRY AUTO CENTERS provides affordable automotive after-market services in the areas of restyling, detailing, accessories and electronics. Our distinctive Auto Boutique format features sunroofs, convertible conversions, mild to wild graphics, ground effects and a full range of installed products and services to make vehicles look better and last longer.

HISTORY: . . . . IFA	FINANCIAL:	FRANCHISOR TRAINING/SUPPORT:
Established in 1988; . . 1st Franchised in 1988	Cash Investment: $30-45K	Financial Assistance Provided: . . . Yes(I)
Company-Owned Units (As of 12/1/1989): . .0	Total Investment: $45-95K	Site Selection Assistance: . . . . . . .Yes
Franchised Units (12/1/1989): 15	Fees: Franchise - $20K	Lease Negotiation Assistance: . . . . .Yes
Total Units (12/1/1989): 15	Royalty: 6%, Advert.: 1%	Co-operative Advertising: . . . . No
Distribution: US-15;Can-0;Overseas-0	Contract Periods (Yrs.): 10/10	Training: . . . . 2 Wks. Headquarters
North America: . . . . .1 State	Area Development Agreement: .No	. . . .
Concentration: . . . . .15 in MI	Sub-Franchise Contract: . . . . .No	On-Going Support: . . . . .B,C,D,E,G,H,I
Registered: . . . . IL,IN,MI	Expand in Territory: . . . . . . .No	Full-Time Franchisor Support Staff: . . . 4
. . . .	Passive Ownership: . . . Discouraged	EXPANSION PLANS:
Average # of Employees: . . . . . 3-4 FT, 2 PT	Encourage Conversions: . . . . . Yes	US: . . . . MI, OH, IN and IL
Prior Industry Experience: . . . . Helpful	Franchisee Purchase(s) Required: Yes	Canada - No, ...Overseas - No

THREE STAR MUFFLER

8090 Hwy. 51 North
Southaven, MS 38671
TEL: (601) 342-2080 C
FAX:
Mr. Ray Zedlitz, President

THREE STAR MUFFLER franchisees are trained to do total under-car repairs, such as exhaust, exhaust emissions, brakes, CV joints, struts, shocks, springs, front and rear wheel alignment, total replacement of front-end replacement parts. Everything that can be computerized is in place.

HISTORY:	FINANCIAL:	FRANCHISOR TRAINING/SUPPORT:
Established in 1971; . . 1st Franchised in 1980	Cash Investment: $90K	Financial Assistance Provided: . . . Yes(I)
Company-Owned Units (As of 12/1/1989): . .3	Total Investment: $100K	Site Selection Assistance: . . . . . . .Yes
Franchised Units (12/1/1989): 10	Fees: Franchise - $15K	Lease Negotiation Assistance: . . . . .Yes
Total Units (12/1/1989): 13	Royalty: 5%, Advert.: 3%	Co-operative Advertising: . . . . .Yes
Distribution: US-13;Can-0;Overseas-0	Contract Periods (Yrs.): 10/10	Training: . . . . 2 Wks. + Headquarters
North America: . . . . 3 States	Area Development Agreement: Yes/10	. . . .
Concentration: . . 11 in TN, 1 in MS, 1 in MO	Sub-Franchise Contract: . . . . .No	On-Going Support: . . A,B,C,D,E,F,G,H,I
Registered: . . . . All Except AB	Expand in Territory: . . . . Yes	Full-Time Franchisor Support Staff: . . . 17
. . . .	Passive Ownership: . . . . . .Allowed	EXPANSION PLANS:
Average # of Employees: . . . . . . 4 FT, 2 PT	Encourage Conversions: . . . . . Yes	US: . . . . .All US
Prior Industry Experience: . . . . Helpful	Franchisee Purchase(s) Required: .No	Canada - Yes, ...Overseas - No

TIDY CAR INTERNATIONAL

P. O. Box 1290
Troy, MI 48007
TEL: (800) TIDY-CAR (313) 583-0170
FAX:
Ms. Judy Houser, Exec. Asst.

Largest auto appearance and detailing specialist, with locations in US, Canada and Europe. We provide complete training and on-going operational support.

HISTORY: . . . . IFA
Established in 1989; . . 1st Franchised in 1989
Company-Owned Units (As of 12/1/1989): . .0
Franchised Units (12/1/1989): 233
Total Units (12/1/1989): 233
Distribution: . . . US-122;Can-53;Overseas-58
North America: . . . . 27 States, 9 Provinces
Concentration: . . . 13 in PA, 9 in NY, 8 in IL
Registered: . . . . FL,MI
. . . .
Average # of Employees: . . . . . . 2 FT, 1 PT
Prior Industry Experience: . . . . Helpful

FINANCIAL:
Cash Investment: $41.7-50K
Total Investment: $41.7-59K
Fees: Franchise - $15K
Royalty: 5-8%, Advert: 5%
Contract Periods (Yrs.): 10/10
Area Development Agreement: . .No
Sub-Franchise Contract: . . . . .No
Expand in Territory: . . . . . . .No
Passive Ownership: . . . Discouraged
Encourage Conversions: . . . . Yes
Franchisee Purchase(s) Required: Yes

FRANCHISOR TRAINING/SUPPORT:
Financial Assistance Provided: . . . . . No
Site Selection Assistance: . . . . . . .Yes
Lease Negotiation Assistance: . . . . . No
Co-operative Advertising: . . . . . . .Yes
Training: . . . . . 2-2.5 Wks. Headquarters,
. . . . On-going in Field
On-Going Support: . . A,B,C,D,E,F,G,H,I
Full-Time Franchisor Support Staff: . . . 4
EXPANSION PLANS:
US: . . . . All US
Canada - Yes, . . . Overseas - Yes

TIRES ONLY

10 Easton Rd.
Brantford, ON N3P1J5 CAN
TEL: (800) 265-9985 (519) 754-1744
FAX: (519) 759-4360
Ms. Gail Kaufman, Mktg. Dir.

Unique, up-scale retail store program, specializing exclusively in tire sales/service and ride control. Full range of brand-name products from major manufacturers. Services include wheel alignment, front-end and suspension, balancing, repairs, custom wheels and accessories.

HISTORY: . . . .
Established in 1985; . . 1st Franchised in 1988
Company-Owned Units (As of 12/1/1989): . .1
Franchised Units (12/1/1989): 6
Total Units (12/1/1989): 7
Distribution: US-0;Can-7;Overseas-0
North America: . . . . 2 Provinces
Concentration: . . . . 6 in ON, 1 in MB
Registered: . . . .
. . . .
Average # of Employees: . . . . .2 FT
Prior Industry Experience: . . . . Helpful

FINANCIAL:
Cash Investment: $25-30K
Total Investment: $75-100K
Fees: Franchise - $10K
Royalty: 2%, Advert: . . . .
Contract Periods (Yrs.): 5/5
Area Development Agreement: Yes/Var
Sub-Franchise Contract: . . . . Yes
Expand in Territory: . . . . . . Yes
Passive Ownership: . . . Discouraged
Encourage Conversions: . . . . . Yes
Franchisee Purchase(s) Required: Yes

FRANCHISOR TRAINING/SUPPORT:
Financial Assistance Provided: . . . Yes(I)
Site Selection Assistance: . . . . . . .Yes
Lease Negotiation Assistance: . . . . .Yes
Co-operative Advertising: . . . . . . .Yes
Training: . . . . .1-2 Wks. Hands-on Train-
. . . . ing at Existing Stores
On-Going Support: . . . .A,B,C,D,E,F,H,I
Full-Time Franchisor Support Staff: . . . 2
EXPANSION PLANS:
US: . . . . All US
Canada - Yes, ...Overseas - No

TRUCKALINE SUSPENSION CENTER

1420 B Hwy. 12 East
Altoona, WI 54720
TEL: (800) 221-2838 (715) 839-9498
FAX:
Mr. Jerry Wolf, Exec. Recruiter

TRUCKALINE is offering a unique franchise opportunity for a highly-demanded service business with virtually no competition. A TRUCKALINE SUSPENSION CENTER is an ultra-modern truck repair facility, specializing in high-quality maintenance, repair and alignment of heavy duty truck suspension systems.

HISTORY: . . . . IFA
Established in 1978; . . 1st Franchised in 1988
Company-Owned Units (As of 12/1/1989): . .1
Franchised Units (12/1/1989): 0
Total Units (12/1/1989): 1
Distribution: US-1;Can-0;Overseas-0
North America: . . . . .1 State
Concentration: . . . . 1 in WI
Registered: . . . . IL,IN,MN,WI
. . . .
Average # of Employees: . . . . 10 FT
Prior Industry Experience: . . . . Helpful

FINANCIAL:
Cash Investment: $200-225K
Total Investment: $550-600K
Fees: Franchise - $25K
Royalty: 7%, Advert: 2%
Contract Periods (Yrs.): 5/5
Area Development Agreement: . .No
Sub-Franchise Contract: . . . . .No
Expand in Territory: . . . . . . Yes
Passive Ownership: . . . . . .Allowed
Encourage Conversions: . . . . .No
Franchisee Purchase(s) Required: .No

FRANCHISOR TRAINING/SUPPORT:
Financial Assistance Provided: . . . Yes(I)
Site Selection Assistance: . . . . . . .Yes
Lease Negotiation Assistance: . . . . .Yes
Co-operative Advertising: . . . . No
Training: . . . . 2 Wks. Headquarters,
. . . . 2 Wks. On-site, On-going Support
On-Going Support: . . .a,B,C,D,E,F,G,H,I
Full-Time Franchisor Support Staff: . . . 4
EXPANSION PLANS:
US: . . . . Midwest
Canada - No, ...Overseas - No

TUFFY SERVICE CENTER

1414 Baronial Plaza Dr.
Toledo, OH 43615
TEL: (800) 228-8339 (419) 865-6900
FAX:
Mr. Eric Schmitt, Dir. Fran. Sales

TUFFY offers a tremendous opportunity for success in the booming automotive aftermarket. Retail sales and installation of exhaust system replacement, brakes, ride control products, steering and front-end. Excellent initial and on-going training. Field support and business management support on an on-going basis.

HISTORY: . . . . IFA
Established in 1970; . . 1st Franchised in 1971
Company-Owned Units (As of 12/1/1989): . 13
Franchised Units (12/1/1989): 99
Total Units (12/1/1989): 112
Distribution: . . . US-112;Can-0;Overseas-0
 North America: . . . . 8 States
 Concentration: . . 51 in MI, 43 in OH, 7 in VA
Registered: . . . FL,IL,IN,MD,MI,MN,VA,WI
 . . . .
Average # of Employees: . . . . . 2-3 FT, 1 PT
Prior Industry Experience: . . . . Helpful

FINANCIAL:
Cash Investment: $50-70K
Total Investment: $140-150K
Fees: Franchise - $18.5K
 Royalty: 5%, Advert: 5%
Contract Periods (Yrs.): 15/10
Area Development Agreement: Yes/10
Sub-Franchise Contract: . . . . . .No
Expand in Territory: . . . . . . Yes
Passive Ownership: . . . Discouraged
Encourage Conversions: . . . . . Yes
Franchisee Purchase(s) Required: .No

FRANCHISOR TRAINING/SUPPORT:
Financial Assistance Provided: . . .Yes(D)
Site Selection Assistance: . . . . . . .Yes
Lease Negotiation Assistance: . . . . .Yes
Co-operative Advertising: . . . . .No
Training: . . . . 4 Wks. Headquarters
 . . . .
On-Going Support: . . . . .B,C,D,E,G,H,I
Full-Time Franchisor Support Staff: . . 33
EXPANSION PLANS:
 US: . . . . . . Midwest, East, Southeast
 Canada - No, ...Overseas - No

TUNEX

556 East 2100 South
Salt Lake City, UT 84106
TEL: (801) 486-8133
FAX:
Mr. Boyd Enniss, Dir. Fran. Ops.

Attractive six- and eight-bay TUNEX CENTERS offer a complete one-stop tune-up service. Specializing in complete analysis and repair of ignition, fuel, cooling and computerized engine control systems, a full service of the automotive air conditioning system and the newly-added lube and oil service, using the latest equipment and skilled technicians. Salesmanship and business background are essential.

HISTORY: . . . . IFA
Established in 1976; . . 1st Franchised in 1977
Company-Owned Units (As of 12/1/1989): . .9
Franchised Units (12/1/1989): 10
Total Units (12/1/1989): 19
Distribution: US-19;Can-0;Overseas-0
 North America: . . . . 5 States
 Concentration: . . .11 in VT, 3 in CO, 2 in NV
Registered: . . . .
 . . . .
Average # of Employees: . . . . .4 FT
Prior Industry Experience: . . . . Helpful

FINANCIAL: OTC-TUNX
Cash Investment: $65K
Total Investment: $90K
Fees: Franchise - $19K
 Royalty: 5%, Advert: . . $750/Mo.
Contract Periods (Yrs.): 10/10
Area Development Agreement: . .No
Sub-Franchise Contract: . . . . . .No
Expand in Territory: . . . . . . Yes
Passive Ownership: . . . . . .Allowed
Encourage Conversions: . . . . . .No
Franchisee Purchase(s) Required: .No

FRANCHISOR TRAINING/SUPPORT:
Financial Assistance Provided: . . . . . No
Site Selection Assistance: . . . . . . .Yes
Lease Negotiation Assistance: . . . . .Yes
Co-operative Advertising: . . . . .No
Training: . . . . . . 1-2 Wks. Headquarters,
 . . . . . .1 Wk. Site, On-going Technical
On-Going Support: . . . . b,C,D,E,f,G,H,I
Full-Time Franchisor Support Staff: . . .5
EXPANSION PLANS:
 US: . . . West, Southwest, Midwest, NW
 Canada - No, ...Overseas - No

WASH ON WHEELS / WOW

5401 S. Bryant Ave.
Sanford, FL 32773
TEL: (800) 345-1969 *432-7088 (FL)
FAX: (407) 321-3409
Mr. H. George Louser, President

WOW franchisees profit from: WOW Power Washing - buildings, trucks, homes. WOW HY-DRY - carpet, upholstery, drapery cleaning. WOW acoustical/vinyl ceiling cleaning. Voted Top 10 small business franchise by Small Business Opportunity Magazine, August, 1989. Received highest rating from Women in Franchising Association in May, 1989.

HISTORY: . . . . IFA/WIF
Established in 1966; . . 1st Franchised in 1987
Company-Owned Units (As of 12/1/1989): . .0
Franchised Units (12/1/1989): 111
Total Units (12/1/1989): 111
Distribution: . . . US-111;Can-0;Overseas-0
 North America: . . . . 25 States
 Concentration: . . . 9 in FL, 8 in GA, 7 in OH
Registered: . . . CA,FL,HI,IL,IN,MD,MI,MN
 . . . . NY,VA,WA,WI
Average # of Employees: . . . . . . 1 FT, 1 PT
Prior Industry Experience: . . . . Helpful

FINANCIAL:
Cash Investment: $5-18K
Total Investment: $13-57K
Fees: Franchise - $3.5-10.5K
 Royalty: 5%, Advert: 1%
Contract Periods (Yrs.): 5/5
Area Development Agreement: Yes/5
Sub-Franchise Contract: . . . . . .No
Expand in Territory: . . . . . . Yes
Passive Ownership: . . . Discouraged
Encourage Conversions: . . . . . Yes
Franchisee Purchase(s) Required: Yes

FRANCHISOR TRAINING/SUPPORT:
Financial Assistance Provided: . . . Yes(I)
Site Selection Assistance: . . . . . . .NA
Lease Negotiation Assistance: . . . . .NA
Co-operative Advertising: . . . . . . .Yes
Training: . . . . 2 Wks. Headquarters
 . . . .
On-Going Support: . . . . c,D,G,H,I
Full-Time Franchisor Support Staff: . . 13
EXPANSION PLANS:
 US: . . . . .All US
 Canada - Yes, . . . Overseas - Yes

WASH-O-TEL

1500 Louisville Ave.
Monroe, LA 71201
TEL: (318) 322-6140
FAX:
Mr. Wayne Williamson, President

Mobile car wash, specializing in fleets and aircraft. Special techniques and chemicals allow for complete wash and dry in 4 minutes with 1/2 gallon of water. Excellent part-time job. Most washes are evenings.

HISTORY: . . . .
Established in 1983; . . 1st Franchised in 1985
Company-Owned Units (As of 12/1/1989): . .0
Franchised Units (12/1/1989): 2
Total Units (12/1/1989): 2
Distribution: US-2;Can-0;Overseas-0
North America: . . . . 2 States
Concentration: . . . . 1 in OK, 1 in LA
Registered: . . . .
. . . .
Average # of Employees: . . . . .3 FT, 2-10 PT
Prior Industry Experience: . . . . Helpful

FINANCIAL:
Cash Investment: $7-16K
Total Investment: $15-26K
Fees: Franchise - $9.6K
   Royalty: 8%, Advert: 2%
Contract Periods (Yrs.): . . . . Infin.
Area Development Agreement: . .No
Sub-Franchise Contract: . . . . . .No
Expand in Territory: . . . . . . Yes
Passive Ownership: . . . Discouraged
Encourage Conversions: . . . . . Yes
Franchisee Purchase(s) Required: Yes

FRANCHISOR TRAINING/SUPPORT:
Financial Assistance Provided: . . . Yes(I)
Site Selection Assistance: . . . . .NA
Lease Negotiation Assistance: . . . . .NA
Co-operative Advertising: . . . . No
Training: . . . . 1 Wk. Headquarters
. . . .
On-Going Support: . . . . . . B,C,D,E,H,I
Full-Time Franchisor Support Staff: . . . 1
EXPANSION PLANS:
US: . . . . All Exc. Restricted States
Canada - No, ...Overseas - No

ZIEBART CAR IMPROVEMENT SPECIALISTS
1290 E. Maple
Troy, MI 48084
TEL: (800) 877-1312 (313) 588-4100
FAX: (313) 588-2513
Mr. Mark Bollegar, Fran. Sales Dir.

ZIEBART, known world-wide for quality automotive protection, now offers a highly-diversified line of vehicle improvement products and services. Sunroofs, running boards, window tinting, auto alarm systems, auto detailing and more have now joined our traditional services, such as rust, paint and fabric protection.

HISTORY: . . . . .IFA
Established in 1962; . . 1st Franchised in 1962
Company-Owned Units (As of 12/1/1989): . 32
Franchised Units (12/1/1989): 533
Total Units (12/1/1989): 565
Distribution: . . US-328;Can-60;Overseas-177
North America: . . . . 30 States, 9 Provinces
Concentration: . . 49 in MI, 39 in IL, 38 in ON
Registered: . . .CA,IL,MD,MI,MN,OR,RI,VA
. . . . WA,WI,AB
Average # of Employees: . . . . . . 3 FT, 1 PT
Prior Industry Experience: . . . . Helpful

FINANCIAL:
Cash Investment: $20-40k
Total Investment: $20-86.2k
Fees: Franchise - $20K
   Royalty: 8%, Advert: 5%
Contract Periods (Yrs.): . . . 10/Var.
Area Development Agreement: Yes/2+
Sub-Franchise Contract: . . . . . .No
Expand in Territory: . . . . . . Yes
Passive Ownership: . . . Discouraged
Encourage Conversions: . . . . . Yes
Franchisee Purchase(s) Required: Yes

FRANCHISOR TRAINING/SUPPORT:
Financial Assistance Provided: . . .Yes(D)
Site Selection Assistance: . . . . .Yes
Lease Negotiation Assistance: . . . . .Yes
Co-operative Advertising: . . . . .Yes
Training: . . . . 3 Wks. Headquarters,
. . . . On-going in Field
On-Going Support: . . A,B,C,D,E,F,G,H,I
Full-Time Franchisor Support Staff: . . . 8
EXPANSION PLANS:
US: . . . . .All US
Canada - Yes, ...Overseas - Yes

SUPPLEMENTAL LISTING OF FRANCHISORS

60 MINUTE TUNE/10 MINUTE LUBE . . . . .11811 NE 1st St., # 208, Bellevue WA 98005
ABT SERVICE CENTERS . . . . .2339 South 2700 West, Salt Lake City UT 84119
ACE QUICK OIL CHANGE . . . . .648 American Legion Hwy., Westport MA 02790
ACTIVE TIRE & AUTO CENTRE . . . . 186 The Queensway, Toronto ON M8Y1J3   CAN
ALAN FARLEY & ASSOCIATES . . . . 14011 Ventura Blvd., # 307, Sherman Oaks CA 91423
ALLSAVE CAR/TRUCK RENTAL SYSTEMS . . . . .8161 Keele St., # 1A, Concord ON L4K1Z3   CAN
APPEARANCE RECONDITIONING CO. . . . . .12833 Industrial Park Blvd., Minneapolis MN 55441
APPLE AUTO GLASS .449 Fenmar Dr., Weston ON M9L2R6   CAN
AUTO CRITIC . . . . 3307 Northland, # 400, Austin TX 78731
AUTO GENICS TOTAL AUTO SERVICE . . . . . .5399 Eglinton Ave. W, # 201, Etobicoke ON M9C5K6   CAN
AUTO GLASS CENTRES . . . . 334 Rowntree Rd. W., Mississauga ON L4L8H2   CAN
AUTO-LIFE . . . . .1430 South Cherokee St., Denver CO 80223
AUTOLIST . . . . 1101 Gulf Breeze Pkwy., # 200+, Gulf Breeze FL 32561

AUTOSPA CORP.	343 Great Neck Rd., Great Neck NY 11021	
AUTOSTOCK	8288 boul. PIE IX, Montreal PQ H1Z3T6	CAN
BATTERY BANK, THE	2053 Johns Drive, Glenview IL 60025	
BRAKE CHECK	11125 - 107 Ave., # 200, Edmonton AB T5M0X9	CAN
BRAKE EXPRESS	17691 Mitchell N., Irvine CA 92714	
BRAKE SHOP, THE	30695 Little Mack, # 400, Roseville MI 48066	
BRAKE WORLD	7700 NW 27th Ave., Miami FL 33147	
BUFF & SHINE	7207 L St., Omaha NE 68127	
BUYRITE AUTO & TRAVEL CONSULTANTS	464 W. 13 Ave., Vancouver BC V5Y1W5	CAN
CAR CHECKERS OF AMERICA	1031 Rte. 22W, # 302, Bridgewater NJ 08807	
CITYWIDE AUTOGLASS FRANCHISING	826 Belmont St., Brockton MA 02401	
CLASSIC SHINE AUTO FITNESS CENTER	428 W. Putnam Ave., Greenwich CT 06830	
COLORCARE CAR PROTECTANT	6272 E. Pacific Coast Hwy., Long Beach CA 90803	
CROSLEY CORP.	P.O. Box 878, Starke FL 32091	
DER WAGEN HAUS	5316 W. Market St., P.O. Box 1842, Greensboro NC 27419	
DRIVE LINE SERVICE	1309 Tradewind Circle, Sacramento CA 95691	
DURATION LUBE CENTERS	4566 Winchester Rd., Memphis TN 38118	
DYNAMIC MOBILE DETAILING	70 West Grove St., Reno NV 89509	
ENGINE SERVICE SPECIALISTS	331 Fulton St., # 1133, Peoria IL 61602	
EXHAUST PRO	11520 Commonwealth Dr., Louisville KY 40299	
EXPRESS 10 MINUTE LUBE	66 Rte. 125, Kingston NH 03858	
EXPRESS LUBE	320 Railroad Ave., Loveland CO 80537	
FAIR MUFFLER SHOPS	531 E. Roosevelt Rd., # 101, Wheaton IL 60187	
FIRESTONE TIRE & RUBBER COMPANY	6275 Eastland Rd., Brook Park OH 44142	
FLEET MOBILE LUBE SERVICE	11020 King St., # 375, Overland Park KS 66210	
G. LEBEAU	8288 boul. PIE IX, Montreal PQ H1Z3T6	CAN
GASCARD CLUB	110 25 N. Tory Pine Rd., La Jolla CA 92038	
GOODEAL DISCOUNT TRANSMISSIONS	P.O. Box 50, National Park NJ 08063	
GOODYEAR TIRE CENTERS	1144 E. Market St., Akron OH 44316	
GUARANTEED MUFFLER	201 Schell Ave., Toronto ON M6E2T4	CAN
HAMILTON RADIATOR	624 Parkdale Ave. N., Hamilton ON L8H7N1	CAN
HANNA CAR WASH SYSTEMS	2000 Hanna Dr., Portland OR 97222	
INSIDE OUT	751 Dundas St. E., Toronto ON M5A2C4	CAN
INTERNATIONAL FLYING COLORS	1285 N. Post Oak, # 190, Houston TX 77055	
KALES COLLISION	11725 Merriman Rd., Livonia MI 48051	
LANOGUARD	34 Grenfell Cres., Ottawa ON K2G0G2	CAN
LUBE ON WHEELS	150 SW 12th Ave., Pompano Beach FL 33069	
LUBE SHOP, THE	205 S. Country Club Dr., Mesa AZ 85202	
MAACO AUTO PAINTING AND BODYWORKS	381 Brooks Rd., King of Prussia PA 19406	
MAACO AUTO PAINTING AND BODYWORKS	5915 Airport Rd., # 330, Mississauga ON L4V1T1	CAN
MAGICAR AUTOMOTIVE APPEARANCE	621 Lakeview Rd., # C, Clearwater FL 34616	
MAM	14019 Beach Blvd., # 938, Jacksonville FL 32250	
MASTER MECHANIC	1989 Dundas St. E., Mississauga ON L4X1M1	CAN
MCQUIK'S OILUBE	P.O. Box 46, Muncie IN 47308	
MEINEKE DISCOUNT MUFFLER SHOPS	Two Robert Speck Pkwy., # 750, Mississauga ON L4Z1H8	CAN
METRO 25 TIRE & CAR CARE CENTRES	51 Covington St., Hamilton ON L8E2Y4	CAN
MIDAS CANADA	105 Commander Blvd., Agincourt ON M1S3X8	CAN
MILEX TUNE UP & BRAKES	4914 N. Lincoln Ave., Chicago IL 60625	
MING AUTO APPEARANCE CENTERS	7526 Metcalf, Overland Park KS 66214	
MINIT-TUNE AUTO CENTRES	497 W. 5th Ave., Vancouver BC V5Y1J9	CAN
MIRACLE AUTO PAINTING/BODY REPAIR	1065 E. Hillsdale Blvd., # 110, Foster City CA 94404	
MISTER FRONT-END	192 N. Queen St., Etobicoke ON M9C1A8	CAN
MOBILE AUTO MAINTENANCE	14019 Beach Blvd., # 938, Jacksonville FL 32250	
MOBILE AUTO SYSTEMS	11883 Dublin Blvd., # A-245, Dublin CA 94568	
MOBILE AUTO TRIM	11460 Garland Rd., P.O. Box 38108, Dallas TX 75238	
MOBILE MECHANIC	4189 Willowview Ave., Memphis TN 38111	
MONSIEUR MUFFLER	8288 boul. PIE IX, Montreal PQ H1Z3T6	CAN
MOTRA TRANSMISSIONS	4912 N. Lincoln Ave., Chicago IL 60625	

MR. LUBE CANADA . . . . .5555 Calgary Trail, # 1410, Edmonton AB T6H4J9   CAN
MR. TRANSMISSION . . . . .400 Harding Industrial Dr., Nashville TN 37211
MR. WINDOW TINTING . . . . 3617A Silverside Rd., Wilmington DE 19810
MR. WIZARD GLASS TINTING . . . . 587 Bay St., P. O. Box 486, Victoria BC V8W2N8   CAN
MUFFLER XPRESS & BRAKE CENTERS . . . . 1307 Roanoke Ave., Roanoke Rapids NC 27870
MULTI-START . . . . P. O. Box 631, Richboro PA 18954
OIL CAN HENRY'S . . . . 1650 NW Front Ave., # 120, Portland OR 97209
OIL GARD ANTI-RUST/CAR CARE . . . . .105 # 130 Meadowbrook Dr., London ON N6L1G4   CAN
OIL PRO LUBE-N-WASH . . . . .1819 E. Southern, Mesa AZ 85204
PAINT MASTER AUTO REFINISHING CENTRES . . . . 835 Valetta St., London ON N6H2Z2   CAN
PERMA-SHINE CAR CARE CENTRES . . . . .1380 Speers Rd., # 4, Oakville ON L6L5V3   CAN
PHOENIX CAR & TRUCK RENTALS . . . . 2499 Dufferin St., Toronto ON M6B3R3   CAN
PIT PROS, THE . . . . .9657 Distribution Ave., San Diego CA 92121
PRECISION TUNE . . . . P.O. Box 379, Sterling VA 22170
PROBLEM SOLVER AUTO SERVICE . . . . .5480 N. Northwest Hwy., Chicago IL 60630
PROMPTO 10 MINUTE OIL, FILTER & LUBE . . . . 13 Scott Dr., Westbrook ME 04092
QUAKER STATE MINIT LUBE . . . . 1385 W. 2200 S., Salt Lake City UT 84119
QUAL KROM FRANCHISING . . . . 301 Florida Ave., Fort Pierce FL 34950
RADIATOR CENTER USA . . . . 1611 Lakeland Ave., Bohemia NY 11716
ROYAL TRANSMISSION . . . . 291 James St., Toronto ON M8W1L6   CAN
SEAT COVERS, U.S.A. .342 Hempstead Tpk., W. Hempstead NY 11552
SECOND OPINION . . . . 34 Grenfell Cres., Ottawa ON K2G0G2   CAN
SENTINEL AUTOMOTIVE CENTERS . . . . .620 Herndon Pkwy., # 200, Herndon VA 22070
SERVICE CENTER PERFORMANCE AUTO PARTS . . . 1530 W. El Segundo Blvd., Gardena CA 90249
SPECIALTY LUBE . . . . .4566 Winchester Rd., Memphis TN 38118
STOP'N STEER SHOPS .80 Manor Rd., St. Thomas ON N5R5N7   CAN
SUN-SCREEN INTERNATIONAL . . . . .1700 S. Valley Mills Dr., Waco TX 76711
SUPERFORMANCE FRANCHISING . . . . 2950 Airway Ave., # A5, Costa Mesa CA 92626
SUPERIOR RUSTPROOFING . . . . .3120 6 Glen Erin Dr., Mississauga ON L5L1R6   CAN
SURE STOP BRAKE . . . . 201 Schell Ave., Toronto ON M6E2T4   CAN
THAT MUFFLER & BRAKE PLACE . . . . 22309 NE 46th St., Redmond WA 98053
TIDY CAR TOTAL APPEARANCE CENTER . . . . 333 Wyecroft Rd., Mississauga ON L6K2H2   CAN
TINT KING MOTORING ACCESSORIES . . . . 1950 Hwy. # 7, Unit 10, Toronto ON L4K3B2   CAN
TKD NORTH AMERICA .1290 E. Maple Rd., # 304, Troy MI 48084
TOTAL AUTO GLASS & SUNROOFS . . . . .5475 Dundas St. W., Islington ON L4W4H9   CAN
TUFF-KOTE DINOL . . . . 25200 Melvina, Warren MI 48089
TUNEOMIZE AUTO CARE CENTERS . . . . 402 A Harding Industrial Dr., Nashville TN 37211
UNIROYAL GOODRICH . . . . 600 S. Main St., Akron OH 44318
USA FAST LUBE SYSTEMS . . . . .P. O. Box 280742, Lakewood CO 80228
VALVOLINE INSTANT OIL CHANGE . . . . .P.O. Box 14046, Lexington KY 40512
VICTORY LANE QUICK OIL CHANGE . . . . 2610 W. Liberty St., # C, Ann Arbor MI 48103
WESTERN AUTO SUPPLY . . . . .2107 Grand Ave., Kansas City MO 64108
WINDSHIELD DOCTOR CANADA . . . . #200 - 17628 - 103 Ave., Edmonton AB T5S1J9   CAN
ZIEBART RUSTPROOFING . . . . 150 Oakdale Rd., Downsview ON M3N1W1   CAN

CHAPTER 5

AUTO / TRUCK TRAILER RENTAL

AIRWAYS RENT A CAR

4025 N. Mannheim
Schiller Park, IL 60176
TEL: (312) 678-2300
FAX:
Mr. Howard Maybloom, Dir. Fran.

Company active in operating auto rental business for 20 years. Franchising last 3 years. Automated reservation system gives access to 20,000 travel agents, corporate travel managers and airline reservationists. Marketing agreement with major auto manufacturers.

HISTORY: . . . . IFA
Established in 1967; . . 1st Franchised in 1985
Company-Owned Units (As of 12/1/1989): . .2
Franchised Units (12/1/1989): 71
Total Units (12/1/1989): 73
Distribution: US-64;Can-0;Overseas-9
 North America: . . . . 14 States
 Concentration: . . . .14 in IL,11 in CT,3 in NJ
Registered: . . . . CA,FL,IL,VA,WA
. . . .
Average # of Employees: . . . . . . 3 FT, 2 PT
Prior Industry Experience: . . . . Helpful

FINANCIAL:
Cash Investment: $100-500K
Total Investment: $100-500K
Fees: Franchise - . . . . $25+K
 Royalty: 7%, Advert: 0%
Contract Periods (Yrs.): 5/5
Area Development Agreement: . .No
Sub-Franchise Contract: . . . . . Yes
Expand in Territory: . . . . Yes
Passive Ownership: . . . . . .Allowed
Encourage Conversions: . . . . . Yes
Franchisee Purchase(s) Required: .No

FRANCHISOR TRAINING/SUPPORT:
Financial Assistance Provided: . . . Yes(I)
Site Selection Assistance: . . . . .Yes
Lease Negotiation Assistance: . . . . .Yes
Co-operative Advertising: . . . . .Yes
Training: . . . . 1 Wk. Headquarters
. . . .
On-Going Support: . . . a,B,c,d,E,F,G,H,I
Full-Time Franchisor Support Staff: . .120
EXPANSION PLANS:
 US: . . . . All US
 Canada - Yes, ...Overseas - Yes

AUTO, TRUCK & TRAILER RENTAL

	1988	1989	1990	Percentage Change 1988-1989	Percentage Change 1989-1990
Number of Establishments:					
Company-Owned	2,392	2,389	2,415	-0.1%	1.1%
Franchisee-Owned	7,153	7,470	8,198	4.4%	9.7%
Total	9,545	9,859	10,613	3.3%	7.6%
% of Total Establishments:					
Company-Owned	25.1%	24.2%	22.8%		
Franchisee-Owned	74.9%	75.8%	77.2%		
Total	100.0%	100.0%	100.0%		
Annual Sales ($000):					
Company-Owned	$3,745,391	$3,861,730	$4,090,930	3.1%	5.9%
Franchisee-Owned	2,871,325	3,089,170	3,486,900	7.6%	12.9%
Total	6,616,716	6,950,900	7,577,830	5.1%	9.0%
% of Total Sales:					
Company-Owned	56.6%	55.6%	54.0%		
Franchisee-Owned	43.4%	44.4%	46.0%		
Total	100.0%	100.0%	100.0%		
Average Sales Per Unit ($000):					
Company-Owned	$1,566	$1,616	$1,694	3.2%	4.8%
Franchisee-Owned	401	414	425	3.0%	2.9%
Total	693	705	714	1.7%	1.3%
Sales Ratio	390.1%	390.9%	398.3%		

	1st Quartile	Median	4th Quartile
Average 1988 Total Investment:			
Company-Owned	N. A.	$150,000	N. A.
Franchisee-Owned	73,750	150,000	275,000
Single Unit Franchise Fee	$3,000	$15,000	$25,000
Multiple Unit Franchise Fee	N. A.	N. A.	N. A.
Franchisee Start-up Cost	25,000	30,000	75,000

	1988	Employees/Unit	Sales/Employee
Employment:			
Company-Owned	32,302	13.5	$115,949
Franchisee-Owned	44,966	6.3	63,855
Total	77,268	8.1	85,633
Employee Performance Ratios		214.8%	181.6%

Source: Franchising In The Economy, 1988 – 1990, IFA Education Foundation & Horwath International, Published January, 1990.

1) 1989 and 1990 data were estimated by respondents.

ALLSTAR RENT-A-CAR

P. O. Box 69027
Seattle, WA 98168
TEL: (800) 426-5243 (206) 433-8923
FAX: (206) 431-9347
Ms. Luata Lawrence, Fran. Sales

ALLSTAR has over 60 locations nationwide. Full-service system for 13 years. We assist with fleet acquisition and group insurance rates. Providing a nationwide reservation network, computer system, national advertising, comprehensive training and on-going support for the life of the franchise.

HISTORY: . . . . .WIF
Established in 1976; . . 1st Franchised in 1981
Company-Owned Units (As of 12/1/1989): . .3
Franchised Units (12/1/1989): 60
Total Units (12/1/1989): 63
Distribution: US-63;Can-0;Overseas-0
North America: . . . . 17 States
Concentration: . 11 in AK, 10 in NY, 8 in WA
Registered: . . . CA,FL,IL,IN,MD,MI,MN,ND
. . . . OR,RI,SD,VA,WA,WI
Average # of Employees: . . . . . . 3 FT, 2 PT
Prior Industry Experience: . . . . Helpful

FINANCIAL:
Cash Investment: . . . . . $55-100K+
Total Investment: . . . . . $70-200K+
Fees: Franchise - $15-50K
Royalty: 6%, Advert: 2%
Contract Periods (Yrs.): 10/10
Area Development Agreement: Yes/10
Sub-Franchise Contract: . . . . . Yes
Expand in Territory: . . . . . . Yes
Passive Ownership: . . . Discouraged
Encourage Conversions: . . . . . Yes
Franchisee Purchase(s) Required: Yes

FRANCHISOR TRAINING/SUPPORT:
Financial Assistance Provided: . . . Yes(I)
Site Selection Assistance: . . . . . . .Yes
Lease Negotiation Assistance: . . . . .Yes
Co-operative Advertising: . . . . . . .Yes
Training: . . . . .1 Wk. Headquarters,
. . . . 1 Wk. Site
On-Going Support: . . . b,C,D,E,F,G,H,I
Full-Time Franchisor Support Staff: . . 11
EXPANSION PLANS:
US: . . . .NE,S,MW,SE,NW & Mid-East
Canada - No, ...Overseas - No

BUDGET RENT A CAR

200 N. Michigan
Chicago, IL 60601
TEL: (312) 580-5000
FAX:
Mr. Rick Santella, AVP, Fran. Acqs.

Daily car and truck rental.

HISTORY: . . . . IFA
Established in 1958; . . 1st Franchised in 1960
Company-Owned Units (As of 12/1/1989): 460
Franchised Units (12/1/1989): 3049
Total Units (12/1/1989): 3509
Distribution: US-1,241;Can-395;Overseas-1,873
North America: . . . . 50 States,12 Provinces
Concentration: . . . .
Registered: . . . . .All
. . . .
Average # of Employees: . . . . .1 FT / 15 Cars
Prior Industry Experience: . . . . Helpful

FINANCIAL:
Cash Investment: $25-150K
Total Investment: $400K
Fees: Franchise - . . . . . . $15K+
Royalty: 5%, Advert: 2.5%
Contract Periods (Yrs.): 5/5
Area Development Agreement: . Yes
Sub-Franchise Contract: . . . . . Yes
Expand in Territory: . . . . . . Yes
Passive Ownership: . . . Discouraged
Encourage Conversions: . . . . . Yes
Franchisee Purchase(s) Required: .No

FRANCHISOR TRAINING/SUPPORT:
Financial Assistance Provided: . . . . .No
Site Selection Assistance: . . . . . . .Yes
Lease Negotiation Assistance: . . . . .Yes
Co-operative Advertising: . . . . . . .Yes
Training: . . . . .1 Wk. Headquarters,
. . . . 1 Wk. Site
On-Going Support: . . . a,b,C,D,E,F,G,h,I
Full-Time Franchisor Support Staff: . .450
EXPANSION PLANS:
US: . . . . .All US
Canada - Yes, . . . Overseas - Yes

FAMILY RENT A CAR

2438 N. Broadwell
Grand Island, NB 68803
TEL: (308) 381-7676
FAX:
Ms. Gale Mettenbrink, President

We have an automobile rental franchise available that can be run in conjunction with an existing business. There are no minimum number of car requirements.

HISTORY: . . . .
Established in 1981; . . 1st Franchised in 1985
Company-Owned Units (As of 12/1/1989): . 12
Franchised Units (12/1/1989): 61
Total Units (12/1/1989): 73
Distribution: US-73;Can-0;Overseas-0
North America: . . . . 14 States
Concentration: . . . 10 in NE, 7 in CO, 4 in MI
Registered: . . . FL,IL,IN,MI,MN,ND,OR,SD
. . . . WA,WI
Average # of Employees: . . . . .1 FT
Prior Industry Experience: . . . . Helpful

FINANCIAL:
Cash Investment: . . . . $2.5K+
Total Investment: . . . . $Varies
Fees: Franchise - . . . . $1.5K+
Royalty: 4%, Advert: 1%
Contract Periods (Yrs.): 1/1
Area Development Agreement: Yes/1
Sub-Franchise Contract: . . . . . Yes
Expand in Territory: . . . . . . Yes
Passive Ownership: . . . . . .Allowed
Encourage Conversions: . . . . . NA
Franchisee Purchase(s) Required: .No

FRANCHISOR TRAINING/SUPPORT:
Financial Assistance Provided: . . . . .No
Site Selection Assistance: . . . . . . .NA
Lease Negotiation Assistance: . . . . .NA
Co-operative Advertising: . . . . . . .Yes
Training: . . . . . 1-3 Days Franchisee Site
. . . .
On-Going Support: . . . . . . .C,D,E,G,H
Full-Time Franchisor Support Staff: . . . 6
EXPANSION PLANS:
US: . . . . .All US
Canada - No, ...Overseas - No

SENSIBLE CAR RENTAL

51 Gerand Ave.
Matawan, NJ 07747
TEL: (800) 367-5159
FAX: (201) 290-8305
Mr. Charles A. Vitale, President

SENSIBLE CAR RENTAL provides the expertise and systems for car rental, which includes formal and/or on-site training, insurance and management support.

HISTORY: . . . .
Established in 1986; . . 1st Franchised in 1986
Company-Owned Units (As of 12/1/1989): . .0
Franchised Units (12/1/1989): 86
Total Units (12/1/1989): 86
Distribution: US-86;Can-0;Overseas-0
North America: . . . . 16 States
Concentration: . .25 in NY, 20 in NJ, 10 in CT
Registered: . . . . .IL,IN,MD,NY
. . . .
Average # of Employees: . . . . .1 FT
Prior Industry Experience: . . . . . .Necessary

FINANCIAL:
Cash Investment: . . . . $Varies
Total Investment: . . . . $Varies
Fees: Franchise - $3.5-7K
Royalty: NA, Advert: . . . . . . NA
Contract Periods (Yrs.): . . . Infin.
Area Development Agreement: . .No
Sub-Franchise Contract: . . . . .No
Expand in Territory: . . . . . . Yes
Passive Ownership: . . . Not Allowed
Encourage Conversions: . . . . .No
Franchisee Purchase(s) Required: .No

FRANCHISOR TRAINING/SUPPORT:
Financial Assistance Provided: . . . . .No
Site Selection Assistance: . . . . . . .No
Lease Negotiation Assistance: . . . . .No
Co-operative Advertising: . . . . .No
Training: . . . . 2 Days Headquarters
. . . .
On-Going Support: . . . . A,B,C,D,E,F,G
Full-Time Franchisor Support Staff: . . . 8
EXPANSION PLANS:
US: . . . . . . .Midwest, West Southwest
Canada - No, ...Overseas - No

U-SAVE AUTO RENTAL

7525 Connelley Dr., # A
Hanover, MD 21076
TEL: (800) 272-8728 (301) 760-8727
FAX: (301) 760-4390
Mr. William Edwards, Natl. Sales Mgr

U-SAVE AUTO RENTAL is a nationwide rental car franchisor, with 489 locations in 44 states. Franchisees are provided with such tools as a comprehensive training and policy manual, a national insurance program, hands-on field support, a bi-monthly newsletter and free operating forms.

HISTORY: . . . .
Established in 19; . . . . 1st Franchised in 19
Company-Owned Units (As of 12/1/1989): . .0
Franchised Units (12/1/1989): 489
Total Units (12/1/1989): 489
Distribution: US-489;Can-0;Overseas-0
North America: . . . . 44 States
Concentration: . . . .
Registered: . . . . All Except AB
. . . .
Average # of Employees: . . . . .3 FT
Prior Industry Experience: . . . . Helpful

FINANCIAL:
Cash Investment: $30-80K
Total Investment: . . . .$
Fees: Franchise - $7.5-15K
Royalty: Varies, Advert: . . . 2%
Contract Periods (Yrs.): 3/5
Area Development Agreement: . . .
Sub-Franchise Contract: . . . . .No
Expand in Territory: . . . . . . Yes
Passive Ownership: . . . Discouraged
Encourage Conversions: . . . . Yes
Franchisee Purchase(s) Required: .No

FRANCHISOR TRAINING/SUPPORT:
Financial Assistance Provided: . . .Yes(D)
Site Selection Assistance: . . . . . . .Yes
Lease Negotiation Assistance: . . . . .NA
Co-operative Advertising: . . . . .Yes
Training: . . . . 3-5 Days On-site,
. . . . 3-5 Days Home Office
On-Going Support: . . . . . C,D,E,F,G,H,I
Full-Time Franchisor Support Staff: . . . .
EXPANSION PLANS:
US: . . . . All US
Canada - No, ...Overseas - No

UGLY DUCKLING RENT-A-CAR

1240 E. Missouri
Phoenix, AZ 85014
TEL: (800) 843-3825 *545-9449
FAX: (602) 277-8074
Mr. Frank Kapilow, President

Premier used car rentals. "America's Second Car." We offer the most economical, reliable and practical alternative to the "Big Guys" in the industry. We provide continuing support and training and the best profit-oriented programs for our licensees. "Our success comes from your success!"

HISTORY: . . . . .IFA
Established in 1977; . . 1st Franchised in 1977
Company-Owned Units (As of 12/1/1989): . .2
Franchised Units (12/1/1989): 300
Total Units (12/1/1989): 302
Distribution: US-302;Can-0;Overseas-0
North America: . . . . 36 States
Concentration: . .25 in CT, 25 in PA, 25 in CA
Registered: . . . . All Except HI and AB
. . . .
Average # of Employees: . . . . .2-5 FT
Prior Industry Experience: . . . . Helpful

FINANCIAL:
Cash Investment: $25-50K
Total Investment: $100-125K
Fees: Franchise - $15-20K
Royalty: 6%, Advert: 2%
Contract Periods (Yrs.): 5
Area Development Agreement: Yes/5
Sub-Franchise Contract: . . . . Yes
Expand in Territory: . . . . . . Yes
Passive Ownership: . . . Discouraged
Encourage Conversions: . . . . .No
Franchisee Purchase(s) Required: .No

FRANCHISOR TRAINING/SUPPORT:
Financial Assistance Provided: . . . . .NA
Site Selection Assistance: . . . . . . .Yes
Lease Negotiation Assistance: . . . . .Yes
Co-operative Advertising: . . . . .Yes
Training: . . . . 2 Days Headquarters
. . . .
On-Going Support: . . . . . b,C,D,e,G,h,i
Full-Time Franchisor Support Staff: . . 12
EXPANSION PLANS:
US: . . . . All US
Canada - Yes, ... Overseas - No

SUPPLEMENTAL LISTING OF FRANCHISORS

ADA RENT A USED CAR . . . . 3035 Keparo Road, Mill Bay BC V0R2P0   CAN
ADDHAIR TECHNOLOGIES CENTERS . . . . 201 Valencia St., San Francisco CA 94103
AFFORDABLE USED CAR RENTAL SYSTEM . . . . 88A West Front St., Keyport NJ 07735
AJAX RENT A CAR COMPANY . . . . 132 S. Rodeo Drive, Beverly Hills CA 90212
ALL $AVE CAR & TRUCK RENTAL . . . . .8161 Keele St., # 1A, Concord ON L4K1Z3   CAN
ALLSTAR RENT-A-CAR . . . . P.O. Box 69027, Seattle WA 98168
AMERICAN INTERNATIONAL RENT A CAR . . . . One Harborside Dr., Boston MA 02128
AUTO MATE . . . . 1661 E. Camelback, # 118, Phoenix AZ 85016
AVIS RENT-A-CAR (CANADA) . . . . 2 Eva Rd., Etobicoke ON M9C2A8   CAN
BUDGET RENT A CAR OF CANADA . . . . .185 The West Mall, # 900, Toronto ON M9C5L5   CAN
CANA RENT A CAR . . . . .3035 Keparo Road, Mill Bay BC V0R2P0   CAN
DISCOUNT CAR AND TRUCK RENTALS . . . . .130 Winges Rd., # 201, Woodbridge ON L4L6B9   CAN
DOLLAR RENT A CAR SYSTEMS . . . . .6141 W. Century Blvd., Los Angeles CA 90045
FANCY FLIVVERS CAR RENTAL . . . . 311 N. Henry St., Alexandria TX 22314
FREEDOM RENT-A-CAR SYSTEM . . . . .P.O. Box 2345, Bartlesville OK 74003
HERTZ SYSTEM . . . . 225 Brae Blvd., Park Ridge NJ 07656
HOJ CAR & TRUCK RENTALS/HOJ LEASING . . . . . . .51 Constellation Ct., Rexdale ON M9W1K4   CAN
HOLIDAY RENT-A-CAR SYSTEM . . . . .5510 Gulfport Blvd., St. Petersburg FL 33707
MR. RENT A CAR/MR. LEASE A CAR . . . . 45 Haverhill St., Andover MA 01810
PAYLESS RENT-A-CAR SYSTEM . . . . .5510 Gulfport Blvd., St. Petersburg FL 33707
PRACTICAL RENT-A-CAR . . . . .901 Walnut Dr., Boulder City NV 89005
RENT-A-DENT . . . . P.O. Box 69027, Seattle WA 98188
RENT-A-WRECK . . . . 6053 W. Century Blvd., # 550, Los Angeles CA 90045
RENT-RITE TRUCK/CAR RENTALS & LEASING . . . . . 404 Meridian Rd., NE, Calgary AB T2A2N6   CAN
RPM RENT-A-CAR . . . . .5138 W. Century Blvd., Inglewood CA 90304
THRIFTY CAR RENTAL . . . . 2233 Argentia Rd., # 114, Mississauga ON L5N2X7   CAN
THRIFTY RENT-A-CAR SYSTEM . . . . 4608 S. Garnett Rd., Tulsa OK 74153

For a full explanation of the data provided in

the Franchisor Format, please refer to Chapter 2,

"How To Use The Data."

CHAPTER 6

BUILDING AND REMODELING

B-DRY SYSTEM

1341 Copley Rd.
Akron, OH 44320
TEL: (800) 321-0985 (216) 876-2576 C
FAX:
Mr. Joe Garfinkel, VP

Basement waterproofing system. Low cash investment - high return on invest-ment. Intensive and continuous training. No high-cost site expenditure. High gross profit. No previous experience necessary. Unique patented system. Full customer warranty for life of structure.

HISTORY: . . . . IFA
Established in 1978;   . . 1st Franchised in 1979
Company-Owned Units (As of 12/1/1989): . .3
Franchised Units (12/1/1989): 72
Total Units (12/1/1989): 75
Distribution: US-74;Can-1;Overseas-0
  North America: . . . . 24 States
  Concentration: . . . . 7 in OH
Registered: . . . IL,IN,MD,MI,MN,NY,RI,VA
. . . . WA,WI
Average # of Employees: . . . . . 6 FT, 1 PT
Prior Industry Experience: . . . . Helpful

FINANCIAL:
Cash Investment: $25-45K
Total Investment: $40-74K
Fees: Franchise - $15-30K
  Royalty: 6%, Advert: 0%
Contract Periods (Yrs.): 5/5
Area Development Agreement: . .No
Sub-Franchise Contract: . . . . .No
Expand in Territory: . . . . . . Yes
Passive Ownership: . . . Discouraged
Encourage Conversions: . . . . .No
Franchisee Purchase(s) Required: .No

FRANCHISOR TRAINING/SUPPORT:
Financial Assistance Provided: . . .Yes(D)
Site Selection Assistance: . . . . .NA
Lease Negotiation Assistance: . . . . .NA
Co-operative Advertising: . . . . .No
Training: . . . . 2 Wks. Headquarters,
. . . . Continuous in Field
On-Going Support: . . . . D,G,H,I
Full-Time Franchisor Support Staff: . . 15
EXPANSION PLANS:
  US: . . . . . . .New Jersey, Pennsylvania
  Canada - Yes, ... Overseas - No

CONSTRUCTION, HOME IMPROVEMENT, MAINTENANCE & CLEANING SERVICES

	1988	1989	1990	Percentage Change 1988–1989	Percentage Change 1989–1990
Number of Establishments:					
Company–Owned	643	614	611	−4.5%	−0.5%
Franchisee–Owned	21,364	24,132	27,659	13.0%	14.6%
Total	22,007	24,746	28,270	12.4%	14.2%
% of Total Establishments:					
Company–Owned	2.9%	2.5%	2.2%		
Franchisee–Owned	97.1%	97.5%	97.8%		
Total	100.0%	100.0%	100.0%		
Annual Sales ($000):					
Company–Owned	$1,424,744	$1,484,588	$1,610,436	4.2%	8.5%
Franchisee–Owned	3,871,351	4,491,270	5,140,946	16.0%	14.5%
Total	5,296,095	5,975,858	6,751,382	12.8%	13.0%
% of Total Sales:					
Company–Owned	26.9%	24.8%	23.9%		
Franchisee–Owned	73.1%	75.2%	76.1%		
Total	100.0%	100.0%	100.0%		
Average Sales Per Unit ($000):					
Company–Owned	$2,216	$2,418	$2,636	9.1%	9.0%
Franchisee–Owned	181	186	186	2.7%	−0.1%
Total	241	241	239	0.3%	−1.1%
Sales Ratio	1222.8%	1299.2%	1418.1%		

	1st Quartile	Median	4th Quartile
Average 1988 Total Investment:			
Company–Owned	$25,000	$40,000	$237,500
Franchisee–Owned	25,000	40,000	75,000
Single Unit Franchise Fee	$10,000	$15,000	$25,000
Multiple Unit Franchise Fee	8,125	20,000	71,875
Franchisee Start–up Cost	15,000	25,000	50,000

	1988	Employees/Unit	Sales/Employee
Employment:			
Company–Owned	14,351	22.3	$99,278
Franchisee–Owned	110,493	5.2	35,037
Total	124,844	5.7	42,422
Employee Performance Ratios		431.5%	283.4%

Source: Franchising In The Economy, 1988 – 1990, IFA Education Foundation & Horwath International, Published January, 1990.

1) 1989 and 1990 data were estimated by respondents.

2) Incl. on–location cleaning services, sewer & drain–cleaning, lawn and garden, maintenance, improvement & repair services.

BASEMENT DE-WATERING / SAFE-AIRE

162 E. Chestnut St.
Canton, IL 61520
TEL: (800) 331-2943 (309) 647-0331 C
FAX:
Mr. William Wherley, Natl. Sales

BASEMENT DE-WATERING/SAFE-AIRE SYSTEMS offer a two-in-one business opportunity through year-round installations. Basement water seepage control and radon gas mitigation are now affordable for homeowners and tremendously profitable for you. Over 130 dealers serving 36 states and Canada exclusively provide our patented systems. Call today for free information!

HISTORY:	FINANCIAL:	FRANCHISOR TRAINING/SUPPORT:
Established in 1978; . . 1st Franchised in 1986	Cash Investment: $11-19K	Financial Assistance Provided: . . .Yes(D)
Company-Owned Units (As of 12/1/1989): . .2	Total Investment: $16-44K	Site Selection Assistance: . . . . .NA
Franchised Units (12/1/1989): 118	Fees: Franchise - $15.9K	Lease Negotiation Assistance: . . . . .NA
Total Units (12/1/1989): 120	Royalty: 0%, Advert: 0%	Co-operative Advertising: . . . . No
Distribution: US-119;Can-1;Overseas-0	Contract Periods (Yrs.): 5/5	Training: . . . . . . 3-5 Days Headquarters
North America: . . . . . 36 States, 1 Province	Area Development Agreement: . .No	. . . .
Concentration: . . . 12 in PA, 10 in IL, 9 in CT	Sub-Franchise Contract: . . . . .No	On-Going Support: . . . . C,D,G,I
Registered: . . . . IL,MI,WI	Expand in Territory: . . . . Yes	Full-Time Franchisor Support Staff: . . 22
. . . .	Passive Ownership: . . . . . .Allowed	EXPANSION PLANS:
Average # of Employees: . . . . . . 3 FT, 1 PT	Encourage Conversions: . . . . . Yes	US: . . . . .All US
Prior Industry Experience: . . . . Helpful	Franchisee Purchase(s) Required: Yes	Canada - Yes, ...Overseas - No

CHISHOLM TRAIL BUILDERS

P.O. Box 335
San Marcos, TX 78667
TEL: (512) 353-5333
FAX:
Mr. Floyd MacKenzie, Treasurer

Construction of pre-designed residential houses for the suburban family. Houses are modestly priced and may be constructed completely or partially. Customer preference.

HISTORY:	FINANCIAL:	FRANCHISOR TRAINING/SUPPORT:
Established in 1983; . . 1st Franchised in 1986	Cash Investment: $15-20K	Financial Assistance Provided: . . . . . No
Company-Owned Units (As of 12/1/1989): . .1	Total Investment: $30-50K	Site Selection Assistance: . . . . .NA
Franchised Units (12/1/1989): 0	Fees: Franchise - $0	Lease Negotiation Assistance: . . . . .NA
Total Units (12/1/1989): 1	Royalty: Flat, Advert: 0%	Co-operative Advertising: . . . . . . .Yes
Distribution: US-1;Can-0;Overseas-0	Contract Periods (Yrs.): 5/5	Training: . . . . . . Continuous at Territory
North America: . . . . .1 State	Area Development Agreement: . .No	. . . .
Concentration: . . . . 1 in TX	Sub-Franchise Contract: . . . . .No	On-Going Support: . . . . a,B,C,D,F,G,h,I
Registered:	Expand in Territory: . . . . Yes	Full-Time Franchisor Support Staff: . . . 3
. . . .	Passive Ownership: . . . Discouraged	EXPANSION PLANS:
Average # of Employees: . . . . . . 2 FT, 10 PT	Encourage Conversions: . . . . . .No	US: . . . . .All US
Prior Industry Experience: . . . . . .Necessary	Franchisee Purchase(s) Required: .No	Canada - Yes, . . . Overseas - Yes

CLASSIC STORAGE

12 Sterling Ln.
Scotts Valley, CA 95066
TEL: (408) 438-2959
FAX: (408) 438-8427
Mr. Bart L. Ross, CEO

CLASSIC STORAGE, the premier builder of quality residential and commercial storage buildings, offers a unique opportunity in owning your own business. No previous experience required, we completely train you in manufacturing, marketing, sales and day-to- day operations. Exclusive territory, sales assistance, technical support, strong on-going marketing support, low investment, low overhead. Take charge of your future.

HISTORY:	FINANCIAL:	FRANCHISOR TRAINING/SUPPORT:
Established in 1988; . . 1st Franchised in 1988	Cash Investment: $24.5-51K	Financial Assistance Provided: . . . . . No
Company-Owned Units (As of 12/1/1989): . .0	Total Investment: $24.5-51K	Site Selection Assistance: . . . . . . .Yes
Franchised Units (12/1/1989): 7	Fees: Franchise - $18.5K	Lease Negotiation Assistance: . . . . .Yes
Total Units (12/1/1989): 7	Royalty: 5-7%, Advert: 3%	Co-operative Advertising: . . . . . . .Yes
Distribution: US-7;Can-0;Overseas-0	Contract Periods (Yrs.): . . . 10/5/5	Training: . . . . .1 Wk. Headquarters,
North America: . . . . .1 State	Area Development Agreement: . .No	. . . . . . 1 Wk. Franchisee's Territory
Concentration: . . . . 7 in CA	Sub-Franchise Contract: . . . . .No	On-Going Support: . . . . B,C,D,E,F,G,H
Registered: . . . . CA	Expand in Territory: . . . . Yes	Full-Time Franchisor Support Staff: . . . 4
. . . .	Passive Ownership: . . . Not Allowed	EXPANSION PLANS:
Average # of Employees: . . . . .2 FT	Encourage Conversions: . . . . . NA	US: . . . . .All US
Prior Industry Experience: . . . . Helpful	Franchisee Purchase(s) Required: .No	Canada - Yes, ...Overseas - No

DORACO

20 E. Herman St.
Philadelphia, PA 19144
TEL: (800) 338-5330 (215) 843-5300
FAX:
Mr. Dan Puleio, President

DORACO is a unique, low-cost opportunity to enter the $100 billion per year remodelling business. With over 18 years of experience, DORACO will show you step-by-step the road to success and independence.

HISTORY: . . . .
Established in 1971; . . 1st Franchised in 1987
Company-Owned Units (As of 12/1/1989): . .6
Franchised Units (12/1/1989): 0
Total Units (12/1/1989): 6
Distribution: US-6;Can-0;Overseas-0
North America: . . . . 3 States
Concentration: . . . 3 in PA, 2 in MD, 1 in NJ
Registered: . . . . .FL
. . . .
Average # of Employees: . . . . .2 FT
Prior Industry Experience: . . . . . . Helpful

FINANCIAL:
Cash Investment: . . . .$
Total Investment: $13-89K
Fees: Franchise - $1-30K
Royalty: 5%, Advert: 2%
Contract Periods (Yrs.): 10/10
Area Development Agreement: . .No
Sub-Franchise Contract: . . . . .No
Expand in Territory: . . . . Yes
Passive Ownership: . . . Discouraged
Encourage Conversions: . . . . . Yes
Franchisee Purchase(s) Required: Yes

FRANCHISOR TRAINING/SUPPORT:
Financial Assistance Provided: . . .Yes(D)
Site Selection Assistance: . . . . . . .Yes
Lease Negotiation Assistance: . . . . .Yes
Co-operative Advertising: . . . . . . .Yes
Training: . . . . 1 Wk. Headquarters
. . . .
On-Going Support: . . . . . . A,B,C,D,E,I
Full-Time Franchisor Support Staff: . . 30
EXPANSION PLANS:
US: . . . . Northeast
Canada - No, ...Overseas - No

EASI-SET INDUSTRIES

P.O. Box 300
Midland, VA 22728
TEL: (703) 439-8911
FAX:
Mr. Ashley Smith, Dir. Fran. Ops

EASI-SET franchises pre-cast concrete buildings, highway safety barriers, Sierra Wall sound/privacy barriers and farm products.

HISTORY: . . . .
Established in 1978; . . 1st Franchised in 1978
Company-Owned Units (As of 12/1/1989): . .0
Franchised Units (12/1/1989): 37
Total Units (12/1/1989): 37
Distribution: US-31;Can-4;Overseas-2
North America: . . . . 16 States, 2 Provinces
Concentration: . . . 5 in VA, 5 in NC, 4 in FL
Registered: . . . .
. . . .
Average # of Employees: . . . . 10 FT
Prior Industry Experience: . . . . . . Helpful

FINANCIAL:
Cash Investment: $20-30K
Total Investment: $30-100K
Fees: Franchise - $15-25K
Royalty: 3-8%, Advert: . . . 3-5%
Contract Periods (Yrs.): 10/10
Area Development Agreement: . .No
Sub-Franchise Contract: . . . . .No
Expand in Territory: . . . . Yes
Passive Ownership: . . . Discouraged
Encourage Conversions: . . . . . Yes
Franchisee Purchase(s) Required: .No

FRANCHISOR TRAINING/SUPPORT:
Financial Assistance Provided: . . . Yes(I)
Site Selection Assistance: . . . . . . .Yes
Lease Negotiation Assistance: . . . . .Yes
Co-operative Advertising: . . . . . . .Yes
Training: . . . . . . 5-8 Days Headquarters,
. . . . 3 Days Site
On-Going Support: . . . . .B,C,D,E,G,h, I
Full-Time Franchisor Support Staff: . . . 4
EXPANSION PLANS:
US: . . . . .All US
Canada - Yes, . . . Overseas - Yes

ELDORADO STONE

P.O. Box 27X
Carnation, WA 98014
TEL: (206) 883-1991 C
FAX:
Mr. John Bennett, President

ELDORADO STONE franchisees manufacture and sell ELDORADO STONE, simulated stone and brick veneer building products. ELDORADO STONE is made of durable, lightweight concrete. It is hard to distinguish from natural stone, yet is much easier to install and much less expensive than natural stone.

HISTORY: . . . .
Established in 1969; . . 1st Franchised in 1969
Company-Owned Units (As of 12/1/1989): . .0
Franchised Units (12/1/1989): 30
Total Units (12/1/1989): 30
Distribution: US-21;Can-4;Overseas-5
North America: . . . . 19 States
Concentration: . . . . 2 in PA
Registered: . . . . .All
. . . .
Average # of Employees: . . . . .6 FT
Prior Industry Experience: . . . . Helpful

FINANCIAL:
Cash Investment: $49-150K
Total Investment: $50-150K
Fees: Franchise - $3.4K
Royalty: 4%, Advert: 0%
Contract Periods (Yrs.): 10/10
Area Development Agreement: . .No
Sub-Franchise Contract: . . . . .No
Expand in Territory: . . . . Yes
Passive Ownership: . . . . . .Allowed
Encourage Conversions: . . . . . Yes
Franchisee Purchase(s) Required: Yes

FRANCHISOR TRAINING/SUPPORT:
Financial Assistance Provided: . . . Yes(I)
Site Selection Assistance: . . . . . . .Yes
Lease Negotiation Assistance: . . . . . No
Co-operative Advertising: . . . . . . .Yes
Training: . . . . 1 Wk. Existing Plant,
. . . . 1 Wk. New Site Plant
On-Going Support: . . . . . . .B,D,E,G,H
Full-Time Franchisor Support Staff: . . 13
EXPANSION PLANS:
US: . . . . .All US
Canada - Yes, . . . Overseas - Yes

FOUR SEASONS GREENHOUSES DESIGN AND REMODELING CENTERS
5005 Veterans Memorial Hwy.
Holbrook, NY 11741
TEL: (516) 563-4000
FAX: (516) 563-4010
Mr. Tony Russo, VP Fran. Sales Dev.

FOUR SEASONS is the largest manufacturer of greenhouses/solariums in the United States. The FOUR SEASONS franchise program is targeted towards the lucrative remodeling and construction industry. We offer our exclusive line of products through our national and international network of franchisees.

HISTORY: . . . . IFA
Established in 1977; . . 1st Franchised in 1984
Company-Owned Units (As of 12/1/1989): . .4
Franchised Units (12/1/1989): 271
Total Units (12/1/1989): 275
Distribution: . . . US-236;Can-23;Overseas-16
 North America: . . . . 46 States, 6 Provinces
 Concentration: . 25 in NY, 22 in CA, 14 in ON
Registered: . . . . .All
. . . .
Average # of Employees: . . . . . . 2 FT, 1 PT
Prior Industry Experience: . . . . Helpful

FINANCIAL:
Cash Investment: $5-20K
Total Investment: $13-100K
Fees: Franchise - $5-20K
 Royalty: Var., Advert: 0%
Contract Periods (Yrs.): 10/10
Area Development Agreement: Yes/Var
Sub-Franchise Contract: . . . . . .No
Expand in Territory: . . . . .No
Passive Ownership: . . . Discouraged
Encourage Conversions: . . . . . Yes
Franchisee Purchase(s) Required: Yes

FRANCHISOR TRAINING/SUPPORT:
Financial Assistance Provided: . . . . . No
Site Selection Assistance: . . . . . . .Yes
Lease Negotiation Assistance: . . . . .Yes
Co-operative Advertising: . . . . . . .Yes
Training: . . . . 2 Wks. Headquarters
. . . .
On-Going Support: . . . A,B,C,D,E,F,G,H
Full-Time Franchisor Support Staff: . .250
EXPANSION PLANS:
 US: . . . . W,MW,S and Rocky Mountain
 Canada - Yes, . . . Overseas - Yes

KITCHEN SAVER OF CANADA

13 Main St. W.
Lambeth, ON N0L1S0 CAN
TEL: (800)265-0933(ON) (519)652-6390
FAX: (519) 652-6898
Mr. Craig Jones, President

KITCHEN SAVER specializes in affordable kitchen remodelling by offering cabinet front replacement (commonly known as refacing) and a line of high-quality, low-cost cabinets. The remodelling service is completed with the addition of custom countertops, sinks, islands and storage options.

HISTORY: . . . .
Established in 1986; . . 1st Franchised in 1986
Company-Owned Units (As of 12/1/1989): . .0
Franchised Units (12/1/1989): 16
Total Units (12/1/1989): 16
Distribution: US-0;Can-16;Overseas-0
 North America: . . . . .1 Province
 Concentration: . . . . 16 in ON
Registered: . . . .
. . . .
Average # of Employees: . . . . .1 FT
Prior Industry Experience: . . . . Helpful

FINANCIAL:
Cash Investment: $20K
Total Investment: $40-50K
Fees: Franchise - $20-30K
 Royalty: 0%, Advert: 0%
Contract Periods (Yrs.): 5/5/5
Area Development Agreement: . .No
Sub-Franchise Contract: . . . . .No
Expand in Territory: . . . . Yes
Passive Ownership: . . . Discouraged
Encourage Conversions: . . . . NA
Franchisee Purchase(s) Required: Yes

FRANCHISOR TRAINING/SUPPORT:
Financial Assistance Provided: . . . Yes(I)
Site Selection Assistance: . . . . . . .NA
Lease Negotiation Assistance: . . . .NA
Co-operative Advertising: . . . . . . .Yes
Training: . . . . . 2 Wks. Headquarters and
. . . . Existing Dealer Location
On-Going Support: . . . . . B,c,d,E,G,H,I
Full-Time Franchisor Support Staff: . . . 8
EXPANSION PLANS:
 US: . . . . No
 Canada - Yes, ...Overseas - No

KITCHEN SOLVERS, THE / KITCHEN SAVERS, THE
715 Rose St.
La Crosse, WI 54603
TEL: (608) 784-2855
FAX:
Mr. Cliff Le Cleir, Dir. Fran.

KITCHEN SAVERS refacing capitalizes on the consumer's desire to go 1st Class for less money. Refacing utilizes existing framework on cabinets by covering with 1/8" oak or laminate and then "new" doors/drawer fronts are custom-built. Franchisee needs strength in sales and management, not woodworking. Gross profits of 30% are expected.

HISTORY: . . . .
Established in 1982; . . 1st Franchised in 1984
Company-Owned Units (As of 12/1/1989): . .1
Franchised Units (12/1/1989): 10
Total Units (12/1/1989): 11
Distribution: US-11;Can-0;Overseas-0
 North America: . . . . 3 States
 Concentration: . . . 9 in WI, 1 in MN, 1 in ND
Registered: . . . . .MN,ND,WI
. . . .
Average # of Employees: . . . . .2 FT
Prior Industry Experience: . . . . Helpful

FINANCIAL:
Cash Investment: $5-15K
Total Investment: $11-40K
Fees: Franchise - $7-12K
 Royalty: 5%, Advert: 0%
Contract Periods (Yrs.): 5/5
Area Development Agreement: Yes/5
Sub-Franchise Contract: . . . . . Yes
Expand in Territory: . . . . Yes
Passive Ownership: . . . Discouraged
Encourage Conversions: . . . . . Yes
Franchisee Purchase(s) Required: .No

FRANCHISOR TRAINING/SUPPORT:
Financial Assistance Provided: . . . Yes(I)
Site Selection Assistance: . . . . . . .Yes
Lease Negotiation Assistance: . . . .Yes
Co-operative Advertising: . . . . No
Training: . . . . . . 3 Days Headquarters, 2
. . .Days Headquarters, Period. Seminars
On-Going Support: . . . . B,C,D,h
Full-Time Franchisor Support Staff: . . .7
EXPANSION PLANS:
 US: . . . . Midwest
 Canada - No, ...Overseas - No

KITCHEN TUNE-UP

131 N. Roosevelt
Aberdeen, SD 57401
TEL: (800) 333-6385 (605) 225-4049 C
FAX:
Mr. David Haglund, President

KITCHEN TUNE-UP offers three franchise businesses for one franchise fee; 1) KITCHEN TUNE-UP Wood Care Specialists, 2) Do-It-Yourself door replacement, and 3) Custom closets. Our franchise is a home-based business that has no inventory requirements and has a low start-up cost.

HISTORY: . . . .
Established in 1988; . . 1st Franchised in 1989
Company-Owned Units (As of 12/1/1989): . .0
Franchised Units (12/1/1989): 54
Total Units (12/1/1989): 54
Distribution: US-54;Can-0;Overseas-0
North America: . . . . 20 States
Concentration: . . 11 in MN, 5 in OH, 4 in PA
Registered: . . . CA,FL,IL,IN,MD,MI,MN,ND
. . . . OR,SD,WA,WI
Average # of Employees: . . . . . . 1 FT, 1 PT
Prior Industry Experience: . . . . . . Helpful

FINANCIAL:
Cash Investment: $11-12K
Total Investment: $11-12K
Fees: Franchise - $10K
Royalty: 7%, Advert: 0%
Contract Periods (Yrs.): 8/24
Area Development Agreement: . .No
Sub-Franchise Contract: . . . . .No
Expand in Territory: . . . . . . Yes
Passive Ownership: . . . Discouraged
Encourage Conversions: . . . . NA
Franchisee Purchase(s) Required: .No

FRANCHISOR TRAINING/SUPPORT:
Financial Assistance Provided: . . . . .NA
Site Selection Assistance: . . . . .NA
Lease Negotiation Assistance: . . . . .NA
Co-operative Advertising: . . . . .NA
Training: . . . . 3 Days Headquarters,
. . . . .2 Days Franchisee Location
On-Going Support: . . . . . . B,C,D,G,h,I
Full-Time Franchisor Support Staff: . . . 4
EXPANSION PLANS:
US: . . . . .All US
Canada - Yes, ...Overseas - No

MR. BUILD

628 Hebron Ave., # 110
Glastonbury, CT 06033
TEL: (800) 242-8453 (203) 657-3607
FAX: (203) 657-3719
Mr. Sherman Tarr, Dir. PR/Advert.

MR. BUILD gives contractors in 50 trades and services an image of quality and dependability. Customers make one call for most residential and business property services. In some regions, MR. BUILD is teamed with a retail home improvement chain to provide installed sales. Also, the MR. BUILD PLUS home improvement showrooms and the MR. BUILD HANDI-MAN services provide another source of leads.

HISTORY: . . . .
Established in 1981; . . 1st Franchised in 1981
Company-Owned Units (As of 12/1/1989): . .0
Franchised Units (12/1/1989): 560
Total Units (12/1/1989): 560
Distribution: . . . US-425;Can-60;Overseas-75
North America: . . . . 19 States, 4 Provinces
Concentration: . 60 in MA, 55 in WA, 30 in IN
Registered: . . . . . CA,FL,IL,IN,MI,WA,AB
. . . .
Average # of Employees: . . . . Varies
Prior Industry Experience: . . . . . . Helpful

FINANCIAL:
Cash Investment: $4-17K
Total Investment: . . . . $Varies
Fees: Franchise - $3-10K
Royalty: Flat, Advert: . . . . . Flat
Contract Periods (Yrs.): 5/5
Area Development Agreement: Yes/25
Sub-Franchise Contract: . . . . Yes
Expand in Territory: . . . . . . Yes
Passive Ownership: . . . Not Allowed
Encourage Conversions: . . . . Yes
Franchisee Purchase(s) Required: .No

FRANCHISOR TRAINING/SUPPORT:
Financial Assistance Provided: . . . Yes(I)
Site Selection Assistance: . . . . .NA
Lease Negotiation Assistance: . . . . .NA
Co-operative Advertising: . . . . .Yes
Training: . . . . On-going By Region
. . . .
On-Going Support: . . . . .D,G,h,I
Full-Time Franchisor Support Staff: . . . 8
EXPANSION PLANS:
US: . . . . .All US
Canada - Yes, . . . Overseas - Yes

ONE STOP KITCHEN SHOP

19 Montgomery Dr.
Erlanger, KY 41018
TEL: (606) 341-1800
FAX:
Mr. George Weidner, Manager

Sales of complete kitchens for new homes and remodeling. Design, layout and installation available to consumers.

HISTORY: . . . .
Established in 1966; . . 1st Franchised in 1982
Company-Owned Units (As of 12/1/1989): . .2
Franchised Units (12/1/1989): 1
Total Units (12/1/1989): 3
Distribution: US-3;Can-0;Overseas-0
North America: . . . . 2 States
Concentration: . . . . 2 in OH, 1 in KY
Registered: . . . .
. . . .
Average # of Employees: . . . . 1-2 FT, 3-5 PT
Prior Industry Experience: . . . . . . Helpful

FINANCIAL:
Cash Investment: $1-50K
Total Investment: $5-50K
Fees: Franchise - . . . . $.5-2K
Royalty: 1.5, Advert: 5%
Contract Periods (Yrs.): 2/2
Area Development Agreement: . .No
Sub-Franchise Contract: . . . . .No
Expand in Territory: . . . . . . Yes
Passive Ownership: . . . . . .Allowed
Encourage Conversions: . . . . Yes
Franchisee Purchase(s) Required: .No

FRANCHISOR TRAINING/SUPPORT:
Financial Assistance Provided: . . . . .No
Site Selection Assistance: . . . . .Yes
Lease Negotiation Assistance: . . . . .No
Co-operative Advertising: . . . . .Yes
Training: . . . . . . 3 Days Cincinnati, OH
. . . .
On-Going Support: . . . . B,H
Full-Time Franchisor Support Staff: . . . 2
EXPANSION PLANS:
US: . . . . NE, SE, Midwest
Canada - No, ...Overseas - No

PERMA-JACK COMPANY

9066 Watson Rd.
St. Louis, MO 63126
TEL: (314) 843-1957
FAX:
Director of Franchising

The PERMA-JACK SYSTEM is a patented Foundation Stabilizing System, using hydraulic pressure to force steel tubing through the Perma-Jack support bracket down to bedrock or equal load-bearing strata. We stabilize your building's foundation and, in many cases, raise it back to near-original position.

HISTORY: . . . .
Established in 1974; . . 1st Franchised in 1975
Company-Owned Units (As of 12/1/1989): . . 0
Franchised Units (12/1/1989): 12
Total Units (12/1/1989): 12
Distribution: US-12;Can-0;Overseas-0
North America: . . . . 7 States
Concentration: . . . 4 in TX, 2 in CA, 2 in MO
Registered: . . .CA,FL,IL,IN,MD,OR,VA,WA
. . . .
Average # of Employees: . . . . .5 FT
Prior Industry Experience: . . . . Helpful

FINANCIAL:
Cash Investment: $7.5-20K
Total Investment: $24-68K
Fees: Franchise - $7-20K
Royalty: 10%, Advert: 0%
Contract Periods (Yrs.): 2/4
Area Development Agreement: . .No
Sub-Franchise Contract: . . . . . .No
Expand in Territory: . . . . . . Yes
Passive Ownership: . . . Not Allowed
Encourage Conversions: . . . .
Franchisee Purchase(s) Required: .No

FRANCHISOR TRAINING/SUPPORT:
Financial Assistance Provided: . . . . . No
Site Selection Assistance: . . . . No
Lease Negotiation Assistance: . . . . . No
Co-operative Advertising: . . . . No
Training: . . . . As Needed at Headquarters
. . . . or Job Site(s)
On-Going Support: . . . . . B,C,D,E,F,H,I
Full-Time Franchisor Support Staff: . . . 5
EXPANSION PLANS:
US: . . . . .All US
Canada - No, ...Overseas - No

SCREEN MACHINE, THE

P. O. Box 1207, 19636 8th St. E.
Sonoma, CA 95476
TEL: (707) 996-5551
FAX:
Mr. Wayne T. Wirick, President

THE SCREEN MACHINE is a mobile window screen and screen door repair and fabrication service. Existing window screens and screen doors are re-screened or new ones fabricated right on the job. You will get complete technical and business training and a complete equipment and supplies package.

HISTORY: . . . .
Established in 1986; . . 1st Franchised in 1988
Company-Owned Units (As of 12/1/1989): . . 1
Franchised Units (12/1/1989): 4
Total Units (12/1/1989): 5
Distribution: US-5;Can-0;Overseas-0
North America: . . . . .1 State
Concentration: . . . . 5 in CA
Registered: . . . . CA
. . . .
Average # of Employees: . . . . .1 FT
Prior Industry Experience: . . . . Helpful

FINANCIAL:
Cash Investment: $25-30K
Total Investment: $30-49K
Fees: Franchise - $13.5K
Royalty: 6%, Advert: 3%
Contract Periods (Yrs.): . . . 10/10
Area Development Agreement: . .No
Sub-Franchise Contract: . . . . . .No
Expand in Territory: . . . . . . Yes
Passive Ownership: . . . Not Allowed
Encourage Conversions: . . . . .No
Franchisee Purchase(s) Required: .No

FRANCHISOR TRAINING/SUPPORT:
Financial Assistance Provided: . . . . . No
Site Selection Assistance: . . . . . . .NA
Lease Negotiation Assistance: . . . .NA
Co-operative Advertising: . . . . . . .NA
Training: . . . . 6 Days Headquarters
. . . .
On-Going Support: . . . . D,G,H,I
Full-Time Franchisor Support Staff: . . . 1
EXPANSION PLANS:
US: . . . . .All US
Canada - No, ...Overseas - No

SOLID / FLUE

370 100th St. SW
Byron Center, MI 49315
TEL: (800) 444-FLUE (616) 877-4900
FAX:
Mr. Doug LeFleur, President

SOLID / FLUE is a national network of chimney relining and repair professionals. The company markets a proprietary product and process that restores damaged chimney lining without dislodging surrrounding brickwork.

HISTORY: . . . . IFA
Established in 1979; . . 1st Franchised in 1989
Company-Owned Units (As of 12/1/1989): . .0
Franchised Units (12/1/1989): 66
Total Units (12/1/1989): 66
Distribution: US-66;Can-0;Overseas-0
North America: . . . .
Concentration: . . . . .MI, NJ
Registered: . . . . All Except AB
. . . .
Average # of Employees: . . . . . . 2 FT, 2 PT
Prior Industry Experience: . . . . Helpful

FINANCIAL:
Cash Investment: $15-35K
Total Investment: $35K
Fees: Franchise - $5K
Royalty: 0%, Advert: 0%
Contract Periods (Yrs.): 10
Area Development Agreement: . .No
Sub-Franchise Contract: . . . . . .No
Expand in Territory: . . . . . . .No
Passive Ownership: . . . Discouraged
Encourage Conversions: . . . . Yes
Franchisee Purchase(s) Required: Yes

FRANCHISOR TRAINING/SUPPORT:
Financial Assistance Provided: . . . Yes(I)
Site Selection Assistance: . . . . . . .NA
Lease Negotiation Assistance: . . . .NA
Co-operative Advertising: . . . . . . .Yes
Training: . . . . 2 Wks. Headquarters
. . . .
On-Going Support: . . . . . B,C,D,F,G,H,I
Full-Time Franchisor Support Staff: . . 10
EXPANSION PLANS:
US: . . . . .All US
Canada - Yes, . . . Overseas - Yes

SUPER SEAMLESS STEEL SIDING
560 Henderson Dr.
Regina, SK S4N5X2 CAN
TEL: (306) 721-8000 C
FAX: (306) 721-2532
Marilyn Lohmeyer, Dir. Fran. Sales

The manufacture and installation of SUPER SEAMLESS STEEL SIDING is done on the job site, providing top-quality, seamless steel siding to the consumer. Product is widely accepted and specified for comercial and residential applications. Available in 24 designer profiles and 10 colors.

HISTORY: . . . .
Established in 1978; . . 1st Franchised in 1985
Company-Owned Units (As of 12/1/1989): . .2
Franchised Units (12/1/1989): 15
Total Units (12/1/1989): 17
Distribution: US-0;Can-17;Overseas-0
 North America: . . . . 8 Provinces
 Concentration: . . . 8 in SK, 2 in MB, 2 in PQ
Registered: . . . . AB
 . . . .
Average # of Employees: . . . . . . 4 FT, 1 PT
Prior Industry Experience: . . . . Helpful

FINANCIAL:
Cash Investment: $20-30K
Total Investment: $65-85K
Fees: Franchise - $7.5K
 Royalty: $1200/Yr, Advert: 1/2-1.5%
Contract Periods (Yrs.): . . . . Infin.
Area Development Agreement: . Yes
Sub-Franchise Contract: . . . . . Yes
Expand in Territory: . . . . Yes
Passive Ownership: . . . Discouraged
Encourage Conversions: . . . . .No
Franchisee Purchase(s) Required: Yes

FRANCHISOR TRAINING/SUPPORT:
Financial Assistance Provided: . . . . . No
Site Selection Assistance: . . . . .NA
Lease Negotiation Assistance: . . . .NA
Co-operative Advertising: . . . . .Yes
Training: . . . . . 5-10 Days Headquarters,
 . . . . 3-6 Days On-site
On-Going Support: . . . . .B,C,D,E,G,H,I
Full-Time Franchisor Support Staff: . . . 5
EXPANSION PLANS:
 US: . . . . .No
 Canada - Yes, ...Overseas - No

WALL-FILL WORLDWIDE
649 Childs St.
Wheaton, IL 60187
TEL: (708) 668-3400
FAX:
Mr. Ed Lowrie, President

WALL-FILL has been in home improvements since 1928. The franchise is a business format franchise. The franchisor is currently interested in Illinois. Maintenance-free home improvement products. Siding, gutters, windows, doors.

HISTORY: . . . .
Established in 1928; . . 1st Franchised in 1988
Company-Owned Units (As of 12/1/1989): . .1
Franchised Units (12/1/1989): 0
Total Units (12/1/1989): 1
Distribution: US-1;Can-0;Overseas-0
 North America: . . . . .1 State
 Concentration: . . . . .1 in IL
Registered: IL
 . . . .
Average # of Employees: . . . . . . 1 FT, 1 PT
Prior Industry Experience: . . . . . . Helpful

FINANCIAL:
Cash Investment: $15-20K
Total Investment: . . . $31.2-64.3K
Fees: Franchise - $13.5K
 Royalty: 7%, Advert: 1%
Contract Periods (Yrs.): 10/5
Area Development Agreement: . .No
Sub-Franchise Contract: . . . . .No
Expand in Territory: . . . . . . Yes
Passive Ownership: . . . Discouraged
Encourage Conversions: . . . . . Yes
Franchisee Purchase(s) Required: .No

FRANCHISOR TRAINING/SUPPORT:
Financial Assistance Provided: . . . . .NA
Site Selection Assistance: . . . . . . .Yes
Lease Negotiation Assistance: . . . . .Yes
Co-operative Advertising: . . . . . . .Yes
Training: . . . . . . 10 Days Headquarters,
 . . . . 5 Days Franchisee Site
On-Going Support: . . . . . . B,C,D,E,F,I
Full-Time Franchisor Support Staff: . . . 5
EXPANSION PLANS:
 US: . . . . .Midwest
 Canada - No, ...Overseas - No

WIMBERLEY HOMES
P.O. Box 8
San Marcos, TX 78667
TEL: (512) 353-5333
FAX:
Mr. F. MacKenzie, Treasurer

Construction and remodeling of residential houses in suburban areas. Factory-designed country houses for the discriminating buyer at a modest price level.

HISTORY: . . . .
Established in 1985; . . 1st Franchised in 1987
Company-Owned Units (As of 12/1/1989): . .1
Franchised Units (12/1/1989): 0
Total Units (12/1/1989): 1
Distribution: US-1;Can-0;Overseas-0
 North America: . . . . .1 State
 Concentration: . . . . 1 in TX
Registered: . . . .
 . . . .
Average # of Employees: . . . . .2 FT
Prior Industry Experience: . . . . . .Necessary

FINANCIAL:
Cash Investment: $1-25K
Total Investment: $35K
Fees: Franchise - $0
 Royalty: Flat, Advert: 0%
Contract Periods (Yrs.): 5/5
Area Development Agreement: . .No
Sub-Franchise Contract: . . . . .No
Expand in Territory: . . . . . . Yes
Passive Ownership: . . . Discouraged
Encourage Conversions: . . . . .No
Franchisee Purchase(s) Required: .No

FRANCHISOR TRAINING/SUPPORT:
Financial Assistance Provided: . . . . . No
Site Selection Assistance: . . . . .NA
Lease Negotiation Assistance: . . . .NA
Co-operative Advertising: . . . . .Yes
Training: . . . . Continuous in
 . . . . Field & Territory
On-Going Support: . . . . a,B,C,D,F,G,h,I
Full-Time Franchisor Support Staff: . . . 1
EXPANSION PLANS:
 US: . . . . All US
 Canada - Yes, ...Overseas - Yes

SUPPLEMENTAL LISTING OF FRANCHISORS

A PLUS STUDENT PAINTERS	100 Mary Croft Ave., # 1, Woodbridge ON L4L5Y4	CAN
ABC SEAMLESS	3001 Fletchner Dr., SW, Fargo ND 58103	
ACRYSYL SALES & SERVICE	P.O. Box 13963, 11 S. 11th St., Reading PA 19612	
ADD-VENTURES OF AMERICA	38 Park St. Station, Medfield MA 02052	
AMERICAN LINCOLN HOMES/AMERLINK	Route 48 North, Battleboro NC 27809	
ARCHADECK	P.O. Box 5185, Richmond VA 23220	
BARN YARD, THE	345 Ella Grasso Tnpk., Rte. 75, Windsor Locks CT 06096	
CABINET WHOLESALERS	360 Georgetown Sq., Wood Dale IL 60191	
CREATIVE CURB	3002 Dow Ave., # 420, Tustin CA 92680	
CUSTOM ONE	3636 N. MacArthur Blvd., # 120, Irving TX 75062	
DEC-K-ING	#72-15515 24th Ave., Surrey BC V4A2J4	CAN
DECK DIRECTORS	1810 W. Price St., Tucson AZ 85705	
DESIGNER CONCRETE COATINGS	1692 Village Green Dr., Port St. Lucie FL 34952	
DIAL ONE INTERNATIONAL	175 S. Third St., # 450, Columbus OH 43215	
EVER DRY WATERPROOFING	365 E. Highland Rd., Macedonia OH 44056	
EXOTIC DECKS	5005 Veterans Memorial Hwy., Holbrook NY 11741	
FERSINA WINDOWS	14201 F & G South Lakes Dr., Charlotte NC 28217	
FIRE SAFE	5694 Ambler Dr., Mississauga ON L4W2K9	CAN
FLEX-SHIELD INTERNATIONAL	P.O. Box 1790, Gilbert AZ 85234	
FOUR SEASONS (CANADA)	506 McNicoll Ave., Willowdale ON M2H2E1	CAN
H.E.L.P.	32 Flagg Pl., Staten Island NY 10304	
HEAT & ENERGY LOSS PREVENTION	32 Flagg Pl., Staten Island NY 10304	
KING FENCE SYSTEMS	60 Shepherd Rd., Oakville ON L6K2G5	CAN
KITCHEN FACELIFTERS	5938 Reed Ave., Columbus GA 31909	
LAVASTONE INDUSTRIES	2633 Dawson St., P.O. Box 26699, Dallas TX 75226	
MACTAVISH RAILROAD SALVAGE	5100 Jefferson Ave., Newport News VA 23605	
MAGNUM PIERING	2A Hilltop Village Ctr., Eureka MO 63025	
MISTER RENOVATOR	622 N. Washington, P. O. Box 1928, Alexandria VA 22320	
MR. RENOVATOR	622 N. Washington, P. O. Box 1928, Alexandria VA 22320	
NEW ENGLAND LOG HOMES FRANCHISING	P.O. Box 5427, Hamden CT 06518	
NORTHERN PRODUCTS LOG HOMES	P.O. Box 616, Bomarc Rd., Bangor ME 04401	
NOVUS PLATE GLASS REPAIR	10425 Hampshire Ave. S., Minneapolis MN 55438	
PAUL DAVIS SYSTEMS (CANADA)	3025 Kennedy Rd., # 1, Scarborough ON M1V1S3	CAN
PERFECT SURFACE	1625 Oak Meadow, Irving TX 75061	
PERMAFLU CHIMNEY LINING SYSTEM	105 W. Merrimack St., #4035, Manchester NH 03108	
PERMAR WINDOWS	10 Dunlop Dr., St. Catharines ON L2R1A2	CAN
PRO PROPERTY IMPROVEMENTS	1300 - 1100 Melville St., Vancouver BC V6E4A6	CAN
RE-SSIDE AMERICA	11002 Park Rd., Fairfax VA 22030	
SCREENMOBILE	457 W. Allen Ave., # 107, San Dimas CA 91773	
SERVICE AMERICA	223 Perimeter Center Pkwy., # 510, Atlanta GA 30346	
SPEED FAB-CRETE	P.O. Box 15580, Fort Worth TX 76119	
TIMBERMILL STORAGE BARNS	One Wolf Run, Glen Ellen CA 95442	
TUFCO FLOORING	34 Grenfell Cres., Ottawa ON K2G0G2	CAN
URO-TILE OF AMERICA	6810 S. Cedar St., #2-B, Lansing MI 48911	
WINDOW MAN, THE	711 Rigsbee Ave., Durham NC 27701	

CHAPTER 7

BUSINESS: ACCOUNTING / CREDIT / COLLECTION

ACCOUNTAX SERVICES

1110 A Wilson Ave., # 202
Toronto, ON M3M1G7 CAN
TEL: (416) 638-1303
FAX: (416) 638-1443
Mr. Vijay Kapur, Marketing Director

The development of each franchisee into a strong, service-oriented professional is based on the effective support in training programs, operational system, marketing support, co-op advertising plan and on-going assistance.

HISTORY: . . . . IFA
Established in 1980; . . 1st Franchised in 1981
Company-Owned Units (As of 12/1/1989): . .1
Franchised Units (12/1/1989): 6
Total Units (12/1/1989): 7
Distribution: US-0;Can-7;Overseas-0
  North America: . . . . 3 Provinces
  Concentration: . . . . 5 in ON
Registered: . . . .
. . . .
Average # of Employees: . . . . .8 FT
Prior Industry Experience: . . . . . .Necessary

FINANCIAL:
Cash Investment: $10K
Total Investment: $10-15K
Fees: Franchise - $10K
  Royalty: 4%, Advert: 2%
Contract Periods (Yrs.): 5/5
Area Development Agreement: Yes/5
Sub-Franchise Contract: . . . . . .No
Expand in Territory: . . . . .No
Passive Ownership: . . . Discouraged
Encourage Conversions: . . . . . .No
Franchisee Purchase(s) Required: . .

FRANCHISOR TRAINING/SUPPORT:
Financial Assistance Provided: . . . Yes(I)
Site Selection Assistance: . . . . .Yes
Lease Negotiation Assistance: . . . . .NA
Co-operative Advertising: . . . . .No
Training: . . . . .1 Month HQ
. . . .
On-Going Support: . . . A,B,C,D,F,G,H,I
Full-Time Franchisor Support Staff: . . .2
EXPANSION PLANS:
  US: . . . . .All US
  Canada - Yes, ...Overseas - Yes

BUSINESS AIDS & SERVICES

	1988	1989	1990	Percentage Change 1988-1989	Percentage Change 1989-1990
Number of Establishments:					
Company–Owned	7,475	7,033	7,493	–5.9%	6.5%
Franchisee–Owned	48,110	52,747	59,778	9.6%	13.3%
Total	55,585	59,780	67,271	7.5%	12.5%
% of Total Establishments:					
Company–Owned	13.4%	11.8%	11.1%		
Franchisee–Owned	86.6%	88.2%	88.9%		
Total	100.0%	100.0%	100.0%		
Annual Sales ($000):					
Company–Owned	$3,253,276	$3,424,911	$3,855,690	5.3%	12.6%
Franchisee–Owned	12,469,288	13,669,104	15,638,077	9.6%	14.4%
Total	15,722,564	17,094,015	19,493,767	8.7%	14.0%
% of Total Sales:					
Company–Owned	20.7%	20.0%	19.8%		
Franchisee–Owned	79.3%	80.0%	80.2%		
Total	100.0%	100.0%	100.0%		
Average Sales Per Unit ($000):					
Company–Owned	$435	$487	$515	11.9%	5.7%
Franchisee–Owned	259	259	262	0.0%	0.9%
Total	283	286	290	1.1%	1.3%
Sales Ratio	167.9%	187.9%	196.7%		

	1st Quartile	Median	4th Quartile
Average 1988 Total Investment:			
Company–Owned	$39,000	$74,000	$145,000
Franchisee–Owned	30,000	59,500	100,000
Single Unit Franchise Fee	$10,000	$15,500	$25,000
Multiple Unit Franchise Fee	7,500	15,000	18,950
Franchisee Start–up Cost	15,000	25,000	50,000

	1988	Employees/Unit	Sales/Employee
Employment:			
Company–Owned	240,842	32.2	$13,508
Franchisee–Owned	466,361	9.7	26,737
Total	707,203	12.7	22,232
Employee Performance Ratios		332.4%	50.5%

Source: Franchising In The Economy, 1988 – 1990, IFA Education Foundation & Horwath International, Published January, 1990.

1) 1989 and 1990 data were estimated by respondents.

2) Includes accounting, credit collections & real estate agencies; employment, tax preparation and printing/copying services.

ACCOUNTING, CREDIT, COLLECTION AGENCIES & GENERAL BUSINESS SYSTEMS

	1988	1989	1990	Percentage Change 1988-1989	Percentage Change 1989-1990
Number of Establishments:					
Company-Owned	25	27	28	8.0%	3.7%
Franchisee-Owned	1,631	1,671	1,831	2.5%	9.6%
Total	1,656	1,698	1,859	2.5%	9.5%
% of Total Establishments:					
Company-Owned	1.5%	1.6%	1.5%		
Franchisee-Owned	98.5%	98.4%	98.5%		
Total	100.0%	100.0%	100.0%		
Annual Sales ($000):					
Company-Owned	$7,198	$8,025	$9,410	11.5%	17.3%
Franchisee-Owned	159,263	178,251	205,030	11.9%	15.0%
Total	166,461	186,276	214,440	11.9%	15.1%
% of Total Sales:					
Company-Owned	4.3%	4.3%	4.4%		
Franchisee-Owned	95.7%	95.7%	95.6%		
Total	100.0%	100.0%	100.0%		
Average Sales Per Unit ($000):					
Company-Owned	$288	$297	$336	3.2%	13.1%
Franchisee-Owned	98	107	112	9.2%	5.0%
Total	101	110	115	9.1%	5.1%
Sales Ratio	294.9%	278.6%	300.1%		

	1st Quartile		Median		4th Quartile
Average 1988 Total Investment:					
Company-Owned	N. A.		N. A.		N. A.
Franchisee-Owned	$20,000		$39,000		$55,000
Single Unit Franchise Fee	$12,000		$20,000		$25,000
Multiple Unit Franchise Fee	N. A.		N. A.		N. A.
Franchisee Start-up Cost	11,250		20,000		24,750

	1988		Employees/Unit		Sales/Employee
Employment:					
Company-Owned	144		5.8		$49,986
Franchisee-Owned	4,448		2.7		35,806
Total	4,592		2.8		36,250
Employee Performance Ratios			211.2%		139.6%

Source: Franchising In The Economy, 1988 – 1990, IFA Education Foundation & Horwath International, Published January, 1990.

1) 1989 and 1990 data were estimated by respondents.

ADVANTAGE PAYROLL SERVICES

800 Center St., P.O. Box 1330
Auburn, ME 04210
TEL: (800) 323-9648 (207) 784-0178
FAX:
Mr. David Friedrich, President

The unique ADVANTAGE franchise relationship allows a proven salesperson with no computer or payroll experience to become self-employed in the computer services industry. ADVANTAGE franchisees provide local personalized service, while using the company's large mainframe computer processing power, sophisticated software and proven payroll tax filing service.

HISTORY: . . . . IFA	FINANCIAL:	FRANCHISOR TRAINING/SUPPORT:
Established in 1967; . . 1st Franchised in 1983	Cash Investment: $10-15K	Financial Assistance Provided: . . .Yes(D)
Company-Owned Units (As of 12/1/1989): . .1	Total Investment: $15-20K	Site Selection Assistance: . . . . .NA
Franchised Units (12/1/1989): 21	Fees: Franchise - $10K	Lease Negotiation Assistance: . . . . .NA
Total Units (12/1/1989): 22	Royalty: 0%, Advert: 0%	Co-operative Advertising: . . . . .Yes
Distribution: US-22;Can-0;Overseas-0	Contract Periods (Yrs.): . . . 10/10	Training: . . . . 2 Wks. Headquarters,
North America: . . . . 12 States	Area Development Agreement: Yes/10	. . . . 10 Days Franchise Territory
Concentration: . . . 6 in ME,2 in NH,2 in MA	Sub-Franchise Contract: · . . . . .No	On-Going Support: . . . . . a,B,C,D,G,H,I
Registered: . . . . All States	Expand in Territory: . . . . .No	Full-Time Franchisor Support Staff: . . 50
	Passive Ownership: . . . Not Allowed	EXPANSION PLANS:
Average # of Employees: . . . . . . 1 FT, 1 PT	Encourage Conversions: . . . . . Yes	US: . . . . .All US
Prior Industry Experience: . . . . Helpful	Franchisee Purchase(s) Required: Yes	Canada - No, ...Overseas - No

COMCHEQ SERVICES LIMITED

298 Garry St.
Winnipeg, MB R3C1H3 CAN
TEL: (204) 947-9400
FAX: (204) 947-9400
Mr. Jerry Butler, Licensee Co-ord.

COMCHEQ is a rapidly-growing payroll service company. COMCHEQ processes 8 million paychecks, totalling $5 billion annually. Individuals established in the financial services industry have an opportunity to expand their product line. Benefits include: non-seasonal, immediate cash flow, new business incentives and on-going support.

HISTORY: . . . . .CFA	FINANCIAL:	FRANCHISOR TRAINING/SUPPORT:
Established in 1968; . . 1st Franchised in 1988	Cash Investment: . . . . $1K+	Financial Assistance Provided: . . .Yes(D)
Company-Owned Units (As of 12/1/1989): . 19	Total Investment: . . . . $1K+	Site Selection Assistance: . . . . .NA
Franchised Units (12/1/1989): 4	Fees: Franchise - . . . . $1K+	Lease Negotiation Assistance: . . . . .NA
Total Units (12/1/1989): 23	Royalty: 15%, Advert: 0%	Co-operative Advertising: . . . . .Yes
Distribution: US-0;Can-23;Overseas-0	Contract Periods (Yrs.): 1/1	Training: . . . . .On-going At Closest
North America: . . . . 9 Provinces	Area Development Agreement: . .No	. . . . .Regional Branch
Concentration: . . . 6 in ON, 5 in MB, 3 in PQ	Sub-Franchise Contract: . . . . .No	On-Going Support: . . . . . A,B,C,D,,G,h
Registered:	Expand in Territory: . . . . Yes	Full-Time Franchisor Support Staff: . .350
	Passive Ownership: . . . Discouraged	EXPANSION PLANS:
Average # of Employees: . . . . . . 1 FT, 2 PT	Encourage Conversions: . . . . . NA	US: . . . . No
Prior Industry Experience: . . . . Helpful	Franchisee Purchase(s) Required: Yes	Canada - Yes, ...Overseas - No

CORRECT CREDIT COMPANY

P. O. Box 865
Oakhurst, NJ 07755
TEL: (201) 517-0077
FAX:
Mr. P. Fasano, President

Over 6 years of success in helping people get a good credit rating.

HISTORY:	FINANCIAL:	FRANCHISOR TRAINING/SUPPORT:
Established in 1983; . . 1st Franchised in 1985	Cash Investment: $30K	Financial Assistance Provided: . . .Yes(D)
Company-Owned Units (As of 12/1/1989): . .3	Total Investment: . . . .$	Site Selection Assistance: . . . . . . .Yes
Franchised Units (12/1/1989): 6	Fees: Franchise - $19.5K	Lease Negotiation Assistance: . . . . .Yes
Total Units (12/1/1989): 9	Royalty: 10%, Advert: 0%	Co-operative Advertising: . . . . .Yes
Distribution: US-9;Can-0;Overseas-0	Contract Periods (Yrs.): . . . 10/10	Training: . . . . 4 Days Headquarters,
North America: . . . . 4 States	Area Development Agreement: Yes/1	. . . . 3 Days Site
Concentration: . . . . 4 in NJ	Sub-Franchise Contract: . . . . . Yes	On-Going Support: . . . . C,d,E,h,I
Registered: . . . . .FL	Expand in Territory: . . . . Yes	Full-Time Franchisor Support Staff: . . . 8
	Passive Ownership: . . . Discouraged	EXPANSION PLANS:
Average # of Employees: . . . . . 2 FT, 3-6 PT	Encourage Conversions: . . . . . Yes	US: . . . . .All US
Prior Industry Experience: . . . . Helpful	Franchisee Purchase(s) Required: .No	Canada - No, ...Overseas - No

CREDIT CLINICS

Box 1941
Venice, CA 90291
TEL: (213) 451-5958
FAX:
Mr. Irv Sylvern, President

Service business for business and/or persons desiring to help others establish good credit or re-establish impaired credit.

HISTORY: . . . . IFA	FINANCIAL:	FRANCHISOR TRAINING/SUPPORT:
Established in 1978; . . 1st Franchised in 1979	Cash Investment: $500	Financial Assistance Provided: . . . . . No
Company-Owned Units (As of 12/1/1989): . .1	Total Investment: $500	Site Selection Assistance: . . . . No
Franchised Units (12/1/1989): 851	Fees: Franchise - $250	Lease Negotiation Assistance: . . . . . No
Total Units (12/1/1989): 852	Royalty: 0%, Advert: 0%	Co-operative Advertising: . . . . .No
Distribution: US-846;Can-5;Overseas-1	Contract Periods (Yrs.): . . . . . Inf.	Training: . . . . .Training By Manual
North America: . . . . 50 States	Area Development Agreement: . .No	. . . .
Concentration:	Sub-Franchise Contract: . . . . .No	On-Going Support: . . . .
Registered: . . . . CA	Expand in Territory: . . . . Yes	Full-Time Franchisor Support Staff: . . . 3
. . . .	Passive Ownership: . . . . . .Allowed	EXPANSION PLANS:
Average # of Employees: . . . . .1 FT	Encourage Conversions: . . . . .No	US: . . . . .All US
Prior Industry Experience: . . . . Helpful	Franchisee Purchase(s) Required: .No	Canada - Yes, . . . Overseas - Yes

EDWIN K. WILLIAMS & CO.

8774 Yates Dr., # 210
Westminster, CO 80030
TEL: (800) 255-2359 (303) 427-4989
FAX: (303) 650-7286
Mr. Sid Gregory, VP

E. K. WILLIAMS is the largest company in the world producing accounting systems, and is also a franchisor of accounting and business management counseling services for small businesses. We have led the field for many years in these products for the retail petroleum industry and for the past 12 years have included all other small businesses. Turn-key computer packages are available to franchisees.

HISTORY:	FINANCIAL:	FRANCHISOR TRAINING/SUPPORT:
Established in 1935; . . 1st Franchised in 1947	Cash Investment: $50-75K	Financial Assistance Provided: . . .Yes(D)
Company-Owned Units (As of 12/1/1989): . .0	Total Investment: $50-75K	Site Selection Assistance: . . . . .No
Franchised Units (12/1/1989): 310	Fees: Franchise - $18.5K	Lease Negotiation Assistance: . . . . .No
Total Units (12/1/1989): 310	Royalty: Var., Advert: 0%	Co-operative Advertising: . . . . .No
Distribution: US-310;Can-0;Overseas-0	Contract Periods (Yrs.): 10/10	Training: . . . . 2 Wks. Headquarters,
North America: . . . . 41 States	Area Development Agreement: . Yes	. . . . 2 Wks. South Bend, IN
Concentration: . . . . Primarily CA, TX & FL	Sub-Franchise Contract: . . . . .No	On-Going Support: . . . . . A,B,C,d,G,h,I
Registered: . . CA,FL,IL,MD,ND,OR,WA,WI	Expand in Territory: . . . . Yes	Full-Time Franchisor Support Staff: . . 27
. . . .	Passive Ownership: . . . Not Allowed	EXPANSION PLANS:
Average # of Employees: . . . . .4 FT	Encourage Conversions: . . . . . Yes	US: . . . . .All US
Prior Industry Experience: . . . . . .Necessary	Franchisee Purchase(s) Required: Yes	Canada - Yes, ...Overseas - No

FINANCIAL EXPRESS

14679 Midway, # 102
Dallas, TX 75244
TEL: (800) 637-3461 (214) 991-9255 C
FAX:
Mr. Tim Terry, President

Our nationally-recognized trademark says it all: efficient, on-site bookkeeping and tax service for the fastest-growing segment of the US -small business. Our client acquisition program, professional service and success record are the distinctives that set us apart. Our mobile offices add efficiencies which equal greater profits.

HISTORY:	FINANCIAL:	FRANCHISOR TRAINING/SUPPORT:
Established in 1986; . . 1st Franchised in 1986	Cash Investment: $30-40K	Financial Assistance Provided: . . . Yes(I)
Company-Owned Units (As of 12/1/1989): . .3	Total Investment: $70-80K	Site Selection Assistance: . . . . .Yes
Franchised Units (12/1/1989): 5	Fees: Franchise - $20K	Lease Negotiation Assistance: . . . . .Yes
Total Units (12/1/1989): 8	Royalty: 8%, Advert: . . . . . . NA	Co-operative Advertising: . . . . .Yes
Distribution: US-8;Can-0;Overseas-0	Contract Periods (Yrs.): 10/5/5	Training: . . . . 2 Wks. Headquarters,
North America: . . . . .1 State	Area Development Agreement: Yes/5	. . . . 1 Wk. Franchisee Site
Concentration: . . . . 8 in TX	Sub-Franchise Contract: . . . . .No	On-Going Support: . . .A,B,C,D,E,F,G,h,I
Registered: . . . . FL,VA	Expand in Territory: . . . . Yes	Full-Time Franchisor Support Staff: . . 10
. . . .	Passive Ownership: . . . . . .Allowed	EXPANSION PLANS:
Average # of Employees: . . . . .2 FT	Encourage Conversions: . . . . . Yes	US: . . . . .All US
Prior Industry Experience: . . . . . .Necessary	Franchisee Purchase(s) Required: Yes	Canada - Yes, ...Overseas - No

NATIONAL ACCOUNTING SERVICE

223 McLeod St., # 200
Ottawa, ON K2P0Z8 CAN
TEL: (613) 563-0287
FAX: (613) 563-0338
Mr. Cliff Bowditch, President

A network of independently-owned accounting/bookkeeping offices across the country, sharing each other's expertise, as well as that of the home office to provide a full service to their clients at a reasonable fee.

HISTORY: . . . .
Established in 1987; . . 1st Franchised in 1988
Company-Owned Units (As of 12/1/1989): . .1
Franchised Units (12/1/1989): 3
Total Units (12/1/1989): 4
Distribution: US-0;Can-4;Overseas-0
 North America: . . . . 3 Provinces
 Concentration: . . . 2 in ON, 1 in PQ, 1 in BC
Registered: . . . .
. . . .
Average # of Employees: . . . . . . 1 FT, 1 PT
Prior Industry Experience: . . . . . .Necessary

FINANCIAL:
Cash Investment: $11.5K
Total Investment: $11.5-15K
Fees: Franchise - $9.5K
 Royalty: $200/Mo., Advert: . . 0%
Contract Periods (Yrs.): 5/5
Area Development Agreement: . .No
Sub-Franchise Contract: . . . . .No
Expand in Territory: . . . . . . Yes
Passive Ownership: . . . Not Allowed
Encourage Conversions: . . . . .No
Franchisee Purchase(s) Required: .No

FRANCHISOR TRAINING/SUPPORT:
Financial Assistance Provided: . . . . .No
Site Selection Assistance: . . . . .Yes
Lease Negotiation Assistance: . . . . .Yes
Co-operative Advertising: . . . . No
Training: . . . . 3 Days Headquarters
. . . .
On-Going Support: . . . . c,d,G,h,I
Full-Time Franchisor Support Staff: . . . 2
EXPANSION PLANS:
 US: . . . . No
 Canada - Yes, ...Overseas - No

PADGETT BUSINESS SERVICES USA

160 Hawthorne Park
Athens, GA 30606
TEL: (800) 323-7292 (404) 543-8537 C
FAX: (404) 543-8537
Mr. Hub Brightwell, VP Mktg.

PBS grants licenses to individuals who desire to operate their own accounting, income tax and business consulting practice, utilizing the unique forms and successful systems of operation developed by the franchisor. The franchisee markets to small owner-operated businesses located in his own territory.

HISTORY: . . . .
Established in 1966; . . 1st Franchised in 1975
Company-Owned Units (As of 12/1/1989): . .0
Franchised Units (12/1/1989): 101
Total Units (12/1/1989): 101
Distribution: US-91;Can-10;Overseas-0
 North America: . . . . 22 States, 2 Provinces
 Concentration: . .22 in GA, 13 in FL, 10 in AL
Registered: . . . . FL,MD
. . . .
Average # of Employees: . . . . . . 1 FT, 2 PT
Prior Industry Experience: . . . . Helpful

FINANCIAL:
Cash Investment: $39K
Total Investment: $39K
Fees: Franchise - $24.5K
 Royalty: 9%, Advert: 0%
Contract Periods (Yrs.): . . . 20/20
Area Development Agreement: Yes/1
Sub-Franchise Contract: . . . . Yes
Expand in Territory: . . . . . . Yes
Passive Ownership: . . . Discouraged
Encourage Conversions: . . . . .No
Franchisee Purchase(s) Required: .No

FRANCHISOR TRAINING/SUPPORT:
Financial Assistance Provided: . . .Yes(D)
Site Selection Assistance: . . . . . . .NA
Lease Negotiation Assistance: . . . . . No
Co-operative Advertising: . . . . No
Training: . . . . . . 2 Wks. Headquarters, 1
 . . . . Wk. Field, 1 Wk. Site
On-Going Support: . . . . C,D,G,H,I
Full-Time Franchisor Support Staff: . . . 5
EXPANSION PLANS:
 US: . . . . .All US
 Canada - Yes, ... Overseas - No

SUPPLEMENTAL LISTING OF FRANCHISORS

ACCOUNTING CORPORATION OF AMERICA . . . . . 1505 Commonwealth Ave., Brighton MA 02135
BINEX CORPORATION . . . . 4441-E Auburn Blvd., E., Sacramento CA 95841
CANADIAN CONSUMER CREDIT CONSULTANTS . . . . 34 Grenfell Cr., Ottawa ON K2G0G2 CAN
COLLATERAL MANAGEMENT CANADA . . . # 104 - 630 Columbia St., New Westminster BC V3M1A5 CAN
COMPREHENSIVE ACCOUNTING SERVICES . . . . 2111 Comprehensive Dr., Aurora IL 60507
DEBIT ONE MOBILE BOOKKEEPING . . . . 4739 Belleview, # 101, Kansas City MO 64112
E. K. WILLIAMS & CO. . . . . 783 Brant St., Burlington ON L7R2J3 CAN
EQUITABLE BUSINESS & FIN. SERVICES . . . . 434 E. Dougherty St., #201, Athens GA 30601
INVESTORS GROUP . . . . 180 Dundas St. W., # 1502, Toronto ON M5G2A3 CAN
M.G.C. SERVICE . . . . P.O. Box 345, Blair NE 68008
PADGETT BUSINESS SERVICES OF CANADA . . . . .5580 Kennedy Rd., # 3, Mississauga ON L4Z2A9 CAN
RAMAR BUREAU . . . . 5206 Benito St., Montclair CA 91763

CHAPTER 8

BUSINESS: ADVERTISING AND PROMOTION

ADTEL MARKETING CENTER

1661 E. Camelback Rd., # 118
Phoenix, AZ 85016
TEL: (602) 263-1225
FAX:
Mr. Kenneth Hollowell, Mktg. Dir.

The ADTEL MARKETING CENTER is a business establishment which will promote and distribute, on a leased basis, professionally audio-taped music and messages which have been customized for playback on telephone systems with "hold" capabilities.

HISTORY: . . . .
Established in 1985;   . . 1st Franchised in 1989
Company-Owned Units (As of 12/1/1989):   . .0
Franchised Units (12/1/1989): 4
Total Units (12/1/1989): 4
Distribution: US-1;Can-3;Overseas-0
  North America: . . . . . .1 State, 2 Provinces
  Concentration: . . . 2 in AB, 1 in BC, 1 in AZ
Registered: . . . .
. . . .
Average # of Employees: . . . . .3 FT
Prior Industry Experience: . . . . Helpful

FINANCIAL:
Cash Investment: $20-25K
Total Investment: $20-25K
Fees: Franchise - $15K
  Royalty: 0%, Advert: 0%
Contract Periods (Yrs.): 10/10
Area Development Agreement: . .No
Sub-Franchise Contract: . . . . . .No
Expand in Territory: . . . . .No
Passive Ownership: . . . Not Allowed
Encourage Conversions: . . . . . .No
Franchisee Purchase(s) Required: Yes

FRANCHISOR TRAINING/SUPPORT:
Financial Assistance Provided: . . . . .No
Site Selection Assistance: . . . . .Yes
Lease Negotiation Assistance: . . . . .Yes
Co-operative Advertising: . . . . .Yes
Training: . . . . 5 Days Headquarters
. . . .
On-Going Support: . . . . . C,D,E,F,G,h,I
Full-Time Franchisor Support Staff: . . . 2
EXPANSION PLANS:
  US: . . . . Southwest
  Canada - Yes, ... Overseas - No

AMERICAN ADVERTISING DISTRIBUTORS
234 S. Extension, P.O. Box AAD 16964
Mesa, AZ 85201
TEL: (800) 528-8249 (602) 964-9393
FAX: (602) 461-0052
Mr. Al Shindelman, Dir. Fran. Ops.

A full-service, professional, direct mail marketing business with trademarked training techniques in establishing a sucessful business, meeting the needs of the local business community. The franchisor handles all aspects of the physical execution of the promotion. The franchise needs good business management and sales skills.

HISTORY: .... IFA	FINANCIAL:	FRANCHISOR TRAINING/SUPPORT:
Established in 1976; . . 1st Franchised in 1977	Cash Investment: . . . . . . $23.5K+	Financial Assistance Provided: . . . . . No
Company-Owned Units (As of 12/1/1989): . .2	Total Investment: $28-50K	Site Selection Assistance: . . . . .NA
Franchised Units (12/1/1989): 111	Fees: Franchise - . . . . . . $23.5K+	Lease Negotiation Assistance: . . . . .NA
Total Units (12/1/1989): 113	Royalty: Flat, Advert: . . . . . Flat	Co-operative Advertising: . . . . .Yes
Distribution: . . . US-113;Can-0;Overseas-0	Contract Periods (Yrs.): 10/5	Training: . . . . .2 Wks. HQ, 1 Wk.
North America: . . . . 29 States	Area Development Agreement: . .No	. . . . Field, 1 Wk. Site
Concentration:	Sub-Franchise Contract: . . . . .No	On-Going Support: . . . . D,G,H,I
Registered: . . . . All States	Expand in Territory: . . . . . . Yes	Full-Time Franchisor Support Staff: . .162
. . . .	Passive Ownership: . . . Discouraged	EXPANSION PLANS:
Average # of Employees:	Encourage Conversions: . . . . Yes	US: . . . . All US
Prior Industry Experience: . . . . . . Helpful	Franchisee Purchase(s) Required: Yes	Canada - No, ...Overseas - No

CREATIVE CARD

2120 S. Green Rd.
Cleveland, OH 44121
TEL: (216) 381-1111
FAX:
Mr. Marshall Mallie, President

A "CREATIVE CARD" franchise provides more leads and referral business for businesses through its "Concepts for Sales" programs. Its products are produced photographically and typographically and include business cards, post cards, note cards, brochures, business reply and mailing pieces. The "Create-a-Shot" program is for school students. "CREATIVE CARD" franchisees are taught every aspect of the business, including photography and sales.

HISTORY:	FINANCIAL:	FRANCHISOR TRAINING/SUPPORT:
Established in 1987; . . 1st Franchised in 1988	Cash Investment: $14-19K	Financial Assistance Provided: . . . Yes(I)
Company-Owned Units (As of 12/1/1989): . .1	Total Investment: $19-31K	Site Selection Assistance: . . . . .NA
Franchised Units (12/1/1989): 1	Fees: Franchise - $13.8K	Lease Negotiation Assistance: . . . . .NA
Total Units (12/1/1989): 2	Royalty: 2%, Advert: 1.5%	Co-operative Advertising: . . . . .NA
Distribution: US-2;Can-0;Overseas-0	Contract Periods (Yrs.): 10/5/5	Training: . . . . . 5-5 1/2 Days HQ, 2 Days
North America: . . . . .1 State	Area Development Agreement: . .No	. .Site, Region. Workshops, Monthly HQ
Concentration: . . . . 2 in OH	Sub-Franchise Contract: . . . . .No	On-Going Support: . . . . C,D,h
Registered: . . . . .CA,FL,IL,MI,NY	Expand in Territory: . . . . . . Yes	Full-Time Franchisor Support Staff: . . . 6
. . . .	Passive Ownership: . . . Not Allowed	EXPANSION PLANS:
Average # of Employees: . . . . . .6+ FT, 4 PT	Encourage Conversions: . . . . .No	US: . . . . . .Midwest,PA,NY,NJ,FL,DE
Prior Industry Experience: . . . . . . Helpful	Franchisee Purchase(s) Required: Yes	Canada - No, ...Overseas - No

GOOD NEWS ADVERTISING

36 C Stoffel Dr.
Rexdale, ON M9W1A8 CAN
TEL: (416) 248-2555
FAX:
Ms. Louise Billet, Fran. Sales Dir.

Bulk mailing of advertising flyers is a fast-growing business serving the business community. At present, 15% per year annual growth is seen due to the fact that the advertising is more effective than any other, on a dollar-for-dollar basis. Franchisees operate this direct mail business from home or office.

HISTORY: . . . . IFA	FINANCIAL:	FRANCHISOR TRAINING/SUPPORT:
Established in 1985; . . 1st Franchised in 1985	Cash Investment: $10-40K	Financial Assistance Provided: . . . . .No
Company-Owned Units (As of 12/1/1989): . .1	Total Investment: $15-50K	Site Selection Assistance: . . . . .NA
Franchised Units (12/1/1989): 3	Fees: Franchise - $10-40K	Lease Negotiation Assistance: . . . . .NA
Total Units (12/1/1989): 4	Royalty: 5%, Advert: 0%	Co-operative Advertising: . . . . .Yes
Distribution: US-1;Can-3;Overseas-0	Contract Periods (Yrs.): 5/5	Training: . . . . . . 2 Wks. Headquarters, 1
North America: . . . . . .1 State, 1 Provinces	Area Development Agreement: . .No	. . . .Wk. On-site, 1 Wk. Staff College
Concentration: . . . . 1 in FL, 3 in ON	Sub-Franchise Contract: . . . . . .No	On-Going Support: . . . . .B,C,D,F,G,H,I
Registered:	Expand in Territory: . . . . . . .No	Full-Time Franchisor Support Staff: . . . 6
. . . .	Passive Ownership: . . . Not Allowed	EXPANSION PLANS:
Average # of Employees: . . . . .2 FT	Encourage Conversions: . . . . Yes	US: . . . . All US
Prior Industry Experience: . . . . . . Helpful	Franchisee Purchase(s) Required: Yes	Canada - Yes, ...Overseas - No

HEADLINES USA

2401 Fountainview, # 900
Houston, TX 77057
TEL: (713) 781-2102 C
FAX: (713) 975-8849
Mr. Jim Rolfe, Dir. Fran. Devel.

The newest advertising media in America. We sell high-class restroom advertising installed on beautiful adboards. Nightclubs, restaurants, sports arenas, race tracks, convention centers are typical locations. Local, regional and national advertisers love us.

HISTORY: . . . .
Established in 1987; . . 1st Franchised in 1988
Company-Owned Units (As of 12/1/1989): . .3
Franchised Units (12/1/1989): 8
Total Units (12/1/1989): 11
Distribution: US-11;Can-0;Overseas-0
North America: . . . . 6 States
Concentration: . . . . 4 in TX, 2 in CA
Registered: . . . . FL,MI
. . . .
Average # of Employees: . . . . . 1-3 FT, 1 PT
Prior Industry Experience: . . . . Helpful

FINANCIAL:
Cash Investment: $27-77K
Total Investment: $27-77K
Fees: Franchise - $7.5-25K
  Royalty: 15%, Advert: 0%
Contract Periods (Yrs.): 5/5
Area Development Agreement: Yes/5
Sub-Franchise Contract: . . . . . .No
Expand in Territory: . . . . . . Yes
Passive Ownership: . . . Discouraged
Encourage Conversions: . . . . .No
Franchisee Purchase(s) Required: .No

FRANCHISOR TRAINING/SUPPORT:
Financial Assistance Provided: . . . . .No
Site Selection Assistance: . . . . . . .Yes
Lease Negotiation Assistance: . . . . .Yes
Co-operative Advertising: . . . . .NA
Training: . . . . .1 Wk. Headquarters,
. . . . .5-15 In Field
On-Going Support: . . A,B,C,D,E,F,G,h,i
Full-Time Franchisor Support Staff: . . . 9
EXPANSION PLANS:
US: . . . . All US
Canada - Yes, . . . Overseas - Yes

MONEY MAILER

15472 Chemical Ln.
Huntington Beach, CA 92649
TEL: (800) 624-5371 (714) 898-9111
FAX: (714) 898-7927
Mr. Steve Olson, VP Fran.

Direct mail advertising franchise, with regional support office for on-going assistance of sales and production. Ranked Number 1 advertising franchise by Entrepreneur. Business suited for the sales/management professional. MONEY MAILER is the leader in Macintosh technology in the advertising industry. Master franchises available.

HISTORY: . . . . IFA/WIF
Established in 1979; . . 1st Franchised in 1980
Company-Owned Units (As of 12/1/1989): . .1
Franchised Units (12/1/1989): 245
Total Units (12/1/1989): 246
Distribution: US-246;Can-0;Overseas-0
North America: . . . . 28 States
Concentration: . 31 in CA, 28 in MD, 24 in FL
Registered: . . . CA,FL,HI,IL,IN,MD,MI,MN
. . . . NY,OR,VA,WA,WI
Average # of Employees: . . . . . . 2 FT, 1 PT
Prior Industry Experience: . . . . Helpful

FINANCIAL:
Cash Investment: $0-15K
Total Investment: $15-59k
Fees: Franchise - $15-32k
  Royalty: 9%, Advert: 0%
Contract Periods (Yrs.): 5/5
Area Development Agreement: . .No
Sub-Franchise Contract: . . . . Yes
Expand in Territory: . . . . . . Yes
Passive Ownership: . . . Not Allowed
Encourage Conversions: . . . . .No
Franchisee Purchase(s) Required: .No

FRANCHISOR TRAINING/SUPPORT:
Financial Assistance Provided: . . . Yes(I)
Site Selection Assistance: . . . . .NA
Lease Negotiation Assistance: . . . . .NA
Co-operative Advertising: . . . . .Yes
Training: . . . . . . .1 Wk. S. CA, 1 Wk.
. . . Regional Office, 1 Wk. Field Train.
On-Going Support: . . . . . . B,D,G,h,I
Full-Time Franchisor Support Staff: . .100
EXPANSION PLANS:
US: . . . . All US
Canada - Yes, . . . Overseas - Yes

NAMCO SYSTEMS

7 Strathmore Rd.
Natick, MA 01760
TEL: (508) 655-0510
FAX:
Ms. Julie Stansky, Fran. Admin.

An exclusive, target-marketed advertising program that guarantees continual exposure day after day in the home. Comprehensive classroom and field training, coupled with on-going support included in a one-time investment. No hidden costs.

HISTORY: . . . .
Established in 1953; . . 1st Franchised in 1982
Company-Owned Units (As of 12/1/1989): . .7
Franchised Units (12/1/1989): 31
Total Units (12/1/1989): 38
Distribution: US-38;Can-0;Overseas-0
North America: . . . . 16 States
Concentration: . . . . 5 in PA, 4 in NY, 4 in IL
Registered: . . . . FL,MI
. . . .
Average # of Employees: . . . . .1 FT
Prior Industry Experience: . . . . Helpful

FINANCIAL:
Cash Investment: $30K
Total Investment: $30K
Fees: Franchise - $24-32K
  Royalty: 15%, Advert: 0%
Contract Periods (Yrs.): . . . 10/10
Area Development Agreement: Yes/10
Sub-Franchise Contract: . . . . . .No
Expand in Territory: . . . . . . .No
Passive Ownership: . . . Not Allowed
Encourage Conversions: . . . . .No
Franchisee Purchase(s) Required: .No

FRANCHISOR TRAINING/SUPPORT:
Financial Assistance Provided: . . . . .No
Site Selection Assistance: . . . . . . .NA
Lease Negotiation Assistance: . . . . .NA
Co-operative Advertising: . . . . .NA
Training: . . . . 4 Days Headquarters,
. . . . 10 Days Site, On-going
On-Going Support: . . . . . . .B,C,D,G,H
Full-Time Franchisor Support Staff: . . . 1
EXPANSION PLANS:
US: . . . . All Except West
Canada - No, ...Overseas - No

SUPER COUPS

180 Bodwell St.
Avon, MA 02322
TEL: (800) 626-2620 (508) 580-4340
FAX: (508) 588-2000
Mr. Ralph Berry, Dir. Fran. Sales

Co-operative direct mail advertising company, servicing the needs of small local merchants and large national advertisers.

HISTORY: . . . .
Established in 1983; . . 1st Franchised in 1983
Company-Owned Units (As of 12/1/1989): . .0
Franchised Units (12/1/1989): 79
Total Units (12/1/1989): 79
Distribution: US-79;Can-0;Overseas-0
North America: . . . . 13 States
Concentration: . . 25 in MA, 19 in NJ, 12 in RI
Registered: . . . . FL,NY,OR,RI,VA
. . . .
Average # of Employees: . . . . .2 FT
Prior Industry Experience: . . . . . . Helpful

FINANCIAL:
Cash Investment: $21.9-35K
Total Investment: $21.9-35K
Fees: Franchise - $21.9K
  Royalty: NA, Advert: . . . . . . NA
Contract Periods (Yrs.): 10/10
Area Development Agreement: . .No
Sub-Franchise Contract: . . . . . Yes
Expand in Territory: . . . . Yes
Passive Ownership: . . . Discouraged
Encourage Conversions: . . . . . Yes
Franchisee Purchase(s) Required: .No

FRANCHISOR TRAINING/SUPPORT:
Financial Assistance Provided: . . . . No
Site Selection Assistance: . . . . . . .Yes
Lease Negotiation Assistance: . . . . .NA
Co-operative Advertising: . . . . . . .Yes
Training: . . . . 5 Days Headquarters,
 . . . . .5 Days Franchised Location
On-Going Support: . . . A,B,C,D,E,G,H,I
Full-Time Franchisor Support Staff: . .150
EXPANSION PLANS:
 US: . . . . .All US
Canada - No, ...Overseas - No

TRIMARK

184 Quigley Blvd., P. O. Box 10530
Wilmington, DE 19850
TEL: (800) 874-6275 (302) 322-2143 C
FAX: (302) 322-2163
Mr. Gilbert Kinch, VP Sales

Co-op advertising and marketing company. Franchisor is a printing and publishing company in the business of co-op direct mail advertising, which consists of mailing advertisements, usually in the form of redeemable coupons and special discount notices, to homes. TRIMARK has refined the co-op concept, which brings together non- competitive business into a single "coupon" package.

HISTORY: . . . . .IFA
Established in 1977; . . 1st Franchised in 1978
Company-Owned Units (As of 12/1/1989): . .0
Franchised Units (12/1/1989): 63
Total Units (12/1/1989): 63
Distribution: US-63;Can-0;Overseas-0
North America: . . . . 26 States
Concentration: . . . 5 in NY, 4 in PA, 3 in MA
Registered: . . . . .FL,OR
. . . .
Average # of Employees: . . . . . . 2 FT, 1 PT
Prior Industry Experience: . . . . Helpful

FINANCIAL:
Cash Investment: . . . . . $Up to 10K
Total Investment: $10-39K
Fees: Franchise - $5-29K
  Royalty: 0%, Advert: 0%
Contract Periods (Yrs.): . . .Negot.
Area Development Agreement: . .No
Sub-Franchise Contract: . . . . .No
Expand in Territory: . . . . Yes
Passive Ownership: . . . Discouraged
Encourage Conversions: . . . . .No
Franchisee Purchase(s) Required: .No

FRANCHISOR TRAINING/SUPPORT:
Financial Assistance Provided: . . . . .No
Site Selection Assistance: . . . . . . .Yes
Lease Negotiation Assistance: . . . .NA
Co-operative Advertising: . . . . . . .Yes
Training: . . . . .1 Wk. Headquarters,
 . . . . 1 Wk. Franchisee's Area
On-Going Support: . . . . A,B,C,D,G,H,I
Full-Time Franchisor Support Staff: . . 70
EXPANSION PLANS:
 US: . . . . .All US
Canada - No, ... Overseas - No

SUPPLEMENTAL LISTING OF FRANCHISORS

BREAD BOX, THE . . . . 1010 South Taylor, Little Rock AR 72204
CARD ETC., THE . . . . 1525 State St., Santa Barbara CA 93101
CIRCUIT CARD . . . . 1661 E. Camelback, # 118, Phoenix AZ 85016
ESP DISCOUNT COUPONS .195 Courtland St., Belleville NJ 07109
FLYER NETWORK . . . . .2201 Brandt St., # 531, Burlington ON L7P3N6   CAN
GREETINGS . . . . P. O. Box 25623, Lexington KY 40524
IDEAL PAK . . . . 32 Andrea Rd., Ajax ON L1S3V7   CAN
LOCAL MERCHANT DISPLAY CENTERS . . . . 4115 Tiverton Rd., Randallstown MD 21133
POINTS FOR PROFIT . . . . .P.O. Box 81026, San Diego CA 92138
SAVINGS TODAY! COUPON MAGAZINE . . . . 1220 44th Ave. E., Bradenton FL 34203
STUFFIT . . . . 12450 Automobile Blvd., Clearwater FL 33520
VAL-PAK DIRECT MARKETING SYSTEMS . . . . 10601 Belcher Rd., Largo FL 34647
VIDEO IMPACT . . . . 34 Grenfell Cres., Ottawa ON K2G0G2   CAN
WHERE THE HEART IS . . . . 125 East St., # 303A, Dedham MA 02026
ZOOM MOBILE ADVERTISING . . . . 528 North 26th St., Allentown PA 18104

CHAPTER 9

BUSINESS: OFFICE SERVICES AND TELECOMMUNICATIONS

ANSWERING SPECIALISTS

119 W. Doty Ave.
Summerville, SC 29483
TEL: (803) 724-6300
FAX:
Mr. Bud Doty, President

ANSWERING SPECIALISTS gives people a truly professional, quality telephone answering service. Provides personalized message and appointment taking for important customer contact. It's a low overhead, easy to manage business. It requires a small investment for a business based on years of development.

HISTORY: . . . .
Established in 1972; . . 1st Franchised in 1988
Company-Owned Units (As of 12/1/1989): . .1
Franchised Units (12/1/1989): 0
Total Units (12/1/1989): 1
Distribution: US-1;Can-0;Overseas-0
  North America: . . . . .1 State
  Concentration: . . . . 1 in SC
Registered: . . . .
. . . .
Average # of Employees: . . . . .4 FT
Prior Industry Experience: . . . . . . Helpful

FINANCIAL:
Cash Investment: $27-45K
Total Investment: $27-45K
Fees: Franchise - $14.5K
  Royalty: $300/Mo., Advert: $75/Mo.
Contract Periods (Yrs.): 5/5
Area Development Agreement: . Yes
Sub-Franchise Contract: . . . . . Yes
Expand in Territory: . . . . Yes
Passive Ownership: . . . . . .Allowed
Encourage Conversions: . . . . . Yes
Franchisee Purchase(s) Required: .No

FRANCHISOR TRAINING/SUPPORT:
Financial Assistance Provided: . . . . .No
Site Selection Assistance: . . . . .Yes
Lease Negotiation Assistance: . . . . .Yes
Co-operative Advertising: . . . . .Yes
Training: . . . . 5 Days Headquarters
. . . .
On-Going Support: . . . . .B,C,D,E,G,H,I
Full-Time Franchisor Support Staff: . . . 9
EXPANSION PLANS:
  US: . . . . .All US
  Canada - Yes, ...Overseas - Yes

COMMUNICATIONS WORLD

14828 W. 6th Ave., # 13B
Golden, CO 80401
TEL: (800) 525-3200 (303) 279-8200
FAX:
Mr. Ron Haines, Fran. Sales

COMMUNICATIONS WORLD franchisees sell telecommuncations equipment (including telephone systems, facsimile, voice mail and call accounting) to small- to medium-sized businesses. Also offer service, moves and maintenance agreements. Leasing and rental programs available.

HISTORY: . . . . IFA	FINANCIAL: OTC-CWIIA	FRANCHISOR TRAINING/SUPPORT:
Established in 1979; . . 1st Franchised in 1982	Cash Investment: $10-25K	Financial Assistance Provided: . . .Yes(D)
Company-Owned Units (As of 12/1/1989): . .3	Total Investment: $25-100K	Site Selection Assistance: . . . . . . .NA
Franchised Units (12/1/1989): 59	Fees: Franchise - $10K	Lease Negotiation Assistance: . . . . .NA
Total Units (12/1/1989): 62	Royalty: 9%, Advert: 1%	Co-operative Advertising: . . . . . . .Yes
Distribution: US-62;Can-0;Overseas-0	Contract Periods (Yrs.): 10/10	Training: . . . . 5 Days Headquarters,
North America: . . . . 16 States	Area Development Agreement: . .No	. . . . Varies at Site, 2-3 Day Seminars
Concentration: . . . 9 in CO, 8 in MN, 7 in AZ	Sub-Franchise Contract: . . . . .No	On-Going Support: . . . . . . B,D,F,G,H,I
Registered: . . CA,IL,IN,MD,MI,MN,VA,WA	Expand in Territory: . . . . .No	Full-Time Franchisor Support Staff: . . 25
	Passive Ownership: . . . Not Allowed	EXPANSION PLANS:
Average # of Employees: . . . . . . 2 FT, 1 PT	Encourage Conversions: . . . . . Yes	US: . . . . .All US
Prior Industry Experience: . . . . Helpful	Franchisee Purchase(s) Required: .No	Canada - No, ...Overseas - No

EXECUTIVE BUSINESS CENTERS / EBC FRANCHISE GROUP

1080 Holcomb Bridge Rd., #100-310
Boswell, GA 30076
TEL: (800) 635-6641 (404) 992-1119
FAX:
Mr. Tom N. Dye, Pres./CEO

EBC Office Centers provide offices and shared services to companies and executives that are efficient, cost-effective and enhance their business image and performance. More than 70% of our office population are executives of national and regional corporations. The balance are entrepreneurs, technical and financial consultants, and businesses in the marketing and service sectors.

HISTORY:	FINANCIAL:	FRANCHISOR TRAINING/SUPPORT:
Established in 1984; . . 1st Franchised in 1988	Cash Investment: $50-100K	Financial Assistance Provided: . . . . .No
Company-Owned Units (As of 12/1/1989): . 15	Total Investment: $176-290K	Site Selection Assistance: . . . . . . .Yes
Franchised Units (12/1/1989): 2	Fees: Franchise - $25K	Lease Negotiation Assistance: . . . . .Yes
Total Units (12/1/1989): 17	Royalty: 4%, Advert: 4%	Co-operative Advertising: . . . . . . .Yes
Distribution: US-17;Can-0;Overseas-0	Contract Periods (Yrs.): 10/5	Training: . . . . . . 2-3 Wks. Headquarters,
North America: . . . . 7 States	Area Development Agreement: Yes/5	. . . . On-going Franchisee Site
Concentration: . . . .8 in GA, 4 in FL, 2 in TN	Sub-Franchise Contract: . . . . .No	On-Going Support: . . . a,b,C,D,E,f,G,H,I
Registered: . . . . VA	Expand in Territory: . . . . Yes	Full-Time Franchisor Support Staff: . . . 9
	Passive Ownership: . . . . . .Allowed	EXPANSION PLANS:
Average # of Employees: . . . . .3-4 FT	Encourage Conversions: . . . . . Yes	US: . . . . .All US
Prior Industry Experience: . . . . . . Helpful	Franchisee Purchase(s) Required: .No	Canada - Yes, ...Overseas - No

FAX-9

1609 S. Murray Blvd.
Colorado Springs, CO 80916
TEL: (800) 727-3299 (719) 380-1133
FAX: (719) 380-1143
Mr. Dave Spahr, Natl Fran. Coord.

FAX-9, a nation-wide network of franchises, offers fax machines for public use. Individuals or businesses can send or receive fax transmissions at any FAX-9 station. Franchises will be located in existing businesses or owned by individuals. Expert technical, advertising and marketing assistance is on-going.

HISTORY:	FINANCIAL: OTC	FRANCHISOR TRAINING/SUPPORT:
Established in 1988; . . 1st Franchised in 1988	Cash Investment: $1.5K	Financial Assistance Provided: . . .Yes(D)
Company-Owned Units (As of 12/1/1989): . .0	Total Investment: . . . . . . $5.5K+	Site Selection Assistance: . . . . . .Yes
Franchised Units (12/1/1989): 425	Fees: Franchise - $3.5K	Lease Negotiation Assistance: . . . . .NA
Total Units (12/1/1989): 425	Royalty: $40/Mo., Advert: . . . 0%	Co-operative Advertising: . . . . . . .Yes
Distribution: US-421;Can-0;Overseas-0	Contract Periods (Yrs.): 7/7	Training: . . . . . 1-2 Days During Install-
North America: . . . . 42 States, 2 Provinces	Area Development Agreement: . .No	. . . . ation at Site
Concentration: . .34 in CA, 24 in CO, 13 in IL	Sub-Franchise Contract: . . . . . Yes	On-Going Support: . . . . B,C,D,G,I
Registered: . . CA,FL,IL,MD,MI,MN,NY,WA	Expand in Territory: . . . . Yes	Full-Time Franchisor Support Staff: . . 14
	Passive Ownership: . . . . . .Allowed	EXPANSION PLANS:
Average # of Employees: . . . . .1 FT	Encourage Conversions: . . . . . Yes	US: . . . . .All US
Prior Industry Experience: . . . . Helpful	Franchisee Purchase(s) Required: .No	Canada - Yes, ...Overseas - No

HQ - HEADQUARTERS COMPANIES

120 Montgomery St., # 1040
San Francisco, CA 94104
TEL: (800) 227-3004 (415) 781-7811
FAX: (415) 781-8034
Ms. Lesley Archer, Dir. Development

Office space, full or part-time; business support services; and telecommunications in a shared office environment with over 90 business centers throughout the US and Europe.

HISTORY: . . . .
Established in 1969; . . 1st Franchised in 1977
Company-Owned Units (As of 12/1/1989): . .0
Franchised Units (12/1/1989): 93
Total Units (12/1/1989): 93
Distribution: US-91;Can-0;Overseas-2
North America: . . . . 20 States
Concentration: . . .35 in CA, 7 in OH, 7 in TX
Registered: . . . CA,FL,IL,IN,MD,MI,MN,NY
. . . . OR,VA,WI
Average # of Employees: . . . . .8 FT
Prior Industry Experience: . . . . . . Helpful

FINANCIAL:
Cash Investment: $250-1,000K
Total Investment: $1MM
Fees: Franchise - . . . . . .$30-50K+
Royalty: 1%, Advert: 5%
Contract Periods (Yrs.): . . . . . NA
Area Development Agreement: Yes/1
Sub-Franchise Contract: . . . . .No
Expand in Territory: . . . . . . Yes
Passive Ownership: . . . Discouraged
Encourage Conversions: . . . . . Yes
Franchisee Purchase(s) Required: .No

FRANCHISOR TRAINING/SUPPORT:
Financial Assistance Provided: . . . . . No
Site Selection Assistance: . . . . No
Lease Negotiation Assistance: . . . . . No
Co-operative Advertising: . . . . . . .Yes
Training: . . . .
On-Going Support: . . . . . . .C,d,e,G,h,I
Full-Time Franchisor Support Staff: . . 10
EXPANSION PLANS:
US: . . . . Midwest, East
Canada - Yes, . . . Overseas - Yes

OFFICE ALTERNATIVE, THE

One SeaGate, # 1001
Toledo, OH 43604
TEL: (800) 262-4181 (419) 247-5400 C
FAX: (419) 247-5421
Ms. Martha Wolff, EVP

Ground-floor opportunity for YOU! Dynamic business support franchise now available in 86 geographic areas. As the owner of your own OFFICE ALTERNATIVE CENTER, you'll offer: personalized telephone answering, secretarial/word processing with laser printing, resumes, wrap/ship, FAX, copying, conference room and office rental and more!

HISTORY: . . . . IFA/WIF
Established in 1983; . . 1st Franchised in 1986
Company-Owned Units (As of 12/1/1989): . .1
Franchised Units (12/1/1989): 17
Total Units (12/1/1989): 18
Distribution: US-18;Can-0;Overseas-0
North America: . . . . 9 States
Concentration: . . . 5 in OH, 4 in GA, 2 in FL
Registered: . . . . FL,IL,IN,MN,ND,RI,SD,WI
. . . .
Average # of Employees: . . . . . . 3 FT, 2 PT
Prior Industry Experience: . . . . . . Helpful

FINANCIAL:
Cash Investment: $44-54K
Total Investment: $44-54K
Fees: Franchise - $15K
Royalty: 5%, Advert: 0%
Contract Periods (Yrs.): 10/10
Area Development Agreement: Yes/5
Sub-Franchise Contract: . . . . . Yes
Expand in Territory: . . . . . . Yes
Passive Ownership: . . . Not Allowed
Encourage Conversions: . . . . . Yes
Franchisee Purchase(s) Required: .No

FRANCHISOR TRAINING/SUPPORT:
Financial Assistance Provided: . . .Yes(D)
Site Selection Assistance: . . . . . . .Yes
Lease Negotiation Assistance: . . . .Yes
Co-operative Advertising: . . . . . . .NA
Training: . . . . . . 3-4 Days Headquarters,
. . . . 3-5 Days On-site
On-Going Support: . . . . . . .C,D,E,G,H,I
Full-Time Franchisor Support Staff: . . . 4
EXPANSION PLANS:
US: . . . . .All US
Canada - Yes, ...Overseas - No

OFFICE ANSWER, THE

8445 Keystone Crossing, # 165
Indianapolis, IN 46240
TEL: (800) 678-2336 (317) 254-9040
FAX:
Mr. Roger Nondorf, VP Mktg/Bus. Dev.

THE OFFICE ANSWER brings computerized technology to the telephone answering industry. Computer-assisted operators offer personalized and professional service to clients. You support the small businessman. Low overhead, recurring revenues, strong customer loyalty. Additional services include mail receiving and sending, word processing and facsimile transmission.

HISTORY: . . . . IFA
Established in 1987; . . 1st Franchised in 1988
Company-Owned Units (As of 12/1/1989): . .0
Franchised Units (12/1/1989): 7
Total Units (12/1/1989): 7
Distribution: US-7;Can-0;Overseas-0
North America: . . . . 3 States
Concentration: . . . . 4 in IN, 2 in DE, 1 in PA
Registered: . . . . FL,IL,IN
. . . .
Average # of Employees: . . . . .1-2 FT
Prior Industry Experience: . . . . Helpful

FINANCIAL:
Cash Investment: $10-15K
Total Investment: $10-25K
Fees: Franchise - $8.5K
Royalty: 5%, Advert: 0%
Contract Periods (Yrs.): 10/10
Area Development Agreement: Yes/10
Sub-Franchise Contract: . . . . . .No
Expand in Territory: . . . . . . .No
Passive Ownership: . . . Discouraged
Encourage Conversions: . . . . . Yes
Franchisee Purchase(s) Required: .No

FRANCHISOR TRAINING/SUPPORT:
Financial Assistance Provided: . . . . .No
Site Selection Assistance: . . . . . . .Yes
Lease Negotiation Assistance: . . . .Yes
Co-operative Advertising: . . . . .No
Training: . . . . . . 1-7 Days Headquarters,
. . . 1-2 Days On-site, On-going Support
On-Going Support: . . . . . . C,D,E,G,H,I
Full-Time Franchisor Support Staff: . . . 4
EXPANSION PLANS:
US: . . . . .All US
Canada - No, ...Overseas - No

TELE - TECH COMMUNICATION

1350 East 4th Ave.
Vancouver, BC V5N1J5 CAN
TEL: (604) 255-5000
FAX: (604) 255-2212
Mr. Ian Abramson, President

An alternative to coin-op payphones - a coilless, cordless payphone brought to customer at restaurants, lounges, clubs, etc. The dealer shares in the revenue.

HISTORY: . . . .
Established in 1987; . . 1st Franchised in 1987
Company-Owned Units (As of 12/1/1989): . .0
Franchised Units (12/1/1989): 12
Total Units (12/1/1989): 12
Distribution: US-0;Can-12;Overseas-0
North America: . . . . 10 Provinces
Concentration: . . . .
Registered: . . . . AB
. . . .
Average # of Employees: . . . . .4 FT
Prior Industry Experience: . . . . . . Helpful

FINANCIAL:
Cash Investment: $5K
Total Investment: $5K
Fees: Franchise - $0
  Royalty: 5%, Advert: 1%
Contract Periods (Yrs.): 3/3
Area Development Agreement: . .No
Sub-Franchise Contract: . . . . .No
Expand in Territory: . . . . . . Yes
Passive Ownership: . . . Discouraged
Encourage Conversions: . . . . .No
Franchisee Purchase(s) Required: .No

FRANCHISOR TRAINING/SUPPORT:
Financial Assistance Provided: . . . . No
Site Selection Assistance: . . . . No
Lease Negotiation Assistance: . . . . No
Co-operative Advertising: . . . . . . .Yes
Training: . . . . . . 2 Days Headquarters
. . . .
On-Going Support: . . . . . A,B,C,D,G,h,I
Full-Time Franchisor Support Staff: . . . 8
EXPANSION PLANS:
US: . . . . .All US
Canada - Yes, . . . Overseas - Yes

VOICE ENTERPRISES /
VOICE-TEL
70 West Streetsboro St.
Hudson, OH 44236
TEL: (800) 247-4237 (216) 656-9366
FAX:
Mr. Joseph McClellan, Fran. Dir.

Offering metro and single-unit franchise voice message service bureaus, providing transmission, storage and retrieval of verbal messages through a communications system and any touch-tone telephone.

HISTORY: . . . . .IFA
Established in 1986; . . 1st Franchised in 1986
Company-Owned Units (As of 12/1/1989): . .0
Franchised Units (12/1/1989): 51
Total Units (12/1/1989): 51
Distribution: US-51;Can-0;Overseas-0
North America: . . . . 8 States
Concentration: . . 11 in OH, 6 in VA, 3 in NC
Registered: . . . . . .All States Exc. ND & SD
. . . .
Average # of Employees: . . . . .3 FT
Prior Industry Experience: . . . . . . Helpful

FINANCIAL:
Cash Investment: $35-75K
Total Investment: $49-210K
Fees: Franchise - $20-75K
  Royalty: 6-10%, Advert: 2%
Contract Periods (Yrs.): . . . 20/10
Area Development Agreement: Yes/20
Sub-Franchise Contract: . . . . .No
Expand in Territory: . . . . . . .No
Passive Ownership: . . . . . .Allowed
Encourage Conversions: . . . . .No
Franchisee Purchase(s) Required: Yes

FRANCHISOR TRAINING/SUPPORT:
Financial Assistance Provided: . . . Yes(I)
Site Selection Assistance: . . . . . . .Yes
Lease Negotiation Assistance: . . . . .Yes
Co-operative Advertising: . . . . . . .Yes
Training: . . . . 10 Days Headquarters
. . . .
On-Going Support: . . . . B,C,D,E,F,G,h,I
Full-Time Franchisor Support Staff: . . . 8
EXPANSION PLANS:
US: . . . . .All US
Canada - No, ...Overseas - Yes

SUPPLEMENTAL LISTING OF FRANCHISORS

CAR PHONE CONNECTION/CPC SYSTEMS . . . . .8 Campus Dr., Parsippany NJ 07054
CARTRONIX . . . . 1031 - 2nd St. South, Hopkins MN 55343
CELLULAND . . . . .10717 Sorrento Valley Rd., San Diego CA 92121
CPC SYSTEMS . . . . .8 Campus Dr., Parsippany NJ 07054
LETTER WRITER, THE . . . . .9357 Haggerty Rd., Plymouth MI 48170
OFFICE PARTNERS RESOURCE CENTERS . . . 4695 MacArthur Ct., # 1420, Newport Beach CA 92660
PMTS SYSTEMS . . . . 4400 Bragdon St., Indianapolis IN 46226
SNC TELECOM PROBLEM SOLVERS . . . . .101 W. Waukau Ave., Oshkosh WI 54901

CHAPTER 10

BUSINESS: PRINTING /
MAIL SERVICES / PACKAGING

AIR SOURCE EXPRESS

3357 Hollenberg Dr.
Bridgeton, MO 63044
TEL: (800) 325-4727 (314) 739-0077
FAX:
Mr. Richard Baum, VP-Finance

A full-service, air express/air courier company providing: local cartage, same-day, overnight, 9 AM and deferred deliveries from 1-? pounds to both large and small business; strong telemarketing and accounting/collection support.

HISTORY: . . . .
Established in 1982; . . 1st Franchised in 1987
Company-Owned Units (As of 12/1/1989): . .0
Franchised Units (12/1/1989): 10
Total Units (12/1/1989): 10
Distribution: US-10;Can-0;Overseas-0
North America: . . . . 9 States
Concentration: . . . 2 in PA, 1 in MO, 1 in NY
Registered: . . . CA,FL,HI,IL,IN,MD,MI,MN
. . . . NY,OR,VA,WA,WI
Average # of Employees: . . . . . . 4 FT, 1 PT
Prior Industry Experience: . . . . Helpful

FINANCIAL:
Cash Investment: $37-121K
Total Investment: $37-121K
Fees: Franchise - $10-60K
  Royalty: 12%, Advert: 1%
Contract Periods (Yrs.): 10/5/5
Area Development Agreement: . .No
Sub-Franchise Contract: . . . . . .No
Expand in Territory: . . . . . . .No
Passive Ownership: . . . Discouraged
Encourage Conversions: . . . . . Yes
Franchisee Purchase(s) Required: .No

FRANCHISOR TRAINING/SUPPORT:
Financial Assistance Provided: . . . . .No
Site Selection Assistance: . . . . .Yes
Lease Negotiation Assistance: . . . . .Yes
Co-operative Advertising: . . . . .Yes
Training: . . . . 2 Wks. Headquarters,
. . . . 1 Wk. On-site
On-Going Support: . . . .A,B,C,D,E,G,h,I
Full-Time Franchisor Support Staff: . . 17
EXPANSION PLANS:
  US: . . . . .All US
  Canada - No, ... Overseas - No

PRINTING & COPYING SERVICES

	1988	1989	1990	Percentage Change 1988-1989	Percentage Change 1989-1990
Number of Establishments:					
Company-Owned	148	158	167	6.8%	5.7%
Franchisee-Owned	5,727	6,291	7,199	9.8%	14.4%
Total	5,875	6,449	7,366	9.8%	14.2%
% of Total Establishments:					
Company-Owned	2.5%	2.4%	2.3%		
Franchisee-Owned	97.5%	97.6%	97.7%		
Total	100.0%	100.0%	100.0%		
Annual Sales ($000):					
Company-Owned	$43,671	$48,765	$54,300	11.7%	11.4%
Franchisee-Owned	1,369,139	1,560,824	1,835,994	14.0%	17.6%
Total	1,412,810	1,609,589	1,890,294	13.9%	17.4%
% of Total Sales:					
Company-Owned	3.1%	3.0%	2.9%		
Franchisee-Owned	96.9%	97.0%	97.1%		
Total	100.0%	100.0%	100.0%		
Average Sales Per Unit ($000):					
Company-Owned	$295	$309	$325	4.6%	5.3%
Franchisee-Owned	239	248	255	3.8%	2.8%
Total	240	250	257	3.8%	2.8%
Sales Ratio	123.4%	124.4%	127.5%		

	1st Quartile	Median	4th Quartile
Average 1988 Total Investment:			
Company-Owned	$61,750	$127,000	$218,750
Franchisee-Owned	91,500	113,500	148,500
Single Unit Franchise Fee	$18,150	$24,000	$34,750
Multiple Unit Franchise Fee	7,500	11,250	17,375
Franchisee Start-up Cost	30,000	47,500	73,000

	1988	Employees/Unit	Sales/Employee
Employment:			
Company-Owned	823	5.6	$53,063
Franchisee-Owned	24,245	4.2	56,471
Total	25,068	4.3	56,359
Employee Performance Ratios		131.4%	94.0%

Source: Franchising In The Economy, 1988 – 1990, IFA Education Foundation & Horwath International, Published January, 1990.

1) 1989 and 1990 data were estimated by respondents.

ALPHAGRAPHICS PRINTSHOPS OF THE FUTURE (CANADA)
455 Milres Ave.
Scarborough, ON M1B2K4 CAN
TEL: (416) 291-3059
FAX:
Mr. Colin Innes, VP Fin. & Ops.

ALPHAGRAPHICS PRINTSHOPS OF THE FUTURE pioneered the concept of desktop publishing made available to everyone. The high-tech, quick-print shops involve offset printing, high-speed and self-serve duplicating and full-service and self-serve typesetting done on our exclusive Lazer Graphics System. Profitable outlets located in 5 different market types.

HISTORY: . . . . CFA
Established in 1986; . . 1st Franchised in 1986
Company-Owned Units (As of 12/1/1989): . .0
Franchised Units (12/1/1989): 15
Total Units (12/1/1989): 15
Distribution: US-0;Can-15;Overseas-0
North America: . . . . 4 Provinces
Concentration: . . . 9 in ON, 3 in AB, 2 in PQ
Registered: . . . . AB
. . . .
Average # of Employees: . . . . . . 6 FT, 2 PT
Prior Industry Experience: . . . . Helpful

FINANCIAL:
Cash Investment: $130-150K
Total Investment: $300-350K
Fees: Franchise - $50K
Royalty: 9-4%, Advert: 1-2%
Contract Periods (Yrs.): 30/30
Area Development Agreement: . Yes
Sub-Franchise Contract: . . . . . .No
Expand in Territory: . . . . Yes
Passive Ownership: . . . Not Allowed
Encourage Conversions: . . . . . Yes
Franchisee Purchase(s) Required: Yes

FRANCHISOR TRAINING/SUPPORT:
Financial Assistance Provided: . . . Yes(I)
Site Selection Assistance: . . . . . . .Yes
Lease Negotiation Assistance: . . . . .Yes
Co-operative Advertising: . . . . .Yes
Training: . . . . 3 Wks. Tucson, AZ, 1 Wk.
. . . . .Mature Store, 2 Wks. Site
On-Going Support: . . . a,B,C,D,E,f,G,h,I
Full-Time Franchisor Support Staff: . . . 7
EXPANSION PLANS:
US: . . . . US Franchisor
Canada - Yes, ...Overseas - No

AMERICAN POST 'N PARCEL

315 W. Pondera St., # F
Lancaster, PA 93534
TEL: (800) 2-PARCEL (805) 949-3990 C
FAX:
Mr. H. E. Klemm, President

A business opportunity whose format has been developed and successfully tested for nearly 2 years prior to offering its first franchise. Every service provided to the consumer has been carefully selected to provide maximum profit potential with a minimum of overhead and special ability requirements.

HISTORY: . . . . IFA
Established in 1988; . . 1st Franchised in 1988
Company-Owned Units (As of 12/1/1989): . .1
Franchised Units (12/1/1989): 5
Total Units (12/1/1989): 6
Distribution: US-6;Can-0;Overseas-0
North America: . . . . 2 States
Concentration: . . . . 5 in CA
Registered: . . . . CA,IL
. . . .
Average # of Employees: . . . . . . 1 FT, 1 PT
Prior Industry Experience: . . . . Helpful

FINANCIAL:
Cash Investment: $40-60K
Total Investment: $48-68K
Fees: Franchise - $15K
Royalty: 5%, Advert: 1%
Contract Periods (Yrs.): 10/10
Area Development Agreement: . .No
Sub-Franchise Contract: . . . . . .No
Expand in Territory: . . . . Yes
Passive Ownership: . . . Discouraged
Encourage Conversions: . . . . . Yes
Franchisee Purchase(s) Required: .No

FRANCHISOR TRAINING/SUPPORT:
Financial Assistance Provided: . . . . .No
Site Selection Assistance: . . . . . . .Yes
Lease Negotiation Assistance: . . . .Yes
Co-operative Advertising: . . . . .NA
Training: . . . . 5 Days Headquarters
. . . .
On-Going Support: . . . . . C,d,E,F,G,H,I
Full-Time Franchisor Support Staff: . . . 4
EXPANSION PLANS:
US: . . . . .All US
Canada - Yes, . . . Overseas - Yes

AMERICAN SPEEDY PRINTING CENTERS
2555 S. Telegraph Rd.
Bloomfield Hills, MI 48013
TEL: (800) 548-9050 (313) 335-6200
FAX: (313) 335-0267
Ms. Maggie Flood, Development Coord.

Typically located in a strip center or business park, our owners are prepared to provide offset printing and related services to area businesses. High-speed copying, desktop publishing, facsimile, design services, pick-up and delivery are other services in this high-margin business.

HISTORY: . . . . IFA/WIF
Established in 1977; . . 1st Franchised in 1977
Company-Owned Units (As of 12/1/1989): . .0
Franchised Units (12/1/1989): 681
Total Units (12/1/1989): 681
Distribution: . . . US-651;Can-20;Overseas-10
North America: . . . . 42 States, 2 Provinces
Concentration: . 118 in MI, 73 in CA,55 in FL
Registered: . . . . All Except AB
. . . .
Average # of Employees: . . . . . . 2 FT, 1 PT
Prior Industry Experience: . . . . Helpful

FINANCIAL:
Cash Investment: $5-30K
Total Investment: $135-150K
Fees: Franchise - $19.5K
Royalty: 6%, Advert: 1-2%
Contract Periods (Yrs.): 20/20
Area Development Agreement: Yes/Var
Sub-Franchise Contract: . . . . . Yes
Expand in Territory: . . . . Yes
Passive Ownership: . . . Discouraged
Encourage Conversions: . . . . . Yes
Franchisee Purchase(s) Required: .No

FRANCHISOR TRAINING/SUPPORT:
Financial Assistance Provided: . . . Yes(I)
Site Selection Assistance: . . . . . . .Yes
Lease Negotiation Assistance: . . . .Yes
Co-operative Advertising: . . . . .Yes
Training: . . . . 2 Wks. Headquarters,
. . . 1 Wk. On-site, 3 Days Installation
On-Going Support: . . . . .B,C,D,E,G,H,I
Full-Time Franchisor Support Staff: . .124
EXPANSION PLANS:
US: . . . . .All US
Canada - Yes, . . . Overseas - Yes

AMERICAN WHOLESALE THERMOGRAPHERS / AWT
P.O. Box 777
Cypress, TX 77429
TEL: (800) 231-1304 (713) 373-3535 C
FAX: (800) 542-8539
Director of Franchise Sales

AMERICAN WHOLESALE THERMOGRAPHERS (AWT) is a wholesale, raised printing franchise. Franchise includes training and support. Franchising since 1981 with approximately 19 centers. The franchise fee is $38,500.

HISTORY: . . . . .IFA
Established in 1980; . . 1st Franchised in 1981
Company-Owned Units (As of 12/1/1989): . .0
Franchised Units (12/1/1989): 19
Total Units (12/1/1989): 19
Distribution: US-16; Can-3; Overseas-0
North America: . . . . . 13 States, 1 Province
Concentration: . . . 3 in TX, 3 in ON, 2 in CA
Registered: . . . . .All
. . . .
Average # of Employees: . . . . . . 3 FT, 1 PT
Prior Industry Experience: . . . . . . Helpful

FINANCIAL:
Cash Investment: . . . . $~50K
Total Investment: $169-188K
Fees: Franchise - $38.5K
Royalty: 5%, Advert: 0%
Contract Periods (Yrs.): 25/25
Area Development Agreement: . .No
Sub-Franchise Contract: . . . . .No
Expand in Territory: . . . . . . .No
Passive Ownership: . . . Not Allowed
Encourage Conversions: . . . . .No
Franchisee Purchase(s) Required: .No

FRANCHISOR TRAINING/SUPPORT:
Financial Assistance Provided: . . . Yes(I)
Site Selection Assistance: . . . . . . .Yes
Lease Negotiation Assistance: . . . . .Yes
Co-operative Advertising: . . . . . . .NA
Training: . . . . . . 2 Wks. Headquarters, 2
. . . . . Wks. Existing Site(s), 1 Wk. Site
On-Going Support: . . . . .B,C,D,E,G,H,I
Full-Time Franchisor Support Staff: . .126
EXPANSION PLANS:
US: . . . . .All US
Canada - Yes, . . . Overseas - Yes

BOX SHOPPE, THE

7165 E. 87th St.
Indianapolis, IN 46256
TEL: (317) 842-4120
FAX:
Mr. Duke Smith, President

THE BOX SHOPPE is a one-stop source for most every packaging need - for moving and storage, gifts, home or office, packing and shipping, or almost any other special need. Operated from a retail store environment, the store sells at both retail and wholesale levels.

HISTORY: . . . .
Established in 1984; . . 1st Franchised in 1985
Company-Owned Units (As of 12/1/1989): . .4
Franchised Units (12/1/1989): 63
Total Units (12/1/1989): 67
Distribution: US-67; Can-0; Overseas-0
North America: . . . . 7 States
Concentration: . . .23 in IN, 17 in OH, 6 in MI
Registered: . . . . IL,IN,MI
. . . .
Average # of Employees: . . . . . . 1 FT, 1 PT
Prior Industry Experience: . . . . . . Helpful

FINANCIAL:
Cash Investment: $35K
Total Investment: $35-50K
Fees: Franchise - $13.5K
Royalty: 2%, Advert: 2%
Contract Periods (Yrs.): 5/5
Area Development Agreement: . .No
Sub-Franchise Contract: . . . . .No
Expand in Territory: . . . . . . Yes
Passive Ownership: . . . Not Allowed
Encourage Conversions: . . . . .No
Franchisee Purchase(s) Required: .No

FRANCHISOR TRAINING/SUPPORT:
Financial Assistance Provided: . . .Yes(D)
Site Selection Assistance: . . . . . . .Yes
Lease Negotiation Assistance: . . . . .Yes
Co-operative Advertising: . . . . . . .Yes
Training: . . . . 3 Days Minimum at Head-
. . . . quarters
On-Going Support: . . A,B,C,D,E,F,G,H,I
Full-Time Franchisor Support Staff: . . 30
EXPANSION PLANS:
US: . . . . Southeast and Midwest
Canada - No, ...Overseas - No

BOXWORKS, THE

1420 Donelson Pike, A-3
Nashville, TN 37217
TEL: (615) 360-8400
FAX: (615) 360-8490
Mr. Henry Zoller, President

Attractive, up-scale retail/wholesale stores, offering gifts, stationery, party goods, quality designer paper and packaging products, specialty boxes, giftwrap, bags, containers, corrugated moving & utility boxes & packaging materials. Custom imprinting, computer calligraphy & laser printing, exquisite gift wrapping & packaging and worldwide shipping services.

HISTORY: . . . . .IFA
Established in 1986; . . 1st Franchised in 1987
Company-Owned Units (As of 12/1/1989): . .0
Franchised Units (12/1/1989): 35
Total Units (12/1/1989): 35
Distribution: US-35; Can-0; Overseas-0
North America: . . . . 9 States
Concentration: . . . 10 in CA, 6 in TN, 4 in NJ
Registered: . . .CA,FL,IL,MD,MI,NY,VA,WI
. . . .
Average # of Employees: . . . . .2 FT
Prior Industry Experience: . . . . . . Helpful

FINANCIAL:
Cash Investment: $73-122K
Total Investment: $73-122K
Fees: Franchise - $15K
Royalty: 4.5%, Advert: 1%
Contract Periods (Yrs.): . . . 10/10
Area Development Agreement: Yes/10
Sub-Franchise Contract: . . . . .No
Expand in Territory: . . . . . . Yes
Passive Ownership: . . . Not Allowed
Encourage Conversions: . . . . Yes
Franchisee Purchase(s) Required: .No

FRANCHISOR TRAINING/SUPPORT:
Financial Assistance Provided: . . . Yes(I)
Site Selection Assistance: . . . . . . .Yes
Lease Negotiation Assistance: . . . . .Yes
Co-operative Advertising: . . . . . . .Yes
Training: . . . . . . .14 Days Headquarters
. . . .
On-Going Support: . . . A,B,C,D,E,F,G,H
Full-Time Franchisor Support Staff: . . .6
EXPANSION PLANS:
US: . . . . .All US
Canada - Yes, . . . Overseas - Yes

BUSINESS CARD EXPRESS

2555 S. Telegraph
Bloomfield Hills, MI 48013
TEL: (800) 438-4786 (313) 338-7711
FAX:
Mr. C. Glynn Culver, VP

Each B.C.E. franchise produces high-quality raised letter printing products (thermography) on a wholesale only basis to the retail and commercial printing industry. Only 70 to 100 B.C.E. franchises will be awarded in the US, thus offering major market exclusivity.

HISTORY: . . . . IFA	FINANCIAL:	FRANCHISOR TRAINING/SUPPORT:
Established in 1981; . . 1st Franchised in 1984	Cash Investment: $75K	Financial Assistance Provided: . . . Yes(I)
Company-Owned Units (As of 12/1/1989): . .0	Total Investment: $270K	Site Selection Assistance: . . . . . . .Yes
Franchised Units (12/1/1989): 30	Fees: Franchise - $48.5K	Lease Negotiation Assistance: . . . . .Yes
Total Units (12/1/1989): 30	Royalty: 5%, Advert: 1%	Co-operative Advertising: . . . . . . .Yes
Distribution: US-30;Can-0;Overseas-0	Contract Periods (Yrs.): 20/20	Training: . . . . 1 Wk. Headquarters, 1 Wk.
North America: . . . . 13 States	Area Development Agreement: . .No	. . . . .OJT, 2 Wks. On-site
Concentration: . . . . 2 in MI, 2 in IL, 2 in CA	Sub-Franchise Contract: . . . . .No	On-Going Support: . . A,B,C,D,E,F,G,H,I
Registered: . . . . All States	Expand in Territory: . . . . Yes	Full-Time Franchisor Support Staff: . . 12
. . . .	Passive Ownership: . . . Not Allowed	EXPANSION PLANS:
Average # of Employees: . . . . 6-10 FT	Encourage Conversions: . . . . .No	US: . . . . .All US
Prior Industry Experience: . . . . . . Helpful	Franchisee Purchase(s) Required: .No	Canada - Yes, . . . Overseas - Yes

BUSINESS CARDS TOMORROW / BCT

3000 NE 30th Place
Ft. Lauderdale, FL 33306
TEL: (305) 563-1224
FAX:
Mr. Skip Day, President

BUSINESS CARDS TOMORROW is the world's largest wholesale thermography franchise supplying the retail printing industry. We offer site selection and full training, with on-going support.

HISTORY:	FINANCIAL: OTC-BUSC	FRANCHISOR TRAINING/SUPPORT:
Established in 1975; . . 1st Franchised in 1975	Cash Investment: $85K	Financial Assistance Provided: . . .Yes(D)
Company-Owned Units (As of 12/1/1989): . .0	Total Investment: $150K	Site Selection Assistance: . . . . . . .Yes
Franchised Units (12/1/1989): 99	Fees: Franchise - $60K	Lease Negotiation Assistance: . . . . .Yes
Total Units (12/1/1989): 99	Royalty: 6%, Advert: 0%	Co-operative Advertising: . . . . . . .Yes
Distribution: US-89;Can-10;Overseas-0	Contract Periods (Yrs.): 25/10	Training: . . . . 2 Wks. Ft. Lauderdale, FL
North America: . . . . 14 States, 2 Provinces	Area Development Agreement: . .No	. . . . Continuing On-site
Concentration: . . 17 in CA, 10 in FL, 8 in ON	Sub-Franchise Contract: . . . . .No	On-Going Support: . . . . . C,D,E,F,G,h,I
Registered: . . . . .All	Expand in Territory: . . . . Yes	Full-Time Franchisor Support Staff: . . 25
. . . .	Passive Ownership: . . . Not Allowed	EXPANSION PLANS:
Average # of Employees: . . . . .7 FT	Encourage Conversions: . . . . . Yes	US: . . . . .All US
Prior Industry Experience: . . . . . . Helpful	Franchisee Purchase(s) Required: .No	Canada - Yes, . . . Overseas - Yes

COPIES NOW

23131 Verdugo Dr.
Laguna Hills, CA 92653
TEL: (800) 752-7537
FAX: (714) 458-1297
Mr. Dave Collins, VP

COPIES NOW is a high-speed duplicating, desktop publishing, presentation graphics and other business communication center.

HISTORY: . . . . IFA	FINANCIAL:	FRANCHISOR TRAINING/SUPPORT:
Established in 1983; . . 1st Franchised in 1984	Cash Investment: $30K	Financial Assistance Provided: . . . Yes(I)
Company-Owned Units (As of 12/1/1989): . .0	Total Investment: $95K	Site Selection Assistance: . . . . . . .Yes
Franchised Units (12/1/1989): 55	Fees: Franchise - $27.5K	Lease Negotiation Assistance: . . . . .Yes
Total Units (12/1/1989): 55	Royalty: 4-6%, Advert: 2%	Co-operative Advertising: . . . . . . .Yes
Distribution: US-55;Can-0;Overseas-0	Contract Periods (Yrs.): 20/20	Training: . . . . 2 Wks. Headquarters,
North America: . . . . 10 States	Area Development Agreement: Yes/20	. . . . 1-2 Wks. On-site
Concentration:	Sub-Franchise Contract: . . . . .No	On-Going Support: . . . . .B,C,D,E,G,H,I
Registered: . . . . .All	Expand in Territory: . . . . Yes	Full-Time Franchisor Support Staff: . . 65
. . . .	Passive Ownership: . . . Discouraged	EXPANSION PLANS:
Average # of Employees: . . . . .2 FT	Encourage Conversions: . . . . . Yes	US: . . . . .All US
Prior Industry Experience: . . . . . . Helpful	Franchisee Purchase(s) Required: .No	Canada - Yes, . . . Overseas - Yes

COPYMAT

2000 Powell St.
Emeryville, CA 94608
TEL: (415) 655-3513
FAX: (415) 654-2568
Mr. Ken Campbell, SR VP, COO

Our regionally-dominant firm is the leading electronic document processing service in the West. We provide photocopying and desktop publishing services in a distinctive, professional environment which emphasizes service and easy access to proven, leading edge technology.

HISTORY: . . . .
Established in 1974; . . 1st Franchised in 1984
Company-Owned Units (As of 12/1/1989): . .0
Franchised Units (12/1/1989): 68
Total Units (12/1/1989): 68
Distribution: US-68;Can-0;Overseas-0
North America: . . . . .1 State
Concentration: . . . . 68 in CA
Registered: . . . . CA,HI,OR,WA
. . . .
Average # of Employees: . . . . . . 4 FT, 2 PT
Prior Industry Experience: . . . . Helpful

FINANCIAL:
Cash Investment: $150K
Total Investment: $300K
Fees: Franchise - $40K
 Royalty: 7-4%, Advert: 0%
Contract Periods (Yrs.): 15/10
Area Development Agreement: Yes/5
Sub-Franchise Contract: . . . . .No
Expand in Territory: . . . . Yes
Passive Ownership: . . . Discouraged
Encourage Conversions: . . . . . Yes
Franchisee Purchase(s) Required: .No

FRANCHISOR TRAINING/SUPPORT:
Financial Assistance Provided: . . . . . No
Site Selection Assistance: . . . . .Yes
Lease Negotiation Assistance: . . . . . No
Co-operative Advertising: . . . . No
Training: . . . . 3 Wks. Headquarters
. . . .
On-Going Support: . . . . .B,C,D,E,G,H,I
Full-Time Franchisor Support Staff: . . 17
EXPANSION PLANS:
US: . . . . West Coast Only
Canada - No, ...Overseas - No

DYNAMIC AIR FREIGHT

2120 Walnut Hill Ln., # 222
Irvine, TX 75038
TEL: (800) 736-0011 (214) 751-0011
FAX: (214) 550=8662
Mr. Ed McGuire, Dir. Fran. Dev.

Domestic and international air freight forwarding.

HISTORY: . . . .
Established in 1978; . . 1st Franchised in 1985
Company-Owned Units (As of 12/1/1989): . .2
Franchised Units (12/1/1989): 18
Total Units (12/1/1989): 20
Distribution: . . . . US-;Can-;Overseas-
North America: . . . .
Concentration: . . . .
Registered: . . . .
. . . .
Average # of Employees: . . . .
Prior Industry Experience: . . . . . .Necessary

FINANCIAL:
Cash Investment: . . . .$
Total Investment: $36-120K
Fees: Franchise - $10-50K
 Royalty: 14%, Advert: 5%
Contract Periods (Yrs.): 10/10
Area Development Agreement: . .No
Sub-Franchise Contract: . . . . .No
Expand in Territory: . . . . Yes
Passive Ownership: . . . Discouraged
Encourage Conversions: . . . . . Yes
Franchisee Purchase(s) Required: .No

FRANCHISOR TRAINING/SUPPORT:
Financial Assistance Provided: . . . Yes(I)
Site Selection Assistance: . . . . No
Lease Negotiation Assistance: . . . . . No
Co-operative Advertising: . . . . No
Training: . . . . .2 Wks. Dallas, TX
. . . . a,B,C,d,e,f,G,H
On-Going Support: . . . .
Full-Time Franchisor Support Staff: . . . .
EXPANSION PLANS:
US: . . . . .All US
Canada - Yes, . . . Overseas - Yes

EXPRESS POSTAL CENTERS

6475 28th St. SE
Grand Rapids, MI 49506
TEL: (616) 949-7567
FAX:
Mr. Scott Fenstemacher, VP

EXPRESS POSTAL CENTERS are neighborhood service centers that combine the services of the Post Office, major express couriers and parcel systems, all under one roof.

HISTORY: . . . . .IFA
Established in 1987; . . 1st Franchised in 1987
Company-Owned Units (As of 12/1/1989): . .0
Franchised Units (12/1/1989): 11
Total Units (12/1/1989): 11
Distribution: US-11;Can-0;Overseas-0
North America: . . . . 3 States
Concentration: . . . . 8 in MI, 2 in FL, 1 in SC
Registered: . . . . FL,IL,MI,VA
. . . .
Average # of Employees: . . . . . 1 FT, Var. PT
Prior Industry Experience: . . . . Helpful

FINANCIAL:
Cash Investment: $25K
Total Investment: $39-47K
Fees: Franchise - $15K
 Royalty: %, Advert: 2%
Contract Periods (Yrs.): 10/10
Area Development Agreement: . .No
Sub-Franchise Contract: . . . . .No
Expand in Territory: . . . . Yes
Passive Ownership: . . . Discouraged
Encourage Conversions: . . . . . .No
Franchisee Purchase(s) Required: .No

FRANCHISOR TRAINING/SUPPORT:
Financial Assistance Provided: . . . Yes(I)
Site Selection Assistance: . . . . . . .Yes
Lease Negotiation Assistance: . . . . .Yes
Co-operative Advertising: . . . . .NA
Training: . . . . 2 Wks. Headquarters,
. . . . 1 Wk. On-site
On-Going Support: . . . . . . .C,D,E,G,H
Full-Time Franchisor Support Staff: . . .5
EXPANSION PLANS:
US: . . . . .All US
Canada - No, ...Overseas - No

GNOMON COPY

154 Sandown Rd.
Chester, NH 03036
TEL: (603) 887-3030
FAX: (603) 887-2737
Mr. James A. Sutherland, President

Full-service copy center, offering high-speed copying, binding, facsimile, self-service copying and other services. Locate franchises near major colleges and universities. Only franchisor in the US to offer franchise to sole-ownership program. Own your own business (not just a franchise) with the support of an experienced franchisor.

HISTORY: . . . . IFA
Established in 1966; . . 1st Franchised in 1980
Company-Owned Units (As of 12/1/1989): . .0
Franchised Units (12/1/1989): 16
Total Units (12/1/1989): 16
Distribution: US-16;Can-0;Overseas-0
North America: . . . . 5 States
Concentration: . .11 in MAm 2 in NH, 1 in PA
Registered: . . . .
. . . .
Average # of Employees: . . . . . . 1 FT, 3 PT
Prior Industry Experience: . . . . . . Helpful

FINANCIAL:
Cash Investment: $40-58K
Total Investment: $83-107K
Fees: Franchise - $17.5K
Royalty: 0-7%, Advert: 0-4%
Contract Periods (Yrs.): 10/1
Area Development Agreement: . .No
Sub-Franchise Contract: . . . . .No
Expand in Territory: . . . . Yes
Passive Ownership: . . . Discouraged
Encourage Conversions: . . . . . Yes
Franchisee Purchase(s) Required: .No

FRANCHISOR TRAINING/SUPPORT:
Financial Assistance Provided: . . .Yes(D)
Site Selection Assistance: . . . . . . .Yes
Lease Negotiation Assistance: . . . . .Yes
Co-operative Advertising: . . . . No
Training: . . . . 2 Wks.+ On-site,
. . . . . . On-going As Needed On-site
On-Going Support: . . . . B,C,D,E,F,G,I
Full-Time Franchisor Support Staff: . . . 2
EXPANSION PLANS:
US: . . . . .Eastern US
Canada - Yes, ...Overseas - No

HANDLE WITH CARE
PACKAGING STORE

5675 DTC Parkway, # 280
Englewood, CO 80111
TEL: (800) 525-6309 (303) 741-6626
FAX:
Mr. Richard Godwin, President

THE PACKAGING STORE is a megatrend business that is meeting growing consumer and commercial service needs. Minimum cash outlay, easy to operate, great public demand. The PACKAGING STORE offers an unusual opportunity for return on investment. Site selection assistance, in-store training, inventory discounts and an on-going marketing program for maximum profitability.

HISTORY: . . . . IFA
Established in 1980; . . 1st Franchised in 1984
Company-Owned Units (As of 12/1/1989): . .0
Franchised Units (12/1/1989): 320
Total Units (12/1/1989): 320
Distribution: US-320;Can-0;Overseas-0
North America: . . . . 38 States
Concentration: . 47 in CA, 24 in CO, 19 in MI
Registered: . . . . .All
. . . .
Average # of Employees: . . . . . . 1 FT, 1 PT
Prior Industry Experience: . . . . . . Helpful

FINANCIAL:
Cash Investment: $25-40K
Total Investment: $25-40K
Fees: Franchise - $15.5K
Royalty: 5%, Advert: 1-3%
Contract Periods (Yrs.): . . . Infin.
Area Development Agreement: . Yes
Sub-Franchise Contract: . . . . .No
Expand in Territory: . . . . Yes
Passive Ownership: . . . Discouraged
Encourage Conversions: . . . . . Yes
Franchisee Purchase(s) Required: .No

FRANCHISOR TRAINING/SUPPORT:
Financial Assistance Provided: . . . Yes(I)
Site Selection Assistance: . . . . .Yes
Lease Negotiation Assistance: . . . . .No
Co-operative Advertising: . . . . No
Training: . . . . . 1 Wk. Regional Training
. . . . Center
On-Going Support: . . . . . . C,D,E,G,H,I
Full-Time Franchisor Support Staff: . . . 4
EXPANSION PLANS:
US: . . . . All US
Canada - Yes, ...Overseas - No

INK WELL, THE

2323 Lake Club Dr.
Columbus, OH 43232
TEL: (800)235-2221 (800)862-2662(OH)
FAX: (614) 864-4028
Mr. Gerard Ales, VP Development

High-quality, short-run commercial printing centers owned and operated by business people serving a business clientele. Positioned in this growth industry to deliver on customer's increasing demands. All start-up and on-going support provided. Our well is brimming with what you need to realize your dream of independence.

HISTORY: . . . . IFA
Established in 1972; . . 1st Franchised in 1981
Company-Owned Units (As of 12/1/1989): . .1
Franchised Units (12/1/1989): 51
Total Units (12/1/1989): 52
Distribution: US-52;Can-0;Overseas-0
North America: . . . . 7 States
Concentration: . . . . .39 in OH, 6 in FL
Registered: . . . . .FL,IL,IN,MI,MN,VA,WI
. . . .
Average # of Employees: . . . . .3 FT
Prior Industry Experience: . . . . . . Helpful

FINANCIAL:
Cash Investment: $30-40K
Total Investment: $132-168K
Fees: Franchise - $28K
Royalty: 6%, Advert: 2.5%
Contract Periods (Yrs.): . . . 20/20
Area Development Agreement: . Yes
Sub-Franchise Contract: . . . . .No
Expand in Territory: . . . . Yes
Passive Ownership: . . . Discouraged
Encourage Conversions: . . . . . No
Franchisee Purchase(s) Required: .No

FRANCHISOR TRAINING/SUPPORT:
Financial Assistance Provided: . . . Yes(I)
Site Selection Assistance: . . . . . . .Yes
Lease Negotiation Assistance: . . . . .Yes
Co-operative Advertising: . . . . .Yes
Training: . . . . 2 Wks. Headquarters,
. . . . 2 Wks. + 3 Days On-site
On-Going Support: . . . . .B,C,D,E,G,H,I
Full-Time Franchisor Support Staff: . . 20
EXPANSION PLANS:
US: . . . . All US
Canada - No, ... Overseas - No

KWIK KOPY PRINTING (CANADA)

35 Riviera Dr., # 12
Markham, ON L358N4 CAN
TEL: (800) 387-9725
FAX:
Mr. John Johnson, Natl. Mktg. Mgr.

KWIK KOPY PRINTING offers complete printing and photocopying services. We are the largest instant print franchisor in Canada, providing coast-to-coast support services. The integrity of our franchisees is our strength - the service they provide is the difference. Join us at the top.

HISTORY: . . . . IFA
Established in 1978; . . 1st Franchised in 1978
Company-Owned Units (As of 12/1/1989): . .0
Franchised Units (12/1/1989): 110
Total Units (12/1/1989): 110
Distribution: US-0;Can-110;Overseas-0
North America: . . . . 10 Provinces
Concentration: . . . . .61 in ON, 8 in PQ
Registered: . . . . AB
. . . .
Average # of Employees: . . . . . . 6 FT, 1 PT
Prior Industry Experience: . . . . Helpful

FINANCIAL:
Cash Investment: $70K
Total Investment: $150K
Fees: Franchise - $49.5K
Royalty: 6%, Advert: 3%
Contract Periods (Yrs.): 25
Area Development Agreement: . .No
Sub-Franchise Contract: . . . . .No
Expand in Territory: . . . . Yes
Passive Ownership: . . . Not Allowed
Encourage Conversions: . . . . .No
Franchisee Purchase(s) Required: .No

FRANCHISOR TRAINING/SUPPORT:
Financial Assistance Provided: . . .Yes(D)
Site Selection Assistance: . . . . . . .Yes
Lease Negotiation Assistance: . . . . .Yes
Co-operative Advertising: . . . . Yes
Training: . . . . .3 Wks. Houston, TX
. . . .
On-Going Support: . . . . . . C,D,E,G,H,I
Full-Time Franchisor Support Staff: . . 20
EXPANSION PLANS:
US: .No
Canada - Yes, ...Overseas - No

KWIK-KOPY PRINTING CENTERS

One Kwik-Kopy Ln.
Cypress, TX 77429
TEL: (800) 231-1304 (713) 373-3535 C
FAX: *542-8539
Director of Franchise Sales

KWIK-KOPY is a full-service printing franchise. Franchise includes training and support and is using techniques of modern technology. Franchising since 1969 with approximately 1,000 centers. The franchise fee is $22,000 plus $23,000 for start-up program and pre-paid operating costs.

HISTORY: . . . . IFA
Established in 1967; . . 1st Franchised in 1969
Company-Owned Units (As of 12/1/1989): . .1
Franchised Units (12/1/1989): 1003
Total Units (12/1/1989): 1004
Distribution: US-1004;Can-0;Overseas-0
North America: . . . .
Concentration: . . .176 in TX, 63 in CA, 46 IL
Registered: . . . . .All
. . . .
Average # of Employees: . . . . . . 3 FT, 1 PT
Prior Industry Experience: . . . . Helpful

FINANCIAL:
Cash Investment: $45-50K
Total Investment: $138-177K
Fees: Franchise - $22K
Royalty: 4-8%, Advert: 0%
Contract Periods (Yrs.): 25/25
Area Development Agreement: . .No
Sub-Franchise Contract: . . . . .No
Expand in Territory: . . . . Yes
Passive Ownership: . . . Discouraged
Encourage Conversions: . . . . .No
Franchisee Purchase(s) Required: .No

FRANCHISOR TRAINING/SUPPORT:
Financial Assistance Provided: . . . Yes(I)
Site Selection Assistance: . . . . . . .Yes
Lease Negotiation Assistance: . . . .Yes
Co-operative Advertising: . . . . No
Training: . . . . 3 Wks. Headquarters
. . . . 7 Days Franchisee Site
On-Going Support: . . . . . . B,D,E,G,h,I
Full-Time Franchisor Support Staff: . .126
EXPANSION PLANS:
US: . . . . .All US
Canada - Yes, . . . Overseas - Yes

MAIL BOXES ETC. (CANADA)

200 Consumers rd., # 405
Willowdale, ON M2J4R4 CAN
TEL: (800) 387-6108 (416) 495-0181
FAX: (416) 495-1867
Mr. Bill Pump, Franchise Sales

Postal, business and communications service centers. A nationwide network of centers providing: MinuteMail Fax and Telex; custom packing and shipping via UPS, Emery, etc; Western Union services; word processing; notary; office supplies; mail box rentals and many other business-oriented services.

HISTORY: . . . . IFA
Established in 1982; . . 1st Franchised in 1982
Company-Owned Units (As of 12/1/1989): . .0
Franchised Units (12/1/1989): 1200
Total Units (12/1/1989): 1200
Distribution: . . US-1180;Can-10;Overseas-10
North America: . . . . 50 States, 2 Provinces
Concentration: . . . .
Registered: . . . . .All
. . . .
Average # of Employees: . . . . . . 1 FT, 1 PT
Prior Industry Experience: . . . . Helpful

FINANCIAL: NASD-MBE
Cash Investment: $40-60K
Total Investment: $80-140K
Fees: Franchise - $25K
Royalty: 5%, Advert: 3%
Contract Periods (Yrs.): 10/10
Area Development Agreement: Yes/10
Sub-Franchise Contract: . . . . .No
Expand in Territory: . . . . Yes
Passive Ownership: . . . Discouraged
Encourage Conversions: . . . . . Yes
Franchisee Purchase(s) Required: Yes

FRANCHISOR TRAINING/SUPPORT:
Financial Assistance Provided: . . . . .NA
Site Selection Assistance: . . . . . . .Yes
Lease Negotiation Assistance: . . . .Yes
Co-operative Advertising: . . . . . . .Yes
Training: . . . . 2 Wks. Headquarters
. . . .
On-Going Support: . . . a,B,C,D,E,F,G,h,I
Full-Time Franchisor Support Staff: . .100
EXPANSION PLANS:
US: . . . . .All US
Canada - Yes, . . . Overseas - Yes

MAIL BOXES, ETC.

5555 Oberline Dr., # 100
San Diego, CA 92121
TEL: (800) 456-0414 (619) 452-1553
FAX: (619) 452-9937
Franchise Development Dept.

MAIL BOXES ETC. is the largest and most successful network of postal, business and communication services. Lessen the risk of going into business for yourself, and go with the leader.

HISTORY: . . . . IFA
Established in 1980; . . 1st Franchised in 1980
Company-Owned Units (As of 12/1/1989): . . 1
Franchised Units (12/1/1989): 1018
Total Units (12/1/1989): 1019
Distribution: . . . US-1007;Can-10;Overseas-2
North America: . . . . 44 States, 2 Provinces
Concentration: . . . . CA, FL, TX
Registered: . . . . All
. . . .
Average # of Employees: . . . . . . 1 FT, 2 PT
Prior Industry Experience: . . . . Helpful

FINANCIAL: OTC-MAIL
Cash Investment: $55K
Total Investment: $75K
Fees: Franchise - $19.5K
  Royalty: 5%, Advert: 2%
Contract Periods (Yrs.): 10/10
Area Development Agreement: Yes/10
Sub-Franchise Contract: . . . . . No
Expand in Territory: . . . . Yes
Passive Ownership: . . . Discouraged
Encourage Conversions: . . . . . Yes
Franchisee Purchase(s) Required: .No

FRANCHISOR TRAINING/SUPPORT:
Financial Assistance Provided: . . .Yes(D)
Site Selection Assistance: . . . . Yes
Lease Negotiation Assistance: . . . . . Yes
Co-operative Advertising: . . . . Yes
Training: . . . . . . 2 Wks. Headquarters,
. . . . 1 Wk. Franchisee Site
On-Going Support: . . . A,B,C,d,E,f,G,H,I
Full-Time Franchisor Support Staff: . . . .
EXPANSION PLANS:
US: . . . . All US
Canada - Yes, . . . Overseas - Yes

MAIL CENTER USA

12734 Cimarron Path, # 104
San Antonio, TX 78249
TEL: (800) 969-MAIL (512) 699-0311
FAX: (512) 699-3419
Mr. Brian G. Bearden, Dir. Fran.

MAIL CENTER USA offers a unique approach to the postal and business center concept. It's a comprehensive approach that helps our stores serve thousands of customers with packaging, shipping, postal box rental, office supplies, FAX, direct mail marketing and printing. Comprehensive training program provided.

HISTORY: . . . .
Established in 1983; . . 1st Franchised in 1987
Company-Owned Units (As of 12/1/1989): . . 3
Franchised Units (12/1/1989): 22
Total Units (12/1/1989): 25
Distribution: US-25;Can-0;Overseas-0
North America: . . . .
Concentration: . . . .
Registered: . . . . All
. . . .
Average # of Employees: . . . . . . 2 FT, 1 PT
Prior Industry Experience: . . . . Helpful

FINANCIAL:
Cash Investment: $35-60K
Total Investment: $35-60K
Fees: Franchise - $17.5K
  Royalty: 6%, Advert: 0%
Contract Periods (Yrs.): . . 10/Varies
Area Development Agreement: Yes/Var
Sub-Franchise Contract: . . . . . No
Expand in Territory: . . . . Yes
Passive Ownership: . . . Not Allowed
Encourage Conversions: . . . . . Yes
Franchisee Purchase(s) Required: .No

FRANCHISOR TRAINING/SUPPORT:
Financial Assistance Provided: . . . . .NA
Site Selection Assistance: . . . . .Yes
Lease Negotiation Assistance: . . . . .Yes
Co-operative Advertising: . . . . .Yes
Training: . . . . 2 Wks. Headquarters,
. . . . 1 Wk. Franchisee Store
On-Going Support: . . A,B,C,D,E,F,G,H,I
Full-Time Franchisor Support Staff: . . . 5
EXPANSION PLANS:
US: . . . . All US
Canada - No, ...Overseas - No

MINUTEMAN PRESS

1640 New Highway
Farmingdale, NY 11735
TEL: (800) 645-9840 (516) 249-1370
FAX: (516) 249-5618
Mr. Robert Titus, Sr. VP

MINUTEMAN PRESS is a full-service, total graphics, printing center, in a retail format, with 19 regional support offices across North America, servicing over 900 MINUTEMAN PRESS franchises.

HISTORY: . . . . IFA
Established in 1973; . . 1st Franchised in 1975
Company-Owned Units (As of 12/1/1989): . . 0
Franchised Units (12/1/1989): 900
Total Units (12/1/1989): 900
Distribution: US-850;Can-50;Overseas-0
North America: . . . . . 44 States, 3 Provinces
Concentration: . . 100 in CA, 50 in TX, 50 ON
Registered: . . . . All Except AB
. . . .
Average # of Employees: . . . . 3+ FT
Prior Industry Experience: . . . . Helpful

FINANCIAL:
Cash Investment: $27.5-37.5K
Total Investment: $85-112L
Fees: Franchise - $27.5K
  Royalty: 6%, Advert: 0%
Contract Periods (Yrs.): 35/35
Area Development Agreement: . . No
Sub-Franchise Contract: . . . . . No
Expand in Territory: . . . . Yes
Passive Ownership: . . . Not Allowed
Encourage Conversions: . . . . . No
Franchisee Purchase(s) Required: .No

FRANCHISOR TRAINING/SUPPORT:
Financial Assistance Provided: . . . Yes(I)
Site Selection Assistance: . . . . .Yes
Lease Negotiation Assistance: . . . . .Yes
Co-operative Advertising: . . . . No
Training: . . . . Min. 2 Wks. Headquarters
. . . .
On-Going Support: . . . . . b,C,D,E,G,H,I
Full-Time Franchisor Support Staff: . .100
EXPANSION PLANS:
US: . . . . All US
Canada - Yes, ...Overseas - No

MR. SHIP N' CHEK

2323 W. 14th St., # 409
Tempe, AZ 85281
TEL: (800) 828-4257 (602) 437-3353
FAX: (602) 470-0465
Mr. Gary Smith, President

MR. SHIP N' CHEK capitalizes on convenience by uniquely combining three franchises into one! Franchisees have the luxury of the shipping/mailing, office support systems and check cashing services under one roof. Both business and the private sectors benefit from this unique marriage of services.

HISTORY: . . . .
Established in 1988; . . 1st Franchised in 1988
Company-Owned Units (As of 12/1/1989): . .4
Franchised Units (12/1/1989): 6
Total Units (12/1/1989): 10
Distribution: US-10;Can-0;Overseas-0
North America: . . . . .1 State
Concentration: . . . . 10 in AZ
Registered: . . . . CA
. . . .
Average # of Employees: . . . . .2 FT
Prior Industry Experience: . . . . Helpful

FINANCIAL:
Cash Investment: $40K
Total Investment: $60K
Fees: Franchise - $20K
Royalty: 5%, Advert: 2%
Contract Periods (Yrs.): 10/10
Area Development Agreement: Yes/10
Sub-Franchise Contract: . . . . . Yes
Expand in Territory: . . . . .No
Passive Ownership: . . . Discouraged
Encourage Conversions: . . . . . Yes
Franchisee Purchase(s) Required: Yes

FRANCHISOR TRAINING/SUPPORT:
Financial Assistance Provided: . . . Yes(I)
Site Selection Assistance: . . . . . . .Yes
Lease Negotiation Assistance: . . . . .Yes
Co-operative Advertising: . . . . . . .Yes
Training: . . . . 5 Days Mesa, AZ
. . . .
On-Going Support: . . . . . C,D,E,F,G,h,I
Full-Time Franchisor Support Staff: . . 16
EXPANSION PLANS:
US: . . . . Southwest
Canada - Yes, ...Overseas - No

P.K.G.'s

4394 Glendale-Milford Rd.
Cincinnati, OH 45242
TEL: (800) 543-7547 (513) 733-8778 C
FAX: (513) 733-8760
Mr. Stephen Karales, Dir. Fran.

P.K.G.'S - "The Leader of the Pack!" Enter business as the established leader in a fast-growing new industry with the world's most complete retail packaging and shipping service. P.K.G.'S, the industry's leader, provides a complete program that includes residential and commercial customer base, state-of-the-art equipment, exclusive turn-key installation, comprehensive training/operations support, advertising/marketing programs, and much more.

HISTORY: . . . . .IFA/CFA
Established in 1983; . . 1st Franchised in 1983
Company-Owned Units (As of 12/1/1989): . 15
Franchised Units (12/1/1989): 70
Total Units (12/1/1989): 85
Distribution: US-85;Can-0;Overseas-0
North America: . . . . 20 States
Concentration: . . 18 in FL, 15 in OH, 7 in GA
Registered: . . . . FL,IL,IN,MD,MI
. . . .
Average # of Employees: . . . . . . 1 FT, 1 PT
Prior Industry Experience: . . . . Helpful

FINANCIAL:
Cash Investment: $25K
Total Investment: $45K
Fees: Franchise - $15.5K
Royalty: 5%, Advert: 3%
Contract Periods (Yrs.): 10/10
Area Development Agreement: Yes/Var
Sub-Franchise Contract: . . . . . .No
Expand in Territory: . . . . Yes
Passive Ownership: . . . . . .Allowed
Encourage Conversions: . . . . . Yes
Franchisee Purchase(s) Required: Yes

FRANCHISOR TRAINING/SUPPORT:
Financial Assistance Provided: . . . Yes(I)
Site Selection Assistance: . . . . . . .Yes
Lease Negotiation Assistance: . . . . .Yes
Co-operative Advertising: . . . . . . .Yes
Training: . . . . . . 1 Wk. Headquarters, 1 Wk.
. . . .Site, Continuous On-going Support
On-Going Support: . . A,B,C,D,E,F,G,H,I
Full-Time Franchisor Support Staff: . . . 2
EXPANSION PLANS:
US: . . . . .All US
Canada - Yes, . . . Overseas - Yes

PACK 'N' MAIL
MAILING CENTER
5701 Slide Rd., # C
Lubbock, TX 79414
TEL: (800) 759-2424 (806) 797-3400
FAX: (806) 797-8142
Mr. Mike Gallagher, President

We are a complete mailing and shipping center (UPS, US Mail, overnight services, fax, copier, Western Union, furniture shipping and box rental). We ship anything anywhere. Complete training, site location, lease negotiations. No royalties and, of course, on-going assistance.

HISTORY: . . . .
Established in 1981; . . 1st Franchised in 1987
Company-Owned Units (As of 12/1/1989): . .3
Franchised Units (12/1/1989): 82
Total Units (12/1/1989): 85
Distribution: US-85;Can-0;Overseas-0
North America: . . . . 30 States
Concentration: . . . 48 in TX, 15 in IL, 8 in NJ
Registered: . . . . All States
. . . .
Average # of Employees: . . . . . . 2 FT, 1 PT
Prior Industry Experience: . . . . Helpful

FINANCIAL:
Cash Investment: $44K
Total Investment: $49K
Fees: Franchise - $10-17.5K
Royalty: 0%, Advert: 0%
Contract Periods (Yrs.): . . . 10/10
Area Development Agreement: Yes/5
Sub-Franchise Contract: . . . . . Yes
Expand in Territory: . . . . Yes
Passive Ownership: . . . . . .Allowed
Encourage Conversions: . . . . . Yes
Franchisee Purchase(s) Required: .No

FRANCHISOR TRAINING/SUPPORT:
Financial Assistance Provided: . . .Yes(D)
Site Selection Assistance: . . . . . . .Yes
Lease Negotiation Assistance: . . . . .Yes
Co-operative Advertising: . . . . . . .Yes
Training: . . . . . .10 Days - 2 Wks. Head-
. . . . . .quarters of Newport News, VA
On-Going Support: . . . .B,C,D,E,F,G,H,I
Full-Time Franchisor Support Staff: . . 10
EXPANSION PLANS:
US: . . . . .All US
Canada - Yes, . . . Overseas - Yes

PACKAGING PLUS SERVICES

20 S. Terminal Dr.
Plainview, NY 11803
TEL: (800) 922-PACK (516) 349-1300
FAX:
Mr. Bill Reichert, Dir. Fran. Devel.

PACKAGING PLUS SERVICES is engaged in franchising service centers which offer convenient packaging, shipping, mailing and communication services to businesses, retailers, professionals and residential customers. PPS offers all convenient services that a full-service department would provide to a large corporation, but on an "as needed" basis, and at a fraction of the cost.

HISTORY: . . . . IFA	FINANCIAL: OTC-3PPSS	FRANCHISOR TRAINING/SUPPORT:
Established in 1985; . . 1st Franchised in 1986	Cash Investment: $25K	Financial Assistance Provided: . . . Yes(I)
Company-Owned Units (As of 12/1/1989): . .	Total Investment: $48-71K	Site Selection Assistance: . . . . .Yes
Franchised Units (12/1/1989): 98	Fees: Franchise - $19.5K	Lease Negotiation Assistance: . . . . .Yes
Total Units (12/1/1989): 98	Royalty: 4%, Advert: 2%	Co-operative Advertising: . . . . .Yes
Distribution: US-98;Can-0;Overseas-0	Contract Periods (Yrs.): 10/5	Training: . . . . 2 Wks. Headquarters,
North America: . . . . 14 States	Area Development Agreement: Yes/10	. . . . . .3 Days In-store Grand Opening
Concentration: . . 45 in NY, 29 in NJ, 7 in PA	Sub-Franchise Contract: . . . . .No	On-Going Support: . . . a,B,C,D,E,f,G,H,I
Registered: . . . . All States	Expand in Territory: . . . . Yes	Full-Time Franchisor Support Staff: . . 22
. . . .	Passive Ownership: . . . Discouraged	EXPANSION PLANS:
Average # of Employees: . . . . . . 1 FT, 1 PT	Encourage Conversions: . . . . . Yes	US: . . . . .All US
Prior Industry Experience: . . . . . . Helpful	Franchisee Purchase(s) Required: .No	Canada - Yes, . . . Overseas - Yes

PAK MAIL CENTERS

10555 E. Dartmouth Ave., # 360
Aurora, CO 80014
TEL: (800) 833-2821 (303) 752-3500
FAX: (303) 755-9721
Mr. Ron Brown, VP Mktg.

Private mail box rental, packaging, shipping services for residential and commercial accounts. Specialty crating and shipping, a very profitable part of the business. Business support services, such as FAX and voice mail included. Ranked by Venture Magazine in Top 100 and Entrepreneur Magazine in Top 25 US franchises.

HISTORY: . . . . IFA	FINANCIAL: OTC	FRANCHISOR TRAINING/SUPPORT:
Established in 1983; . . 1st Franchised in 1984	Cash Investment: $30-40K	Financial Assistance Provided: . . .Yes(D)
Company-Owned Units (As of 12/1/1989): . .1	Total Investment: $50-60K	Site Selection Assistance: . . . . .Yes
Franchised Units (12/1/1989): 260	Fees: Franchise - $17.5K	Lease Negotiation Assistance: . . . . .Yes
Total Units (12/1/1989): 261	Royalty: 5%, Advert: 1%	Co-operative Advertising: . . . . .Yes
Distribution: US-230;Can-31;Overseas-0	Contract Periods (Yrs.): 5/1	Training: . . . . . . 5 Days Headquarters,
North America: . . . . 31 States, 2 Provinces	Area Development Agreement: Yes/5	. . . . .3 Days On-site
Concentration: . . 35 in CA, 18 in IL, 16 in CO	Sub-Franchise Contract: . . . . . Yes	On-Going Support: . . . . .B,C,D,E,G,H,I
Registered: . . . . .All	Expand in Territory: . . . . Yes	Full-Time Franchisor Support Staff: . . 15
. . . .	Passive Ownership: . . . . . .Allowed	EXPANSION PLANS:
Average # of Employees: . . . . . . 1 FT, 1 PT	Encourage Conversions: . . . . . .No	US: . . . . .All US
Prior Industry Experience: . . . . . . Helpful	Franchisee Purchase(s) Required: .No	Canada - Yes, . . . Overseas - Yes

PARCEL PLUS

1410 Forest Dr., # 28
Annapolis, MD 21403
TEL: (800) 662-5553 (301) 268-2944
FAX: (301) 263-3892
Mr. David G. Campbell, President

PARCEL PLUS is the only franchise of its type with high-level management transportation experience. Our franchisees are trained as retail transportation consultants. Our trademarked slogan "We Do Everything First Class" is reflected in our committment to excellence in people, site selection and training.

HISTORY: . . . . IFA	FINANCIAL:	FRANCHISOR TRAINING/SUPPORT:
Established in 1986; . . 1st Franchised in 1988	Cash Investment: $40-58K	Financial Assistance Provided: . . . Yes(I)
Company-Owned Units (As of 12/1/1989): . .2	Total Investment: $48-68K	Site Selection Assistance: . . . . .Yes
Franchised Units (12/1/1989): 24	Fees: Franchise - $13.5K	Lease Negotiation Assistance: . . . . .Yes
Total Units (12/1/1989): 26	Royalty: 3.5%, Advert: 1%	Co-operative Advertising: . . . . .Yes
Distribution: US-26;Can-0;Overseas-0	Contract Periods (Yrs.): 5/5	Training: . . . . 5 Days Headquarters,
North America: . . . . 7 States	Area Development Agreement: . .No	. . . . .5 Days On-site
Concentration: . . 12 in MD, 6 in VA, 3 in NH	Sub-Franchise Contract: . . . . .No	On-Going Support: . . . .B,C,D,E,F,G,H,I
Registered: . . . . .CA,FL,MD,VA	Expand in Territory: . . . . Yes	Full-Time Franchisor Support Staff: . . . 6
. . . .	Passive Ownership: . . . Not Allowed	EXPANSION PLANS:
Average # of Employees: . . . . .2 FT	Encourage Conversions: . . . . . .No	US: . . . . . Mid-Atlantic, New Eng.,CA
Prior Industry Experience: . . . . . . Helpful	Franchisee Purchase(s) Required: .No	Canada - No, ...Overseas - No

PIP PRINTING

27001 Agoura Rd.
Agoura Hills, CA 91301
TEL: (800) 421-4634 (818) 880-3800
FAX:
Mr. Keith Emerson, Dir. Bus. Devel.

PIP PRINTING is the world's largest business printer. Services include color printing, desktop publishing, forms, high-speed duplicating, etc. Franchisees are supported with a comprehensive marketing program, including national TV advertising, radio, yellow pages, direct mail and in-store display materials.

HISTORY: . . . . IFA	FINANCIAL:	FRANCHISOR TRAINING/SUPPORT:
Established in 1964; . . 1st Franchised in 1968	Cash Investment: . . . . . . $67K+	Financial Assistance Provided: . . .Yes(D)
Company-Owned Units (As of 12/1/1989): . 17	Total Investment: $125.9K	Site Selection Assistance: . . . . . . .Yes
Franchised Units (12/1/1989): 1143	Fees: Franchise - $40K	Lease Negotiation Assistance: . . . . .Yes
Total Units (12/1/1989): 1160	Royalty: 6-8%, Advert: 1%	Co-operative Advertising: . . . . . . .Yes
Distribution: . . . US-1096;Can-4;Overseas-64	Contract Periods (Yrs.): 20/20	Training: . . . . 2 Wks. Headquarters
North America: . . . . 49 States	Area Development Agreement: Yes/20	. . . .
Concentration: . . 260 in CA, 90 in FL, 65 NY	Sub-Franchise Contract: . . . . . Yes	On-Going Support: . . . . B,C,D,E,f,G,h,I
Registered: . . . . .All	Expand in Territory: . . . . Yes	Full-Time Franchisor Support Staff: . .121
. . . .	Passive Ownership: . . . Discouraged	EXPANSION PLANS:
Average # of Employees: . . . . .3 FT	Encourage Conversions: . . . . . Yes	US: . . . . .All US
Prior Industry Experience: . . . . Helpful	Franchisee Purchase(s) Required: .No	Canada - Yes, ...Overseas - No

PONY MAILBOX & BUSINESS CENTER

13110 NE 177 Place
Woodinville, WA 98072
TEL: (206) 483-0360
FAX: (206) 486-6495
Mr. Robert Howell, President

A commercial mail receiving business, with private post office boxes in addition to Western Union, UPS, word processing, copying, business cards, wedding announcements, answering service, FAX, cartons, packaging materials, rubber stamps. A one-stop business center, which allows franchisees to add their own business service concepts to meet local demand needs.

HISTORY:	FINANCIAL:	FRANCHISOR TRAINING/SUPPORT:
Established in 1981; . . 1st Franchised in 1986	Cash Investment: $48-57K	Financial Assistance Provided: . . . . .No
Company-Owned Units (As of 12/1/1989): . .1	Total Investment: $48-57K	Site Selection Assistance: . . . . . . .Yes
Franchised Units (12/1/1989): 15	Fees: Franchise - $32.9K	Lease Negotiation Assistance: . . . . .Yes
Total Units (12/1/1989): 16	Royalty: Flat, Advert: 0%	Co-operative Advertising: . . . . . . .NA
Distribution: . . . US-16;Can-0;Overseas-0	Contract Periods (Yrs.): 6/5	Training: . . . . . . 4-5 Days Headquarters
North America: . . . . 6 States	Area Development Agreement: . Yes	. . . .
Concentration: . . . .7 in WA, 3 in FL, 2 in NJ	Sub-Franchise Contract: . . . . . Yes	On-Going Support: . . . . .C,D,E,G
Registered: . . . . CA,FL,IL,OR,WA	Expand in Territory: . . . . Yes	Full-Time Franchisor Support Staff: . . .5
. . . .	Passive Ownership: . . . . . .Allowed	EXPANSION PLANS:
Average # of Employees: . . . . .1 FT	Encourage Conversions: . . . . . Yes	US: . . . . .NE and Midwest
Prior Industry Experience: . . . . Helpful	Franchisee Purchase(s) Required: .No	Canada - Yes, . . . Overseas - Yes

POSTALANNEX+

9050 Friars Rd., # 400
San Diego, CA 92108
TEL: (800) 456-1525 (619) 563-4800 C
FAX: (619) 563-9850
Mr. Ralph Boden, Dir. Fran. Devel.

You can become the "Home Office" for entrepreneurs, small businesses, active retired, as well as the business needs of the homemaker. We support you from day one to help you grow, with site selection, design, construction, classroom and in-store training. Area franchises and unit franchises available.

HISTORY: . . . . IFA	FINANCIAL:	FRANCHISOR TRAINING/SUPPORT:
Established in 1986; . . 1st Franchised in 1986	Cash Investment: $49-66K	Financial Assistance Provided: . . . Yes(I)
Company-Owned Units (As of 12/1/1989): . .0	Total Investment: $59-75K	Site Selection Assistance: . . . . . . .Yes
Franchised Units (12/1/1989): 75	Fees: Franchise - $17.5K	Lease Negotiation Assistance: . . . . .Yes
Total Units (12/1/1989): 75	Royalty: 5%, Advert: 2%	Co-operative Advertising: . . . . . . .Yes
Distribution: US-75;Can-0;Overseas-0	Contract Periods (Yrs.): 10/10	Training: . . . . 2 Wks. Headquarters
North America: . . . . 4 States	Area Development Agreement: Yes/10	. . . .
Concentration: . . .71 in CA, 2 in NV, 2 in FL	Sub-Franchise Contract: . . . . . Yes	On-Going Support: . . . a,b,C,D,E,f,G,h,I
Registered: . . . . CA	Expand in Territory: . . . . . . .No	Full-Time Franchisor Support Staff: . . 14
. . . .	Passive Ownership: . . . Discouraged	EXPANSION PLANS:
Average # of Employees: . . . . . 2-3 FT, 2 PT	Encourage Conversions: . . . . . Yes	US: . . . . .All US
Prior Industry Experience: . . . . Helpful	Franchisee Purchase(s) Required: .No	Canada - No, ...Overseas - No

PRINT SHACK

500 N. Westshore Blvd., # 610
Tampa, FL 33609
TEL: (800) 237-5167
FAX:
Mr. Frank Sorrentino, President

PRINT SHACK has combined the specialty advertising and printing industries into a unique dual profit center. We offer you the ability to open two stores in your exclusive area, on-going support, site selection and 4 weeks of training before you open your center.

HISTORY: . . . . IFA	FINANCIAL: OTC-BUSC	FRANCHISOR TRAINING/SUPPORT:
Established in 1982; . . 1st Franchised in 1983	Cash Investment: $45K	Financial Assistance Provided: . . .Yes(D)
Company-Owned Units (As of 12/1/1989): . .0	Total Investment: $100K	Site Selection Assistance: . . . . . . .Yes
Franchised Units (12/1/1989): 123	Fees: Franchise - $17.5K	Lease Negotiation Assistance: . . . . .Yes
Total Units (12/1/1989): 123	Royalty: 6%, Advert: 0%	Co-operative Advertising: . . . . . . .Yes
Distribution: US-123;Can-0;Overseas-0	Contract Periods (Yrs.): . . . 20/20	Training: . . . . 2 Wks. Headquarters,
North America: . . . . 30 States	Area Development Agreement: . .No	. . . . .2 Wks. On-site
Concentration: . . 20 in FL, 10 in CA, 8 in TX	Sub-Franchise Contract: . .No	On-Going Support: . . . . C,D,E,F,G,h,I
Registered: . . . . .All	Expand in Territory: . . . . Yes	Full-Time Franchisor Support Staff: . . 25
. . . .	Passive Ownership: . . . Not Allowed	EXPANSION PLANS:
Average # of Employees: . . . . .3-5 FT	Encourage Conversions: . . . . . Yes	US: . . . . All US
Prior Industry Experience: . . . . Helpful	Franchisee Purchase(s) Required: .No	Canada - Yes, . . . Overseas - Yes

PRINT THREE

184 Shorting Rd.
Scarborough, ON M1S3S7 CAN
TEL: (800) 268-4177 (416) 754-8700
FAX: (416) 754-8441
Mr. Lynn Barrett, VP PR/Comm.

Full-service electronic printing center, featuring a Leading Edge desk-top publishing system, utilizing proprietary laser printing equipment with superior resolution of 1200 x 600 DPI. A high-tech operation with print-link communications, offering transmittal of text, data and graphics across the continent.

HISTORY: . . . . IFA	FINANCIAL:	FRANCHISOR TRAINING/SUPPORT:
Established in 1970; . . 1st Franchised in 1983	Cash Investment: $200K	Financial Assistance Provided: . . .Yes(D)
Company-Owned Units (As of 12/1/1989): . .0	Total Investment: $50K	Site Selection Assistance: . . . . . . .Yes
Franchised Units (12/1/1989): 165	Fees: Franchise - $35K	Lease Negotiation Assistance: . . . . .Yes
Total Units (12/1/1989): 165	Royalty: 6%, Advert: 3%	Co-operative Advertising: . . . . . . .Yes
Distribution: US-25;Can-140;Overseas-0	Contract Periods (Yrs.): . . . 10/10	Training: . . . . 3 Wks. Headquarters,
North America: . . . . . . 19 States, 8 Provinces	Area Development Agreement: . .No	. . . . . . On-going at Franchisee Center
Concentration: . . .62 in ON, 5 in PQ, 4 in AB	Sub-Franchise Contract: . .No	On-Going Support: . . . . . C,D,E,F,G,H,I
Registered: . . . . .All	Expand in Territory: . . . . Yes	Full-Time Franchisor Support Staff: . . 25
. . . .	Passive Ownership: . . . Not Allowed	EXPANSION PLANS:
Average # of Employees: . . . . . . 2 FT, 1 PT	Encourage Conversions: . . . . . NA	US: . . . . All US
Prior Industry Experience: . . . . Helpful	Franchisee Purchase(s) Required: .No	Canada - Yes, ...Overseas - No

PRINTING NETWORK

156 Willowdale Ave.
North York, ON M2N4Y6 CAN
TEL: (416) 250-0241 C
FAX: (416) 250-0275
Mr. Joe Osiel, President

PRINTING NETWORK offers the latest in electronic color and black and white printing, with the absolute latest in the state-of-the-art of laser desk-top publishing. 4 weeks' training program, plus 1 week at franchisee's location. Help in marketing, sales, advertising, etc. Full-service franchise.

HISTORY:	FINANCIAL:	FRANCHISOR TRAINING/SUPPORT:
Established in 1989; . . 1st Franchised in 1989	Cash Investment: $50-60K	Financial Assistance Provided: . . .Yes(D)
Company-Owned Units (As of 12/1/1989): . .1	Total Investment: $171K	Site Selection Assistance: . . . . . . .Yes
Franchised Units (12/1/1989): 3	Fees: Franchise - $36K	Lease Negotiation Assistance: . . . . .Yes
Total Units (12/1/1989): 4	Royalty: 5%, Advert: 4%	Co-operative Advertising: . . . . . . .Yes
Distribution: US-0;Can-4;Overseas-0	Contract Periods (Yrs.): . . . 10/10	Training: . . . . 4 Wks. Headquarters,
North America: . . . . .1 Province	Area Development Agreement: Yes/10	. . . . 1 Wk. at Franchisee Location
Concentration: . . . . .4 in IN	Sub-Franchise Contract: . . . . . Yes	On-Going Support: . . . . .B,C,D,E,G,H,I
Registered:	Expand in Territory: . . . . Yes	Full-Time Franchisor Support Staff: . . .5
. . . .	Passive Ownership: . . . Not Allowed	EXPANSION PLANS:
Average # of Employees: . . . . .3 FT	Encourage Conversions: . . . . . Yes	US: . . . . All US
Prior Industry Experience: . . . . Helpful	Franchisee Purchase(s) Required: .No	Canada - Yes, . . . Overseas - Yes

PRINTMASTERS

370 S. Crenshaw Blvd., # E100
Torrance, CA 90503
TEL: (800) 221-8945 (213) 328-0303
FAX: (213) 533-4826
Mr. Lou Novak, Natl. Sales Mgr.

PRINTMASTERS - Full-Service Printing. Top-quality, single- and multi-color printing, bindery services including typesetting and graphics with a fast turn-around. Both retail and commercial. Owner needs no printing experience. Expansion nationwide.

HISTORY: . . . . IFA
Established in 1976; . . 1st Franchised in 1976
Company-Owned Units (As of 12/1/1989): . .0
Franchised Units (12/1/1989): 110
Total Units (12/1/1989): 110
Distribution: US-110;Can-0;Overseas-0
North America: . . . . 4 States
Concentration: . . 105 in CA, 2 in AZ, 1 in OR
Registered: . . . . CA,OR
. . . .
Average # of Employees: . . . . .3 FT
Prior Industry Experience: . . . . Helpful

FINANCIAL:
Cash Investment: $35K
Total Investment: $133-140K
Fees: Franchise - $34K
  Royalty: 4%, Advert: 2%
Contract Periods (Yrs.): 20/20
Area Development Agreement: . .No
Sub-Franchise Contract: . . . . .No
Expand in Territory: . . . . Yes
Passive Ownership: . . . Not Allowed
Encourage Conversions: . . . . .No
Franchisee Purchase(s) Required: Yes

FRANCHISOR TRAINING/SUPPORT:
Financial Assistance Provided: . . . Yes(I)
Site Selection Assistance: . . . . .Yes
Lease Negotiation Assistance: . . . . .Yes
Co-operative Advertising: . . . . .Yes
Training: . . . . 2 Wks. Headquarters,
. . . . .2 Wks. Franchisee Center
On-Going Support: . . . . .C,D,E,F,G,H,I
Full-Time Franchisor Support Staff: . . 10
EXPANSION PLANS:
  US: . . . . .All US
  Canada - No, ...Overseas - No

PROFESSOR PRINT
COPY CENTRES
36 C Stoffel Dr.
Rexdale, ON M9W1A8 CAN
TEL: (416) 248-5558
FAX:
Mr. Peter Quire, Fran. Sales Dir.

PROFESSOR PRINT operates copy centres and satellite printing outlets with optional stock of office supplies. Telemarketing, advertising and personal calls are used to build presence. Computer graphics and laser printing plus fax transmission lets central staff do the more technical work.

HISTORY: . . . . IFA
Established in 1985; . . 1st Franchised in 1985
Company-Owned Units (As of 12/1/1989): . .1
Franchised Units (12/1/1989): 7
Total Units (12/1/1989): 8
Distribution: US-0;Can-8;Overseas-0
North America: . . . . .1 Province
Concentration: . . . . 8 in ON
Registered: . . . .
. . . .
Average # of Employees: . . . . .2 FT
Prior Industry Experience: . . . . Helpful

FINANCIAL:
Cash Investment: $10K
Total Investment: $30-120K
Fees: Franchise - $10K
  Royalty: 4%, Advert: 2%
Contract Periods (Yrs.): 5/5
Area Development Agreement: . .No
Sub-Franchise Contract: . . . . .No
Expand in Territory: . . . . .No
Passive Ownership: . . . Not Allowed
Encourage Conversions: . . . . . Yes
Franchisee Purchase(s) Required: Yes

FRANCHISOR TRAINING/SUPPORT:
Financial Assistance Provided: . . . . . No
Site Selection Assistance: . . . . .Yes
Lease Negotiation Assistance: . . . . .Yes
Co-operative Advertising: . . . . .Yes
Training: . . . . 4 Wks. Headquarters,
. . . . 4 Wks. Operating Store
On-Going Support: . . . . .B,C,D,F,G,H,I
Full-Time Franchisor Support Staff: . . .8
EXPANSION PLANS:
  US: . . . . No
  Canada - Yes, ...Overseas - No

QUIK PRINT

3445 N. Webb Rd.
Wichita, KS 67226
TEL: (800) 825-COPY (316) 636-5666
FAX: (316) 636-5678
Mr. Johnny Tarrant, Sr. VP

Nationwide fast offset printing and copying network; est. 1963; expanding to offer additional related services (typesetting, facsimile, thermography, etc.). Complete professional training and support program (site selection, advertising, bookkeeping, improvements, etc.) both at home office and on-site continues beyond initial opening as needed.

HISTORY: . . . .
Established in 1963; . . 1st Franchised in 1967
Company-Owned Units (As of 12/1/1989): . 67
Franchised Units (12/1/1989): 135
Total Units (12/1/1989): 202
Distribution: US-202;Can-0;Overseas-0
North America: . . . . 26 States
Concentration: . 45 in TX, 26 in CA, 20 in CO
Registered: . . . . CA,FL,IL,MN,VA
. . . .
Average # of Employees: . . . . .3-5 FT
Prior Industry Experience: . . . . Helpful

FINANCIAL:
Cash Investment: $75-100K
Total Investment: $125K
Fees: Franchise - $15K
  Royalty: 5%, Advert: 0%
Contract Periods (Yrs.): 25/25
Area Development Agreement: Yes/25
Sub-Franchise Contract: . . . . .No
Expand in Territory: . . . . Yes
Passive Ownership: . . . Discouraged
Encourage Conversions: . . . . .No
Franchisee Purchase(s) Required: .No

FRANCHISOR TRAINING/SUPPORT:
Financial Assistance Provided: . . .Yes(D)
Site Selection Assistance: . . . . .Yes
Lease Negotiation Assistance: . . . . .Yes
Co-operative Advertising: . . . . .No
Training: . . . . 4 Wks. Headquarters,
. . . . .2 Wks. On-site
On-Going Support: . . . .B,C,D,E,F,G,H,I
Full-Time Franchisor Support Staff: . . 35
EXPANSION PLANS:
  US: . . . . .All US
  Canada - No, ...Overseas - No

SHIPPING CONNECTION

7220 W. Jefferson Ave.
Denver, CO 80235
TEL: (303) 980-9595
FAX: (303) 985-1982
Ms. Betty Russotti, VP

A packaging and shipping franchise that was founded by ex-UPS management personnel. We can provide you with 3 weeks of training and the latest techniques in packaging and shipping. Dealing with both business and individual customers, you can literally ship anything, anywhere in the world.

HISTORY: . . . . IFA
Established in 1982; . . 1st Franchised in 1986
Company-Owned Units (As of 12/1/1989): . . 1
Franchised Units (12/1/1989): 19
Total Units (12/1/1989): 20
Distribution: US-20;Can-0;Overseas-0
North America: . . . . 5 States
Concentration: . . . .8 in OH, 6 in CO, 2 in NJ
Registered: . . . . . . FL,HI,MD,MN,NY,VA
. . . .
Average # of Employees: . . . . .5 FT
Prior Industry Experience: . . . . . . Helpful

FINANCIAL:
Cash Investment: $25-46K
Total Investment: $25-46K
Fees: Franchise - $14.5K
Royalty: 5%, Advert: 2%
Contract Periods (Yrs.): 10/5
Area Development Agreement: Yes/5
Sub-Franchise Contract: . . . . .No
Expand in Territory: . . . . . . .No
Passive Ownership: . . . Discouraged
Encourage Conversions: . . . . . Yes
Franchisee Purchase(s) Required: .No

FRANCHISOR TRAINING/SUPPORT:
Financial Assistance Provided: . . . . .No
Site Selection Assistance: . . . . .Yes
Lease Negotiation Assistance: . . . . .Yes
Co-operative Advertising: . . . . .Yes
Training: . . . . 2 Wks. Headquarters,
. . . . 1 Wk. Site
On-Going Support: . . . . B,C,D,E,G,H
Full-Time Franchisor Support Staff: . . . 1
EXPANSION PLANS:
US: . . . . .All US
Canada - No, ...Overseas - No

SHIPPING DEPARTMENT, THE

5800 Siegen Ln, # G
Baton Rouge, LA 70809
TEL: (504) 295-1085
FAX:
Mr. Robert Hafele, President

Packing and shipping experts, specializing in household and industrial shipments under 2,100 pounds (filling the market void between UPS and major moving lines). We provide the means to move a small household at the most affordable price.

HISTORY: . . . .
Established in 1985; . . 1st Franchised in 1989
Company-Owned Units (As of 12/1/1989): . . 1
Franchised Units (12/1/1989): 0
Total Units (12/1/1989): 1
Distribution: US-1;Can-0;Overseas-0
North America: . . . . .1 State
Concentration: . . . . 1 in LA
Registered: . . . .
. . . .
Average # of Employees: . . . . . . 2 FT, 1 PT
Prior Industry Experience: . . . . Helpful

FINANCIAL:
Cash Investment: $20-24K
Total Investment: $24K
Fees: Franchise - $12K
Royalty: 5%, Advert: 1%
Contract Periods (Yrs.): 5/5
Area Development Agreement: . .No
Sub-Franchise Contract: . . . . .No
Expand in Territory: . . . . Yes
Passive Ownership: . . . Discouraged
Encourage Conversions: . . . . . Yes
Franchisee Purchase(s) Required: .No

FRANCHISOR TRAINING/SUPPORT:
Financial Assistance Provided: . . . . .No
Site Selection Assistance: . . . . .Yes
Lease Negotiation Assistance: . . . . .Yes
Co-operative Advertising: . . . . .Yes
Training: . . . . . . 1-2 Wks. Headquarters

On-Going Support: . . . . . . C,D,E,F,I
Full-Time Franchisor Support Staff: . . . 1
EXPANSION PLANS:
US: . . . . .All US
Canada - No, ...Overseas - No

SIGNAL GRAPHICS

848 Broadway
Denver, CO 80203
TEL: (800) 852-6336 (303) 837-9998 C
FAX:
Mr. Steve Morris, President

A full range of services places SIGNAL GRAPHICS ahead of the competition. Our franchising program will equip the owner having no previous printing experience to market quick printing, copying, typesetting and high-quality commercial printing to a wide range of customers in the business community.

HISTORY: . . . . IFA
Established in 1974; . . 1st Franchised in 1982
Company-Owned Units (As of 12/1/1989): . .0
Franchised Units (12/1/1989): 19
Total Units (12/1/1989): 19
Distribution: US-19;Can-0;Overseas-0
North America: . . . . 5 States
Concentration: . . . . 11 in CO
Registered: . . . . .CA,FL,HI
. . . .
Average # of Employees: . . . . . . 4 FT, 1 PT
Prior Industry Experience: . . . . Helpful

FINANCIAL:
Cash Investment: $35-65K
Total Investment: $160K
Fees: Franchise - $28K
Royalty: 5-0%, Advert: 0%
Contract Periods (Yrs.): 20/20
Area Development Agreement: . .No
Sub-Franchise Contract: . . . . .No
Expand in Territory: . . . . Yes
Passive Ownership: . . . Discouraged
Encourage Conversions: . . . . . NA
Franchisee Purchase(s) Required: .No

FRANCHISOR TRAINING/SUPPORT:
Financial Assistance Provided: . . . Yes(I)
Site Selection Assistance: . . . . .Yes
Lease Negotiation Assistance: . . . . .Yes
Co-operative Advertising: . . . . .Yes
Training: . . . . 3 Wks. Headquarters,
. . . . 1 Wk. Site
On-Going Support: . . . . B,C,d,E,G,H,I
Full-Time Franchisor Support Staff: . . . 4
EXPANSION PLANS:
US: . . . . .All US
Canada - No, ...Overseas - No

SIR SPEEDY

23131 Verdugo Dr.
Laguna Hills, CA 92653
TEL: (800) 854-3321 (714) 472-0330
FAX:
Mr. Dave Collins, VP Sales

SIR SPEEDY PRINTING is a leader in high-tech printing. Nation-wide, fast fax transmittal service. Nation's largest system of desktop publishing, computer graphics, laser printing. High-speed copying. Full-service printing. SBA financing. As low as $50,000 cash needed, including working capital.

HISTORY: . . . . IFA	FINANCIAL:	FRANCHISOR TRAINING/SUPPORT:
Established in 1968; . . 1st Franchised in 1968	Cash Investment: $50K	Financial Assistance Provided: . . . Yes(I)
Company-Owned Units (As of 12/1/1989): . .0	Total Investment: $170K	Site Selection Assistance: . . . . . . .Yes
Franchised Units (12/1/1989): 865	Fees: Franchise - $40K	Lease Negotiation Assistance: . . . . .Yes
Total Units (12/1/1989): 865	Royalty: 6%, Advert: 2%	Co-operative Advertising: . . . . . . .Yes
Distribution: . . . US-840;Can-15;Overseas-10	Contract Periods (Yrs.): 20/20	Training: . . . . 2 Wks. Headquarters,
North America: . . . . 45 States,12 Provinces	Area Development Agreement: Yes/20	. . . . 2.5 Wks. at Location
Concentration: . . 175 in CA, 90 in FL,55 in IL	Sub-Franchise Contract: . . . . . .No	On-Going Support: C
Registered: . . . . .All	Expand in Territory: . . . . Yes	Full-Time Franchisor Support Staff: . . 65
. . . .	Passive Ownership: . . . Discouraged	EXPANSION PLANS:
Average # of Employees: . . . . .3 FT	Encourage Conversions: . . . . . Yes	US: . . . . .All US
Prior Industry Experience: . . . . . . Helpful	Franchisee Purchase(s) Required: .No	Canada - Yes, . . . Overseas - Yes

SPEEDY PRINTING CENTERS

5799 Yonge St., # 705
Willowdale, ON M2M3V3 CAN
TEL: (800) 668-0119 (416) 733-4455 C
FAX: (416) 395-0456
Mr. Tom Davidson, President

SPEEDY PRINTING CENTERS - the Canadian arm of American Speedy Printing Centers, offer a full-service business center, including printing, copying, desktop publishing, fax, typesetting and related services.

HISTORY: . . . . .IFA/CFA	FINANCIAL:	FRANCHISOR TRAINING/SUPPORT:
Established in 1986; . . 1st Franchised in 1987	Cash Investment: $30-80K	Financial Assistance Provided: . . . Yes(D)
Company-Owned Units (As of 12/1/1989): . .0	Total Investment: $150-190K	Site Selection Assistance: . . . . . . .Yes
Franchised Units (12/1/1989): 20	Fees: Franchise - $42.5K	Lease Negotiation Assistance: . . . . .Yes
Total Units (12/1/1989): 20	Royalty: 6%, Advert: 2%	Co-operative Advertising: . . . . . . .Yes
Distribution: US-0;Can-20;Overseas-0	Contract Periods (Yrs.): 20/20	Training: . . . . . . .2 Wks. Detroit, 1 Wk.
North America: . . . . 2 Provinces	Area Development Agreement: Yes/20	. . . . . Existing Center, 1 Wk. On-site
Concentration: . . . . 16 in ON, 4 in BC	Sub-Franchise Contract: . . . . . Yes	On-Going Support: . . . . . . C,D,E,G,H,I
Registered:	Expand in Territory: . . . . Yes	Full-Time Franchisor Support Staff: . . . 5
. . . .	Passive Ownership: . . . Discouraged	EXPANSION PLANS:
Average # of Employees: . . . . .3 FT	Encourage Conversions: . . . . . Yes	US: . . . . .No
Prior Industry Experience: . . . . . . Helpful	Franchisee Purchase(s) Required: .No	Canada - Yes, ...Overseas - No

UNISHIPPERS ASSOCIATION

1045 E. 4500 South
Salt Lake City, UT 84117
TEL: (800) 999-8721 (801) 262-3300
FAX: (801) 261-4839
Mr. Steve Nelson, Dir. Fran. Sales

Overnight air express franchise, acting as a marketing and billing agent for Airborne Express to businesses. A built-in profit margin is in each shipment that your customers send. Airborne handles pick-up and delivery. You handle marketing and billing.

HISTORY: . . . . IFA	FINANCIAL:	FRANCHISOR TRAINING/SUPPORT:
Established in 1987; . . 1st Franchised in 1987	Cash Investment: $5-50K	Financial Assistance Provided: . . . Yes(I)
Company-Owned Units (As of 12/1/1989): . .5	Total Investment: $10-75K	Site Selection Assistance: . . . . . . .Yes
Franchised Units (12/1/1989): 22	Fees: Franchise - $5-50K	Lease Negotiation Assistance: . . . . .NA
Total Units (12/1/1989): 27	Royalty: 4%, Advert: 0%	Co-operative Advertising: . . . . . . .Yes
Distribution: US-27;Can-0;Overseas-0	Contract Periods (Yrs.): 20	Training: . . . . 1 Wk. Headquarters
North America: . . . . 18 States	Area Development Agreement: .No	. . . .
Concentration: . . . .8 in FL, 7 in CA, 3 in TX	Sub-Franchise Contract: . . . . . .No	On-Going Support: . . . . . . B,C,D,G,H,I
Registered: . . .CA,FL,IL,MD,MI,MN,OR,VA	Expand in Territory: . . . . Yes	Full-Time Franchisor Support Staff: . . 12
. . . . WA,WI	Passive Ownership: . . . Discouraged	EXPANSION PLANS:
Average # of Employees: . . . . .2 FT	Encourage Conversions: . . . . . NA	US: . . . . .All US
Prior Industry Experience: . . . . . . Helpful	Franchisee Purchase(s) Required: .No	Canada - No, ...Overseas - No

UNITED PRINTING UNLIMITED

P.O. Box 3378
Sarasota, FL 34230
TEL: (813) 922-3937
FAX:
Mr. Jack Swat

Training, support, support after opening. 90% financing available.

HISTORY: . . . .
Established in 1984; . . 1st Franchised in 1984
Company-Owned Units (As of 12/1/1989): . .1
Franchised Units (12/1/1989): 7
Total Units (12/1/1989): 8
Distribution: US-8;Can-0;Overseas-0
 North America: . . . .
 Concentration: . . . .
Registered: . . . . .FL
. . . .
Average # of Employees: . . . . . . 1 FT, 2 PT
Prior Industry Experience: . . . . Helpful

FINANCIAL:
Cash Investment: . . . . . . $12.5K+
Total Investment: $75K
Fees: Franchise - $25K
 Royalty: 5%, Advert: 0%
Contract Periods (Yrs.): 20/20
Area Development Agreement: Yes/20
Sub-Franchise Contract: . . . . Yes
Expand in Territory: . . . . . . Yes
Passive Ownership: . . . . . .Allowed
Encourage Conversions: . . . . Yes
Franchisee Purchase(s) Required: Yes

FRANCHISOR TRAINING/SUPPORT:
Financial Assistance Provided: . . .Yes(D)
Site Selection Assistance: . . . . .Yes
Lease Negotiation Assistance: . . . . .Yes
Co-operative Advertising: . . . . .Yes
Training: . . . . 3 Wks. Headquarters
. . . .
On-Going Support: . . . . . B,C,D,E,F,G,I
Full-Time Franchisor Support Staff: . . . 5
EXPANSION PLANS:
US: . . . . All US
Canada - Yes, . . . Overseas - Yes

UPMOST, POST & PARCEL CENTERS

16981 Via Tazon, # O
San Diego, CA 92127
TEL: (619) 592-9903 C
FAX:
Mr. Frank Walter

Packaging and mail-receiving franchise operation. Includes state-of-the-art computerized UPS manifest system, including automated label, customer receipt and franchisee income statements. Automated mailbox and money order management. Centers offer complete business and communication services, emphasizing customer service and convenience.

HISTORY: . . . . .IFA
Established in 1983; . . 1st Franchised in 1987
Company-Owned Units (As of 12/1/1989): . .1
Franchised Units (12/1/1989): 6
Total Units (12/1/1989): 7
Distribution: US-7;Can-0;Overseas-0
 North America: . . . . .1 State
 Concentration: . . . . 7 in CA
Registered: . . . . .CA,FL,HI
. . . .
Average # of Employees: . . . . . . 1 FT, 1 PT
Prior Industry Experience: . . . . Helpful

FINANCIAL:
Cash Investment: $35-45K
Total Investment: $50-65K
Fees: Franchise - $18K
 Royalty: 5%, Advert: 2%
Contract Periods (Yrs.): 10/10
Area Development Agreement: Yes/10
Sub-Franchise Contract: . . . . Yes
Expand in Territory: . . . . . . Yes
Passive Ownership: . . . . . .Allowed
Encourage Conversions: . . . . Yes
Franchisee Purchase(s) Required: .No

FRANCHISOR TRAINING/SUPPORT:
Financial Assistance Provided: . . .Yes(D)
Site Selection Assistance: . . . . .Yes
Lease Negotiation Assistance: . . . .Yes
Co-operative Advertising: . . . . .Yes
Training: . . . . .1 Wk. Headquarters,
 . . . . . 1 Wk. Franchisee Site, On-going
On-Going Support: . . A,B,C,D,E,F,G,H,I
Full-Time Franchisor Support Staff: . . . 5
EXPANSION PLANS:
US: . . . . All US
Canada - Yes, ...Overseas - Yes

SUPPLEMENTAL LISTING OF FRANCHISORS

A. I. M. MAIL CENTERS	26861 Trabuco Rd., # E-1, Mission Viejo CA 92691	
ACCESS PRINT AND COPY CENTRES	831 Glencarin Ave., Toronto ON M6B2A4	CAN
ACTIONFAX	6390 LBJ Frwy., # 105, Dallas TX 75240	
ADS & TYPE OVERNIGHT	Dept. FH, P. O. Box F133, Fairview NJ 07022	
ALPHAGRAPHICS PRINTSHOPS	3760 N. Commerce Dr., Tucson AZ 85705	
AMATEUR SPORTS JOURNAL	P.O. Box 6996, Hollywood FL 33081	
ASSOCIATED AIR FREIGHT	3333 New Hyde Park Rd., New Hyde Park NY 11042	
BCX PRINTING CENTER	613 E. Indian School Rd., Phoenix AZ 85017	
BEKINS BOXSTORE	777 Flower St., Glendale CA 91201	
BOX BROS.	7050 Owensmouth Ave., # 200, Canoga Park CA 91303	
BOXES PLUS	6450 W. Hanna Avenue, Indianapolis IN 46241	
BUSINESS CARDS TOMORROW	105 Gordon Baker Rd., # 220, Willowdale ON M2H3P8	CAN
CAN-MAIL	200 Consumers Rd., # 405, Willowdale ON M2J4R4	CAN
CANADA POST CORPORATION	Sir Alex. Campbell Bldg., # 319, Ottawa ON K1AOB1	CAN

CARIBBEAN CLEAR . . . . 220 Executive Ctr. Dr., # 310, Columbia SC 29210
EXPRESS POSTAL CENTERS . . . . .6475 28th St. SE, Grand Rapids MI 49506
FAXTYME OF CANADA . . . . 20 Bevshire Cir., # 1, Thornhill ON L4V5B3   CAN
FRANCOR PRINTING . . . . 518 Beatty St., 5th Fl., Vancouver BC V6B2L3   CAN
FRANKLIN'S PRINTING & OFFICE SUPPLY . . . . .135 International Blvd., NWQ, Atlanta GA 30303
FRANKLINS SYSTEMS . . . . .40 Wynford Dr., # 315, Don Mills ON M3C1J5   CAN
HURRICANE OFFICE SUPPLY & PRINTING . . . . .65 Spencer Hwy., South Houston TX 77587
INSTANT COPY PRINTING/COPYING/COMM. . . . . 232 W. Wayne St., Fort Wayne IN 46802
INSTY-PRINTS PRINTING CENTERS . . . . .1010 S. Seventh St., # 450, Minneapolis MN 55415
KOPY KING PRINTING CENTERS . . . . P.O. Box 6996, Hollywood FL 33081
KOPY-RITE . . . . P.O. Box 6996, Hollywood FL 33081
KP COPY CENTRES . . . . .89 Glen Cameron Rd., Thornhill ON L3T1N8   CAN
MAIL SERV . . . . 17911 Fitch Ave., Irvine CA 92714
MAIL-IT-QUIK POSTAL CENTERS . . . . 13013 Lee Jackson Hwy., #1400, Fairfax VA 22033
MINUTEMAN PRESS OF CANADA COMPANY . . . . 6299 Airport Rd., # 704, Mississauga ON L4V1N3   CAN
MR. SHIP N' CHECK . . . . .4355 University, # 107, Mesa AZ 85205
PACKAGE & WRAP . . . . .17 Linwood Ave., Newton NJ 07860
PACKAGE SHIPPERS . . . . P.O. Box 82184, Tampa FL 33682
PACKAGING DEPOT . . . . 5524 Cambrie St., Vancouver BC V5Z3A2   CAN
PACKY THE SHIPPER . . . . 409 Main St., Racine WI 53403
PACK 'N SHIP . . . . 409 Main St., Racine WI 53403
PNS . . . . 409 Main St., Racine WI 53403
PAK MAIL CENTERS . . . . 3405 America Dr., # 1, Mississauga ON L4V1T6 CAN
PRINT THREE . . . . 3305 W. Spring Mountian Rd., # 60, Las Vegas NV 89102
PRINTHOUSE EXPRESS . . . . .2 Pidgeon Hill Dr., Sterling VA 22170
SIGNED, SEALED AND REMEMBERED . . . . P.O. Box 68324, Tucson AZ 85737
SIR SPEEDY PRINTING (CANADA) . . . . 4 Director Ct., # 202, Woodbridge ON L4L3Z5   CAN
SQP COPY CENTERS . . . . .1825 Rockbridge Rd., Stone Mountain GA 30087
STRICTLY COPIES . . . . 34 Grenfell Cres., Ottawa ON K2G0G2   CAN
THERMOGRAFIX . . . . .201 Consumers Rd., # 205, Toronto ON M2J4G8   CAN
TRANSAMERICA PRINTING . . . . 1286-F Citizens Pkwy., Morrow GA 30260
U-DESIGN . . . . 201 Ann St., Hartford CT 06103
W.P. TEAM . . . . 34 Grenfell Cres., Ottawa ON K2G0G2   CAN
WRAP & SHIP . . . . 538 Conner Creek Dr., Noblesville IN 46060
ZIPPY PRINT . . . . 1455 W. Georgia St., 4th Fl., Vancouver BC V6G2T6   CAN
ZIPPY PRINT CANADA . . . . 5800 Ambler Dr., # 114, Mississauga ON L4W4J4 CAN

For a full explanation of the data provided in

the Franchisor Format, please refer to Chapter 2,

"How To Use The Data."

CHAPTER 11

BUSINESS: TAX PREPARATION

AFTE BUSINESS ANALYSTS

13831 Northwest Fwy., # 335
Houston, TX 77040
TEL: (800) 683-2383 (713) 462-7855
FAX:
Mr. Ken Jaeger, VP

An AFTE franchise provides a total bookkeeping and tax service as the financial answer for a small business. We use a complete computerized bookkeeping tax service and business consulting concept - one of the top three growth franchise industries in the US. We offer a unique method of getting clients and an established system to control a large-volume practice.

HISTORY: . . . .
Established in 1978; . . 1st Franchised in 1986
Company-Owned Units (As of 12/1/1989): . .0
Franchised Units (12/1/1989): 12
Total Units (12/1/1989): 12
Distribution: US-12;Can-0;Overseas-0
  North America: . . . . 7 States
  Concentration: . . . . 6 in TX
Registered: . . . . FL
. . . .
Average # of Employees: . . . . . . 1 FT, 1 PT
Prior Industry Experience: . . . . Helpful

FINANCIAL:
Cash Investment: $3.5K
Total Investment: $5K
Fees: Franchise - $2K
  Royalty: 7%, Advert: 0%
Contract Periods (Yrs.): 15/15
Area Development Agreement: . .No
Sub-Franchise Contract: . . . . .No
Expand in Territory: . . . . . . Yes
Passive Ownership: . . . . . .Allowed
Encourage Conversions: . . . . . Yes
Franchisee Purchase(s) Required: .No

FRANCHISOR TRAINING/SUPPORT:
Financial Assistance Provided: . . .Yes(D)
Site Selection Assistance: . . . . .Yes
Lease Negotiation Assistance: . . . . .Yes
Co-operative Advertising: . . . . .Yes
Training: . . . . 2 Wks. Headquarters
. . . .
On-Going Support: . . . . . C,D,e,F,G,h,I
Full-Time Franchisor Support Staff: . . . 6
EXPANSION PLANS:
  US: . . . . All US
  Canada - No, ... Overseas - No

TAX PREPARATION SERVICES

	1988	1989	1990	Percentage Change 1988–1989	Percentage Change 1989–1990
Number of Establishments:					
Company–Owned	3,536	3,364	3,421	–4.9%	1.7%
Franchisee–Owned	4,767	4,857	5,039	1.9%	3.7%
Total	8,303	8,221	8,460	–1.0%	2.9%
% of Total Establishments:					
Company–Owned	42.6%	40.9%	40.4%		
Franchisee–Owned	57.4%	59.1%	59.6%		
Total	100.0%	100.0%	100.0%		
Annual Sales ($000):					
Company–Owned	$332,032	$354,690	$382,615	6.8%	7.9%
Franchisee–Owned	276,140	298,715	325,715	8.2%	9.0%
Total	608,172	653,405	708,330	7.4%	8.4%
% of Total Sales:					
Company–Owned	54.6%	54.3%	54.0%		
Franchisee–Owned	45.4%	45.7%	46.0%		
Total	100.0%	100.0%	100.0%		
Average Sales Per Unit ($000):					
Company–Owned	$94	$105	$112	12.3%	6.1%
Franchisee–Owned	58	62	65	6.2%	5.1%
Total	73	79	84	8.5%	5.3%
Sales Ratio	162.1%	171.4%	173.0%		

	1st Quartile	Median	4th Quartile
Average 1988 Total Investment:			
Company–Owned	N. A.	$10,000	N. A.
Franchisee–Owned	N. A.	10,000	N. A.
Single Unit Franchise Fee	$2,750	$5,000	$10,000
Multiple Unit Franchise Fee	N. A.	11,250	N. A.
Franchisee Start–up Cost	N. A.	N. A.	N. A.

	1988	Employees/Unit	Sales/Employee
Employment:			
Company–Owned	41,882	11.8	$7,928
Franchisee–Owned	37,447	7.9	7,374
Total	79,329	9.6	7,666
Employee Performance Ratios		150.8%	107.5%

Source: Franchising In The Economy, 1988 – 1990, IFA Education Foundation & Horwath International, Published January, 1990.

1) 1989 and 1990 data were estimated by respondents.

H & R BLOCK

4410 Main St.
Kansas City, MO 64111
TEL: (816) 753-6900
FAX:
Franchise Information

An H & R BLOCK franchise prepares individual, partnership and corporate tax returns under the name of the world's largest tax preparation firm.

HISTORY: . . . . IFA
Established in 1955; . . 1st Franchised in 1957
Company-Owned Units (As of 12/1/1989): 3886
Franchised Units (12/1/1989): 4892
Total Units (12/1/1989): 8778
Distribution: . US-7458;Can-926;Overseas-394
 North America: . . . . All States, All Prov.
 Concentration: .582 in CA, 524 in TX, 402 NY
Registered: . . . . .All
. . . .
Average # of Employees: . . . . . . 2 FT, 2 PT
Prior Industry Experience: . . . . . . Helpful

FINANCIAL: NYSE-HRB
Cash Investment: $4-6K
Total Investment: $4-6K
Fees: Franchise - $0
 Royalty: Var., Advert: 0%
Contract Periods (Yrs.): 5/5
Area Development Agreement: .No
Sub-Franchise Contract: . . . . .No
Expand in Territory: . . . . Yes
Passive Ownership: . . . Discouraged
Encourage Conversions: . . . . . NA
Franchisee Purchase(s) Required: .No

FRANCHISOR TRAINING/SUPPORT:
Financial Assistance Provided: . . . . .No
Site Selection Assistance: . . . . . . .Yes
Lease Negotiation Assistance: . . . . .Yes
Co-operative Advertising: . . . . .NA
Training: . . . . . 1-2 Days Field Mana., 75
 . . . . Hrs. Field Tax, As Needed on Site
On-Going Support: . . . . . . b,C,D,G,h,I
Full-Time Franchisor Support Staff: . .750
EXPANSION PLANS:
US: . . . . .All US
Canada - Yes, . . . Overseas - Yes

JACKSON HEWITT TAX SERVICE

224 Groveland Rd.
Virginia Beach, VA 23452
TEL: (800) 234-1040 (804) 463-3300
FAX: (804) 463-8612
Mr. Walter J. Ewell, VP Fran. Devel.

A JACKSON HEWITT TAX SERVICE franchise will offer computerized (IBM PC compatible) income tax preparation, electronic filing (incl. refund anticipation loans), bookkeeping and other related services. Franchisees are provided proprietary software, accounting packages, merchandising equipment selection, advertising, sales and promotional techniques.

HISTORY: . . . . IFA
Established in 1960; . . 1st Franchised in 1986
Company-Owned Units (As of 12/1/1989): . 14
Franchised Units (12/1/1989): 232
Total Units (12/1/1989): 246
Distribution: US-246;Can-0;Overseas-0
 North America: . . . . 22 States
 Concentration: . 40 in CA, 39 in VA, 34 in NY
Registered: . . . . .FL,MD,NY,VA
. . . .
Average # of Employees: . . . . . . 1 FT, 7 PT
Prior Industry Experience: . . . . . . Helpful

FINANCIAL:
Cash Investment: $15-23K
Total Investment: $15-23K
Fees: Franchise - $10K
 Royalty: 12%, Advert: 6%
Contract Periods (Yrs.): 5/5
Area Development Agreement: Yes/Var
Sub-Franchise Contract: . . . . .No
Expand in Territory: . . . . Yes
Passive Ownership: . . . Discouraged
Encourage Conversions: . . . . . .No
Franchisee Purchase(s) Required: .No

FRANCHISOR TRAINING/SUPPORT:
Financial Assistance Provided: . . . . .No
Site Selection Assistance: . . . . . . .Yes
Lease Negotiation Assistance: . . . . .Yes
Co-operative Advertising: . . . . . . .Yes
Training: . . . . .1 Wk. Headquarters,
 . . . . 2 Days/Yr. Update HQ
On-Going Support: . . . . .B,C,D,E,G,H,I
Full-Time Franchisor Support Staff: . . 40
EXPANSION PLANS:
US: . . . . . .All US/Montgomery Wards
Canada - No, ...Overseas - No

NATIONWIDE INCOME TAX SERVICE

14507 W. Warren
Dearborn, MI 48126
TEL: (313) 584-7640
FAX:
Mr. Carl K. Gilbert, President

Preparation of federal, state and local tax returns.

HISTORY: . . . .
Established in 1964; . . 1st Franchised in 1966
Company-Owned Units (As of 12/1/1989): . .8
Franchised Units (12/1/1989): 32
Total Units (12/1/1989): 40
Distribution: US-40;Can-0;Overseas-0
 North America: . . . . .1 State
 Concentration: . . . . .40 in MI
Registered: . . . . .MI
. . . .
Average # of Employees: . . . . 1-2 FT, 2-6 PT
Prior Industry Experience: . . . . Helpful

FINANCIAL:
Cash Investment: $10-15K
Total Investment: $10-30K
Fees: Franchise - $5K
 Royalty: 7-10%, Advert: . . 5-10%
Contract Periods (Yrs.): 10/10
Area Development Agreement: .No
Sub-Franchise Contract: . . . . .No
Expand in Territory: . . . . Yes
Passive Ownership: . . . Discouraged
Encourage Conversions: . . . . . Yes
Franchisee Purchase(s) Required: .No

FRANCHISOR TRAINING/SUPPORT:
Financial Assistance Provided: . . . . .No
Site Selection Assistance: . . . . . . .Yes
Lease Negotiation Assistance: . . . . .Yes
Co-operative Advertising: . . . . . . .Yes
Training: . . . . . . 1-2 Wks. Headquarters
. . . .
On-Going Support: . . . . .B,C,d,E,G,H,I
Full-Time Franchisor Support Staff: . . .5
EXPANSION PLANS:
US: . . . . .All US
Canada - No, ...Overseas - No

PINNACLE 1 INTERNATIONAL

3350 Lenape St.
N. Charleston, SC 29405
TEL: (803) 744-5861
FAX:
Mr. Bob Roe, CEO

Complete tax/bookkeeping system using computers - free electronic filing. Clients provided.

HISTORY: . . . . IFA		
Established in 1981; . . 1st Franchised in 1981		
Company-Owned Units (As of 12/1/1989): . .0		
Franchised Units (12/1/1989): 52		
Total Units (12/1/1989): 52		
Distribution: US-52;Can-0;Overseas-0		
North America: . . . . 5 States		
Concentration: . . 35 in SC, 12 in NC, 2 in GA		
Registered: . . . . .FL		
. . . .		
Average # of Employees: . . . . . . 2 FT, 1 PT		
Prior Industry Experience: . . . . Helpful		

FINANCIAL:
Cash Investment: $7.5K
Total Investment: $25-35K
Fees: Franchise - $15K
   Royalty: 7%, Advert: 3%
Contract Periods (Yrs.): 10/5
Area Development Agreement: Yes/10
Sub-Franchise Contract: . . . . . .No
Expand in Territory: . . . . Yes
Passive Ownership: . . . Discouraged
Encourage Conversions: . . . . . Yes
Franchisee Purchase(s) Required: .No

FRANCHISOR TRAINING/SUPPORT:
Financial Assistance Provided: . . . . .Yes
Site Selection Assistance: . . . . . . .Yes
Lease Negotiation Assistance: . . . . .Yes
Co-operative Advertising: . . . . .No
Training: . . . . 5 Days Headquarters
. . . .
On-Going Support: . . . . . . .C,D,G,H,I
Full-Time Franchisor Support Staff: . . 14
EXPANSION PLANS:
US: . . . . .All US
Canada - No, ...Overseas - No

TRIPLE CHECK INCOME TAX SERVICE

727 S. Main St.
Burbank, CA 91506
TEL: (800) 733-1040 (213) 849-2273
FAX: (818) 840-9309
Mr. David Lieberman, President

Franchisor offers full range of support services to independent tax practitioners, including training, technical (hotline), marketing (including group referral programs), proprietary worksheet schedule system and reduced computer costs. Through a sister company (Triple Check Financial Services), franchisees have an opportunity to engage in financial and investment planning services.

HISTORY: . . . . IFA		
Established in 1941; . . 1st Franchised in 1979		
Company-Owned Units (As of 12/1/1989): . .0		
Franchised Units (12/1/1989): 285		
Total Units (12/1/1989): 285		
Distribution: . . . US-285;Can-0;Overseas-0		
North America: . . . . 44 States		
Concentration: . . 112 in CA, 16 in FL, 14 CO		
Registered: . . . . . .All States Exc. ND & SD		
. . . .		
Average # of Employees: . . . . Varies		
Prior Industry Experience: . . . . . .Necessary		

FINANCIAL:
Cash Investment: $0-5K
Total Investment: $0-5K
Fees: Franchise - $0
   Royalty: Varies, Advert: . . Varies
Contract Periods (Yrs.): 5/5
Area Development Agreement: .No
Sub-Franchise Contract: . . . . .No
Expand in Territory: . . . . . . Yes
Passive Ownership: . . . Discouraged
Encourage Conversions: . . . . Yes
Franchisee Purchase(s) Required: .No

FRANCHISOR TRAINING/SUPPORT:
Financial Assistance Provided: . . . Yes(I)
Site Selection Assistance: . . . . No
Lease Negotiation Assistance: . . . . . No
Co-operative Advertising: . . . . .Yes
Training: . . . . 80 Hrs. on Tape
. . . .
On-Going Support: . . . . . . .a,b,C,G,h,I
Full-Time Franchisor Support Staff: . . 25
EXPANSION PLANS:
US: . . . . .All US
Canada - No, ...Overseas - No

U & R TAX SERVICES

1345 Pembina Hwy.
Winnipeg, MB R3T2B6 CAN
TEL: (204) 284-1806
FAX: (204) 284-8954
Mr. Donald Jacks, Fran. Mgr.

Income tax preparation, tax discounting, bookkeeping and related services. Ideal for operation in storefront locations, shopping mall kiosks and is compatible with other service businesses. Includes administrative and tax training, advertising, supplies, central checking, processing and information services, errors and omissions insurance and on-going supervision. Currently available in Canada only.

HISTORY:		
Established in 1972; . . 1st Franchised in 1973		
Company-Owned Units (As of 12/1/1989): . 37		
Franchised Units (12/1/1989): 73		
Total Units (12/1/1989): 110		
Distribution: . . . US-0;Can-110;Overseas-0		
North America: . . . . 10 Provinces		
Concentration: . 53 in MB, 18 in ON, 18 in SK		
Registered: . . . . AB		
. . . .		
Average # of Employees: . . . . . . 1 FT, 2 PT		
Prior Industry Experience: . . . . Helpful		

FINANCIAL:
Cash Investment: $5-10K
Total Investment: $5-10K
Fees: Franchise - $4.5-7.5K
   Royalty: 3-50%, Advert: 0%
Contract Periods (Yrs.): 5/5
Area Development Agreement: .No
Sub-Franchise Contract: . . . . .No
Expand in Territory: . . . . . . Yes
Passive Ownership: . . . . . .Allowed
Encourage Conversions: . . . . Yes
Franchisee Purchase(s) Required: .No

FRANCHISOR TRAINING/SUPPORT:
Financial Assistance Provided: . . . . .No
Site Selection Assistance: . . . . . . .Yes
Lease Negotiation Assistance: . . . .Yes
Co-operative Advertising: . . . . .Yes
Training: . . . . .12 Wks. At Home,
. . . . 4-5 Days Headquarters
On-Going Support: . . A,B,C,D,E,F,G,H,I
Full-Time Franchisor Support Staff: . .216
EXPANSION PLANS:
US: . . . . .No
Canada - Yes, ... Overseas - No

SUPPLEMENTAL LISTING OF FRANCHISORS

CEN-TA GROUP . . . . 201 - 935 Marine Dr., N. Vancouver BC V7P1S3   CAN
H & R BLOCK CANADA . . . . 3440 Pharmacy Ave., # 3, Scarborough ON M1W2P8   CAN
K & W COMPUTERIZED TAX SERVICE . . . . 225 N. 7th St., Kansas City KS 66101
SOLUTION 2000 . . . . 1985 est, rue Beaubien, Montreal PQ H2G1L8   CAN
TAX CENTERS OF AMERICA . . . . 77 Arkay Dr., # B1, Hauppage NY 11788
TAX MAN . . . . .674 Massachusetts Ave., Cambridge MA 02139
TAX OFFICES OF AMERICA/HEALTH CLUBS . . . . Box 4098, Waterbury CT 06704
TAX TIME SERVICES . . . . 1304 Speers Rd., Oakville ON L6L2X4   CAN

CHAPTER 12

BUSINESS: MISCELLANEOUS

AMERICA ONE

2214 University Park Dr.
Okemos, MI 48864
TEL: (517) 349-1988
FAX:
Ms. Joanne Dillman, VP Operations

AMERICA ONE offers licensed casualty insurance agents the opportunity to own and operate their own agency. We provide markets, bookkeeping systems and monthly meetings and on-going support.

HISTORY: . . . .
Established in 1980;   . . 1st Franchised in 1982
Company-Owned Units (As of 12/1/1989):   . .0
Franchised Units (12/1/1989):   30
Total Units (12/1/1989):   30
Distribution: US-30;Can-0;Overseas-0
  North America: . . . . .1 State
  Concentration: . . . . .30 in MI
Registered: . . . . .MI
  . . . .
Average # of Employees: . . . . .2 FT
Prior Industry Experience: . . . . . .Necessary

FINANCIAL:
Cash Investment: $10-18K
Total Investment: $10K
Fees: Franchise - $10K
  Royalty: 15%, Advert: 2%
Contract Periods (Yrs.): 10/10
Area Development Agreement: . .No
Sub-Franchise Contract: . . . . .No
Expand in Territory: . . . . .No
Passive Ownership: . . . Not Allowed
Encourage Conversions: . . . . .No
Franchisee Purchase(s) Required: .No

FRANCHISOR TRAINING/SUPPORT:
Financial Assistance Provided: . . . . .No
Site Selection Assistance: . . . . .Yes
Lease Negotiation Assistance: . . . . .Yes
Co-operative Advertising: . . . . .Yes
Training: . . . . 10 Days Home Office
  . . . .
On-Going Support: . . . . . . B,C,D,E,H,I
Full-Time Franchisor Support Staff: . . . 3
EXPANSION PLANS:
  US: . . . . Michigan Only
  Canada - No, ... Overseas - No

MISCELLANEOUS BUSINESS SYSTEMS

	1988	1989	1990	Percentage Change	
				1988-1989	1989-1990
Number of Establishments:					
Company-Owned	782	716	818	-8.4%	14.2%
Franchisee-Owned	17,180	20,099	24,261	17.0%	20.7%
Total	17,962	20,815	25,079	15.9%	20.5%
% of Total Establishments:					
Company-Owned	4.4%	3.4%	3.3%		
Franchisee-Owned	95.6%	96.6%	96.7%		
Total	100.0%	100.0%	100.0%		
Annual Sales ($000):					
Company-Owned	$353,666	$408,565	$492,173	15.5%	20.5%
Franchisee-Owned	2,596,948	2,968,306	3,652,780	14.3%	23.1%
Total	2,950,614	3,376,871	4,144,953	14.4%	22.7%
% of Total Sales:					
Company-Owned	12.0%	12.1%	11.9%		
Franchisee-Owned	88.0%	87.9%	88.1%		
Total	100.0%	100.0%	100.0%		
Average Sales Per Unit ($000):					
Company-Owned	$452	$571	$602	26.2%	5.4%
Franchisee-Owned	151	148	151	-2.3%	1.9%
Total	164	162	165	-1.2%	1.9%
Sales Ratio	299.2%	386.4%	399.6%		

	1st Quartile	Median	4th Quartile
Average 1988 Total Investment:			
Company-Owned	$25,000	$60,000	$150,000
Franchisee-Owned	30,000	50,000	100,000
Single Unit Franchise Fee	$10,000	$17,000	$25,000
Multiple Unit Franchise Fee	10,200	15,000	25,925
Franchisee Start-up Cost	15,000	25,000	50,000

	1988	Employees/Unit	Sales/Employee
Employment:			
Company-Owned	15,599	19.9	$22,672
Franchisee-Owned	50,450	2.9	51,476
Total	66,049	3.7	44,673
Employee Performance Ratios		679.3%	44.0%

Source: Franchising In The Economy, 1988 – 1990, IFA Education Foundation & Horwath International, Published January, 1990.

1) 1989 and 1990 data were estimated by respondents.

AMERICAN DOCUMENT SHREDDING

1180 Spring Ctr. South Blvd., # 115
Altamonte Springs, FL 32714
TEL: (800) 445-5238 (407) 862-2223
FAX:
Mr. William Olday, President

Franchisees provide mobile and on-site shredding of confidential documents that companies and individuals desire to have destroyed. Computers are churning out mountains of information that is confidential to the customer's business. Customers are banks, doctors, manufacturers, distributors, government agencies and more.

HISTORY: . . . .
Established in 1989; . . 1st Franchised in 1989
Company-Owned Units (As of 12/1/1989): . .1
Franchised Units (12/1/1989): 0
Total Units (12/1/1989): 1
Distribution: US-1;Can-0;Overseas-0
North America: . . . . .1 State
Concentration: . . . . 1 in FL
Registered: . . . . .FL
. . . .
Average # of Employees: . . . . . . 1 FT, 1 PT
Prior Industry Experience: . . . . Helpful

FINANCIAL:
Cash Investment: $5-14K
Total Investment: $8-20K
Fees: Franchise - $5.9-9.5K
    Royalty: 7%, Advert: 0%
Contract Periods (Yrs.): 7/7
Area Development Agreement: Yes/7
Sub-Franchise Contract: . . . . .No
Expand in Territory: . . . . Yes
Passive Ownership: . . . Discouraged
Encourage Conversions: . . . . . NA
Franchisee Purchase(s) Required: Yes

FRANCHISOR TRAINING/SUPPORT:
Financial Assistance Provided: . . .Yes(D)
Site Selection Assistance: . . . . .Yes
Lease Negotiation Assistance: . . . . .NA
Co-operative Advertising: . . . . .Yes
Training: . . . . . . 3-5 Days Headquarters
. . . .
On-Going Support: . . . . a,b,c,d,G,I
Full-Time Franchisor Support Staff: . . . 3
EXPANSION PLANS:
US: . . . . .All US
Canada - Yes, ...Overseas - No

AMERICAN INSTITUTE OF SMALL BUSINESS

7515 Wayzata Blvd., # 201
Minneapolis, MN 55426
TEL: (800) 328-2906 (612) 545-7001
FAX:
Mr. Max Fallek, Director

THE AMERICAN INSTITUTE OF SMALL BUSINESS provides educational materials, including books and newsletters, on Small Business and Entrepreneurship. It also provides a seminar for training people on how to set up and operate their own small business. The Institute also supplies business software sold by franchisees.

HISTORY: . . . .
Established in 1985; . . 1st Franchised in 1988
Company-Owned Units (As of 12/1/1989): . .1
Franchised Units (12/1/1989): 4
Total Units (12/1/1989): 5
Distribution: US-5;Can-0;Overseas-0
North America: . . . . 2 States
Concentration: . . . . 3 in MN, 2 in CO
Registered: . . . .
. . . .
Average # of Employees: . . . . . . 1 FT, 1 PT
Prior Industry Experience: . . . . Helpful

FINANCIAL:
Cash Investment: $5K
Total Investment: $5K
Fees: Franchise - $5K
    Royalty: 2%, Advert: 0%
Contract Periods (Yrs.): 2/2
Area Development Agreement: . .No
Sub-Franchise Contract: . . . . .No
Expand in Territory: . . . . Yes
Passive Ownership: . . . . .Allowed
Encourage Conversions: . . . .
Franchisee Purchase(s) Required: Yes

FRANCHISOR TRAINING/SUPPORT:
Financial Assistance Provided: . . . . .No
Site Selection Assistance: . . . . . . .Yes
Lease Negotiation Assistance: . . . .NA
Co-operative Advertising: . . . . . . .NA
Training: . . . . 2 Days Headquarters
. . . .
On-Going Support: . . . . C,d,e,I
Full-Time Franchisor Support Staff: . . . 8
EXPANSION PLANS:
US: . . . . .All US
Canada - No, ...Overseas - No

BARTER EXCHANGE

1106 Clayton Ln., # 480 W.
Austin, TX 78723
TEL: (800) 44-TRADE (512) 467-9989
FAX:
Franchise Department

BARTER EXCHANGE is the fastest-growing national trade network in a booming $600 billion industry. An established company, a proven franchised business . . . this all adds up to one thing, the most exciting and profitable business opportunity available anywhere.

HISTORY: . . . .
Established in 1983; . . 1st Franchised in 1984
Company-Owned Units (As of 12/1/1989): . .3
Franchised Units (12/1/1989): 12
Total Units (12/1/1989): 15
Distribution: US-15;Can-0;Overseas-0
North America: . . . . 14 States
Concentration: . . . .
Registered: . . . . CA,FL,MI,OR
. . . .
Average # of Employees: . . . . . .13 FT, 4 PT
Prior Industry Experience: . . . . Helpful

FINANCIAL:
Cash Investment: $30-90K
Total Investment: $60-90K
Fees: Franchise - $60K
    Royalty: 0%, Advert: $1K
Contract Periods (Yrs.): 5/5
Area Development Agreement: . .No
Sub-Franchise Contract: . . . . .No
Expand in Territory: . . . . Yes
Passive Ownership: . . . . .Allowed
Encourage Conversions: . . . . . Yes
Franchisee Purchase(s) Required: .No

FRANCHISOR TRAINING/SUPPORT:
Financial Assistance Provided: . . .Yes(D)
Site Selection Assistance: . . . . . . .Yes
Lease Negotiation Assistance: . . . .NA
Co-operative Advertising: . . . . . . .Yes
Training: . . . . . . 5 Days Headquarters,
    . . . . 5 Days Field Off., 5 Days Site Off.
On-Going Support: . . . A,C,D,E,F,G,H,I
Full-Time Franchisor Support Staff: . . 30
EXPANSION PLANS:
US: . . . . .All US
Canada - No, ...Overseas - No

BUSINESS AMERICA

300 Cedar Blvd.
Pittsburgh, PA 15228
TEL: (412) 833-1910
FAX:
Mr. Thomas Atkins, President

Complete line of business and franchise brokerage. Confidential handling of businesses and buyers. Referral agents for franchises. Commissions earned on sale of business or acceptance of licensee on franchise.

HISTORY: . . . . IFA
Established in 1984; . . 1st Franchised in 1985
Company-Owned Units (As of 12/1/1989): . .0
Franchised Units (12/1/1989): 4
Total Units (12/1/1989): 4
Distribution: US-4;Can-0;Overseas-0
North America: . . . . 1 States
Concentration: . . . . 4 in PA
Registered: . . . .
. . . .
Average # of Employees: . . . . 2 Ft, 2 PT
Prior Industry Experience: . . . . Helpful

FINANCIAL:
Cash Investment: $40K
Total Investment: $55K
Fees: Franchise - $25K
Royalty: 6%, Advert: 2%
Contract Periods (Yrs.): 5/5
Area Development Agreement: . .No
Sub-Franchise Contract: . . . . .No
Expand in Territory: . . . . . . .No
Passive Ownership: . . . Not Allowed
Encourage Conversions: . . . . . NA
Franchisee Purchase(s) Required: .No

FRANCHISOR TRAINING/SUPPORT:
Financial Assistance Provided: . . . . .No
Site Selection Assistance: . . . . . . .Yes
Lease Negotiation Assistance: . . . . .Yes
Co-operative Advertising: . . . . . . .Yes
Training: . . . . .1 Wk. Headquarters,
. . . . 1 Wk. On-site
On-Going Support: . . . . c,D,E,f,h,i
Full-Time Franchisor Support Staff: . . . .
EXPANSION PLANS:
US: . . . . .All US
Canada - Yes, . . . Overseas - Yes

CA$H PLUS

4020 Chicago Ave.
Riverside, CA 92507
TEL: (714) 682-2274 C
FAX:
Mr. Jerry E. Todd, President

For those of you looking for the ideal business, look no further! With a CA$H PLUS check cashing franchise, there are no accounts receivable, no returns, no spoilage, no inventory, low overhead and high returns.

HISTORY: . . . .
Established in 1984; . . 1st Franchised in 1988
Company-Owned Units (As of 12/1/1989): . .1
Franchised Units (12/1/1989): 9
Total Units (12/1/1989): 10
Distribution: US-10;Can-0;Overseas-0
North America: . . . . 3 States
Concentration: . . . 6 in CA, 1 in NV, 1 in OK
Registered: . . . . All States
. . . .
Average # of Employees: . . . . . . 2 FT, 1 PT
Prior Industry Experience: . . . . Helpful

FINANCIAL:
Cash Investment: $25-30K
Total Investment: $30-35K
Fees: Franchise - $5K
Royalty: 6%, Advert: 0%
Contract Periods (Yrs.): 5/5
Area Development Agreement: Yes/5
Sub-Franchise Contract: . . . . Yes
Expand in Territory: . . . . . . Yes
Passive Ownership: . . . Discouraged
Encourage Conversions: . . . . Yes
Franchisee Purchase(s) Required: Yes

FRANCHISOR TRAINING/SUPPORT:
Financial Assistance Provided: . . . . .No
Site Selection Assistance: . . . . . . .Yes
Lease Negotiation Assistance: . . . . .Yes
Co-operative Advertising: . . . . . . .No
Training: . . . . . Period Varies at Head-
. . . . quarters
On-Going Support: . . . .B,C,D,E,F,G,H,I
Full-Time Franchisor Support Staff: . . . 4
EXPANSION PLANS:
US: . . . . .All US
Canada - No, ...Overseas - No

CHECK EXPRESS U.S.A.

4300 W. Cypress, # 451
Tampa, FL 33607
TEL: (800) 521-8211 (813) 874-6069
FAX: (813) 873-3684
Mr. J. J. Moran, EVP

An exclusive, computerized system for check verification. We cash all types of checks - payroll, government, welfare, personal and 2nd and 3rd party, out-of-town, insurance drafts. Protected territory, site selection. 2 weeks training. Radio, TV and direct mail programs.

HISTORY: . . . .
Established in 1981; . . 1st Franchised in 1988
Company-Owned Units (As of 12/1/1989): . 20
Franchised Units (12/1/1989): 32
Total Units (12/1/1989): 52
Distribution: US-52;Can-0;Overseas-0
North America: . . . . 10 States
Concentration: . . . . .Primarily FL, MI & KS
Registered: . . .CA,FL,HI,IN,MD,MI,MN,ND
. . . . OR,RI,SD,VA,WA,WI
Average # of Employees: . . . . .3 FT
Prior Industry Experience: . . . . Helpful

FINANCIAL: 0TC-CEI
Cash Investment: $100K
Total Investment: $110-120K
Fees: Franchise - $19.5K
Royalty: 5%, Advert: 3%
Contract Periods (Yrs.): 15/5
Area Development Agreement: Yes/10
Sub-Franchise Contract: . . . . .No
Expand in Territory: . . . . . . Yes
Passive Ownership: . . . . . .Allowed
Encourage Conversions: . . . . Yes
Franchisee Purchase(s) Required: .No

FRANCHISOR TRAINING/SUPPORT:
Financial Assistance Provided: . . . . .No
Site Selection Assistance: . . . . . . .Yes
Lease Negotiation Assistance: . . . . .Yes
Co-operative Advertising: . . . . . . .Yes
Training: . . . . 2 Wks. Headquarters
. . . .
On-Going Support: . . A,B,C,D,E,F,G,H,I
Full-Time Franchisor Support Staff: . .100
EXPANSION PLANS:
US: . . . . .All US
Canada - No, ...Overseas - No

CHECK-X-CHANGE CORP.

111 SW Columbia, # 1080
Portland, OR 97201
TEL: (800) 432-3371 (503) 241-1800
FAX:
Mr. Jeff Voss, Chairman

CHECK-X-CHANGE stores cash checks for a fee. Estimates are that 25% of the adult population does not have a banking relationship. Always liquid (cash) inventory. Estimated US market is 59 billion dollars. Complete training, territory protection, name recognition, field support and backing of the largest chain in the industry.

HISTORY: . . . .
Established in 1982; . . 1st Franchised in 1984
Company-Owned Units (As of 12/1/1989): . .0
Franchised Units (12/1/1989): 137
Total Units (12/1/1989): 137
Distribution: . . . US-137;Can-0;Overseas-0
North America: . . . . 24 States
Concentration: . 27 in WA, 20 in FL, 16 in CA
Registered: . . . .CA,FL,HI,IN,MD,MI,OR,RI
. . . . WA,WI
Average # of Employees: . . . . .3 FT
Prior Industry Experience: . . . . Helpful

FINANCIAL:
Cash Investment: $75-100K
Total Investment: $75-100K
Fees: Franchise - $19.7K
Royalty: $915/Mo., Advert: Varies
Contract Periods (Yrs.): . . . 10/10
Area Development Agreement: . .No
Sub-Franchise Contract: . . . . .No
Expand in Territory: . . . . . . Yes
Passive Ownership: . . . Discouraged
Encourage Conversions: . . . . . Yes
Franchisee Purchase(s) Required: .No

FRANCHISOR TRAINING/SUPPORT:
Financial Assistance Provided: . . . . .No
Site Selection Assistance: . . . . . . .Yes
Lease Negotiation Assistance: . . . . .Yes
Co-operative Advertising: . . . . . . .Yes
Training: . . . . 2 Wks. Headquarters
. . . .
On-Going Support: . . . .B,C,D,E,F,G,H,I
Full-Time Franchisor Support Staff: . . 16
EXPANSION PLANS:
US: . . . . .All US
Canada - Yes, . . . Overseas - Yes

CHECKCARE SYSTEMS

3907 Macon Rd.
Columbus, GA 31907
TEL: (404) 563-3721 C
FAX:
Mr. F. Steve Taylor, President

CHECKCARE SYSTEMS is a check protection agency for retail business. This unique program guarantees bad checks for merchants within 15 days with no phone calls or special equipment. Outstanding cash flow.

HISTORY: . . . .
Established in 1982; . . 1st Franchised in 1984
Company-Owned Units (As of 12/1/1989): . .1
Franchised Units (12/1/1989): 25
Total Units (12/1/1989): 26
Distribution: US-26;Can-0;Overseas-0
North America: . . . . 6 States
Concentration: . . . .7 in GA, 6 in FL, 4 in TN
Registered: . . . . .FL,IL,MN
. . . .
Average # of Employees: . . . . .4-8 FT
Prior Industry Experience: . . . . Helpful

FINANCIAL:
Cash Investment: $45-75K
Total Investment: $45-75K
Fees: Franchise - $10-50K
Royalty: 4-5%, Advert: 0%
Contract Periods (Yrs.): . . . 10/10
Area Development Agreement: . .No
Sub-Franchise Contract: . . . . .No
Expand in Territory: . . . . . . Yes
Passive Ownership: . . . Discouraged
Encourage Conversions: . . . . .No
Franchisee Purchase(s) Required: .No

FRANCHISOR TRAINING/SUPPORT:
Financial Assistance Provided: . . . . .No
Site Selection Assistance: . . . . . . .Yes
Lease Negotiation Assistance: . . . . .No
Co-operative Advertising: . . . . . . .Yes
Training: . . . . 1 Wk. Headquarters, 2-3
. . . Days Another Franchise, On-going
On-Going Support: . . . . .c,d,H
Full-Time Franchisor Support Staff: . . 14
EXPANSION PLANS:
US: . . . . .All US
Canada - No, ...Overseas - No

CORPORATE FINANCE ASSOCIATES

600 17th St., # 700
Denver, CO 80202
TEL: (303) 623-5600
FAX:
Mr. James Sorensen, President

We assist mid-sized businesses with strategic decisions, sell-merge-finance decisions and help to improve profit. We do acquisition search work for companies seeking expansion. We prepare companies for sale or merger.

HISTORY: . . . .
Established in 1956; . . 1st Franchised in 1960
Company-Owned Units (As of 12/1/1989): . .0
Franchised Units (12/1/1989): 47
Total Units (12/1/1989): 47
Distribution: US-44;Can-1;Overseas-2
North America: . . . . 27 States, 1 Province
Concentration: . . . 6 in CA, 4 in OH, 3 in PA
Registered: . . .CA,IL,IN,MD,MI,MN,NY,OR
. . . . VA,WA,WI
Average # of Employees: . . . . . . 3 FT, 1 PT
Prior Industry Experience: . . . . Helpful

FINANCIAL:
Cash Investment: $15-100K
Total Investment: $15-100K
Fees: Franchise - $15K
Royalty: 7%, Advert: 0%
Contract Periods (Yrs.): 1/1
Area Development Agreement: . .No
Sub-Franchise Contract: . . . . .No
Expand in Territory: . . . . . . .No
Passive Ownership: . . . Not Allowed
Encourage Conversions: . . . .
Franchisee Purchase(s) Required: .No

FRANCHISOR TRAINING/SUPPORT:
Financial Assistance Provided: . . . . .No
Site Selection Assistance: . . . . . . .NA
Lease Negotiation Assistance: . . . .NA
Co-operative Advertising: . . . . . . .NA
Training: . . . . . 3 Days Headquarters, 2
. . . .Days/Yr. Region, 3 Days/Yr. Nat'l.
On-Going Support: . . . . . .A,B,C,D,H,I
Full-Time Franchisor Support Staff: . . 10
EXPANSION PLANS:
US: . . . . .All US
Canada - Yes, . . . Overseas - Yes

DOCU-PREP CENTER

925 S. Gilbert Rd., # 207
Mesa, AZ 85204
TEL: (602) 263-1225
FAX:
Mr. Kenneth Hollowell, Mktg. Mgr.

The DOCU-PREP CENTER is a business establishment which will prepare uncontested legal documents such as bankruptcy, divorce, legal separation, living trust, living will, name change, power of attorney, quit claim deed, etc.

HISTORY: . . . . IFA	FINANCIAL: OTC	FRANCHISOR TRAINING/SUPPORT:
Established in 1989; . . 1st Franchised in 1989	Cash Investment: $5-10K	Financial Assistance Provided: . . . . . No
Company-Owned Units (As of 12/1/1989): . .0	Total Investment: $15-20K	Site Selection Assistance: . . . . .Yes
Franchised Units (12/1/1989): 4	Fees: Franchise - $5K	Lease Negotiation Assistance: . . . . .Yes
Total Units (12/1/1989): 4	Royalty: 6%, Advert: 2%	Co-operative Advertising: . . . . . . .Yes
Distribution: US-4;Can-0;Overseas-0	Contract Periods (Yrs.): . . . 10/10	Training: . . . . 3 Days Headquarters
North America: . . . . .1 State	Area Development Agreement: . .No	
Concentration: . . . . 4 in AZ	Sub-Franchise Contract: . . . . .No	On-Going Support: . . . . A,C,D,E,F,G,h,I
Registered:	Expand in Territory: . . . . . . .No	Full-Time Franchisor Support Staff: . . .2
. . . .	Passive Ownership: . . . Discouraged	EXPANSION PLANS:
Average # of Employees: . . . . .2 FT	Encourage Conversions: . . . . .No	US: . . . . Southwest
Prior Industry Experience: . . . . . . Helpful	Franchisee Purchase(s) Required: Yes	Canada - No, ...Overseas - No

FILTERFRESH

Trimex Bldg., Route 11
Mooers, NY 12958
TEL: (800) 361-0443 (514) 676-3819 C
FAX: (514) 676-9348
Mr. Leslie Allan, Fran. Sales Mgr.

High-tech office coffee service, using a patented single-cup coffeemaker. FIL-TERFRESH brews coffee by-the-cup from fresh-ground coffee in seconds. Choice exclusive territories are available. The FILTERFRESH franchise provides access to patented equipment, detailed training in sales and service, on-going support and supply services.

HISTORY: . . . . IFA	FINANCIAL: Yes(I)	FRANCHISOR TRAINING/SUPPORT:
Established in 1986; . . 1st Franchised in 1987	Cash Investment: $50-90k	Financial Assistance Provided: . . . .
Company-Owned Units (As of 12/1/1989): . .0	Total Investment: $250-500k	Site Selection Assistance: . . . . .NA
Franchised Units (12/1/1989): 23	Fees: Franchise - $24.5k	Lease Negotiation Assistance: . . . . .No
Total Units (12/1/1989): 23	Royalty: 5%, Advert: 2%	Co-operative Advertising: . . . . .Yes
Distribution: US-23;Can-0;Overseas-0	Contract Periods (Yrs.): . . . 10/10	Training: . . . . 8 Days Headquarters,
North America: . . . . 15 States	Area Development Agreement: . .No	. . . . . 3-4 Days On-site, On-going Site
Concentration: . . . .4 in NY, 2 in NJ, 2 in CT	Sub-Franchise Contract: . . . . .No	On-Going Support: . . A,B,C,D,E,F,G,H,I
Registered: . . . CA,FL,IL,IN,MD,MI,MN,NY	Expand in Territory: . . . . Yes	Full-Time Franchisor Support Staff: . . 10
. . . . OR,RI,VA,WA,WI	Passive Ownership: . . . Not Allowed	EXPANSION PLANS:
Average # of Employees: . . . . . . 4 FT, 2 PT	Encourage Conversions: . . . . . NA	US: . . . . .All US
Prior Industry Experience: . . . . . . Helpful	Franchisee Purchase(s) Required: Yes	Canada - No, ...Overseas - No

FRANCHISE CENTREX

79 Parkingway, P. O. Box 7169
Quincy, MA 02169
TEL: (617) 773-0530
FAX:
Mr. Leo Meady, President

All-inclusive franchise consulting firm. Potential investors pay $12.00 annual membership fees for newsletters, work-shops, etc. Major income derived from $5,000 "finder's fee" paid by franchisors selling franchises to our members. Also produce franchise packages for budget-minded companies wanting to franchise their product.

HISTORY:	FINANCIAL:	FRANCHISOR TRAINING/SUPPORT:
Established in 1988; . . 1st Franchised in 1990	Cash Investment: $38-45K	Financial Assistance Provided: . . . . .No
Company-Owned Units (As of 12/1/1989): . .1	Total Investment: $38-45K	Site Selection Assistance: . . . . . . .Yes
Franchised Units (12/1/1989): 1	Fees: Franchise - $15K	Lease Negotiation Assistance: . . . .Yes
Total Units (12/1/1989): 1	Royalty: 6%, Advert: 0%	Co-operative Advertising: . . . . . . .Yes
Distribution: US-1;Can-0;Overseas-0	Contract Periods (Yrs.): 10/10	Training: . . . . . . .1 Wk. Headquarters.
North America: . . . . .1 State	Area Development Agreement: . .No	. . . . 2-3 2-day Sessions Franchisee Site
Concentration: . . . . .1 in MA	Sub-Franchise Contract: . . . . .No	On-Going Support: . . . . . . D,E,G,H,I
Registered:	Expand in Territory: . . . . . . .No	Full-Time Franchisor Support Staff: . . .2
. . . .	Passive Ownership: . . . Discouraged	EXPANSION PLANS:
Average # of Employees: . . . . . . 1 FT, 6 PT	Encourage Conversions: . . . . .No	US: . . . . .All US
Prior Industry Experience: . . . . . . Helpful	Franchisee Purchase(s) Required: .No	Canada - Yes, ...Overseas - No

FRANCHISE SYSTEMS NETWORK

15600-20 San Carlos Blvd.
Ft. Myers, FL 33908
TEL: (800) 633-4608
FAX: (813) 433-0383
Mr. Ron Greene, Managing Principal

New concept offering expert franchise-related services: marketing, consulting, UFOC preparation, sales brochures, operations manuals, site selection, lease negotiation and training programs. Complete program development for new franchisors. Services to franchisors, franchisees, would-be franchisors and would-be franchisees. Regional Training Directors to assist our franchisees.

HISTORY: . . . . IFA	FINANCIAL:	FRANCHISOR TRAINING/SUPPORT:
Established in 1989; . . 1st Franchised in 1989	Cash Investment: . . . .$	Financial Assistance Provided: . . .Yes(D)
Company-Owned Units (As of 12/1/1989): . . 1	Total Investment: . . . .$	Site Selection Assistance: . . . . . . .Yes
Franchised Units (12/1/1989): 16	Fees: Franchise - $17.5K	Lease Negotiation Assistance: . . . . .Yes
Total Units (12/1/1989): 17	Royalty: 20%, Advert: 0%	Co-operative Advertising: . . . . . . .Yes
Distribution: US-17;Can-0;Overseas-0	Contract Periods (Yrs.): 10/10	Training: . . . . .5 Days Franchisee's
North America: . . . . 11 States	Area Development Agreement: . .No	. . . . .Location
Concentration: . . . . .5 in PA, 2 in FL	Sub-Franchise Contract: . . . . . .No	On-Going Support: . . . . .C,D,E,F,G,H,I
Registered: . . . . .FL	Expand in Territory: . . . . Yes	Full-Time Franchisor Support Staff: . . . 3
. . . .	Passive Ownership: . . . . . .Allowed	EXPANSION PLANS:
Average # of Employees: . . . . .2 FT	Encourage Conversions: . . . . . Yes	US: . . . . .All US
Prior Industry Experience: . . . . Helpful	Franchisee Purchase(s) Required: .No	Canada - Yes, . . . Overseas - Yes

FRANKLIN TRAFFIC SERVICE

P. O. Box 100
Ransomville, NY 14131
TEL: (716) 731-3131
FAX:
Mr. Richard L. Dearborn, Sales Mgr.

Our clientele ships, receives, and/or manufactures at locations all over the country. With the changes in the law during 1980 and 1981, a new facet of our business has emerged: complete traffic management, physically being a client's entire traffic department.

HISTORY:	FINANCIAL:	FRANCHISOR TRAINING/SUPPORT:
Established in 1969; . . . 1st Franchised in 19	Cash Investment: $25-30K	Financial Assistance Provided: . . .Yes(D)
Company-Owned Units (As of 12/1/1989): . .0	Total Investment: $25-30K	Site Selection Assistance: . . . . .NA
Franchised Units (12/1/1989): 4	Fees: Franchise - $25-30K	Lease Negotiation Assistance: . . . . .NA
Total Units (12/1/1989): 4	Royalty: Varies, Advert: . . Varies	Co-operative Advertising: . . . . .Yes
Distribution: US-4;Can-0;Overseas-0	Contract Periods (Yrs.): . . . .Varies	Training: . . . . 3 Wks. Headquarters
North America: . . . . 2 States	Area Development Agreement: . .No	. . . .
Concentration: . . . . 3 in NY, 1 in GA	Sub-Franchise Contract: . . . . . .No	On-Going Support: . . . . .A,B,C,D
Registered:	Expand in Territory: . . . . .No	Full-Time Franchisor Support Staff: . . 70
. . . .	Passive Ownership: . . . Not Allowed	EXPANSION PLANS:
Average # of Employees: . . . . .1-2 FT	Encourage Conversions: . . . . . NA	US: . . . . Southeast
Prior Industry Experience: . . . . . .Necessary	Franchisee Purchase(s) Required: .No	Canada - No, ...Overseas - No

GENERAL BUSINESS SERVICES

20271 Goldenrod Ln.
Germantown, MD 20874
TEL: (800) 638-7940 (301) 428-1040
FAX: (301) 428-0916
Mr. Tom Palazzo, Fran. Sales Dir.

Your ambition and ability to help others solve business problems is the key to running a successful business yourself. We'll train you to become a skilled advisor in financial management, business and tax counseling to small business owners and professionals. Field and headquarters support and assist in business development.

HISTORY: . . . . IFA	FINANCIAL:	FRANCHISOR TRAINING/SUPPORT:
Established in 1962; . . 1st Franchised in 1962	Cash Investment: $25K	Financial Assistance Provided: . . . . . No
Company-Owned Units (As of 12/1/1989): . .0	Total Investment: . . . . $25K+	Site Selection Assistance: . . . . . . .NA
Franchised Units (12/1/1989): 449	Fees: Franchise - $25K	Lease Negotiation Assistance: . . . . .NA
Total Units (12/1/1989): 449	Royalty: 7%, Advert: 0%	Co-operative Advertising: . . . . .NA
Distribution: US-449;Can-0;Overseas-0	Contract Periods (Yrs.): 5/5	Training: . . . . 9 Days Headquarters,
North America: . . . . 49 States	Area Development Agreement: . .No	. . . . .5 Days Field
Concentration: . 55 in CA, 24 in FL, 21 in MD	Sub-Franchise Contract: . . . . .No	On-Going Support: . . . . A,B,C,D,G,H,I
Registered: . . . . All Except AB	Expand in Territory: . . . . Yes	Full-Time Franchisor Support Staff: . . 93
. . . .	Passive Ownership: . . . Not Allowed	EXPANSION PLANS:
Average # of Employees: . . . . . . 1 FT, 1 PT	Encourage Conversions: . . . . . Yes	US: . . . . .All US
Prior Industry Experience: . . . . Helpful	Franchisee Purchase(s) Required: Yes	Canada - No, ...Overseas - No

INTERNATIONAL INSURANCE BROKERS
3524 16th St., # B
Metairie, LA 70002
TEL: (800)445-4754(LA) (504)888-0324
FAX: (504) 888-0369
Mr. Otto Mehrgut, CEO

Brokeraged and retail sales of homeowners, life, health and auto insurance. IIB provides a complete software system that operates the entire insurance agency. Our unique system invites all insurance agents to broker through our insurance underwriters.

HISTORY: . . . . IFA	FINANCIAL: VSE	FRANCHISOR TRAINING/SUPPORT:
Established in 1986; . . 1st Franchised in 1987	Cash Investment: $10K	Financial Assistance Provided: . . . . . No
Company-Owned Units (As of 12/1/1989): . .6	Total Investment: $20K	Site Selection Assistance: . . . . Yes
Franchised Units (12/1/1989): 5	Fees: Franchise - $5-7.5K	Lease Negotiation Assistance: . . . . .Yes
Total Units (12/1/1989): 11	Royalty: 2%, Advert: 1%	Co-operative Advertising: . . . . . . .Yes
Distribution: US-11;Can-0;Overseas-0	Contract Periods (Yrs.): 10/5	Training: . . . . 1 Wk. Headquarters
North America: . . . . .1 State	Area Development Agreement: . .No	. . . .
Concentration: . . . . 11 in LA	Sub-Franchise Contract: . . . . .No	On-Going Support: . . . . a,B,C,d,E,f,G,H
Registered:	Expand in Territory: . . . . Yes	Full-Time Franchisor Support Staff: . . . 6
. . . .	Passive Ownership: . . . Discouraged	EXPANSION PLANS:
Average # of Employees: . . . . . . 1 FT, 1 PT	Encourage Conversions: . . . . . NA	US: . . . . Louisiana, Alabama,Tennessee
Prior Industry Experience: . . . . Helpful	Franchisee Purchase(s) Required: .No	Canada - No, ...Overseas - No

INTERNATIONAL MERGERS & ACQUISITIONS
8100 E. Indian School Rd., # 7 W
Scottsdale, AZ 85251
TEL: (602) 990-3899
FAX:
Mr. Neil Lewis, President

National affiliation of members engaged in the profession of serving merger and acquisition-minded companies, offering consulting services, financing, mergers and acquisitions and other services of a distinctive nature.

HISTORY:	FINANCIAL:	FRANCHISOR TRAINING/SUPPORT:
Established in 1969; . . 1st Franchised in 1979	Cash Investment: $10K	Financial Assistance Provided: . . . . . No
Company-Owned Units (As of 12/1/1989): . .0	Total Investment: $20-25K	Site Selection Assistance: . . . . .NA
Franchised Units (12/1/1989): 38	Fees: Franchise - $10K	Lease Negotiation Assistance: . . . . .NA
Total Units (12/1/1989): 38	Royalty: 3%, Advert: 1%	Co-operative Advertising: . . . . . . .NA
Distribution: US-38;Can-0;Overseas-0	Contract Periods (Yrs.): 5/5	Training: . . . . . As Needed Headquarters,
North America: . . . . 13 States	Area Development Agreement: . .No	. . . . If Necessary Site
Concentration: . . . 7 in AZ, 3 in CO, 3 in SD	Sub-Franchise Contract: . . . . .No	On-Going Support: . . . . D,G,H,I
Registered: . . . . All States	Expand in Territory: . . . . . . .No	Full-Time Franchisor Support Staff: . . .2
. . . .	Passive Ownership: . . . Discouraged	EXPANSION PLANS:
Average # of Employees: . . . . .1 FT	Encourage Conversions: . . . . . .No	US: . . . . .All US
Prior Industry Experience: . . . . . . Helpful	Franchisee Purchase(s) Required: .No	Canada - Yes, . . . Overseas - Yes

NATIONAL FINANCIAL COMPANY

7332 Caverna Dr.
Hollywood, CA 90068
TEL: (213) 856-0100
FAX:
Mr. Leonard VanderBie, President

Computer matches client's capital needs with sources of capital. Data base contains over 15,000 variable sources of capital. Consultants licensed by company have access to data base for their own clients, who are in need of capital. Consultants earn both retainer and finder's fees.

HISTORY:	FINANCIAL:	FRANCHISOR TRAINING/SUPPORT:
Established in 1957; . . 1st Franchised in 1957	Cash Investment: $18K	Financial Assistance Provided: . . . . . No
Company-Owned Units (As of 12/1/1989): . .1	Total Investment: $18K	Site Selection Assistance: . . . . .Yes
Franchised Units (12/1/1989): 445	Fees: Franchise - $18K	Lease Negotiation Assistance: . . . . .Yes
Total Units (12/1/1989): 446	Royalty: 0%, Advert: 0%	Co-operative Advertising: . . . . .No
Distribution: US-401;Can-0;Overseas-45	Contract Periods (Yrs.): 4/4	Training: . . . . 3 Days Site
North America: . . . . 50 States	Area Development Agreement: . .No	. . . .
Concentration:	Sub-Franchise Contract: . . . . .No	On-Going Support: . . . . A,F,G,I
Registered:	Expand in Territory: . . . . Yes	Full-Time Franchisor Support Staff: . . 14
. . . .	Passive Ownership: . . . Not Allowed	EXPANSION PLANS:
Average # of Employees: . . . . 14 FT	Encourage Conversions: . . . . . .No	US: . . . . .All US
Prior Industry Experience: . . . . Helpful	Franchisee Purchase(s) Required: Yes	Canada - Yes, . . . Overseas - Yes

NETWORK LEASING

100 Westmore Dr., # 11B
Rexdale, ON M9V5C3 CAN
TEL: (800) 387-7434 (416) 745-7880 C
FAX:
Mr. Scott Hinsperger, Fran. Coord.

NETWORK LEASING provides leasefunding to businesses, professionals and consumers for all types of equipment and vehicles. Leases are tailor-made to suit the client's financial needs. Franchisees enjoy high profits in a prestigious business with excellent growth potential.

HISTORY: . . . . .CFA	FINANCIAL:	FRANCHISOR TRAINING/SUPPORT:
Established in 1971; . . 1st Franchised in 1987	Cash Investment: . . . .$	Financial Assistance Provided: . . . Yes(I)
Company-Owned Units (As of 12/1/1989): . .1	Total Investment: $95-105K	Site Selection Assistance: . . . . .NA
Franchised Units (12/1/1989): 15	Fees: Franchise - $40K	Lease Negotiation Assistance: . . . . .NA
Total Units (12/1/1989): 16	Royalty: Flat, Advert: . . . . . . %	Co-operative Advertising: . . . . .Yes
Distribution: US-0;Can-16;Overseas-0	Contract Periods (Yrs.): 5/5	Training: . . . . .1 Wk. Headquarters,
North America: . . . . .1 Province	Area Development Agreement: . .No	. . . . 1 Wk. Franchisee's Office
Concentration: . . . . 16 in ON	Sub-Franchise Contract: . . . . .No	On-Going Support: . . . . A,B,C,D,G,H,I
Registered:	Expand in Territory: . . . . Yes	Full-Time Franchisor Support Staff: . . . 8
. . . .	Passive Ownership: . . . Not Allowed	EXPANSION PLANS:
Average # of Employees: . . . . . . 1 FT, 1 PT	Encourage Conversions: . . . . . Yes	US: . . . . Michigan, New York
Prior Industry Experience: . . . . Helpful	Franchisee Purchase(s) Required: .No	Canada - Yes, ...Overseas - No

PARSON-BISHOP SERVICES

7870 Camargo Rd.
Cincinnati, OH 45243
TEL: (800) 543-0468 (513) 561-5560
FAX:
Mr. Lou Bishop, President

Creative plans and systems which help corporations increase cash flow and reduce billing/collection costs associated with accounts receivable. Excellent long-term repeat business. Professional business service franchise for the sales-oriented business executive.

HISTORY: . . . . IFA	FINANCIAL:	FRANCHISOR TRAINING/SUPPORT:
Established in 1973; . . 1st Franchised in 1986	Cash Investment: $23-29K	Financial Assistance Provided: . . . . . No
Company-Owned Units (As of 12/1/1989): . .0	Total Investment: $23-29K	Site Selection Assistance: . . . . .NA
Franchised Units (12/1/1989): 58	Fees: Franchise - $23-29K	Lease Negotiation Assistance: . . . . .NA
Total Units (12/1/1989): 58	Royalty: 0%, Advert: 0%	Co-operative Advertising: . . . . .Yes
Distribution: US-58;Can-0;Overseas-0	Contract Periods (Yrs.): 5/5	Training: . . . . . . .1 Wk. Headquarters, 3
North America: . . . . 21 States	Area Development Agreement: . .No	. . . . Days On-site, 3 Days On-site
Concentration: . . . 5 in OH, 5 in NY, 4 in FL	Sub-Franchise Contract: . . . . .No	On-Going Support: . . . . A,B,C,D,G,H,I
Registered: . . . FL,IL,IN,MD,MI,MN,NY,VA	Expand in Territory: . . . . Yes	Full-Time Franchisor Support Staff: . . 25
. . . . WA	Passive Ownership: . . . Not Allowed	EXPANSION PLANS:
Average # of Employees: . . . . .1 PT	Encourage Conversions: . . . . . .No	US: . . . . .All US Except CA
Prior Industry Experience: . . . . Helpful	Franchisee Purchase(s) Required: .No	Canada - No, ...Overseas - No

PAUL DAVIS SYSTEMS

244 Roswell St., # 300
Marietta, GA 30060
TEL: (404) 427-7220
FAX:
Ms. Linda Edwards, Fran. Sales Dir.

PDS provides a unique, computerized property damage estimating service and restoration management program to all major insurance companies and their property owners. Operates on a fixed cost tied to fixed selling price.

HISTORY:	FINANCIAL:	FRANCHISOR TRAINING/SUPPORT:
Established in 1966; . . 1st Franchised in 1970	Cash Investment: . . . . . $30K+WC	Financial Assistance Provided: . . .Yes(D)
Company-Owned Units (As of 12/1/1989): . .0	Total Investment: $65K	Site Selection Assistance: . . . . . . .Yes
Franchised Units (12/1/1989): 130	Fees: Franchise - $47K	Lease Negotiation Assistance: . . . . .NA
Total Units (12/1/1989): 130	Royalty: 2.5%, Advert: 0%	Co-operative Advertising: . . . . .NA
Distribution: US-117;Can-13;Overseas-0	Contract Periods (Yrs.): 5/1	Training: . . . .4 Wks. Home Office, 1 Wk.
North America: . . . . 32 States, 3 Provinces	Area Development Agreement: . .No	. . . . . Internship Field, 1 Wk. On-site
Concentration: . . . 20 in FL, 8 in TX, 8 in OH	Sub-Franchise Contract: . . . . .No	On-Going Support: . . . .A,b,C,D,E,G,H,I
Registered: . . . . All Except HI	Expand in Territory: . . . . Yes	Full-Time Franchisor Support Staff: . . 20
. . . .	Passive Ownership: . . . Not Allowed	EXPANSION PLANS:
Average # of Employees: . . . . .3 FT	Encourage Conversions: . . . . . .No	US: . . . . .All US Esp. West & NE
Prior Industry Experience: . . . . Helpful	Franchisee Purchase(s) Required: .No	Canada - Yes, ...Overseas - No

PROFORMA

4705 Van Epps Rd.
Cleveland, Oh 44131
TEL: (800) 825-1525 (216) 741-0400
FAX: (216) 741-8887
Mr. John Campbell, Dir. Fran. Dev.

Distributor of business forms, commercial printing, office/computer supplies, office furniture and micro-computers. Not a retail business. Seeking owner/operator with strong marketing and management background to develop this business through a sales force and distribution facility. $250,000 minimum net worth required.

HISTORY:	IFA
Established in 1978; 1st Franchised in 1985	
Company-Owned Units (As of 12/1/1989):	1
Franchised Units (12/1/1989):	90
Total Units (12/1/1989):	91
Distribution:	US-91;Can-0;Overseas-0
North America:	29 States
Concentration:	6 in OH, 6 in NJ, 6 in NC
Registered:	CA,FL,IL,IN,MD,MI,MN,NY OR,RI,VA,WA,WI
Average # of Employees:	1-2 FT Initially
Prior Industry Experience:	Helpful

FINANCIAL:	
Cash Investment:	$39.5K
Total Investment:	$43.2-46.2K
Fees: Franchise -	$39.5K
Royalty: 7%, Advert:	1%
Contract Periods (Yrs.):	10/Lease
Area Development Agreement:	No
Sub-Franchise Contract:	No
Expand in Territory:	Yes
Passive Ownership:	Not Allowed
Encourage Conversions:	No
Franchisee Purchase(s) Required:	No

FRANCHISOR TRAINING/SUPPORT:	
Financial Assistance Provided:	No
Site Selection Assistance:	No
Lease Negotiation Assistance:	No
Co-operative Advertising:	Yes
Training:	1 Wk. Headquarters, 2-4 Days in Field
On-Going Support:	A,B,C,D,F,G,H,I
Full-Time Franchisor Support Staff:	60
EXPANSION PLANS:	
US:	All US
Canada - Yes, Overseas - No	

PROVE

4806 Shelly Dr.
Wilmington, NC 28405
TEL: (800) 442-5393 (919) 392-2550
FAX: (919) 395-4075
Ms. Lorraine G. Taylor, President

National network of locally-owned, professional Mystery Shopping agencies. Largest organization of its kind. Provides services to business owners, including: evaluation of employees as regards customer service, salesmanship, cash handling procedures and adherence to prescribed company policies. Evaluation of location in regards to appearance, maintenance and security/insurance hazards. Awards programs. Seminars.

HISTORY:	IFA
Established in 1974; 1st Franchised in 1987	
Company-Owned Units (As of 12/1/1989):	0
Franchised Units (12/1/1989):	35
Total Units (12/1/1989):	35
Distribution:	US-35;Can-0;Overseas-0
North America:	15 States
Concentration:	7 in NC, 6 in FL, 5 in SC
Registered:	All States
Average # of Employees:	2 FT, PT As Needed
Prior Industry Experience:	Helpful

FINANCIAL:	
Cash Investment:	$14.5K+
Total Investment:	$16.5K
Fees: Franchise -	$14.5K+
Royalty: 8%, Advert:	0%
Contract Periods (Yrs.):	20/10
Area Development Agreement:	No
Sub-Franchise Contract:	No
Expand in Territory:	Yes
Passive Ownership:	Discouraged
Encourage Conversions:	NA
Franchisee Purchase(s) Required:	Yes

FRANCHISOR TRAINING/SUPPORT:	
Financial Assistance Provided:	Yes(D)
Site Selection Assistance:	NA
Lease Negotiation Assistance:	NA
Co-operative Advertising:	No
Training:	10 Days Headquarters
On-Going Support:	C,D,G,h,I
Full-Time Franchisor Support Staff:	
EXPANSION PLANS:	
US:	All US
Canada - Yes, Overseas - No	

PROVENTURE BUSINESS BROKERS

79 Parkingway
Quincy, MA 02169
TEL: (617) 773-0530
FAX:
Mr. Leo Meady, Chairman

PROVENTURE is an all-inclusive business brokerage. We list and sell going businesses (up to $2 million). We also sell franchise opportunities for client companies. Also offered is a moderate-priced consulting service for new franchisors.

HISTORY:	IFA
Established in 1981; 1st Franchised in 1981	
Company-Owned Units (As of 12/1/1989):	1
Franchised Units (12/1/1989):	7
Total Units (12/1/1989):	8
Distribution:	US-8;Can-0;Overseas-0
North America:	2 States
Concentration:	7 in MA, 1 in NJ
Registered:	
Average # of Employees:	2 FT, 5 PT
Prior Industry Experience:	Helpful

FINANCIAL:	
Cash Investment:	$45K
Total Investment:	$45K
Fees: Franchise -	$15K (Incl.)
Royalty: 6%, Advert:	0%
Contract Periods (Yrs.):	10/10
Area Development Agreement:	No
Sub-Franchise Contract:	No
Expand in Territory:	Yes
Passive Ownership:	Discouraged
Encourage Conversions:	Yes
Franchisee Purchase(s) Required:	No

FRANCHISOR TRAINING/SUPPORT:	
Financial Assistance Provided:	No
Site Selection Assistance:	Yes
Lease Negotiation Assistance:	Yes
Co-operative Advertising:	Yes
Training:	1 Wk. Headquarters, 1 Wk. Site
On-Going Support:	C,D,E,h,I
Full-Time Franchisor Support Staff:	3
EXPANSION PLANS:	
US:	All US
Canada - No, Overseas - No	

SPECIAL SELECTIONS PERSONAL SHOPPING SERVICE
P. O. Box 3243
Boise, ID 83703
TEL: (208) 343-3629
FAX:
Ms. Roxanne Overton, President

Personal shopping service for busy executives and professionals. We purchase both personal and business gifts. Clients are signed under specialized marketing techniques and merchandise is purchased at below retail prices to enhance profits. We don't cater to the general public.

HISTORY: . . . . IFA	FINANCIAL:	FRANCHISOR TRAINING/SUPPORT:
Established in 1988; . . 1st Franchised in 1989	Cash Investment: $9-18K	Financial Assistance Provided: . . . Yes(I)
Company-Owned Units (As of 12/1/1989): . .1	Total Investment: $9-18K	Site Selection Assistance: . . . . .No
Franchised Units (12/1/1989): 1	Fees: Franchise - $5-8.5K	Lease Negotiation Assistance: . . . . .No
Total Units (12/1/1989): 2	Royalty: 5%, Advert: 1%	Co-operative Advertising: . . . . . . .Yes
Distribution: US-2;Can-0;Overseas-0	Contract Periods (Yrs.): . . . .Varies	Training: . . . . 4 Days Headquarters
North America: . . . . .1 State	Area Development Agreement: . .No	
Concentration: . . . . .2 in ID	Sub-Franchise Contract: . . . . .No	On-Going Support: . . . . .C,G,h,i
Registered: . . . . CA,IN,OR,WA	Expand in Territory: . . . . Yes	Full-Time Franchisor Support Staff: . . . 1
. . . .	Passive Ownership: . . . Discouraged	EXPANSION PLANS:
Average # of Employees: . . . . .1 FT	Encourage Conversions: . . . . .No	US: . . . . Emphasis on Northwest
Prior Industry Experience: . . . . . . Helpful	Franchisee Purchase(s) Required: .No	Canada - Yes, ...Overseas - No

VR BUSINESS BROKERS

230 Western Ave.
Boston, MA 02134
TEL: (800) 343-4416 (617) 254-4100
FAX: (617) 783-1940
Marketing Director

America's largest network of franchised business brokerage offices, specializing in small to mid-sized business sales. Computer-based networking includes customized software package for business evaluations, national listing exchanges, buyer tracking and sales management stats. Since 1987, VR has been a member of the Christie Group, England's leading business brokerage and related services company.

HISTORY: . . . . IFA	FINANCIAL: LONDON	FRANCHISOR TRAINING/SUPPORT:
Established in 1979; . . 1st Franchised in 1979	Cash Investment: $70-80K	Financial Assistance Provided: . . . . No
Company-Owned Units (As of 12/1/1989): . .0	Total Investment: $79.5-118K	Site Selection Assistance: . . . . . . .Yes
Franchised Units (12/1/1989): 151	Fees: Franchise - $35K	Lease Negotiation Assistance: . . . .Yes
Total Units (12/1/1989): 151	Royalty: 6%, Advert: 2%	Co-operative Advertising: . . . . . . .Yes
Distribution: US-149;Can-2;Overseas-0	Contract Periods (Yrs.): 5/5	Training: . . . . 2 Wks. Headquarters
North America: . . . . . 34 States, 2 Provinces	Area Development Agreement: . .No	
Concentration: . . 17 in TX, 14 in IL, 12 in CA	Sub-Franchise Contract: . . . . .No	On-Going Support: . . . A,B,C,D,E,G,H,I
Registered: . . . CA,FL,HI,IL,IN,MD,MI,MN	Expand in Territory: . . . . Yes	Full-Time Franchisor Support Staff: . . 26
. . . . .NY,OR,RI,VA,WA,WI	Passive Ownership: . . . Discouraged	EXPANSION PLANS:
Average # of Employees: . . . . 8-10 FT	Encourage Conversions: . . . . . Yes	US: . . . . .All US
Prior Industry Experience: . . . . . . Helpful	Franchisee Purchase(s) Required: .No	Canada - Yes, ...Overseas - No

WALL STREET FINANCIAL CENTERS

18881 Von Karman, Ground Fl.
Irvine, CA 92715
TEL: (714) 756-8100
FAX: (714) 756-0261
Mr. Kenneth A. Ziskin, President

WALL STREET FINANCIAL CENTERS, a subsidiary of Wall Street Financial Corporation, is a community banking network designed to assist community banks to compete with larger banks, savings and loans and financial service entities throughout the US.

HISTORY: . . . . IFA	FINANCIAL: OTC-WSFC	FRANCHISOR TRAINING/SUPPORT:
Established in 1986; . . 1st Franchised in 1988	Cash Investment: $25-30K	Financial Assistance Provided: . . . . . No
Company-Owned Units (As of 12/1/1989): . .0	Total Investment: $25-30K	Site Selection Assistance: . . . . . . .NA
Franchised Units (12/1/1989): 0	Fees: Franchise - $25-45K	Lease Negotiation Assistance: . . . . .No
Total Units (12/1/1989): 0	Royalty: 1.5%, Advert: 1%	Co-operative Advertising: . . . . . . .Yes
Distribution: US-0;Can-0;Overseas-0	Contract Periods (Yrs.): 5/5	Training: . . . . . . 4 Days Franchisee Site
North America:	Area Development Agreement: . .No	
Concentration:	Sub-Franchise Contract: . . . . .No	On-Going Support: . . . . . C,D,e,G,h,I
Registered: . . . . CA	Expand in Territory: . . . . Yes	Full-Time Franchisor Support Staff: . . .7
. . . .	Passive Ownership: . . . Not Allowed	EXPANSION PLANS:
Average # of Employees: . . . . . .30-100 FT	Encourage Conversions: . . . . . Yes	US: . . . . .All US
Prior Industry Experience: . . . . . .Necessary	Franchisee Purchase(s) Required: .No	Canada - Yes, . . . Overseas - Yes

WESTERN APPRAISERS

P.O. Box 5211
El Dorado Hills, CA 95630
TEL: (916) 933-2148
FAX:
Mr. Bert McMillan, EVP

WESTERN APPRAISERS services our insurance company clients by providing repair appraisals and total loss evaluations of their insureds' damaged automobiles, trucks and off-road farm and construction equipment. WESTERN APPRAISERS also furnishes evaluation appraisals for lenders, attorneys and fleet owners.

HISTORY: . . . .
Established in 1960; . . 1st Franchised in 1978
Company-Owned Units (As of 12/1/1989): . .0
Franchised Units (12/1/1989): 33
Total Units (12/1/1989): 33
Distribution: US-33;Can-0;Overseas-0
North America: . . . . 7 States
Concentration: . . .22 in CA, 3 in OR, 3 in AZ
Registered: . . . . .CA,OR,WA
. . . .
Average # of Employees: . . . . .1-8 FT
Prior Industry Experience: . . . . . .Necessary

FINANCIAL:
Cash Investment: $7-15K
Total Investment: $17-30K
Fees: Franchise - $7-15K
Royalty: 5%, Advert: 0%
Contract Periods (Yrs.): 10/10
Area Development Agreement: . .No
Sub-Franchise Contract: . . . . .No
Expand in Territory: . . . . . . Yes
Passive Ownership: . . . Not Allowed
Encourage Conversions: . . . . .No
Franchisee Purchase(s) Required: .No

FRANCHISOR TRAINING/SUPPORT:
Financial Assistance Provided: . . . Yes(I)
Site Selection Assistance: . . . . . . .NA
Lease Negotiation Assistance: . . . . .NA
Co-operative Advertising: . . . . . . .Yes
Training: . . . . 2-4 Wks. San Jose,
. . . . 1 Wk. Site
On-Going Support: . . . . . . B,C,D,E,H,I
Full-Time Franchisor Support Staff: . . .2
EXPANSION PLANS:
US: . . . . West & Midwest
Canada - No, ...Overseas - No

WORLDWIDE CANADIAN MANAGE-MENT CONSULTANTS

P. O. Box 639
Pickering, ON L1V3T3 CAN
TEL: (416) 686-1152
FAX:
Mr. Kelly Rogers, Admin. Dir.

Excellent opportunity for retired or near-retired personnel. Services include: business planning, market planning, business system analysis and design, staff training and professional placement services.

HISTORY: . . . .
Established in 1976; . . 1st Franchised in 1980
Company-Owned Units (As of 12/1/1989): . .2
Franchised Units (12/1/1989): 35
Total Units (12/1/1989): 37
Distribution: US-0;Can-2;Overseas-35
North America: . . . . .1 Province
Concentration: . . . . 2 in ON
Registered: . . . .
. . . .
Average # of Employees: . . . . . . 1 FT, 2 PT
Prior Industry Experience: . . . . . .Necessary

FINANCIAL:
Cash Investment: $36K
Total Investment: $120K
Fees: Franchise - $16K
Royalty: 8%, Advert: 0%
Contract Periods (Yrs.): 5/10
Area Development Agreement: . .No
Sub-Franchise Contract: . . . . .No
Expand in Territory: . . . . . . .No
Passive Ownership: . . . Not Allowed
Encourage Conversions: . . . . .No
Franchisee Purchase(s) Required: Yes

FRANCHISOR TRAINING/SUPPORT:
Financial Assistance Provided: . . . Yes(I)
Site Selection Assistance: . . . . . . .Yes
Lease Negotiation Assistance: . . . . . No
Co-operative Advertising: . . . . No
Training: . . . . . On-the-job for 6 Months
. . . . in Major US Cities
On-Going Support: . . . . .H
Full-Time Franchisor Support Staff: . . .5
EXPANSION PLANS:
US: . . . . .All US
Canada - Yes, ...Overseas - Yes

SUPPLEMENTAL LISTING OF FRANCHISORS

ADAM GROUP . . . . 81 N. Chicago St., # 105, Joliet IL 60431
AMERI-CK . . . . 5800 E. Skelly Dr., # 918, Tulsa OK 74135
AMERICAN BUSINESS ASSOCIATES . . . . 475 Park Ave. South, New York NY 10016
AMERICAN INVENTORY SERVICE .P.O. Box 9045, Jackson TN 38314
AMERICAN LENDERS SERVICE CO. . . . . P.O. Box 4855, Odessa TX 79760
BLUE CHIP BUSINESS CENTRES . . . . 710 Dorval Dr., # 518, Oakville ON L6K3V7   CAN
CAREER EXCHANGE NETWORK . . . . 6992 El Camino Real, # 104-439, Carlsbad CA 92008
CASHLAND CHECK CASHING . . . . .451 - 2nd St., Solvang CA 93463
CHECK MART . . . . .1555 S. Havana, Unit 43, Aurora CO 80012
CHECKCHANGERS . . . . 2 W. Madison, # 200, Oak Park IL 60302
COMPUSURANCE INSURANCE AGENCIES . . . . 2136 Danforth Ave., Toronto ON M4C1J9   CAN
CONCEPT III INTERNATIONAL . . . . 9200 Shelbyville Rd., Louisville KY 40222
CONVENIENCE MONEY CENTERS . . . . 1555 S. Havana, Unit 43, Aurora CO 80012
CREATIVE ASSET MANAGEMENT . . . . 65 Jackson Dr., # 2000, Cranford NJ 07016

DATAGAS . . . . .P.O. Box 1110, Oskaloosa IA 52577
DELIVEREX SERVICE CENTERS . . . . 2025 Gateway Pl., # 318, San Jose CA 95110
EMPIRE BUSINESS BROKERS . . . . 3806 Union Rd., Cheektowaga NY 14225
FACS RECORDS CENTRE . . . . 1701 Powell St., Vancouver BC V5L1H6   CAN
FINANCIAL MANAGEMENT . . . . .402 Barker Circle, P.O. Box 2364, West Chester PA 19380
INSURORS GROUP . . . . 100 Pine St., # 1700, San Francisco CA 94111
INTERNATIONAL FRANCHISE SALES NETWORK . . . . 34 Grenfell Cres., Ottawa ON K2G0G2   CAN
ISU . . . . 100 Pine St., # 1700, San Francisco CA 94111
InFORMerific . . . . .P.O. Box 2833, Charleston WV 25330
LCA INTERNATIONAL .575 Fifth Ave., 21st Fl., New York NY 10017
LEASE MART SYSTEMS . . . . 1750 Steeles Ave., W., # 219, Concord ON L4K2L7   CAN
MACHINERY WHOLESALERS . . . . 3510 Biscayne Blvd., Miami FL 33137
MARCOIN BUSINESS SERVICES . . . . .2001 Sixth Ave., # 2501, Seattle WA 98121
MARTIN-ROCHE ASSOCIATES . . . . 64 Division Ave., Levittown NY 11756
MONEY CONCEPTS (CANADA) . . . . 190 Attwell Dr., # 204, Rexdale ON M9W6H8   CAN
MONEY CONCEPTS INTERNATIONAL . . . 1 Golden Bear Pl., 11760 US Hwy., N. Palm Beach FL 33408
PARALEGAL ASSOCIATES . . . . 2000 Argentia Rd., Pl. 1, # 306, Mississauga ON L5N1P7   CAN
PRICECHECK SERVICES . . . . 32 Sixth St., Toronto ON M8V3A2   CAN
PROTOCOL MESSAGE MGT. CENTERS . . . . 12200 Sunrise Valley Dr., Reston VA 22091
SAFEGUARD BUSINESS SYSTEMS . . . . .5789 Coopers Ave., Mississauga ON L4Z1R9   CAN
SECURITY TRUSTCO MANAGEMENT . . . . .701 W. Georgia, # 1500, Vancouver BC V7Y1A1   CAN
STAPLES DIRECT OFFICE SUPPLY . . . . .4400 Amon Carter Blvd., # 110, Ft. Worth TX 76155
SUCCESS CENTERS INTERNATIONAL . . . . 681 Marshall Rd., Rochester NY 14624
TAX RESULTS/USA . . . . P.O. Box 15448, Baton Rouge LA 70895
TAYLOR GROUP, THE . . . . 4806 Shelly Dr., Wilmington NC 28405
TBC BUSINESS BROKERS .61 Dewey Ave., Warwick RI 02886
TELECHECK SERVICES .5299 DTC Blvd., Englewood CO 80111
TGIF PAPERWORKS . . . . P.O. Box 828, Old Lyme CT 06371
TGIF PEOPLEWORKS . . . . P.O. Box 828, Old Lyme CT 06371
TGT FRANCHISE SERVICES . . . . 5799 Yonge St., # 705, Willowdale ON M2M3V3   CAN
UBI BUSINESS BROKERS . . . . .18663 Ventura Blvd., # 223, Tarzana CA 91356
UNITED SERVICE NETWORK . . . . .3657 Oak Grove Dr., Sarasota FL 34243
VENTURE FRONTIERS CORP. . . . . .402 Barker Cr., # 5, West Chester PA 19380
VR BUSINES BROKERS (CANADA) . . . . 2201 Warden Ave., # 202, Toronto ON M1T1V5   CAN
WORD HANDLERS . . . . 7580 E. Camino del Rio, Tucson AZ 85715

CHAPTER 13

CONVENIENCE STORES / SUPER-MARKETS / DRUGS

6-TWELVE CONVENIENT MART

18757 N. Frederick Rd.
Gaithersburg, MD 20879
TEL: (301) 840-8559
FAX: (301) 840-5965
Mr. George Palmer, Franchise Dir.

Up-scale convenience store, featuring a deli, as well as a bakery. 6-TWELVE offers more grocery selections at lower prices. Store may also offer: beer, wine, gas and dry cleaning. Some have car washes. Fully computerized.

HISTORY: . . . . IFA
Established in 1984; . . 1st Franchised in 1986
Company-Owned Units (As of 12/1/1989): . .1
Franchised Units (12/1/1989): 70
Total Units (12/1/1989): 71
Distribution: US-71;Can-0;Overseas-0
  North America: . . . . 3 States
  Concentration: . .37 in MD, 30 in VA, 4 in DC
Registered: . . . . .CA,FL,MD,MI,VA

. . . .
Average # of Employees: . . . . . 5 FT, 5-7 PT
Prior Industry Experience: . . . . Helpful

FINANCIAL:
Cash Investment: $50-80K
Total Investment: $150-305K
Fees: Franchise - $30K
  Royalty: 5%, Advert: 2%
Contract Periods (Yrs.): . . . 10/5+5
Area Development Agreement: Yes/20
Sub-Franchise Contract: . . . . .No
Expand in Territory: . . . . . . .No
Passive Ownership: . . . Not Allowed
Encourage Conversions: . . . . . Yes
Franchisee Purchase(s) Required: .No

FRANCHISOR TRAINING/SUPPORT:
Financial Assistance Provided: . . . Yes(I)
Site Selection Assistance: . . . . . . .Yes
Lease Negotiation Assistance: . . . . .Yes
Co-operative Advertising: . . . . .Yes
Training: . . . .5 Weeks HQ, 1-3 Wks. Site

On-Going Support: . . A,B,C,D,E,F,G,H,I
Full-Time Franchisor Support Staff: . . 20
EXPANSION PLANS:
  US: . . . .Units-Mid-Atlant;Area Dev-US
  Canada - No, ... Overseas - No

CONVENIENCE STORES

	1988	1989	1990	Percentage Change 1988-1989	Percentage Change 1989-1990
Number of Establishments:					
Company-Owned	10,794	10,948	10,880	1.4%	-0.6%
Franchisee-Owned	6,417	6,341	6,587	-1.2%	3.9%
Total	17,211	17,289	17,467	0.5%	1.0%
% of Total Establishments:					
Company-Owned	62.7%	63.3%	62.3%		
Franchisee-Owned	37.3%	36.7%	37.7%		
Total	100.0%	100.0%	100.0%		
Annual Sales ($000):					
Company-Owned	$9,247,960	$9,415,650	$9,572,172	1.8%	1.7%
Franchisee-Owned	4,647,980	4,634,840	4,846,287	-0.3%	4.6%
Total	13,895,940	14,050,490	14,418,459	1.1%	2.6%
% of Total Sales:					
Company-Owned	66.6%	67.0%	66.4%		
Franchisee-Owned	33.4%	33.0%	33.6%		
Total	100.0%	100.0%	100.0%		
Average Sales Per Unit ($000):					
Company-Owned	$857	$860	$880	0.4%	2.3%
Franchisee-Owned	724	731	736	0.9%	0.7%
Total	807	813	825	0.7%	1.6%
Sales Ratio	118.3%	117.7%	119.6%		

	1st Quartile	Median	4th Quartile
Average 1988 Total Investment:			
Company-Owned	$81,250	$250,000	$750,000
Franchisee-Owned	100,000	180,000	450,000
Single Unit Franchise Fee	$7,125	$7,500	$39,725
Multiple Unit Franchise Fee	N. A.	N. A.	N. A.
Franchisee Start-up Cost	28,750	46,500	92,500

	1988	Employees/Unit	Sales/Employee
Employment:			
Company-Owned	117,863	10.9	$78,464
Franchisee-Owned	31,287	4.9	148,559
Total	149,150	8.7	93,168
Employee Performance Ratios		224.0%	52.8%

Source: Franchising In The Economy, 1988 – 1990, IFA Education Foundation & Horwath International, Published January, 1990.

1) 1989 and 1990 data were estimated by respondents.

7-ELEVEN FOOD STORES

2711 N. Haskell Ave.
Dallas, TX 75204
TEL: (800) 255-0711 (214) 828-7763
FAX:
Mr. E. G. White-Swift, Mgr. Stores

7-ELEVEN offers an extended hour retail convenience store, providing groceries, take-out foods and beverages, dairy products, non-food merchandise, specialty items and selected services which emphasize convenience to the customer.

HISTORY: . . . . IFA	FINANCIAL:	FRANCHISOR TRAINING/SUPPORT:
Established in 1927; . . 1st Franchised in 1964	Cash Investment: $13-229K	Financial Assistance Provided: . . .Yes(D)
Company-Owned Units (As of 12/1/1989): 3550	Total Investment: $13-229K	Site Selection Assistance: . . . . .NA
Franchised Units (12/1/1989): 8098	Fees: Franchise - $0-92.7K	Lease Negotiation Assistance: . . . . .NA
Total Units (12/1/1989): 11648	Royalty: NA, Advert: . . . . . . NA	Co-operative Advertising: . . . . .NA
Distribution: US-6966;Can-519;Overseas-4451	Contract Periods (Yrs.): . . 10/Lease	Training: . . . . 5 Days San Diego, 5 Days
North America: . . . . 36 States, 5 Provinces	Area Development Agreement: . .No	. . Bethlehem, PA, 10 Days On Location
Concentration: .1300 in CA,700 in TX,680 VA	Sub-Franchise Contract: . . . . . .No	On-Going Support: . . A,B,C,D,E,F,G,H,I
Registered: . . . CA,IL,IN,MD,NY,OR,RI,VA	Expand in Territory: . . . . Yes	Full-Time Franchisor Support Staff: . . 90
. . . . WA	Passive Ownership: . . . Not Allowed	EXPANSION PLANS:
Average # of Employees: . . . . . . 4 FT, 4 PT	Encourage Conversions: . . . . . NA	US: . . . . .East/West Coast, Great Lakes
Prior Industry Experience: . . . . Helpful	Franchisee Purchase(s) Required: .No	Canada - No, ...Overseas - No

BECKER MILK COMPANY

671 Warden Ave.
Scarborough, ON M1L3Z7 CAN
TEL: (416) 698-2591
FAX: (416) 698-2907
Mr. H. R. Keene, VP

Convenience store chain located in some 200 communities within Ontario.

HISTORY: . . . . IFA	FINANCIAL: TSE-BKR B	FRANCHISOR TRAINING/SUPPORT:
Established in 1957; . . 1st Franchised in 1974	Cash Investment: $150K	Financial Assistance Provided: . . . Yes(I)
Company-Owned Units (As of 12/1/1989): 675	Total Investment: . . . .$	Site Selection Assistance: . . . . . . .Yes
Franchised Units (12/1/1989): 100	Fees: Franchise - $25K	Lease Negotiation Assistance: . . . . .Yes
Total Units (12/1/1989): 775	Royalty: 5%, Advert: 0%	Co-operative Advertising: . . . . No
Distribution: US-0;Can-775;Overseas-0	Contract Periods (Yrs.): 5/5	Training: . . . . .3 Wks. On-site
North America: . . . . .1 Province	Area Development Agreement: . .No	
Concentration: . . . . .775 in ON	Sub-Franchise Contract: . . . . . .No	On-Going Support: . . .a,B,C,D,E,F,G,H,I
Registered:	Expand in Territory: . . . . Yes	Full-Time Franchisor Support Staff: . .500
. . . .	Passive Ownership: . . . Not Allowed	EXPANSION PLANS:
Average # of Employees: . . . . . . 2 FT, 2 PT	Encourage Conversions: . . . . . NA	US: . . . . .No
Prior Industry Experience: . . . . Helpful	Franchisee Purchase(s) Required: Yes	Canada - Yes, ...Overseas - No

CRUISERS SHOP AROUND

619 Divesadero St.
Fresno, CA 93701
TEL: (901) 761-3086 (209) 237-3345 C
FAX:
Mr. G. A. Prath, Sales Dept.

Walkin' or Rollin', shopping is AUTO-matic with the ultimate in convenience. The drive-thru with everything. Our food store is the future of this mobile society. Join our team of stores on the cutting edge of technology. It's here at C.S.A. drive-thru food stores.

HISTORY:	FINANCIAL:	FRANCHISOR TRAINING/SUPPORT:
Established in 1986; . . 1st Franchised in 1988	Cash Investment: $40K	Financial Assistance Provided: . . . . .No
Company-Owned Units (As of 12/1/1989): . .1	Total Investment: $40-200K	Site Selection Assistance: . . . . . . .Yes
Franchised Units (12/1/1989): 0	Fees: Franchise - $10K	Lease Negotiation Assistance: . . . . .No
Total Units (12/1/1989): 1	Royalty: 3%, Advert: 2.5%	Co-operative Advertising: . . . . .Yes
Distribution: US-1;Can-0;Overseas-0	Contract Periods (Yrs.): 10	Training: . . . . 2 Wks. Headquarters
North America: . . . . .1 State	Area Development Agreement: . Yes	. . . .
Concentration: . . . . 1 in CA	Sub-Franchise Contract: . . . . . .No	On-Going Support: . . . . .C,E,I
Registered:	Expand in Territory: . . . . Yes	Full-Time Franchisor Support Staff: . . .1
. . . .	Passive Ownership: . . . . . .Allowed	EXPANSION PLANS:
Average # of Employees: . . . . . . 3 FT, 5 PT	Encourage Conversions: . . . . . Yes	US: . . . . .All US
Prior Industry Experience: . . . . Helpful	Franchisee Purchase(s) Required: .No	Canada - No, ...Overseas - No

DRUG EMPORIUM

7760 Olentangy River Rd.
Columbus, OH 43235
TEL: (800) 284-3784 (614) 888-6876
FAX: (614) 888-3689
Mr. R. Patrick Hiller, VP Fran.

Deep discount drug store, featuring health and beauty aids, cosmetics, greeting cards, pharmacy and sundries. We are a large, high-volume, low-margin, specialty drug store, dealing with name-brand merchandise.

HISTORY: . . . . IFA/CFA
Established in 1977; . . 1st Franchised in 1979
Company-Owned Units (As of 12/1/1989): . 65
Franchised Units (12/1/1989): 129
Total Units (12/1/1989): 194
Distribution: US-194;Can-0;Overseas-0
North America: . . . . 29 States
Concentration: . 20 in PA, 19 in GA, 11 in AZ
Registered: . . . . All States
. . . .
Average # of Employees: . . . . 35 FT
Prior Industry Experience: . . . . . .Necessary

FINANCIAL:
Cash Investment: $700K
Total Investment: . . . . $.7-1.05MM
Fees: Franchise - $25K
Royalty: 1-3%, Advert: 01%
Contract Periods (Yrs.): 25/5
Area Development Agreement: Yes/20
Sub-Franchise Contract: . . . . .No
Expand in Territory: . . . . . . Yes
Passive Ownership: . . . Not Allowed
Encourage Conversions: . . . . . Yes
Franchisee Purchase(s) Required: .No

FRANCHISOR TRAINING/SUPPORT:
Financial Assistance Provided: . . . . .No
Site Selection Assistance: . . . . . . .Yes
Lease Negotiation Assistance: . . . . .Yes
Co-operative Advertising: . . . . . . .Yes
Training: . . . . 6 Wks. Headquarters

On-Going Support: . . . A,C,D,E,F,G,H,I
Full-Time Franchisor Support Staff: . . 45
EXPANSION PLANS:
US: . . . . .All US
Canada - Yes, . . . Overseas - Yes

JR. FOOD MART

P. O. Box 3500
Jackson, MS 39207
TEL: (601) 944-0873
FAX:
Mr. Jack Parker, Dir. Fran. Sales

Convenience food store, selling groceries, gasoline and a variety of fast foods (both take-out and eat-in).

HISTORY: . . . .
Established in 1919; . . 1st Franchised in 1921
Company-Owned Units (As of 12/1/1989): . 60
Franchised Units (12/1/1989): 440
Total Units (12/1/1989): 500
Distribution: US-500;Can-0;Overseas-0
North America: . . . . 19 States
Concentration: . . . . MS, AL, LA
Registered: . . . . FL,IL,IN,VA
. . . .
Average # of Employees: . . . . . .10 FT, 6 PT
Prior Industry Experience: . . . . . . Helpful

FINANCIAL:
Cash Investment: $60K
Total Investment: $60-150K
Fees: Franchise - $10-35K
Royalty: 1.5%, Advert: 0%
Contract Periods (Yrs.): 15/5
Area Development Agreement: Yes/15
Sub-Franchise Contract: . . . . .No
Expand in Territory: . . . . . . Yes
Passive Ownership: . . . Discouraged
Encourage Conversions: . . . . . .No
Franchisee Purchase(s) Required: Yes

FRANCHISOR TRAINING/SUPPORT:
Financial Assistance Provided: . . .Yes(D)
Site Selection Assistance: . . . . . . .Yes
Lease Negotiation Assistance: . . . . .Yes
Co-operative Advertising: . . . . No
Training: . . . . 3 Wks. Headquarters
. . . .
On-Going Support: . . .a,B,C,D,E,F,G,H,I
Full-Time Franchisor Support Staff: . . 80
EXPANSION PLANS:
US: . . . . . Northeast, Northwest,Central
Canada - Yes, . . . Overseas - Yes

LI'L PEACH

101 Billerica Ave.
N. Billerica, MA 01862
TEL: (617) 721-0000
FAX: (508) 671-1609
Mr. David P. Kearns, Dir. Fran.

LI'L PEACH operates convenience stores in the state of Mass. We offer a turn-key operation, complete site selection, full training and excellent follow-up. Services provided include sales/marketing assistance, loss prevention assistance, operational follow-up, payroll and finance.

HISTORY: . . . .
Established in 1971; . . 1st Franchised in 1974
Company-Owned Units (As of 12/1/1989): . .2
Franchised Units (12/1/1989): 63
Total Units (12/1/1989): 65
Distribution: US-65;Can-0;Overseas-0
North America: . . . . .1 State
Concentration: . . . . 65 in MA
Registered: . . . .
. . . .
Average # of Employees: . . . . . . 1 FT, 7 PT
Prior Industry Experience: . . . . . . Helpful

FINANCIAL:
Cash Investment: $20-50K
Total Investment: $40-50K
Fees: Franchise - $2-20K
Royalty: 15.5%, Advert: 0%
Contract Periods (Yrs.): 5
Area Development Agreement: . .No
Sub-Franchise Contract: . . . . .No
Expand in Territory: . . . . . . .No
Passive Ownership: . . . Not Allowed
Encourage Conversions: . . . . . Yes
Franchisee Purchase(s) Required: .No

FRANCHISOR TRAINING/SUPPORT:
Financial Assistance Provided: . . .Yes(D)
Site Selection Assistance: . . . . . . .Yes
Lease Negotiation Assistance: . . . . .Yes
Co-operative Advertising: . . . . . . .Yes
Training: . . . . 3 Wks. Headquarters,
. . . . .3 Wks. Follow Up
On-Going Support: . . . A,C,D,E,F,G,H,I
Full-Time Franchisor Support Staff: . . 40
EXPANSION PLANS:
US: . . . . .Massachusetts Only
Canada - No, ...Overseas - No

MEDICAP PHARMACY

10202 Douglas Ave.
Des Moines, IA 50322
TEL: (800) 445-2244 (515) 276-5491 C
FAX:
Mr. Calvin James, VP Fran. Dev.

MEDICAP PHARMACIES are convenient and low-cost professional pharmacies. They typically operate in a 700-1,000 SF location with 80-90% of the business being the filling of prescriptions. Providing over-the-counter, medically-oriented product is 10-20% of the business. New store start-up and conversion of full-line drug stores and independent pharmacies to the MEDICAP concept.

HISTORY: . . . . IFA
Established in 1971; . . 1st Franchised in 1974
Company-Owned Units (As of 12/1/1989): . .0
Franchised Units (12/1/1989): 82
Total Units (12/1/1989): 82
Distribution: US-82;Can-0;Overseas-0
North America: . . . . 16 States
Concentration: . . . 51 in IA, 8 in MO, 4 in IL
Registered: . . . . . . .IL,MN,MO,ND,SD,WI
. . . .
Average # of Employees: . . . . .2 FT
Prior Industry Experience: . . . . . . Necessary

FINANCIAL:
Cash Investment: $25-30K
Total Investment: $95-110K
Fees: Franchise - $15K
Royalty: 4%, Advert: 1%
Contract Periods (Yrs.): 20/20
Area Development Agreement: . .No
Sub-Franchise Contract: . . . . .No
Expand in Territory: . . . . Yes
Passive Ownership: . . . Not Allowed
Encourage Conversions: . . . . . Yes
Franchisee Purchase(s) Required: . .

FRANCHISOR TRAINING/SUPPORT:
Financial Assistance Provided: . . . Yes(I)
Site Selection Assistance: . . . . . . .Yes
Lease Negotiation Assistance: . . . . .Yes
Co-operative Advertising: . . . . . . .Yes
Training: . . . . 3 Days Headquarters,
. . . . 3 Days Computer Training
On-Going Support: . . . . . .C,D,E,F,G,H
Full-Time Franchisor Support Staff: . . 16
EXPANSION PLANS:
US: . . . . . Midwest, E, SE, S, West Cst.
Canada - No, ...Overseas - No

MEDICINE SHOPPE, THE

1100 N. Lindbergh Blvd.
St. Louis, MO 63132
TEL: (800) 325-1397 (314) 993-6000
FAX:
Mr. Mike M. Eicher, VP Franchising

MEDICINE SHOPPE is the largest and fastest-growing chain of franchised pharmacies in the US. Our stores are apothecary-style, 1,000 SF stores owned and operated by pharmacists. We have over 150 stores waiting to open in the US.

HISTORY: . . . . IFA
Established in 1970; . . 1st Franchised in 1971
Company-Owned Units (As of 12/1/1989): . .0
Franchised Units (12/1/1989): 805
Total Units (12/1/1989): 805
Distribution: US-805;Can-0;Overseas-0
North America: . . . . 48 States
Concentration: . . 84 in PA, 80 in CA, 43 in IL
Registered: . . . . All States Except HI
. . . .
Average # of Employees: . . . . . . 1 FT, 2 PT
Prior Industry Experience: . . . . . .Necessary

FINANCIAL: OTC-MSII
Cash Investment: $18-29K
Total Investment: $78-88K
Fees: Franchise - $18K
Royalty: 5.5%, Advert: 2%
Contract Periods (Yrs.): 20/10
Area Development Agreement: . .No
Sub-Franchise Contract: . . . . . Yes
Expand in Territory: . . . . . . .No
Passive Ownership: . . . Discouraged
Encourage Conversions: . . . . . Yes
Franchisee Purchase(s) Required: Yes

FRANCHISOR TRAINING/SUPPORT:
Financial Assistance Provided: . . .Yes(D)
Site Selection Assistance: . . . . . . .Yes
Lease Negotiation Assistance: . . . . .Yes
Co-operative Advertising: . . . . . . .Yes
Training: . . . . . 1 Wk. Headquarters, 5-7
. . . . Days/Yr. Natl./Regional Meetings
On-Going Support: . . A,B,C,D,E,F,G,H,I
Full-Time Franchisor Support Staff: . .145
EXPANSION PLANS:
US: . . . . .All US
Canada - No, ...Overseas - No

SUNSHINE FAST MARTS

P.O. Box 1467
Thousand Oaks, CA 91358
TEL: (805) 497-3576
FAX:
Mr. Geoffrey C. Prouse, VP

Franchisor of convenience stores and mini-marts.

HISTORY: . . . .
Established in 1983; . . 1st Franchised in 1983
Company-Owned Units (As of 12/1/1989): . .0
Franchised Units (12/1/1989): 6
Total Units (12/1/1989): 6
Distribution: US-6;Can-0;Overseas-0
North America: . . . . .1 State
Concentration: . . . . 6 in CA
Registered: . . . . CA
. . . .
Average # of Employees: . . . . . . 4 FT, 4 PT
Prior Industry Experience: . . . . Helpful

FINANCIAL:
Cash Investment: $70K
Total Investment: $145K
Fees: Franchise - $15K
Royalty: 4%, Advert: 0%
Contract Periods (Yrs.): 10/10
Area Development Agreement: . .No
Sub-Franchise Contract: . . . . .No
Expand in Territory: . . . . . . .No
Passive Ownership: . . . . . .Allowed
Encourage Conversions: . . . . . Yes
Franchisee Purchase(s) Required: .No

FRANCHISOR TRAINING/SUPPORT:
Financial Assistance Provided: . . . Yes(I)
Site Selection Assistance: . . . . . . .Yes
Lease Negotiation Assistance: . . . . .Yes
Co-operative Advertising: . . . . . . .Yes
Training: . . . . 4 Wks. Headquarters
. . . .
On-Going Support: . . . . . . A,B,C,D,E,f
Full-Time Franchisor Support Staff: . . 10
EXPANSION PLANS:
US: . . . . California Only
Canada - No, ...Overseas - No

WHITE HEN PANTRY

660 Industrial Dr.
Elmhurst, IL 60126
TEL: (708) 833-3100
FAX: (708) 833-0292
Mr. James O. Williams, Fran. Mgr.

A WHITE HEN PANTRY is a convenience store, specializing in full-service deli, fresh sandwiches, produce and bakery. Typical stores are 2,400 - 2,500 SF and operate extended hours, 365 days/yr. WHITE HEN PANTRY stores are franchised to area residents who become owner/operators of this "Family Business."

HISTORY: . . . . IFA
Established in 1965; . . 1st Franchised in 1965
Company-Owned Units (As of 12/1/1989): . .3
Franchised Units (12/1/1989): 375
Total Units (12/1/1989): 378
Distribution: US-378;Can-0;Overseas-0
North America: . . . . 5 States
Concentration: . .287 in IL, 62 in MA,14 in IN
Registered: . . . . .IL,IN,RI,WI
. . . .
Average # of Employees: . . . . .2 FT, 7-15 PT
Prior Industry Experience: . . . . Helpful

FINANCIAL:
Cash Investment: $20-30K
Total Investment: $45-55K
Fees: Franchise - $10K
  Royalty: 13.5%, Advert: 0%
Contract Periods (Yrs.): 10/10
Area Development Agreement: . .No
Sub-Franchise Contract: . . . . .No
Expand in Territory: . . . . . . .No
Passive Ownership: . . . Not Allowed
Encourage Conversions: . . . . .No
Franchisee Purchase(s) Required: .No

FRANCHISOR TRAINING/SUPPORT:
Financial Assistance Provided: . . .Yes(D)
Site Selection Assistance: . . . . .NA
Lease Negotiation Assistance: . . . .NA
Co-operative Advertising: . . . . . . .Yes
Training: . . . . 2 Wks. Headquarters
. . . .
On-Going Support: . . . A,C,D,E,F,G,H,I
Full-Time Franchisor Support Staff: . .235
EXPANSION PLANS:
  US: . . . . Midwest, Northeast
  Canada - No, ... Overseas - No

SUPPLEMENTAL LISTING OF FRANCHISORS

AM/PM MINI-MARKET . . . . 515 S. Flower St., Los Angeles CA 90071
CONVENIENT FOOD MART . . . . 9701 W. Higgins Rd., # 850, Rosemont IL 60018
CUMBERLAND DRUGS . . . . 4700 Prince of Wales, Montreal PQ H4B2L3 CAN
DAIRY MART CONVENIENCE STORES . . . . 240 South Rd., Enfield CT 06082
DRUG CASTLE FRANCHISES . . . . 810 East High St., Springfield OH 45505
FLYING J TRAVEL PLAZA . . . . P. O. Box 678, Brigham City UT 84302
FOOD GIANT . . . . 170 Attwell Dr., Rexdale ON M9W6A3 CAN
FOOD-N-FUEL . . . . 8500 Lexington Ave. N, Circle Pines MN 55014
GATEWAY CIGAR STORES . . . . 30 E. Beavercreek Rd., # 206, Richmond Hill ON L4B1J2 CAN
GIANT TIGER STORES . . . . .98 George St., Ottawa ON K1N5W2 CAN
HASTY MARKET . . . . 22 St. Clair Ave. E., # 201, Toronto ON M4T2S5 CAN
HEALTH MART . . . . .1220 Senlac Dr., Carrollton TX 75006
IGA . . . . 170 Attwell Dr., Rexdale ON M9W6A3 CAN
IGA CANADA LIMITED . . . . 170 Attwell Dr., Rexdale ON M9W6A3 CAN
J.T.'S GENERAL STORE . . . . .511 Lake Zurich Rd., Barrington IL 60010
JUG CITY . . . . 6355 Viscount Rd., Mississauga ON L4V1W2 CAN
MAC'S CONVENIENCE STORES . . . . 10 Commander Blvd., Scarborough ON M1S3T2 CAN
MAYFAIR . . . . 170 Attwell Dr., Rexdale ON M9W6A3 CAN
NEXT DOOR FOOD STORES . . . . 5115 E. Pickard St., Mt. Pleasant MI 48858
OPEN PANTRY FOOD MARTS . . . . 817 S. Main St., Racine WI 53403
PROVI-SOIR . . . . 3100 Cote Vertu, # 560, Ville St. Laurent PQ H4R2J8 CAN
RED ROOSTER . . . . 170 Attwell Dr., Rexdale ON M9W6A3 CAN
SAV-A-STEP FOOD MART . . . . 4165 Roosevelt Ave., Louisville KY 40213
SHELL PRODUCTS CANADA . . . . # 708 - 1155 W. Pender St., Vancouver BC V6E2P4 CAN
SHOPPERS DRUG MART . . . . .225 Yorkland Blvd., Willowdale ON M2J4Y7 CAN
SUPER VALU STORES . . . . .P.O. Box 990, Minneapolis MN 55440
TRAILSIDE GENERAL STORE . . . . Box 667, Centerville UT 84014
WINKS CONVENIENCE STORES . . . . 5938 Ambler Dr., Mississauga ON L4W2N3 CAN

CHAPTER 14

CHILD DEVELOPMENT / EDUCATION / PRODUCTS

A CHOICE NANNY

8950 Rte. 108, Gorman Plaza, # 217
Columbia, MD 21045
TEL: (301) 730-2356
FAX: (301) 964-5726
Ms. Tess Granlund, Asst. Dir. Fran.

Buy into the Baby Boom! Own your own child-care referral service. Recruit, screen and train private nannies for working parents seeking quality in-home care. Franchise fee includes computer system, classroom and on-the-job training, advertising and public relations package, plus on-going support.

HISTORY:	. . . . IFA
Established in 1983;	. . 1st Franchised in 1988
Company-Owned Units (As of 12/1/1989):	. .1
Franchised Units (12/1/1989):	 21
Total Units (12/1/1989):	 22
Distribution:	US-22;Can-0;Overseas-0
North America:	. . . . 5 States
Concentration: . . .	6 in MD, 5 in VA, 4 in PA
Registered:	. . . . FL,MD,VA

. . . .

Average # of Employees: . . . . . . 1 FT, 1 PT
Prior Industry Experience: . . . . Helpful

FINANCIAL:
Cash Investment: $34-38K
Total Investment: $34-38K
Fees: Franchise - $21.9K
   Royalty: 10%, Advert: 3%
Contract Periods (Yrs.): 10/10
Area Development Agreement: . .No
Sub-Franchise Contract: . . . . . Yes
Expand in Territory: . . . . . . .No
Passive Ownership: . . . Discouraged
Encourage Conversions: . . . . . Yes
Franchisee Purchase(s) Required: .No

FRANCHISOR TRAINING/SUPPORT:
Financial Assistance Provided: . . . . .No
Site Selection Assistance: . . . . . . .Yes
Lease Negotiation Assistance: . . . . .Yes
Co-operative Advertising: . . . . .Yes
Training: . . . . 1 Wk. HQ Before Opening,
   . . . 1 Wk. HQ After Opening - 2 People
On-Going Support: . . . . . A,b,C,D,e,G,h
Full-Time Franchisor Support Staff: . . . .
EXPANSION PLANS:
US: . . . . East Coast & Mid-west
  Canada - Yes, ...Overseas - Yes

BELLINI JUVENILE DESIGNER FURNITURE
15 Engle St., # 304
Englewood, NJ 07631
TEL: (800) 332-2229 (201) 871-0370
FAX: (201) 871-7168
Mr. John Sterns, Sales Manager

BELLINI is an up-scale, one-stop baby boutique, offering exclusive, European-designed furniture and accessories. Each store is staffed with knowledgeable personnel to aid parents in selecting all their nursery needs.

HISTORY: . . . . IFA	FINANCIAL:	FRANCHISOR TRAINING/SUPPORT:
Established in 1982; . . 1st Franchised in 1982	Cash Investment: $50K	Financial Assistance Provided: . . . Yes(I)
Company-Owned Units (As of 12/1/1989): . .5	Total Investment: $130-150K	Site Selection Assistance: . . . . .Yes
Franchised Units (12/1/1989): 49	Fees: Franchise - $25K	Lease Negotiation Assistance: . . . . .Yes
Total Units (12/1/1989): 54	Royalty: 5%, Advert: 0%	Co-operative Advertising: . . . . .Yes
Distribution: US-54;Can-0;Overseas-0	Contract Periods (Yrs.): 10/10	Training: . . . . .2 Wks. Cedarhurst, NY or
North America: . . . . 16 States	Area Development Agreement: . .No	. . . . Sherman Oaks, CA, 1 Wk. On-site
Concentration: . . . 13 in CA, 8 in NY, 4 in NJ	Sub-Franchise Contract:	On-Going Support: . . . . . . C,D,E,G,H,I
Registered: . . CA,FL,IL,MD,MI,MN,NY,VA	Expand in Territory: . . . . Yes	Full-Time Franchisor Support Staff: . . .7
. . . . WA	Passive Ownership: . . . Discouraged	EXPANSION PLANS:
Average # of Employees: . . . . . . 2 FT, 1 PT	Encourage Conversions: . . . . .No	US: . . . . All US
Prior Industry Experience: . . . . Helpful	Franchisee Purchase(s) Required: Yes	Canada - Yes, . . . Overseas - Yes

BOOMER CLUB, THE

57 King St. W.
Kitchener, ON N2G1A1 CAN
TEL: (519) 576-9300
FAX: (519) 576-7229
Mr. Doug Marr, President

THE BOOMER CLUB carries children's and youth's activewear up to size 20.

HISTORY:	FINANCIAL:	FRANCHISOR TRAINING/SUPPORT:
Established in 1986; . . 1st Franchised in 1986	Cash Investment: . . . .$NA	Financial Assistance Provided: . . . . . No
Company-Owned Units (As of 12/1/1989): . 14	Total Investment: . . . .$NA	Site Selection Assistance: . . . . . . .Yes
Franchised Units (12/1/1989): 6	Fees: Franchise - . . . .$NA	Lease Negotiation Assistance: . . . .Yes
Total Units (12/1/1989): 20	Royalty: 3%, Advert: 1%	Co-operative Advertising: . . . . . . .Yes
Distribution: US-0;Can-20;Overseas-0	Contract Periods (Yrs.): 10/5	Training: . . . . Varies
North America: . . . . 2 Provinces	Area Development Agreement: . Yes	
Concentration: . . . . 19 in ON, 1 in AB	Sub-Franchise Contract: . . . . .No	On-Going Support: . . . . d,e,H,I
Registered: . . . . AB	Expand in Territory: . . . . Yes	Full-Time Franchisor Support Staff: . . 14
. . . .	Passive Ownership: . . . Discouraged	EXPANSION PLANS:
Average # of Employees: . . . . . . 1 FT, 3 PT	Encourage Conversions: . . . . . NA	US: . . . . No
Prior Industry Experience: . . . . Helpful	Franchisee Purchase(s) Required: .No	Canada - Yes, ...Overseas - No

COMPUTERTOTS

P.O. Box 408
Great Falls, VA 22066
TEL: (703) 759-2556
FAX: (703) 759-1938
Ms. Karen Marshall, President

COMPUTERTOTS offers unique, discovery-oriented computer classes for children ages 3-8. These classes are offered on-site at day care centers and private pre-schools. This home-managed opportunity is targeted toward individuals wishing to offer an exciting educational experience while maintaining flexibility and freedom.

HISTORY: . . . . IFA/WIF	FINANCIAL:	FRANCHISOR TRAINING/SUPPORT:
Established in 1983; . . 1st Franchised in 1988	Cash Investment: $12-20K	Financial Assistance Provided: . . . . . No
Company-Owned Units (As of 12/1/1989): . .1	Total Investment: $12-20K	Site Selection Assistance: · . . . . . . .NA
Franchised Units (12/1/1989): 8	Fees: Franchise - $12K	Lease Negotiation Assistance: . . . .NA
Total Units (12/1/1989): 9	Royalty: 6%, Advert: 1%	Co-operative Advertising: . . . . . . .NA
Distribution: US-9;Can-0;Overseas-0	Contract Periods (Yrs.): 5/5	Training: . . . . . . 3-5 Days Headquarters
North America: . . . . 5 States	Area Development Agreement: Yes/5	
Concentration: . . . 3 in MD, 2 in GA, 1 in NC	Sub-Franchise Contract: . . . . .No	On-Going Support: . . . . . .B,C,D,G,H,I
Registered: . . . . FL,MD	Expand in Territory: . . . . Yes	Full-Time Franchisor Support Staff: . . .4
. . . .	Passive Ownership: . . . Discouraged	EXPANSION PLANS:
Average # of Employees: . . . . . . 1 FT, 5 PT	Encourage Conversions:	US: . . . . All US
Prior Industry Experience: . . . . Helpful	Franchisee Purchase(s) Required: .No	Canada - No, ...Overseas - No

FIT BY FIVE

1606 Penfield Rd.
Rochester, NY 14625
TEL: (716) 586-7980
FAX:
Ms. Betty Perkins-Carpenter, Pres.

FIT BY FIVE is an athletically-oriented pre-school program for children 2 1/2 to 5 years. It is the alternative to nursery school. Children are exposed to sport activities, and all pre-school readiness skills are taught through sports, games, activities and movement that enhance physical, emotional and social development.

HISTORY: . . . .
Established in 1969; . . 1st Franchised in 1984
Company-Owned Units (As of 12/1/1989): . .1
Franchised Units (12/1/1989): 4
Total Units (12/1/1989): 5
Distribution: US-5;Can-0;Overseas-0
North America: . . . . 3 States
Concentration: . . . 2 in NY, 2 in MD, 1 in IL
Registered: . . . . MD,NY
. . . .
Average # of Employees: . . . . . . 1 FT, 5 PT
Prior Industry Experience: . . . . . . Helpful

FINANCIAL:
Cash Investment: $25K
Total Investment: $40-46K
Fees: Franchise - $15K
Royalty: 2%, Advert: 0%
Contract Periods (Yrs.): 10/10
Area Development Agreement: Yes/5
Sub-Franchise Contract: . . . . . .No
Expand in Territory: . . . . Yes
Passive Ownership: . . . Discouraged
Encourage Conversions: . . . . .No
Franchisee Purchase(s) Required: Yes

FRANCHISOR TRAINING/SUPPORT:
Financial Assistance Provided: . . . . .No
Site Selection Assistance: . . . . . . .Yes
Lease Negotiation Assistance: . . . .Yes
Co-operative Advertising: . . . . . . .Yes
Training: . . . . . . 1-2 Wks. Headquarters
. . . .
On-Going Support: . . . . . . .C,D,E,G,H
Full-Time Franchisor Support Staff: . . 16
EXPANSION PLANS:
US: . . . . Northeast, SW and Midwest
Canada - No, ...Overseas - No

GODDARD EARLY LEARNING CENTER

381 Brooks Rd.
King of Prussia, PA 19406
TEL: (215) 265-5015 C
FAX: (215) 337-6113
Ms. Jill Panetta, Fran. Admin.

GODDARD EARLY LEARNING CENTERS has begun to franchise a chain of high-quality child care facilities to meet one of the most challenging problems of the 1990's. The same expertise that has made MAACO a giant in the franchising world is being combined with experts in the field of child care to search for a corps of men and women with the skills and talents to build a child care chain with a competitive edge on other services throughout the country.

HISTORY: . . . . IFA
Established in 1986; . . 1st Franchised in 1988
Company-Owned Units (As of 12/1/1989): . .2
Franchised Units (12/1/1989): 3
Total Units (12/1/1989): 5
Distribution: US-5;Can-0;Overseas-0
North America: . . . . .1 State
Concentration: . . . . 5 in PA
Registered: . . . . MD,VA
. . . .
Average # of Employees: . . . . 10 FT
Prior Industry Experience: . . . . . . Helpful

FINANCIAL:
Cash Investment: $30-40K
Total Investment: $100-140K
Fees: Franchise - $25K
Royalty: 7%, Advert: 4%
Contract Periods (Yrs.): 15/5
Area Development Agreement: Yes/15
Sub-Franchise Contract: . . . . . .No
Expand in Territory: . . . . .No
Passive Ownership: . . . Not Allowed
Encourage Conversions: . . . . . Yes
Franchisee Purchase(s) Required: .No

FRANCHISOR TRAINING/SUPPORT:
Financial Assistance Provided: . . . Yes(I)
Site Selection Assistance: . . . . . . .Yes
Lease Negotiation Assistance: . . . .Yes
Co-operative Advertising: . . . . . . .Yes
Training: . . . . 3 Wks. Headquarters
. . . .
On-Going Support: . . A,B,C,D,E,F,G,H,I
Full-Time Franchisor Support Staff: . . . .
EXPANSION PLANS:
US: . . . . .Northeast and Southeast
Canada - No, ...Overseas - No

GYMBOREE

577 Airport Blvd., # 400
Burlingame, CA 94010
TEL: (415) 579-0600
FAX: (415) 579-1733
Mr. Bob Campbell, Dir. Fran. Sales

GYMBOREE, the world's largest development play program, offers weekly classes to parents and their children, aged 3 months through 4 years, on custom-designed equipment for infants, toddlers and pre-schoolers. The program is based on sensory integration theory, positive parenting, child development principles and the importance of play.

HISTORY: . . . . IFA
Established in 1976; . . 1st Franchised in 1986
Company-Owned Units (As of 12/1/1989): . .5
Franchised Units (12/1/1989): 369
Total Units (12/1/1989): 374
Distribution: . . . US-331;Can-13;Overseas-20
North America: . . . . 35 States, 3 Provinces
Concentration: . . . . .CA, NY, NJ
Registered: . . . CA,FL,HI,IL,IN,MD,MI,MN
. . . . NY,OR,RI,VA,WA,AB
Average # of Employees: . . . . . . 1 FT, 1 PT
Prior Industry Experience: . . . . Helpful

FINANCIAL:
Cash Investment: $30-45K
Total Investment: $30-45K
Fees: Franchise - $8-18K
Royalty: 6%, Advert: 1.8%
Contract Periods (Yrs.): . . . 10/10
Area Development Agreement: . Yes
Sub-Franchise Contract: . . . . Yes
Expand in Territory: . . . . . . .No
Passive Ownership: . . . Discouraged
Encourage Conversions: . . . . .No
Franchisee Purchase(s) Required: .No

FRANCHISOR TRAINING/SUPPORT:
Financial Assistance Provided: . . . . .No
Site Selection Assistance: . . . . . . .Yes
Lease Negotiation Assistance: . . . .No
Co-operative Advertising: . . . . . . .Yes
Training: . . . . 9 Days Headquarters
. . . .
On-Going Support: . . . . . B,C,D,F,G,h,I
Full-Time Franchisor Support Staff: . . .3
EXPANSION PLANS:
US: . . . . .All US
Canada - Yes, . . . Overseas - Yes

GYMSTERS

5468 Castle Glen Ave.
San Jose, CA 95129
TEL: (408) 996-8955
FAX:
Ms. Harli Rabow, President

GYMSTERS offers a physical education service to children from age 2 through junior high, which is delivered to them on site. GYMSTERS brings its own unique sports skills and motor development program to the child's school, utilizing specialized equipment and methods.

HISTORY:	FINANCIAL:	FRANCHISOR TRAINING/SUPPORT:
Established in 1980; . . 1st Franchised in 1983	Cash Investment: $13-15K	Financial Assistance Provided: . . . . . No
Company-Owned Units (As of 12/1/1989): . . .2	Total Investment: $13-15K	Site Selection Assistance: . . . . .Yes
Franchised Units (12/1/1989): 6	Fees: Franchise - $11K	Lease Negotiation Assistance: . . . . .Yes
Total Units (12/1/1989): 8	Royalty: 9%, Advert: 1%	Co-operative Advertising: . . . . .Yes
Distribution: US-8;Can-0;Overseas-0	Contract Periods (Yrs.): . . . 10/10	Training: . . . . 3 Days Headquarters,
North America: . . . . 2 States	Area Development Agreement: Yes/10	. . . . .3-5 Days Franchisee's Area
Concentration: . . . . 7 in CA, 1 in NV	Sub-Franchise Contract: . . . . .No	On-Going Support: . . .A,B,C,D,E,F,G,h,I
Registered: . . . . CA	Expand in Territory: . . . . . . Yes	Full-Time Franchisor Support Staff: . . .2
. . . .	Passive Ownership: . . . . . .Allowed	EXPANSION PLANS:
Average # of Employees: . . . . .1 FT	Encourage Conversions: . . . . NA	US: . . . . .All US
Prior Industry Experience: . . . . . . Helpful	Franchisee Purchase(s) Required: Yes	Canada - Yes, . . . Overseas - Yes

HAMMETT'S LEARNING WORLD

P.O. Box 9057, Hammett Place
Braintree, MA 02184
TEL: (800) 225-5467 (617) 848-1000
FAX: (617) 843-4901
Mr. Richard A. Krause, VP

HAMMETT'S LEARNING WORLD retail stores serve teachers, parents, businesses, hobbyists and "whiz kids" with educational products, games, toys and office and art supplies. The complete line includes 7,000 items of retail stock supported by a catalog offering 14,000 additional items.

HISTORY:	FINANCIAL:	FRANCHISOR TRAINING/SUPPORT:
Established in 1900; . . 1st Franchised in 1986	Cash Investment: $40-62K	Financial Assistance Provided: . . . . . No
Company-Owned Units (As of 12/1/1989): . 21	Total Investment: $121-189K	Site Selection Assistance: . . . . .Yes
Franchised Units (12/1/1989): 5	Fees: Franchise - $25K	Lease Negotiation Assistance: . . . . .Yes
Total Units (12/1/1989): 26	Royalty: 6%, Advert: 1%	Co-operative Advertising: . . . . .Yes
Distribution: US-26;Can-0;Overseas-0	Contract Periods (Yrs.): . . . 10/5/5	Training: . . . . .1 Wk. Headquarters,
North America: . . . . 10 States	Area Development Agreement: . .No	. . . . .1 Wk. Retail Store
Concentration: . . . 5 in NJ, 4 in MA, 4 in VA	Sub-Franchise Contract: . . . . .No	On-Going Support: . . . .B,C,D,E,F,G,H,I
Registered: . . . . FL,IL,IN,MI,NY	Expand in Territory: . . . . . . Yes	Full-Time Franchisor Support Staff: . . 13
. . . .	Passive Ownership: . . . Discouraged	EXPANSION PLANS:
Average # of Employees: . . . . 2 FT, 4-6 PT	Encourage Conversions: . . . . .No	US: . . . . . . Southeast & Midwest Only
Prior Industry Experience: . . . . . . Helpful	Franchisee Purchase(s) Required: Yes	Canada - No, ...Overseas - No

KINDERDANCE INTERNATIONAL

2150 Atlantic St., P. O. Box 510881
Melbourne Beach, FL 32951
TEL: (800) 666-1595 (407) 723-1595 C
FAX:
Mr. Bernard Friedman, VP

A unique educational dance and motor development program that increases pre-schoolers' perceptual motor skills, enhances psychomotor development, as well as expanding intellectual capacity. The program is designed specifically for boys and girls, 3-5 years of age and is taught in child care centers and other viable locations. The KINDERDANCE program is welcomed by children and parents, as well as owners and directors of child care centers.

HISTORY: . . . . .WIF	FINANCIAL:	FRANCHISOR TRAINING/SUPPORT:
Established in 1979; . . 1st Franchised in 1985	Cash Investment: $7K	Financial Assistance Provided: . . . . . No
Company-Owned Units (As of 12/1/1989): . .0	Total Investment: $7K	Site Selection Assistance: . . . . .NA
Franchised Units (12/1/1989): 19	Fees: Franchise - $5K	Lease Negotiation Assistance: . . . . .NA
Total Units (12/1/1989): 19	Royalty: 15%, Advert: 3%	Co-operative Advertising: . . . . .NA
Distribution: US-19;Can-0;Overseas-0	Contract Periods (Yrs.): . . . 10/10	Training: . . . . 7 Days Home Office
North America: . . . . 9 States	Area Development Agreement: . .No	. . . .
Concentration: . . . .6 in FL, 5 in TX, 2 in AZ	Sub-Franchise Contract: . . . . .No	On-Going Support: . . . . . .C,D,E,G,H,I
Registered: . . . . CA,FL,IL,IN,MI	Expand in Territory: . . . . . . Yes	Full-Time Franchisor Support Staff: . . .2
. . . .	Passive Ownership: . . . Discouraged	EXPANSION PLANS:
Average # of Employees: . . . . .1 FT	Encourage Conversions: . . . . .No	US: . . . . .All US
Prior Industry Experience: . . . . . . Helpful	Franchisee Purchase(s) Required: .No	Canada - Yes, ...Overseas - No

LOLLIPOP LANE PRE-SCHOOL AND CHILD CARE CENTERS

7031 E. Camelback Rd., # 379
Scottsdale, AZ 85251
TEL: (602) 423-0802
FAX: (602) 423-5142
Mr. Jerry Scali, President

Pre-schools and child care centers, specifically tailored to children 6 weeks of age to 5 years of age. Excellent kindergarten preparation curriculum. We do not run vans for after-school children, nor do we accept children older than 5 years of age. We stress lower staff/child ratios, manners, grooming, social graces, basic educational skills, computers and an emphasis on "care of the child."

HISTORY:	FINANCIAL: VSE-LLP	FRANCHISOR TRAINING/SUPPORT:
Established in 1981; . . 1st Franchised in 1987	Cash Investment: $70-100K	Financial Assistance Provided: . . . Yes(I)
Company-Owned Units (As of 12/1/1989): . .3	Total Investment: $70-100K	Site Selection Assistance: . . . . . . .Yes
Franchised Units (12/1/1989): 1	Fees: Franchise - $35K	Lease Negotiation Assistance: . . . . .Yes
Total Units (12/1/1989): 4	Royalty: 6%, Advert: 1%	Co-operative Advertising: . . . . . . .Yes
Distribution: US-4;Can-0;Overseas-0	Contract Periods (Yrs.): 10/10	Training: . . . . . 10 Days Phoenix, 5 Days
North America: . . . . 3 States	Area Development Agreement: Yes/10	. . . . . . .Pre-Opening School Location
Concentration: . . . 2 in AZ, 1 in CA, 1 in MO	Sub-Franchise Contract: . . . . . .No	On-Going Support: . . . . . b,C,D,E,G,h,I
Registered:	Expand in Territory: . . . . Yes	Full-Time Franchisor Support Staff: . . . 4
. . . .	Passive Ownership: . . . . . .Allowed	EXPANSION PLANS:
Average # of Employees: . . . . . . 6 FT, 6 PT	Encourage Conversions: . . . . Yes	US: . . . . .All US
Prior Industry Experience: . . . . Helpful	Franchisee Purchase(s) Required: .No	Canada - Yes, . . . Overseas - Yes

PEE WEE WORKOUT

5568A Bramble Ct.
Willoughby, OH 44094
TEL: (216) 946-7888
FAX:
Ms. Margi Carr, President

PEE WEE WORKOUT teaches healthy living to pre-schoolers. The 30-minute classes consist of 20 minutes of movement set to original music that covers all components of fitness with 10 minutes of a heart/anatomy/nutrition lesson. Trained instructors have weekly visits to day/pre-schools, athletic departments.

HISTORY:	FINANCIAL:	FRANCHISOR TRAINING/SUPPORT:
Established in 1986; . . 1st Franchised in 1988	Cash Investment: $1-2K	Financial Assistance Provided: . . . . .No
Company-Owned Units (As of 12/1/1989): . .1	Total Investment: $1-2K	Site Selection Assistance: . . . . .No
Franchised Units (12/1/1989): 17	Fees: Franchise - $750-1.5K	Lease Negotiation Assistance: . . . . .No
Total Units (12/1/1989): 18	Royalty: 10-20%, Advert: . . . 0%	Co-operative Advertising: . . . . .No
Distribution: US-18;Can-0;Overseas-0	Contract Periods (Yrs.): 5/3	Training: . . . . .Video Based
North America: . . . . .1 State	Area Development Agreement: .No	. . . .
Concentration: . . . . 18 in OH	Sub-Franchise Contract: . . . . . .No	On-Going Support: . . . . .G,I
Registered:	Expand in Territory: . . . . Yes	Full-Time Franchisor Support Staff: . . . 2
. . . .	Passive Ownership: . . . Discouraged	EXPANSION PLANS:
Average # of Employees: . . . . .1 FT	Encourage Conversions:	US: . . . . .All US
Prior Industry Experience: . . . . Helpful	Franchisee Purchase(s) Required: Yes	Canada - Yes, . . . Overseas - Yes

PLAYORENA

125 Mineola Ave.
Rosyln Heights, NY 11577
TEL: (516) 621-7529
FAX:
Mr. Fred Jaroslow, EVP

PLAYORENA is a recreational and exercise program for children 3 months - 4 years old who attend weekly sessions with a parent. Activities and equipment are custom-designed and time-tested for the rapidly-shifting stages of motor development. Program is based on learning through natural play.

HISTORY:	FINANCIAL:	FRANCHISOR TRAINING/SUPPORT:
Established in 1981; . . 1st Franchised in 1984	Cash Investment: $25-30K	Financial Assistance Provided: . . . . .NA
Company-Owned Units (As of 12/1/1989): . 38	Total Investment: $25-30K	Site Selection Assistance: . . . . . . .Yes
Franchised Units (12/1/1989): 21	Fees: Franchise - $7-14K	Lease Negotiation Assistance: . . . . .Yes
Total Units (12/1/1989): 59	Royalty: 6%, Advert: 0%	Co-operative Advertising: . . . . .NA
Distribution: US-58;Can-0;Overseas-1	Contract Periods (Yrs.): 10/10	Training: . . . . 8 Days Headquarters
North America: . . . . 4 States	Area Development Agreement: .No	. . . .
Concentration: . . 34 in NY, 13 in NJ, 6 in CT	Sub-Franchise Contract: . . . . . Yes	On-Going Support: . . . . B,C,G,H,I
Registered: . . . . CA,IL,MD,NY,RI,VA	Expand in Territory: . . . . Yes	Full-Time Franchisor Support Staff: . . . 8
. . . .	Passive Ownership: . . . Not Allowed	EXPANSION PLANS:
Average # of Employees: . . . . .3 PT	Encourage Conversions: . . . . . NA	US: . . . . .All US
Prior Industry Experience: . . . . Helpful	Franchisee Purchase(s) Required: .No	Canada - Yes, . . . Overseas - Yes

PRIMARY PREP

1601 Forum Pl., # 802
W. Palm Beach, FL 33401
TEL: (800) 940-5900 (407) 640-5800
FAX: (407) 640-5804
Ms. Pauline A. McKee, President

Child care - pre-school. **PRIMARY PREP** is committed to a quality learning and educational environment. Our training director is Barbara Wallis, who holds a master's degree in early childhood curriculum. **PRIMARY PREP** provides a solid-growth curriculum, incorporating cognitive, physical, social and emotional development. Excellent training program.

HISTORY: . . . .
Established in 1984; . . 1st Franchised in 1984
Company-Owned Units (As of 12/1/1989): . .0
Franchised Units (12/1/1989): 14
Total Units (12/1/1989): 14
Distribution: US-14;Can-0;Overseas-0
North America: . . . . .1 State
Concentration: . . . . .14 in FL
Registered: . . . .
. . . .
Average # of Employees: . . . . Varies
Prior Industry Experience: . . . . . . Helpful

FINANCIAL:
Cash Investment: $64-74K
Total Investment: $64-74K
Fees: Franchise - $24.5K
Royalty: 4%, Advert: 1%
Contract Periods (Yrs.): 10/10
Area Development Agreement: Yes/10
Sub-Franchise Contract: . . . . . .No
Expand in Territory: . . . . Yes
Passive Ownership: . . . Discouraged
Encourage Conversions: . . . . . Yes
Franchisee Purchase(s) Required: .No

FRANCHISOR TRAINING/SUPPORT:
Financial Assistance Provided: . . . Yes(I)
Site Selection Assistance: . . . . . . .Yes
Lease Negotiation Assistance: . . . . .Yes
Co-operative Advertising: . . . . . . .Yes
Training: . . . . . Minimum 2-3 Wks. in FL
. . . . . . Depending Upon Experience
On-Going Support: . . . . . B,C,D,E,H,I
Full-Time Franchisor Support Staff: . . . 6
EXPANSION PLANS:
US: . . . . All US
Canada - Yes, . . . Overseas - Yes

SPORTASTIKS

2901 Watterson Ct.
Champaign, IL 61821
TEL: (217) 352-4269
FAX: (217) 352-4350
Mr. Jim Wilkins, VP

Children's fitness and gymnastics centers, for children aged 18 months through high school. No gymnastics experience required. We acquire existing gymnastics facilities for absentee investors or passive owners. SPORTASTIKS provides management for franchisees through personal visits, phone consultations, newsletters, daily reports faxed in, etc.

HISTORY: . . . .
Established in 1979; . . 1st Franchised in 1986
Company-Owned Units (As of 12/1/1989): . .2
Franchised Units (12/1/1989): 14
Total Units (12/1/1989): 16
Distribution: US-16;Can-0;Overseas-0
North America: . . . . 7 States
Concentration: . . . .5 in IL, 3 in WA, 3 in SC
Registered: . . . . .IL,IN,WA
. . . .
Average # of Employees: . . . . . .2 FT, 10 PT
Prior Industry Experience: . . . . . . Helpful

FINANCIAL:
Cash Investment: $30-40K
Total Investment: $130-180K
Fees: Franchise - $25K
Royalty: 6.5%, Advert: 2%
Contract Periods (Yrs.): 5/5/5
Area Development Agreement: . .No
Sub-Franchise Contract: . . . . . .No
Expand in Territory: . . . . Yes
Passive Ownership: . . . . . .Allowed
Encourage Conversions: . . . . . Yes
Franchisee Purchase(s) Required: Yes

FRANCHISOR TRAINING/SUPPORT:
Financial Assistance Provided: . . . . .NA
Site Selection Assistance: . . . . . . .Yes
Lease Negotiation Assistance: . . . . .Yes
Co-operative Advertising: . . . .
Training: . . . . .5-7 Days at Either
. . . . .Headquarters or On-site
On-Going Support: . . . . a,B,C,D,E,G,H
Full-Time Franchisor Support Staff: . . . 9
EXPANSION PLANS:
US: . . . . . Northwest, Southeast, SW
Canada - No, ...Overseas - No

WEE WATCH PRIVATE HOME DAY CARE

25 Valleywood Dr.
Markham, ON L3R5L9 CAN
TEL: (416) 479-4274 C
FAX:
Mr. Terry Fullerton, VP

WEE WATCH is a private, home day care agency, catering to children aged 6 weeks and older. Full-time and part-time. The care takes place in fully-inspected home containing a trained provider.

HISTORY: . . . .
Established in 1984; . . 1st Franchised in 1986
Company-Owned Units (As of 12/1/1989): . .0
Franchised Units (12/1/1989): 24
Total Units (12/1/1989): 24
Distribution: US-0;Can-24;Overseas-0
North America: . . . . 2 Provinces
Concentration: . . . . 22 in ON, 2 in BC
Registered: . . . .
. . . .
Average # of Employees: . . . . . . 1 FT, 1 PT
Prior Industry Experience: . . . . Helpful

FINANCIAL:
Cash Investment: $15K
Total Investment: $15K
Fees: Franchise - $5K
Royalty: 6%, Advert: 2%
Contract Periods (Yrs.): 25/5
Area Development Agreement: . .No
Sub-Franchise Contract: . . . . . .No
Expand in Territory: . . . . .No
Passive Ownership: . . . Not Allowed
Encourage Conversions: . . . . . Yes
Franchisee Purchase(s) Required: .No

FRANCHISOR TRAINING/SUPPORT:
Financial Assistance Provided: . . . . . No
Site Selection Assistance: . . . . . . .NA
Lease Negotiation Assistance: . . . . .NA
Co-operative Advertising: . . . . . . .Yes
Training: . . . . 3 Days Headquarters
. . . .
On-Going Support: . . . . . . B,C,D,G,h,I
Full-Time Franchisor Support Staff: . . . 5
EXPANSION PLANS:
US: . . . . All US
Canada - Yes, ...Overseas - No

YOUTHLAND ACADEMY

4392 Windsor Oaks Circle
Marietta, GA 30066
TEL: (404) 591-1110
FAX: (404) 924-8672
Ms. Jan Schmitt, CEO

YOUTHLAND ACADEMY is a full-service child care facility. Children from ages 6 weeks through 12 years receive the ultimate in quality care. State-of-the-art programs are provided for stimulation, education and socialization. Additionally, premier locations are available to the right franchisee.

HISTORY: . . . . IFA	FINANCIAL:	FRANCHISOR TRAINING/SUPPORT:
Established in 1982; . . 1st Franchised in 1985	Cash Investment: $50-80K	Financial Assistance Provided: . . . . . No
Company-Owned Units (As of 12/1/1989): . .1	Total Investment: $65K	Site Selection Assistance: . . . . . . .Yes
Franchised Units (12/1/1989): 13	Fees: Franchise - $27.5K	Lease Negotiation Assistance: . . . . .Yes
Total Units (12/1/1989): 14	Royalty: 5%, Advert: $250	Co-operative Advertising: . . . . .Yes
Distribution: US-14;Can-0;Overseas-0	Contract Periods (Yrs.): 10/5	Training: . . . . . .10 Days Cincinnati, OH
North America: . . . . 4 States	Area Development Agreement: . Yes	. . . .
Concentration: . . . 9 in OH, 2 in FL, 2 in GA	Sub-Franchise Contract: . . . . . Yes	On-Going Support: . . . . .b,C,D,E,F,G,H
Registered: . . . . FL,IL,IN,VA	Expand in Territory: . . . . Yes	Full-Time Franchisor Support Staff: . . .5
. . . .	Passive Ownership: . . . Discouraged	EXPANSION PLANS:
Average # of Employees: . . . . . .15 FT, 5 PT	Encourage Conversions:	US: . . . . All US
Prior Industry Experience: . . . . Helpful	Franchisee Purchase(s) Required: .No	Canada - Yes, ...Overseas - Yes

SUPPLEMENTAL LISTING OF FRANCHISORS

4 BABYS ONLY . . . . 16800 E. Gale Blvd., City of Industry CA 91745
ANY SITUATION .4920 City Avenue, Philadelphia PA 19131
BABY NEWS . . . . 23521 Foley St., Hayward CA 94545
BABY TOYTOWN . . . . 16800 E. Gale Blvd., City of Industry CA 91745
BABY'S ROOM USA . . . . 752 N. Larch Ave, Elmhurst IL 60126
CAROUSEL SYSTEMS . . . . 381 Brooks Rd., King of Prussia PA 19406
CHAD'S RAINBOW . . . . 2801 Apple Valley, Garland TX 75043
CHILDREN'S ORCHARD .253 Low St., Newburyport MA 01950
LAURETT'S JUST 4 KIDS . . . . 6439 Ridge Manor Ave., San Diego CA 92120
LEWIS OF LONDON . . . . 25 Power Dr., Hauppage NY 11788
LI'L GUYS 'N' GALS DAYCARE . . . . 10850 N. 90th St., Scottsdale AZ 85260
MASTERMIND EDUCATIONAL TECHNOLOGIES . . . 465 Milner Ave., # 7, Scarborough ON M1B2K4   CAN
PLAYFUL PARENTING . . . . 145 Maple Dr., New Holland PA 17557
PRIMROSE SCHOOLS . . . . 5131 Roswell Rd., NE, Marietta GA 30062
QUINBY'S FOR THE CURIOUS CHILD . . . . 425 Brannan St., # 200, San Francisco CA 94107
STORK NEWS . . . . 5075 Morgantown Rd., # 12A, Fayetteville NC 28304
SUPERCLUB SPORTS & FITNESS FOR KIDS . . . . . . .Reflections II, # 117, Virginia Beach VA 23452
TEGELER TIME DAY CARE . . . . 10 Forbes Rd., Braintree MA 02184
TOYBRARY, THE LENDING LIBRARY OF TOYS . . . . Box 583, Main St., Norwich VT 05055
WONDERS OF WISDOM CHILDREN'S CENTER .3114 Golansky Blvd., # 201, Prince William VA 22192

CHAPTER 15

EDUCATION / PERSONAL
DEVELOPMENT / TRAINING

ACADEMY OF LEARNING

300 John St., # 504
Thornhill, ON L3T5W4 CAN
TEL: (416) 886-8973 C
FAX: (416) 886-8591
Mr. Max Lacob, President

ACADEMY OF LEARNING Skills Development Centres offer computer, office and secretarial training courses. Our centres use unique audio/visual methods unmatched by others in the industry. We offer the most flexible form of self-paced learning on the market. Students work at their own time and pace and receive recognized certificates of achievement upon successful completion of their program.

HISTORY: . . . .
Established in 1986; . . 1st Franchised in 1987
Company-Owned Units (As of 12/1/1989): . .1
Franchised Units (12/1/1989): 21
Total Units (12/1/1989): 22
Distribution: US-0;Can-22;Overseas-0
   North America: . . . . 2 Provinces
   Concentration: . . . . 21 in ON, 1 in NB
Registered: . . . .
. . . .
Average # of Employees: . . . . . . 1 FT, 1 PT
Prior Industry Experience: . . . . Helpful

FINANCIAL:
Cash Investment: $20-30K
Total Investment: $30-75K
Fees: Franchise - $20-30K
   Royalty: None, Advert: 4%
Contract Periods (Yrs.): 10/10
Area Development Agreement: . .No
Sub-Franchise Contract: . . . . . .No
Expand in Territory: . . . . Yes
Passive Ownership: . . . Discouraged
Encourage Conversions: . . . . . NA
Franchisee Purchase(s) Required: Yes

FRANCHISOR TRAINING/SUPPORT:
Financial Assistance Provided: . . . Yes(I)
Site Selection Assistance: . . . . .Yes
Lease Negotiation Assistance: . . . . .Yes
Co-operative Advertising: . . . . .Yes
Training: . . . . .As Required Head Office,
. . . . .Other Centres & on-site
On-Going Support: . . . A,B,C,D,E,G,H,I
Full-Time Franchisor Support Staff: . . . 7
EXPANSION PLANS:
   US: . . . . .No
   Canada - Yes, ... Overseas - No

EDUCATIONAL PRODUCTS & SERVICES

	1988	1989	1990	Percentage Change 1988-1989	Percentage Change 1989-1990
Number of Establishments:					
Company–Owned	656	601	664	–8.4%	10.5%
Franchisee–Owned	10,914	11,291	12,601	3.5%	11.6%
Total	11,570	11,892	13,265	2.8%	11.5%
% of Total Establishments:					
Company–Owned	5.7%	5.1%	5.0%		
Franchisee–Owned	94.3%	94.9%	95.0%		
Total	100.0%	100.0%	100.0%		
Annual Sales ($000):					
Company–Owned	$471,438	$539,760	$617,793	14.5%	14.5%
Franchisee–Owned	1,228,930	1,385,551	1,704,652	12.7%	23.0%
Total	1,700,368	1,925,311	2,322,445	13.2%	20.6%
% of Total Sales:					
Company–Owned	27.7%	28.0%	26.6%		
Franchisee–Owned	72.3%	72.0%	73.4%		
Total	100.0%	100.0%	100.0%		
Average Sales Per Unit ($000):					
Company–Owned	$719	$898	$930	25.0%	3.6%
Franchisee–Owned	113	123	135	9.0%	10.2%
Total	147	162	175	10.2%	8.1%
Sales Ratio	638.2%	731.9%	687.8%		

	1st Quartile	Median	4th Quartile
Average 1988 Total Investment:			
Company–Owned	$25,750	$80,000	$187,500
Franchisee–Owned	25,000	50,000	100,000
Single Unit Franchise Fee	$12,000	$18,750	$26,125
Multiple Unit Franchise Fee	N. A.	20,375	N. A.
Franchisee Start–up Cost	15,000	25,000	75,000

	1988	Employees/Unit	Sales/Employee
Employment:			
Company–Owned	19,209	29.3	$24,543
Franchisee–Owned	41,714	3.8	29,461
Total	60,923	5.3	27,910
Employee Performance Ratios		766.1%	83.3%

Source: Franchising In The Economy, 1988 – 1990, IFA Education Foundation & Horwath International, Published January, 1990.

1) 1989 and 1990 data were estimated by respondents.

2) Includes diet and weight control centers, learning centers (especially for children), trade schools and day–care centers.

AUSTRALIAN/AMERICAN LEARNING ACADEMY

1661 E. Camelback Rd., # 118
Phoenix, AZ 85016
TEL: (602) 263-1225
FAX:
Mr. Kenneth Hollowell, Mktg. Dir.

THE AUSTRALIAN/AMERICAN LEARNING ACADEMY is a business establishment which will provide personnel skill training programs and workshop training programs in effective speed reading, memory and comprehension.

HISTORY:	FINANCIAL:	FRANCHISOR TRAINING/SUPPORT:
Established in 1989; . . 1st Franchised in 1989	Cash Investment: $10-15K	Financial Assistance Provided: . . . . .No
Company-Owned Units (As of 12/1/1989): . .0	Total Investment: $55-78K	Site Selection Assistance: . . . . . . .Yes
Franchised Units (12/1/1989): 1	Fees: Franchise - $15K	Lease Negotiation Assistance: . . . . .Yes
Total Units (12/1/1989): 1	Royalty: 6%, Advert: 2%	Co-operative Advertising: . . . . . . .Yes
Distribution: US-1;Can-0;Overseas-0	Contract Periods (Yrs.): 10/10	Training: . . . . 5 Days Headquarters
North America: . . . . .1 State	Area Development Agreement: . .No	. . . .
Concentration: . . . . 1 in AZ	Sub-Franchise Contract: . . . . .No	On-Going Support: . . . . B,C,D,E,F,G,h,I
Registered:	Expand in Territory: . . . . Yes	Full-Time Franchisor Support Staff: . . .2
. . . .	Passive Ownership: . . . Not Allowed	EXPANSION PLANS:
Average # of Employees: . . . . . . 1 FT, 2 PT	Encourage Conversions: . . . . .No	US: . . . . Southwest
Prior Industry Experience: . . . . Helpful	Franchisee Purchase(s) Required: Yes	Canada - Yes, . . . Overseas - Yes

BARBIZON SCHOOL

950 Third Ave.
New York, NY 10022
TEL: (212) 371-4300
FAX:
Mr. B. Wolff, President

Proprietary, private schools of modeling, personal improvement and related creative arts.

HISTORY: . . . . .IFA	FINANCIAL:	FRANCHISOR TRAINING/SUPPORT:
Established in 1939; . . 1st Franchised in 1968	Cash Investment: $35-45K	Financial Assistance Provided: . . .Yes(D)
Company-Owned Units (As of 12/1/1989): . .0	Total Investment: $60K	Site Selection Assistance: . . . . . . .Yes
Franchised Units (12/1/1989): 96	Fees: Franchise - $19-35K	Lease Negotiation Assistance: . . . . .Yes
Total Units (12/1/1989): 96	Royalty: 7.5%, Advert: 2%	Co-operative Advertising: . . . . . . .NA
Distribution: US-90;Can-2;Overseas-4	Contract Periods (Yrs.): 10	Training: . . . . .Continuous Training
North America: . . . . 40 States	Area Development Agreement: . .No	. . . .
Concentration: . . . 11 in CA, 7 in NY, 6 in FL	Sub-Franchise Contract: . . . . .No	On-Going Support: . . . . .C,D,G,H
Registered: . . . . .CA,IL,NY	Expand in Territory: . . . . Yes	Full-Time Franchisor Support Staff: . . 11
. . . .	Passive Ownership: . . . Discouraged	EXPANSION PLANS:
Average # of Employees: . . . . . .5 FT, 10 PT	Encourage Conversions: . . . . .No	US: . . . . .All US
Prior Industry Experience: . . . . Helpful	Franchisee Purchase(s) Required: .No	Canada - Yes, . . . Overseas - Yes

BUTLER LEARNING SYSTEMS

1325 W. Dorothy Ln.
Dayton, OH 45409
TEL: (513) 298-7462
FAX:
Mr. Don Butler, President

Choose from 25 proven audio-visual, multi-media, training programs for managers, supervisors, sales professionals and workers. Sell programs and seminars to business, industry, banks, hospitals and public sector. Supplement consulting or build a business. Training available.

HISTORY:	FINANCIAL:	FRANCHISOR TRAINING/SUPPORT:
Established in 1959; . . 1st Franchised in 1977	Cash Investment: $10K	Financial Assistance Provided: . . . . .No
Company-Owned Units (As of 12/1/1989): . .1	Total Investment: $15K	Site Selection Assistance: . . . . . . .NA
Franchised Units (12/1/1989): 54	Fees: Franchise - $500	Lease Negotiation Assistance: . . . . .NA
Total Units (12/1/1989): 55	Royalty: 10%, Advert: 0%	Co-operative Advertising: . . . . . . .No
Distribution: US-42;Can-7;Overseas-6	Contract Periods (Yrs.): . . . . 1/Inf.	Training: . . . . . 1 Wk. HQ, Yearly at HQ
North America: . . . . 21 States, 6 Provinces	Area Development Agreement: . .No	. . . .
Concentration: . . . . 5 in OH, 3 in CA	Sub-Franchise Contract: . . . . .No	On-Going Support: . . . . .D,G,H
Registered:	Expand in Territory: . . . . Yes	Full-Time Franchisor Support Staff: . . 13
. . . .	Passive Ownership: . . . . . .Allowed	EXPANSION PLANS:
Average # of Employees: . . . . . . 1 FT, 1 PT	Encourage Conversions: . . . . Yes	US: . . . . .All US
Prior Industry Experience: . . . . Helpful	Franchisee Purchase(s) Required: Yes	Canada - Yes, . . . Overseas - Yes

COMPUCOLLEGE SCHOOL OF BUSINESS
5650 Yonge St., # 1400
North York, ON M2M4G3 CAN
TEL: (416) 733-4452
FAX:
Mr. J. Stressel, VP Mktg.

COMPUCOLLEGE BUSINESS SCHOOLS are private schools offering career training at the post-secondary school level. The courses range from general business and accounting to travel, fashion merchandising, etc. The curriculum gives each student the necessary knowledge to gain an entry-level position in his/her chosen field.

HISTORY: . . . . IFA
Established in 1976; . . 1st Franchised in 1983
Company-Owned Units (As of 12/1/1989): . . 4
Franchised Units (12/1/1989): 20
Total Units (12/1/1989): 24
Distribution: US-0;Can-24;Overseas-0
North America: . . . . 4 Provinces
Concentration: . . . 11 in ON, 5 in BC, 3 in SK
Registered: . . . .
. . . .
Average # of Employees: . . . . 10-15 FT, 4 PT
Prior Industry Experience: . . . . . . Helpful

FINANCIAL:
Cash Investment: $75-125K
Total Investment: $250-350K
Fees: Franchise - $75K
Royalty: 7%, Advert: . . . . . Var.
Contract Periods (Yrs.): 5-10
Area Development Agreement: Yes/Var
Sub-Franchise Contract: . . . . . Yes
Expand in Territory: . . . . Yes
Passive Ownership: . . . Not Allowed
Encourage Conversions: . . . . .No
Franchisee Purchase(s) Required: .No

FRANCHISOR TRAINING/SUPPORT:
Financial Assistance Provided: . . . . .No
Site Selection Assistance: . . . . . . .Yes
Lease Negotiation Assistance: . . . . .Yes
Co-operative Advertising: . . . . . . .Yes
Training: . . . . . . 2 Wks. Headquarters,
. . . . Varies On-site
On-Going Support: . . . . . . a,C,D,G,h,I
Full-Time Franchisor Support Staff: . . 15
EXPANSION PLANS:
US: . . . . .All US
Canada - Yes, . . . Overseas - Yes

CPA CLUB, THE
462 Stevens Ave., # 100
Solana Beach, CA 92075
TEL: (800) 622-8593 (619) 792-5556
FAX: (619) 792-9623
Mr. David P. Rhame, Dir. Franchises

THE CPA CLUB is designed to provide the franchisee with a unique networking system that will generate clients from the CPA community in a chosen territory. The franchisee must be a licensed financial consultant, such as a securities registered representative.

HISTORY: . . . .
Established in 1989; . . 1st Franchised in 1989
Company-Owned Units (As of 12/1/1989): . . 1
Franchised Units (12/1/1989): 17
Total Units (12/1/1989): 18
Distribution: US-18;Can-0;Overseas-0
North America: . . . . 14 States
Concentration: . . . 2 in AR, 2 in MS, 2 in TX
Registered: . . . . FL,IN,MI,ND,RI
. . . .
Average # of Employees: . . . . .2 PT
Prior Industry Experience: . . . . . .Necessary

FINANCIAL:
Cash Investment: $2.5-5K
Total Investment: $2.5-5K
Fees: Franchise - $2.5-4K
Royalty: 0%, Advert: 0%
Contract Periods (Yrs.): 2/2
Area Development Agreement: .No
Sub-Franchise Contract: . . . . .No
Expand in Territory: . . . . Yes
Passive Ownership: . . . Not Allowed
Encourage Conversions: . . . . NA
Franchisee Purchase(s) Required: Yes

FRANCHISOR TRAINING/SUPPORT:
Financial Assistance Provided: . . . . .No
Site Selection Assistance: . . . . . . .NA
Lease Negotiation Assistance: . . . . .NA
Co-operative Advertising: . . . . . . .NA
Training: . . . . Not Applicable
. . . .
On-Going Support: . . . . .G,h,I
Full-Time Franchisor Support Staff: . . . 5
EXPANSION PLANS:
US: . . . . All US Exc. Registration
Canada - No, ...Overseas - No

EXECUTRAIN
100 Abernathy Rd., # 400
Atlanta, GA 30328
TEL: (800) 843-6984 (404) 396-9200 C
FAX: (404) 698-9180
Mr. Tom Lang, Dir. Franchising

EXECUTRAIN, the nation's leading personal computer training franchise, offers exclusive franchise opportunities in the $47 billion training industry. EXECUTRAIN has trained well over 100,000 business people how to use Lotus 1-2-3 and other popular computer programs.

HISTORY: . . . .
Established in 1984; . . 1st Franchised in 1986
Company-Owned Units (As of 12/1/1989): . .2
Franchised Units (12/1/1989): 23
Total Units (12/1/1989): 25
Distribution: US-25;Can-0;Overseas-0
North America: . . . . 20 States
Concentration: . . . .3 in FL, 2 in TN, 2 in CA
Registered: . . . CA,FL,IL,IN,MD,MI,MN,NY
. . . . OR,RI,VA,WA,WI
Average # of Employees: . . . . .5 FT
Prior Industry Experience: . . . . . . Helpful

FINANCIAL:
Cash Investment: $50-60K
Total Investment: $100-150K
Fees: Franchise - $30K
Royalty: 6-9%, Advert: 1%
Contract Periods (Yrs.): 7/14
Area Development Agreement: .No
Sub-Franchise Contract: . . . . .No
Expand in Territory: . . . . Yes
Passive Ownership: . . . Not Allowed
Encourage Conversions: . . . . .No
Franchisee Purchase(s) Required: .No

FRANCHISOR TRAINING/SUPPORT:
Financial Assistance Provided: . . .Yes(D)
Site Selection Assistance: . . . . . . .Yes
Lease Negotiation Assistance: . . . . .Yes
Co-operative Advertising: . . . . . . .No
Training: . . . . . . 4 Wks. Headquarters,
. . . . 1 Wk. Franchise Location
On-Going Support: . . . A,B,C,D,E,G,H,I
Full-Time Franchisor Support Staff: . . 18
EXPANSION PLANS:
US: . . . . .All US
Canada - Yes, . . . Overseas - Yes

JOHN CASABLANCAS MODELING AND CAREER CENTER
111 E. 22nd St.
New York, NY 10010
TEL: (212) 420-0655
FAX:
Ms. Nita Boyle, Sales Mgr.

MMI franchises the JOHN CASABLANCAS MODELING & CAREER CENTERS. They offer a complete franchise package that includes course manuals, operations manuals, advertising and promotional materials and audio-visuals, on-going guidance and promotional/placement link with Elite, the world's leading model agency and its president, John Casablancas.

HISTORY: . . . .
Established in 1979;   . . 1st Franchised in 1979
Company-Owned Units (As of 12/1/1989):   . .0
Franchised Units (12/1/1989): 72
Total Units (12/1/1989): 72
Distribution: US-65;Can-5;Overseas-2
  North America: . . . . 32 States, 4 Provinces
  Concentration: . . . 7 in CA, 5 in FL, 4 in NY
Registered: . . . . .All
. . . .
Average # of Employees: . . . . . .6 FT, 25 PT
Prior Industry Experience: . . . . Helpful

FINANCIAL:
Cash Investment: $22-88K
Total Investment: $22-88K
Fees: Franchise - $6-27K
  Royalty: 7%, Advert: 3%
Contract Periods (Yrs.): 10/10
Area Development Agreement: . .No
Sub-Franchise Contract: . . . . . Yes
Expand in Territory: . . . . Yes
Passive Ownership: . . . . . .Allowed
Encourage Conversions: . . . . . Yes
Franchisee Purchase(s) Required: .No

FRANCHISOR TRAINING/SUPPORT:
Financial Assistance Provided: . . . . .No
Site Selection Assistance: . . . . . . .Yes
Lease Negotiation Assistance: . . . . .Yes
Co-operative Advertising: . . . . . . .Yes
Training: . . . . 3 Days Headquarters,
. . . . 2 Days Site
On-Going Support: . . A,B,C,D,E,F,G,H,I
Full-Time Franchisor Support Staff: . . 13
EXPANSION PLANS:
US: . . . . All US (Pending Regist.)
Canada - Yes,   . . . Overseas - Yes

JOHN ROBERT POWERS

175 Andover St.
Danvers, MA 01923
TEL: (800) 954 (508) 777-8677
FAX: (508) 777-7120
Mr. Richard Ciummei, President

Schools specializing in training for men and women in America and internationally. Specializing in the following areas: self-improvement modeling, executive grooming, drama, fashion merchandising, interior design, flight attendant, make-up artistry, pageant and convention training.

HISTORY: . . . . IFA
Established in 1923;   . . 1st Franchised in 1950
Company-Owned Units (As of 12/1/1989):   . .1
Franchised Units (12/1/1989): 64
Total Units (12/1/1989): 65
Distribution: US-54;Can-0;Overseas-11
  North America: . . . . 22 States
  Concentration: . . . 17 in CA, 4 in FL, 4 in OH
Registered: . . . . CA,FL,IL,MD,VA
. . . .
Average # of Employees: . . . . . . 4 FT, 10 PT
Prior Industry Experience: . . . . Helpful

FINANCIAL:
Cash Investment: $25-75K
Total Investment: $50-125K
Fees: Franchise - $15-30K
  Royalty: 10%, Advert: . . . . Flat
Contract Periods (Yrs.): 5/1
Area Development Agreement: . .No
Sub-Franchise Contract: . . . . . .No
Expand in Territory: . . . . Yes
Passive Ownership: . . . Discouraged
Encourage Conversions: . . . . . Yes
Franchisee Purchase(s) Required: Yes

FRANCHISOR TRAINING/SUPPORT:
Financial Assistance Provided: . . . . .No
Site Selection Assistance: . . . . . . .Yes
Lease Negotiation Assistance: . . . . .Yes
Co-operative Advertising: . . . . . . .Yes
Training: . . . . 3 Wks. Headquarters,
. . . . 2-3 Days On-site
On-Going Support: . . . . .B,C,D,E,G,H,I
Full-Time Franchisor Support Staff: . . . 5
EXPANSION PLANS:
US: . . . . .All US
Canada - Yes,   . . . Overseas - Yes

MAC TAY AQUATIC SCHOOLS

P. O. Box 753
Champaign, IL 61824
TEL: (217) 352-1561 C
FAX:
Ms. Karen N. Taylor, President

A full, comprehensive learn-to-swim program for all ages from infants to adults, as well as classes for the special populations. MAC TAY AQUATIC SCHOOL was designed by a professional educator, based upon flexible teaching techniques and a unique, self-motivated approach to swim instruction.

HISTORY: . . . .
Established in 1977;   . . 1st Franchised in 1985
Company-Owned Units (As of 12/1/1989):   . .1
Franchised Units (12/1/1989): 3
Total Units (12/1/1989): 4
Distribution: US-4;Can-0;Overseas-0
  North America: . . . . 2 States
  Concentration: . . . .
Registered: . . . . .IL,IN,MI,MN,WI
. . . .
Average # of Employees: . . . . . 2 FT, 6-8 PT
Prior Industry Experience: . . . . . . Necessary

FINANCIAL:
Cash Investment: $7.5K
Total Investment: $25.5-29.5K
Fees: Franchise - $20K
  Royalty: 5%, Advert: 2.5%
Contract Periods (Yrs.): 10/7
Area Development Agreement: . .No
Sub-Franchise Contract: . . . . .No
Expand in Territory: . . . . Yes
Passive Ownership: . . . Not Allowed
Encourage Conversions: . . . . .No
Franchisee Purchase(s) Required: .No

FRANCHISOR TRAINING/SUPPORT:
Financial Assistance Provided: . . .Yes(D)
Site Selection Assistance: . . . . . . .Yes
Lease Negotiation Assistance: . . . . .Yes
Co-operative Advertising: . . . . . . .Yes
Training: . . . . . 10-15 Days Headquarters
. . . .
On-Going Support: . . . . . . C,D,E,G,h,i
Full-Time Franchisor Support Staff: . . 16
EXPANSION PLANS:
US: . . . . Midwest
Canada - No, ...Overseas - No

PAT BOND SCHOOL OF CLIMBING

4703 Crofton Rd.
Louisville, KY 40207
TEL: (800) HRD-ROCK (502) 893-5436
FAX: (502) 893-3322
Ms. Lee Bond, VP Fran. Ops.

Former Mt. Everest team member and nationally-recognized free-climbing expert has developed unique course methods to teach young and old alike the thrills of recreational climbing - free-climbing, rope climbing, spelunking and free falling (bungee cord). Safety and proper technique are paramount. Novice to technical classes. Only highly-experienced and technically proficient franchisees/instructors selected. Unique ground-floor opportunity.

HISTORY: . . . .
Established in 1984; . . 1st Franchised in 1987
Company-Owned Units (As of 12/1/1989): . .2
Franchised Units (12/1/1989): 2
Total Units (12/1/1989): 4
Distribution: US-4;Can-0;Overseas-0
North America: . . . . 3 States
Concentration: . . 2 in KY, 1 in CO, 1 IN WA
Registered: . . . . CA,WA
. . . .
Average # of Employees: . . . . . . 1 FT, 1 PT
Prior Industry Experience: . . . . . . Required

FINANCIAL:
Cash Investment: $20-40K
Total Investment: $75-125K
Fees: Franchise - $22.5K
Royalty: 5%, Advert: 0%
Contract Periods (Yrs.): 5/5
Area Development Agreement: . .No
Sub-Franchise Contract: . . . . . .No
Expand in Territory: . . . . Yes
Passive Ownership: . . . Not Allowed
Encourage Conversions: . . . . . Yes
Franchisee Purchase(s) Required: .No

FRANCHISOR TRAINING/SUPPORT:
Financial Assistance Provided: . . . . .No
Site Selection Assistance: . . . . . . .Yes
Lease Negotiation Assistance: . . . . .Yes
Co-operative Advertising: . . . . . . .Yes
Training: . . . . 2 Wks. Headquarters,
. . . . 2 Wks. Mt. Ranier, 2 Wks. On-site
On-Going Support: . . . . B,D,F,G,i
Full-Time Franchisor Support Staff: . . . 5
EXPANSION PLANS:
US: . . . . . Areas with Mountain Ranges
Canada - Yes, ...Overseas - No

PRIORITY MANAGEMENT

500 - 108th Ave. NE
Bellevue, WA 98004
TEL: (800) 221-9031 (206) 454-7686
FAX: *367-4743
Mr. Jonathon Harshaw, VP Fran. Sales

Work with business professionals in the area of effective management skills. This includes meeting management, project planning, decision making, delegation, organization and communication skills development. Both corporate and individual clients are taught a unique process that includes workshops as well as one-on-one consultation.

HISTORY: . . . . IFA
Established in 1984; . . 1st Franchised in 1984
Company-Owned Units (As of 12/1/1989): . .0
Franchised Units (12/1/1989): 215
Total Units (12/1/1989): 215
Distribution: . . . US-131;Can-48;Overseas-36
North America: . . . . 33 States,10 Provinces
Concentration: . 15 in TX, 13 in CA, 10 in ON
Registered: . . . . .All
. . . .
Average # of Employees: . . . . . . 3 FT, 1 PT
Prior Industry Experience: . . . . . . Helpful

FINANCIAL:
Cash Investment: $30-35K
Total Investment: $30-45K
Fees: Franchise - $29.5K
Royalty: 9%, Advert: 1%
Contract Periods (Yrs.): 5/5
Area Development Agreement: . .No
Sub-Franchise Contract: . . . . . .No
Expand in Territory: . . . . Yes
Passive Ownership: . . . . . .Allowed
Encourage Conversions: . . . . NA
Franchisee Purchase(s) Required: .No

FRANCHISOR TRAINING/SUPPORT:
Financial Assistance Provided: . . . . . No
Site Selection Assistance: . . . . . . .NA
Lease Negotiation Assistance: . . . .NA
Co-operative Advertising: . . . . . . .NA
Training: . . . . . 7 Days Vancouver, BC, 4
. . . . . Days in Field, 5 Days in Region
On-Going Support: . . . . C,D,G,H,I
Full-Time Franchisor Support Staff: . . 28
EXPANSION PLANS:
US: . . . . .All US
Canada - No, ... Overseas - Yes

SANDLER SYSTEMS

10411 Stevenson Village
Stevenson, MD 21153
TEL: (800) 638-5686 *727-4754
FAX: (301) 358-7858
Mr. Bruce Seidman, VP

SANDLER SYSTEMS offers a unique style of sales and sales management training. With over 59 franchised offices, we deliver local and national, on-going sales training and reinforcement to small, medium and large companies. Built-in repeat business. SANDLER SELLING SYSTEMS is controversially opposite and uniquely more effective than traditional sales training methods.

HISTORY: . . . .
Established in 1967; . . 1st Franchised in 1983
Company-Owned Units (As of 12/1/1989): . .1
Franchised Units (12/1/1989): 59
Total Units (12/1/1989): 60
Distribution: US-60;Can-0;Overseas-0
North America: . . . . 22 States
Concentration: . . . 8 in NY, 7 in PA, 4 in MA
Registered: . . . CA,FL,IL,IN,MD,MI,MN,NY
. . . . VA
Average # of Employees: . . . . . . 2 FT, 5 PT
Prior Industry Experience: . . . . Helpful

FINANCIAL:
Cash Investment: $23K
Total Investment: $23K
Fees: Franchise - $23K
Royalty: $825/Mo., Advert: . . 0%
Contract Periods (Yrs.): 5/5
Area Development Agreement: . .No
Sub-Franchise Contract: . . . . . .No
Expand in Territory: . . . . Yes
Passive Ownership: . . . . . .Allowed
Encourage Conversions: . . . . NA
Franchisee Purchase(s) Required: Yes

FRANCHISOR TRAINING/SUPPORT:
Financial Assistance Provided: . . . . .Yes
Site Selection Assistance: . . . . . . .NA
Lease Negotiation Assistance: . . . .NA
Co-operative Advertising: . . . . . . .Yes
Training: . . . . . . 3 Days Each Quarter at
. . . . Headquarters
On-Going Support: . . . . C,D,G,H,I
Full-Time Franchisor Support Staff: . . 12
EXPANSION PLANS:
US: . . . . .All US
Canada - Yes, . . . Overseas - Yes

SYLVAN LEARNING CORP.

2400 Presidents Dr.
Montgomery, AL 36116
TEL: (800) 284-8214 (205) 277-7720
FAX: (205) 272-3719
Ms. Charlotte Bentley, Fran. Sales

Diagnostic and prescriptive reading, math, writing, college prep, algebra, study skills and readiness instruction for students (K-adult). All after-school teaching with 3-1 ratio, highly motivational with guaranteed success.

HISTORY: . . . . IFA
Established in 1979; . . 1st Franchised in 1980
Company-Owned Units (As of 12/1/1989): . 25
Franchised Units (12/1/1989): 452
Total Units (12/1/1989): 477
Distribution: US-449;Can-27;Overseas-1
North America: . . . . 45 States, 4 Provinces
Concentration: . .44 in CA, 44 in TX, 35 in FL
Registered: . . . . .All
. . . .
Average # of Employees: . . . . . . 2 FT, 4 PT
Prior Industry Experience: . . . . Helpful

FINANCIAL: NASD-KIND
Cash Investment: $25-70K
Total Investment: $56-115K
Fees: Franchise - $19.5-35K
Royalty: 8-10%, Advert: . . . 1.5%
Contract Periods (Yrs.): . . . 10/10
Area Development Agreement: . .No
Sub-Franchise Contract: . . . . .No
Expand in Territory: . . . . Yes
Passive Ownership: . . . . . .Allowed
Encourage Conversions: . . . . Yes
Franchisee Purchase(s) Required: Yes

FRANCHISOR TRAINING/SUPPORT:
Financial Assistance Provided: . . .Yes(D)
Site Selection Assistance: . . . . .Yes
Lease Negotiation Assistance: . . . . .Yes
Co-operative Advertising: . . . . .Yes
Training: . . . . 2 Wks. Headquarters
. . . .
On-Going Support: . . .A,B,C,d,E,G,H,h,I
Full-Time Franchisor Support Staff: . .135
EXPANSION PLANS:
US: . . . . .All US
Canada - Yes, . . . Overseas - Yes

TECNIC DRIVING SCHOOL / GROUPE TECNIC

1265 Berri, # 300
Montreal, PQ H2L4C6 CAN
TEL: (514) 844-4318
FAX:
M. Guylaine Handfield, Comm. Dir.

Driving school for autos, trucks, motorcycles, buses and adapted vehicles for handicapped drivers. The most advanced and reliable teaching method, with qualified teachers.

HISTORY: . . . .
Established in 1985; . . 1st Franchised in 1985
Company-Owned Units (As of 12/1/1989): . .5
Franchised Units (12/1/1989): 115
Total Units (12/1/1989): 120
Distribution: US-0;Can-120;Overseas-0
North America: . . . . 2 Provinces
Concentration: . . . . . . 117 in PQ, 3 in ON
Registered: . . . .
. . . .
Average # of Employees: . . . .
Prior Industry Experience: . . . . . . Helpful

FINANCIAL:
Cash Investment: $15K
Total Investment: $20K
Fees: Franchise - $12.5K
Royalty: 3%, Advert: 2.5%
Contract Periods (Yrs.): 5/5
Area Development Agreement: . .No
Sub-Franchise Contract: . . . . .No
Expand in Territory: . . . . Yes
Passive Ownership: . . . .
Encourage Conversions: . . . . Yes
Franchisee Purchase(s) Required: Yes

FRANCHISOR TRAINING/SUPPORT:
Financial Assistance Provided: . . . . .No
Site Selection Assistance: . . . . .Yes
Lease Negotiation Assistance: . . . . .Yes
Co-operative Advertising: . . . . .Yes
Training: . . . . 2 Wks. Headquarters
. . . .
On-Going Support: . . . . . a,b,d,E,F,G,H
Full-Time Franchisor Support Staff: . . 15
EXPANSION PLANS:
US: . . . . .All US
Canada - Yes, . . . Overseas - Yes

TELLER TRAINING INSTITUTE

2033 6th Ave., # 400, UAL Bldg.
Seattle, WA 98121
TEL: (206) 448-7100
FAX:
Mr. David Lonay, President

TELLER TRAINING INSTITUTES recruit, train, and provide job placement for persons seeking entry-level careers in financial institutions. 55,000 graduates nationwide. No competition. No banking or eductional experience is necessary to successfully and profitably operate a franchise. Complete franchisee training is provided.

HISTORY: . . . . IFA
Established in 1975; . . 1st Franchised in 1976
Company-Owned Units (As of 12/1/1989): . .4
Franchised Units (12/1/1989): 14
Total Units (12/1/1989): 18
Distribution: US-18;Can-0;Overseas-0
North America: . . . . 22 States
Concentration: . . .3 in CA, 3 in WA, 2 in MO
Registered: . . . . CA,IL,MD,OR,VA
. . . .
Average # of Employees: . . . . . . 3 FT, 1 PT
Prior Industry Experience: . . . . Helpful

FINANCIAL:
Cash Investment: $40-60K
Total Investment: $40-60K
Fees: Franchise - $20-30K
Royalty: 8%, Advert: . . . 0%
Contract Periods (Yrs.): . . . 15/15
Area Development Agreement: . .No
Sub-Franchise Contract: . . . . .No
Expand in Territory: . . . . Yes
Passive Ownership: . . . Not Allowed
Encourage Conversions: . . . . Yes
Franchisee Purchase(s) Required: Yes

FRANCHISOR TRAINING/SUPPORT:
Financial Assistance Provided: . . . . .No
Site Selection Assistance: . . . . .Yes
Lease Negotiation Assistance: . . . . .Yes
Co-operative Advertising: . . . . .Yes
Training: . . . . 2 Wks. Headquarters,
. . . . 2 Wks. St. Louis, MO
On-Going Support: . . . . A,B,C,D,E,G,H
Full-Time Franchisor Support Staff: . . 12
EXPANSION PLANS:
US: . . . . .East Coast, Midwest
Canada - No, ...Overseas - No

TIME MASTERS - MANAGEMENT TOOLS AND SEMINARS

36C Stoffel Dr.
Rexdale, ON M9W1A8 CAN
TEL: (800) 284-2987 (416) 248-5555
FAX: (416) 248-5558
Mr. Thom Tyson, President

TIME MASTERS markets exclusive Time Management Tools and in-house and public seminars. Clients are taught how to improve effectiveness in business, social and personal life. Clients include business, governments and individuals. Audio visual presentations are used, and participants get personal follow-up, manuals, newsletters, and cassettes. Franchisees provide management tools, sell books, cassettes and training courses.

HISTORY: . . . . IFA
Established in 1984; . . 1st Franchised in 1987
Company-Owned Units (As of 12/1/1989): . .2
Franchised Units (12/1/1989): 24
Total Units (12/1/1989): 26
Distribution: US-2;Can-24;Overseas-0
North America: . . . . . 2 States, 5 Provinces
Concentration: . . .21 in ON, 3 in SK, 2 in AB
Registered: . . . . .FL,AB
. . . .
Average # of Employees: . . . . .2 FT
Prior Industry Experience: . . . . Helpful

FINANCIAL:
Cash Investment: $10-20K
Total Investment: $10-20K
Fees: Franchise - $10K
 Royalty: 3%, Advert: 3%
Contract Periods (Yrs.): 10/10
Area Development Agreement: Yes/1
Sub-Franchise Contract: . . . . . Yes
Expand in Territory: . . . . Yes
Passive Ownership: . . . Discouraged
Encourage Conversions: . . . . . Yes
Franchisee Purchase(s) Required: Yes

FRANCHISOR TRAINING/SUPPORT:
Financial Assistance Provided: . . . . . No
Site Selection Assistance: . . . . .NA
Lease Negotiation Assistance: . . . . .NA
Co-operative Advertising: . . . . .Yes
Training: . . . . 5 Days Toronto
. . . .
On-Going Support: . . . .B,C,D,E,F,G,h,I
Full-Time Franchisor Support Staff: . . 12
EXPANSION PLANS:
 US: . . . . .All US
 Canada - Yes, ...Overseas - No

TOWNSEND LEARNING CENTER

210 Bell St.
Chagrin Falls, OH 44022
TEL: (216) 247-8300
FAX:
Ms. Sarah Littlefield, Exec. Dir.

TOWNSEND LEARNING CENTERS offer professional educational services to the community. These include diagnostic testing, college preparation and study skills. TOWNSEND LEARNING CENTERS offer programs in schools and corporations, as well as their home office.

HISTORY: . . . . IFA
Established in 1969; . . 1st Franchised in 1987
Company-Owned Units (As of 12/1/1989): . .3
Franchised Units (12/1/1989): 2
Total Units (12/1/1989): 5
Distribution: US-5;Can-0;Overseas-0
North America: . . . . .1 State
Concentration: . . . . 5 in OH
Registered: . . . .
. . . .
Average # of Employees: . . . . . 2 FT, 3-6 PT
Prior Industry Experience: . . . . Helpful

FINANCIAL:
Cash Investment: $30-75K
Total Investment: $50-100K
Fees: Franchise - $10-25K
 Royalty: 8.5%, Advert: 4%
Contract Periods (Yrs.):
Area Development Agreement: . .No
Sub-Franchise Contract: . . . . .No
Expand in Territory: . . . . Yes
Passive Ownership: . . . Not Allowed
Encourage Conversions: . . . . .No
Franchisee Purchase(s) Required: Yes

FRANCHISOR TRAINING/SUPPORT:
Financial Assistance Provided: . . .Yes(D)
Site Selection Assistance: . . . . .Yes
Lease Negotiation Assistance: . . . . .Yes
Co-operative Advertising: . . . . No
Training: . . . . . . .10 Days Headquarters
. . . .
On-Going Support: . . . . b,C,E,G,h
Full-Time Franchisor Support Staff: . . .2
EXPANSION PLANS:
 US: . . . . Ohio Only
 Canada - No, ...Overseas - No

TRAVEL PROFESSIONALS INSTITUTE

10172 Linn Station Rd.
Louisville, KY 40223
TEL: (800) 628-2208 (502) 423-9900
FAX: (502) 423-9914
Mr. John E. Boyce, Dir. Fran. Sales

TRAVEL PROFESSIONALS INSTITUTE provides professional educational training to individuals seeking employment in the travel industry. The curriculum has a long history of a consistently high level of acceptance of its graduates by the industry.

HISTORY: . . . .
Established in 1989; . . 1st Franchised in 1989
Company-Owned Units (As of 12/1/1989): . .1
Franchised Units (12/1/1989): 0
Total Units (12/1/1989): 1
Distribution: US-1;Can-0;Overseas-0
North America: . . . . .1 State
Concentration: . . . . 1 in KY
Registered: . . . . .FL
. . . .
Average # of Employees: . . . . . . 1 FT, 3 PT
Prior Industry Experience: . . . . Helpful

FINANCIAL:
Cash Investment: $61K
Total Investment: $61K
Fees: Franchise - $27.5K
 Royalty: 7%, Advert: 0%
Contract Periods (Yrs.): 10/10
Area Development Agreement: . .No
Sub-Franchise Contract: . . . . . Yes
Expand in Territory: . . . . Yes
Passive Ownership: . . . Discouraged
Encourage Conversions: . . . . . Yes
Franchisee Purchase(s) Required: .No

FRANCHISOR TRAINING/SUPPORT:
Financial Assistance Provided: . . . . . No
Site Selection Assistance: . . . . .Yes
Lease Negotiation Assistance: . . . . .Yes
Co-operative Advertising: . . . . No
Training: . . . . . 5 Days Louisville, KY or
. . . . Denver, CO
On-Going Support: . . . . . B,C,D,E,H,I
Full-Time Franchisor Support Staff: . . . 4
EXPANSION PLANS:
 US: . . . . .All US
 Canada - No, ...Overseas - No

TRAVEL TRADE SCHOOL

7921 Southpark Plaza, # 105
Littleton, CO 80120
TEL: (303) 795-1825
FAX:
Ms. Adonna Hipple, President

Travel industry training, using live airline computers in the classroom. Preparing graduates for entry-level positions in the travel industry. Airlines, (reservationist) tour companies and travel agencies.

HISTORY:	. . . . IFA
Established in 1980;	. . 1st Franchised in 1981
Company-Owned Units (As of 12/1/1989):	. .1
Franchised Units (12/1/1989):	5
Total Units (12/1/1989):	6
Distribution:	. . . . . . US-6;Can-0;Overseas-0
North America:	. . . . .1 State
Concentration:	. . . . 6 in CO
Registered:	. . . .
. . . .	
Average # of Employees:	. . . . . .1 FT, 1 PT
Prior Industry Experience:	. . . . Helpful

FINANCIAL:	
Cash Investment:	. . . . $40K
Total Investment:	. . . . $40K
Fees: Franchise -	. . . . $25K
Royalty: 7%, Advert:	. . . . . . 0%
Contract Periods (Yrs.):	. . . . 10/10
Area Development Agreement:	. .No
Sub-Franchise Contract:	. . . . .No
Expand in Territory:	. . . . . . Yes
Passive Ownership:	. . . Discouraged
Encourage Conversions:	. . . . . NA
Franchisee Purchase(s) Required:	Yes

FRANCHISOR TRAINING/SUPPORT:	
Financial Assistance Provided:	. . . . .No
Site Selection Assistance:	. . . . . . .Yes
Lease Negotiation Assistance:	. . . . .Yes
Co-operative Advertising:	. . . . .No
Training:	. . . . .Up to 8 Wks. HQ for Dir-
. . . . . .ectors, Unlimited at Site w/ Fee	
On-Going Support:	. . . .B,C,D,E,F,G,H,I
Full-Time Franchisor Support Staff:	. . . 3
EXPANSION PLANS:	
US:	. . . . .All US
Canada - Yes,	. . . . . .Overseas - Yes

SUPPLEMENTAL LISTING OF FRANCHISORS

ACHIEVERS INTERNATIONAL	. . . . 550 - 1500 W. Georgia, Vancouver BC V6G2Z6	CAN
AMERICAN COLLEGE PLANNING SERVICE	. . . . 94-B Jefryn Blvd., E, Deer Park NY 11729	
BETTER BIRTH FOUNDATION	. . . . .733 Main St., Stone Mt. GA 30083	
EDUCATIONAL RESOURCE CENTERS	. . . . .315 Golfview Dr., # 203, Boca Raton FL 33432	
ELS INTERNATIONAL	. . . . .5761 Buckingham Parkway, Culver City CA 90230	
FUTURE SEARCH	. . . . 15 Engle St., # 304, Englewood NJ 07631	
HUNTINGTON LEARNING CENTERS	. . . . 660 Kinderkamack Rd., Oradell NJ 07649	
INFORMATION DEPOT OPEN UNIVERSITY	. . . . 13784 Graber Ave., Sylmar CA 91342	
INSTITUTE OF READING DEVELOPMENT	. . . . 5 Saddle Ln., Novato CA 94949	
INTERNATIONAL BUSINESS SCHOOLS	. . . . .5650 Yonge St., # 1400, North York ON M2M4G3	CAN
INTERNATIONAL TRAINING COURSES	. . . . 303 E. Ohio St., # 2718, Chicago IL 60611	
PERSONAL COMPUTER LEARNING CENTERS	. . . . .230 Park Ave., New York NY 10169	
PRINCETON REVIEW	. . . . .606 Columbus Ave., # 201, New York NY 10024	
PRIORITY MANAGEMENT TRAINING	. . . . .M5-601 W. Broadway, Vancouver BC V5Z4C2	CAN
PROVO COLLEGE	. . . . 1275 N. University, # 2, Provo UT 84604	
QUICK START LEARNING CENTRES	. . . . .One Nicholas St., # 512, Ottawa ON K1N7B7	CAN
SEXTON EDUCATIONAL CENTERS	. . . . .443 East 3rd Ave., Roselle NJ 07203	
SMI INTERNATIONAL	. . . . 5000 Lakewood Dr., Waco TX 76710	
SYNDRAX TRAINING	. . . . .P. O. Box 13351, Kanata ON K2K1X5	CAN
TIME ON MY SIDE	. . . . 1470 Don Mills Rd., # 206, Don Mills ON M3B2X9	CAN
TIME ON MY SIDE	. . . . .P. O. Box 54, Westmount PQ H3Z2T1	CAN
TORONTO SCHOOL OF BUSINESS	. . . . .5650 Yonge St., # 1400, North York ON M2M4G3	CAN
TRAINING CORPORATION, THE	. . . . .3000 Steeles Ave. E., # 308, Markham ON L3R4T9	CAN

CHAPTER 16

EMPLOYMENT AND PERSONNEL

AAA EMPLOYMENT

410 K Creekside Dr.
Clearwater, FL 34620
TEL: (800)237-2853 (800)282-2847(FL)
FAX:
Ms. Stacy Mabhu, Fran. Ops. Dir.

AAA EMPLOYMENT is a general employment agency, specializing in permanent placement at all levels of employment. Applicant-paid and employer-paid positons are handled. Low placement fee with convenient terms sets AAA EMPLOYMENT apart from other agencies, giving them a competitive edge in the employment industry.

HISTORY: . . . .
Established in 1957; . . 1st Franchised in 1977
Company-Owned Units (As of 12/1/1989): . 83
Franchised Units (12/1/1989): 48
Total Units (12/1/1989): 131
Distribution: US-131;Can-0;Overseas-0
 North America: . . . . 19 States
 Concentration: . . 59 in FL,15 in TN,12 IN GA
Registered: . . .CA,IL,IN,MD,MI,MN,NY,OR
 . . . . VA,WA,WI
Average # of Employees: . . . . .1-2 FT
Prior Industry Experience: . . . . Helpful

FINANCIAL:
Cash Investment: $8-19K
Total Investment: $14-34K
Fees: Franchise - $10-30K
 Royalty: 10%, Advert: 0%
Contract Periods (Yrs.): 10/1
Area Development Agreement: . .No
Sub-Franchise Contract: . . . . .No
Expand in Territory: . . . . Yes
Passive Ownership: . . . . . .Allowed
Encourage Conversions: . . . .
Franchisee Purchase(s) Required: .No

FRANCHISOR TRAINING/SUPPORT:
Financial Assistance Provided: . . .Yes(D)
Site Selection Assistance: . . . . .Yes
Lease Negotiation Assistance: . . . . .Yes
Co-operative Advertising: . . . . .Yes
Training: . . . . 2-4 Wks. Corp. HQ,
 . . . . . 1 Wk. Site, On-going As Needed
On-Going Support: . . . . . .C,D,E,G,H,I
Full-Time Franchisor Support Staff: . . 10
EXPANSION PLANS:
 US: . . . . All US Except Southeast
 Canada - No, ... Overseas - No

EMPLOYMENT SERVICES

	1988	1989	1990	Percentage Change	
				1988-1989	1989-1990
Number of Establishments:					
Company-Owned	2,842	2,650	2,940	-6.8%	10.9%
Franchisee-Owned	3,653	3,999	4,611	9.5%	15.3%
Total	6,495	6,649	7,551	2.4%	13.6%
% of Total Establishments:					
Company-Owned	43.8%	39.9%	38.9%		
Franchisee-Owned	56.2%	60.1%	61.1%		
Total	100.0%	100.0%	100.0%		
Annual Sales ($000):					
Company-Owned	$2,450,045	$2,536,351	$2,843,552	3.5%	12.1%
Franchisee-Owned	2,211,185	2,486,879	2,941,773	12.5%	18.3%
Total	4,661,230	5,023,230	5,785,325	7.8%	15.2%
% of Total Sales:					
Company-Owned	52.6%	50.5%	49.2%		
Franchisee-Owned	47.4%	49.5%	50.8%		
Total	100.0%	100.0%	100.0%		
Average Sales Per Unit ($000):					
Company-Owned	$862	$957	$967	11.0%	1.1%
Franchisee-Owned	605	622	638	2.7%	2.6%
Total	718	755	766	5.3%	1.4%
Sales Ratio	142.4%	153.9%	151.6%		

	1st Quartile	Median	4th Quartile
Average 1988 Total Investment:			
Company-Owned	$62,500	$100,000	$146,250
Franchisee-Owned	51,250	70,000	98,000
Single Unit Franchise Fee	$15,000	$15,000	$25,000
Multiple Unit Franchise Fee	4,750	15,000	82,500
Franchisee Start-up Cost	22,750	28,500	50,000

	1988	Employees/Unit	Sales/Employee
Employment:			
Company-Owned	179,812	63.3	$13,626
Franchisee-Owned	154,888	42.4	14,276
Total	334,700	51.5	13,927
Employee Performance Ratios		149.2%	95.4%

Source: Franchising In The Economy, 1988 – 1990, IFA Education Foundation & Horwath International, Published January, 1990.

1) 1989 and 1990 data were estimated by respondents.

ACCOUNTANTS ON CALL

95 Route 17 S.
Paramus, NJ 07652
TEL: (800) 545-0006 (201) 843-0006
FAX:
Mr. Richard C. Pittius, VP Fran.

ACCOUNTANTS ON CALL is a specialized temporary help service, engaged in providing a full service to the financial area. Placing accounting, bookkeeping and financial personnel to clients on a temporary and permanent basis. We offer exclusive territory, payroll for the temporaries, computerized operational systems and manuals, on-going consulting and training.

HISTORY: . . . . IFA/WIF	FINANCIAL: NYSE	FRANCHISOR TRAINING/SUPPORT:
Established in 1979; . . 1st Franchised in 1979	Cash Investment: $90K	Financial Assistance Provided: . . .Yes(D)
Company-Owned Units (As of 12/1/1989): . 33	Total Investment: $105K	Site Selection Assistance: . . . . . . .Yes
Franchised Units (12/1/1989): 21	Fees: Franchise - $25K	Lease Negotiation Assistance: . . . . .Yes
Total Units (12/1/1989): 54	Royalty: 7-10%, Advert: 0%	Co-operative Advertising: . . . . .No
Distribution: US-53;Can-1;Overseas-0	Contract Periods (Yrs.): 20/20	Training: . . . . .12 Days HQ, 2 Wks. Site,
North America: . . . . 18 States	Area Development Agreement: . .No	. . .2 Daysx3/Yr. Region, Field Training
Concentration: . . . . . .Primarily CA, NJ, FL	Sub-Franchise Contract: . . . . .No	On-Going Support: . . . A,B,C,D,E,G,H,I
Registered: . . . . .CA,HI,IL,IN,MD,NY	Expand in Territory: . . . . Yes	Full-Time Franchisor Support Staff: . . 32
. . . .	Passive Ownership: . . . . . .Allowed	EXPANSION PLANS:
Average # of Employees: . . . . .4 FT	Encourage Conversions: . . . . Yes	US: . . . . .All US
Prior Industry Experience: . . . . Helpful	Franchisee Purchase(s) Required: .No	Canada - No, ...Overseas - No

ALPHA PERSONNEL SYSTEM

535 Fifth Ave.
New York, NY 10017
TEL: (800) 343-8518 (212) 557-4900 C
FAX: (212) 972-5367
Mr. Collin Gaffney, Dir. Fran. Dev.

Firmly entrenched permanent and temporary personnel services provided to client companies and applicants in the tri-state area. Over 25 years of name recognition and service satisfaction.

HISTORY: . . . . IFA	FINANCIAL: AMER-WRS	FRANCHISOR TRAINING/SUPPORT:
Established in 1961; . . 1st Franchised in 1964	Cash Investment: $45-60K	Financial Assistance Provided: . . .Yes(D)
Company-Owned Units (As of 12/1/1989): . .0	Total Investment: $70-85K	Site Selection Assistance: . . . . . . .Yes
Franchised Units (12/1/1989): 4	Fees: Franchise - $25K	Lease Negotiation Assistance: . . . . .No
Total Units (12/1/1989): 4	Royalty: 7%, Advert: 0%	Co-operative Advertising: . . . . .Yes
Distribution: US-4;Can-0;Overseas-0	Contract Periods (Yrs.): 5/5	Training: . . . . 2 Wks. Headquarters
North America: . . . . .1 State	Area Development Agreement: . .No	. . . .
Concentration: . . . . 4 in NY	Sub-Franchise Contract: . . . . .No	On-Going Support: . . . . . . .C,D,E,G,H,I
Registered: . . . . NY,RI,VA,WA	Expand in Territory: . . . . Yes	Full-Time Franchisor Support Staff: . . 12
. . . .	Passive Ownership: . . . Not Allowed	EXPANSION PLANS:
Average # of Employees: . . . . .4 FT	Encourage Conversions: . . . . Yes	US: . . . . NY, CT and NJ Only
Prior Industry Experience: . . . . Helpful	Franchisee Purchase(s) Required: .No	Canada - No, ...Overseas - No

ANY SITUATION

4920 City Ave.
Philadlphia, PA 19131
TEL: (215) 247-8001
FAX:
Ms. Helen Tucker, President

ANY SITUATION is a nanny placement service, catering to the child-care needs of professional parents. The company provides long-term, live-out nannies and short-term subscription back-up child care.

HISTORY:	FINANCIAL:	FRANCHISOR TRAINING/SUPPORT:
Established in 1985; . . 1st Franchised in 1989	Cash Investment: $20K	Financial Assistance Provided: . . .Yes(D)
Company-Owned Units (As of 12/1/1989): . .1	Total Investment: $18.5-22K	Site Selection Assistance: . . . . . . .Yes
Franchised Units (12/1/1989): 0	Fees: Franchise - $15.5K	Lease Negotiation Assistance: . . . . .Yes
Total Units (12/1/1989): 1	Royalty: 7%, Advert: . . . $45/MO.	Co-operative Advertising: . . . . .No
Distribution: US-1;Can-0;Overseas-0	Contract Periods (Yrs.): 10/10	Training: . . . . 2 Wks. Headquarters
North America: . . . . .1 State	Area Development Agreement: . .No	. . . .
Concentration: . . . . 1 in PA	Sub-Franchise Contract: . . . . .No	On-Going Support: . . . . .H,I
Registered:	Expand in Territory: . . . . .No	Full-Time Franchisor Support Staff: . . .2
. . . .	Passive Ownership: . . . Discouraged	EXPANSION PLANS:
Average # of Employees: . . . . . . 1 FT, 1 PT	Encourage Conversions: . . . . .No	US: . . . . All US, Especially NE
Prior Industry Experience: . . . . Helpful	Franchisee Purchase(s) Required: .No	Canada - No, ...Overseas - No

ATLANTIC PERSONNEL SERVICES

4806 Shelly Dr.
Wilmington, NC 28405
TEL: (919) 392-2550
FAX:
Mr. Jim Smith, EVP

Concepts: targeted toward entry level through middle management. Professional resume production. Resume certification - networking. In-house financing.

HISTORY: . . . . IFA	FINANCIAL:	FRANCHISOR TRAINING/SUPPORT:
Established in 1983; . . 1st Franchised in 1985	Cash Investment: $8-14K	Financial Assistance Provided: . . . . .Yes
Company-Owned Units (As of 12/1/1989): . .2	Total Investment: $13-24K	Site Selection Assistance: . . . . . . .Yes
Franchised Units (12/1/1989): 32	Fees: Franchise - $14K	Lease Negotiation Assistance: . . . . .Yes
Total Units (12/1/1989): 34	Royalty: 7-8%, Advert: 1%	Co-operative Advertising: . . . . .NA
Distribution: US-34;Can-0;Overseas-0	Contract Periods (Yrs.): 10/10	Training: . . . . 1 Wk. Site, 1 Wk.
North America: . . . . 3 States	Area Development Agreement: Yes/10	. . . . Site, 2 Days HQ
Concentration: . . . 24 in NC,9 in SC,1 in GA	Sub-Franchise Contract: . . . . . Yes	On-Going Support: . . . .a,B,C,D,E,G,H,I
Registered: . . . . .FL	Expand in Territory: . . . . . . Yes	Full-Time Franchisor Support Staff: . . . 8
	Passive Ownership: . . . Not Allowed	EXPANSION PLANS:
. . . .	Encourage Conversions: . . . . . Yes	US: . . . . All US
Average # of Employees: . . . . .3-5 FT	Franchisee Purchase(s) Required: .No	Canada - No, ...Overseas - No
Prior Industry Experience: . . . . Helpful		

BAILEY EMPLOYMENT SERVICE

51 Shelton Rd.
Monroe, CT 06468
TEL: (203) 261-2908
FAX:
Mr. S. Leighton, Presient

Recruitment and placement of professionally-skilled individuals in salary ranges from $30,000-100,000. The BAILEY franchise includes unlimited training on computers, which will be positioned in the office to instantly network with Bailey computers in system. Franchisee has immediate access to job order and candidate resources. A 100%-financed temp service is available.

HISTORY:	FINANCIAL:	FRANCHISOR TRAINING/SUPPORT:
Established in 1960; . . 1st Franchised in 1972	Cash Investment: $40K	Financial Assistance Provided: . . .Yes(D)
Company-Owned Units (As of 12/1/1989): . .2	Total Investment: $55-60K	Site Selection Assistance: . . . . . . .NA
Franchised Units (12/1/1989): 16	Fees: Franchise - $40K	Lease Negotiation Assistance: . . . . .Yes
Total Units (12/1/1989): 18	Royalty: 8%, Advert: 0%	Co-operative Advertising: . . . . .No
Distribution: US-18;Can-0;Overseas-0	Contract Periods (Yrs.): . . . . . Inf.	Training: . . . . Unlimited HQ
North America: . . . . 3 States	Area Development Agreement: . .No	. . . . As Needed Site
Concentration: . . . . .11 in CT	Sub-Franchise Contract: . . . . .No	On-Going Support: . . . . . .A,C,D,G,H,I
Registered:	Expand in Territory: . . . . . . Yes	Full-Time Franchisor Support Staff: . . . 5
	Passive Ownership: . . . Discouraged	EXPANSION PLANS:
. . . .	Encourage Conversions: . . . . .No	US: . . . . East Coast
Average # of Employees: . . . . . . 4 FT, 1 PT	Franchisee Purchase(s) Required: .No	Canada - No, ...Overseas - No
Prior Industry Experience: . . . . Helpful		

CAREER ADVANCEMENT SCIENCES

Six Market Square
Pittsburgh, PA 15222
TEL: (412) 281-2005
FAX: (412) 281-2057
Mr. R. D. Hindman, President

C.A.S. is the only firm of its kind. We provide complete job search assistance services for individuals and corporations, including professional resume preparation, computerized employer research, executive marketing programs, job search consulting and corporate outplacement. All offices are electronically linked to HQ's writing, research and support staff.

HISTORY:	FINANCIAL:	FRANCHISOR TRAINING/SUPPORT:
Established in 1962; . . 1st Franchised in 1972	Cash Investment: $0	Financial Assistance Provided: . . . . .No
Company-Owned Units (As of 12/1/1989): . 12	Total Investment: $0	Site Selection Assistance: . . . . . . .Yes
Franchised Units (12/1/1989): 30	Fees: Franchise - $0	Lease Negotiation Assistance: . . . . .Yes
Total Units (12/1/1989): 42	Royalty: 0%, Advert: 0%	Co-operative Advertising: . . . . . . .Yes
Distribution: US-42;Can-0;Overseas-0	Contract Periods (Yrs.): . . . Infinite	Training: . . . . 1 Wk. Headquarters
North America: . . . . 18 States	Area Development Agreement: . .No	. . . .
Concentration:	Sub-Franchise Contract: . . . . .No	On-Going Support: . . . . .A,B,C,D,G,h,I
Registered:	Expand in Territory: . . . . Yes	Full-Time Franchisor Support Staff: . . 12
	Passive Ownership: . . . Discouraged	EXPANSION PLANS:
. . . .	Encourage Conversions: . . . . . Yes	US: . . . . All US
Average # of Employees:	Franchisee Purchase(s) Required: .No	Canada - Yes, . . . Overseas - Yes
Prior Industry Experience: . . . . Helpful		

CAREER BLAZERS

590 Fifth Ave.
New York, NY 10036
TEL: (800) 284-3232 (212) 719-3232
FAX: (212) 921-1827
Ms. Patricia Bavaro, Dir. Fran.

We offer a personnel service franchise that capitalizes on the financial advantages and natural synergy of a permanent placement agency and a temporary service. Our franchises provide office, clerical and light industrial workers to a wide variety of businessess, government agencies and non-profit organizations.

HISTORY: . . . . IFA
Established in 1949; . . 1st Franchised in 1987
Company-Owned Units (As of 12/1/1989): . .7
Franchised Units (12/1/1989): 4
Total Units (12/1/1989): 11
Distribution: US-11;Can-0;Overseas-0
North America: . . . . .5 State
Concentration: . . . .6 in NY, 2 in NJ, 1 in CT
Registered: . . . . MD,NY,RI,VA
. . . .
Average # of Employees: . . . . .7 FT
Prior Industry Experience: . . . . Helpful

FINANCIAL:
Cash Investment: $70-85K
Total Investment: $95-129K
Fees: Franchise - $15-18K
Royalty: 7%, Advert: 1%
Contract Periods (Yrs.): 5/5
Area Development Agreement: . .No
Sub-Franchise Contract: . . . . . .No
Expand in Territory: . . . . Yes
Passive Ownership: . . . Discouraged
Encourage Conversions: . . . . . Yes
Franchisee Purchase(s) Required: .No

FRANCHISOR TRAINING/SUPPORT:
Financial Assistance Provided: . . . Yes(I)
Site Selection Assistance: . . . . . . .Yes
Lease Negotiation Assistance: . . . . .Yes
Co-operative Advertising: . . . . . . .Yes
Training: . . . . . . 15 Days Headquarters,
. . . . .5 Days Site, On-going
On-Going Support: . . . . . A,B,C,D,E,h,I
Full-Time Franchisor Support Staff: . . 18
EXPANSION PLANS:
US: . . . . Northeast
Canada - No, ...Overseas - No

CAREERS U.S.A

1825 JFK Blvd.
Philadelphia, PA 19103
TEL: (215) 561-3800 C
FAX: (215) 387-8990
Mr. George Ounjian, President

CAREERS USA is a temporary and permanent placement franchise that offers complete training and support of its franchise owners. CAREERS USA offers a fully-automated computer system that helps franchisees manage their businesses financially and operationally.

HISTORY: . . . . IFA
Established in 1981; . . 1st Franchised in 1987
Company-Owned Units (As of 12/1/1989): . 12
Franchised Units (12/1/1989): 11
Total Units (12/1/1989): 23
Distribution: US-23;Can-0;Overseas-0
North America: . . . . 5 States
Concentration: . . . . PA, GA, NJ
Registered: . . . . All States
. . . .
Average # of Employees: . . . . .3 FT
Prior Industry Experience: . . . . Helpful

FINANCIAL:
Cash Investment: $15K
Total Investment: $115-145K
Fees: Franchise - $15K
Royalty: 9.5%, Advert: 4%
Contract Periods (Yrs.): 10
Area Development Agreement: . .No
Sub-Franchise Contract: . . . . . .No
Expand in Territory: . . . . .No
Passive Ownership: . . . Discouraged
Encourage Conversions: . . . . . Yes
Franchisee Purchase(s) Required: .No

FRANCHISOR TRAINING/SUPPORT:
Financial Assistance Provided: . . . Yes(I)
Site Selection Assistance: . . . . . . .Yes
Lease Negotiation Assistance: . . . . .Yes
Co-operative Advertising: . . . . . . .Yes
Training: . . . . 2 Wks. Headquarters,
. . . . 1 Wk. Franchisee's Location
On-Going Support: . . . A,B,C,D,E,F,G,H
Full-Time Franchisor Support Staff: . . 58
EXPANSION PLANS:
US: . . . . .All US
Canada - No, ...Overseas - No

DIVISION 10

535 Fifth Ave.
New York, NY 10017
TEL: (800) 343-8518 (212) 557-4900 C
FAX: (212) 972-5367
Mr. Collin Gaffney, Dir. Fran. Dev.

Permanent and temporary personnel services provided to client companies and applicants in the accounting, finance, office clerical and office support fields. Temporary payroll 100% financed. Computerized for ease of operation. Training conducted by experts in the field.

HISTORY: . . . . IFA
Established in 1979; . . 1st Franchised in 1979
Company-Owned Units (As of 12/1/1989): . .1
Franchised Units (12/1/1989): 10
Total Units (12/1/1989): 11
Distribution: US-11;Can-0;Overseas-0
North America: . . . . 8 States
Concentration: . . . . 4 in NJ
Registered: . . . . NY,RI,VA,WA
. . . .
Average # of Employees: . . . . Varies
Prior Industry Experience: . . . . Helpful

FINANCIAL: AMER-WRS
Cash Investment: $35-50K
Total Investment: $75-100K
Fees: Franchise - $15K
Royalty: 8%, Advert: 0%
Contract Periods (Yrs.): 5/10
Area Development Agreement: . .No
Sub-Franchise Contract: . . . . . .No
Expand in Territory: . . . . Yes
Passive Ownership: . . . Not Allowed
Encourage Conversions: . . . . . Yes
Franchisee Purchase(s) Required: .No

FRANCHISOR TRAINING/SUPPORT:
Financial Assistance Provided: . . .Yes(D)
Site Selection Assistance: . . . . . . .Yes
Lease Negotiation Assistance: . . . . . No
Co-operative Advertising: . . . . . . .Yes
Training: . . . . . . 5 Wks. During 1st Year
. . . . at Headquarters or Existing Office
On-Going Support: . . . . . . C,D,E,G,H,I
Full-Time Franchisor Support Staff: . . 12
EXPANSION PLANS:
US: . . . . .All US
Canada - Yes, ...Overseas - No

DYNAMIC TEMPORARY SERVICES

3091 Maple Dr. NE,
Atlanta, GA 30305
TEL: (800) 525-7443 (404) 266-2256
FAX:
Mr. Ike Steele, Franchise Manager

A division of a $500 million temporary help industry leader, specializing in providing office automation temporary personnel. Program offers full support, including funding and processing, billing, temporary employee bonding and liability insurance, accounting reports, marketing analysis, direct mail, training and pre- opening consultation.

HISTORY: . . . . IFA
Established in 1987; . . 1st Franchised in 1987
Company-Owned Units (As of 12/1/1989): . . 3
Franchised Units (12/1/1989): 7
Total Units (12/1/1989): 10
Distribution: US-10;Can-0;Overseas-0
North America: . . . . 7 States + DC
Concentration: . . . . 3 in DC, 2 in IL
Registered: . . . . . CA,FL,IL,MD,MI,NY,VA
. . . .
Average # of Employees: . . . . 3 FT
Prior Industry Experience: . . . . Helpful

FINANCIAL:
Cash Investment: $50-90K
Total Investment: $50-90K
Fees: Franchise - $0
 Royalty: Varies, Advert: . . . . . .
Contract Periods (Yrs.): 15
Area Development Agreement: . .No
Sub-Franchise Contract: . . . . . No
Expand in Territory: . . . . Yes
Passive Ownership: . . . Not Allowed
Encourage Conversions: . . . . . No
Franchisee Purchase(s) Required: .No

FRANCHISOR TRAINING/SUPPORT:
Financial Assistance Provided: . . . . . No
Site Selection Assistance: . . . . Yes
Lease Negotiation Assistance: . . . . . Yes
Co-operative Advertising: . . . . Yes
Training: . . . . 1-2 Wks. Field,
. . . . On-going at Home Office
On-Going Support: . . . .A,b,C,D,E,G,H,I
Full-Time Franchisor Support Staff: . . . 7
EXPANSION PLANS:
US: . . . . Major US Cities
Canada - No, ... Overseas - No

EXPRESS SERVICES

6300 NW Expressway
Oklahoma City, OK 73132
TEL: (800) 652-6400 (405) 840-5000
FAX:
Mr. Thomas Gunderson, Fran. Dir.

3 divisions, permanent and temporary placement and executive search offer complete coverage of the employment field. With 130 franchises in 33 states, each franchise receives total advertising plus superior training. Complete financing of temporary payroll. Rated in Venture Magazine as 1 of the 10 "best bets" in franchising.

HISTORY: . . . . IFA
Established in 1983; . . 1st Franchised in 1985
Company-Owned Units (As of 12/1/1989): . . 0
Franchised Units (12/1/1989): 130
Total Units (12/1/1989): 130
Distribution: . . . US-130;Can-0;Overseas-0
North America: . . . . 33 States
Concentration: . . . 9 in WA, 9 in CO, 8 in OR
Registered: . . .CA,FL,IL,IN,MD,MN,NY,ND
. . . . OR,SD,WA,WI
Average # of Employees: . . . . 3 FT
Prior Industry Experience: . . . . Helpful

FINANCIAL:
Cash Investment: . . . . $
Total Investment: . . . . $
Fees: Franchise - $12-15K
 Royalty: 8%, Advert: 0%
Contract Periods (Yrs.): 5/5
Area Development Agreement: Yes/5
Sub-Franchise Contract: . . . . . No
Expand in Territory: . . . . Yes
Passive Ownership: . . . Discouraged
Encourage Conversions: . . . . . Yes
Franchisee Purchase(s) Required: .No

FRANCHISOR TRAINING/SUPPORT:
Financial Assistance Provided: . . . . . No
Site Selection Assistance: . . . . Yes
Lease Negotiation Assistance: . . . . . Yes
Co-operative Advertising: . . . . Yes
Training: . . . . 11 Days Headquarters
. . . .
On-Going Support: . . . A,b,C,D,e,f,G,h,I
Full-Time Franchisor Support Staff: . . 50
EXPANSION PLANS:
US: . . . . SE, Southern CA
Canada - No, ... Overseas - No

FIVE STAR TEMPORARIES

1415 Elbridge Payne, # 255
Chesterfield, MO 63017
TEL: (314) 532-2777
FAX:
Mr. Arthur Harter, Jr., President

Temporary employment services, including laborers, clerical, data processing, technical and professional employees. We own offices in St. Louis (3) and Indianapolis. We offer a ground-floor opportunity to join a successful firm. We are interested in franchisees managing multiple offices.

HISTORY: . . . .
Established in 1979; . . 1st Franchised in 1990
Company-Owned Units (As of 12/1/1989): . . 4
Franchised Units (12/1/1989): 0
Total Units (12/1/1989): 4
Distribution: US-4;Can-0;Overseas-0
North America: . . . . 2 States
Concentration: . . . . 3 in MO, 1 in IN
Registered: . . . .
. . . .
Average # of Employees: . . . . . . 10 FT, 1 PT
Prior Industry Experience: . . . . Helpful

FINANCIAL:
Cash Investment: . . . . . . $50K+
Total Investment: . . . . . . $75K+
Fees: Franchise - $5K
 Royalty: 6%, Advert: 1%
Contract Periods (Yrs.): . . . None
Area Development Agreement: . .No
Sub-Franchise Contract: . . . . . No
Expand in Territory: . . . . Yes
Passive Ownership: . . . Not Allowed
Encourage Conversions: . . . . . Yes
Franchisee Purchase(s) Required: .No

FRANCHISOR TRAINING/SUPPORT:
Financial Assistance Provided: . . . . . No
Site Selection Assistance: . . . . Yes
Lease Negotiation Assistance: . . . . . Yes
Co-operative Advertising: . . . . Yes
Training: . . . . 2 Wks. Headquarters
. . . . 2 Wks. Site
On-Going Support: . . A,B,C,D,E,F,G,H,I
Full-Time Franchisor Support Staff: . . 17
EXPANSION PLANS:
US: . . . . All, Prefer MW
Canada - No, ... Overseas - No

HANDI-MAN /
PRO-TEM
260 Cochituate Rd., # 109
Framingham, MA 01701
TEL: (508) 875-1341 C
FAX:
Mr. G. A. Powers, President

We offer a low-cost opportunity, which is restricted to individuals having a minimum of 2 years' successful experience in the sales/management of temporary help services.

HISTORY: . . . .
Established in 1970; . . 1st Franchised in 1975
Company-Owned Units (As of 12/1/1989): . 12
Franchised Units (12/1/1989): 4
Total Units (12/1/1989): 16
Distribution: US-16;Can-0;Overseas-0
North America: . . . . 5 States
Concentration: . . . . .10 in FL
Registered: . . . .
. . . .
Average # of Employees: . . . . . . 1 FT, 1 PT
Prior Industry Experience: . . . . . .Necessary

FINANCIAL:
Cash Investment: $15-35K
Total Investment: $15-35K
Fees: Franchise - $0
Royalty: Varies, Advert: . . Varies
Contract Periods (Yrs.): 5/5
Area Development Agreement: . .No
Sub-Franchise Contract: . . . . . .No
Expand in Territory: . . . . Yes
Passive Ownership: . . . Not Allowed
Encourage Conversions: . . . . . Yes
Franchisee Purchase(s) Required: .No

FRANCHISOR TRAINING/SUPPORT:
Financial Assistance Provided: . . .Yes(D)
Site Selection Assistance: . . . . .Yes
Lease Negotiation Assistance: . . . . .Yes
Co-operative Advertising: . . . . .No
Training: . . . . 5 Days Site
. . .
On-Going Support: . . . . . . .A,B,C,D,E
Full-Time Franchisor Support Staff: . . 35
EXPANSION PLANS:
US: . . . . .All US
Canada - No, ...Overseas - No

HAYES GROUP

3020 E. Camelback Rd.
Phoenix, AZ 85216
TEL: (602) 956-9010
FAX:
Mr. David Hayes, President

THE HAYES GROUP offers the expertise in permanent, temporary and executive search without the penalty of on-going royalties or the restriction of geographical growth. In addition to the intensive initial training, you can choose our affiliation program on a one-year contract, renewable by your choice.

HISTORY: . . . .
Established in 1976; . . 1st Franchised in 1981
Company-Owned Units (As of 12/1/1989): . .1
Franchised Units (12/1/1989): 5
Total Units (12/1/1989): 6
Distribution: US-5;Can-0;Overseas-1
North America: . . . . 3 States
Concentration: . . . 2 in CO, 1 in AZ, 1 in TX
Registered: . . . .
. . . .
Average # of Employees: . . . . .2 FT
Prior Industry Experience: . . . . . . Helpful

FINANCIAL:
Cash Investment: $7.5K
Total Investment: $40K
Fees: Franchise - $7.5K
Royalty: 0%, Advert: 0%
Contract Periods (Yrs.): 1/1
Area Development Agreement: . .No
Sub-Franchise Contract: . . . . . .No
Expand in Territory: . . . . Yes
Passive Ownership: . . . . . .Allowed
Encourage Conversions: . . . . . Yes
Franchisee Purchase(s) Required: .No

FRANCHISOR TRAINING/SUPPORT:
Financial Assistance Provided: . . . . . No
Site Selection Assistance: . . . . .Yes
Lease Negotiation Assistance: . . . . .Yes
Co-operative Advertising: . . . . .No
Training: . . . . . 1-3 Wks. Headquarters or
. . . . .Site
On-Going Support: . . . . .B,C,D,E,G,H,I
Full-Time Franchisor Support Staff: . . .4
EXPANSION PLANS:
US: . . . . .All US
Canada - Yes, . . . Overseas - Yes

HEALTH FORCE

1600 Stewart Ave., # 700
Westbury, NY 11590
TEL: (516) 683-6000 C
FAX: (516) 683-1640
Mr. Michael Ward, Dir. Fran. Devel.

HEALTH FORCE is a leader in the growing temporary health care business. The company has experienced exceptional growth by furnishing home health care nursing services to patients, and supplemental staffing to institutions.

HISTORY: . . . . .IFA
Established in 1977; . . 1st Franchised in 1982
Company-Owned Units (As of 12/1/1989): . 12
Franchised Units (12/1/1989): 38
Total Units (12/1/1989): 50
Distribution: US-50;Can-0;Overseas-0
North America: . . . . 13 States
Concentration: . . .13 in NY, 9 in FL, 7 in CA
Registered: . . . . .All
. . . .
Average # of Employees: . . . . . . 2 FT, 1 Pt
Prior Industry Experience: . . . . . . Helpful

FINANCIAL: NYSE-BAW
Cash Investment: $103-134K
Total Investment: $103-134K
Fees: Franchise - $39.5K
Royalty: 12-8.5%, Advert: . . 1/2%
Contract Periods (Yrs.): 10/5/5
Area Development Agreement: . .No
Sub-Franchise Contract: . . . . . .No
Expand in Territory: . . . . Yes
Passive Ownership: . . . Discouraged
Encourage Conversions: . . . . . Yes
Franchisee Purchase(s) Required: .No

FRANCHISOR TRAINING/SUPPORT:
Financial Assistance Provided: . . .Yes(D)
Site Selection Assistance: . . . . . . .Yes
Lease Negotiation Assistance: . . . .Yes
Co-operative Advertising: . . . . .No
Training: . . . . 2 Wks. Headquarters,
. . . . . . 2 Wks. Local Office, On-going
On-Going Support: . . . . A,B,C,D,E,G,H
Full-Time Franchisor Support Staff: . .200
EXPANSION PLANS:
US: . . . . .All US
Canada - No, ...Overseas - No

JOBMATE

P. O. Drawer 959
Ridgeland, MS 39158
TEL: (800) 347-JOBY (601) 856-5010
FAX: (601) 856-5092
Mr. Thurman Boykin, President

Employee leasing is the future trend in business-to-business services. JOBMATE is the first national franchisor. Low overhead, marketing, reduce small business paperwork and high benefits cost headaches.

HISTORY: . . . . IFA	FINANCIAL:	FRANCHISOR TRAINING/SUPPORT:
Established in 1986; . . 1st Franchised in 1989	Cash Investment: $45-60K	Financial Assistance Provided: . . . . . No
Company-Owned Units (As of 12/1/1989): . .1	Total Investment: $45K	Site Selection Assistance: . . . . No
Franchised Units (12/1/1989): 1	Fees: Franchise - $35-50K	Lease Negotiation Assistance: . . . . . No
Total Units (12/1/1989): 2	Royalty: 3%, Advert: 2%	Co-operative Advertising: . . . . .Yes
Distribution: US-2;Can-0;Overseas-0	Contract Periods (Yrs.): 10/5	Training: . . . . 1 Wk. Headquarters
North America: . . . . 2 States	Area Development Agreement: . Yes	. . . .
Concentration: . . . . 1 in MS, 1 in GA	Sub-Franchise Contract: . . . . .No	On-Going Support: . . . . C,D,E,H,I
Registered:	Expand in Territory: . . . . Yes	Full-Time Franchisor Support Staff: . . . 8
. . . .	Passive Ownership: . . . Discouraged	EXPANSION PLANS:
Average # of Employees: . . . . .2 FT	Encourage Conversions: . . . . NA	US: . . . . All US
Prior Industry Experience: . . . . Helpful	Franchisee Purchase(s) Required: Yes	Canada - No, ...Overseas - No

LABOR WORLD OF AMERICA

5444 N. Federal Hwy.
Boca Raton, FL 33434
TEL: (407) 994-9255
FAX:
Mr. Alan Schubert, President

Supply temporary industrial laborers to business and industry.

HISTORY:	FINANCIAL:	FRANCHISOR TRAINING/SUPPORT:
Established in 1974; . . 1st Franchised in 1982	Cash Investment: $100-150K	Financial Assistance Provided: . . . . .Yes
Company-Owned Units (As of 12/1/1989): . 22	Total Investment: $150-200K	Site Selection Assistance: . . . . . . .Yes
Franchised Units (12/1/1989): 22	Fees: Franchise - $20K	Lease Negotiation Assistance: . . . . .Yes
Total Units (12/1/1989): 44	Royalty: 4%, Advert: 1%	Co-operative Advertising: . . . . . . .Yes
Distribution: US-44;Can-0;Overseas-0	Contract Periods (Yrs.): 15/15	Training: . . . . 2 Wks. Headquarters,
North America: . . . . 9 States	Area Development Agreement: . .No	. . . . 2 Wks. Site
Concentration: . . . .11 in FL, 4 in IL, 2 in TX	Sub-Franchise Contract: . . . . .No	On-Going Support: . . . . . b,C,D,E,G,H,I
Registered: . . . . All States	Expand in Territory: . . . . Yes	Full-Time Franchisor Support Staff: . .110
. . . .	Passive Ownership: . . . Not Allowed	EXPANSION PLANS:
Average # of Employees: . . . . .4 FT	Encourage Conversions: . . . . Yes	US: . . . . All US
Prior Industry Experience: . . . . Helpful	Franchisee Purchase(s) Required: .No	Canada - No, ...Overseas - No

LEGALSTAFF

1415 21st St.
Sacramento, CA 95814
TEL: (916) 446-7792 C
FAX:
Mr. Steven K. Greene, Fran. Dir.

LEGALSTAFF offers a unique, specialized employment agency franchise which provides placement services for all legal personnel, including legal secretaries, paralegals, law clerks and attorneys. The LEGALSTAFF franchisee can meet all law office or legal department staffing needs by providing personnel on either a temporary or permanent basis. A "white collar" business where the franchisee can work with highly-qualified applicants and clients.

HISTORY:	FINANCIAL:	FRANCHISOR TRAINING/SUPPORT:
Established in 1973; . . 1st Franchised in 1988	Cash Investment: $35-45K	Financial Assistance Provided: . . . Yes(I)
Company-Owned Units (As of 12/1/1989): . .4	Total Investment: $50-75K	Site Selection Assistance: . . . . . . .Yes
Franchised Units (12/1/1989): 5	Fees: Franchise - $25K	Lease Negotiation Assistance: . . . . .Yes
Total Units (12/1/1989): 9	Royalty: 4-8%, Advert: 0%	Co-operative Advertising: . . . . . . .Yes
Distribution: US-9;Can-0;Overseas-0	Contract Periods (Yrs.): 10/5/5	Training: . . . . 2 Wks. Headquarters,
North America: . . . . 3 States	Area Development Agreement: . .No	. . . . 1 Wk. Franchisee's Office
Concentration: . . . 7 in CA, 1 in TX, 1 in PA	Sub-Franchise Contract: . . . . .No	On-Going Support: . . . . . B,C,D,E,G,H,I
Registered: . . . . CA,IL,NY,OR	Expand in Territory: . . . . Yes	Full-Time Franchisor Support Staff: . . . 9
. . . .	Passive Ownership: . . . . . .Allowed	EXPANSION PLANS:
Average # of Employees: . . . . . 1-2 FT, 1 PT	Encourage Conversions: . . . . .No	US: . . . . All US
Prior Industry Experience: . . . . Helpful	Franchisee Purchase(s) Required: .No	Canada - No, ...Overseas - No

LIFETIME MEDICAL

P.O. Box 1468
Pawtucket, RI 02862
TEL: (800) 333-6877 (401) 728-9898
FAX:
Ms. Marie Issa, President

LIFETIME MEDICAL assists qualified individuals with a system of business ownership that has had a successful track record in the field of nursing personnel placement.

HISTORY: . . . . IFA	FINANCIAL:	FRANCHISOR TRAINING/SUPPORT:
Established in 1979; . . 1st Franchised in 1986	Cash Investment: $50-100K	Financial Assistance Provided: . . . . . No
Company-Owned Units (As of 12/1/1989): . .1	Total Investment: $50-100K	Site Selection Assistance: . . . . .Yes
Franchised Units (12/1/1989): 5	Fees: Franchise - $16K	Lease Negotiation Assistance: . . . . .Yes
Total Units (12/1/1989): 6	Royalty: 4.5%, Advert: 0%	Co-operative Advertising: . . . . No
Distribution: US-6;Can-0;Overseas-0	Contract Periods (Yrs.): 10/10	Training: . . . . 2 Wks. Headquarters
North America: . . . . 4 States	Area Development Agreement: . .No	. . . .
Concentration: . . . 3 in MA, 1 in CT, 1 in NH	Sub-Franchise Contract: . . . . . .No	On-Going Support: . . . . .C,D,I
Registered: . . . CA,FL,HI,MD,MI,OR,RI,VA	Expand in Territory: . . . . Yes	Full-Time Franchisor Support Staff: . . 25
. . . . .WI	Passive Ownership: . . . Discouraged	EXPANSION PLANS:
Average # of Employees: . . . . 2-5 FT, 1-3 PT	Encourage Conversions: . . . . . Yes	US: . . . . All US
Prior Industry Experience: . . . . Helpful	Franchisee Purchase(s) Required: .No	Canada - No, ...Overseas - No

MANAGEMENT RECRUITERS

1127 Euclid Ave., # 1400
Cleveland, OH 44115
TEL: (800) 366-6744 (216) 696-1122 C
FAX: (216) 696-3221
Mr. Robert Angell, VP Fran. Mktg.

MAGAGEMENT RECRUITERS is the world's largest and most professional contingency search firm. Our slogan is apt - "the search and recruiting specialists." Our market is mid-management and professional, the entire gamut of positions from $25,000 - $75,000 per annum and higher.

HISTORY: . . . . .IFA/CFA	FINANCIAL: NY-CDI	FRANCHISOR TRAINING/SUPPORT:
Established in 1957; . . 1st Franchised in 1965	Cash Investment: $35-62K	Financial Assistance Provided: . . . . . No
Company-Owned Units (As of 12/1/1989): . 28	Total Investment: $35-62K	Site Selection Assistance: . . . . .Yes
Franchised Units (12/1/1989): 381	Fees: Franchise - $20-30K	Lease Negotiation Assistance: . . . . .Yes
Total Units (12/1/1989): 409	Royalty: 7%, Advert: 5%	Co-operative Advertising: . . . . No
Distribution: US-409;Can-0;Overseas-0	Contract Periods (Yrs.): 5-10	Training: . . . . 3 Wks. Headquarters
North America: . . . . . . 45 States and DC	Area Development Agreement: . .No	. . . .
Concentration: . 34 in CA, 26 in OH, 24 in FL	Sub-Franchise Contract: . . . . . .No	On-Going Support: . . . . . C,D,E,G,H,I
Registered: . . . . All Except AB	Expand in Territory: . . . . Yes	Full-Time Franchisor Support Staff: . . 75
. . . .	Passive Ownership: . . . Discouraged	EXPANSION PLANS:
Average # of Employees: . . . . .4-6 FT	Encourage Conversions: . . . . . Yes	US: . . . . All US
Prior Industry Experience: . . . . Helpful	Franchisee Purchase(s) Required: .No	Canada - Yes, . . . Overseas - Yes

MEDICAL PERSONNEL POOL

2050 Spectrum Blvd.
Ft. Lauderdale, FL 33432
TEL: (800) 937-7665 (305) 938-7600
FAX: (305) 938-7775
Mr. Tom Camplese, Dir. Fran. Sales

MEDICAL PERSONNEL POOL is an international provider of quality medical care professionals to hospitals, nursing homes and private patients in the home.

HISTORY: . . . . IFA	FINANCIAL: NYSE-BLKHR	FRANCHISOR TRAINING/SUPPORT:
Established in 1946; . . 1st Franchised in 1966	Cash Investment: $50-75K	Financial Assistance Provided: . . . . . No
Company-Owned Units (As of 12/1/1989): . 81	Total Investment: $100-125K	Site Selection Assistance: . . . . .Yes
Franchised Units (12/1/1989): 207	Fees: Franchise - $15-25K	Lease Negotiation Assistance: . . . . .Yes
Total Units (12/1/1989): 288	Royalty: 5%, Advert: 0%	Co-operative Advertising: . . . . .Yes
Distribution: US-283;Can-5;Overseas-0	Contract Periods (Yrs.): 5/10	Training: . . . . 2 Wks. Headquarters,
North America: . . . . 44 States, 3 Provinces	Area Development Agreement: . .No	. . . . 2 Wks. Site Opening
Concentration: . 35 in FL, 21 in CA, 17 in NY	Sub-Franchise Contract: . . . . . .No	On-Going Support: . . . a,B,C,D,E,F,G,H,I
Registered: . . . . .All	Expand in Territory: . . . . Yes	Full-Time Franchisor Support Staff: . .215
. . . .	Passive Ownership: . . . Discouraged	EXPANSION PLANS:
Average # of Employees: . . . . . . 2 FT, 1 PT	Encourage Conversions: . . . . . Yes	US: . . . . All US
Prior Industry Experience: . . . . Helpful	Franchisee Purchase(s) Required: .No	Canada - Yes, . . . Overseas - Yes

MURPHY GROUP, THE

1211 W. 22nd St.
Oak Brook, IL 60521
TEL: (312) 571-1088
FAX:
Mr. William Murphy, President

Recruiting and placing administrative, sales and professional candidates and office staff. Audio tape, video tape, and training manuals. Computerized job order network running in Illinois and available in other areas with at least 7 other franchisees at additional cost.

HISTORY: . . . .
Established in 1957; . . 1st Franchised in 1967
Company-Owned Units (As of 12/1/1989): . .3
Franchised Units (12/1/1989): 8
Total Units (12/1/1989): 11
Distribution: US-11;Can-0;Overseas-0
  North America: . . . . .1 State
  Concentration: . . . . 11 in IL
  Registered: IL
. . . .
Average # of Employees: . . . . .4 FT
Prior Industry Experience: . . . . Helpful

FINANCIAL:
Cash Investment: $45-50K
Total Investment: $45-50K
Fees: Franchise - $15K
  Royalty: 7-10%, Advert: 0%
Contract Periods (Yrs.): 3/20
Area Development Agreement: . .No
Sub-Franchise Contract: . . . . .No
Expand in Territory: . . . . Yes
Passive Ownership: . . . Not Allowed
Encourage Conversions: . . . . . Yes
Franchisee Purchase(s) Required: .No

FRANCHISOR TRAINING/SUPPORT:
Financial Assistance Provided: . . . . . No
Site Selection Assistance: . . . . . . .NA
Lease Negotiation Assistance: . . . . .Yes
Co-operative Advertising: . . . . . . .Yes
Training: . . . . . . 3-4 Wks. Headquarters
. . . .
On-Going Support: . . . . A,B,H,I
Full-Time Franchisor Support Staff: . . .7
EXPANSION PLANS:
  US: . . . . .All US
  Canada - No, ...Overseas - No

NORRELL SERVICES

3535 Piedmont Rd. NE
Atlanta, GA 30305
TEL: (800) 334-9694 (404) 240-3370 C
FAX:
Mr. Stan Anderson, Fran. Devel.

A consultative approach to the temporary help industry, catering to the office automation, banking, retailing, manufacturing and insurance industries. Implementing programs specifically designed for the client company's changing personnel needs. Our regional, district and pre-opening managers assist in all phases of growth and business development.

HISTORY: . . . . IFA/WIF
Established in 1961; . . 1st Franchised in 1967
Company-Owned Units (As of 12/1/1989): 134
Franchised Units (12/1/1989): 141
Total Units (12/1/1989): 275
Distribution: US-268;Can-7;Overseas-0
  North America: . . . . 41 States, 2 Provinces
  Concentration: . 30 in CA, 25 in FL, 22 in GA
  Registered: . . . . .All
. . . .
Average # of Employees: . . . . .3 FT
Prior Industry Experience: . . . . . . Helpful

FINANCIAL:
Cash Investment: $50-80K
Total Investment: $50-80K
Fees: Franchise - $0
  Royalty: Var., Advert: 0%
Contract Periods (Yrs.): 15/15
Area Development Agreement: . .No
Sub-Franchise Contract: . . . . .No
Expand in Territory: . . . . Yes
Passive Ownership: . . . Not Allowed
Encourage Conversions: . . . . .No
Franchisee Purchase(s) Required: .No

FRANCHISOR TRAINING/SUPPORT:
Financial Assistance Provided: . . . . . No
Site Selection Assistance: . . . . . . .Yes
Lease Negotiation Assistance: . . . . .Yes
Co-operative Advertising: . . . . . . .Yes
Training: . . . . . . 2 Wks. Headquarters, 1
  . . . Wk. Field Training, On-going Field
On-Going Support: . . . . .A,C,D,E,G,H,I
Full-Time Franchisor Support Staff: . . 50
EXPANSION PLANS:
  US: . . . . .All US
  Canada - Yes, ...Overseas - No

NURSEFINDERS

1200 Copeland Rd., # 200
Arlington, TX 76011
TEL: (800 445-0459
FAX: (817) 861-8185
Ms. Debra Ebel, Dir. Fran. Sales

NURSEFINDERS' offices provide supplemental staffing to health care facilities, private duty care to patients in health care facilities and home health care services to patients in their homes. Franchisees receive thorough training, proven business systems and strong home office support.

HISTORY: . . . .
Established in 1974; . . 1st Franchised in 1978
Company-Owned Units (As of 12/1/1989): . 34
Franchised Units (12/1/1989): 105
Total Units (12/1/1989): 139
Distribution: US-139;Can-0;Overseas-0
  North America: . . . . 39 States
  Concentration: . . 21 in FL, 13 in IL, 10 in CA
  Registered: . . . . All Except AB
. . . .
Average # of Employees: . . . . . 4-6 FT, 1 PT
Prior Industry Experience: . . . . Helpful

FINANCIAL:
Cash Investment: $90-235K
Total Investment: $90-235K
Fees: Franchise - $15-55K
  Royalty: 5%, Advert: 0%
Contract Periods (Yrs.): 5/5
Area Development Agreement: Yes/2
Sub-Franchise Contract: . . . . .No
Expand in Territory: . . . . Yes
Passive Ownership: . . . Not Allowed
Encourage Conversions: . . . . .No
Franchisee Purchase(s) Required: .No

FRANCHISOR TRAINING/SUPPORT:
Financial Assistance Provided: . . . . .No
Site Selection Assistance: . . . . . . .Yes
Lease Negotiation Assistance: . . . . .No
Co-operative Advertising: . . . . .No
Training: . . . . 2 Wks. Field, 2 Wks.
  . . . . . . Home Office, 2 Wks. On-site
On-Going Support: . . . . .B,C,D,E,G,H,I
Full-Time Franchisor Support Staff: . . 52
EXPANSION PLANS:
  US: . . . . .All US
  Canada - No, ... Overseas - No

PROFESSIONAL DYNAMETRIC PROGRAMS / PDP

400 W. Highway 24, # 201, Box 5289
Woodland Park, CO 80866
TEL: (719) 687-6074
FAX:
Mr. Bruce Hubby, President

The PDP System is used for the motivation, communication and understanding of people. PDP products encompass profile analysis, objective screening, team building and performance evaluation. The Profile Analysis product (PRO SCAN) is a heavily-researched data base (1 MM) of stimuli-generated behavioral predictions. Persons experienced in upper management and sales have quicker success rate.

HISTORY: . . . .
Established in 1978; . . 1st Franchised in 1979
Company-Owned Units (As of 12/1/1989): . .1
Franchised Units (12/1/1989): 25
Total Units (12/1/1989): 26
Distribution: US-21;Can-4;Overseas-1
North America: . . . . 11 States, 2 Provinces
Concentration: . . . 5 in CA, 2 in BC, 2 in PA
Registered: . . . . .CA,FL
. . . .
Average # of Employees: . . . . . . 2 FT, 2 PT
Prior Industry Experience: . . . . Helpful

FINANCIAL:
Cash Investment: $25-27.5K
Total Investment: $40-60K
Fees: Franchise - $25-27.5K
  Royalty: 30%, Advert: 0%
Contract Periods (Yrs.): 7/3
Area Development Agreement: . .No
Sub-Franchise Contract: . . . . .No
Expand in Territory: . . . . Yes
Passive Ownership: . . . Not Allowed
Encourage Conversions: . . . . . .No
Franchisee Purchase(s) Required: Yes

FRANCHISOR TRAINING/SUPPORT:
Financial Assistance Provided: . . . Yes(I)
Site Selection Assistance: . . . . .NA
Lease Negotiation Assistance: . . . . .NA
Co-operative Advertising: . . . . .Yes
Training: . . . . 1 Wk. Headquarters
. . . .
On-Going Support: . . . . .G,H,I
Full-Time Franchisor Support Staff: . . . 5
EXPANSION PLANS:
US: . . . . All US
Canada - Yes, . . . Overseas - Yes

R. Ph. STAFFING

P.O. Box 23743
Tigard, OR 97223
TEL: (503) 244-2426 C
FAX:
Ms. Karen M. Freier, GM/Owner

We are a temporary service, providing pharmacists to all types of pharmacies, including retail, hospital and medical clinics, encompassing all aspects of pharmacy. Future plans will incorporate support personnel for pharmacies.

HISTORY: . . . .
Established in 1983; . . 1st Franchised in 1986
Company-Owned Units (As of 12/1/1989): . .1
Franchised Units (12/1/1989): 0
Total Units (12/1/1989): 1
Distribution: US-1;Can-0;Overseas-0
North America: . . . . .1 State
Concentration: . . . . 1 in OR
Registered: . . . . CA,OR,WI
. . . .
Average # of Employees: . . . . . . 1 FT, 6 PT
Prior Industry Experience: . . . . Helpful

FINANCIAL:
Cash Investment: $20K
Total Investment: $20K
Fees: Franchise - $10-15K
  Royalty: 4.5%, Advert: 1/2%
Contract Periods (Yrs.): 7/7
Area Development Agreement: Yes/7
Sub-Franchise Contract: . . . . . Yes
Expand in Territory: . . . . Yes
Passive Ownership: . . . . . .Allowed
Encourage Conversions: . . . . . .No
Franchisee Purchase(s) Required: .No

FRANCHISOR TRAINING/SUPPORT:
Financial Assistance Provided: . . . . .No
Site Selection Assistance: . . . . .Yes
Lease Negotiation Assistance: . . . . .NA
Co-operative Advertising: . . . . .Yes
Training: . . . . 5 Days Headquarters,
. . . . 5 Days Franchisee Site
On-Going Support: . . . . C,D,G,h
Full-Time Franchisor Support Staff: . . . 1
EXPANSION PLANS:
US: . . . . All US
Canada - No, ...Overseas - No

REMEDYTEMP

32122 Camino Capistrano
San Juan Capistrano, CA 92675
TEL: (800) 722-8376 (714) 661-1211
FAX: (714) 248-0813
Mr. Jerry Rhydderch, VP Fran. Devel.

REMEDYTEMP's franchise program provides entrepreneurs with an opportunity to develop a profitable and substantial business in an exclusive market using the proven system, training, marketing and on-going support of one of California's most established and respected temporary help companies.

HISTORY: . . . . IFA
Established in 1968; . . 1st Franchised in 1987
Company-Owned Units (As of 12/1/1989): . 46
Franchised Units (12/1/1989): 17
Total Units (12/1/1989): 63
Distribution: US-63;Can-0;Overseas-0
North America: . . . . 14 States
Concentration: . . .43 in CA, 4 in AZ, 3 in VA
Registered: . . . CA,FL,HI,IL,IN,MD,MI,MN
. . . . .NY,OR,RI,VA,WA,WI
Average # of Employees: . . . . . . 3 FT, 1 PT
Prior Industry Experience: . . . . Helpful

FINANCIAL:
Cash Investment: $35-50K
Total Investment: $90-125K
Fees: Franchise - $15K
  Royalty: 6.5%, Advert: 1/2%
Contract Periods (Yrs.): 10/10
Area Development Agreement: . .No
Sub-Franchise Contract: . . . . .No
Expand in Territory: . . . . Yes
Passive Ownership: . . . Discouraged
Encourage Conversions: . . . . . Yes
Franchisee Purchase(s) Required: .No

FRANCHISOR TRAINING/SUPPORT:
Financial Assistance Provided: . . . . .No
Site Selection Assistance: . . . . .Yes
Lease Negotiation Assistance: . . . . .Yes
Co-operative Advertising: . . . . .Yes
Training: . . . . 5 Days Headquarters, 5
. . . . .Days Branch
On-Going Support: . . . A,B,C,D,E,G,H,I
Full-Time Franchisor Support Staff: . . . 6
EXPANSION PLANS:
US: . . . . All US
Canada - No, ...Overseas - No

RETAIL RECRUITERS / SPECTRA PROFESSIONAL SEARCH

100 Foxborough Blvd., # 201
Foxboro, MA 02035
TEL: (800) 323-0501 (508) 543-0400 C
FAX: (508) 543-6276
Mr. Jacques Lapointe, President

RETAIL RECRUITERS / SPECTRA PROFESSIONAL SEARCH specialize in executive recruiting in permanent placement on a continuing basis. Offers complete state-of-the-art training plus 8 video tapes on recruiting business. Offers strong management training to help new franchisees get off to a strong start.

HISTORY: . . . . .WIF
Established in 1973; . . 1st Franchised in 1976
Company-Owned Units (As of 12/1/1989): . .0
Franchised Units (12/1/1989): 40
Total Units (12/1/1989): 40
Distribution: US-40;Can-0;Overseas-0
North America: . . . .
Concentration: . . .11 in CA, 3 in FL, 3 in MA
Registered: . . . . .CA,FL,MD,MI,NY,RI,VA
. . . .
Average # of Employees: . . . . .4-6 FT
Prior Industry Experience: . . . . . . Helpful

FINANCIAL:
Cash Investment: $70-80K
Total Investment: $70-80K
Fees: Franchise - $30-35K
Royalty: 7%, Advert: 1%
Contract Periods (Yrs.): 10/5
Area Development Agreement: . .No
Sub-Franchise Contract: . . . . .No
Expand in Territory: . . . . . . Yes
Passive Ownership: . . . Not Allowed
Encourage Conversions: . . . . . Yes
Franchisee Purchase(s) Required: .No

FRANCHISOR TRAINING/SUPPORT:
Financial Assistance Provided: . . .Yes(I)
Site Selection Assistance: . . . . . . .Yes
Lease Negotiation Assistance: . . . . .Yes
Co-operative Advertising: . . . . . . .Yes
Training: . . . . 2 Wks. Headquarters,
. . . . .2 Wks. On-site
On-Going Support: . . . . .C,D,E,F,G,H,I
Full-Time Franchisor Support Staff: . . 12
EXPANSION PLANS:
US: . . . . .All US
Canada - Yes, ...Overseas - No

RETIREE SKILLS

1475 W. Prince Rd.
Tucson, AZ 85705
TEL: (800) 888-9851 (602) 888-8310
FAX:
Mr. Robert Rheinhart, President

A temporary help service, specializing in the "over 50" worker. Over 12 years in business. With the "over 50" age group being the fastest-growing segment of our populaton, the success should explode in the 90's.

HISTORY: . . . .
Established in 1978; . . 1st Franchised in 1990
Company-Owned Units (As of 12/1/1989): . .1
Franchised Units (12/1/1989): 1
Total Units (12/1/1989): 2
Distribution: US-2;Can-0;Overseas-0
North America: . . . . .1 State
Concentration: . . . . .2 in NM
Registered: . . . .
. . . .
Average # of Employees: . . . . . 2 FT, 1 PT
Prior Industry Experience: . . . . . . Helpful

FINANCIAL:
Cash Investment: $30K
Total Investment: $30K
Fees: Franchise - $15K
Royalty: 5%, Advert: 1%
Contract Periods (Yrs.): . . . 10/10
Area Development Agreement: . .No
Sub-Franchise Contract: . . . . .No
Expand in Territory: . . . . . . Yes
Passive Ownership: . . . Not Allowed
Encourage Conversions: . . . . . .No
Franchisee Purchase(s) Required: .No

FRANCHISOR TRAINING/SUPPORT:
Financial Assistance Provided: . . . . .No
Site Selection Assistance: . . . . . . .Yes
Lease Negotiation Assistance: . . . . .Yes
Co-operative Advertising: . . . . . . .Yes
Training: . . . . . . 5 Working Days Head-
. . . . .quarters
On-Going Support: . . . . D,E
Full-Time Franchisor Support Staff: . . .3
EXPANSION PLANS:
US: . . . . . .Non-reg. States W. of Miss.
Canada - No, ...Overseas - No

ROMAC AND ASSOCIATES

183 Middle St., P.O. Box 7469 DTS
Portland, ME 04112
TEL: (800) 341-0263 (207) 773-6298 C
FAX: (207) 773-5633
Mr. Rick Sandler, Dir. Mktg.

Executive recruiting offices, specializing in the permanent and temporary placement of accounting, banking and financial services personnel. ROMAC offers one of the best training programs in the industry, as well as on-going training support.

HISTORY: . . . .
Established in 1966; . . 1st Franchised in 1978
Company-Owned Units (As of 12/1/1989): . .2
Franchised Units (12/1/1989): 39
Total Units (12/1/1989): 41
Distribution: US-41;Can-0;Overseas-0
North America: . . . . 23 States
Concentration: . . . .4 in FL, 3 in CT, 3 in NY
Registered: . . .CA,IL,IN,MI,MN,NY,OR,VA
. . . . WA,WI
Average # of Employees: . . . . .4 FT
Prior Industry Experience: . . . . . . Helpful

FINANCIAL:
Cash Investment: $100-125K
Total Investment: $100-125K
Fees: Franchise - $40K
Royalty: 8%, Advert: 1%
Contract Periods (Yrs.): 15/15
Area Development Agreement: . .No
Sub-Franchise Contract: . . . . .No
Expand in Territory: . . . . . . Yes
Passive Ownership: . . . Not Allowed
Encourage Conversions: . . . . . Yes
Franchisee Purchase(s) Required: .No

FRANCHISOR TRAINING/SUPPORT:
Financial Assistance Provided: . . .Yes(D)
Site Selection Assistance: . . . . . . .Yes
Lease Negotiation Assistance: . . . . .Yes
Co-operative Advertising: . . . . . . .Yes
Training: . . . . 5 Days Headquarters,
. . . . 15 Days Site
On-Going Support: . . . .A,B,C,D,E,G,h,I
Full-Time Franchisor Support Staff: . . 18
EXPANSION PLANS:
US: . . . . West, Midwest
Canada - No, ...Overseas - No

ROTH YOUNG

535 Fifth Ave.
New York, NY 10017
TEL: (800) 343-8518 (212) 557-4900 C
FAX: (212) 972-5367
Mr. Collin Gaffney, Dir. Fran. Dev.

25 years of growth and productivity in the recruitment of executives for the hospitality, retail, food, clerical and health care industries. Computerized "interchange" system provides nationwide referral network for major client companies and applicants.

HISTORY: . . . . IFA	FINANCIAL: AMER-WRS	FRANCHISOR TRAINING/SUPPORT:
Established in 1964; . . 1st Franchised in 1967	Cash Investment: $35-50K	Financial Assistance Provided: . . .Yes(D)
Company-Owned Units (As of 12/1/1989): . .1	Total Investment: $75-100K	Site Selection Assistance: . . . . . . .Yes
Franchised Units (12/1/1989): 29	Fees: Franchise - $50K	Lease Negotiation Assistance: . . . . .Yes
Total Units (12/1/1989): 30	Royalty: 8%, Advert: 0%	Co-operative Advertising: . . . . .Yes
Distribution: US-30;Can-0;Overseas-0	Contract Periods (Yrs.): 10/10	Training: . . . . 2 Wks. Headquarters
North America: . . . . 23 States	Area Development Agreement: . .No	. . . .
Concentration: . . . .3 in TX, 2 in FL, 2 in OH	Sub-Franchise Contract: . . . . .No	On-Going Support: . . . . . .C,D,E,G,H,I
Registered: . . . . .NY,RI,VA,WA	Expand in Territory: . . . . . . Yes	Full-Time Franchisor Support Staff: . . 12
. . . .	Passive Ownership: . . . Not Allowed	EXPANSION PLANS:
Average # of Employees: . . . . .4 FT	Encourage Conversions: . . . . Yes	US: . . . . .All US
Prior Industry Experience: . . . . Helpful	Franchisee Purchase(s) Required: .No	Canada - Yes, ...Overseas - No

SALES CONSULTANTS

1127 Euclid Ave.
Cleveland, OH 44115
TEL: (800) 366-6744 (216) 696-1122 C
FAX: (216) 696-3221
Mr. Robert Angell, VP Fran. Mktg.

Our slogan says it all, "Finding and placing sales, sales management and marketing talent is our only business." SALES CONSULTANTS is the world's largest and most professional organization specializing in the search, recruitment and placement of salesmen, saleswomen, sales managers and marketing staff.

HISTORY: . . . . .IFA/CFA	FINANCIAL: NYSE-CDI	FRANCHISOR TRAINING/SUPPORT:
Established in 1957; . . 1st Franchised in 1966	Cash Investment: $35-62K	Financial Assistance Provided: . . . . . No
Company-Owned Units (As of 12/1/1989): . 31	Total Investment: $35-62K	Site Selection Assistance: . . . . .Yes
Franchised Units (12/1/1989): 134	Fees: Franchise - $20-30K	Lease Negotiation Assistance: . . . . .Yes
Total Units (12/1/1989): 165	Royalty: 7%, Advert: 1/2%	Co-operative Advertising: . . . . No
Distribution: US-165;Can-0;Overseas-0	Contract Periods (Yrs.): . . . 5-20/10	Training: . . . . 3 Wks. Headquarters
North America: . . . . 37 States + DC	Area Development Agreement: . .No	. . . .
Concentration: . . 21 in CA, 15 in NJ, 11 in FL	Sub-Franchise Contract: . . . . .No	On-Going Support: . . . . . .C,D,E,G,H,I
Registered: . . . . All States	Expand in Territory: . . . . . . Yes	Full-Time Franchisor Support Staff: . . 75
. . . .	Passive Ownership: . . . Discouraged	EXPANSION PLANS:
Average # of Employees: . . . . .4-6 FT	Encourage Conversions: . . . . Yes	US: . . . . .All US
Prior Industry Experience: . . . . Helpful	Franchisee Purchase(s) Required: .No	Canada - Yes, . . . Overseas - Yes

SANFORD ROSE ASSOCIATES

265 S. Main St.
Akron, OH 44308
TEL: (800) 759-7673 (216) 762-6211
FAX:
Mr. Doug Eilertson, EVP

"Executive Search" is distinct within the SRA organization! We provide a highly-reliable service to fill critical openings with our corporate clients. Only the most qualified candidates are presented. Our adaptability allows us to work at virtually all professional levels developing repeat business!

HISTORY: . . . . IFA	FINANCIAL:	FRANCHISOR TRAINING/SUPPORT:
Established in 1959; . . 1st Franchised in 1970	Cash Investment: $40-50K	Financial Assistance Provided: . . .Yes(D)
Company-Owned Units (As of 12/1/1989): . .1	Total Investment: $50-75K	Site Selection Assistance: . . . . . . .Yes
Franchised Units (12/1/1989): 87	Fees: Franchise - $29.5K	Lease Negotiation Assistance: . . . . .Yes
Total Units (12/1/1989): 88	Royalty: 8-3%, Advert: 0%	Co-operative Advertising: . . . . .NA
Distribution: US-88;Can-0;Overseas-0	Contract Periods (Yrs.): . . . . Infin.	Training: . . . . 3 Wks. Headquarters,
North America: . . . . 25 States	Area Development Agreement: . .No	. . . . .2 Wks. On-site
Concentration: . . . 18 in OH, 9 in PA, 5 in FL	Sub-Franchise Contract: . . . . .No	On-Going Support: . . A,B,C,D,E,F,G,H,I
Registered: . . . CA,FL,IL,IN,MD,MI,MN,NY	Expand in Territory: . . . . . . Yes	Full-Time Franchisor Support Staff: . . . .
. . . . OR,RI,VA,WA,WI	Passive Ownership: . . . Not Allowed	EXPANSION PLANS:
Average # of Employees: . . . . .1-10 FT, 1 PT	Encourage Conversions: . . . . .No	US: . . . . .All US
Prior Industry Experience: . . . . . .Necessary	Franchisee Purchase(s) Required: Yes	Canada - No, ...Overseas - No

SARA CARE

1612 Lee Trevino, # A
El Paso, TX 79936
TEL: (800) 351-CARE
FAX: (915) 591-2579
Ms. Sara Addis, Sales Rep.

In-home personal support services from coast-to-coast and Japan. SARA CARE offers home health care, companion care for the elderly, baby/child care and house/pet care, all of which make up a major, dominant growth industry - home care.

HISTORY: . . . . IFA	FINANCIAL:	FRANCHISOR TRAINING/SUPPORT:
Established in 1978; . . 1st Franchised in 1982	Cash Investment: $28-40K	Financial Assistance Provided: . . . . . No
Company-Owned Units (As of 12/1/1989): . . 1	Total Investment: $28-40K	Site Selection Assistance: . . . . .Yes
Franchised Units (12/1/1989): 6	Fees: Franchise - $7.5-12.5K	Lease Negotiation Assistance: . . . . .Yes
Total Units (12/1/1989): 7	Royalty: 7%, Advert: 2%	Co-operative Advertising: . . . . .No
Distribution: US-6;Can-0;Overseas-1	Contract Periods (Yrs.): 10/10	Training: . . . . .1 Wk. Headquarters.
North America: . . . . 4 States	Area Development Agreement: Yes/1	. . . . 1 Wk. On-site
Concentration: . . . .3 in FL, 1 in CA, 1 in KS	Sub-Franchise Contract: . . . . .No	On-Going Support: . . . . . . C,d,E,G,H,I
Registered: . . . . CA	Expand in Territory: . . . . Yes	Full-Time Franchisor Support Staff: . . . 6
. . . .	Passive Ownership: . . . Discouraged	EXPANSION PLANS:
Average # of Employees: . . . . .2 FT	Encourage Conversions: . . . . . NA	US: . . . . .All US
Prior Industry Experience: . . . . Helpful	Franchisee Purchase(s) Required: .No	Canada - Yes, ...Overseas - No

---

SITTERS UNLIMITED

23015 Del Lago, D2-152
Laguna Hills, CA 92653
TEL: (714) 380-8733
FAX:
Ms. Nancy Ann Van Wie, President

The nation's largest and only coast-to-coast child care agency which provides in-home care on both a part-time and full-time basis. In addition to sitters and nannies, we also provide child care services on a nationwide basis for hotels and major conventions.

HISTORY:	FINANCIAL:	FRANCHISOR TRAINING/SUPPORT:
Established in 1979; . . 1st Franchised in 1982	Cash Investment: $13-25K	Financial Assistance Provided: . . . . . No
Company-Owned Units (As of 12/1/1989): . .0	Total Investment: $16-28K	Site Selection Assistance: . . . . .NA
Franchised Units (12/1/1989): 22	Fees: Franchise - $13-28K	Lease Negotiation Assistance: . . . . .NA
Total Units (12/1/1989): 22	Royalty: 5%, Advert: 1%	Co-operative Advertising: . . . . .Yes
Distribution: US-22;Can-0;Overseas-0	Contract Periods (Yrs.): 5/5	Training: . . . . .1 Wk. Headquarters
North America: . . . . 8 States	Area Development Agreement: Yes/Inf	. . . .
Concentration: . . . . .5 in IL, 5 in CA	Sub-Franchise Contract: . . . . Yes	On-Going Support: . . . . . . .b,c,d,G,H,I
Registered: . . . . . CA,FL,HI,IL,MD,NY,VA	Expand in Territory: . . . . Yes	Full-Time Franchisor Support Staff: . . . 1
. . . .	Passive Ownership: . . . Discouraged	EXPANSION PLANS:
Average # of Employees: . . . . . . 1 FT, 1 PT	Encourage Conversions: . . . . .No	US: . . . . .All US
Prior Industry Experience: . . . . Helpful	Franchisee Purchase(s) Required: .No	Canada - Yes, . . . Overseas - Yes

---

SNELLING AND SNELLING / SNELLING TEMPORARIES

4000 S. Tamiami Trail
Sarasota, FL 34231
TEL: (800) 237-9475 (813) 922-9616
FAX: (813) 921-1527
Mr. Richard Spragins, Sr. VP

SNELLING AND SNELLING, America's Personnel System, offers existing & exciting opportunities nationwide in the permanent placement and temporary help industries. With over 38 years of experience in today's competitive marketplace, franchisor offers strong brand-name recognition, proven operating system and excellent training and on-going support.

HISTORY: . . . . IFA	FINANCIAL: OTC-SNEL	FRANCHISOR TRAINING/SUPPORT:
Established in 1951; . . 1st Franchised in 1956	Cash Investment: $50-165K	Financial Assistance Provided: . . . Yes(I)
Company-Owned Units (As of 12/1/1989): . .0	Total Investment: $50-165K	Site Selection Assistance: . . . . .Yes
Franchised Units (12/1/1989): 531	Fees: Franchise - $10-14K	Lease Negotiation Assistance: . . . . .Yes
Total Units (12/1/1989): 531	Royalty: 4.5-7%, Advert: . . 1/2-3%	Co-operative Advertising: . . . . .NA
Distribution: US-526;Can-2;Overseas-3	Contract Periods (Yrs.): . . . .Varies	Training: . . . . 2 Wks. Headquarters,
North America: . . . . 47 States	Area Development Agreement: . .No	. . . . 2 Wks. Franchisee Site
Concentration: . .42 in TX, 42 in CA, 40 in NJ	Sub-Franchise Contract: . . . . .No	On-Going Support: . . . . D,G
Registered: . . . . All States	Expand in Territory: . . . . Yes	Full-Time Franchisor Support Staff: . .130
. . . .	Passive Ownership: . . . Discouraged	EXPANSION PLANS:
Average # of Employees: . . . . .3-8 FT	Encourage Conversions: . . . . . Yes	US: . . . . .All US
Prior Industry Experience: . . . . Helpful	Franchisee Purchase(s) Required: .No	Canada - Yes, . . . Overseas - Yes

STAFF BUILDERS

1981 Marcus Ave.
Lake Success, NY 11042
TEL: (800) 342-5782
FAX:
Mr. Fred Nicholas, Dir. Fran.

Full-service personnel services, providing both temporary and permanent employment. Two separate franchises - one for health care - second for business/industry. Benefits of financing temporary payroll and accounts receivable, initial and continuous training, computerization, centralized management and risk control.

HISTORY: . . . . IFA
Established in 1961; . . 1st Franchised in 1966
Company-Owned Units (As of 12/1/1989): 100
Franchised Units (12/1/1989): 50
Total Units (12/1/1989): 150
Distribution: US-150;Can-0;Overseas-0
North America: . . . . 29 States
Concentration: . 27 in NY, 21 in CA, 14 in OH
Registered: . . . . All States
. . . .
Average # of Employees: . . . . . . 3 FT, 1 PT
Prior Industry Experience: . . . . Helpful

FINANCIAL: NASD-SBLI
Cash Investment: $15-50K
Total Investment: $75-115K
Fees: Franchise - $15K
Royalty: Var., Advert: 0%
Contract Periods (Yrs.): 10/5
Area Development Agreement: . .No
Sub-Franchise Contract: . . . . . .No
Expand in Territory: . . . . Yes
Passive Ownership: . . . Discouraged
Encourage Conversions: . . . . . Yes
Franchisee Purchase(s) Required: Yes

FRANCHISOR TRAINING/SUPPORT:
Financial Assistance Provided: . . . . . No
Site Selection Assistance: . . . . .Yes
Lease Negotiation Assistance: . . . . .Yes
Co-operative Advertising: . . . . .No
Training: . . . . . . 2-3 Wks. Headquarters
. . . .
On-Going Support: . . . . A,b,C,D,E,G,h,I
Full-Time Franchisor Support Staff: . . . .
EXPANSION PLANS:
US: . . . . .All US
Canada - No, ...Overseas - No

T.L.C. NURSING CENTER

P. O. Box 767519
Roswell, GA 30076
TEL: (404) 396-2273
FAX:
Mr. Bill Wimbish, President

The T.L.C. NURSING CENTER is a private-duty, nurse-placement service devoted to the home health care market primarily, but which is fully capable of furnishing staffing assistance to doctors, hospitals and other institutions. Each Center maintains a Registry of nurses, homemakers, sitters, etc. to which it sub-contracts positions it has obtained through advertising and marketing of its services.

HISTORY: . . . .
Established in 1984; . . 1st Franchised in 1984
Company-Owned Units (As of 12/1/1989): . .1
Franchised Units (12/1/1989): 5
Total Units (12/1/1989): 6
Distribution: US-6;Can-0;Overseas-0
North America: . . . . 2 States
Concentration: . . . . 5 in GA, 1 in PA
Registered: . . . . FL,MI
. . . .
Average # of Employees: . . . . . . 1 FT, 1 PT
Prior Industry Experience: . . . . . Helpful

FINANCIAL:
Cash Investment: $12-35K
Total Investment: $20-50K
Fees: Franchise - $5-20K
Royalty: 8%, Advert: 2%
Contract Periods (Yrs.): 5/5
Area Development Agreement: Yes/5
Sub-Franchise Contract: . . . . . .No
Expand in Territory: . . . . Yes
Passive Ownership: . . . . . .Allowed
Encourage Conversions: . . . . . Yes
Franchisee Purchase(s) Required: .No

FRANCHISOR TRAINING/SUPPORT:
Financial Assistance Provided: . . .Yes(D)
Site Selection Assistance: . . . . . . .Yes
Lease Negotiation Assistance: . . . . .Yes
Co-operative Advertising: . . . . . . .Yes
Training: . . . . .1 Wk. Headquarters,
. . . . .1 Wk. Operating Center
On-Going Support: . . . . .c,d,h
Full-Time Franchisor Support Staff: . . .3
EXPANSION PLANS:
US: . . . . .All US
Canada - Yes, ...Overseas - No

TALENT FORCE TEMPORARIES

2970 Clairmont Rd., # 1000
Atlanta, GA 30329
TEL: (800) 777-5455
FAX: (404) 325-2911
Ms. Rebecca Johnson, Mktg. Dir.

Industry innovator with 14 years' experience as Atlanta's #1 temporary help service, provides you with opportunity for success in the country's fastest-growing industry. TALENT FORCE provides a well-rounded scope of support for our franchisees that includes receivables financing, on-going training, total marketing support and more.

HISTORY: . . . . IFA
Established in 1976; . . 1st Franchised in 1987
Company-Owned Units (As of 12/1/1989): . 10
Franchised Units (12/1/1989): 3
Total Units (12/1/1989): 13
Distribution: US-13;Can-0;Overseas-0
North America: . . . . 4 States
Concentration: . . .10 in GA, 1 in NC, 1 in TN
Registered: . . . . FL,VA
. . . .
Average # of Employees: . . . . .2-3 FT
Prior Industry Experience: . . . . Helpful

FINANCIAL:
Cash Investment: $50-120K
Total Investment: $50-100K
Fees: Franchise - $7.5-17K
Royalty: Varies, Advert: 0%
Contract Periods (Yrs.): 5/5
Area Development Agreement: Yes/5
Sub-Franchise Contract: . . . . . .No
Expand in Territory: . . . . Yes
Passive Ownership: . . . Discouraged
Encourage Conversions: . . . . . Yes
Franchisee Purchase(s) Required: .No

FRANCHISOR TRAINING/SUPPORT:
Financial Assistance Provided: . . .Yes(D)
Site Selection Assistance: . . . . . . .Yes
Lease Negotiation Assistance: . . . . .Yes
Co-operative Advertising: . . . . . . .Yes
Training: . . . . 2 Wks. Headquarters,
. . . . On-going On-site
On-Going Support: . . . . A,B,C,D,E,G,h,I
Full-Time Franchisor Support Staff: . . 52
EXPANSION PLANS:
US: . . . . Southeast
Canada - No, ...Overseas - No

TEMP FORCE

1600 Stewart Ave.
Westbury, NY 11590
TEL: (516) 683-6000 C
FAX: (516) 683-1540
Mr. Michael Ward, Dir. Fran. Dev.

TEMP FORCE, temporary help services, specializes in office, clerical, light industrial, technical and professional personnel. We offer franchise payroll funding, computer management data, bookkeeping services, promotional aids, extensive training and field support, pre-opening site selection, office layout and staffing assistance.

HISTORY: . . . . IFA	FINANCIAL: LONDON-PLC	FRANCHISOR TRAINING/SUPPORT:
Established in 1960; . . . 1st Franchised in 19	Cash Investment: $85-105K	Financial Assistance Provided: . . .Yes(D)
Company-Owned Units (As of 12/1/1989): . .7	Total Investment: $85-105K	Site Selection Assistance: . . . . .Yes
Franchised Units (12/1/1989): 52	Fees: Franchise - $25K	Lease Negotiation Assistance: . . . . .Yes
Total Units (12/1/1989): 59	Royalty: Varies, Advert: . . . 1/2%	Co-operative Advertising: . . . . .Yes
Distribution: US-59;Can-0;Overseas-0	Contract Periods (Yrs.): . . . .Varies	Training: . . . . 2 Wks. Headquarters,
North America: . . . . 26 States	Area Development Agreement: . .No	. . . . 1 Wk. On-site, On-going
Concentration: . . .16 in NY, 4 in PA, 4 in CA	Sub-Franchise Contract: . . . . .No	On-Going Support: . . . A,B,C,D,E,G,H,I
Registered: . . . . All States	Expand in Territory: . . . . . . Yes	Full-Time Franchisor Support Staff: . .200
. . . .	Passive Ownership: . . . Discouraged	EXPANSION PLANS:
Average # of Employees: . . . . .3 FT	Encourage Conversions: . . . . . Yes	US: . . . . .All US
Prior Industry Experience: . . . . . . Helpful	Franchisee Purchase(s) Required: .No	Canada - No, ...Overseas - No

TEMPS & CO.

245 Peachtree Center Ave., # 2500
Atlanta, GA 30303
TEL: (800) 331-3586 (404) 659-5236
FAX: (404) 659-7139
Mr. A. R. "Al" French, Dir. Mktg.

TEMPS & CO. allows you the opportunity to stand out in both temporary and permanent placement. We offer unique service concepts to compete in this high-growth, dynamic industry. Ours is one of the fastest-growing industries in the US today. Call for informaton.

HISTORY: . . . . .WIF	FINANCIAL:	FRANCHISOR TRAINING/SUPPORT:
Established in 1972; . . 1st Franchised in 1988	Cash Investment: . . . .$NA	Financial Assistance Provided: . . .Yes(D)
Company-Owned Units (As of 12/1/1989): . 16	Total Investment: $50-80K	Site Selection Assistance: . . . . .Yes
Franchised Units (12/1/1989): 17	Fees: Franchise - $12.5K	Lease Negotiation Assistance: . . . . .Yes
Total Units (12/1/1989): 33	Royalty: Var., Advert: . . . Var.	Co-operative Advertising: . . . . .Yes
Distribution: US-32;Can-0;Overseas-1	Contract Periods (Yrs.): . . . 5/Indef.	Training: . . . . 2 Wks. Headquarters,
North America: . . . . 11 States	Area Development Agreement: . .No	. . . 1 Wk. On-site, 2 Days Exist. Office
Concentration: . . . 10 in GA, 5 in TX, 3 in FL	Sub-Franchise Contract: . . . . .No	On-Going Support: . . . . .A,C,D,E,G,H,I
Registered: . . . . .FL	Expand in Territory: . . . . . . Yes	Full-Time Franchisor Support Staff: . . .8
. . . .	Passive Ownership: . . . . . .Allowed	EXPANSION PLANS:
Average # of Employees: . . . . .2 FT	Encourage Conversions: . . . . Yes	US: . . . . .All US
Prior Industry Experience: . . . . . . Helpful	Franchisee Purchase(s) Required: .No	Canada - No, ...Overseas - No

TIME SERVICES /
TIME TEMPORARIES

6422 Lima Rd.
Ft. Wayne, IN 46818
TEL: (219) 489-2020
FAX:
Mr. Bob Busch, VP Admin.

Temporary employment - technical, clerical and industrial. TIME TEMPORARIES is a growth company offering franchisees exclusive territories in major markets. Specialization is in the technical fields - i.e. engineers and programmers. On-line operations, search and retrieval systems and centralized payroll and billing.

HISTORY:	FINANCIAL:	FRANCHISOR TRAINING/SUPPORT:
Established in 1981; . . 1st Franchised in 1982	Cash Investment: $50-75K	Financial Assistance Provided: . . . . .No
Company-Owned Units (As of 12/1/1989): . .6	Total Investment: $50-75K	Site Selection Assistance: . . . . .Yes
Franchised Units (12/1/1989): 2	Fees: Franchise - $15K	Lease Negotiation Assistance: . . . . .Yes
Total Units (12/1/1989): 8	Royalty: 50%, Advert: . . . . NA	Co-operative Advertising: . . . . .Yes
Distribution: US-8;Can-0;Overseas-0	Contract Periods (Yrs.): . . . 5/5/5	Training: . . . . 2 Wks. Headquarters,
North America: . . . . 3 States	Area Development Agreement: . .No	. . . .1 Wk. Grand Opening, 2 Days/Mo.
Concentration: . . . . 5 in IN, 2 in OH, 1 in MI	Sub-Franchise Contract: . . . . .No	On-Going Support: . . . a,b,C,D,E,F,G,H,
Registered: . . . . .FL,IN,VA	Expand in Territory: . . . . . . Yes	Full-Time Franchisor Support Staff: . . 30
. . . .	Passive Ownership: . . . . . .Allowed	EXPANSION PLANS:
Average # of Employees: . . . . .4 FT	Encourage Conversions: . . . . .No	US: . . . . Midwest and Florida
Prior Industry Experience: . . . . . . Helpful	Franchisee Purchase(s) Required: Yes	Canada - No, ...Overseas - No

TODAYS TEMPORARY

18111 Preston Rd., # 800
Dallas, TX 75252
TEL: (800) 822-7868 (214) 380-9380
FAX: (214) 250-3732
Ms. Jennifer Allen, Mktg. Coord.

TODAYS TEMPORARY is a national company offering franchisees an exclusive territory in a major market. Franchise owners control profitability by providing only office-related assistance to clients, emphasizing quality service. TODAYS TEMPORARY has been listed in INC. Magazine's 500 fastest-growing companies in 1987 and 1988.

HISTORY: . . . . IFA
Established in 1982; . . 1st Franchised in 1983
Company-Owned Units (As of 12/1/1989): . 13
Franchised Units (12/1/1989): 26
Total Units (12/1/1989): 39
Distribution: US-39;Can-0;Overseas-0
North America: . . . . 14 States
Concentration: . . . 11 in TX, 7 in FL, 4 in NJ
Registered: . . . . . .All States Exc. ND & SD
. . . .
Average # of Employees: . . . . .2 FT
Prior Industry Experience: . . . . . . Helpful

FINANCIAL:
Cash Investment: $60-100K
Total Investment: $60-100K
Fees: Franchise - $0
Royalty: 25%, Advert: 0%
Contract Periods (Yrs.): 5/5/5
Area Development Agreement: . .No
Sub-Franchise Contract: . . . . .No
Expand in Territory: . . . . Yes
Passive Ownership: . . . Not Allowed
Encourage Conversions: . . . . . Yes
Franchisee Purchase(s) Required: .No

FRANCHISOR TRAINING/SUPPORT:
Financial Assistance Provided: . . . Yes(I)
Site Selection Assistance: . . . . . . .Yes
Lease Negotiation Assistance: . . . . .Yes
Co-operative Advertising: . . . . . . .Yes
Training: . . . . 2 Wks. Headquarters,
. . . . . .1-2 Wks. Est. Office, On-going
On-Going Support: . . A,B,C,D,E,F,G,H,I
Full-Time Franchisor Support Staff: . . 50
EXPANSION PLANS:
US: . . . . .All US
Canada - No, ...Overseas - No

TRC TEMPORARY SERVICES

100 Ashford Center N., # 500
Atlanta, GA 30338
TEL: (404) 392-1411
FAX: (404) 393-2742
Mr. Robert Gallagher, VP Fran. Div.

TRC is a full-service, national temporary help company, offering a support program second to none, with exceptional markets available. We specialize in the placement of temporary employees in secretarial, clerical, light industrial, data processing, word processing and more.

HISTORY: . . . . IFA
Established in 1980; . . 1st Franchised in 1984
Company-Owned Units (As of 12/1/1989): . 28
Franchised Units (12/1/1989): 17
Total Units (12/1/1989): 45
Distribution: US-45;Can-0;Overseas-0
North America: . . . . 13 States
Concentration: . . .12 in GA, 8 in TX, 2 in CA
Registered: . . . CA,FL,IL,IN,MD,MI,NY,OR
. . . . RI,VA,WA
Average # of Employees: . . . . .4 FT
Prior Industry Experience: . . . . . . Helpful

FINANCIAL:
Cash Investment: . . . .$
Total Investment: $50-125K
Fees: Franchise - $0
Royalty: 45%, Advert: 0%
Contract Periods (Yrs.): 30
Area Development Agreement: . .No
Sub-Franchise Contract: . . . . .No
Expand in Territory: . . . . Yes
Passive Ownership: . . . Not Allowed
Encourage Conversions: . . . . . Yes
Franchisee Purchase(s) Required: .No

FRANCHISOR TRAINING/SUPPORT:
Financial Assistance Provided: . . .Yes(D)
Site Selection Assistance: . . . . . . .Yes
Lease Negotiation Assistance: . . . . .No
Co-operative Advertising: . . . . . . .Yes
Training: . . . . . . .23 Days Site, 21 Days
. . . . .Headquarters, 3 Days/Qtr.
On-Going Support: . . . . A,B,C,D,E,G,H
Full-Time Franchisor Support Staff: . .130
EXPANSION PLANS:
US: . . . . .All US
Canada - No, ...Overseas - No

V.I.P COMPANION-CARE

4914 W. Genesee St.
Camillus, NY 13031
TEL: (315) 468-5500
FAX:
Mr. Girdon E. Buck, President

V.I.P COMPANION-CARE is a professional service, providing care and companionship to the elderly in their own homes. Our services are of great value to the frail elderly and their families. Through our Live-In and Sitter Companion programs, they may postpone or even avoid the distress of institutionalization. The elderly person can remain at home and retain a sense of dignity and independence.

HISTORY: . . . .
Established in 1984; . . 1st Franchised in 1989
Company-Owned Units (As of 12/1/1989): . .1
Franchised Units (12/1/1989): 2
Total Units (12/1/1989): 3
Distribution: US-3;Can-0;Overseas-0
North America: . . . . 3 States
Concentration: . . . . .1 in PA, 1 in NJ
Registered: . . . . .FL
. . . .
Average # of Employees: . . . . .3 FT
Prior Industry Experience: . . . . . . Helpful

FINANCIAL:
Cash Investment: $100-150K
Total Investment: $100-150K
Fees: Franchise - $35K
Royalty: 7%, Advert: 5%
Contract Periods (Yrs.): . . . 10/10
Area Development Agreement: . .No
Sub-Franchise Contract: . . . . .No
Expand in Territory: . . . . . . Yes
Passive Ownership: . . . Discouraged
Encourage Conversions: . . . . . Yes
Franchisee Purchase(s) Required: .No

FRANCHISOR TRAINING/SUPPORT:
Financial Assistance Provided: . . . Yes(I)
Site Selection Assistance: . . . . . . .Yes
Lease Negotiation Assistance: . . . .Yes
Co-operative Advertising: . . . . . . .Yes
Training: . . . . 1 Wk. Headquarters

On-Going Support: . . . . C,D,E,I
Full-Time Franchisor Support Staff: . . 12
EXPANSION PLANS:
US: . . . . Northeast
Canada - No, ...Overseas - No

WESTERN TEMPORARY SERVICES

301 Lennon Ln.
Walnut Creek, CA 94598
TEL: (800)USA-TEMP (800)FOR-TEMP(CA)
FAX:
Mr. Terry Slocum, Sr. VP

WESTERN provides a full range of temporary help. We finance the temporary payroll and the accounts receivable, provide all insurance coverage, handle invoicing, provide start-up financial incentives, supply advertising and direct mail material and promotional support at no charge to local office.

HISTORY: . . . .
Established in 1948; . . 1st Franchised in 1960
Company-Owned Units (As of 12/1/1989) 225
Franchised Units (12/1/1989): 125
Total Units (12/1/1989): 350
Distribution: US-291;Can-0;Overseas-59
North America: . . . . 45 States
Concentration: . . 65 in CA, 19 in NJ, 15 in IL
Registered: . . .CA,FL,IL,IN,MD,MN,NY,ND
. . . . .RI,SD,VA,WI
Average # of Employees: . . . . . 2 FT, 1 PT
Prior Industry Experience: . . . . . . Helpful

FINANCIAL:
Cash Investment: $15-50K
Total Investment: $15-100K
Fees: Franchise - $10-25K
Royalty: Share GP, Advert: . . 0%
Contract Periods (Yrs.): . . . 5/Infin.
Area Development Agreement: . .No
Sub-Franchise Contract: . . . . .No
Expand in Territory: . . . . . . Yes
Passive Ownership: . . . Not Allowed
Encourage Conversions: . . . . . Yes
Franchisee Purchase(s) Required: .No

FRANCHISOR TRAINING/SUPPORT:
Financial Assistance Provided: . . .Yes(D)
Site Selection Assistance: . . . . No
Lease Negotiation Assistance: . . . . .Yes
Co-operative Advertising: . . . . . . .Yes
Training: . . . . . . 5 Days Headquarters, 2
. . . . Days Field, 2-3 Days Local Office
On-Going Support: . . . . A,B,C,D,E,G,H
Full-Time Franchisor Support Staff: . .550
EXPANSION PLANS:
US: . . . . All US
Canada - No, ...Overseas - No

WOODBURY PERSONNEL ASSOCIATES

375 N. Broadway
Jericho, NY 11753
TEL: (800) 342-2140 (516) 938-7910 C
FAX:
Mr. Louis Copt, President

Search and recruiting in all facets of business, with an emphasis in the banking and finance fields. The franchise fee includes the option of opening a second recruiting firm, CJK Associates, within the same territory for no additional franchise fee, thereby potentially doubling the business penetration.

HISTORY: . . . . .IFA
Established in 1976; . . 1st Franchised in 1986
Company-Owned Units (As of 12/1/1989): . .5
Franchised Units (12/1/1989): 0
Total Units (12/1/1989): 5
Distribution: US-5;Can-0;Overseas-0
North America: . . . . 2 States
Concentration: . . . . 3 in NY, 2 in MA
Registered: . . . . NY
. . . .
Average # of Employees: . . . . .4-5 FT
Prior Industry Experience: . . . . . . Helpful

FINANCIAL:
Cash Investment: $30-50K
Total Investment: $60-105K
Fees: Franchise - $25K
Royalty: 7%, Advert: 1%
Contract Periods (Yrs.): 10/10
Area Development Agreement: . .No
Sub-Franchise Contract: . . . . .No
Expand in Territory: . . . . . . Yes
Passive Ownership: . . . Not Allowed
Encourage Conversions: . . . . . Yes
Franchisee Purchase(s) Required: .No

FRANCHISOR TRAINING/SUPPORT:
Financial Assistance Provided: . . . Yes(I)
Site Selection Assistance: . . . . .Yes
Lease Negotiation Assistance: . . . . .Yes
Co-operative Advertising: . . . . . . .Yes
Training: . . . . 2 Wks. Headquarters,
. . . . 5 Days Site Opening
On-Going Support: . . . .b,C,D,E,F,G,H,I
Full-Time Franchisor Support Staff: . . 37
EXPANSION PLANS:
US: . . . . .East Coast, Midwest
Canada - No, ... Overseas - No

SUPPLEMENTAL LISTING OF FRANCHISORS

COSMOPOLITAN PERSONNEL SERVICES . . . . .330 Seventh Ave., New York NY 10001
DENTAL POWER . . . . 5530 Wisconsin Ave., # 741, Chevy Chase MD 20815
DIVISION 10 TEMPS . . . . .535 Fifth Avenue, New York NY 10017
DR. PERSONNEL . . . . .4179 E. Peakview Cr., Littleton CO 80121
DRAKE OFFICE OVERLOAD . . . . 10866 Wilshire Blvd., # 925, Los Angeles CA 90024
DRAKE OVERLOAD . . . . .150 Bloor St., W., Toronto ON M5S2X9   CAN
DUNHILL PERSONNEL . . . . One Old Country Rd., Carle Place NY 11514
EDP SEARCH . . . . .277 Fairfield Rd., Fairfield NJ 07006
EMPLOYERS OVERLOAD . . . . 8040 Cedar Ave. South, Minneapolis MN 55420
FORTUNE PERSONNEL CONSULTANTS . . . . 655 Third Ave., New York NY 10017
GEROTOGA ENTERPRISES . . . . 211 Park Ave., Scotch Plains NJ 07076
HEALTHCARE RECRUITERS INTERNATIONAL . . . . . . 5420 LBJ Freeway, LB 4, Dallas TX 75240
HOMECALL . . . . .30 E. Patrick St., Frederick MD 21701
HOUSESITTERS, THE . . . . 530 Queen St., E., Toronto ON M5A1V2   CAN
HUNT PERSONNEL . . . . 1240 Bay St., # 202, Toronto ON M5R2A7   CAN
INTELLIDEX CONTRAC CORP. . . . . One Sheraton Plaza, # 702, New Rochelle NY 10801
J.O.B.S. . . . . .3560 Shoreline Circle, Palm Harbor FL 34684
LALONDE-GEORGE CAREERS . . . . #511 - 1505 Baseline Rd., Ottawa ON K2C3L4   CAN
LLOYD PERSONNEL CONSULTANTS . . . . 10 Cuttermill Rd., Great Neck NY 11021
MANPOWER TEMPORARY SERVICES . . . . 5301 N. Ironwood Rd., Milwaukee WI 53201
MANPOWER TEMPORARY SERVICES(CANADA) . . . . . 124 Eglinton St. W., Toronto ON M4P2H2   CAN
MDL PERSONNEL SYSTEM . . . . .919 W. Highway 436, # 270, Altamonte Springs FL 32714
MEDICAL POWER . . . . 5530 Wisconsin Ave., # 741, Chevy Chase MD 20815
MTS . . . . Box 5677, Knoxville TN 37918
NAT'L. INST. OF SANITATION & MAINTEN. . . . . . .1512 Western Ave., Box 1273, Seattle WA 98111
NATIONAL NANNY CORP. . . . . 2136 Danforth Ave., Toronto ON M4C1J9   CAN
NETREX INTERNATIONAL . . . . .5420 LBJ Freeway, # 575, Dallas TX 75240
NORRELL SERVICES . . . . .5925 Airport Rd., # 752, Mississauga ON L4V1W1   CAN
OFFICE ASSISTANCE . . . . .734 - 1055 Dunsmuir, Box 49292, Vancouver BC V7X1P5   CAN
OFFICE OVERLOAD . . . . .150 Bloor St., W., Toronto ON M5S2X9   CAN
OMNIWORKS! . . . . 2465 Ridgecrest Ave., Orange Park FL 32065
PERSONAL RESUMES INTERNATL. . . . . . . #907-Barron Bldg., 610 8th Ave.,S, Calgary AB T2A2A6   CAN
PLACE MART FRANCHISING . . . . .277 Fairfield Rd., Fairfield NJ 07006
PREFERRED TEMPORARY SERVICES . . . . .245 Peachtree Ctr. Ave., # 2500, Atlanta GA 30303
REGIONAL NETWORK OF PERSONNEL CONSULT. . . . 1211 W. 22nd St., #200, Oakbrook IL 60521
SEARCH AMERICA . . . . .1917 N. 2nd St., Sheboygan WI 53081
SENIOR SITTERS ASSOCIATES . . . . .4230 Dewey Ave., Rochester NY 14616
SULLIVAN & COGLIANO . . . . .230 Second Ave., Waltham MA 02154
TAYLOR REVIEW . . . . 4806 Shelly Dr., Wilmington NC 28405
TEMPORARILY YOURS . . . . 1240 Bay St., # 202, Toronto ON M5R2A7   CAN
TEMPOSITIONS . . . . 150 Post St., San Francisco CA 94108
UNIFORCE TEMPORARY SERVICES . . . . .1335 Jericho Tpk., New Hyde Park NY 11040
UNITED TEMPORARY PERSONNEL SYST. . . . . 555 Pointe Dr., Bldg. 3-300, Brea CA 92621
WE CARE HEALTH SERVICES . . . . 42 MacTavish Ave., E., Brandon MB R7A2B2   CAN

CHAPTER 17

RETAIL FOOD:
DONUTS / COOKIES / BAKERY

ALL MY MUFFINS

P.O. Box 852
Hillside, IL 60162
TEL: (708) 691-7033
FAX:
Mr. Paul Bernstein, VP

ALL MY MUFFINS offers an assortment of "Gourmet Muffins" from our rotating list of over 250 varieties, from raisin bran to blueberry to raspberry with white chocolate. We also feature expresso, cappucino, our blend of gourmet coffee, fresh juices and smoothies.

HISTORY: . . . .
Established in 1985; . . 1st Franchised in 1986
Company-Owned Units (As of 12/1/1989): . .
Franchised Units (12/1/1989): 3
Total Units (12/1/1989): 3
Distribution: US-3;Can-0;Overseas-0
  North America: . . . . 2 States
  Concentration: . . . . 2 in MI, 1 in IL
Registered: . . . CA,FL,IL,MI,MN,NY,OR,SD
. . . . WA,WI
Average # of Employees: . . . . .8 PT
Prior Industry Experience: . . . . Helpful

FINANCIAL:
Cash Investment: . . . . . . $Varies
Total Investment: $95-190K
Fees: Franchise - $20K
  Royalty: 6%, Advert: 2-4%
Contract Periods (Yrs.): . . . 10/Var.
Area Development Agreement: Yes/Var
Sub-Franchise Contract: . . . . .No
Expand in Territory: . . . . . . Yes
Passive Ownership: . . . . .Allowed
Encourage Conversions: . . . .
Franchisee Purchase(s) Required: .No

FRANCHISOR TRAINING/SUPPORT:
Financial Assistance Provided: . . . . . No
Site Selection Assistance: . . . . . . .Yes
Lease Negotiation Assistance: . . . . .Yes
Co-operative Advertising: . . . . . . .Yes
Training: . . . . .1 Wk. Field, 10 Days Site
. . . .
On-Going Support: . . . .B,C,D,E,F,G,H,I
Full-Time Franchisor Support Staff: . . .5
EXPANSION PLANS:
  US: . . . . .All US
  Canada - Yes, ...Overseas - Yes

RETAILING – FOOD (NON–C0NVENIENCE)

	1988	1989	1990	Percentage Change	
				1988-1989	1989-1990
Number of Establishments:					
Company–Owned	4,364	4,198	4,316	–3.8%	2.8%
Franchisee–Owned	17,292	18,826	21,058	8.9%	11.9%
Total	21,656	23,024	25,374	6.3%	10.2%
% of Total Establishments:					
Company–Owned	20.2%	18.2%	17.0%		
Franchisee–Owned	79.8%	81.8%	83.0%		
Total	100.0%	100.0%	100.0%		
Annual Sales ($000):					
Company–Owned	$2,303,802	$2,342,917	$2,523,039	1.7%	7.7%
Franchisee–Owned	7,879,864	8,530,348	9,366,679	8.3%	9.8%
Total	10,183,666	10,873,265	11,889,718	6.8%	9.3%
% of Total Sales:					
Company–Owned	22.6%	21.5%	21.2%		
Franchisee–Owned	77.4%	78.5%	78.8%		
Total	100.0%	100.0%	100.0%		
Average Sales Per Unit ($000):					
Company–Owned	$528	$558	$585	5.7%	4.7%
Franchisee–Owned	456	453	445	–0.6%	–1.8%
Total	470	472	469	0.4%	–0.8%
Sales Ratio	115.8%	123.2%	131.4%		

	1st Quartile	Median	4th Quartile
Average 1988 Total Investment:			
Company–Owned	$100,000	$127,500	$180,000
Franchisee–Owned	100,000	115,000	175,000
Single Unit Franchise Fee	$15,000	$19,500	$22,500
Multiple Unit Franchise Fee	10,000	15,500	25,000
Franchisee Start–up Cost	40,000	50,000	75,000

	1988	Employees/Unit	Sales/Employee
Employment:			
Company–Owned	41,908	9.6	$54,973
Franchisee–Owned	185,689	10.7	42,436
Total	227,597	10.5	44,744
Employee Performance Ratios		89.4%	129.5%

Source: Franchising In The Economy, 1988 – 1990, IFA Education Foundation & Horwath International, Published January, 1990.

1) 1989 and 1990 data were estimated by respondents.

2) Includes ice cream and yogurt stores, donut shops, nut shops, cookie stores, cinnamon bun retailers and other food specialties.

CHEESECAKE, ETC.

400 Swallow Dr.
Miami Springs, FL 33166
TEL: (305) 887-0258
FAX:
Mr. Bill Wolar, President

CHEESECAKE, ETC. is a retail/wholesale franchise opportunity. The beautifully decorated retail area allows patrons to dine in or take home. All flavors and varieties of cheesecake, Florida Key Lime pie and other specialty dessert items are created by CHEESECAKE, ETC. No previous business ownership or baking experience necessary.

HISTORY: . . . .
Established in 1974; . . 1st Franchised in 1986
Company-Owned Units (As of 12/1/1989): . .1
Franchised Units (12/1/1989): 4
Total Units (12/1/1989): 5
Distribution: US-5;Can-0;Overseas-0
North America: . . . . 2 States
Concentration: . . . . .4 in FL, 1 in CT
Registered: . . . . CA,NY,OR,WA
. . . .
Average # of Employees: . . . . .2 FT
Prior Industry Experience: . . . . . . Helpful

FINANCIAL:
Cash Investment: $10-25K
Total Investment: $55-65K
Fees: Franchise - $22.5K
  Royalty: 0%, Advert: . . $150/Mo.
Contract Periods (Yrs.): 10/10
Area Development Agreement: Yes/10
Sub-Franchise Contract: . . . . .No
Expand in Territory: . . . . Yes
Passive Ownership: . . . Discouraged
Encourage Conversions: . . . . . Yes
Franchisee Purchase(s) Required: Yes

FRANCHISOR TRAINING/SUPPORT:
Financial Assistance Provided: . . . Yes(I)
Site Selection Assistance: . . . . .Yes
Lease Negotiation Assistance: . . . . .Yes
Co-operative Advertising: . . . . . . .Yes
Training: . . . . .7-10 Days HQ
. . . . 5 Days Site
On-Going Support: . . . . . . B,C,D,E,F,I
Full-Time Franchisor Support Staff: . . . 8
EXPANSION PLANS:
US: . . . . .All US
Canada - No, ...Overseas - No

CINDY'S CINNAMON ROLLS

1432 S. Mission
Fallbrook, CA 92028
TEL: (619) 723-1121
FAX: (619) 723-4143
Mr. Tom Harris, President

Fresh-baked cinnamon rolls and muffins. All shops in major shopping malls. Great family business. All products made in the shop and baked fresh all day.

HISTORY: . . . .
Established in 1985; . . 1st Franchised in 1986
Company-Owned Units (As of 12/1/1989): . .0
Franchised Units (12/1/1989): 44
Total Units (12/1/1989): 44
Distribution: US-42;Can-2;Overseas-0
North America: . . . . 18 States, 2 Provinces
Concentration: . . . 5 in CA, 4 in NY, 4 in GA
Registered: . . . . .All
. . . .
Average # of Employees: . . . . . .10 FT, 4 PT
Prior Industry Experience: . . . . . . Helpful

FINANCIAL:
Cash Investment: $140K
Total Investment: $140K
Fees: Franchise - $25K
  Royalty: 5%, Advert: 0%
Contract Periods (Yrs.): 10/10
Area Development Agreement: . .No
Sub-Franchise Contract: . . . . .No
Expand in Territory: . . . . Yes
Passive Ownership: . . . Discouraged
Encourage Conversions: . . . . . Yes
Franchisee Purchase(s) Required: Yes

FRANCHISOR TRAINING/SUPPORT:
Financial Assistance Provided: . . . . .No
Site Selection Assistance: . . . . . . .Yes
Lease Negotiation Assistance: . . . . .Yes
Co-operative Advertising: . . . . .No
Training: . . . . 1 Wk. Atlanta, GA or
. . . . Syracuse, NY
On-Going Support: . . . . . .C,D,E,F,G,H
Full-Time Franchisor Support Staff: . . . .
EXPANSION PLANS:
US: . . . . .All US
Canada - Yes, . . . Overseas - Yes

CINNABON

936 N. 34th, # 206
Seattle, WA 98103
TEL: (206) 548-1032
FAX: (206) 632-3533
Mr. James Radloff, VP Franchising

Our bakeries provide a unique eating experience for our guests which entails producing (on premise) and serving our World Famous CINNABON cinnamon rolls. CINNABON bakeries are usually found in large shopping malls and are easily identified by their unique design and irresistible aroma.

HISTORY: . . . .
Established in 1969; . . 1st Franchised in 1986
Company-Owned Units (As of 12/1/1989): . 67
Franchised Units (12/1/1989): 58
Total Units (12/1/1989): 125
Distribution: . . . US-105;Can-20;Overseas-0
North America: . . . . 22 States, 4 Provinces
Concentration: . . 10 in AB, 7 in PA, 7 in MD
Registered: . . CA,FL,HI,MD,MI,MN,NY,OR
. . . . WA
Average # of Employees: . . . . 20 FT
Prior Industry Experience: . . . . . . Helpful

FINANCIAL:
Cash Investment: $135-245K
Total Investment: . . . . . . $Varies
Fees: Franchise - . . $10-12K/Bakery
  Royalty: 5%, Advert: . . . . Varies
Contract Periods (Yrs.): 10/5/5
Area Development Agreement: Yes/3
Sub-Franchise Contract: . . . . .No
Expand in Territory: . . . . Yes
Passive Ownership: . . . Discouraged
Encourage Conversions: . . . . .No
Franchisee Purchase(s) Required: .No

FRANCHISOR TRAINING/SUPPORT:
Financial Assistance Provided: . . . . .No
Site Selection Assistance: . . . . . . .Yes
Lease Negotiation Assistance: . . . . .Yes
Co-operative Advertising: . . . . . . .Yes
Training: . . . . . 3 Wks. in Various Locations As Training Bakeries
On-Going Support: . . . . b,C,D,E,H
Full-Time Franchisor Support Staff: . . .2
EXPANSION PLANS:
US: . . . . .All US
Canada - No, ...Overseas - No

COMPANY'S COMING SNACK BARS

#440 - 1121 Centre St. N.
Calgary, AB T2E7K6 CAN
TEL: (403) 230-1151 C
FAX: (403) 230-2182
Mr. Don Schafer, President

The sale of freshly-baked goods and gourmet beverages.

HISTORY: . . . . .CFA
Established in 1986; . . 1st Franchised in 1988
Company-Owned Units (As of 12/1/1989): . .2
Franchised Units (12/1/1989): 6
Total Units (12/1/1989): 8
Distribution: US-0;Can-8;Overseas-0
North America: . . . . 4 Provinces
Concentration: . . . 5 in AB, 1 in SK, 1 in BC
Registered: . . . . AB
. . . .
Average # of Employees: . . . . . . 2 FT, 4 PT
Prior Industry Experience: . . . . Helpful

FINANCIAL: ALB-CSO.B
Cash Investment: $110-140K
Total Investment: $110-140K
Fees: Franchise - $25K
Royalty: 8%, Advert: 0%
Contract Periods (Yrs.): . . . .Varies
Area Development Agreement: . .No
Sub-Franchise Contract: . . . . . Yes
Expand in Territory: . . . . Yes
Passive Ownership: . . . Not Allowed
Encourage Conversions: . . . . . Yes
Franchisee Purchase(s) Required: .No

FRANCHISOR TRAINING/SUPPORT:
Financial Assistance Provided: . . . . .No
Site Selection Assistance: . . . . .Yes
Lease Negotiation Assistance: . . . . .Yes
Co-operative Advertising: . . . . .Yes
Training: . . . . . 7-10 Days Headquarters,
. . . . .3 Days On-site
On-Going Support: . . . . . . .C,D,E,,G,h
Full-Time Franchisor Support Staff: . . . 6
EXPANSION PLANS:
US: .No
Canada - Yes, ...Overseas - No

CRUMBLES MUFFINS

237 Dougall Ave.
Windsor, ON N9A4P3 CAN
TEL: (519) 973-1942
FAX:
Mr. John D. Sheridan, VP

Offering exclusive, unique, low-sugar, natural muffins, over 100 varieties, including the original line of yogurt muffins. Internationally acclaimed by shopping centre developers as the best muffin chain in the business. The system provides the highest relative sales volume and the best bottom line.

HISTORY: . . . . IFA
Established in 1982; . . 1st Franchised in 1986
Company-Owned Units (As of 12/1/1989): . .6
Franchised Units (12/1/1989): 7
Total Units (12/1/1989): 13
Distribution: US-4;Can-9;Overseas-0
North America: . . . . . 3 States, 2 Provinces
Concentration: . . . 8 in ON, 3 in NE, 1 in NY
Registered: . . . . MI,NY,WI
. . . .
Average # of Employees: . . . . . . 3 FT, 2 PT
Prior Industry Experience: . . . . Helpful

FINANCIAL:
Cash Investment: $125K
Total Investment: $40K
Fees: Franchise - $18K
Royalty: 6%, Advert: 2%
Contract Periods (Yrs.): 10/5
Area Development Agreement: Yes/20
Sub-Franchise Contract: . . . . . Yes
Expand in Territory: . . . . Yes
Passive Ownership: . . . Not Allowed
Encourage Conversions: . . . . . .No
Franchisee Purchase(s) Required: .No

FRANCHISOR TRAINING/SUPPORT:
Financial Assistance Provided: . . . Yes(I)
Site Selection Assistance: . . . . .Yes
Lease Negotiation Assistance: . . . . . No
Co-operative Advertising: . . . . .Yes
Training: . . . . 1 Wk. Headquarters
. . . .
On-Going Support: . . . . .a,B,C,D,E,F,G
Full-Time Franchisor Support Staff: . . 30
EXPANSION PLANS:
US: . . . . .All US
Canada - Yes, ...Overseas - No

DAWN DONUT SYSTEMS

G-4300 W. Pierson Rd.
Flint, MI 48504
TEL: (313) 733-0760
FAX: (313) 733-0210
Mr. Bill Morin, Dir. Franchising

DAWN DONUTS emphasizes quality donuts, cookies and baked goods and believes in simplicity. Most new units have retail gasoline and convenience operations, but this is not mandatory. The concept fits nicely into existing gas/convenience store operations and offers wholesale business opportunities.

HISTORY: . . . .
Established in 1956; . . 1st Franchised in 1956
Company-Owned Units (As of 12/1/1989): . 15
Franchised Units (12/1/1989): 45
Total Units (12/1/1989): 60
Distribution: US-60;Can-0;Overseas-0
North America: . . . . 2 States
Concentration: . . . . 59 in MI, 1 in IN
Registered: . . . . .MI
. . . .
Average # of Employees: . . . . . .10 FT, 5 PT
Prior Industry Experience: . . . . Helpful

FINANCIAL:
Cash Investment: $50-250K
Total Investment: $250-750K
Fees: Franchise - $15K
Royalty: 4.5%, Advert: . . . 3.5%
Contract Periods (Yrs.): . . . 15/15
Area Development Agreement: Yes/15
Sub-Franchise Contract: . . . . . .No
Expand in Territory: . . . . Yes
Passive Ownership: . . . Discouraged
Encourage Conversions: . . . . . Yes
Franchisee Purchase(s) Required: .No

FRANCHISOR TRAINING/SUPPORT:
Financial Assistance Provided: . . . Yes(I)
Site Selection Assistance: . . . . .Yes
Lease Negotiation Assistance: . . . . .Yes
Co-operative Advertising: . . . . .Yes
Training: . . . . 3 Wks. Headquarters,
. . . . .3 Wks. On-site
On-Going Support: . . . . .B,C,D,E,G,H,I
Full-Time Franchisor Support Staff: . . . .
EXPANSION PLANS:
US: . . . . Midwest
Canada - No, ...Overseas - No

DONUT DELITE CAFE

77 Bessemer Rd., # 19
London, ON N6E1P9 CAN
TEL: (519) 668-6868
FAX: (519) 668-1127
Mr. Joe Garagozzo, President

Excellent turn-key donut operation to include light lunches and soups.

HISTORY: . . . .
Established in 1984; . . 1st Franchised in 1985
Company-Owned Units (As of 12/1/1989): . .2
Franchised Units (12/1/1989): 28
Total Units (12/1/1989): 30
Distribution: US-0;Can-30;Overseas-0
North America: . . . . .1 Province
Concentration: . . . . 30 in ON
Registered: . . . .
. . . .
Average # of Employees: . . . . . . 6 FT, 4 PT
Prior Industry Experience: . . . . Helpful

FINANCIAL:
Cash Investment: $50K
Total Investment: $120-150K
Fees: Franchise - $20K
Royalty: 5%, Advert: 2%
Contract Periods (Yrs.): 10/5
Area Development Agreement: . .No
Sub-Franchise Contract: . . . . .No
Expand in Territory: . . . . Yes
Passive Ownership: . . . Discouraged
Encourage Conversions: . . . . . NA
Franchisee Purchase(s) Required: Yes

FRANCHISOR TRAINING/SUPPORT:
Financial Assistance Provided: . . . Yes(I)
Site Selection Assistance: . . . . .Yes
Lease Negotiation Assistance: . . . . .Yes
Co-operative Advertising: . . . . .Yes
Training: . . . . . 3 Wks. or Until Ready at
. . . . Franchisee Site
On-Going Support: . . .a,B,C,D,E,F,G,H,I
Full-Time Franchisor Support Staff: . . .7
EXPANSION PLANS:
US: . . . . Michigan Only
Canada - Yes, ...Overseas - No

DONUT HOLE, THE

W. Industrial Park, RR1, Box 704
Dickinson, ND 58601
TEL: (701) 225-4444
FAX: (701) 225-7981
Mr. Guy M. Moos, Dir. Fran.

The commissary concept is used where we do the measuring, mixing and initial preparation for your donut shop. Products are delivered to you ready to bake or fry. No fumbling with ingredients at midnight or hiring high-priced bakers. The result - consistent, top-quality donuts.

HISTORY: . . . . IFA
Established in 1956; . . 1st Franchised in 1977
Company-Owned Units (As of 12/1/1989): . .2
Franchised Units (12/1/1989): 15
Total Units (12/1/1989): 17
Distribution: US-17;Can-0;Overseas-0
North America: . . . . 3 States
Concentration: . . . 9 in ND, 5 in MT, 3 in SD
Registered: . . . . MN,ND,SD
. . . .
Average # of Employees: . . . . . . 5 FT, 4 PT
Prior Industry Experience: . . . . Helpful

FINANCIAL:
Cash Investment: $40K
Total Investment: $115K
Fees: Franchise - $14.5K
Royalty: 3%, Advert: 1%
Contract Periods (Yrs.): 10/10
Area Development Agreement: . .No
Sub-Franchise Contract: . . . . .No
Expand in Territory: . . . . Yes
Passive Ownership: . . . Not Allowed
Encourage Conversions: . . . . . Yes
Franchisee Purchase(s) Required: Yes

FRANCHISOR TRAINING/SUPPORT:
Financial Assistance Provided: . . . . .No
Site Selection Assistance: . . . . .Yes
Lease Negotiation Assistance: . . . . .Yes
Co-operative Advertising: . . . . .Yes
Training: . . . . 2 Wks. Headquarters,
. . . . . .1 Wk. On-site, 2 Wks. Opening
On-Going Support: . . . a,B,C,D,E,f,G,H,I
Full-Time Franchisor Support Staff: . . . 5
EXPANSION PLANS:
US: . . . . Upper Midwest, Plains
Canada - Yes, ...Overseas - No

GREAT AMERICAN COOKIE

4685 Frederick Dr., SW
Atlanta, GA 30336
TEL: (404) 696-1700
FAX:
Ms. Betty W. Ansley, VP

A license to own a store in the fastest-growing cookie company in America. An attractive store design that permits high-volume and efficient operation. On-going and continuing training and help. On-going marketing and advertising support, including grand opening promotion, logos, point-of-purchase displays and advertising materials.

HISTORY: . . . . IFA
Established in 1977; . . 1st Franchised in 1978
Company-Owned Units (As of 12/1/1989): 300
Franchised Units (12/1/1989): 300
Total Units (12/1/1989): 600
Distribution: . . . US-600;Can-0;Overseas-0
North America: . . . .
Concentration: . . . . .TX, FL, GA
Registered: . . .CA,IL,IN,MI,MN,NY,ND,OR
. . . . .RI,SD,VA,WI
Average # of Employees: . . . . .Varies
Prior Industry Experience: . . . . Helpful

FINANCIAL:
Cash Investment: $130-150K
Total Investment: $130-150K
Fees: Franchise - $25K
Royalty: 7%, Advert: 0%
Contract Periods (Yrs.): . . . . Lease
Area Development Agreement: . .No
Sub-Franchise Contract: . . . . .No
Expand in Territory: . . . . Yes
Passive Ownership: . . . . . .Allowed
Encourage Conversions: . . . . . NA
Franchisee Purchase(s) Required: Yes

FRANCHISOR TRAINING/SUPPORT:
Financial Assistance Provided: . . . . .No
Site Selection Assistance: . . . . .Yes
Lease Negotiation Assistance: . . . . .Yes
Co-operative Advertising: . . . .
Training: . . . . 2 Wks. Headquarters,
. . . . . On-going at Franchisee Location
On-Going Support: . . . .B,C,D,E,F,G,H,I
Full-Time Franchisor Support Staff: . . . .
EXPANSION PLANS:
US: . . . . .All US
Canada - Yes, . . . Overseas - Yes

GREAT HARVEST FRANCHISING

Box 488
Dillon, MT 59725
TEL: (800) 442-0424 (406) 683-6800
FAX:
Mr. John Wendt, Admin. Asst.

Specialty whole wheat bakeries, using premium whole wheat, stoneground fresh daily on premises for highest quality bread.

HISTORY: . . . . IFA	FINANCIAL:	FRANCHISOR TRAINING/SUPPORT:
Established in 1970; . . 1st Franchised in 1978	Cash Investment: $65-75K	Financial Assistance Provided: . . . . . No
Company-Owned Units (As of 12/1/1989): . .1	Total Investment: $65-75K	Site Selection Assistance: . . . . . . .Yes
Franchised Units (12/1/1989): 31	Fees: Franchise - $20K	Lease Negotiation Assistance: . . . . .Yes
Total Units (12/1/1989): 32	Royalty: 6%, Advert: 2%	Co-operative Advertising: . . . . . . .NA
Distribution: US-32;Can-0;Overseas-0	Contract Periods (Yrs.): 5/5	Training: . . . . .3 Days Bakery, 1 Day
North America: . . . . 18 States	Area Development Agreement: . .No	. . . . Each of 3 Bakeries, 8 Days On-site
Concentration: . . .4 in MT, 4 in WA, 3 in OR	Sub-Franchise Contract: . . . . . .No	On-Going Support: . . . . . . B,C,D,E,G,I
Registered: . . .CA,FL,IN,MI,MN,ND,OR,VA	Expand in Territory: . . . . Yes	Full-Time Franchisor Support Staff: . . . 6
. . . . WA,WI	Passive Ownership: . . . Not Allowed	EXPANSION PLANS:
Average # of Employees: . . . . . . 2 FT, 4 PT	Encourage Conversions: . . . . . .No	US: .All US
Prior Industry Experience: . . . . Helpful	Franchisee Purchase(s) Required: .No	Canada - Yes, . . . Overseas - Yes

HOL 'N ONE DONUT HOUSE / HOL 'N ONE CAFE

6390 Beresford St.
Burnaby, BC V5E1B6 CAN
TEL: (604) 435-4242
FAX:
Mr. Larry Seller, Mgr. Ops.

Outlets specialize in donuts, muffins and a menu consisting of home-style hamburgers, sandwiches and soups.

HISTORY:	FINANCIAL:	FRANCHISOR TRAINING/SUPPORT:
Established in 1955; . . 1st Franchised in 1965	Cash Investment: $30-40K	Financial Assistance Provided: . . . . . No
Company-Owned Units (As of 12/1/1989): . .5	Total Investment: $150K	Site Selection Assistance: . . . . . . .Yes
Franchised Units (12/1/1989): 5	Fees: Franchise - $20K	Lease Negotiation Assistance: . . . . .Yes
Total Units (12/1/1989): 10	Royalty: 3%, Advert: 1%	Co-operative Advertising: . . . . . . .Yes
Distribution: US-0;Can-10;Overseas-0	Contract Periods (Yrs.): 10/10	Training: . . . . .1 Wk. Company
North America: . . . . .1 Province	Area Development Agreement: . .No	. . . . .Store
Concentration: . . . . 10 in BC	Sub-Franchise Contract: . . . . . .No	On-Going Support: . . . . .B,C,d,e,f
Registered: . . . . AB	Expand in Territory: . . . . Yes	Full-Time Franchisor Support Staff: . . . 6
. . . .	Passive Ownership: . . . Discouraged	EXPANSION PLANS:
Average # of Employees: . . . . . . 3 FT, 4 PT	Encourage Conversions: . . . . . Yes	US: .No
Prior Industry Experience: . . . . Helpful	Franchisee Purchase(s) Required: Yes	Canada - Yes, ...Overseas - No

KATIE MCGUIRE'S PIE & BAKE SHOPPE

17682 Sampson Ln.
Huntington Beach, CA 92647
TEL: (714) 847-0325
FAX:
Ms. Janie Stine, Fran. Development

Home-style pies, muffins, cookies, cheesecakes, plus small cafe of quiche, chicken pot pies, soups and sandwiches. Products supplied from a central commissary to be freshly baked in store. No baking experience is required.

HISTORY:	FINANCIAL:	FRANCHISOR TRAINING/SUPPORT:
Established in 1982; . . 1st Franchised in 1984	Cash Investment: $60K	Financial Assistance Provided: . . . . . No
Company-Owned Units (As of 12/1/1989): . .0	Total Investment: $100-150K	Site Selection Assistance: . . . . . . .Yes
Franchised Units (12/1/1989): 15	Fees: Franchise - $22.5K	Lease Negotiation Assistance: . . . . .Yes
Total Units (12/1/1989): 15	Royalty: 6%, Advert: 2%	Co-operative Advertising: . . . . . . .No
Distribution: US-15;Can-0;Overseas-0	Contract Periods (Yrs.): 10/5	Training: . . . . .1 Wk. Headquarters,
North America: . . . . .1 State	Area Development Agreement: Yes/10	. . . . 2 Wks. Site
Concentration: . . . . 15 in CA	Sub-Franchise Contract: . . . . . .No	On-Going Support: . . . .B,C,D,E,F,G,H,I
Registered: . . . . CA	Expand in Territory: . . . . Yes	Full-Time Franchisor Support Staff: . . . 4
. . . .	Passive Ownership: . . . Discouraged	EXPANSION PLANS:
Average # of Employees: . . . . 12 FT	Encourage Conversions: . . . . Yes	US: . . . . California Only
Prior Industry Experience: . . . . Helpful	Franchisee Purchase(s) Required: Yes	Canada - No, ...Overseas - No

LE MUFFIN PLUS

P. O. Box 888760
Atlanta, GA 30356
TEL: (404) 876-3858
FAX: (404) 394-5096
Mr. Albert Brull, President

America's newest muffin, cookie and coffee concept. Menu designed to maximize sales during breakfast, lunch and dinner.

HISTORY: . . . .
Established in 1985; . . 1st Franchised in 1986
Company-Owned Units (As of 12/1/1989): . .1
Franchised Units (12/1/1989): 17
Total Units (12/1/1989): 18
Distribution: US-1;Can-17;Overseas-0
 North America: . . . . . . 1 State, 1 Province
 Concentration: . . . . .17 in PQ, 1 in GA
Registered: . . . .
 . . . .
Average # of Employees: . . . . Varies
Prior Industry Experience: . . . . . . Helpful

FINANCIAL:
Cash Investment: . . . . . . $Varies
Total Investment: . . . . $Varies
Fees: Franchise - $25K
 Royalty: 8%, Advert: 0-2%
Contract Periods (Yrs.): . . . . Lease
Area Development Agreement: . .No
Sub-Franchise Contract: . . . . .No
Expand in Territory: . . . . . . Yes
Passive Ownership: . . . Discouraged
Encourage Conversions: . . . . .No
Franchisee Purchase(s) Required: .No

FRANCHISOR TRAINING/SUPPORT:
Financial Assistance Provided: . . . . . No
Site Selection Assistance: . . . . .Yes
Lease Negotiation Assistance: . . . . .Yes
Co-operative Advertising: . . . . .NA
Training: . . . . . .1-2 Wks. Company Store,
 . . . . .As Required Franchisee Location
On-Going Support: . . . . C,D,E,H,I
Full-Time Franchisor Support Staff: . . . 5
EXPANSION PLANS:
US: . . . . Southeast
Canada - Yes, ...Overseas - No

LES BOULANGERIE CANTOR BAKERY

8575 8th Ave.
Montreal, PQ H1Z2X2 CAN
TEL: (514) 374-2700
FAX:
Ms. Gail Cantor, GM

Be the owner/operator of a CANTOR BAKERY, a European-style bakery/convenience food store selling a full line of fresh-daily bakery products, plus a full line of convenience items, including deli and dairy items.

HISTORY: . . . .
Established in 1956; . . 1st Franchised in 1963
Company-Owned Units (As of 12/1/1989): . .5
Franchised Units (12/1/1989): 75
Total Units (12/1/1989): 80
Distribution: US-0;Can-80;Overseas-0
 North America: . . . . 2 Provinces
 Concentration: . . . . . . 60 in PQ, 20 in ON
Registered: . . . .
 . . . .
Average # of Employees: . . . . . . 4 FT, 3 PT
Prior Industry Experience: . . . . Helpful

FINANCIAL:
Cash Investment: $25-30K
Total Investment: $125-150K
Fees: Franchise - $0
 Royalty: 2%, Advert: 0%
Contract Periods (Yrs.): . . . . Lease
Area Development Agreement: . .No
Sub-Franchise Contract: . . . . .No
Expand in Territory: . . . . . . Yes
Passive Ownership: . . . . . .Allowed
Encourage Conversions: . . . . Yes
Franchisee Purchase(s) Required: Yes

FRANCHISOR TRAINING/SUPPORT:
Financial Assistance Provided: . . . Yes(I)
Site Selection Assistance: . . . . .Yes
Lease Negotiation Assistance: . . . . .Yes
Co-operative Advertising: . . . . .Yes
Training: . . . . 2-4 Wks. Company-Owned
 . . . . Unit
On-Going Support: . . . . C,D,E,F,I
Full-Time Franchisor Support Staff: . .200
EXPANSION PLANS:
US: . . . . .No
Canada - Yes, ...Overseas - No

MISTER DONUT OF AMERICA

Multifoods Twr., P.O. Box 2942
Minneapolis, MN 55402
TEL: (800) 328-8304 (612) 340-6693
FAX: (612) 340-3306
Mr. John A. Fox, Dir. Development

Retailing of over 55 varieties of donuts, muffins, baked goods/pastries and related beverages - primarily coffee and soft drinks. Features drive-thru and walk-in franchised units.

HISTORY: . . . . IFA
Established in 1955; . . 1st Franchised in 1956
Company-Owned Units (As of 12/1/1989): . .0
Franchised Units (12/1/1989): 570
Total Units (12/1/1989): 570
Distribution: US-482;Can-88;Overseas-0
 North America: . . . 29 States, 5 Provinces
 Concentration: . . 113 in PA, 56 in FL, 55 ON
Registered: . . . IL,IN,MD,MI,MN,NY,RI,VA
 . . . . .WI
Average # of Employees: . . . . . . 8 FT, 20 PT
Prior Industry Experience: . . . . Helpful

FINANCIAL: NY-INTMULT
Cash Investment: $65-75K
Total Investment: $313-503K
Fees: Franchise - $25K
 Royalty: 4.9%, Advert: 5%
Contract Periods (Yrs.): . . . 20/10
Area Development Agreement: Yes/Var
Sub-Franchise Contract: . . . . .No
Expand in Territory: . . . . . . Yes
Passive Ownership: . . . Not Allowed
Encourage Conversions: . . . . Yes
Franchisee Purchase(s) Required: .No

FRANCHISOR TRAINING/SUPPORT:
Financial Assistance Provided: . . . . . No
Site Selection Assistance: . . . . .Yes
Lease Negotiation Assistance: . . . . .Yes
Co-operative Advertising: . . . . .Yes
Training: . . . . 4 Wks. Headquarters
 . . . .
On-Going Support: . . . . B,C,D,E,F,G,H
Full-Time Franchisor Support Staff: . . 50
EXPANSION PLANS:
US: . . . . . . .NE, SE, SW and Midwest
Canada - Yes, ...Overseas - No

MR. MUGS

196 Dalhousie St., Box 124
Brantford, ON N3T5M3 CAN
TEL: (519) 752-9890
FAX: (519) 752-0978
Mr. Ron Hewitt, Dir. Fran.

An exciting concept in the coffee and donut industry, offering the customer a deli-bar section, featuring made-from-scratch chili, soups, salads and sandwiches. Fresh muffins and baked goods prepared daily. All locations show exceptional acceptance of product lines and store design concept.

HISTORY: . . . .
Established in 1984; . . 1st Franchised in 1986
Company-Owned Units (As of 12/1/1989): . .1
Franchised Units (12/1/1989): 18
Total Units (12/1/1989): 19
Distribution: US-0;Can-19;Overseas-0
North America: . . . . 2 Provinces
Concentration: . . . . .17 in ON, 2 in PQ
Registered: . . . . CA,FL,NY
. . . .
Average # of Employees: . . . . . . 9 FT, 7 PT
Prior Industry Experience: . . . . Helpful

FINANCIAL:
Cash Investment: $50-70K
Total Investment: $180-195K
Fees: Franchise - $20K
  Royalty: 4%, Advert: 2%
Contract Periods (Yrs.): 10/10
Area Development Agreement: Yes/10
Sub-Franchise Contract: . . . . . .No
Expand in Territory: . . . . Yes
Passive Ownership: . . . Discouraged
Encourage Conversions: . . . . . Yes
Franchisee Purchase(s) Required: .No

FRANCHISOR TRAINING/SUPPORT:
Financial Assistance Provided: . . . . . No
Site Selection Assistance: . . . . . . .Yes
Lease Negotiation Assistance: . . . . .Yes
Co-operative Advertising: . . . . . . .Yes
Training: . . . . 4 Wks. Headquarters,
. . . . 2 Wks. Franchisee Site
On-Going Support: . . . .B,C,D,E,F,G,H,I
Full-Time Franchisor Support Staff: . . 10
EXPANSION PLANS:
US: . . . . All US
Canada - Yes, ...Overseas - No

MY FAVORITE MUFFIN

15 Engle St., # 304
Englewood, NJ 07631
TEL: (800) 332-2229 (201) 871-0370
FAX: (201) 871-7168
Mr. John Sterns, Sales Manager

MY FAVORITE MUFFIN is a unique specialty baked goods franchise, offering over 100 varieties of gourmet muffins to meet the tastes of the food-conscious, health-conscious American. We also offer our own gourmet coffee selection and frozen yogurt.

HISTORY: . . . .
Established in 1987; . . 1st Franchised in 1987
Company-Owned Units (As of 12/1/1989): . .1
Franchised Units (12/1/1989): 11
Total Units (12/1/1989): 12
Distribution: US-12;Can-0;Overseas-0
North America: . . . . 6 States
Concentration: . . . . 4 in NJ, 1 in FL, 1 in NY
Registered: . . . . NY,VA
. . . .
Average # of Employees: . . . . . . 3 FT, 2 PT
Prior Industry Experience: . . . . Helpful

FINANCIAL:
Cash Investment: $50-75K
Total Investment: $130-180K
Fees: Franchise - $20K
  Royalty: 5%, Advert: 0%
Contract Periods (Yrs.): 10/10
Area Development Agreement: . .No
Sub-Franchise Contract: . . . . . .No
Expand in Territory: . . . . Yes
Passive Ownership: . . . . . .Allowed
Encourage Conversions: . . . . . .No
Franchisee Purchase(s) Required: .No

FRANCHISOR TRAINING/SUPPORT:
Financial Assistance Provided: . . . Yes(I)
Site Selection Assistance: . . . . . . .Yes
Lease Negotiation Assistance: . . . .Yes
Co-operative Advertising: . . . . . . .Yes
Training: . . . . 2 Wks. Princeton, NJ,
. . . . 1 Wk. On-site
On-Going Support: . . . . . . C,D,E,G,H,I
Full-Time Franchisor Support Staff: . . . 5
EXPANSION PLANS:
US: . . . . All US
Canada - No, ...Overseas - No

SAINT CINNAMON BAKE SHOPPES

7030 Woodbine Ave., # 103
Markham, ON L3R1A2 CAN
TEL: (416) 470-1517
FAX: (416) 470-8112
Mr. Bob Forsey, VP

Fresh cinnamon rolls prepared from scratch in full view of customers. All ingredients are of the finest quality. The enticing and irresistible aroma defies you to pass up this great cinnamon treat.

HISTORY: . . . .
Established in 1986; . . 1st Franchised in 1986
Company-Owned Units (As of 12/1/1989): . .2
Franchised Units (12/1/1989): 55
Total Units (12/1/1989): 57
Distribution: US-0;Can-57;Overseas-0
North America: . . . . 8 Provinces
Concentration: . . . 30 in ON, 9 in PQ, 4 in NS
Registered: . . . . AB
. . . .
Average # of Employees: . . . . . . 4 FT, 6 PT
Prior Industry Experience: . . . . Helpful

FINANCIAL:
Cash Investment: $40-60K
Total Investment: $125-160K
Fees: Franchise - $25K
  Royalty: 6%, Advert: 3%
Contract Periods (Yrs.): . . . 10/Var.
Area Development Agreement: Yes/Var
Sub-Franchise Contract: . . . . . Yes
Expand in Territory: . . . . Yes
Passive Ownership: . . . Discouraged
Encourage Conversions: . . . . . Yes
Franchisee Purchase(s) Required: Yes

FRANCHISOR TRAINING/SUPPORT:
Financial Assistance Provided: . . . . .NA
Site Selection Assistance: . . . . . . .Yes
Lease Negotiation Assistance: . . . .Yes
Co-operative Advertising: . . . . . . .Yes
Training: . . . . 3 Wks. Headquarters
. . . .
On-Going Support: . . . . .B,C,D,E,G,H,I
Full-Time Franchisor Support Staff: . . 14
EXPANSION PLANS:
US: . . . . All US
Canada - Yes, ...Overseas - No

SPROLL'S OLD COUNTRY BREAD

35 Alexandra Blvd.
Toronto, ON M4R1L8 CAN
TEL: (416) 488-3687 C
FAX:
Mr. S. MacKneson, President

Our quality breads are baked from old-country recipes using no fat, sugar, milk, preservatives or colouring; and for the coffee table, Danish, cheesecake, apple strudel are baked from traditional German recipes. No bakery experience needed because our bakery concept provides complete training.

HISTORY: . . . .
Established in 1979; . . 1st Franchised in 1989
Company-Owned Units (As of 12/1/1989): . .2
Franchised Units (12/1/1989): 3
Total Units (12/1/1989): 5
Distribution: US-0;Can-5;Overseas-0
North America: . . . . .1 Province
Concentration: . . . . 5 in ON
Registered: . . . .
. . . .
Average # of Employees: . . . . . . 3 FT, 3 PT
Prior Industry Experience: . . . . Helpful

FINANCIAL:
Cash Investment: $65K
Total Investment: $147K
Fees: Franchise - $25K
Royalty: 5%, Advert: 2%
Contract Periods (Yrs.): . . . 10/10
Area Development Agreement: Yes/10
Sub-Franchise Contract: . . . . . Yes
Expand in Territory: . . . . . . Yes
Passive Ownership: . . . Discouraged
Encourage Conversions: . . . . . Yes
Franchisee Purchase(s) Required: .No

FRANCHISOR TRAINING/SUPPORT:
Financial Assistance Provided: . . . Yes(I)
Site Selection Assistance: . . . . . . .Yes
Lease Negotiation Assistance: . . . . .Yes
Co-operative Advertising: . . . . . . .Yes
Training: . . . . 3 Wks. Headquarters,
. . . . 2 Wks. Franchisee's Site
On-Going Support: . . A,B,C,D,E,F,G,H,I
Full-Time Franchisor Support Staff: . . .9
EXPANSION PLANS:
US: . . . . .All US
Canada - Yes, ...Overseas - No

T. J. CINNAMONS

1010 W. 39th St.
Kansas City, MO 64111
TEL: (816) 931-9341
FAX:
Mr. James Dwyer, VP Sales/RE

T. J. CINNAMONS is a unique bakery concept, specializing in cinnamon roll products. These products are baked fresh throughout the day and in full view of the consumer. This is accomplished in a bakery design that is both attractive and flexible enough to meet a variety of facility configurations.

HISTORY: . . . . .IFA
Established in 1985; . . 1st Franchised in 1985
Company-Owned Units (As of 12/1/1989): . .6
Franchised Units (12/1/1989): 220
Total Units (12/1/1989): 226
Distribution: US-229;Can-6;Overseas-0
North America: . . . . 38 States
Concentration: . 17 in MO, 11 in TX, 10 in FL
Registered: . . . . . . .All Except NY and VA
. . . .
Average # of Employees: . . . . .5+ FT , 5+ PT
Prior Industry Experience: . . . . Helpful

FINANCIAL:
Cash Investment: $100-150K
Total Investment: $100-150K
Fees: Franchise - $25K
Royalty: 5%, Advert: 2%
Contract Periods (Yrs.): . . . .Varies
Area Development Agreement: Yes/Var
Sub-Franchise Contract: . . . . .No
Expand in Territory: . . . . . . Yes
Passive Ownership: . . . Discouraged
Encourage Conversions: . . . . .No
Franchisee Purchase(s) Required: .No

FRANCHISOR TRAINING/SUPPORT:
Financial Assistance Provided: . . . . .No
Site Selection Assistance: . . . . . . .Yes
Lease Negotiation Assistance: . . . . .No
Co-operative Advertising: . . . . . . .Yes
Training: . . . . 2 Wks. Headquarters,
. . . . 4 Days Site
On-Going Support: . . . .B,C,D,E,F,G,H,I
Full-Time Franchisor Support Staff: . . 51
EXPANSION PLANS:
US: . . . . .All US, Especially West
Canada - Yes, ...Overseas - No

TIM HORTON DONUTS

874 Sinclair Rd.
Oakville, ON L6K2Y1 CAN
TEL: (416) 845-6511
FAX:
Ms. Louise Harris, Dir. Fran.

Coffee and donuts/baked goods chain.

HISTORY: . . . .
Established in 1964; . . 1st Franchised in 1965
Company-Owned Units (As of 12/1/1989): . 20
Franchised Units (12/1/1989): 420
Total Units (12/1/1989): 440
Distribution: US-7;Can-433;Overseas-0
North America: . . . . 3 States, 10 Provinces
Concentration: . 225 in ON, 45 in PQ,30 in NS
Registered: . . . . AB
. . . .
Average # of Employees: . . . . 22 FT
Prior Industry Experience: . . . . Helpful

FINANCIAL:
Cash Investment: $80K
Total Investment: $215-230K
Fees: Franchise - . . . .$
Royalty: 3%, Advert: 4%
Contract Periods (Yrs.): . . . 10/10
Area Development Agreement: .No
Sub-Franchise Contract: . . . . .No
Expand in Territory: . . . . . . Yes
Passive Ownership: . . . Not Allowed
Encourage Conversions: . . . . . Yes
Franchisee Purchase(s) Required: Yes

FRANCHISOR TRAINING/SUPPORT:
Financial Assistance Provided: . . . Yes(I)
Site Selection Assistance: . . . . . . .Yes
Lease Negotiation Assistance: . . . . .Yes
Co-operative Advertising: . . . . . . .Yes
Training: . . . . . .8-10 Wks. Headquarters
. . . .
On-Going Support: . . . .B,C,D,E,F,G,H,I
Full-Time Franchisor Support Staff: . .220
EXPANSION PLANS:
US: . . . . .No
Canada - Yes, ...Overseas - No

WHOLE DONUT, THE

894 New Britain Ave.
Hartford, CT 06106
TEL: (203) 953-3569 C
FAX: (203) 953-1692
Mr. Frank Gencarelli, President

WHOLE DONUT SHOPS are approximately 1,800 SF. All products are made on premises. Donuts, cookies, muffins, fruit squares and other baked goods. The WHOLE DONUT also serves deli sandwiches, hot dogs, chili salad platters and soups. Most new shops have drive-thru windows.

HISTORY: . . . .
Established in 1981; . . 1st Franchised in 1984
Company-Owned Units (As of 12/1/1989): . 12
Franchised Units (12/1/1989): 27
Total Units (12/1/1989): 39
Distribution: US-39;Can-0;Overseas-0
North America: . . . . 4 States
Concentration: . . . . NY, New England
Registered: . . . . NY
. . . .
Average # of Employees: . . . . . . 4 FT, 7 PT
Prior Industry Experience: . . . . . . Helpful

FINANCIAL:
Cash Investment: $80-100K
Total Investment: $165K
Fees: Franchise - $20K
 Royalty: 5%, Advert: 2%
Contract Periods (Yrs.): 8/8
Area Development Agreement: Yes/10
Sub-Franchise Contract: . . . . . .No
Expand in Territory: . . . . Yes
Passive Ownership: . . . Not Allowed
Encourage Conversions: . . . . .No
Franchisee Purchase(s) Required: .No

FRANCHISOR TRAINING/SUPPORT:
Financial Assistance Provided: . . . . . No
Site Selection Assistance: . . . . .Yes
Lease Negotiation Assistance: . . . . .Yes
Co-operative Advertising: . . . . .Yes
Training: . . . . 6 Wks. Headquarters
. . . .
On-Going Support: . . . . b,E,F,G,H
Full-Time Franchisor Support Staff: . . .7
EXPANSION PLANS:
US: . . . . .New England and NY
Canada - No, ... Overseas - No

SUPPLEMENTAL LISTING OF FRANCHISORS

BAGELMANIA OF AMERICA	1050 Ali Baba Ave., Miami FL 33054	
BAKER'S DOZEN DONUTS	1224 Dundas St. E., # 13, Mississauga ON L4Y4A2	CAN
BLUE CHIP COOKIES	124 Beale St., # 401, San Francisco CA 94105	
BOSA DONUTS	P. O. Box 2636, Pinetop AZ 85935	
BREAD BASKET, THE	Rte. 130 & Browning Rd., Brooklawn NJ 08030	
BREAD KING BAKERIES	103 Guildwood Pkwy., Scarborough ON M1E1P1	CAN
BUN KING BAKERIES	1173 N. Service Rd., E., Oakville ON L6H1A7	CAN
BUNS MASTER BAKERY SYSTEMS CORP.	6065 E. Mississauga Rd., N., Mississauga ON L5N1A6	CAN
BUSKETT BAKERY	3029 Dundas St., W., Toronto ON M9P1Z3	CAN
CINNAMON SAM'S BAKERY/CAFE	P. O. Box 633, Moberly KS 65270	
COFFEE WAY, THE	1910 Kipling Ave., # 1, Rexdale ON M9W4J1	CAN
COOKIE FACTORY BAKERY	651 E. Butterfield, # 503, Lombard IL 60148	
COOKIE STORE	4198 N. Cherry St., Winston-Salem NC 27105	
COOKIES BY GEORGE	200 - 1508 W. 2nd Ave., Vancouver BC V6J1H2	CAN
COUNTRY STYLE DONUTS	2 E. Beaver Creek Rd., Bldg. #1, Richmond Hill ON L4B2N3	CAN
COUNTRY STYLE DONUTS	380 Kenmore Ave., Buffalo NY 14223	
CREATIVE CROISSANTS	3111 Camino Del Rio N., # 1100, San Diego CA 92108	
CROISSANT 'N MORE	7001 Mumford Rd., #3030, Twr. 2, Halifax NS B3L4R3	CAN
CROISSANT + PLUS	6818 est, Jarry rue, St-Leonard PQ H1P1W3	CAN
DAVID'S COOKIES	1511 Forum Pl., # 100, W. Palm Beach FL 33401	
DIXIE CREAM DONUT SHOP	P.O. Box 180, St. Louis MO 63166	
DONUT INN	6355 Topanga Canyon Blvd., # 403, Woodland Hills CA 91367	
DONUTLAND	P. O. Box 409, Marion IA 53202	
DONUTS & THINGS INTERNATIONAL	51 Toro Rd., Downsview ON M3J2A4	CAN
DONUTS GALORE	115 E. Glenside Ave., # 14, Glenside PA 19038	
DONUTS N' COFFEE	2222 State St., Columbus IN 47201	
DUNKIN' DONUTS (CANADA)	10620 Cote de Liesse, Lachine PQ H8T1A5	CAN
DUNKIN' DONUTS OF AMERICA	P.O. Box 317, Randolph MA 02368	
DUTCH MASTER DONUTS	747 Don Mills Rd., Toronto ON M3C1L7	CAN
ENGLISH BAY PIE COMPANY	708 - 1155 W. Pender St., Vancouver BC V6E2P4	CAN
FAMOUS AMOS	750 Battery St., # 440, San Francisco CA 94111	
FLOUR POT BOUTIQUES	10 Piedmont Ctr., # 700, Atlanta GA 30305	
FRENCH BAKER	651 E. Butterfield Rd., # 503, Lombard IL 60148	
GRANDMA LEE'S BAKERY/EATING PLACE	25 Watline Ave., # 402, Mississauga ON L4Z2Z1	CAN

HEALTH BREAD	1125 Finch Ave., W., Toronto ON M3J2E8	CAN
HEAVENLY MUFFINS LTD.	13541 - 102nd Ave., # 207, Surrey BC V3T4X8	CAN
HOW'S FRESH HOT CINNAMON ROLLS	430 East Ave., Scarborough ON M1C2W8	CAN
JOLLY PIRATE DONUTS & COFFEE SHOPS	3923 E. Broad St., Columbus OH 43213	
KING DONUTS	278 Bunting Rd., St. Catharines ON L2M7M2	CAN
LEON'S FOOD ENTERPRISES	1000 Universal Dr., North Haven CT 06473	
MANHATTAN BAGEL CO.	1665 Stelton Rd., Piscataway NJ 08854	
MICHEL'S BAGUETTE	1 Dundas St. W., # 2306, Toronto ON M4G1Z3	CAN
MISTER C'S DONUTS & MORE	8261 Woodbine Ave., Markham ON L3R8Z5	CAN
MISTER DONUT OF CANADA	1035 McNicoll Ave. E., # 302, Scarborough ON M1W3W6	CAN
MMMARVELOUS MMMUFFINS	1 Dundas St. W., # 2306, Toronto ON M4G1Z3	CAN
MOM'S CINNAMON ROLL SHOPS/BAKERY	8100 S. Quebec, #B-206, Englewood CO 80231	
MRS. POWELL'S CINNAMON ROLLS	500 Franklin Village Dr., # 106, Franklin MA 02038	
MUFFIN BREAK CANADA	310 - 1656 Martin Dr., Surrey BC V4A6E7	CAN
NEAL'S COOKIES	5700 Savoy, Houston TX 77036	
NECTAR DONUTS	350 Lincoln St., Welland ON L3B4N4	CAN
O'DONUTS COFFEE SHOPS	2373 Bloor St., W., Toronto ONP M6P1P6	CAN
OPEN WINDOW BAKERY	1125 Finch Ave., W., Toronto ON M3J2E8	CAN
PARIS CROISSANT	1450 rue Nobel, # 12, Boucherville PQ J4V5H3	CAN
ROBIN'S DONUTS	906 Victoria Ave. E., Thunder Bay ON P7C1B4	CAN
SPUDNUTS	742 Hampshire, # B, Westlake CA 91361	
SWEET ROSIE'S COOKIES	2-A Wellesley St., W., Toronto ON M4Y1E7	CAN
TASTEE DONUTS	5600 Mournes St., Harahan LA 70123	
TREATS	121 Bloor St. East, # 810, Toronto ON M4W3M5	CAN
TROLL'S FISH	13541 - 102nd Ave., # 207, Surrey BC V3T4X8	CAN
U.S.A. TREATS	11365 Ventura Blvd., # 307, Studio City CA 91604	
VIE DE FRANCE BAKERIES	651 E. Butterfield Rd., # 503, Lombard IL 60148	
WINCHELL'S DONUT HOUSE	16424 Valley View Ave., La Mirada CA 90637	
YUM YUM DONUTS	18830 E. San Jose Ave., City of Industry CA 91748	

For a full explanation of the data provided in the Franchisor Format, please refer to Chapter 2, *"How To Use The Data."*

CHAPTER 18

RETAIL FOOD:
ICE CREAM / YOGURT / GELATO

**ALL AMERICAN FROZEN
YOGURT SHOPS**
4800 SW Macadam Ave., # 301
Portland, OR 97201
TEL: (503) 224-6199 C
FAX: (503) 224-5042
Mr. C. R. Duffie, Jr., President

Regional mall and specialty center based up-scale franchisor. Shops in Western half of US. Looking for owner/operators in US and Canada for major shopping centers and specialty retail centers. Great "add-on" business for existing food and/or service operation.

HISTORY: . . . . IFA
Established in 1986;   . . 1st Franchised in 1988
Company-Owned Units (As of 12/1/1989):   . 15
Franchised Units (12/1/1989): 9
Total Units (12/1/1989): 24
Distribution: US-24;Can-0;Overseas-0
  North America: . . . . 6 States
  Concentration: . . .9 in WA, 6 in OR, 4 in CO
Registered: . . . . .CA,OR,WA

. . . .
Average # of Employees: . . . . . 1 FT, 6-8 PT
Prior Industry Experience: . . . . Helpful

FINANCIAL: OTC
Cash Investment: $20-35K
Total Investment: $100-132K
Fees: Franchise - $16-20K
  Royalty: 5%, Advert: 1%
Contract Periods (Yrs.): 10/10
Area Development Agreement: Yes/Var
Sub-Franchise Contract: . . . . . .No
Expand in Territory: . . . . Yes
Passive Ownership: . . . Discouraged
Encourage Conversions: . . . . . Yes
Franchisee Purchase(s) Required: .No

FRANCHISOR TRAINING/SUPPORT:
Financial Assistance Provided: . . . Yes(I)
Site Selection Assistance: . . . . .Yes
Lease Negotiation Assistance: . . . . .Yes
Co-operative Advertising: . . . . .Yes
Training: . . . . . . 1 Wk. in Headquarters,
  . . . . 1 Wk, Store Location
On-Going Support: . . . . B,C,D,E,F,G,H
Full-Time Franchisor Support Staff: . . 25
EXPANSION PLANS:
  US: . . . . All US
  Canada - Yes, ...Overseas - Yes

BASKIN-ROBBINS ICE CREAM OF CANADA
91 Skyway Ave., # 200
Rexdale, ON M9W6R5 CAN
TEL: (416) 675-3131
FAX:
Mr. Stan White, VP Development

First worldwide fast-food franchisor of top-quality ice cream.

HISTORY: . . . . IFA	FINANCIAL: Yes	FRANCHISOR TRAINING/SUPPORT:
Established in 1970; . . 1st Franchised in 1970	Cash Investment: $50-60K	Financial Assistance Provided: . . . . .No
Company-Owned Units (As of 12/1/1989): . 10	Total Investment: $130-175K	Site Selection Assistance: . . . . .Yes
Franchised Units (12/1/1989): 190	Fees: Franchise - $25K	Lease Negotiation Assistance: . . . . .Yes
Total Units (12/1/1989): 200	Royalty: .05%, Advert: 4%	Co-operative Advertising: . . . . .Yes
Distribution: . . . US-0;Can-200;Overseas-0	Contract Periods (Yrs.): 10/5	Training: . . . . .17 Days Burbank, CA
North America:	Area Development Agreement: .No	. . . .
Concentration:	Sub-Franchise Contract: . . . . .No	On-Going Support: . . . . A,B,C,D,E,G,H
Registered: . . . . AB	Expand in Territory: . . . . .No	Full-Time Franchisor Support Staff: . . 65
. . . .	Passive Ownership: . . . Discouraged	EXPANSION PLANS:
Average # of Employees: . . . . . .2 FT, 4+ PT	Encourage Conversions: . . . . . Yes	US: . . . . .NA
Prior Industry Experience: . . . . Helpful	Franchisee Purchase(s) Required: Yes	Canada - Yes, ...Overseas - No

BOY BLUE OF AMERICA

10919 W. Janesville Rd.
Hales Corners, WI 53130
TEL: (414) 425-5160
FAX:
Mr. Earl J. Phillips, Consultant

Excellent, high-quality soft-serve formula, sold only by BOY BLUE franchisees. Also yogurt and sandwiches.

HISTORY:	FINANCIAL:	FRANCHISOR TRAINING/SUPPORT:
Established in 1967; . . 1st Franchised in 1973	Cash Investment: $50K	Financial Assistance Provided: . . . . .No
Company-Owned Units (As of 12/1/1989): . .0	Total Investment: $75-95K	Site Selection Assistance: . . . . .Yes
Franchised Units (12/1/1989): 14	Fees: Franchise - $10K	Lease Negotiation Assistance: . . . . .Yes
Total Units (12/1/1989): 14	Royalty: 5%, Advert: 1.5%	Co-operative Advertising: . . . . No
Distribution: US-14;Can-0;Overseas-0	Contract Periods (Yrs.): 15/15	Training: . . . . 10 Days Training
North America: . . . . .1 State	Area Development Agreement: Yes/15	. . . .
Concentration: . . . . .14 in WI	Sub-Franchise Contract: . . . . .No	On-Going Support: . . . . .E,H,I
Registered: . . . . .WI	Expand in Territory: . . . . . . Yes	Full-Time Franchisor Support Staff: . . .3
. . . .	Passive Ownership: . . . Not Allowed	EXPANSION PLANS:
Average # of Employees: . . . . . . 3 FT, 6 PT	Encourage Conversions: . . . . .No	US: . . . . .All US
Prior Industry Experience: . . . . Helpful	Franchisee Purchase(s) Required: Yes	Canada - No, ...Overseas - No

BRODY'S YOGURT COMPANY

112 NW 33rd Ct.
Gainesville, FL 32607
TEL: (904) 377-0774
FAX:
Mr. John Chambers, Dir. of Franchise

BRODY'S YOGURT COMPANY offers a premium frozen yogurt and fresh fruit products to the health-conscious consumer. BRODY'S specializes in serving its frozen yogurt, fruit salads, fruit shakes, smoothies and other specialty products through regional mall locations.

HISTORY:	FINANCIAL:	FRANCHISOR TRAINING/SUPPORT:
Established in 1984; . . 1st Franchised in 1984	Cash Investment: $40-80K	Financial Assistance Provided: . . . . No
Company-Owned Units (As of 12/1/1989): . 16	Total Investment: $80-140K	Site Selection Assistance: . . . . .Yes
Franchised Units (12/1/1989): 5	Fees: Franchise - $10K	Lease Negotiation Assistance: . . . . .Yes
Total Units (12/1/1989): 21	Royalty: 4%, Advert: 0-1%	Co-operative Advertising: . . . . No
Distribution: US-21;Can-0;Overseas-0	Contract Periods (Yrs.): 20/5	Training: . . . . .1 Wk. Headquarters,
North America: . . . . 8 States	Area Development Agreement: . .No	. . . . 5 Days In Store
Concentration: . . . 6 in FL, 5 in NC, 4 in OH	Sub-Franchise Contract: . . . . .No	On-Going Support: . . . . b,C,D,E,G,H,I
Registered: . . . . FL,MI	Expand in Territory: . . . . . . Yes	Full-Time Franchisor Support Staff: . . 26
. . . .	Passive Ownership: . . . . . .Allowed	EXPANSION PLANS:
Average # of Employees: . . . . . . 2 FT, 6 PT	Encourage Conversions: . . . . Yes	US: . . . . . . .East Coast and Midwest
Prior Industry Experience: . . . . Helpful	Franchisee Purchase(s) Required: .No	Canada - No, ...Overseas - No

CALIFORNIA YOGURT COMPANY

2401 Vista Way, # E
Oceanside, CA 92054
TEL: (619) 439-5650
FAX:
Mr. Roy Ring, Franchise Development

CALIFORNIA YOGURT COMPANY is a limited-menu food business, featuring frozen yogurt desserts and beverage creations. Top-quality food ingredients and products, state-of-the-art design and equipment and our continuing support make CALIFORNIA YOGURT COMPANY an exceptional opportunity.

HISTORY: . . . .
Established in 1981; . . 1st Franchised in 1986
Company-Owned Units (As of 12/1/1989): . .3
Franchised Units (12/1/1989): 34
Total Units (12/1/1989): 37
Distribution: US-8;Can-0;Overseas-29
 North America: . . . . .1 State
 Concentration: . . . . 8 in CA
Registered: . . . . .CA,HI

. . . .
Average # of Employees: . . . . 1-2 FT, 3-5 PT
Prior Industry Experience: . . . . . . Helpful

FINANCIAL:
Cash Investment: $75-100K
Total Investment: $155-185K
Fees: Franchise - $20K
 Royalty: 4%, Advert: 3%
Contract Periods (Yrs.): 10/5
Area Development Agreement: Yes/15
Sub-Franchise Contract: . . . . . Yes
Expand in Territory: . . . . .No
Passive Ownership: . . . Not Allowed
Encourage Conversions: . . . . .No
Franchisee Purchase(s) Required: .No

FRANCHISOR TRAINING/SUPPORT:
Financial Assistance Provided: . . . Yes(I)
Site Selection Assistance: . . . . . . .Yes
Lease Negotiation Assistance: . . . . .Yes
Co-operative Advertising: . . . . .Yes
Training: . . . . 5 Days Headquarters,
 . . . . 5 Days Site
On-Going Support: . . . . . . B,C,D,E,G,I
Full-Time Franchisor Support Staff: . . .3
EXPANSION PLANS:
 US: . . . . East Coast and South
 Canada - Yes, . . . Overseas - Yes

DOUBLE RAINBOW ICE CREAM & DESSERT CAFE

275 S. Van Ness Ave.
San Francisco, CA 94103
TEL: (415) 861-5858
FAX:
Ms. Leslie Cass, Fran. Co-ord.

DOUBLE RAINBOW ICE CREAM & DESSERT CAFES feature award-winning gourmet ice creams, fine coffees and expressos, old-fashioned fountain specialties and delicious pastries. Additionally, some locations offer frozen yogurt, custom-made ice cream cakes and gourmet-grilled sandwiches.

HISTORY: . . . .
Established in 1976; . . 1st Franchised in 1982
Company-Owned Units (As of 12/1/1989): . .3
Franchised Units (12/1/1989): 28
Total Units (12/1/1989): 31
Distribution: US-31;Can-0;Overseas-0
 North America: . . . . 3 States
 Concentration: . . 29 in CA, 1 in AZ, 1 in NM
Registered: . . . . .CA,HI

. . . .
Average # of Employees: . . . . . . 2 FT, 2 PT
Prior Industry Experience: . . . . . . Helpful

FINANCIAL:
Cash Investment: $75-125K
Total Investment: $155-245K
Fees: Franchise - $30K
 Royalty: 2%, Advert: 2%
Contract Periods (Yrs.): 10/10
Area Development Agreement: .No
Sub-Franchise Contract: . . . . .No
Expand in Territory: . . . . Yes
Passive Ownership: . . . Not Allowed
Encourage Conversions: . . . . . NA
Franchisee Purchase(s) Required: Yes

FRANCHISOR TRAINING/SUPPORT:
Financial Assistance Provided: . . . . . No
Site Selection Assistance: . . . . .Yes
Lease Negotiation Assistance: . . . .Yes
Co-operative Advertising: . . . . .Yes
Training: . . . . 9 Days Headquarters
 . . . .
On-Going Support: . . . . A,C,E,H,I
Full-Time Franchisor Support Staff: . . .3
EXPANSION PLANS:
 US: . . . . .CA, AZ,NM and HI
 Canada - No, ...Overseas - No

FLAMINGO'S FROZEN YOGURT

11033 Montgomery Rd.
Cincinnati, OH 45249
TEL: (800) 446-0808 (513) 984-4380
FAX: (513) 984-4385
Mr. John J. Granito, Dir. Fran.

FLAMINGO'S unique approach goes far beyond that of the average frozen yogurt store. Step into a FLAMINGO'S and experience an ambiance not duplicated in the industry. While some are just selling frozen yogurt as a commodity, FLAMINGO'S is marketing a concept of gourmet enjoyment with their focus on fun and quality in an obviously superior presentation.

HISTORY: . . . .
Established in 1987; . . 1st Franchised in 1988
Company-Owned Units (As of 12/1/1989): . .2
Franchised Units (12/1/1989): 40
Total Units (12/1/1989): 42
Distribution: US-42;Can-0;Overseas-0
 North America: . . . . 8 States
 Concentration: . . . 5 IN OH, 2 in PA, 1 in KY
Registered: . . . . FL,IN,MI,OR

. . . .
Average # of Employees: . . . . . . 2 FT, 6 PT
Prior Industry Experience: . . . . . . Helpful

FINANCIAL:
Cash Investment: $30-40K
Total Investment: $122-205K
Fees: Franchise - $20K
 Royalty: 4%, Advert: 4%
Contract Periods (Yrs.): . . 10/10/10
Area Development Agreement: . Yes
Sub-Franchise Contract: . . . . .No
Expand in Territory: . . . . Yes
Passive Ownership: . . . Discouraged
Encourage Conversions: . . . . . Yes
Franchisee Purchase(s) Required: .No

FRANCHISOR TRAINING/SUPPORT:
Financial Assistance Provided: . . . Yes(I)
Site Selection Assistance: . . . . . . .Yes
Lease Negotiation Assistance: . . . .Yes
Co-operative Advertising: . . . . .Yes
Training: . . . . . . 14 Days Headquarters,
 . . . . .7 Days On-site
On-Going Support: . . . . . C,D,E,F,G,H,I
Full-Time Franchisor Support Staff: . . .7
EXPANSION PLANS:
 US: . . . . All US
 Canada - No, ...Overseas - No

FRESHENS PREMIUM YOGURT

2849 Paces Ferry Rd., # 750
Atlanta, GA 30339
TEL: (404) 433-0983
FAX: (404) 431-9081
Ms. Laurie Lanser, Dir. Fran. Dev.

FRESHENS is positioned as "America's Premium Yogurt" with a proprietary line of low-fat, non-fat and sugar-free non-fat yogurts. FRESHENS sells only premium yogurt and yogurt-related products in malls and shopping centers throughout the US and is America's fastest-growing yogurt chain.

HISTORY: . . . .
Established in 1985; . . 1st Franchised in 1985
Company-Owned Units (As of 12/1/1989): . .2
Franchised Units (12/1/1989): 152
Total Units (12/1/1989): 154
Distribution: . . . US-154;Can-0;Overseas-0
North America: . . . . 30 States
Concentration: . 27 in FL, 19 in GA, 16 in VA
Registered: . . . .CA,FL,IL,IN,MI,NY,VA,WI
. . . .
Average # of Employees: . . . . . . 1 FT, 6 PT
Prior Industry Experience: . . . . Helpful

FINANCIAL:
Cash Investment: $35-50K
Total Investment: $125-165K
Fees: Franchise - $20K
  Royalty: 4%, Advert: 4%
Contract Periods (Yrs.): 10/10
Area Development Agreement: Yes/Var
Sub-Franchise Contract: . . . . .No
Expand in Territory: . . . . . . .No
Passive Ownership: . . . Not Allowed
Encourage Conversions: . . . . Yes
Franchisee Purchase(s) Required: Yes

FRANCHISOR TRAINING/SUPPORT:
Financial Assistance Provided: . . . . . No
Site Selection Assistance: . . . . .Yes
Lease Negotiation Assistance: . . . . .Yes
Co-operative Advertising: . . . . .Yes
Training: . . . . 7 Days Headquarters
. . . .
On-Going Support: . . . . B,C,D,E,F,G,h,I
Full-Time Franchisor Support Staff: . . 16
EXPANSION PLANS:
US: . . . . All US
Canada - No, ...Overseas - No

FRUSEN GLADJE

200 Andover Bus. Park Dr., # 1000
Andover, MA 01810
TEL: (508) 975-1283
FAX: (508) 686-2390
Mr. Michael Newport, VP

Ice cream manufacturer and franchisor of ice cream stores.

HISTORY: . . . .
Established in 1981; . . 1st Franchised in 1981
Company-Owned Units (As of 12/1/1989): . .0
Franchised Units (12/1/1989): 15
Total Units (12/1/1989): 15
Distribution: US-15;Can-0;Overseas-0
North America: . . . . 11 States
Concentration: . . . 7 in FL, 3 in NY, 2 in CA
Registered: . . . .
. . . .
Average # of Employees: . . . .
Prior Industry Experience: . . . . Helpful

FINANCIAL:
Cash Investment: . . . .$
Total Investment: $125-175K
Fees: Franchise - $25K
  Royalty: 0%, Advert: 1.5%
Contract Periods (Yrs.): 10/10
Area Development Agreement: . .No
Sub-Franchise Contract: . . . . .No
Expand in Territory: . . . .
Passive Ownership: . . . Discouraged
Encourage Conversions: . . . . Yes
Franchisee Purchase(s) Required: Yes

FRANCHISOR TRAINING/SUPPORT:
Financial Assistance Provided: . . . .
Site Selection Assistance: . . . . .Yes
Lease Negotiation Assistance: . . . . .Yes
Co-operative Advertising: . . . .
Training: . . . .
. . . .
On-Going Support: I
Full-Time Franchisor Support Staff: . . . .
EXPANSION PLANS:
US: . . . . All US
Canada - No, ...Overseas - No

GELATO AMARE

11504 Hyde Pl.
Raleigh, NC 27614
TEL: (919) 847-4435
FAX:
Mr. John Franklin, President

GELATO AMARE stores feature delicious, all-natural, low-calorie frozen yogurt. We serve over 45 flavors, 25 of which have no fat and no cholesterol. Many stores also serve homemade superpremium, low-fat Italian-style ice cream, salads and sandwiches. All stores serve shakes, smoothies, Hurricanes, sundaes, homemade cones and many other treats.

HISTORY: . . . .
Established in 1983; . . 1st Franchised in 1986
Company-Owned Units (As of 12/1/1989): . .1
Franchised Units (12/1/1989): 4
Total Units (12/1/1989): 5
Distribution: US-5;Can-0;Overseas-0
North America: . . . . .3 State
Concentration: . . . .3 in NC, 1 in FL, 1 in MI
Registered: . . . . CA,FL,HI,IL,MI,NY
. . . .
Average # of Employees: . . . . . . 1 FT, 6 PT
Prior Industry Experience: . . . . Helpful

FINANCIAL:
Cash Investment: $30-50K
Total Investment: $75-130K
Fees: Franchise - $18.9K
  Royalty: 5%, Advert: 3%
Contract Periods (Yrs.): 10/5/5
Area Development Agreement: Yes/10
Sub-Franchise Contract: . . . . . Yes
Expand in Territory: . . . . Yes
Passive Ownership: . . . . . .Allowed
Encourage Conversions: . . . . . Yes
Franchisee Purchase(s) Required: .No

FRANCHISOR TRAINING/SUPPORT:
Financial Assistance Provided: . . . Yes(I)
Site Selection Assistance: . . . . .Yes
Lease Negotiation Assistance: . . . . .Yes
Co-operative Advertising: . . . . .Yes
Training: . . . . 2 Wks. Headquarters
. . . .
On-Going Support: . . . . . . B,C,D,E,H,I
Full-Time Franchisor Support Staff: . . .4
EXPANSION PLANS:
US: . . . . All US
Canada - Yes, . . . Overseas - Yes

GORIN'S HOMEMADE ICE CREAM

158 Oak St.
Avondale Estates, GA 30002
TEL: (404) 292-0043
FAX:
Mr. Stan Adelman, Fran. Dir.

Up-scale ice cream and deli sandwich shop. Additionally, serving quiche, soups and salads.

HISTORY: . . . .
Established in 1981; . . 1st Franchised in 1982
Company-Owned Units (As of 12/1/1989): . .3
Franchised Units (12/1/1989): 30
Total Units (12/1/1989): 33
Distribution: US-33;Can-0;Overseas-0
North America: . . . . 4 States
Concentration: . . . . GA, AL, NC, SC
Registered: . . . .

. . . .
Average # of Employees: . . . . 2-4 FT, 3-5 PT
Prior Industry Experience: . . . . Helpful

FINANCIAL:
Cash Investment: . . . . . . $50+K
Total Investment: . . . .$125+K
Fees: Franchise - $21K
Royalty: 5%, Advert: 1%
Contract Periods (Yrs.): . . . . Open
Area Development Agreement: . Yes
Sub-Franchise Contract: . . . .No
Expand in Territory: . . . . . . Yes
Passive Ownership: . . . Discouraged
Encourage Conversions: . . . . .No
Franchisee Purchase(s) Required: Yes

FRANCHISOR TRAINING/SUPPORT:
Financial Assistance Provided: . . . . .No
Site Selection Assistance: . . . . . . .Yes
Lease Negotiation Assistance: . . . . .Yes
Co-operative Advertising: . . . . . . .Yes
Training: . . . . . . 3-4 Wks. Headquarters

. . . .
On-Going Support: . . A,B,C,D,E,F,G,H,I
Full-Time Franchisor Support Staff: . . . .
EXPANSION PLANS:
US: . . . . Southeast
Canada - No, ...Overseas - No

HIGH WHEELER ICE CREAM PARLOUR/RESTAURANT

5192 West Main St.
Kalamazoo, MI 49009
TEL: (616) 345-4500
FAX:
Mr. Roger Buchholtz, President

Large turn-of-the-century, family-oriented ice cream parlour restaurants, featuring an extensive ice cream creation menu and over 45 flavors of ice cream, gourmet hamburgers, lunches and dinners. Further enhanced by an old-fashioned candy and bake shoppe where fudge, chocolates, candies, brownies, cookies and breads are made in view of the customers.

HISTORY: . . . .
Established in 1975; . . 1st Franchised in 1986
Company-Owned Units (As of 12/1/1989): . .2
Franchised Units (12/1/1989): 4
Total Units (12/1/1989): 6
Distribution: US-6;Can-0;Overseas-0
North America: . . . . 3 States
Concentration: . . . . 2 in MI, 2 in FL, 2 in IL
Registered: . . . .

. . . .
Average # of Employees: . . . . . .3 FT, 50 PT
Prior Industry Experience: . . . . Helpful

FINANCIAL:
Cash Investment: $100K
Total Investment: $1MM
Fees: Franchise - $35K
Royalty: 4%, Advert: 1%
Contract Periods (Yrs.): . . . 20/20
Area Development Agreement: Yes/10
Sub-Franchise Contract: . . . .No
Expand in Territory: . . . . . . Yes
Passive Ownership: . . . Discouraged
Encourage Conversions: . . . . . Yes
Franchisee Purchase(s) Required: Yes

FRANCHISOR TRAINING/SUPPORT:
Financial Assistance Provided: . . . Yes(I)
Site Selection Assistance: . . . . . . .Yes
Lease Negotiation Assistance: . . . .Yes
Co-operative Advertising: . . . . . . .Yes
Training: . . . . 8 Wks. Headquarters

. . . .
On-Going Support: . . a,B,C,D,E,F,G,H,I
Full-Time Franchisor Support Staff: . . 20
EXPANSION PLANS:
US: . . . . .Midwest, SE
Canada - Yes, ...Overseas - No

HILLARY'S GOURMET ICE CREAM

838 Sussex Blvd.
Broomall, PA 19008
TEL: (800) 365-6111 (215) 328-6111
FAX: (215) 328-4259
Mr. Lou Termini, President

America's finest and most exclusive gourmet ice cream parlours. HILLARY'S ice cream and yogurt is only available in HILLARY'S PARLOURS and not in supermarkets or convenience stores. Parlour designs in marble, chrome and neon are high-grossing operations and a favorite of shopping mall developers.

HISTORY: . . . .
Established in 1976; . . 1st Franchised in 1979
Company-Owned Units (As of 12/1/1989): . .1
Franchised Units (12/1/1989): 34
Total Units (12/1/1989): 35
Distribution: US-35;Can-0;Overseas-0
North America: . . . . 6 States
Concentration: . . . 20 in PA, 6 in NJ, 3 in VA
Registered: . . . . .FL,MD,MI,NY,VA

. . . .
Average # of Employees: . . . . . . 10-15 PT
Prior Industry Experience: . . . . Helpful

FINANCIAL:
Cash Investment: . . . . . . $70K+
Total Investment: $100-160K
Fees: Franchise - $25K
Royalty: 4%, Advert: . . . $7.8/Yr.
Contract Periods (Yrs.): 10
Area Development Agreement: Yes/10
Sub-Franchise Contract: . . . . . .No
Expand in Territory: . . . . . . Yes
Passive Ownership: . . . Discouraged
Encourage Conversions: . . . . . Yes
Franchisee Purchase(s) Required: Yes

FRANCHISOR TRAINING/SUPPORT:
Financial Assistance Provided: . . . Yes(I)
Site Selection Assistance: . . . . . . .Yes
Lease Negotiation Assistance: . . . .Yes
Co-operative Advertising: . . . . . . .Yes
Training: . . . . . . 2 Wks. + Headquarters,
. . 10-14 Days + On Location, On-going
On-Going Support: . . . .B,C,D,E,F,G,H,I
Full-Time Franchisor Support Staff: . . 12
EXPANSION PLANS:
US: . . . . . . .Midwest and East Coast
Canada - Yes, . . . Overseas - Yes

HUCKLEBERRY THIN

123 Franklin Corner Rd., # 203
Lawrenceville, NJ 08648
TEL: (800) 343-5087 (609) 895-9676
FAX: (609) 895-1035
Mr. George P. Irish, VP

HUCKLEBERRY THIN store's primary product is frozen yogurt, marketed as a meal, not a dessert. The customer is presented with an attractive array of toppings. Your HUCKLEBERRY THIN store will offer fresh fruit salads and fruit juices, healthy and calorie-conscious entrees, pita bread sandwiches and healthy fruit salads.

HISTORY: . . . .
Established in 1988; . . 1st Franchised in 1989
Company-Owned Units (As of 12/1/1989): . . 1
Franchised Units (12/1/1989): 0
Total Units (12/1/1989): 1
Distribution: US-1;Can-0;Overseas-0
North America: . . . . .1 State
Concentration: . . . . 1 in NJ
Registered: . . . .

Average # of Employees: . . . . . .6 FT, 10 PT
Prior Industry Experience: . . . . Helpful

FINANCIAL:
Cash Investment: $65K
Total Investment: $165-250K
Fees: Franchise - $17.5K
Royalty: 6%, Advert: 3%
Contract Periods (Yrs.): 10/10
Area Development Agreement: Yes/Var
Sub-Franchise Contract: . . . . . .No
Expand in Territory: . . . . Yes
Passive Ownership: . . . Discouraged
Encourage Conversions: . . . . . Yes
Franchisee Purchase(s) Required: Yes

FRANCHISOR TRAINING/SUPPORT:
Financial Assistance Provided: . . . Yes(I)
Site Selection Assistance: . . . . . . .Yes
Lease Negotiation Assistance: . . . . .Yes
Co-operative Advertising: . . . . . . .Yes
Training: . . . . 10 Business Days At
. . . . Headquarters
On-Going Support: . . . A,C,D,E,F,G,H,I
Full-Time Franchisor Support Staff: . . .2
EXPANSION PLANS:
US: . . . . Northeast
Canada - No, ...Overseas - No

I LOVE YOGURT

12770 Coit Rd., # 1115
Dallas, TX 75251
TEL: (214) 788-1580 C
FAX: (214) 788-1570
Mr. Robert J. Schultz, VP Devel.

I LOVE YOGURT SHOPPES offer a franchisee a varied product line which eliminates some of the seasonality that is associated with frozen yogurt shoppes. Our shoppes combine our frozen yogurt and toppings with menu items like fresh-baked cookies, soups salads and sandwiches. Everything is high quality and pre-prepared.

HISTORY: . . . .
Established in 1980; . . 1st Franchised in 1986
Company-Owned Units (As of 12/1/1989): . 12
Franchised Units (12/1/1989): 8
Total Units (12/1/1989): 20
Distribution: US-20;Can-0;Overseas-0
North America: . . . . 4 States
Concentration: . . .13 in TX, 3 in OK, 2 in KS
Registered: . . . . .CA,FL

Average # of Employees: . . . . . 2-3 FT, 4 PT
Prior Industry Experience: . . . . Helpful

FINANCIAL:
Cash Investment: $35-40K
Total Investment: $85-135K
Fees: Franchise - $20K
Royalty: 4%, Advert: 1%
Contract Periods (Yrs.): 10/5
Area Development Agreement: Yes/Var
Sub-Franchise Contract: . . . . . .No
Expand in Territory: . . . . Yes
Passive Ownership: . . . . . .Allowed
Encourage Conversions: . . . . . Yes
Franchisee Purchase(s) Required: .No

FRANCHISOR TRAINING/SUPPORT:
Financial Assistance Provided: . . . . .NA
Site Selection Assistance: . . . . . . .Yes
Lease Negotiation Assistance: . . . . .Yes
Co-operative Advertising: . . . . . . .Yes
Training: . . . . .1 Wk. Headquarters
. . . .
On-Going Support: . . . . . B,C,D,E,F,G,I
Full-Time Franchisor Support Staff: . . .7
EXPANSION PLANS:
US: . . . . .All US
Canada - Yes, . . . Overseas - Yes

KILWIN'S CHOCOLATES AND ICE CREAM

355 N. Division Rd.
Petoskey, MI 49770
TEL: (616) 347-3800
FAX: (616) 347-6951
Mr. H. Wayne Rose, President

KILWIN'S CHOCOLATES AND ICE CREAM is a family of confectionary stores that give old-fashioned enjoyment to customers by providing quality products, turn-of-the-century store atmosphere and over 40 years of experience. Modern business systems provide efficiency and simplicity of operation while knowledgeable, experienced franchise personnel are committed to your success.

HISTORY: . . . . .IFA
Established in 1946; . . 1st Franchised in 1981
Company-Owned Units (As of 12/1/1989): . .1
Franchised Units (12/1/1989): 24
Total Units (12/1/1989): 25
Distribution: US-25;Can-0;Overseas-0
North America: . . . . 7 States
Concentration: . . .14 in MI, 2 in NC, 1 in FL
Registered: . . . . .FL,IL,IN,MI,RI,WI

Average # of Employees: . . . . . . 3 FT, 5 PT
Prior Industry Experience: . . . . Helpful

FINANCIAL:
Cash Investment: $50-100K
Total Investment: $80-160K
Fees: Franchise - $20K
Royalty: 5%, Advert: 0%
Contract Periods (Yrs.): 10/10
Area Development Agreement: Yes/2
Sub-Franchise Contract: . . . . . .No
Expand in Territory: . . . . Yes
Passive Ownership: . . . Not Allowed
Encourage Conversions: . . . . . .No
Franchisee Purchase(s) Required: .No

FRANCHISOR TRAINING/SUPPORT:
Financial Assistance Provided: . . . . .No
Site Selection Assistance: . . . . . . .Yes
Lease Negotiation Assistance: . . . . .Yes
Co-operative Advertising: . . . . . . .Yes
Training: . . . . 5 Days Headquarters,
. . . . .5 Days Franchisee's Store
On-Going Support: . . . . . . .C,D,E,G,H,I
Full-Time Franchisor Support Staff: . . .4
EXPANSION PLANS:
US: . . . . . Midwest, East and Southeast
Canada - No, ...Overseas - No

LARRY'S ICE CREAM & YOGURT

14550 McCormick Dr.
Tampa, FL 33626
TEL: (800) ICE-KREM (813) 855-0481
FAX: (813) 854-1317
Mr. Roger Kumar, COO

Super-premium ice cream, with unique yogurt operation. We blend fresh fruit, cookies or candy with vanilla yogurt - e.g. strawberry-banana yogurt is made with fresh whole strawberries and banana. Flavors are unlimited in number and scope - e.g. apple pie yogurt is fresh slices of apple with cinnamon powder.

HISTORY: . . . . IFA
Established in 1981; . . 1st Franchised in 1982
Company-Owned Units (As of 12/1/1989): . .4
Franchised Units (12/1/1989): 44
Total Units (12/1/1989): 48
Distribution: US-48;Can-0;Overseas-0
North America: . . . . 3 States
Concentration: . . . 46 in FL, 1 in GA, 1 in SC
Registered: . . . . FL
. . . .
Average # of Employees: . Varies With Volume
Prior Industry Experience: . . . . Helpful

FINANCIAL: OTC-LARY
Cash Investment: . . . .$
Total Investment: $75-92K
Fees: Franchise - $15K
  Royalty: 2%, Advert: 4%
Contract Periods (Yrs.): 10/10
Area Development Agreement: Yes/Var
Sub-Franchise Contract: . . . . . Yes
Expand in Territory: . . . . . . Yes
Passive Ownership: . . . Discouraged
Encourage Conversions: . . . . Yes
Franchisee Purchase(s) Required: Yes

FRANCHISOR TRAINING/SUPPORT:
Financial Assistance Provided: . . . . .No
Site Selection Assistance: . . . . . . .Yes
Lease Negotiation Assistance: . . . . .Yes
Co-operative Advertising: . . . . . . .Yes
Training: . . . . . . 1 Wk. Company-owned
. . . . Stores in Tampa Bay Area
On-Going Support: . . . . . B,C,D,E,G,H
Full-Time Franchisor Support Staff: . . 40
EXPANSION PLANS:
US: . . . . Southeast
Canada - No, ...Overseas - No

LEE'S HOMEMADE ICE CREAM

1125 DeSoto Rd.
Baltimore, MD 21223
TEL: (301) 525-2224
FAX: (310) 525-8320
Mr. Scott Garfield, Dir. Fran.

LEE'S HOMEMADE ICE CREAM is a super-premium, gourmet product. Our award-winning ice cream is recognized as an unparalleled dessert. We offer a line of delicious cookies, in addition to other dessert items.

HISTORY: . . . .
Established in 1979; . . 1st Franchised in 1985
Company-Owned Units (As of 12/1/1989): . .2
Franchised Units (12/1/1989): 9
Total Units (12/1/1989): 11
Distribution: US-11;Can-0;Overseas-0
North America: . . . . 4 States
Concentration: . . . 6 in MD, 3 in VA, 1 in DC
Registered: . . . . MD
. . . .
Average # of Employees: . . . . . .2 FT, 15 PT
Prior Industry Experience: . . . . Helpful

FINANCIAL:
Cash Investment: $110K
Total Investment: $220K
Fees: Franchise - $30K
  Royalty: 0%, Advert: 4%
Contract Periods (Yrs.): . . . 10/10
Area Development Agreement: . .No
Sub-Franchise Contract: . . . . .No
Expand in Territory: . . . . . . Yes
Passive Ownership: . . . Discouraged
Encourage Conversions: . . . . NA
Franchisee Purchase(s) Required: Yes

FRANCHISOR TRAINING/SUPPORT:
Financial Assistance Provided: . . . . .No
Site Selection Assistance: . . . . . . .Yes
Lease Negotiation Assistance: . . . . .Yes
Co-operative Advertising: . . . . . . .Yes
Training: . . . . . . 2 Wks. Company Store,
. . . . 2 Wks. Co. office, 2 Wks. On-site
On-Going Support: . . . . . . B,C,D,E,F,I
Full-Time Franchisor Support Staff: . . . 6
EXPANSION PLANS:
US: . . Mid-Atlantic(PA,MD,DC,NY,NJ)
Canada - No, ...Overseas - No

LOVE'S YOGURT

1830 Techny Ct.
Northbrook, IL 60062
TEL: (708) 480-9200
FAX: (708) 480-0280
Mr. Rovert Silverstein, President

LOVE'S YOGURT AND SALADS offers a unique soft-serve frozen yogurt and salad bar concept. The emphasis is toward healthy, quality foods with prepared salads prepared daily, in addition to soups, chili, baked potatoes with toppings, and freshly-baked muffins. Personalized service is our specialty.

HISTORY: . . . .
Established in 1987; . . 1st Franchised in 1988
Company-Owned Units (As of 12/1/1989): . .3
Franchised Units (12/1/1989): 6
Total Units (12/1/1989): 9
Distribution: US-9;Can-0;Overseas-0
North America: . . . . 2 States
Concentration: . . . . 8 in IL, 1 in IN
Registered: . . . . IL,IN
. . . .
Average # of Employees: . . . . . . 3 FT, 3 PT
Prior Industry Experience: . . . . Helpful

FINANCIAL:
Cash Investment: $100K
Total Investment: $160-200K
Fees: Franchise - $20K
  Royalty: 4%, Advert: 2%
Contract Periods (Yrs.): 15/15
Area Development Agreement: . .No
Sub-Franchise Contract: . . . . .No
Expand in Territory: . . . . . . Yes
Passive Ownership: . . . Not Allowed
Encourage Conversions: . . . . .No
Franchisee Purchase(s) Required: .No

FRANCHISOR TRAINING/SUPPORT:
Financial Assistance Provided: . . . Yes(I)
Site Selection Assistance: . . . . . . .Yes
Lease Negotiation Assistance: . . . . .Yes
Co-operative Advertising: . . . . . . .Yes
Training: . . . . .1 Wk. Headquarters,
. . . . 1 Wk. Site, 1 Wk. Franchisee Site
On-Going Support: . . . . . B,C,D,E,F,H,I
Full-Time Franchisor Support Staff: . . 10
EXPANSION PLANS:
US: . . . . Midwest
Canada - No, ... Overseas - Yes

MS MUFFET'S YOGURT SHOPS

P. O. Box 447
Wrightsville Beach, NC 28480
TEL: (919) 256-2900
FAX:
Mr. Bernie J. Pisczek, VP

Full-line frozen yogurt shops, offering 9 different flavors (from list of 45) and 35 toppings. Developed by food industry pros to yield maximum profitability and quick return on investment. Superior taste, innovative operating systems and liberal development terms make this the best yogurt opportunity available.

HISTORY: . . . . IFA	FINANCIAL:	FRANCHISOR TRAINING/SUPPORT:
Established in 1984; . . 1st Franchised in 1989	Cash Investment: $20-50K	Financial Assistance Provided: . . . Yes(I)
Company-Owned Units (As of 12/1/1989): . .6	Total Investment: $80-130K	Site Selection Assistance: . . . . . . .Yes
Franchised Units (12/1/1989): 12	Fees: Franchise - $17.5	Lease Negotiation Assistance: . . . . .Yes
Total Units (12/1/1989): 18	Royalty: 4%, Advert: 3%	Co-operative Advertising: . . . . . . .Yes
Distribution: US-18;Can-0;Overseas-0	Contract Periods (Yrs.): 15/15	Training: . . . . .1 Wk. Headquarters,
North America: . . . . 3 States	Area Development Agreement: Yes/Var	. . . . 1 Wk. Franchisee's Shop
Concentration: . . .16 in NC, 1 in SC, 1 in VA	Sub-Franchise Contract: . . . . .No	On-Going Support: . . . . a,B,C,D,E,F,H,I
Registered: . . . . FL,VA	Expand in Territory: . . . . . . Yes	Full-Time Franchisor Support Staff: . . . 7
. . . .	Passive Ownership: . . . . . .Allowed	EXPANSION PLANS:
Average # of Employees: . . . . . . 2 FT, 4 PT	Encourage Conversions: . . . . NA	US: . . . . .All US
Prior Industry Experience: . . . . Helpful	Franchisee Purchase(s) Required: Yes	Canada - Yes, ...Overseas - No

NATURALLY YOGURT / SPEEDSTERS CAFE

1 Annabel Ln. # 207
San Ramon, CA 94583
TEL: (415) 866-6768
FAX: (415) 866-2918
Mr. Sheldon Feinberg, VP

NATURALLY YOGURT is a quality, fresh frozen yogurt operation. Clean, high-tech graphics in a unique presentation offering a wide range of toppings, sundaes, shakes, smoothies and other specialty items. SPEEDSTERS is an expanded menu concept in keeping with today's yuppie movement, offering fresh salads, homemade soups, baked potatoes and a complete yogurt presentation that leads up to the tag line "Fun, Fast, First Class."

HISTORY:	FINANCIAL:	FRANCHISOR TRAINING/SUPPORT:
Established in 1983; . . 1st Franchised in 1985	Cash Investment: $65-100K	Financial Assistance Provided: . . . . . No
Company-Owned Units (As of 12/1/1989): . .0	Total Investment: $155-180K	Site Selection Assistance: . . . . .Yes
Franchised Units (12/1/1989): 15	Fees: Franchise - $20K	Lease Negotiation Assistance: . . . . .Yes
Total Units (12/1/1989): 15	Royalty: Var., Advert: 0%	Co-operative Advertising: . . . . .NA
Distribution: US-15;Can-0;Overseas-0	Contract Periods (Yrs.): 15/10	Training: . . . . . 2 Wks. Company-Owned
North America: . . . . .1 State	Area Development Agreement: Yes/15	. . . . .Store
Concentration: . . . . 15 in CA	Sub-Franchise Contract: . . . . . Yes	On-Going Support: . . . . . .B,C,D,E,F,G
Registered: . . . . CA	Expand in Territory: . . . . . . Yes	Full-Time Franchisor Support Staff: . . . 4
. . . .	Passive Ownership: . . . Discouraged	EXPANSION PLANS:
Average # of Employees: . . . . . . 1 FT, 6 PT	Encourage Conversions: . . . . . Yes	US: . . . . .All US
Prior Industry Experience: . . . . . . Helpful	Franchisee Purchase(s) Required: .No	Canada - Yes, . . . Overseas - Yes

PENGUIN'S PLACE FROZEN YOGURT

325 E. Hillcrest Dr., # 130
Thousand Oaks, CA 91360
TEL: (805) 495-3608
FAX: (805) 495-6247
Mr. Doug Frank, Dir. Fran.

Highest volume frozen yogurt retail stores. Black and white, contemporary decor with broad, bountiful presentation of toppings and upbeat environment. Proprietary yogurt with unique, smooth, creamy taste. Incomparable marketing program. Successful franchisees.

HISTORY:	FINANCIAL:	FRANCHISOR TRAINING/SUPPORT:
Established in 1984; . . 1st Franchised in 1985	Cash Investment: $75-100K	Financial Assistance Provided: . . . . . No
Company-Owned Units (As of 12/1/1989): . .7	Total Investment: $150-200K	Site Selection Assistance: . . . . .Yes
Franchised Units (12/1/1989): 113	Fees: Franchise - $25K	Lease Negotiation Assistance: . . . . .Yes
Total Units (12/1/1989): 120	Royalty: 4%, Advert: 4%	Co-operative Advertising: . . . . . . .No
Distribution: US-120;Can-0;Overseas-0	Contract Periods (Yrs.): 10/10	Training: . . . . . 14 Days Chatsworth, CA,
North America: . . . . 6 States	Area Development Agreement: Yes/3	. . . . . . .4 Days Thousand Oaks, CA
Concentration: . . 99 in CA, 10 in CO, 6 in HI	Sub-Franchise Contract: . . . . .No	On-Going Support: . . . .B,C,D,E,F,G,H,I
Registered: . . . . CA,FL,HI,OR,WA	Expand in Territory: . . . . . . Yes	Full-Time Franchisor Support Staff: . . 35
. . . .	Passive Ownership: . . . Discouraged	EXPANSION PLANS:
Average # of Employees: . . . . . .1 FT, 10 PT	Encourage Conversions: . . . . . .No	US: . . . . Sunbelt and Northwest
Prior Industry Experience: . . . . Helpful	Franchisee Purchase(s) Required: Yes	Canada - No, ...Overseas - No

SPATZ FROZEN YOGURT EMPORIUM

11 Belfield Rd.
Rexdale, ON M9W1E8 CAN
TEL: (416) 247-1408
FAX:
Mr. Alan Aston, President

Frozen yogurt and related health-oriented products.

HISTORY: . . . .
Established in 1987; . . 1st Franchised in 1988
Company-Owned Units (As of 12/1/1989): . .1
Franchised Units (12/1/1989): 2
Total Units (12/1/1989): 3
Distribution: US-0;Can-3;Overseas-0
North America: . . . . 2 Provinces
Concentration: . . . . 2 in ON, 1 in SK
Registered: . . . .

. . . .
Average # of Employees: . . . . . . 1 FT, 2 PT
Prior Industry Experience: . . . . Helpful

FINANCIAL:
Cash Investment: $50-75K
Total Investment: $135-150K
Fees: Franchise - $25K
Royalty: 5%, Advert: 3%
Contract Periods (Yrs.): 10/10
Area Development Agreement: Yes/5
Sub-Franchise Contract: . . . . . Yes
Expand in Territory: . . . . . . Yes
Passive Ownership: . . . Discouraged
Encourage Conversions: . . . . .No
Franchisee Purchase(s) Required: .No

FRANCHISOR TRAINING/SUPPORT:
Financial Assistance Provided: . . .Yes(D)
Site Selection Assistance: . . . . .Yes
Lease Negotiation Assistance: . . . . .Yes
Co-operative Advertising: . . . . . . .Yes
Training: . . . . 1-2 Wks. on Location

. . . .
On-Going Support: . . . .A,B,C,D,E,F,H,I
Full-Time Franchisor Support Staff: . . .3
EXPANSION PLANS:
US: . . . . .All US
Canada - Yes, . . . Overseas - Yes

STEVE'S HOMEMADE ICE CREAM

200 Andover Bus. Park Dr., # 1000
Andover, MA 01810
TEL: (508) 975-1283
FAX:
Mr. Michael Newport, VP Devel.

STEVE'S offers the highest-quality, super-premium ice cream in over 50 flavors, yet still maintaining the old-fashioned store look.

HISTORY: . . . .
Established in 1973; . . 1st Franchised in 1985
Company-Owned Units (As of 12/1/1989): . .6
Franchised Units (12/1/1989): 51
Total Units (12/1/1989): 57
Distribution: US-27;Can-0;Overseas-30
North America: . . . . 16 States
Concentration: . . . 8 in MA, 5 in NY, 5 in TX
Registered: . . . .

. . . .
Average # of Employees: . . . .
Prior Industry Experience: . . . . Helpful

FINANCIAL: NYSE
Cash Investment: . . . .$
Total Investment: $125-175K
Fees: Franchise - $25K
Royalty: 6%, Advert: 1%
Contract Periods (Yrs.): 10/10
Area Development Agreement: . Yes
Sub-Franchise Contract: . . . .
Expand in Territory: . . . . . . Yes
Passive Ownership: . . . Discouraged
Encourage Conversions: . . . . . Yes
Franchisee Purchase(s) Required: Yes

FRANCHISOR TRAINING/SUPPORT:
Financial Assistance Provided: . . . Yes(I)
Site Selection Assistance: . . . . .Yes
Lease Negotiation Assistance: . . . . .Yes
Co-operative Advertising: . . . .
Training: . . . . . . 1-2 Wks. Headquarters

. . . .
On-Going Support: . . . .
Full-Time Franchisor Support Staff: . . . .
EXPANSION PLANS:
US: . . . . .All US
Canada - No, ... Overseas - Yes

STRAWBERRY HILL ICE CREAM

8456 Castleton Corner Dr.
Indianapolis, IN 46250
TEL: (317) 849-4165
FAX:
Mr. Paul Clayton, Fran. Sales. Dir.

STRAWBERRY HILL is a retailer, offering a unique mix of the finest ice cream, yogurt and frozen novelties available under one roof. STRAWBERRY HILL prides itself on its all-American image and its sparkling clean stores. Exclusive territories allow franchisee wholesaling opportunities and other extras.

HISTORY: . . . .
Established in 1983; . . 1st Franchised in 1989
Company-Owned Units (As of 12/1/1989): . .1
Franchised Units (12/1/1989): 4
Total Units (12/1/1989): 5
Distribution: US-5;Can-0;Overseas-0
North America: . . . . .1 State
Concentration: . . . . .5 in IN
Registered: . . . . .IN

. . . .
Average # of Employees: . . . . . .2 FT, 12 PT
Prior Industry Experience: . . . . Helpful

FINANCIAL:
Cash Investment: $80-100K
Total Investment: $80-100K
Fees: Franchise - $12K
Royalty: 0%, Advert: 0%
Contract Periods (Yrs.): 10/10
Area Development Agreement: . Yes
Sub-Franchise Contract: . . . . .No
Expand in Territory: . . . . . . Yes
Passive Ownership: . . . . . .Allowed
Encourage Conversions: . . . . . Yes
Franchisee Purchase(s) Required: Yes

FRANCHISOR TRAINING/SUPPORT:
Financial Assistance Provided: . . . . . No
Site Selection Assistance: . . . . .Yes
Lease Negotiation Assistance: . . . . .Yes
Co-operative Advertising: . . . . . . .Yes
Training: . . . . 2 Wks. Headquarters

. . . .
On-Going Support: . . . . .C,D,E,F,G,H,I
Full-Time Franchisor Support Staff: . . .6
EXPANSION PLANS:
US: . . . . Midwest Only
Canada - No, ...Overseas - No

SWENSON'S ICE CREAM

200 Andover Bus. Pk.,#1000,River Rd.
Andover, MA 01810
TEL: (508) 975-1283
FAX:
Mr. Michael J. Newport, VP Devel.

SWENSEN'S ICE CREAM - high atop Russian Hill in San Francisco, along one of the city's famous cable car routes, customers still flock to the original Swensen's Ice Cream factory. It's from this small store that SWENSEN'S ICE CREAM has expanded to encompass an international chain of ice cream parlours and restaurants. SWENSEN'S offers an all-natural product, containing no artificial flavoring or other additives.

HISTORY: . . . .
Established in 1948; . . 1st Franchised in 1964
Company-Owned Units (As of 12/1/1989): . .3
Franchised Units (12/1/1989): 272
Total Units (12/1/1989): 276
Distribution: . . . US-199;Can-15;Overseas-62
North America: . . . . 40 States
Concentration: . 84 in CA, 20 in AZ, 18 in TX
Registered: . . . CA,HI,IL,IN,MD,MI,NY,VA
. . . .
Average # of Employees: . . . 12-24 FT, 2-6 PT
Prior Industry Experience: . . . . . . Helpful

FINANCIAL: NY-STEVC
Cash Investment: $50K
Total Investment: $150-200K
Fees: Franchise - $20-25K
Royalty: 6%, Advert: 1%
Contract Periods (Yrs.): 10/10
Area Development Agreement: . .No
Sub-Franchise Contract: . . . . . Yes
Expand in Territory: . . . . Yes
Passive Ownership: . . . Discouraged
Encourage Conversions: . . . . . Yes
Franchisee Purchase(s) Required: Yes

FRANCHISOR TRAINING/SUPPORT:
Financial Assistance Provided: . . . Yes(I)
Site Selection Assistance: . . . . .Yes
Lease Negotiation Assistance: . . . . .Yes
Co-operative Advertising: . . . . No
Training: . . . . . 3 Wks. + 1 Day Phoenix,
. . . . .AZ
On-Going Support: . . . . C,E,G,H,I
Full-Time Franchisor Support Staff: . .
EXPANSION PLANS:
US: . . . . All US
Canada - Yes, . . . Overseas - Yes

TASTES YOGURT EMPORIUM

300 John St.
Thornhill, ON L3T5W4 CAN
TEL: (416) 731-7175 C
FAX:
Mr. Arthur J. Clabby, President

TASTES YOGURT EMPORIUM sells both frozen yogurt that is blended with frozen fruit in our "Tastes Creator" and soft frozen yogurt where we keep on tap the most popular flavors. We have a complete line of delicious and nutritious shakes, such as the Northern Breeze and The Power. We have cakes and pies made with frozen yogurt, fresh fruit salads, vegetable salads and yogurt dips.

HISTORY: . . . .
Established in 1987; . . 1st Franchised in 1989
Company-Owned Units (As of 12/1/1989): . .2
Franchised Units (12/1/1989): 2
Total Units (12/1/1989): 4
Distribution: US-0;Can-4;Overseas-0
North America: . . . . .1 Province
Concentration: . . . . 4 in ON
Registered: . . . .
. . . .
Average # of Employees: . . . . . 1 FT, 1-3 PT
Prior Industry Experience: . . . . Helpful

FINANCIAL:
Cash Investment: $50-75K
Total Investment: $100-175K
Fees: Franchise - $20-35K
Royalty: 5%, Advert: 1%
Contract Periods (Yrs.): 10/10
Area Development Agreement: Yes/10
Sub-Franchise Contract: . . . . . .No
Expand in Territory: . . . . Yes
Passive Ownership: . . . Discouraged
Encourage Conversions: . . . . . NA
Franchisee Purchase(s) Required: .No

FRANCHISOR TRAINING/SUPPORT:
Financial Assistance Provided: . . . Yes(I)
Site Selection Assistance: . . . . .Yes
Lease Negotiation Assistance: . . . . .Yes
Co-operative Advertising: . . . . .Yes
Training: . . . . .1 Wk. Headquarters.
. . . . .1 Wk. On-site, 1-2 Days Training
On-Going Support: . . . .a,b,C,D,E,f,G,h,i
Full-Time Franchisor Support Staff: . . . 4
EXPANSION PLANS:
US: . . . . No
Canada - Yes, ...Overseas - No

TCBY - THE COUNTRY'S BEST YOGURT

1100 TCBY Tower, 425 W. Capitol
Little Rock, AR 72201
TEL: (501) 688-8229
FAX: (501) 688-8294
Mr. Roger Harrod, VP Fran. Dev.

TCBY's own brand of distinctive frozen yogurt that is served in a variety of specialty desserts. Attractive decor and successful marketing programs enhance repeat business.

HISTORY: . . . . .IFA
Established in 1981; . . 1st Franchised in 1982
Company-Owned Units (As of 12/1/1989): 136
Franchised Units (12/1/1989): 1357
Total Units (12/1/1989): 1493
Distribution: . . . US-1465;Can-23;Overseas-5
North America: . . . . 50 States
Concentration: . . . .
Registered: . . . . . . All Except FL and AB
. . . .
Average # of Employees: . . . . Varies By Unit
Prior Industry Experience: . . . . Helpful

FINANCIAL: NYSE-TBY
Cash Investment: . . . . $Varies
Total Investment: $102-182K
Fees: Franchise - $20K
Royalty: 4%, Advert: 3%
Contract Periods (Yrs.): 10/10
Area Development Agreement: . .No
Sub-Franchise Contract: . . . . . .No
Expand in Territory: . . . . Yes
Passive Ownership: . . . Discouraged
Encourage Conversions: . . . . . Yes
Franchisee Purchase(s) Required: Yes

FRANCHISOR TRAINING/SUPPORT:
Financial Assistance Provided: . . . . .No
Site Selection Assistance: . . . . .Yes
Lease Negotiation Assistance: . . . . . No
Co-operative Advertising: . . . . .Yes
Training: . . . . .10 Days Headquarters
On-Going Support: . . . . B,C,D,E,F,G,H
Full-Time Franchisor Support Staff: . . . .
EXPANSION PLANS:
US: . . . . All US
Canada - Yes, . . . Overseas - Yes

WHIRLA-WHIP SYSTEMS

9359 G Court
Omaha, NE 68127
TEL: (402) 592-7799
FAX: (402) 592-7499
Mr. Duke Fischer, EVP/GM

WHIRLA-WHIP SYSTEMS invented the original blending machine over 40 years ago. The WHIRLA-WHIP machine allows the retailer to blend fresh fruits, candy bars, cookies, candies and nuts into ice cream or yogurt. Offering the customer hundreds of flavors in as little as 100 SF.

HISTORY:	FINANCIAL:	FRANCHISOR TRAINING/SUPPORT:
Established in 1981; . . 1st Franchised in 1981	Cash Investment: $60K	Financial Assistance Provided: . . . . . No
Company-Owned Units (As of 12/1/1989): . . 0	Total Investment: $13-60K	Site Selection Assistance: . . . . Yes
Franchised Units (12/1/1989): 254	Fees: Franchise - $10K	Lease Negotiation Assistance: . . . . . Yes
Total Units (12/1/1989): 254	Royalty: 5%, Advert: 1%	Co-operative Advertising: . . . . Yes
Distribution: . . . US-120;Can-50;Overseas-84	Contract Periods (Yrs.): 5/5	Training: . . . . Varies On-site
North America: . . . . 11 States, 2 Provinces	Area Development Agreement: Yes/5	
Concentration: . . 43 in ON, 17 in NE, 7 in AB	Sub-Franchise Contract: . . . . . Yes	On-Going Support: . . . . B,C,D,E,F
Registered: . . . . All	Expand in Territory: . . . . Yes	Full-Time Franchisor Support Staff: . . . 4
. . . .	Passive Ownership: . . . . . .Allowed	EXPANSION PLANS:
Average # of Employees: . . . . . . 1 FT, 6 PT	Encourage Conversions: . . . . . Yes	US: . . . . All US
Prior Industry Experience: . . . . . . Helpful	Franchisee Purchase(s) Required: Yes	Canada - Yes, . . . Overseas - Yes

WHITE MOUNTAIN CREAMERY

1576 Bardstown Rd.
Louisville, KY 40205
TEL: (502) 456-2663
FAX:
Mr. Charles G. Ducas, Fran. Sales

WHITE MOUNTAIN CREAMERY is a unique dessert concept, featuring the on-site production of super-premium ice cream, yogurt and gourmet bakery goods. Come grow with us; we offer three fast-moving product lines under one roof. Also, we have Area Development commitments for 100+ stores.

HISTORY:	FINANCIAL:	FRANCHISOR TRAINING/SUPPORT:
Established in 1983; . . 1st Franchised in 1983	Cash Investment: $40-75K	Financial Assistance Provided: . . . Yes(I)
Company-Owned Units (As of 12/1/1989): . . 2	Total Investment: $10-190K	Site Selection Assistance: . . . . Yes
Franchised Units (12/1/1989): 26	Fees: Franchise - $20K	Lease Negotiation Assistance: . . . . . Yes
Total Units (12/1/1989): 28	Royalty: 4%, Advert: 1%	Co-operative Advertising: . . . . Yes
Distribution: US-28;Can-0;Overseas-0	Contract Periods (Yrs.): 10/10	Training: . . . . 12 Days Headquarters
North America: . . . . 8 States	Area Development Agreement: Yes/Var	. . . .
Concentration: . . . 6 in KY, 4 in MA, 4 in PA	Sub-Franchise Contract: . . . . . .No	On-Going Support: . . . . B,C,D,E,F,G,H
Registered: . . . . . .CA,FL,HI,IL,IN,MD,NY	Expand in Territory: . . . . Yes	Full-Time Franchisor Support Staff: . . . 9
. . . .	Passive Ownership: . . . Not Allowed	EXPANSION PLANS:
Average # of Employees: . . . . . 1 FT, 6-8 PT	Encourage Conversions: . . . . . Yes	US: . . . . Southeast, Midwest, NE & CA
Prior Industry Experience: . . . . . . Helpful	Franchisee Purchase(s) Required: Yes	Canada - No, ...Overseas - No

YOGEN FRUZ

7500 Woodbine Ave., # 303
Markham, ON L3R1A8 CAN
TEL: (416) 479-8762
FAX: (416) 479-5235
Mr. Tom Bryant, Dir. Franchising

Canada's largest and fastest-growing frozen yogurt company. With a unique and modern design, YOGEN FRUZ offers the least expensive frozen yogurt franchise out in the market today. With a 100% track record, YOGEN FRUZ can offer you a future in the frozen yogurt industry.

HISTORY: . . . . IFA/CFA	FINANCIAL:	FRANCHISOR TRAINING/SUPPORT:
Established in 1986; . . 1st Franchised in 1987	Cash Investment: $30-35K	Financial Assistance Provided: . . . . .NA
Company-Owned Units (As of 12/1/1989): . . 2	Total Investment: $80-110K	Site Selection Assistance: . . . . Yes
Franchised Units (12/1/1989): 92	Fees: Franchise - $25K	Lease Negotiation Assistance: . . . . . Yes
Total Units (12/1/1989): 94	Royalty: 6%, Advert: 2%	Co-operative Advertising: . . . . Yes
Distribution: US-4;Can-88;Overseas-2	Contract Periods (Yrs.): 10/10	Training: . . . . 2 Wks. Store Level,
North America: . . . . . 2 States, 3 Provinces	Area Development Agreement: Yes/20	. . . . 1 Wk. Corporate Office
Concentration: . . . . .ON, PQ, BC	Sub-Franchise Contract: . . . . . Yes	On-Going Support: . . . . B,C,D,E,F,g,H,I
Registered: . . . . FL,MD,RI,AB	Expand in Territory: . . . . Yes	Full-Time Franchisor Support Staff: . . 24
. . . .	Passive Ownership: . . . Discouraged	EXPANSION PLANS:
Average # of Employees: . . . . . 1 FT, 2-3 PT	Encourage Conversions: . . . . . .No	US: . . . . All US
Prior Industry Experience: . . . . . . Helpful	Franchisee Purchase(s) Required: .No	Canada - Yes, . . . Overseas - Yes

YOGURT STATION, THE

618 W. Arrow Hwy.
San Dimas, CA 91774
TEL: (714) 592-2564
FAX:
Ms. Patricia Beaty, VP

THE YOGURT STATION specializes in serving premium-quality frozen yogurt and treats. The extensive training program familiarizes the franchisee with the entire operation and offers an enjoyable family business at an affordable start-up cost. Come join the hottest business sweeping the country today!

HISTORY: . . . . IFA
Established in 1981; . . 1st Franchised in 1988
Company-Owned Units (As of 12/1/1989): . .6
Franchised Units (12/1/1989): 4
Total Units (12/1/1989): 10
Distribution: US-10;Can-0;Overseas-0
North America: . . . . .1 State
Concentration: . . . . 10 in CA
Registered: . . . . CA
. . . .
Average # of Employees: . . . . . .1 FT, 10 PT
Prior Industry Experience: . . . . . . Helpful

FINANCIAL:
Cash Investment: $45-175K
Total Investment: $125-175K
Fees: Franchise - $18.5K
Royalty: 5-3%, Advert: 2%
Contract Periods (Yrs.): 5/5
Area Development Agreement: . .No
Sub-Franchise Contract: . . . . . .No
Expand in Territory: . . . . Yes
Passive Ownership: . . . Discouraged
Encourage Conversions: . . . . . .No
Franchisee Purchase(s) Required: Yes

FRANCHISOR TRAINING/SUPPORT:
Financial Assistance Provided: . . . . .No
Site Selection Assistance: . . . . . . .Yes
Lease Negotiation Assistance: . . . . .Yes
Co-operative Advertising: . . . . . . .Yes
Training: . . . . 2 Wks. Headquarters,
. . . . 1 Wk. Franchise Facility
On-Going Support: . . . . . .C,D,E,G,H,I
Full-Time Franchisor Support Staff: . . . 4
EXPANSION PLANS:
US: . . . . Southwest
Canada - Yes, . . . Overseas - Yes

YOGURTY'S YOGURT DISCOVERY

91 Skyway Ave., # 205
Rexdale, ON M9W6R5 CAN
TEL: (416) 674-8553
FAX: (416) 675-9398
Mr. David G. Seebach, Dir. Fran.

Soft-serve frozen yogurt franchise, specializing in frozen yogurt desserts, fountain items, sundaes, hot and cold beverages and fashion apparel.

HISTORY: . . . . .IFA/CFA
Established in 1987; . . 1st Franchised in 1988
Company-Owned Units (As of 12/1/1989): . 17
Franchised Units (12/1/1989): 20
Total Units (12/1/1989): 37
Distribution: US-0;Can-37;Overseas-0
North America: . . . . 5 Provinces
Concentration: . . 24 in ON, 5 in BC, 4 in MB
Registered: . . . . AB
. . . .
Average # of Employees: . . . 1-2 FT, 10-15 PT
Prior Industry Experience: . . . . . . Helpful

FINANCIAL: TORON-SIL
Cash Investment: $40-55K
Total Investment: $135-170K
Fees: Franchise - $25K
Royalty: 4%, Advert: 2%
Contract Periods (Yrs.): . . . 10/10
Area Development Agreement: Yes/10
Sub-Franchise Contract: . . . . . .No
Expand in Territory: . . . . Yes
Passive Ownership: . . . . . .Allowed
Encourage Conversions: . . . . . Yes
Franchisee Purchase(s) Required: .No

FRANCHISOR TRAINING/SUPPORT:
Financial Assistance Provided: . . . Yes(I)
Site Selection Assistance: . . . . . . .Yes
Lease Negotiation Assistance: . . . . .Yes
Co-operative Advertising: . . . . . . .Yes
Training: . . . . . . .14 Days Headquarters
. . . .
On-Going Support: . . . . B,C,D,E,F,G,H
Full-Time Franchisor Support Staff: . . . 8
EXPANSION PLANS:
US: . . . . .No
Canada - Yes, ...Overseas - No

ZACK'S FAMOUS FROZEN YOGURT

P.O. Box 8522
Metairie, LA 70011
TEL: (504) 887-6407
FAX:
Mr. Steven A. Watts, President

ZACK'S offers a franchise food product so healthy and flavorful, you'd serve it to your children. Our delicious and nutritious frozen yogurt is sold through attractive, up-scale stores in cones, cups, shakes, sundaes, malts and pies. ZACK'S also offers cookies, brownies, breads and related products.

HISTORY: . . . . IFA
Established in 1977; . . 1st Franchised in 1978
Company-Owned Units (As of 12/1/1989): . 10
Franchised Units (12/1/1989): 205
Total Units (12/1/1989): 215
Distribution: . . . US-160;Can-45;Overseas-10
North America: . . . . 27 States, 4 Provinces
Concentration: . .37 in LA, 26 in FL, 20 in ON
Registered: . . . CA,FL,HI,IL,IN,MD,MI,MN
. . . . .NY,RI,VA,WA
Average # of Employees: . . . . . . 2 FT, 3 PT
Prior Industry Experience: . . . . . . Helpful

FINANCIAL:
Cash Investment: $30-50K
Total Investment: $106-143K
Fees: Franchise - $20K
Royalty: 5%, Advert: 3%
Contract Periods (Yrs.): . . . 20/20
Area Development Agreement: Yes/5
Sub-Franchise Contract: . . . . . Yes
Expand in Territory: . . . . Yes
Passive Ownership: . . . Discouraged
Encourage Conversions: . . . . . .No
Franchisee Purchase(s) Required: Yes

FRANCHISOR TRAINING/SUPPORT:
Financial Assistance Provided: . . . . .No
Site Selection Assistance: . . . . . . .Yes
Lease Negotiation Assistance: . . . . .Yes
Co-operative Advertising: . . . . . . .Yes
Training: . . . . .1 Wk. New Orleans,
. . . . 3 Days In Store
On-Going Support: . . . . . B,C,D,E,G,H
Full-Time Franchisor Support Staff: . . 39
EXPANSION PLANS:
US: . . . . .All US
Canada - Yes, ...Overseas - Yes

SUPPLEMENTAL LISTING OF FRANCHISORS

APPLE A DAY YOGURT . . . . .1056 Gage St., Winnetka IL 60093
ASHLEY'S ICE CREAM . . . . 196 College St., New Haven CT 06510
BASKIN-ROBBINS ICE CREAM . . . . 31 Baskin-Robbins Pl., Glendale CA 91201
BEN & JERRY'S (CANADA) . . . . .598 Lauder Ave., # 3, Toronto ON M6E3J6   CAN
BEN AND JERRY'S . . . . .P.O. Box 240, Route 100, Waterbury VT 05676
BLOOMER'S ICE CREAM . . . . 5900 N. Port Washington Rd., Milwaukee WI 53217
BO DEE'S YUMMIES . . . . .3520 Hwy. 6, South, Sugarland TX 77478
BRESLER'S ICE CREAM & YOGURT SHOPS . . . . 999 E. Touhy, # 333, Des Plaines IL 60018
BUZZIE'S ICE CREAM . . . . .4516 N. Sterling Ave., # 440, Peoria IL 61615
CARBERRY'S HOMEMADE ICE CREAM PARLORS . . . . .42 Rose St., Merritt Island FL 32953
CARVEL CORPORATION . . . . 201 Saw Mill River Rd., Yonkers NY 10701
CHRISTY'S FROZEN YOGURT AND BAKERY . . . . .3211 Knox St., Dallas TX 75205
DANDY'S YOGURT . . . . 2225 Buchanan Rd., # H, Antioch CA 94509
DIPPER DAN ICE CREAM & SWEET SHOPPES . . . . P.O. Box 47068, St. Petersburg FL 33743
EMACK & BOLIO'S . . . . 75 Lawrence St., Brockton MA 02402
FRUSEN GLADJE .200 Andover Bus. Park Dr., # 1000, Andover MA 01810
HAAGEN-DAZS . . . . Glenpointe Centre E., Teaneck NJ 07666
HAWAIIAN FREEZE . . . . 2403 E. Waco Dr., Waco TX 76705
HEALTHY DELI . . . . 5858 NE 87th Ave., Portland OR 97220
HEIDI'S FROZEN YOGURT SHOPPES . . . . P.O. Box 9008, Andover MA 01810
HELEN HUTCHLEYS .P.O. Box 80995, Station C, Canton OH 44708
I CAN'T BELIEVE ITS YOGURT . . . . P. O. Box 791908, Dallas TX 75379
ICE CREAM CHURN . . . . 2222 Kalakaua Ave., # 1200, Honolulu HI 96815
ICE CREAM CLUB, THE .278 S. Ocean Blvd., Manalapan FL 33462
ISLAND FREEZE . . . . 2222 Kalakaua Ave., # 1200, Honolulu HI 96815
ISLAND SNOW HAWAII .P.O. Box 80957, Las Vegas NV 89180
IT'S YOGURT! . . . . 3829 E. Tamiami Trail, Naples FL 33962
J. HIGBY'S . . . . 11030 White Rock Rd., #210, Rancho Cordova CA 95670
L'OURS POLAIRE . . . . .4221 rue Garlock, Sherbrooke PQ J1L2L8   CAN
LEATHERBY'S FAMILY CREAMERY . . . . .3939 Cambridge Rd., #100, Cameron Park CA 95682
MALIBU MAGIC FROZEN TREATS . . . . 1 Hartfield Blvd., # 204, East Windsor CT 06088
MARBLE SLAB CREAMERY . . . . 3100 S. Gessner, # 230, Houston TX 77063
MOTHER'S ICE CREAM . . . . Northway Mall, Marshfield WI 54449
MOUNTAIN SMOW . . . . .948 Riverview Dr., Morgantown WV 26505
NIBBLE-LO'S . . . . 5300 W. Atlantic Ave., # 408, Delray Beach FL 33484
NIELSEN'S FROZEN CUSTARD . . . . .P.O. Box 731, Bountiful UT 84010
OASIS ICE CREAM & FROZEN YOGURT . . . . .1512 Business Loop 70 W., Columbia MO 65202
PERKITS YOGURT SHOPS . . . . .P.O. Box 4700, Cleveland TN 37320
REAL RICH ICE CREAM SHOPS . . . . .8730 Georgia Ave., # 500, Silver Spring MD 20910
SKINNY DIP . . . . 1218 Fox Run Dr., Charlotte NC 28212
SMOOTHIE KING . . . . 2725 Mississippi Ave., # 7, Metairie LA 70003
STEVE'S HOMEMADE ICE CREAM . . . . .P. O. Box 9008, Andover MA 01810
SWENSON'S ICE CREAM . . . . 200 Andover Bus. Pk.,#1000, Andover MA 01810
TCBY THE COUNTRY'S BEST YOGURT . . . . 17 Four Seasons Pl., Etobicoke ON M9B6E6   CAN
TWISTEE TREAT . . . . 2445 Pine Island Rd. W., Cape Coral FL 33991
UNCLE GAYLORD'S ICE CREAM CAFE . . . . 824 S. Petaluma Blvd., Petaluma CA 94952
WHIPPER'S ICE CREAM & FROZEN YOGURT . . . . P.O. Box 871, Greenville TX 75401
WHIRLA-WHIP SYSTEMS CANADA . . . . 288 Wildcat Rd., Downsview ON M3J2N5   CAN
WILD WALLY'S FROZEN YOGURT . . . . .7035 Maxwell Rd., # 3, Mississauga ON L5S1R5   CAN
YOGURT FANTASTIK . . . . 1936 County Line Rd., Huntington Valley PA 19006
YOGURT STAND . . . . 5858 NE 87th Ave., Portland OR 97220
YUMMY YOGURT . . . . 4211 Evergreen Ln., Annandale VA 22003

CHAPTER 19

RETAIL FOOD: SPECIALTY FOODS

BOARDWALK PEANUT SHOPPE, THE

P.O. Box 749, 10th St. & Boardwalk
Ocean City, NJ 08226
TEL: (800) 527-2430
FAX: (609) 398-3546
Mr. Leo Yeager, III, President

"Something for Everyone" is the motto at THE BOARDWALK PEANUT SHOPPE. In addition to hot roasted peanuts and the most popular nuts, we sell dried fruits, popcorn, hand-dipped chocolates, candy and unique gift items. This product mix gives you the widest market appeal.

HISTORY: . . . .
Established in 1971; . . 1st Franchised in 1987
Company-Owned Units (As of 12/1/1989): . .3
Franchised Units (12/1/1989): 4
Total Units (12/1/1989): 7
Distribution: US-7;Can-0;Overseas-0
North America: . . . . .1 State
Concentration: . . . . 7 in NJ
Registered: . . . .

. . . .
Average # of Employees: . . . . . . 2 FT, 4 PT
Prior Industry Experience: . . . . Helpful

FINANCIAL:
Cash Investment: $12K
Total Investment: $45-75K
Fees: Franchise - $12K
  Royalty: 5%, Advert: 1%
Contract Periods (Yrs.): 10/10
Area Development Agreement: . .No
Sub-Franchise Contract: . . . . . .No
Expand in Territory: . . . . . . Yes
Passive Ownership: . . . Not Allowed
Encourage Conversions: . . . . . Yes
Franchisee Purchase(s) Required: .No

FRANCHISOR TRAINING/SUPPORT:
Financial Assistance Provided: . . . Yes(I)
Site Selection Assistance: . . . . .Yes
Lease Negotiation Assistance: . . . . .Yes
Co-operative Advertising: . . . . No
Training: . . . . 1 Wk. Headquarters
. . . .
On-Going Support: . . .A,B,C,D,E,F,G,h,I
Full-Time Franchisor Support Staff: . . 12
EXPANSION PLANS:
US: . . . . Mid-Atlantic States
Canada - No, ...Overseas - Yes

CALIFORNIA SMOOTHIE

1700 Rte. 23
Wayne, NJ 07470
TEL: (201) 696-7200
FAX: (201) 696-2123
Mr. Mike Flynn, VP Development

Positioned as the healthy foods alternative, CALIFORNIA SMOOTHIE offers frozen yogurt, fruit blends, salads, pita sandwiches, soups and home-made breads. Operates in high-volume malls, festive market-places and downtown locations. . . .For The Health Of It!

HISTORY: . . . . IFA	FINANCIAL:	FRANCHISOR TRAINING/SUPPORT:
Established in 1973; . . 1st Franchised in 1981	Cash Investment: $60K	Financial Assistance Provided: . . . . . No
Company-Owned Units (As of 12/1/1989): . 16	Total Investment: $150-200K	Site Selection Assistance: . . . . .Yes
Franchised Units (12/1/1989): 22	Fees: Franchise - $25K	Lease Negotiation Assistance: . . . . .Yes
Total Units (12/1/1989): 38	Royalty: 5%, Advert: 2%	Co-operative Advertising: . . . . . . .Yes
Distribution: US-38;Can-0;Overseas-0	Contract Periods (Yrs.): 10/10	Training: . . . . 8 Days Headquarters
North America: . . . . 6 States	Area Development Agreement: Yes/10	. . . .
Concentration: . . . 11 in FL, 8 in NJ, 4 in NY	Sub-Franchise Contract: . . . . . .No	On-Going Support: . . . B,C,D,E,F,G,H
Registered: . . . . CA,FL,MD,NY,VA	Expand in Territory: . . . . Yes	Full-Time Franchisor Support Staff: . . 16
. . . .	Passive Ownership: . . . . . .Allowed	EXPANSION PLANS:
Average # of Employees: . . . . . . 3 FT, 4 PT	Encourage Conversions: . . . . . Yes	US: . . . . East
Prior Industry Experience: . . . . Helpful	Franchisee Purchase(s) Required: .No	Canada - No, ...Overseas - No

CAROLE'S CHEESECAKE COMPANY

1272 Castlefield Ave.
Toronto, ON M6B1G3 CAN
TEL: (416) 256-0000
FAX:
Mr. Michael Ch. Ogus, EVP

Manufacturer and retailer of premium-brand of 85 flavors of cheesecakes, plus a dozen other baked gourmet desserts. Exclusive importer and retailer of hand-made Belgian chocolates from the House of Nihoul, Brussels.

HISTORY:	FINANCIAL:	FRANCHISOR TRAINING/SUPPORT:
Established in 1979; . . 1st Franchised in 1980	Cash Investment: $27-35K	Financial Assistance Provided: . . .Yes(D)
Company-Owned Units (As of 12/1/1989): . .3	Total Investment: $85-115K	Site Selection Assistance: . . . . . . .Yes
Franchised Units (12/1/1989): 13	Fees: Franchise - $15-35K	Lease Negotiation Assistance: . . . .Yes
Total Units (12/1/1989): 16	Royalty: 0%, Advert: . . . . . ~1%	Co-operative Advertising: . . . . . . .Yes
Distribution: US-0;Can-16;Overseas-0	Contract Periods (Yrs.): . . . . Lease	Training: . . . . .1 Wk. Headquarters,
North America: . . . . 2 Provinces	Area Development Agreement: . .No	. . . . 1 Wk. On-site
Concentration: . . . . . . 15 in ON, 1 in BC	Sub-Franchise Contract: . . . . . .No	On-Going Support: . . . .B,C,D,E,F,G,H,I
Registered:	Expand in Territory: . . . . Yes	Full-Time Franchisor Support Staff: . . 30
. . . .	Passive Ownership: . . . Discouraged	EXPANSION PLANS:
Average # of Employees: . . . . . . 2 FT, 1 PT	Encourage Conversions: . . . . . .No	US: . . . . .All US
Prior Industry Experience: . . . . Helpful	Franchisee Purchase(s) Required: Yes	Canada - Yes, . . . Overseas - Yes

COFFEE BEANERY, THE

G-3429 Pierson Pl.
Flushing, MI 48433
TEL: (800) 537-2326 (313) 733-1020 C
FAX: (313) 733-1536
Mr. Kevin Shaw, Fran. Dir.

THE COFFEE BEANERY is an up-scale, gourmet coffee and tea store in high demand by major malls. We use only top-quality, fresh-roasted (by Company) coffees, gold foil packaging to maintain the Godiva Image. The stores have a better than average gross profit margin.

HISTORY: . . . . IFA	FINANCIAL:	FRANCHISOR TRAINING/SUPPORT:
Established in 1975; . . 1st Franchised in 1985	Cash Investment: $40-90K	Financial Assistance Provided: . . . Yes(I)
Company-Owned Units (As of 12/1/1989): . .5	Total Investment: $90-210K	Site Selection Assistance: . . . . . . .Yes
Franchised Units (12/1/1989): 26	Fees: Franchise - $17.5K	Lease Negotiation Assistance: . . . .Yes
Total Units (12/1/1989): 31	Royalty: 6%, Advert: 1%	Co-operative Advertising: . . . . . . .Yes
Distribution: US-31;Can-0;Overseas-0	Contract Periods (Yrs.): 5/5	Training: . . . . . . 1 Wk. Training Center,
North America: . . . . 6 States	Area Development Agreement: Yes/5	. . . 1 Wk. Corp. Store, 2 Wks. New Site
Concentration: . . 20 in MI, 4 in OH, 2 in MD	Sub-Franchise Contract: . . . . . .No	On-Going Support: . . .B,C,D,E,F,G,H,I
Registered: . . . CA,FL,IL,IN,MD,MI,MN,OR	Expand in Territory: . . . . Yes	Full-Time Franchisor Support Staff: . . 25
. . . . VA,WI	Passive Ownership: . . . . . .Allowed	EXPANSION PLANS:
Average # of Employees: . . . .2-3 FT, 3-12 PT	Encourage Conversions: . . . . . .No	US: . . . . .All US
Prior Industry Experience: . . . . Helpful	Franchisee Purchase(s) Required: Yes	Canada - No, ...Overseas - No

FOREMOST LIQUOR STORES

5252 N. Broadway
Chicago, IL 60640
TEL: (800) 621-5150 (312) 334-0077
FAX: (312) 334-2438
Ms. Gail Zelitzky, President

FOREMOST LIQUORS is a full-service discount wine, liquor and beer supermarket appealing to today's cost-conscious, up-scale consumer. FOREMOST LIQUORS & GRAPERIE is also a full-service discount wine, liquor, and beer supermarket, but featuring a temperature-controlled wine room with customer storage that caters to the most sophisticated wine connoisseur. Heavy emphasis on gifts and customized gift packaging.

HISTORY: . . . .
Established in 1949; . . 1st Franchised in 1949
Company-Owned Units (As of 12/1/1989): . .0
Franchised Units (12/1/1989): 120
Total Units (12/1/1989): 120
Distribution: . . . US-120;Can-0;Overseas-0
North America: . . . . 2 States
Concentration: . . . . .85 in FL, 35 in IL
Registered: IL

. . . .
Average # of Employees: . . . . . . 3 FT, 6 PT
Prior Industry Experience: . . . . Helpful

FINANCIAL:
Cash Investment: $150-350K
Total Investment: $300-550K
Fees: Franchise - $1-25K
   Royalty: 0-2.5%, Advert: 0%
Contract Periods (Yrs.): 1-10
Area Development Agreement: . .No
Sub-Franchise Contract: . . . . .No
Expand in Territory: . . . . Yes
Passive Ownership: . . . Discouraged
Encourage Conversions: . . . . . Yes
Franchisee Purchase(s) Required: Yes

FRANCHISOR TRAINING/SUPPORT:
Financial Assistance Provided: . . . Yes(I)
Site Selection Assistance: . . . . . . .Yes
Lease Negotiation Assistance: . . . . .Yes
Co-operative Advertising: . . . . No
Training: . . . . . Pre-Opening at Corporate
   . . . . Office, Continuous on Site
On-Going Support: . . . . . C,D,E,F,G,H,I
Full-Time Franchisor Support Staff: . . 11
EXPANSION PLANS:
US: . . . . All US, Where Legal
Canada - No, ...Overseas - No

FRONTIER FRUIT & NUT Co.

3823 Wadsworth Rd.
Norton, OH 44203
TEL: (216) 825-7835
FAX:
Mr. Raymond J. Karee, President

Retail sale of dried fruits, nuts and candies. All stores located in regional malls.

HISTORY: . . . .
Established in 1976; . . 1st Franchised in 1977
Company-Owned Units (As of 12/1/1989): 116
Franchised Units (12/1/1989): 32
Total Units (12/1/1989): 148
Distribution: . . . US-89;Can-59;Overseas-0
North America: . . . 12 States, 8 Provinces
Concentration: . 34 in ON, 21 in OH, 14 in MI
Registered: . . . FL,IL,IN,MI,MN,NY,VA,AB

. . . .
Average # of Employees: . . . . . . 2 FT, 3 PT
Prior Industry Experience: . . . . Helpful

FINANCIAL:
Cash Investment: $20-60K
Total Investment: $40-120K
Fees: Franchise - $15K
   Royalty: 6%, Advert: 0%
Contract Periods (Yrs.): 5/5
Area Development Agreement: . .No
Sub-Franchise Contract: . . . . .No
Expand in Territory: . . . . Yes
Passive Ownership: . . . Discouraged
Encourage Conversions: . . . . . Yes
Franchisee Purchase(s) Required: .No

FRANCHISOR TRAINING/SUPPORT:
Financial Assistance Provided: . . . . .No
Site Selection Assistance: . . . . . . .Yes
Lease Negotiation Assistance: . . . . .Yes
Co-operative Advertising: . . . . No
Training: . . . . 3 Days Headquarters,
   . . . . .1 Wk. In Store
On-Going Support: . . . . C,D,E,G,I
Full-Time Franchisor Support Staff: . . . 8
EXPANSION PLANS:
US: . . . . East of Mississippi
Canada - Yes, ...Overseas - No

FUDGE COMPANY, THE

103 Belvedere Ave.
Charlevoix, MI 49720
TEL: (616) 547-4612 C
FAX:
Mr. Paul Hoffman, Fran. Dir.

FUDGE CO.'s all-natural, homemade fudge is delicious! Our candy is cooked in copper kettles and "creamed" on marble slabs, in full view of public. The showmanship of making fudge provides unique, enjoyable and profitable operation. FUDGE CO. provides equipment, franchisee provides building/location.

HISTORY: . . . .
Established in 1977; . . 1st Franchised in 1983
Company-Owned Units (As of 12/1/1989): . .1
Franchised Units (12/1/1989): 7
Total Units (12/1/1989): 8
Distribution: US-8;Can-0;Overseas-0
North America: . . . . 5 States
Concentration: . . . 1 in TX, 1 in AK, 1 in AZ
Registered: . . . .

. . . .
Average # of Employees: . . . . . 1 FT, 3-4 PT
Prior Industry Experience: . . . . Helpful

FINANCIAL:
Cash Investment: $15-35K
Total Investment: $25-45K
Fees: Franchise - $12-15K
   Royalty: 3%, Advert: 0%
Contract Periods (Yrs.): . . . 10/10
Area Development Agreement: Yes/10
Sub-Franchise Contract: . . . . . Yes
Expand in Territory: . . . . Yes
Passive Ownership: . . . Discouraged
Encourage Conversions: . . . . . Yes
Franchisee Purchase(s) Required: . .

FRANCHISOR TRAINING/SUPPORT:
Financial Assistance Provided: . . . Yes(I)
Site Selection Assistance: . . . . . . .Yes
Lease Negotiation Assistance: . . . .Yes
Co-operative Advertising: . . . . . . .NA
Training: . . . . . . 1-2 Wks. Headquarters,
   . . . . .7-10 Days Site
On-Going Support: . . . . D,E
Full-Time Franchisor Support Staff: . . . 4
EXPANSION PLANS:
US: . . . . .All US
Canada - Yes, . . . Overseas - Yes

GIULIANO'S DELICATESSEN & BAKERY
1117 E. Walnut St.
Carson, CA 90746
TEL: (213) 537-7700
FAX:
Mr. John Kidde, President

Retail specialty food store, offering a full-service delicatessen; a take-out menu; fresh bread and pastry; catering; wine and beer; and specialty groceries.

HISTORY:	FINANCIAL:	FRANCHISOR TRAINING/SUPPORT:
Established in 1974; . . 1st Franchised in 1978	Cash Investment: $150K	Financial Assistance Provided: . . . . . No
Company-Owned Units (As of 12/1/1989): . .5	Total Investment: $550K	Site Selection Assistance: . . . . . . .Yes
Franchised Units (12/1/1989): 6	Fees: Franchise - $30K	Lease Negotiation Assistance: . . . . .Yes
Total Units (12/1/1989): 11	Royalty: 3-5%, Advert: 1.5%	Co-operative Advertising: . . . . . . .Yes
Distribution: US-11;Can-0;Overseas-0	Contract Periods (Yrs.): 20/5/5	Training: . . . . . .8-12 Wks. Southern CA
North America: . . . . .1 State	Area Development Agreement: . Yes	. . . .
Concentration: . . . . 11 in CA	Sub-Franchise Contract: . . . . Yes	On-Going Support: . . .B,C,D,E,F,G,H,I
Registered: . . . . CA	Expand in Territory: . . . . . . Yes	Full-Time Franchisor Support Staff: . .180
. . . .	Passive Ownership: . . . Discouraged	EXPANSION PLANS:
Average # of Employees: . . . . . 15 FT,10 PT	Encourage Conversions: . . . . Yes	US: . . . . .Southern CA
Prior Industry Experience: . . . . . . Helpful	Franchisee Purchase(s) Required: Yes	Canada - No, ...Overseas - No

GLORIA JEAN'S COFFEE BEAN

12 West College Dr.
Arlington Heights, IL 60004
TEL: (800) 333-0050 (708) 253-0580 C
FAX: (708) 253-3730
Mr. Jim Ludwig, VP Fran. Sales

America's largest retail gourmet coffee franchisor, offers the highest-quality gourmet coffees, teas and accessories. Our unique store design and exclusive coffee bean counter are the focal points of our nationally-honored company. Each store has up to 64 varieties of coffees, plus a complete line of signature teas, along with a complete line of state-of-the-art coffee and tea accessories.

HISTORY: . . . . IFA	FINANCIAL:	FRANCHISOR TRAINING/SUPPORT:
Established in 1979; . . 1st Franchised in 1986	Cash Investment: $60-70K	Financial Assistance Provided: . . . Yes(I)
Company-Owned Units (As of 12/1/1989): . .3	Total Investment: $118-200K	Site Selection Assistance: . . . . . . .Yes
Franchised Units (12/1/1989): 120	Fees: Franchise - $19.5K	Lease Negotiation Assistance: . . . . .Yes
Total Units (12/1/1989): 123	Royalty: 6%, Advert: 1%	Co-operative Advertising: . . . . . . .Yes
Distribution: US-123;Can-0;Overseas-0	Contract Periods (Yrs.): . . . . Lease	Training: . . . . . . 10 Days Headquarters,
North America: . . . . 22 States	Area Development Agreement: Yes/Var	. . . . 9 Days Pre-opening
Concentration: . . .17 in IL, 15 in CA, 6 in TX	Sub-Franchise Contract: . . . . .No	On-Going Support: . . A,B,C,D,E,F,G,H,I
Registered: . . . . All States	Expand in Territory: . . . . . . Yes	Full-Time Franchisor Support Staff: . . 18
. . . .	Passive Ownership: . . . Discouraged	EXPANSION PLANS:
Average # of Employees: . . . . . . 2 FT, 3 PT	Encourage Conversions: . . . . Yes	US: . . . . All US
Prior Industry Experience: . . . . . . Helpful	Franchisee Purchase(s) Required: Yes	Canada - Yes, . . . Overseas - Yes

GOURMET CUP, THE

P.O. Box 490, 2265 W. Railway St
Abbotsford, BC V2S5Z5 CAN
TEL: (604) 852-8771
FAX: (604) 859-1711
Mr. Wolfgang Lehmann, President

THE GOURMET CUP is a specialty retail store, offering the finest coffees, teas; merchandise such as mugs, brewing equipment, etc; serving specially-blended coffee, tea, cocoa, cappuccino, expresso; spices; individually-wrapped baked goods. The stores are turn-key operations, fixtured, stocked and ready for business.

HISTORY:	FINANCIAL:	FRANCHISOR TRAINING/SUPPORT:
Established in 1985; . . 1st Franchised in 1986	Cash Investment: $35-55K	Financial Assistance Provided: . . . . .No
Company-Owned Units (As of 12/1/1989): . .8	Total Investment: $80-140K	Site Selection Assistance: . . . . . . .NA
Franchised Units (12/1/1989): 30	Fees: Franchise - $25K	Lease Negotiation Assistance: . . . .Yes
Total Units (12/1/1989): 38	Royalty: 6%, Advert: 2%	Co-operative Advertising: . . . . . . .No
Distribution: US-0;Can-38;Overseas-0	Contract Periods (Yrs.): . . . .Varies	Training: . . . . ~ 1 Wk. On-site
North America: . . . . 8 Provinces	Area Development Agreement: . .No	. . . .
Concentration: . . . 9 in AB, 9 in ON, 9 in BC	Sub-Franchise Contract: . . . . .No	On-Going Support: . . . . . . C,D,E,G,I
Registered: . . . . AB	Expand in Territory: . . . . . . Yes	Full-Time Franchisor Support Staff: . . .9
. . . .	Passive Ownership: . . . Discouraged	EXPANSION PLANS:
Average # of Employees: . . . . . . 1 FT, 2 PT	Encourage Conversions: . . . . .No	US: . . . . .No
Prior Industry Experience: . . . . . . Helpful	Franchisee Purchase(s) Required: .No	Canada - Yes, ...Overseas - No

HEAVENLY HAM

8800 Roswell Rd., # 135
Atlanta, GA 30350
TEL: (404) 993-2232
FAX: (404) 587-3529
Mr. R. Hutch Hodgson, President

Paradise Food franchises retail HEAVENLY HAM STORES, selling fully-baked, spiral sliced, honey and spice glazed HEAVENLY HAM with "a taste that is out of this world." The stores also sell smoked turkey, ribs, condiments and delicious take-away sandwiches. Call today for information!

HISTORY: . . . . IFA
Established in 1984; . . 1st Franchised in 1984
Company-Owned Units (As of 12/1/1989): . . 0
Franchised Units (12/1/1989): 36
Total Units (12/1/1989): 36
Distribution: US-36;Can-0;Overseas-0
North America: . . . . 16 States
Concentration: . . . 7 in SC, 5 in MD, 4 in FL
Registered: . . . . . FL,IL,IN,MD,MI,NY,VA
. . . .
Average # of Employees: . . . . . . 2 FT, 2 PT
Prior Industry Experience: . . . . Helpful

FINANCIAL:
Cash Investment: $30-60K
Total Investment: $84-134K
Fees: Franchise - $25K
  Royalty: 5%, Advert: 1%
Contract Periods (Yrs.): 10/10
Area Development Agreement: Yes/10
Sub-Franchise Contract: . . . . .No
Expand in Territory: . . . . . . Yes
Passive Ownership: . . . Not Allowed
Encourage Conversions: . . . . .No
Franchisee Purchase(s) Required: Yes

FRANCHISOR TRAINING/SUPPORT:
Financial Assistance Provided: . . . . .No
Site Selection Assistance: . . . . . . .Yes
Lease Negotiation Assistance: . . . . .Yes
Co-operative Advertising: . . . . .No
Training: . . . . . . .1 Wk. Headquarters,
. . . . .5 Days Site, On-going
On-Going Support: . . . . . .C,D,E,F,G,H
Full-Time Franchisor Support Staff: . . .5
EXPANSION PLANS:
US: . . . . . . SE,NE,MW,NW and SW
Canada - No, ...Overseas - No

HICKORY FARMS

1505 Holland Rd., P. O. Box 219
Maumee, OH 43615
TEL: (419) 893-7611
FAX: (419) 893-0164
Mr. Kelvin Friesen, Dir. Fran. Ops.

Gourmet/specialty food and gift retailer.

HISTORY: . . . .
Established in 1959; . . 1st Franchised in 1960
Company-Owned Units (As of 12/1/1989): 153
Franchised Units (12/1/1989): 113
Total Units (12/1/1989): 266
Distribution: US-265;Can-1;Overseas-0
North America: . . . . . 44 States, 1 Province
Concentration: . .42 in CA, 21 in PA, 16 in FL
Registered: . . . .
. . . .
Average # of Employees: . . . . . . 1 FT, 5 PT
Prior Industry Experience: . . . . Helpful

FINANCIAL:
Cash Investment: . . . .$
Total Investment: $160-230K
Fees: Franchise - $20K
  Royalty: 6%, Advert: 2%
Contract Periods (Yrs.): . . 10/Varies
Area Development Agreement: Yes/10
Sub-Franchise Contract: . . . . .No
Expand in Territory: . . . . . . Yes
Passive Ownership: . . . Not Allowed
Encourage Conversions: . . . . .No
Franchisee Purchase(s) Required: .No

FRANCHISOR TRAINING/SUPPORT:
Financial Assistance Provided: . . . . .No
Site Selection Assistance: . . . . . . .Yes
Lease Negotiation Assistance: . . . . .Yes
Co-operative Advertising: . . . . .Yes
Training: . . . . 7 Days Headquarters
. . . .
On-Going Support: . . . . .B,C,D,E,G,H,I
Full-Time Franchisor Support Staff: . . . 1
EXPANSION PLANS:
US: . . . . .All US
Canada - No, ...Overseas - No

JAKE'S TAKE N' BAKE PIZZA

620 High St.
San Luis Obispo, CA 93401
TEL: (805) 543-3339 C
FAX:
Mr. Willis Reeser, President

Make and sell fresh, unbaked pizzas - dough is made fresh every day.

HISTORY: . . . .
Established in 1984; . . 1st Franchised in 1986
Company-Owned Units (As of 12/1/1989): . . 0
Franchised Units (12/1/1989): 20
Total Units (12/1/1989): 20
Distribution: US-20;Can-0;Overseas-0
North America: . . . . .1 State
Concentration: . . . . 14 in CA
Registered: . . . . CA
. . . .
Average # of Employees: . . . . . . 6 FT, 2 PT
Prior Industry Experience: . . . . Helpful

FINANCIAL:
Cash Investment: $25-40K
Total Investment: $25-40K
Fees: Franchise - $10K
  Royalty: 3%, Advert: 1%
Contract Periods (Yrs.): 10/5
Area Development Agreement: .No
Sub-Franchise Contract: . . . . .No
Expand in Territory: . . . . . . .No
Passive Ownership: . . . Discouraged
Encourage Conversions: . . . . .No
Franchisee Purchase(s) Required: Yes

FRANCHISOR TRAINING/SUPPORT:
Financial Assistance Provided: . . . . .No
Site Selection Assistance: . . . . . . .Yes
Lease Negotiation Assistance: . . . . .Yes
Co-operative Advertising: . . . . .Yes
Training: . . . . . . 14 Days Headquarters,
. . . . .5 Days Franchisee Store
On-Going Support: . . . . B,C,D,E,F
Full-Time Franchisor Support Staff: . . .3
EXPANSION PLANS:
US: . . . . .All US
Canada - No, ...Overseas - No

KAYSERS HEALTH BARS

3890 La Cumbre Plaza Ln.
Santa Barbara, CA 93105
TEL: (800)242-FLIP(CA) (805)563-2007
FAX: (805) 682-8444
Mr. Jack C. Onyett, EVP

Healthy and gourmet shakes, smoothies and frapees, blended in front of customer with fresh, nutritious ingredients. Tasty, nutritious impulse food items and vitamins and minerals. 38-year proven products provide health-conscious America an alternative to fast food.

HISTORY: . . . .
Established in 1951; . . 1st Franchised in 1987
Company-Owned Units (As of 12/1/1989): . .2
Franchised Units (12/1/1989): 4
Total Units (12/1/1989): 6
Distribution: US-6;Can-0;Overseas-0
North America: . . . . .1 State
Concentration: . . . . 6 in CA
Registered: . . . . CA
. . . .
Average # of Employees: . . . . . 1 FT, 3-5 PT
Prior Industry Experience: . . . . Helpful

FINANCIAL:
Cash Investment: $40-100K
Total Investment: $70-150K
Fees: Franchise - $15K
  Royalty: 4%, Advert: 1%
Contract Periods (Yrs.): 10/5/5
Area Development Agreement: Yes/Var
Sub-Franchise Contract: . . . . . .No
Expand in Territory: . . . . Yes
Passive Ownership: . . . Discouraged
Encourage Conversions: . . . . . Yes
Franchisee Purchase(s) Required: Yes

FRANCHISOR TRAINING/SUPPORT:
Financial Assistance Provided: . . . Yes(I)
Site Selection Assistance: . . . . . . .Yes
Lease Negotiation Assistance: . . . . .Yes
Co-operative Advertising: . . . . . . .Yes
Training: . . . . 2 Wks. Headquarters
. . . .
On-Going Support: . . . . . .C,D,E,G,H,I
Full-Time Franchisor Support Staff: . . . 4
EXPANSION PLANS:
US: . . . . CA and the West
Canada - No, ...Overseas - No

KID'S KORNER PIZZA

P.O. Box 9288
Waukegan, IL 60079
TEL: (708) 249-8606
FAX:
Mr. K. Gulko, VP

We offer an extremely affordable opportunity in one of the fastest growing segments of our economy. We are the originator of the unique "We make 'em, you bake 'em at home" concept with an exceptionally broad customer base. Highest-quality product at a very low price.

HISTORY: . . . . IFA
Established in 1977; . . 1st Franchised in 1978
Company-Owned Units (As of 12/1/1989): . .0
Franchised Units (12/1/1989): 27
Total Units (12/1/1989): 27
Distribution: US-27;Can-;Overseas-
North America: . . . .
Concentration: . . . 21 in WI, 3 in MN, 2 in IL
Registered: . . . CA,FL,IL,IN,MI,MN,ND,SD
. . . . VA,WI
Average # of Employees: . . . . . .1 FT,3-5 PT
Prior Industry Experience: . . . . Helpful

FINANCIAL:
Cash Investment: $25-35K
Total Investment: $25-35K
Fees: Franchise - $12.5K
  Royalty: 4%, Advert: 1.5%
Contract Periods (Yrs.): 10/10
Area Development Agreement: Yes/10
Sub-Franchise Contract: . . . . . .No
Expand in Territory: . . . . Yes
Passive Ownership: . . . . . .Allowed
Encourage Conversions: . . . . . Yes
Franchisee Purchase(s) Required: Yes

FRANCHISOR TRAINING/SUPPORT:
Financial Assistance Provided: . . . . .No
Site Selection Assistance: . . . . . . .Yes
Lease Negotiation Assistance: . . . . .Yes
Co-operative Advertising: . . . . . . .Yes
Training: . . . . 3-7 Days Headquarters,
. . . . 3-7 Days Site
On-Going Support: . . . . . C,D,E,F,G,H,I
Full-Time Franchisor Support Staff: . . . 4
EXPANSION PLANS:
US: . . . . .Most US
Canada - Yes, ...Overseas - No

MANHATTAN FRIES

124 Rubidge St.
Peterborough, ON K9J3N4 CAN
TEL: (705) 742-5947 C
FAX: (705) 742-8132
Mr. Ken Purvey, President

Fresh-cut (skin on) french fries, finger foods, such as cajun shrimp, clam strips, chicken and fish fingers, gravy, soft drinks, etc.

HISTORY: . . . . .CFA
Established in 1987; . . 1st Franchised in 1987
Company-Owned Units (As of 12/1/1989): . .3
Franchised Units (12/1/1989): 12
Total Units (12/1/1989): 15
Distribution: US-0;Can-15;Overseas-0
North America: . . . . 3 Provinces
Concentration: . . 12 in ON, 2 in MB, 1 in NS
Registered: . . . .
. . . .
Average # of Employees: . . . . . . 2 FT, 4 PT
Prior Industry Experience: . . . . Helpful

FINANCIAL:
Cash Investment: $50-65K
Total Investment: $100-130K
Fees: Franchise - $25K
  Royalty: 6%, Advert: 0-2%
Contract Periods (Yrs.): 10/5/5
Area Development Agreement: . .No
Sub-Franchise Contract: . . . . . .No
Expand in Territory: . . . . Yes
Passive Ownership: . . . Discouraged
Encourage Conversions: . . . . . .No
Franchisee Purchase(s) Required: .No

FRANCHISOR TRAINING/SUPPORT:
Financial Assistance Provided: . . . Yes(I)
Site Selection Assistance: . . . . . . .Yes
Lease Negotiation Assistance: . . . . .Yes
Co-operative Advertising: . . . . . . .Yes
Training: . . . . . . 6 Days Minimun Head-
. . . . quarters
On-Going Support: . . . .A,B,C,D,E,F,G,I
Full-Time Franchisor Support Staff: . . . 4
EXPANSION PLANS:
US: . . . . No
Canada - Yes, ...Overseas - No

MR. BULKY'S

755 W. Big Beaver, # 1600
Troy, MI 48084
TEL: (313) 244-9000
FAX:
Mr. Richard Zimmer, Dir. Fran. Serv.

MISTER BULKY'S is a retail bulk food franchise, providing the consumer with the opportunity to purchase over 700 items of bulk food, such as candies, nuts, coffees, snacks, giftware, etc. at an attractive price, providing the ability to purchase a little or a lot, depending on the consumer's needs. Stores operate primarily in major malls.

HISTORY: . . . .
Established in 1984; . . 1st Franchised in 1984
Company-Owned Units (As of 12/1/1989): . 14
Franchised Units (12/1/1989): 54
Total Units (12/1/1989): 68
Distribution: US-68;Can-0;Overseas-0
North America: . . . . 18 States
Concentration: . . .15 in MI, 14 in OH, 6 in IL
Registered: . . . IL,IN,MD,MI,MN,NY,RI,VA
. . . .
Average # of Employees: . . . . . . 2 FT, 8 PT
Prior Industry Experience: . . . . . . Helpful

FINANCIAL:
Cash Investment: . . . .$
Total Investment: $135-245K
Fees: Franchise - $30K
Royalty: 5%, Advert: 0%
Contract Periods (Yrs.): 10/5
Area Development Agreement: Yes/10
Sub-Franchise Contract: . . . . . .No
Expand in Territory: . . . . Yes
Passive Ownership: . . . Discouraged
Encourage Conversions: . . . . . .No
Franchisee Purchase(s) Required: .No

FRANCHISOR TRAINING/SUPPORT:
Financial Assistance Provided: . . . Yes(I)
Site Selection Assistance: . . . . .Yes
Lease Negotiation Assistance: . . . . .Yes
Co-operative Advertising: . . . . No
Training: . . . . 14 Days at Franchisee
. . . . .Location Prior to Opening
On-Going Support: . . . . . .C,D,E,G,H
Full-Time Franchisor Support Staff: . . 25
EXPANSION PLANS:
US: . . . . .All US
Canada - No, ...Overseas - No

NEW YORK FRIES

1220 Yonge St., # 400
Toronto, ON M4T1W1 CAN
TEL: (416) 963-5005
FAX: (416) 963-4920
Mr. Don Landon, EVP

NEW YORK FRIES offers the consumer a fresh-cut, gourmet french fry. We offer our franchisees an up-scale concept that is simple to operate, successful and rewarding. Our product line is limited so we can put out a high-quality product.

HISTORY: . . . .
Established in 1984; . . . 1st Franchised in 1985
Company-Owned Units (As of 12/1/1989): . .5
Franchised Units (12/1/1989): 41
Total Units (12/1/1989): 46
Distribution: US-1;Can-45;Overseas-0
North America: . . . . . .1 State, 6 Provinces
Concentration: . . 28 in ON, 5 in AB, 1 in WA
Registered: . . . . WA,AB
. . . .
Average # of Employees: . . . . . 3 FT, 4-6 PT
Prior Industry Experience: . . . . Helpful

FINANCIAL:
Cash Investment: . . . .$
Total Investment: $125-160K
Fees: Franchise - $25K
Royalty: 6%, Advert: 1.5%
Contract Periods (Yrs.): 1-/5/5
Area Development Agreement: Yes/10
Sub-Franchise Contract: . . . . . .No
Expand in Territory: . . . . Yes
Passive Ownership: . . . Discouraged
Encourage Conversions: . . . . . Yes
Franchisee Purchase(s) Required: .No

FRANCHISOR TRAINING/SUPPORT:
Financial Assistance Provided: . . . . . No
Site Selection Assistance: . . . . .Yes
Lease Negotiation Assistance: . . . . .Yes
Co-operative Advertising: . . . . No
Training: . . . . 1 Wk. Headquarters
. . . .
On-Going Support: . . . . . . B,C,d,E,G,h
Full-Time Franchisor Support Staff: . . . .
EXPANSION PLANS:
US: . . . . .California, New York,Florida
Canada - Yes, ...Overseas - No

NUT KETTLE CANDY KITCHEN, THE

P. O. Box 1072
Palm Springs, CA 92263
TEL: (800) 456-3533 (619) 324-3533
FAX:
Mr. Keith Culverhouse, Chairman

THE NUT KETTLE CANDY KITCHEN offers the opportunity to produce the world's finest popcorn confections of unequalled flavor and quality. Other Kitchen-fresh products are fudges, chocolate specialties and nuts. Imported coffee beans and candies complete high-impulse product mix. Your customers "Never Had It So Good!"

HISTORY: . . . .
Established in 1968; . . 1st Franchised in 1987
Company-Owned Units (As of 12/1/1989): . .1
Franchised Units (12/1/1989): 3
Total Units (12/1/1989): 4
Distribution: US-4;Can-0;Overseas-0
North America: . . . . 3 States
Concentration: . . . 2 in CA, 1 in VA, 1 in PA
Registered: . . . . CA,VA
. . . .
Average # of Employees: . . . . . . 2 FT, 3 PT
Prior Industry Experience: . . . . Helpful

FINANCIAL:
Cash Investment: $125-150K
Total Investment: $125-150K
Fees: Franchise - $20K
Royalty: 5%, Advert: 0%
Contract Periods (Yrs.): 10/10
Area Development Agreement: . .No
Sub-Franchise Contract: . . . . . .No
Expand in Territory: . . . . Yes
Passive Ownership: . . . Discouraged
Encourage Conversions: . . . . . .No
Franchisee Purchase(s) Required: .No

FRANCHISOR TRAINING/SUPPORT:
Financial Assistance Provided: . . . . . No
Site Selection Assistance: . . . . .Yes
Lease Negotiation Assistance: . . . . . No
Co-operative Advertising: . . . . No
Training: . . . . . . 1 Wk. - 10 Days Head-
. . . . quarters, 1 Wk. On-site
On-Going Support: . . . . .D,E,I
Full-Time Franchisor Support Staff: . . .4
EXPANSION PLANS:
US: . . . . California
Canada - Yes, ...Overseas - No

PAPA ALDO'S INTERNATIONAL

9600 SW Capitol Hwy.
Portland, OR 97219
TEL: (800) 537-3902 (503) 246-7272
FAX: (503) 245-3654
Mr. Dennis Steinman, VP

Team up with PAPA ALDO'S, the world's largest Take & Bake pizza chain, in the $20 billion pizza industry's newest dimension. We create fresh pizza that customers take home and bake in less than 15 minutes. PAPA ALDO'S shops offer quality, convenience and price.

HISTORY:	FINANCIAL:	FRANCHISOR TRAINING/SUPPORT:
Established in 1981; . . 1st Franchised in 1981	Cash Investment: $30-35K	Financial Assistance Provided: . . . Yes(I)
Company-Owned Units (As of 12/1/1989): . .1	Total Investment: $81-140K	Site Selection Assistance: . . . . . . .Yes
Franchised Units (12/1/1989): 90	Fees: Franchise - $17.5K	Lease Negotiation Assistance: . . . . .Yes
Total Units (12/1/1989): 91	Royalty: 5%, Advert: 2%	Co-operative Advertising: . . . . .Yes
Distribution: US-83;Can-6;Overseas-2	Contract Periods (Yrs.): 10/5	Training: . . . . .1 Wk. Headquarters,
North America: . . . . . 7 States, 2 Provinces	Area Development Agreement: Yes/10	. . . . .1 Wk. On-site at Opening
Concentration: . .45 in OR, 29 in WA, 5 in BC	Sub-Franchise Contract: . . . . . Yes	On-Going Support: . . .B,C,D,E,F,G,H,I
Registered: . . . . CA,FL,HI,MI,OR,WA	Expand in Territory: . . . . .No	Full-Time Franchisor Support Staff: . . 20
. . . .	Passive Ownership: . . . Discouraged	EXPANSION PLANS:
Average # of Employees: . . . . . . 1 FT, 5 PT	Encourage Conversions: . . . . . Yes	US: . . . . .All US
Prior Industry Experience: . . . . . . Helpful	Franchisee Purchase(s) Required: .No	Canada - Yes, . . . Overseas - Yes

PERFECT PORTIONS FROZEN FOODS

440 Niagara St.
Welland, ON L3C1L5 CAN
TEL: (416) 735-2000
FAX: (416) 735-5825
Mr. Andre Champagne, President

Retail/wholesale frozen foods - portion control, sizes individually wrapped. Oven-ready, micro-wavable or BBQ ready. Saves families and singles time and money purchasing in this way. Vegetables, meats, seafoods, finger foods, specialty items, etc. No line ups at supermarket. Excellent quality foods. Credit cards accepted. Turn-key.

HISTORY: . . . . .CFA	FINANCIAL:	FRANCHISOR TRAINING/SUPPORT:
Established in 1984; . . 1st Franchised in 1985	Cash Investment: $60K	Financial Assistance Provided: . . . Yes(I)
Company-Owned Units (As of 12/1/1989): . .1	Total Investment: $140-170K	Site Selection Assistance: . . . . . . .Yes
Franchised Units (12/1/1989): 11	Fees: Franchise - $25K	Lease Negotiation Assistance: . . . . .Yes
Total Units (12/1/1989): 12	Royalty: 4%, Advert: 4%	Co-operative Advertising: . . . . .Yes
Distribution: US-0;Can-12;Overseas-0	Contract Periods (Yrs.): 10/10	Training: . . . . 1 Wk. Corporate Store
North America: . . . . .1 Province	Area Development Agreement: .No	. . . .
Concentration: . . . . 12 in ON	Sub-Franchise Contract: . . . . . .No	On-Going Support: . . . . B,C,D,E,F,G,H
Registered:	Expand in Territory: . . . . Yes	Full-Time Franchisor Support Staff: . . .7
. . . .	Passive Ownership: . . . Not Allowed	EXPANSION PLANS:
Average # of Employees: . . . . . . 2 FT, 3 PT	Encourage Conversions: . . . . . Yes	US: . . . . .No
Prior Industry Experience: . . . . . . Helpful	Franchisee Purchase(s) Required: Yes	Canada - Yes, ...Overseas - No

ROCKY MOUNTAIN CHOCOLATE FACTORY

P. O. Box 2408
Durango, CO 81302
TEL: (303) 259-0554
FAX:
Mr. Franklin Crail, President

On-site candy making, done in front of the customer to generate interest and excitement. An entire line of American-made assorted chocolates in both bulk and pre-pack is offered in addition to an extensive holiday and specialty line.

HISTORY:	FINANCIAL: OTC-RMCF	FRANCHISOR TRAINING/SUPPORT:
Established in 1981; . . 1st Franchised in 1982	Cash Investment: $30-50K	Financial Assistance Provided: . . . . .No
Company-Owned Units (As of 12/1/1989): . .3	Total Investment: $80-130K	Site Selection Assistance: . . . . . . .Yes
Franchised Units (12/1/1989): 67	Fees: Franchise - $19.5K	Lease Negotiation Assistance: . . . . .Yes
Total Units (12/1/1989): 70	Royalty: 5%, Advert: 1%	Co-operative Advertising: . . . . .Yes
Distribution: US-67;Can-3;Overseas-0	Contract Periods (Yrs.): 5/5	Training: . . . . 10 Days Headquarters
North America: . . . . 21 States	Area Development Agreement: .No	. . . .
Concentration: . .27 in CA, 19 in CO, 4 in NM	Sub-Franchise Contract: . . . . . .No	On-Going Support: . . . .B,C,D,E,F,G,H,I
Registered: . . . .CA,FL,HI,IL,MD,MI,NY,RI	Expand in Territory: . . . . Yes	Full-Time Franchisor Support Staff: . . 12
. . . . .WA	Passive Ownership: . . . Discouraged	EXPANSION PLANS:
Average # of Employees: . . . . . . 2 FT, 2 PT	Encourage Conversions: . . . . . Yes	US: . . . . .All US
Prior Industry Experience: . . . . . . Helpful	Franchisee Purchase(s) Required: Yes	Canada - No, ...Overseas - No

SANGSTER'S HEALTH CENTRE

P.O. Box 996
Yorkton, SK S3N2X3 CAN
TEL: (306) 783-9177 C
FAX:
Mr. R. Sangster, President

SANGSTER'S HEALTH CENTRES offer quality, name-brand vitamins along with assorted bulk nuts and candies. All major health companies are also carried. Increased buying power gives maximum profits.

HISTORY:	FINANCIAL:	FRANCHISOR TRAINING/SUPPORT:
Established in 1971; . . 1st Franchised in 1978	Cash Investment: $10K	Financial Assistance Provided: . . . . . No
Company-Owned Units (As of 12/1/1989): . .4	Total Investment: $50-75K	Site Selection Assistance: . . . . .Yes
Franchised Units (12/1/1989): 4	Fees: Franchise - $15K	Lease Negotiation Assistance: . . . . .Yes
Total Units (12/1/1989): 8	Royalty: 5%, Advert: 2%	Co-operative Advertising: . . . . . . .Yes
Distribution: US-0;Can-8;Overseas-0	Contract Periods (Yrs.): 5/5	Training: . . . . .1-2 Wks.
North America: . . . . 3 Provinces	Area Development Agreement: . .No	. . . .
Concentration: . . . 6 in SK, 1 in AB, 1 in MB	Sub-Franchise Contract: . . . . . .No	On-Going Support: . . . . . . B,D,E,F,G,I
Registered: . . . . AB	Expand in Territory: . . . . Yes	Full-Time Franchisor Support Staff: . . 20
. . . .	Passive Ownership: . . . Discouraged	EXPANSION PLANS:
Average # of Employees: . . . . . . 1 FT, 2 PT	Encourage Conversions: . . . . . Yes	US: . . . . .No
Prior Industry Experience: . . . . Helpful	Franchisee Purchase(s) Required: Yes	Canada - Yes, ...Overseas - No

STUFF 'N TURKEY

15 Engle St., # 304
Englewood, NJ 07631
TEL: (800) 332-2229 (201) 871-0370
FAX: (201) 871-7168
Mr. John Sterns, Sales Manager

Specialty deli operation, offering home-cooked turkey and glazed ham dishes. Fast food with a home-cooked taste, geared for the health-conscious American.

HISTORY:	FINANCIAL:	FRANCHISOR TRAINING/SUPPORT:
Established in 1986; . . 1st Franchised in 1988	Cash Investment: $50K	Financial Assistance Provided: . . . Yes(I)
Company-Owned Units (As of 12/1/1989): . .5	Total Investment: $130-180K	Site Selection Assistance: . . . .
Franchised Units (12/1/1989): 6	Fees: Franchise - $25K	Lease Negotiation Assistance: . . . .
Total Units (12/1/1989): 11	Royalty: 5%, Advert: 3%	Co-operative Advertising: . . . .
Distribution: US-11;Can-0;Overseas-0	Contract Periods (Yrs.): . . 10/10/10	Training: . . . . 2 Wks. Company Location,
North America: . . . . 6 States	Area Development Agreement: . .No	. . . . 1-2 Wks. On-site
Concentration: . . . 4 in FL, 2 in MD, 2 in MA	Sub-Franchise Contract: . . . . . .No	On-Going Support: . . . . . B,C,D,E,F,G,I
Registered: . . . . .FL,MD,NY,VA	Expand in Territory: . . . . Yes	Full-Time Franchisor Support Staff: . . . 6
. . . .	Passive Ownership: . . . . . .Allowed	EXPANSION PLANS:
Average # of Employees: . . . . . . 2 FT, 3 PT	Encourage Conversions: . . . . .No	US: . . . . .All US
Prior Industry Experience: . . . . Helpful	Franchisee Purchase(s) Required: .No	Canada - Yes, ... Overseas - No

SUPPLEMENTAL LISTING OF FRANCHISORS

ALTERNATIVES NATURAL FOOD MARKET . . . . .453 Reynolds St., Oakville ON L6J3M6	CAN
BARNIE'S COFFEE & TEA COMPANY . . . . .340 N. Primrose Dr., Orlando FL 32803	
BIG ORANGE FRANCHISE . . . . P. O. Box 2620, Ft. Walton Beach FL 32549	
BIN & BARREL . . . . .9950 Westpark, # 110, Houston TX 77063	
BROWNEE POINTS GIFTS & GIFT DELIVERY . . . . . 6298 Hamilton Rd., # 2-D, Columbus GA 31909	
CANDY WRAPPERS . . . . 312 Rideau St., Ottawa ON K1N5Y5	CAN
CARAWAY DELICATESSEN RESTAURANT . . . . . . .252 Sandringham Dr., Downsview ON M3H1G3	CAN
CHEESE SHOP INTERNATIONAL . . . . .5301 Belt Line Rd., # 2032, Dallas TX 75240	
CHEF'S CUISINE EXPRESS . . . . 50 Burnhamthorpe Rd., W., Mississauga ON L5B3C2	CAN
CHEZ CHOCOLATE . . . . .5170 Indiana Ave., # A, Winston-Salem NC 27106	
COFFEE TREE, THE . . . . 110 Berkeley St., Toronto ON M5A2W7	CAN
COFFEE, TEA & THEE . . . . P.O. Box 11025, Winston-Salem NC 27116	
CONNOISSEUR, THE . . . . 201 Torance Blvd., Redondo Beach CA 90277	

COOK'S CORNER . . . . .2277 Boca St., Carlsbad CA 92009
DR POPCORN . . . . 3021 Rigel Ave., Las Vegas NV 89102
FIGARO'S FRESH-TO-BAKE PIZZA & MORE . . . . .P. O. Box 12575, Salem OR 97309
GENERAL NUTRITION CENTRE . . . . 4001, cote Vertu, Ville St-Laurent PQ H4R1R5   CAN
GRANNY FEELGOOD'S NATURAL FOOD . . . . 190 SE 1st Ave., Miami FL 33131
GREAT EARTH VITAMIN STORE . . . . P.O. Box 1993, Santa Ana CA 92702
GREAT SAN FRANCISCO SEAFOOD CO. . . . . .8962 E. Hampden Ave., # 189, Denver CO 80231
HAM SUPREME SHOPS . . . . .P.O. Box 07009, Detroit MI 48207
HOUSE OF ALMONDS . . . . P.O. Box 11178, Bakersfield CA 93389
JO-ANN'S NUT HOUSE . . . . 5170 Indiana Ave., # A, Winston-Salem NC 27106
JO-ANN'S NUT HOUSE . . . . 5170 Indiana Ave., # A, Winston-Salem NC 27106
JOHNNY QUIK . . . . .7955 N. Cedar Ave., Fresno CA 93710
KARMELKORN . . . . P.O. Box 35286, Minneapolis MN 55435
KELLY'S COFFEE & FUDGE FACTORY . . . . .23232 Peralta, # 102, Laguna Hills CA 92653
KERNELS . . . . .40 Eglinton Ave. E., # 250, Toronto ON M4P3A2   CAN
LE CHOCOLATE BELGE DANIEL . . . . .124 W. 3rd Ave., Vancouver BC V5Y1E9   CAN
LIBERTY PRODUCTS . . . . .71 College Dr., Orange Park FL 32065
LOGAN FARMS HONEY BRAND HAMS . . . . 10001 Westheimer, # 1040, Houston TX 77042
M & M MEAT SHOPS . . . . 421 Greenbrook Dr., Kitchener ON N2M4K1   CAN
MCBEANS . . . . 214 - 1595 McKenzie Ave., Victoria BC V8N1A4   CAN
MORROW NUT HOUSE .5051 Edison, Chino CA 91710
MORROW NUT HOUSE . . . . P.O. Box 11178, Bakersfield CA 93389
MRS. EMM'S ALL NATURAL HEALTH STORES . . . . .1907 Greentree Rd., Cherry Hill NJ 08003
MRS. GEE'S HOMEMADE EGGROLLS . . . . . RR # 7, Box 11, 35 Scissions Rd., Nepean ON K2H7V2   CAN
MURPHY'S PIZZA TAKE 'N' BAKE . . . . 1301 Redwood Way, # 245, Petaluma CA 94952
NATIONAL MEAT & SEAFOOD COMPANY . . . . 1006 Branch Dr., Alpharetta GA 30201
NUTTER'S FRUIT & NUT CO. . . . . .107 - 1601 Dunmore Rd., SE, Medicine Hat AB T1A1Z8   CAN
PEANUT SHACK . . . . 4198 N. Cherry St., Winston-Salem NC 27105
PEANUT SHACK . . . . P.O. Box 11025, Winston-Salem NC 27116
PHANNYS EMPORIUM . . . . 1525 W. Orangegrove Ave., # A, Orange CA 92668
PICOLO'S . . . . 15 Oregon Ave., # 106, Tacoma WA 98409
POPS-U-BAKE PIZZA TO GO . . . . .7955 N. Cedar Ave., Fresno CA 93710
RANELLI'S DELI & SANDWICH SHOP . . . . .2134 Warrior Rd., Birmingham AL 35208
RIVERSIDE CHOCOLATE FACTORY . . . . .1335 N. Riverside Dr., McHenry IL 60050
SECOND CUP, THE . . . . 293 Church St., Oakville ON L6J1N9   CAN
SNACKPACKER . . . . P.O. Box 33488, Raleigh NC 27636
STEAK SHOP, THE . . . . .320 N. Queen St., # 130, Etobicoke ON M9C5K4   CAN
STRICTLY SUGARLESS CANDIES . . . . 6827 Grand Ave., Hammond IN 46323
SWISS COLONY STORES . . . . 1 Alpine Ln., Monroe WI 53566
TEA MASTERS-AN INTERNATIONAL CAFE . . . . 789 Don Mills Rd., # 606, Don Mills ON M3C1T5   CAN
THINNY DELITES . . . . 426 Pennsylvania Ave., # 3, Ft. Washington PA 19034
TIMOTHY'S COFFEES OF THE WORLD . . . . 1230 Yonge St., Toronto ON M4T1W3   CAN
TRUFFLES CHOCOLATIER . . . . P. O. Box 369, Stillwater MN 55082
U-TAKE & BAKE PIZZA . . . . 2030 A Drew St., Clearwater FL 34625
UNITED SNACKS . . . . P.O. Box 33488, Raleigh NC 27636
VOGEL NATURAL FOODS . . . . .4001 Cote Vertu, Ville St. Laurent PQ H4R1R5   CAN

CHAPTER 20

RETAIL FOOD:
QUICK SERVICE / TAKE-OUT

1 POTATO 2

5640 International Pkwy.
New Hope, MN 55428
TEL: (800) 328-8467 (612) 537-3833
FAX: (612) 537-4241
Mr. Todd D. King, Franchise Dir.

1 POTATO 2 owns and franchises restaurants specializing in baked potato entrees with a variety of hot toppings and also snack potato items. The restaurants are located exclusively in regional shopping malls and downtown office centers.

HISTORY: . . . . IFA
Established in 1977; . . 1st Franchised in 1984
Company-Owned Units (As of 12/1/1989): . 33
Franchised Units (12/1/1989): 39
Total Units (12/1/1989): 72
Distribution: US-69;Can-0;Overseas-3
North America: . . . . 23 States
Concentration: . . . 12 in CA, 7 in MN, 5 in IL
Registered: . . . CA,FL,IL,IN,MD,MI,MN,NY
. . . . OR,RI,VA,WA,WI
Average # of Employees: . . . . 1-2 FT, 6-8 PT
Prior Industry Experience: . . . . Helpful

FINANCIAL:
Cash Investment: $40-80K
Total Investment: $110-160K
Fees: Franchise - $20K
Royalty: 6%, Advert: 0%
Contract Periods (Yrs.): 5/5
Area Development Agreement: Yes/5
Sub-Franchise Contract: . . . . . Yes
Expand in Territory: . . . . Yes
Passive Ownership: . . . Discouraged
Encourage Conversions: . . . . . Yes
Franchisee Purchase(s) Required: .No

FRANCHISOR TRAINING/SUPPORT:
Financial Assistance Provided: . . . Yes(I)
Site Selection Assistance: . . . . .Yes
Lease Negotiation Assistance: . . . . .Yes
Co-operative Advertising: . . . . .NA
Training: . . . . 14 Days HQ
. . . .
On-Going Support: . . . .B,C,D,E,F,G,H,I
Full-Time Franchisor Support Staff: . . 30
EXPANSION PLANS:
US: . . . . .All US
Canada - Yes, ...Overseas - Yes

RESTAURANTS – ALL TYPES

	1988	1989	1990	Percentage Change 1988-1989	Percentage Change 1989-1990
Number of Establishments:					
Company–Owned	27,305	27,761	29,313	1.7%	5.6%
Franchisee–Owned	63,040	66,524	72,822	5.5%	9.5%
Total	90,345	94,285	102,135	4.4%	8.3%
% of Total Establishments:					
Company–Owned	30.2%	29.4%	28.7%		
Franchisee–Owned	69.8%	70.6%	71.3%		
Total	100.0%	100.0%	100.0%		
Annual Sales ($000):					
Company–Owned	22,276,989	23,438,938	25,688,238	5.2%	9.6%
Franchisee–Owned	42,003,446	45,655,170	50,827,883	8.7%	11.3%
Total	64,280,435	69,094,108	76,516,121	7.5%	10.7%
% of Total Sales:					
Company–Owned	34.7%	33.9%	33.6%		
Franchisee–Owned	65.3%	66.1%	66.4%		
Total	100.0%	100.0%	100.0%		
Average Sales Per Unit ($000):					
Company–Owned	$816	$844	$876	3.5%	3.8%
Franchisee–Owned	666	686	698	3.0%	1.7%
Total	711	733	749	3.0%	2.2%
Sales Ratio	122.4%	123.0%	125.6%		

	1st Quartile	Median	4th Quartile
Average 1988 Total Investment:			
Company–Owned	$150,000	$337,500	$642,500
Franchisee–Owned	130,000	250,000	500,000
Single Unit Franchise Fee	$15,000	$20,000	$25,000
Multiple Unit Franchise Fee	10,000	15,000	27,625
Franchisee Start-up Cost	50,000	80,000	125,000

	1988	Employees/Unit	Sales/Employee
Employment:			
Company–Owned	855,180	31.3	$26,049
Franchisee–Owned	1,871,425	29.7	22,445
Total	2,726,605	30.2	23,575
Employee Performance Ratios		105.5%	116.1%

Source: Franchising In The Economy, 1988 – 1990, IFA Education Foundation & Horwath International, Published January, 1990.

1) 1989 and 1990 data were estimated by respondents.

RESTAURANT – DISTRIBUTION BY MENU THEME
(PROJECTED 1990)

	Establish- ments	Sales ($000)	% of Total Sales	Avg. Sales /Yr. /Unit	Sales Ratio
Chicken:					
Company–Owned	2,868	$1,977,410	34.9%	$689,474	116.7%
Franchisee–Owned	6,244	3,689,020	65.1%	$590,810	
Total	9,112	5,666,430	100.0%	$621,865	
Hamburgers					
Company–Owned	9,018	$9,245,350	24.6%	$1,025,211	116.7%
Franchisee–Owned	32,231	28,324,955	75.4%	$878,811	
Total	41,249	37,570,305	100.0%	$910,817	
Pizza					
Company–Owned	7,337	$4,578,639	39.9%	$624,048	132.0%
Franchisee–Owned	14,617	6,908,880	60.1%	$472,661	
Total	21,954	11,487,519	100.0%	$523,254	
Mexican					
Company–Owned	2,074	$1,773,825	52.3%	$855,268	150.9%
Franchisee–Owned	2,852	1,615,975	47.7%	$566,611	
Total	4,926	3,389,800	100.0%	$688,145	
Seafood					
Company–Owned	695	$470,632	56.2%	$677,168	109.1%
Franchisee–Owned	590	366,095	43.8%	$620,500	
Total	1,285	836,727	100.0%	$651,149	
Pancakes/Waffles					
Company–Owned	511	$556,607	35.6%	$1,089,250	151.2%
Franchisee–Owned	1,397	1,006,574	64.4%	$720,525	
Total	1,908	1,563,181	100.0%	$819,277	
Steak (Full Menu)					
Company–Owned	6,329	$6,864,211	50.2%	$1,084,565	115.0%
Franchisee–Owned	7,236	6,822,970	49.8%	$942,920	
Total	13,565	13,687,181	100.0%	$1,009,007	
Sandwich & Other					
Company–Owned	481	$221,564	9.6%	$460,632	168.4%
Franchisee–Owned	7,655	2,093,414	90.4%	$273,470	
Total	8,136	2,314,978	100.0%	$284,535	
Grand Total	102,135	$76,516,121			

Source: Franchising In The Economy, 1988 – 1990, IFA Education Foundation & Horwath International, Published January, 1990.

1) 1990 data was estimated by respondents.

A & W FOOD SERVICES OF CANADA

171 W. Esplanade, # 300
N. Vancouver, BC V7M3K9 CAN
TEL: (800) 663-4473 (604) 988-2141
FAX: (604) 988-0553
Mr. Richard C. Murray, Dir. Fran.

Unique ground-floor opportunity to join established franchisor with internationally-recognized trademark. Single and/or multiple unit franchises available in most areas. Menu features world famous "A & W Root Beer," root beer floats, hamburgers, hot dogs, "Coney Dogs," low calorie/cholesterol grilled chicken sandwiches, etc.

HISTORY: . . . . .CFA	FINANCIAL:	FRANCHISOR TRAINING/SUPPORT:
Established in 1956; . . 1st Franchised in 1957	Cash Investment: . . . . $Varies	Financial Assistance Provided: . . . . .No
Company-Owned Units (As of 12/1/1989): 136	Total Investment: $200-650K	Site Selection Assistance: . . . . .Yes
Franchised Units (12/1/1989): 238	Fees: Franchise - $35K	Lease Negotiation Assistance: . . . . .Yes
Total Units (12/1/1989): 374	Royalty: 2.5%, Advert: 3.5%	Co-operative Advertising: . . . . . . .Yes
Distribution: US-0;Can-374;Overseas-0	Contract Periods (Yrs.): 20	Training: . . . . 4 Weeks
North America: . . . . 10 Provinces	Area Development Agreement: . .No	. . . .
Concentration: . 89 in ON, 71 in AB, 65 in BC	Sub-Franchise Contract: . . . . .No	On-Going Support: . . . . .A,B,C,D,G,h,I
Registered: . . . . AB	Expand in Territory: . . . . Yes	Full-Time Franchisor Support Staff: . 1144
. . . .	Passive Ownership: . . . Not Allowed	EXPANSION PLANS:
Average # of Employees:	Encourage Conversions: . . . . . Yes	US: . . . . .No
Prior Industry Experience: . . . . . . Helpful	Franchisee Purchase(s) Required: .No	Canada - Yes, ...Overseas - No

A & W RESTAURANTS

17197 N. Laurel Park Dr., # 500
Livonia, MI 48152
TEL: (800) 222-2337 (313) 462-0029
FAX:
Franchise Sales Department

Unique ground floor opportunity to join established franchisor with internationally-recognized trademark. Single and/or multiple unit franchises available in most areas. Menu features world famous "A & W Root Beer," root beer floats, hamburgers, hot dogs, "Coney Dogs," low calorie/cholesterol grilled chicken sandwiches, etc.

HISTORY: . . . . IFA	FINANCIAL:	FRANCHISOR TRAINING/SUPPORT:
Established in 1919; . . 1st Franchised in 1925	Cash Investment: $150-300K	Financial Assistance Provided: . . . . .No
Company-Owned Units (As of 12/1/1989): . 10	Total Investment: $150-1.0M	Site Selection Assistance: . . . . .Yes
Franchised Units (12/1/1989): 526	Fees: Franchise - $15K	Lease Negotiation Assistance: . . . . .Yes
Total Units (12/1/1989): 536	Royalty: 4%, Advert: 4%	Co-operative Advertising: . . . . . . .Yes
Distribution: US-477;Can-0;Overseas-59	Contract Periods (Yrs.): 20/20	Training: . . . . 10 Days HQ
North America: . . . . 37 States	Area Development Agreement: Yes/Var	. . . .
Concentration: . . 74 in WI,69 in CA,67 in MI	Sub-Franchise Contract: . . . . . .No	On-Going Support: . . . . .B,C,D,E,G,H,I
Registered: . . . CA,FL,IL,IN,MD,MI,MN,NY	Expand in Territory: . . . . .No	Full-Time Franchisor Support Staff: . . 89
. . . . .OR,VA,WA,WI	Passive Ownership: . . . Discouraged	EXPANSION PLANS:
Average # of Employees:	Encourage Conversions: . . . . . Yes	US: . . . . Midwest
Prior Industry Experience: . . . . . . Helpful	Franchisee Purchase(s) Required: .No	Canada - No, ... Overseas - Yes

A.L. VAN HOUTTE

6045 Boul. Des Grandes Prairies
St. Leonard, PQ H1P1A5 CAN
TEL: (800) 361-5628 (514) 327-3110
FAX:
Ms. Sonia Lepage, Asst. Dir. Fran.

The A.L. VAN HOUTTE CAFE-BISTROS offer light meals and the usual selection of A.L. Van Houtte coffees. The menu includes soups, quiches, salads and a selection of sandwiches and pastries.

HISTORY:	FINANCIAL: Mont-VHOUT	FRANCHISOR TRAINING/SUPPORT:
Established in 1919; . . 1st Franchised in 1981	Cash Investment: $90-100K	Financial Assistance Provided: . . . Yes(I)
Company-Owned Units (As of 12/1/1989): . .4	Total Investment: $225-250K	Site Selection Assistance: . . . . .Yes
Franchised Units (12/1/1989): 77	Fees: Franchise - $35K	Lease Negotiation Assistance: . . . . .Yes
Total Units (12/1/1989): 81	Royalty: 5%, Advert: 2%	Co-operative Advertising: . . . . . . .Yes
Distribution: US-0;Can-81;Overseas-0	Contract Periods (Yrs.): 10/5	Training: . . . . . . 5 Wks. "School Store"
North America: . . . . 2 Provinces	Area Development Agreement: . .No	. . . . 1-3 Wks. at Site
Concentration: . . . . .77 in PQ, 4 in ON	Sub-Franchise Contract: . . . . . .No	On-Going Support: . . . . .C,D,E,F,G,H,I
Registered:	Expand in Territory: . . . . Yes	Full-Time Franchisor Support Staff: . . 49
. . . .	Passive Ownership: . . . Discouraged	EXPANSION PLANS:
Average # of Employees: . . . . . . 6 FT, 8 PT	Encourage Conversions: . . . . . .No	US: . . . . .No
Prior Industry Experience: . . . . Helpful	Franchisee Purchase(s) Required: Yes	Canada - Yes, ...Overseas - No

AL'S CHICAGO'S #1 ITALIAN BEEF

22 W. 140 North Ave.
Glen Ellyn, IL 60137
TEL: (708) 858-9090
FAX:
Mr. Terry G. Pacelli, President

Fast-food sandwiches, fries, drinks. Famous in the Chicago area for our Italian beef sandwiches and fresh-cut fries.

HISTORY: . . . .
Established in 1984; . . 1st Franchised in 1985
Company-Owned Units (As of 12/1/1989): . . 0
Franchised Units (12/1/1989): 7
Total Units (12/1/1989): 7
Distribution: US-7;Can-0;Overseas-0
North America: . . . . 1 State
Concentration: . . . . 7 in IL
Registered: . . . . IL,IN
. . . .
Average # of Employees: . . . . . . 2 FT, 11 PT
Prior Industry Experience: . . . . Helpful

FINANCIAL:
Cash Investment: $115-150K
Total Investment: . . . .$
Fees: Franchise - $20K
Royalty: 4%, Advert: 2%
Contract Periods (Yrs.): . . . 10/10
Area Development Agreement: . . .
Sub-Franchise Contract: . . . . Yes
Expand in Territory: . . . . Yes
Passive Ownership: . . . . . .Allowed
Encourage Conversions: . . . . Yes
Franchisee Purchase(s) Required: Yes

FRANCHISOR TRAINING/SUPPORT:
Financial Assistance Provided: . . . . .No
Site Selection Assistance: . . . . .Yes
Lease Negotiation Assistance: . . . . .Yes
Co-operative Advertising: . . . . No
Training: . . . . 6 Wks. Chicago, IL
. . . .
On-Going Support: . . . . . . a,C,D,E,H,i
Full-Time Franchisor Support Staff: . . . .
EXPANSION PLANS:
US: . . . . Only Illinois Currently
Canada - No, ...Overseas - No

ARBY'S

10 Piedmont Center, # 700
Atlanta, GA 30305
TEL: (800) 554-1388 (404) 262-2729
FAX: (404) 262-3089
Mr. Jim Squire, Group VP Fran.

ARBY'S is fast becoming one of the world's most favorite food restaurant chains, specializing in roast beef sandwiches, with over 2,000 locations domestically and internationally. The 25-year old company has established itself as a leader in the fast-food industry through innovation, marketing, operations and customer service.

HISTORY: . . . . IFA
Established in 1964; . . 1st Franchised in 1965
Company-Owned Units (As of 12/1/1989): 214
Franchised Units (12/1/1989): 1954
Total Units (12/1/1989): 2168
Distribution: . . US-2069;Can-84;Overseas-15
North America: . . . . 50 States, 6 Provinces
Concentration: .143 in TX, 122 in OH, 115 CA
Registered: . . . . .All
. . . .
Average # of Employees: . . . . . 35 FT, 20 PT
Prior Industry Experience: . . . . Helpful

FINANCIAL:
Cash Investment: $200-300K
Total Investment: $525-850K
Fees: Franchise - $25-37K
Royalty: 3.5-4.0%, Advert: . . 0.1%
Contract Periods (Yrs.): . . . 20/20
Area Development Agreement: Yes/Var
Sub-Franchise Contract: . . . . Yes
Expand in Territory: . . . . Yes
Passive Ownership: . . . Discouraged
Encourage Conversions: . . . . . Yes
Franchisee Purchase(s) Required: .No

FRANCHISOR TRAINING/SUPPORT:
Financial Assistance Provided: . . . Yes(I)
Site Selection Assistance: . . . . .Yes
Lease Negotiation Assistance: . . . . .Yes
Co-operative Advertising: . . . . .Yes
Training: . . . . 2 Wks. HQ (Owner),
. . .6 Wks. Various Locations (Operator)
On-Going Support: . . . . .B,C,D,E,G,H,I
Full-Time Franchisor Support Staff: . .360
EXPANSION PLANS:
US: . . . . .All US
Canada - Yes, . . . Overseas - Yes

BAACO PIZZA SYSTEMS

5620 104 St.
Edmonton, AB T0H2K2 CAN
TEL: (403) 434-8486
FAX: (403) 436-2475
Mr. Byron Watt, President

Pick-up and home delivery. Also "pizza by the slice" kiosks.

HISTORY: . . . . .CFA
Established in 1978; . . 1st Franchised in 1979
Company-Owned Units (As of 12/1/1989): . .0
Franchised Units (12/1/1989): 26
Total Units (12/1/1989): 26
Distribution: US-0;Can-26;Overseas-0
North America: . . . . 2 Provinces
Concentration: . . . . . . .15 in AB, 11 in MN
Registered: . . . . AB
. . . .
Average # of Employees: . . . . .3-5 FT, 10 PT
Prior Industry Experience: . . . . Helpful

FINANCIAL:
Cash Investment: $30-50K
Total Investment: $50-80K
Fees: Franchise - $14.7K
Royalty: 6%, Advert: 6%
Contract Periods (Yrs.): 10/10
Area Development Agreement: Yes/10
Sub-Franchise Contract: . . . . Yes
Expand in Territory: . . . . Yes
Passive Ownership: . . . Discouraged
Encourage Conversions: . . . . . Yes
Franchisee Purchase(s) Required: .No

FRANCHISOR TRAINING/SUPPORT:
Financial Assistance Provided: . . . . .No
Site Selection Assistance: . . . . .Yes
Lease Negotiation Assistance: . . . . .Yes
Co-operative Advertising: . . . . .Yes
Training: . . . . . . 4-6 Wks. Headquarters
. . . .
On-Going Support: . . . . .B,C,D,E,F,G,h
Full-Time Franchisor Support Staff: . . . 4
EXPANSION PLANS:
US: . . . . Northwest and Southwest
Canada - Yes, ...Overseas - No

BACK YARD BURGERS

4245 Cherry Ctr. Dr., # 4
Memphis, TN 38118
TEL: (901) 367-0888
FAX: (901) 367-0956
Mr. Charles Saba, VP Fran. Devel.

Double drive-thru, char-broiled gourmet hamburgers and chicken breasts. Our 1/3 lb. patties are ground fresh daily and topped with fresh, quality condiments. We offer 19 sandwiches, 2 varieties of fries, cobbler, hand-dipped shakes and much more. BACK YARD BURGERS is "fresh gourmet fast!"

HISTORY: . . . .
Established in 1986; . . 1st Franchised in 1987
Company-Owned Units (As of 12/1/1989): . .3
Franchised Units (12/1/1989): 12
Total Units (12/1/1989): 15
Distribution: US-15;Can-0;Overseas-0
North America: . . . . 4 States
Concentration: . . . .6 in MS, 4 in TN, 2 in FL
Registered: . . . . .CA,FL
. . . .
Average # of Employees: . . . . . .8 FT, 15 PT
Prior Industry Experience: . . . . Helpful

FINANCIAL:
Cash Investment: $50-80K
Total Investment: $180-250K
Fees: Franchise - $16K
   Royalty: 4%, Advert: 3%
Contract Periods (Yrs.): 10/5
Area Development Agreement: Yes/10
Sub-Franchise Contract: . . . . . Yes
Expand in Territory: . . . . . . Yes
Passive Ownership: . . . . . .Allowed
Encourage Conversions: . . . . . .No
Franchisee Purchase(s) Required: Yes

FRANCHISOR TRAINING/SUPPORT:
Financial Assistance Provided: . . . Yes(I)
Site Selection Assistance: . . . . .Yes
Lease Negotiation Assistance: . . . . .Yes
Co-operative Advertising: . . . . .Yes
Training: . . . . . 4 Wks. HQ for Operator,
   . . . . . . 1 Wk. Headquarters for Owner
On-Going Support: . . . a,B,C,D,E,F,G,h,i
Full-Time Franchisor Support Staff: . . 11
EXPANSION PLANS:
US: . . . . .All US
Canada - Yes, ...Overseas - No

BALDINOS GIANT JERSEY SUBS

760 Elaine St.
Hinesville, GA 31313
TEL: (912) 368-2822
FAX:
Mr. Bill Baer, President/CEO

Quality submarine sandwiches with in-store bakery. All subs sliced fresh as ordered in full view of customer, served on freshly-baked rolls. Built for volume business at a "fast food" pace by use of multi-production lines. Variety of 20 hot and cold subs and freshly-baked gourmet cookies.

HISTORY: . . . .
Established in 1975; . . 1st Franchised in 1984
Company-Owned Units (As of 12/1/1989): . .6
Franchised Units (12/1/1989): 17
Total Units (12/1/1989): 23
Distribution: US-23;Can-0;Overseas-0
North America: . . . . 3 States
Concentration: . . 12 in GA, 10 in NC, 1 in SC
Registered: . . . . .FL
. . . .
Average # of Employees: . . . . . .8 FT, 12 PT
Prior Industry Experience: . . . . Helpful

FINANCIAL:
Cash Investment: $50-75K
Total Investment: $90-150K
Fees: Franchise - $10K
   Royalty: 4.5%, Advert: 5%
Contract Periods (Yrs.): 15/10
Area Development Agreement:Yes/15+
Sub-Franchise Contract: . . . . . Yes
Expand in Territory: . . . . . . Yes
Passive Ownership: . . . Discouraged
Encourage Conversions: . . . . . Yes
Franchisee Purchase(s) Required: .No

FRANCHISOR TRAINING/SUPPORT:
Financial Assistance Provided: . . . . . No
Site Selection Assistance: . . . . .Yes
Lease Negotiation Assistance: . . . . .Yes
Co-operative Advertising: . . . . .Yes
Training: . . . . 4 Wks. Headquarters
. . . .
On-Going Support: . . . .B,C,D,E,F,G,H,I
Full-Time Franchisor Support Staff: . . . 4
EXPANSION PLANS:
US: . . . . Southeast
Canada - No, ...Overseas - No

BEEFY'S HAMBURGERS

107 Music City Circle, # 305
Nashville, TN 37214
TEL: (800) 548-0352 (615) 889-4766
FAX:
Mr. E.F. Griswold, Dir. Fran. Serv.

Six years of solid growth and expertise in double drive-thru, limited menu field. Units open in 7 states and more opening soon. System, marketing support and training to help you grow with us. For complete information, call or write.

HISTORY: . . . .
Established in 1984; . . 1st Franchised in 1985
Company-Owned Units (As of 12/1/1989): . .9
Franchised Units (12/1/1989): 23
Total Units (12/1/1989): 32
Distribution: US-32;Can-0;Overseas-0
North America: . . . . 7 States
Concentration: . . .15 in TN, 6 in KY, 4 in AL
Registered: . . . . .CA,FL,IL,IN,MI,NY,VA
. . . .
Average # of Employees: . . . . . .5 FT, 10 PT
Prior Industry Experience: . . . . Helpful

FINANCIAL:
Cash Investment: $35-58K
Total Investment: $160-193K
Fees: Franchise - $10K
   Royalty: 3%, Advert: 1%
Contract Periods (Yrs.): 20/10
Area Development Agreement: Yes/20
Sub-Franchise Contract: . . . . . Yes
Expand in Territory: . . . . . . Yes
Passive Ownership: . . . Discouraged
Encourage Conversions: . . . . . .No
Franchisee Purchase(s) Required: .No

FRANCHISOR TRAINING/SUPPORT:
Financial Assistance Provided: . . . . . No
Site Selection Assistance: . . . . .Yes
Lease Negotiation Assistance: . . . . .Yes
Co-operative Advertising: . . . . .Yes
Training: . . . . 3 Wks. Headquarters
. . . .
On-Going Support: . . . . C,D,E,G,I
Full-Time Franchisor Support Staff: . . 10
EXPANSION PLANS:
US: . . . . All Registered States
Canada - No, ...Overseas - No

BERT'S HAMBURGERS AND FRIES

700 S. University Parks Rd., # 690
Waco, TX 76706
TEL: (817) 757-2378
FAX:
Mr. Bob Pryor, Franchise Sales

A proven money-maker, BERT'S HAMBURGERS AND FRIES is the ultimate fast food restaurant. A simple system that serves high-quality, great-tasting hamburgers at affordable prices. BERT's is well known for its double drive-thru kiosks and mall units. The staff provides site selection, complete training and on-going support.

HISTORY: . . . . .IFA	FINANCIAL:	FRANCHISOR TRAINING/SUPPORT:
Established in 1987; . . 1st Franchised in 1988	Cash Investment: $35K	Financial Assistance Provided: . . . . .No
Company-Owned Units (As of 12/1/1989): . .2	Total Investment: $140K	Site Selection Assistance: . . . . . . .Yes
Franchised Units (12/1/1989): 11	Fees: Franchise - $19.6K	Lease Negotiation Assistance: . . . . .Yes
Total Units (12/1/1989): 13	Royalty: 5%, Advert: 0%	Co-operative Advertising: . . . . .NA
Distribution: US-13;Can-0;Overseas-0	Contract Periods (Yrs.): 10/10	Training: . . . . .1 Month Hewitt, TX
North America: . . . . 3 States	Area Development Agreement: Yes/10	. . . .
Concentration: . . .10 in TX, 2 in LA, 1 in MS	Sub-Franchise Contract: . . . . .No	On-Going Support: . . . . . . A,C,D,E,F,I
Registered:	Expand in Territory: . . . . Yes	Full-Time Franchisor Support Staff: . . 10
. . . .	Passive Ownership: . . . Discouraged	EXPANSION PLANS:
Average # of Employees: . . . . . .3 FT, 10 PT	Encourage Conversions: . . . . . Yes	US: . . . . Southwest
Prior Industry Experience: . . . . Helpful	Franchisee Purchase(s) Required: .No	Canada - No, ...Overseas - No

BLIMPIE

740 Broadway
New York, NY 10003
TEL: (800) SAN-WICH (212) 673-5900
FAX: (212) 995-2560
Mr. Pat O'Brien, Sales

BLIMPIE, "America's Best Dressed Sandwich," is a limited-menu, fast-food submarine sandwich and salad chain, offering cold and hot sandwiches. In 1989, Blimpie added Lites - 4 salads and pita sandwiches designed and approved by the Diet Workshop. Low investment and no cooking. Call today!

HISTORY:	FINANCIAL:	FRANCHISOR TRAINING/SUPPORT:
Established in 1964; . . 1st Franchised in 1971	Cash Investment: $35-50K	Financial Assistance Provided: . . . Yes(I)
Company-Owned Units (As of 12/1/1989): . .0	Total Investment: $70-100K	Site Selection Assistance: . . . . . . .Yes
Franchised Units (12/1/1989): 332	Fees: Franchise - $15-18K	Lease Negotiation Assistance: . . . . .Yes
Total Units (12/1/1989): 332	Royalty: 6%, Advert: 3%	Co-operative Advertising: . . . . .Yes
Distribution: US-332;Can-0;Overseas-0	Contract Periods (Yrs.): 20/5	Training: . . . . . 1 Wk. Atlanta, 80 Hrs. in
North America: . . . . 17 States	Area Development Agreement: Yes/50	. . .Area Opening Store, 10-14 Days Site
Concentration: . 120 in NY,90 in NJ, 75 in GA	Sub-Franchise Contract: . . . . . Yes	On-Going Support: . . . . B,C,D,E,F,G,H
Registered: . . . . CA,FL,IL,NY,OR,RI	Expand in Territory: . . . . Yes	Full-Time Franchisor Support Staff: . . 50
. . . .	Passive Ownership: . . . . . .Allowed	EXPANSION PLANS:
Average # of Employees: . . . . . .3 FT, 10 PT	Encourage Conversions: . . . . . Yes	US: . . . . .All US
Prior Industry Experience: . . . . Helpful	Franchisee Purchase(s) Required: .No	Canada - No, ...Overseas - No

BOARDWALK FRIES

8307 Main St.
Ellicott City, MD 21043
TEL: (301) 465-5020
FAX: (301) 465-5213
Mr. Jack Csicsek, VP Fran./Leasing

Established since 1981, BOARDWALK FRIES is a nationally-known, fast-food chain, currently franchised in 18 states with 56 locations. BOARDWALK FRIES provides site location, lease negotiations, training, operational support, product development and the establishment of national accounts for services and products.

HISTORY: . . . . .IFA	FINANCIAL:	FRANCHISOR TRAINING/SUPPORT:
Established in 1981; . . 1st Franchised in 1983	Cash Investment: $110-190K	Financial Assistance Provided: . . . Yes(I)
Company-Owned Units (As of 12/1/1989): . .5	Total Investment: $110-190K	Site Selection Assistance: . . . . . . .Yes
Franchised Units (12/1/1989): 67	Fees: Franchise - $20K	Lease Negotiation Assistance: . . . . .Yes
Total Units (12/1/1989): 72	Royalty: 7%, Advert: 2%	Co-operative Advertising: . . . . .NA
Distribution: US-72;Can-0;Overseas-0	Contract Periods (Yrs.): 10/10	Training: . . . . 12 Days Hunt Valley Mall,
North America: . . . . 18 States	Area Development Agreement: Yes/10	. . . . Hunt Valley, MD
Concentration: . . . 8 in FL, 7 in MD, 5 in CA	Sub-Franchise Contract: . . . . . .No	On-Going Support: . . . . . .B,C,E,F,G,H
Registered: . . . . All States	Expand in Territory: . . . . Yes	Full-Time Franchisor Support Staff: . . 15
. . . .	Passive Ownership: . . . Discouraged	EXPANSION PLANS:
Average # of Employees: . . . . . . 2 FT, 5 PT	Encourage Conversions: . . . . . .No	US: . . . . .All US
Prior Industry Experience: . . . . Helpful	Franchisee Purchase(s) Required: .No	Canada - No, ... Overseas - Yes

BOONDOGGLES HAMBURGER STATION

937 - C St. James St.
Winnipeg, MB R3H0X2 CAN
TEL: (204) 774-6638
FAX:
Mr. Barry Greenberg, Fran. Dir.

BOONDOGGLES is Canada's first double drive-thru. Over 3 years of research and development has gone into making double drive-thru viable in a colder climate. We can do it all for you! We are successful, established and ready to expand. Ground floor opportunity!

HISTORY: . . . .
Established in 1987; . . 1st Franchised in 1990
Company-Owned Units (As of 12/1/1989): . .2
Franchised Units (12/1/1989): 0
Total Units (12/1/1989): 2
Distribution: US-0;Can-2;Overseas-0
North America: . . . . .1 Province
Concentration: . . . . 2 in MB
Registered: . . . .
. . . .
Average # of Employees: . . . . . . 4 FT, 6 PT
Prior Industry Experience: . . . . Helpful

FINANCIAL:
Cash Investment: $30-50K
Total Investment: $180-190K
Fees: Franchise - $2.5K
Royalty: 4%, Advert: 1%
Contract Periods (Yrs.): 20/10
Area Development Agreement: Yes/10
Sub-Franchise Contract: . . . . . Yes
Expand in Territory: . . . . . . Yes
Passive Ownership: . . . Discouraged
Encourage Conversions: . . . . .No
Franchisee Purchase(s) Required: Yes

FRANCHISOR TRAINING/SUPPORT:
Financial Assistance Provided: . . . Yes(I)
Site Selection Assistance: . . . . . . .Yes
Lease Negotiation Assistance: . . . . .Yes
Co-operative Advertising: . . . . . . .Yes
Training: . . . . 4 Wks. Headquarters,
. . . . .2 Wks. On-site
On-Going Support: . . . . a,C,D,E,F,G,H,I
Full-Time Franchisor Support Staff: . . . 8
EXPANSION PLANS:
US: . . . . .No
Canada - Yes, ...Overseas - No

BREADEAUX PISA

P. O. Box 158 Fairleigh Station
St. Joseph, MO 64506
TEL: (816) 364-1088
FAX: (816) 364-3739
Mr. J. Charles Zimmermann, VP

BREADEAUX PISA is a rapidly growing, carry-out pizza franchise, utilizing the Buy One, Get One Free concept. Pizzas are made with a unique french bread style crust and all-natural ingredients. Menu includes gourmet and dessert pizzas. Average investment is one of the lowest in the industry.

HISTORY: . . . . IFA
Established in 1985; . . 1st Franchised in 1985
Company-Owned Units (As of 12/1/1989): . 11
Franchised Units (12/1/1989): 88
Total Units (12/1/1989): 99
Distribution: US-99;Can-0;Overseas-0
North America: . . . . 6 States
Concentration: . 58 in IA, 20 in NE, 14 in MO
Registered: . . . . IL,MN,SD,WI
. . . .
Average # of Employees: . . . .2-4 FT, 6-10 PT
Prior Industry Experience: . . . . Helpful

FINANCIAL:
Cash Investment: $35-50K
Total Investment: $65-100K
Fees: Franchise - $15K
Royalty: 5%, Advert: 2%
Contract Periods (Yrs.): 10/10
Area Development Agreement: . Yes
Sub-Franchise Contract: . . . . .No
Expand in Territory: . . . . . . Yes
Passive Ownership: . . . Not Allowed
Encourage Conversions: . . . . NA
Franchisee Purchase(s) Required: .No

FRANCHISOR TRAINING/SUPPORT:
Financial Assistance Provided: . . . Yes(I)
Site Selection Assistance: . . . . . . .Yes
Lease Negotiation Assistance: . . . . No
Co-operative Advertising: . . . . No
Training: . . . . . . .1 Wk. Headquarters,
. . . . 1 Wk. Site, On-going
On-Going Support: . . . a,B,C,D,E,F,G,H
Full-Time Franchisor Support Staff: . . . .
EXPANSION PLANS:
US: . . . . .IA,MN,NE,KS,IL,CO,SD,WI
Canada - No, ...Overseas - No

BRIGHAM'S

30 Mill St.
Arlington, MA 02174
TEL: (800) BRIGHAM (617) 648-9000 C
FAX: (617) 646-0507
Mr. Clark Merrill, III, Dir. Fran.

We are Boston's best premium ice cream and restaurant, targeting a quick-service market with a rich 1940's dining look. We offer a ground-floor franchising opportunity to investors and owner-operators. 75-year track record.

HISTORY: . . . . IFA
Established in 1914; . . 1st Franchised in 1977
Company-Owned Units (As of 12/1/1989): . 16
Franchised Units (12/1/1989): 48
Total Units (12/1/1989): 64
Distribution: US-64;Can-0;Overseas-0
North America: . . . . 3 States
Concentration: . . 63 in MA, 1 in NH, 1 in NY
Registered: . . . . .NY,RI
. . . .
Average # of Employees: . . . . . . 4 FT, 15 PT
Prior Industry Experience: . . . . . .Necessary

FINANCIAL:
Cash Investment: $100-400K
Total Investment: $200-600K
Fees: Franchise - $31.5K
Royalty: 5%, Advert: 1%
Contract Periods (Yrs.): 4/5
Area Development Agreement: Yes/5
Sub-Franchise Contract: . . . . .No
Expand in Territory: . . . . . . Yes
Passive Ownership: . . . Discouraged
Encourage Conversions: . . . . .No
Franchisee Purchase(s) Required: Yes

FRANCHISOR TRAINING/SUPPORT:
Financial Assistance Provided: . . . . .No
Site Selection Assistance: . . . . . . .Yes
Lease Negotiation Assistance: . . . . .Yes
Co-operative Advertising: . . . . . . .Yes
Training: . . . . . . 10 Days Headquarters,
. . . . 2-4 Wks. Site
On-Going Support: . . . . . B,C,D,E,F,G,I
Full-Time Franchisor Support Staff: . . 25
EXPANSION PLANS:
US: . . . . . . .New England, NY and NJ
Canada - No, ...Overseas - No

BROWNIES HOLDINGS

406-4190 Lougheed Hwy.
Burnaby, BC V5C6A8 CAN
TEL: (604) 291-6060
FAX:
Mr. David McFaul, Mktg. Mgr.

During the past 20 years, BROWNIES recipe fried chicken has built a tremendous customer loyalty based on our unique cooking process and secret blend of ingredients. Franchisees benefit from a winning product, proven system and the on-going support of an experienced franchise team.

HISTORY:	FINANCIAL:	FRANCHISOR TRAINING/SUPPORT:
Established in 1968; . . 1st Franchised in 1968	Cash Investment: $60K	Financial Assistance Provided: . . . Yes(I)
Company-Owned Units (As of 12/1/1989): . .5	Total Investment: $100K	Site Selection Assistance: . . . . .Yes
Franchised Units (12/1/1989): 55	Fees: Franchise - $25K	Lease Negotiation Assistance: . . . . .Yes
Total Units (12/1/1989): 60	Royalty: 4%, Advert: 3%	Co-operative Advertising: . . . . . . .Yes
Distribution: US-0;Can-48;Overseas-12	Contract Periods (Yrs.): 5/5	Training: . . . . .Training Provided in New
North America: . . . . 3 Provinces	Area Development Agreement: . Yes	. . . .& Existing Units - Variable Length
Concentration: . . .38 in BC, 3 in ON, 2 in SA	Sub-Franchise Contract: . . . . . Yes	On-Going Support: . . . . B,C,D,E,F,G,h,I
Registered:	Expand in Territory: . . . . Yes	Full-Time Franchisor Support Staff: . . .6
	Passive Ownership: . . . . . .Allowed	EXPANSION PLANS:
Average # of Employees: . . . . . . 2 FT, 6 PT	Encourage Conversions: . . . . Yes	US: . . . . . . All US - Master Franchises
Prior Industry Experience: . . . . . . Helpful	Franchisee Purchase(s) Required: .No	Canada - Yes, . . . Overseas - Yes

BURGER KING (CANADA)

201 City Centre Dr., 8th Fl.
Mississauga, ON L5B2T4 CAN
TEL: (416) 273-5000
FAX: (416) 896-6928
Mr. W. F. Reid, Franchise Department

BURGER KING is the second largest hamburger chain in the world, with a presence in 35 foreign countries. As a wholly-owned subsidiary of the Burger King Corporation, it is also part of the world's largest food organization. BURGER KING continues in their commitment to give customers the best meal and best meal time experience for their money. 5,500 units in the US.

HISTORY: . . . . IFA	FINANCIAL:	FRANCHISOR TRAINING/SUPPORT:
Established in 1954; . . 1st Franchised in 1968	Cash Investment: $350K	Financial Assistance Provided: . . . . .No
Company-Owned Units (As of 12/1/1989): . 56	Total Investment: $700-800K	Site Selection Assistance: . . . . .No
Franchised Units (12/1/1989): 149	Fees: Franchise - $40K	Lease Negotiation Assistance: . . . . .No
Total Units (12/1/1989): 205	Royalty: 4%, Advert: 4%	Co-operative Advertising: . . . . . . .Yes
Distribution: US-0;Can-205;Overseas-0	Contract Periods (Yrs.): . . 20/Varies	Training: . . . . . . 8 Wks. In Store - Head
North America: . . . . 10 Provinces	Area Development Agreement: . .No	. . . . Office
Concentration: . . . Primarily ON, PQ and BC	Sub-Franchise Contract: . . . . .No	On-Going Support: . . A,B,C,D,E,F,G,H,I
Registered: . . . . AB	Expand in Territory: . . . . Yes	Full-Time Franchisor Support Staff: . . . .
	Passive Ownership: . . . Not Allowed	EXPANSION PLANS:
Average # of Employees: . . . . . 10 FT, 50 PT	Encourage Conversions: . . . . .No	US: . . . . .No
Prior Industry Experience: . . . . Helpful	Franchisee Purchase(s) Required: Yes	Canada - Yes, ...Overseas - No

C. J. CARYL'S INTERNATIONAL

10585 N. Meridian, # 245
Indianapolis, IN 46290
TEL: (317) 573-4825
FAX: (317) 573-4826
Mr. Jim Petsas, VP

C. J. CARYL'S offers Tendairlite chicken cooked, with a patented cooking process. A lite alternative offering meals, snacks and group gatherings a choice of healthful products - the choice of the nineties. The flavor is chicken, pure and simple.

HISTORY: . . . . IFA	FINANCIAL:	FRANCHISOR TRAINING/SUPPORT:
Established in 1985; . . 1st Franchised in 1987	Cash Investment: $50-150K	Financial Assistance Provided: . . . Yes(I)
Company-Owned Units (As of 12/1/1989): . .3	Total Investment: . . . .$	Site Selection Assistance: . . . . . . .Yes
Franchised Units (12/1/1989): 2	Fees: Franchise - $9.5K	Lease Negotiation Assistance: . . . . .Yes
Total Units (12/1/1989): 5	Royalty: 4%, Advert: 1%	Co-operative Advertising: . . . . . . .Yes
Distribution: US-3;Can-0;Overseas-2	Contract Periods (Yrs.): 10/10	Training: . . . . 2 Wks. Headquarters
North America: . . . . .1 State	Area Development Agreement: Yes/10	. . . .
Concentration: . . . . .3 in IN	Sub-Franchise Contract: . . . . . Yes	On-Going Support: . . . .B,C,D,E,F,G,H,I
Registered: . . . . FL,IN,MI	Expand in Territory: . . . . Yes	Full-Time Franchisor Support Staff: . . 12
	Passive Ownership: . . . Not Allowed	EXPANSION PLANS:
Average # of Employees: . . . . . .4 FT, 10 PT	Encourage Conversions: . . . . Yes	US: . . . . .All US
Prior Industry Experience: . . . . Helpful	Franchisee Purchase(s) Required: Yes	Canada - Yes, . . . Overseas - Yes

CAFFE CLASSICO

369 Pine St., # 900
San Francisco, CA 94104
TEL: (415) 433-3111
FAX:
Ms. Janet Willis, Manager

European cafe, serving wonderful expresso coffee drinks and pastries in the morning, delicious sandwiches, soups and salads at lunch and award-winning gelato, sorbetto and frozen yogurt. A concept which maximizes revenues by providing sales from early morning to late evening. Member IFA.

HISTORY: . . . . IFA
Established in 1976; . . 1st Franchised in 1982
Company-Owned Units (As of 12/1/1989): . .3
Franchised Units (12/1/1989): 41
Total Units (12/1/1989): 44
Distribution: US-44;Can-0;Overseas-0
North America: . . . . 8 States
Concentration: . . . 21 in CA, 6 in IL, 4 in AZ
Registered: . . .CA,FL,HI,IL,MN,NY,VA,WA
. . . .
Average # of Employees: . . . . . . 2 FT, 4 PT
Prior Industry Experience: . . . . . . Helpful

FINANCIAL:
Cash Investment: $45-75K
Total Investment: $90-175K
Fees: Franchise - $25K
  Royalty: 4%, Advert: 2%
Contract Periods (Yrs.): 10/10
Area Development Agreement: Yes/10
Sub-Franchise Contract: . . . . . .No
Expand in Territory: . . . . Yes
Passive Ownership: . . . Not Allowed
Encourage Conversions: . . . . . Yes
Franchisee Purchase(s) Required: Yes

FRANCHISOR TRAINING/SUPPORT:
Financial Assistance Provided: . . . Yes(I)
Site Selection Assistance: . . . . . . .Yes
Lease Negotiation Assistance: . . . . .Yes
Co-operative Advertising: . . . . .No
Training: . . . . . . 10 Days San Francisco
. . . .
On-Going Support: . . . . B,C,D,E,F,G,H
Full-Time Franchisor Support Staff: . . 15
EXPANSION PLANS:
US: . . . . .All US
Canada - Yes, . . . Overseas - Yes

CAP'N TACO

P.O. Box 415
North Olmsted, OH 44070
TEL: (216) 676-9100
FAX:
Mr. Raymond Brown, Dir. Fran. Devel.

CAP'N TACO has developed a unique niche in fast-food marketing: our service is 35 seconds, our dining room is full-service, our price structure is competitive with the quick-service segment. We are Mexican, however, and our restaurants are theme-oriented - multi-TV's, pictures, games, promotions. Our food is also different from most - we use only white mild cheese and a unique blend of secret spices that makes our beef "spreadable."

HISTORY: . . . .
Established in 1976; . . 1st Franchised in 1987
Company-Owned Units (As of 12/1/1989): . .3
Franchised Units (12/1/1989): 0
Total Units (12/1/1989): 3
Distribution: US-3;Can-0;Overseas-0
North America: . . . . .1 State
Concentration: . . . . 2 in OH
Registered: . . . .
. . . .
Average # of Employees: . . . . . . 2 FT, 4 PT
Prior Industry Experience: . . . . . . Helpful

FINANCIAL:
Cash Investment: $7.5-15K
Total Investment: $65-100K
Fees: Franchise - $15K
  Royalty: 5%, Advert: 2%
Contract Periods (Yrs.): 10/10
Area Development Agreement: . .No
Sub-Franchise Contract: . . . . . .No
Expand in Territory: . . . . Yes
Passive Ownership: . . . Discouraged
Encourage Conversions: . . . . . Yes
Franchisee Purchase(s) Required: .No

FRANCHISOR TRAINING/SUPPORT:
Financial Assistance Provided: . . . . .No
Site Selection Assistance: . . . . . . .Yes
Lease Negotiation Assistance: . . . . .Yes
Co-operative Advertising: . . . . .Yes
Training: . . . . . . .2 Wks. Brook Park, OH
. . . . .Plus Annual Classes
On-Going Support: . . A,B,C,D,E,F,G,H,I
Full-Time Franchisor Support Staff: . . 15
EXPANSION PLANS:
US: . . . . .All US
Canada - No, ... Overseas - Yes

CAPT. SUBMARINE

69 Viceroy Rd.
Concord, ON L4K2L6 CAN
TEL: (416) 669-6966
FAX: (416) 660-7421
Mr. Jack Goldstein, President

Fit our concept into your town/area.

HISTORY: . . . .
Established in 1972; . . 1st Franchised in 1972
Company-Owned Units (As of 12/1/1989): . .4
Franchised Units (12/1/1989): 23
Total Units (12/1/1989): 27
Distribution: US-0;Can-27;Overseas-0
North America: . . . . 5 Provinces
Concentration: . . .11 in ON, 6 in NB, 2 in PQ
Registered: . . . .
. . . .
Average # of Employees: . . . . . 3 FT, 5-6 PT
Prior Industry Experience: . . . . . . Helpful

FINANCIAL:
Cash Investment: $40-50K
Total Investment: $100-125K
Fees: Franchise - $10K
  Royalty: 5%, Advert: 3%
Contract Periods (Yrs.): 5/5
Area Development Agreement: . .No
Sub-Franchise Contract: . . . .
Expand in Territory: . . . . Yes
Passive Ownership: . . . Discouraged
Encourage Conversions: . . . .
Franchisee Purchase(s) Required: Yes

FRANCHISOR TRAINING/SUPPORT:
Financial Assistance Provided: . . . Yes(I)
Site Selection Assistance: . . . . . . .Yes
Lease Negotiation Assistance: . . . . .Yes
Co-operative Advertising: . . . . .Yes
Training: . . . . . . .2 Wks.-1 Yr. Existing
. . . . .Location
On-Going Support: . . . . . . B,C,E,F,h,I
Full-Time Franchisor Support Staff: . . .3
EXPANSION PLANS:
US: . . . . .No
Canada - Yes, ...Overseas - No

CAPTAIN D'S SEAFOOD

1727 Elm Hill Pike
Nashville, TN 37210
TEL: (615) 391-5201
FAX:
Jeffrey L. Heston, Dir. Fran. Devel.

Quick-service seafood restaurant with drive-thru service.

HISTORY: . . . . IFA	FINANCIAL: OTC-SHONC	FRANCHISOR TRAINING/SUPPORT:
Established in 1969; . . 1st Franchised in 1969	Cash Investment: $50K	Financial Assistance Provided: . . . . . No
Company-Owned Units (As of 12/1/1989): 349	Total Investment: $572K	Site Selection Assistance: . . . . . . .Yes
Franchised Units (12/1/1989): 260	Fees: Franchise - $12.5K	Lease Negotiation Assistance: . . . . .Yes
Total Units (12/1/1989): 609	Royalty: 3%, Advert: 6%	Co-operative Advertising: . . . . . . .Yes
Distribution: . . . US-609;Can-0;Overseas-0	Contract Periods (Yrs.): 20/20	Training: . . . . . . 4-7 Wks. Headquarters
North America:	Area Development Agreement: Yes/Var	
Concentration:	Sub-Franchise Contract: . . . . . .No	On-Going Support: . . . .a,b,C,d,e,F,G,h,I
Registered: . . . . All States	Expand in Territory: . . . . Yes	Full-Time Franchisor Support Staff: . . . .
. . . .	Passive Ownership: . . . Not Allowed	EXPANSION PLANS:
Average # of Employees: . . . . 25 FT	Encourage Conversions: . . . . . .No	US: . . . . .NE, NW and West
Prior Industry Experience: . . . . . .Necessary	Franchisee Purchase(s) Required: Yes	Canada - Yes, . . . Overseas - Yes

CAPTAIN TONY'S PIZZA & PASTA EMPORIUM

2990 Culver Rd.
Rochester, NY 14622
TEL: (800) 332-TONY (716) 467-2250 C
FAX: (716) 467-0784
Mr. Michael Martella, President

Pizza and pasta dine-in, take-out and delivery.

HISTORY:	FINANCIAL: OTC	FRANCHISOR TRAINING/SUPPORT:
Established in 1985; . . 1st Franchised in 1986	Cash Investment: $50K	Financial Assistance Provided: . . . . . No
Company-Owned Units (As of 12/1/1989): . .1	Total Investment: $200K	Site Selection Assistance: . . . . .Yes
Franchised Units (12/1/1989): 14	Fees: Franchise - $15K	Lease Negotiation Assistance: . . . . .No
Total Units (12/1/1989): 15	Royalty: 3%, Advert: 2-.5%	Co-operative Advertising: . . . . . . .Yes
Distribution: US-14;Can-0;Overseas-1	Contract Periods (Yrs.): 10/10	Training: . . . . .3 Weeks New York,
North America: . . . . . .5 States, 1 Province	Area Development Agreement: Yes/10	. . . . .5-10 Days On-site
Concentration: . . . 8 in NY, 3 in CA, 3 in OH	Sub-Franchise Contract: . . . . . . Yes	On-Going Support: . . . . . b,C,D,E,F,G,I
Registered: . . . CA,FL,IL,IN,MD,MI,NY,OR	Expand in Territory: . . . . Yes	Full-Time Franchisor Support Staff: . . . 3
. . . . VA	Passive Ownership: . . . Discouraged	EXPANSION PLANS:
Average # of Employees: . . . 4-8 FT, 10-20 PT	Encourage Conversions: . . . . . Yes	US: . . . . .All US
Prior Industry Experience: . . . . Helpful	Franchisee Purchase(s) Required: Yes	Canada - Yes, . . . Overseas - Yes

CENTRAL PARK USA

6100 Bldg., #3800, Eastgate Ctr.
Chattanooga, TN 37411
TEL: (615) 892-9753
FAX:
Ms. Diana Akers, Franchise Co-ord.

CENTRAL PARK is the originator of the limited menu, double drive-thru concept. After several years of successfully operating company stores in Tennessee, we are identifying this year owner-operators to run 1-3 stores in the following Southern states: NC, SC, GA, AL, MS, AR, and North FL.

HISTORY: . . . . IFA	FINANCIAL:	FRANCHISOR TRAINING/SUPPORT:
Established in 1982; . . 1st Franchised in 1986	Cash Investment: $50K	Financial Assistance Provided: . . . Yes(I)
Company-Owned Units (As of 12/1/1989): . 18	Total Investment: $150-200K	Site Selection Assistance: . . . . . . .Yes
Franchised Units (12/1/1989): 32	Fees: Franchise - $15K	Lease Negotiation Assistance: . . . . .Yes
Total Units (12/1/1989): 50	Royalty: 3-4%, Advert: 0-2%	Co-operative Advertising: . . . . .No
Distribution: US-50;Can-0;Overseas-0	Contract Periods (Yrs.): 15/15	Training: . . . . 3 Wks. Headquarters
North America: . . . . 8 States	Area Development Agreement: . .No	. . . .
Concentration: . . .22 in TN, 5 in GA, 5 in SC	Sub-Franchise Contract: . . . . . .No	On-Going Support: . . . . . . B,C,d,E,f,G
Registered: . . . . FL,IL,IN,MD	Expand in Territory: . . . . Yes	Full-Time Franchisor Support Staff: . . 21
. . . .	Passive Ownership: . . . Not Allowed	EXPANSION PLANS:
Average # of Employees: . . . . . .5 FT, 12 PT	Encourage Conversions: . . . . . .No	US: . . . . Southeast
Prior Industry Experience: . . . . Helpful	Franchisee Purchase(s) Required: .No	Canada - No, ...Overseas - No

CHECKERBOARD PIZZA

12891 73rd Ave. N.
Maple Grove, MN 55369
TEL: (612) 424-5814
FAX: (612) 645-5532
Mr. Jim Provinzino, President

CHECKERBOARD PIZZA - SUBS AND RIBS. Take-out and delivery. No experience necessary, low initial investment, complete training, site selection and on-going support. Call (612) 424-5814.

HISTORY: . . . .
Established in 1986; . . 1st Franchised in 1987
Company-Owned Units (As of 12/1/1989): . .0
Franchised Units (12/1/1989): 12
Total Units (12/1/1989): 12
Distribution: US-12;Can-0;Overseas-0
North America: . . . . 5 States
Concentration:
Registered: . . . . CA,MN,WI
. . . .
Average # of Employees: . . . . 15-20 FT
Prior Industry Experience: . . . . Helpful

FINANCIAL: Local
Cash Investment: . . . .$
Total Investment: . . . .$
Fees: Franchise - $15K
　Royalty: 5%, Advert: 2%
Contract Periods (Yrs.): 10/10
Area Development Agreement: . .No
Sub-Franchise Contract: . . . . . Yes
Expand in Territory: . . , ... Yes
Passive Ownership: . . . . . .Allowed
Encourage Conversions: . . . . . Yes
Franchisee Purchase(s) Required: Yes

FRANCHISOR TRAINING/SUPPORT:
Financial Assistance Provided: . . . Yes(I)
Site Selection Assistance: . . . . . . .Yes
Lease Negotiation Assistance: . . . . .Yes
Co-operative Advertising: . . . . . . .Yes
Training: . . . . 2 Wks. St. Paul, MN
. . . .
On-Going Support: . . . . B,C,D,E,F,G,h,I
Full-Time Franchisor Support Staff: . . 10
EXPANSION PLANS:
US: . . . . .Northwest, Southwest
Canada - No, ...Overseas - No

CHICAGO'S PIZZA

1111 N. Broadway
Greenfield, IN
TEL: (317) 462-9878
FAX:
Mr. Robert L. McDonald, CEO

Franchise designed for owner/operator. Flexibility allowed to ensure success. Can be adapted to large and small operations. Inside dining/carry-out/delivery.

HISTORY: . . . .
Established in 1979; . . 1st Franchised in 1981
Company-Owned Units (As of 12/1/1989): . .1
Franchised Units (12/1/1989): 9
Total Units (12/1/1989): 10
Distribution: US-10;Can-0;Overseas-0
North America: . . . . .1 State
Concentration: . . . . 10 in IN
Registered: . . . . IN
. . . .
Average # of Employees: . . . .
Prior Industry Experience: . . . . Helpful

FINANCIAL:
Cash Investment: $50K
Total Investment: $300K
Fees: Franchise - $7K
　Royalty: 4%, Advert: 2%
Contract Periods (Yrs.): 10/10
Area Development Agreement: Yes/1
Sub-Franchise Contract: . . . . .No
Expand in Territory: . . . . . . Yes
Passive Ownership: . . . Not Allowed
Encourage Conversions: . . . . . Yes
Franchisee Purchase(s) Required: .No

FRANCHISOR TRAINING/SUPPORT:
Financial Assistance Provided: . . . . .No
Site Selection Assistance: . . . . . . .Yes
Lease Negotiation Assistance: . . . .Yes
Co-operative Advertising: . . . . . . .Yes
Training: . . . . . . 4 Wks. Indianapolis, IN
. . . .
On-Going Support: . . . . C,D,E,F,I
Full-Time Franchisor Support Staff: . . . 4
EXPANSION PLANS:
US: . . . . .Indiana Only
Canada - No, ...Overseas - No

CHICKEN DELIGHT

395 Berry St.
Winnipeg, MB 53J1N6 CAN
TEL: (204) 885-7570
FAX: (204) 831-6176
Mr. Robert J. Ritchie, Dir. Mktg.

Dine-in, take-out, delivery and catering of world-famous, deep-pressure fried chicken pieces, plus fresh-dough pizza, ribs, shrimp, fish, cole slaw, fries, salads, desserts and beverages. A proven system of serving popular foods profitably. Over 35 years of experience.

HISTORY: . . . . IFA
Established in 1952; . . 1st Franchised in 1952
Company-Owned Units (As of 12/1/1989): . .3
Franchised Units (12/1/1989): 71
Total Units (12/1/1989): 74
Distribution: . . . US-33;Can-39;Overseas-2
North America: . . . . 4 States, 4 Provinces
Concentration: . 32 in MB, 20 in NY, 12 in CA
Registered: . . . . . . .CA,MI,NY,ND,OR,AB
. . . .
Average # of Employees: . . . . . 10 FT, 8 PT
Prior Industry Experience: . . . . Helpful

FINANCIAL:
Cash Investment: $70-225K
Total Investment: $125-650K
Fees: Franchise - $15-25K
　Royalty: 5%, Advert: 2%
Contract Periods (Yrs.): 10/10
Area Development Agreement: Yes/10
Sub-Franchise Contract: . . . . .No
Expand in Territory: . . . . . . Yes
Passive Ownership: . . . Discouraged
Encourage Conversions: . . . . . Yes
Franchisee Purchase(s) Required: Yes

FRANCHISOR TRAINING/SUPPORT:
Financial Assistance Provided: . . . Yes(I)
Site Selection Assistance: . . . . . . .Yes
Lease Negotiation Assistance: . . . .Yes
Co-operative Advertising: . . . . . . .Yes
Training: . . . . . . .30 Days Headquarters
. . . .
On-Going Support: . . . . . B,C,D,E,G,H
Full-Time Franchisor Support Staff: . . 20
EXPANSION PLANS:
US: . . . . .All US
Canada - Yes, . . . Overseas - Yes

CLARK'S SUBMARINE SANDWICHES

417 University Ave.
St. Paul, MN 55103
TEL: (612) 291-1374
FAX: (612) 291-1373
Mr. Clark Armstead, President

30 years in business selling submarine sandwiches.

HISTORY:	FINANCIAL:	FRANCHISOR TRAINING/SUPPORT:
Established in 1959; . . 1st Franchised in 1989	Cash Investment: $60-80K	Financial Assistance Provided: . . . . .Yes
Company-Owned Units (As of 12/1/1989): . 18	Total Investment: $80-100K	Site Selection Assistance: . . . . . . .Yes
Franchised Units (12/1/1989): 0	Fees: Franchise - $10K	Lease Negotiation Assistance: . . . . .Yes
Total Units (12/1/1989): 18	Royalty: 5%, Advert: 4%	Co-operative Advertising: . . . . . . .Yes
Distribution: US-18;Can-0;Overseas-0	Contract Periods (Yrs.): . . . 10/10	Training: . . . . . . 1 Wk. General Offices,
North America: . . . . .1 State	Area Development Agreement: . .No	. . . . .1 Wk. Co. Store, 1 Wk. On-site
Concentration: . . . . 18 in MN	Sub-Franchise Contract: . . . . .No	On-Going Support: . . . . . .a,B,C,D,E,F
Registered: . . . . MN	Expand in Territory: . . . . Yes	Full-Time Franchisor Support Staff: . .150
	Passive Ownership: . . . Not Allowed	EXPANSION PLANS:
. . . .	Encourage Conversions: . . . . . Yes	US: . . . . Minnesota Only
Average # of Employees: . . . . . . 7 FT, 8 PT	Franchisee Purchase(s) Required: .No	Canada - No, ...Overseas - No
Prior Industry Experience: . . . . Helpful		

COUSINS SUBMARINES

N93 W16112 Megal Dr.
Menomonee Falls, WI 53051
TEL: (414) 255-3942
FAX: (414) 255-4892
Mr. David K. Kilby, VP

Uniquely-developed submarine sandwich operation with over 17 years' experience. Volume-oriented, fast-service concept in an up-scale, in-line strip or free-standing location - some with drive-up windows. Outstanding fresh-baked bread and the finest-quality ingredients go into our hot subs, delicious soups and garden-fresh salads. Now franchising opportunities for a select group of single and multi-unit franchise owners.

HISTORY: IFA	FINANCIAL:	FRANCHISOR TRAINING/SUPPORT:
Established in 1972; . . 1st Franchised in 1985	Cash Investment: $50-100K	Financial Assistance Provided: . . . Yes(I)
Company-Owned Units (As of 12/1/1989): . 37	Total Investment: $160-360K	Site Selection Assistance: . . . . . . .Yes
Franchised Units (12/1/1989): 16	Fees: Franchise - $18.5K	Lease Negotiation Assistance: . . . . .Yes
Total Units (12/1/1989): 53	Royalty: 6%, Advert: 2%	Co-operative Advertising: . . . . . . .Yes
Distribution: US-53;Can-0;Overseas-0	Contract Periods (Yrs.): . . . 15/15	Training: . . . . 4 Wks. Headquarters,
North America: . . . . 2 States	Area Development Agreement: Yes/Var	. . . 10 Days (2 People) New Restaurant
Concentration: . . . . .37 in WI	Sub-Franchise Contract: . . . . .No	On-Going Support: . . . .B,C,D,E,G,H,I
Registered: . . . . .FL,IL,MN,WI	Expand in Territory: . . . . . . Yes	Full-Time Franchisor Support Staff: . . . .
	Passive Ownership: . . . Not Allowed	EXPANSION PLANS:
. . . .	Encourage Conversions: . . . . .No	US: . . . . Northwest
Average # of Employees: . . . . . .6 FT, 14 PT	Franchisee Purchase(s) Required: .No	Canada - No, ...Overseas - No
Prior Industry Experience: . . . . Helpful		

CREPENCORE

35 Alexandra Blvd.
Toronto, ON M4R1L8 CAN
TEL: (416) 488-3687 C
FAX:
Director of Franchising

Tender and delicate French crepes made from all-natural ingredients, plain or stuffed with a wide variety of fillings, frozen or fresh. One automatic crepe system for an exclusive region will supply fast food and retail outlets.

HISTORY:	FINANCIAL:	FRANCHISOR TRAINING/SUPPORT:
Established in 1985; . . 1st Franchised in 1988	Cash Investment: $95K	Financial Assistance Provided: . . . . . No
Company-Owned Units (As of 12/1/1989): . .1	Total Investment: $180K	Site Selection Assistance: . . . . . . .Yes
Franchised Units (12/1/1989): 4	Fees: Franchise - $25K	Lease Negotiation Assistance: . . . . .Yes
Total Units (12/1/1989): 5	Royalty: 5%, Advert: 2%	Co-operative Advertising: . . . . No
Distribution: US-4;Can-0;Overseas-1	Contract Periods (Yrs.): . . . 15/15	Training: . . . . .1 Wk. Europe,
North America:	Area Development Agreement: Yes/15	. . . . .1 Wk. Site
Concentration:	Sub-Franchise Contract: . . . . .No	On-Going Support: . . . . . .B,D,F,G,H,I
Registered:	Expand in Territory: . . . . . . Yes	Full-Time Franchisor Support Staff: . . . 4
	Passive Ownership: . . . . . .Allowed	EXPANSION PLANS:
. . . .	Encourage Conversions: . . . . .No	US: . . . . .All US
Average # of Employees: . . . . . . 3 FT, 2 PT	Franchisee Purchase(s) Required: Yes	Canada - Yes, . . . Overseas - Yes
Prior Industry Experience: . . . . Helpful		

CRUSTY'S USA / DINO'S
100 E. Six Forks, Rd., # 309
Raleigh, NC 27609
TEL: (919) 781-4611
FAX:
Mr. John E. Ray, President

CRUSTY'S pizza offers 30 years of success and experience in the fast-food pizza delivery business. Franchisees receive the support of a proven management and training program. CRUSTY'S is an award-winning pizza operation.

HISTORY: . . . . IFA	FINANCIAL:	FRANCHISOR TRAINING/SUPPORT:
Established in 1957; . . 1st Franchised in 1962	Cash Investment: . . . . $35K+	Financial Assistance Provided: . . . Yes(I)
Company-Owned Units (As of 12/1/1989): . .2	Total Investment: $70-150K	Site Selection Assistance: . . . . .Yes
Franchised Units (12/1/1989): 192	Fees: Franchise - $15K	Lease Negotiation Assistance: . . . . .Yes
Total Units (12/1/1989): 194	Royalty: 5%, Advert: 4%	Co-operative Advertising: . . . . . . .Yes
Distribution: US-194;Can-0;Overseas-0	Contract Periods (Yrs.): 10/5	Training: . . . . . . 300 Hrs. Total, 2 Wks.
North America: . . . . 17 States	Area Development Agreement: Yes/10	. . . . . Headquarters, 4 Wks. Site/Field
Concentration: . 6O IN FL, 40 in MI, 10 in NC	Sub-Franchise Contract: . . . . . .No	On-Going Support: . . A,B,C,D,E,F,G,H,I
Registered: . . . . .FL,IL,IN,MD,MI,VA	Expand in Territory: . . . . Yes	Full-Time Franchisor Support Staff: . . 20
. . . .	Passive Ownership: . . . Discouraged	EXPANSION PLANS:
Average # of Employees: . . . . . .12 FT, 3 PT	Encourage Conversions: . . . . Yes	US: . . . . East of Mississippi
Prior Industry Experience: . . . . Helpful	Franchisee Purchase(s) Required: Yes	Canada - No, ...Overseas - No

CULTURES FRESH FOOD RESTAURANTS
145 Davenport Rd.
Toronto, ON M5RIJ1 CAN
TEL: (416) 968-1440
FAX:
Ms. Barb N. Anderson, Fran. Co-ord.

"Fresh" food concept, in which all products are prepared fresh on the premises every day. Salad, soup, quiche, sandwiches, a wide variety of baked goods and frozen yogurt specialties make up a "healthy" menu.

HISTORY:	FINANCIAL:	FRANCHISOR TRAINING/SUPPORT:
Established in 1977; . . 1st Franchised in 1978	Cash Investment: $70-140K	Financial Assistance Provided: . . . Yes(I)
Company-Owned Units (As of 12/1/1989): . 18	Total Investment: $200-400K	Site Selection Assistance: . . . . .Yes
Franchised Units (12/1/1989): 52	Fees: Franchise - $35K	Lease Negotiation Assistance: . . . .Yes
Total Units (12/1/1989): 70	Royalty: 5%, Advert: 2%	Co-operative Advertising: . . . . . . .Yes
Distribution: US-0;Can-70;Overseas-0	Contract Periods (Yrs.): 10	Training: . . . . . . 6 Wks. Headquarters
North America: . . . . 6 Provinces	Area Development Agreement: . .No	
Concentration: . . .51 in ON, 3 in AB, 2 in BC	Sub-Franchise Contract: . . . . . .No	On-Going Support: . . . . B,C,D,E,F,G,H
Registered: . . . . AB	Expand in Territory: . . . . .No	Full-Time Franchisor Support Staff: . . . .
. . . .	Passive Ownership: . . . Not Allowed	EXPANSION PLANS:
Average # of Employees: . . . .2-8 FT, 6-12 PT	Encourage Conversions: . . . . .No	US: . . . . .No
Prior Industry Experience: . . . . . . Helpful	Franchisee Purchase(s) Required: .No	Canada - Yes, ...Overseas - No

DADDY-O'S EXPRESS DRIVE-THRU

1496 Old Henderson Rd.
Columbus, OH 43220
TEL: (614) 459-3250
FAX:
Mr. James D. Brockman, President

DADDY-O'S EXPRESS DRIVE-THRU "puts the fast back in fast food." With the demands of today's fast-paced lifestyles, the need for a quick-service, good price/value restaurant is evident. DADDY-O'S meets this demand with its double drive-thru format and represents a future growth trend in the restaurant industry.

HISTORY: . . . . IFA	FINANCIAL:	FRANCHISOR TRAINING/SUPPORT:
Established in 1987; . . 1st Franchised in 1987	Cash Investment: $20-35K	Financial Assistance Provided: . . . . .No
Company-Owned Units (As of 12/1/1989): . .1	Total Investment: $135-250K	Site Selection Assistance: . . . . .Yes
Franchised Units (12/1/1989): 2	Fees: Franchise - $20K	Lease Negotiation Assistance: . . . .Yes
Total Units (12/1/1989): 3	Royalty: 4%, Advert: 4%	Co-operative Advertising: . . . . . . .Yes
Distribution: US-3;Can-0;Overseas-0	Contract Periods (Yrs.): . . . 10/Var	Training: . . . . 2 Wks. Headquarters
North America:	Area Development Agreement: . .No	
Concentration:	Sub-Franchise Contract: . . . . . Yes	On-Going Support: . . . . B,C,D,E,F,G,H
Registered:	Expand in Territory:	Full-Time Franchisor Support Staff: . . 12
. . . .	Passive Ownership: . . . Discouraged	EXPANSION PLANS:
Average # of Employees: . . . . 20 PT	Encourage Conversions: . . . . . .No	US: . . . . .All US
Prior Industry Experience: . . . . Helpful	Franchisee Purchase(s) Required: .No	Canada - No, ...Overseas - No

DAIRY QUEEN

P. O. Box 35286
Minneapolis, MN 55435
TEL: (800) 634-4384 (612) 830-0312
FAX: (612) 830-0270
Mr. John P. Hyduke, VP Fran. Dev.

The DAIRY QUEEN name has been synonymous with high quality for fifty years. We are known world-wide as the largest retailer of frozen dairy desserts. We continue to develop new products for our licensees - i.e. no-fat frozen yogurt, waffle cone sundaes. Join a system that intends to stay number one!

HISTORY: . . . . IFA
Established in 1940; . . 1st Franchised in 1944
Company-Owned Units (As of 12/1/1989): . .5
Franchised Units (12/1/1989): 5062
Total Units (12/1/1989): 5067
Distribution: . . US-4661;Can-406;Overseas-0
 North America: . . . . 49 States, 8 Provinces
 Concentration: . 802 in TX, 261 in IL,253 MN
Registered: . . . . .All
 . . . .
Average # of Employees: . . . . . 4 FT, 30 PT
Prior Industry Experience: . . . . Helpful

FINANCIAL: NASD-INDOA
Cash Investment: . . . .$
Total Investment: . . . .$
Fees: Franchise - . . . .$
 Royalty: , Advert: . . . .
Contract Periods (Yrs.): . . . .Varies
Area Development Agreement: . .No
Sub-Franchise Contract: . . . . . Yes
Expand in Territory: . . . . Yes
Passive Ownership: . . . . . .Allowed
Encourage Conversions: . . . . . Yes
Franchisee Purchase(s) Required: .No

FRANCHISOR TRAINING/SUPPORT:
Financial Assistance Provided: . . .Yes(D)
Site Selection Assistance: . . . . . . .Yes
Lease Negotiation Assistance: . . . . .No
Co-operative Advertising: . . . . .No
Training: . . . . 2 Wks. Headquarters,
 . . . . .3 Wks. Franchisee's Store
On-Going Support: . . . . B,C,D,E,G,H
Full-Time Franchisor Support Staff: . . . .
EXPANSION PLANS:
 US: . . . . .All US
 Canada - Yes, . . . Overseas - Yes

DEL'S LEMONADE AND REFRESHMENTS

1260 Oaklawn Ave.
Cranston, RI 02920
TEL: (800) 274-DELS (401) 463-6190
FAX: (401) 463-7931
Mr. Joe Padula, VP

All natural, soft frozen lemonade, as well as low-calorie, soft-frozen lemonade, snack foods, pretzels, nacho's, popcorn, pizza, bagel cheddar dogs (i.e. zappers), etc.

HISTORY: . . . .
Established in 1948; . . 1st Franchised in 1962
Company-Owned Units (As of 12/1/1989): . .3
Franchised Units (12/1/1989): 25
Total Units (12/1/1989): 28
Distribution: US-28;Can-0;Overseas-0
 North America: . . . . 8 States
 Concentration: . . . 17 in RI, 2 in MA, 1 in TX
Registered: . . . . . . CA,MD,MN,RI,VA,WI
 . . . .
Average # of Employees: . . . . . . 1 FT, 2 PT
Prior Industry Experience: . . . . Helpful

FINANCIAL:
Cash Investment: $25-30K
Total Investment: $65-100K
Fees: Franchise - $9.5-25K
 Royalty: 6%, Advert: 4%
Contract Periods (Yrs.): 10/5/5
Area Development Agreement: Yes/Var
Sub-Franchise Contract: . . . . . Yes
Expand in Territory: . . . . Yes
Passive Ownership: . . . Discouraged
Encourage Conversions: . . . . . Yes
Franchisee Purchase(s) Required: Yes

FRANCHISOR TRAINING/SUPPORT:
Financial Assistance Provided: . . . . .No
Site Selection Assistance: . . . . .Yes
Lease Negotiation Assistance: . . . .Yes
Co-operative Advertising: . . . . .Yes
Training: . . . . . . Minimum 1 Wk. Head-
 . . . . quarters or Closest Franchise
On-Going Support: . . .A,B,C,D,E,F,G,h,I
Full-Time Franchisor Support Staff: . . . 7
EXPANSION PLANS:
 US: . . . . .All US
 Canada - Yes, . . . Overseas - Yes

DOMINO'S PIZZA

30 Frank Lloyd Wright Dr., Box 997
Ann Arbor, MI 48106
TEL: (313) 668-6055
FAX:
Deborah S. Sargent, Dir. Fran. Serv.

Pizza delivery and carry-out.

HISTORY: . . . . .IFA
Established in 1960; . . 1st Franchised in 1967
Company-Owned Units (As of 12/1/1989): 1400
Franchised Units (12/1/1989): 3593
Total Units (12/1/1989): 4993
Distribution: . US-4663;Can-138;Overseas-192
 North America: . . . . 50 States
 Concentration: .467 in CA, 254 in OH, 285 TX
Registered: . . . . .All
 . . . .
Average # of Employees: . . .1-6 FT, 10-30 PT
Prior Industry Experience: . . . . . .Necessary

FINANCIAL:
Cash Investment: $10-30K
Total Investment: $75-150K
Fees: Franchise - $1-3K
 Royalty: 5.5%, Advert: 3%
Contract Periods (Yrs.): 10/10
Area Development Agreement: . Yes
Sub-Franchise Contract: . . . . . Yes
Expand in Territory: . . . . Yes
Passive Ownership: . . . Not Allowed
Encourage Conversions: . . . . . Yes
Franchisee Purchase(s) Required: Yes

FRANCHISOR TRAINING/SUPPORT:
Financial Assistance Provided: . . . Yes(I)
Site Selection Assistance: . . . . .No
Lease Negotiation Assistance: . . . . .No
Co-operative Advertising: . . . . .Yes
Training: . . . . 4 Days Headquarters
 . . . .
On-Going Support: . . . . a,b,C,D,e,G,H,I
Full-Time Franchisor Support Staff: . . . .
EXPANSION PLANS:
 US: . . . . Not Actively Seeking
 Canada - Yes, ...Overseas - Yes

DRUSILLA SEAFOOD CAFE

8133 Jefferson Hwy.
Baton Rouge, LA 70809
TEL: (504) 927-8844
FAX:
Mr. Frank J. Fresina, EVP Sales

DRUSILLA SEAFOOD CAFE offers a distinctive and delicious seafood menu featuring salads, gumbos, po-boys, dinners and specials. Quick-service dining and carry-out in high-traffic malls with a Louisiana bayou atmosphere. Franchisee becomes a distributor of DRUSILLA SEAFOODS product line of seasonings and spices.

HISTORY: . . . .
Established in 1979; . . 1st Franchised in 1986
Company-Owned Units (As of 12/1/1989): . .4
Franchised Units (12/1/1989): 8
Total Units (12/1/1989): 12
Distribution: US-12;Can-0;Overseas-0
North America: . . . . 4 States
Concentration: . . . 8 in LA, 2 in TX, 1 in AL
Registered: . . . . FL,MD,VA
. . . .
Average # of Employees: . . . . . . 6 FT, 6 PT
Prior Industry Experience: . . . . Helpful

FINANCIAL:
Cash Investment: $123-190K
Total Investment: $123-190K
Fees: Franchise - $35K
  Royalty: 4%, Advert: 3%
Contract Periods (Yrs.): 10/10
Area Development Agreement: Yes/10
Sub-Franchise Contract: . . . . . Yes
Expand in Territory: . . . . Yes
Passive Ownership: . . . . . .Allowed
Encourage Conversions: . . . . . Yes
Franchisee Purchase(s) Required: Yes

FRANCHISOR TRAINING/SUPPORT:
Financial Assistance Provided: . . . Yes(I)
Site Selection Assistance: . . . . . . .Yes
Lease Negotiation Assistance: . . . . .Yes
Co-operative Advertising: . . . . . . .Yes
Training: . . . . 2 Wks. On Location/
. . . . .Home Office
On-Going Support: . . A,B,C,D,E,F,G,H,I
Full-Time Franchisor Support Staff: . . 12
EXPANSION PLANS:
US: . . . . Southwest and Southeast
Canada - No, ...Overseas - No

ENTREES ON-TRAYS

3 Lombardy Terrace
Ft. Worth, TX 76132
TEL: (817) 735-8558
FAX:
Mr. Don Shipe, Owner

A dinner delivery service participating with more than 150 of the finest restaurants in the Ft. Worth-Dallas metroplex. Represented by 4 franchises operated from respective homes, complete with chef-uniformed drivers, mobile radios and special insulated carriers.

HISTORY: . . . .
Established in 1986; . . 1st Franchised in 1988
Company-Owned Units (As of 12/1/1989): . .1
Franchised Units (12/1/1989): 3
Total Units (12/1/1989): 4
Distribution: US-4;Can-0;Overseas-0
North America: . . . . .1 State
Concentration: . . . . 4 in TX
Registered: . . . .
. . . .
Average # of Employees: . . . . .1 PT
Prior Industry Experience: . . . . Helpful

FINANCIAL:
Cash Investment: $12.5K
Total Investment: $17.5K
Fees: Franchise - $10K
  Royalty: 10%, Advert: 0%
Contract Periods (Yrs.): 5/5
Area Development Agreement: Yes/5
Sub-Franchise Contract: . . . . .No
Expand in Territory: . . . . . . .No
Passive Ownership: . . . Not Allowed
Encourage Conversions: . . . . .No
Franchisee Purchase(s) Required: .No

FRANCHISOR TRAINING/SUPPORT:
Financial Assistance Provided: . . . . .No
Site Selection Assistance: . . . . .NA
Lease Negotiation Assistance: . . . . .NA
Co-operative Advertising: . . . . .No
Training: . . . . . . 1-2 Days Headquarters,
. . . 1-2 days Site at Franchisee Expense
On-Going Support: . . . . A,B,C,D,G,H,I
Full-Time Franchisor Support Staff: . . . .
EXPANSION PLANS:
US: . . . . Southwest
Canada - No, ...Overseas - No

EVERYTHING YOGURT/BANANAS

304 Port Richmond Ave.
Staten Island, NY 10302
TEL: (718) 816-7800
FAX:
Ms. Lois Nicotra, VP

EVERYTHING YOGURT offers more than just yogurt. We also feature cold pasta salads, quiche, pita sandwiches. Our tandem unit, "BANANAS," features frosty fruit shakes and fresh fruit cups. This concept adds to sales, not overhead. Our services include architectural drawings and specifications for equipment, training and overall operational support.

HISTORY: . . . . IFA
Established in 1976; . . 1st Franchised in 1981
Company-Owned Units (As of 12/1/1989): . .6
Franchised Units (12/1/1989): 262
Total Units (12/1/1989): 268
Distribution: US-268;Can-0;Overseas-0
North America: . . . . 30 States
Concentration: . .60 in NY, 28 in NJ, 19 in CA
Registered: . . . CA,FL,IL,IN,MD,MI,MN,NY
. . . . RI,VA,WA,WI
Average # of Employees: . . . . . .2 FT, 15 PT
Prior Industry Experience: . . . . Helpful

FINANCIAL:
Cash Investment: $56K
Total Investment: $200-225K
Fees: Franchise - $30K
  Royalty: 5%, Advert: 1%
Contract Periods (Yrs.): 10/10
Area Development Agreement: Yes/10
Sub-Franchise Contract: . . . . .No
Expand in Territory: . . . . Yes
Passive Ownership: . . . Discouraged
Encourage Conversions: . . . . . Yes
Franchisee Purchase(s) Required: .No

FRANCHISOR TRAINING/SUPPORT:
Financial Assistance Provided: . . . Yes(I)
Site Selection Assistance: . . . . . . .Yes
Lease Negotiation Assistance: . . . . .Yes
Co-operative Advertising: . . . . . . .Yes
Training: . . . . 1 Wk. Heradquarters,
. . . . 1 Wk. Site, On-going
On-Going Support: . . . . B,C,D,E,F,G,H
Full-Time Franchisor Support Staff: . . 33
EXPANSION PLANS:
US: . . . . All US
Canada - Yes, . . . Overseas - Yes

FAJITA JUNCTION

9801 McCullough
San Antonio, TX 78216
TEL: (512) 340-8989
FAX:
Mr. Gerry Telle, President

A multi-unit, fast-food Mexican restaurant that offers a quality product with its trademark product being beef and chicken fajitas. The philosophy or system established provides quality product on a consistent basis. It's back to the basics - quality food, speed of service, friendliness of employees and cleanliness of stores.

HISTORY: . . . .
Established in 1986; . . 1st Franchised in 1987
Company-Owned Units (As of 12/1/1989): . 41
Franchised Units (12/1/1989): 8
Total Units (12/1/1989): 49
Distribution: US-49;Can-0;Overseas-0
North America: . . . . 3 States
Concentration: . . . . 41 in CA, 5 in CA
Registered: . . . . CA,IL

. . . .
Average # of Employees: . . . . 40 FT
Prior Industry Experience: . . . . . .Necessary

FINANCIAL:
Cash Investment: $175-280K
Total Investment: $1.5-2.5MM
Fees: Franchise - $17.5K
Royalty: 4%, Advert: 4%
Contract Periods (Yrs.): 20
Area Development Agreement: Yes/20
Sub-Franchise Contract: . . . . . .No
Expand in Territory: . . . . Yes
Passive Ownership: . . . . . .Allowed
Encourage Conversions: . . . . . Yes
Franchisee Purchase(s) Required: .No

FRANCHISOR TRAINING/SUPPORT:
Financial Assistance Provided: . . . . . No
Site Selection Assistance: . . . . No
Lease Negotiation Assistance: . . . . . No
Co-operative Advertising: . . . . .NA
Training: . . . . 6 Wks. Headquarters
. . . .
On-Going Support: . . . .B,C,D,E,F,G,H,I
Full-Time Franchisor Support Staff: . . 25
EXPANSION PLANS:
US: . . . . .All US
Canada - Yes, . . . Overseas - Yes

FLOOKYS HOT DOGS

7921 Canoga Ave., # A
Canoga Park, CA 91304
TEL: (818) 992-3422 C
FAX:
Mr. Stan Houston, VP Sales

FLOOKY'S is the all-American hot dog, burger, family-oriented restaurant. The meals are easy to make, low cost, small square footage and small number of employees - giving you big, big profit potential. Mainly in California. $30,000 cash can get you started in business today.

HISTORY: . . . .
Established in 1927; . . 1st Franchised in 1983
Company-Owned Units (As of 12/1/1989): . .0
Franchised Units (12/1/1989): 5
Total Units (12/1/1989): 5
Distribution: US-5;Can-0;Overseas-0
North America: . . . . .1 State
Concentration: . . . . 5 in CA
Registered: . . . . CA

. . . .
Average # of Employees: . . . . . . 4 FT, 2 PT
Prior Industry Experience: . . . . Helpful

FINANCIAL:
Cash Investment: . . . . $30K+
Total Investment: $50-142K
Fees: Franchise - $7.5-25K
Royalty: 5%, Advert: 3%
Contract Periods (Yrs.): 15/10
Area Development Agreement: Yes/15
Sub-Franchise Contract: . . . . . Yes
Expand in Territory: . . . . Yes
Passive Ownership: . . . Discouraged
Encourage Conversions: . . . . . Yes
Franchisee Purchase(s) Required: .No

FRANCHISOR TRAINING/SUPPORT:
Financial Assistance Provided: . . . Yes(I)
Site Selection Assistance: . . . . .Yes
Lease Negotiation Assistance: . . . . .Yes
Co-operative Advertising: . . . . .Yes
Training: . . . . . 2-4 Wks. Headquarters or
. . . . .Closest Store
On-Going Support: . . . . . C,D,E,F,G,H,I
Full-Time Franchisor Support Staff: . . . 4
EXPANSION PLANS:
US: . . . . Western Region Only
Canada - No, ...Overseas - No

FOSTERS FREEZE

1052 Grand Ave., # C, P.O. Box 266
Arroyo Grande, CA 93421
TEL: (800) 628-5600 (805) 481-9577
FAX: (805) 481-3791
Mr. Dennis Poletti, Fran. Devel.

FOSTERS FREEZE is a quick-service restaurant with drive-thru and take-out service. This 44-year old, California-based franchise chain features a quality menu with full fountain service with made-to-order shakes, sundaes, cones, hamburgers, hot dogs and specialty sandwiches.

HISTORY: . . . . IFA
Established in 1946; . . 1st Franchised in 1948
Company-Owned Units (As of 12/1/1989): . .3
Franchised Units (12/1/1989): 176
Total Units (12/1/1989): 179
Distribution: US-177;Can-0;Overseas-2
North America: . . . . 2 States
Concentration: . . . . . . 175 in CA, 2 in AZ
Registered: . . . . CA

. . . .
Average # of Employees: . . . . 25 FT
Prior Industry Experience: . . . . Helpful

FINANCIAL:
Cash Investment: $150K
Total Investment: $600K
Fees: Franchise - $40K
Royalty: 4%, Advert: 3%
Contract Periods (Yrs.): 20/20
Area Development Agreement: . .No
Sub-Franchise Contract: . . . . . .No
Expand in Territory: . . . . .No
Passive Ownership: . . . Discouraged
Encourage Conversions: . . . . . .No
Franchisee Purchase(s) Required: Yes

FRANCHISOR TRAINING/SUPPORT:
Financial Assistance Provided: . . . Yes(I)
Site Selection Assistance: . . . . .Yes
Lease Negotiation Assistance: . . . . .Yes
Co-operative Advertising: . . . . .Yes
Training: . . . . . 8 Wks. Santa Clarita, CA
. . . .
On-Going Support: . . A,B,C,D,E,F,G,H,I
Full-Time Franchisor Support Staff: . . 12
EXPANSION PLANS:
US: . . . . .AZ, NV and CA
Canada - No, ... Overseas - Yes

FOUR STAR PIZZA

P. O. Box 1370
Washington, PA 15301
TEL: (800) 477-STAR (412) 228-6040
FAX: (412) 228-6051
Ms. Susan Anderson, Mktg./PR Rep.

FOUR STAR PIZZA'S commitment to quality, evident in the fresh, wholesome ingredients used in our pizza and specialty sandwiches, as well as our outstanding national average delivery time of 18 minutes, carries over into the franchise program. Through the franchise program at FOUR STAR PIZZA, you can experience the satisfaction of operating your own business, while having access to the services and support of an experienced and progressive franchisor.

HISTORY: . . . . IFA
Established in 1981; . . 1st Franchised in 1985
Company-Owned Units (As of 12/1/1989): . .0
Franchised Units (12/1/1989): 90
Total Units (12/1/1989): 90
Distribution: US-83;Can-0;Overseas-7
North America: . . . . 10 States
Concentration: . . 40 in PA, 8 in MD, 6 in OH
Registered: . . . . CA,FL,HI,MD,VA

Average # of Employees: . . . . . 5-7 FT,10 PT
Prior Industry Experience: . . . . . . Helpful

FINANCIAL: NASD-CUTC
Cash Investment: $28-35K
Total Investment: $65-165K
Fees: Franchise - $9K
Royalty: 5%, Advert: 1%
Contract Periods (Yrs.): 10/10
Area Development Agreement: . Yes
Sub-Franchise Contract: . . . . Yes
Expand in Territory: . . . . . . Yes
Passive Ownership: . . . Discouraged
Encourage Conversions: . . . . Yes
Franchisee Purchase(s) Required: Yes

FRANCHISOR TRAINING/SUPPORT:
Financial Assistance Provided: . . . Yes(I)
Site Selection Assistance: . . . . . . .Yes
Lease Negotiation Assistance: . . . . .Yes
Co-operative Advertising: . . . . . . .Yes
Training: . . . . 2 Wks. Headquarters,
. . . . .100 Hours in Field
On-Going Support: . . . . B,C,D,E,F,G,H
Full-Time Franchisor Support Staff: . . 10
EXPANSION PLANS:
US: . . . . .All US
Canada - No, ... Overseas - Yes

FOX'S PIZZA DEN

3243 Old Frankstown Rd.
Pittsburgh, PA 15239
TEL: (412) 733-7888
FAX:
Mr. James Fox, President

FOX'S PIZZA DEN believes in the philosophy . . . You earned it, you keep it! No percentage charged. FOX's gives you a pizza franchise, a sandwich franchise and wedgie franchise - all for one low price. FOX's truely gives you the opportunity to be your own boss.

HISTORY: . . . .
Established in 1971; . . 1st Franchised in 1974
Company-Owned Units (As of 12/1/1989): . .0
Franchised Units (12/1/1989): 118
Total Units (12/1/1989): 118
Distribution: US-118;Can-0;Overseas-0
North America: . . . . 5 States
Concentration: . 84 in PA, 11 in MD, 10 in WV
Registered: . . . . MD,VA

Average # of Employees: . . . . . . 2 FT, 8 PT
Prior Industry Experience: . . . . . . Helpful

FINANCIAL:
Cash Investment: $40-60K
Total Investment: $10-20K
Fees: Franchise - $8K
Royalty: $200/Mo., Advert: . . 0%
Contract Periods (Yrs.): 5/5
Area Development Agreement: Yes/3
Sub-Franchise Contract: . . . . Yes
Expand in Territory: . . . . . . Yes
Passive Ownership: . . . Discouraged
Encourage Conversions: . . . . Yes
Franchisee Purchase(s) Required: Yes

FRANCHISOR TRAINING/SUPPORT:
Financial Assistance Provided: . . . Yes(I)
Site Selection Assistance: . . . . . . .Yes
Lease Negotiation Assistance: . . . .Yes
Co-operative Advertising: . . . . . . .Yes
Training: . . . . 10 Days on Site
On-Going Support: . . . .B,C,D,E,F,G,H,I
Full-Time Franchisor Support Staff: . . .5
EXPANSION PLANS:
US: . . . . Northeast
Canada - No, ...Overseas - No

GIFF'S SUB SHOP

634 NE Eglin Pkwy.
Ft. Walton Beach, FL 32548
TEL: (904) 863-9011
FAX:
Mr. Rick Arnette, Dir. of Operations

GIFF'S SUB SHOP is an opportunity to take a proven method, work hard and make a good living. We feature over 30 subs, specializing in steaksubs with our world famous "Fighter Pilot" sub. We believe that good food, prepared to the customer's taste, at a good price, will be successful.

HISTORY: . . . .
Established in 1977; . . 1st Franchised in 1979
Company-Owned Units (As of 12/1/1989): . .1
Franchised Units (12/1/1989): 11
Total Units (12/1/1989): 12
Distribution: US-12;Can-0;Overseas-0
North America: . . . . 1 State
Concentration: . . . . .12 in FL
Registered: . . . . .FL

Average # of Employees: . . . . . . 2 FT, 1 PT
Prior Industry Experience: . . . . . . Helpful

FINANCIAL:
Cash Investment: $25-30K
Total Investment: $25-30K
Fees: Franchise - $10.5K
Royalty: 4%, Advert: 2%
Contract Periods (Yrs.): 10/10
Area Development Agreement: Yes/10
Sub-Franchise Contract: . . . . . .No
Expand in Territory: . . . . . . Yes
Passive Ownership: . . . Discouraged
Encourage Conversions: . . . . . .No
Franchisee Purchase(s) Required: .No

FRANCHISOR TRAINING/SUPPORT:
Financial Assistance Provided: . . .Yes(D)
Site Selection Assistance: . . . . . . .Yes
Lease Negotiation Assistance: . . . .Yes
Co-operative Advertising: . . . . . . .Yes
Training: . . . . 1 Wk. Home Office
On-Going Support: . . . . . C,D,E,F,G,I
Full-Time Franchisor Support Staff: . . .3
EXPANSION PLANS:
US: . . . . .Southeast and South
Canada - No, ...Overseas - No

GODFATHER'S PIZZA

9140 W. Dodge Rd.
Omaha, NE 68114
TEL: (800) 456-8347 (402) 391-1452
FAX: (402) 392-2357
Mr. Bruce Cannon, Dir. Fran. Devel.

GODFATHER'S PIZZA is consistently recognized by consumers and independent research as having a superior quality product. Couple this with consistent operations, innovative new products, attention to service and full support services and GODFATHER'S PIZZA is positioned to retain its reputation for high quality and service.

HISTORY: . . . .
Established in 1973; . . 1st Franchised in 1974
Company-Owned Units (As of 12/1/1989): 171
Franchised Units (12/1/1989): 340
Total Units (12/1/1989): 511
Distribution: US-508;Can-3;Overseas-0
North America: . . . . 39 States
Concentration: . 72 in WA, 47 in IA, 45 in MN
Registered: . . . HI,IL,MD,MI,MN,ND,SD,WI
. . . .
Average # of Employees: . . . 6-8 FT, 12-20 PT
Prior Industry Experience: . . . . . . Helpful

FINANCIAL:
Cash Investment: $55-120K
Total Investment: $72-291K
Fees: Franchise - $7.5-15K
  Royalty: 5%, Advert: 0%
Contract Periods (Yrs.): 15/10
Area Development Agreement: Yes/1-5
Sub-Franchise Contract: . . . . . .No
Expand in Territory: . . . . Yes
Passive Ownership: . . . Discouraged
Encourage Conversions: . . . . . Yes
Franchisee Purchase(s) Required: .No

FRANCHISOR TRAINING/SUPPORT:
Financial Assistance Provided: . . . . . No
Site Selection Assistance: . . . . .Yes
Lease Negotiation Assistance: . . . . . .No
Co-operative Advertising: . . . . .Yes
Training: . . . . . 4-5 Wks. Training Center
. . . .
On-Going Support: . . . . .C,D,E,F,G,H,I
Full-Time Franchisor Support Staff: . . 20
EXPANSION PLANS:
US: . . . . .All US
Canada - No, ...Overseas - No

GOLDEN FRIED CHICKEN

4835 LBJ Freeway, # 525
Dallas, TX 75244
TEL: (214) 458-9555 C
FAX:
Mr. Mark Parmerlee, President

GOLDEN FRIED CHICKEN is a fast-food fried chicken restaurant, offering indoor dining, drive-thru and carry-out service. GFC's menu consists of fresh Golden Fried Chicken, Golden Tenders, country-style biscuits, gravy, french fries, cole-slaw, mashed potatoes, corn on the cob and fountain soft drinks.

HISTORY: . . . . IFA
Established in 1967; . . 1st Franchised in 1972
Company-Owned Units (As of 12/1/1989): . .3
Franchised Units (12/1/1989): 69
Total Units (12/1/1989): 72
Distribution: US-72;Can-0;Overseas-0
North America: . . . . 3 States
Concentration: . . .68 in TX, 3 in OK, 1 in AR
Registered: . . . .
. . . .
Average # of Employees: . . . . . 3 FT, 6-8 PT
Prior Industry Experience: . . . . . . Helpful

FINANCIAL:
Cash Investment: $25-50K
Total Investment: $280-500K
Fees: Franchise - $10K
  Royalty: 4%, Advert: 25%
Contract Periods (Yrs.): 20/0
Area Development Agreement: Yes/Var
Sub-Franchise Contract: . . . . . .No
Expand in Territory: . . . . Yes
Passive Ownership: . . . Discouraged
Encourage Conversions: . . . . . Yes
Franchisee Purchase(s) Required: .No

FRANCHISOR TRAINING/SUPPORT:
Financial Assistance Provided: . . . . . No
Site Selection Assistance: . . . . .Yes
Lease Negotiation Assistance: . . . . .Yes
Co-operative Advertising: . . . . .Yes
Training: . . . . .1 Wk. In Store
. . . .
On-Going Support: . . . . . B,C,D,E,G,H
Full-Time Franchisor Support Staff: . . . 8
EXPANSION PLANS:
US: . . . . Southwest
Canada - No, ...Overseas - No

GOURMET'S QUICHE BY THE PIECE

201 - 1252 Burrard St.
Vancouver, BC V6Z1Z6 CAN
TEL: (604) 687-2900
FAX:
Mr. Donald Burdeny, President

Quiche baked in a large pan. Minimum of 7 varieties. Sold by the piece or whole! Locations readily available. No competition. Master franchises only available.

HISTORY: . . . .
Established in 1985; . . 1st Franchised in 1989
Company-Owned Units (As of 12/1/1989): . .1
Franchised Units (12/1/1989): 0
Total Units (12/1/1989): 1
Distribution: US-0;Can-1;Overseas-0
North America: . . . . .1 Province
Concentration: . . . . 1 in BC
Registered: . . . .
. . . .
Average # of Employees: . . . . .2 FT
Prior Industry Experience: . . . . . . Helpful

FINANCIAL:
Cash Investment: . . . . $35+K
Total Investment: $20K
Fees: Franchise - $15K
  Royalty: 6%, Advert: 5%
Contract Periods (Yrs.): 3/3
Area Development Agreement: Yes/3
Sub-Franchise Contract: . . . . Yes
Expand in Territory: . . . . . . .No
Passive Ownership: . . . Discouraged
Encourage Conversions: . . . . Yes
Franchisee Purchase(s) Required: .No

FRANCHISOR TRAINING/SUPPORT:
Financial Assistance Provided: . . . . . No
Site Selection Assistance: . . . . .Yes
Lease Negotiation Assistance: . . . .Yes
Co-operative Advertising: . . . . .Yes
Training: . . . . Headquarters
. . . .
On-Going Support: . . .a,B,C,D,E,F,G,H,I
Full-Time Franchisor Support Staff: . . . 2
EXPANSION PLANS:
US: . . . . Master Franchises Only
Canada - Yes, . . . Overseas - Yes

GRAND JUNCTION HAMBURGER STATION
771 Corporate Dr., # 400
Lexington, KY 40503
TEL: (606) 223-2541
FAX:
Mr. James Hoff, Fran. Dir.

GRAND JUNCTION HAMBURGER STATIONS offer both the consumer and franchise investor a system of fast food at affordable prices. The small, double-drive thru facilities require low investment for land, building and up-keep, thereby allowing the consumer to enjoy quality fast food at prices approximately 25% less that those of major franchisors. Limited menu.

HISTORY: . . . .
Established in 1984; . . 1st Franchised in 1987
Company-Owned Units (As of 12/1/1989): . .9
Franchised Units (12/1/1989): 24
Total Units (12/1/1989): 33
Distribution: US-33;Can-0;Overseas-0
North America: . . . . 5 States
Concentration: . . .14 in KY, 4 in OH, 2 in SC
Registered: . . . . FL,IL,IN
. . . .
Average # of Employees: . . . . . 10 FT, 15 PT
Prior Industry Experience: . . . . Helpful

FINANCIAL:
Cash Investment: $60-150K
Total Investment: $210-295K
Fees: Franchise - $20K
Royalty: 4%, Advert: 4%
Contract Periods (Yrs.): 15/5/5
Area Development Agreement: Yes/5
Sub-Franchise Contract: . . . . .No
Expand in Territory: . . . . . . Yes
Passive Ownership: . . . Discouraged
Encourage Conversions: . . . . .No
Franchisee Purchase(s) Required: .No

FRANCHISOR TRAINING/SUPPORT:
Financial Assistance Provided: . . . . .No
Site Selection Assistance: . . . . . . .Yes
Lease Negotiation Assistance: . . . . .Yes
Co-operative Advertising: . . . . . . .Yes
Training: . . . . 3 Wks. Headquarters
. . . .
On-Going Support: . . . . . .C,D,E,F,G,H
Full-Time Franchisor Support Staff: . . .6
EXPANSION PLANS:
US: . . . . Southeast
Canada - No, ...Overseas - No

GREAT GRUNTS

8545 Lookout Mtn.
Los Angeles, CA 90046
TEL: (213) 654-2189
FAX: (213) 654-4444
Mr. Kurt T. Antonius, President

GREAT GRUNTS prides itself on offering excellent food, served in attractive surroundings, at resonable prices. By using the state-of-the-art technology in convection cooking and portion control, we are able to minimize the investment in capital, significantly reduce preparation time, and serve a consistently great meal.

HISTORY: . . . .
Established in 1981; . . 1st Franchised in 1981
Company-Owned Units (As of 12/1/1989): . .2
Franchised Units (12/1/1989): 4
Total Units (12/1/1989): 6
Distribution: US-6;Can-0;Overseas-0
North America: . . . . .2 States
Concentration: . . . . 3 in CA, 3 in WA
Registered: . . . . CA,WA
. . . .
Average # of Employees: . . . . . . 2 FT, 4 PT
Prior Industry Experience: . . . . Helpful

FINANCIAL:
Cash Investment: $30K
Total Investment: $185K
Fees: Franchise - $15K
Royalty: 5%, Advert: 3%
Contract Periods (Yrs.): 10/5
Area Development Agreement: . .No
Sub-Franchise Contract: . . . . .No
Expand in Territory: . . . . . . Yes
Passive Ownership: . . . . . .Allowed
Encourage Conversions: . . . . Yes
Franchisee Purchase(s) Required: Yes

FRANCHISOR TRAINING/SUPPORT:
Financial Assistance Provided: . . . Yes(I)
Site Selection Assistance: . . . . . . .Yes
Lease Negotiation Assistance: . . . . .Yes
Co-operative Advertising: . . . . . . .Yes
Training: . . . . 3 Wks. Headquarters
. . . . 2 Wks. Site, On-going
On-Going Support: . . .a,B,C,D,E,F,G,H,I
Full-Time Franchisor Support Staff: . . .6
EXPANSION PLANS:
US: . . . . West Coast Only
Canada - Yes, ...Overseas - No

GRINNER'S /
GRECO PIZZA DONAIR
105 Walker St., P. O. Box 1040
Truro, NS B2N5G9 CAN
TEL: (800) 565-4389 (902) 893-4141
FAX: (902) 895-7635
Mr. Chris Robertson, General Manager

Atlantic Canada's largest home-delivery pizza chain.

HISTORY: . . . . .CFA
Established in 1977; . . 1st Franchised in 1977
Company-Owned Units (As of 12/1/1989): . .0
Franchised Units (12/1/1989): 50
Total Units (12/1/1989): 50
Distribution: US-0;Can-50;Overseas-0
North America: . . . . 4 Provinces
Concentration: . . 23 in NS, 19 in NB, 5 in NF
Registered: . . . .
. . . .
Average # of Employees: . . . . . .5 FT, 15 PT
Prior Industry Experience: . . . . Helpful

FINANCIAL:
Cash Investment: $35K
Total Investment: $130K
Fees: Franchise - $15K
Royalty: 5%, Advert: 3%
Contract Periods (Yrs.): 10/5
Area Development Agreement: . .No
Sub-Franchise Contract: . . . . .No
Expand in Territory: . . . . . . Yes
Passive Ownership: . . . Discouraged
Encourage Conversions: . . . . Yes
Franchisee Purchase(s) Required: Yes

FRANCHISOR TRAINING/SUPPORT:
Financial Assistance Provided: . . . Yes(I)
Site Selection Assistance: . . . . . . .Yes
Lease Negotiation Assistance: . . . . .Yes
Co-operative Advertising: . . . . . . .Yes
Training: . . . . . 3 Wks. Correspondence,
. . . .3 Wks. Oper. Unit, 3 Wks. On-site
On-Going Support: . . .a,B,C,D,E,F,G,H,I
Full-Time Franchisor Support Staff: . . 20
EXPANSION PLANS:
US: . . . . .No
Canada - Yes, ...Overseas - No

HAPPY JOE'S PIZZA AND ICE CREAM PARLOR

2705 Commerce Dr.
Bettendorf, IA 52722
TEL: (319) 332-8811
FAX: (319) 332-5822
Mr. Larry Whitty, Fran. Dir.

Pizza and ice cream in a fun, family atmosphere. Special program for birthdays. Very involved with special programs for youth in the community. Diversified pizza, pasta, sandwiches, salad bar and ice cream menu, candy, soft drinks and beer.

HISTORY: . . . .
Established in 1972; . . 1st Franchised in 1972
Company-Owned Units (As of 12/1/1989): . 17
Franchised Units (12/1/1989): 65
Total Units (12/1/1989): 82
Distribution: US-82;Can-0;Overseas-0
North America: . . . . 7 States
Concentration: . . 41 in IA, 15 in IL, 10 in WI
Registered: . . . . IL,WI
. . . .
Average # of Employees: . . . . 31 FT
Prior Industry Experience: . . . . Helpful

FINANCIAL:
Cash Investment: . . . . $75K+
Total Investment: . . . . $160K+
Fees: Franchise - $10K
Royalty: 6%, Advert: 3%
Contract Periods (Yrs.): 15/10
Area Development Agreement: Yes/15
Sub-Franchise Contract: . . . . . .No
Expand in Territory: . . . . Yes
Passive Ownership: . . . Discouraged
Encourage Conversions: . . . . . Yes
Franchisee Purchase(s) Required: .No

FRANCHISOR TRAINING/SUPPORT:
Financial Assistance Provided: . . . . .No
Site Selection Assistance: . . . . . . .Yes
Lease Negotiation Assistance: . . . . .Yes
Co-operative Advertising: . . . . .Yes
Training: . . . . 6 Wks. Headquarters
. . . .
On-Going Support: . . A,B,C,D,E,F,G,H,I
Full-Time Franchisor Support Staff: . . 31
EXPANSION PLANS:
US: . . . . Midwest
Canada - No, ...Overseas - No

HARDEE'S FOOD SYSTEMS

1233 Hardee's Blvd.
Rocky Mount, NC 27802
TEL: (919) 977-2000
FAX:
Mr. Roger Attanas, Natl. Dir. Sales

HARDEE'S FOOD SYSTEMS is among the world's leading hamburger chains in terms of store count and average store volumes. Our principle objective is to be a consumer-driven company. Our plan is to be the best, not the biggest restaurant chain. We will do this by providing customers with a superior eating experience each time they stop at HARDEE'S.

HISTORY: . . . . IFA
Established in 1960; . . 1st Franchised in 1962
Company-Owned Units (As of 12/1/1989): 1018
Franchised Units (12/1/1989): 2222
Total Units (12/1/1989): 3240
Distribution: . . . US-3206;Can-0;Overseas-34
North America: . . . . 38 States
Concentration: . 336 in NC, 219 in GA, 193 IL
Registered: . . . FL,HI,IL,IN,MD,MI,MN,NY
. . . . ND,RI,SD,VA,WI
Average # of Employees: . . . . 3 FT, 25-50 PT
Prior Industry Experience: . . . . Helpful

FINANCIAL: TOR-IMASCO
Cash Investment: . . . . $.15-1.4MM
Total Investment: . . . . . $.7-1.6MM
Fees: Franchise - $15K
Royalty: 3.5+%, Advert: 5%
Contract Periods (Yrs.): 20/5/5
Area Development Agreement: Yes/Var
Sub-Franchise Contract: . . . . . .No
Expand in Territory: . . . . Yes
Passive Ownership: . . . Not Allowed
Encourage Conversions: . . . . . Yes
Franchisee Purchase(s) Required: Yes

FRANCHISOR TRAINING/SUPPORT:
Financial Assistance Provided: . . . Yes(I)
Site Selection Assistance: . . . . . . .Yes
Lease Negotiation Assistance: . . . . . No
Co-operative Advertising: . . . . .Yes
Training: . . . . . . 4 Wks. Field Training,
. . . . On-going
On-Going Support: . . . .B,C,D,E,F,G,H,I
Full-Time Franchisor Support Staff: . . . .
EXPANSION PLANS:
US: . . . . All Exc. Northeast, West
Canada - No, ... Overseas - Yes

HARTZ CHICKEN

14409 Cornerstone Village Dr.
Houston, TX 77014
TEL: (713) 583-0020
FAX: (713) 580-3752
Mr. Steve Jaspersen, VP Franchising

Initially, HARTZ CHICKEN was take-out/quick-service, and within the last 5 years has evolved into not only quick-service/take-out, but an all-you-can-eat buffet, featuring not only our mainstay Krispy Chicken, but also mesquite roasted chicken and over a dozen steamed vegetables, along with made-from-scratch yeast rolls.

HISTORY: . . . .
Established in 1972; . . 1st Franchised in 1975
Company-Owned Units (As of 12/1/1989): . 14
Franchised Units (12/1/1989): 37
Total Units (12/1/1989): 51
Distribution: US-51;Can-0;Overseas-0
North America: . . . . 4 States
Concentration: . . .46 in TX, 2 in AL, 2 in MS
Registered: . . . .
. . . .
Average # of Employees: . . .5-7 FT, 10-15 PT
Prior Industry Experience: . . . . Helpful

FINANCIAL:
Cash Investment: $100-200K
Total Investment: $380-420K
Fees: Franchise - $10K
Royalty: 4%, Advert: 0-2%
Contract Periods (Yrs.): . . 10/10/10
Area Development Agreement: Yes/10
Sub-Franchise Contract: . . . . . Yes
Expand in Territory: . . . . Yes
Passive Ownership: . . . Not Allowed
Encourage Conversions: . . . . . Yes
Franchisee Purchase(s) Required: .No

FRANCHISOR TRAINING/SUPPORT:
Financial Assistance Provided: . . . . .No
Site Selection Assistance: . . . . . . .Yes
Lease Negotiation Assistance: . . . . . No
Co-operative Advertising: . . . . .Yes
Training: . . . . . . .2 Wks. Company Store,
. 1 Wk. HQ, 2 Wks. Co-Store, On-Going
On-Going Support: . . . . . .C,D,E,G,H,I
Full-Time Franchisor Support Staff: . . 15
EXPANSION PLANS:
US: . . . . . Currently TX and Bordering
Canada - No, ...Overseas - No

HEAVENLY HOT DOGS

2804 Del Prado Blvd.
Cape Coral, FL 33904
TEL: (800) 476-8221 (813) 945-2300
FAX: (813) 945-2631
Franchising Department

Retail sale of Vienna and Chicago-style hot dogs and related products. Stores and mobile units are specially designed to be owned, operated by and/or employ the physically challenged.

HISTORY: . . . . IFA	FINANCIAL: OTC	FRANCHISOR TRAINING/SUPPORT:
Established in 1987; . . 1st Franchised in 1989	Cash Investment: . . . . $20K+	Financial Assistance Provided: . . . . . No
Company-Owned Units (As of 12/1/1989): . .3	Total Investment: $55-175K	Site Selection Assistance: . . . . .Yes
Franchised Units (12/1/1989): 1	Fees: Franchise - $6K	Lease Negotiation Assistance: . . . . .Yes
Total Units (12/1/1989): 4	Royalty: 6%, Advert: 3%	Co-operative Advertising: . . . . .Yes
Distribution: US-4;Can-0;Overseas-0	Contract Periods (Yrs.): 10/5	Training: . . . . 2 Wks. Headquarters/
North America: . . . . 2 States	Area Development Agreement: Yes/10	. . . . Company Store
Concentration: . . . . 3 in FL, 1 in CO	Sub-Franchise Contract: . . . . . Yes	On-Going Support: . . . . c,d,E,f,h
Registered: . . . . .CA,FL,IL,MI,NY	Expand in Territory: . . . . Yes	Full-Time Franchisor Support Staff: . . .6
	Passive Ownership: . . . Discouraged	EXPANSION PLANS:
. . . .	Encourage Conversions: . . . . . Yes	US: . . . . . . Sunbelt, IL, MI, Northeast
Average # of Employees:	Franchisee Purchase(s) Required: Yes	Canada - No, ...Overseas - No
Prior Industry Experience: . . . . Helpful		

HOP TOO'S

3500 Gateway Dr., # 201
Pompano Beach, FL 33069
TEL: (305) 968-4300
FAX:
Mr. Joseph P. Piazza, EVP

Take-out and delivery of Great Chinese Food, freshly prepared to order, then conveniently delivered to the home or workplace. HOP TOO'S uses only fresh vegetables, high-quality meats and flavorful sauces, with never a hint of MSG.

HISTORY:	FINANCIAL:	FRANCHISOR TRAINING/SUPPORT:
Established in 1987; . . 1st Franchised in 1988	Cash Investment: $40-125K	Financial Assistance Provided: . . . . . No
Company-Owned Units (As of 12/1/1989): . .1	Total Investment: $100-125K	Site Selection Assistance: . . . . .Yes
Franchised Units (12/1/1989): 9	Fees: Franchise - $25K	Lease Negotiation Assistance: . . . . .Yes
Total Units (12/1/1989): 10	Royalty: 5%, Advert: 5%	Co-operative Advertising: . . . . .Yes
Distribution: US-10;Can-0;Overseas-0	Contract Periods (Yrs.): 10/10	Training: . . . . 4 Wks. Headquarters
North America: . . . . 2 States	Area Development Agreement: Yes/10	. . . .
Concentration: . . . . 7 in FL, 3 in MA	Sub-Franchise Contract: . . . . . .No	On-Going Support: . . . .B,C,D,E,F,G,H,I
Registered: . . . . .FL	Expand in Territory: . . . . Yes	Full-Time Franchisor Support Staff: . . 10
	Passive Ownership: . . . Discouraged	EXPANSION PLANS:
. . . .	Encourage Conversions: . . . . . Yes	US: . . . . .Northeast and Southeast
Average # of Employees: . . . . . 10 FT, 10 PT	Franchisee Purchase(s) Required: Yes	Canada - Yes, ...Overseas - No
Prior Industry Experience: . . . . Helpful		

HUBB'S PUB

P.O. Box 150279
Altamonte, FL 32715
TEL: (407) 260-5190
FAX:
Mr. Dave Ungar, VP

Largest selection of draft beers in the world - 31; colossal sandwiches; a place you always meet a "friend."

HISTORY:	FINANCIAL:	FRANCHISOR TRAINING/SUPPORT:
Established in 1982; . . 1st Franchised in 1986	Cash Investment: $75K	Financial Assistance Provided: . . .Yes(D)
Company-Owned Units (As of 12/1/1989): . .2	Total Investment: $200K	Site Selection Assistance: . . . . .Yes
Franchised Units (12/1/1989): 2	Fees: Franchise - $25K	Lease Negotiation Assistance: . . . . .Yes
Total Units (12/1/1989): 4	Royalty: 0%, Advert: 0%	Co-operative Advertising: . . . . .Yes
Distribution: US-4;Can-0;Overseas-0	Contract Periods (Yrs.): 20/20	Training: . . . . 6 Wks. Headquarters
North America: . . . . .1 State	Area Development Agreement: Yes/10	. . . .
Concentration: . . . . 4 in FL	Sub-Franchise Contract: . . . . . .No	On-Going Support: . . . a,b,C,D,E,F,G,H,I
Registered: . . . . .FL	Expand in Territory: . . . . Yes	Full-Time Franchisor Support Staff: . . .5
	Passive Ownership: . . . . . .Allowed	EXPANSION PLANS:
. . . .	Encourage Conversions: . . . . .No	US: . . . . .All US
Average # of Employees: . . . . . .4 FT, 10 PT	Franchisee Purchase(s) Required: .No	Canada - No, ... Overseas - Yes
Prior Industry Experience: . . . . Helpful		

HUNGRY HOWIE'S PIZZA & SUBS

35301 Schoolcraft Rd.
Livonia, MI 48150
TEL: (313) 422-1717
FAX: (313) 427-2713
Mr. Albert T. Abdou, Dir. Fran. Dev.

HUNGRY HOWIE'S offers 8 varieties of their unique Flavored Crust pizza, plus subs and salads. Our stores are designed for fast, efficient carry-out and delivery service. Franchise owners also have the advantage of HUNGRY HOWIE'S commissary. America's 12th largest pizza franchise.

HISTORY: . . . .
Established in 1973; . . 1st Franchised in 1982
Company-Owned Units (As of 12/1/1989): . 20
Franchised Units (12/1/1989): 140
Total Units (12/1/1989): 160
Distribution: US-160;Can-0;Overseas-0
North America: . . . . 3 States
Concentration: . .75 in FL, 60 in MI, 10 in GA
Registered: . . . . CA,FL,IL,IN,MI
. . . .
Average # of Employees: . . . . 4 FT, 6 -10 PT
Prior Industry Experience: . . . . Helpful

FINANCIAL:
Cash Investment: $50K
Total Investment: $70-113K
Fees: Franchise - $7.5K
Royalty: 3-5%, Advert: 3%
Contract Periods (Yrs.): 20/20
Area Development Agreement: . Yes
Sub-Franchise Contract: . . . . . Yes
Expand in Territory: . . . . . . Yes
Passive Ownership: . . . Not Allowed
Encourage Conversions: . . . . Yes
Franchisee Purchase(s) Required: Yes

FRANCHISOR TRAINING/SUPPORT:
Financial Assistance Provided: . . . Yes(I)
Site Selection Assistance: . . . . .Yes
Lease Negotiation Assistance: . . . . .Yes
Co-operative Advertising: . . . . .Yes
Training: . . . . 4 Wks. Headquarters,
. . . . 1 Wk. On-site, On-going
On-Going Support: . . . . b,C,D,E,F,G,H,I
Full-Time Franchisor Support Staff: . . 10
EXPANSION PLANS:
US: . . . . Midwest and Southeast
Canada - No, ...Overseas - No

INTERSTATE DAIRY QUEEN

2135 Wisconsin Ave. NW
Washington, DC 20007
TEL: (202) 338-8313 C
FAX: (202) 342-7102
Mr. Walt Tellegen, President

Fast food franchisor. DAIRY QUEEN, a system of over 5,000 stores worldwide, commands over 50% of snack sales by chains. Home of the "Blizzard." Interstate is "DAIRY QUEEN" system's fastest-growing territory operator, with stores from Maine to New Mexico. Both on and off the Interstate Highways.

HISTORY: . . . .
Established in 1977; . . 1st Franchised in 1977
Company-Owned Units (As of 12/1/1989): . .3
Franchised Units (12/1/1989): 74
Total Units (12/1/1989): 77
Distribution: US-77;Can-0;Overseas-0
North America: . . . . 23 States
Concentration: . .13 in GA, 11 in FL, 11 in SC
Registered: . . . .CA,FL,IL,IN,MD,MI,NY,RI
. . . .
Average # of Employees: . . . 2-3 FT, 20-25 PT
Prior Industry Experience: . . . . . . Helpful

FINANCIAL:
Cash Investment: $100-110K
Total Investment: $400-525K
Fees: Franchise - $25K
Royalty: 4%, Advert: 3-5%
Contract Periods (Yrs.): . . . . Infin.
Area Development Agreement: . .No
Sub-Franchise Contract: . . . . .No
Expand in Territory: . . . . . . Yes
Passive Ownership: . . . . . .Allowed
Encourage Conversions: . . . . . Yes
Franchisee Purchase(s) Required: .No

FRANCHISOR TRAINING/SUPPORT:
Financial Assistance Provided: . . . Yes(I)
Site Selection Assistance: . . . . .Yes
Lease Negotiation Assistance: . . . . .Yes
Co-operative Advertising: . . . . No
Training: . . . . 2 Wks. Headquarters,
. . . . 2 Wks. Store (Not Covered in Fee)
On-Going Support: . . . .B,C,D,E,F,G,H,I
Full-Time Franchisor Support Staff: . . 12
EXPANSION PLANS:
US: . . . . .All US
Canada - No, ...Overseas - No

JACK IN THE BOX

9330 Balboa Ave.
San Diego, CA 92123
TEL: (800) 876-5225 (619) 571-2200
FAX: (619) 277-9788
Mr. Jerry K. Prinds, Dir. Fran. Sale

Exciting up-scale, fast-food hamburger restaurants, offering a variety, from hamburgers to Mexican, specialty salads and snacks. First with breakfast, we now serve lunch and dinner, appealing to a wide variety of customer tastes. Opportunities available to develop new units.

HISTORY: . . . . .IFA
Established in 1950; . . 1st Franchised in 1982
Company-Owned Units (As of 12/1/1989): 605
Franchised Units (12/1/1989): 382
Total Units (12/1/1989): 987
Distribution: US-987;Can-0;Overseas-0
North America: . . . . 15 States
Concentration: . 181 in CA, 106 in TX, 41 AZ
Registered: . . . . Exempt
. . . .
Average # of Employees: . . . . . .3 FT, 35 PT
Prior Industry Experience: . . . . Helpful

FINANCIAL:
Cash Investment: $25K
Total Investment: $750K
Fees: Franchise - $25K
Royalty: 4%, Advert: 5%
Contract Periods (Yrs.): . . 20/Varies
Area Development Agreement: Yes/Var
Sub-Franchise Contract: . . . . .No
Expand in Territory: . . . . . . Yes
Passive Ownership: . . . Not Allowed
Encourage Conversions: . . . . . Yes
Franchisee Purchase(s) Required: .No

FRANCHISOR TRAINING/SUPPORT:
Financial Assistance Provided: . . . Yes(I)
Site Selection Assistance: . . . . .Yes
Lease Negotiation Assistance: . . . . .Yes
Co-operative Advertising: . . . . No
Training: . . . . 10 Wks. HQ/Training Ctr.,
. . . . . .5 Days Franchisee Restaurant
On-Going Support: . . . . B,C,D,E,F,G,h,I
Full-Time Franchisor Support Staff: . . . .
EXPANSION PLANS:
US: . . . . . Southwest, TX, MO and WA
Canada - No, ... Overseas - Yes

JACK'S FAMOUS DELI

1150 Lombard St.
Baltimore, MD 21202
TEL: (301) 522-4002
FAX:
Mr. George M. Palmer, Fran. Dir.

JACK'S is an up-scale concept targeted towards office buildings and business parks which features a captive market. JACK'S menu includes: sandwiches, salads, frozen treats, breakfast items and numerous carry-out items. Self-service salad bars are featured in many franchised units.

HISTORY:
Established in 1953; . . 1st Franchised in 1987
Company-Owned Units (As of 12/1/1989): . .5
Franchised Units (12/1/1989): 15
Total Units (12/1/1989): 20
Distribution: US-20;Can-0;Overseas-0
North America: . . . . 20 States
Concentration: . . 18 in MD, 1 in VA, 1 in DC
Registered: . . . . FL,MD,VA
. . . .
Average # of Employees: . . . . 1-2 FT, 3-5 PT
Prior Industry Experience: . . . . Helpful

FINANCIAL:
Cash Investment: $35-50K
Total Investment: $85-150K
Fees: Franchise - $25K
Royalty: 5%, Advert: 2%
Contract Periods (Yrs.): 20/20
Area Development Agreement: Yes/Var
Sub-Franchise Contract: . . . . . .No
Expand in Territory: . . . . . . .No
Passive Ownership: . . . Discouraged
Encourage Conversions: . . . . . Yes
Franchisee Purchase(s) Required: Yes

FRANCHISOR TRAINING/SUPPORT:
Financial Assistance Provided: . . . Yes(I)
Site Selection Assistance: . . . . . . .Yes
Lease Negotiation Assistance: . . . . .Yes
Co-operative Advertising: . . . . . . .Yes
Training: . . . . 2 Wks. Headquarters,
. . . . .1 Wk. Franchisee Site
On-Going Support: . . . b,C,D,E,F,G,H,I
Full-Time Franchisor Support Staff: . . . 8
EXPANSION PLANS:
US: . . . . . All US-Bus Parks/Major City
Canada - No, ...Overseas - No

JAKE'S PIZZA

1204 Carnegie St.
Rolling Meadows, IL 60008
TEL: (708) 398-2200 C
FAX: (708) 398-0193
Mr. James J. Banks, EVP

JAKE'S PIZZA specializes in serving premium and gourmet thin crust pizza. All ingredients are made fresh daily and the pizza is created and cooked in a kitchen that is open to the customer's view. Also served are salads, Italian sandwiches and pasta.

HISTORY:
Established in 1961; . . 1st Franchised in 1964
Company-Owned Units (As of 12/1/1989): . .0
Franchised Units (12/1/1989): 22
Total Units (12/1/1989): 22
Distribution: US-22;Can-0;Overseas-0
North America: . . . . .1 State
Concentration: . . . . 22 in IL
Registered: IL
. . . .
Average # of Employees: . . . . . . 2 FT, 6 PT
Prior Industry Experience: . . . . Helpful

FINANCIAL:
Cash Investment: $78-422K
Total Investment: $78-422K
Fees: Franchise - $15K
Royalty: 4%, Advert: 2%
Contract Periods (Yrs.): 5/5
Area Development Agreement: . .No
Sub-Franchise Contract: . . . . . .No
Expand in Territory: . . . . . . .No
Passive Ownership: . . . Discouraged
Encourage Conversions: . . . . . Yes
Franchisee Purchase(s) Required: Yes

FRANCHISOR TRAINING/SUPPORT:
Financial Assistance Provided: . . . . .No
Site Selection Assistance: . . . . . . .Yes
Lease Negotiation Assistance: . . . . .Yes
Co-operative Advertising: . . . . . . .Yes
Training: . . . . . . 4-6 Wks. Headquarters
. . . .
On-Going Support: . . . . . .B,C,D,E,F,H
Full-Time Franchisor Support Staff: . . . 8
EXPANSION PLANS:
US: . . . . Midwest Only
Canada - No, ...Overseas - No

JARED'S PIZZA

P. O. Box 305
Noble, OK 73068
TEL: (405) 872-5170
FAX:
Mr. Floyd Taber, President

Pizza priced 2 for 1. The best pizza, any way you want it! Complete training and support to help you grow with us. With our Master Franchise program, you can become a sub-franchisor. Rare opportunity, convert your present unit to a JARED'S PIZZA RESTAURANT.

HISTORY:
Established in 1989; . . 1st Franchised in 1989
Company-Owned Units (As of 12/1/1989): . .1
Franchised Units (12/1/1989): 0
Total Units (12/1/1989): 1
Distribution: US-1;Can-0;Overseas-0
North America: . . . . .1 State
Concentration: . . . . 1 in OK
Registered:
. . . .
Average # of Employees: . . . . . . 4 FT, 6 PT
Prior Industry Experience: . . . . Helpful

FINANCIAL:
Cash Investment: $15K
Total Investment: $25K
Fees: Franchise - $2.5-5K
Royalty: 5%, Advert: . . . . Varies
Contract Periods (Yrs.): 5/5
Area Development Agreement: Yes/5
Sub-Franchise Contract: . . . . . Yes
Expand in Territory: . . . . . . Yes
Passive Ownership: . . . . . .Allowed
Encourage Conversions: . . . . . Yes
Franchisee Purchase(s) Required: .No

FRANCHISOR TRAINING/SUPPORT:
Financial Assistance Provided: . . . Yes(I)
Site Selection Assistance: . . . . . . .Yes
Lease Negotiation Assistance: . . . . .Yes
Co-operative Advertising: . . . . . . .Yes
Training: . . . . . .1-2 Wks. Training Store
. . . .
On-Going Support: . . . A,C,d,E,F,G,H,I
Full-Time Franchisor Support Staff: . . . 1
EXPANSION PLANS:
US: . . . . .All US
Canada - No, ...Overseas - No

JOHNNY ROCKETS

1145 Gayley Ave., # 315
Los Angeles, CA
TEL: (213) 208-1322
FAX:
Mr. C. Jeffers VP Franchising

Limited menu with great food, counter seating, interesting decor. A fun place!

HISTORY:	FINANCIAL:	FRANCHISOR TRAINING/SUPPORT:
Established in 1986; . . 1st Franchised in 1987	Cash Investment: $300-400K	Financial Assistance Provided: . . . . . No
Company-Owned Units (As of 12/1/1989): . .4	Total Investment: $300-400K	Site Selection Assistance: . . . . .Yes
Franchised Units (12/1/1989): 7	Fees: Franchise - $39K	Lease Negotiation Assistance: . . . . . No
Total Units (12/1/1989): 11	Royalty: 5%, Advert: 2%	Co-operative Advertising: . . . . .Yes
Distribution: US-11;Can-0;Overseas-0	Contract Periods (Yrs.): 10/10	Training: . . . . 5 Wks. Headquarters
North America: . . . . 4 States	Area Development Agreement: Yes/10	. . . .
Concentration: . . . .5 in CA, 3 in GA, 2 in IL	Sub-Franchise Contract: . . . . .No	On-Going Support: . . . . .D,E,F,I
Registered: . . . . All States	Expand in Territory: . . . . Yes	Full-Time Franchisor Support Staff: . . 11
. . . .	Passive Ownership: . . . Not Allowed	EXPANSION PLANS:
Average # of Employees: . . . . . 18 FT, 12 PT	Encourage Conversions: . . . . . .No	US: . . . . .All US
Prior Industry Experience: . . . . . . Helpful	Franchisee Purchase(s) Required: .No	Canada - Yes, . . . Overseas - Yes

JR.'S HOT DOGS INTERNATIONAL

1661 N. Swan, # 234
Tucson, AZ 85715
TEL: (602) 322-3644
FAX:
Mr. Roy VanderWall, Sr., President

Specializing in a top-quality "Chicago-style" hot dog. Additional menu items include chili dogs, cheese dogs, Polish sausage, Italian beef and sausage and french fries. JR'S is a fast-food concept with carry-out, drive-thru and limited seating. Options available. Regional franchises also available.

HISTORY: . . . . IFA/WIF	FINANCIAL:	FRANCHISOR TRAINING/SUPPORT:
Established in 1970; . . 1st Franchised in 1976	Cash Investment: $60-100K	Financial Assistance Provided: . . . . . No
Company-Owned Units (As of 12/1/1989): . .4	Total Investment: $100-400K	Site Selection Assistance: . . . . .Yes
Franchised Units (12/1/1989): 20	Fees: Franchise - $12-18K	Lease Negotiation Assistance: . . . . .Yes
Total Units (12/1/1989): 24	Royalty: 5%, Advert: 4%	Co-operative Advertising: . . . . .Yes
Distribution: US-24;Can-0;Overseas-0	Contract Periods (Yrs.): 15/5	Training: . . . . 1 Day Orientation-Region,
North America: . . . . 2 States	Area Development Agreement: .No	. . . . 2 Wks. Operations On-site
Concentration: . . . . 20 in IL, 4 in CA	Sub-Franchise Contract: . . . . . Yes	On-Going Support: . . . . B,C,D,E,F,h,I
Registered: . . . . CA,FL,IL,IN,WI	Expand in Territory: . . . . Yes	Full-Time Franchisor Support Staff: . . . .
. . . .	Passive Ownership: . . . Discouraged	EXPANSION PLANS:
Average # of Employees: . . . . . . 3 FT, 6 PT	Encourage Conversions: . . . . . .No	US: . . . . .All US
Prior Industry Experience: . . . . . . Helpful	Franchisee Purchase(s) Required: .No	Canada - No, ...Overseas - No

JUST BURGERS

1523 Ludington St.
Escanaba, MI 49829
TEL: (800) 678-1225 (517) 694-2800
FAX:
Mr. Edward Gillespie, VP Mktg.

The JUST BURGERS RESTAURANT is a drive-thru restaurant that offers a "back to the basics" approach to serving hamburgers, french fries and soft drinks. Their success is based on their limited menu, being of high quality, large quantity, fast service and low prices. Complete turnkey package at one price available.

HISTORY:	FINANCIAL:	FRANCHISOR TRAINING/SUPPORT:
Established in 1987; . . 1st Franchised in 1987	Cash Investment: $40K	Financial Assistance Provided: . . . . . No
Company-Owned Units (As of 12/1/1989): . .0	Total Investment: $315-400K	Site Selection Assistance: . . . . .Yes
Franchised Units (12/1/1989): 4	Fees: Franchise - $20K	Lease Negotiation Assistance: . . . . .Yes
Total Units (12/1/1989): 4	Royalty: 4%, Advert: 2%	Co-operative Advertising: . . . . .Yes
Distribution: US-4;Can-0;Overseas-0	Contract Periods (Yrs.): 10/10	Training: . . . . .10 Days Site
North America: . . . . 2 States	Area Development Agreement: Yes/10	. . . .
Concentration: . . . . .3 in MI, 1 in WI	Sub-Franchise Contract: . . . . . .No	On-Going Support: . . . .B,C,D,E,F,G,H,I
Registered: . . . . .MI,WI	Expand in Territory: . . . . Yes	Full-Time Franchisor Support Staff: . . . 5
. . . .	Passive Ownership: . . . . . .Allowed	EXPANSION PLANS:
Average # of Employees: . . . . 14 FT	Encourage Conversions: . . . . Yes	US: . . . . .All US
Prior Industry Experience: . . . . Helpful	Franchisee Purchase(s) Required: .No	Canada - Yes, ...Overseas - No

KENTUCKY FRIED CHICKEN

P. O. Box 32070
Louisville, KY 40232
TEL: (800) 544-5774 (502) 456-8673
FAX: (502) 456-8360
Mr. Walter J. Simon, VP Fran. Dev.

KENTUCKY FRIED CHICKEN is the industry leader in the quick-service chicken segment. With over 30 years' experience in restaurant franchising, KFC is considered one of the world's premier franchise companies. New build and acquisition opportunities are available throughout the KFC worldwide franchise system.

HISTORY: . . . . IFA
Established in 1952; . . 1st Franchised in 1952
Company-Owned Units (As of 12/1/1989): 1329
Franchised Units (12/1/1989): 3600
Total Units (12/1/1989): 4929
Distribution: US-4929;Can-0;Overseas-0
North America: . . . . 47 States
Concentration: . . .494 in CA,179 OH, 169 FL
Registered: . . . . .All
. . . .
Average # of Employees: . . . . . .3 FT, 24 PT
Prior Industry Experience: . . . . Helpful

FINANCIAL: NYSE-PEP
Cash Investment: $150K
Total Investment: $600-800K
Fees: Franchise - $20K
Royalty: 4%, Advert: 4.5%
Contract Periods (Yrs.): 20/10
Area Development Agreement: . .No
Sub-Franchise Contract: . . . . .No
Expand in Territory: . . . . Yes
Passive Ownership: . . . Not Allowed
Encourage Conversions: . . . . . Yes
Franchisee Purchase(s) Required: Yes

FRANCHISOR TRAINING/SUPPORT:
Financial Assistance Provided: . . . . .No
Site Selection Assistance: . . . . . . .Yes
Lease Negotiation Assistance: . . . . .No
Co-operative Advertising: . . . . . . .Yes
Training: . . . . 3 Months KFC Restaurant,
. . . . 2 Wks. KFC Chicken University
On-Going Support: . . . . B,C,d,E,F,G,H,I
Full-Time Franchisor Support Staff: . . 12
EXPANSION PLANS:
US: . . . . .All US
Canada - Yes, . . . Overseas - Yes

LE CROISSANT SHOP

227 W. 40th St.
New York, NY 10018
TEL: (212) 719-5940
FAX: (212) 944-0269
Mr. Jacques Pelletier, VP

French bakery cafe - specialty croissants, bread, soups, french sandwiches and gourmet salads.

HISTORY: . . . . IFA
Established in 1981; . . 1st Franchised in 1984
Company-Owned Units (As of 12/1/1989): . .6
Franchised Units (12/1/1989): 31
Total Units (12/1/1989): 37
Distribution: US-19;Can-0;Overseas-18
North America: . . . . 4 States
Concentration: . . . 16 in NY, 1 in PA, 1 in FL
Registered: . . . .
. . . .
Average # of Employees: . . . . 10 FT
Prior Industry Experience: . . . . Helpful

FINANCIAL:
Cash Investment: $100K
Total Investment: $200-300K
Fees: Franchise - $22.5K
Royalty: 5%, Advert: 2%
Contract Periods (Yrs.): 10/5/5
Area Development Agreement: Yes/10
Sub-Franchise Contract: . . . . . .
Expand in Territory: . . . .
Passive Ownership: . . . .
Encourage Conversions: . . . .
Franchisee Purchase(s) Required: .No

FRANCHISOR TRAINING/SUPPORT:
Financial Assistance Provided: . . . .
Site Selection Assistance: . . . .
Lease Negotiation Assistance: . . . .
Co-operative Advertising: . . . .
Training: . . . . 4 Wks. Headquarters
. . . .
On-Going Support: . . . .
Full-Time Franchisor Support Staff: . . . .
EXPANSION PLANS:
US: . . . . East Coast
Canada - No, ...Overseas - No

LEE'S FAMOUS RECIPE
COUNTRY CHICKEN
1727 Elm Hill Pike
Nashville, TN 37210
TEL: (615) 391-5201
FAX:
Jeffrey L. Heston, Dir. Fran. Devel.

Sit-down/take-out chicken restaurant.

HISTORY: . . . . IFA
Established in 1966; . . 1st Franchised in 1966
Company-Owned Units (As of 12/1/1989): . 48
Franchised Units (12/1/1989): 235
Total Units (12/1/1989): 283
Distribution: US-283;Can-0;Overseas-0
North America: . . . .
Concentration: . . . .
Registered: . . . . All States
. . . .
Average # of Employees: . . . . 20 FT
Prior Industry Experience: . . . . . .Necessary

FINANCIAL: OTC-SHONC
Cash Investment: $50K
Total Investment: $529K
Fees: Franchise - $10K
Royalty: 3%, Advert: 9%
Contract Periods (Yrs.): . . . 20/20
Area Development Agreement: Yes/Var
Sub-Franchise Contract: . . .No
Expand in Territory: . . . . Yes
Passive Ownership: . . . Not Allowed
Encourage Conversions: . . . . .No
Franchisee Purchase(s) Required: Yes

FRANCHISOR TRAINING/SUPPORT:
Financial Assistance Provided: . . . . .No
Site Selection Assistance: . . . . . . .Yes
Lease Negotiation Assistance: . . . .Yes
Co-operative Advertising: . . . . . . .Yes
Training: . . . . 5 Wks. Headquarters
. . . .
On-Going Support: . . . . a,b,C,d,e,F,G,h,I
Full-Time Franchisor Support Staff: . . . .
EXPANSION PLANS:
US: . . . . .NE, NW and West
Canada - Yes, . . . Overseas - Yes

LITTLE CAESARS PIZZA

2211 Woodward Ave., Fox Office Ctr.
Detroit, MI 48201
TEL: (800) 444-1544 (313) 983-6000
FAX: (313) 983-6390
Mr. Robert Massey, VP Fran. Sales

LITTLE CAESARS PIZZA is the world's largest carry-out pizza chain, as well as one of the fastest-growing companies in the industry. The LITTLE CAESARS system developed over 30 years of experience in the restaurant business, and gives its franchisees the means to provide their customers with a quality product, great value and fast service.

HISTORY: . . . .
Established in 1959; . . 1st Franchised in 1961
Company-Owned Units (As of 12/1/1989): 713
Franchised Units (12/1/1989): 1887
Total Units (12/1/1989): 2600
Distribution: . . US-2504;Can-82;Overseas-14
North America: . . . .
Concentration: . . . .
Registered: . . . .
. . . .
Average # of Employees: . . . .
Prior Industry Experience: . . . . . . Helpful

FINANCIAL:
Cash Investment: $50-70K
Total Investment: $120-180K
Fees: Franchise - $15K
　Royalty: 5%, Advert: 6.5%
Contract Periods (Yrs.): . . . .
Area Development Agreement: . .No
Sub-Franchise Contract: . . . . .No
Expand in Territory: . . . . Yes
Passive Ownership: . . . Discouraged
Encourage Conversions: . . . .
Franchisee Purchase(s) Required: . .

FRANCHISOR TRAINING/SUPPORT:
Financial Assistance Provided: . . . Yes(I)
Site Selection Assistance: . . . . . . .Yes
Lease Negotiation Assistance: . . . . .Yes
Co-operative Advertising: . . . . . . .Yes
Training: . . . . 8 Wks. Headquarters
. . . .
On-Going Support: . . . . .B,C,D,E,G,H,I
Full-Time Franchisor Support Staff: . .
EXPANSION PLANS:
　US: . . . . .All US
Canada - Yes, . . . Overseas - Yes

LITTLE KING

11811 "I" St.
Omaha, NE 68137
TEL: (800) 248-2148 (402) 330-5030 C
FAX:
Ms. Rebecca Bishop, Dir. Fran. Dev.

LITLE KING RESTAURANT is a successful Hero sandwich/deli-pizza concept. Emphasis on fresh food, fast, with products of freshest ingredients prepared in full view of customer. Bread baked daily on premises and special 300 calorie or less "Lite Menu." Over 20 years' experience.

HISTORY: . . . . .IFA
Established in 1968; . . 1st Franchised in 1978
Company-Owned Units (As of 12/1/1989): . 28
Franchised Units (12/1/1989): 38
Total Units (12/1/1989): 66
Distribution: US-66;Can-0;Overseas-0
North America: . . . . 17 States
Concentration: . . . . 9 in NE, 5 in KS, 4 in IA
Registered: . . . CA,FL,IL,IN,MD,MI,MN,ND
. . . . .SD,VA,WA,WI
Average # of Employees: . . . . .2-3 FT, 6+ PT
Prior Industry Experience: . . . . . . Helpful

FINANCIAL:
Cash Investment: $39-125K
Total Investment: $69-125K
Fees: Franchise - $9.5K
　Royalty: 6%, Advert: . . . .
Contract Periods (Yrs.): 15/15
Area Development Agreement: Yes/15
Sub-Franchise Contract: . . . . .No
Expand in Territory: . . . . Yes
Passive Ownership: . . . Discouraged
Encourage Conversions: . . . . . Yes
Franchisee Purchase(s) Required: .No

FRANCHISOR TRAINING/SUPPORT:
Financial Assistance Provided: . . . Yes(I)
Site Selection Assistance: . . . . . . .Yes
Lease Negotiation Assistance: . . . . .Yes
Co-operative Advertising: . . . . . . .Yes
Training: . . . . . . 15 Days Headquarters,
. . . . 2 Wks. Site
On-Going Support: . . . .B,C,D,E,F,G,H,I
Full-Time Franchisor Support Staff: . . 73
EXPANSION PLANS:
　US: . . . . .All US
Canada - Yes, . . . Overseas - Yes

LONG JOHN SILVER'S SEAFOOD SHOPPES

P.O. Box 11988
Lexington, KY 40579
TEL: (606) 263-6000
FAX:
Mr. Eugene Getchell, VP Fran.

LONG JOHN SILVER'S SEAFOOD SHOPPES, the dominant seafood restaurant chain in the world, offers a standardized, limited menu consisting of fish, chicken, shrimp, seafood, salads and a variety of side items.

HISTORY: . . . . .IFA
Established in 1969; . . 1st Franchised in 1970
Company-Owned Units (As of 12/1/1989): 1022
Franchised Units (12/1/1989): 471
Total Units (12/1/1989): 1493
Distribution: US-1460;Can-5;Overseas-5
North America: . . . . 36 States
Concentration: . 202 in TX,115 in OH,97 in IN
Registered: . . . . All States
. . . .
Average # of Employees: . . . . 3-4 FT,7-10 PT
Prior Industry Experience: . . . . . . Helpful

FINANCIAL: OTC-JERR
Cash Investment: . . . .$
Total Investment: $600-900K
Fees: Franchise - $20K
　Royalty: 4%, Advert: 5%
Contract Periods (Yrs.): 15/5/5
Area Development Agreement: Yes/4
Sub-Franchise Contract: . . . . .No
Expand in Territory: . . . . Yes
Passive Ownership: . . . . . .Allowed
Encourage Conversions: . . . . . Yes
Franchisee Purchase(s) Required: Yes

FRANCHISOR TRAINING/SUPPORT:
Financial Assistance Provided: . . . . .No
Site Selection Assistance: . . . . . . .Yes
Lease Negotiation Assistance: . . . . .No
Co-operative Advertising: . . . . . . .Yes
Training: . . . . 3 Wks. Site, 3 Wks.
. . . . .Site, 2 Wks. Basic Mgmt.
On-Going Support: . . . .B,C,D,E,G,H,I
Full-Time Franchisor Support Staff: . . . .
EXPANSION PLANS:
　US: . . . . .All US
Canada - Yes, ... Overseas - No

LOS RIOS MEXICAN FOODS

835 Supertest Rd., # 200
North York, ON M3J2M9 CAN
TEL: (416) 665-4077
FAX: (416) 665-1483
Mr. Nick Lattanzio, Fran. Dir.

LOS RIOS, an original Canadian concept in its 7th year, is a unique Mexican fast-food restaurant. Designed to provide today's consumer with a delicious food alternative, consisting of high-quality foods prepared fresh on site. LOS RIOS is continuing expansion through high-volume food court locations.

HISTORY: . . . .
Established in 1983; . . 1st Franchised in 1985
Company-Owned Units (As of 12/1/1989): . .3
Franchised Units (12/1/1989): 17
Total Units (12/1/1989): 20
Distribution: US-0;Can-20;Overseas-0
North America: . . . . 2 Provinces
Concentration: . . . . .16 in ON, 4 in PQ
Registered: . . . .
. . . .
Average # of Employees: . . . . . 3-4 FT, 6 PT
Prior Industry Experience: . . . . Helpful

FINANCIAL:
Cash Investment: $50K
Total Investment: $150K
Fees: Franchise - $25K
Royalty: 6%, Advert: 2%
Contract Periods (Yrs.): 10/5
Area Development Agreement: Yes/10
Sub-Franchise Contract: . . . . .No
Expand in Territory: . . . . . . Yes
Passive Ownership: . . . Not Allowed
Encourage Conversions: . . . . Yes
Franchisee Purchase(s) Required: .No

FRANCHISOR TRAINING/SUPPORT:
Financial Assistance Provided: . . . Yes(I)
Site Selection Assistance: . . . . . . .Yes
Lease Negotiation Assistance: . . . . .Yes
Co-operative Advertising: . . . . .Yes
Training: . . . . . . 4-6 Wks. Headquarters,
. . . . 4-6 Wks. Existing New Unit
On-Going Support: . . . . .C,D,E,F,G,H,I
Full-Time Franchisor Support Staff: . . 20
EXPANSION PLANS:
US: . . . . Northwest
Canada - Yes, . . . Overseas - Yes

MADE IN JAPAN JAPANESE RESTAURANTS

2133 Royal Windsor Dr., # 23
Mississauga, ON L5J1K5 CAN
TEL: (416) 823-8883
FAX:
Mr. Lou Donato, President

Fresh-food restaurants, located primarily in food courts of regional shopping malls, specializing in freshly-prepared Japanese-style foods prepared in front of customers. For example: teriyaki steak, chicken or shrimp with freshly-grilled vegetables and steamed rice.

HISTORY: . . . . IFA
Established in 1986; . . 1st Franchised in 1987
Company-Owned Units (As of 12/1/1989): . .3
Franchised Units (12/1/1989): 30
Total Units (12/1/1989): 33
Distribution: US-0;Can-33;Overseas-0
North America: . . . . 5 Provinces
Concentration: . . .24 in ON, 6 in PQ, 1 in AB
Registered: . . . . AB
. . . .
Average # of Employees: . . . . . . 3 FT, 5 PT
Prior Industry Experience: . . . . Helpful

FINANCIAL:
Cash Investment: $40-50K
Total Investment: $150-175K
Fees: Franchise - $25K
Royalty: 6%, Advert: 3.5%
Contract Periods (Yrs.): 10/5
Area Development Agreement: . Yes
Sub-Franchise Contract: . . . . . Yes
Expand in Territory: . . . . . . Yes
Passive Ownership: . . . Not Allowed
Encourage Conversions: . . . . Yes
Franchisee Purchase(s) Required: .No

FRANCHISOR TRAINING/SUPPORT:
Financial Assistance Provided: . . .Yes(D)
Site Selection Assistance: . . . . . . .Yes
Lease Negotiation Assistance: . . . .Yes
Co-operative Advertising: . . . . . . .Yes
Training: . . . . . . .2 Wks. Toronto Eaton
. . . . Centre
On-Going Support: . . . . . . C,D,E,F,h,I
Full-Time Franchisor Support Staff: . . 15
EXPANSION PLANS:
US: . . . . .All US
Canada - Yes, . . . Overseas - Yes

MARCO'S PIZZA

5254 Monroe St.
Toledo, OH 43623
TEL: (419) 885-4844
FAX:
Mr. Ken Switzer, Dir. Admin.

MARCO'S PIZZA sells the most popular pizza in its Ohio and Michigan markets due to its product quality, conscientious service and strong image. The quality taste, which can not be duplicated, is due to MARCO's unique blend of the finest ingredients available.

HISTORY: . . . .
Established in 1978; . . 1st Franchised in 1979
Company-Owned Units (As of 12/1/1989): . 16
Franchised Units (12/1/1989): 24
Total Units (12/1/1989): 40
Distribution: US-40;Can-0;Overseas-0
North America: . . . . 2 States
Concentration: . . . . . . .38 in OH, 2 in MI
Registered: . . . . .MI
. . . .
Average # of Employees: . . . . . .8 FT, 14 PT
Prior Industry Experience: . . . . . . Helpful

FINANCIAL:
Cash Investment: $25-50K
Total Investment: $75-125K
Fees: Franchise - $12K
Royalty: 5%, Advert: 1.5%
Contract Periods (Yrs.): 10/10
Area Development Agreement: Yes/10
Sub-Franchise Contract: . . . . .No
Expand in Territory: . . . . . . Yes
Passive Ownership: . . . Not Allowed
Encourage Conversions: . . . . .No
Franchisee Purchase(s) Required: .No

FRANCHISOR TRAINING/SUPPORT:
Financial Assistance Provided: . . . Yes(I)
Site Selection Assistance: . . . . . . .Yes
Lease Negotiation Assistance: . . . .Yes
Co-operative Advertising: . . . . . . .Yes
Training: . . . . . 8 Wks.+ Training Stores,
. . . 3 Wks. Headquarters, 1 Wk. On-site
On-Going Support: . . . . .b,C,D,E,G,H,I
Full-Time Franchisor Support Staff: . . 14
EXPANSION PLANS:
US: . . . . .All US
Canada - No, ...Overseas - No

MARY BROWN'S FRIED CHICKEN

500 Champagne Dr.
Downsview, ON M3J2T9 CAN
TEL: (416) 635-2900
FAX:
Mr. Nigel Beattie, VP Fran. Dev.

Franchisor of MARY BROWN'S FRIED CHICKEN, which specializes in a superior brand of fried chicken cooked in peanut oil. Also associated food products.

HISTORY: . . . . .CFA	FINANCIAL:	FRANCHISOR TRAINING/SUPPORT:
Established in 1978; . . 1st Franchised in 1978	Cash Investment: $65-105K	Financial Assistance Provided: . . . . . No
Company-Owned Units (As of 12/1/1989): . .0	Total Investment: $165-205K	Site Selection Assistance: . . . . . . .Yes
Franchised Units (12/1/1989): 83	Fees: Franchise - $20K	Lease Negotiation Assistance: . . . . .Yes
Total Units (12/1/1989): 83	Royalty: 4%, Advert: 5%	Co-operative Advertising: . . . . . . .Yes
Distribution: US-0;Can-83;Overseas-0	Contract Periods (Yrs.): 15/10	Training: . . . . 3 Wks. Headquarters
North America: . . . . 7 Provinces	Area Development Agreement: . .No	. . . .
Concentration: . . . . 38 in ON, 32 in NF	Sub-Franchise Contract: . . . . .No	On-Going Support: . . . .B,C,D,E,F,G,H,I
Registered:	Expand in Territory: . . . . Yes	Full-Time Franchisor Support Staff: . . 24
. . . .	Passive Ownership: . . . Discouraged	EXPANSION PLANS:
Average # of Employees: . . . . . .3 FT, 10 PT	Encourage Conversions: . . . . . Yes	US: . . . . No
Prior Industry Experience: . . . . Helpful	Franchisee Purchase(s) Required: .No	Canada - Yes, ...Overseas - No

MCDONALD'S CORPORATION

Kroc Dr.
Oak Brook, IL 60521
TEL: (708) 575-6196
FAX:
Licensing Department

World's leading food service organization, serving 22 million customers a day, with annual sales of over $16 billion. 75% of MCDONALD'S restaurants are franchised. Restaurants are franchised by 2 methods: Conventional purchase or leasing program, depending on amount of funds available to invest.

HISTORY: . . . . IFA	FINANCIAL: NYSE-MCD	FRANCHISOR TRAINING/SUPPORT:
Established in 1955; . . 1st Franchised in 1955	Cash Investment: $40-250K	Financial Assistance Provided: . . . . . No
Company-Owned Units (As of 12/1/1989): 3350	Total Investment: $575K	Site Selection Assistance: . . . . . . .NA
Franchised Units (12/1/1989): 7553	Fees: Franchise - $22.5K	Lease Negotiation Assistance: . . . . .NA
Total Units (12/1/1989): 10903	Royalty: 3.5%, Advert: 4%	Co-operative Advertising: . . . . . . .Yes
Distribution: US-8130;Can-592;Overseas-2181	Contract Periods (Yrs.): 20	Training: . . . . . .2 Yrs. Local Restaurant,
North America: . . . . 50 States	Area Development Agreement: . .No	. . .3 Wks. Regional Offices, 2 Wks. HQ
Concentration:	Sub-Franchise Contract: . . . . .No	On-Going Support: . . . . B,C,D,E,F,G,H
Registered: . . . . .All	Expand in Territory: . . . . . . .No	Full-Time Franchisor Support Staff: . . 99
. . . .	Passive Ownership: . . . Not Allowed	EXPANSION PLANS:
Average # of Employees: . . . 6-8 FT, 60-80 PT	Encourage Conversions: . . . . .No	US: . . . . .All US
Prior Industry Experience: . . . . Helpful	Franchisee Purchase(s) Required: .No	Canada - Yes, . . . Overseas - Yes

MR. HERO / MR. PHILLY

6902 Pearl Rd.
Cleveland, OH 44130
TEL: (800) 366-1555 (216) 842-6000
FAX: (216) 884-2638
Mr. Bill Plautz, VP Bus. Devel.

Fast food, featuring Philly-style cheesesteak sandwich, Romanburger - gourmet hamburgers, selection of cold subs, cross-cut french fries, fresh salads and beverages.

HISTORY:	FINANCIAL:	FRANCHISOR TRAINING/SUPPORT:
Established in 1965; . . 1st Franchised in 1970	Cash Investment: $75K	Financial Assistance Provided: . . . . .No
Company-Owned Units (As of 12/1/1989): . 21	Total Investment: $170-200K	Site Selection Assistance: . . . . . . .Yes
Franchised Units (12/1/1989): 112	Fees: Franchise - $21.5K	Lease Negotiation Assistance: . . . . .Yes
Total Units (12/1/1989): 133	Royalty: 5%, Advert: 2.6%	Co-operative Advertising: . . . . . . .Yes
Distribution: US-133;Can-0;Overseas-0	Contract Periods (Yrs.): 20/20	Training: . . . . 4 Wks. Headquarters,
North America: . . . . 10 States	Area Development Agreement: . .No	. . . . 7 Days New Store Opening
Concentration: . . 88 in OH, 10 in IL, 8 in CA	Sub-Franchise Contract: . . . . .No	On-Going Support: . . . . . .C,D,E,G,H,I
Registered: . . . . .IL,MI,NY,VA	Expand in Territory: . . . . Yes	Full-Time Franchisor Support Staff: . . 25
. . . .	Passive Ownership: . . . Discouraged	EXPANSION PLANS:
Average # of Employees: . . . . . . 4 FT, 7 PT	Encourage Conversions: . . . . . Yes	US: . . . . .Midwest
Prior Industry Experience: . . . . Helpful	Franchisee Purchase(s) Required: .No	Canada - No, ...Overseas - No

MR. SUBMARINE

300 - 720 Spadina Ave.
Toronto, ON M4V2C1 CAN
TEL: (416) 962-6232
FAX: (416) 962-9995
Mr. Thanos Dimitrakopoulos

Sit-down and take-out service, vending a large variety of hot and cold submarine sandwiches, salads and soft drinks, juices, milk, coffee, milkshakes, cheesecakes and danish. A multi-media advertising program is used, as well as national promotions and local marketing.

HISTORY: . . . . .CFA
Established in 1968; . . 1st Franchised in 1972
Company-Owned Units (As of 12/1/1989): . 17
Franchised Units (12/1/1989): 303
Total Units (12/1/1989): 320
Distribution: US-0;Can-320;Overseas-0
North America: . . . . 9 Provinces
Concentration: . . 228 in ON, 37 in AB, 19 SK
Registered: . . . . AB
. . . .
Average # of Employees: . . . . . .3 Ft, 3-4 PT
Prior Industry Experience: . . . . . . Helpful

FINANCIAL:
Cash Investment: $50K
Total Investment: $130-160K
Fees: Franchise - $15K
  Royalty: 5%, Advert: 3%
Contract Periods (Yrs.): 10/10
Area Development Agreement: . .No
Sub-Franchise Contract: . . . . .No
Expand in Territory: . . . . Yes
Passive Ownership: . . . Not Allowed
Encourage Conversions: . . . . . Yes
Franchisee Purchase(s) Required: .No

FRANCHISOR TRAINING/SUPPORT:
Financial Assistance Provided: . . . Yes(I)
Site Selection Assistance: . . . . . . .Yes
Lease Negotiation Assistance: . . . . .Yes
Co-operative Advertising: . . . . . . .Yes
Training: . . . . 3 Wks. Headquarters
. . . .
On-Going Support: . . . . B,C,D,E,F,G,H
Full-Time Franchisor Support Staff: . . 56
EXPANSION PLANS:
US: . . . . All US-Licensees Only
Canada - Yes, . . . Overseas - Yes

MRS. VANELLI'S RESTAURANTS

2133 Royal Windsor Dr., # 23
Mississauga, ON L5J1K5 CAN
TEL: (416) 823-8883
FAX:
Mr. Lou Donato, President

Fresh-food restaurants, located primarily in food courts of regional shopping malls, specializing in freshly-prepared pizza, pasta, salads, etc.

HISTORY: . . . . IFA
Established in 1981; . . 1st Franchised in 1984
Company-Owned Units (As of 12/1/1989): . .7
Franchised Units (12/1/1989): 56
Total Units (12/1/1989): 63
Distribution: US-0;Can-63;Overseas-0
North America:
Concentration: . . .40 in ON, 9 in BC, 7 in AB
Registered: . . . . AB
. . . .
Average # of Employees: . . . . . . 2 FT, 2 PT
Prior Industry Experience: . . . . . . Helpful

FINANCIAL:
Cash Investment: $40-50K
Total Investment: $175-225K
Fees: Franchise - $25K
  Royalty: 6%, Advert: 1%
Contract Periods (Yrs.): 10/5
Area Development Agreement: Yes/15
Sub-Franchise Contract: . . . . Yes
Expand in Territory: . . . . Yes
Passive Ownership: . . . Not Allowed
Encourage Conversions: . . . . . Yes
Franchisee Purchase(s) Required: .No

FRANCHISOR TRAINING/SUPPORT:
Financial Assistance Provided: . . .Yes(D)
Site Selection Assistance: . . . . . . .Yes
Lease Negotiation Assistance: . . . .Yes
Co-operative Advertising: . . . . . . .Yes
Training: . . . . . 2 Wks. Mall in Hamilton
. . . .
On-Going Support: . . . . . . C,D,E,F,h,I
Full-Time Franchisor Support Staff: . . 31
EXPANSION PLANS:
US: . . . . .All US
Canada - Yes, ...Overseas - No

NATHAN'S FAMOUS

1400 Old Country Rd.
Westbury, NY 11590
TEL: (800) NATH-ANS (516) 338-8500
FAX: (516) 338-7220
Mr. Carl Paley, VP Fran. Devel.

NATHAN'S - featuring expandable menu and seven prototypes, including malls, food courts, free-standing and shopping centers. Quality food, highly supportive company with professional staff to guide and assist.

HISTORY: . . . . IFA
Established in 1916; . . 1st Franchised in 1979
Company-Owned Units (As of 12/1/1989): . 14
Franchised Units (12/1/1989): 42
Total Units (12/1/1989): 56
Distribution: US-56;Can-0;Overseas-0
North America: . . . .
Concentration: . . . . NY, NJ, FL
Registered: . . CA,FL,IL,MD,MI,MN,NY,ND
. . . . RI,VA,WA,WI
Average # of Employees: . . . .
Prior Industry Experience: . . . . Helpful

FINANCIAL:
Cash Investment: $150-250K
Total Investment: $300-600K
Fees: Franchise - $30K
  Royalty: 4%, Advert: 3%
Contract Periods (Yrs.): 20/15
Area Development Agreement: Yes/20
Sub-Franchise Contract: . . . . . .No
Expand in Territory: . . . . .No
Passive Ownership: . . . Discouraged
Encourage Conversions: . . . . . NA
Franchisee Purchase(s) Required: .No

FRANCHISOR TRAINING/SUPPORT:
Financial Assistance Provided: . . . . .NA
Site Selection Assistance: . . . . .Yes
Lease Negotiation Assistance: . . . .Yes
Co-operative Advertising: . . . . . . .NA
Training: . . . . 2 Wks. New York
. . . .
On-Going Support: . . .B,C,D,E,F,G,H,I
Full-Time Franchisor Support Staff: . . 40
EXPANSION PLANS:
US: . . . . East Coast, FL - New England
Canada - No, ...Overseas - No

NEW YORK BURRITO

165 S. Union Blvd., # 710
Lakewood, CO 80228
TEL: (800) 456-8705 (303) 980-5118
FAX: (303) 980-5323
Mr. Robert Palmer, Dir. Fran.

Southwestern-style Mexican fast food, served with New York flair. The concept is designed to serve an outstanding and unique Mexican-style menu, delivered with special emphasis on the overall decor, which is best described as "art deco" and exciting!

HISTORY: . . . .
Established in 1988; . . 1st Franchised in 1990
Company-Owned Units (As of 12/1/1989): . .2
Franchised Units (12/1/1989): 0
Total Units (12/1/1989): 2
Distribution: US-2;Can-0;Overseas-0
North America: . . . . .1 State
Concentration: . . . . 2 in CO
Registered: . . . .
. . . .
Average # of Employees: . . . . . . 4 FT, 3 PT
Prior Industry Experience: . . . . . . Helpful

FINANCIAL:
Cash Investment: $40-60K
Total Investment: $66.9-90.5K
Fees: Franchise - $12.5K
Royalty: 5%, Advert: 2.5%
Contract Periods (Yrs.): 10/10
Area Development Agreement: Yes/5
Sub-Franchise Contract: . . . . . .No
Expand in Territory: . . . . . . .No
Passive Ownership: . . . . . .Allowed
Encourage Conversions: . . . . . .No
Franchisee Purchase(s) Required: .No

FRANCHISOR TRAINING/SUPPORT:
Financial Assistance Provided: . . . Yes(I)
Site Selection Assistance: . . . . . . .Yes
Lease Negotiation Assistance: . . . . .Yes
Co-operative Advertising: . . . . No
Training: . . . . . . 1-2 Wks. Headquarters,
. . . . .5 Days On-site
On-Going Support: . . . . . . C,D,E,G,H,I
Full-Time Franchisor Support Staff: . . . 3
EXPANSION PLANS:
US: . . . . All US
Canada - Yes, . . . Overseas - Yes

NYPD - NEW YORK PIZZA DEPT.

9449 Balboa Ave., # 212
San Diego, CA 92123
TEL: (619) 292-9111
FAX:
Mr. Daniel Crotta, President

Arrestingly delicious pizza delivered from your precinct theme restaurant in Squad Cars! Marketing uniqueness plus quality. Pizza delivery is the fastest-growing segment and most preferred fast food (Gallup poll). For consumer awareness, in the #1 industry, join the ground floor opportunities with "New York's Finest." Multi-unit areas.

HISTORY: . . . .
Established in 1972; . . 1st Franchised in 1984
Company-Owned Units (As of 12/1/1989): . .4
Franchised Units (12/1/1989): 3
Total Units (12/1/1989): 7
Distribution: US-7;Can-0;Overseas-0
North America: . . . . .1 State
Concentration: . . . . 7 in CA
Registered: . . . . CA
. . . .
Average # of Employees: . . . . . .3 FT, 15 PT
Prior Industry Experience: . . . . . . Helpful

FINANCIAL:
Cash Investment: $50-100K
Total Investment: $100-170K
Fees: Franchise - $9.5K
Royalty: 5%, Advert: 3%
Contract Periods (Yrs.): 10/10
Area Development Agreement: Yes/10
Sub-Franchise Contract: . . . . . .No
Expand in Territory: . . . . . . Yes
Passive Ownership: . . . Discouraged
Encourage Conversions: . . . . . .No
Franchisee Purchase(s) Required: Yes

FRANCHISOR TRAINING/SUPPORT:
Financial Assistance Provided: . . . Yes(I)
Site Selection Assistance: . . . . . . .Yes
Lease Negotiation Assistance: . . . . .Yes
Co-operative Advertising: . . . . . . .Yes
Training: . . . . . . 4-6 Wks. Headquarters
. . . .
On-Going Support: . . . . B,C,D,E,f,G,H,I
Full-Time Franchisor Support Staff: . . . 4
EXPANSION PLANS:
US: . . . . Southwest
Canada - No, ... Overseas - Yes

OLD FLORIDA BAR-B-Q

1388 E. Oakland Park Blvd.
Ft. Lauderdale, FL 33334
TEL: (305) 561-1882
FAX:
Mr. Bill Claus, President

Take-out and delivery only, with optional drive-thru. Authentic southern Bar-B-Q. Limited cholesterol-conscious menu. Baby back ribs, pork, beef brisket, chicken and chicken wings at moderate prices fill the menu. Catering boosts sales and free advertising.

HISTORY: . . . .
Established in 1985; . . 1st Franchised in 1987
Company-Owned Units (As of 12/1/1989): . .1
Franchised Units (12/1/1989): 0
Total Units (12/1/1989): 1
Distribution: US-1;Can-0;Overseas-0
North America: . . . . .1 State
Concentration: . . . . 1 in FL
Registered: . . . . . FL,IL,IN,MD,MI,NY,RI
. . . .
Average # of Employees: . . . . . . 8 FT, 2 PT
Prior Industry Experience: . . . . . . Helpful

FINANCIAL:
Cash Investment: $40K
Total Investment: $50-80K
Fees: Franchise - $5K
Royalty: 5%, Advert: 2%
Contract Periods (Yrs.): . . . 10/5/5/
Area Development Agreement: Yes/5
Sub-Franchise Contract: . . . . . .No
Expand in Territory: . . . . . . Yes
Passive Ownership: . . . Discouraged
Encourage Conversions: . . . . . Yes
Franchisee Purchase(s) Required: .No

FRANCHISOR TRAINING/SUPPORT:
Financial Assistance Provided: . . . . . No
Site Selection Assistance: . . . . . . .Yes
Lease Negotiation Assistance: . . . . .Yes
Co-operative Advertising: . . . . . . .Yes
Training: . . . . 3 Wks. Headquarters
. . . .
On-Going Support: . . . . C,D,E,F,H
Full-Time Franchisor Support Staff: . . 10
EXPANSION PLANS:
US: . . . . All US
Canada - Yes, . . . Overseas - Yes

OLGA'S KITCHEN

1940 Northwood Dr.
Troy, MI 48084
TEL: (313) 362-0001
FAX: (313) 362-2013
Mr. Robert McRae, VP

Specialty restaurant with quick table service at moderate prices, and featuring "The Olga," a unique menu of gourmet sandwiches with secret recipe bread that's cooked fresh every order. OLGA'S is perfectly positioned to answer the increasing demand for fast-food alternatives.

HISTORY: . . . . IFA
Established in 1975; . . 1st Franchised in 1985
Company-Owned Units (As of 12/1/1989): . 50
Franchised Units (12/1/1989): 15
Total Units (12/1/1989): 65
Distribution: US-65;Can-0;Overseas-0
North America: . . . . 12 States
Concentration: . . . 30 in MI, 4 in CA, 3 in OH
Registered: . . . CA,FL,IL,IN,MD,MI,MN,NY
. . . . RI,VA,WI
Average # of Employees: . . . . . 20 FT, 20 PT
Prior Industry Experience: . . . . Helpful

FINANCIAL:
Cash Investment: $150-200K
Total Investment: $450-650K
Fees: Franchise - $25K
Royalty: 5%, Advert: 3%
Contract Periods (Yrs.): 10/5
Area Development Agreement: Yes/Var
Sub-Franchise Contract: . . . . . .No
Expand in Territory: . . . . Yes
Passive Ownership: . . . Discouraged
Encourage Conversions: . . . . . Yes
Franchisee Purchase(s) Required: .No

FRANCHISOR TRAINING/SUPPORT:
Financial Assistance Provided: . . . . . No
Site Selection Assistance: . . . . .Yes
Lease Negotiation Assistance: . . . . .Yes
Co-operative Advertising: . . . . No
Training: . . . . 6 Wks. Headquarters
. . . .
On-Going Support: . . A,B,C,D,E,F,G,H,I
Full-Time Franchisor Support Staff: . . 30
EXPANSION PLANS:
US: . . . . .All US
Canada - Yes, ...Overseas - No

OLIVERIO'S PIZZA / OLIVER'S PIZZA

28580 Orchard Lake Rd.
Farmington Hills, MI 48018
TEL: (800) 422-0707 (313) 737-4800
FAX: (313) 737-2503
Mr. Blake J. Discher, VP Fran. Dev.

Join the hottest growth segment of fast food. We feature 2-for-1 round and square deep-dish pizza, submarine sandwiches and salads for carry-out and delivery. High-quality ingredients and great-tasting product is our emphasis. Stores are colorful, bright and upscale in appearance.

HISTORY: . . . .
Established in 1982; . . 1st Franchised in 1984
Company-Owned Units (As of 12/1/1989): . .1
Franchised Units (12/1/1989): 67
Total Units (12/1/1989): 68
Distribution: US-68;Can-0;Overseas-0
North America: . . . . 6 States
Concentration: . . . 36 in MI, 3 in TX, 2 in FL
Registered: . . . . FL,IL,MI
. . . .
Average # of Employees: . . . . . .5 FT, 12 PT
Prior Industry Experience: . . . . Helpful

FINANCIAL:
Cash Investment: $40-45K
Total Investment: $85-135K
Fees: Franchise - $7.5K
Royalty: 5%, Advert: 3%
Contract Periods (Yrs.): 10/10
Area Development Agreement: Yes/4
Sub-Franchise Contract: . . . . . Yes
Expand in Territory: . . . . Yes
Passive Ownership: . . . Discouraged
Encourage Conversions: . . . . . Yes
Franchisee Purchase(s) Required: .No

FRANCHISOR TRAINING/SUPPORT:
Financial Assistance Provided: . . . Yes(I)
Site Selection Assistance: . . . . .Yes
Lease Negotiation Assistance: . . . . . No
Co-operative Advertising: . . . . .Yes
Training: . . . . . . 4-6 Wks. Field, 2 Days
. . . . . . .Headquarters, 5 Days On-site
On-Going Support: . . . .B,C,D,E,F,G,H,I
Full-Time Franchisor Support Staff: . . 14
EXPANSION PLANS:
US: . . . . .All US
Canada - Yes, ...Overseas - No

ORIGINAL PANZEROTTO & PIZZA

234 Parliament St.
Toronto, ON M5A3A4 CAN
TEL: (416) 362-5555
FAX: (416) 362-4916
Mr. Joe Schiavone, Fran. Dir.

We are a growing fast-food chain, specializing in pizzas and other Italian food. Our main goal is to provide a premium, quality product and at the same time offer fast, efficient service to our customers.

HISTORY: . . . .
Established in 1976; . . 1st Franchised in 1979
Company-Owned Units (As of 12/1/1989): . .1
Franchised Units (12/1/1989): 23
Total Units (12/1/1989): 24
Distribution: US-0;Can-24;Overseas-0
North America: . . . . .1 Province
Concentration: . . . . 24 in ON
Registered: . . . .
. . . .
Average # of Employees: . . . . . . 2 FT, 3 PT
Prior Industry Experience: . . . . Helpful

FINANCIAL:
Cash Investment: . . . .$
Total Investment: $120-150K
Fees: Franchise - $25K
Royalty: 5%, Advert: 3%
Contract Periods (Yrs.): 5/5
Area Development Agreement: Yes/10
Sub-Franchise Contract: . . . . . Yes
Expand in Territory: . . . . Yes
Passive Ownership: . . . . . .Allowed
Encourage Conversions: . . . . . Yes
Franchisee Purchase(s) Required: .No

FRANCHISOR TRAINING/SUPPORT:
Financial Assistance Provided: . . . Yes(I)
Site Selection Assistance: . . . . .Yes
Lease Negotiation Assistance: . . . . .Yes
Co-operative Advertising: . . . . .Yes
Training: . . . . 5 Days Headquarters,
. . . . .3 Wks. On-site
On-Going Support: . . A,B,C,D,E,F,G,H,I
Full-Time Franchisor Support Staff: . . 17
EXPANSION PLANS:
US: . . . . Northeast
Canada - Yes, ...Overseas - No

PAPA GINO'S OF AMERICA

600 Providence Hwy.
Dedham, MA 02026
TEL: (617) 461-1200
FAX: (617) 461-1896
Mr. Paul LaRose, Dir. Fran.

PAPA GINO'S offers its legendary pizza, complemented by an expansive menu, including pasta entrees, a generous salad bar, and overstuffed submarine sandwiches, along with an abundance of beverages, desserts and ice cream. PAPA GINO'S also offers eat-in or take-out services with delivery available in most locations.

HISTORY: . . . .
Established in 1963; . . 1st Franchised in 1989
Company-Owned Units (As of 12/1/1989): 215
Franchised Units (12/1/1989): 0
Total Units (12/1/1989): 215
Distribution: US-215;Can-0;Overseas-0
North America: . . . . 8 States
Concentration: . .156 in MA, 23 in NH, 19 CT
Registered: . . . . .FL,NY,RI
. . . .
Average # of Employees: . . . . . .6 FT, 19 PT
Prior Industry Experience: . . . . . .Necessary

FINANCIAL:
Cash Investment: $80-275K
Total Investment: $439-559K
Fees: Franchise - $25K
Royalty: 4.5%, Advert: 4.5%
Contract Periods (Yrs.): . . 10/Lease
Area Development Agreement: Yes/Var
Sub-Franchise Contract: . . . . .No
Expand in Territory: . . . . Yes
Passive Ownership: . . . Discouraged
Encourage Conversions: . . . . .No
Franchisee Purchase(s) Required: Yes

FRANCHISOR TRAINING/SUPPORT:
Financial Assistance Provided: . . . . .No
Site Selection Assistance: . . . . .No
Lease Negotiation Assistance: . . . .Yes
Co-operative Advertising: . . . . . . .Yes
Training: . . . . 4 Wks. Headquarters
. . . .
On-Going Support: . . . . . .a,b,C,D,E,f,I
Full-Time Franchisor Support Staff: . . .3
EXPANSION PLANS:
US: . . . . .Mid-Atlantic, Southeast
Canada - No, ...Overseas - No

PENN STATION STEAK & SUB

7516 Heatherwood Ln.
Cincinnati, OH 45244
TEL: (513) 231-0181
FAX:
Mr. Jeff Osterfeld, President

PENN STATION specializes in quality food, prepared fresh before your eyes. We sell original "Philadelphia cheesesteaks," fresh-cut fries, fresh-squeezed lemonade and over-stuffed cold subs. Store locations include strip centers, shopping malls, downtown areas and college campuses.

HISTORY: . . . .
Established in 1983; . . 1st Franchised in 1988
Company-Owned Units (As of 12/1/1989): . .0
Franchised Units (12/1/1989): 6
Total Units (12/1/1989): 6
Distribution: US-6;Can-0;Overseas-0
North America: . . . . 2 States
Concentration: . . . . .5 in OH, 1 in IN
Registered: . . . .
. . . .
Average # of Employees: . . . . . . 4 FT, 8 PT
Prior Industry Experience: . . . . . . Helpful

FINANCIAL:
Cash Investment: $90-125K
Total Investment: $90-125K
Fees: Franchise - $17.5K
Royalty: 6%, Advert: 0%
Contract Periods (Yrs.): 10/10
Area Development Agreement: Yes/10
Sub-Franchise Contract: . . . . .No
Expand in Territory: . . . . Yes
Passive Ownership: . . . Discouraged
Encourage Conversions: . . . . . Yes
Franchisee Purchase(s) Required: .No

FRANCHISOR TRAINING/SUPPORT:
Financial Assistance Provided: . . . . .No
Site Selection Assistance: . . . . . . .Yes
Lease Negotiation Assistance: . . . .Yes
Co-operative Advertising: . . . . . . .Yes
Training: . . . . . . .10 Days Headquarters
. . . .
On-Going Support: . . . . . B,C,D,E,F,H,I
Full-Time Franchisor Support Staff: . . .3
EXPANSION PLANS:
US: . . . . .All US
Canada - No, ...Overseas - No

PHILADELPHIA STEAK & SUB

1700 Rte. 23
Wayne, NJ 07470
TEL: (201) 696-7200
FAX:
Mr. Mike Flynn, VP Dev.

Authentic South Philly-style cheesesteaks and sub sandwiches. First store opened in 1974 in Philadelphia. Operations in high-volume malls, festive marketplaces and downtown locations. "We stand behind our sandwiches."

HISTORY: . . . . IFA
Established in 1974; . . 1st Franchised in 1984
Company-Owned Units (As of 12/1/1989): . 11
Franchised Units (12/1/1989): 5
Total Units (12/1/1989): 16
Distribution: US-16;Can-0;Overseas-0
North America: . . . . 4 States
Concentration: . . . 4 in NJ, 4 in NY, 3 in VA
Registered: . . . . FL,NY,VA
. . . .
Average # of Employees: . . . . . .4 FT, 12 PT
Prior Industry Experience: . . . . . . Helpful

FINANCIAL:
Cash Investment: $45-95K
Total Investment: $135-200K
Fees: Franchise - $25K
Royalty: 5%, Advert: 2%
Contract Periods (Yrs.): 10/10
Area Development Agreement: Yes/10
Sub-Franchise Contract: . . . . .No
Expand in Territory: . . . . Yes
Passive Ownership: . . . Not Allowed
Encourage Conversions: . . . . . Yes
Franchisee Purchase(s) Required: .No

FRANCHISOR TRAINING/SUPPORT:
Financial Assistance Provided: . . . . .No
Site Selection Assistance: . . . . . . .Yes
Lease Negotiation Assistance: . . . .Yes
Co-operative Advertising: . . . . . . .Yes
Training: . . . . . . 6 Days Training Store,
. . . . . 2 Days Office, 7 Days On-site
On-Going Support: . . . .B,C,D,E,F,G,H,I
Full-Time Franchisor Support Staff: . . 16
EXPANSION PLANS:
US: . . . . .East Coast, Ohio
Canada - No, ...Overseas - No

PIONEER CHICKEN

7301 Topanga Canyon Blvd., # 200
Canoga Park, CA 91303
TEL: (818) 716-5500
FAX: (818) 715-0815
Mr. Robert Singer, President

Franchisor was formed in 9/89 to purchase the assets of Pioneer Take Out Corp., the former franchisor of fast-food restaurants specializing in chicken products. Franchises are currently being offered to former PTOC franchisees. New franchisees will be offered to the general public in mid-1990.

HISTORY: . . . .
Established in 1989; . . 1st Franchised in 1989
Company-Owned Units (As of 12/1/1989): . 24
Franchised Units (12/1/1989): 145
Total Units (12/1/1989): 169
Distribution: US-169;Can-0;Overseas-0
North America: . . . . 2 States
Concentration: . . . . 168 in CA, 1 in AZ
Registered: . . . . CA
. . . .
Average # of Employees: . . . . . . 1 FT, 15 PT
Prior Industry Experience: . . . . . . Helpful

FINANCIAL:
Cash Investment: $100-500K
Total Investment: $100-500K
Fees: Franchise - $35K
  Royalty: 4%, Advert: 4.9%
Contract Periods (Yrs.): 20/10
Area Development Agreement: . .No
Sub-Franchise Contract: . . . . . .No
Expand in Territory: . . . . . . Yes
Passive Ownership: . . . . . .Allowed
Encourage Conversions: . . . . Yes
Franchisee Purchase(s) Required: .No

FRANCHISOR TRAINING/SUPPORT:
Financial Assistance Provided: . . . . . No
Site Selection Assistance: . . . . .NA
Lease Negotiation Assistance: . . . . .NA
Co-operative Advertising: . . . . .Yes
Training: . . . . 8 Wks. Headquarters
. . . .
On-Going Support: . . . . . .A,C,D,G,H,I
Full-Time Franchisor Support Staff: . . 45
EXPANSION PLANS:
US: . . . . . . .West of Mississippi River
Canada - No, ... Overseas - Yes

PIZZA FACTORY

P.O. Box 989
Oakhurst, CA 93644
TEL: (209) 683-3377
FAX:
Mr. Ron Willey, VP

We Toss 'Em, They're Awesome. PIZZA FACTORY has a proven track record with 55 restaurants in 7 states, The franchisee has a strong support system which includes site location, negotiating lease, on-site training and on-going support from headquarters. Call for brochure.

HISTORY: . . . .
Established in 1979; . . 1st Franchised in 1985
Company-Owned Units (As of 12/1/1989): . .4
Franchised Units (12/1/1989): 51
Total Units (12/1/1989): 55
Distribution: US-55;Can-0;Overseas-0
North America: . . . . 7 States
Concentration: . . 46 in CA, 3 in AZ, 2 in WA
Registered: . . . . .CA,FL,OR,WA
. . . .
Average # of Employees: . . . . 2 FT, 12-15 PT
Prior Industry Experience: . . . . . . Helpful

FINANCIAL:
Cash Investment: $50-65K
Total Investment: $65-95K
Fees: Franchise - $20K
  Royalty: 3%, Advert: 1%
Contract Periods (Yrs.): 15/10
Area Development Agreement: Yes/Var
Sub-Franchise Contract: . . . . .No
Expand in Territory: . . . . . . Yes
Passive Ownership: . . . Discouraged
Encourage Conversions: . . . . Yes
Franchisee Purchase(s) Required: Yes

FRANCHISOR TRAINING/SUPPORT:
Financial Assistance Provided: . . . . .No
Site Selection Assistance: . . . . . . .Yes
Lease Negotiation Assistance: . . . .Yes
Co-operative Advertising: . . . . . . .Yes
Training: . . . . 325 Hours Training Stores
. . . .
On-Going Support: . . . . . .C,D,E,G,H,I
Full-Time Franchisor Support Staff: . . . 1
EXPANSION PLANS:
US: . . . . .All US
Canada - No, ...Overseas - No

PIZZA LITE

9951 SW 142 Ave.
Miami, FL 33186
TEL: (800) 228-LITE (305) 386-7878
FAX:
Mr. Robert Friesmuth, President

PIZZA LITE is a unique pizza take-out and delivery concept that specializes in high-quality, fresh pizza that contains less fat and cholesterol. PIZZA LITE also offers garden-fresh salads, Haagen-Dazs ice cream, etc.

HISTORY: . . . .
Established in 1985; . . 1st Franchised in 1988
Company-Owned Units (As of 12/1/1989): . .1
Franchised Units (12/1/1989): 10
Total Units (12/1/1989): 11
Distribution: US-11;Can-0;Overseas-0
North America: . . . . 5 States
Concentration: . . . .4 in FL, 3 in GA, 2 in TN
Registered: . . . . CA,FL,MN
. . . .
Average # of Employees: . . . . . . 4 FT, 12 PT
Prior Industry Experience: . . . . . . Helpful

FINANCIAL:
Cash Investment: $30-60K
Total Investment: $65-100K
Fees: Franchise - $15K
  Royalty: $160/Wk., Advert: $40/Wk.
Contract Periods (Yrs.): 20/10
Area Development Agreement: Yes/20
Sub-Franchise Contract: . . . . Yes
Expand in Territory: . . . . . . Yes
Passive Ownership: . . . . . .Allowed
Encourage Conversions: . . . . .No
Franchisee Purchase(s) Required: Yes

FRANCHISOR TRAINING/SUPPORT:
Financial Assistance Provided: . . . Yes(I)
Site Selection Assistance: . . . . . . .Yes
Lease Negotiation Assistance: . . . .Yes
Co-operative Advertising: . . . . . . .Yes
Training: . . . . 5 Days Headquarters,
. . . . . . .5-7 Days Franchisee Location
On-Going Support: . . . B,C,D,E,F,G,h,I
Full-Time Franchisor Support Staff: . . .4
EXPANSION PLANS:
US: . . . . .All US
Canada - No, ...Overseas - No

PIZZA PIT

2154 Atwood Ave.
Madison, WI 53704
TEL: (608) 241-2163
FAX:
Mr. Kerry Cook, VP

Free home delivery and carry-out of handcrafted pizzas and specialty sandwiches. Units also adaptable to inside seating with prepared salads, expanded menu and/or pizza by the slice. Single and multiple-unit programs available.

HISTORY: . . . .
Established in 1969; . . 1st Franchised in 1982
Company-Owned Units (As of 12/1/1989): . 12
Franchised Units (12/1/1989): 8
Total Units (12/1/1989): 20
Distribution: US-20;Can-0;Overseas-0
North America: . . . . 2 States
Concentration: . . . . 16 in WI, 3 in IA
Registered: . . . . FL,IL,IN,WI
. . . .
Average # of Employees: . . . . . . 6 FT, 9 PT
Prior Industry Experience: . . . . . . Helpful

FINANCIAL:
Cash Investment: $40-50K
Total Investment: $100-230K
Fees: Franchise - $14-15K
Royalty: 4.5%, Advert: 1%
Contract Periods (Yrs.): . . . 15/10
Area Development Agreement: Yes/15
Sub-Franchise Contract: . . . . .No
Expand in Territory: . . . . . . Yes
Passive Ownership: . . . Discouraged
Encourage Conversions: . . . . Yes
Franchisee Purchase(s) Required: .No

FRANCHISOR TRAINING/SUPPORT:
Financial Assistance Provided: . . . . .No
Site Selection Assistance: . . . . . . .Yes
Lease Negotiation Assistance: . . . . .Yes
Co-operative Advertising: . . . . . . .Yes
Training: . . . . . . 4-6 Wks. Headquarters
. . . .
On-Going Support: . . . . B,C,D,E,F,G,H
Full-Time Franchisor Support Staff: . .125
EXPANSION PLANS:
US: . . . . .West and Midwest
Canada - No, ...Overseas - No

PIZZA PIZZA

580 Jarvis St.
Toronto, ON M4Y2H9 CAN
TEL: (416) 967-0177
FAX: (416) 967-0891
Mr. Roman Solek, Fran. Sales

Fast-food take-out and delivery. Computerized one number system.

HISTORY: . . . . IFA
Established in 1968; . . 1st Franchised in 1975
Company-Owned Units (As of 12/1/1989): . 10
Franchised Units (12/1/1989): 195
Total Units (12/1/1989): 205
Distribution: . . . US-0;Can-205;Overseas-0
North America: . . . . 2 Provinces
Concentration: . . . . . . 147 in ON, 9 in PQ
Registered: . . . .
. . . .
Average # of Employees: . . . . . 5 FT, 3-4 PT
Prior Industry Experience: . . . . . . Helpful

FINANCIAL:
Cash Investment: $53K
Total Investment: $175K
Fees: Franchise - $20K
Royalty: 6%, Advert: 6%
Contract Periods (Yrs.): 20/5
Area Development Agreement: . .No
Sub-Franchise Contract: . . . . .No
Expand in Territory: . . . . . . Yes
Passive Ownership: . . . Not Allowed
Encourage Conversions: . . . . Yes
Franchisee Purchase(s) Required: Yes

FRANCHISOR TRAINING/SUPPORT:
Financial Assistance Provided: . . .Yes(D)
Site Selection Assistance: . . . . . . .Yes
Lease Negotiation Assistance: . . . . .Yes
Co-operative Advertising: . . . . . . .Yes
Training: . . . . 12 Wks. Headquarters
. . . .
On-Going Support: . . . A,B,C,D,E,F,G,H
Full-Time Franchisor Support Staff: . .300
EXPANSION PLANS:
US: . . . . No
Canada - Yes, ...Overseas - No

PORT OF SUBS

100 Washington St., # 200
Reno, NV 89503
TEL: (800) 245-0245 (702) 322-7901 C
FAX: (702) 322-6093
Mr. Pat Larsen, President

A fast-service restaurant, offering a wide variety of submarine-type sandwiches, hot sandwiches and related items. Sandwiches are made-to-order to customer's specifications, using the freshest ingredients, including the highest-quality meats and cheeses and fresh bread baked on the premises.

HISTORY: . . . . IFA
Established in 1972; . . 1st Franchised in 1986
Company-Owned Units (As of 12/1/1989): . .7
Franchised Units (12/1/1989): 47
Total Units (12/1/1989): 54
Distribution: US-54;Can-0;Overseas-0
North America: . . . . 4 States
Concentration: . . 30 in NV, 18 in CA, 4 in AZ
Registered: . . . . CA,HI,WA
. . . .
Average # of Employees: . . . . . . 1 FT, 4 PT
Prior Industry Experience: . . . . . . Helpful

FINANCIAL:
Cash Investment: $40-50K
Total Investment: $100-158K
Fees: Franchise - $16K
Royalty: 5.5%, Advert: . . . 1%
Contract Periods (Yrs.): . . . 10/10
Area Development Agreement: Yes/Var
Sub-Franchise Contract: . . . . .No
Expand in Territory: . . . . . . Yes
Passive Ownership: . . . . . .Allowed
Encourage Conversions: . . . . Yes
Franchisee Purchase(s) Required: .No

FRANCHISOR TRAINING/SUPPORT:
Financial Assistance Provided: . . . Yes(I)
Site Selection Assistance: . . . . . . .Yes
Lease Negotiation Assistance: . . . . .Yes
Co-operative Advertising: . . . . . . .Yes
Training: . . . . 2 Wks. Headquarters
. . . .
On-Going Support: . . . . B,C,D,E,F,G,h,I
Full-Time Franchisor Support Staff: . . 12
EXPANSION PLANS:
US: . . . . .West
Canada - No, ...Overseas - No

POTTS' HOT DOG

16305 San Carlos Blvd.
Ft. Myers, FL 33908
TEL: (813) 466-7747 C
FAX:
Mr. Michael Potts, VP/Secty.

POTTS' HOT DOG is a fast-growing franchise, which specializes in POTTS' exclusively-made hot dogs and chili. Our stores are fast, clean, friendly and reasonable. Due to the nation's love for a great hot dog, we believe that there is no area that would be wrong for a POTTS' DOGGIE SHOP.

HISTORY: . . . .
Established in 1965; . . 1st Franchised in 1985
Company-Owned Units (As of 12/1/1989): . .5
Franchised Units (12/1/1989): 10
Total Units (12/1/1989): 15
Distribution: US-15;Can-0;Overseas-0
  North America: . . . . 3 States
  Concentration: . . . 10 in PA, 4 in FL, 1 in NJ
Registered: . . . . .FL
. . . .
Average # of Employees: . . . . . . 4 FT, 4 PT
Prior Industry Experience: . . . . Helpful

FINANCIAL:
Cash Investment: $30K
Total Investment: $30-50K
Fees: Franchise - $15K
  Royalty: 4%, Advert: 2%
Contract Periods (Yrs.): 5/5
Area Development Agreement: Yes/5
Sub-Franchise Contract: . . . . .No
Expand in Territory: . . . . . . Yes
Passive Ownership: . . . Discouraged
Encourage Conversions: . . . . .No
Franchisee Purchase(s) Required: Yes

FRANCHISOR TRAINING/SUPPORT:
Financial Assistance Provided: . . . . .No
Site Selection Assistance: . . . . . . .Yes
Lease Negotiation Assistance: . . . . .Yes
Co-operative Advertising: . . . . . . .Yes
Training: . . . . 100 Hrs.+ Bethlehem, PA,
. . . . .100 Hrs.+ Headquarters
On-Going Support: . . . . D,E,G,H,I
Full-Time Franchisor Support Staff: . . . .
EXPANSION PLANS:
US: . . . . .PA, FL and NJ
Canada - No, ...Overseas - No

PRO PORTION FOODS

45 Jefryn Blvd. W.
Deer Park, NY 11729
TEL: (516) 667-4500
FAX:
Ms.Janet Micheletti, Fran. Ops. Mgr.

Low-calorie "ice cream" and food cafe, featuring a naturally-sweetened Soft-serve (21 flavors) and full menu. Everything we serve for sit-down or feature in our take-out section is calorie-controlled with exchange information provided. "Counting calories was never so delicious."

HISTORY: . . . .
Established in 1975; . . 1st Franchised in 1984
Company-Owned Units (As of 12/1/1989): . .0
Franchised Units (12/1/1989): 12
Total Units (12/1/1989): 12
Distribution: US-12;Can-0;Overseas-0
  North America: . . . . 3 States
  Concentration: . . . .9 in NY, 2 in FL, 1 in WI
Registered: . . . . FL,NY,WI
. . . .
Average # of Employees: . . . . . . 4 FT, 10 PT
Prior Industry Experience: . . . . Helpful

FINANCIAL:
Cash Investment: . . . .$
Total Investment: $219K
Fees: Franchise - $22.5K
  Royalty: 4%, Advert: 2%
Contract Periods (Yrs.): 25/25
Area Development Agreement: Yes/Var
Sub-Franchise Contract: . . . . . Yes
Expand in Territory: . . . . . . Yes
Passive Ownership: . . . . . .Allowed
Encourage Conversions: . . . . . Yes
Franchisee Purchase(s) Required: Yes

FRANCHISOR TRAINING/SUPPORT:
Financial Assistance Provided: . . . Yes(I)
Site Selection Assistance: . . . . . . .Yes
Lease Negotiation Assistance: . . . . .Yes
Co-operative Advertising: . . . . . . .Yes
Training: . . . . .2-4 Wks. or As Needed at
. . . . Existing Stores
On-Going Support: . . . .B,C,D,E,F,G,H,I
Full-Time Franchisor Support Staff: . . . 8
EXPANSION PLANS:
US: . . . . NY, FL, WI and NJ
Canada - No, ...Overseas - No

PUDGIES PIZZA & SUB SHOPS

524-530 N. Main St.
Elmira, NY 14901
TEL: (607) 734-7419
FAX:
Mr. Michael Cleary, Officer

High-volume units - very successful. Emphasis on quality and value. Innovators in the pizza/sub industry. Often imitated, strong identity. Professional pizza-pleasing people.

HISTORY: . . . .
Established in 1963; . . 1st Franchised in 1972
Company-Owned Units (As of 12/1/1989): . .3
Franchised Units (12/1/1989): 29
Total Units (12/1/1989): 32
Distribution: US-32;Can-0;Overseas-0
  North America: . . . . 2 States
  Concentration: . . . . . . .32 in NY, 6 in PA
Registered: . . . .
. . . .
Average # of Employees: . . . . . 20 FT, 10 PT
Prior Industry Experience: . . . . Helpful

FINANCIAL:
Cash Investment: $100-150K
Total Investment: $400-600K
Fees: Franchise - $20K
  Royalty: 4%, Advert: 0%
Contract Periods (Yrs.): 15/10
Area Development Agreement: . Yes
Sub-Franchise Contract: . . . . .No
Expand in Territory: . . . . . . Yes
Passive Ownership: . . . Discouraged
Encourage Conversions: . . . . Yes
Franchisee Purchase(s) Required: .No

FRANCHISOR TRAINING/SUPPORT:
Financial Assistance Provided: . . . . .No
Site Selection Assistance: . . . . . . .Yes
Lease Negotiation Assistance: . . . . .Yes
Co-operative Advertising: . . . . . . .Yes
Training: . . . . . . 2-3 Wks. Headquarters
. . . .
On-Going Support: . . A,B,C,D,e,F,G,H,I
Full-Time Franchisor Support Staff: . . . .
EXPANSION PLANS:
US: . . . . Northeast Only
Canada - No, ...Overseas - No

QUIZNO'S AMERICA

190 E. 9th, # 190
Denver, CO 80203
TEL: (303) 860-7222
FAX:
Mr. Todd C. Disner, President

Provides an up-scale product served in up-scale surroundings. Over-stuffed and oven-baked sub-style sandwiches. We use proprietary dressings and sauces to provide a sandwich unlike any in the industry.

HISTORY: . . . .
Established in 1981; . . 1st Franchised in 1983
Company-Owned Units (As of 12/1/1989): . .5
Franchised Units (12/1/1989): 20
Total Units (12/1/1989): 25
Distribution: US-25;Can-0;Overseas-0
North America: . . . . 3 States
Concentration: . . 22 in CO, 2 in CA, 1 in NM
Registered: . . . . CA
. . . .
Average # of Employees: . . . . . . 8 FT, 5 PT
Prior Industry Experience: . . . . Helpful

FINANCIAL:
Cash Investment: . . . . $35K+
Total Investment: $100-600K
Fees: Franchise - $15K
  Royalty: 4%, Advert: 3%
Contract Periods (Yrs.): 15/5
Area Development Agreement: Yes/Var
Sub-Franchise Contract: . . . . . .No
Expand in Territory: . . . . Yes
Passive Ownership: . . . Discouraged
Encourage Conversions: . . . . . Yes
Franchisee Purchase(s) Required: .No

FRANCHISOR TRAINING/SUPPORT:
Financial Assistance Provided: . . . . . No
Site Selection Assistance: . . . . .Yes
Lease Negotiation Assistance: . . . . .Yes
Co-operative Advertising: . . . . .Yes
Training: . . . . 2 Wks. Headquarters
. . . .
On-Going Support: . . . .a,B,C,D,E,f,G,H
Full-Time Franchisor Support Staff: . . 10
EXPANSION PLANS:
  US: . . . . .All US
  Canada - Yes, . . . Overseas - Yes

RALLY'S HAMBURGERS

10002 Shelbyville Rd., # 150
Louisville, KY 40223
TEL: (502) 245-8900
FAX:
Mr. Edward C. Binzel, Sr. VP

Double drive-thru hamburger restaurant. Includes walk-up windows and outside seating.

HISTORY: . . . . IFA
Established in 1984; . . 1st Franchised in 1986
Company-Owned Units (As of 12/1/1989): . 67
Franchised Units (12/1/1989): 105
Total Units (12/1/1989): 172
Distribution: US-172;Can-0;Overseas-0
North America: . . . . 23 States
Concentration: . . . .
Registered: . . . CA,FL,IL,IN,MI,MD,MN,NY
. . . . OR,RI,VA,WI
Average # of Employees: . . . .
Prior Industry Experience: . . . . . .Necessary

FINANCIAL:
Cash Investment: . . . .$
Total Investment: . . . .$
Fees: Franchise - . . . .$
  Royalty: 4%, Advert: 4%
Contract Periods (Yrs.): 15
Area Development Agreement: Yes/Var
Sub-Franchise Contract: . . . . . .No
Expand in Territory: . . . . Yes
Passive Ownership: . . . .
Encourage Conversions: . . . .
Franchisee Purchase(s) Required: .No

FRANCHISOR TRAINING/SUPPORT:
Financial Assistance Provided: . . . . . No
Site Selection Assistance: . . . . .Yes
Lease Negotiation Assistance: . . . . . No
Co-operative Advertising: . . . .
Training: . . . .
. . . .
On-Going Support: . . . . . . .B,C,D,E,G
Full-Time Franchisor Support Staff: . . 15
EXPANSION PLANS:
  US: . . . . .All US
  Canada - Yes, ...Overseas - No

RAX RESTAURANTS

1266 Dublin Rd.
Columbus, OH 43215
TEL: (614) 486-3669
FAX: (614) 486-5113
Mr. Mark Koschny, Dir. Fran.

Quick-service restaurants, offering a broad menu of specialty sandwiches, hot-topped potatoes, shakes and a 50+ item salad bar with your own Mexican entrees, hot pastas and salads.

HISTORY: . . . .
Established in 1978; . . 1st Franchised in 1978
Company-Owned Units (As of 12/1/1989): 150
Franchised Units (12/1/1989): 350
Total Units (12/1/1989): 500
Distribution: US-497;Can-3;Overseas-0
North America: . . . 29 States, 2 Provinces
Concentration: . . 108 in OH, 57 in FL, 54 PA
Registered: . . . . .All
. . . .
Average # of Employees: . . . . 2-3 FT, 30+ PT
Prior Industry Experience: . . . . Helpful

FINANCIAL: NASD-RAX
Cash Investment: $50-125K
Total Investment: $550-800K
Fees: Franchise - $30K
  Royalty: 4%, Advert: 4%
Contract Periods (Yrs.): 20
Area Development Agreement: Yes/3-5
Sub-Franchise Contract: . . . . . .No
Expand in Territory: . . . . Yes
Passive Ownership: . . . Not Allowed
Encourage Conversions: . . . . . Yes
Franchisee Purchase(s) Required: .No

FRANCHISOR TRAINING/SUPPORT:
Financial Assistance Provided: . . . Yes(I)
Site Selection Assistance: . . . . .Yes
Lease Negotiation Assistance: . . . . .Yes
Co-operative Advertising: . . . . .Yes
Training: . . . . 5 Wks. in Columbus,
. . . . .St. Louis or Orlando
On-Going Support: . . .B,C,D,E,G,H,I
Full-Time Franchisor Support Staff: . . .3
EXPANSION PLANS:
  US: . . . . . Midwest, FL, Pacific N'west
  Canada - Yes, . . . Overseas - Yes

RENZIOS

P. O. Box 2190, 701 W. Hampden Ave.
Englewood, CO 80150
TEL: (800) 888-3139 (303) 781-3441
FAX:
Mr. Thomas D. Rentzios, President

Unique Greek fast-food restaurants operating in mall food courts and strip malls. RENZIOS fills the space between typical fast-food and the full-service restaurant, offering traditional Greek recipes and featuring the wholesome Gyros Sandwich. For those who want more in a meal, there are lean meat platters, Gyros Salad or lamb kabob. Authentic Greek pastries. You'll have all the right ingredients for success.

HISTORY: . . . .
Established in 1985; . . 1st Franchised in 1989
Company-Owned Units (As of 12/1/1989): . .6
Franchised Units (12/1/1989): 1
Total Units (12/1/1989): 7
Distribution: US-7;Can-0;Overseas-0
 North America: . . . . 3 States
 Concentration: . . . 4 in CO, 2 in MT, 1 in NV
Registered: . . . . WA
. . . .
Average # of Employees: . . . . . . 2 FT, 5 PT
Prior Industry Experience: . . . . Helpful

FINANCIAL:
Cash Investment: $20-30K
Total Investment: $80-150K
Fees: Franchise - $18K
 Royalty: 5%, Advert: 0%
Contract Periods (Yrs.): 10/5/5
Area Development Agreement: Yes/5
Sub-Franchise Contract: . . . . .No
Expand in Territory: . . . . . . Yes
Passive Ownership: . . . . . .Allowed
Encourage Conversions: . . . . Yes
Franchisee Purchase(s) Required: .No

FRANCHISOR TRAINING/SUPPORT:
Financial Assistance Provided: . . . Yes(I)
Site Selection Assistance: . . . . . . .Yes
Lease Negotiation Assistance: . . . . .Yes
Co-operative Advertising: . . . . . . .Yes
Training: . . . . . . 21 Days Headquarters,
 . . . . .7 Days Franchisee Location
On-Going Support: . . . . . C,D,E,F,G,H,I
Full-Time Franchisor Support Staff: . . . 3
EXPANSION PLANS:
US: . . . . .All Exc. Not Registered
Canada - No, ...Overseas - No

ROLI BOLI

15 Engle St., # 304
Englewood, NJ 07631
TEL: (800) 332-2229 (201) 871-0370
FAX: (201) 871-7168
Mr. John Sterns, Sales Manager

A unique food concept which combines a light, crispy french dough recipe, and choice of 24 fresh ingredients for delicious filling.

HISTORY: . . . .
Established in 1987; . . 1st Franchised in 1989
Company-Owned Units (As of 12/1/1989): . .4
Franchised Units (12/1/1989): 1
Total Units (12/1/1989): 5
Distribution: US-5;Can-0;Overseas-0
 North America: . . . . 2 States
 Concentration: . . . . .4 in NJ, 1 in CT
Registered: . . . . FL,NY
. . . .
Average # of Employees: . . . . . . 2 FT, 2 PT
Prior Industry Experience: . . . . Helpful

FINANCIAL:
Cash Investment: $50-75K
Total Investment: $130-185K
Fees: Franchise - $20K
 Royalty: 5%, Advert: 3%
Contract Periods (Yrs.): . . 10/10/10
Area Development Agreement: . .No
Sub-Franchise Contract: . . . . .No
Expand in Territory: . . . . . . Yes
Passive Ownership: . . . . . .Allowed
Encourage Conversions: . . . . .No
Franchisee Purchase(s) Required: .No

FRANCHISOR TRAINING/SUPPORT:
Financial Assistance Provided: . . . Yes(I)
Site Selection Assistance: . . . . . . .Yes
Lease Negotiation Assistance: . . . . .Yes
Co-operative Advertising: . . . . . . .NA
Training: . . . . . . 2 Wks. Company Store,
 . . . . 1 Wk. On-site
On-Going Support: . . . . . B,C,D,E,F,G,I
Full-Time Franchisor Support Staff: . . . 6
EXPANSION PLANS:
US: . . . . .All US
Canada - Yes, ...Overseas - No

ROY ROGERS RESTAURANTS

1 Marriott Dr., # 202
Washington, DC 20058
TEL: (800) 638-6707 (301) 251-6128
FAX: (301) 279-2384
Mr. Richard Kelly, Dir. Licensing

ROY ROGERS provides the brand name, operating system and on-going support to capture market share. We offer 2 advantages that other fast-food franchisors can't provide - the popularity of both fried chicken and burgers with 20 years of successful operations.

HISTORY: . . . . IFA
Established in 1927; . . 1st Franchised in 1969
Company-Owned Units (As of 12/1/1989): 395
Franchised Units (12/1/1989): 240
Total Units (12/1/1989): 635
Distribution: . . . US-635;Can-0;Overseas-0
 North America: . . . . 13 States
 Concentration: . 135 in MD, 130 in NJ, 92 NY
Registered: . . . . MD,VA
. . . .
Average # of Employees: . . . . 10 FT, 45 PT
Prior Industry Experience: . . . . . .Necessary

FINANCIAL: NYSE-MHS
Cash Investment: $300-500K
Total Investment: . . . $475-1,675K
Fees: Franchise - $30K
 Royalty: 4%, Advert: 5%
Contract Periods (Yrs.): 20/20
Area Development Agreement: . .No
Sub-Franchise Contract: . . . . .No
Expand in Territory: . . . . . . Yes
Passive Ownership: . . . Not Allowed
Encourage Conversions: . . . . Yes
Franchisee Purchase(s) Required: .No

FRANCHISOR TRAINING/SUPPORT:
Financial Assistance Provided: . . . . . No
Site Selection Assistance: . . . . . . .Yes
Lease Negotiation Assistance: . . . . .Yes
Co-operative Advertising: . . . . . . .Yes
Training: . . . . 2 Wks. Headquarters,
 . . . . 7-8 Wks. On-site
On-Going Support: . . . . . .b,C,D,E,G,H
Full-Time Franchisor Support Staff: . .228
EXPANSION PLANS:
US: . . . . Northeast
Canada - No, ... Overseas - No

RUSTY'S PIZZA PARLOR

1027 Garden St.
Santa Barbara, CA 93101
TEL: (805) 963-9127
FAX: (805) 962-5054
Mr. Roger Duncan, President

RUSTY'S PIZZA PARLORS - pizza, subs and salads in an up-scale, self-service dining room or a "delivery-only" concept. We offer training and support to help you grow with us. Single or multi-unit areas available in 1989 for California only. Call RUSTY at (805) 963-9127.

HISTORY: . . . .
Established in 1968; . . 1st Franchised in 1980
Company-Owned Units (As of 12/1/1989): . 11
Franchised Units (12/1/1989): 3
Total Units (12/1/1989): 14
Distribution: US-14;Can-0;Overseas-0
North America: . . . . .1 State
Concentration: . . . . 14 in CA
Registered: . . . . CA
. . . .
Average # of Employees: . . . . 5 FT, 12-15 PT
Prior Industry Experience: . . . . Helpful

FINANCIAL:
Cash Investment: $150-350K
Total Investment: $150-350K
Fees: Franchise - $15K
  Royalty: 5%, Advert: 3%
Contract Periods (Yrs.): 20/10
Area Development Agreement: . .No
Sub-Franchise Contract: . . . . .No
Expand in Territory: . . . . Yes
Passive Ownership: . . . Not Allowed
Encourage Conversions: . . . . . Yes
Franchisee Purchase(s) Required: .No

FRANCHISOR TRAINING/SUPPORT:
Financial Assistance Provided: . . . . .No
Site Selection Assistance: . . . . .Yes
Lease Negotiation Assistance: . . . . .Yes
Co-operative Advertising: . . . . No
Training: . . . . . . .500 Hrs. Headquarters
. . . .
On-Going Support: . . . . C,D,G
Full-Time Franchisor Support Staff: . . 41
EXPANSION PLANS:
  US: . . . . California Only
  Canada - No, ...Overseas - No

SAKURA JAPANESE FAST FOOD

645 Sir Richards Rd.
Mississauga, ON L5C1A3 CAN
TEL: (416) 897-8795
FAX: (416) 897-1794
Mr. Ken Ough, President

Genuine Japanese home cuisine, which includes teriyaki, sukiyaki, katsu, domburi, tempura (shrimp), udon (noodle soup) and sushi (limited).

HISTORY: . . . .
Established in 1979; . . 1st Franchised in 1987
Company-Owned Units (As of 12/1/1989): . .1
Franchised Units (12/1/1989): 5
Total Units (12/1/1989): 6
Distribution: US-0;Can-6;Overseas-0
North America: . . . . .1 Province
Concentration: . . . . 6 in On
Registered: . . . . .IL,NY
. . . .
Average # of Employees: . . . . . . 3 FT, 1 PT
Prior Industry Experience: . . . . . . Helpful

FINANCIAL:
Cash Investment: . . . .$145K+
Total Investment: . . . . . . $145K+
Fees: Franchise - $25K
  Royalty: 5%, Advert: 2%
Contract Periods (Yrs.): 15/15
Area Development Agreement: . .No
Sub-Franchise Contract: . . . . .No
Expand in Territory: . . . . Yes
Passive Ownership: . . . Not Allowed
Encourage Conversions: . . . . . NA
Franchisee Purchase(s) Required: Yes

FRANCHISOR TRAINING/SUPPORT:
Financial Assistance Provided: . . . . .No
Site Selection Assistance: . . . . .Yes
Lease Negotiation Assistance: . . . . .Yes
Co-operative Advertising: . . . . .Yes
Training: . . . . 2 Wks. Headquarters
. . . .
On-Going Support: . . . . C,D,E
Full-Time Franchisor Support Staff: . . 20
EXPANSION PLANS:
  US: . . . . Illinois, New York, Calif.
  Canada - Yes, . . . Overseas - Yes

SAM THE CHICKEN MAN

310 E. Burlington, # 9
Iowa City, IA 52240
TEL: (319) 337-9365
FAX:
Mr. James McNulty, President

SAM THE CHICKEN MAN offers a unique concept aimed at the enormously growing home delivery market. SAM's specializes in the delivery of Southern fried chicken and BBQ ribs. This concept is attractive for strip centers or locations of 1,000-1,500 SF. Carry-out and eat-in facilities also.

HISTORY: . . . .
Established in 1986; . . 1st Franchised in 1986
Company-Owned Units (As of 12/1/1989): . .0
Franchised Units (12/1/1989): 2
Total Units (12/1/1989): 2
Distribution: US-2;Can-0;Overseas-0
North America: . . . . .1 State
Concentration: . . . . .2 in IL
Registered: IL
. . . .
Average # of Employees: . . . . . . 3 FT, 7 PT
Prior Industry Experience: . . . . . . Helpful

FINANCIAL:
Cash Investment: $55-85K
Total Investment: $55-85K
Fees: Franchise - $15K
  Royalty: 8%, Advert: 2%
Contract Periods (Yrs.): . . . 20/10
Area Development Agreement: Yes/10
Sub-Franchise Contract: . . . . . Yes
Expand in Territory: . . . . Yes
Passive Ownership: . . . Discouraged
Encourage Conversions: . . . . . Yes
Franchisee Purchase(s) Required: .No

FRANCHISOR TRAINING/SUPPORT:
Financial Assistance Provided: . . . Yes(I)
Site Selection Assistance: . . . . .Yes
Lease Negotiation Assistance: . . . . .Yes
Co-operative Advertising: . . . . .Yes
Training: . . . . . . 1 Wk. Corporate Store,
. . . . 1-2 Wks. Site
On-Going Support: . . . . B,C,D,E,F,h
Full-Time Franchisor Support Staff: . . .3
EXPANSION PLANS:
  US: . . . . .All US
  Canada - Yes, . . . Overseas - Yes

**SCHLOTZSKY'S SANDWICH
RESTAURANTS**
200 W. Fourth St.
Austin, TX 78701
TEL: (800) 950-8419 (512) 480-9871
FAX: (512) 477-2897
Mr. Kelly Arnold, Natl. Sales Mgr.

SCHLOTZSKY'S are franchised restaurants serving a menu of sandwiches, pizza and salads on SCHLOTZSKY'S baked-fresh daily sourdough bread. Restaurants are designed to provide fresh, clean environments incorporating in-store baking. The design will cost $120,000 with a sales to investment ratio in excess of 2.5 to 1.

HISTORY: . . . .
Established in 1971; . . 1st Franchised in 1977
Company-Owned Units (As of 12/1/1989): . 23
Franchised Units (12/1/1989): 224
Total Units (12/1/1989): 247
Distribution: US-246;Can-1;Overseas-0
North America: . . . . 25 States
Concentration: . .124 in TX, 17 in OK, 13 NM
Registered: . . . . All States
. . . .
Average # of Employees: . . . . . .2 FT, 10 PT
Prior Industry Experience: . . . . . . Helpful

FINANCIAL:
Cash Investment: $30-60K
Total Investment: $120-160K
Fees: Franchise - $15-25K
Royalty: 4%, Advert: 1%
Contract Periods (Yrs.): 20/10
Area Development Agreement: Yes/Var
Sub-Franchise Contract: . . . . .No
Expand in Territory: . . . . Yes
Passive Ownership: . . . Not Allowed
Encourage Conversions: . . . . . Yes
Franchisee Purchase(s) Required: .No

FRANCHISOR TRAINING/SUPPORT:
Financial Assistance Provided: . . .Yes(D)
Site Selection Assistance: . . . . . . .Yes
Lease Negotiation Assistance: . . . . . No
Co-operative Advertising: . . . . . . .Yes
Training: . . . . 2 Wks. Headquarters
. . . .
On-Going Support: . . . . . B,C,D,E,G,H
Full-Time Franchisor Support Staff: . . 28
EXPANSION PLANS:
US: . . . . Midwest and Southeast
Canada - No, ...Overseas - No

SEAFOOD AMERICA

645 Mearns Rd.
Warminster, PA 18974
TEL: (215) 672-2211
FAX:
Mr. Robert Brennan, Fran. Dir.

SEAFOOD AMERICA is a fast-food, take-out seafood store unique in both product and design. The products are primarily seafood items designed for quick service and maximum profits. Some products are prepared on the premises, but most are commissary-based.

HISTORY: . . . . .IFA
Established in 1979; . . 1st Franchised in 1980
Company-Owned Units (As of 12/1/1989): . .1
Franchised Units (12/1/1989): 19
Total Units (12/1/1989): 20
Distribution: US-20;Can-0;Overseas-0
North America: . . . . 2 States
Concentration: . . . . 17 in PA, 3 in NJ
Registered: . . . .
. . . .
Average # of Employees: . . . . . . 2 FT, 8 PT
Prior Industry Experience: . . . . Helpful

FINANCIAL:
Cash Investment: $40-60K
Total Investment: $100-130K
Fees: Franchise - $10K
Royalty: 1%, Advert: 1%
Contract Periods (Yrs.): 10/10
Area Development Agreement: Yes/20
Sub-Franchise Contract: . . . . .No
Expand in Territory: . . . . . . .No
Passive Ownership: . . . Discouraged
Encourage Conversions: . . . . .No
Franchisee Purchase(s) Required: Yes

FRANCHISOR TRAINING/SUPPORT:
Financial Assistance Provided: . . . Yes(I)
Site Selection Assistance: . . . . . . .Yes
Lease Negotiation Assistance: . . . .Yes
Co-operative Advertising: . . . . . . .Yes
Training: . . . . . . .2 Wks. Existing Store,
. . . . 4 Wks. Site
On-Going Support: . . . a,B,C,D,E,F,h,I
Full-Time Franchisor Support Staff: . . .6
EXPANSION PLANS:
US: . . . . .NJ,PA & DE Only
Canada - No, ...Overseas - No

SEAWEST SUB SHOPS

One Lake Bellevue Dr., # 107
Bellevue, WA 98005
TEL: (206) 453-5216
FAX: (206) 454-7951
Mr. Bernie Kane

Total investment of $36,550 - 65,000. We do not manage hours or take a royalty percentage. Your annual costs are fixed at: Year One - $500/Quarter ($2,000/Year); Year Two - $750/Quarter ($3,000/Year); Year Three through Ten - $333.33/Month ($4,000/Year). Your yearly advertising fee is from $1,000 - 3,000.

HISTORY: . . . .
Established in 1980; . . 1st Franchised in 1985
Company-Owned Units (As of 12/1/1989): . .0
Franchised Units (12/1/1989): 75
Total Units (12/1/1989): 75
Distribution: US-75;Can-0;Overseas-0
North America: . . . . 13 States
Concentration: . 26 in WA, 14 in OR, 5 in OH
Registered: . . . . CA,FL,IL,OR,WA
. . . .
Average # of Employees: . . . . . 2 FT, 4-5 PT
Prior Industry Experience: . . . . Helpful

FINANCIAL:
Cash Investment: $36-65K
Total Investment: $36-65K
Fees: Franchise - $15K
Royalty: 2-4K/Yr., Advert: 1-3K/Yr.
Contract Periods (Yrs.): 10/10
Area Development Agreement: Yes/10
Sub-Franchise Contract: . . . . . Yes
Expand in Territory: . . . . . . Yes
Passive Ownership: . . . . . .Allowed
Encourage Conversions: . . . . . Yes
Franchisee Purchase(s) Required: .No

FRANCHISOR TRAINING/SUPPORT:
Financial Assistance Provided: . . . . .Yes
Site Selection Assistance: . . . . . . .Yes
Lease Negotiation Assistance: . . . .Yes
Co-operative Advertising: . . . . . . .Yes
Training: . . . . . . 2 Wks. Regional Shop,
. . . . 2 Wks. Headquarters
On-Going Support: . . .B,C,D,E,F,G,H,I
Full-Time Franchisor Support Staff: . . .4
EXPANSION PLANS:
US: . . . . All US
Canada - Yes, . . . Overseas - Yes

SELECT SANDWICH

50 Gervais Dr., # 506
Toronto, ON M3C1Z3 CAN
TEL: (416) 391-1244
FAX: (416) 391-5244
Ms. Carol Kahn, Dir. Franchising

Custom-made sandwiches, soups, salads, on-premises baked muffins. Daily hot specials. Catering to business. Breakfast and lunch. Easy operation, 5-day week, 7 AM - 6 PM.

HISTORY: . . . .
Established in 1981; . . 1st Franchised in 1983
Company-Owned Units (As of 12/1/1989): . .4
Franchised Units (12/1/1989): 31
Total Units (12/1/1989): 35
Distribution: US-0;Can-35;Overseas-0
North America: . . . . .1 Province
Concentration: . . . . 35 in ON
Registered: . . . .
. . . .
Average # of Employees: . . . . . . 5 FT, 4 PT
Prior Industry Experience: . . . . Helpful

FINANCIAL:
Cash Investment: $75-120K
Total Investment: $220-290K
Fees: Franchise - $30K
Royalty: 6%, Advert: 2%
Contract Periods (Yrs.): 10/5/5
Area Development Agreement: . .No
Sub-Franchise Contract: . . . . .No
Expand in Territory: . . . . . . Yes
Passive Ownership: . . . Not Allowed
Encourage Conversions: . . . . .No
Franchisee Purchase(s) Required: .No

FRANCHISOR TRAINING/SUPPORT:
Financial Assistance Provided: . . . Yes(I)
Site Selection Assistance: . . . . .NA
Lease Negotiation Assistance: . . . . .NA
Co-operative Advertising: . . . . .Yes
Training: . . . . .4 Wks. Corporate Store in
. . . . Toronto
On-Going Support: . . . . . . C,E,F,G,H,I
Full-Time Franchisor Support Staff: . . 29
EXPANSION PLANS:
US: . . . . .All US
Canada - Yes, . . . Overseas - Yes

SOBIK'S SUBS

753 N. 17-92
Longwood, FL 32750
TEL: (407) 699-4644
FAX: (407) 699-1815
Mr. William Parker, Mgr. Fran. Dev.

SOBIK'S SUBS is a fast-food restaurant concept, featuring submarine and specialty sandwiches and salads for eat-in or take-out. We have 40+ SOBIK'S SUB SHOPS in Central Florida and have just sold our first Master Franchise for the Southwest Coast of Florida. Our concept stresses quality, ease of operation and speed of service.

HISTORY: . . . .
Established in 1969; . . 1st Franchised in 1981
Company-Owned Units (As of 12/1/1989): . .6
Franchised Units (12/1/1989): 37
Total Units (12/1/1989): 43
Distribution: US-43;Can-0;Overseas-0
North America: . . . . .1 State
Concentration: . . . . 43 in FL
Registered: . . . . .FL
. . . .
Average # of Employees: . . . . . . 2 FT, 4 PT
Prior Industry Experience: . . . . Helpful

FINANCIAL:
Cash Investment: $20-40K
Total Investment: $65-90K
Fees: Franchise - $15K
Royalty: 4%, Advert: 4%
Contract Periods (Yrs.): 10/10
Area Development Agreement: Yes/10
Sub-Franchise Contract: . . . . . Yes
Expand in Territory: . . . . . . Yes
Passive Ownership: . . . Discouraged
Encourage Conversions: . . . . .No
Franchisee Purchase(s) Required: Yes

FRANCHISOR TRAINING/SUPPORT:
Financial Assistance Provided: . . . . .No
Site Selection Assistance: . . . . .Yes
Lease Negotiation Assistance: . . . . .Yes
Co-operative Advertising: . . . . .Yes
Training: . . . . 2 Wks. Orlando, FL
. . . .
On-Going Support: . . . . . B,C,D,E,G,H
Full-Time Franchisor Support Staff; . . 10
EXPANSION PLANS:
US: . . . . .Florida Only
Canada - No, ...Overseas - No

SONIC DRIVE IN

120 Robert S. Kerr Ave.
Oklahoma City, OK 73102
TEL: (800) 458-8778 (405) 232-4334
FAX: (405) 236-4128
Mr. Robert P. Flack, VP Corp. Devel.

Fast-food, drive-in restaurants featuring hamburgers, coney dogs, french fries and onion rings.

HISTORY: . . . . .IFA
Established in 1959; . . 1st Franchised in 1959
Company-Owned Units (As of 12/1/1989): . 88
Franchised Units (12/1/1989): 917
Total Units (12/1/1989): 1005
Distribution: US-1005;Can-0;Overseas-0
North America: . . . . 21 States
Concentration: . 314 in TX, 147 in OK, 75 AR
Registered: . . . . .CA,FL,IN,VA
. . . .
Average # of Employees: . . . . . 35 Combined
Prior Industry Experience: . . . . Helpful

FINANCIAL:
Cash Investment: $38-68K
Total Investment: $300-550K
Fees: Franchise - $15K
Royalty: 1-4%, Advert: 3/4%
Contract Periods (Yrs.): 15/15
Area Development Agreement: Yes/Var
Sub-Franchise Contract: . . . . .No
Expand in Territory: . . . . . . Yes
Passive Ownership: . . . Discouraged
Encourage Conversions: . . . . . Yes
Franchisee Purchase(s) Required: .No

FRANCHISOR TRAINING/SUPPORT:
Financial Assistance Provided: . . . Yes(I)
Site Selection Assistance: . . . . .Yes
Lease Negotiation Assistance: . . . . .Yes
Co-operative Advertising: . . . . .Yes
Training: . . . . 6 Days Headquarters,
. . . . .4 Wks. On-the-job Training
On-Going Support: . . .a,B,C,D,E,F,G,H,I
Full-Time Franchisor Support Staff: . . 71
EXPANSION PLANS:
US: . . . . . . Southeast and Southwest
Canada - No, ...Overseas - No

SPAGHETTI SHOP, THE

P. O. Box 1807
Champaign, IL 61824
TEL: (217) 356-4200
FAX: (217) 356-4231
Mr. James A. Teaters, President

THE SPAGHETTI SHOP serves a variety of Italian cuisine in a fast-food format, including Fettuccine Alfredo, spaghetti with meat sauce, lasagna, ravioli, fresh-baked bread and sandwiches. Our authentic products are available eat-in, carry-out or through our drive-up.

HISTORY: . . . . IFA
Established in 1985; . . 1st Franchised in 1987
Company-Owned Units (As of 12/1/1989): . .4
Franchised Units (12/1/1989): 25
Total Units (12/1/1989): 29
Distribution: US-29;Can-0;Overseas-0
North America: . . . . 5 States
Concentration: . . . .13 in IN, 5 in KY, 5 in IL
Registered: . . . . IL,IN,MI
. . . .
Average # of Employees: . . . . . . 4 FT, 12 Pt
Prior Industry Experience: . . . . Helpful

FINANCIAL:
Cash Investment: $100-200K
Total Investment: $147-313K
Fees: Franchise - $20K
  Royalty: 4$, Advert: 2%
Contract Periods (Yrs.): 10/10
Area Development Agreement: Yes/5
Sub-Franchise Contract: . . . . . Yes
Expand in Territory: . . . . Yes
Passive Ownership: . . . Discouraged
Encourage Conversions: . . . . . Yes
Franchisee Purchase(s) Required: .No

FRANCHISOR TRAINING/SUPPORT:
Financial Assistance Provided: . . . Yes(I)
Site Selection Assistance: . . . . . . .Yes
Lease Negotiation Assistance: . . . . .Yes
Co-operative Advertising: . . . . . . .Yes
Training: . . . . 3 Wks. Headquarters
. . . .
On-Going Support: . . . . B,C,D,E,F,G,H
Full-Time Franchisor Support Staff: . . 15
EXPANSION PLANS:
US: . . . . .Midwest
Canada - No, ...Overseas - No

SPINNER'S PIZZA & SUBS

910 KCK Way
Cedar Hill, TX 75104
TEL: (214) 299-5656 C
FAX:
Mr. Ernest Hagler, VP

SPINNER'S PIZZA is seeking individuals to become owner/operators of delivery/take-out units specializing in the highest-quality products with an emphasis on superior customer service. Our strength is training individuals without business/food experience and making them a part of our success. People-oriented!

HISTORY: . . . .
Established in 1983; . . 1st Franchised in 1986
Company-Owned Units (As of 12/1/1989): . .8
Franchised Units (12/1/1989): 30
Total Units (12/1/1989): 38
Distribution: US-38;Can-0;Overseas-0
North America: . . . . .1 State
Concentration: . . . . 38 in TX
Registered: . . . .
. . . .
Average # of Employees: . . . 3-5 FT, 10-20 PT
Prior Industry Experience: . . . . Helpful

FINANCIAL:
Cash Investment: $35-40K
Total Investment: $50-75K
Fees: Franchise - $15K
  Royalty: 4%, Advert: 2%
Contract Periods (Yrs.): 5/5
Area Development Agreement: Yes/5
Sub-Franchise Contract: . . . . .No
Expand in Territory: . . . . Yes
Passive Ownership: . . . Discouraged
Encourage Conversions: . . . . . Yes
Franchisee Purchase(s) Required: .No

FRANCHISOR TRAINING/SUPPORT:
Financial Assistance Provided: . . . Yes(I)
Site Selection Assistance: . . . . . . .Yes
Lease Negotiation Assistance: . . . .Yes
Co-operative Advertising: . . . . . . .Yes
Training: . . . .~ 500 Hrs. Dallas/Fort
. . . . Worth Area
On-Going Support: . . . . . . b,C,D,E,G,h
Full-Time Franchisor Support Staff: . . 30
EXPANSION PLANS:
US: . . . . . . TX, OK, NM, LA and AR
Canada - No, ...Overseas - No

STEAK ESCAPE, THE

1265 Neil Ave.
Columbus, OH 43201
TEL: (614) 297-8860
FAX: (614) 297-8820
Mr. Kennard Smith, Chairman

THE GREAT ESCAPE specializes in genuine Philadelphia cheesesteak sandwiches, freshly-cut french fries and freshly-squeezed lemonade. Use all fresh ingredients and practice exhibition-style cooking. Incredibly tasty food. Typically located in food courts and highly-travelled retail projects.

HISTORY: . . . .
Established in 1982; . . 1st Franchised in 1983
Company-Owned Units (As of 12/1/1989): . .2
Franchised Units (12/1/1989): 60
Total Units (12/1/1989): 62
Distribution: US-61;Can-0;Overseas-1
North America: . . . . 19 States
Concentration: . . . .7 in OH, 6 in TN, 5 in FL
Registered: . . . CA,FL,IL,IN,MD,MI,MN,NY
. . . . .VA,WA,WI
Average # of Employees: . . . . . 12 FT, 6 PT
Prior Industry Experience: . . . . Helpful

FINANCIAL:
Cash Investment: $50-100K
Total Investment: $170-220K
Fees: Franchise - $27K
  Royalty: 8%, Advert: 0%
Contract Periods (Yrs.): 5/5
Area Development Agreement: . .No
Sub-Franchise Contract: . . . . .No
Expand in Territory: . . . . . . .No
Passive Ownership: . . . Not Allowed
Encourage Conversions: . . . . . Yes
Franchisee Purchase(s) Required: .No

FRANCHISOR TRAINING/SUPPORT:
Financial Assistance Provided: . . . . .No
Site Selection Assistance: . . . . . . .Yes
Lease Negotiation Assistance: . . . .Yes
Co-operative Advertising: . . . . . . .Yes
Training: . . . . . . 4-6 Wks. Headquarters,
. . . . .2 Wks. Franchisee Location
On-Going Support: . . . . B,C,D,E,G,h,I
Full-Time Franchisor Support Staff: . . 17
EXPANSION PLANS:
US: . . . . .All US
Canada - Yes, . . . Overseas - Yes

STEAK-OUT

P.O. Box 5981
Huntsville, AL 35814
TEL: (800) 234-2114 (205) 539-7900
FAX:
Mr. David Martin, President

We specialize in DELIVERING charbroiled steaks, burgers and chicken; and if you're wondering, the food is always piping hot - we guarantee it. People absolutely love our combination of quality food and free delivery.

HISTORY: . . . .
Established in 1986; . . 1st Franchised in 1988
Company-Owned Units (As of 12/1/1989): . .2
Franchised Units (12/1/1989): 6
Total Units (12/1/1989): 8
Distribution: US-8;Can-0;Overseas-0
North America: . . . . 3 States
Concentration: . . . 3 in TX, 2 in AL, 2 in GA
Registered: . . . . .FL,OR

. . . .
Average # of Employees: . . . . . .5 FT, 14 PT
Prior Industry Experience: . . . . Helpful

FINANCIAL:
Cash Investment: $70-105K
Total Investment: $79-108K
Fees: Franchise - $7.5K
  Royalty: 3%, Advert: 2%
Contract Periods (Yrs.): 10/10
Area Development Agreement: Yes/Var
Sub-Franchise Contract: . . . . . .No
Expand in Territory: . . . . Yes
Passive Ownership: . . . Discouraged
Encourage Conversions: . . . . . .No
Franchisee Purchase(s) Required: Yes

FRANCHISOR TRAINING/SUPPORT:
Financial Assistance Provided: . . . . .No
Site Selection Assistance: . . . . . . .Yes
Lease Negotiation Assistance: . . . . .Yes
Co-operative Advertising: . . . . .No
Training: . . . . . . 6-8 Wks. Headquarters
. . . .
On-Going Support: . . . . b,C,D,E,I
Full-Time Franchisor Support Staff: . . .6
EXPANSION PLANS:
US: . . . . .All US
Canada - No, ...Overseas - No

STEWART'S DRIVE-IN

114 W. Atlantic Ave.
Clementon, NJ 08021
TEL: (609) 346-1300
FAX:
Mr. Michael Fessler, President

A STEWART'S DRIVE-IN is designed for the independent business person. With STEWART'S, there are no franchise, royalty or advertising fees. All necessary services are available at set fees. A limited menu featuring/specializing in chili dogs and frosted mugs of STEWART'S root beer served by car-hops.

HISTORY: . . . .
Established in 1925; . . 1st Franchised in 1931
Company-Owned Units (As of 12/1/1989): . .0
Franchised Units (12/1/1989): 57
Total Units (12/1/1989): 57
Distribution: US-57;Can-0;Overseas-0
North America: . . . . 7 States
Concentration: . . 36 in NJ, 12 in WV, 5 in OH
Registered: . . . .

. . . .
Average # of Employees: . . . . . .7 FT, 12 PT
Prior Industry Experience: . . . . Helpful

FINANCIAL:
Cash Investment: $75K
Total Investment: $225K
Fees: Franchise - $0
  Royalty: 0%, Advert: 0%
Contract Periods (Yrs.): 15/5
Area Development Agreement: . .No
Sub-Franchise Contract: . . . . . .No
Expand in Territory: . . . . Yes
Passive Ownership: . . . Discouraged
Encourage Conversions: . . . . . Yes
Franchisee Purchase(s) Required: .No

FRANCHISOR TRAINING/SUPPORT:
Financial Assistance Provided: . . . Yes(I)
Site Selection Assistance: . . . . . . .Yes
Lease Negotiation Assistance: . . . . .Yes
Co-operative Advertising: . . . . .No
Training: . . . . 7 Days New Jersey
. . . .
On-Going Support: . . . . c,d,e,f,h
Full-Time Franchisor Support Staff: . . .7
EXPANSION PLANS:
US: . . . . KY, WV and OH
Canada - No, ...Overseas - No

STUFT PIZZA

26875 Calle Hermosa, # 3
Capistrano Beach, CA 92624
TEL: (714) 661-2996
FAX:
Mr. Bill Boie, VP

STUFT PIZZA takes pizza to gourmet quality. STUFT uses only the freshest vegetables, highest-quality mozzarella and premium meats. The dough is made fresh daily and hand thrown for each order. Completing the popular pie is STUFT'S special sauce of secret ingredients developed by founder Jack Bertram.

HISTORY: . . . .
Established in 1976; . . 1st Franchised in 1985
Company-Owned Units (As of 12/1/1989): . .3
Franchised Units (12/1/1989): 29
Total Units (12/1/1989): 32
Distribution: US-32;Can-0;Overseas-0
North America: . . . . .1 State
Concentration: . . . . 27 in CA
Registered: . . . . CA

. . . .
Average # of Employees: . . . . . .4 FT, 18 PT
Prior Industry Experience: . . . . Helpful

FINANCIAL:
Cash Investment: $103-542K
Total Investment: $103-542K
Fees: Franchise - $25K
  Royalty: 3%, Advert: 1%
Contract Periods (Yrs.): 20/5
Area Development Agreement: . .No
Sub-Franchise Contract: . . . . . .No
Expand in Territory: . . . . Yes
Passive Ownership: . . . . . .Allowed
Encourage Conversions: . . . . . .No
Franchisee Purchase(s) Required: Yes

FRANCHISOR TRAINING/SUPPORT:
Financial Assistance Provided: . . . . .No
Site Selection Assistance: . . . . . . .Yes
Lease Negotiation Assistance: . . . . .Yes
Co-operative Advertising: . . . . .Yes
Training: . . . . 2 Wks. Field,
. . . . 5 Days Site
On-Going Support: . . . . C,D,E,G,h
Full-Time Franchisor Support Staff: . . .4
EXPANSION PLANS:
US: . . . . .CA
Canada - No, ...Overseas - No

SUB STATION II

425 N. Main St.
Sumter, SC 29150
TEL: (803) 773-4711
FAX: (803) 775-2220
Ms. Susan L. Hackett, VP

SUB STATION II is a chain of restaurants specializing in the preparation of submarine and deli-style sandwiches. The company began operation in 1976 in South Carolina and now has 123 units operating in 13 states and plans to double in the next few years.

HISTORY: . . . .
Established in 1976; . . 1st Franchised in 1976
Company-Owned Units (As of 12/1/1989): . .2
Franchised Units (12/1/1989): 121
Total Units (12/1/1989): 123
Distribution: US-123;Can-0;Overseas-0
North America: . . . . 13 States
Concentration: . 32 in SC, 23 in NC, 19 in GA
Registered: . . . . CA,FL,IL,MI,NY,VA
. . . .
Average # of Employees: . . . . . . 3 FT, 8 PT
Prior Industry Experience: . . . . Helpful

FINANCIAL:
Cash Investment: $50-90K
Total Investment: $65-90K
Fees: Franchise - $10.5-14.5K
Royalty: 3-4%, Advert: 2%
Contract Periods (Yrs.): . . . 10/10
Area Development Agreement: . .No
Sub-Franchise Contract: . . . . Yes
Expand in Territory: . . . . . . Yes
Passive Ownership: . . . . .Allowed
Encourage Conversions: . . . . Yes
Franchisee Purchase(s) Required: .No

FRANCHISOR TRAINING/SUPPORT:
Financial Assistance Provided: . . . Yes(I)
Site Selection Assistance: . . . . . . .Yes
Lease Negotiation Assistance: . . . . .Yes
Co-operative Advertising: . . . . .Yes
Training: . . . .7-10 Days Company-owned
. . . . Store, 7-14 Days On-site
On-Going Support: . . . . C,D,E,G,h
Full-Time Franchisor Support Staff: . . 10
EXPANSION PLANS:
US: . . . . .All US
Canada - No, ...Overseas - No

TACO CASA

P.O. Box 4542
Topeka, KS 66604
TEL: (913) 267-2548
FAX:
Mr. James Reiter, President

TACO CASA offers Mexican fast-food restaurants, serving tacos, tostadas, burritos, sanchos, enchiladas, sachiladas, chili, chili burritos and various other entree items. Operates primarily in enclosed mall shopping centers. Free-standing units have drive-thru facilities. The attractive initial investment greatly enhances the return on investment.

HISTORY: . . . .
Established in 1964; . . 1st Franchised in 1976
Company-Owned Units (As of 12/1/1989): . .1
Franchised Units (12/1/1989): 24
Total Units (12/1/1989): 25
Distribution: US-20;Can-0;Overseas-5
North America: . . . . . .7 States, 1 Province
Concentration: . . . 6 in KY, 5 in MS, 3 in KS
Registered: . . . . .FL
. . . .
Average # of Employees: . . . . . . 3 FT, 7 PT
Prior Industry Experience: . . . . . . Helpful

FINANCIAL:
Cash Investment: $30-70K
Total Investment: $90-350K
Fees: Franchise - $15K
Royalty: 4%, Advert: 1.5%
Contract Periods (Yrs.): . . . 20/10
Area Development Agreement: Yes/10
Sub-Franchise Contract: . . . . .No
Expand in Territory: . . . . . . Yes
Passive Ownership: . . . Discouraged
Encourage Conversions: . . . . Yes
Franchisee Purchase(s) Required: Yes

FRANCHISOR TRAINING/SUPPORT:
Financial Assistance Provided: . . . . . No
Site Selection Assistance: . . . . . . .Yes
Lease Negotiation Assistance: . . . .Yes
Co-operative Advertising: . . . . . . .Yes
Training: . . . . 2 Wks. Headquarters,
. . . . . .5 Days Site Opening, On-going
On-Going Support: . . . a,b,C,D,E,F,G,h,I
Full-Time Franchisor Support Staff: . . . 4
EXPANSION PLANS:
US: . . . . Southeast
Canada - No, ... Overseas - Yes

TACO GRANDE

P. O. Box 780066
Wichita, KS 67278
TEL: (316) 688-1757
FAX: (316) 688-0715
Mr. John Wylie, President

TACO GRANDE offers a limited-menu Mexican restaurant, featuring drive-thru service. Our recipes are authentic Mexican recipes and we have been in successful operation for over 29 years. We offer excellent products, training and a cost-efficient and labor-saving building design.

HISTORY: . . . .
Established in 1960; . . 1st Franchised in 1966
Company-Owned Units (As of 12/1/1989): . .9
Franchised Units (12/1/1989): 15
Total Units (12/1/1989): 24
Distribution: US-24;Can-0;Overseas-0
North America: . . . . 5 States
Concentration: . . . 16 in KS, 5 in IN, 1 in MI
Registered: . . . . IN,MI
. . . .
Average # of Employees: . . . . 10 FT, 20 PT
Prior Industry Experience: . . . . . .Necessary

FINANCIAL:
Cash Investment: $45K
Total Investment: $250-450K
Fees: Franchise - $20K
Royalty: 3%, Advert: 2%
Contract Periods (Yrs.): . . . 15/15
Area Development Agreement: Yes/5
Sub-Franchise Contract: . . . . Yes
Expand in Territory: . . . . . . Yes
Passive Ownership: . . . Discouraged
Encourage Conversions: . . . . .No
Franchisee Purchase(s) Required: Yes

FRANCHISOR TRAINING/SUPPORT:
Financial Assistance Provided: . . . . .No
Site Selection Assistance: . . . . . . .Yes
Lease Negotiation Assistance: . . . . No
Co-operative Advertising: . . . . .Yes
Training: . . . . 4 Wks. Headquarters
On-Going Support: . . . . C,D,E,G,h
Full-Time Franchisor Support Staff: . . . 4
EXPANSION PLANS:
US: . . . . .All US
Canada - No, ...Overseas - No

TACO MAKER, THE

2302 Washington Blvd., # 400
Ogden, UT 84401
TEL: (801) 621-7486 C
FAX: (801) 621-0139
Mr. Wayne Webster, EVP

Mexican fast-food franchisor. Locations already approved around US, low cash investment, 23 years of experience. Join our successful franchising program in the fastest-growing segment of the fast-food industry.

HISTORY: . . . .
Established in 1976; . . 1st Franchised in 1977
Company-Owned Units (As of 12/1/1989): . .5
Franchised Units (12/1/1989): 88
Total Units (12/1/1989): 93
Distribution: US-91;Can-1;Overseas-1
North America: . . . . . 14 States, 1 Province
Concentration: . . . .8 in NY, 7 in UT, 4 in NJ
Registered: . . CA,FL,MD,MN,NY,OR,RI,WA

. . . .
Average # of Employees: . . . . 3 FT, 10-12 PT
Prior Industry Experience: . . . . Helpful

FINANCIAL:
Cash Investment: $40-70K
Total Investment: $90-150K
Fees: Franchise - $22.5K
 Royalty: 5%, Advert: 3%
Contract Periods (Yrs.): 15/10
Area Development Agreement: Yes/15
Sub-Franchise Contract: . . . . . Yes
Expand in Territory: . . . . . . Yes
Passive Ownership: . . . Discouraged
Encourage Conversions: . . . . . Yes
Franchisee Purchase(s) Required: .No

FRANCHISOR TRAINING/SUPPORT:
Financial Assistance Provided: . . . . .NA
Site Selection Assistance: . . . . . . .Yes
Lease Negotiation Assistance: . . . . .Yes
Co-operative Advertising: . . . . No
Training: . . . . . . .30 Days Headquarters
. . . .
On-Going Support: . . . a,b,C,D,E,F,G,h,I
Full-Time Franchisor Support Staff: . . 12
EXPANSION PLANS:
 US: . . . . .All US
Canada - Yes, . . . Overseas - Yes

TACO MAYO

10405 Greenbriar Pl.
Oklahoma City, OK 73159
TEL: (405) 691-8226
FAX:
Mr. Randy K. Earhart, President

Mexican-style fast food. Pleasant inside dining and fast, efficient drive-thru service. Low start-up, with 3% on-going royalties. Continuing advisory, in-depth training. Franchises available in 8 Southwestern states.

HISTORY: . . . .
Established in 1978; . . 1st Franchised in 1980
Company-Owned Units (As of 12/1/1989): . 18
Franchised Units (12/1/1989): 36
Total Units (12/1/1989): 54
Distribution: US-54;Can-0;Overseas-0
North America: . . . . 5 States
Concentration: . . .37 in OK, 8 in TX, 3 in AR
Registered: . . . .

. . . .
Average # of Employees: . . . . . .8 FT, 12 PT
Prior Industry Experience: . . . . Helpful

FINANCIAL:
Cash Investment: $30-50K
Total Investment: $80-300K
Fees: Franchise - $7.5K
 Royalty: 3%, Advert: 2-3%
Contract Periods (Yrs.): 10/10
Area Development Agreement: Yes/10
Sub-Franchise Contract: . . . . . .No
Expand in Territory: . . . . Yes
Passive Ownership: . . . Not Allowed
Encourage Conversions: . . . . . Yes
Franchisee Purchase(s) Required: .No

FRANCHISOR TRAINING/SUPPORT:
Financial Assistance Provided: . . . . .No
Site Selection Assistance: . . . . . . .Yes
Lease Negotiation Assistance: . . . . .Yes
Co-operative Advertising: . . . . .Yes
Training: . . . . . 3-4 Wks. Company Unit,
. . . . 2-4 Wks. On-site
On-Going Support: . . . . . .B,C,E,F,G,H
Full-Time Franchisor Support Staff: . . .7
EXPANSION PLANS:
 US: . . . . Southwest Only
Canada - No, ...Overseas - No

TACO TABER

P. O. Box 305
Noble, OK 73068
TEL: (405) 872-5170
FAX:
Mr. Floyd Taber, President

Taco's priced at $.49. "The best Mexican food around." Complete training and support to help you grow with us. With our Master Franchise program, you can become a sub-franchisor. Rare opportunity - convert your present unit to a TACO TABER restaurant.

HISTORY: . . . .
Established in 1983; . . 1st Franchised in 1988
Company-Owned Units (As of 12/1/1989): . .0
Franchised Units (12/1/1989): 1
Total Units (12/1/1989): 1
Distribution: US-1;Can-0;Overseas-0
North America: . . . . .1 State
Concentration: . . . . 1 in OK
Registered: . . . .

. . . .
Average # of Employees: . . . . . 2 FT, 6-8 PT
Prior Industry Experience: . . . . Helpful

FINANCIAL:
Cash Investment: $15K
Total Investment: $30K
Fees: Franchise - $2.5-5K
 Royalty: 5%, Advert: . . . . Varies
Contract Periods (Yrs.): 5/5
Area Development Agreement: Yes/5
Sub-Franchise Contract: . . . . . Yes
Expand in Territory: . . . . Yes
Passive Ownership: . . . . . .Allowed
Encourage Conversions: . . . . . Yes
Franchisee Purchase(s) Required: .No

FRANCHISOR TRAINING/SUPPORT:
Financial Assistance Provided: . . . Yes(I)
Site Selection Assistance: . . . . . . .Yes
Lease Negotiation Assistance: . . . . .Yes
Co-operative Advertising: . . . . .Yes
Training: . . . . . .1-2 Wks. Training Store
. . . .
On-Going Support: . . . .A,C,d,E,F,G,H,I
Full-Time Franchisor Support Staff: . . .1
EXPANSION PLANS:
 US: . . . . .All US
Canada - No, ...Overseas - No

TACOTIME

3880 W. 11th Ave.
Eugene, OR 97402
TEL: (800) 547-8907 (503) 687-8222 C
FAX: (503) 343-5208
Mr. Jim Thomas, VP Fran. Devel.

TACOTIME is a dynamic leader in the Mexican fast-food business. Outstanding food products feature quality-fresh ingredients and exciting menu items. New 1,700 SF solarium-enhanced prototype unit is highly efficient and attractively designed to encourage high volume and lower break-even point. High-quality food and new product development has made TACOTIME a favorite in the US, Canada, Venezuela, UK and Japan.

HISTORY: . . . . IFA
Established in 1959; . . 1st Franchised in 1961
Company-Owned Units (As of 12/1/1989): . 22
Franchised Units (12/1/1989): 267
Total Units (12/1/1989): 289
Distribution: . . US-188;Can-179;Overseas-22
North America: . . . . 21 States, 5 Provinces
Concentration: . 61 in OR, 39 in UT, 27 in AB
Registered: . . . . .All
. . . . All Except RI
Average # of Employees: . . . . . . 3 FT, 15 PT
Prior Industry Experience: . . . . Helpful

FINANCIAL:
Cash Investment: $70K
Total Investment: $129-203K
Fees: Franchise - $18K
  Royalty: 5%, Advert: 5%
Contract Periods (Yrs.): 15/10
Area Development Agreement: Yes/5
Sub-Franchise Contract: . . . . . Yes
Expand in Territory: . . . . . . .No
Passive Ownership: . . . Discouraged
Encourage Conversions: . . . . Yes
Franchisee Purchase(s) Required: .No

FRANCHISOR TRAINING/SUPPORT:
Financial Assistance Provided: . . . . .No
Site Selection Assistance: . . . . . . .Yes
Lease Negotiation Assistance: . . . . .No
Co-operative Advertising: . . . . . . .Yes
Training: . . . . 5 Wks. Headquarters
. . . .
On-Going Support: . . . . .B,C,E,F,G,H,I
Full-Time Franchisor Support Staff: . . 37
EXPANSION PLANS:
  US: . . . . .All US
  Canada - Yes, . . . Overseas - Yes

TASTEE FREEZ

1151 Montrose Pl.
Kelowna, BC V1Y3M4 CAN
TEL: (614) 763-0595
FAX:
Mr. R. Watson, President

TASTEE FREEZ FAMILY RESTAURANTS are located in small towns and cities throughout Western Canada, serving breakfast menu, burgers, chicken and TASTEE FREEZ ice cream products. We favor free-standing buildings with drive-thru service.

HISTORY: . . . . .CFA
Established in 1972; . . 1st Franchised in 1974
Company-Owned Units (As of 12/1/1989): . .1
Franchised Units (12/1/1989): 12
Total Units (12/1/1989): 14
Distribution: US-0;Can-14;Overseas-0
North America: . . . . 2 Provinces
Concentration: . . . . . . .13 in BC, 1 in AB
Registered: . . . . AB
. . . .
Average # of Employees: . . . . . . 5 FT, 8 PT
Prior Industry Experience: . . . . . . Helpful

FINANCIAL:
Cash Investment: $170K
Total Investment: $170K
Fees: Franchise - $20K
  Royalty: 4%, Advert: 0%
Contract Periods (Yrs.): 10/5
Area Development Agreement: . .No
Sub-Franchise Contract: . . . . .No
Expand in Territory: . . . . . . Yes
Passive Ownership: . . . Discouraged
Encourage Conversions: . . . . Yes
Franchisee Purchase(s) Required: Yes

FRANCHISOR TRAINING/SUPPORT:
Financial Assistance Provided: . . . Yes(I)
Site Selection Assistance: . . . . . . .Yes
Lease Negotiation Assistance: . . . . .Yes
Co-operative Advertising: . . . . . . .Yes
Training: . . . . 1 Wk. Kamloops, BC
On-Going Support: . . . . .B,C,D,E,F,G
Full-Time Franchisor Support Staff: . . .3
EXPANSION PLANS:
  US: . . . . .No
  Canada - Yes, ...Overseas - No

TASTEE-FREEZ INTERNATIONAL

8345 Hall Rd., Box 162
Utica, MI 48019
TEL: (313) 739-5520
FAX:
Mr. James Brasier, VP

TASTEE-FREEZ offers its traditional menu of soft-serve desserts along with a core menu of hamburgers, hot dogs and fries (optional fried chicken and breakfast programs). Most recently, this menu has been augmented with a 14% gourmet dipped ice cream manufactured in the store. TASTEE-FREEZ is entering its 40th year of franchising.

HISTORY: . . . . IFA
Established in 1950; . . 1st Franchised in 1950
Company-Owned Units (As of 12/1/1989): . .0
Franchised Units (12/1/1989): 400
Total Units (12/1/1989): 400
Distribution: US-388;Can-12;Overseas-0
North America: . . . . 38 States, 4 Provinces
Concentration: . . 34 in IL, 33 in VA, 29 in PA
Registered: . . . . FL,IN,MI,ND,VA
. . . .
Average # of Employees: . . . .
Prior Industry Experience: . . . . Helpful

FINANCIAL:
Cash Investment: $50-150K
Total Investment: $125-450K
Fees: Franchise - $10-25K
  Royalty: 4%, Advert: 2%
Contract Periods (Yrs.): 10/10
Area Development Agreement: . .No
Sub-Franchise Contract: . . . . . Yes
Expand in Territory: . . . .
Passive Ownership: . . . Discouraged
Encourage Conversions: . . . . Yes
Franchisee Purchase(s) Required: .No

FRANCHISOR TRAINING/SUPPORT:
Financial Assistance Provided: . . . Yes(I)
Site Selection Assistance: . . . . . . .Yes
Lease Negotiation Assistance: . . . . .Yes
Co-operative Advertising: . . . . . . .Yes
Training: . . . . . . 3-4 Days Headquarters,
. . . . 10-14 Days On-site
On-Going Support: . . . . . . .C,D,E,G,H
Full-Time Franchisor Support Staff: . . 15
EXPANSION PLANS:
  US: . . . . .All US
  Canada - Yes, . . . Overseas - Yes

TIPPY'S TACO HOUSE

Box 665
Winnsboro, TX 75494
TEL: (214) 629-7800
FAX: (214) 342-5882
Mr. W. W. Locklier, Owner-Consultant

Excellent "Tex-Mex" food packaged to go or eat in. We give owner-operator a lot of leeway to use his own drive and initiative to be innovative within guidelines laid out by parent company. We are available at any time for advice or guidance.

HISTORY: . . . .
Established in 1958; . . 1st Franchised in 1968
Company-Owned Units (As of 12/1/1989): . .0
Franchised Units (12/1/1989): 22
Total Units (12/1/1989): 22
Distribution: US-22;Can-0;Overseas-0
North America: . . . . 5 States
Concentration: . . . .
Registered: . . . .
. . . .
Average # of Employees: . . . . .5 FT
Prior Industry Experience: . . . . Helpful

FINANCIAL:
Cash Investment: $30-50K
Total Investment: $100K
Fees: Franchise - $15K
Royalty: 3%, Advert: 0%
Contract Periods (Yrs.): . . . 20/20
Area Development Agreement: Yes/Var
Sub-Franchise Contract: . . . . . Yes
Expand in Territory: . . . . . . Yes
Passive Ownership: . . . Discouraged
Encourage Conversions: . . . . Yes
Franchisee Purchase(s) Required: Yes

FRANCHISOR TRAINING/SUPPORT:
Financial Assistance Provided: . . . . .No
Site Selection Assistance: . . . . . . .Yes
Lease Negotiation Assistance: . . . .Yes
Co-operative Advertising: . . . . No
Training: . . . . .Variable at
. . . . Nearest Operating Unit
On-Going Support: . . . . . . .C,D,E,F,G
Full-Time Franchisor Support Staff: . . . 4
EXPANSION PLANS:
US: . . . . All US
Canada - Yes, . . . Overseas - Yes

TOGO'S EATERY

900 E. Campbell, # 1
Campbell, CA 95008
TEL: (408) 377-1754
FAX:
Ms. Valerie Konomos, Fran. Coord.

We are an operation specializing in high-quality, fast-service sandwich restaurants. Unique in style, service and decor with a product that offers more variety and quality than traditional fast-food, with an emphasis on healthy food.

HISTORY: . . . .
Established in 1972; . . 1st Franchised in 1977
Company-Owned Units (As of 12/1/1989): . .7
Franchised Units (12/1/1989): 118
Total Units (12/1/1989): 125
Distribution: . . . US-125;Can-0;Overseas-0
North America: . . . . 3 States
Concentration: . . 118 in CA, 1 in NV, 1 in OR
Registered: . . . . .CA,OR,WA
. . . .
Average # of Employees: . . . . . .2 FT, 25 PT
Prior Industry Experience: . . . . . . Helpful

FINANCIAL:
Cash Investment: $90-160K
Total Investment: . . . .$
Fees: Franchise - $10-25K
Royalty: 5%, Advert: 2%
Contract Periods (Yrs.): . . . 10/10
Area Development Agreement: Yes/5
Sub-Franchise Contract: . . . . .No
Expand in Territory: . . . . . . Yes
Passive Ownership: . . . Not Allowed
Encourage Conversions: . . . . .No
Franchisee Purchase(s) Required: .No

FRANCHISOR TRAINING/SUPPORT:
Financial Assistance Provided: . . . . No
Site Selection Assistance: . . . . . . .Yes
Lease Negotiation Assistance: . . . .Yes
Co-operative Advertising: . . . . . . .Yes
Training: . . . . . . 2 Wks. Headquarters, 2
. . . . Wks. in Store
On-Going Support: . . . . . . .C,D,E,G,H
Full-Time Franchisor Support Staff: . . 18
EXPANSION PLANS:
US: . . . . .Northwest, Southwest
Canada - No, ...Overseas - No

VERN'S DOG HOUSE

1257 NYS Rte. 96N
Waterloo, NY 13165
TEL: (315) 539-3379
FAX:
Mr. Vern Sessler, President

VERN'S DOG HOUSE is a high-quality, fast-food restaurant that specializes in German-style franks (hot dogs) with 6 hot toppings and various condiments, all for one price, on a soft side bread roll. Side dishes include homemade macaroni salad, salt potatoes and various soft drinks with free refills. All toppings and drinks are self-serve. Seasonal operation with outside seating under umbrellas.

HISTORY: . . . .
Established in 1985; . . 1st Franchised in 1988
Company-Owned Units (As of 12/1/1989): . .5
Franchised Units (12/1/1989): 1
Total Units (12/1/1989): 6
Distribution: US-6;Can-0;Overseas-0
North America: . . . . .1 State
Concentration: . . . . 6 in NY
Registered: . . . . FL,NY,VA
. . . .
Average # of Employees: . . . . . . 3 FT, 2 PT
Prior Industry Experience: . . . . . . .Helpful

FINANCIAL:
Cash Investment: . . . .$
Total Investment: $60K
Fees: Franchise - $10K
Royalty: 3%, Advert: 1%
Contract Periods (Yrs.): 5/Var
Area Development Agreement: Yes/2
Sub-Franchise Contract: . . . . . Yes
Expand in Territory: . . . . . . .No
Passive Ownership: . . . Discouraged
Encourage Conversions: . . . . .No
Franchisee Purchase(s) Required: Yes

FRANCHISOR TRAINING/SUPPORT:
Financial Assistance Provided: . . . . No
Site Selection Assistance: . . . . . . .Yes
Lease Negotiation Assistance: . . . . No
Co-operative Advertising: . . . . . . .Yes
Training: . . . . Up to 2 Wks. Headquarters
. . . . . . Up to 2 Wks. Franchisee Site
On-Going Support: . . . . . .b,C,D,E,F,G,h
Full-Time Franchisor Support Staff: . . 15
EXPANSION PLANS:
US: . . . . East of Mississippi
Canada - No, ...Overseas - No

WENDY'S OLD FASHIONED HAMBURGERS
4288 W. Dublin-Granville Rd.
Dublin, OH 43017
TEL: (614) 764-3100
FAX: (614) 764-6894
Mr. David Simmerman, Dir. Fran. Aps.

Quick-service restaurant, specializing in hamburgers.

HISTORY: . . . . IFA	FINANCIAL: NYSE-WEN	FRANCHISOR TRAINING/SUPPORT:
Established in 1969; . . 1st Franchised in 1972	Cash Investment: . . . . . . $~250K	Financial Assistance Provided: . . . . . No
Company-Owned Units (As of 12/1/1989): 1146	Total Investment: . . . . . $.7-1.3MM	Site Selection Assistance: . . . . .Yes
Franchised Units (12/1/1989): 2579	Fees: Franchise - $25-30K	Lease Negotiation Assistance: . . . . .Yes
Total Units (12/1/1989): 3725	Royalty: 4%, Advert: 4%	Co-operative Advertising: . . . . .Yes
Distribution: . US-3489;Can-130;Overseas-106	Contract Periods (Yrs.): 20/5	Training: . . . . 10 Wks. Closest Store
North America: . . . . 50 States,10 Provinces	Area Development Agreement: Yes/20	. . . .
Concentration: . 290 in OH, 264 in FL,221 TX	Sub-Franchise Contract: . . . . .No	On-Going Support: . . . . .B,C,D,E,G,H,I
Registered: . . . . .All	Expand in Territory: . . . . Yes	Full-Time Franchisor Support Staff: . . 12
	Passive Ownership: . . . Not Allowed	EXPANSION PLANS:
Average # of Employees: . . . 3-5 FT, 25-30 PT	Encourage Conversions: . . . . . .No	US: . . . . .All US
Prior Industry Experience: . . . . . . Helpful	Franchisee Purchase(s) Required: .No	Canada - Yes, . . . Overseas - Yes

WENDY'S RESTAURANTS OF CANADA

6303 Airport Rd., # 500
Mississauga, ON L4V1R8 CAN
TEL: (416) 677-7023
FAX: (416) 677-5297
Mr. George Lathouras, VP

Consumers have voted WENDY'S the best-tasting hamburgers in the business in our industry time and time again. We are the only national chain to use fresh, 100% pure domestic beef. Our hamburgers are served hot-off-the-grill, with the customer's choice of toppings. It's this kind of old-fashioned quality that you'll find throughout the WENDY'S family of top-quality products.

HISTORY: . . . . .IFA/CFA	FINANCIAL: NYSE-WEN	FRANCHISOR TRAINING/SUPPORT:
Established in 1975; . . . 1st Franchised in 19	Cash Investment: $200-500K	Financial Assistance Provided: . . .Yes(D)
Company-Owned Units (As of 12/1/1989): . 87	Total Investment: . . . . . $.4-1.0MM	Site Selection Assistance: . . . . .Yes
Franchised Units (12/1/1989): 44	Fees: Franchise - $40K	Lease Negotiation Assistance: . . . . .Yes
Total Units (12/1/1989): 131	Royalty: 4%, Advert: 2%	Co-operative Advertising: . . . . .Yes
Distribution: US-0;Can-131;Overseas-0	Contract Periods (Yrs.): . . 20/Varies	Training: . . . . 8 Wks. Regional,
North America: . . . . 10 Provinces	Area Development Agreement: Yes/Var	. . . . 2 Wks. Headquarters
Concentration: . 72 in ON, 20 in BC, 16 in AB	Sub-Franchise Contract: . . . . .No	On-Going Support: . . . . .B,C,D,E,G,H,I
Registered: . . . . AB	Expand in Territory: . . . . Yes	Full-Time Franchisor Support Staff: . .710
	Passive Ownership: . . . Not Allowed	EXPANSION PLANS:
Average # of Employees: . . . . . 4 FT, 60 PT	Encourage Conversions: . . . . Yes	US: . . . . Have Separate US Parent
Prior Industry Experience: . . . . . . Helpful	Franchisee Purchase(s) Required: Yes	Canada - Yes, . . . Overseas - Yes

WHATABURGER RESTAURANT

4600 Parkdale Dr.
Corpus Christi, TX 78411
TEL: (512) 878-0650
FAX: (512) 878-0427
Mr. Joe Middendorf, Sr. VP

Fast-food restaurants, emphasizing excellent quality and service. Units provide dining room and drive-through service, featuring made-to-order hamburgers, chicken and fish sandwiches. Most open 24 hours, offering breakfast, lunch and dinner. 443 restaurants now in operation in TX, OK, LA, AZ, NM, AL and FL, GA and TN. New franchises available in these states.

HISTORY: . . . . IFA	FINANCIAL:	FRANCHISOR TRAINING/SUPPORT:
Established in 1950; . . 1st Franchised in 1953	Cash Investment: $100K	Financial Assistance Provided: . . . . .No
Company-Owned Units (As of 12/1/1989): 279	Total Investment: $500-800K	Site Selection Assistance: . . . . . . .Yes
Franchised Units (12/1/1989): 164	Fees: Franchise - $15K	Lease Negotiation Assistance: . . . .Yes
Total Units (12/1/1989): 443	Royalty: 5%, Advert: 4%	Co-operative Advertising: . . . . . . .Yes
Distribution: US-443;Can-0;Overseas-0	Contract Periods (Yrs.): 10/5	Training: . . . . 4 Wks. Headquarters
North America: . . . . 9 States	Area Development Agreement: Yes/Var	
Concentration: . . 371 in TX, 29 in AZ, 14 OK	Sub-Franchise Contract: . . . . .No	On-Going Support: . . . . . B,C,D,E,G,H
Registered: . . . . .FL	Expand in Territory: . . . . Yes	Full-Time Franchisor Support Staff: . . .6
	Passive Ownership: . . . Discouraged	EXPANSION PLANS:
Average # of Employees: . . . . .6 FT	Encourage Conversions: . . . . Yes	US: . . . . TX, OK, LA, AR, FL, GA, TN
Prior Industry Experience: . . . . . . Helpful	Franchisee Purchase(s) Required: .No	Canada - No, ...Overseas - No

WIENERSCHNITZEL

4440 Von Karman Ave.
Newport Beach, CA 92660
TEL: (800) 854-6143 *432-3316 (CA)
FAX:
Mr. Alan F. Gallup, Dir. Fran. Sales

WIENERSCHNITZEL is the segment leader in hot dogs and the most successful full-menu hot dog franchise in the country. WIENERSCHNITZEL possesses high name recognition with generally lower entry costs than other major chains.

HISTORY: . . . . IFA
Established in 1961; . . 1st Franchised in 1964
Company-Owned Units (As of 12/1/1989): . 92
Franchised Units (12/1/1989): 204
Total Units (12/1/1989): 296
Distribution: US-296;Can-0;Overseas-0
North America: . . . . 15 States
Concentration: . . . . . Primarily CA, TX, AZ
Registered: . . . . CA,IL,WA
. . . .
Average # of Employees: . . . . . .5 FT, 15 PT
Prior Industry Experience: . . . . Helpful

FINANCIAL:
Cash Investment: $60-150K
Total Investment: $500-800K
Fees: Franchise - $30K
Royalty: 5%, Advert: 4%
Contract Periods (Yrs.): . . 20/Varies
Area Development Agreement: Yes/Var
Sub-Franchise Contract: . . . . . No
Expand in Territory: . . . . . . Yes
Passive Ownership: . . . Discouraged
Encourage Conversions: . . . . . Yes
Franchisee Purchase(s) Required: .No

FRANCHISOR TRAINING/SUPPORT:
Financial Assistance Provided: . . . Yes(I)
Site Selection Assistance: . . . . .Yes
Lease Negotiation Assistance: . . . . .Yes
Co-operative Advertising: . . . . .Yes
Training: . . . . 6 Wks. Headquarters
. . . .
On-Going Support: . . . . A,B,C,D,e,G,h,I
Full-Time Franchisor Support Staff: . . 80
EXPANSION PLANS:
US: . . . . Southwest
Canada - No, ...Overseas - No

YOUR PIZZA SHOP

1177 S. Main St.
North Canton, OH 44720
TEL: (216) 499-1177
FAX:
Mr. John Purney, President

Carry-out, dining room operation, with salad bar and/or smorgasbord available.

HISTORY: . . . .
Established in 1957; . . 1st Franchised in 1962
Company-Owned Units (As of 12/1/1989): . .3
Franchised Units (12/1/1989): 17
Total Units (12/1/1989): 20
Distribution: US-20;Can-0;Overseas-0
North America: . . . . 2 States
Concentration: . . . . .19 in OH, 1 in FL
Registered: . . . . .FL
. . . .
Average # of Employees: . . . . . . 7 FT, 7 PT
Prior Industry Experience: . . . . Helpful

FINANCIAL:
Cash Investment: $40-50K
Total Investment: $60-75K
Fees: Franchise - $10K
Royalty: 2%, Advert: 2%
Contract Periods (Yrs.): 5/5
Area Development Agreement: Yes/5
Sub-Franchise Contract: . . . . . No
Expand in Territory: . . . . . . Yes
Passive Ownership: . . . Discouraged
Encourage Conversions: . . . . . Yes
Franchisee Purchase(s) Required: .No

FRANCHISOR TRAINING/SUPPORT:
Financial Assistance Provided: . . . . .No
Site Selection Assistance: . . . . .Yes
Lease Negotiation Assistance: . . . . .Yes
Co-operative Advertising: . . . . .Yes
Training: . . . . 4 Wks. Field,
. . . . .4 Wks. On-site
On-Going Support: . . . . . . .B,C,D,E,H
Full-Time Franchisor Support Staff: . . 45
EXPANSION PLANS:
US: . . . . All US
Canada - No, ... Overseas - No

SUPPLEMENTAL LISTING OF FRANCHISORS

241 PIZZA	2000 Weston Rd., #300, Weston ON M9N1X3	CAN
ACADIA CAFE	353 Courthouse Rd., Gulfport MS 39501	
ALIMENTATION COUCHE TARD	1600 est, boul. St-Martin, B-280, Laval PQ H7G4S7	CAN
ALL AMERICAN HERO	110 E. Broward Blvd., # 650, Ft. Lauderdale FL 33301	
ALL V'S SANDWICHES	26 W. Dry Creek Circle, # 390, Littleton CO 80120	
AMERICAN DAIRY QUEEN	P.O. Box 35286, Minneapolis MN 55435	
APPETITO'S	5517 N. 27th Ave., Phoenix AZ 85013	
ARBY'S	3090 Kingston Rd., #402, Scarborough ON M1M1P2	CAN
ARTHUR TREACHER'S FISH & CHIPS	5121 Mahoning Ave., Youngstown OH 44515	
ATLANTIC CONCESSIONS SYSTEMS	P.O. Box 11339, Ft. Lauderdale FL 33339	
AUNT CHILOTTA TACOS	133 Coon Rapids Blvd., Coon Rapids MN 55433	
BAMBOLINO'S	214 N. Nagle, Houston TX 77003	
BENNETT'S PIT BAR-B-QUE	6635 S. Dayton, # 330, Englewood CO 80111	

BIG CHEESE PIZZA CORPORATION	1877 N. Rock Rd., Wichita KS 67208	
BIG FRANK'S CHICAGO STYLE HOT DOGS	3131 Alabama, # 309, Houston TX 77098	
BLIMPIE COMPANY	1775 The Exchange, # 215, Atlanta GA 30339	
BLUEBERRY HILL RESTAURANTS	2036 Sheppard Ave., E., Willowdale ON M2J5B3	CAN
BOBBY'S KASTLE	18547 Collins St., # B-34, Tarzana CA 91356	
BOJANGLES' OF AMERICA	4421 Stuart Andrew, # 500, Charlotte NC 28217	
BOZ HOT DOGS	770 E. 142nd St., Dolton IL 60419	
BROWN'S CHICKEN	377 E. Butterfield Rd., Lombard IL 60148	
BTG EXPRESS	P. O. Box 1313, Battle Creek MI 49016	
BUBBA'S BREAKAWAY	2738 9 W. College Ave., State College PA 16801	
BUCKY'S BURGERS	2528 Donegal Dr., Racine WI 53405	
BUMPERS OF AMERICA	P.O. Box 700, Greenwood MS 38930	
BURGER BOX SYSTEMS	2002 Roosevelt - B, Arlington TX 76013	
BURGER BROTHERS	456 Main St., Penticton BC V2A5C5	CAN
BURGER INN	19th & Pioneer, # 301, Cheyenne WY 82001	
BURGER KING	P.O. Box 520783, General Mail Cen, Miami FL 33152	
BURGERS DIRECT	1160 Broadway Blvd., Ann Arbor MI 48105	
BUSCEMI'S PIZZA & SUB SHOPPE	30362 Gratiot Ave., Roseville MI 48066	
CAJUN JOE'S	325 Bic Dr., Milford CT 06460	
CAPT'N NEMOS	7367 N. Clark St., Chicago IL 60626	
CARA OPERATIONS LTD.	230 Bloor St. W., Toronto ON M5S1T8	CAN
CASA BONITA/TACO BUENO	8115 Preston Rd., Dallas TX 75225	
CASSANO'S PIZZA & SUBS	1700 E. Stroop Rd., Kettering OH 45429	
CATFISH SHAKS OF AMERICA	353 Courthouse Rd., Gulfport MS 39501	
CHANTECLER CHAR-B.Q. CHICKEN 'N' RIB	39 Pinnacle Rd., Willowdale ON M2L2V6	CAN
CHATEAU ST. JEROME BAR-B-QUE & RIBS	7001 Mumford Rd., # 3030-2, Halifax NS B3L4R3	CAN
CHECKERS DRIVE-IN RESTAURANT	P.O. Box 2907, Mobile AL 36652	
CHEEZ & CHOPSTIX	900 W. 16th St., N. Vancouver BC	CAN
CHEF'S TAKEOUT	111 N. Victory, Burbank CA 91502	
CHESTERFRIED CHICKEN	Industrial Park, P.O. Box 500, Carbonear NF A0A1T0	CAN
CHICK-N-JOY SYSTEMS	P.O. Box 327, West Hill ON M1E4R8	CAN
CHICKEN COOP	2010 Winters Dr., Kalamazoo MI 49002	
CHOWDER'S FAMOUS FISH & SEAFOOD	247 Airport N. Office Park, Ft. Wayne IN 46825	
CHURCH'S FRIED CHICKEN	1333 S. Clearview Pkwy., Jefferson LA 70121	
CIRCLES PIZZA BISTRO	310 Bay Ridge Ave., Bay Ridge NY 11220	
CITY SUBMARINE	812 - 1661 Portage Ave., Winnipeg MB R3J3T7	CAN
CLUB SANDWICH	107 Cherry St., New Canaan CT 06840	
CLUCK IN A BUCKET SKINLESS CHICKEN	2335 Honolulu Ave., Montrose CA 91020	
COCK OF THE WALK	P.O. Box 806, Natchez MS 39120	
CONFUCIUS SAYS	1001 - 805 W. Broadway, Vancouver BC V5Z1K1	CAN
CONFUCIUS SAYS	3901 MacArthur Blvd., # 200, Newport Beach CA 92660	
COPELANDS	1333 S. Clearview Pkwy., # 413, Jefferson LA 70121	
COUCH'S BBQ	5323 27-E Nettleton Ave., Jonesboro AR 72410	
COVERED WAGON CAFE	15 Bellfield Rd., # C, Rexdale ON M9W1E8	CAN
CULTURES, FRESH FOOD RESTAURANTS	145 Davenport Rd., Toronto ON M5RIJ1	CAN
D'LITES EMPORIUM	9760 W. Sample Rd., Coral Springs FL 33065	
DAFFY'S DONAIRS	30 Hockley Path, Brampton ON L6V3R3	CAN
DAIRY QUEEN CANADA	5245 Harvester Rd., P.O. Box 430, Burlington ON L7R3Y3	CAN
DAVE'S PIZZA	#6 - 5579 - 47 St., Red Deer AB T4N1S1	CAN
DEL TACO	1801 Royal Ln., # 902, Dallas TX 75229	
DELICORP FOODSERVICE	55 Avenue Rd., # 2950, Toronto ON M5R3L2	CAN
DEXTER'S SUBS	1516 W. Mound St., Columbus OH 43223	
DIMARTINO'S NEW ORLEANS MUFFULETTAS	1788 Carol Sue Ave., Gretna LA 70056	
DOG N SUDS RESTAURANTS	P.O. Box 162, Utica MI 48087	
DOMINO'S PIZZA OF CANADA	969 Derry Rd. E., # 112, Mississauga ON L5T2T7	CAN
DOUBLE DEAL PIZZA	2646 Palma Dr., Ventura CA 93003	
DUBBLES DRIVE THRU RESTAURANTS	669 N. Main St., Marion OH 44302	
EAT-A-BURGER	3760 S. Highland Dr., # 405, Salt Lake City UT 84106	

EDWARDO'S NATURAL PIZZA RESTAURANT . . . . . . 4415 W. Harrison St., # 510, Hillside IL 60162
EGG ROLL EXPRESS . . . . 6625 S. Lewis Ave., Tulsa OK 74136
EXPRESS BURGER . . . . 1814 Pioneer Ave., # 301, Cheyenne WY 82001
FAMILIES ORIGINAL GOURMET SANDWICHES   6760 Corporate Dr., #300, Colorado Springs CO 80919
FAMOUS DILL BURGER . . . . .600 5th Ave. Plaza, Des Moines IA 50309
FAST TRACK USA . . . . 138 McGehee Dr., Baton Rouge LA 70815
FATBURGER . . . . 123 N. San Vincente, # 124, Beverly Hills CA 90211
FATSO'S . . . . .102 Bloor St. W., Toronto ON M5S1M8   CAN
FATSO'S CANADA . . . . 102 Bloor St. W., # 1100, Toronto ON M5S1M8   CAN
FRANCHISE CHEZ BETTER . . . . 4384, boul. St-Laurent, Montreal PQ H2W1Z5   CAN
FRANK & STEIN DOGS & DRAFTS . . . . P.O. Box 20608, Roanoke VA 24018
FRENCHY'S CREOLE FRIED CHICKEN . . . . 6830 Mykawa Rd., Houston TX 77033
FRESHY'S PIZZA . . . . P.O. Box 324, Cedarburg WI 53012
GALLUCCI'S PIZZERIA . . . . .2845 NW Hwy., # 101, Lincoln City OR 97367
GODFATHER CORP. . . . . .101 Meadowbrook Dr., # 125, Lambeth ON N6L1C7   CAN
GOLD STAR CHILI . . . . 5204 Beechmont Ave., Cincinnati OH 45230
GOLDEN SKILLET FRIED CHICKEN . . . . 310 Turner Rd., #1, Richmond VA 23225
GRANDMA'S FRIED CHICKEN . . . . 3310 S. Broadway, # 202, Tyler TX 75701
GRANDY'S . . . . .997 Grandy Ln., Lewisville TX 75067
GRANNY'S . . . . 201 North Front St., # 1001, Sarnia ON N7T7T9   CAN
GRANNY'S CHICKEN COOP . . . . .P.O. Box 611290, Port Huron MI 48061
GREAT AMERICAN TREATS . . . . 4005 Merel Hay Rd., Des Moines IA 50301
GROUPE ST-HUBERT . . . . .2, Place Laval, # 500, Chomedey, Laval PQ H7N5N6   CAN
GYRO WRAP . . . . .150 Oak St., Avondale Estate GA 30002
HARVEST INN . . . . 15463 - 104th Ave., # 202, Surrey BC V3R1N9   CAN
HEAVY DUTY PIZZA . . . . 113 - 115 Cushman Rd., Unit 21, St. Catharines ON L2M6S9   CAN
HENNY O'ROURKES . . . . .7516 Heatherwood Ln., Cincinnati OH 45244
HIENIE'S . . . . 8331 W. 145th Pl., Orland Park IL 60462
HIP POCKET . . . . 3804 Country Club Dr., Irving TX 75038
HO-LEE . . . . 177 Danforth Ave., # 302, Toronto ON M4K1N2   CAN
HOOKERS HAMBURGERS . . . . 1130 Cleveland St., Clearwater FL 34615
HOTLICKS . . . . 8 Dinnell Dr., Pittsburgh PA 15221
HUNKY BILL'S HOUSE OF PEROGIES . . . . .207 - 96 E. Broadway, Vancouver BC V5T4N9   CAN
IN 'N' OUT FOOD STORES . . . . .19215 W. Eight Mile Rd., Detroit MI 48219
INTERNATIONAL DAIRY QUEEN . . . . P.O. Box 35286, Minneapolis MN 55435
IZZY'S PIZZA RESTAURANTS . . . . .110 3rd Ave., SE, Albany OR 97321
J. J. HOOKERS . . . . 1130 Cleveland St., Clearwater FL 34615
JASON'S DELI . . . . 112 Gateway, Beaumont TX 77701
JERRY'S SUBS & PIZZA . . . . .15942 Shady Grove Rd., Gaithersburg MD 20877
JERSEY MIKE'S SUBMARINES & SALADS . . . . .2627 Hwy. 70, Manasquan (Wall) NJ 08736
JIMBOY'S TACOS . . . . 1560 B Juliesse Ave., Sacramento CA 95815
JIMMY THE GREEK . . . . 9 Laredo Ct., Willowdale ON M2N4H7   CAN
JOYCE'S SUBS & PIZZA . . . . 14001 E. Iliff Ave., # 701, Aurora CO 80014
JRECK SUBS . . . . P.O. Box 6, Watertown NY 13601
JV'S FISH& CHIPS . . . . 3395 Pony Trail Dr., # 401, Mississauga ON K4Y3R7   CAN
KEN'S PIZZA . . . . 4441 S. 72nd E. Ave., Tulsa OK 74145
KENTUCKY FRIED CHICKEN (CANADA) . . . . .10 Carlson Court, # 300, Rexdale ON M9W6L2   CAN
KOYA JAPAN . . . . 812 - 1661 Portage Ave., Winnipeg MB R3J3T7   CAN
KRUMBLY BURGERS . . . . .101 Tymes Square, Troy MI 63379
KRYSTAL KWIK . . . . One Union Square, Chattanooga TN 37402
LE CAFE . . . . 519 E. First St., Los Angeles CA 90012
LEE'S HOAGIE HOUSE . . . . .600 W. Broadway, # 320, Glendale CA 91204
LES PRES . . . . 1801 McGill College Ave., # 1050, Montreal PQ H3A2N4   CAN
LINDY - GERTIS'S . . . . 8437 Park Ave., Burr Ridge IL 60521
LITTLE CEASAR OF CANADA . . . . 5665 McLaughlin Rd., Mississauga ON L5R3K5   CAN
LOEB . . . . 400 Industrial Ave., Ottawa ON K1G3K8   CAN
LONDON FISH N' CHIPS . . . . .306 S. Maple Ave., S. San Francisco CA 94080
LONG JOHN SILVER'S SEAFOOD SHOPPES . . . . 520 Hespeler Rd., Cambridge ON N1R3H3   CAN

M CORP	903 Gratton St., Ville-St-Laurent PQ H4M2G6	CAN
MAID-RITE	3112 University Ave., Des Moines IA 50311	
MANCHU WOK	2900 John St., # 2, Markham ON L3R5G3	CAN
MAZZIO'S PIZZA	4441 S. 72nd E. Ave., Tulsa OK 74145	
MCCARTHY'S	8331 W. 145th Pl., Orland Park IL 60462	
MCDONALD'S RESTAURANTS OF CANADA	McDonalds Place, Toronto ON M3C3L4	CAN
MINUTE MAN OF AMERICA	P.O. Box 828, Little Rock AR 72203	
MISSISSIPPI JACKS	74-090 El Paseo Dr., # 101, Palm Desert CA 92260	
MR. CHICKEN	P.O. Box 23271, Cleveland OH 44123	
MR. HERO	6902 Pearl Rd., Cleveland OH 44130	
MR. JIM'S PIZZERIA CORPORATION	2817 Rugal, # 108, Plano TX 75075	
MR. PHILLY	6902 Pearl Rd., Cleveland OH 44130	
MR. TACO	718 N. Porter, # 220, Norman OK 73071	
NATHAN'S FAMOUS	1400 Old Country Rd., Westbury NY 11590	
NEW ORLEANS FAMOUS FRIED CHICKEN	P.O. Box 700, Greenwood MS 38930	
NEW YORK PICKLE DELI	976 Sullivan Ave., South Windsor CT 06074	
NUTRI FRESH RESTAURANTS	3338 Homark Dr., Mississauga ON L4Y2K4	CAN
O! DELI	65 Battery St., San Francisco CA 94111	
OLDE STYLE HAMBURGERS	107 Evant Rd., Raymore MO 64083	
OLIVER'S PIZZA/OLIVERIO'S PIZZA	28580 Orchard Lake Rd., Farmington Hills MI 48018	
ORANGE JULIUS CANADA	5245 Harvester Rd., Burlington ON L7R3Y3	CAN
ORANGE JULIUS OF AMERICA	P.O. Box 35286, Minneapolis MN 55435	
OREAN THE HEALTH EXPRESS	1320 North Vine, Hollywood CA 90028	
ORIGINAL HAMBURGER STAND	4440 Von Karman Ave., Newport Beach CA 92660	
OTTOMANELLI'S CAFE	1549 York Ave., New York NY 10028	
P-WEE'S, PIZZA, PASTA & MORE	P.O. Box 4381, Postal Sta. D, Hamilton ON L8V4L8	CAN
PACIFIC TASTEE FREEZ	721 Brea Canyon Rd., # 3, Walnut CA 91789	
PANZEROTTO & PIZZA	234 Parliament St., Toronto ON M5A3A4	CAN
PAPA JOHN'S FRESH PIZZA & SUBS	119 W. Sherman Ave., Ft. Atkinson WI 53538	
PAPA RICARDOS	Main St. Plaza, # 600, Voorhees NJ 08043	
PASQUALE PIZZA & PASTA	19 W. Oxmoor Rd., Birmingham AL 35209	
PASTEL	#1150 - 355 Burrard St., Vancouver BC V6C2G8	CAN
PAUL REVERE'S PIZZA	1652 - 42nd St. NE, # C, Cedar Rapids IA 52402	
PEACHY'S PIZZA PARLORS	Box # 1, Suite # 30, RR # 4, Sudbury ON P3E4M9	CAN
PENGUIN POINT FRANCHISE SYSTEMS	P.O. Box 975, Warsaw IN 46580	
PHILLY'S FINEST RESTAURANT	5056 E. Broadway, Tucson AZ 85711	
PITA FEAST INTERNATIONAL	11660 Olympic Blvd., Los Angeles CA 90064	
PIZZA DELIGHT	1530 Markham Rd., # 400, Scarborough ON M1B3G4	CAN
PIZZA DEPOT	10059 Sandmeyer Ln., Bldg. C, Philadelphia PA 19116	
PIZZA EXPRESS	P.O. Box 305, Noble OK 73068	
PIZZA MAN, HE DELIVERS	6930-1/2 Tujunga Ave., North Hollywood CA 91605	
PIZZA MOVERS	1300 Mercantile Ln., # 198, Landover MD 20785	
PIZZA NOVA TAKE-OUT	2100 Elsmere Rd., # 300, Scarborough ON M1H3B7	CAN
PIZZA RACK FRANCHISE SYSTEMS	2130 Market Ave. N., Canton OH 44714	
PIZZA, PASTA & MORE	P.O. Box 4381, Station D, Hamilton ON L8V4L8	CAN
PIZZAVILLE-PIZZA & PANZEROTTO	741 Rowntree Dairy Rd., Woodbridge ON L4L5T9	CAN
PLUS 1 PIZZA	P.O. Box 516, 1354 Clark St., Cambridge OH 43725	
POPEYES FAMOUS FRIED CHICKEN	1333 S. Clearview Pkwy., # 413, Jefferson LA 70121	
POR-PORTIONS	1801 McGill College Ave., # 1050, Montreal PQ H3A2N4	CAN
PROVENDER	177 Danforth Ave., # 302, Toronto ON M4K1N2	CAN
REGGIES SANDWICHES	45 Dunlop St. E., Barrie ON L4M1A2	CAN
RESTAURANTS LES PRES (CANADA)	1585, boul. del Laurentide, Chomedey, Laval PQ H7N4Y6	CAN
RIBBY'S EXPRESS BARBECUE	8080 N. Central Expy., # 500, Box, Dallas TX 75206	
RICKY'S DAIRY BAR	34500 Doreka Dr., Fraser MI 48026	
RICKY'S PANCAKE HOUSE	12354 S. Park Crescent, Surrey BC V3W9X4	CAN
RUFFAGE	#1150 - 355 Burrard St., Vancouver BC V6C2G8	CAN
RUNZA DRIVE-INNS OF AMERICA	P.O. Box 6042, Lincoln NE 68506	
SAILOR'S STEAMER HOTDOG	1110 Center St., N, # 202, Calgary AB T2E252	CAN

SANDWICH FACTORY, THE	5498 Mahoning Ave., Youngstown OH 44515	
SAUCY'S PIZZA & YOGURT BAR	2930 Wetmore Ave., # 908, Everett WA 98201	
SBARRO OF CANADA	300 John St., # 324, Thornhill ON	CAN
SCOOTER'S	4441 S. 72nd E. Ave., Tulsa OK 74145	
SCOTTO PIZZA	1895 Greentree Rd., Cherry Hill NJ 08003	
SENOR WIMPY'S	1010 Turquoise St., # 201, San Diego CA 92109	
SICILY'S PIZZA	4635 S. Sherwood Forest Blvd., Baton Rouge LA 70816	
SIR PIZZA INTERNATIONAL	15311 NW 60th Ave., Miami Lakes FL 33014	
SISTER'S CHICKEN & BISCUITS	25000 Country Club Blvd., # 440, N. Olmsted OH 44070	
SIZZLING WOK	P.O. Box 1038, Saskatoon SK S7K4R6	CAN
SKIPPER'S	14450 NE 29th Pl., # 200, Bellevue WA 98007	
SKOLNIKS BAGEL BAKERY	10801 Electron Dr., # 308, Louisville KY 40299	
SMITHFIELD CHICKEN & BAR-B-Q	Gum Branch Sq. II, # 130, Jacksonville NC 28540	
SNACK SHACK	Industrial Park, P.O. Box 500, Carbonear NF A0A1T0	CAN
SOME PLACE ELSE	1863 Apple Ave., Muskegon MI 49442	
SOUTHERN STYLE CATFISH	409 Old Highway 40, O'Fallon MO 63366	
SR. WIMPY'S	1010 Turquoise St., # 201, San Diego CA 92109	
SUB & STUFF SANDWICH SHOP	412 First National Center, Hutchinson KS 67501	
SUB / URBAN	520 Fellowship Rd., Mt. Laurel NJ 08054	
SUB STATION II	P. O. Box 2260, Sumter SC 29150	
T.G. QUICKLY BAR-B-Q	77 Progress Ave., # 102, Scarborough ON M1P2Y7	CAN
TACO BELL CORPORATION	17901 Von Karman, Irvine CA 92714	
TACO JOHN'S	808 W. 20th St., Cheyenne WY 82001	
TACO TICO	7610 Stemmons Fwy., # 140, Dallas TX 75247	
TACO VIA	1100 Main St., # 109, Kansas City MO 64105	
TAQUITOS REAL	3601 E. Broadway, # 112A, Box 438, Tucson AZ 85733	
TARK'S CLAM STAND	2116 Sherman St., Hollywood FL 33020	
TOMS HOUSE OF PIZZA	7730 MacLeod Trail S., Calgary AB T2H0L9	CAN
TRAK-AIRE	7108 S. Alton Way, # J, Englewood CO 80112	
TUBBY'S SUB SHOPS	34500 Doreka Dr., Fraser MI 48026	
UMBERTINO'S RESTAURANTS	4305 Dawson St., Vancouver BC V5C4B4	CAN
VALENTINE	6495 boul. Choquette, St-Hyacinthe PQ J2S8L2	CAN
VISTA RESTAURANTS	1911 Tuttle Creek Blvd., Manhattan KS 66502	
VITO'S NEW YORK PIZZA CO.	732 W. New Orleans, Broken Arrow OK 74011	
WAT-A-PIZZA	19 Ingram Dr., Toronto ON M3J2X5	CAN
WEE-BAG-IT DELIVERY EMPORIUMS	1 SW 129th Ave., Pembroke Pines FL 33027	
WESTERN PIZZA & BBQ CHICKEN	1107 Rae St., Regina SK S4T2B9	CAN
WILBUR'S WIENER WORKS	8290 Hubbard Rd., Auburn CA 95603	
WING MACHINE	1925 Yonge St., 2nd Fl., Toronto ON M4S1Z3	CAN
YU-CHU'S	4141 Yonge St., # 301, Willowdale ON M2P2A8	CAN
YUMMIES COFFEE HOUSE	1701 Woodward Dr., Ottawa ON K2C0R4	CAN
ZAB'S BACKYARD HOTS	Box 305 A, Rt. 6, Andover CT 06232	
ZACK'S FAMOUS FROZEN YOGURT	236 King St. E., # 300, Toronto ON M5A1K1	CAN
ZIPPS HAMBURGERS	393 N. Euclid Ave., St. Louis MO 63108	
ZOOMZ	P.O. Box 1060, Columbus OH 43215	

CHAPTER 21

CHAPTER 21

RETAIL FOOD:
RESTAURANT / FAMILY-STYLE

ABC FAMILY RESTAURANTS

#202 - 15373 Fraser Hwy.
Surrey, BC V3R3P3 CAN
TEL: (604) 583-2919
FAX: (604) 583-8488
Mr. Ron Martens, President

ABC FAMILY RESTAURANTS offer the BEST in family dining. Menu features over 150 quality homestyle, delicious food dishes. Courteous, efficient service is provided in a contemporary, relaxing environment. High emphasis placed on in-store bakeries, which have made ABC "The Famous Pie Place" restaurants.

HISTORY: . . . . .CFA
Established in 1976; . . 1st Franchised in 1976
Company-Owned Units (As of 12/1/1989): . .1
Franchised Units (12/1/1989): 12
Total Units (12/1/1989): 13
Distribution: US-0;Can-13;Overseas-0
  North America: . . . . .1 Province
  Concentration: . . . . 13 in BC
Registered: . . . . AB
. . . .
Average # of Employees: . . . . . 40 FT, 20 PT
Prior Industry Experience: . . . . Helpful

FINANCIAL:
Cash Investment: $150-300K
Total Investment: $250-300K
Fees: Franchise - $35K
  Royalty: 4%, Advert: 1%
Contract Periods (Yrs.): . . . 10/10
Area Development Agreement: . .No
Sub-Franchise Contract: . . . . . .No
Expand in Territory: . . . . . . Yes
Passive Ownership: . . . Not Allowed
Encourage Conversions: . . . . . .No
Franchisee Purchase(s) Required: Yes

FRANCHISOR TRAINING/SUPPORT:
Financial Assistance Provided: . . . Yes(I)
Site Selection Assistance: . . . . . . .Yes
Lease Negotiation Assistance: . . . . .Yes
Co-operative Advertising: . . . . . . .Yes
Training: . . . . . . 8 Wks. Training Center
. . . .
On-Going Support: . . .a,B,C,D,E,F,G,H,I
Full-Time Franchisor Support Staff: . . .6
EXPANSION PLANS:
  US: . . . . .No
  Canada - Yes, ... Overseas - No

AMERICAN CAFE, THE

7911 Braygreen Rd.
Laurel, MD 20707
TEL: (301) 497-6921
FAX:
Mr. Regis T. Robbins, Dir. Fran.

Full-service, casual dining restaurant and gourmet carry-out deli. Concept takes advantage of pouch cooking technology to reduce labor and simplify kitchen.

HISTORY: . . . . IFA
Established in 1970; . . . 1st Franchised in 19
Company-Owned Units (As of 12/1/1989): . 13
Franchised Units (12/1/1989): 0
Total Units (12/1/1989): 13
Distribution: US-13;Can-0;Overseas-0
North America: . . . . 3 States
Concentration: . . . 5 in DC,4 in VA, 4 in MD
Registered: . . . . .MD,NY,VA
. . . .
Average # of Employees: . . . . . .4 FT, 45 PT
Prior Industry Experience: . . . . Helpful

FINANCIAL: NYSE-GRA
Cash Investment: $300-600K
Total Investment: $700-1,000K
Fees: Franchise - $35-45K
Royalty: 4%, Advert: 1.5%
Contract Periods (Yrs.): 10/5
Area Development Agreement: . Yes
Sub-Franchise Contract: . . . . . .No
Expand in Territory: . . . . Yes
Passive Ownership: . . . . . .Allowed
Encourage Conversions: . . . . . Yes
Franchisee Purchase(s) Required: Yes

FRANCHISOR TRAINING/SUPPORT:
Financial Assistance Provided: . . . . .No
Site Selection Assistance: . . . . . . .Yes
Lease Negotiation Assistance: . . . . .No
Co-operative Advertising: . . . . . . .Yes
Training: . . . . . 8 Wks. Washington, DC,
. . . . .2 Wks. Opening Restaurant
On-Going Support: . . . . B,C,D,E,F,G,H
Full-Time Franchisor Support Staff: . .140
EXPANSION PLANS:
US: . . . . . . CT,NY,NJ,PA,VA and NC
Canada - No, ...Overseas - No

BEEFSTEAK CHARLIE'S

17 W. 32nd St.
New York, NY 10001
TEL: (212) 465-1188
FAX: (212) 465-1506
Mr. Scott J. Kriger, Sr. VP Ops.

BEEFSTEAK CHARLIE'S sets itself apart from the crowd by offering the unique selling proposition of a warm, comfortable atmosphere where diners can enjoy a variety of beef, ribs, chicken or fish entrees that include UNLIMITED SHRIMP, SALAD BAR AND DRINKS, all at a very affordable price. This "winning recipe" gives BEEFSTEAK CHARLIE'S an unusually large and diverse market appeal.

HISTORY: . . . .
Established in 1972; . . 1st Franchised in 1972
Company-Owned Units (As of 12/1/1989): . 10
Franchised Units (12/1/1989): 14
Total Units (12/1/1989): 24
Distribution: US-24;Can-0;Overseas-0
North America: . . . . 7 States
Concentration: . . .13 in NY, 4 in FL, 2 in MD
Registered: . . . . FL,MD,NY
. . . .
Average # of Employees: . . . . . 15 FT, 20 PT
Prior Industry Experience: . . . . . .Necessary

FINANCIAL:
Cash Investment: $150-200K
Total Investment: $300-375K
Fees: Franchise - $25K
Royalty: 5%, Advert: 3%
Contract Periods (Yrs.): . . . 10/10
Area Development Agreement: Yes/10
Sub-Franchise Contract: . . . . . Yes
Expand in Territory: . . . . Yes
Passive Ownership: . . . Not Allowed
Encourage Conversions: . . . . . Yes
Franchisee Purchase(s) Required: .No

FRANCHISOR TRAINING/SUPPORT:
Financial Assistance Provided: . . . . .No
Site Selection Assistance: . . . . . . .Yes
Lease Negotiation Assistance: . . . .Yes
Co-operative Advertising: . . . . . . .Yes
Training: . . . 4 Wks. Sheepshead Bay, NY
. . . .
On-Going Support: . . . . . a,C,D,e,f,G,H
Full-Time Franchisor Support Staff: . . 15
EXPANSION PLANS:
US: . . . . .All US
Canada - Yes, . . . Overseas - Yes

BENIHANA OF TOKYO

8685 NW 53 Terrace, P.O. Box 020210
Miami, FL 33102
TEL: (305) 593-0770
FAX:
Mr. Michael W. Kata, Dir. Licensing

Japanese steakhouse, featuring teppanyaki-style cooking. Meals are prepared by skilled chefs on electric or gas-heated stainless steel grills that form part of the dining room. Menu selections include steak, chicken and seafood.

HISTORY: . . . .
Established in 1964; . . 1st Franchised in 1970
Company-Owned Units (As of 12/1/1989): . 39
Franchised Units (12/1/1989): 11
Total Units (12/1/1989): 50
Distribution: US-47;Can-1;Overseas-2
North America: . . . . . 22 States, 1 Province
Concentration: . . . 12 in CA, 6 in FL, 3 in NY
Registered: . . . . CA,HI,NY
. . . .
Average # of Employees: . . . . . 25 FT, 10 PT
Prior Industry Experience: . . . . Helpful

FINANCIAL: OTC-BNHN
Cash Investment: $450-500K
Total Investment: $1.2-1.6M
Fees: Franchise - $50K
Royalty: 6%, Advert: 5%
Contract Periods (Yrs.): . . 15/Varies
Area Development Agreement: Yes/15
Sub-Franchise Contract: . . . . . .No
Expand in Territory: . . . . .No
Passive Ownership: . . . Discouraged
Encourage Conversions: . . . . . Yes
Franchisee Purchase(s) Required: Yes

FRANCHISOR TRAINING/SUPPORT:
Financial Assistance Provided: . . . . .No
Site Selection Assistance: . . . . . . .Yes
Lease Negotiation Assistance: . . . .Yes
Co-operative Advertising: . . . . . . .Yes
Training: . . . . . . .12-15 Wks. at Various
. . . . .Locations Throughout US
On-Going Support: . . . a,C,d,E,F,G,H,I
Full-Time Franchisor Support Staff: . . .2
EXPANSION PLANS:
US: . PA,MD,MI,OH,AZ,NY (exc. NYC)
Canada - No, ... Overseas - Yes

BINO'S FAMILY RESTAURANT

6962 Buller Ave.
Burnaby, BC V5J4S3 CAN
TEL: (604) 435-3044
FAX:
Mr. Kevin Turner, Development

Family restaurant with versatile menu, serving breakfast, lunch or dinner - 24 hours per day.

HISTORY: . . . .
Established in 1972; . . 1st Franchised in 1977
Company-Owned Units (As of 12/1/1989): . .0
Franchised Units (12/1/1989): 18
Total Units (12/1/1989): 18
Distribution: US-0;Can-18;Overseas-0
North America: . . . . .1 Province
Concentration: . . . . 18 in BC
Registered: . . . .

. . . .
Average # of Employees: . . . . .12+FT,10+PT
Prior Industry Experience: . . . . . . Helpful

FINANCIAL:
Cash Investment: $150K
Total Investment: $300-350K
Fees: Franchise - $25K
 Royalty: 4%, Advert: 1%
Contract Periods (Yrs.): . . . . . Var.
Area Development Agreement: . .No
Sub-Franchise Contract: . . . . . .No
Expand in Territory: . . . . . . .No
Passive Ownership: . . . Discouraged
Encourage Conversions: . . . . . Yes
Franchisee Purchase(s) Required: Yes

FRANCHISOR TRAINING/SUPPORT:
Financial Assistance Provided: . . . . .No
Site Selection Assistance: . . . . . . .Yes
Lease Negotiation Assistance: . . . . .Yes
Co-operative Advertising: . . . . .NA
Training: . . . . 1 Wk. HQ
. . . . 6 Wks. Site
On-Going Support: . . . . . . b,C,D,E,h
Full-Time Franchisor Support Staff: . . .7
EXPANSION PLANS:
US: . . . . No
Canada - Yes, ...Overseas - No

BOBBY RUBINO'S PLACE FOR RIBS

900 NE 26th Ave.
Ft. Lauderdale, FL 33304
TEL: (305) 565-1888
FAX: (305) 565-9771
Mr. Jerry Moniz, Dir. of Operations

BOBBY RUBINO'S PLACE FOR RIBS is a leader in the family barbecue dinnerhouse segment, meeting the needs of today's consumers by adhering to the practice of serving the best barbecue ribs, chicken and shrimp, steak, prime rib and more, in a clean and friendly environment at reasonable prices. BOBBY RUBINO'S is committed to producing maximum results in everything we do, a commitment that will enhance a franchisee's investment.

HISTORY: . . . . IFA
Established in 1978; . . 1st Franchised in 1982
Company-Owned Units (As of 12/1/1989): . 11
Franchised Units (12/1/1989): 8
Total Units (12/1/1989): 19
Distribution: US-18;Can-1;Overseas-0
North America: . . . . . .4 States, 1 Province
Concentration: . . 12 in FL, 4 in NY, 1 in PA
Registered: . . . . CA,FL,NY

. . . .
Average # of Employees: . . . . . 50 FT, 10 PT
Prior Industry Experience: . . . . . .Necessary

FINANCIAL:
Cash Investment: . . . . . . $.5-1.5M
Total Investment: . . . . . $.5-1.5M
Fees: Franchise - $50K
 Royalty: 4%, Advert: 2%
Contract Periods (Yrs.): 15/10
Area Development Agreement: Yes/15
Sub-Franchise Contract: . . . . . .No
Expand in Territory: . . . . Yes
Passive Ownership: . . . Not Allowed
Encourage Conversions: . . . . . Yes
Franchisee Purchase(s) Required: .No

FRANCHISOR TRAINING/SUPPORT:
Financial Assistance Provided: . . . . .No
Site Selection Assistance: . . . . . . .Yes
Lease Negotiation Assistance: . . . . .NA
Co-operative Advertising: . . . . . . .Yes
Training: . . . . 4 Wks. Headquarters
. . . .
On-Going Support: . . . . C,D,E,F
Full-Time Franchisor Support Staff: . . . 6
EXPANSION PLANS:
US: . . . . .All US
Canada - Yes, . . . Overseas - Yes

BOSTON PIZZA

212 - 6011 Westminster Hwy.
Richmond, BC V7C4V4 CAN
TEL: (604) 270-1108
FAX: (614) 270-4168
Mr. Bob Meister, Franchise Sales

We are an up-scale pizza and pasta restaurant that is unique in as much as we appeal to four sectors of the general public: 1) the families for early evening business, 2) business people in a hurry at lunch, 3) after the movies or show for cocktails and finger foods and 4) take-out and delivery of most items. All at reasonable prices.

HISTORY: . . . . IFA
Established in 1963; . . 1st Franchised in 1968
Company-Owned Units (As of 12/1/1989): . .1
Franchised Units (12/1/1989): 95
Total Units (12/1/1989): 96
Distribution: US-0;Can-92;Overseas-4
North America: . . . . 5 Provinces
Concentration: . . 43 in AB, 30 in BC, 9 in ON
Registered: . . . . AB

. . . .
Average # of Employees: . . . . . 20 FT, 30 PT
Prior Industry Experience: . . . . . . Helpful

FINANCIAL:
Cash Investment: $225-250K
Total Investment: $575-700K
Fees: Franchise - $30K
 Royalty: 7%, Advert: 2.5%
Contract Periods (Yrs.): 10/5
Area Development Agreement: . Yes
Sub-Franchise Contract: . . . . . .No
Expand in Territory: . . . . Yes
Passive Ownership: . . . Not Allowed
Encourage Conversions: . . . . . .No
Franchisee Purchase(s) Required: .No

FRANCHISOR TRAINING/SUPPORT:
Financial Assistance Provided: . . . Yes(I)
Site Selection Assistance: . . . . . . .Yes
Lease Negotiation Assistance: . . . . .Yes
Co-operative Advertising: . . . . . . .Yes
Training: . . . Minimum 6 Wks. Corporate
. . . . Store, Richmond, BC
On-Going Support: . . A,B,C,D,E,F,G,H
Full-Time Franchisor Support Staff: . . 23
EXPANSION PLANS:
US: . . . . .All US
Canada - Yes, . . . Overseas - Yes

BRICK OVEN BEANERY

433 Park Point Dr., # 250
Golden, CO 80401
TEL: (303) 526-1888
FAX:
Mr. Ross Johnson, President

"Honest Fast Food" - traditional American cuisine made from scratch and served in a fast-food style, in a warm, comfortable environment. The investment is based on converting existing restaurants. Consequently, the start-up costs are low and the return on investment high.

HISTORY: . . . .
Established in 1984; . . 1st Franchised in 1984
Company-Owned Units (As of 12/1/1989): . .1
Franchised Units (12/1/1989): 3
Total Units (12/1/1989): 4
Distribution: US-4;Can-0;Overseas-0
North America: . . . . 3 States
Concentration: . . . . .3 in CO, 1 in ID
Registered: . . . .

. . . .
Average # of Employees: . . . .
Prior Industry Experience: . . . . Helpful

FINANCIAL:
Cash Investment: $60K
Total Investment: $150-180K
Fees: Franchise - $20K
Royalty: 4%, Advert: 3%
Contract Periods (Yrs.): . . . .
Area Development Agreement: . Yes
Sub-Franchise Contract: . . . . .No
Expand in Territory: . . . . . . Yes
Passive Ownership: . . . Discouraged
Encourage Conversions: . . . . . Yes
Franchisee Purchase(s) Required: .No

FRANCHISOR TRAINING/SUPPORT:
Financial Assistance Provided: . . . . . No
Site Selection Assistance: . . . . .Yes
Lease Negotiation Assistance: . . . . . No
Co-operative Advertising: . . . . .Yes
Training: . . . . 21 Days Denver, CO,
. . . . . .2 Wks. Franchisee's Restaurant
On-Going Support: . . . . a,C,D,E
Full-Time Franchisor Support Staff: . . . .
EXPANSION PLANS:
US: . . . . .All US
Canada - No, ...Overseas - No

BRIDGEMAN'S ORIGINAL ICE CREAM RESTAURANT

6009 Wayzata Blvd., # 113
Minneapolis, MN 55416
TEL: (612) 593-1455
FAX: (612) 541-1101
Mr. John P. Taft, Fran. Sales Mgr.

BRIDGEMAN'S, a full-service, family-style restaurant, featuring our famous ice cream specialty treats. Bridgeman's will also award franchise opportunities based on our "Dip Shoppe" concept. The Dip Shoppe, strong in a food court setting, offers ice cream treats along with a limited sandwich menu.

HISTORY: . . . . IFA
Established in 1936; . . 1st Franchised in 1950
Company-Owned Units (As of 12/1/1989): . .9
Franchised Units (12/1/1989): 15
Total Units (12/1/1989): 24
Distribution: US-24;Can-0;Overseas-0
North America: . . . . 2 States
Concentration: . . . . 21 in MN, 3 in WI
Registered: . . . . MN,WI

. . . .
Average # of Employees: . . 5-10 FT, 20-35 PT
Prior Industry Experience: . . . . . . Helpful

FINANCIAL:
Cash Investment: $100K
Total Investment: $130-630K
Fees: Franchise - $9-25K
Royalty: 4%, Advert: 2%
Contract Periods (Yrs.): 10/10
Area Development Agreement: . .No
Sub-Franchise Contract: . . . . .No
Expand in Territory: . . . . . . .No
Passive Ownership: . . . Discouraged
Encourage Conversions: . . . . . Yes
Franchisee Purchase(s) Required: Yes

FRANCHISOR TRAINING/SUPPORT:
Financial Assistance Provided: . . . . . No
Site Selection Assistance: . . . . .Yes
Lease Negotiation Assistance: . . . . . No
Co-operative Advertising: . . . . .Yes
Training: . . . . . . 4-8 Wks. Headquarters
. . . .
On-Going Support: . . . .a,B,C,D,E,f,G,H
Full-Time Franchisor Support Staff: . . 20
EXPANSION PLANS:
US: . . . . MN,WI,SD,ND and IA
Canada - No, ...Overseas - No

CASEY'S

3228 S. Service Rd., # 133 W.
Burlington, ON L7N3H8 CAN
TEL: (416) 681-1296
FAX: (416) 333-4488
Mr. Caz Wisniewski, EVP

We are a leading force in the restaurant/bar concept in Canada. We pride ourselves on the quality of food we serve in the dining room, as well as the energetic atmosphere created in the bar area. Dance floor, DJ and stand-up bar are an integral part of the package.

HISTORY: . . . . .CFA
Established in 1980; . . 1st Franchised in 1982
Company-Owned Units (As of 12/1/1989): . .0
Franchised Units (12/1/1989): 26
Total Units (12/1/1989): 26
Distribution: US-0;Can-26;Overseas-0
North America: . . . . .1 Province
Concentration: . . . . 26 in ON
Registered: . . . .

. . . .
Average # of Employees: . . . . . 25 FT, 50 PT
Prior Industry Experience: . . . . Helpful

FINANCIAL:
Cash Investment: $250-300K
Total Investment: $540-690K
Fees: Franchise - $40K
Royalty: 5%, Advert: 2%
Contract Periods (Yrs.): . . . .Varies
Area Development Agreement: . .No
Sub-Franchise Contract: . . . . .No
Expand in Territory: . . . . . . .No
Passive Ownership: . . . Not Allowed
Encourage Conversions: . . . . . Yes
Franchisee Purchase(s) Required: .No

FRANCHISOR TRAINING/SUPPORT:
Financial Assistance Provided: . . . Yes(I)
Site Selection Assistance: . . . . .Yes
Lease Negotiation Assistance: . . . . .Yes
Co-operative Advertising: . . . . .Yes
Training: . . . . 12 Wks. Site
. . . .
On-Going Support: . . . A,B,C,D,E,F,G,H
Full-Time Franchisor Support Staff: . . 30
EXPANSION PLANS:
US: . . . . No
Canada - Yes, ...Overseas - No

CHARLIE BARLIE'S DOWNHOME RESTAURANT
3214 Marion Ct.
Louisville, KY 40206
TEL: (502) 893-2158
FAX:
Mr. Charles Willis, President

A truly unique dining experience, specializing in Mom's frizzled beef, wonderful Southern fried chicken, creamed sweetbreads and many other family recipes - all served in elegant Southern style. 16 units currently operating in Kentucky and Tennessee, with 5 additional units under construction. Unparalleled support from home office before and after opening. "You can't beat Mom's cooking and hospitality."

HISTORY: . . . .
Established in 1984; . . 1st Franchised in 1986
Company-Owned Units (As of 12/1/1989): . .4
Franchised Units (12/1/1989): 12
Total Units (12/1/1989): 16
Distribution: US-16;Can-0;Overseas-0
North America: . . . . 2 States
Concentration: . . . . 10 in KY, 4 in TN
Registered: . . . .
. . . .
Average # of Employees: . . . . . .7 FT, 23 PT
Prior Industry Experience: . . . . . . Helpful

FINANCIAL:
Cash Investment: $110-240K
Total Investment: $225-425K
Fees: Franchise - $25K
　Royalty: 6%, Advert: 1%
Contract Periods (Yrs.): 10/10
Area Development Agreement: Yes/10
Sub-Franchise Contract: . . . . . .No
Expand in Territory: . . . . . . .No
Passive Ownership: . . . Not Allowed
Encourage Conversions: . . . . . Yes
Franchisee Purchase(s) Required: .No

FRANCHISOR TRAINING/SUPPORT:
Financial Assistance Provided: . . . Yes(I)
Site Selection Assistance: . . . . . . .Yes
Lease Negotiation Assistance: . . . . .Yes
Co-operative Advertising: . . . . . . .Yes
Training: . . . . 8 Wks. Headquarters,
. . . . . . 3 Wks. Pre-Opening, On-going
On-Going Support: . . A,B,C,D,E,F,G,H,I
Full-Time Franchisor Support Staff: . . 21
EXPANSION PLANS:
US: . . . . .South and Southeast
Canada - No, ...Overseas - No

CLASSIC QUICHE CAFE

330 Queen Anne Rd.
Teaneck, NJ 07666
TEL: (201) 692-0150 C
FAX: (201) 692-7968
Mr. Michael Malloy, President

European-style cafe, featuring 25 varieties of quiche, 15 types of salads, soups, specials.

HISTORY: . . . .
Established in 1980; . . 1st Franchised in 1988
Company-Owned Units (As of 12/1/1989): . .1
Franchised Units (12/1/1989): 1
Total Units (12/1/1989): 2
Distribution: US-2;Can-0;Overseas-0
North America: . . . . .1 State
Concentration: . . . . 2 in NJ
Registered: . . . .
. . . .
Average # of Employees: . . . . . . 4 FT, 3 PT
Prior Industry Experience: . . . . . . Helpful

FINANCIAL:
Cash Investment: $30-60K
Total Investment: $60K
Fees: Franchise - $10K
　Royalty: 5%, Advert: 2%
Contract Periods (Yrs.): 5
Area Development Agreement: . . .
Sub-Franchise Contract: . . . . . Yes
Expand in Territory: . . . . . . Yes
Passive Ownership: . . . Discouraged
Encourage Conversions: . . . . . Yes
Franchisee Purchase(s) Required: Yes

FRANCHISOR TRAINING/SUPPORT:
Financial Assistance Provided: . . . . .No
Site Selection Assistance: . . . . . . .Yes
Lease Negotiation Assistance: . . . .Yes
Co-operative Advertising: . . . . . . .Yes
Training: . . . . . . 1-2 Wks. Headquarters
. . . .
On-Going Support: . . . .B,C,D,E,F,G,H,I
Full-Time Franchisor Support Staff: . . .7
EXPANSION PLANS:
US: . . . . .All US
Canada - No, ...Overseas - No

CUCOS MEXICAN RESTAURANTE

3009 25th St
Metairie, LA 70002
TEL: (800) 888-CUCO (504) 835-0306
FAX:
Mr. Charley Coffey, VP Devel.

CUCOS is a full-service, specialty restaurant chain, offering moderately-priced, Sonoran-style Mexican appetizers, entrees and complementing alcoholic beverages.

HISTORY: . . . . .IFA
Established in 1981; . . 1st Franchised in 1983
Company-Owned Units (As of 12/1/1989): . 10
Franchised Units (12/1/1989): 18
Total Units (12/1/1989): 28
Distribution: US-28;Can-0;Overseas-0
North America: . . . . 9 States
Concentration: . . . .8 in LA, 6 in FL, 5 in AL
Registered: . . . .
. . . .
Average # of Employees: . . . . . 50 FT, 50 PT
Prior Industry Experience: . . . . . . Helpful

FINANCIAL: OTC-CUCO
Cash Investment: $100-200K
Total Investment: $430-750K
Fees: Franchise - $30K
　Royalty: 4%, Advert: 5%
Contract Periods (Yrs.): 20/20
Area Development Agreement: Yes/Var
Sub-Franchise Contract: . . . . . .No
Expand in Territory: . . . . . . Yes
Passive Ownership: . . . Discouraged
Encourage Conversions: . . . . . Yes
Franchisee Purchase(s) Required: Yes

FRANCHISOR TRAINING/SUPPORT:
Financial Assistance Provided: . . . . .No
Site Selection Assistance: . . . . . . .Yes
Lease Negotiation Assistance: . . . .Yes
Co-operative Advertising: . . . . . . .Yes
Training: . . . .9-11 Wks. Co-Owned Rest-
. . . . aurant
On-Going Support: . . . . .C,D,E,F,G,H,I
Full-Time Franchisor Support Staff: . . . 1
EXPANSION PLANS:
US: . . . . Southeast and Midwest
Canada - No, ...Overseas - No

DIAMOND DAVE'S TACO COMPANY

1933 Keokuk St.
Iowa City, IA 52240
TEL: (319) 337-7690
FAX: (319) 337-4707
Mr. Stanley J. White, President

DIAMOND DAVE'S TACO COMPANY is a regional restaurant chain, featuring great family-priced Mexican/American cuisine. Opportunities include full-service restaurant/bar concept and fast-food concept. Locations available in enclosed regional malls, strip centers and free-standing units.

HISTORY: . . . .
Established in 1980; . . 1st Franchised in 1982
Company-Owned Units (As of 12/1/1989): . . .0
Franchised Units (12/1/1989): 29
Total Units (12/1/1989): 29
Distribution: US-29;Can-0;Overseas-0
North America: . . . . 5 States
Concentration: . . . . .9 in WI, 9 in IL 6 in IA
Registered: . . . . IL,IN,WI
. . . .
Average # of Employees: . . . . . .5 FT, 10 PT
Prior Industry Experience: . . . . Helpful

FINANCIAL:
Cash Investment: $25-75K
Total Investment: $100-200K
Fees: Franchise - $15K
 Royalty: 4%, Advert: 1%
Contract Periods (Yrs.): 10/10
Area Development Agreement: . Yes
Sub-Franchise Contract: . . . . .No
Expand in Territory: . . . . . . Yes
Passive Ownership: . . . Discouraged
Encourage Conversions: . . . . Yes
Franchisee Purchase(s) Required: Yes

FRANCHISOR TRAINING/SUPPORT:
Financial Assistance Provided: . . . . .NA
Site Selection Assistance: . . . . .Yes
Lease Negotiation Assistance: . . . . .Yes
Co-operative Advertising: . . . . .Yes
Training: . . . . 2-4 Wks. Local Restaurant
. . . .
On-Going Support: . . . . .C,D,E,F,G,H,I
Full-Time Franchisor Support Staff: . . .2
EXPANSION PLANS:
US: . . . . Midwest Only
Canada - No, ...Overseas - No

EAST SIDE MARIO'S

3228 S. Service Rd., # 133 W
Burlington, ON L7N3H8 CAN
TEL: (416) 681-1296
FAX: (416) 333-4488
Mr. Caz Wisniewski, EVP

EAST SIDE MARIO'S is inspired by Little Italy in the East Side of New York. The concept offers a wide selection of authentic American-Italian menu items, moderate prices and a convivial family atmosphere. The parent company, Prime Restaurant Systems, expects EAST SIDE MARIO'S to be a significant expansion vehicle into the 1990's.

HISTORY: . . . . .CFA
Established in 1986; . . 1st Franchised in 1986
Company-Owned Units (As of 12/1/1989): . . .0
Franchised Units (12/1/1989): 6
Total Units (12/1/1989): 6
Distribution: US-1;Can-5;Overseas-0
North America: . . . . . . 1 State, 1 Province
Concentration: . . . . 1 in FL, 5 in ON
Registered: . . . . .FL
. . . .
Average # of Employees: . . . . . 25 FT, 50 PT
Prior Industry Experience: . . . . . . Helpful

FINANCIAL:
Cash Investment: $200-300K
Total Investment: $450-540K
Fees: Franchise - $40K
 Royalty: 5%, Advert: 2%
Contract Periods (Yrs.): . . . . Lease
Area Development Agreement: . .No
Sub-Franchise Contract: . . . . .No
Expand in Territory: . . . . . . .No
Passive Ownership: . . . Not Allowed
Encourage Conversions: . . . . . Yes
Franchisee Purchase(s) Required: .No

FRANCHISOR TRAINING/SUPPORT:
Financial Assistance Provided: . . . Yes(I)
Site Selection Assistance: . . . . .Yes
Lease Negotiation Assistance: . . . . .Yes
Co-operative Advertising: . . . . .Yes
Training: . . . . 12 Wks. On-site
. . . .
On-Going Support: . . . A,B,C,D,E,F,G,H
Full-Time Franchisor Support Staff: . . 30
EXPANSION PLANS:
US: . . . . .All US
Canada - Yes, ...Overseas - No

EDO JAPAN

602 Manitou Rd., SE
Calgary, AB T2G4C5 CAN
TEL: (403) 287-3822
FAX:
Mr. S.K. Ituka, President

Fresh!! Nutritious!! and Healthy Food!! Showmanship chefs cook before your eyes on a Teppan grill. Generous servings. Served with our secret sauce. No MSG.

HISTORY: . . . .
Established in 1978; . . 1st Franchised in 1986
Company-Owned Units (As of 12/1/1989): . . .6
Franchised Units (12/1/1989): 38
Total Units (12/1/1989): 44
Distribution: US-2;Can-42;Overseas-0
North America: . . . . . .1 State, 4 Provinces
Concentration: . . .20 in AB, 6 in ON, 4 in BC
Registered: . . . . CA,AB
. . . .
Average # of Employees: . . . . . . 3 FT, 2 PT
Prior Industry Experience: . . . . Helpful

FINANCIAL:
Cash Investment: . . . .$
Total Investment: $150K
Fees: Franchise - $20K
 Royalty: 6%, Advert: 0%
Contract Periods (Yrs.): 10/5
Area Development Agreement: Yes/10
Sub-Franchise Contract: . . . . Yes
Expand in Territory: . . . . . . Yes
Passive Ownership: . . . . . .Allowed
Encourage Conversions: . . . . .No
Franchisee Purchase(s) Required: Yes

FRANCHISOR TRAINING/SUPPORT:
Financial Assistance Provided: . . . . .No
Site Selection Assistance: . . . . . . .Yes
Lease Negotiation Assistance: . . . . .Yes
Co-operative Advertising: . . . . .No
Training: . . . . 1 Wk. Headquarters
. . . .
On-Going Support: . . . . B,C,D,E
Full-Time Franchisor Support Staff: . . 12
EXPANSION PLANS:
US: . . . . Southwest Only
Canada - Yes, ...Overseas - No

EL CHICO

12200 Stemmons Fwy., # 100
Dallas, TX 75234
TEL: (800) 877-1985 (214) 241-5500
FAX: (214) 888-8198
Mr. Wes Jablonski, Dir. Fran.

Full-service, mid-priced, Mexican food restaurant with alcoholic beverage service, featuring authentic Tex-Mex recipes prepared fresh daily. Environment is authentic Mexican, with variability to individual market needs.

HISTORY: . . . . IFA
Established in 1940; . . 1st Franchised in 1969
Company-Owned Units (As of 12/1/1989): . 57
Franchised Units (12/1/1989): 29
Total Units (12/1/1989): 86
Distribution: US-86;Can-0;Overseas-0
North America: . . . . 12 States
Concentration: . . 40 in TX, 14 in OK, 8 in LA
Registered: . . . . FL,IL
. . . .
Average # of Employees: . . . . 20 FT, 30 PT
Prior Industry Experience: . . . . . Necessary

FINANCIAL: OTC-ELC
Cash Investment: $202-300K
Total Investment: . . . $1.4-1.8MM
Fees: Franchise - $35K
Royalty: 4%, Advert: 1%
Contract Periods (Yrs.): . . . 15/10
Area Development Agreement: . .No
Sub-Franchise Contract: . . . . .No
Expand in Territory: . . . . . . .No
Passive Ownership: . . . Discouraged
Encourage Conversions: . . . . . Yes
Franchisee Purchase(s) Required: Yes

FRANCHISOR TRAINING/SUPPORT:
Financial Assistance Provided: . . . . .No
Site Selection Assistance: . . . . . . .Yes
Lease Negotiation Assistance: . . . . .No
Co-operative Advertising: . . . . .Yes
Training: . . . . 12-16 Wks. Various
. . . . .Regional Training Facilities
On-Going Support: . . . . . B,C,d,E,G,h,I
Full-Time Franchisor Support Staff: . . . 1
EXPANSION PLANS:
US: . . . . Southeast, Southwest,Midwest
Canada - No, ...Overseas - No

FAT BOY'S BARBECUE

1550 W. King St.
Cocoa, FL 32926
TEL: (407) 636-1000
FAX:
Mr. Ray Konar, VP Mktg.

FAT BOY'S BARBECUE restaurants are full-service, sit-down type restaurants. Over 30 years in business, using secret recipes for beef, ribs, pork, chicken plus many other specialty items, including world-famous barbecue beans. Open for breakfast, lunch and dinner. Building is Southwestern adobe style.

HISTORY: . . . .
Established in 1958; . . 1st Franchised in 1968
Company-Owned Units (As of 12/1/1989): . .1
Franchised Units (12/1/1989): 26
Total Units (12/1/1989): 27
Distribution: US-27;Can-0;Overseas-1
North America: . . . . .1 State
Concentration: . . . . .27 in FL
Registered: . . . FL,IL,IN,MD,MI,MN,NY,ND
. . . . VA
Average # of Employees: . . . . . 15 FT, 10 PT
Prior Industry Experience: . . . . Helpful

FINANCIAL:
Cash Investment: $75-150K
Total Investment: $250-800K
Fees: Franchise - $25K
Royalty: 3%, Advert: 1%
Contract Periods (Yrs.): . . . 20/20
Area Development Agreement: . .No
Sub-Franchise Contract: . . . . .No
Expand in Territory: . . . . . . Yes
Passive Ownership: . . . Not Allowed
Encourage Conversions: . . . . . Yes
Franchisee Purchase(s) Required: Yes

FRANCHISOR TRAINING/SUPPORT:
Financial Assistance Provided: . . . Yes(I)
Site Selection Assistance: . . . . . . .Yes
Lease Negotiation Assistance: . . . . .Yes
Co-operative Advertising: . . . . .Yes
Training: . . . . . . .400 Hrs. Headquarters
. . . .
On-Going Support: . . . . . .B,C,D,E,F,H
Full-Time Franchisor Support Staff: . . . 8
EXPANSION PLANS:
US: . . . . .All US
Canada - No, ...Overseas - No

FRED P. OTT'S BAR & GRILL

4210 Shawnee Mission Pkwy., # 300A
Shawnee Mission, KS 66205
TEL: (913) 384-4700
FAX:
Mr. Avery Murray, VP Fran.

Appropriate for business lunches or late night gatherings, FRED P. OTT'S BAR & GRILL works because of its uncomplicated, speedy menu, a whimsical decor of unusual artifacts and TVs and game area set into a high-energy atmosphere. The concept is backed by a team of nationally-recognized professionals.

HISTORY: . . . . IFA
Established in 1976; . . 1st Franchised in 1988
Company-Owned Units (As of 12/1/1989): . .3
Franchised Units (12/1/1989): 3
Total Units (12/1/1989): 6
Distribution: US-6;Can-0;Overseas-0
North America: . . . . .1 State
Concentration: . . . . .6 in MO
Registered: . . . . IL,MD,VA
. . . .
Average # of Employees: . . . . . .6 FT, 18 PT
Prior Industry Experience: . . . . Helpful

FINANCIAL:
Cash Investment: $100K
Total Investment: $300-600K
Fees: Franchise - $30K
Royalty: 5-3%, Advert: 5-2
Contract Periods (Yrs.): . . . 10/10
Area Development Agreement: . Yes
Sub-Franchise Contract: . . . . .No
Expand in Territory: . . . . . . Yes
Passive Ownership: . . . Discouraged
Encourage Conversions: . . . . . Yes
Franchisee Purchase(s) Required: .No

FRANCHISOR TRAINING/SUPPORT:
Financial Assistance Provided: . . . . .No
Site Selection Assistance: . . . . . . .Yes
Lease Negotiation Assistance: . . . . .Yes
Co-operative Advertising: . . . . .Yes
Training: . . . . . 3 Wks. Kansas City, MO,
. . . . 1 Wk. Franchisee Location
On-Going Support: . . . . .B,C,D,E,G,H,I
Full-Time Franchisor Support Staff: . . 18
EXPANSION PLANS:
US: . . . . .Midwest, East Coast
Canada - No, ... Overseas - Yes

FUDDRUCKERS

Two Lakeside Office Park
Wakefield, MA 01880
TEL: (617) 245-2233
FAX: (617) 245-3573
Mr. Leo H. Skellchock, VP Fran. Dev.

A family restaurant serving upscale 1/3 and 1/2 pound hamburgers, fish and chicken sandwiches, hot dogs, salads and fun foods, on-premise butcher shop and bakery to insure freshness. Full produce bar allows guests to fix entrees as they like it.

HISTORY: . . . .
Established in 1980; . . 1st Franchised in 1983
Company-Owned Units (As of 12/1/1989): . 46
Franchised Units (12/1/1989): 67
Total Units (12/1/1989): 113
Distribution: US-101;Can-7;Overseas-5
North America: . . . . 26 States, 4 Provinces
Concentration: . . 23 in TX, 11 in CA, 8 in FL
Registered: . . . .
. . . .
Average # of Employees: . . . . Total About 50
Prior Industry Experience: . . . . Helpful

FINANCIAL: NASD-DKAI
Cash Investment: $450-750K
Total Investment: $1-2MM
Fees: Franchise - $50K
Royalty: 5%, Advert: . . . . Varies
Contract Periods (Yrs.): . . . 10/10
Area Development Agreement: . .No
Sub-Franchise Contract: . . . . .No
Expand in Territory: . . . . Yes
Passive Ownership: . . . Discouraged
Encourage Conversions: . . . . Yes
Franchisee Purchase(s) Required: .No

FRANCHISOR TRAINING/SUPPORT:
Financial Assistance Provided: . . . . . No
Site Selection Assistance: . . . . No
Lease Negotiation Assistance: . . . . . No
Co-operative Advertising: . . . . .Yes
Training: . . . . .6 Wks. Houston, TX
. . . .
On-Going Support: . . . . B,C,d,E,F,G,h,i
Full-Time Franchisor Support Staff: . . . .
EXPANSION PLANS:
US: . . . . .All US
Canada - Yes, . . . Overseas - Yes

GIORGIO RESTAURANTS

222 St. Lawrence Blvd.
Montreal, PQ H2Y2Y3 CAN
TEL: (514) 845-4221
FAX:
Ms. Sylvie Paradis, Fran. Dir.

GIORGIO is a chain of Italian restaurants. The concept was developed towards the end of the 1970's in the specialty restaurant field. It positions itself as a responsive and innovative approach to new-style dining in a relaxing and comfortable environment. GIORGIO means quality, low price, quantity, ambiance and speedy service.

HISTORY: . . . .
Established in 1977; . . 1st Franchised in 1985
Company-Owned Units (As of 12/1/1989): . .9
Franchised Units (12/1/1989): 21
Total Units (12/1/1989): 30
Distribution: US-0;Can-30;Overseas-0
North America: . . . . .1 Province
Concentration: . . . . 30 on PQ
Registered: . . . .
. . . .
Average # of Employees: . . . . . 25 FT,25 PT
Prior Industry Experience: . . . . Helpful

FINANCIAL:
Cash Investment: $200-300K
Total Investment: . . . . . . $1.2 MM
Fees: Franchise - $30K
Royalty: 5%, Advert: 4%
Contract Periods (Yrs.): . . . 10/10
Area Development Agreement: . .No
Sub-Franchise Contract: . . . . .No
Expand in Territory: . . . . Yes
Passive Ownership: . . . Discouraged
Encourage Conversions: . . . . Yes
Franchisee Purchase(s) Required: Yes

FRANCHISOR TRAINING/SUPPORT:
Financial Assistance Provided: . . . . . No
Site Selection Assistance: . . . . .Yes
Lease Negotiation Assistance: . . . . .Yes
Co-operative Advertising: . . . . .Yes
Training: . . . .
. . . .
On-Going Support: . . . . C,d,e,G,h
Full-Time Franchisor Support Staff: . . 30
EXPANSION PLANS:
US: . . . . .All US
Canada - Yes, ...Overseas - No

GOOD EARTH RESTAURANT & BAKERY

23133 Hawthorne Blvd., # 301
Torrance, CA 90505
TEL: (213) 373-1326
FAX:
Mr. John F. Ranhofer, Broker

THE GOOD EARTH has a unique and presently unchallenged market niche. It offers food and baked goods for an economical price, with large portions, so no one ever leaves hungry. The company is on the cutting edge of consumers' demand for better/more nutritious foods.

HISTORY: . . . .
Established in 1976; . . 1st Franchised in 1976
Company-Owned Units (As of 12/1/1989): . .8
Franchised Units (12/1/1989): 29
Total Units (12/1/1989): 37
Distribution: US-37;Can-0;Overseas-0
North America: . . . . 6 States
Concentration: . . 28 in CA, 3 in MN, 1 in AZ
Registered: . . . . CA,FL,MD,OR,WA
. . . .
Average # of Employees: . . . . . . 4 FT, 70 PT
Prior Industry Experience: . . . . Helpful

FINANCIAL:
Cash Investment: $150K
Total Investment: $600K
Fees: Franchise - $40K
Royalty: 4%, Advert: 4%
Contract Periods (Yrs.): . . . 20/20
Area Development Agreement: Yes/20
Sub-Franchise Contract: . . . . . .No
Expand in Territory: . . . . Yes
Passive Ownership: . . . Discouraged
Encourage Conversions: . . . . Yes
Franchisee Purchase(s) Required: Yes

FRANCHISOR TRAINING/SUPPORT:
Financial Assistance Provided: . . . Yes(I)
Site Selection Assistance: . . . . .Yes
Lease Negotiation Assistance: . . . . .Yes
Co-operative Advertising: . . . . .Yes
Training: . . . .5 Wks. Headquarters,2 Wks
. . Pre-Opening, 1 Month+ Post-Opening
On-Going Support: . . . . . B,C,D,E,F,H,I
Full-Time Franchisor Support Staff: . . 65
EXPANSION PLANS:
US: . . . . .South and East
Canada - No, ...Overseas - No

GROUND ROUND, THE

10 Woodbridge Center Dr.
Woodbridge, NJ 07097
TEL: (617) 331-7005
FAX:
Mr. Jack Crawford, Dir. Franchising

THE GROUND ROUND offers a full-service family restaurant franchise opportunity with over 20 years of established experience, operational support, proven products, unrivaled training programs and computerized financial control systems.

HISTORY: . . . .
Established in 1969; . . 1st Franchised in 1970
Company-Owned Units (As of 12/1/1989): 176
Franchised Units (12/1/1989): 40
Total Units (12/1/1989): 216
Distribution: . . . US-216;Can-0;Overseas-0
North America: . . . . 22 States
Concentration: . 48 in NY, 23 in OH, 19 in MA
Registered: . . . . .MI,MN,NY,ND,RI,VA,WI
. . . .
Average # of Employees: . . . . . 70 FT, 50 PT
Prior Industry Experience: . . . . . .Necessary

FINANCIAL: AMER-PRO
Cash Investment: . . . . : $400-700K
Total Investment: $1.3-2.0MM
Fees: Franchise - $30K
Royalty: 3%, Advert: 2%
Contract Periods (Yrs.): 20/10
Area Development Agreement: Yes/Var
Sub-Franchise Contract: . . . . .No
Expand in Territory: . . . . . . Yes
Passive Ownership: . . . Not Allowed
Encourage Conversions: . . . . . Yes
Franchisee Purchase(s) Required: .No

FRANCHISOR TRAINING/SUPPORT:
Financial Assistance Provided: . . . Yes(I)
Site Selection Assistance: . . . . . . .Yes
Lease Negotiation Assistance: . . . . .Yes
Co-operative Advertising: . . . . . . .Yes
Training: . . . . . 6-8 Wks. Regional Unit,
. .11 Member Training Team 3 Wks. Site
On-Going Support: . . . . . B,C,D,E,G,H
Full-Time Franchisor Support Staff: . . . 4
EXPANSION PLANS:
US: . . . . All US
Canada - Yes, ...Overseas - No

HACIENDA MEXICAN RESTAURANT

3302 Mishawaka Ave.
South Bend, IN 46615
TEL: (800) 541-3227 (219) 234-3700
FAX:
Mr. Gary White, Dir. Fran. Dev.

HACIENDA is a full-service, Mexican dinnerhouse chain, with the benefit of relatively low entry costs. A quality menu, moderate prices and a fun and festive atmosphere attract HACIENDA customers and keep them coming back for more. Specialties include our famous frozen margarita and our incomparable Wet Burrito and Nachos Fiesta.

HISTORY: . . . . IFA
Established in 1978; . . 1st Franchised in 1988
Company-Owned Units (As of 12/1/1989): . .8
Franchised Units (12/1/1989): 2
Total Units (12/1/1989): 10
Distribution: US-10;Can-0;Overseas-0
North America: . . . . 2 States
Concentration: . . . . 8 in IN, 2 in MI
Registered: . . . . FL, IL,IN,MI,OR
. . . .
Average # of Employees: . . . . . 30 FT, 45 PT
Prior Industry Experience: . . . . Helpful

FINANCIAL:
Cash Investment: $50-200K
Total Investment: $233-559K
Fees: Franchise - $20K
Royalty: 5-2%, Advert: . . . .
Contract Periods (Yrs.): 15/5/5
Area Development Agreement: . .No
Sub-Franchise Contract: . . . . .No
Expand in Territory: . . . . . . Yes
Passive Ownership: . . . . . .Allowed
Encourage Conversions: . . . . . Yes
Franchisee Purchase(s) Required: .No

FRANCHISOR TRAINING/SUPPORT:
Financial Assistance Provided: . . . . .No
Site Selection Assistance: . . . . . . .Yes
Lease Negotiation Assistance: . . . . .Yes
Co-operative Advertising: . . . . . . .Yes
Training: . . . . . . .30 Days Headquarters
. . . .
On-Going Support: . . . . . . C,D,E,G,H,I
Full-Time Franchisor Support Staff: . . . 8
EXPANSION PLANS:
US: . . . . Midwest Only
Canada - No, ...Overseas - No

HUDDLE HOUSE

2969 E. Ponce De Leon Ave.
Decatur, GA 30030
TEL: (800) 476-4833 (404) 377-5700
FAX: (404) 377-0497
Ms. Sandra Law, Fran. Sales Dept.

A system of 24-hour family restaurants, specializing in the sale of breakfast items, but offering a full range of lunch and dinner entrees, such as steaks, seafoods and sandwiches. Franchises are offered for individual units in locations throughout the Southeastern US.

HISTORY: . . . . IFA
Established in 1964; . . 1st Franchised in 1966
Company-Owned Units (As of 12/1/1989): . .8
Franchised Units (12/1/1989): 162
Total Units (12/1/1989): 170
Distribution: . . . US-170;Can-0;Overseas-0
North America: . . . . 10 States
Concentration: . 89 in GA, 43 in SC, 15 in AL
Registered: . . . . .FL
. . . .
Average # of Employees: . . . . . .14 FT, 6 PT
Prior Industry Experience: . . . . Helpful

FINANCIAL:
Cash Investment: $47.7-53.4K
Total Investment: $47.7-470K
Fees: Franchise - $15-25K
Royalty: 4%, Advert: 0%
Contract Periods (Yrs.): 15/5/5
Area Development Agreement: . .No
Sub-Franchise Contract: . . . . .No
Expand in Territory: . . . . . . .No
Passive Ownership: . . . Discouraged
Encourage Conversions: . . . . . .No
Franchisee Purchase(s) Required: Yes

FRANCHISOR TRAINING/SUPPORT:
Financial Assistance Provided: . . . . .No
Site Selection Assistance: . . . . . . .Yes
Lease Negotiation Assistance: . . . . .Yes
Co-operative Advertising: . . . . . . .No
Training: . . . . 4 Days Headquarters,
. . . . 10 Days Training Ctr., 7 Days Site
On-Going Support: . . . . B,C,D,E,F,G,H
Full-Time Franchisor Support Staff: . .100
EXPANSION PLANS:
US: . . . . Southeast
Canada - No, ...Overseas - No

HUMPTY'S EGG PLACE

Box 364, Station T
Calgary, AB T2H2G9 CAN
TEL: (403) 269-4675 C
FAX:
Mr. Don Koenig, Fran. Co-ord.

Family restaurant, open 24 hours, specializing in breakfast, but also offering dinner entrees, gourmet burgers and deli sandwiches.

HISTORY: . . . .
Established in 1978; . . 1st Franchised in 1982
Company-Owned Units (As of 12/1/1989): . . 3
Franchised Units (12/1/1989): 21
Total Units (12/1/1989): 24
Distribution: US-0;Can-24;Overseas-0
North America: . . . . 4 Provinces
Concentration: . . . 18 in AB, 2 in BC, 3 in SK
Registered: . . . . AB
. . . .
Average # of Employees: . . . . . 15 FT, 17 PT
Prior Industry Experience: . . . . Helpful

FINANCIAL:
Cash Investment: $60-100K
Total Investment: $175-250K
Fees: Franchise - $25K
Royalty: 5%, Advert: 2%
Contract Periods (Yrs.): 10/5
Area Development Agreement: Yes/20
Sub-Franchise Contract: . . . . . .No
Expand in Territory: . . . .
Passive Ownership: . . . Not Allowed
Encourage Conversions: . . . . Yes
Franchisee Purchase(s) Required: Yes

FRANCHISOR TRAINING/SUPPORT:
Financial Assistance Provided: . . . Yes(I)
Site Selection Assistance: . . . . .Yes
Lease Negotiation Assistance: . . . . .Yes
Co-operative Advertising: . . . . .Yes
Training: . . . . 3 Wks. Headquarters
. . . .
On-Going Support: . . A,B,C,D,E,F,G,H,i
Full-Time Franchisor Support Staff: . . 10
EXPANSION PLANS:
US: . . . . .All US
Canada - Yes, ...Overseas - No

J. T. CROC 'N BERRYS BAR & GRILL

3333 S. Pasadena Ave.
S. Pasadena, FL 33707
TEL: (813) 360-6931
FAX:
Mr. Jud Scott

It's fun! It's beautiful! Great service! Fantastic food and super beverages! Catch your favorite sport on 4 TVs or relax to terrific live music. We stand alone when it comes to quality and service and good times!

HISTORY: . . . .
Established in 1975; . . 1st Franchised in 1981
Company-Owned Units (As of 12/1/1989): . . 1
Franchised Units (12/1/1989): 8
Total Units (12/1/1989): 9
Distribution: US-9;Can-0;Overseas-0
North America: . . . . 3 States
Concentration: . . . 7 in FL, 1 in PA, 1 in WA
Registered: . . . . FL,WA
. . . .
Average # of Employees: . . . . . 25 FT, 25 PT
Prior Industry Experience: . . . . Helpful

FINANCIAL:
Cash Investment: $250-500K
Total Investment: . . . $400-1,000K
Fees: Franchise - $35K
Royalty: 3%, Advert: 0%
Contract Periods (Yrs.): 30
Area Development Agreement: Yes/10
Sub-Franchise Contract: . . . . . .No
Expand in Territory: . . . . Yes
Passive Ownership: . . . Discouraged
Encourage Conversions: . . . . . Yes
Franchisee Purchase(s) Required: .No

FRANCHISOR TRAINING/SUPPORT:
Financial Assistance Provided: . . . . .No
Site Selection Assistance: . . . . .Yes
Lease Negotiation Assistance: . . . . .Yes
Co-operative Advertising: . . . . .Yes
Training: . . . . 8 Wks. Headquarters
. . . .
On-Going Support: . . . . .B,C,D,E,F,G,H,I
Full-Time Franchisor Support Staff: . . 50
EXPANSION PLANS:
US: . . . . . . FL,PA,WA,GA,NC,SC,AL
Canada - Yes, . . . Overseas - Yes

MACAYO MEXICAN RESTAURANT

4001 N. Central
Phoenix, AZ 85012
TEL: (800) 622-4797 (602) 264-1831
FAX: (602) 277-1795
Mr. Stephen Johnson, President

Full-service Mexican food restaurant, established 45 years ago. Products made fresh daily. Unique menu items and very vibrant decor and building characteristics.

HISTORY: . . . .
Established in 1946; . . 1st Franchised in 1986
Company-Owned Units (As of 12/1/1989): . 14
Franchised Units (12/1/1989): 0
Total Units (12/1/1989): 14
Distribution: US-14;Can-0;Overseas-0
North America: . . . . 2 States
Concentration: . . . . 7 in AZ, 7 in NV
Registered: . . . . . CA,MI,MN,OR,SD,VA
. . . .
Average # of Employees: . . . . . 80 FT, 20 PT
Prior Industry Experience: . . . . . .Necessary

FINANCIAL:
Cash Investment: $200-500K
Total Investment: $1.1-1.5MM
Fees: Franchise - $45K
Royalty: 4%, Advert: 5%
Contract Periods (Yrs.): 20/20
Area Development Agreement: Yes/20
Sub-Franchise Contract: . . . . . .No
Expand in Territory: . . . . Yes
Passive Ownership: . . . Not Allowed
Encourage Conversions: . . . . . Yes
Franchisee Purchase(s) Required: Yes

FRANCHISOR TRAINING/SUPPORT:
Financial Assistance Provided: . . . Yes(I)
Site Selection Assistance: . . . . .Yes
Lease Negotiation Assistance: . . . . .Yes
Co-operative Advertising: . . . . .NA
Training: . . . . 4 Wks. Headquarters
. . . .
On-Going Support: . . . . . . b,C,d,E,F,g
Full-Time Franchisor Support Staff: . . 10
EXPANSION PLANS:
US: . . . . .Southwest, Northwest,Central
Canada - No, ...Overseas - No

MARITA'S CANTINA

210 Carnegie Center, # 103
Princeton, NJ 08540
TEL: (609) 452-2838
FAX:
Mr. Kevin C. Kruse, Dir. of Ops.

A MARITA'S CANTINA franchise caters to the growing Mexican dinnerhouse market. In addition, the lower costs attainable with the proper production of Mexican food, and sales of the increasingly popular and profitable Margaritas and Mexican beers, all combine to produce an interesting, fun and profitable business.

HISTORY: . . . .
Established in 1977; . . 1st Franchised in 1980
Company-Owned Units (As of 12/1/1989): . . 1
Franchised Units (12/1/1989): 12
Total Units (12/1/1989): 13
Distribution: US-13;Can-0;Overseas-0
North America: . . . . 2 States
Concentration: . . . . 8 in NJ, 5 in PA
Registered: . . . .
. . . .
Average # of Employees: . . . . . 12 FT, 23 PT
Prior Industry Experience: . . . . Helpful

FINANCIAL:
Cash Investment: $150-250K
Total Investment: $250-775K
Fees: Franchise - $17.5K
Royalty: 4%, Advert: 2%
Contract Periods (Yrs.): 15/15
Area Development Agreement: . .No
Sub-Franchise Contract: . . . . .No
Expand in Territory: . . . . . . .No
Passive Ownership: . . . . .Allowed
Encourage Conversions: . . . . Yes
Franchisee Purchase(s) Required: Yes

FRANCHISOR TRAINING/SUPPORT:
Financial Assistance Provided: . . . . .No
Site Selection Assistance: . . . . . . .Yes
Lease Negotiation Assistance: . . . . .Yes
Co-operative Advertising: . . . . . . .Yes
Training: . . . . 4 Wks. Site
. . . .
On-Going Support: . . . . B,C,D,E,F,G,H
Full-Time Franchisor Support Staff: . . . 3
EXPANSION PLANS:
US: . . . . . . Mid-Atl., MD, Northeast
Canada - No, ...Overseas - No

MIFFY'S RESTAURANT

Box 540
Don Mills, ON M3C2T6 CAN
TEL: (416) 587-3001
FAX: (416) 431-9397
Mr. Ernest Ng, Marketing Manager

Your "atypical" oriental dining room, serving freshly-prepared oriental dishes in a casual atmosphere. Home of the MIFFIN and MIFTIZER.

HISTORY: . . . .
Established in 1988; . . 1st Franchised in 1989
Company-Owned Units (As of 12/1/1989): . . 1
Franchised Units (12/1/1989): 0
Total Units (12/1/1989): 1
Distribution: US-0;Can-1;Overseas-0
North America: . . . . .1 Province
Concentration: . . . . 1 in ON
Registered: . . . .
. . . .
Average # of Employees: . . . . . . 3 FT, 2 PT
Prior Industry Experience: . . . . Helpful

FINANCIAL:
Cash Investment: . . . . $75K+
Total Investment: . . . . $Varies
Fees: Franchise - . . . . .$Negotiable
Royalty: Negot., Advert: . . . 10%
Contract Periods (Yrs.): 5/5
Area Development Agreement: . .No
Sub-Franchise Contract: . . . . .No
Expand in Territory: . . . . . . Yes
Passive Ownership: . . . Not Allowed
Encourage Conversions: . . . . Yes
Franchisee Purchase(s) Required: Yes

FRANCHISOR TRAINING/SUPPORT:
Financial Assistance Provided: . . . Yes(I)
Site Selection Assistance: . . . . . . .Yes
Lease Negotiation Assistance: . . . . .Yes
Co-operative Advertising: . . . . . . .Yes
Training: . . . .
. . . .
On-Going Support: . . . .
Full-Time Franchisor Support Staff: . . . 2
EXPANSION PLANS:
US: . . . . Completely Negotiable
Canada - Yes, ...Overseas - No

MIKES RESTAURANTS

8250 Decarie Blvd.
Montreal, PQ H4P2P5 CAN
TEL: (514) 341-5544
FAX: (514) 341-5635
Mr. Neil Zeidel, Dir. Fran. Dev.

MIKES RESTAURANTS, a wholly-owned subsidiary of M-Corp, Inc., is a franchise management company, operating through licensees, 112 family-style Italian restaurants, featuring pizza, hot submarine sandwiches and pastas, and offering a full turn-key to new franchisees.

HISTORY: . . . . .IFA/CFA
Established in 1967; . . 1st Franchised in 1972
Company-Owned Units (As of 12/1/1989): . .0
Franchised Units (12/1/1989): 112
Total Units (12/1/1989): 112
Distribution: . . . US-0;Can-112;Overseas-0
North America: . . . . 2 Provinces
Concentration: . . . . . . 111 in PQ, 1 in ON
Registered: . . . .
. . . .
Average # of Employees: . . . . . 15 FT, 20 PT
Prior Industry Experience: . . . . Helpful

FINANCIAL: TORON-MCI
Cash Investment: $75-175K
Total Investment: $225-525K
Fees: Franchise - $40K
Royalty: 5%, Advert: 3%
Contract Periods (Yrs.): 20
Area Development Agreement: Yes/20
Sub-Franchise Contract: . . . . .No
Expand in Territory: . . . . . . Yes
Passive Ownership: . . . Not Allowed
Encourage Conversions: . . . . .No
Franchisee Purchase(s) Required: .No

FRANCHISOR TRAINING/SUPPORT:
Financial Assistance Provided: . . . Yes(I)
Site Selection Assistance: . . . . . . .Yes
Lease Negotiation Assistance: . . . . .Yes
Co-operative Advertising: . . . . . . .Yes
Training: . . . . . . .6 Wks. Training Rest.,
. . . . 2 Wks. New Restaurant
On-Going Support: . . . . . .C,D,E,F,G,H
Full-Time Franchisor Support Staff: . . 39
EXPANSION PLANS:
US: . . . . .No
Canada - Yes, ...Overseas - No

MR. MIKE'S FAMILY STEAKHOUSE

8615 Granville St.
Vancouver, BC V6P5A2 CAN
TEL: (604) 263-1404
FAX: (604) 263-8411
Mr. Jack Gordon, Dir. Operations

Medium-priced family steakhouse, featuring a 60+ item food bar, 28-day aged steaks, burgers, chicken and ice cream bar.

HISTORY: . . . .
Established in 1964; . . 1st Franchised in 1968
Company-Owned Units (As of 12/1/1989): . .0
Franchised Units (12/1/1989): 30
Total Units (12/1/1989): 30
Distribution: US-0;Can-30;Overseas-0
North America: . . . . 3 Provinces
Concentration: . 28 in BC, 1 in YK, 1 in NWT
Registered: . . . . AB
. . . .
Average # of Employees: . . . . . . 10 FT, 6 PT
Prior Industry Experience: . . . . . . Helpful

FINANCIAL:
Cash Investment: $50-75K
Total Investment: $175-200K
Fees: Franchise - $25K
 Royalty: 4%, Advert: 4%
Contract Periods (Yrs.): 10/10
Area Development Agreement: Yes/10
Sub-Franchise Contract: . . . . . Yes
Expand in Territory: . . . . Yes
Passive Ownership: . . . Not Allowed
Encourage Conversions: . . . . . Yes
Franchisee Purchase(s) Required: Yes

FRANCHISOR TRAINING/SUPPORT:
Financial Assistance Provided: . . . . .No
Site Selection Assistance: . . . . . . .Yes
Lease Negotiation Assistance: . . . . .Yes
Co-operative Advertising: . . . . . . .Yes
Training: . . . . 4 Wks. Pre-Opening,
. . . . 2-3 Wks. On-site
On-Going Support: . . A,B,C,D,E,F,G,H,I
Full-Time Franchisor Support Staff: . . 12
EXPANSION PLANS:
US: . . . . .No
Canada - Yes, ...Overseas - No

NOBLE ROMAN'S PIZZA

333 N. Pennsylvania, # 800
Indianapolis, IN
TEL: (317) 634-3377
FAX:
Mr. John West, VP

Restaurant selling pizza, pasta, sandwiches and salads for dine-in and carry-out consumption. Restaurants also serve beer and wine.

HISTORY: . . . .
Established in 1972; . . 1st Franchised in 1972
Company-Owned Units (As of 12/1/1989): . 19
Franchised Units (12/1/1989): 69
Total Units (12/1/1989): 88
Distribution: US-88;Can-0;Overseas-0
North America: . . . . 4 States
Concentration: . . 68 in IN, 16 in OH, 3 in MO
Registered: . . . . IN
. . . .
Average # of Employees: . . . . . . 6 FT, 20 PT
Prior Industry Experience: . . . . Helpful

FINANCIAL: OTC-NROM
Cash Investment: $75-100K
Total Investment: $250-450K
Fees: Franchise - $12.5K
 Royalty: 4%, Advert: 0%
Contract Periods (Yrs.): 20/20
Area Development Agreement: Yes/Var
Sub-Franchise Contract: . . . . . .No
Expand in Territory: . . . . Yes
Passive Ownership: . . . Discouraged
Encourage Conversions: . . . . . Yes
Franchisee Purchase(s) Required: .No

FRANCHISOR TRAINING/SUPPORT:
Financial Assistance Provided: . . . . .No
Site Selection Assistance: . . . . . . .Yes
Lease Negotiation Assistance: . . . . .Yes
Co-operative Advertising: . . . . . . .Yes
Training: . . . . . . 3-5 Wks. Headquarters
. . . .
On-Going Support: . . . . C,D,E,h
Full-Time Franchisor Support Staff: . . . .
EXPANSION PLANS:
US: . . . . Midwest
Canada - No, ...Overseas - No

NOODLE DELIGHT

85 W. Wilmot St., # 6
Richmond Hill, ON L4B1K7 CAN
TEL: (416) 886-9700/(416) 886-9701
FAX: (416) 886-9702
Mr. Alfred P. Lam, VP/Exec. Dir.

We offer authentic Chinese noodle and rice dishes in a Western convenience setting (all our restaurants seat over 90). Special feature is our Open Kitchen, where patrons can watch their food being cooked in front of them in giant woks and served piping hot.

HISTORY: . . . . .CFA
Established in 1983; . . . 1st Franchised in 1986
Company-Owned Units (As of 12/1/1989): . .2
Franchised Units (12/1/1989): 3
Total Units (12/1/1989): 5
Distribution: US-0;Can-5;Overseas-0
North America: . . . . .1 Province
Concentration: . . . . 5 in ON
Registered: . . . .
. . . .
Average # of Employees: . . . . . 7-8 FT, 6 PT
Prior Industry Experience: . . . . Helpful

FINANCIAL:
Cash Investment: $200K
Total Investment: $350K
Fees: Franchise - $25K
 Royalty: 5%, Advert: 3%
Contract Periods (Yrs.): 10/10
Area Development Agreement: Yes/Var
Sub-Franchise Contract: . . . . . Yes
Expand in Territory: . . . . Yes
Passive Ownership: . . . Discouraged
Encourage Conversions: . . . . . .No
Franchisee Purchase(s) Required: Yes

FRANCHISOR TRAINING/SUPPORT:
Financial Assistance Provided: . . . Yes(I)
Site Selection Assistance: . . . . . . .Yes
Lease Negotiation Assistance: . . . . .Yes
Co-operative Advertising: . . . . . . .Yes
Training: . . . . . .Minimum 4 Wks. Head-
. . . . quarters
On-Going Support: . . . . a,b,C,D,E,F,G,h
Full-Time Franchisor Support Staff: . . . .
EXPANSION PLANS:
US: . . . . .All US
Canada - Yes, ... Overseas - No

NUMERO UNO PIZZA & ITALIAN RESTAURANTS
8214 Van Nuys Blvd.
Panorama City, CA 91402
TEL: (818) 781-4448
FAX:
Mr. Rod Read, Dir. Mktg.

NUMERO UNO PASTA & PIZZA is a casual Italian restaurant, featuring a unique, award-winning deep-dish pizza and a full line of pastas. The concept offers table service with beer and wine in an eclectic, casual atmosphere. It has been rated the top pizza chain in Southern California each of the past 5 years.

HISTORY: . . . . IFA	FINANCIAL:	FRANCHISOR TRAINING/SUPPORT:
Established in 1974; . . 1st Franchised in 1975	Cash Investment: $50-100K	Financial Assistance Provided: . . . Yes(D)
Company-Owned Units (As of 12/1/1989): . .3	Total Investment: $200-400K	Site Selection Assistance: . . . . Yes
Franchised Units (12/1/1989): 57	Fees: Franchise - $10-25K	Lease Negotiation Assistance: . . . . . Yes
Total Units (12/1/1989): 60	Royalty: 5.5%, Advert: 4.5%	Co-operative Advertising: . . . . Yes
Distribution: US-57;Can-0;Overseas-3	Contract Periods (Yrs.): 10/10	Training: . . . . . 4-6 Wks. Training Center
North America: . . . . .1 State	Area Development Agreement: Yes/20	. . . .
Concentration: . . . . 57 in CA	Sub-Franchise Contract: . . . . . Yes	On-Going Support: . . . a,B,C,D,E,F,G,H
Registered: . . . . CA	Expand in Territory: . . . . Yes	Full-Time Franchisor Support Staff: . . 12
. . . .	Passive Ownership: . . . Discouraged	EXPANSION PLANS:
Average # of Employees: . . . . 2 FT, 12-15 PT	Encourage Conversions: . . . . . Yes	US: . . . . .CA Only
Prior Industry Experience: . . . . . .Necessary	Franchisee Purchase(s) Required: .No	Canada - Yes, . . . Overseas - Yes

O'TOOLE'S ROADHOUSE RESTAURANT
585 Aero Dr.
Buffalo, NY 14225
TEL: (716) 686-6537
FAX: (716) 685-1558
Mr. Stephen F. Leous, Dir. Fran.

O'TOOLE'S is a warm, comfortable gathering place, combining aspects of an English pub and an American neighborhood restaurant/bar. Its low-to-moderately priced menu offers a variety of American fare. Seating approximately 200, the restaurant is outfitted with brick, wood and various memorabilia. At night, the casual dining atmosphere is transformed into an active nightspot, complete with dancing and a disc jockey.

HISTORY:	FINANCIAL: TORONTO-OT	FRANCHISOR TRAINING/SUPPORT:
Established in 1983; . . 1st Franchised in 1983	Cash Investment: $150-250K	Financial Assistance Provided: . . . Yes(I)
Company-Owned Units (As of 12/1/1989): . .5	Total Investment: $600-750K	Site Selection Assistance: . . . . Yes
Franchised Units (12/1/1989): 83	Fees: Franchise - $35K	Lease Negotiation Assistance: . . . . . Yes
Total Units (12/1/1989): 88	Royalty: 6%, Advert: 1.5%	Co-operative Advertising: . . . . NA
Distribution: US-15;Can-73;Overseas-0	Contract Periods (Yrs.): 10/10	Training: . . . . 2 Wks. HQ, 2 Wks. On-site
North America: . . . . . 8 States, 4 Provinces	Area Development Agreement: Yes/10	. . . .Pre-Opening, 2 Wks. Post-Opening
Concentration: . . 64 in ON, 5 in NY, 4 in VA	Sub-Franchise Contract: . . . . . NA	On-Going Support: . . . . . .C,D,E,F,G,H
Registered: . . . . . . .CA,FL,MD,MI,NY,VA	Expand in Territory:	Full-Time Franchisor Support Staff: . . 18
. . . .	Passive Ownership: . . . Not Allowed	EXPANSION PLANS:
Average # of Employees: . . . . 60-70 FT	Encourage Conversions: . . . . . Yes	US: . . . . NE, South, Midwest, Mid-Atl.
Prior Industry Experience: . . . . Helpful	Franchisee Purchase(s) Required: .No	Canada - Yes, . . . Overseas - UK

PACINI
910 Belanger Est
Montreal, PQ H2S3P4 CAN
TEL: (514) 276-5818
FAX:
Mr. Alain Villeneuve, VP Development

Italian-style, full-service family restaurant. Attractive atmosphere. Very popular concept in province of Quebec. Expanding in Ontario.

HISTORY: . . . . IFA	FINANCIAL:	FRANCHISOR TRAINING/SUPPORT:
Established in 1980; . . 1st Franchised in 1986	Cash Investment: $250K	Financial Assistance Provided: . . . Yes(I)
Company-Owned Units (As of 12/1/1989): . 21	Total Investment: $650K	Site Selection Assistance: . . . . Yes
Franchised Units (12/1/1989): 7	Fees: Franchise - $35K	Lease Negotiation Assistance: . . . . . Yes
Total Units (12/1/1989): 28	Royalty: 5%, Advert: 4%	Co-operative Advertising: . . . . Yes
Distribution: US-0;Can-28;Overseas-0	Contract Periods (Yrs.): 10/10	Training: . . . . 7 Wks. Montreal Location,
North America: . . . . .1 Province	Area Development Agreement: . Yes	. . . . .3 Wks. Franchisee Location
Concentration: . . . . .28 in PQ	Sub-Franchise Contract: . . . . .No	On-Going Support: . . . . a,B,C,D,E,F,H,I
Registered:	Expand in Territory: . . . . . . .No	Full-Time Franchisor Support Staff: . . . .
. . . .	Passive Ownership: . . . Not Allowed	EXPANSION PLANS:
Average # of Employees: . . . . . 20 FT, 15 PT	Encourage Conversions: . . . . . Yes	US: . . . . .No
Prior Industry Experience: . . . . Helpful	Franchisee Purchase(s) Required: .No	Canada - Yes, ...Overseas - No

PANCAKE COTTAGE FAMILY RESTAURANTS
P.O. Box 1909
N. Massapequa, NY 11758
TEL: (516) 795-0978
FAX: (516) 795-8732
Mr. Chris Levano, Fran. Devel.

PANCAKE COTTAGE is a full-service family restaurant, specializing in pancakes and waffles. Famous for our breakfast, we also offer a wide variety for lunch and dinner. Established in 1964, and a franchise system since 1971. COTTAGE is currently seeking franchisees in the New England area.

HISTORY: . . . . IFA
Established in 1964; . . 1st Franchised in 1971
Company-Owned Units (As of 12/1/1989): . .0
Franchised Units (12/1/1989): 20
Total Units (12/1/1989): 20
Distribution: US-20;Can-0;Overseas-0
North America: . . . . .1 State
Concentration: . . . . 20 in NY
Registered: . . . . NY
. . . .
Average # of Employees: . . . . . 25 FT, 10 PT
Prior Industry Experience: . . . . Helpful

FINANCIAL:
Cash Investment: . . . .$~175K
Total Investment: $450-550K
Fees: Franchise - $25K
Royalty: 5%, Advert: 3%
Contract Periods (Yrs.): 10/10
Area Development Agreement: . .No
Sub-Franchise Contract: . . . . .No
Expand in Territory: . . . . Yes
Passive Ownership: . . . . . .Allowed
Encourage Conversions: . . . . Yes
Franchisee Purchase(s) Required: .No

FRANCHISOR TRAINING/SUPPORT:
Financial Assistance Provided: . . . Yes(I)
Site Selection Assistance: . . . . .Yes
Lease Negotiation Assistance: . . . . .Yes
Co-operative Advertising: . . . . No
Training: . . . . . .~ 3 Months at Company
. . . . Store or Franchised Unit
On-Going Support: . . . . . B,C,D,E,G,H
Full-Time Franchisor Support Staff: . . .9
EXPANSION PLANS:
US: . . . . New England Area
Canada - No, ...Overseas - No

PANTRY FAMILY RESTAURANTS

202 - 15463 104th Ave.
Surrey, BC V3R1N9 CAN
TEL: (604) 584-4115
FAX:
Mr. M. Hoffmann, President

A full-service family restaurant franchise. A turn-key operation - franchisor responsible for site selection, restaurant layout, construction, equipment selection, training - including initial hiring and training of staff, bookkeeping procedures and negotiations with food suppliers to get best prices and maintain quality control on food.

HISTORY: . . . . IFA
Established in 1975; . . 1st Franchised in 1977
Company-Owned Units (As of 12/1/1989): . .3
Franchised Units (12/1/1989): 15
Total Units (12/1/1989): 18
Distribution: US-0;Can-18;Overseas-0
North America: . . . . .1 Province
Concentration: . . . . 18 in BC
Registered: . . . .
. . . .
Average # of Employees: . . . . . .35 FT or PT
Prior Industry Experience: . . . . Helpful

FINANCIAL:
Cash Investment: $300-350K
Total Investment: . . . .$
Fees: Franchise - $40K
Royalty: 4.5%, Advert: 2.5%
Contract Periods (Yrs.): . . . .Varies
Area Development Agreement: Yes/5+
Sub-Franchise Contract: . . . . . .No
Expand in Territory: . . . . .No
Passive Ownership: . . . Not Allowed
Encourage Conversions: . . . . .No
Franchisee Purchase(s) Required: .No

FRANCHISOR TRAINING/SUPPORT:
Financial Assistance Provided: . . . . . No
Site Selection Assistance: . . . . .Yes
Lease Negotiation Assistance: . . . . .Yes
Co-operative Advertising: . . . . .Yes
Training: . . . . 3 Wks. Minimum
. . . .
On-Going Support: . . . .
Full-Time Franchisor Support Staff: . . . 6
EXPANSION PLANS:
US: . . . . .No
Canada - Yes, ...Overseas - No

PAT AND MARIO'S

3228 S. Service Rd., # 133 W
Burlington, ON L7N3H8 CAN
TEL: (416) 681-1296
FAX: (416) 333-4488
Mr. Caz Wisniewski, EVP

PAT AND MARIO'S combines the Irish Pub and the Italian eatery, with specialty wood oven pizza, fresh pasta and great finger foods dominating the menu. This concept has a more urban, up-scale image and was designed to appeal to a more affluent up-town patron.

HISTORY: . . . . .CFA
Established in 1979; . . 1st Franchised in 1981
Company-Owned Units (As of 12/1/1989): . .0
Franchised Units (12/1/1989): 14
Total Units (12/1/1989): 14
Distribution: US-0;Can-14;Overseas-0
North America: . . . . .1 Province
Concentration: . . . . 14 in ON
Registered: . . . .
. . . .
Average # of Employees: . . . . . 25 FT, 50 PT
Prior Industry Experience: . . . . Helpful

FINANCIAL:
Cash Investment: $250-300
Total Investment: $690-790K
Fees: Franchise - $40K
Royalty: 5%, Advert: 2%
Contract Periods (Yrs.): . . . . Lease
Area Development Agreement: . .No
Sub-Franchise Contract: . . . . . .No
Expand in Territory: . . . . .No
Passive Ownership: . . . Not Allowed
Encourage Conversions: . . . . . Yes
Franchisee Purchase(s) Required: Yes

FRANCHISOR TRAINING/SUPPORT:
Financial Assistance Provided: . . . Yes(I)
Site Selection Assistance: . . . . .Yes
Lease Negotiation Assistance: . . . . .Yes
Co-operative Advertising: . . . . .Yes
Training: . . . . 12 Wks. On-site
. . . .
On-Going Support: . . . A,B,C,D,E,F,G,H
Full-Time Franchisor Support Staff: . . 30
EXPANSION PLANS:
US: . . . . .No
Canada - Yes, ...Overseas - No

PERKINS FAMILY RESTAURANTS

6075 Poplar Ave., # 800
Memphis, TN 38119
TEL: (901) 766-6475
FAX:
Mr. Phil Joseph, Sr. Director

PERKINS FAMILY RESTAURANTS is a full-service, family-style restaurant, offering a broad menu of breakfast, lunch and dinner entrees. The stores are open 24 hours a day, 7 days a week.

HISTORY: . . . . IFA
Established in 1958; . . 1st Franchised in 1958
Company-Owned Units (As of 12/1/1989): 114
Franchised Units (12/1/1989): 227
Total Units (12/1/1989): 341
Distribution: US-340;Can-1;Overseas-0
North America: . . . . . 26 States, 1 Province
Concentration: . 59 in MN, 49 in OH, 33 in PA
Registered: . . . FL,IL,IN,MD,MI,MN,NY,ND
. . . . SD,VA,WA,WI
Average # of Employees: . . . . . 5 FT, 40+ PT
Prior Industry Experience: . . . . Helpful

FINANCIAL: NYSE-PERKF
Cash Investment: $150K
Total Investment: . . . . . $.9-1.4MM
Fees: Franchise - $30K
Royalty: 4%, Advert: 4%
Contract Periods (Yrs.): 20/10
Area Development Agreement: Yes/Var
Sub-Franchise Contract: . . . . . .No
Expand in Territory: . . . . Yes
Passive Ownership: . . . Discouraged
Encourage Conversions: . . . . . Yes
Franchisee Purchase(s) Required: Yes

FRANCHISOR TRAINING/SUPPORT:
Financial Assistance Provided: . . . Yes(I)
Site Selection Assistance: . . . . . . .Yes
Lease Negotiation Assistance: . . . . . .Yes
Co-operative Advertising: . . . . . . .Yes
Training: . . . . Varies
. . . .
On-Going Support: . . . . b,C,D,e,F,G,H,I
Full-Time Franchisor Support Staff: . . . 4
EXPANSION PLANS:
US: . . . . SE, SW and Midwest
Canada - Yes, ...Overseas - No

PETER PIPER PIZZA

2321 W. Royal Palm Rd.
Phoenix, AZ 85021
TEL: (602) 995-1975
FAX: (602) 995-8857
Mr. John Baillon, Dir. Fran. Sales

PETER PIPER PIZZA fills a unique niche in the fast-food industry pizza segment. PETER PIPER PIZZA offers take-out or casual dine-in, with a variety of games and fun for the family. Quality pizza, at a great value. Menu includes regular, pan and express lunch pizza, salad, beer and soft drinks.

HISTORY: . . . .
Established in 1973; . . 1st Franchised in 1977
Company-Owned Units (As of 12/1/1989): . 40
Franchised Units (12/1/1989): 72
Total Units (12/1/1989): 112
Distribution: US-112;Can-0;Overseas-0
North America: . . . . 8 States
Concentration: . 46 in AZ, 32 in TX, 10 in UT
Registered: . . . . CA,VA
. . . .
Average # of Employees: . . . . . .5 FT, 25 PT
Prior Industry Experience: . . . . . . Helpful

FINANCIAL:
Cash Investment: $110-180K
Total Investment: $325-510K
Fees: Franchise - $25K
Royalty: 5%, Advert: 5%
Contract Periods (Yrs.): 10/10
Area Development Agreement: Yes/Var
Sub-Franchise Contract: . . . . . .No
Expand in Territory: . . . .
Passive Ownership: . . . Discouraged
Encourage Conversions: . . . . . Yes
Franchisee Purchase(s) Required: .No

FRANCHISOR TRAINING/SUPPORT:
Financial Assistance Provided: . . . . . No
Site Selection Assistance: . . . . .Yes
Lease Negotiation Assistance: . . . .Yes
Co-operative Advertising: . . . . . . .Yes
Training: . . . . 2-3 Wks. Minimum Head-
. . . . quarters
On-Going Support: . . . . . B,C,D,E,F,H,I
Full-Time Franchisor Support Staff: . . 30
EXPANSION PLANS:
US: . .Southwest-AZ,CO,NM,TX,UT,NV
Canada - No, ...Overseas - No

PIZZA INN

2930 Stemmons Fwy.
Dallas, TX 75247
TEL: (800) 677-4872 *284-2527
FAX: (214) 634-8506
Mr. Monty Whitehurst, VP Franchising

Dine-in, carry-out or delivery. 3 styles of pizza crusts - thin, pan and New York-style. Menu carries pizza, pasta, sandwiches, desserts. Lunch and dinner buffets. Marketing, advertising, site selection and training assistance/programs.

HISTORY: . . . . IFA
Established in 1960; . . 1st Franchised in 1963
Company-Owned Units (As of 12/1/1989): 150
Franchised Units (12/1/1989): 427
Total Units (12/1/1989): 577
Distribution: US-554;Can-0;Overseas-23
North America: . . . . 25 States, NC, TX, MI
Concentration: . . . . FL,VA
Registered: . . . .
. . . .
Average # of Employees: . . . . . 30 FT, 10 PT
Prior Industry Experience: . . . . . .Necessary

FINANCIAL:
Cash Investment: $75-150K
Total Investment: $150-300K
Fees: Franchise - $17.5K
Royalty: 4%, Advert: 1.5%
Contract Periods (Yrs.): 20/20
Area Development Agreement: Yes/Var
Sub-Franchise Contract: . . . . . .No
Expand in Territory: . . . . Yes
Passive Ownership: . . . . . .Allowed
Encourage Conversions: . . . . . Yes
Franchisee Purchase(s) Required: Yes

FRANCHISOR TRAINING/SUPPORT:
Financial Assistance Provided: . . . . . No
Site Selection Assistance: . . . . .Yes
Lease Negotiation Assistance: . . . . No
Co-operative Advertising: . . . . . . .Yes
Training: . . . . 5 Wks. at Certified
. . . . Training Stores Closest Franchisee
On-Going Support: . . . . . . B,C,D,E,H,I
Full-Time Franchisor Support Staff: . .100
EXPANSION PLANS:
US: . . . . Midwest, South, East
Canada - Yes, . . . Overseas - Yes

PONDEROSA STEAKHOUSE

P.O. Box 578
Dayton, OH 45401
TEL: (800) 543-9670
FAX:
Mr. Edward Day, Dir. Fran. Sales

The franchisor's primary business is a modified self-service, family-style steak-house restaurant, open 7 days a week for lunch and dinner. The restaurant features a reasonably-priced menu which includes beef entrees, seafood entrees, chicken and the Grand Buffet. Many PONDEROSA STEAKHOUSES offer breakfast.

HISTORY: . . . .
Established in 1965; . . 1st Franchised in 1966
Company-Owned Units (As of 12/1/1989):   398
Franchised Units (12/1/1989): 341
Total Units (12/1/1989): 739
Distribution: . . . US-707;Can-10;Overseas-22
North America: . . . . 34 States, 4 Provinces
Concentration: . . 122 in OH, 75 in IN, 74 NY
Registered: . . . . All States
. . . .
Average # of Employees: . . . . . 15 FT, 60 PT
Prior Industry Experience: . . . . Helpful

FINANCIAL:
Cash Investment: $100-300K
Total Investment: . . . . . $.8-1.3MM
Fees: Franchise - $25K
   Royalty: 4%, Advert: 4%
Contract Periods (Yrs.): . . . 20/20
Area Development Agreement: Yes/3+
Sub-Franchise Contract: . . . . . .No
Expand in Territory: . . . . . . Yes
Passive Ownership: . . . Not Allowed
Encourage Conversions: . . . . . Yes
Franchisee Purchase(s) Required: .No

FRANCHISOR TRAINING/SUPPORT:
Financial Assistance Provided: . . . Yes(I)
Site Selection Assistance: . . . . .Yes
Lease Negotiation Assistance: . . . . . No
Co-operative Advertising: . . . . .Yes
Training: . . . . . . 5 Wks. in Field, 1 Wk.
. . . . Headquarters, 3 Wks. Field
On-Going Support: . . . . .B,C,D,E,G,H,I
Full-Time Franchisor Support Staff: . . .5
EXPANSION PLANS:
   US: . . . . .All US
   Canada - Yes, . . . Overseas - Yes

RED ROBIN BURGER & SPIRITS EMPORIUMS

9 Executive Circle, # 190
Irvine, CA 92714
TEL: (714) 756-2121
FAX:
Mr. Madison Jobe, Dir. Fran.

RED ROBIN is an exciting, vibrant concept, offering an appealing and inviting array of fresh, healthy, high-quality foods and refreshing beverages in a full-ser-vice restaurant. Our Master Mixologists serve concoctions that are unique in name, appearance and taste.

HISTORY: . . . . IFA
Established in 1969; . . 1st Franchised in 1979
Company-Owned Units (As of 12/1/1989): . 21
Franchised Units (12/1/1989): 38
Total Units (12/1/1989): 59
Distribution: US-50;Can-9;Overseas-0
North America: . . . . 11 States, 2 Provinces
Concentration: . .17 in CA, 15 in WA, 6 in BC
Registered: . . . . CA,FL,MI,NY,OR,WA,AB
. . . .
Average # of Employees: . . . . . 30 FT, 40 PT
Prior Industry Experience: . . . . Helpful

FINANCIAL:
Cash Investment: $100-400K
Total Investment: $1.0-2.5MM
Fees: Franchise - $30-50K
   Royalty: 4%, Advert: 5%
Contract Periods (Yrs.): . . . 20/10
Area Development Agreement: Yes/15
Sub-Franchise Contract: . . . . . .No
Expand in Territory: . . . . . . Yes
Passive Ownership: . . . Discouraged
Encourage Conversions: . . . . . Yes
Franchisee Purchase(s) Required: Yes

FRANCHISOR TRAINING/SUPPORT:
Financial Assistance Provided: . . . . . No
Site Selection Assistance: . . . . .Yes
Lease Negotiation Assistance: . . . . .Yes
Co-operative Advertising: . . . . .Yes
Training: . . . . 3 Days Headquarters,
. . . . . 12 Wks. Corporate Restaurants
On-Going Support: . . . . C,d,E,G,H
Full-Time Franchisor Support Staff: . . 55
EXPANSION PLANS:
   US: . . . . NE, SE and Midwest
   Canada - No, ... Overseas - Yes

ROUND TABLE PIZZA

655 Montgomery St.
San Francisco, CA 94111
TEL: (415) 392-7500
FAX:
Mr. Bob Veeneman, Dir. Fran. Dev.

ROUND TABLE FRANCHISE CORPORATION offers franchises to establish and operate a ROUND TABLE PIZZA RESTAURANT, which provides the public with pizza and related products in a wholesome, family restaurant setting.

HISTORY: . . . .
Established in 1959; . . 1st Franchised in 1962
Company-Owned Units (As of 12/1/1989): . .0
Franchised Units (12/1/1989): 540
Total Units (12/1/1989): 540
Distribution: US-540;Can-0;Overseas-1
North America: . . . . .12 States
Concentration: . . . . .450 in CA
Registered: . . . . CA,HI,OR,WA
. . . .
Average # of Employees: . . . . . .4 FT, 16 PT
Prior Industry Experience: . . . . Helpful

FINANCIAL:
Cash Investment: $100K
Total Investment: $300K
Fees: Franchise - $25K
   Royalty: 4%, Advert: 3%
Contract Periods (Yrs.): 15/15
Area Development Agreement: Yes/Var
Sub-Franchise Contract: . . . . . Yes
Expand in Territory: . . . . . . Yes
Passive Ownership: . . . Discouraged
Encourage Conversions: . . . . . Yes
Franchisee Purchase(s) Required: .No

FRANCHISOR TRAINING/SUPPORT:
Financial Assistance Provided: . . . . . No
Site Selection Assistance: . . . . .Yes
Lease Negotiation Assistance: . . . . .Yes
Co-operative Advertising: . . . . .Yes
Training: . . . . . .4 Wks. Culver City, CA
. . . .
On-Going Support: . . . . . . C,D,e,F,G,h
Full-Time Franchisor Support Staff: . .100
EXPANSION PLANS:
   US: . . . . W, SW and NW
   Canada - No, ... Overseas - Yes

SALADELLY RESTAURANTS

Coulter Ave. & St. James St.
Ardmore, PA 19003
TEL: (215) 642-0453
FAX:
Mr. Steve Byer, Chairman

Limited-menu, full-service restaurant, featuring a superb SALADELLY Saladbar and a limited selection of hot, grilled entrees. SALADELLY'S average about 110 seats in attractive, comfortable dining settings.

HISTORY: . . . .
Established in 1978; . . 1st Franchised in 1986
Company-Owned Units (As of 12/1/1989): . .7
Franchised Units (12/1/1989): 2
Total Units (12/1/1989): 9
Distribution: US-9;Can-0;Overseas-0
North America: . . . . .1 State
Concentration: . . . . 9 in PA
Registered: . . . .
. . . .
Average # of Employees: . . . . . 10 FT, 20 PT
Prior Industry Experience: . . . . Helpful

FINANCIAL:
Cash Investment: $100-150K
Total Investment: $275K
Fees: Franchise - $15K
Royalty: 4%, Advert: 2%
Contract Periods (Yrs.): 10/5
Area Development Agreement: Yes/Var
Sub-Franchise Contract: . . . . Yes
Expand in Territory: . . . . . . Yes
Passive Ownership: . . . Not Allowed
Encourage Conversions: . . . . Yes
Franchisee Purchase(s) Required: .No

FRANCHISOR TRAINING/SUPPORT:
Financial Assistance Provided: . . . . . No
Site Selection Assistance: . . . . . . .Yes
Lease Negotiation Assistance: . . . . .Yes
Co-operative Advertising: . . . . .Yes
Training: . . . . 6 Wks. Headquarters
. . . .
On-Going Support: . . . . C,D,E
Full-Time Franchisor Support Staff: . .100
EXPANSION PLANS:
US: . . . . Northeast
Canada - No, ...Overseas - No

SANDWICH TREE RESTAURANTS

602 - 535 Thurlow St.
Vancouver, BC V6E3L2 CAN
TEL: (604) 684-3314 C
FAX:
Mr. George Moen, President

Famous for our custom sandwiches, creative salads, hearty soups and much more, SANDWICH TREE is a limited-hours operation located in shopping centres, commerical towers and industrial centres. Our quality food, served in our attractive surroundings, make SANDWICH TREE a number one investment opportunity.

HISTORY: . . . .
Established in 1977; . . 1st Franchised in 1979
Company-Owned Units (As of 12/1/1989): . .2
Franchised Units (12/1/1989): 68
Total Units (12/1/1989): 70
Distribution: US-0;Can-70;Overseas-0
North America: . . . . 8 Provinces
Concentration: . . .35 in BC, 9 in ON, 9 in NS
Registered: . . . . AB
. . . .
Average # of Employees: . . . . . . 4 FT, 7 PT
Prior Industry Experience: . . . . Helpful

FINANCIAL:
Cash Investment: $35-55K
Total Investment: $100-165K
Fees: Franchise - $27.5K
Royalty: 4.5%, Advert: 3%
Contract Periods (Yrs.): 10/10
Area Development Agreement: Yes/10
Sub-Franchise Contract: . . . . Yes
Expand in Territory: . . . . . . Yes
Passive Ownership: . . . Discouraged
Encourage Conversions: . . . . Yes
Franchisee Purchase(s) Required: .No

FRANCHISOR TRAINING/SUPPORT:
Financial Assistance Provided: . . . Yes(I)
Site Selection Assistance: . . . . . . .Yes
Lease Negotiation Assistance: . . . . .Yes
Co-operative Advertising: . . . . .Yes
Training: . . . . 3 Wks. Headquarters,
. . . . 1 Wk. Toronto, 1 Wk. Halifax, NS
On-Going Support: . . . a,B,C,D,E,F,G,H
Full-Time Franchisor Support Staff: . . 14
EXPANSION PLANS:
US: . . . . No
Canada - Yes, ...Overseas - No

SHONEY'S RESTAURANTS -
AMERICA'S DINNER TABLE
1727 Elm Hill Pike
Nashville, TN 37210
TEL: (615) 391-5201
FAX:
Mr. Jeffrey Heston, Dir. Fran. Dev.

Full-service, family restaurant, featuring original breakfast bar.

HISTORY: . . . . IFA
Established in 1959; . . 1st Franchised in 1971
Company-Owned Units (As of 12/1/1989): 281
Franchised Units (12/1/1989): 402
Total Units (12/1/1989): 683
Distribution: US-683;Can-0;Overseas-0
North America: . . . .
Concentration: . . . .
Registered: . . . . All States
. . . .
Average # of Employees: . . . . 70 FT
Prior Industry Experience: . . . . . .Necessary

FINANCIAL: OTC-SHONC
Cash Investment: $75K
Total Investment: $900K
Fees: Franchise - $25K
Royalty: 3%, Advert: 5%
Contract Periods (Yrs.): 20/20
Area Development Agreement: Yes/Var
Sub-Franchise Contract: . . . . .No
Expand in Territory: . . . . . . Yes
Passive Ownership: . . . Not Allowed
Encourage Conversions: . . . . .No
Franchisee Purchase(s) Required: Yes

FRANCHISOR TRAINING/SUPPORT:
Financial Assistance Provided: . . . . . No
Site Selection Assistance: . . . . . . .Yes
Lease Negotiation Assistance: . . . . .Yes
Co-operative Advertising: . . . . .Yes
Training: . . . . . . 4-7 Wks. Headquarters
. . . .
On-Going Support: . . . .a,b,C,d,e,F,G,h,I
Full-Time Franchisor Support Staff: . . . .
EXPANSION PLANS:
US: . . . . .NE, NW and West
Canada - Yes, . . . Overseas - Yes

SHOOTERS ON THE WATER

3033 NE 32nd Ave.
Ft. Lauderdale, FL 33308
TEL: (305) 566-2855
FAX: (305) 566-2953
Mr. Melvin Burge, EVP

Up-scale, waterfront family-type restaurant and entertainment complex, catering to singles, family and boating clientele, offering valet service for boat docking and auto's. Outside dining patio, swimming pool, plus over 120 menu items.

HISTORY: . . . .
Established in 1982; . . 1st Franchised in 1985
Company-Owned Units (As of 12/1/1989): . .3
Franchised Units (12/1/1989): 4
Total Units (12/1/1989): 7
Distribution: US-7;Can-0;Overseas-0
North America: . . . . 3 States
Concentration: . . . 3 in OH, 3 in FL, 1 in NY
Registered: . . . . . .CA,FL,IL,MI,NY,RI,VA
. . . .
Average # of Employees: . . . . 210 FT
Prior Industry Experience: . . . . . .Necessary

FINANCIAL:
Cash Investment: . . . .$
Total Investment: $1.1-1.5MM
Fees: Franchise - $50K
Royalty: 5%, Advert: 1%
Contract Periods (Yrs.): . . . 15/10
Area Development Agreement: . .No
Sub-Franchise Contract: . . . . .No
Expand in Territory: . . . . Yes
Passive Ownership: . . . . . .Allowed
Encourage Conversions: . . . . . Yes
Franchisee Purchase(s) Required: .No

FRANCHISOR TRAINING/SUPPORT:
Financial Assistance Provided: . . . . .No
Site Selection Assistance: . . . . .Yes
Lease Negotiation Assistance: . . . . .Yes
Co-operative Advertising: . . . . .Yes
Training: . . . . . 2-3 Months Headquarters
. . . .
On-Going Support: . . . . . . .C,D,E,F,H
Full-Time Franchisor Support Staff: . . 15
EXPANSION PLANS:
US: . . . . .All US
Canada - Yes, . . . Overseas - Yes

SHOWBIZ PIZZA PLACE / CHUCK E. CHEESE

4441 W. Airport Fwy.
Irving, TX 75061
TEL: (214) 258-8507
FAX: (214) 258-8545
Mr. Robert Ortegel, Dir. Fran. Dev.

The franchisor operates and sells franchises for family-oriented restaurants, featuring pizza and other food and beverages, entertainment by 3-dimensional, computer-controlled amimated characters, a kiddie area and skill game area with coin and/or token-operated games and rides and the sale of related novelty products.

HISTORY: . . . . .IFA
Established in 1980; . . 1st Franchised in 1981
Company-Owned Units (As of 12/1/1989): 130
Franchised Units (12/1/1989): 126
Total Units (12/1/1989): 256
Distribution: US-247;Can-7;Overseas-2
North America: . . . . 44 States, 3 Provinces
Concentration: . . .15 in CA, 7 in TN, 5 in NY
Registered: . . . . .All
. . . .
Average # of Employees: . . . . . .4 FT, 35 PT
Prior Industry Experience: . . . . Helpful

FINANCIAL: OTC-SHBZ
Cash Investment: $250-300K
Total Investment: . . . . . $.7-1.0MM
Fees: Franchise - $25K
Royalty: 3.8%, Advert: 3%
Contract Periods (Yrs.): . . . 15/15
Area Development Agreement: Yes/15
Sub-Franchise Contract: . . . . . .No
Expand in Territory: . . . . Yes
Passive Ownership: . . . Discouraged
Encourage Conversions: . . . . . Yes
Franchisee Purchase(s) Required: .No

FRANCHISOR TRAINING/SUPPORT:
Financial Assistance Provided: . . . . .No
Site Selection Assistance: . . . . No
Lease Negotiation Assistance: . . . . .Yes
Co-operative Advertising: . . . . .Yes
Training: . . . . . 3-4 Wks. Company Units
. . . .
On-Going Support: . . . . . . .C,D,E,G,h
Full-Time Franchisor Support Staff: . . . .
EXPANSION PLANS:
US: . . . . .All US
Canada - Yes, ...Overseas - No

SIRLOIN STOCKADE FAMILY STEAKHOUSES

9 Compound Dr.
Hutchinson, KS 67502
TEL: (316) 669-9372
FAX:
Ms. Judy Froese, Dir. Fran. Devel.

SIRLOIN STOCKADE FAMILY STEAKHOUSES feature a selection of top-quality steaks, chicken and fish, and a self-service salad, hot food and dessert bar, at affordable prices. Free-standing buildings of 6,000-7,400 SF, seating 240-320; 50,000 SF of land required.

HISTORY: . . . . .IFA
Established in 1984; . . 1st Franchised in 1984
Company-Owned Units (As of 12/1/1989): . .6
Franchised Units (12/1/1989): 63
Total Units (12/1/1989): 69
Distribution: US-69;Can-0;Overseas-0
North America: . . . . 12 States
Concentration: . . 20 in TX, 13 in KS, 9 in OK
Registered: . . . . . . .CA,IL,IN,SD,VA,WI
. . . .
Average # of Employees: . . . . . 20 FT, 30 PT
Prior Industry Experience: . . . . Helpful

FINANCIAL:
Cash Investment: $150-250K
Total Investment: . . . . . $.7-1/0MM
Fees: Franchise - $15K
Royalty: 3%, Advert: 1%
Contract Periods (Yrs.): . . . 15/15
Area Development Agreement: Yes/Var
Sub-Franchise Contract: . . . . . .No
Expand in Territory: . . . . .No
Passive Ownership: . . . Discouraged
Encourage Conversions: . . . . . .No
Franchisee Purchase(s) Required: .No

FRANCHISOR TRAINING/SUPPORT:
Financial Assistance Provided: . . . . .No
Site Selection Assistance: . . . . .Yes
Lease Negotiation Assistance: . . . . .No
Co-operative Advertising: . . . . .No
Training: . . . . . 6 Wks. Training Store,
. . . Opening Wk. at Site, On-going Site
On-Going Support: . . . . . B,C,D,E,G,h,i
Full-Time Franchisor Support Staff: . . 13
EXPANSION PLANS:
US: . . . . .All US
Canada - No, ...Overseas - No

SIZZLER RESTAURANTS INTERNATIONAL
12655 W. Jefferson Blvd.
Los Angeles, CA 90066
TEL: (800) 759-0059 (213) 827-2300
FAX: (213) 822-5786
Mr. Gregg Williams, Lic. Development

SIZZLER RESTAURANTS operates moderately-priced, self-service, limited-menu restaurants. Our trend-setting concept encompasses steak and seafood entrees, along with our famous salad bar. Some units serve beer/wine. Our concept continues to evolve along with customer needs, as witnessed in the pasta, muffin and tostada bars.

HISTORY: . . . .
Established in 1959; . . 1st Franchised in 1968
Company-Owned Units (As of 12/1/1989): 205
Franchised Units (12/1/1989): 450
Total Units (12/1/1989): 655
Distribution: US-642;Can-2;Overseas-11
North America: . . . .
Concentration: . . . .
Registered: . . . . All Except ND and SD
. . . .
Average # of Employees: . . . . . .8 FT, 50 PT
Prior Industry Experience: . . . . Helpful

FINANCIAL: NASD-SIZZ
Cash Investment: $300K
Total Investment: $1.1MM
Fees: Franchise - $30K
Royalty: 4.5%, Advert: 4.5%
Contract Periods (Yrs.): . . 20/Lease
Area Development Agreement: Yes/Var
Sub-Franchise Contract: . . . . . Yes
Expand in Territory: . . . .
Passive Ownership: . . . .
Encourage Conversions: . . . . . Yes
Franchisee Purchase(s) Required: .No

FRANCHISOR TRAINING/SUPPORT:
Financial Assistance Provided: . . . . .No
Site Selection Assistance: . . . . .Yes
Lease Negotiation Assistance: . . . . .Yes
Co-operative Advertising: . . . . .Yes
Training: . . . . . . 13 Wks. Training Unit,
. . . . 1 Wk. Corporate Office
On-Going Support: . . . . .B,C,D,E,G,H,I
Full-Time Franchisor Support Staff: . . . 5
EXPANSION PLANS:
US: . . . . . Northeast, Southeast,Central
Canada - Yes, . . . Overseas - Yes

SMITTY'S PANCAKE HOUSE

600-501 18th Ave. SW
Calgary, AB T2S0C7 CAN
TEL: (403) 229-3838
FAX:
Mr. W. Chan, President

Family restaurant, specializing in pancakes and waffles. Featuring lunch and dinner items, as well as a full-license lounge.

HISTORY: . . . .
Established in 1960; . . 1st Franchised in 1960
Company-Owned Units (As of 12/1/1989): . 20
Franchised Units (12/1/1989): 128
Total Units (12/1/1989): 148
Distribution: US-2;Can-146;Overseas-0
North America: . . . .
Concentration: . . . .
Registered: . . . .
. . . .
Average # of Employees: . . . . . 30 FT,10 PT
Prior Industry Experience: . . . . Helpful

FINANCIAL:
Cash Investment: $300-400K
Total Investment: $300-400K
Fees: Franchise - $35K
Royalty: 5%, Advert: 3%
Contract Periods (Yrs.): 20/10
Area Development Agreement: .No
Sub-Franchise Contract: . . . . .No
Expand in Territory: . . . . . . Yes
Passive Ownership: . . . Not Allowed
Encourage Conversions: . . . . . Yes
Franchisee Purchase(s) Required: .No

FRANCHISOR TRAINING/SUPPORT:
Financial Assistance Provided: . . . . .No
Site Selection Assistance: . . . . .Yes
Lease Negotiation Assistance: . . . . .No
Co-operative Advertising: . . . . .No
Training: . . . . . . 2-3 Wks. Headquarters
. . . .
On-Going Support: . . . . C,D,E,F,H
Full-Time Franchisor Support Staff: . . 20
EXPANSION PLANS:
US: . . . . .No
Canada - Yes, ...Overseas - No

SONNY'S REAL PIT BAR B Q

3631 SW Archer Rd.
Gainesville, FL 32608
TEL: (904) 376-9721
FAX: (904) 372-7847
Mr. Frank Scharf, Dir. Mktg.

SONNY'S REAL PIT BAR B Q offers licenses for full-service barbeque restaurants. Family dining with a 40-item salad bar, children's menu and catering a variety of lunch specials and diet plates. Take-out/service also available.

HISTORY: . . . . IFA
Established in 1968; . . 1st Franchised in 1977
Company-Owned Units (As of 12/1/1989): . .0
Franchised Units (12/1/1989): 80
Total Units (12/1/1989): 80
Distribution: US-80;Can-0;Overseas-0
North America: . . . . 7 States
Concentration: . . 55 in FL, 15 in GA, 3 in NC
Registered: . . . . FL,IL,OR
. . . .
Average # of Employees: . . . . . 15 FT, 10 PT
Prior Industry Experience: . . . . Helpful

FINANCIAL:
Cash Investment: $150-250K
Total Investment: $350-950K
Fees: Franchise - $35K
Royalty: 4%, Advert: 1.5%
Contract Periods (Yrs.): 20/5
Area Development Agreement: Yes/Var
Sub-Franchise Contract: . . . . .No
Expand in Territory: . . . . . . Yes
Passive Ownership: . . . Discouraged
Encourage Conversions: . . . . Yes
Franchisee Purchase(s) Required: .No

FRANCHISOR TRAINING/SUPPORT:
Financial Assistance Provided: . . . . .No
Site Selection Assistance: . . . . . . .Yes
Lease Negotiation Assistance: . . . . .No
Co-operative Advertising: . . . . .Yes
Training: . . . .400 Hrs HQ (General Mgr.)
. . . . . . 150 Hrs. HQ (Kitchen Mgr.)
On-Going Support: . . . . . B,C,D,E,G,H
Full-Time Franchisor Support Staff: . . 35
EXPANSION PLANS:
US: . . . . Mid-Atlantic, SE, NE,Midwest
Canada - No, ... Overseas - Yes

ST-HUBERT B-B-Q

2 Place Laval, # 500
Laval, PQ H7N5N6 CAN
TEL: (514) 668-4500
FAX: (514) 668-9037
Mr. Normand Pregent, VP Devel./RE

ST-HUBERT is a family-style restaurant, offering roasted chicken and Bar-B-Q ribs. Table service, take-out and home delivery in certain areas.

HISTORY:	FINANCIAL:	FRANCHISOR TRAINING/SUPPORT:
Established in 1951; . . 1st Franchised in 1967	Cash Investment: $200-400K	Financial Assistance Provided: . . . Yes(I)
Company-Owned Units (As of 12/1/1989): . 26	Total Investment: . . . . . $.7-1.3MM	Site Selection Assistance: . . . . .Yes
Franchised Units (12/1/1989): 90	Fees: Franchise - $40K	Lease Negotiation Assistance: . . . . . No
Total Units (12/1/1989): 116	Royalty: 4%, Advert: 3%	Co-operative Advertising: . . . . .Yes
Distribution: US-0;Can-116;Overseas-0	Contract Periods (Yrs.): . . . 20/10	Training: . . . . .7 Wks. Montreal
North America: . . . . 4 Provinces	Area Development Agreement: Yes/10	. . . .
Concentration: . . 82 in PQ, 28 in ON, 5 in NB	Sub-Franchise Contract: . . . . .No	On-Going Support: . . . . . .b,c,d,e,G,H,I
Registered:	Expand in Territory: . . . . . . Yes	Full-Time Franchisor Support Staff: . . 30
. . . .	Passive Ownership: . . . Not Allowed	EXPANSION PLANS:
Average # of Employees: . . . . . 23 FT, 32 PT	Encourage Conversions: . . . . Yes	US: . . . . .No
Prior Industry Experience: . . . . Helpful	Franchisee Purchase(s) Required: Yes	Canada - Yes, ...Overseas - No

STASH & STELLA'S

585 Aero Dr.
Buffalo, NY 14222
TEL: (716) 633-9771
FAX:
Mr. Stephen F. Leous, Dir. Fran.

A classic 1950's-style American diner, featuring home-style food served quickly and in a friendly environment. Vintage pieces of memorabilia remind customers of the way America used to look. A varied and moderately-priced menu appeals to the demographic needs of young and old alike, whether seated in a booth or at the lunch counter.

HISTORY:	FINANCIAL: TORONT0-OT	FRANCHISOR TRAINING/SUPPORT:
Established in 1983; . . 1st Franchised in 1989	Cash Investment: $100-250K	Financial Assistance Provided: . . . Yes(I)
Company-Owned Units (As of 12/1/1989): . .6	Total Investment: $550-600K	Site Selection Assistance: . . . . .Yes
Franchised Units (12/1/1989): 0	Fees: Franchise - $35K	Lease Negotiation Assistance: . . . . .Yes
Total Units (12/1/1989): 6	Royalty: 6%, Advert: 1.5%	Co-operative Advertising: . . . . .NA
Distribution: US-6;Can-0;Overseas-0	Contract Periods (Yrs.): . . . 10/10	Training: . . . . 2 Wks. Headquarters,
North America: . . . . .1 State	Area Development Agreement: Yes/10	. . 2 Wks. On-site, 2 Wks. Post-Opening
Concentration: . . . . 6 in NY	Sub-Franchise Contract: . . . . . NA	On-Going Support: . . . . . .C,D,E,F,G,H
Registered: . . . . NY	Expand in Territory:	Full-Time Franchisor Support Staff: . . 18
. . . .	Passive Ownership: . . . Not Allowed	EXPANSION PLANS:
Average # of Employees: . . . . 50 FT	Encourage Conversions: . . . . .No	US: . . . .NE, S, Midwest, Mid-AtlantNo
Prior Industry Experience: . . . . Helpful	Franchisee Purchase(s) Required: .No	Canada - No, ...Overseas - No

STRAW HAT PIZZA

6400 Village Pkwy.
Dublin, CA 94568
TEL: (415) 829-1500
FAX:
Mr. Jack T. Wood, President

THE STRAW HAT co-operative is unique because we are offering memberships, where the franchisees own the franchisor. The benefits are: you will be a member; you will have more flexibility in running your restaurant; you will pay very low assessment and marketing fees; you will receive a broad package of support services. Growth will come from new owners willing to devote considerable time, energy and resources to build a successful business.

HISTORY:	FINANCIAL:	FRANCHISOR TRAINING/SUPPORT:
Established in 1987; . . 1st Franchised in 1987	Cash Investment: $50-100L	Financial Assistance Provided: . . . . . No
Company-Owned Units (As of 12/1/1989): . .0	Total Investment: $50-400K	Site Selection Assistance: . . . . No
Franchised Units (12/1/1989): 76	Fees: Franchise - $10K	Lease Negotiation Assistance: . . . . . No
Total Units (12/1/1989): 76	Royalty: 1%, Advert: 5%	Co-operative Advertising: . . . . .Yes
Distribution: US-76;Can-0;Overseas-0	Contract Periods (Yrs.):	Training: . . . . 30 Days California
North America: . . . . 3 States	Area Development Agreement: . .No	. . . .
Concentration: . . 70 in CA, 5 in NV, 1 in WA	Sub-Franchise Contract: . . . . .No	On-Going Support: . . . . . .C,D,E,F,G,H
Registered: . . . . CA	Expand in Territory: . . . . . . Yes	Full-Time Franchisor Support Staff: . . . 4
. . . .	Passive Ownership: . . . Discouraged	EXPANSION PLANS:
Average # of Employees: . . . 4-8 FT, 10-20 PT	Encourage Conversions: . . . . . Yes	US: . . . . CA, NV AND WA
Prior Industry Experience: . . . . Helpful	Franchisee Purchase(s) Required: .No	Canada - No, ...Overseas - No

SUBWAY SANDWICHES & SALADS

325 Bic Dr.
Milford, CT 06460
TEL: (800) 888-4848 (203) 877-4281
FAX: (203) 878-7493
Mr. George Shea, Asst. VP Mktg.

The world's largest submarine sandwich chain, SUBWAY SANDWICHES & SALADS is also the fastest-growing fast food chain. With over 4,000 units in development, SUBWAY has a simple, reasonable system of success that will impress you. Call today for a free franchise brochure.

HISTORY: . . . . IFA
Established in 1965; . . 1st Franchised in 1974
Company-Owned Units (As of 12/1/1989): . 30
Franchised Units (12/1/1989): 3970
Total Units (12/1/1989): 4000
Distribution: . . US-3857;Can-130;Overseas-13
North America: . . . 49 States, 10 Province
Concentration: . 252 in FL,201 in CA,87 in IN
Registered: . . . . .All
. . . .
Average # of Employees: . . . . 8-10 FT
Prior Industry Experience: . . . . . . Helpful

FINANCIAL:
Cash Investment: $35-65K
Total Investment: $39.9K
Fees: Franchise - $7.5K
 Royalty: 8%, Advert: 2.5%
Contract Periods (Yrs.): 20/20
Area Development Agreement: . Yes
Sub-Franchise Contract: . . . . . Yes
Expand in Territory: . . . . . . Yes
Passive Ownership: . . . Discouraged
Encourage Conversions: . . . . . NA
Franchisee Purchase(s) Required: .No

FRANCHISOR TRAINING/SUPPORT:
Financial Assistance Provided: . . .Yes(D)
Site Selection Assistance: . . . . . . .Yes
Lease Negotiation Assistance: . . . . .Yes
Co-operative Advertising: . . . . . . .Yes
Training: . . . . 2 Wks. Headquarters
On-Going Support: . . . A,C,D,E,F,G,h,I
Full-Time Franchisor Support Staff: . .250
EXPANSION PLANS:
US: . . . . .All US
Canada - Yes, . . . Overseas - Yes

T.G.I. FRIDAY'S / DALTS

P.O. Box 809062
Dallas, TX 75080
TEL: (214) 450-5599
FAX:
Mr. Randy M. Clifton, VP Fran. Dev.

Full-service, casual-theme restaurants T.G.I. FRIDAY'S and DALTS.

HISTORY: . . . . IFA
Established in 1965; . . 1st Franchised in 1970
Company-Owned Units (As of 12/1/1989): 134
Franchised Units (12/1/1989): 30
Total Units (12/1/1989): 164
Distribution: US-159;Can-0;Overseas-5
North America: . . . . 33 States
Concentration: . .22 in FL, 18 in TX, 17 in CA
Registered: . . . . All States
. . . .
Average # of Employees: . . . . 90-115 Total
Prior Industry Experience: . . . . . .Necessary

FINANCIAL: OTC-TGI
Cash Investment: $1.0MM
Total Investment: . . . $2.0-2.5MM
Fees: Franchise - $50K
 Royalty: 4%, Advert: 2-4%
Contract Periods (Yrs.): . . 20/Var
Area Development Agreement: . Yes
Sub-Franchise Contract: . . . . .No
Expand in Territory: . . . . . . Yes
Passive Ownership: . . . Not Allowed
Encourage Conversions: . . . . .No
Franchisee Purchase(s) Required: .No

FRANCHISOR TRAINING/SUPPORT:
Financial Assistance Provided: . . . . .No
Site Selection Assistance: . . . . . . .Yes
Lease Negotiation Assistance: . . . . .No
Co-operative Advertising: . . . . . . .NA
Training: . . . . .1 Wk. Headquarters,
 . . . . .18 Wks. Local Units
On-Going Support: . . . . . b,C,D,E,G,H,I
Full-Time Franchisor Support Staff: . .200
EXPANSION PLANS:
US: . . . . Most US Markets
Canada - Yes, . . . Overseas - Yes

TEK'S SEAFOODS RESTAURANT

218 Lakeside Dr.
North Bay, ON P1A3E3 CAN
TEL: (705) 472-8685
FAX:
Mr. Bert Teklenburg, President

Family-style seafood restaurant. Also take-out and fresh fish retail and live lobsters.

HISTORY: . . . .
Established in 1957; . . 1st Franchised in 1975
Company-Owned Units (As of 12/1/1989): . .0
Franchised Units (12/1/1989): 2
Total Units (12/1/1989): 2
Distribution: US-0;Can-2;Overseas-0
North America: . . . .
Concentration: . . . .
Registered: . . . .
. . . .
Average # of Employees: . . . . . . 6 FT, 6 PT
Prior Industry Experience: . . . . Helpful

FINANCIAL:
Cash Investment: . . . .$100K+
Total Investment: . . . .$
Fees: Franchise - $8K
 Royalty: 5%, Advert: 0%
Contract Periods (Yrs.): 10/10
Area Development Agreement: . .No
Sub-Franchise Contract: . . . .No
Expand in Territory: . . . . . . Yes
Passive Ownership: . . . Not Allowed
Encourage Conversions: . . . . .No
Franchisee Purchase(s) Required: Yes

FRANCHISOR TRAINING/SUPPORT:
Financial Assistance Provided: . . . . .No
Site Selection Assistance: . . . . . . .Yes
Lease Negotiation Assistance: . . . .Yes
Co-operative Advertising: . . . . . . .Yes
Training: . . . . 4 Wks. Headquarters
On-Going Support: . . .a,B,C,D,E,F,G,H,i
Full-Time Franchisor Support Staff: . . . 2
EXPANSION PLANS:
US: . . . . .All US, Especially Southwest
Canada - Yes, . . . Overseas - Yes

TEXAS LOOSEY'S CHILI PARLOR AND SALOON

P. O. Box 1697
Temecula, CA 92390
TEL: (714) 676-0323
FAX: (714) 699-6963
Mr. Ron Walton, President

This unique, family-style specialty restaurant features mesquite-smoked ribs, chicken, 1/2 lb. hamburgers, Mexican food (Tex-Mex) and Texas red chili, set in western motif with lots of stained glass, brass and oak woods, with waitresses clad in custom western chap outfits.

HISTORY: . . . .
Established in 1987; . . 1st Franchised in 1987
Company-Owned Units (As of 12/1/1989): . .5
Franchised Units (12/1/1989): 2
Total Units (12/1/1989): 7
Distribution: US-7;Can-0;Overseas-0
North America: . . . . .1 State
Concentration: . . . . 7 in CA
Registered: . . . . CA
. . . .
Average # of Employees: . . . . . 20 FT, 30 PT
Prior Industry Experience: . . . . Helpful

FINANCIAL:
Cash Investment: $500K
Total Investment: $500K
Fees: Franchise - $30K
Royalty: 5%, Advert: 2%
Contract Periods (Yrs.): 10/10
Area Development Agreement: . .No
Sub-Franchise Contract: . . . . .No
Expand in Territory: . . . . Yes
Passive Ownership: . . . . . .Allowed
Encourage Conversions: . . . . Yes
Franchisee Purchase(s) Required: .No

FRANCHISOR TRAINING/SUPPORT:
Financial Assistance Provided: . . . Yes(I)
Site Selection Assistance: . . . . .Yes
Lease Negotiation Assistance: . . . . .Yes
Co-operative Advertising: . . . . .Yes
Training: . . . . . . 4-5 Wks. Fullerton, CA
. . . .
On-Going Support: . . .a,B,C,D,E,F,G,H,I
Full-Time Franchisor Support Staff: . . . 6
EXPANSION PLANS:
US: . . . . Southwest
Canada - Yes, . . . Overseas - Yes

TONY ROMA'S - A PLACE FOR RIBS

10,000 North Central Expy., # 900
Dallas, TX 75231
TEL: (214) 891-7600
FAX:
Mr. Dale Ross, VP Fran. Dev.

TONY ROMA'S is the largest dinnerhouse chain specializing in BBQ ribs and chicken, famous onion loaf. We have a special niche in the industry. Great price/value relationship, high-quality food products, with full bar service. Also offering take-out and delivery.

HISTORY: . . . . IFA
Established in 1972; . . 1st Franchised in 1979
Company-Owned Units (As of 12/1/1989): . 17
Franchised Units (12/1/1989): 116
Total Units (12/1/1989): 133
Distribution: . . . US-105;Can-9;Overseas-19
North America: . . . . 17 States, 5 Provinces
Concentration: . 36 in CA, 19 in FL, 10 in NY
Registered: . . . . .All
. . . .
Average # of Employees: . . . . . 50 FT,10 PT
Prior Industry Experience: . . . . .Necessary

FINANCIAL:
Cash Investment: $300K
Total Investment: $600-900K
Fees: Franchise - $50K
Royalty: 4%, Advert: 1/2%
Contract Periods (Yrs.): 20/20
Area Development Agreement: Yes/Var
Sub-Franchise Contract: . . . . .No
Expand in Territory: . . . . Yes
Passive Ownership: . . . Discouraged
Encourage Conversions: . . . . . Yes
Franchisee Purchase(s) Required: .No

FRANCHISOR TRAINING/SUPPORT:
Financial Assistance Provided: . . . . .No
Site Selection Assistance: . . . . .Yes
Lease Negotiation Assistance: . . . . .Yes
Co-operative Advertising: . . . . .Yes
Training: . . . . 6 Wks. Headquarters,
. . . . . . 6 Wks. LA, 10-12 Days Site
On-Going Support: . . . . .C,D,E,F,G,H,I
Full-Time Franchisor Support Staff: . . 65
EXPANSION PLANS:
US: . . . . .Midwest, East Coast
Canada - No, ... Overseas - Yes

VILLAGE INN RESTAURANT

400 W. 48th Ave.
Denver, CO 80216
TEL: (303) 296-2121
FAX:
Mr. Robert Kaltenbach, EVP

Full-service, mid-size restaurant, offering a variety of menu items, with emphasis on breakfast served all day.

HISTORY: . . . .
Established in 1958; . . 1st Franchised in 1961
Company-Owned Units (As of 12/1/1989): 132
Franchised Units (12/1/1989): 101
Total Units (12/1/1989): 233
Distribution: US-233;Can-0;Overseas-0
North America: . . . . 25 States
Concentration: . .51 in CO, 39 in FL, 25 in AZ
Registered: . . . . CA,FL,MI,MN,ND,SD,WA
. . . .
Average # of Employees: . . . . . 35 FT, 15 PT
Prior Industry Experience: . . . . Helpful

FINANCIAL: OTC-VICORP
Cash Investment: . . . .$dK
Total Investment: . . . . $.8-1.2MM
Fees: Franchise - $25K
Royalty: 5%, Advert: 0%
Contract Periods (Yrs.): 15/20
Area Development Agreement: Yes/5
Sub-Franchise Contract: . . . . .No
Expand in Territory: . . . . Yes
Passive Ownership: . . . Discouraged
Encourage Conversions: . . . . . Yes
Franchisee Purchase(s) Required: .No

FRANCHISOR TRAINING/SUPPORT:
Financial Assistance Provided: . . . . .No
Site Selection Assistance: . . . . .Yes
Lease Negotiation Assistance: . . . . .No
Co-operative Advertising: . . . . .No
Training: . . . . .10-14 Wks. Headquarters,
. . . . 2-3 Wks. Site Location
On-Going Support: . . . . . . C,d,E,G,h,I
Full-Time Franchisor Support Staff: . . .9
EXPANSION PLANS:
US: . . . . SW, Pac. NW, Midwest & FL
Canada - No, ...Overseas - No

WAFFLETOWN U.S.A.

3 Koger Ctr., # 103
Norfolk, VA 23502
TEL: (804) 455-5658
FAX:
Mr. Tim Mathas, President

WAFFLETOWN U.S.A. is a family-style restaurant, specializing in breakfast, lunch and dinner. Breakfast is one of the most profitable food items sold in the restaurant business. You will be given 4 to 6 weeks' training in one of the stores before opening up one of your own and then WAFFLETOWN will supply someone to work with you for 2 to 4 weeks in your store.

HISTORY:	FINANCIAL:	FRANCHISOR TRAINING/SUPPORT:
Established in 1980; . . 1st Franchised in 1980	Cash Investment: $50-100K	Financial Assistance Provided: . . . . . No
Company-Owned Units (As of 12/1/1989): . .1	Total Investment: $125-190K	Site Selection Assistance: . . . . .Yes
Franchised Units (12/1/1989): 7	Fees: Franchise - $15K	Lease Negotiation Assistance: . . . . .Yes
Total Units (12/1/1989): 8	Royalty: 3%, Advert: 3%	Co-operative Advertising: . . . . .Yes
Distribution: US-8;Can-0;Overseas-0	Contract Periods (Yrs.): 20/20	Training: . . . . . .2 Wks. Each in Virginia
North America: . . . . .1 State	Area Development Agreement: . .No	. Beach, Portsmouth and Chesapeake,VA
Concentration: . . . . 8 in VA	Sub-Franchise Contract: . . . . .No	On-Going Support: . . . . C,D,E,H,I
Registered: . . . . VA	Expand in Territory: . . . . Yes	Full-Time Franchisor Support Staff: . . . 1
. . . .	Passive Ownership: . . . Not Allowed	EXPANSION PLANS:
Average # of Employees: . . . . . 30 FT, 12 PT	Encourage Conversions: . . . . . Yes	US: . . . . Southeast
Prior Industry Experience: . . . . . . Helpful	Franchisee Purchase(s) Required: .No	Canada - No, ...Overseas - No

WESTERN STEER FAMILY STEAKHOUSE / WSMP

WSMP Dr., P. O. Box 399
Claremont, NC 28610
TEL: (800) 438-9207
FAX:
Mr. Kenneth L. Moser, VP Fran.

WESTERN STEER FAMILY STEAKHOUSE is an economy steak restaurant establishment that serves US Choice steak and steak dishes, certain specialty items and side dishes, and features a large food bar serving salads, hot vegetables and dessert.

HISTORY: . . . . IFA	FINANCIAL: OTC-WSMP	FRANCHISOR TRAINING/SUPPORT:
Established in 1972; . . 1st Franchised in 1978	Cash Investment: $850K	Financial Assistance Provided: . . . . . No
Company-Owned Units (As of 12/1/1989): . 50	Total Investment: $1.2MM	Site Selection Assistance: . . . . .Yes
Franchised Units (12/1/1989): 138	Fees: Franchise - $25K	Lease Negotiation Assistance: . . . . .Yes
Total Units (12/1/1989): 188	Royalty: 3%, Advert: 2%	Co-operative Advertising: . . . . .Yes
Distribution: US-188;Can-0;Overseas-0	Contract Periods (Yrs.): 20/20	Training: . . . . 4 Wks. Pre-opening Train-
North America: . . . . 12 States	Area Development Agreement: Yes/3	. . . . ing, 2 Wks. Franchisee Site
Concentration: . 87 in NC, 19 in GA, 18 in SC	Sub-Franchise Contract: . . . . .No	On-Going Support: . . . . .a,B,C,d,E,G,H
Registered: . . . . FL,MD,VA	Expand in Territory: . . . . Yes	Full-Time Franchisor Support Staff: . . 60
. . . .	Passive Ownership: . . . Not Allowed	EXPANSION PLANS:
Average # of Employees: . . . . . 25 FT, 25 PT	Encourage Conversions: . . . . .No	US: . . . . . . Eastern & Southeastern US
Prior Industry Experience: . . . . . . Helpful	Franchisee Purchase(s) Required: Yes	Canada - No, ... Overseas - No

SUPPLEMENTAL LISTING OF FRANCHISORS

ABC FAMILY RESTAURANTS . . . . #303 - 33695 S. Fraser Way, Abbotsford BC V2S2C1   CAN
APPLEBEE'S . . . . .1801 Royal Ln., # 902, Dallas TX 75229
BACALLS CAFE . . . . .6118 Hamilton Ave., # 200, Cincinnati OH 45224
BARN'RDS INTERNATIONAL . . . . 307 1st National Bank Bldg., Council Bluffs IA 51501
BIG BOY FAMILY RESTAURANT SYSTEMS . . . . 4199 Marcy St., Warren MI 48091
BIG SCOOP FAMILY RESTAURANTS . . . . #203 - 1965 W. 4th Ave., Vancouver BC V6T1M8   CAN
BISCO BAR . . . . 1010 Sherbrooke W., # 1604, Montreal PQ H3A2R7   CAN
BJ'S KOUNTRY KITCHEN . . . . 600 W. Shaw Ave., # 160, Fresno CA 93704
BOLL WEEVIL SYSTEMS .2044 1st Ave., San Diego CA 92101
BONANZA (CANADA) . . . . 310 - 1600 Ness Ave., Winnipeg MB R3J3W7   CAN
BONANZA RESTAURANTS . . . . 8080 N. Central Expwy., #500, Box, Dallas TX 75206
BRANDYBERRY'S HOUSE OF PRIME RIB . . . . 133 Coon Rapids Blvd., Coon Rapids MN 55433
BROOKHILL . . . . 2246 E. Date Ave., Fresno CA 93706

CALICO JACK'S	1025 Miller Dr., Altamonte Springs FL 32701	
CARL'S JR. RESTAURANTS	1200 N. Harbor Blvd., Anaheim CA 92803	
CASA OLE RESTAURANT & CANTINA	1050 Edgebrook, Houston TX 77034	
CHAMPIONS SPORTS BAR	150 S. Washington St., # 200, Falls Church VA 22046	
CHARLIE BUBBLES RESTAURANTS	1936 Ridge Rd. W., Rochester NY 14626	
CHELSEA STREET PUBS	P.O. Box 9989, Austin TX 78766	
CHICKEN CORRAL RESTAURANTS	P.O. Box 447, Neepawa MB R0J1H0	CAN
CHILI'S GRILL & BAR	6820 LBJ Fwy., # 200, Dallas TX 75240	
CHOWDER POT, THE	2 Market Yard, Freehold NJ 07728	
COOKER CONCEPTS	2440 Grinstead Dr., Louisville KY 40204	
COUNTRY KITCHEN (CANADA)	1 1st Canadian Pl., # 5900, Toronto ON M5X1K2	CAN
COUNTRY KITCHEN INTERNATIONAL	7800 Metro Pkwy., Minneapolis MN 55425	
CREATIVE FOOD 'N FUN	1801 Royal Ln., # 902, Dallas TX 75229	
CREATIVE FOOD 'N FUN	1801 Royal Ln., # 902, Dallas TX 75229	
DE DUTCH PANNEKOEK HOUSE	1534 Main St., Vancouver BC V6A2W8	CAN
DELI-STOP RESTAURANTS	# 10 - 1080 Waverley St., Winnipeg MB R3T5S4	CAN
DENNY'S	16417 Berwyn, Cerritos CA 90701	
DIETWORKS RESTAURANTS, THE	30 W. Mt. Pleasant Ave., Livingston NJ 07039	
DIXIE LEE CHICKEN & SEAFOOD	820 Flint Rd., Downsview ON M3J2J5	CAN
DRUTHER'S INTERNATIONAL	2440 Grinstead Dr., Louisville KY 40204	
EL POLLO ASADO	3420 E. Shea Blvd., # 150, Phoenix AZ 85028	
ELEPHANT AND CASTLE, THE	P.O. Box 10240, Pacific Centre, Vancouver BC V7Y1E7	CAN
ELMER'S PANCAKE & STEAK HOUSE	11802 SE Stark St., Portland OR 97216	
FAT ALBERT'S RESTAURANT	150 Montreal Rd., # 305, Ottawa ON K1L8H2	CAN
FAT BELLY DELI	111 Hazard Ave., Enfield CT 06082	
FISH & CHIP SHOPPE, THE	481 N. Service Rd. W., # 16, Oakville ON L6M2V6	CAN
FLAKEY JAKE'S	2351 W. NW Hwy., # 2101, Dallas TX 75220	
GARFIELD'S	3240 W. Britton Rd., Bldg. 2S,# 2, Oklahoma City OK 73120	
GERACI'S PASTA, SEAFOOD & SALAD	273 W. Audubon Dr., Fresno CA 93711	
GLASS OVEN BAKERY & CAFE	1640 New Highway, Farmingdale NY 11735	
GOLDEN CORRAL	P.O. Box 29502, Raleigh NC 27626	
GOLDEN GRIDDLE PANCAKE HOUSE	505 Consumers Rd., # 1000, Willowdale ON M2J4V8	CAN
GOLDIE'S PATIO GRILL	8332 E. 73rd St., S., Tulsa OK 74133	
GREAT TEXAS RESTAURANTS	7079 Torbram Rd., Mississauga ON L4T1G7	CAN
GREEK'S PIZZERIA	1600 University Ave., Muncie IN 47303	
GREENSTREETS HAMBURGER GRILL & BAR	72 Garden Dr., Burnsville MN 55337	
HAPPY STEAK	2246 E. Date Ave., Fresno CA 93706	
HARVEY'S RESTAURANTS	230 Bloor St., W., Toronto ON M5S1T8	CAN
HOUSE OF YAKATORI JAPANESE REST.	5975 N. Academy Blvd., # 210, Colorado Springs CO 80907	
IHOP	6837 Lankershim Blvd., North Hollywood CA 91605	
IN ZONE LOUNGES & RESTAURANTS	3601 W. Sahara Ave., # 201, Las Vegas NV 89102	
INTERNATIONAL HOUSE OF PANCAKES	6837 Lankershim Blvd., North Hollywood CA 91605	
JAMCO LTD.	P.O. Box 9006, 2329 W. Main, Littleton CO 80120	
JAN DRAKES	2700 Post Oak Blvd., # 1820, Houston TX 77056	
JOHNNY APPLESEED RESTAURANTS	537 Warrenton Rd., Falmouth VA 22405	
K-BOB'S	5307 E. Mockingbird, # 710, Dallas TX 75206	
KELSEYS ROAD HOUSE	450 S. Service Rd., Oakville ON L6K2H4	CAN
KETTLE RESTAURANTS	P.O. Box 2964, Houston TX 77252	
KRACKER SEAFOOD	7515 NCNB Bank Tower, # 300, Dallas TX 75231	
LA MAISON DE CROISSANT	695 Yonge St., Toronto ON M4Y2B2	CAN
LAROSA'S PIZZERIAS	5870 Belmont Ave., Cincinnati OH 45224	
LE PEEP RESTAURANTS	4 W. Dry Creek Circle, Littleton CO 80120	
MALIBU JACK'S CALIFORNIA FOOD EPIC	162 Metcalfe St., Ottawa ON K2P1P2	CAN
MARIE CALLENDER PIE SHOPS	1100 Town & Country Rd., #1300, Orange CA 92668	
MAVERICK STEAK HOUSE	1752 W. Jefferson, Springfield IL 62702	
MELTING POT, THE	P.O. Box 270059, Tampa FL 33688	
MOTHERS PIZZA-PASTA RESTAURANT	5665 McLaughlin Rd., Mississauga ON L7L5L1	CAN
MOUNTAIN MIKE'S PIZZA	1975 Hamilton Ave., # 30, San Jose CA 95125	

MR. FRANKFURT RESTAURANT COMPANY . . . . .893 Queen St., E., Toronto ON M4M1J4   CAN
MR. GATTI'S . . . . 220 Foremost Dr., Austin TX 78745
MR. STEAK .P. O. Box 9006, 2329 W. Main St., Littleton CO 80160
OLDE WORLD CHEESE SHOP . . . . 3333 S. Pasadena Ave., S. Pasadena FL 33707
ONION CROCK . . . . 4485 Plainfield, N.E., Box 2088, Grand Rapids MI 49501
OYSTER KRACKER SEAFOOD . . . . 7515 NCNB Bank Tower, # 300, Dallas TX 75231
PANNEKOEKEN HUIS FAMILY RESTAURANTS . . . . 6517 Cecilia Circle, Edina MN 55435
PANTERA'S PIZZA . . . . .11933 Westline Industrial Dr., St. Louis MO 63146
PAPACHINO'S RISTORANTE & PIZZA . . . . .7940 Silverton Ave., # 103, San Diego CA 92126
PEPE'S MEXICAN RESTAURANTS . . . . 1325 W. 15th St., Chicago IL 60608
PERKO'S . . . . 2246 E. Date Ave., Fresno CA 93706
PEWTER MUG . . . . 207 Frankfort Ave., Cleveland OH 44113
PIZZA DELIGHT/PIZZA PATIO . . . . .Box 2070, Station A, Moncton NB E1C8H7   CAN
PIZZA HUT . . . . .P.O. Box 428, Wichita KS 67201
PIZZA HUT (CANADA . . . . 10 Four Seasons Pl., # 500, Etobicoke ON M9B6H7   CAN
PIZZERIA UNO . . . . .100 Charles Park Rd., W. Roxbury MA 02132
PJ'S CASA FIESTA . . . . .23696 El Toro Rd., El Toro CA 92630
PLUSH PIPPIN REST./PIE SHOPS . . . . 31620 23rd Ave. S., # 318, Federal Way WA 98003
POFOLKS . . . . P. O. Box 17406, Nashville TN 37217
POUR LA FRANCE! CAFE & BAKERY . . . . .303-H, AABC, Aspen CO 81611
PRIMO'S DELI CAFE . . . . 2700 Post Oak Blvd., # 1820, Houston TX 77056
RALPH'S DINING . . . . 150 Montreal Rd., # 305, Ottawa ON K1L8H2   CAN
RITZY'S - AMERICAN FOOD FAVORITES . . . . .1496 Old Henderson Rd., Columbus OH 43220
ROCKY ROCOCO RESTAURANTS . . . . .340 W. Washington Ave., Madison WI 53703
SBARRO THE ITALIAN EATERY . . . . .763 Larkfield Rd., Commack NY 11725
SEAFOOD JUBILEE . . . . 7920 Beltlima Rd., Lock Box 107, Dallas TX 75240
SHAKEY'S . . . . 651 Gateway Blvd., # 1200, South San Francisco CA 94080
SKYLINE CHILI RESTAURANTS . . . . 109 Illinios Ave., Cincinnati OH 45215
SOUP AND SALAD SYSTEMS . . . . .2645 Financial Ct., # A, San Diego CA 92117
SPOONS RESTAURANTS . . . . 4410 El Camino Real, # 204, Los Altos CA 94022
STEAK & BURGER . . . . 230 Bloor St. W., Toronto ON M5S1T8   CAN
STREETS OF NEW YORK . . . . .7500 N. Dreamy Draw Dr., # 234, Phoenix AZ 85020
STRINGS . . . . .2880 Sunrise Blvd., # 308, Sacramento CA 95742
STUDEBAKER'S . . . . .1418 Wakehurst Cres., Oakville ON L6J6P8   CAN
SWISS CHALET . . . . .230 Bloor St., W., Toronto ON M5S1T8   CAN
TACO BELL (CANADA) . . . . 10 Four Seasons Pl., # 500, Etobicoke ON M9B6H7   CAN
TACO DEL SOL MEXICAN REST. . . . . 101 North 4th St., # 8, Norfolk NE 68701
TEQUILABERRY CALIFORNIA REST. . . . . 133 Coon Rapids Blvd., Coon Rapids MN 55433
UNCLE TONY'S PIZZA & PASTA . . . . 27 Airport Plaza, 1800 Post Rd., Warwick RI 02886
WAITERS TO YOU . . . . .6137 N. 17th Ave., Phoenix AZ 85015
WARD'S RESTAURANTS . . . . 1145 10th Ave., Hattiesburg MD 39403
WOODY'S BAR-B-Q . . . . 1626 Atlantic Univ. Circle, Jacksonville FL 32207
YOUR PLACE RESTAURANTS . . . . .2133 Lincoln Hwy. E., Lancaster PA 17538

CHAPTER 22

FURNITURE / APPLIANCE REFINISHING AND REPAIR

BATCHCREST

2425 S. Progress Dr.
Salt Lake City, UT 84119
TEL: (800) 826-6790 (801) 972-1110
FAX: (801) 977-0328
Mr. Scott Peterson, President

BATHCREST has developed a revolutionary new method of porcelain resurfacing. Tested and proven, BATHCREST's methods and products provide a welcome alternative to expensive bathroom remodeling. BATHCREST services hotels, motels, apartment houses, homeowners and contractors. With BATHCREST, you will be in business for yourself, but not by yourself.

HISTORY: . . . . IFA
Established in 1979; . . 1st Franchised in 1985
Company-Owned Units (As of 12/1/1989): . . 1
Franchised Units (12/1/1989): 143
Total Units (12/1/1989): 144
Distribution: US-143;Can-1;Overseas-0
 North America: . . . . . 35 States, 1 Province
 Concentration: . . 21 in CA, 14 in FL, 10 in NJ
Registered: . . . .CA,FL,HI,IL,IN,MD,MI,NY
 .OR,VA,WA
Average # of Employees: . . . . .3 FT
Prior Industry Experience: . . . . Helpful

FINANCIAL:
Cash Investment: $24.5K
Total Investment: $24.5K
Fees: Franchise - $3.5K
 Royalty: 0%, Advert: 0%
Contract Periods (Yrs.): . . On-going
Area Development Agreement: Yes/1
Sub-Franchise Contract: . . . . .No
Expand in Territory: . . . . . . Yes
Passive Ownership: . . . Discouraged
Encourage Conversions: . . . .
Franchisee Purchase(s) Required: Yes

FRANCHISOR TRAINING/SUPPORT:
Financial Assistance Provided: . . . . .No
Site Selection Assistance: . . . . .NA
Lease Negotiation Assistance: . . . . .NA
Co-operative Advertising: . . . . .NA
Training: . . . . 5 Days Headquarters
 . . . .
On-Going Support: . . . . . . b,C,D,G,H,I
Full-Time Franchisor Support Staff: . . 13
EXPANSION PLANS:
US: . . . . .All US
Canada - Yes, ... Overseas - No

DIP 'N STRIP

2141 S. Platte River Dr.
Denver, Co 80223
TEL: (303) 781-8300
FAX:
Mr. E. Roger Schuyler, President

Franchised operations assisting the household, community, antique dealers, furniture refinishers, industrial and commericial accounts in the removal of finishes from wood and metal. Operation requires approximately 2,000 SF of warehouse space with concrete floor, drain, cold water tap, 220 V power, overhead door and small office space. Removals accomplished with cold stripping formula in chemical solutions, with 3 large tanks.

HISTORY: . . . . IFA
Established in 1970; . . 1st Franchised in 1972
Company-Owned Units (As of 12/1/1989): . . 1
Franchised Units (12/1/1989): 219
Total Units (12/1/1989): 220
Distribution: . . . US-146;Can-16;Overseas-58
   North America: . . . . . 31 States, 4 Provinces
   Concentration: . . 10 in PA, 10 in ON, 7 in OK
Registered: . . . . CA
. . . .
Average # of Employees: . . . . .2 FT
Prior Industry Experience: . . . . Helpful

FINANCIAL:
Cash Investment: $12.5K
Total Investment: $16K
Fees: Franchise - $0
   Royalty: 6%, Advert: 0%
Contract Periods (Yrs.): 5/5
Area Development Agreement: .No
Sub-Franchise Contract: . . . . .No
Expand in Territory: . . . . . . Yes
Passive Ownership: . . . Discouraged
Encourage Conversions: . . . . . Yes
Franchisee Purchase(s) Required: Yes

FRANCHISOR TRAINING/SUPPORT:
Financial Assistance Provided: . . .Yes(D)
Site Selection Assistance: . . . . .Yes
Lease Negotiation Assistance: . . . . . No
Co-operative Advertising: . . . . .Yes
Training: . . . . .7 Days On-site
. . . .
On-Going Support: . . . . B,E,G
Full-Time Franchisor Support Staff: . . . 4
EXPANSION PLANS:
   US: . . . . .All US
   Canada - No, ... Overseas - Yes

DR. VINYL & ASSOCIATES

13665 E. 42nd St. South
Independence, MO 64055
TEL: (800) 531-6600 (816) 478-0800
FAX:
Mr. Tom Buckley, Jr., President

Vinyl, leather, velour, coloring and dyeing; auto windshield and dash repair. Vinyl and stainless auto striping. Wheel well and door edge guards, etc. Join the nation's largest mobile franchisor to new and used auto and truck dealers, fast food restaurants, motels, hotels, schools, boats, planes. We are the alternative to replacement.

HISTORY: . . . . IFA
Established in 1972; . . 1st Franchised in 1981
Company-Owned Units (As of 12/1/1989): . .6
Franchised Units (12/1/1989): 92
Total Units (12/1/1989): 98
Distribution: US-98;Can-0;Overseas-0
   North America: . . . . 31 States
   Concentration: . . . .
Registered: . . . CA,FL,HI,IL,IN,MD,MI,MN
. . . . NY,RI,VA,WI
Average # of Employees: . . . . .1-2 FT
Prior Industry Experience: . . . . Helpful

FINANCIAL:
Cash Investment: $20-40K
Total Investment: $35-40K
Fees: Franchise - $20K
   Royalty: 4-7%, Advert: 1%
Contract Periods (Yrs.): . . . 10/10
Area Development Agreement: Yes/10
Sub-Franchise Contract: . . . . Yes
Expand in Territory: . . . . . . Yes
Passive Ownership: . . . Discouraged
Encourage Conversions: . . . . . Yes
Franchisee Purchase(s) Required: .No

FRANCHISOR TRAINING/SUPPORT:
Financial Assistance Provided: . . . Yes(I)
Site Selection Assistance: . . . . . . .NA
Lease Negotiation Assistance: . . . . .NA
Co-operative Advertising: . . . . .Yes
Training: . . . . 2 Wks. Headquarters,
. . . . 5 Wks. on Location
On-Going Support: . . A,B,C,D,E,F,G,H,I
Full-Time Franchisor Support Staff: . . 11
EXPANSION PLANS:
   US: . . . . .All US
   Canada - Yes, . . . Overseas - Yes

MIRACLE METHOD BATHROOM RESTORATION

3732 W. Century Blvd., # 6
Inglewood, CA 90303
TEL: (800) 444-8827 (213) 671-4995
FAX: (213) 671-1146
Mr. Brian Pearce, President

Homes, apartments and hotels need improvements to their fixtures and tile in bathrooms and kitchens. Replacement costs thousands, refinishing costs hundreds! Plus, 30-50% of all fixtures are damaged during construction. YOU can fill this existing demand in your area. Earn a great income and pay all expenses from day one of operation.

HISTORY: . . . .
Established in 1978; . . 1st Franchised in 1979
Company-Owned Units (As of 12/1/1989): . .0
Franchised Units (12/1/1989): 109
Total Units (12/1/1989): 109
Distribution: US-54;Can-0;Overseas-55
   North America: . . . . 16 States
   Concentration: . . 29 in CA, 3 in MA, 2 in TX
Registered: . . . . CA,IL,OR,RI
. . . .
Average # of Employees: . . . . .4 FT
Prior Industry Experience: . . . . Helpful

FINANCIAL: NA
Cash Investment: $35K
Total Investment: $35K
Fees: Franchise - $20K
   Royalty: 7.5%, Advert: 3%
Contract Periods (Yrs.): 5/5
Area Development Agreement: .No
Sub-Franchise Contract: . . . . Yes
Expand in Territory: . . . . . . .No
Passive Ownership: . . . Not Allowed
Encourage Conversions: . . . . . Yes
Franchisee Purchase(s) Required: .No

FRANCHISOR TRAINING/SUPPORT:
Financial Assistance Provided: . . . . .No
Site Selection Assistance: . . . . . . .Yes
Lease Negotiation Assistance: . . . . .NA
Co-operative Advertising: . . . . No
Training: . . . . . . 1-3 Wks. Headquarters,
. . . . 2-3 Wks. On-site
On-Going Support: . . . . . . C,d,E,G,h,I
Full-Time Franchisor Support Staff: . . . 3
EXPANSION PLANS:
   US: . . . . .All US
   Canada - Yes, . . . Overseas - Yes

MOBILE TRIM TEAM

1239 Braselton Hwy.
Lawrenceville, GA 30243
TEL: (404) 339-1086 C
FAX:
Mr. Ken Clark, President

MOBILE TRIM TEAM franchisees offer the widest variety of repair services and complete upholstery to new and used car dealers, restaurants, motels, hotels, hospitals and wherever there is work to be done.

HISTORY: . . . .
Established in 1972; . . 1st Franchised in 1985
Company-Owned Units (As of 12/1/1989): . . 2
Franchised Units (12/1/1989): 18
Total Units (12/1/1989): 20
Distribution: US-20;Can-0;Overseas-0
North America: . . . . 12 States
Concentration: . . . 8 in TN, 2 in GA, 2 in MS
Registered: . . . . FL,RI
. . . .
Average # of Employees: . . . . .1 FT
Prior Industry Experience: . . . . Helpful

FINANCIAL:
Cash Investment: . . . .$
Total Investment: $22.5-28.5K
Fees: Franchise - $17.5K
Royalty: 5%, Advert: 1%
Contract Periods (Yrs.): . . . 10/10
Area Development Agreement: . Yes
Sub-Franchise Contract: . . . . .No
Expand in Territory: . . . . Yes
Passive Ownership: . . . Discouraged
Encourage Conversions: . . . . . NA
Franchisee Purchase(s) Required: .No

FRANCHISOR TRAINING/SUPPORT:
Financial Assistance Provided: . . . Yes(I)
Site Selection Assistance: . . . . . . .Yes
Lease Negotiation Assistance: . . . . .No
Co-operative Advertising: . . . . . . .Yes
Training: . . . . 2 Wks. Memphis, TN
. . . .
On-Going Support: . . . . .b,C,D,E,G,H,I
Full-Time Franchisor Support Staff: . . . 5
EXPANSION PLANS:
US: . . . . .All US
Canada - Yes, . . . Overseas - Yes

PERMA-GLAZE

132 S. Sherwood Village Dr.
Tucson, AZ 85710
TEL: (800) 332-7397 (602) 722-9718
FAX: (602) 296-4393
Ms. Joan Gucciardo, Exec. Secty.

Specialize in restoration/refinishing bathroom/kitchen fixtures, wall tile, appliances, etc. Refinishable materials include porcelain, fiberglass, acrylic, cultered marble, formica, appliances, shower enclosures, most building materials. 32 colors available. All work under warranty, residential or commercial. Services include chip repairs, fiberglass/acrylic repairs.

HISTORY: . . . . IFA
Established in 1978; . . 1st Franchised in 1981
Company-Owned Units (As of 12/1/1989): . . 1
Franchised Units (12/1/1989): 70
Total Units (12/1/1989): 71
Distribution: US-67;Can-2;Overseas-2
North America: . . . . 22 States
Concentration: . . 17 in CA, 10 in TX, 4 in PA
Registered: . . . . . CA,FL,IL,MI,NY,WA,WI
. . . .
Average # of Employees: . . . . .1 FT
Prior Industry Experience: . . . . Helpful

FINANCIAL:
Cash Investment: $24.5K
Total Investment: $24.5K
Fees: Franchise - $24.5K
Royalty: 0%, Advert: 0%
Contract Periods (Yrs.): . . . . Life
Area Development Agreement: . .No
Sub-Franchise Contract: . . . . .No
Expand in Territory: . . . . Yes
Passive Ownership: . . . . . .Allowed
Encourage Conversions: . . . . .No
Franchisee Purchase(s) Required: Yes

FRANCHISOR TRAINING/SUPPORT:
Financial Assistance Provided: . . . Yes(I)
Site Selection Assistance: . . . . .No
Lease Negotiation Assistance: . . . . .No
Co-operative Advertising: . . . . .No
Training: . . . . 5 Days Headquarters
. . . .
On-Going Support: . . . . .b,G,I
Full-Time Franchisor Support Staff: . . . 5
EXPANSION PLANS:
US: . . . . .All US
Canada - Yes, . . . Overseas - Yes

PROFUSION SYSTEMS

2851 S. Parker Rd., # 650
Aurora, CO 80015
TEL: (800) 777-FUSE (313) 337-1949
FAX: (313) 337-0790
Mr. William E. Gabbard, President

Selected as the No. 1 vinyl repair franchise by Entrepreneur Magazine in 1989. PROFUSION SYSTEMS services a $ 20 billion industry, including vinyl, leather and velour materials.

HISTORY: . . . . IFA
Established in 1980; . . 1st Franchised in 1984
Company-Owned Units (As of 12/1/1989): . .0
Franchised Units (12/1/1989): 154
Total Units (12/1/1989): 154
Distribution: US-150;Can-2;Overseas-2
North America: . . . . . 25 States, 1 Province
Concentration: . . . . OH, CA, ON
Registered: . . . . All Except AB
. . . .
Average # of Employees: . . . . .2 FT
Prior Industry Experience: . . . . Helpful

FINANCIAL:
Cash Investment: . . . .$
Total Investment: . . . .$
Fees: Franchise - $20.5K
Royalty: 6%, Advert: 5%
Contract Periods (Yrs.): 20/5
Area Development Agreement: . .No
Sub-Franchise Contract: . . . . .No
Expand in Territory: . . . . Yes
Passive Ownership: . . . Discouraged
Encourage Conversions: . . . . . NA
Franchisee Purchase(s) Required: Yes

FRANCHISOR TRAINING/SUPPORT:
Financial Assistance Provided: . . . . .No
Site Selection Assistance: . . . . . . .Yes
Lease Negotiation Assistance: . . . . .Yes
Co-operative Advertising: . . . . . . .Yes
Training: . . . . 2 Wks. Denver, CO
. . . .
On-Going Support: . . . .B,C,D,E,G,H,I
Full-Time Franchisor Support Staff: . . 10
EXPANSION PLANS:
US: . . . . .All US
Canada - Yes, . . . Overseas - Yes

SPR COUNTERTOPS & BATHTUB

3398 Sanford Dr.
Marietta, GA 30066
TEL: (404) 429-0232
FAX:
Mr. Larry Stevens, Sr., President

Repair, refinishing and touch-up of bathtubs, sinks, countertops, tile, appliances, fiberglass, acrylic spas, porcelain, cultured and natural marble. Complete training and operating and service and market manuals and on-going phone consultation. An Area Development Program to achieve financial independence through sub-dealers. Factory warranty for all major manufacturers.

HISTORY: . . . . IFA
Established in 1973; . . 1st Franchised in 1974
Company-Owned Units (As of 12/1/1989): . .2
Franchised Units (12/1/1989): 18
Total Units (12/1/1989): 20
Distribution: US-19;Can-1;Overseas-0
North America: . . . . . .9 States, 1 Province
Concentration: . . . 3 in VA, 2 in FL, 2 in MT
Registered: . . . .

Average # of Employees: . . . . .2-4 FT
Prior Industry Experience: . . . . . . Helpful

FINANCIAL:
Cash Investment: . . . .$
Total Investment: . . . .$
Fees: Franchise - $20K
  Royalty: 5%, Advert: 0%
Contract Periods (Yrs.): . . . . Infin.
Area Development Agreement: Yes/Inf
Sub-Franchise Contract: . . . . . Yes
Expand in Territory: . . . . Yes
Passive Ownership: . . . Discouraged
Encourage Conversions: . . . . . Yes
Franchisee Purchase(s) Required: Yes

FRANCHISOR TRAINING/SUPPORT:
Financial Assistance Provided: . . .Yes(D)
Site Selection Assistance: . . . . .Yes
Lease Negotiation Assistance: . . . . .No
Co-operative Advertising: . . . . . . .Yes
Training: . . . . 2 Wks. Headquarters
. . . .
On-Going Support: . . . . . .B,C,D,G,H,I
Full-Time Franchisor Support Staff: . . . 4
EXPANSION PLANS:
US: . . . . All US
Canada - Yes, . . . Overseas - Yes

SPR MARBLE RESTORATION

P. O. Box 830275
Stone Mountain, GA 30083
TEL: (404) 297-8944
FAX:
Mr. Rubin Cruz, Jr., President

Marble refinishing, repair and polishing of floors, walls, sculptured art, furniture, bathrooms and countertops. Restore marble, granite, travertine and terrazo stones in commercial and residential properties. Refinishing, repairing cracks, scratches, stains, worn and dull marble. Complete training, high-tech equipment, marketing and advertising sources available. Phone consultation. Lucrative work.

HISTORY: . . . .
Established in 1973; . . 1st Franchised in 1989
Company-Owned Units (As of 12/1/1989): . .2
Franchised Units (12/1/1989): 18
Total Units (12/1/1989): 20
Distribution: US-19;Can-1;Overseas-0
North America: . . . .
Concentration: . . . . .GA, NC, FL
Registered: . . . .

Average # of Employees: . . . . .2-4 FT
Prior Industry Experience: . . . . Helpful

FINANCIAL:
Cash Investment: $25K
Total Investment: $25K
Fees: Franchise - . . . .$
  Royalty: 25%, Advert: 0%
Contract Periods (Yrs.): . . Perpetual
Area Development Agreement: . Yes
Sub-Franchise Contract: . . . . . Yes
Expand in Territory: . . . . Yes
Passive Ownership: . . . Not Allowed
Encourage Conversions: . . . . . Yes
Franchisee Purchase(s) Required: Yes

FRANCHISOR TRAINING/SUPPORT:
Financial Assistance Provided: . . . . .NA
Site Selection Assistance: . . . . .Yes
Lease Negotiation Assistance: . . . .NA
Co-operative Advertising: . . . . .Yes
Training: . . . . . . .2-4 Wks. Atlanta, GA
. . . .
On-Going Support: . . . . . B,C,D,f,G,h,I
Full-Time Franchisor Support Staff: . . .2
EXPANSION PLANS:
US: . . . . All US
Canada - Yes, ...Overseas - No

SURFACE SPECIALISTS

2362 175th Ln., NW
Andover, MN 55304
TEL: (612) 753-2807 C
FAX: (612) 753-4943
Mr. Wayne McClosky, President

Repair, refinishing, recoloring of acrylic spas, formica countertops, cultured marble, fiberglass tubs and showers, porcelain tubs, PVC units. Factory authorized warranty service for over 30 manufacturers, service work for apartment complexes and major hotel/motel chains. Excellent opportunity.

HISTORY: . . . .
Established in 1981; . . 1st Franchised in 1982
Company-Owned Units (As of 12/1/1989): . .1
Franchised Units (12/1/1989): 11
Total Units (12/1/1989): 12
Distribution: US-11;Can-1;Overseas-0
North America: . . . . . .8 States, 1 Province
Concentration: . . . . 2 in IL, 2 in WI
Registered: . . . . FL,IL,ND,WI

Average # of Employees: . . . . .4 FT
Prior Industry Experience: . . . . Helpful

FINANCIAL:
Cash Investment: $9-20K
Total Investment: $9-20K
Fees: Franchise - $9-16.5K
  Royalty: 5%, Advert: 1%
Contract Periods (Yrs.): 10/10
Area Development Agreement: .No
Sub-Franchise Contract: . . . . .No
Expand in Territory: . . . . Yes
Passive Ownership: . . . Discouraged
Encourage Conversions: . . . . . Yes
Franchisee Purchase(s) Required: Yes

FRANCHISOR TRAINING/SUPPORT:
Financial Assistance Provided: . . .Yes(D)
Site Selection Assistance: . . . . .NA
Lease Negotiation Assistance: . . . .NA
Co-operative Advertising: . . . . . . .Yes
Training: . . . . . . 2-3 Wks. Headquarters
. . . .
On-Going Support: . . . . . . B,D,F,G,h,I
Full-Time Franchisor Support Staff: . . .9
EXPANSION PLANS:
US: . . . . All US
Canada - Yes, . . . Overseas - Yes

WORLDWIDE REFINISHING SYSTEMS / GNU
508 Lake Air Dr.
Waco, TX 76710
TEL: (800) 369-9361 (817) 776-4701
FAX:
Mr. Don Dwyer, President

We have mastered the ability to refinish, repair and recolor both modern and antique bath and kitchen fixtures using the exclusive GNU TUB Process. Save your customers up to 80% of replacement costs on porcelain, fiberglass, tile, marble, formica, china, acrylic and appliances. Government tested and approved.

HISTORY:	. . . . IFA
Established in 1970;	. . 1st Franchised in 1972
Company-Owned Units (As of 12/1/1989):	. . 1
Franchised Units (12/1/1989):	 190
Total Units (12/1/1989):	 191
Distribution:	. . . . US-187;Can-1;Overseas-3
North America:	. . . . 20 States
Concentration:	. . .19 in TX, 5 in OH, 5 in AZ
Registered:	. . . . All States
Average # of Employees:	. . . . .1 FT
Prior Industry Experience:	. . . . . . Helpful

FINANCIAL:
Cash Investment: $7.5-50K
Total Investment: $10.5-53.5K
Fees: Franchise - $7.5K
Royalty: 5%, Advert: 2%
Contract Periods (Yrs.): 10/10
Area Development Agreement: Yes/10
Sub-Franchise Contract: . . . . . .No
Expand in Territory: . . . . Yes
Passive Ownership: . . . . . .Allowed
Encourage Conversions: . . . . . Yes
Franchisee Purchase(s) Required: Yes

FRANCHISOR TRAINING/SUPPORT:
Financial Assistance Provided: . . . . .No
Site Selection Assistance: . . . . . . .NA
Lease Negotiation Assistance: . . . . .NA
Co-operative Advertising: . . . . . . .NA
Training: . . . . .1 Wk. Headquarters,
. . . . . .On-going Support and Training
On-Going Support: . . . . D,F,H,I
Full-Time Franchisor Support Staff: . . 20
EXPANSION PLANS:
US: . . . . .All US
Canada - Yes, ...Overseas - Yes

SUPPLEMENTAL LISTING OF FRANCHISORS

BATHTUB DOCTOR . . . . 631-B Dunedin St., Victoria BC V8T2L7 CAN
CHAKRAS . . . . 3814 Bloor St. W., Etobicoke ON M9B6C2 CAN
CROSSLAND FURNITURE RESTORATION . . . . 5679 Monroe St., # 208, Sylvania OH 43560
DOCTEUR BAIGNOIRE . . . . 631-B Dunedin St., Victoria BC V8T2L7 CAN
MARBLELIFE . . . . 39 Olde Ridgebury Rd., # F, Danbury CT 06817
PERMA CERAM ENTERPRISES . . . . 327 Village Place, Wyckoff NJ 07481
PERMA-BRITE . . . . P.O. Box 369, 88 Pierson Ln, Windsor CT 06095
SPEEDY VINYL . . . . 2 Sheppard Ave., E., # 900, Willowdale ON M2N5Y7 CAN
SPR STONE ART . . . . .3800 Wendell Dr., # 302, Atlanta GA 30336
WESTERN VINYL REPAIR . . . . 2851 S. Parker Rd., # 650, Aurora CO 80014

For a full explanation of the data provided in the Franchisor Format, please refer to Chapter 2, *"How To Use The Data."*

CHAPTER 23

HAIRSTYLING SALONS

ACCENT HAIR SALONS

211 S. Main St., # 1130
Dayton, OH 45402
TEL: (513) 461-0394 C
FAX:
Mr. Claude Patmon, President

America's #1 choice for total black hair care, featuring convenient walk-in service, prompt service, attractive mall location, affordable prices and a full range of black hair care service. A carefully-planned salon system, designed with today's black woman in mind.

HISTORY: . . . . IFA
Established in 1981; . . 1st Franchised in 1987
Company-Owned Units (As of 12/1/1989): . .2
Franchised Units (12/1/1989): 7
Total Units (12/1/1989): 9
Distribution: US-9;Can-0;Overseas-0
 North America: . . . . 5 States
 Concentration: . . .4 in OH, 2 in MD, 1 in GA
Registered: . . . . MD,MI
. . . .
Average # of Employees: . . . . 19 FT
Prior Industry Experience: . . . . Helpful

FINANCIAL:
Cash Investment: $35-40K
Total Investment: $125K
Fees: Franchise - $20K
 Royalty: 5%, Advert: 5%
Contract Periods (Yrs.): 10/10
Area Development Agreement: Yes/5
Sub-Franchise Contract: . . . . .No
Expand in Territory: . . . . . . Yes
Passive Ownership: . . . Discouraged
Encourage Conversions: . . . . .No
Franchisee Purchase(s) Required: .No

FRANCHISOR TRAINING/SUPPORT:
Financial Assistance Provided: . . . Yes(I)
Site Selection Assistance: . . . . . . .Yes
Lease Negotiation Assistance: . . . . .Yes
Co-operative Advertising: . . . . . . .Yes
Training: . . . . 3 Wks. Headquarters,
. . . . 2 Wks. Franchised Unit
On-Going Support: . . . . . . .C,D,E,F,H
Full-Time Franchisor Support Staff: . . .5
EXPANSION PLANS:
 US: . . . . .All US
 Canada - No, ... Overseas - No

CITY LOOKS By THE BARBERS

300 Industrial Blvd., NE
Minneapolis, MN 55413
TEL: (612) 331-8500
FAX: (612) 331-2821
Ms. Judie Johnson, Sales/RE Admin.

CITY LOOKS By THE BARBERS provides private, individual consultation and styling in tasteful, comfortable surroundings, filling a need for clients who place a strong emphasis on full-service, personalized hair care. CITY LOOKS franchise generates deep customer loyalty and up-scale sales.

HISTORY: . . . . IFA
Established in 1963; . . 1st Franchised in 1968
Company-Owned Units (As of 12/1/1989): . .8
Franchised Units (12/1/1989): 84
Total Units (12/1/1989): 92
Distribution: US-92;Can-0;Overseas-0
North America: . . . . 11 States
Concentration: . . 58 in MN, 10 in IA, 9 in WI
Registered: . . . . .All Except FL
. . . .
Average # of Employees: . . . . . . 4 FT, 5 PT
Prior Industry Experience: . . . . Helpful

FINANCIAL: OTC
Cash Investment: $5-18K
Total Investment: $37-155K
Fees: Franchise - $12.5K
    Royalty: 4%, Advert: 4%
Contract Periods (Yrs.): 15/5
Area Development Agreement: Yes/Var
Sub-Franchise Contract: . . . . .No
Expand in Territory: . . . . Yes
Passive Ownership: . . . . . .Allowed
Encourage Conversions: . . . . . Yes
Franchisee Purchase(s) Required: .No

FRANCHISOR TRAINING/SUPPORT:
Financial Assistance Provided: . . . Yes(I)
Site Selection Assistance: . . . . . . .Yes
Lease Negotiation Assistance: . . . .Yes
Co-operative Advertising: . . . . . . .Yes
Training: . . . . 5 Days At Site,
. . . . 5 Days Headquarters
On-Going Support: . . . .B,C,D,E,F,G,h,I
Full-Time Franchisor Support Staff: . . 63
EXPANSION PLANS:
US: . . . . .All US
Canada - Yes, . . . Overseas - Yes

COST CUTTERS FAMILY
HAIR CARE SHOPS

300 Industrial Blvd. NE
Minneapolis, MN 55413
TEL: (612) 331-8500
FAX: (612) 331-2821
Ms. Judie Johnson, Sales/RE Admin.

COST CUTTERS franchises provide low-cost, no-frills, hair services for the family, with each service being offered at a separate price. The franchisor created COST CUTTERS to meet the demand for providing the public with quality hair services and products at a moderate price.

HISTORY: . . . . IFA
Established in 1963; . . 1st Franchised in 1982
Company-Owned Units (As of 12/1/1989): . .4
Franchised Units (12/1/1989): 358
Total Units (12/1/1989): 362
Distribution: US-360;Can-2;Overseas-0
North America: . . . . . 23 States, 1 Province
Concentration: . 79 in MN, 72 in WI, 30 in CO
Registered: . . . . .All Except FL
. . . .
Average # of Employees: . . . . . . 4 FT, 8 PT
Prior Industry Experience: . . . . Helpful

FINANCIAL: OTC
Cash Investment: $5-18K
Total Investment: $28-95K
Fees: Franchise - $19.5K
    Royalty: 6%, Advert: 4%
Contract Periods (Yrs.): 15/5
Area Development Agreement: Yes/Var
Sub-Franchise Contract: . . . . .No
Expand in Territory: . . . . Yes
Passive Ownership: . . . . .Allowed
Encourage Conversions: . . . . . Yes
Franchisee Purchase(s) Required: .No

FRANCHISOR TRAINING/SUPPORT:
Financial Assistance Provided: . . . Yes(I)
Site Selection Assistance: . . . . . . .Yes
Lease Negotiation Assistance: . . . .Yes
Co-operative Advertising: . . . . . . .Yes
Training: . . . . 5 Days Headquarters,
. . . . 5 Days Site
On-Going Support: . . . .B,C,D,E,F,G,h,I
Full-Time Franchisor Support Staff: . . 63
EXPANSION PLANS:
US: . . . . .All US
Canada - Yes, . . . Overseas - Yes

CUSTOM CUTS

13850 Manchester
St. Louis, MO 63011
TEL: (314) 391-1717
FAX: (314) 227-9208
Mr. Bob Hanson, President

Family haircare at popular prices in prime locations that must meet our requirements in terms of population count in a 3-mile radius, auto traffic count and specific anchor requirements.

HISTORY: . . . .
Established in 1985; . . 1st Franchised in 1985
Company-Owned Units (As of 12/1/1989): . .6
Franchised Units (12/1/1989): 6
Total Units (12/1/1989): 12
Distribution: US-12;Can-0;Overseas-0
North America: . . . . 2 States
Concentration: . . . . 11 in MO, 1 in IL
Registered: . . . .
. . . .
Average # of Employees: . . . . 11 FT
Prior Industry Experience: . . . . Helpful

FINANCIAL:
Cash Investment: $80-110K
Total Investment: $80-110K
Fees: Franchise - $25K
    Royalty: 6%, Advert: 6%
Contract Periods (Yrs.): 10/10
Area Development Agreement: .No
Sub-Franchise Contract: . . . . .No
Expand in Territory: . . . . . . Yes
Passive Ownership: . . . . . .Allowed
Encourage Conversions: . . . . NA
Franchisee Purchase(s) Required: .No

FRANCHISOR TRAINING/SUPPORT:
Financial Assistance Provided: . . . . .No
Site Selection Assistance: . . . . . . .Yes
Lease Negotiation Assistance: . . . .Yes
Co-operative Advertising: . . . . . . .Yes
Training: . . . . 10 Days - 2 Wks. at
. . . . Headquarters
On-Going Support: . . . .A,B,C,D,E,F,H,I
Full-Time Franchisor Support Staff: . . .1
EXPANSION PLANS:
US: . . . . .All US
Canada - No, ...Overseas - No

EASY HAIR

1257-H Kennestone Circle
Marietta, GA 30066
TEL: (404) 426-0254
FAX:
Mr. Don Westbrook, President

EASY HAIR offers a unique system of operations and support which drastically reduces the risks faced by all new businesses. This system makes it possible for people with many varied experience levels to efficiently own and operate an EASY HAIR.

HISTORY: . . . .
Established in 1984; . . 1st Franchised in 1986
Company-Owned Units (As of 12/1/1989): . .1
Franchised Units (12/1/1989): 10
Total Units (12/1/1989): 11
Distribution: US-11;Can-0;Overseas-0
   North America: . . . . .1 State
   Concentration: . . . . 11 in GA
Registered: . . . .
. . . .
Average # of Employees: . . . . . . 8 FT, 2 PT
Prior Industry Experience: . . . . Helpful

FINANCIAL:
Cash Investment: $25-35K
Total Investment: $80-110K
Fees: Franchise - $20K
   Royalty: 5%, Advert: 2%
Contract Periods (Yrs.): 20/20
Area Development Agreement: Yes/20
Sub-Franchise Contract: . . . . .No
Expand in Territory: . . . . . . Yes
Passive Ownership: . . . Discouraged
Encourage Conversions: . . . . .No
Franchisee Purchase(s) Required: .No

FRANCHISOR TRAINING/SUPPORT:
Financial Assistance Provided: . . . Yes(I)
Site Selection Assistance: . . . . . . .Yes
Lease Negotiation Assistance: . . . .Yes
Co-operative Advertising: . . . . . . .Yes
Training: . . . 1 Wk. Headquarters, 1 Wk.
. . . . Field, 1 Wk. Site
On-Going Support: . . . . .a,B,C,D,E,F,H
Full-Time Franchisor Support Staff: . . . 4
EXPANSION PLANS:
   US: . . . . Southeast
   Canada - No, ...Overseas - No

FAMILY HAIRCUT STORE

398 Hebron Ave.
Glastonbury, CT 06033
TEL: (800)822-2557(CT) (203)659-1430
FAX:
Mr. Randall Gibbons, President

Quality haircare with the convenience of fast service, seven days, five nights a week, with no appointment necessary.

HISTORY: . . . . IFA
Established in 1985; . . 1st Franchised in 1987
Company-Owned Units (As of 12/1/1989): . .3
Franchised Units (12/1/1989): 24
Total Units (12/1/1989): 27
Distribution: US-27;Can-0;Overseas-0
   North America: . . . . 2 States
   Concentration: . . . . . . 25 in CT, 2 in MA
Registered: . . . .
. . . .
Average # of Employees: . . . . 5-8 FT, 2-4 PT
Prior Industry Experience: . . . . Helpful

FINANCIAL:
Cash Investment: $77-123K
Total Investment: $77-123K
Fees: Franchise - $23K
   Royalty: 6%, Advert: 0%
Contract Periods (Yrs.): 10
Area Development Agreement: Yes/10
Sub-Franchise Contract: . . . . . Yes
Expand in Territory: . . . . . . Yes
Passive Ownership: . . . . . .Allowed
Encourage Conversions: . . . . .No
Franchisee Purchase(s) Required: Yes

FRANCHISOR TRAINING/SUPPORT:
Financial Assistance Provided: . . . . No
Site Selection Assistance: . . . . . . .Yes
Lease Negotiation Assistance: . . . .Yes
Co-operative Advertising: . . . . . . .Yes
Training: . . . . .1 Wk. Headquarters,
. . . . .3 Days Site (Start-Up)
On-Going Support: . . . . B,C,D,E,I
Full-Time Franchisor Support Staff: . . . 5
EXPANSION PLANS:
   US: . . . . Northeast
   Canada - No, ...Overseas - No

FANTASTIC SAM'S, THE ORIGINAL FAMILY HAIRCUTTERS

3180 Old Getwell Rd.
Memphis, TN 38118
TEL: (800) 621-5307 (901) 363-8624 C
FAX: (901) 363-8946
Mr. John Lewis, President

FANTASTIC SAM'S is the largest and fastest-growing family haircare franchise in the world. We offer retail private label products for sale in the stores, flat weekly license and advertising fees (not % based) and extensive training for every member of the FANTASTIC SAM'S team.

HISTORY: . . . . IFA
Established in 1974; . . 1st Franchised in 1976
Company-Owned Units (As of 12/1/1989): . .1
Franchised Units (12/1/1989): 1337
Total Units (12/1/1989): 1338
Distribution: . . US-1218;Can-72;Overseas-48
   North America: . . . . 46 States, 8 Provinces
   Concentration: . .218 in CA, 110 in FL, 70 TX
Registered: . . . . .ALL
. . . .
Average # of Employees: . . . . . . 6 FT, 3 PT
Prior Industry Experience: . . . . Helpful

FINANCIAL:
Cash Investment: $20K
Total Investment: $59-123K
Fees: Franchise - $20-30K
   Royalty: 152/Wk., Advert: $70/Wk.
Contract Periods (Yrs.): 10/10
Area Development Agreement: .No
Sub-Franchise Contract: . . . . Yes
Expand in Territory: . . . . . . Yes
Passive Ownership: . . . Discouraged
Encourage Conversions: . . . . .No
Franchisee Purchase(s) Required: .No

FRANCHISOR TRAINING/SUPPORT:
Financial Assistance Provided: . . . . No
Site Selection Assistance: . . . . . . .Yes
Lease Negotiation Assistance: . . . .Yes
Co-operative Advertising: . . . . . . .Yes
Training: . . . . 8 Days Headquarters
. . . .
On-Going Support: . . . . . . B,C,D,E,h,I
Full-Time Franchisor Support Staff: . . 35
EXPANSION PLANS:
   US: . . . . .All US
   Canada - Yes, . . . Overseas - Yes

FIRST CHOICE HAIRCUTTERS

6465 Millcreek Dr., # 205
Mississauga, ON L5N5R3 CAN
TEL: (800) 387-8335 (416) 567-4180
FAX: (416) 567-5335
George Kostopoulos, Dir. Fran. Dev.

We are a chain of price-value, full-service family haircare shops, offering excellent franchisee service in areas of training, advertising, management expertise, R & D and field support. Our proven concept offers exclusive territories, excellent growth potential, a cash business with virtually no inventory and a strong corporate base of over 70 stores.

HISTORY: . . . . .IFA/CFA
Established in 1980; . . 1st Franchised in 1982
Company-Owned Units (As of 12/1/1989): . 75
Franchised Units (12/1/1989): 170
Total Units (12/1/1989): 245
Distribution: US-53;Can-192;Overseas-0
North America: . . . . . 3 States, 9 Provinces
Concentration: . . 109 in ON, 29 in OH, 19 FL
Registered: . . . . FL,IL,AB
. . . .
Average # of Employees: . . . . 4-6 FT, 2-4 PT
Prior Industry Experience: . . . . . . Helpful

FINANCIAL:
Cash Investment: $35-40K
Total Investment: $75-80K
Fees: Franchise - $25K
  Royalty: 6-10%, Advert: 2%
Contract Periods (Yrs.): 10/5
Area Development Agreement: Yes/15
Sub-Franchise Contract: . . . . . .No
Expand in Territory: . . . . Yes
Passive Ownership: . . . Discouraged
Encourage Conversions: . . . . . Yes
Franchisee Purchase(s) Required: .No

FRANCHISOR TRAINING/SUPPORT:
Financial Assistance Provided: . . . Yes(I)
Site Selection Assistance: . . . . .Yes
Lease Negotiation Assistance: . . . . .Yes
Co-operative Advertising: . . . . .Yes
Training: . . . . 1-2 Wks. Headquarters,
. . . . . . 10-13 Days Franchisee Store
On-Going Support: . . . . .B,C,D,E,G,H,I
Full-Time Franchisor Support Staff: . . 43
EXPANSION PLANS:
US: . . . .Northeast, Southeast,Midwest
Canada - Yes, . . . Overseas - Yes

GREAT CLIPS

3601 Minnesota Dr.
Minneapolis, MN 55435
TEL: (800) 999-5959 (612) 893-9088
FAX:
Ms. Carolyn Jensen, Fran. Devel.

High-volume haircutting salon, specializing in haircuts for entire family. Unique, attractive decor, with quality, comprehensive advertising programs. Strong, hands-on support to franchisees, excellent training programs. We offer real value to our customers. Tremendous growth opportunities.

HISTORY: . . . .
Established in 1982; . . 1st Franchised in 1983
Company-Owned Units (As of 12/1/1989): . .0
Franchised Units (12/1/1989): 197
Total Units (12/1/1989): 197
Distribution: US-197;Can-0;Overseas-0
North America: . . . . 12 States
Concentration: .50 in MN, 39 in CO, 28 in MO
Registered: . . . . FL,IL,IN,MN,WI
. . . .
Average # of Employees: . . . .6-10 FT, 2-4 PT
Prior Industry Experience: . . . . . . Helpful

FINANCIAL:
Cash Investment: $16-25K
Total Investment: $65-87.5K
Fees: Franchise - $12.5K
  Royalty: 6%, Advert: 5%
Contract Periods (Yrs.): 10/10
Area Development Agreement: . .No
Sub-Franchise Contract: . . . . . .No
Expand in Territory: . . . . Yes
Passive Ownership: . . . . . .Allowed
Encourage Conversions: . . . . . Yes
Franchisee Purchase(s) Required: .No

FRANCHISOR TRAINING/SUPPORT:
Financial Assistance Provided: . . . . .No
Site Selection Assistance: . . . . .Yes
Lease Negotiation Assistance: . . . . .Yes
Co-operative Advertising: . . . . .Yes
Training: . . . . . 3 Days HQ or Home For
. . . Franchisee, 4-5 Days Market Others
On-Going Support: . . . . . . .C,D,E,G,H
Full-Time Franchisor Support Staff: . . 17
EXPANSION PLANS:
US: . . . . Midwest, Southwest,Southeast
Canada - No, ... Overseas - Yes

GREAT EXPECTATIONS / HAIRCRAFTERS

125 S. Service Rd., P.O. Box 265
Jericho, NY 11753
TEL: (800) 992-0139 (516) 334-8400
FAX:
Mr. Don vonLiebermann, President

Full-service hair care salon that appeals to and attracts an 18-50 year-old image and fashion-conscious clientele. Salons offer contemporary hair care services, including precision haircuts, perms and coloring in a distinctive establishment. Franchise package offers a thoroughly modern, attractively-designed shop, streamlined equipment, operational support, advertising materials and assistance, personnel recruitment and training.

HISTORY: . . . . .IFA
Established in 1955; . . 1st Franchised in 1967
Company-Owned Units (As of 12/1/1989): . 28
Franchised Units (12/1/1989): 147
Total Units (12/1/1989): 185
Distribution: US-185;Can-0;Overseas-0
North America: . . . . 40 States
Concentration: . 34 in CA, 16 in NY, 16 in TX
Registered: . . . . All States
. . . .
Average # of Employees: . . . . 5-7 FT, 3-5 PT
Prior Industry Experience: . . . . . . Helpful

FINANCIAL: OTC-CUTC
Cash Investment: $50K
Total Investment: $83-176.5K
Fees: Franchise - $20K
  Royalty: 6%, Advert: 0%
Contract Periods (Yrs.): 15/5
Area Development Agreement: Yes/15
Sub-Franchise Contract: . . . . . Yes
Expand in Territory: . . . . Yes
Passive Ownership: . . . Discouraged
Encourage Conversions: . . . . . .No
Franchisee Purchase(s) Required: .No

FRANCHISOR TRAINING/SUPPORT:
Financial Assistance Provided: . . .Yes(D)
Site Selection Assistance: . . . . .Yes
Lease Negotiation Assistance: . . . . .Yes
Co-operative Advertising: . . . . .Yes
Training: . . . . . .7-10 Days Pre-Opening,
. . . . 7 Days Field
On-Going Support: . . . .B,C,D,E,F,G,H,I
Full-Time Franchisor Support Staff: . . 60
EXPANSION PLANS:
US: . . . . .All US
Canada - Yes, ...Overseas - No

LEMON TREE, A UNISEX HAIRCUTTING ESTABLISHMENT
3301 Hempstead Tnpk.
Long Island, NY 11756
TEL: (800) 345-9156 (516) 735-2828
FAX: (516) 735-1851
Mr. John Wagner, VP

LEMON TREE FAMILY HAIRCUTTERS offers complete haircare and grooming services to men, women and children at affordable prices. LEMON TREE offers franchise opportunities to individuals who have a strong desire to become financially independent. LEMON TREE offers some financing on the initial franchise fee and a portion of the equipment package. For a total investment of $26,000 - 35,000, a dream can become a reality.

HISTORY: . . . . .WIF
Established in 1974; . . 1st Franchised in 1976
Company-Owned Units (As of 12/1/1989): . .0
Franchised Units (12/1/1989): 63
Total Units (12/1/1989): 63
Distribution: US-63;Can-0;Overseas-0
North America: . . . . 3 States
Concentration: . . . 60 in NY, 2 in NJ, 1 in CT
Registered: . . . . FL,NY
. . . .
Average # of Employees: . . . . . . 5 FT, 2 PT
Prior Industry Experience: . . . . . . Helpful

FINANCIAL:
Cash Investment: $19-26K
Total Investment: $26.5-33.5K
Fees: Franchise - $7.5K
Royalty: 6%, Advert: . . $400/Wk.
Contract Periods (Yrs.): . . . 15/15
Area Development Agreement: . .No
Sub-Franchise Contract: . . . . .No
Expand in Territory: . . . . . . Yes
Passive Ownership: . . . . . .Allowed
Encourage Conversions: . . . . . Yes
Franchisee Purchase(s) Required: .No

FRANCHISOR TRAINING/SUPPORT:
Financial Assistance Provided: . . .Yes(D)
Site Selection Assistance: . . . . . . .Yes
Lease Negotiation Assistance: . . . .Yes
Co-operative Advertising: . . . . . . .Yes
Training: . . . . 5 Days Headquarters,
. . . . .5 Days On-site
On-Going Support: . . . . .C,D,E,F,G,H,I
Full-Time Franchisor Support Staff: . . .6
EXPANSION PLANS:
US: . . . . NY, NJ and CT
Canada - No, ...Overseas - No

MARYANN'S HAIRCRAFT

1581 W. Main St.
Willimantic, CT 06226
TEL: (203) 228-1987 C
FAX: (203) 228-1987
Mr. Louis Haddad, Jr., President

MARYANN'S HAIRCRAFT offers a complete image enhancement center. Easy to operate, multi-level profit centers integrate to yield high margins, client and staff loyalty and unparalleled opportunity. Emphasis on core services and products. Custom training in systems that generate success in a full-price environment.

HISTORY: . . . .
Established in 1977; . . 1st Franchised in 1987
Company-Owned Units (As of 12/1/1989): . .3
Franchised Units (12/1/1989): 0
Total Units (12/1/1989): 3
Distribution: US-3;Can-0;Overseas-0
North America: . . . . .1 State
Concentration: . . . . 4 in CT
Registered: . . . . .FL
. . . .
Average # of Employees: . . . . . . 5 FT, 3 PT
Prior Industry Experience: . . . . . . Helpful

FINANCIAL:
Cash Investment: $15-50K
Total Investment: $50-100K
Fees: Franchise - $15K
Royalty: 5%, Advert: 2.5%
Contract Periods (Yrs.): . . . 10/10
Area Development Agreement: Yes/10
Sub-Franchise Contract: . . . . . Yes
Expand in Territory: . . . . . . Yes
Passive Ownership: . . . . . .Allowed
Encourage Conversions: . . . . . Yes
Franchisee Purchase(s) Required: .No

FRANCHISOR TRAINING/SUPPORT:
Financial Assistance Provided: . . . Yes(I)
Site Selection Assistance: . . . . . . .Yes
Lease Negotiation Assistance: . . . .Yes
Co-operative Advertising: . . . . . . .Yes
Training: . . . . 2 Wks. Headquarters
. . . .
On-Going Support: . . . . a,B,C,D,E,F,g,I
Full-Time Franchisor Support Staff: . . 35
EXPANSION PLANS:
US: . . . . . . .Northeast and Southeast
Canada - No, ...Overseas - No

PRO-CUTS

3716 Rufe Snow Dr.
Fort Worth, TX 76180
TEL: (800) 542-2887 (817) 595-4171
FAX:
Mr. Donald H. Stone, Exec. Director

Professional haircuts for the whole family at affordable prices. PRO-CUTS exhibits a friendly, yet professional, atmosphere. Franchisees are provided with support in all phases of operation, as well as on-going training for employees.

HISTORY: . . . .
Established in 1982; . . 1st Franchised in 1984
Company-Owned Units (As of 12/1/1989): . 22
Franchised Units (12/1/1989): 72
Total Units (12/1/1989): 94
Distribution: US-94;Can-0;Overseas-0
North America: . . . . 4 States
Concentration: . . 74 in TX, 5 in OK, 4 in NM
Registered: . . . .
. . . .
Average # of Employees: . . . . .6 FT
Prior Industry Experience: . . . . . . Helpful

FINANCIAL:
Cash Investment: $10-25K
Total Investment: $35-85K
Fees: Franchise - $15-25K
Royalty: 6%, Advert: 5%
Contract Periods (Yrs.): . . . 10/10
Area Development Agreement: . Yes
Sub-Franchise Contract: . . . . .No
Expand in Territory: . . . . . . Yes
Passive Ownership: . . . . . .Allowed
Encourage Conversions: . . . . NA
Franchisee Purchase(s) Required: .No

FRANCHISOR TRAINING/SUPPORT:
Financial Assistance Provided: . . .Yes(D)
Site Selection Assistance: . . . . . . .Yes
Lease Negotiation Assistance: . . . .Yes
Co-operative Advertising: . . . . . . .Yes
Training: . . . . . . Varies at Headquarters
. . . .
On-Going Support: . . . .A,B,C,d,E,G,H,I
Full-Time Franchisor Support Staff: . . 22
EXPANSION PLANS:
US: . . . . Southwest
Canada - No, ...Overseas - No

SUPERCUTS

555 Northgate Dr.
San Rafael, CA 94903
TEL: (800) 999-2887 (415) 472-1170
FAX: (415) 472-1170
Ms. Deborah Steinberg, VP Fra. Dev.

SUPERCUTS shops provide affordable, stylish, custom haircare for men, women and children. SUPERCUTS' success is founded on the simple concept of the precision, mistake-proof, guaranteed haircut made possible by technical advances pioneered by SUPERCUTS and supported by a training program unrivaled in the industry.

HISTORY: . . . . IFA
Established in 1975; . . 1st Franchised in 1979
Company-Owned Units (As of 12/1/1989): 518
Franchised Units (12/1/1989): 35
Total Units (12/1/1989): 553
Distribution: US-553;Can-0;Overseas-0
North America: . . . . 36 States
Concentration: . . 169 in CA, 77 in TX, 46 FL
Registered: . . . .CA,FL,HI,IL,IN,MD,MI,NY
. . . . .OR,VA,WA,WI
Average # of Employees: . . . . 10-15 FT
Prior Industry Experience: . . . . . . Helpful

FINANCIAL:
Cash Investment: $50-100K
Total Investment: $54-133K
Fees: Franchise - $0-25K
Royalty: 10%, Advert: 5%
Contract Periods (Yrs.): 10/10
Area Development Agreement: Yes/Var
Sub-Franchise Contract: . . . . .No
Expand in Territory: . . . . Yes
Passive Ownership: . . . Discouraged
Encourage Conversions: . . . . . Yes
Franchisee Purchase(s) Required: .No

FRANCHISOR TRAINING/SUPPORT:
Financial Assistance Provided: . . . Yes(I)
Site Selection Assistance: . . . . . . .Yes
Lease Negotiation Assistance: . . . . .Yes
Co-operative Advertising: . . . . No
Training: . . . . . .5 Days Owner Training,
. . . . 5 Days Employee Training
On-Going Support: . . . . .B,C,D,E,G,H,I
Full-Time Franchisor Support Staff: . .175
EXPANSION PLANS:
US: . . . . NE, SE, S and Midwest
Canada - No, ...Overseas - No

WE CARE HAIR

7323 W. 90th St.
Bridgeview, IL 60455
TEL: (800) 323-8309 (312) 430-2552
FAX: (708) 430-8237
Mr. Anthony Siciliano, VP Fran. Dev.

Moderately-priced hair care centers. We provide assistance with real estate, site selection, construction and equipment, on-going operational support, financial assistance and advertising within the corporate structure.

HISTORY: . . . . IFA
Established in 1986; . . 1st Franchised in 1987
Company-Owned Units (As of 12/1/1989): . .3
Franchised Units (12/1/1989): 19
Total Units (12/1/1989): 22
Distribution: US-22;Can-0;Overseas-0
North America: . . . . 12 States
Concentration: . . . . 7 in IL, 5 in LA, 1 in VA
Registered: . . . . CA,FL,IL,MD,MI,VA
. . . .
Average # of Employees: . . . . . . 5 FT, 6 PT
Prior Industry Experience: . . . . . . Helpful

FINANCIAL:
Cash Investment: $55-80K
Total Investment: $55-80K
Fees: Franchise - $7.5K
Royalty: 8%, Advert: 4%
Contract Periods (Yrs.): 10/10
Area Development Agreement: . .No
Sub-Franchise Contract: . . . . .No
Expand in Territory: . . . . Yes
Passive Ownership: . . . . . .Allowed
Encourage Conversions: . . . . .No
Franchisee Purchase(s) Required: .No

FRANCHISOR TRAINING/SUPPORT:
Financial Assistance Provided: . . .Yes(D)
Site Selection Assistance: . . . . . . .Yes
Lease Negotiation Assistance: . . . . .Yes
Co-operative Advertising: . . . . . . .Yes
Training: . . . . 2 Wks. Headquarters
. . . .
On-Going Support: . . A,B,C,D,E,F,G,H,I
Full-Time Franchisor Support Staff: . .250
EXPANSION PLANS:
US: . . . . All US
Canada - Yes, ...Overseas - Yes

SUPPLEMENTAL LISTING OF FRANCHISORS

BARBERS, HAIRSTYLING FOR MEN & WOMEN . . . . 300 Industrial Blvd. NE, Minneapolis MN 55413
C.A.P. CENTERS . . . . 15 Engle St., # 304, Englewood NJ 07631
COMMAND PERFORMANCE . . . . .Baldwin Park II, 7 Alfred St., Woburn MA 01801
DAVID ALAN'S CUTS FOR KIDS . . . . 15 Engle St., # 304, Englewood NJ 07631
FAMILY HAIRCUT STORE . . . . 398 Hebron Ave., Glastonbury CT 06033
FANTASTIC SAM'S . . . . 55 Milner Ave., Scarborough ON M1S3P6   CAN
FOR PEANUTS ONLY . . . . .427 St. Paul Ave., Brantford ON N3R4N8   CAN
GREAT CUTS . . . . 3223 Crow Canyon Rd., # 220, San Ramon CA 94583
HAIR BEARS . . . . P.O. Box 1415, Mt. Pleasant SC 29465
HAIR PERFORMERS, THE . . . . 7327 W. 90th St., Bridgeview IL 60455
HAIRCRAFTERS . . . . 125 S. Service Rd., P.O. Box 265, Jericho NY 11753
HOUSE OF LORDS . . . . 639 Yonge St., Toronto ON M4Y1Z9   CAN
JOSEPH'S HAIR SALONS . . . . 22 Bobwhite Cres., Willowdale ON M2L2E1   CAN

LORD'S & LADY'S HAIR SALONS . . . . .450 Belgrade Ave., Boston MA 02132
MAGICUTS . . . . .2105 Midland Ave., # 1, Scarborough ON M1P3E3   CAN
MANTRAP INTERNATIONAL . . . . .8640 Seminole Blvd., Seminole FL 34642
SHAMPOO-CHEZ . . . . 1378 Soquel Ave., Santa Cruz CA 95062
THIRD DIMENSION CUTS . . . . 8015 Broadway, Everett WA 98203

CHAPTER 24

HEALTH / FITNESS / BEAUTY

AMERICAN MEDICAL WEIGHT ASSOCIATION
1735 Merriman Rd.
Akron, OH 44313
TEL: (800) 321-9517 (216) 869-0222
FAX:
Mr. Norb Meadows, Fran. Dir.

AMERICAN MEDICAL WEIGHT ASSOCIATION offers a proven, medically-supervised weight loss franchise. Includes counseling, behavior modification techniques and an exclusive product line of Diet Plus Supplement. Emphasis on franchise support and on-going training. Entrepreneurs and serious investor inquiries welcome.

HISTORY: . . . .
Established in 1979; . . 1st Franchised in 1980
Company-Owned Units (As of 12/1/1989): . . .0
Franchised Units (12/1/1989): 16
Total Units (12/1/1989): 16
Distribution: US-16;Can-0;Overseas-0
  North America: . . . . 4 States
  Concentration: . . .11 in OH, 2 in AL, 2 in VA
Registered: . . . . .FL
. . . .
Average # of Employees: . . . . . . 2 FT, 2 PT
Prior Industry Experience: . . . . Helpful

FINANCIAL:
Cash Investment: $40K
Total Investment: $40K
Fees: Franchise - $16.5K
  Royalty: 7%, Advert: 0%
Contract Periods (Yrs.): 5/5
Area Development Agreement: Yes/5
Sub-Franchise Contract: . . . . . .No
Expand in Territory: . . . . Yes
Passive Ownership: . . . Discouraged
Encourage Conversions: . . . . . Yes
Franchisee Purchase(s) Required: Yes

FRANCHISOR TRAINING/SUPPORT:
Financial Assistance Provided: . . . . .No
Site Selection Assistance: . . . . . . .Yes
Lease Negotiation Assistance: . . . . .Yes
Co-operative Advertising: . . . . .No
Training: . . . . 5 Days Headquarters
. . . . 2 Days Site
On-Going Support: . . . . . .C,D,E,G,H,I
Full-Time Franchisor Support Staff: . . .4
EXPANSION PLANS:
  US: . . . . .All US
  Canada - Yes, ...Overseas - Yes

CAROL BLOCK

7701 Bull Valley Rd.
McHenry, IL 60050
TEL: (815) 344-0488
FAX: (815) 344-2503
Mr. Neal Rohr, EVP

D'Plume is the state-of-the-art in equipment that removes superfluous hair permanently. D'Plume removes hair with lazer-like technology, high intensity light, - no needles - no pain - no scarring. In the age of AIDS, D'Plume eliminates the risk of infection from needle stick injuries.

HISTORY: . . . . IFA/CFA	FINANCIAL:	FRANCHISOR TRAINING/SUPPORT:
Established in 1937; . . 1st Franchised in 1988	Cash Investment: $35-40K	Financial Assistance Provided: . . . Yes(I)
Company-Owned Units (As of 12/1/1989): . 14	Total Investment: $60-100K	Site Selection Assistance: . . . . .Yes
Franchised Units (12/1/1989): 5	Fees: Franchise - $30K	Lease Negotiation Assistance: . . . . .Yes
Total Units (12/1/1989): 19	Royalty: 10%, Advert.: 3%	Co-operative Advertising: . . . . .NA
Distribution: US-14;Can-0;Overseas-5	Contract Periods (Yrs.): 10/5	Training: . . . . 6 Wks. Headquarters
North America: . . . . 2 States	Area Development Agreement: Yes/10	. . . .
Concentration: . . . . 14 in IL, 1 in WI	Sub-Franchise Contract: . . . . . Yes	On-Going Support: . . A,B,C,D,E,F,G,H,I
Registered: IL	Expand in Territory: . . . . Yes	Full-Time Franchisor Support Staff: . . 32
. . . .	Passive Ownership: . . . . . .Allowed	EXPANSION PLANS:
Average # of Employees: . . . . .3 FT	Encourage Conversions: . . . . . Yes	US: . . . . .All US
Prior Industry Experience: . . . . . . Helpful	Franchisee Purchase(s) Required: Yes	Canada - Yes, . . . Overseas - Yes

DOCTORS & NURSES WEIGHT CONTROL CENTERS

1600 N. Palafox
Pensacola, FL 32501
TEL: (800) 367-6391 (904) 438-7592
FAX:
Mr. Marty Uranker, Dir. Operations

Professionally-supervised weight control program, utilizing store-bought foods and nutritional, high-energy weight control supplements.

HISTORY:	FINANCIAL:	FRANCHISOR TRAINING/SUPPORT:
Established in 1987; . . 1st Franchised in 1987	Cash Investment: $25.5-35K	Financial Assistance Provided: . . . Yes(I)
Company-Owned Units (As of 12/1/1989): . .1	Total Investment: $35-66K	Site Selection Assistance: . . . . .Yes
Franchised Units (12/1/1989): 29	Fees: Franchise - $25.5K	Lease Negotiation Assistance: . . . . .Yes
Total Units (12/1/1989): 30	Royalty: 10%, Advert.: 2%	Co-operative Advertising: . . . . .Yes
Distribution: US-30;Can-0;Overseas-0	Contract Periods (Yrs.): 5/5	Training: . . . . 2 Wks. Headquarters
North America: . . . . 7 States	Area Development Agreement: Yes/5	. . . .
Concentration: . . . .7 in FL, 6 in GA, 3 in TN	Sub-Franchise Contract: . . . . . Yes	On-Going Support: . . . . B,C,d,E,F,G,h,I
Registered: . . . . .CA,VA,WA	Expand in Territory: . . . . Yes	Full-Time Franchisor Support Staff: . . 17
. . . .	Passive Ownership: . . . Discouraged	EXPANSION PLANS:
Average # of Employees: . . . . . . 2 FT, 1 PT	Encourage Conversions: . . . . . Yes	US: . . . . .All US
Prior Industry Experience: . . . . . . Helpful	Franchisee Purchase(s) Required: Yes	Canada - Yes, ...Overseas - No

FIFTH SEASON, THE

18518 Detroit Ave.
Lakewood, OH 44107
TEL: (216) 228-SUNY
FAX:
Mr. Mike Matynka, President

At FIFTH SEASON Tanning and Toning, we want to help each of our patrons to look and feel his/her absolute best. That's why we offer more than just a great tan. To achieve and maintain a healthy-looking appearance, we offer suntanning, daily aerobic program, exterior design body sculpting and massage therapy.

HISTORY:	FINANCIAL:	FRANCHISOR TRAINING/SUPPORT:
Established in 1984; . . 1st Franchised in 1988	Cash Investment: $70-82K	Financial Assistance Provided: . . . . . No
Company-Owned Units (As of 12/1/1989): . .1	Total Investment: . . . . . . $70-82 K	Site Selection Assistance: . . . . .Yes
Franchised Units (12/1/1989): 0	Fees: Franchise - $15K	Lease Negotiation Assistance: . . . .Yes
Total Units (12/1/1989): 1	Royalty: 10%, Advert.: 5%	Co-operative Advertising: . . . . .Yes
Distribution: US-1;Can-0;Overseas-0	Contract Periods (Yrs.): 10/10	Training: . . . . 2 Wks. Headquarters
North America: . . . . .1 State	Area Development Agreement: . .No	. . . .
Concentration: . . . . 1 in OH	Sub-Franchise Contract: . . . . . .No	On-Going Support: . . . . B,C,D,E,F,G,h,I
Registered:	Expand in Territory: . . . . Yes	Full-Time Franchisor Support Staff: . . . 2
. . . .	Passive Ownership: . . . Not Allowed	EXPANSION PLANS:
Average # of Employees: . . . . . . 1 FT, 1 PT	Encourage Conversions: . . . . . Yes	US: . . . . Ohio Only
Prior Industry Experience: . . . . . . Helpful	Franchisee Purchase(s) Required: .No	Canada - No, ...Overseas - No

GENERAL NUTRITION

921 Penn Ave.
Pittsburgh, PA 15222
TEL: (800) 223-2824 (412) 288-4600
FAX:
Mr. Jim Shallcross, GM Franchising

GENERAL NUTRITION is committed to becoming the leading provider of products, services and information in the self-care and personal health enhancement markets.

HISTORY: . . . . IFA	FINANCIAL: NYSE-GNC	FRANCHISOR TRAINING/SUPPORT:
Established in 1936; . . 1st Franchised in 1988	Cash Investment: $60K	Financial Assistance Provided: . . .Yes(D)
Company-Owned Units (As of 12/1/1989): 1100	Total Investment: $125K	Site Selection Assistance: . . . . . . .Yes
Franchised Units (12/1/1989): 27	Fees: Franchise - $15K	Lease Negotiation Assistance: . . . . .Yes
Total Units (12/1/1989): 1127	Royalty: 4%, Advert: 1%	Co-operative Advertising: . . . . . . .NA
Distribution: US-1127;Can-0;Overseas-0	Contract Periods (Yrs.): 10/5	Training: . . . . 2 Wks. Headquarters
North America: . . . . 49 States	Area Development Agreement: Yes/Var	. . . .
Concentration: . 115 in CA, 90 in PA,87 in FL	Sub-Franchise Contract: . . . . .No	On-Going Support: . . . . . B,C,D,E,G,h,I
Registered: . . . . All States	Expand in Territory: . . . . Yes	Full-Time Franchisor Support Staff: . . . 6
. . . .	Passive Ownership: . . . Not Allowed	EXPANSION PLANS:
Average # of Employees: . . . . . . 2 FT, 2 PT	Encourage Conversions: . . . . . Yes	US: . . . . All US
Prior Industry Experience: . . . . Helpful	Franchisee Purchase(s) Required: Yes	Canada - No, ... Overseas - Yes

GODDESSE OF LAS VEGAS NAIL SUPPLY SPECIALTY SHOPS

P.O. Box 71536
Las Vegas, NV 89170
TEL: (800) NAIL-BIS (702) 361-4544
FAX:
Ms. Marilyn Clark, President

The nail care revolution has become a world-wide business that is growing by leaps and bounds, and with it the demand for convenient, one-stop supply shops that have over 5,000 products for nails, hands and feet, along with nail services. Selling at both the wholesale and retail levels assures a great profit picture.

HISTORY:	FINANCIAL:	FRANCHISOR TRAINING/SUPPORT:
Established in 1970; . . 1st Franchised in 1984	Cash Investment: $40-50K	Financial Assistance Provided: . . . . .No
Company-Owned Units (As of 12/1/1989): . .3	Total Investment: $40-50K	Site Selection Assistance: . . . . . . .Yes
Franchised Units (12/1/1989): 5	Fees: Franchise - $15K	Lease Negotiation Assistance: . . . . .Yes
Total Units (12/1/1989): 8	Royalty: 5.5%, Advert: 3%	Co-operative Advertising: . . . . . . .Yes
Distribution: US-8;Can-0;Overseas-0	Contract Periods (Yrs.): 10/10	Training: . . . . .1-2 Wks. Denver, CO,
North America: . . . . 5 States	Area Development Agreement: . Yes	. . . . 2-4 Days On-site
Concentration:	Sub-Franchise Contract: . . . . . Yes	On-Going Support: . . . . .b,C,D,E,G,H,I
Registered: . . . . .MI	Expand in Territory: . . . . Yes	Full-Time Franchisor Support Staff: . . 15
. . . .	Passive Ownership: . . . Discouraged	EXPANSION PLANS:
Average # of Employees: . . . . . . 1 FT, 1 PT	Encourage Conversions: . . . . . Yes	US: . . . . All US
Prior Industry Experience: . . . . Helpful	Franchisee Purchase(s) Required: .No	Canada - Yes, . . . Overseas - Yes

GOUBAUD

280 Smith St.
Farmingdale, NY 11735
TEL: (516) 420-8000
FAX:
Ms. Maryann Backstrom, GM

Skin care and cosmetics.

HISTORY:	FINANCIAL:	FRANCHISOR TRAINING/SUPPORT:
Established in 1946; . . 1st Franchised in 1950	Cash Investment: $10-20K	Financial Assistance Provided: . . . . .No
Company-Owned Units (As of 12/1/1989): . .2	Total Investment: $20-40K	Site Selection Assistance: . . . . . . .Yes
Franchised Units (12/1/1989): 40	Fees: Franchise - $0	Lease Negotiation Assistance: . . . . .No
Total Units (12/1/1989): 42	Royalty: 0%, Advert: 5%	Co-operative Advertising: . . . . . . .Yes
Distribution: US-42;Can-0;Overseas-0	Contract Periods (Yrs.): . . . . 1/Inf.	Training: . . . . As Necessary Headquarters
North America:	Area Development Agreement: . .No	
Concentration:	Sub-Franchise Contract: . . . . .No	. . . .
Registered:	Expand in Territory: . . . . Yes	On-Going Support: . . A,B,C,D,E,F,G,H,I
. . . .	Passive Ownership: . . . . . .Allowed	Full-Time Franchisor Support Staff: . . 10
Average # of Employees: . . . . . . 1 FT, 2 PT	Encourage Conversions: . . . . . Yes	EXPANSION PLANS:
Prior Industry Experience: . . . . Helpful	Franchisee Purchase(s) Required: Yes	US: . . . . All US
		Canada - Yes, . . . Overseas - Yes

**HAIR REPLACEMENT SYSTEMS /
HAIR ASSOCIATES**
P.O. Box 939
Waitsfield, VT 05673
TEL: (800) 451-4580 (802) 496-5830
FAX: (802) 496-6604
Mr. Leo Benjamin, VP Fran. Dev.

Sales and service of non-surgical men's and women's hair replacement procedures.

HISTORY: . . . . IFA
Established in 1981; . . 1st Franchised in 1983
Company-Owned Units (As of 12/1/1989): . .0
Franchised Units (12/1/1989): 50
Total Units (12/1/1989): 50
Distribution: US-47;Can-3;Overseas-0
North America: . . . . 20 States, 2 Provinces
Concentration: . . . 9 in NY, 5 in PA, 4 in NC
Registered: . . . . CA,FL,IL,IN,MI,NY,RI,VA
. . . . .WI
Average # of Employees: . . . . . . 3 FT, 1 PT
Prior Industry Experience: . . . . Helpful

FINANCIAL:
Cash Investment: $25-100K
Total Investment: $25-100K
Fees: Franchise - . . . . $6.5K+
 Royalty: 6%, Advert: 0%
Contract Periods (Yrs.): 5/5
Area Development Agreement: .No
Sub-Franchise Contract: . . . . .No
Expand in Territory: . . . . Yes
Passive Ownership: . . . Discouraged
Encourage Conversions: . . . . Yes
Franchisee Purchase(s) Required: Yes

FRANCHISOR TRAINING/SUPPORT:
Financial Assistance Provided: . . . Yes(I)
Site Selection Assistance: . . . . . . .Yes
Lease Negotiation Assistance: . . . .Yes
Co-operative Advertising: . . . . . . .Yes
Training: . . . . .5 Days Phila., PA,
 . . . 5 Days Portland, ME, 5 Days Miami
On-Going Support: . . . . .B,C,D,E,G,H,I
Full-Time Franchisor Support Staff: . . 10
EXPANSION PLANS:
 US: . . . . .All US
Canada - Yes, ...Overseas - No

I NATURAL COSMETICS

355 Middlesex Ave.
Wilmington, MA 01887
TEL: (800) 9-MAKEUP (508) 658-8921
FAX:
Mr. Robert Greenberg, Chmn.

Unique retail cosmetic shop, specializing in skin care treatments and emphasizing customer education. Located primarily in major regional fashion malls. Merchandising includes out-of-shop demonstrations and classes. Most shops offer beauty services, facials, manicures, nail sculpturing, color consulting, ear piercing, hair removal, etc.

HISTORY: . . . . IFA/WIF
Established in 1970; . . 1st Franchised in 1972
Company-Owned Units (As of 12/1/1989): . .2
Franchised Units (12/1/1989): 84
Total Units (12/1/1989): 86
Distribution: US-74;Can-0;Overseas-12
North America: . . . . 25 States
Concentration: . . 13 in CA, 8 in MA, 7 in NC
Registered: . . . CA,FL,IL,IN,MD,MI,MN,VA
. . . . .WA
Average # of Employees: . . . . . . 3 FT, 6 PT
Prior Industry Experience: . . . . Helpful

FINANCIAL:
Cash Investment: $25-30K
Total Investment: $50-90K
Fees: Franchise - . . . .$NA
 Royalty: NA, Advert: . . . . . NA
Contract Periods (Yrs.): 10/5
Area Development Agreement: . Yes
Sub-Franchise Contract: . . . . .No
Expand in Territory: . . . . Yes
Passive Ownership: . . . Discouraged
Encourage Conversions: . . . . Yes
Franchisee Purchase(s) Required: Yes

FRANCHISOR TRAINING/SUPPORT:
Financial Assistance Provided: . . . . .No
Site Selection Assistance: . . . . . . .Yes
Lease Negotiation Assistance: . . . .Yes
Co-operative Advertising: . . . . . . .Yes
Training: . . . . 7 Days Site
. . . .
On-Going Support: . . A,B,C,D,E,F,G,H,I
Full-Time Franchisor Support Staff: . . 30
EXPANSION PLANS:
 US: . . . . .All US
Canada - Yes, . . . Overseas - Yes

**INCHES-A-WEIGH WEIGHT
LOSS CENTERS**
P. O. Box 550297
Birmingham, AL 35205
TEL: (205) 879-8663 C
FAX:
Mr. Scott Simcik, President

INCHES-A-WEIGH WEIGHT LOSS CENTERS offers a complete "Figure Correction" program for ladies 30-95 years of age. We provide Stage I (a nutritionally-sound, family-oriented weight loss with a compatible food line). State II (we reshape/redevelop the musculature of the 4 problem areas). Stage III (we finally tone the muscle group).

HISTORY: . . . .
Established in 1985; . . 1st Franchised in 1986
Company-Owned Units (As of 12/1/1989): . .4
Franchised Units (12/1/1989): 15
Total Units (12/1/1989): 19
Distribution: US-14;Can-0;Overseas-5
North America: . . . . 3 States
Concentration: . . . . .AL, GA, PR
Registered: . . . .
. . . .
Average # of Employees: . . . . . . 2 FT, 2 PT
Prior Industry Experience: . . . . Helpful

FINANCIAL:
Cash Investment: $25-40K
Total Investment: $25-40K
Fees: Franchise - $10K
 Royalty: 2%, Advert: 0%
Contract Periods (Yrs.): 3/3
Area Development Agreement: Yes/5
Sub-Franchise Contract: . . . . Yes
Expand in Territory: . . . . . . Yes
Passive Ownership: . . . Discouraged
Encourage Conversions: . . . . Yes
Franchisee Purchase(s) Required: Yes

FRANCHISOR TRAINING/SUPPORT:
Financial Assistance Provided: . . . .Yes
Site Selection Assistance: . . . . . . .Yes
Lease Negotiation Assistance: . . . .Yes
Co-operative Advertising: . . . . . . .Yes
Training: . . . . . . 1-2 Wks. Headquarters
. . . .
On-Going Support: . . . . .C,D,E,G
Full-Time Franchisor Support Staff: . .105
EXPANSION PLANS:
 US: . . . . .All US
Canada - Yes, . . . Overseas - Yes

JAZZERCISE

2808 Roosevelt St.
Carlsbad, CA 92008
TEL: (800) FIT IS IT (619) 434-2101
FAX:
Ms. Maureen Waldorf, Training

JAZZERCISE is the #1 Fitness Program in the world. All routines are choreographed by Judi Sheppard Misset and screened by an in-house exercise physiologist for safety and effectiveness. All JAZZERCISE instructors are pre-screened and carefully trained in dance technique, marketing and business operations. All instructors are certified by JAZZERCISE, INC.

HISTORY: . . . .
Established in 1969; . . 1st Franchised in 1983
Company-Owned Units (As of 12/1/1989): . .0
Franchised Units (12/1/1989): 4100
Total Units (12/1/1989): 4100
Distribution: . US-3800;Can-150;Overseas-150
North America: . . . . 50 States, 5 Provinces
Concentration: . . . .
Registered: . . . . .All
. . . .
Average # of Employees: . . . . . 1 FT, 1-2 PT
Prior Industry Experience: . . . . Helpful

FINANCIAL:
Cash Investment: $2K
Total Investment: $2K
Fees: Franchise - $500
  Royalty: 20%, Advert: 0%
Contract Periods (Yrs.): 5/5
Area Development Agreement: Yes/Var
Sub-Franchise Contract: . . . . . Yes
Expand in Territory: . . . . Yes
Passive Ownership: . . . Not Allowed
Encourage Conversions: . . . . . .No
Franchisee Purchase(s) Required: Yes

FRANCHISOR TRAINING/SUPPORT:
Financial Assistance Provided: . . . . .No
Site Selection Assistance: . . . . . . .Yes
Lease Negotiation Assistance: . . . . .No
Co-operative Advertising: . . . . . . .Yes
Training: . . . .3 Days Workshop Preceded
. . . . .by Video Training
On-Going Support: . . . . C,D,G,H,I
Full-Time Franchisor Support Staff: . .110
EXPANSION PLANS:
US: . . . . .All US
Canada - Yes, . . . Overseas - Yes

JENNY CRAIG WEIGHT LOSS
CENTRES

445 Marine View Dr., # 300
Del Mar, CA 92014
TEL: (619) 259-7000
FAX: (619) 259-2812
Mr. Gary Hawk, VP Franchising

JENNY CRAIG offers a proven structure for success in the dynamic weight loss industry. Our progarm provides personal counselling, great-tasting Jenny's Cuisine and a supportive, motivating environment. Seeking franchisees with a proven record of developing and motivating talent, dedication to client service and making a profit.

HISTORY: . . . . .IFA
Established in 1983; . . 1st Franchised in 1986
Company-Owned Units (As of 12/1/1989): 306
Franchised Units (12/1/1989): 109
Total Units (12/1/1989): 415
Distribution: . . . US-277;Can-0;Overseas-138
North America: . . . . 20 States
Concentration: . . . 110 in CA, 38 in IL, 14 FL
Registered: . . . . All Except AB
. . . .
Average # of Employees: . . . . . .10 FT, 2 PT
Prior Industry Experience: . . . . Helpful

FINANCIAL:
Cash Investment: $150-600K
Total Investment: . . . $150-1,000K
Fees: Franchise - $50K
  Royalty: 7%, Advert: 0%
Contract Periods (Yrs.): 10/10
Area Development Agreement: Yes/20
Sub-Franchise Contract: . . . . . .No
Expand in Territory: . . . . Yes
Passive Ownership: . . . Not Allowed
Encourage Conversions: . . . . . NA
Franchisee Purchase(s) Required: Yes

FRANCHISOR TRAINING/SUPPORT:
Financial Assistance Provided: . . . . .No
Site Selection Assistance: . . . . . . .Yes
Lease Negotiation Assistance: . . . . .No
Co-operative Advertising: . . . . . . .No
Training: . . . . 6 Wks. in San Diego,
. . . . .Los Angeles or Chicago
On-Going Support: . . . . A,B,C,D,E,F,H
Full-Time Franchisor Support Staff: . .100
EXPANSION PLANS:
US: . . . . Midwest, South and East
Canada - Yes, ...Overseas - No

LADY OF AMERICA

25231 Grogans Mill Rd., # 510
Woodlands, TX 77380
TEL: (713) 367-8880
FAX: (713) 292-1206
Mr. Roger Wittenberns, President

This chain of ultra-modern fitness centers positions its locations in neighborhood retail centers. The company features collection of monthly dues from its members by electronic funds transfer. Often referred to as the McDonald's of fitness.

HISTORY: . . . .
Established in 1984; . . 1st Franchised in 1986
Company-Owned Units (As of 12/1/1989): . .9
Franchised Units (12/1/1989): 31
Total Units (12/1/1989): 40
Distribution: US-40;Can-0;Overseas-0
North America: . . . . .1 State
Concentration: . . . . 40 in TX
Registered: . . . .
. . . .
Average # of Employees: . . . . . . 2 FT, 7 PT
Prior Industry Experience: . . . . Helpful

FINANCIAL:
Cash Investment: $40K
Total Investment: $99K
Fees: Franchise - $25K
  Royalty: 10-5%, Advert: . . . 2-5%
Contract Periods (Yrs.): 10/5
Area Development Agreement: Yes/1
Sub-Franchise Contract: . . . . . .No
Expand in Territory: . . . . Yes
Passive Ownership: . . . . . .Allowed
Encourage Conversions: . . . . . Yes
Franchisee Purchase(s) Required: .No

FRANCHISOR TRAINING/SUPPORT:
Financial Assistance Provided: . . .Yes(D)
Site Selection Assistance: . . . . . . .Yes
Lease Negotiation Assistance: . . . . .Yes
Co-operative Advertising: . . . . . . .Yes
Training: . . . . 35 Hrs. Headquarters,
. . . . . 30 Days Pre-sale Site, On-going
On-Going Support: . . . . . .a,c,d,E,G,H,I
Full-Time Franchisor Support Staff: . . 38
EXPANSION PLANS:
US: . . . . .All US
Canada - No, ...Overseas - No

LEAN LINE

151 New World Way
South Plainfield, NJ 07080
TEL: (201) 757-7677
FAX:
Ms. Lorraine Wurtzel, Co-Director

The LEAN LINE weight loss program provides nutritional, psychological, inspirational and image building techniques, supervised by Drs. Arnold Lazarus and Hans Fisher of Rutgers Univ. The "point system" diet adjusts to comtemporary life styles and tastes. Four franchisees, nationwide sales began 1/88.

HISTORY:	FINANCIAL:	FRANCHISOR TRAINING/SUPPORT:
Established in 1968; . . 1st Franchised in 1969	Cash Investment: $10-25K	Financial Assistance Provided: . . . . . No
Company-Owned Units (As of 12/1/1989): . . 1	Total Investment: $10-15K	Site Selection Assistance: . . . . Yes
Franchised Units (12/1/1989): 3	Fees: Franchise - $5-15K	Lease Negotiation Assistance: . . . . . Yes
Total Units (12/1/1989): 4	Royalty: 10%, Advert: 10%	Co-operative Advertising: . . . . Yes
Distribution: US-4;Can-0;Overseas-0	Contract Periods (Yrs.): 5/15	Training: . . . . 2 Wks. Initially,
North America: . . . . 2 States	Area Development Agreement: . .No	. . . . On-going As Needed
Concentration: . . . . 3 in NJ, 1 in NY	Sub-Franchise Contract: . . . . . .No	On-Going Support: . . . . . B,c,d,e,G,H,I
Registered: . . . . NY	Expand in Territory: . . . . Yes	Full-Time Franchisor Support Staff: . . 30
. . . .	Passive Ownership: . . . Not Allowed	EXPANSION PLANS:
Average # of Employees:	Encourage Conversions: . . . . . .No	US: . . . . All US
Prior Industry Experience: . . . . Helpful	Franchisee Purchase(s) Required: Yes	Canada - No, ... Overseas - No

LIFE TREND WEIGHT LOSS/ EXERCISE CENTERS

106 W. 31st
Independence, MO 64055
TEL: (800) 821-3126 (816) 254-0805
FAX: (816) 254-1557
Mr. Glen Henson, VP

Our LIFE TREND WEIGHT LOSS PROGRAM is combined with a small exercise center, which leads to permanent weight loss. We provide many options, I.E., Isokinetic exercisers, treadmills and bikes, toning tables, body wraps and tanning beds. We provide full training and follow-up.

HISTORY:	FINANCIAL:	FRANCHISOR TRAINING/SUPPORT:
Established in 1977; . . 1st Franchised in 1979	Cash Investment: $20-30K	Financial Assistance Provided: . . . Yes(D)
Company-Owned Units (As of 12/1/1989): . . 0	Total Investment: $25-35K	Site Selection Assistance: . . . . No
Franchised Units (12/1/1989): 350	Fees: Franchise - $15K	Lease Negotiation Assistance: . . . . . No
Total Units (12/1/1989): 350	Royalty: 0%, Advert: 0%	Co-operative Advertising: . . . . No
Distribution: . . . US-300;Can-20;Overseas-30	Contract Periods (Yrs.): 10/10	Training: . . . . 3 Days Headquarters
North America: . . . . . . 30 States, 5 Provinces	Area Development Agreement: . .No	. . . .
Concentration: . 40 in ME, 30 in KS, 26 in NE	Sub-Franchise Contract: . . . . . .No	On-Going Support: . . . . E,G,H,I
Registered: . . . . .All	Expand in Territory: . . . . Yes	Full-Time Franchisor Support Staff: . . . 6
. . . .	Passive Ownership: . . . Discouraged	EXPANSION PLANS:
Average # of Employees: . . . . . . 1 FT, 2 PT	Encourage Conversions: . . . . . .No	US: . . . . All US
Prior Industry Experience: . . . . . Necessary	Franchisee Purchase(s) Required: .No	Canada - Yes, . . . Overseas - Yes

NUTRI/SYSTEM

3901 Commerce Ave.
Willow Grove, PA 19090
TEL: (800) UR-NUTRI (215) 784-5600
FAX:
Mr. Joel D. Rosen, Dir. Fran. Dev.

No industry is as dynamic and full of opportunity as the weight loss industry. Reasons for wanting to lose weight are more compelling than ever. Medical information says it is healthier to be thinner. The population continues to age. NUTRI/SYSTEM is the leader in the industry and plans to continue.

HISTORY: IFA	FINANCIAL:	FRANCHISOR TRAINING/SUPPORT:
Established in 1971; . . 1st Franchised in 1973	Cash Investment: $75-125K	Financial Assistance Provided: . . . . . No
Company-Owned Units (As of 12/1/1989): 233	Total Investment: $75-200K	Site Selection Assistance: . . . . No
Franchised Units (12/1/1989): 1243	Fees: Franchise - $13-60K	Lease Negotiation Assistance: . . . . . No
Total Units (12/1/1989): 1476	Royalty: 7%, Advert: 0%	Co-operative Advertising: . . . . Yes
Distribution: . . US-1282;Can-179;Overseas-15	Contract Periods (Yrs.): 10/10	Training: . . . . .1 Wk. Headquarters,
North America: . . . . 50 States, 9 Provinces	Area Development Agreement: . .No	. . . . 1 Wk. Franchisee Location
Concentration:	Sub-Franchise Contract: . . . . . .No	On-Going Support: . . . . . C,D,E,G,H,I
Registered: . . . . .All	Expand in Territory: . . . . Yes	Full-Time Franchisor Support Staff: . . . 4
. . . .	Passive Ownership: . . . Discouraged	EXPANSION PLANS:
Average # of Employees: . . . . . . 1 FT, 6 PT	Encourage Conversions: . . . . . .No	US: . . . . Midwest and South
Prior Industry Experience: . . . . Helpful	Franchisee Purchase(s) Required: Yes	Canada - Yes, . . . Overseas - Yes

PAT'S PLACE

1356 Muirlands Vista
La Jolla, CA 92037
TEL: (800) CLOS-CUT (619) 459-7266
FAX: (619) 459-3286
Mr. Pat Curran, President

Unique opportunity in the highly profitable, growth business of removing unwanted facial and body hair. Specializing in "Pat's Bikini Cuts," guaranteed to last 3 months. Custom merkin fitting. Free initial consultation. Average customer spends $225 per year for services. Great customer loyalty. Complete turn-key operation. Initial investment under $25,000. Learn from the pros!

HISTORY: . . . .
Established in 1982; . . 1st Franchised in 1986
Company-Owned Units (As of 12/1/1989): . .3
Franchised Units (12/1/1989): 4
Total Units (12/1/1989): 7
Distribution: US-6;Can-1;Overseas-0
North America: . . . . . .3 States, 1 Province
Concentration: . . . 3 in CA, 1 in KY, 1 in TN
Registered: . . . . CA,OR,AB
. . . .
Average # of Employees: . . . . . . 2 FT, 3 PT
Prior Industry Experience: . . . . Helpful

FINANCIAL: OTC-RUDI
Cash Investment: $25-45K
Total Investment: $35-75K
Fees: Franchise - $12K
 Royalty: 4%, Advert: 1%
Contract Periods (Yrs.): 10/10
Area Development Agreement: Yes/10
Sub-Franchise Contract: . . . . . .No
Expand in Territory: . . . . .No
Passive Ownership: . . . Discouraged
Encourage Conversions: . . . . Yes
Franchisee Purchase(s) Required: Yes

FRANCHISOR TRAINING/SUPPORT:
Financial Assistance Provided: . . .Yes(D)
Site Selection Assistance: . . . . . . .Yes
Lease Negotiation Assistance: . . . .Yes
Co-operative Advertising: . . . . . . .Yes
Training: . . . . 4 Wks. Headquarters,
 . . . . 2 Wks. Site
On-Going Support: . . . . . .A,C,D,G,H,I
Full-Time Franchisor Support Staff: . . . 5
EXPANSION PLANS:
 US: . . . . All US
 Canada - Yes, . . . Overseas - Yes

PHYSICIANS WEIGHT LOSS CENTRES OF CANADA

1235 Bay St., # 400
Toronto, ON M5R3K4 CAN
TEL: (416) 921-7952
FAX: (416) 966-5040
Ms. Jeannie Butler, Dir. CAN Ops.

PHYSICIANS WEIGHT LOSS CENTRES was established in 1979 by Mr. Charles Sekeres. We offer a medically-supervised weight loss and weight maintenance program, offering fast, safe and guaranteed weight loss.

HISTORY: . . . . .IFA/CFA
Established in 1979; . . 1st Franchised in 1987
Company-Owned Units (As of 12/1/1989): . 30
Franchised Units (12/1/1989): 407
Total Units (12/1/1989): 437
Distribution: US-426;Can-11;Overseas-0
North America: . . . . 35 States, 2 Provinces
Concentration: . 34 in FL, 34 in GA, 28 in VA
Registered: . . . . FL,IL,IN,MI,RI,VA
. . . .
Average # of Employees: . . . . .5 FT
Prior Industry Experience: . . . . Helpful

FINANCIAL:
Cash Investment: $25-50K
Total Investment: $70-110K
Fees: Franchise - $25K
 Royalty: 10%, Advert: . . . $2,500
Contract Periods (Yrs.): 3/5
Area Development Agreement: . .No
Sub-Franchise Contract: . . . . . .No
Expand in Territory: . . . . Yes
Passive Ownership: . . . Not Allowed
Encourage Conversions: . . . . Yes
Franchisee Purchase(s) Required: Yes

FRANCHISOR TRAINING/SUPPORT:
Financial Assistance Provided: . . .Yes(D)
Site Selection Assistance: . . . . . . .Yes
Lease Negotiation Assistance: . . . .Yes
Co-operative Advertising: . . . . . . .Yes
Training: . . . . 3 Wks. Akron, OH
. . . .
On-Going Support: . . . .A,b,C,D,E,G,H,I
Full-Time Franchisor Support Staff: . . 76
EXPANSION PLANS:
 US: . . . . Northeast
 Canada - Yes, ...Overseas - No

SLENDER CENTER

6515 Grand Teton Pl., # 241
Madison, WI 53719
TEL: (608) 833-1477 C
FAX:
Ms. Jean Geurink, President

SLENDER CENTER offers a new program for the 90's. Innovative program for clients using regular foods and education in "self-talk" behavior modification with use of audio tapes. Marketing and advertising are innovative. Full support to franchisee in training, sales, nutritional and psychological education. Tried and tested, celebrating 10 years!

HISTORY: . . . .
Established in 1979; . . 1st Franchised in 1981
Company-Owned Units (As of 12/1/1989): . .2
Franchised Units (12/1/1989): 33
Total Units (12/1/1989): 35
Distribution: US-35;Can-0;Overseas-0
North America: . . . . 7 States
Concentration: . . . 24 in WI, 4 in MI, 3 in NY
Registered: . . . . . IL,MI,MN,NY,RI,VA,WI
. . . .
Average # of Employees: . . . . . 1-2 FT, 2 PT
Prior Industry Experience: . . . . Helpful

FINANCIAL:
Cash Investment: $23-50K
Total Investment: $23-50K
Fees: Franchise - $12-27K
 Royalty: 5%, Advert: . . . . . . NA
Contract Periods (Yrs.): 5/5
Area Development Agreement: . .No
Sub-Franchise Contract: . . . . . .No
Expand in Territory: . . . . .No
Passive Ownership: . . . . . .Allowed
Encourage Conversions: . . . . .No
Franchisee Purchase(s) Required: Yes

FRANCHISOR TRAINING/SUPPORT:
Financial Assistance Provided: . . . . . No
Site Selection Assistance: . . . . . . .Yes
Lease Negotiation Assistance: . . . .Yes
Co-operative Advertising: . . . . . . .No
Training: . . . . 5 Days Headquarters,
. . . . 5 Days Site
On-Going Support: . . . . . .b,C,D,E,G,H
Full-Time Franchisor Support Staff: . . . 7
EXPANSION PLANS:
 US: . . . . . Midwest, Southeast, S & E
 Canada - No, ...Overseas - No

SLIM TAN TOTAL BEAUTY CARE

8040 E. Mill Plain Blvd.
Vancouver, WA 98661
TEL: (206) 693-4118 C
FAX:
Ms. Marie Bell, Owner

Exclusive weight and inch loss method. Hair care, nail care and sculptured nails. Make-up. Electrolysis hair removal (skin care). Tanning. Hot tubbing and massage therapy.

HISTORY: . . . .
Established in 1985; . . 1st Franchised in 1986
Company-Owned Units (As of 12/1/1989): . . 1
Franchised Units (12/1/1989): 3
Total Units (12/1/1989): 4
Distribution: US-4;Can-0;Overseas-0
North America: . . . . 2 States
Concentration: . . . . .3 in WA, 1 in OR
Registered: . . . . OR,WA
. . . .
Average # of Employees: . . . . . . 3 FT, 2 PT
Prior Industry Experience: . . . . . . Helpful

FINANCIAL:
Cash Investment: $35-50K
Total Investment: $35-75K
Fees: Franchise - $15K
Royalty: 3%, Advert: . . . .
Contract Periods (Yrs.): 10/10
Area Development Agreement: Yes/10
Sub-Franchise Contract: . . . . . .No
Expand in Territory: . . . . Yes
Passive Ownership: . . . . . .Allowed
Encourage Conversions: . . . . . Yes
Franchisee Purchase(s) Required: Yes

FRANCHISOR TRAINING/SUPPORT:
Financial Assistance Provided: . . . . . No
Site Selection Assistance: . . . . . . .Yes
Lease Negotiation Assistance: . . . . .Yes
Co-operative Advertising: . . . . .Yes
Training: . . . . . .Minimum 2 Wks. Head-
. . . . quarters
On-Going Support: . . . . .B,C,D,E,G,H,I
Full-Time Franchisor Support Staff: . . . 6
EXPANSION PLANS:
US: . . . . Northwest
Canada - No, ...Overseas - No

STOP SMOKING PLAN

P.O. Box 232
E. Amherst, NY 14051
TEL: (716) 688-4573
FAX:
Mr. Fredrica P. Nixon, President

We offer a 10-day stop smoking program which makes it easy to quit. Specifically suited for corporate teaching, which is a big market today. Also, we have a kit which you can retail for $19.95 for additional profit. We teach you how to capture the corporate market!

HISTORY: . . . .
Established in 1981; . . 1st Franchised in 1988
Company-Owned Units (As of 12/1/1989): . .2
Franchised Units (12/1/1989): 4
Total Units (12/1/1989): 6
Distribution: US-6;Can-0;Overseas-0
North America: . . . . 6 States
Concentration: . . . .
Registered: . . . .
. . . .
Average # of Employees: . . . . . . 2 FT, 1 PT
Prior Industry Experience: . . . . . . Helpful

FINANCIAL:
Cash Investment: $1.5-5K
Total Investment: $6K
Fees: Franchise - $1.5-5K
Royalty: 0%, Advert: 0%
Contract Periods (Yrs.): . . . .
Area Development Agreement: . Yes
Sub-Franchise Contract: . . . . . Yes
Expand in Territory: . . . . Yes
Passive Ownership: . . . . . .Allowed
Encourage Conversions: . . . . .No
Franchisee Purchase(s) Required: .No

FRANCHISOR TRAINING/SUPPORT:
Financial Assistance Provided: . . .Yes(D)
Site Selection Assistance: . . . . . . .Yes
Lease Negotiation Assistance: . . . . .Yes
Co-operative Advertising: . . . . .Yes
Training: . . . . . . 2 Days Buffalo, NY or
. . . . .Through Training Manual
On-Going Support: . . . . h,I
Full-Time Franchisor Support Staff: . . . 3
EXPANSION PLANS:
US: . . . . All US
Canada - Yes, ...Overseas - No

SUNBANQUE ISLAND TANNING

2533A Yonge St.
Toronto, ON M4P2H9 CAN
TEL: (416) 488-5838 C
FAX:
Mr. Joel Giusto, President

SUNBANQUE ISLAND TANNING is a full-service suntan salon with complete and exclusive inventory control and management.

HISTORY: . . . .
Established in 1983; . . 1st Franchised in 1984
Company-Owned Units (As of 12/1/1989): . .4
Franchised Units (12/1/1989): 11
Total Units (12/1/1989): 15
Distribution: US-7;Can-8;Overseas-0
North America: . . . . . 1 State, 1 Province
Concentration: . . . . .8 in MA, 7 in ON
Registered: . . . .
. . . .
Average # of Employees: . . . . . . 1 FT, 1 PT
Prior Industry Experience: . . . . . . Helpful

FINANCIAL:
Cash Investment: $10-20K
Total Investment: $30-40K
Fees: Franchise - . . . .$
Royalty: Flat, Advert: 3%
Contract Periods (Yrs.): 5/5
Area Development Agreement: Yes/5
Sub-Franchise Contract: . . . . .No
Expand in Territory: . . . . Yes
Passive Ownership: . . . Discouraged
Encourage Conversions: . . . . . Yes
Franchisee Purchase(s) Required: .No

FRANCHISOR TRAINING/SUPPORT:
Financial Assistance Provided: . . .Yes(D)
Site Selection Assistance: . . . . . . .Yes
Lease Negotiation Assistance: . . . . .Yes
Co-operative Advertising: . . . . .Yes
Training: . . . . 1 Wk. Headquarters
. . . .
On-Going Support: . . . . . . B,C,D,E,F,I
Full-Time Franchisor Support Staff: . . . 8
EXPANSION PLANS:
US: . . . . All US
Canada - Yes, . . . Overseas - Yes

TRANSFORM WEIGHT LOSS & WELLNESS CENTER
29634 Ramsey Ct.
Temecula, CA 92390
TEL: (714) 699-5274 C
FAX:
Mr. William Prouty, VP

A unique and powerful system that uses the latest in technology and breakthrough systems. Many entertainment and sports celebrities will endorse. Fast and strong cash flow, with outstanding return on investment. High level of repeat business for excellent profitability. Pioneering the 1990's age of wellness.

HISTORY: . . . .
Established in 1989; . . 1st Franchised in 1990
Company-Owned Units (As of 12/1/1989): . .3
Franchised Units (12/1/1989): 0
Total Units (12/1/1989): 3
Distribution: US-3;Can-0;Overseas-0
North America: . . . . .1 State
Concentration: . . . . 3 in CA
Registered: . . . . CA
. . . .
Average # of Employees: . . . . . . 3 FT, 5 PT
Prior Industry Experience: . . . . Helpful

FINANCIAL:
Cash Investment: $15-20K
Total Investment: $37.5K
Fees: Franchise - $22.5K
  Royalty: $200/Mo., Advert:$100/Mo.
Contract Periods (Yrs.): 7/7
Area Development Agreement: . .No
Sub-Franchise Contract: . . . . .No
Expand in Territory: . . . . Yes
Passive Ownership: . . . Discouraged
Encourage Conversions: . . . . .No
Franchisee Purchase(s) Required: Yes

FRANCHISOR TRAINING/SUPPORT:
Financial Assistance Provided: . . . Yes(I)
Site Selection Assistance: . . . . . . .Yes
Lease Negotiation Assistance: . . . . . No
Co-operative Advertising: . . . . No
Training: . . . . 5 Days Headquarters
. . . .
On-Going Support: . . . A,B,C,D,e,F,G,h,I
Full-Time Franchisor Support Staff: . . .7
EXPANSION PLANS:
US: . . . . .All US
Canada - Yes, ...Overseas - No

WOMEN AT LARGE FITNESS SALON
1020 S. 48th Ave.
Yakima, WA 98908
TEL: (509) 965-0115
FAX:
Ms. Sharlyne Powell, Pres./CEO

Physical fitness, image development, wellness system for the larger woman with a market base of 35-40 million women in the US alone. No other program is geared to this clientele base, which has been completely overlooked in the fitness world. Sophisticated programming, training and operations.

HISTORY: . . . .
Established in 1983; . . 1st Franchised in 1986
Company-Owned Units (As of 12/1/1989): . .1
Franchised Units (12/1/1989): 26
Total Units (12/1/1989): 27
Distribution: US-20;Can-7;Overseas-0
North America: . . . . 11 States, 2 Provinces
Concentration: . . . 5 in CA, 3 in WA, 3 in AB
Registered: . . . . .All
. . . .
Average # of Employees: . . . . . . 1 FT, 6 PT
Prior Industry Experience: . . . . Helpful

FINANCIAL:
Cash Investment: $20K
Total Investment: $60K
Fees: Franchise - $14-19K
  Royalty: 6%, Advert: 0%
Contract Periods (Yrs.): . . . 10/5/5
Area Development Agreement: Yes/10
Sub-Franchise Contract: . . . . .No
Expand in Territory: . . . . . . .No
Passive Ownership: . . . . . .Allowed
Encourage Conversions: . . . . .No
Franchisee Purchase(s) Required: Yes

FRANCHISOR TRAINING/SUPPORT:
Financial Assistance Provided: . . . . . No
Site Selection Assistance: . . . . . . .Yes
Lease Negotiation Assistance: . . . . . No
Co-operative Advertising: . . . . No
Training: . . . . 2 Wks. Headquarters
. . . .
On-Going Support: . . . . .B,C,D,E,G,H,I
Full-Time Franchisor Support Staff: . . 16
EXPANSION PLANS:
US: . . . . .All US
Canada - Yes, . . . Overseas - Yes

WOMEN'S WORKOUT WORLD
5811 W. Dempster St.
Morton Grove, IL 60053
TEL: (708) 965-1551
FAX: (708) 965-1664
Mr. Robert Morley, President

WOMEN'S WORKOUT WORLD offers a unique exercise program for women at an extremely affordable price. Our program offers the finest exercise equipment and continuous aerobic classes within a modern health club setting. We take great pride in offering exemplary service and sparkling clean facilities.

HISTORY: . . . .
Established in 1969; . . 1st Franchised in 1986
Company-Owned Units (As of 12/1/1989): . 15
Franchised Units (12/1/1989): 12
Total Units (12/1/1989): 27
Distribution: US-27;Can-0;Overseas-0
North America: . . . . 2 States
Concentration: . . . . 21 in IL, 3 in MN
Registered: . . . . .IL,MI,MN,WI
. . . .
Average # of Employees: . . . . . 2 FT, 20 PT
Prior Industry Experience: . . . . Helpful

FINANCIAL:
Cash Investment: $150-225K
Total Investment: $150-225K
Fees: Franchise - $35K
  Royalty: 10%, Advert: 0%
Contract Periods (Yrs.): . . . 20/20
Area Development Agreement: Yes/5
Sub-Franchise Contract: . . . . .No
Expand in Territory: . . . . Yes
Passive Ownership: . . . Not Allowed
Encourage Conversions: . . . . .No
Franchisee Purchase(s) Required: .No

FRANCHISOR TRAINING/SUPPORT:
Financial Assistance Provided: . . . . .No
Site Selection Assistance: . . . . . . .Yes
Lease Negotiation Assistance: . . . . .Yes
Co-operative Advertising: . . . . . . .Yes
Training: . . . . 2 Wks. Headquarters,
. . . . 1 Month On-site
On-Going Support: . . . . . B,C,D,E,G,H
Full-Time Franchisor Support Staff: . . 30
EXPANSION PLANS:
US: . . . . . . Midwest, Southeast, East
Canada - No, ...Overseas - No

SUPPLEMENTAL LISTING OF FRANCHISORS

ALOETTE COSMETICS	345 Lancaster Ave., Malvern PA 19355	
ALOETTE COSMETICS OF CANADA	89 Edilcan Dr., Concord ON L4K3S6	CAN
BEAUX VISAGES	90 State St., # 536, Albany NY 12207	
BEVERLY HILLS WEIGHT LOSS CLINIC	4400 Plank Rd., # 102, Fredericksburg VA 22401	
BODY INTERNATIONAL, THE	11000 Richmond, Houston TX 77042	
BODY SHOP, THE	15 Prince Andrew Pl., Don Mills ON M3C2H2	CAN
CARYL BAKER VISAGE	801 Eglinton Ave., W., Toronto ON M5N1E3	CAN
CLEAN & LEAN	743 Shadowridge Dr., Vista CA 92083	
COLOURS	173 Carlton St., Toronto ON M5A2K3	CAN
COSMETIC DESIGN CENTER	P.O. Box 522, Hudson OH 44236	
DIET CENTER	220 S. 2nd West, Rexburg ID 83440	
DIET WORKSHOP, THE	10 Brooklinw Pl. W., # 300, Brookline MA 02146	
DOCTORS WEIGHT LOSS	4400 Bayou Blvd., # 49, Pensacola FL 32503	
DOMINELLI JUVENIS CENTRES	#700 - 1140 W. Pender St., Vancouver BC V6E2P6	CAN
EMS WEIGHT LOSS CENTERS	211 Yonge St., Toronto ON M5B1M4	CAN
EUROPEAN TANSPA	5002 Main St., Downers Grove IL 60515	
FEMINIME WAY, THE	24 Inglewood Dr., Hamilton ON L8P2T5	CAN
FORMU-3 INTERNATIONAL	4790 Douglas Circle, NW, Canton OH 44718	
FORTUNATE LIFE WEIGHT LOSS CENTERS	1600 Quail Run Rd., Charlottesville VA 22901	
HEALTH CLUBS OF AMERICA	Box 4098, Waterville CT 06714	
HEAVENLY BODY'S FITNESS SALON	P.O. Box 3, S. Easton MA 02375	
HOME FITNESS STUDIO	6600 NW 12 Ave., # 217, Ft. Lauderdale FL 33309	
INTRIWEB HAIR DEVELOPMENT CENTER	415 1/2 Cedar Ln., Teaneck NJ 07666	
JENEAL INT'L SKIN CORRECTION	3798 West Chase, Houston TX 77042	
LA FOUNTAINE SPA	1248 Yonge St., Toronto ON M4T1W5	CAN
LASER CONCEPT	246 Blakie Rd., # 134, London ON N6L1G5	CAN
LIFE TRENDS WEIGHT LOSS	106 W. 31st St., Independence MO 64055	
LIFESTYLE 2000 STUDIOS	1790 Albion Rd., # 207, Rexdale ON M9V1C2	CAN
LOOK INTERNATIONAL	1886 Marine Dr., # 80, North Vancouver BC V7P1V5	CAN
MED+WAY MEDICAL WEIGHT MANAGEMENT	1375 S. Voss Rd., Houston TX 77057	
NAIL QUEEN	1425 Dundas St. E., # 210, Mississauga ON L4X1L3	CAN
NAIL SHOPPE, THE	29 Elm St., Toronto ON M5G1H1	CAN
NAILS 'N LASHES STUDIO	Box 340, Sharon ON L0G1V0	CAN
NATIONAL HEALTH ENHANCEMENT	3200 North Central Ave., #1750, Phoenix AZ 85012	
NEURO-VISION APPETITE/SMOKING CONTR.	1951 Colonial Blvd., Fort Myers FL 33907	
NU-CONCEPT BODY WRAP	603 Cleveland St., Elyria OH 44035	
NUDEX NAILS	20 Edgecliffe Golf Way, # 816, Don Mills ON M3C3A4	CAN
NUTRA BOLIC WEIGHT REDUCTION	4790 Douglas Circle NW, Canton OH 44718	
OUR WEIGH	3340 Poplar, # 136, Memphis TN 38111	
PERFECT LIFE DEVELOPMENT CENTER	2001 E. Locust Ct., Ontario CA 91761	
PERMANENT WEIGHT CONTROL CENTERS	99 Cherry St., # B, Milford CT 06460	
PHYSICIANS BARIATRIC CLINIC	3585 Kori Rd., Jacksonville FL 32257	
PHYSICIANS WEIGHT LOSS CENTERS	30 Springside Dr., Akron OH 44313	
POTIONS & LOTIONS	10201 N. 21st Ave., # 8, Phoenix AZ 85021	
PROFESSIONAL WEIGHT LOSS CLINICS	204 - 1220 W. 6th Ave., Vancouver BC V6H1A5	CAN
R.X. SOLEIL	4881 Jarry East, # 280, Montreal PQ H1R1Y1	CAN
SLIMTAN SYSTEMS TOTAL BEAUTY CENTER	8040 E. Mill Plain Blvd., Vancouver WA 98661	
SPACE AGE THERAPY CENTRE	294 Portage Ave., Winnipeg MB R3C0B9	CAN
SUDDENLY SUN & FIRM	25000 G N Corp. Ctr., # 452, N. Olmsted OH 44070	
SUNRAY LASERTHERAPY CENTRES	363 Broadway, # 850, Winnipeg MB R3C3N9	CAN
SUNSPOT SOLARIUM	2152 Yonge St., Toronto ON M4S2A8	CAN
TAN & TONE FITNESS CENTERS	3114 Weatherford Rd., Independence MO 64055	
TOP OF THE LINE COSMETICS	515 Bath Ave., Long Beach NJ 07740	

TOTAL LIFESTYLE CENTER . . . . P.O. Box 636, Millington TN 38053
TRIM AND TONE . . . . 3114 Weatherford Rd., Independence MO 64055
WEIGH TO GO . . . . .2311 205th St., # 103, Torrance CA 90501
WIGGY'S NAIL PLACE . . . . 20 Edgecliffe Golf Way, # 816, Don Mills ON M3C3A4   CAN
YVES ROCHER . . . . 6250 rue Marivaux, St-Leonard PQ H1P3K3   CAN

CHAPTER 25

LAUNDRY AND DRY CLEANING

CLEAN 'N' PRESS

7301 N. 16th St., # 101
Phoenix, AZ 85020
TEL: (800) 262-4114 (602) 943-9737
FAX: (602) 943-9605
Mr. Robert J. Gottschalk, Pres./CEO

Quality discount dry cleaning business, with emphasis on 4 main components: 1) quality product, 2) dramatic discount pricing, 3) multi-store/central plant structure and 4) marketing superiority. CLEAN 'N' PRESS franchisees aren't dry cleaners! They focus on marketing, business management, customer service and new store developement.

HISTORY: . . . . IFA
Established in 1985;   . . 1st Franchised in 1987
Company-Owned Units (As of 12/1/1989): . .5
Franchised Units (12/1/1989): 67
Total Units (12/1/1989): 72
Distribution: US-72;Can-0;Overseas-0
 North America: . . . . 5 States
 Concentration: . 32 in MN, 18 in CA, 14 in AZ
Registered: . . . . CA,FL,IL,MI,MN,WI
. . . .
Average # of Employees: . . . . . . 8 FT, 6 PT
Prior Industry Experience: . . . . Helpful

FINANCIAL:
Cash Investment: $85-100K
Total Investment: $277-295K
Fees: Franchise - $25K
 Royalty: 5%, Advert: 1-3%
Contract Periods (Yrs.): 10/10
Area Development Agreement: Yes/5
Sub-Franchise Contract: . . . . . .No
Expand in Territory: . . . . Yes
Passive Ownership: . . . Discouraged
Encourage Conversions: . . . . . .No
Franchisee Purchase(s) Required: .No

FRANCHISOR TRAINING/SUPPORT:
Financial Assistance Provided: . . . Yes(I)
Site Selection Assistance: . . . . .Yes
Lease Negotiation Assistance: . . . . .Yes
Co-operative Advertising: . . . . .Yes
Training: . . . . 2 Days Headquarters,
 . . . . . . 7 Days On-site Grand Opening
On-Going Support: . . . . .B,C,D,E,G,H,I
Full-Time Franchisor Support Staff: . . . 6
EXPANSION PLANS:
 US: . . . . . .Northeast, CA and Midwest
 Canada - No, ... Overseas - No

LAUNDRY & DRY CLEANING

	1988	1989	1990	Percentage Change 1988–1989	Percentage Change 1989–1990
Number of Establishments:					
Company–Owned	126	136	141	7.9%	3.7%
Franchisee–Owned	2,155	2,336	2,488	8.4%	6.5%
Total	2,281	2,472	2,629	8.4%	6.4%
% of Total Establishments:					
Company–Owned	5.5%	5.5%	5.4%		
Franchisee–Owned	94.5%	94.5%	94.6%		
Total	100.0%	100.0%	100.0%		
Annual Sales ($000):					
Company–Owned	$33,152	$36,627	$40,200	10.5%	9.8%
Franchisee–Owned	238,390	266,245	294,655	11.7%	10.7%
Total	271,542	302,872	334,855	11.5%	10.6%
% of Total Sales:					
Company–Owned	12.2%	12.1%	12.0%		
Franchisee–Owned	87.8%	87.9%	88.0%		
Total	100.0%	100.0%	100.0%		
Average Sales Per Unit ($000):					
Company–Owned	$263	$269	$285	2.4%	5.9%
Franchisee–Owned	111	114	118	3.0%	3.9%
Total	119	123	127	2.9%	4.0%
Sales Ratio	237.8%	236.3%	240.7%		

	1st Quartile	Median	4th Quartile
Average 1988 Total Investment:			
Company–Owned	N. A.	$150,000	N. A.
Franchisee–Owned	125,000	150,000	191,250
Single Unit Franchise Fee	N. A.	$16,500	N. A.
Multiple Unit Franchise Fee	N. A.	9,500	N. A.
Franchisee Start–up Cost	20,000	50,000	70,000

	1988	Employees/Unit	Sales/Employee
Employment:			
Company–Owned	920	7.3	$36,035
Franchisee–Owned	8,145	3.8	29,268
Total	9,065	4.0	29,955
Employee Performance Ratios		193.2%	123.1%

Source: Franchising In The Economy, 1988 – 1990, IFA Education Foundation & Horwath International, Published January, 1990.

1) 1989 and 1990 data were estimated by respondents.

DRYCLEAN - U.S.A.

9100 S. Dadeland Blvd.
Miami, FL 33156
TEL: (305) 667-3488
FAX:
Mr. Kenneth Moll, VP

DRYCLEAN - USA, America's great drycleaning/laundry stores, include a complete "turn key" franchise program from site selection to grand opening. DRYCLEAN - USA has received many plant design awards for efficient planning, state-of-the-art equipment, quality work, inviting and attention-getting decor, personal service, attractive packaging and creative merchandising.

HISTORY: . . . . IFA
Established in 1973; . . 1st Franchised in 1977
Company-Owned Units (As of 12/1/1989): . 83
Franchised Units (12/1/1989): 220
Total Units (12/1/1989): 313
Distribution: US-313;Can-0;Overseas-0
North America: . . . .
Concentration: . . . .
Registered: . . . . All Except Alberta
. . . .
Average # of Employees: . . . . . . 3 FT, 2 PT
Prior Industry Experience: . . . . Helpful

FINANCIAL:
Cash Investment: $50-70K
Total Investment: $180-240K
Fees: Franchise - . . . .$
  Royalty: 3-5%, Advert: 2%
Contract Periods (Yrs.): . . . . Lease
Area Development Agreement: . .No
Sub-Franchise Contract: . . . . .No
Expand in Territory: . . . . . . Yes
Passive Ownership: . . . Discouraged
Encourage Conversions: . . . . .No
Franchisee Purchase(s) Required: .No

FRANCHISOR TRAINING/SUPPORT:
Financial Assistance Provided: . . . Yes(I)
Site Selection Assistance: . . . . . . .Yes
Lease Negotiation Assistance: . . . .Yes
Co-operative Advertising: . . . . . . .Yes
Training: . . . . .4-6 Wks. Florida
. . . .
On-Going Support: . . . . B,C,D,E,F,G,H
Full-Time Franchisor Support Staff: . . 75
EXPANSION PLANS:
US: . . . . .All US
Canada - No, ...Overseas - No

DUDS 'N SUDS

3401 101st St., # E
Des Moines, IA 50322
TEL: (515) 270-3837
FAX:
Mr. Philip Akim, CEO

The leader in franchise laundry centers. DUDS 'N SUDS is a combination self-service laundry and snack bar entertainment center.

HISTORY: . . . . IFA
Established in 1983; . . 1st Franchised in 1984
Company-Owned Units (As of 12/1/1989): . .0
Franchised Units (12/1/1989): 65
Total Units (12/1/1989): 65
Distribution: US-65;Can-0;Overseas-0
North America: . . . . 30 States
Concentration: . . 11 in IA, 10 in CO, 6 in MO
Registered: . . . . .All
. . . .
Average # of Employees: . . . . . . 4 FT, 3 PT
Prior Industry Experience: . . . . Helpful

FINANCIAL:
Cash Investment: $20-50K
Total Investment: $140-200K
Fees: Franchise - $15K
  Royalty: 3%, Advert: 1%
Contract Periods (Yrs.): 10/10
Area Development Agreement: . Yes
Sub-Franchise Contract: . . . . Yes
Expand in Territory: . . . . . . Yes
Passive Ownership: . . . Discouraged
Encourage Conversions: . . . . Yes
Franchisee Purchase(s) Required: Yes

FRANCHISOR TRAINING/SUPPORT:
Financial Assistance Provided: . . . . .Yes
Site Selection Assistance: . . . . . . .Yes
Lease Negotiation Assistance: . . . .Yes
Co-operative Advertising: . . . . No
Training: . . . . .1 Wk. Headquarters,
. . . . 1 Wk. in Store
On-Going Support: . . . .B,C,D,E,F,G,H,I
Full-Time Franchisor Support Staff: . . .4
EXPANSION PLANS:
US: . . . . .All US
Canada - Yes, . . . Overseas - Yes

EXECUTIVE IMAGE CLEANERS

1333 W. 120th Ave., # 222
Denver, CO 80234
TEL: (303) 457-2700
FAX:
Mr. Chuck Yerbic, President

EXECUTIVE IMAGE CLEANERS (EIC) serves the busy executive and office employee at their places of business. With the ever-increasing two income families, time becomes a very important factor in their lives. The office professional can eliminate those extra steps to the local dry cleaner because EIC brings the dry cleaning plant to the employee. EIC is a unique business that features quality, convenience and hand-finished garments.

HISTORY: . . . .
Established in 1988; . . 1st Franchised in 1988
Company-Owned Units (As of 12/1/1989): . .0
Franchised Units (12/1/1989): 8
Total Units (12/1/1989): 8
Distribution: US-8;Can-0;Overseas-0
North America: . . . . 3 States
Concentration: . . . 4 in OH, 3 in PA, 1 in CO
Registered: . . . . FL,HI,MI
. . . .
Average # of Employees: . . . . . . 1 FT, 1 PT
Prior Industry Experience: . . . . Helpful

FINANCIAL:
Cash Investment: $35-40K
Total Investment: $100-120K
Fees: Franchise - $18K
  Royalty: 5%, Advert: 3%
Contract Periods (Yrs.): 10/5
Area Development Agreement: . .No
Sub-Franchise Contract: . . . . .No
Expand in Territory: . . . . . . .No
Passive Ownership: . . . . . .Allowed
Encourage Conversions: . . . . . Yes
Franchisee Purchase(s) Required: .No

FRANCHISOR TRAINING/SUPPORT:
Financial Assistance Provided: . . . Yes(I)
Site Selection Assistance: . . . . . . .Yes
Lease Negotiation Assistance: . . . .Yes
Co-operative Advertising: . . . . No
Training: . . . . .1 Wk. Headquarters,
. . . . . . Minimum 5 Days at Opening
On-Going Support: . . . . . . .B,C,D,E,H
Full-Time Franchisor Support Staff: . . .3
EXPANSION PLANS:
US: . . . . .All US
Canada - No, ...Overseas - No

HIS AND HERS IRONING SERVICE

10841 W. 155th Terrace
Overland Park, KS 66221
TEL: (913) 897-5757 C
FAX:
Mr. Kenneth Mairs, President

HIS AND HERS IRONING SERVICE is a personalized ironing and laundry business with pick-up and delivery. This truly unique service business has excellent growth potential, low overhead and virtually no competition.

HISTORY: . . . .
Established in 1983; . . 1st Franchised in 1985
Company-Owned Units (As of 12/1/1989): . .1
Franchised Units (12/1/1989): 1
Total Units (12/1/1989): 2
Distribution: US-2;Can-0;Overseas-0
North America: . . . . 2 States
Concentration: . . . . 1 in KS, 1 in MO
Registered: . . . .
. . . .
Average # of Employees: . . . . .2 FT
Prior Industry Experience: . . . . Helpful

FINANCIAL:
Cash Investment: $20-40K
Total Investment: $20-40K
Fees: Franchise - $10K
Royalty: 5%, Advert: 2%
Contract Periods (Yrs.): 15/5
Area Development Agreement: Yes/15
Sub-Franchise Contract: . . . . Yes
Expand in Territory: . . . . . . .No
Passive Ownership: . . . Discouraged
Encourage Conversions: . . . . .No
Franchisee Purchase(s) Required: .No

FRANCHISOR TRAINING/SUPPORT:
Financial Assistance Provided: . . . . .No
Site Selection Assistance: . . . . . . .NA
Lease Negotiation Assistance: . . . .NA
Co-operative Advertising: . . . . . . .Yes
Training: . . . . 1 Wk. Headquarters
. . . .
On-Going Support: . . . . . . .a,b,c,d,E,f
Full-Time Franchisor Support Staff: . . .2
EXPANSION PLANS:
US: . . . . Midwest and South
Canada - No, ...Overseas - No

JIM DANDY DISCOUNT DRY CLEANERS

15155 Stagg St.
Van Nuys, CA 91405
TEL: (800) 635-0516 (818) 782-8166
FAX: (818) 782-4749
President

JIM DANDY INTERNATIONAL allows entry into the multi-billion dollar dry cleaning industry. A unique opportunity in "Profit-Based Discount Dry Cleaning." This franchise was organized for the explicit purpose of satisfying consumer demand for convenient, quality dry cleaning, coupled with discount pricing.

HISTORY: . . . .
Established in 1986; . . 1st Franchised in 1989
Company-Owned Units (As of 12/1/1989): . 12
Franchised Units (12/1/1989): 0
Total Units (12/1/1989): 12
Distribution: US-12;Can-0;Overseas-0
North America: . . . .
Concentration: . . . .
Registered: . . . . CA,FL,OR
. . . .
Average # of Employees: . . . . .6 FT
Prior Industry Experience: . . . . Helpful

FINANCIAL:
Cash Investment: $75K
Total Investment: $195K
Fees: Franchise - $20K
Royalty: 3%, Advert: 1%
Contract Periods (Yrs.): 10/5
Area Development Agreement: . .No
Sub-Franchise Contract: . . . . .No
Expand in Territory: . . . . . . Yes
Passive Ownership: . . . Discouraged
Encourage Conversions: . . . . .No
Franchisee Purchase(s) Required: .No

FRANCHISOR TRAINING/SUPPORT:
Financial Assistance Provided: . . . . .No
Site Selection Assistance: . . . . . . .Yes
Lease Negotiation Assistance: . . . .Yes
Co-operative Advertising: . . . . . . .No
Training: . . . . .1 Wk. Headquarters,
. . . . .2 Wks. On-site
On-Going Support: . . . . . .C,D,E,F,H,I
Full-Time Franchisor Support Staff: . . . 5
EXPANSION PLANS:
US: . . . . . . .Northwest and Southwest
Canada - No, ... Overseas - Yes

OASIS LAUNDRY, THE

100 Homeland Ct.
Santa Clara, CA 95051
TEL: (408) 452-0106 C
FAX: (408) 452-1161
Ms. Joan Young, VP Fran. Sales

OASIS LAUNDRY provides premium laundry services. Customers are offered clean, comfortable environments; full-time customer service attendants; snack bars; big-screen TV; convenient drop-off service and agency dry cleaning. OASIS is a superior alternative to the traditional laundromat, consistently rated #1 by the media.

HISTORY: . . . . IFA
Established in 1987; . . 1st Franchised in 1988
Company-Owned Units (As of 12/1/1989): . .3
Franchised Units (12/1/1989): 28
Total Units (12/1/1989): 31
Distribution: US-31;Can-0;Overseas-0
North America: . . . . .1 State
Concentration: . . . . 31 in CA
Registered: . . . . CA
. . . .
Average # of Employees: . . . . .4 PT
Prior Industry Experience: . . . . Helpful

FINANCIAL:
Cash Investment: $75-100K
Total Investment: $275-350K
Fees: Franchise - $25K
Royalty: 5%, Advert: 2%
Contract Periods (Yrs.): 10/5
Area Development Agreement: . Yes
Sub-Franchise Contract: . . . . .No
Expand in Territory: . . . . . . Yes
Passive Ownership: . . . Discouraged
Encourage Conversions: . . . . .No
Franchisee Purchase(s) Required: .No

FRANCHISOR TRAINING/SUPPORT:
Financial Assistance Provided: . . . Yes(I)
Site Selection Assistance: . . . . . . .Yes
Lease Negotiation Assistance: . . . .Yes
Co-operative Advertising: . . . . . . .No
Training: . . . . 4 Days San Jose, CA,
. . . . .5 Days Franchisee Location
On-Going Support: . . . . . .C,D,e,G,H,I
Full-Time Franchisor Support Staff: . . 10
EXPANSION PLANS:
US: . . . . . All US, Primarily West, NW
Canada - No, ...Overseas - No

ONE HOUR MARTINIZING

2005 Ross Ave.
Cincinnati, OH 45212
TEL: (800) 827-0207 (513) 351-6211
FAX:
Mr. Jerry Laesser, VP

World's largest dry cleaning franchise. Complete start-up assistance, comprehensive training program, location/site assistance with NDS computerized demographics capabilities, grand opening marketing package and on-going local store and nationwide promotional programs, field and operations assistance.

HISTORY: . . . . IFA
Established in 1949; . . 1st Franchised in 1949
Company-Owned Units (As of 12/1/1989): . .0
Franchised Units (12/1/1989): 905
Total Units (12/1/1989): 905
Distribution: . . . US-814;Can-59;Overseas-32
 North America: . . . . 48 States
 Concentration: . .126 in CA, 101 in MI, 89 TX
Registered: . . . . All States
 . . . .
Average # of Employees: . . . . .3 FT
Prior Industry Experience: . . . . Helpful

FINANCIAL:
Cash Investment: $50K
Total Investment: $150-200K
Fees: Franchise - $20K
 Royalty: 4%, Advert: 4%
Contract Periods (Yrs.): . . . 10/10
Area Development Agreement: Yes/Var
Sub-Franchise Contract: . . . . .No
Expand in Territory: . . . . . . Yes
Passive Ownership: . . . . . .Allowed
Encourage Conversions: . . . . Yes
Franchisee Purchase(s) Required: .No

FRANCHISOR TRAINING/SUPPORT:
Financial Assistance Provided: . . . Yes(I)
Site Selection Assistance: . . . . . . .Yes
Lease Negotiation Assistance: . . . . .Yes
Co-operative Advertising: . . . . . . .Yes
Training: . . . . 3 Wks. Headquarters
 . . . .
On-Going Support: . . . . . . C,d,E,G,H,I
Full-Time Franchisor Support Staff: . . 15
EXPANSION PLANS:
US: . . . . .All US
Canada - Yes, . . . Overseas - Yes

PILGRIM CLEANERS & LAUNDERERS

4201 Laneland Ave. N.
Minneapolis, MN 55422
TEL: (612) 533-1293
FAX:
Mr. Gene J. Bemel, VP

Quality-oriented, full-service dry cleaner and shirt launderer.

HISTORY: . . . .
Established in 1940; . . 1st Franchised in 1988
Company-Owned Units (As of 12/1/1989): . 17
Franchised Units (12/1/1989): 13
Total Units (12/1/1989): 30
Distribution: US-30;Can-0;Overseas-0
 North America: . . . . .1 State
 Concentration: . . . . 30 in MN
Registered: . . . . . . IL,MI,MN,ND,SD,WI
 . . . .
Average # of Employees: . . . . .4 FT
Prior Industry Experience: . . . . . . Helpful

FINANCIAL:
Cash Investment: $75K
Total Investment: $150-175K
Fees: Franchise - $17.5-24.9K
 Royalty: 4.75%, Advert: . . 2.5%
Contract Periods (Yrs.): . . . 10/10
Area Development Agreement: Yes/10
Sub-Franchise Contract: . . . . .No
Expand in Territory: . . . . . . Yes
Passive Ownership: . . . Discouraged
Encourage Conversions: . . . . Yes
Franchisee Purchase(s) Required: .No

FRANCHISOR TRAINING/SUPPORT:
Financial Assistance Provided: . . . Yes(I)
Site Selection Assistance: . . . . . . .Yes
Lease Negotiation Assistance: . . . .Yes
Co-operative Advertising: . . . . . . .Yes
Training: . . . . 2 Wks. Headquarters,
 . . . . 1 Wk. Franchisee Site
On-Going Support: . . . . B,C,E,F
Full-Time Franchisor Support Staff: . . .2
EXPANSION PLANS:
US: . . . . .Midwest
Canada - No, ...Overseas - No

WEDDING GOWN SPECIALISTS / RESTORATION LABS

1799 Briarcliff Rd. NE
Atlanta, GA 30306
TEL: (800) 543-8987 (404) 875-5773 C
FAX:
Mr. Gary Webster, President

For established professional dry cleaners, an added specialty of restoring yellowed/stained wedding gowns to true color. No additional equipment, space or staffing required for those already handling wedding gowns. Restoration is just one more step to your current procedure. Each unit operates under license to provide services under national trade name and logo.

HISTORY: . . . .
Established in 1987; . . 1st Franchised in 1987
Company-Owned Units (As of 12/1/1989): . .1
Franchised Units (12/1/1989): 53
Total Units (12/1/1989): 54
Distribution: US-49;Can-5;Overseas-0
 North America: . . . . 20 States, 3 Provinces
 Concentration: . . . . 5 in CA, 3 in TN, 3 in IL
Registered: . . . . .All
 . . . .
Average # of Employees: . . . . .1 FT
Prior Industry Experience: . . . . Helpful

FINANCIAL:
Cash Investment: $1-30K
Total Investment: $1-30K
Fees: Franchise - $1-30K
 Royalty: 20%, Advert: 0%
Contract Periods (Yrs.): 1/1
Area Development Agreement: .No
Sub-Franchise Contract: . . . . .No
Expand in Territory: . . . . . . Yes
Passive Ownership: . . . Discouraged
Encourage Conversions: . . . . .No
Franchisee Purchase(s) Required: .No

FRANCHISOR TRAINING/SUPPORT:
Financial Assistance Provided: . . . . .No
Site Selection Assistance: . . . . . . .No
Lease Negotiation Assistance: . . . . .No
Co-operative Advertising: . . . . . . .Yes
Training: . . . . .Written and Taped
 . . . . Training
On-Going Support: . . . . .G,H,I
Full-Time Franchisor Support Staff: . . .4
EXPANSION PLANS:
US: . . . . .All US
Canada - Yes, ...Overseas - Yes

SUPPLEMENTAL LISTING OF FRANCHISORS

ALPINE CLEANERS . . . . 3501 Chateau Blvd., Kenner LA 70065
CACHE CLEANERS . . . . 1333 W. 120th Ave., # 222, Denver CO 80234
CHATEL VOTRE NETTOYEUR . . . . 1200 boul. Rome Local D, Brossard PQ J4W3H3   CAN
CLASSIC CORPORATION OF COLUMBIA . . . . 1330 Lady St., Keenan Bldg., Columbia SC 29201
CLEAN DUDS . . . . .P.O. Box B, Welch Station, Ames IA 50010
DRY CLEANERS-POSTAL CTRS. OF AMERICA . . 13013 Lee Jackson Hwy., #1400, Fairfax VA 22033
DRY CLEANING WORLD/LAUNDRY WORLD . . . . 1234 Brittain Rd., Akron OH 44310
FIRST CHOICE DRY CLEANING . . . . .1310 Dundas St. E., # 210, Mississauga ON L4Y2C1   CAN
NETTOYEURS MICHEL FORGET . . . . 8 ouest, rue Prouix, Pont-Vizu, Laval PQ H7N1N1   CAN
OLD WEST WASH HOUSE . . . . .P.O. Box 835, Somerset PA 15501
SKETCHLEY CLEANERS . . . . .1 Concord Gate, # 600, North York ON M3C3N6   CAN
SOAP OPERA . . . . .5757 Corporate Blvd., # 300, Baton Rouge LA 70808
SOAPARAMA . . . . 729 Boylston St., # 208, Boston MA 02116
WINDSOR VALET . . . . 24 Woodstream Blvd., Woodbridge ON L4L8C4   CAN

CHAPTER 26

LAWN AND GARDEN

BAREFOOT GRASS LAWN SERVICE

1018 Proprietors Rd.
Worthington, OH 43085
TEL: (614) 846-1800
FAX:
Mr. Mark Long, Franchise Mgr.

A BAREFOOT GRASS franchise covers an entire metropolitan area (Ex. Lexington, KY). You provide lawn services: aeration, fertilization, crabgrass control, weed control and insect control. Technical knowledge important. A fine growth opportunity for experienced lawn care specialists.

HISTORY: . . . .
Established in 1975; . . 1st Franchised in 1977
Company-Owned Units (As of 12/1/1989): . 16
Franchised Units (12/1/1989): 34
Total Units (12/1/1989): 50
Distribution: US-46;Can-1;Overseas-0
 North America: . . . . . 22 States, 1 Province
 Concentration: . . . 8 in OH, 4 in WI,3 in NC
Registered: . . . . . IL,IN,MI,MN,NY,VA,WI

. . . .
Average # of Employees: . . . . . . 1 FT, 1 PT
Prior Industry Experience: . . . . . .Necessary

FINANCIAL:
Cash Investment: $15-50K
Total Investment: $20-100K
Fees: Franchise - $15-60K
 Royalty: 10%, Advert: 0%
Contract Periods (Yrs.): 10/10
Area Development Agreement: . .No
Sub-Franchise Contract: . . . . .No
Expand in Territory: . . . . . . Yes
Passive Ownership: . . . Discouraged
Encourage Conversions: . . . . . Yes
Franchisee Purchase(s) Required: .No

FRANCHISOR TRAINING/SUPPORT:
Financial Assistance Provided: . . . . .No
Site Selection Assistance: . . . . . . .NA
Lease Negotiation Assistance: . . . .NA
Co-operative Advertising: . . . . . . .NA
Training: . . . . 2 Days Headquarters,
 . . . . 2 Days Site
On-Going Support: . . . . . . A,B,C,G,h,i
Full-Time Franchisor Support Staff: . . 25
EXPANSION PLANS:
 US: . . . . East of Rockies
 Canada - No, ... Overseas - No

CLINTAR GROUNDSKEEPING SERVICES
4210 Midland Ave.
Scarborough, ON M1V4S6 CAN
TEL: (416) 291-1611
FAX:
Mr. Robert C. Wilton, President

CLINTAR provides high-quality groundskeeping services to Fortune 500 clients. Our year-round services include landscape maintenance, snow removal, power sweeping and light construction to a select group of image-conscious customers. Intensive support, marketing and training.

HISTORY:	FINANCIAL:	FRANCHISOR TRAINING/SUPPORT:
Established in 1973; . . 1st Franchised in 1984	Cash Investment: $34-45K	Financial Assistance Provided: . . . Yes(I)
Company-Owned Units (As of 12/1/1989): . .1	Total Investment: $80-90K	Site Selection Assistance: . . . . . . .Yes
Franchised Units (12/1/1989): 9	Fees: Franchise - $25K	Lease Negotiation Assistance: . . . . .Yes
Total Units (12/1/1989): 10	Royalty: 8%, Advert: 0%	Co-operative Advertising: . . . . . . .Yes
Distribution: US-0;Can-10;Overseas-0	Contract Periods (Yrs.): 10/5	Training: . . . . . . 4 Months Headquarters
North America: . . . . .1 Province	Area Development Agreement: . .No	
Concentration: . . . . 10 in ON	Sub-Franchise Contract: . . . . .No	On-Going Support: . . .a,B,C,D,E,F,G,H,I
Registered:	Expand in Territory: . . . . Yes	Full-Time Franchisor Support Staff: . . 10
. . . .	Passive Ownership: . . . Not Allowed	EXPANSION PLANS:
Average # of Employees: . . . . . .6 FT, 10 PT	Encourage Conversions: . . . . . Yes	US: . . . . Northeast
Prior Industry Experience: . . . . Helpful	Franchisee Purchase(s) Required: .No	Canada - Yes, ...Overseas - No

EMERALD GREEN LAWN CARE

5300 Dupont Circle
Milford, OH 45150
TEL: (800) 543-5296 (513) 248-0981
FAX: (513) 831-1428
Mr. Jim Miller, General Manager

With an EMERALD GREEN franchise, you can count on being backed by our superior lawn care system - a system that will build your business through time. It only takes a modest equipment cost and a small franchise fee to share the EMERALD GREEN success formula.

HISTORY:	FINANCIAL:	FRANCHISOR TRAINING/SUPPORT:
Established in 1984; . . 1st Franchised in 1985	Cash Investment: $20-40K	Financial Assistance Provided: . . . . . No
Company-Owned Units (As of 12/1/1989): . .3	Total Investment: $50-70K	Site Selection Assistance: . . . . .NA
Franchised Units (12/1/1989): 15	Fees: Franchise - $7.5-10K	Lease Negotiation Assistance: . . . . .Yes
Total Units (12/1/1989): 18	Royalty: 8.5%, Advert: 0%	Co-operative Advertising: . . . . . . .Yes
Distribution: US-18;Can-0;Overseas-0	Contract Periods (Yrs.): 15/1	Training: . . . . . 1 Wk. Co-owned Branch,
North America: . . . . 8 States	Area Development Agreement: . .No	. . . . As Needed On-site
Concentration: . . .6 in OH, 3 in PA, 3 in NJ	Sub-Franchise Contract: . . . . .No	On-Going Support: . . . . . B,C,F,G,H,I
Registered: . . . . IL,IN,MI,RI,VA,WI	Expand in Territory: . . . . Yes	Full-Time Franchisor Support Staff: . . 10
. . . .	Passive Ownership: . . . Not Allowed	EXPANSION PLANS:
Average # of Employees: . . . 3 FT, Various PT	Encourage Conversions: . . . . . Yes	US: . . . . East of Mississippi
Prior Industry Experience: . . . . Helpful	Franchisee Purchase(s) Required: Yes	Canada - Yes, ...Overseas - No

FAS GRAS INTERNATIONAL

13751 Travilah Rd.
Rockville, MD 20850
TEL: (301) 424-7333
FAX: (301) 424-2581
Mr. Robert Hamilton, VP

FAS GRAS is a patented processs that can establish a lawn (seeded to form a stand of grass) in just 3-5 days. After it has been seeded with FAS GRAS, it is mowable in about 3 weeks. A product that sells for about 1/2 the cost of sod.

HISTORY: . . . . .IFA	FINANCIAL:	FRANCHISOR TRAINING/SUPPORT:
Established in 1980; . . 1st Franchised in 1981	Cash Investment: $100K	Financial Assistance Provided: . . . .NA
Company-Owned Units (As of 12/1/1989): . .6	Total Investment: $160K	Site Selection Assistance: . . . . . . .Yes
Franchised Units (12/1/1989): 8	Fees: Franchise - $25K	Lease Negotiation Assistance: . . . .Yes
Total Units (12/1/1989): 14	Royalty: 6%, Advert: 0%	Co-operative Advertising: . . . . . . .NA
Distribution: US-14;Can-0;Overseas-0	Contract Periods (Yrs.): 20/10	Training: . . . . . . 3-4 Wks. Headquarters,
North America: . . . . 2 States + DC	Area Development Agreement: . .No	. . . . . . .3 Wks. on Site, On-going Site
Concentration: . . . . .MD, VA	Sub-Franchise Contract: . . . . .No	On-Going Support: . . . .B,C,D,E,F,G,H,I
Registered: . . . . .MD,VA	Expand in Territory: . . . . . . .No	Full-Time Franchisor Support Staff: . .150
. . . .	Passive Ownership: . . . Discouraged	EXPANSION PLANS:
Average # of Employees: . . . . . . 4 FT, 6 PT	Encourage Conversions: . . . . . .No	US: . . . . . . .Northeast and Southeast
Prior Industry Experience: . . . . Helpful	Franchisee Purchase(s) Required: Yes	Canada - Yes, . . . Overseas - Yes

GREENS ALIVE INTERNATIONAL

35 Alexandra Blvd.
Toronto, ON M4R1L8 CAN
TEL: (416) 488-3687 C
FAX:
Mr. Stephen MacKneson, Fran. Dir.

Environmentally-controlled greenhouses with patented high-tech growing systems for the production of gourmet-quality salad vegetables, which are harvested and delivered twice weekly, year-round. Since we use no pesticides, herbicides or sprays of any kind, our salad greens need not be washed.

HISTORY:	FINANCIAL:	FRANCHISOR TRAINING/SUPPORT:
Established in 1987; . . 1st Franchised in 1988	Cash Investment: $150K	Financial Assistance Provided: . . . Yes(I)
Company-Owned Units (As of 12/1/1989): . .1	Total Investment: $267K	Site Selection Assistance: . . . . .Yes
Franchised Units (12/1/1989): 2	Fees: Franchise - $40K	Lease Negotiation Assistance: . . . . .Yes
Total Units (12/1/1989): 3	Royalty: 7.5%, Advert: 2%	Co-operative Advertising: . . . . .Yes
Distribution: US-0;Can-3;Overseas-0	Contract Periods (Yrs.): 10/10	Training: . . . . 3 Wks. Headquarters,
North America: . . . . .1 Province	Area Development Agreement: . .No	. . . . 2 Wks. Site
Concentration: . . . . 1 in ON	Sub-Franchise Contract: . . . . .No	On-Going Support: . . . A,B,C,D,F,G,H,I
Registered:	Expand in Territory: . . . . . . .No	Full-Time Franchisor Support Staff: . . 12
. . . .	Passive Ownership: . . . Discouraged	EXPANSION PLANS:
Average # of Employees: . . . . . . 2 FT, 6 PT	Encourage Conversions: . . . . .No	US: . . . . .All US
Prior Industry Experience: . . . . Helpful	Franchisee Purchase(s) Required: Yes	Canada - Yes, . . . Overseas - Yes

LAWN DOCTOR

142 Hwy. 34, Box 512
Matawan, NJ 07747
TEL: (800) 631-5660 (201) 583-4700 C
FAX:
Mr. Edward Reid, Fran. Sales Dir.

The largest franchised automated lawn care company in the US. The business is operated by utilizing the company's business format system methods, specifications, standards, operating procedures, assistance and know-how to provide the best analysis of lawn problems and to create a healthy, beautiful lawn for the consumer.

HISTORY: . . . . IFA	FINANCIAL:	FRANCHISOR TRAINING/SUPPORT:
Established in 1967; . . 1st Franchised in 1967	Cash Investment: $25.5K	Financial Assistance Provided: . . .Yes(D)
Company-Owned Units (As of 12/1/1989): . .1	Total Investment: $30.5K	Site Selection Assistance: . . . . .NA
Franchised Units (12/1/1989): 290	Fees: Franchise - $0	Lease Negotiation Assistance: . . . . .NA
Total Units (12/1/1989): 291	Royalty: 10%, Advert: 0%	Co-operative Advertising: . . . . .Yes
Distribution: US-291;Can-0;Overseas-0	Contract Periods (Yrs.): 20/20	Training: . . . . . . 2 Wks. Headquarters
North America: . . . . 28 States	Area Development Agreement: . .No	. . . .
Concentration: . .67 in NJ, 65 in NY, 29 in PA	Sub-Franchise Contract: . . . . .No	On-Going Support: . . . . A,B,C,D,G,H,I
Registered: . . . FL,IL,MD,MI,MN,NY,RI,SD	Expand in Territory: . . . . . . .No	Full-Time Franchisor Support Staff: . . 50
. . . . VA	Passive Ownership: . . . . . .Allowed	EXPANSION PLANS:
Average # of Employees: . . . . .3 PT	Encourage Conversions: . . . . .No	US: . . . . .All US Except CA
Prior Industry Experience: . . . . Helpful	Franchisee Purchase(s) Required: .No	Canada - No, ...Overseas - No

LIQUI-GREEN LAWN CARE

9601 N. Allen Rd.
Peoria, IL 61615
TEL: (800) 255-2255 (309) 243-5211
FAX:
Mr. C.M. Dailey, Director

LIQUI-GREEN is a complete lawn and tree care company with a whole family of products. Completely equipped 1-ton truck with 2-hose system, electric start rewind reels and tree injection system along with tree spraying.

HISTORY:	FINANCIAL:	FRANCHISOR TRAINING/SUPPORT:
Established in 1953; . . 1st Franchised in 1971	Cash Investment: $8K	Financial Assistance Provided: . . .Yes(D)
Company-Owned Units (As of 12/1/1989): . .1	Total Investment: $25K	Site Selection Assistance: . . . . .Yes
Franchised Units (12/1/1989): 29	Fees: Franchise - $5K	Lease Negotiation Assistance: . . . . .No
Total Units (12/1/1989): 30	Royalty: Flat Fee, Advert:	Co-operative Advertising: . . . . .Yes
Distribution: US-30;Can-0;Overseas-0	Contract Periods (Yrs.): 10/5	Training: . . . . OJT, 2 Seminars,
North America: . . . . 4 States	Area Development Agreement: . .No	. . . . .2 Days Each
Concentration: . . . .23 in IL, 5 in IA, 1 in TX	Sub-Franchise Contract: . . . . Yes	On-Going Support: . . . . . . .B,C,D,G,H
Registered: IL	Expand in Territory: . . . . . . Yes	Full-Time Franchisor Support Staff: . . .1
. . . .	Passive Ownership: . . . . . .Allowed	EXPANSION PLANS:
Average # of Employees: . . . . .3 FT	Encourage Conversions: . . . . .No	US: . . . . Central and Southeast
Prior Industry Experience: . . . . Helpful	Franchisee Purchase(s) Required: Yes	Canada - No, ...Overseas - No

NUTRITE

P. O. Box 1000
Brossard, PQ J4Z3N2 CAN
TEL: (514) 462-2555 C
FAX: (514) 462-3634
M. Jacques Cardinal, Mktg. Mgr.

Your venture . . . If you dream of starting your own business, or want to add new services to an existing business, you should think seriously about owning a NUTRITE LAWN CARE franchise. The bottom line is . . . A NUTRITE franchise is a wise investment. Join the NUTRITE group now!

HISTORY: . . . .
Established in 1967; . . 1st Franchised in 1984
Company-Owned Units (As of 12/1/1989): . . .0
Franchised Units (12/1/1989): 38
Total Units (12/1/1989): 38
Distribution: US-0;Can-38;Overseas-0
  North America: . . . . 3 Provinces
  Concentration: . . . 30 in PQ, 7 in ON, 1 in NS
Registered: . . . . CA
  . . . .
Average # of Employees: . . . . .2 FT
Prior Industry Experience: . . . . Helpful

FINANCIAL:
Cash Investment: $40K
Total Investment: $40K
Fees: Franchise - $10K
  Royalty: $3.5K/Yr, Advert: . . . 0%
Contract Periods (Yrs.): 5/5
Area Development Agreement: . .No
Sub-Franchise Contract: . . . . .No
Expand in Territory: . . . . .No
Passive Ownership: . . . . . .Allowed
Encourage Conversions: . . . . . Yes
Franchisee Purchase(s) Required: Yes

FRANCHISOR TRAINING/SUPPORT:
Financial Assistance Provided: . . . . .No
Site Selection Assistance: . . . . .Yes
Lease Negotiation Assistance: . . . . .No
Co-operative Advertising: . . . . .No
Training: . . . . . . .No Limit On Location
. . . .
On-Going Support: . . . .A,B,C,D,F,G,h,i
Full-Time Franchisor Support Staff: . . 30
EXPANSION PLANS:
  US: . . . . No
  Canada - Yes, ...Overseas - No

SPRING-GREEN LAWN AND TREE CARE

11927 Spaulding School Dr.
Plainfield, IL 60544
TEL: (800) 435-4051 (815) 436-8777 C
FAX: (815) 436-9056
Mr. Joseph Nubie, Dir. Fran.Devel.

SPRING-GREEN LAWN CARE offers high-quality, professional lawn, tree and shrub care services to residential and commercial customers. Primary focus is on highly-efficient application processes for fertilization and other lawn health and beautification services. SPRING-GREEN's on-going support and training focuses on getting and keeping customers, emphasizing a unique computer system for efficiency.

HISTORY: . . . . IFA
Established in 1977; . . 1st Franchised in 1977
Company-Owned Units (As of 12/1/1989): . 10
Franchised Units (12/1/1989): 133
Total Units (12/1/1989): 143
Distribution: US-143;Can-0;Overseas-0
  North America: . . . . 22 States
  Concentration: . . 35 in IL, 21 in WI, 25 in PA
Registered: . . . CA,FL,IL,IN,MD,MI,MN,NY
. . . . OR,RI,VA,WA,WI
Average # of Employees: . . . . . 2 FT, 3 PT
Prior Industry Experience: . . . . . . Helpful

FINANCIAL:
Cash Investment: $13-20K
Total Investment: $20-45K
Fees: Franchise - $12.9K
  Royalty: 6-9%, Advert: 2%
Contract Periods (Yrs.): 10/10
Area Development Agreement: . .No
Sub-Franchise Contract: . . . . .No
Expand in Territory: . . . . Yes
Passive Ownership: . . . Discouraged
Encourage Conversions: . . . . . Yes
Franchisee Purchase(s) Required: .No

FRANCHISOR TRAINING/SUPPORT:
Financial Assistance Provided: . . . Yes(I)
Site Selection Assistance: . . . . . . .Yes
Lease Negotiation Assistance: . . . . .Yes
Co-operative Advertising: . . . . . . .Yes
Training: . . . . .30-Hr Pre-training Course
. . . . . 1 Wk. Natl. Ctr., 4 Days On-site
On-Going Support: . . A,B,C,D,E,F,G,H,I
Full-Time Franchisor Support Staff: . . 15
EXPANSION PLANS:
  US: . . . . .All US
  Canada - No, ...Overseas - No

SUPER LAWNS

9100 Aldershot Dr., P. O. Box 34278
Bethesda, MD 20817
TEL: (301) 365-4740 C
FAX:
Mr. Ron Miller, President

Our system offers a modern, profitable approach to lawn care. One person, or many, dependent upon your desire for growth. We'll teach you to be "one step above" the competition.

HISTORY: . . . .
Established in 1976; . . 1st Franchised in 1976
Company-Owned Units (As of 12/1/1989): . .2
Franchised Units (12/1/1989): 23
Total Units (12/1/1989): 25
Distribution: US-25;Can-0;Overseas-0
  North America: . . . . 4 States
  Concentration: . . .11 in MD, 6 in VA, 3 in NJ
Registered: . . . . CA,MD,NY,VA
. . . .
Average # of Employees: . . . . .2 FT
Prior Industry Experience: . . . . Helpful

FINANCIAL:
Cash Investment: $30-50K
Total Investment: $50K
Fees: Franchise - $17.5K
  Royalty: 10%, Advert: 0%
Contract Periods (Yrs.): 20/5
Area Development Agreement: . .No
Sub-Franchise Contract: . . . . .No
Expand in Territory: . . . . Yes
Passive Ownership: . . . Not Allowed
Encourage Conversions: . . . . . NA
Franchisee Purchase(s) Required: .No

FRANCHISOR TRAINING/SUPPORT:
Financial Assistance Provided: . . . Yes(I)
Site Selection Assistance: . . . . . . .Yes
Lease Negotiation Assistance: . . . .NA
Co-operative Advertising: . . . . .No
Training: . . . . . As Needed Home Office
. . . .
On-Going Support: . . . . . b,C,D,E,F,H,I
Full-Time Franchisor Support Staff: . . . 2
EXPANSION PLANS:
  US: . . . . East of Mississippi
  Canada - Yes, ...Overseas - No

U. S. LAWNS

2300 Maitland Center Pkwy., # 116
Maitland, FL 32751
TEL: (407) 875-1433
FAX:
Mr. Bill Neetz, VP & GM

A unique franchise opportunity. The professional approach to the multi-billion dollar commercial landscape maintenance industry. Complete training and support provided by top industry professionals. Talk with our franchisees about our profitable, proven business system.

HISTORY: . . . .
Established in 1986; . . 1st Franchised in 1987
Company-Owned Units (As of 12/1/1989): . . .0
Franchised Units (12/1/1989): 14
Total Units (12/1/1989): 14
Distribution: US-14;Can-0;Overseas-0
North America: . . . . 4 States
Concentration: . . 10 in FL, 2 in MO, 2 in MD
Registered: . . . . .FL
. . . .
Average # of Employees: . . . 3-50 FT, 2-20 PT
Prior Industry Experience: . . . . Helpful

FINANCIAL:
Cash Investment: $20-40K
Total Investment: $35-55K
Fees: Franchise - $15-40K
   Royalty: 4%, Advert: 2%
Contract Periods (Yrs.): 5/15
Area Development Agreement: . .No
Sub-Franchise Contract: . . . . .No
Expand in Territory: . . . . Yes
Passive Ownership: . . . Discouraged
Encourage Conversions: . . . . . Yes
Franchisee Purchase(s) Required: .No

FRANCHISOR TRAINING/SUPPORT:
Financial Assistance Provided: . . . . .No
Site Selection Assistance: . . . . .NA
Lease Negotiation Assistance: . . . . .NA
Co-operative Advertising: . . . . .NA
Training: . . . . .1 Wk. Headquarters,
. . . . 1 Wk. Franchisee Location
On-Going Support: . . . . . . B,C,D,G,H,I
Full-Time Franchisor Support Staff: . . .7
EXPANSION PLANS:
   US: . . . . Southeast
Canada - No, ...Overseas - No

WEED MAN

2399 Royal Windsor Dr.
Mississauga, ON L5J1K9 CAN
TEL: (416) 823-8550
FAX: (416) 823-4594
Mr. Kent Jackson, Natl. Mktg Mgr.

WEED MAN is Canada's largest lawn care organization. We offer complete training and professional support for this highly-profitable, seasonal business.

HISTORY: . . . . .CFA
Established in 1970; . . 1st Franchised in 1976
Company-Owned Units (As of 12/1/1989): . .1
Franchised Units (12/1/1989): 100
Total Units (12/1/1989): 101
Distribution: US-1;Can-101;Overseas-00
North America: . . . . . .1 State, 9 Provinces
Concentration: . 63 in ON, 10 in BC, 10 in PQ
Registered: . . . . AB
. . . .
Average # of Employees: . . . . . . 4 FT, 6 PT
Prior Industry Experience: . . . . Helpful

FINANCIAL:
Cash Investment: $45-55K
Total Investment: $60K
Fees: Franchise - $33K
   Royalty: Flat, Advert: . . . . . Flat
Contract Periods (Yrs.): 10/10
Area Development Agreement: . .No
Sub-Franchise Contract: . . . . . Yes
Expand in Territory: . . . . . . .No
Passive Ownership: . . . Discouraged
Encourage Conversions: . . . . .No
Franchisee Purchase(s) Required: .No

FRANCHISOR TRAINING/SUPPORT:
Financial Assistance Provided: . . . . .No
Site Selection Assistance: . . . . .NA
Lease Negotiation Assistance: . . . . .Yes
Co-operative Advertising: . . . . .Yes
Training: . . . . 1 Wk. Headquarters
. . . .
On-Going Support: . . . . .B,C,D,E,G,H,I
Full-Time Franchisor Support Staff: . . 11
EXPANSION PLANS:
   US: . . . . No
Canada - Yes, ...Overseas - Yes

SUPPLEMENTAL LISTING OF FRANCHISORS

A-PERM-O-GREEN LAWN . . . . P.O. Box 561687, Dallas TX 75356
LAWN SPECIALTIES . . . . 5 N. Conahan Dr., Butler Ind. Par, Hazleton PA 18201
LAWN-A-MAT OF CANADA . . . ., Conestogo ON N0B1N0   CAN
MACLAWN SPRAY . . . . P.O. Box 364 North Service Rd., Beamsville ON L0R1BO   CAN
NITRO-GREEN PROFESSIONAL LAWN & TREE . . . . P.O. Box M, Fort Collins CO 80522
NUTRI-LAWN INTERNATIONAL . . . . 2319 McGillvary Blvd., Winnipeg MB R0G0R0   CAN
SERVICEMASTER LAWNCARE . . . . 888 Ridge Lake Blvd., Memphis TN 38119

CHAPTER 27

MAID SERVICES AND HOME CLEANING

CLASSY MAIDS

1180 S. Spring Ctr. Blvd., # 115
Altamount Springs, FL 32714
TEL: (800) 445-5238 (407) 862-2223 C
FAX:
Mr. William Olday, President

Professional home cleaning service with latest state-of-the-art computer management program. Proven training and marketing program. Protected territory. Grand Opening Program gets you off to fast start. Carpet cleaning and commercial cleaning. Training films, brochures, annual marketing program. No experience needed.

HISTORY: . . . .
Established in 1980; . . 1st Franchised in 1985
Company-Owned Units (As of 12/1/1989): . .1
Franchised Units (12/1/1989): 28
Total Units (12/1/1989): 29
Distribution: US-29;Can-0;Overseas-0
North America: . . . . 8 States
Concentration: . . . 6 in WI, 3 in MN, 5 in FL
Registered: . . . . . . FL,MD,MI,MN,VA,WI

. . . .
Average # of Employees: 2 FT, 12 PT as Needed
Prior Industry Experience: . . . . Helpful

FINANCIAL:
Cash Investment: $6-10K
Total Investment: $8-14K
Fees: Franchise - $6-10K
  Royalty: 6%, Advert: 0%
Contract Periods (Yrs.): 7/7
Area Development Agreement: Yes/7
Sub-Franchise Contract: . . . . . .No
Expand in Territory: . . . . Yes
Passive Ownership: . . . Discouraged
Encourage Conversions: . . . . . .No
Franchisee Purchase(s) Required: .No

FRANCHISOR TRAINING/SUPPORT:
Financial Assistance Provided: . . .Yes(D)
Site Selection Assistance: . . . . .NA
Lease Negotiation Assistance: . . . . .NA
Co-operative Advertising: . . . . .Yes
Training: . . . . 1 Wk. Headquarters
. . . .
On-Going Support: . . . . . . B,C,d,G,H,I
Full-Time Franchisor Support Staff: . . . 3
EXPANSION PLANS:
US: . . . . .All US
Canada - No, ... Overseas - No

CUSTOM MAID

1608 N. Miller Rd., # 5
Scottsdale, AZ 85257
TEL: (800) 888-6876 (602) 941-2993
FAX:
Mr. Frank E. Hronek, Sales Director

CUSTOM MAID provides quality home cleaning on a regularly-scheduled basis. The maids learn CUSTOM MAID methods and procedures, which optimize efficiency and help assure quality. CUSTOM MAID offers you a complete package of operating manuals, office forms and 5 days of comprehensive training.

HISTORY: . . . .
Established in 1985; . . 1st Franchised in 1989
Company-Owned Units (As of 12/1/1989): . .1
Franchised Units (12/1/1989): 0
Total Units (12/1/1989): 1
Distribution: US-1;Can-0;Overseas-0
 North America: . . . . .1 State
 Concentration: . . . . 1 in AZ
Registered: . . . .

. . . .
Average # of Employees: . . . . .1 FT, 2-24 PT
Prior Industry Experience: . . . . . . Helpful

FINANCIAL:
Cash Investment: $500-5K
Total Investment: $500-5K
Fees: Franchise - $2.9K
 Royalty: 0%, Advert: 0%
Contract Periods (Yrs.): . . . . Indef.
Area Development Agreement: . .No
Sub-Franchise Contract: . . . . .No
Expand in Territory: . . . . Yes
Passive Ownership: . . . . . .Allowed
Encourage Conversions: . . . . . Yes
Franchisee Purchase(s) Required: .No

FRANCHISOR TRAINING/SUPPORT:
Financial Assistance Provided: . . . . . No
Site Selection Assistance: . . . . .NA
Lease Negotiation Assistance: . . . . . No
Co-operative Advertising: . . . . .NA
Training: . . . . 5 Days Headquarters
. . . .
On-Going Support: I
Full-Time Franchisor Support Staff: . . .2
EXPANSION PLANS:
 US: . . . . .All US
 Canada - No, ...Overseas - No

CUSTOM MAID

30455 Greenfield Rd.
Southfield, MI 48076
TEL: (313) 258-6243 C
FAX:
Mr. Robert Toliver, President

A CUSTOM MAID franchise is a maid service business for both domestic and commercial applications in the marketplace. What sets CUSTOM MAID apart is our proven, time-tested system and our dedication to the "old fashioned" tradition of quality maid service, extensive training and support program, a computerized or manual operations and management system.

HISTORY: . . . .
Established in 1982; . . 1st Franchised in 1987
Company-Owned Units (As of 12/1/1989): . .1
Franchised Units (12/1/1989): 1
Total Units (12/1/1989): 2
Distribution: US-2;Can-0;Overseas-0
 North America: . . . . .1 State
 Concentration: . . . . 2 in MI
Registered: . . . . IL,MD,MI,NY,VA

. . . .
Average # of Employees: . . . . .3 FT
Prior Industry Experience: . . . . . . Helpful

FINANCIAL:
Cash Investment: $20K
Total Investment: $28K
Fees: Franchise - $12.5K
 Royalty: 8%, Advert: 1-3%
Contract Periods (Yrs.): 10/10
Area Development Agreement: . .No
Sub-Franchise Contract: . . . . .No
Expand in Territory: . . . . Yes
Passive Ownership: . . . Discouraged
Encourage Conversions: . . . . . Yes
Franchisee Purchase(s) Required: .No

FRANCHISOR TRAINING/SUPPORT:
Financial Assistance Provided: . . . . . No
Site Selection Assistance: . . . . .Yes
Lease Negotiation Assistance: . . . . .Yes
Co-operative Advertising: . . . . .Yes
Training: . . . . 2 Wks. Headquarters,
. . . . 1 Wk. Franchisee Location
On-Going Support: . . . a,B,c,D,E,F,G,h,i
Full-Time Franchisor Support Staff: . . .3
EXPANSION PLANS:
 US: . . . . .All US
 Canada - No, ...Overseas - No

DIAL-A-MAID

753 1/2 Harry L. Dr.
Johnson City, NY 13790
TEL: (607) 798-8871 C
FAX:
Mr. Dennis Coughlin, President

DIAL-A-MAID is a professional house cleaning service which tailors cleanings to individual client's needs. DIAL-A-MAID performs both regularly-scheduled cleanings and specialized Spring-type cleanings. Expansion is encouraged into small commercial accounts and full-service residential cleaning. Founders are a family with over 26 years of cleaning experience.

HISTORY: . . . .
Established in 1983; . . 1st Franchised in 1986
Company-Owned Units (As of 12/1/1989): . .1
Franchised Units (12/1/1989): 5
Total Units (12/1/1989): 6
Distribution: US-6;Can-0;Overseas-0
 North America: . . . . 2 States
 Concentration: . . . . 3 in NY, 3 in PA
Registered: . . . . NY

. . . .
Average # of Employees: . . . . 10 FT
Prior Industry Experience: . . . . . . Helpful

FINANCIAL:
Cash Investment: $0
Total Investment: $14-21K
Fees: Franchise - $5-9.5K
 Royalty: 6%, Advert: 2%
Contract Periods (Yrs.): 10/5
Area Development Agreement: Yes/5
Sub-Franchise Contract: . . . . . Yes
Expand in Territory: . . . . . . .No
Passive Ownership: . . . Discouraged
Encourage Conversions: . . . . . Yes
Franchisee Purchase(s) Required: .No

FRANCHISOR TRAINING/SUPPORT:
Financial Assistance Provided: . . . Yes(I)
Site Selection Assistance: . . . . . . .Yes
Lease Negotiation Assistance: . . . .Yes
Co-operative Advertising: . . . . No
Training: . . . . . 3-5 Days Headquarters,
. . . . 1-7 Days Site
On-Going Support: . . . . .B,C,D,E,G,H,I
Full-Time Franchisor Support Staff: . . .4
EXPANSION PLANS:
 US: . . . . .All US
 Canada - Yes, ...Overseas - No

GUARANTEE GIRLS

6210 Hollyfield Dr.
Baton Rouge, LA 70810
TEL: (800) 735-4475 (504) 293-8682 C
FAX: (504) 296-3910
Ms. Ellen K. Folks, President

Full-service residential and commercial cleaning, carpet cleaning and disaster clean-up from water and fire damage, all for the one low franchise fee. Two weeks' training. Unique method of cleaning residential homes to produce top profits. Management, marketing training. 800 #.

HISTORY: . . . .
Established in 1984; . . 1st Franchised in 1986
Company-Owned Units (As of 12/1/1989): . .1
Franchised Units (12/1/1989): 3
Total Units (12/1/1989): 4
Distribution: US-4;Can-0;Overseas-0
North America: . . . . 3 States
Concentration: . . . 2 in LA, 1 in TX, 1 in TN
Registered: . . . .
. . . .
Average # of Employees: . . . . . .10 FT, 5 PT
Prior Industry Experience: . . . . Helpful

FINANCIAL:
Cash Investment: $10-20K
Total Investment: $15-20K
Fees: Franchise - $10K
  Royalty: 5%, Advert: 2%
Contract Periods (Yrs.): 10/10
Area Development Agreement: . .No
Sub-Franchise Contract: . . . . . .No
Expand in Territory: . . . . . . Yes
Passive Ownership: . . . Discouraged
Encourage Conversions: . . . . . Yes
Franchisee Purchase(s) Required: .No

FRANCHISOR TRAINING/SUPPORT:
Financial Assistance Provided: . . .Yes(D)
Site Selection Assistance: . . . . . . .NA
Lease Negotiation Assistance: . . . .NA
Co-operative Advertising: . . . . . . .No
Training: . . . . 2 Wks. Headquarters
. . . .
On-Going Support: . . . . . . B,D,E,G,H,I
Full-Time Franchisor Support Staff: . . 25
EXPANSION PLANS:
US: . . . . Southeast
Canada - No, ...Overseas - No

HOME CLEANING CENTERS OF AMERICA

1111 W. 95th St., # 219
Overland Park, KS 66214
TEL: (800) 767-1118 (913) 599-6453
FAX:
Mr. Mike Calhoon, President

Primarily a conventional home cleaning service for the two income family, with secondary emphasis on carpet, window and small office cleaning. Strong appeal to franchisees who are looking for an individualized business plan which will yield predictable results.

HISTORY: . . . .
Established in 1981; . . 1st Franchised in 1984
Company-Owned Units (As of 12/1/1989): . .1
Franchised Units (12/1/1989): 9
Total Units (12/1/1989): 10
Distribution: US-10;Can-0;Overseas-0
North America: . . . . 5 States
Concentration: . . . . 4 in MO, 3 in KS
Registered: . . . . .IN
. . . .
Average # of Employees: . . . . 10 FT
Prior Industry Experience: . . . . . . Helpful

FINANCIAL:
Cash Investment: $20-30K
Total Investment: $20-30K
Fees: Franchise - $11K
  Royalty: 4.5-5%, Advert: 0%
Contract Periods (Yrs.): . . 10/Varies
Area Development Agreement: Yes/Var
Sub-Franchise Contract: . . . . . .No
Expand in Territory: . . . . . . Yes
Passive Ownership: . . . Discouraged
Encourage Conversions: . . . . NA
Franchisee Purchase(s) Required: .No

FRANCHISOR TRAINING/SUPPORT:
Financial Assistance Provided: . . . Yes(I)
Site Selection Assistance: . . . . . . .Yes
Lease Negotiation Assistance: . . . .Yes
Co-operative Advertising: . . . . . . .Yes
Training: . . . . 5 Days Headquarters
. . . .
On-Going Support: . . . . . B,C,D,E,G,H
Full-Time Franchisor Support Staff: . . . 3
EXPANSION PLANS:
US: . . . . .All US
Canada - No, ...Overseas - No

MAID BRIGADE SERVICES

850 Indian Trail, Box 1901
Lilburn, GA 30226
TEL: (800) 772-MAID (404) 564-2400
FAX:
Mr. Don Hay, President

MAID BRIGADE's unique approach to franchise success is through a support system of Business Development Officers located in regional offices throughout the nation. Their sole, full-time function is to work with their franchisees from the day they return from the initial training program.

HISTORY: . . . . .IFA
Established in 1979; . . 1st Franchised in 1980
Company-Owned Units (As of 12/1/1989): . .5
Franchised Units (12/1/1989): 210
Total Units (12/1/1989): 215
Distribution: . . . US-110;Can-105;Overseas-0
North America: . . . . 23 States, 8 Provinces
Concentration: . 18 in FL, 16 in VA, 13 in ON
Registered: . . .CA,FL,HI,IN,MD,MI.MN.OR
. . . . RI,VA,WA,WI
Average # of Employees: . . . . 12 FT
Prior Industry Experience: . . . . . . Helpful

FINANCIAL:
Cash Investment: $25-28K
Total Investment: $25-28K
Fees: Franchise - $14K
  Royalty: 7%, Advert: 2%
Contract Periods (Yrs.): 10/10
Area Development Agreement: . .No
Sub-Franchise Contract: . . . . Yes
Expand in Territory: . . . . . . .No
Passive Ownership: . . . Discouraged
Encourage Conversions: . . . . Yes
Franchisee Purchase(s) Required: .No

FRANCHISOR TRAINING/SUPPORT:
Financial Assistance Provided: . . . . .No
Site Selection Assistance: . . . . . . .Yes
Lease Negotiation Assistance: . . . .NA
Co-operative Advertising: . . . . . . .Yes
Training: . . . . 5 Days Headquarters,
. . . . .2 Days On-site
On-Going Support: . . . . . .B,C,D,G,H,I
Full-Time Franchisor Support Staff: . . 19
EXPANSION PLANS:
US: . . . . .All US
Canada - No, ...Overseas - No

MAID EASY

33 Pratt St.
Glastonbury, CT 06033
TEL: (203) 659-2953
FAX:
Mr. Pat Brubaker, President

Very low overhead, low start-up costs and a totally unique method of placing expert and professional personnel in home cleaning positions makes MAID EASY your choice for a residential cleaning franchise. MAID EASY can be home-based and, as such, is a business well-suited for women who wish to remain in the home while fulfilling their career objective and customer demand for quality service.

HISTORY: . . . . IFA
Established in 1981; . . 1st Franchised in 1987
Company-Owned Units (As of 12/1/1989): . .1
Franchised Units (12/1/1989): 2
Total Units (12/1/1989): 3
Distribution: US-3;Can-0;Overseas-0
North America: . . . . .1 State
Concentration: . . . . 3 in CT
Registered: . . . . FL,MD
. . . .
Average # of Employees: . . . . .1 FT
Prior Industry Experience: . . . . Helpful

FINANCIAL:
Cash Investment: $9K
Total Investment: $17K
Fees: Franchise - $8.5K
Royalty: Flat, Advert: 2%
Contract Periods (Yrs.): 10/10
Area Development Agreement: . Yes
Sub-Franchise Contract: . . . . .No
Expand in Territory: . . . . . . .No
Passive Ownership: . . . Not Allowed
Encourage Conversions: . . . . Yes
Franchisee Purchase(s) Required: .No

FRANCHISOR TRAINING/SUPPORT:
Financial Assistance Provided: . . . Yes(I)
Site Selection Assistance: . . . . . . .NA
Lease Negotiation Assistance: . . . . .NA
Co-operative Advertising: . . . . . . .NA
Training: . . . . 5 Days Headquarters
. . . .
On-Going Support: . . . . .b,d,G,H,i
Full-Time Franchisor Support Staff: . . .1
EXPANSION PLANS:
US: . . . . .All US
Canada - No, ...Overseas - No

MAIDS ELITE

310 S. Main St., P. O. Box 381998
Duncanville, TX 75138
TEL: (214) 709-1900
FAX:
Mr. Charles Smith, CEO

MAIDS ELITE's systematic, professional approach to cleaning, training and management rank it among the nation's fastest-growing franchises. MAIDS ELITE provides the most comprehensive franchise support and equipment and supply packages in the industry. Attractive financing is provided.

HISTORY: . . . .
Established in 1986; . . 1st Franchised in 1988
Company-Owned Units (As of 12/1/1989): . .1
Franchised Units (12/1/1989): 4
Total Units (12/1/1989): 5
Distribution: US-5;Can-0;Overseas-0
North America: . . . . .1 State
Concentration: . . . . 5 in TX
Registered: . . . .
. . . .
Average # of Employees: . . . . .8 FT
Prior Industry Experience: . . . . Helpful

FINANCIAL:
Cash Investment: $6-9K
Total Investment: $6-9K
Fees: Franchise - $4.9K
Royalty: 4-6%, Advert: 2%
Contract Periods (Yrs.): 10/5
Area Development Agreement: Yes/5
Sub-Franchise Contract: . . . . .No
Expand in Territory: . . . . . . Yes
Passive Ownership: . . . Discouraged
Encourage Conversions: . . . . Yes
Franchisee Purchase(s) Required: .No

FRANCHISOR TRAINING/SUPPORT:
Financial Assistance Provided: . . . Yes(I)
Site Selection Assistance: . . . . . . .Yes
Lease Negotiation Assistance: . . . .Yes
Co-operative Advertising: . . . . . . .Yes
Training: . . . . 2 Wks. Headquarters
. . . . 1 Wk. On-site, On-going
On-Going Support: . . . .B,C,D,E,G,H,I
Full-Time Franchisor Support Staff: . . .4
EXPANSION PLANS:
US: . . . . Southwest
Canada - No, ...Overseas - No

MAIDS, THE -
AMERICA'S MAID SERVICE

4820 Dodge St.
Omaha, NE 68132
TEL: (800) THE-MAID (402) 558-5555
FAX:
Ms. Danielle Bishop, Fran. Dev.

THE MAIDS - AMERICA'S MAID SERVICE has the most professional maid service/house cleaning program available today. Complete programs for advertising, insurance, extensive training, computerized management system, equipment, automobile and supplies. All programs, seminars and annual meetings are designed for maximum support for each franchise operation.

HISTORY: . . . . IFA
Established in 1979; . . 1st Franchised in 1981
Company-Owned Units (As of 12/1/1989): . .0
Franchised Units (12/1/1989): 187
Total Units (12/1/1989): 187
Distribution: . . . US-182;Can-5;Overseas-0
North America: . . . . 38 States, 2 Provinces
Concentration: . . .10 in CA, 8 in NY, 6 in PA
Registered: . . . . .All
. . . .
Average # of Employees: . . . . 1 FT, 12-20 PT
Prior Industry Experience: . . . . Helpful

FINANCIAL:
Cash Investment: $20-30K
Total Investment: $40-50K
Fees: Franchise - $15.9K
Royalty: 4-7%, Advert: . . . 2%
Contract Periods (Yrs.): 5/5
Area Development Agreement: Yes/5
Sub-Franchise Contract: . . . . .No
Expand in Territory: . . . . . . Yes
Passive Ownership: . . . Discouraged
Encourage Conversions: . . . . .No
Franchisee Purchase(s) Required: .No

FRANCHISOR TRAINING/SUPPORT:
Financial Assistance Provided: . . . Yes(I)
Site Selection Assistance: . . . . . . .Yes
Lease Negotiation Assistance: . . . . .No
Co-operative Advertising: . . . . . . .Yes
Training: . . . . .1 Wk. Headquarters
. . . .
On-Going Support: . . . A,B,C,D,E,G,H,I
Full-Time Franchisor Support Staff: . . . .
EXPANSION PLANS:
US: . . . . .All US
Canada - Yes, ...Overseas - No

MCMAID

10 W. Kinzie St.
Chicago, IL 60610
TEL: (800) 444-6250 (312) 321-6250
FAX: (312) 321-9716
Mr. Anthony Foster, Natl. Fran. Dir.

Professional team cleaning, with the emphasis on franchisees having large territories (75,000 - 125,000 households), thereby creating greater opportunity for smaller group.

HISTORY: . . . . IFA
Established in 1975; . . 1st Franchised in 1988
Company-Owned Units (As of 12/1/1989): . . 5
Franchised Units (12/1/1989): 10
Total Units (12/1/1989): 15
Distribution: US-15;Can-0;Overseas-0
North America: . . . . 4 States
Concentration: . . . .9 in Il, 2 in MA, 2 in MN
Registered: . . . . All Except AB
. . . .
Average # of Employees: . . . . 20 FT
Prior Industry Experience: . . . . Helpful

FINANCIAL:
Cash Investment: $18-35K
Total Investment: $18-50K
Fees: Franchise - $5-25K
Royalty: 6%, Advert: 2%
Contract Periods (Yrs.): 10/5/5
Area Development Agreement: . .No
Sub-Franchise Contract: . . . . .No
Expand in Territory: . . . . Yes
Passive Ownership: . . . Discouraged
Encourage Conversions: . . . . NA
Franchisee Purchase(s) Required: .No

FRANCHISOR TRAINING/SUPPORT:
Financial Assistance Provided: . . .Yes(D)
Site Selection Assistance: . . . . .NA
Lease Negotiation Assistance: . . . . .Yes
Co-operative Advertising: . . . . .Yes
Training: . . . . 2 Wks. Headquarters
. . . .
On-Going Support: . . . . . . B,C,D,G,H,I
Full-Time Franchisor Support Staff: . . . 6
EXPANSION PLANS:
US: . . . . .All US
Canada - No, ...Overseas - No

MERRY MAIDS

11117 Mill Valley Rd.
Omaha, NE 68154
TEL: (800) 345-5535 (402) 498-0331 C
FAX: (402) 498-0142
Mr. Bob Burdge, Fran. Sales Dir.

MERRY MAIDS is the largest and most successful company in the maid service industry. The company's commitment to training and on-going support is unmatched. MERRY MAIDS is ranked among the nation's hottest and fastest-growing franchises in Success, Venture and Entrepreneur. MERRY MAIDS provides the most comprehensive computer software package and equipment and supply package in the industry.

HISTORY: . . . . IFA
Established in 1979; . . 1st Franchised in 1980
Company-Owned Units (As of 12/1/1989): . .2
Franchised Units (12/1/1989): 498
Total Units (12/1/1989): 500
Distribution: US-494;Can-1;Overseas-5
North America: . . . . . 45 States, 1 Province
Concentration: . . . . .72 in CA, IL, MA
Registered: . . . . All Except AB
. . . .
Average # of Employees: . . . . . . 2 FT, 1 PT
Prior Industry Experience: . . . . . . Helpful

FINANCIAL: NYSE-SVM
Cash Investment: $25-32.5K
Total Investment: $25-32.5K
Fees: Franchise - $18.5K
Royalty: 7-5%, Advert: 0%
Contract Periods (Yrs.): 5/10
Area Development Agreement: . .No
Sub-Franchise Contract: . . . . .No
Expand in Territory: . . . . Yes
Passive Ownership: . . . Discouraged
Encourage Conversions: . . . . NA
Franchisee Purchase(s) Required: .No

FRANCHISOR TRAINING/SUPPORT:
Financial Assistance Provided: . . .Yes(D)
Site Selection Assistance: . . . .
Lease Negotiation Assistance: . . . . .Yes
Co-operative Advertising: . . . . .No
Training: . . . . .1 Wk. Headquarters,
. . 4 Days Field, 4Wks. + Buddy System
On-Going Support: . . . . A,B,C,D,G,H,I
Full-Time Franchisor Support Staff: . . 33
EXPANSION PLANS:
US: . . . . .All US
Canada - Yes, . . . Overseas - Yes

MINI MAID SERVICES

1855 Piedmont Rd., # 100
Marietta, GA 30066
TEL: (800) 627-6464 (404) 973-3271
FAX:
Mr. Gary R. Latz, COO

MINI MAID founded the team cleaning industry and has franchised longer than anyone else. Our unique flat rate royalty system rewards you for your success and makes MINI MAID the best value and lowest risk in our industry. We continue to be operated by our Founder and are a true Franchise Family, not a factory.

HISTORY: . . . .
Established in 1973; . . 1st Franchised in 1976
Company-Owned Units (As of 12/1/1989): . .0
Franchised Units (12/1/1989): 117
Total Units (12/1/1989): 117
Distribution: US-117;Can-0;Overseas-0
North America: . . . . 23 States
Concentration: . . .17 in GA, 7 in PA, 7 in NY
Registered: . . . . CA,MI
. . . .
Average # of Employees: . . . . 10 FT
Prior Industry Experience: . . . . Helpful

FINANCIAL:
Cash Investment: $15-21K
Total Investment: $15-21K
Fees: Franchise - $12.5K
Royalty: Flat/Mo., Advert: . . . 0%
Contract Periods (Yrs.): 5/5
Area Development Agreement: . .No
Sub-Franchise Contract: . . . . Yes
Expand in Territory: . . . . Yes
Passive Ownership: . . . Discouraged
Encourage Conversions: . . . . Yes
Franchisee Purchase(s) Required: .No

FRANCHISOR TRAINING/SUPPORT:
Financial Assistance Provided: . . . . .No
Site Selection Assistance: . . . . . . .Yes
Lease Negotiation Assistance: . . . .NA
Co-operative Advertising: . . . . .Yes
Training: . . . . . 1 Wk. Corporate Offices
. . . .
On-Going Support: . . . . b,C,d,G,h
Full-Time Franchisor Support Staff: . . . 4
EXPANSION PLANS:
US: . . . . .All US
Canada - Yes, . . . Overseas - Yes

MINI MAID/MINI MENAGE SERVICE SYSTEMS
188 Shorting Rd.
Scarborough, ON M1S3S7 CAN
TEL: (416) 298-7288
FAX:
Mr. Fred Romito, President

Team of 4 maids clean, using own supplies and equipment. All fully-trained, uniformed, insured and bonded.

HISTORY: . . . .
Established in 1979; . . 1st Franchised in 1979
Company-Owned Units (As of 12/1/1989): . 36
Franchised Units (12/1/1989): 65
Total Units (12/1/1989): 101
Distribution: US-0;Can-101;Overseas-0
North America: . . . . 7 Provinces
Concentration: . . 20 in ON, 14 in BC, 9 in PQ
Registered: . . . . AB
. . . .
Average # of Employees: . . . . 6 FT
Prior Industry Experience: . . . . Helpful

FINANCIAL:
Cash Investment: \$17K
Total Investment: \$20K
Fees: Franchise - \$17K
Royalty: 6-4%, Advert: 2%
Contract Periods (Yrs.): 5/5
Area Development Agreement: Yes/5
Sub-Franchise Contract: . . . . . Yes
Expand in Territory: . . . . . . Yes
Passive Ownership: . . . Not Allowed
Encourage Conversions: . . . . . No
Franchisee Purchase(s) Required: .No

FRANCHISOR TRAINING/SUPPORT:
Financial Assistance Provided: . . . . . No
Site Selection Assistance: . . . . .NA
Lease Negotiation Assistance: . . . . .NA
Co-operative Advertising: . . . . .Yes
Training: . . . . 1 Wk. Headquarters
. . . .
On-Going Support: . . . . B,C,G,H,I
Full-Time Franchisor Support Staff: . . . 5
EXPANSION PLANS:
US: . . . . No
Canada - Yes, . . . Overseas - Yes

MOLLY MAID

3001 S. State St.
Ann Arbor, MI 48108
TEL: (800) 289-4600 (313) 996-1555
FAX: (313) 996-1906
Ms. Dena Ott, Fran. Sales Mgr.

MOLLY MAID is the premier residential cleaning service company, currently operating in 7 countries. MOLLY MAID is distinguished by its unique, high-profile image. English-style maid uniforms and navy blue business suits and blue/pink imaged company cars speak of professionalism. It's an image that instills customer confidence - an image that sells! Our nurturing approach to building franchisee success is unequalled.

HISTORY: . . . . IFA/WIF
Established in 1978; . . 1st Franchised in 1979
Company-Owned Units (As of 12/1/1989): . .0
Franchised Units (12/1/1989): 350
Total Units (12/1/1989): 350
Distribution: . . US-142;Can-161;Overseas-47
North America: . . . . 30 States, 8 Provinces
Concentration: . 81 in ON, 21 in CA, 17 in MI
Registered: . . . CA,FL,IL,IN,MD,MI,MN,NY
. . . . OR,VA,WA,WI,AB
Average # of Employees: . . . . 12 FT
Prior Industry Experience: . . . . . . Helpful

FINANCIAL:
Cash Investment: \$23-28K
Total Investment: \$23-28K
Fees: Franchise - \$16.9K
Royalty: 7-4%, Advert: 2%
Contract Periods (Yrs.): . . . 10/10
Area Development Agreement: .No
Sub-Franchise Contract: . . . . .No
Expand in Territory: . . . . . . Yes
Passive Ownership: . . . Not Allowed
Encourage Conversions: . . . . .No
Franchisee Purchase(s) Required: .No

FRANCHISOR TRAINING/SUPPORT:
Financial Assistance Provided: . . . . No
Site Selection Assistance: . . . . . . .Yes
Lease Negotiation Assistance: . . . . . No
Co-operative Advertising: . . . . .Yes
Training: . . . . 1 Wk. Headquarters, 2 Day
. . . . . . .Quarterly Seminars in Region
On-Going Support: . . . . . . C,D,E,G,H,I
Full-Time Franchisor Support Staff: . . 35
EXPANSION PLANS:
US: . . . . All US
Canada - Yes, ...Overseas - Yes

SUPPLEMENTAL LISTING OF FRANCHISORS

CLEANBUSTERS . . . . 3709 W. Chester Pike, Newtown Square PA 19073
CLEANING GENIE, THE . . . . 5763 Talmadge Rd., Toledo OH 43623
CONSUMER CARE BY BODI . . . . 6029 - 104 St., Edmonton AB T6H2K9   CAN
DAISY FRESH . . . . 7807 Wakeley Plaza, Omaha NE 68114
DOMESTICAIDE . . . . 6400 W. 110 St., # 205, Overland Park KS 66211
GREAT MAIDS . . . . 1155 C Chess Dr., # 1, Foster City CA 94404
HOME MAID SERVICES . . . . 563 W. 500 South, # 300, Bountiful UT 84010
MAID CONVENIENT . . . . 69 Queen St. S., Hamilton ON L8P3R6   CAN
MAID ELITE . . . . .310 S. Main St., P. O. Box 381998, Duncanville TX 75138
MAID MASTERS . . . . .18002 Irvine Blvd., # 202, Tustin CA 92680
MAID OF GOLD . . . . 917 W. America Circle, # 101, Mobile AL 36609
MAID WITH PRIDE . . . . P. O. Box 1006, Streetsville ON L5M2C5   CAN
MAIDCO INTERNATIONAL . . . . 2 Bloor St. W., # 700, Toronto ON M4W3R1   CAN

MOLLY MAID . . . . 100 Bronte Rd., Oakville ON L6L3B8   CAN
MR. MOM'S MAID SERVICE . . . . .P. O. Box 4342, Gainesville FL 32613
PROFESSIONALS MAID SERVICE . . . . .1401 Johnson Ferry Rd., #328 D-2, Marietta GA 30062
SOLUFEED LAWN CARE . . . . 2600 John St., # 101, Markham ON L3R3W3   CAN
SUN SERVICES WINDOW CLEANING .35 High St., Belfast ME 04915
TREND TIDY'S MAID SERVICE . . . . 380 Esna Park Dr., Markham ON L3R1H5   CAN

CHAPTER 28

MAINTENANCE / CLEANING SANITATION

**AMERICAN LEAK DETECTION /
LEAK BUSTERS**
P.O. Box 1701, 1750 E. Arenas, #7
Palm Springs, CA 92263
TEL: (619) 320-9991
FAX:
Mr. Daniel Frazier, Fran./Sales Dir.

With the use of highly sophisticated electronic equipment, locate concealed water and gas leaks in swimming pools, spas, fountains, under concrete slabs, roadways and parking lots. With the use of thermography, we locate building heating and cooling losses, roof leaks and electrical malfunctions.

HISTORY: . . . . IFA
Established in 1975; . . 1st Franchised in 1984
Company-Owned Units (As of 12/1/1989): . .0
Franchised Units (12/1/1989): 95
Total Units (12/1/1989): 95
Distribution: US-93;Can-0;Overseas-2
North America: . . . . 10 States
Concentration: . . . . .CA, AZ, TX
Registered: . . . CA,FL,HI,IL,IN,MD,MI,MN
. . . . .NY,OR,VA
Average # of Employees: . . . . . . 1 FT, 1 PT
Prior Industry Experience: . . . . Helpful

FINANCIAL:
Cash Investment: $20K
Total Investment: $40K
Fees: Franchise - $20K
 Royalty: 8-10%, Advert: 0%
Contract Periods (Yrs.): 10/5
Area Development Agreement: . .No
Sub-Franchise Contract: . . . . .No
Expand in Territory: . . . . . . Yes
Passive Ownership: . . . Not Allowed
Encourage Conversions: . . . . . Yes
Franchisee Purchase(s) Required: Yes

FRANCHISOR TRAINING/SUPPORT:
Financial Assistance Provided: . . . . .Yes
Site Selection Assistance: . . . . .NA
Lease Negotiation Assistance: . . . . .NA
Co-operative Advertising: . . . . .No
Training: . . . . . . 3-6 Wks. Headquarters
. . . .
On-Going Support: . . . . . . .b,C,D,G,H
Full-Time Franchisor Support Staff: . . .7
EXPANSION PLANS:
US: . . . . .All US
Canada - Yes, ...Overseas - Yes

AMERICLEAN

6602 S. Frontage Rd.
Billings, MT 59101
TEL: (800) 827-9111 (406) 652-1960
FAX:
Mr. Jim Pearson, VP Fran. Develop.

Serving the multi-billion dollar insurance claims industry, AMERICLEAN is seeking responsible owners to operate high-volume Disaster Restoration Centers. Provide fire and flood damage, repair and deodorization, liquid dry-cleaning of carpets, upholstery & drapery, ceiling and specialty cleaning services. Demonstrated leadership and business acumen required.

HISTORY: . . . . IFA
Established in 1979; . . 1st Franchised in 1981
Company-Owned Units (As of 12/1/1989): . .1
Franchised Units (12/1/1989): 20
Total Units (12/1/1989): 21
Distribution: US-21;Can-0;Overseas-0
North America: . . . . 8 States
Concentration: . . . . 4 in FL, 4 in MT, 4 in ID
Registered: . . . . .All
. . . .
Average # of Employees: . . . . . . 5 FT, 4 PT
Prior Industry Experience: . . . . Helpful

FINANCIAL:
Cash Investment: $13-79K
Total Investment: $28-124K
Fees: Franchise - $15-45K
  Royalty: 1-8.5%, Advert: 0%
Contract Periods (Yrs.): 10/5
Area Development Agreement: Yes/10
Sub-Franchise Contract: . . . . . .No
Expand in Territory: . . . . Yes
Passive Ownership: . . . Discouraged
Encourage Conversions: . . . . Yes
Franchisee Purchase(s) Required: .No

FRANCHISOR TRAINING/SUPPORT:
Financial Assistance Provided: . . .Yes(D)
Site Selection Assistance: . . . . .Yes
Lease Negotiation Assistance: . . . . .Yes
Co-operative Advertising: . . . . .NA
Training: . . . . 2 Wks. HQ,
. . . . . 3 Days + at Franchisee Location
On-Going Support: . . A,B,C,D,E,F,G,H,I
Full-Time Franchisor Support Staff: . . 20
EXPANSION PLANS:
  US: . . . . .All US
  Canada - No, ...Overseas - No

BIO-CARE

2105 S. Bascom Ave., # 240
Campbell, CA 95008
TEL: (800) 421-9740 *468-5655 (CA)
FAX: (408) 559-7590
Franchise Development Dept.

BIO-CARE offers a unique preventative maintenance service to restaurants, providing complete drain line and grease trap inspection backed by a complete guarantee to handle any service problems which may arise between visits. The franchisee sells the service and hires service techs to perform the service, applying the BIO- CARE patented process bacteria to the system.

HISTORY: . . . . IFA
Established in 1985; . . 1st Franchised in 1989
Company-Owned Units (As of 12/1/1989): . .6
Franchised Units (12/1/1989): 8
Total Units (12/1/1989): 14
Distribution: US-14;Can-0;Overseas-0
North America: . . . . 3 States
Concentration: . . . 9 in CA, 3 in AZ, 2 in CO
Registered: . . . . .All
. . . .
Average # of Employees: . . . . .2-3 FT
Prior Industry Experience: . . . . . . Helpful

FINANCIAL:
Cash Investment: . . . .$
Total Investment: . . . $38.5-46.8K
Fees: Franchise - $20K
  Royalty: 10%, Advert: 0%
Contract Periods (Yrs.): 20/5/5
Area Development Agreement: Yes/20
Sub-Franchise Contract: . . . . . Yes
Expand in Territory: . . . .
Passive Ownership: . . . Not Allowed
Encourage Conversions: . . . . NA
Franchisee Purchase(s) Required: Yes

FRANCHISOR TRAINING/SUPPORT:
Financial Assistance Provided: . . . . . No
Site Selection Assistance: . . . . .NA
Lease Negotiation Assistance: . . . . .NA
Co-operative Advertising: . . . . .NA
Training: . . . . 2 Wks. Headquarters
. . . .
On-Going Support: . . . . C,D,H,I
Full-Time Franchisor Support Staff: . . 18
EXPANSION PLANS:
  US: . . . . . All US + Master Franchisees
  Canada - No, ...Overseas - No

CEILING DOCTOR

2200 Lakeshore Blvd. W., # 105
Toronto, ON M8V1A4 CAN
TEL: (800) 668-6094 (416) 253-4900 C
FAX: (416) 253-9777
Mr. Rob Forrest, Fran. Dir.

Intensive training and on-going support ensure the success of franchisees in their protected franchise areas. Low overhead and high profit margins are key factors which make CEILING DOCTOR a very profitable business.

HISTORY: . . . . IFA
Established in 1985; . . 1st Franchised in 1986
Company-Owned Units (As of 12/1/1989): . .1
Franchised Units (12/1/1989): 51
Total Units (12/1/1989): 52
Distribution: US-16;Can-26;Overseas-10
North America: . . . . 9 States, 10 Provinces
Concentration: . . . 11 in ON, 4 in FL, 3 in MI
Registered: . . . . .All
. . . .
Average # of Employees: . . . . . . 2 FT, 2 PT
Prior Industry Experience: . . . . . . Helpful

FINANCIAL:
Cash Investment: $25K
Total Investment: $25K
Fees: Franchise - $15K
  Royalty: 6%, Advert: 2%
Contract Periods (Yrs.): 5/5
Area Development Agreement: Yes/10
Sub-Franchise Contract: . . . . . Yes
Expand in Territory: . . . . Yes
Passive Ownership: . . . Discouraged
Encourage Conversions: . . . . NA
Franchisee Purchase(s) Required: Yes

FRANCHISOR TRAINING/SUPPORT:
Financial Assistance Provided: . . . Yes(I)
Site Selection Assistance: . . . . .NA
Lease Negotiation Assistance: . . . . .NA
Co-operative Advertising: . . . . .Yes
Training: . . . . 10 Days Head Office
. . . .
On-Going Support: . . . . . .B,C,D,G,H,I
Full-Time Franchisor Support Staff: . . 10
EXPANSION PLANS:
  US: . . . . .All US
  Canada - No, ... Overseas - Yes

CHEM SEAL

1052 W. Foxcroft Dr., #A, Box 762
Camp Hill, PA 17011
TEL: (717) 737-0108 C
FAX:
Mr. Norbert K. Flammang, President

CHEM SEAL has revolutionized the asphalt maintenance industry nationwide by combining a cost-effective sealcoating spray system, superior quality materials and a proprietary bonding adhesive. 5 days of training includes equipment handling, specialized sales/marketing techniques and general business topics. Licensed territory protects your investment.

HISTORY: . . . .
Established in 1986; . . 1st Franchised in 1987
Company-Owned Units (As of 12/1/1989): . .0
Franchised Units (12/1/1989): 24
Total Units (12/1/1989): 24
Distribution: US-24;Can-0;Overseas-0
North America: . . . . 15 States
Concentration: . . . 8 in PA, 5 in NY, 4 in MD
Registered: . . . . All States
. . . .
Average # of Employees: . . . . . . 3 FT, 1 PT
Prior Industry Experience: . . . . Helpful

FINANCIAL:
Cash Investment: $49.5-63.5K
Total Investment: $60-75K
Fees: Franchise - $16K
  Royalty: 5%, Advert: 1%
Contract Periods (Yrs.): 10/10
Area Development Agreement: . .No
Sub-Franchise Contract: . . . . . .No
Expand in Territory: . . . . Yes
Passive Ownership: . . . Not Allowed
Encourage Conversions: . . . . . .No
Franchisee Purchase(s) Required: Yes

FRANCHISOR TRAINING/SUPPORT:
Financial Assistance Provided: . . . Yes(I)
Site Selection Assistance: . . . . . . .Yes
Lease Negotiation Assistance: . . . . .NA
Co-operative Advertising: . . . . .Yes
Training: . . . . .5 Days Reading, PA
. . . .
On-Going Support: . . . . .C,D,E,F,G,H,I
Full-Time Franchisor Support Staff: . . . 1
EXPANSION PLANS:
US: . . . . .All US
Canada - Yes, . . . Overseas - Yes

CHEM-DRY CARPET, DRAPERY & UPHOLSTERY CLEANING

3330 Cameron Park Dr., # 700
Cameron Park, CA 95682
TEL: (800) 841-6583 *821-3240 (CA)
FAX:
Mr. Steven Oldfield, EVP Sales

A unique carpet, drapery and upholstery cleaning service, utilizing a patented, non-toxic cleaning solution which is guaranteed to remove virtually all stains, including the so-called "impossible" stains like red soft drinks, indelible ink, etc. Generally dries in one hour or less.

HISTORY: . . . .
Established in 1977; . . 1st Franchised in 1978
Company-Owned Units (As of 12/1/1989): . .0
Franchised Units (12/1/1989): 3500
Total Units (12/1/1989): 3500
Distribution: US-2000;Can-100;Overseas-1400
North America: . . . . 50 States, 7 Provinces
Concentration: 400 in CA,100 in TX,75 in WA
Registered: . . . . .All
. . . .
Average # of Employees: 1-5FT,1-2PT
Prior Industry Experience: . . . . Helpful

FINANCIAL:
Cash Investment: $3.3-4.9K
Total Investment: $9.9-13.9K
Fees: Franchise - $7.6-7.9K
  Royalty: Flat, Advert: 0%
Contract Periods (Yrs.): 5/5
Area Development Agreement: . .No
Sub-Franchise Contract: . . . . . .No
Expand in Territory: . . . . .No
Passive Ownership: . . . . . .Allowed
Encourage Conversions: . . . . . Yes
Franchisee Purchase(s) Required: Yes

FRANCHISOR TRAINING/SUPPORT:
Financial Assistance Provided: . . .Yes(D)
Site Selection Assistance: . . . . . . .NA
Lease Negotiation Assistance: . . . . .NA
Co-operative Advertising: . . . . .NA
Training: . . . . . . 3-4 Days Headquarters
. . . .
On-Going Support: . . . . d,F,G,H,I
Full-Time Franchisor Support Staff: . . 50
EXPANSION PLANS:
US: . . . . .All US
Canada - Yes, . . . Overseas - Yes

CHEMSTATION INTERNATIONAL

3201 Encrete Ln.
Dayton, OH 45439
TEL: (800) 228-8265 *433-8265 (OH)
FAX:
Mr. Mark O'Connell, VP

CHEMSTATION is engaged in the business of selling franchises for the operation of Chemstation dealerships. The dealerships are "bulk" suppliers of industrial strength cleaners to industrial and commercial clients. Dealerships offer their customers a considerable savings through the use of permanent storage tanks and blending pump. Chemicals are non-hazardous.

HISTORY: . . . . .IFA
Established in 1983; . . 1st Franchised in 1984
Company-Owned Units (As of 12/1/1989): . .1
Franchised Units (12/1/1989): 13
Total Units (12/1/1989): 14
Distribution: US-14;Can-0;Overseas-0
North America: . . . . 5 States
Concentration: . . . . 4 in OH, 3 in MI, 2 in IN
Registered: . . . . IN,MI,WI
. . . .
Average # of Employees: . . . . .5 FT
Prior Industry Experience: . . . . Helpful

FINANCIAL:
Cash Investment: $30-50K
Total Investment: $50-100K
Fees: Franchise - $20K
  Royalty: 4%, Advert: 0%
Contract Periods (Yrs.): 10/5
Area Development Agreement: . .No
Sub-Franchise Contract: . . . . . .No
Expand in Territory: . . . . Yes
Passive Ownership: . . . Discouraged
Encourage Conversions: . . . . . Yes
Franchisee Purchase(s) Required: Yes

FRANCHISOR TRAINING/SUPPORT:
Financial Assistance Provided: . . . . .No
Site Selection Assistance: . . . . . . .Yes
Lease Negotiation Assistance: . . . . .No
Co-operative Advertising: . . . . .No
Training: . . . . .1 Wk. Headquarters,
. . . . 1 Wk. Site
On-Going Support: . . . a,b,C,D,E,f,G,H,I
Full-Time Franchisor Support Staff: . . . 6
EXPANSION PLANS:
US: . . . . .All US
Canada - Yes, ...Overseas - No

CLASSIC CARE OF AMERICA

10190 Belladrum Dr.
Alpharetta, GA 30201
TEL: (404) 664-2010
FAX:
Mr. Bob Lennie, VP/Director

CLASSIC CARE OF AMERICA: This high-margin, 3-in-1 franchise is one of America's home service choices coast-to-coast, providing proven high-tech, hands free-window washing and other needed home services. Using our computerized, on-going support programs, you will fill a void in every community.

HISTORY: . . . . IFA	FINANCIAL:	FRANCHISOR TRAINING/SUPPORT:
Established in 1987; . . 1st Franchised in 1987	Cash Investment: $30-38K	Financial Assistance Provided: . . . Yes(I)
Company-Owned Units (As of 12/1/1989): . .0	Total Investment: $60-68K	Site Selection Assistance: . . . . . . .NA
Franchised Units (12/1/1989): 31	Fees: Franchise - $20K	Lease Negotiation Assistance: . . . . .NA
Total Units (12/1/1989): 31	Royalty: 5%, Advert: 2%	Co-operative Advertising: . . . . . .NA
Distribution: US-31;Can-0;Overseas-0	Contract Periods (Yrs.): 10/10	Training: . . . . 6 Days Atlanta, GA
North America: . . . . 17 States	Area Development Agreement: Yes/10	. . . .
Concentration: . . . 7 in CA,2 in MD, 2 in TN	Sub-Franchise Contract: . . . . . .No	On-Going Support: . . . . . B,C,D,E,G,H
Registered: . . . CA,FL,HI,IL,IN,MD,MI,MN	Expand in Territory: . . . . Yes	Full-Time Franchisor Support Staff: . . .7
. . . . NY,OR,VA,WA,WI	Passive Ownership: . . . . . .Allowed	EXPANSION PLANS:
Average # of Employees: . . . . . 3 FT, 1 PT	Encourage Conversions: . . . . . Yes	US: . . . . .All US
Prior Industry Experience: . . . . . . Helpful	Franchisee Purchase(s) Required: .No	Canada - Yes, . . . Overseas - Yes

---

CLEANSERV INDUSTRIES

3403 Tenth St., 8th Fl.
Riverside, CA 92501
TEL: (800) 942-0073 (714) 781-0220
FAX: (714) 781-3864
Mr. Michael Conti, Dir. Fran. Devel.

CLEANSERV INDUSTRIES' unique programs set us apart from other contract cleaning companies. CSI sells you a business, not a job. Staffed and supported by leading professionals, we teach and support franchisees in managaing and promoting a successful contract cleaning company. Applicants must be committed to success and qualify financially.

HISTORY: . . . . IFA	FINANCIAL:	FRANCHISOR TRAINING/SUPPORT:
Established in 1977; . . 1st Franchised in 1987	Cash Investment: $30K	Financial Assistance Provided: . . . Yes(I)
Company-Owned Units (As of 12/1/1989): . .1	Total Investment: $40K	Site Selection Assistance: . . . . . . .Yes
Franchised Units (12/1/1989): 12	Fees: Franchise - $17.5K	Lease Negotiation Assistance: . . . . .Yes
Total Units (12/1/1989): 13	Royalty: 8%, Advert: 4%	Co-operative Advertising: . . . . . .Yes
Distribution: US-13;Can-0;Overseas-0	Contract Periods (Yrs.): . . . 10/10	Training: . . . . 3 Wks. Headquarters
North America: . . . . .1 State	Area Development Agreement: Yes/10	. . . .
Concentration: . . . . 13 in CA	Sub-Franchise Contract: . . . . Yes	On-Going Support: . . . . .C,D,E,F,G,H,I
Registered: . . . . CA	Expand in Territory: . . . . . . Yes	Full-Time Franchisor Support Staff: . . 20
. . . .	Passive Ownership: . . . Discouraged	EXPANSION PLANS:
Average # of Employees: . . . . .4 PT	Encourage Conversions: . . . . Yes	US: . . . . .All US
Prior Industry Experience: . . . . Helpful	Franchisee Purchase(s) Required: .No	Canada - Yes, ...Overseas - No

---

CLENTECH /
ACOUSTIC CLEAN

2901 Wayzata Blvd.
Minneapolis, MN 55405
TEL: (800) 328-4650 (612) 374-1105
FAX:
Mr. Jim Knudsen, Natl. Sales Mgr.

Oldest, largest and most reputable firm in the growing and underserved acoustical ceiling cleaning industry. Unique technology, proven 11-year history, cleaning all types of ceilings and walls. Low overhead, high margins. Over 400 dealers worldwide have been sold and trained.

HISTORY:	FINANCIAL:	FRANCHISOR TRAINING/SUPPORT:
Established in 1978; . . 1st Franchised in 1982	Cash Investment: $6.8K	Financial Assistance Provided: . . . Yes(I)
Company-Owned Units (As of 12/1/1989): . .1	Total Investment: $11.4K	Site Selection Assistance: . . . . . . .Yes
Franchised Units (12/1/1989): 5	Fees: Franchise - $3-5K	Lease Negotiation Assistance: . . . . .No
Total Units (12/1/1989): 6	Royalty: 0%, Advert: 0%	Co-operative Advertising: . . . . . . .Yes
Distribution: US-4;Can-2;Overseas-0	Contract Periods (Yrs.): 10/10	Training: . . . . 3 Days Headquarters,
North America: . . . . 4 States, 2 Provinces	Area Development Agreement: . .No	. . . . .3 Days Franchisee Location
Concentration: . . . .1 in LA,1 in CA,1 in MN	Sub-Franchise Contract: . . . . .No	On-Going Support: . . . .B,C,D,E,F,G,H,I
Registered: . . . . .CA,FL,MN,NY,OR	Expand in Territory: . . . . . . .No	Full-Time Franchisor Support Staff: . . .8
. . . . VA	Passive Ownership: . . . . . .Allowed	EXPANSION PLANS:
Average # of Employees: . . . . . . 1 FT, 1 PT	Encourage Conversions: . . . . Yes	US: . . . . .All US
Prior Industry Experience: . . . . Helpful	Franchisee Purchase(s) Required: Yes	Canada - Yes, . . . Overseas - Yes

COIT DRAPERY AND CARPET CLEANERS
897 Hinckley
Burlingame, CA 94010
TEL: (800) 243-8797 (415) 697-5471
FAX: (415) 697-6117
Mr. Robert Kearn, VP

COIT is the world's largest specialty cleaners. Major services include drapery, carpet, upholstery and area rug cleaning in both the residential and commercial markets.

HISTORY: . . . .
Established in 1950; . . 1st Franchised in 1964
Company-Owned Units (As of 12/1/1989): . . 8
Franchised Units (12/1/1989): 45
Total Units (12/1/1989): 53
Distribution: US-48;Can-4;Overseas-1
North America: . . . 20 States, 3 Provinces
Concentration: . . 10 in CA, 4 in WA, 4 in OH
Registered: . . . . CA
. . . .
Average # of Employees: . . . . .5 FT
Prior Industry Experience: . . . . . . Helpful

FINANCIAL:
Cash Investment: $20-150K
Total Investment: $50-250K
Fees: Franchise - $10-50K
  Royalty: 5%, Advert: 0%
Contract Periods (Yrs.): 10/5
Area Development Agreement: . .No
Sub-Franchise Contract: . . . . .No
Expand in Territory: . . . . . . .No
Passive Ownership: . . . Discouraged
Encourage Conversions: . . . . Yes
Franchisee Purchase(s) Required: .No

FRANCHISOR TRAINING/SUPPORT:
Financial Assistance Provided: . . . . .No
Site Selection Assistance: . . . . . . .Yes
Lease Negotiation Assistance: . . . . .Yes
Co-operative Advertising: . . . . . . .Yes
Training: . . . . .1-2 Wks. California,
. . . . 1-2 Wks. Toronto, ON
On-Going Support: . . . .B,C,D,E,F,G,H,I
Full-Time Franchisor Support Staff: . . 10
EXPANSION PLANS:
US: . . . . All US
Canada - Yes, ...Overseas - No

COLOR-GLO INTERNATIONAL

7111 Ohms Ln.
Minneapolis, MN 55435
TEL: (800) 328-6347 (612) 835-1338
FAX: (612) 835-1395
Mr. Scott Smith, Dir. Franchising

Low-overhead mobile business, providing exclusive color and surface restoration service for leather, cloth, vinyl, plastic, etc. To auto dealers, fleets, boats, RV's, aircraft, business - anywhere. Savings of up to 98% over replacement. Vast ready market awaits motivated individual desiring extremely high income, full- time or part-time.

HISTORY: . . . . .IFA
Established in 1976; . . 1st Franchised in 1985
Company-Owned Units (As of 12/1/1989): . .3
Franchised Units (12/1/1989): 298
Total Units (12/1/1989): 301
Distribution: US-289;Can-7;Overseas-5
North America: . . . . 50 States, 3 Provinces
Concentration: . . . 8 in FL, 7 in MN, 6 in OH
Registered: . . . . .All
. . . .
Average # of Employees: . . . . .Varies
Prior Industry Experience: . . . . . . Helpful

FINANCIAL:
Cash Investment: $4.9-17K
Total Investment: $5.6-25K
Fees: Franchise - $2.5K
  Royalty: 0%, Advert: 0%
Contract Periods (Yrs.): 10/5
Area Development Agreement: Yes/5
Sub-Franchise Contract: . . . . . Yes
Expand in Territory: . . . . Yes
Passive Ownership: . . . . . .Allowed
Encourage Conversions: . . . . Yes
Franchisee Purchase(s) Required: Yes

FRANCHISOR TRAINING/SUPPORT:
Financial Assistance Provided: . . .Yes(D)
Site Selection Assistance: . . . . . . .Yes
Lease Negotiation Assistance: . . . . .Yes
Co-operative Advertising: . . . . . . .Yes
Training: . . . . .3 Days Central Area
. . . .
On-Going Support: . . . A,B,C,D,F,G,H,I
Full-Time Franchisor Support Staff: . . 11
EXPANSION PLANS:
US: . . . .'. All US
Canada - Yes, . . . Overseas - Yes

COMPU-CLEAN

2512 Caledonia Ave.
N. Vancouver, BC V7G1T9 CAN
TEL: (604) 984-7878 (604) 929-7187
FAX: (604) 984-4390
Mr. Terence Winder, Franchise Dir.

COMPU-CLEAN provides a specialized system for cleaning exterior surfaces and keyboards and allied electronic equipment. Anti-static, anti-bacterial protection is included. Work is done in clients' premises, e.g. banks, universities, major companies, so franchisees may start from home, part-time.

HISTORY: . . . .
Established in 1988; . . 1st Franchised in 1989
Company-Owned Units (As of 12/1/1989): . .3
Franchised Units (12/1/1989): 0
Total Units (12/1/1989): 3
Distribution: US-0;Can-2;Overseas-1
North America: . . . . .1 Province
Concentration: . . . . 2 in BC
Registered: . . . .
. . . .
Average # of Employees: . . . . . . 1 FT, 4 PT
Prior Industry Experience: . . . . . . Helpful

FINANCIAL:
Cash Investment: $7-13K
Total Investment: $9-15K
Fees: Franchise - $5-11K
  Royalty: 10%, Advert: 0%
Contract Periods (Yrs.): 5/5
Area Development Agreement: . .No
Sub-Franchise Contract: . . . . . Yes
Expand in Territory: . . . . Yes
Passive Ownership: . . . . . .Allowed
Encourage Conversions: . . . . .No
Franchisee Purchase(s) Required: Yes

FRANCHISOR TRAINING/SUPPORT:
Financial Assistance Provided: . . . . .No
Site Selection Assistance: . . . . . . .NA
Lease Negotiation Assistance: . . . . .NA
Co-operative Advertising: . . . . . . .NA
Training: . . . . .1 Wk. Headquarters
. . . .
On-Going Support: . . . . B,C,D,F,h,I
Full-Time Franchisor Support Staff: . . 13
EXPANSION PLANS:
US: . . . . All US
Canada - Yes, . . . Overseas - Yes

COUSTIC-GLO INTERNATIONAL

7111 Ohms Ln.
Minneapolis, MN 55435
TEL: (800) 333-8523 (612) 835-1338 C
FAX: (612) 835-1395
Mr. Scott Smith, Fran. Sales Dir.

Providing only complete line of products and services to clean and remove all types of ceiling and wall materials. These exclusive, environmentally-safe products will restore a clean, healthy environment to all buildings, while saving thousands over alternative methods. Very high profit, low overhead business.

HISTORY: . . . . .IFA/CFA	FINANCIAL:	FRANCHISOR TRAINING/SUPPORT:
Established in 1970; . . 1st Franchised in 1980	Cash Investment: $9.8-25K	Financial Assistance Provided: . . .Yes(D)
Company-Owned Units (As of 12/1/1989): . .1	Total Investment: $12-30K	Site Selection Assistance: . . . . . . .Yes
Franchised Units (12/1/1989): 227	Fees: Franchise - $2.5K	Lease Negotiation Assistance: . . . . .Yes
Total Units (12/1/1989): 228	Royalty: 5%, Advert: 1%	Co-operative Advertising: . . . . .Yes
Distribution: US-201;Can-9;Overseas-18	Contract Periods (Yrs.): 10/5	Training: . . . . .2-3 Days Training On-site
North America: . . . . 50 States, 4 Provinces	Area Development Agreement: Yes/10	. . . .
Concentration: . .13 in FL, 11 in PA, 11 in TX	Sub-Franchise Contract: . . . . . Yes	On-Going Support: . . A,B,C,D,E,F,G,H,I
Registered: . . . . .All	Expand in Territory: . . . . Yes	Full-Time Franchisor Support Staff: . . 18
. . . .	Passive Ownership: . . . . . .Allowed	EXPANSION PLANS:
Average # of Employees: . . . . .2 PT	Encourage Conversions: . . . . . Yes	US: . . . . .All US
Prior Industry Experience: . . . . Helpful	Franchisee Purchase(s) Required: Yes	Canada - Yes, . . . Overseas - Yes

COVERALL

3111 Camino Del Rio North, # 1200
San Diego, CA 92108
TEL: (800) 537-3371 (619) 584-1911
FAX: (619) 584-4923
Mr. Alex Roudi, President

COVERALL offers a comprehensive janitorial franchise which includes customer base, equipment and supplies package. Franchisee will provide professional cleaning programs to commercial and industrial buildings. Franchisees can obtain future contracts direct or through coverall. COVERALL also has a few choice markets left for Master Franchisees.

HISTORY: . . . . .IFA	FINANCIAL:	FRANCHISOR TRAINING/SUPPORT:
Established in 1982; . . 1st Franchised in 1982	Cash Investment: $3-200K	Financial Assistance Provided: . . .Yes(D)
Company-Owned Units (As of 12/1/1989): . .7	Total Investment: $4-250K	Site Selection Assistance: . . . . .NA
Franchised Units (12/1/1989): 795	Fees: Franchise - $4-200K	Lease Negotiation Assistance: . . . . .Yes
Total Units (12/1/1989): 802	Royalty: 10%, Advert: 1%	Co-operative Advertising: . . . . .NA
Distribution: US-772;Can-0;Overseas-30	Contract Periods (Yrs.): 10/10	Training: . . . . . . 1-2 Wks. Headquarters,
North America: . . . . 16 States	Area Development Agreement: . .No	. . . . 1-4 Wks. Regional Offices
Concentration: . .250 in CA, 135 in IL, 82 GA	Sub-Franchise Contract: . . . . . Yes	On-Going Support: . . . . A,B,C,D,G,H,I
Registered: . . . CA,FL,IL,MD,MN,RI,VA,WI	Expand in Territory: . . . . Yes	Full-Time Franchisor Support Staff: . . 85
. . . .	Passive Ownership: . . . Discouraged	EXPANSION PLANS:
Average # of Employees: . . . . . . 2 FT, 1 PT	Encourage Conversions: . . . . .No	US: . . . . .All US
Prior Industry Experience: . . . . . . Helpful	Franchisee Purchase(s) Required: .No	Canada - Yes, . . . Overseas - Yes

DURACLEAN

2151 Waukegan Rd.
Deerfield, IL 60015
TEL: (800) 251-7070 (708) 945-2000 C
FAX: (708) 945-2023
Mr. Mike Higgins, Dir. Mkt. Devel

Five different franchise opportunities available, covering carpet, furniture, wall, ceiling cleaning and fire, smoke and water damage restoration services; building maintenance services; master franchise in selected locations. Ask about our "DURACLEAN Difference."

HISTORY: . . . . .IFA	FINANCIAL:	FRANCHISOR TRAINING/SUPPORT:
Established in 1930; . . 1st Franchised in 1945	Cash Investment: $10.9-22.8K	Financial Assistance Provided: . . .Yes(D)
Company-Owned Units (As of 12/1/1989): . .1	Total Investment: $20-50K	Site Selection Assistance: . . . . . . .Yes
Franchised Units (12/1/1989): 619	Fees: Franchise - $5.5-8.2K	Lease Negotiation Assistance: . . . . .NA
Total Units (12/1/1989): 620	Royalty: 2-8%, Advert: 0%	Co-operative Advertising: . . . . .No
Distribution: . . . US-570;Can-30;Overseas-20	Contract Periods (Yrs.): 3/3	Training: . . . . . 6 Days Headquarters, 2+
North America: . . . . 50 States, 8 Provinces	Area Development Agreement: Yes/3	. . .Days Nearby Franchise, Manuals, etc
Concentration: . .52 in CA, 50 in IL, 41 in NY	Sub-Franchise Contract: . . . . .No	On-Going Support: . . . . . .B,C,D,G,H,I
Registered: . . . . .All	Expand in Territory: . . . . Yes	Full-Time Franchisor Support Staff: . . 50
. . . .	Passive Ownership: . . . Discouraged	EXPANSION PLANS:
Average # of Employees: . . . . . . 2 FT, 1 PT	Encourage Conversions: . . . . . Yes	US: . . . . .All US
Prior Industry Experience: . . . . Helpful	Franchisee Purchase(s) Required: Yes	Canada - Yes, . . . Overseas - Yes

FABRI-ZONE CLEANING SYSTEMS

375 Bering Ave.
Toronto, ON M8Z3B1 CAN
TEL: (416) 231-1155 C
FAX: (416) 237-0304
Mr. David Collier, President

FABRIZONE offers a unique licensing concept to start part or full-time, cleaning carpets, upholstery, on-site drapery, ceilings, insurance work and the patented Fab-Restore Carpet Purification Process for as little as $3,000 down. Equipment, chemicals, training, marketing and promotional materials included. Recommended by manufacturers. Technical support center back-up.

HISTORY: . . . .
Established in 1981; . . 1st Franchised in 1985
Company-Owned Units (As of 12/1/1989): . . 1
Franchised Units (12/1/1989): 92
Total Units (12/1/1989): 93
Distribution: US-15;Can-70;Overseas-8
North America: . . . .
Concentration: . . 20 in ON, 14 in AB, 7 in NS
Registered: . . . .
. . . .
Average # of Employees: . . . . . . 1 FT, 2 PT
Prior Industry Experience: . . . . Helpful

FINANCIAL:
Cash Investment: $2K
Total Investment: $5-16K
Fees: Franchise - $0
  Royalty: $100/Mo., Advert: . . 0%
Contract Periods (Yrs.): . . . . Indef.
Area Development Agreement: . .No
Sub-Franchise Contract: . . . . .No
Expand in Territory: . . . . . . Yes
Passive Ownership: . . . . . .Allowed
Encourage Conversions: . . . . NA
Franchisee Purchase(s) Required: Yes

FRANCHISOR TRAINING/SUPPORT:
Financial Assistance Provided: . . . Yes(I)
Site Selection Assistance: . . . . .NA
Lease Negotiation Assistance: . . . . .NA
Co-operative Advertising: . . . . .NA
Training: . . . . . . 1 Wk. Headquarters or
. . . . Regional Office
On-Going Support: . . . . .G,H,I
Full-Time Franchisor Support Staff: . . 15
EXPANSION PLANS:
US: . . . . .All US
Canada - Yes, . . . Overseas - Yes

FLEETCLEANER

3731 Northcrest Rd.
Atlanta, GA 30340
TEL: (404) 458-4157 C
FAX: (404) 458-5365
Mr. Dan Whisenhunt, Sales Manager

FLEETCLEANER creates the most unique equipment and technology combination to take advantage of the growing opportunities in the maintenance and cleaning of truck and bus fleets. Our mobile brush wash machine includes everything needed to get established as a major mobile fleet washing contractor in your area.

HISTORY: . . . .
Established in 1983; . . 1st Franchised in 1986
Company-Owned Units (As of 12/1/1989): . .0
Franchised Units (12/1/1989): 4
Total Units (12/1/1989): 4
Distribution: US-4;Can-0;Overseas-0
North America: . . . .
Concentration: . . . . .CA, TX, FL
Registered: . . . .
. . . .
Average # of Employees: . . . . . . 2 FT, 1 PT
Prior Industry Experience: . . . . Helpful

FINANCIAL:
Cash Investment: $1-5K
Total Investment: $47K
Fees: Franchise - $2K
  Royalty: 0%, Advert: 0%
Contract Periods (Yrs.): 1/1
Area Development Agreement: . .No
Sub-Franchise Contract: . . . . .No
Expand in Territory: . . . . . . Yes
Passive Ownership: . . . Not Allowed
Encourage Conversions: . . . . .No
Franchisee Purchase(s) Required: .No

FRANCHISOR TRAINING/SUPPORT:
Financial Assistance Provided: . . . Yes(I)
Site Selection Assistance: . . . . . . .Yes
Lease Negotiation Assistance: . . . . .Yes
Co-operative Advertising: . . . . . . .Yes
Training: . . . . 2 Days Headquarters,
. . . . .3 Days Franchisee Location
On-Going Support: . . A,B,C,D,E,F,G,H,I
Full-Time Franchisor Support Staff: . . . 8
EXPANSION PLANS:
US: . . . . .All US
Canada - Yes, . . . Overseas - Yes

JANI-KING

4950 Keller Springs, # 190
Dallas, TX 75248
TEL: (800) 552-5264 (214) 991-0900
FAX: (214) 239-7706
Mr. Jerry Crawford, VP Natl. Sales

World's largest janitorial franchisor. Franchise includes a specified amount of initial business, depending on area purchased, supplies and equipment necessary to begin business. Over 20 years in commercial cleaning. Professional training and continuous support while franchisees provide commercial cleaning programs on long-term contract basis.

HISTORY: . . . . .IFA/CFA
Established in 1969; . . 1st Franchised in 1974
Company-Owned Units (As of 12/1/1989): . 14
Franchised Units (12/1/1989): 1509
Total Units (12/1/1989): 1523
Distribution: . . US-1418;Can-105;Overseas-0
North America: . . . .34 States, All Provinc
Concentration: . . . . .411 in CA, 320 in TX
Registered: . . . . .All
. . . .
Average # of Employees: . . . . 10 PT
Prior Industry Experience: . . . . Helpful

FINANCIAL:
Cash Investment: $2-14K
Total Investment: . . . . $2K+
Fees: Franchise - . . . . . . $6.5-14K+
  Royalty: 7-10%, Advert: . . 1/2%
Contract Periods (Yrs.): . . . 20/20
Area Development Agreement: . .No
Sub-Franchise Contract: . . . . Yes
Expand in Territory: . . . . . . .No
Passive Ownership: . . . Discouraged
Encourage Conversions: . . . . Yes
Franchisee Purchase(s) Required: .No

FRANCHISOR TRAINING/SUPPORT:
Financial Assistance Provided: . . .Yes(D)
Site Selection Assistance: . . . . . . .NA
Lease Negotiation Assistance: . . . . .NA
Co-operative Advertising: . . . . . . .NA
Training: . . . . . 30 Hrs. Regional Center,
. . . . 1 Wk. Headquarters, As Requested
On-Going Support: . . . . A,B,C,D,G,H,I
Full-Time Franchisor Support Staff: . .200
EXPANSION PLANS:
US: . . . . .All US
Canada - Yes, ...Overseas - Yes

JANTIZE AMERICA

20300 Superior, # 190
Taylor, MI 48180
TEL: (800) 456-9182 (313) 287-6006
FAX: (313) 287-3230
Mr. Jerry Prins, Mktg. Dir.

You can have the office cleaning franchise of the future for less than the cost of a new car with a JANTIZE commercial cleaning franchise. Computerized procedures, audio/visual training, one-on-one assistance and more!

HISTORY: . . . .
Established in 1986; . . 1st Franchised in 1988
Company-Owned Units (As of 12/1/1989): . .1
Franchised Units (12/1/1989): 8
Total Units (12/1/1989): 9
Distribution: US-9;Can-0;Overseas-0
North America: . . . . 9 States
Concentration: . . . .
Registered: . . . . .MI
. . . .
Average # of Employees: . . . . . 2 FT, 1-5 PT
Prior Industry Experience: . . . . Helpful

FINANCIAL:
Cash Investment: $8.5-12K
Total Investment: $8.5-20K
Fees: Franchise - $8.5K
Royalty: 8%, Advert: 1%
Contract Periods (Yrs.): 7/7
Area Development Agreement: Yes/10
Sub-Franchise Contract: . . . . .No
Expand in Territory: . . . . . . .No
Passive Ownership: . . . Discouraged
Encourage Conversions: . . . . Yes
Franchisee Purchase(s) Required: .No

FRANCHISOR TRAINING/SUPPORT:
Financial Assistance Provided: . . .Yes(D)
Site Selection Assistance: . . . . . . .Yes
Lease Negotiation Assistance: . . . . .NA
Co-operative Advertising: . . . . . . .Yes
Training: . . . . 3 Days Headquarters,
. . . . 3 Days Franchisee Site
On-Going Support: . . . . c,D,G,H,I
Full-Time Franchisor Support Staff: . . . 4
EXPANSION PLANS:
US: . . . . .All US
Canada - Yes, ...Overseas - No

LANGENWALTER DYE CONCEPT

4410 E. La Palma
Anaheim, CA 92807
TEL: (800) 422-4370 (714) 528-7610
FAX:
Mr. John Langenwalter, VP

Complete carpet restoration. The franchisees are professionals in taking care of carpet problems, including sunfading, pet-bleach-chemical stains, etc. and can make complete color changes, saving the customer up to 75% of carpet replacement costs.

HISTORY: . . . .
Established in 1975; . . 1st Franchised in 1981
Company-Owned Units (As of 12/1/1989): . .0
Franchised Units (12/1/1989): 130
Total Units (12/1/1989): 130
Distribution: . . . US-126;Can-2;Overseas-2
North America: . . . . 28 States
Concentration: . . 42 in CA, 5 in OR, 5 in WA
Registered: . . . .
. . . .
Average # of Employees: . . . . 1-2 FT, 2-3 PT
Prior Industry Experience: . . . . . . Helpful

FINANCIAL:
Cash Investment: $16.5K
Total Investment: $17-18K
Fees: Franchise - $16.5K
Royalty: Flat, Advert: 0%
Contract Periods (Yrs.): 3/3
Area Development Agreement: . .No
Sub-Franchise Contract: . . . . Yes
Expand in Territory: . . . . . . Yes
Passive Ownership: . . . Not Allowed
Encourage Conversions: . . . .
Franchisee Purchase(s) Required: .No

FRANCHISOR TRAINING/SUPPORT:
Financial Assistance Provided: . . . . . No
Site Selection Assistance: . . . . NA
Lease Negotiation Assistance: . . . . .NA
Co-operative Advertising: . . . . . . .Yes
Training: . . . . 1 Wk. Headquarters
. . . .
On-Going Support: . . . . .G,H,I
Full-Time Franchisor Support Staff: . . . 6
EXPANSION PLANS:
US: . . . . .All US, Especially Southwest
Canada - Yes, . . . Overseas - Yes

MR. BUILD HANDI-MAN SERVICES

628 Hebron Ave., # 110
Glastonbury, CT 06033
TEL: (800) 242-8453 (203) 657-3607
FAX: (203) 657-3719
Mr. Glenn Cooper, Director

MR. BUILD HANDI-MAN SERVICES offers residential and commercial property owners a central source for small repair, maintenance and renovation work. Each franchisee has a protected territory and is tied into a regional central dispatch by computer.

HISTORY: . . . .
Established in 1989; . . 1st Franchised in 1989
Company-Owned Units (As of 12/1/1989): . .0
Franchised Units (12/1/1989): 8
Total Units (12/1/1989): 8
Distribution: US-6;Can-2;Overseas-0
North America: . . . . .3 States, 1 Province
Concentration: . . . . .3 in IN, 2 in BC
Registered: . . . . CA,FL,IL,IN
. . . .
Average # of Employees: . . . . . . 3 FT, 1 PT
Prior Industry Experience: . . . . Helpful

FINANCIAL:
Cash Investment: $23.9K
Total Investment: $23.9-35K
Fees: Franchise - $23.9K
Royalty: 7%, Advert: 2%
Contract Periods (Yrs.): 20/20
Area Development Agreement: . .No
Sub-Franchise Contract: . . . . Yes
Expand in Territory: . . . . . . Yes
Passive Ownership: . . . Not Allowed
Encourage Conversions: . . . . .No
Franchisee Purchase(s) Required: Yes

FRANCHISOR TRAINING/SUPPORT:
Financial Assistance Provided: . . . . .No
Site Selection Assistance: . . . . . . .NA
Lease Negotiation Assistance: . . . .Yes
Co-operative Advertising: . . . . . . .Yes
Training: . . . . .1 Wk. Headquarters,
. . . . On-going in Region
On-Going Support: . . . A,B,C,D,E,G,H,I
Full-Time Franchisor Support Staff: . . . 8
EXPANSION PLANS:
US: . . . . .All US
Canada - Yes, . . . Overseas - Yes

MR. ROOTER

P. O. Box 3146
Waco, TX 76707
TEL: (800) 950-8003 (817) 755-0055 C
FAX: (817) 752-0661
Mr. Robert Tunmire, VP

MR. ROOTER has developed exclusive equipment and marketing techniques in the sewer and cleaning business. Prior to opening, franchisees will complete a minimum of 5 days' training program at franchisor's headquarters. Franchisee's territory is exclusive.

HISTORY: . . . . IFA	FINANCIAL: NASD-ROOT	FRANCHISOR TRAINING/SUPPORT:
Established in 1972; . . 1st Franchised in 1974	Cash Investment: $18.5-30K	Financial Assistance Provided: . . . Yes(I)
Company-Owned Units (As of 12/1/1989): . .1	Total Investment: $18.5-40K	Site Selection Assistance: . . . . . . .NA
Franchised Units (12/1/1989): 50	Fees: Franchise - $10K	Lease Negotiation Assistance: . . . . .NA
Total Units (12/1/1989): 51	Royalty: 6-3%, Advert: 2%	Co-operative Advertising: . . . . No
Distribution: US-51;Can-0;Overseas-0	Contract Periods (Yrs.): . . . 10/10	Training: . . . . 5 Days Headquarters
North America: . . . . 16 States	Area Development Agreement: . .No	. . . .
Concentration: . . . 11 in TX, 5 in CA, 3 in TN	Sub-Franchise Contract: . . . . . .No	On-Going Support: . . . . .B,C,D,E,G,H,I
Registered: . . . . All Except AB	Expand in Territory: . . . . Yes	Full-Time Franchisor Support Staff: . . .2
. . . .	Passive Ownership: . . . Discouraged	EXPANSION PLANS:
Average # of Employees: . . . . .1 FT	Encourage Conversions: . . . . . Yes	US: . . . . .All US
Prior Industry Experience: . . . . . . Helpful	Franchisee Purchase(s) Required: .No	Canada - Yes, . . . Overseas - Yes

NATIONAL CHEMICALS & SERVICES

691 N. Church Rd.
Elmhurst, IL 60126
TEL: (800) 888-8407 (708) 832-8407
FAX:
Mr. Michael M. Saks, President

Sanitation and deodorization service, using our own 7-step procedure.

HISTORY:	FINANCIAL:	FRANCHISOR TRAINING/SUPPORT:
Established in 1964; . . 1st Franchised in 1967	Cash Investment: . . $8.5K Maximum	Financial Assistance Provided: . . .Yes(D)
Company-Owned Units (As of 12/1/1989): . .1	Total Investment: $3.7-8.5K	Site Selection Assistance: . . . . . . .NA
Franchised Units (12/1/1989): 31	Fees: Franchise - $3.7K	Lease Negotiation Assistance: . . . . .NA
Total Units (12/1/1989): 32	Royalty: 25%, Advert: 2%	Co-operative Advertising: . . . . . . .Yes
Distribution: US-32;Can-0;Overseas-0	Contract Periods (Yrs.): . . . 10/10	Training: . . . . 1 Wk. Headquarters
North America: . . . . 2 States	Area Development Agreement: . .No	. . . .
Concentration: . . . . 28 in Il, 3 in IN	Sub-Franchise Contract: . . . . . .No	On-Going Support: . . . A,B,C,D,F,G,H,I
Registered: . . . . IL,IN	Expand in Territory: . . . . Yes	Full-Time Franchisor Support Staff: . . . 7
. . . .	Passive Ownership: . . . Discouraged	EXPANSION PLANS:
Average # of Employees: . . . . .1 FT	Encourage Conversions: . . . . . NA	US: . . . . .Midwest
Prior Industry Experience: . . . . . . Helpful	Franchisee Purchase(s) Required: Yes	Canada - No, ...Overseas - No

NATIONAL LEAK DETECTION

P. O. Box 3191
Palos Verdes Estate, CA 90274
TEL: (213) 377-2699
FAX:
Mr. Richard Evans, President

NATIONAL LEAK DETECTION is a unique franchise opportunity. We detect and repair hidden water and gas leaks; specializing in swimming pool and spa leaks. We have proprietary leak detection systems and a proprietary "leak-sealing" system and product - AQUA 2000. One of a kind process. No competition.

HISTORY: . . . . IFA	FINANCIAL:	FRANCHISOR TRAINING/SUPPORT:
Established in 1986; . . 1st Franchised in 1989	Cash Investment: $40K	Financial Assistance Provided: . . . Yes(I)
Company-Owned Units (As of 12/1/1989): . .1	Total Investment: $50K	Site Selection Assistance: . . . . . . .NA
Franchised Units (12/1/1989): 1	Fees: Franchise - $20K	Lease Negotiation Assistance: . . . . .NA
Total Units (12/1/1989): 2	Royalty: 8%, Advert: 0%	Co-operative Advertising: . . . . . . .Yes
Distribution: US-2;Can-0;Overseas-0	Contract Periods (Yrs.): 5/5	Training: . . . . 2 Wks. Headquarters
North America: . . . . .1 State	Area Development Agreement: . .No	. . . .
Concentration: . . . . 2 in CA	Sub-Franchise Contract: . . . . . .No	On-Going Support: . . . . .b,C,D,E
Registered: . . . . CA	Expand in Territory: . . . . Yes	Full-Time Franchisor Support Staff: . . . 1
. . . .	Passive Ownership: . . . Discouraged	EXPANSION PLANS:
Average # of Employees: . . . . . . 1 FT, 1 PT	Encourage Conversions: . . . . . NA	US: . . . . Sunbelt States
Prior Industry Experience: . . . . Helpful	Franchisee Purchase(s) Required: Yes	Canada - Yes, . . . Overseas - Yes

NATIONAL MAINTENANCE CONTRACTORS
1801 130th Ave. NE
Bellevue, WA 98005
TEL: (206) 881-0500
FAX:
Mr. Tony Monsaas, Fran. Dir.

NATIONAL offers guaranteed accounts with almost immediate (30 - 60 days) positive cash flow. Our franchisees are given free on-going training with full support from the franchisor to help build their business in the booming janitorial industry.

HISTORY: . . . .
Established in 1970; . . 1st Franchised in 1975
Company-Owned Units (As of 12/1/1989): . .2
Franchised Units (12/1/1989): 247
Total Units (12/1/1989): 249
Distribution: US-249;Can-0;Overseas-0
North America: . . . . 2 States
Concentration: . . . . . . 152 in WA, 95 in OR
Registered: . . . . OR,WA
. . . .
Average # of Employees: . . . . .2 FT
Prior Industry Experience: . . . . Helpful

FINANCIAL:
Cash Investment: $1.6-10K
Total Investment: $2.6-20K
Fees: Franchise - . . . $5xMo.Billings
Royalty: 20%, Advert: 0%
Contract Periods (Yrs.): 5/5
Area Development Agreement: . .No
Sub-Franchise Contract: . . . . .No
Expand in Territory: . . . . . . Yes
Passive Ownership: . . . Not Allowed
Encourage Conversions: . . . . Yes
Franchisee Purchase(s) Required: .No

FRANCHISOR TRAINING/SUPPORT:
Financial Assistance Provided: . . .Yes(D)
Site Selection Assistance: . . . . .NA
Lease Negotiation Assistance: . . . . .NA
Co-operative Advertising: . . . . .No
Training: . . . . . . .3 Days Bellevue, WA,
. . . . 3 Days Tigard, OR
On-Going Support: . . . . A,B,C,D,G,H,I
Full-Time Franchisor Support Staff: . . 30
EXPANSION PLANS:
US: . . . . Northwest
Canada - No, ... Overseas - Yes

O.P.E.N. CLEANING SYSTEMS

2390 E. Camelback Rd.
Phoenix, AZ 85016
TEL: (800) 777-6736 (602) 224-0594 C
FAX: (602) 468-3788
Mr. Eric Roudi, President

O.P.E.N. provides the opportunity for the small investor to enter the highly profitable and growing field of office cleaning. Each O.P.E.N. franchisee will receive initial cleaning contracts, plus training and full support from the franchisor.

HISTORY: . . . .
Established in 1983; . . 1st Franchised in 1983
Company-Owned Units (As of 12/1/1989): . .1
Franchised Units (12/1/1989): 245
Total Units (12/1/1989): 246
Distribution: US-246;Can-0;Overseas-0
North America: . . . . 3 States
Concentration: . .140 in AZ, 90 in WA, 10 CA
Registered: . . . . CA,WA
. . . .
Average # of Employees: . . . . . . 1 FT, 3 PT
Prior Industry Experience: . . . . Helpful

FINANCIAL:
Cash Investment: $1.7-9K
Total Investment: $2.5-11K
Fees: Franchise - $3-15K
Royalty: 10%, Advert: 0%
Contract Periods (Yrs.): . . . 10/10
Area Development Agreement: Yes/10
Sub-Franchise Contract: . . . . . Yes
Expand in Territory: . . . . . . Yes
Passive Ownership: . . . Discouraged
Encourage Conversions: . . . . Yes
Franchisee Purchase(s) Required: .No

FRANCHISOR TRAINING/SUPPORT:
Financial Assistance Provided: . . .Yes(D)
Site Selection Assistance: . . . . .NA
Lease Negotiation Assistance: . . . . .NA
Co-operative Advertising: . . . . .NA
Training: . . . . 3 Days Headquarters,
. . . 3 Days Seattle, 3 Days Los Angeles
On-Going Support: . . . . .A,b,C,D,G,H,I
Full-Time Franchisor Support Staff: . . 32
EXPANSION PLANS:
US: . . . . .All US
Canada - Yes, . . . Overseas - Yes

PROFESSIONAL CARPET SYSTEMS

5182 Old Dixie Hwy.
Forest Park, GA 30050
TEL: (800) 735-5055 (404) 361-9362
FAX: (404) 361-4937
Ms. Gail Dungan, Dir. Mktg.

PROFESSIONAL CARPET SYSTEMS is the leader in "on-site" carpet redyeing, servicing thousands of apartment complexes, hotels and motels worldwide. Services also include carpet cleaning, rejuvenation, repair, water and flood damage restoration and "guaranteed odor control." A total carpet care concept.

HISTORY: . . . . IFA
Established in 1978; . . 1st Franchised in 1979
Company-Owned Units (As of 12/1/1989): . .4
Franchised Units (12/1/1989): 356
Total Units (12/1/1989): 360
Distribution: US-341;Can-14;Overseas-5
North America: . . . .
Concentration: . . . .
Registered: . . . . .All Exc. ND
. . . .
Average # of Employees: . . . . . 2+ FT, 2+ PT
Prior Industry Experience: . . . . Helpful

FINANCIAL:
Cash Investment: $8.5K
Total Investment: $13-22K
Fees: Franchise - $8.5K
Royalty: 5%, Advert: . . . .
Contract Periods (Yrs.): . . . 10/10
Area Development Agreement: . .No
Sub-Franchise Contract: . . . . .No
Expand in Territory: . . . . . . Yes
Passive Ownership: . . . Not Allowed
Encourage Conversions: . . . . .No
Franchisee Purchase(s) Required: Yes

FRANCHISOR TRAINING/SUPPORT:
Financial Assistance Provided: . . .Yes(D)
Site Selection Assistance: . . . . . . .Yes
Lease Negotiation Assistance: . . . . .NA
Co-operative Advertising: . . . . .NA
Training: . . . . 2 Wks. Headquarters
. . . .
On-Going Support: . . . . .G,h,I
Full-Time Franchisor Support Staff: . . 75
EXPANSION PLANS:
US: . . . . All US
Canada - Yes, . . . Overseas - Yes

PROPERTY DAMAGE APPRAISERS

6100 Western Pl., # 900
Fort Worth, TX 76107
TEL: (817) 731-5555
FAX:
Mr. John R. Tate, Sr. VP, Fran. Ops.

PROPERTY DAMAGE APPRAISERS offers the potential franchisee a complete insurance appraisal business to include administration, accounting, marketing and direct sales assistance. No initial franchise fee is required. A royalty on completed business.

HISTORY: . . . . IFA	FINANCIAL:	FRANCHISOR TRAINING/SUPPORT:
Established in 1963; . . 1st Franchised in 1963	Cash Investment: $0	Financial Assistance Provided: . . . . . No
Company-Owned Units (As of 12/1/1989): . .0	Total Investment: $0-10K	Site Selection Assistance: . . . . . . .Yes
Franchised Units (12/1/1989): 180	Fees: Franchise - $0	Lease Negotiation Assistance: . . . . . No
Total Units (12/1/1989): 180	Royalty: 20%, Advert: 0%	Co-operative Advertising: . . . . . . .Yes
Distribution: US-180;Can-0;Overseas-0	Contract Periods (Yrs.): 5/5	Training: . . . . 1 Wk. On-site
North America:	Area Development Agreement: . .No	. . . .
Concentration: . .16 in TX, 15 in CA, 10 in FL	Sub-Franchise Contract: . . . . . .No	On-Going Support: . . . .A,C,D,E,F,G,h,I
Registered: . . . . All States	Expand in Territory: . . . . Yes	Full-Time Franchisor Support Staff: . . 31
. . . .	Passive Ownership: . . . Not Allowed	EXPANSION PLANS:
Average # of Employees: . . . . .Varies	Encourage Conversions: . . . . . Yes	US: . . . . All US
Prior Industry Experience: . . . . . .Necessary	Franchisee Purchase(s) Required: .No	Canada - No, ...Overseas - No

ROTO-ROOTER

300 Ashworth Rd.
West Des Moines, IA 50265
TEL: (515) 223-1343
FAX: (515) 223-4220
Mr. Paul Carter, Dir. Fran. Admin.

The nation's largest and most experienced sewer and drain cleaning franchisor.

HISTORY: . . . . IFA	FINANCIAL: OTC-ROTO	FRANCHISOR TRAINING/SUPPORT:
Established in 1935; . . 1st Franchised in 1935	Cash Investment: $14-75K	Financial Assistance Provided: . . . . . No
Company-Owned Units (As of 12/1/1989): . 50	Total Investment: $15-75K	Site Selection Assistance: . . . . No
Franchised Units (12/1/1989): 655	Fees: Franchise - $1K	Lease Negotiation Assistance: . . . . . No
Total Units (12/1/1989): 705	Royalty: Var., Advert: . . . . Var.	Co-operative Advertising: . . . . .Yes
Distribution: US-679;Can-23;Overseas-3	Contract Periods (Yrs.): 5/5	Training: . . . Training in Co-Owned Site
North America: . . . . 50 States, 5 Provinces	Area Development Agreement: . .No	. . . . or Near-by Site As Required
Concentration: . 50 in CA, 36 in TX, 29 in OH	Sub-Franchise Contract: . . . . . .No	On-Going Support: . . . . . . b,C,D,G,h,I
Registered: . . . . All Except RI and AB	Expand in Territory: . . . . Yes	Full-Time Franchisor Support Staff: . . 24
. . . .	Passive Ownership: . . . Discouraged	EXPANSION PLANS:
Average # of Employees: . . . . . . 3 FT, 1 PT	Encourage Conversions: . . . . . Yes	US: . . . . . . Scattered Rural Areas Only
Prior Industry Experience: . . . . Helpful	Franchisee Purchase(s) Required: .No	Canada - Yes, . . . Overseas - Yes

ROTO-STATIC INTERNATIONAL

6810-1 Kitimat Rd., # 1
Mississauga, ON L5N5M2 CAN
TEL: (416) 858-8410
FAX: (416) 827-7330
Mr. Gerry Whelan, VP

Unique system of carpet cleaning, using "static attraction" principle. Eliminates all problems of other systems (no shrinkage, no split seams, no soil-attracting soaps). Complete training in Toronto for carpet and upholstery cleaning, fabric protectors and many other services. 13 years of growth through repeat and referral business - that tells the story!

HISTORY:	FINANCIAL:	FRANCHISOR TRAINING/SUPPORT:
Established in 1977; . . 1st Franchised in 1977	Cash Investment: $25.7K	Financial Assistance Provided: . . . . . No
Company-Owned Units (As of 12/1/1989): . .0	Total Investment: $25.7K	Site Selection Assistance: . . . . .NA
Franchised Units (12/1/1989): 110	Fees: Franchise - $5.7K	Lease Negotiation Assistance: . . . . .NA
Total Units (12/1/1989): 110	Royalty: 5%, Advert: 0%	Co-operative Advertising: . . . . .NA
Distribution: US-0;Can-110;Overseas-0	Contract Periods (Yrs.): 50	Training: . . . . 2 Days Toronto
North America: . . . . 9 Provinces	Area Development Agreement: . .No	. . . .
Concentration: . . . . .ON, PQ, BC	Sub-Franchise Contract: . . . . .No	On-Going Support: . . . . C,G,H
Registered: . . . . AB	Expand in Territory: . . . . Yes	Full-Time Franchisor Support Staff: . . . 8
. . . .	Passive Ownership: . . . Discouraged	EXPANSION PLANS:
Average # of Employees: . . . . .1-2 FT	Encourage Conversions:	US: . . . . . . Master Franchisors Sought
Prior Industry Experience: . . . . Helpful	Franchisee Purchase(s) Required: Yes	Canada - Yes, . . . Overseas - Yes

RUG DOCTOR PRO

2788 N. Larkin Ave.
Fresno, CA 93727
TEL: (800) 678-7844 (209) 291-5511
FAX: (209) 291-9963
Mr. Art Tosti, Regional Sales Mgr.

Potential franchisees have choice of Dual Vac Auto Fill/Discharge with original vibrating brush floor tool or RUG DOCTOR PRO Nissan-powered truck mount. Only school in country that qualifies students for IICUC certification. Presently is ground-floor opportunity with 18-year old company.

HISTORY: . . . . IFA
Established in 1971; . . 1st Franchised in 1987
Company-Owned Units (As of 12/1/1989): . . 1
Franchised Units (12/1/1989): 22
Total Units (12/1/1989): 23
Distribution: US-23;Can-0;Overseas-0
North America: . . . . 4 States
Concentration: . . . . 17 in CA, 2 in NM
Registered: . . . CA,FL,IL,IN,MD,MI,MN,OR
. . . . VA,WA
Average # of Employees: . . . . 1 FT
Prior Industry Experience: . . . . . . Helpful

FINANCIAL:
Cash Investment: $5-12K
Total Investment: $17-60K
Fees: Franchise - . . . . $5K+
Royalty: 6-3%, Advert: 2%
Contract Periods (Yrs.): 10/5
Area Development Agreement: . .No
Sub-Franchise Contract: . . . . .No
Expand in Territory: . . . . . . .No
Passive Ownership: . . . Not Allowed
Encourage Conversions: . . . . .No
Franchisee Purchase(s) Required: .No

FRANCHISOR TRAINING/SUPPORT:
Financial Assistance Provided: . . . Yes(I)
Site Selection Assistance: . . . . .NA
Lease Negotiation Assistance: . . . . .Yes
Co-operative Advertising: . . . . . . .Yes
Training: . . . . 5 Days Headquarters,
. . . . .2 Days On-site
On-Going Support: . . . . B,D,G,H,I
Full-Time Franchisor Support Staff: . . . 5
EXPANSION PLANS:
US: . . . . .All US
Canada - No, ... Overseas - Yes

SERV U-1ST

10175 SW Barbur Blvd., Bldg.B-100BA
Portland, OR 97219
TEL: (503) 244-7628
FAX:
Mr. Bob Rosenkranz, President

SERV U-1ST owners clean up with know-how. We serve you with on-going instruction in janitorial services for buildings. We teach proven technologies for procuring, servicing and keeping your clients. We offer 20 years' experience and our honest reputation.

HISTORY: . . . .
Established in 1988; . . 1st Franchised in 1988
Company-Owned Units (As of 12/1/1989): . .0
Franchised Units (12/1/1989): 3
Total Units (12/1/1989): 3
Distribution: US-3;Can-0;Overseas-0
North America: . . . . .1 State
Concentration: . . . . 3 in OR
Registered: . . . . OR
. . . .
Average # of Employees: . . . . .Varies
Prior Industry Experience: . . . . . . Helpful

FINANCIAL:
Cash Investment: . . . . $.5-8K
Total Investment: $2-8K
Fees: Franchise - $1-3K
Royalty: Var., Advert: 0%
Contract Periods (Yrs.): 2/2
Area Development Agreement: . .No
Sub-Franchise Contract: . . . . Yes
Expand in Territory: . . . . . . Yes
Passive Ownership: . . . Not Allowed
Encourage Conversions: . . . . Yes
Franchisee Purchase(s) Required: .No

FRANCHISOR TRAINING/SUPPORT:
Financial Assistance Provided: . . .Yes(D)
Site Selection Assistance: . . . . .Yes
Lease Negotiation Assistance: . . . . .NA
Co-operative Advertising: . . . . .NA
Training: . . . . .2 Days Headquarters, On-
. . going as Needed,8 Group Sessions/Yr
On-Going Support: . . . . .C,D,E,H
Full-Time Franchisor Support Staff: . . . 1
EXPANSION PLANS:
US: . . . . .Oregon Only
Canada - No, ...Overseas - No

SERVICE-TECH CORPORATION

21012 Aurora Rd.
Warrensville Hts., OH 44146
TEL: (800) 992-9302 (216) 663-2600 C
FAX: (216) 663-8804
Mr. Alan Sutton, President

Indoor Air Quality. Opportunity to join 30 years of experience in solving the growing concerns of indoor air pollution. Services offered include air duct cleaning, kitchen exhaust cleaning, vacuum cleaning and specialized cleaning, plus more, to industrial and commercial customers.

HISTORY: . . . .
Established in 1960; . . 1st Franchised in 1988
Company-Owned Units (As of 12/1/1989): . .4
Franchised Units (12/1/1989): 1
Total Units (12/1/1989): 5
Distribution: US-5;Can-0;Overseas-0
North America: . . . . 2 States
Concentration: . . . . 4 in OH, 1 in MI
Registered: . . . . IL,IN
. . . .
Average # of Employees: . . . . . . 4 FT, 2 PT
Prior Industry Experience: . . . . . . Helpful

FINANCIAL:
Cash Investment: $20-50K
Total Investment: $59-89K
Fees: Franchise - $39K
Royalty: 4-6%, Advert: 1%
Contract Periods (Yrs.): . . . 10/10+
Area Development Agreement: . .No
Sub-Franchise Contract: . . . . .No
Expand in Territory: . . . . . . Yes
Passive Ownership: . . . Not Allowed
Encourage Conversions: . . . . NA
Franchisee Purchase(s) Required: .No

FRANCHISOR TRAINING/SUPPORT:
Financial Assistance Provided: . . . Yes(I)
Site Selection Assistance: . . . . .NA
Lease Negotiation Assistance: . . . . .NA
Co-operative Advertising: . . . . . . .NA
Training: . . . . 2 Wks. Headquarters,
. . . . 1 Wk. Fanchise Location
On-Going Support: . . . . . . B,C,D,H,I
Full-Time Franchisor Support Staff: . . 35
EXPANSION PLANS:
US: . . . . .All US
Canada - No, ...Overseas - No

SERVPRO

575 Airport Blvd.
Gallatin, TN 37066
TEL: (800) 826-9586 (615) 451-0200
FAX: (615) 451-0291
Mr. Richard Isaacson, VP Mktg.

A complete cleaning and restoration business, specializing in profit center development. Full-service disaster restoration; commercial and residential development is the major focus. SERVPRO teaches effective business management skills. Our focus is on quality franchisees that become profitable business owners. If you want to be the best, join the best team - SERVPRO.

HISTORY: . . . . IFA
Established in 1967; . . 1st Franchised in 1969
Company-Owned Units (As of 12/1/1989): . .0
Franchised Units (12/1/1989): 710
Total Units (12/1/1989): 710
Distribution: US-710;Can-0;Overseas-0
North America: . . . . 47 States
Concentration: . 91 in CA, 59 in FL, 42 in GA
Registered: . . . . All States
. . . .
Average # of Employees: . . . .6-8 FT, 4-10 PT
Prior Industry Experience: . . . . Helpful

FINANCIAL:
Cash Investment: $15-20K
Total Investment: $40-45K
Fees: Franchise - $18-32K
Royalty: 10-3%, Advert: 0%
Contract Periods (Yrs.): 5/5
Area Development Agreement: Yes/5
Sub-Franchise Contract: . . . . . Yes
Expand in Territory: . . . . . . Yes
Passive Ownership: . . . Discouraged
Encourage Conversions: . . . . Yes
Franchisee Purchase(s) Required: Yes

FRANCHISOR TRAINING/SUPPORT:
Financial Assistance Provided: . . .Yes(D)
Site Selection Assistance: . . . . . . .NA
Lease Negotiation Assistance: . . . . .NA
Co-operative Advertising: . . . . . . .Yes
Training: . . . 2 Wks. Home Study, 2 Wks.
. . . . OJT, 3 Days Opening, 1 Wk. Natl.
On-Going Support: . . A,B,C,D,E,F,G,H,I
Full-Time Franchisor Support Staff: . . 45
EXPANSION PLANS:
US: . . . . All US
Canada - No, ...Overseas - No

SPARKLE WASH INTERNATIONAL

26851 Richmond Rd.
Cleveland, OH 44146
TEL: (800) 321-0770 (216) 464-4212 C
FAX:
Sales Department

High-quality, reliable mobile power cleaning and restoration services to a diverse range of industrial and residential customers. Factory-trained and supported franchisees employ the unique, patented mobile equipment and proven (since 1965) processes to reach levels of quality and efficiency unavailable with other systems.

HISTORY: . . . .
Established in 1965; . . 1st Franchised in 1967
Company-Owned Units (As of 12/1/1989): . .1
Franchised Units (12/1/1989): 179
Total Units (12/1/1989): 180
Distribution: US-175;Can-3;Overseas-2
North America: . . . . 30 States, 2 Provinces
Concentration: . .20 in PA, 20 in OH, 15 in FL
Registered: . . . CA,FL,IL,IN,MD,MI,MN,NY
. . . . .RI,VA,WA,WI, AB
Average # of Employees: . . . . . . 3 FT, 3 PT
Prior Industry Experience: . . . . Helpful

FINANCIAL:
Cash Investment: $15K
Total Investment: $50-65K
Fees: Franchise - $13-50K
Royalty: 5%, Advert: 0%
Contract Periods (Yrs.): 5/5
Area Development Agreement: Yes/15
Sub-Franchise Contract: . . . . . Yes
Expand in Territory: . . . . . . Yes
Passive Ownership: . . . . . .Allowed
Encourage Conversions: . . . . Yes
Franchisee Purchase(s) Required: .No

FRANCHISOR TRAINING/SUPPORT:
Financial Assistance Provided: . . .Yes(D)
Site Selection Assistance: . . . . . . .NA
Lease Negotiation Assistance: . . . . .NA
Co-operative Advertising: . . . . . . .NA
Training: . . . . 5 Days Headquarters,
. . . . 3 Days in Territory
On-Going Support: . . . . .B,C,D,F,G,H,I
Full-Time Franchisor Support Staff: . . 15
EXPANSION PLANS:
US: . . . . All US
Canada - Yes, . . . Overseas - Yes

SPOTLESS OFFICE SERVICES

4040 Brockton Cr.
North Vancouver, BC V7G1E6 CAN
TEL: (604) 929-4432
FAX:
Mr. Bob Mussio, President

Building Maintenance Broker. No investment in trucks or janitorial equipment. Equipment is owned by janitors. Office cleaning is our specialty.

HISTORY: . . . .
Established in 1978; . . 1st Franchised in 1980
Company-Owned Units (As of 12/1/1989): . .1
Franchised Units (12/1/1989): 116
Total Units (12/1/1989): 117
Distribution: US-2;Can-115;Overseas-0
North America: . . . .
Concentration: . . . .
Registered: . . . .
. . . .
Average # of Employees: . . . . 10 PT
Prior Industry Experience: . . . . Helpful

FINANCIAL:
Cash Investment: $3K
Total Investment: $3K
Fees: Franchise - $3K
Royalty: 5%, Advert: 0%
Contract Periods (Yrs.): 1/1
Area Development Agreement: . .No
Sub-Franchise Contract: . . . . .No
Expand in Territory: . . . . . . .No
Passive Ownership: . . . . . .Allowed
Encourage Conversions: . . . .
Franchisee Purchase(s) Required: .No

FRANCHISOR TRAINING/SUPPORT:
Financial Assistance Provided: . . . . .No
Site Selection Assistance: . . . . . . .Yes
Lease Negotiation Assistance: . . . .
Co-operative Advertising: . . . .
Training: . . . . 1 Wk. Headquarters
. . . .
On-Going Support: . . . . . . C,D,E,G,H,I
Full-Time Franchisor Support Staff: . . 10
EXPANSION PLANS:
US: . . . . All US
Canada - Yes, . . . Overseas - Yes

STANLEY STEEMER CARPET CLEANER

5500 Stanley Steemer Pkwy.
Dublin, OH 43017
TEL: (800) 848-7496 (614) 764-2007
FAX:
Mr. Philip Ryser, VP Fran.

Carpet and upholstery cleaning and related services for both residential and commercial customers. Provide additional services, such as deodorizing, carpet protection, static electricity control and water extraction.

HISTORY: . . . . IFA
Established in 1947; . . 1st Franchised in 1972
Company-Owned Units (As of 12/1/1989): . 18
Franchised Units (12/1/1989): 220
Total Units (12/1/1989): 238
Distribution: US-238;Can-0;Overseas-0
North America: . . . . 37 States
Concentration: . . 34 in FL, 21 in OH, 15 in IN
Registered: . . . . All States Except FL
. . . .
Average # of Employees: . . . . 10-12 FT
Prior Industry Experience: . . . . . . Helpful

FINANCIAL:
Cash Investment: $42-200K
Total Investment: $42-200K
Fees: Franchise - . . . . $20K+
Royalty: 7%, Advert: 0%
Contract Periods (Yrs.): 20/10
Area Development Agreement: . .No
Sub-Franchise Contract: . . . . .No
Expand in Territory: . . . . . . Yes
Passive Ownership: . . . . . .Allowed
Encourage Conversions: . . . . .No
Franchisee Purchase(s) Required: Yes

FRANCHISOR TRAINING/SUPPORT:
Financial Assistance Provided: . . .Yes(D)
Site Selection Assistance: . . . . . . .NA
Lease Negotiation Assistance: . . . . .No
Co-operative Advertising: . . . . . . .Yes
Training: . . . . 2 Wks. Headquarters,
. . . . As Needed Site
On-Going Support: . . . . . . B,C,D,G,h,I
Full-Time Franchisor Support Staff: . . 80
EXPANSION PLANS:
US: . . . . .All US
Canada - Yes, . . . Overseas - Yes

TOWN & COUNTRY CLEANING CONTRACTORS

2580 San Ramon Blvd., #B-208
San Ramon, CA 94583
TEL: (415) 867-3850
FAX: (916) 362-1380
Mr. Ted Prince, President

State-of-the-art dry extraction carpet cleaning system. Easy to use. The plan provides for routinely-scheduled commercial contracts. Office cleaning also included with complete training. Customers are provided.

HISTORY: . . . .
Established in 1971; . . 1st Franchised in 1986
Company-Owned Units (As of 12/1/1989): . .0
Franchised Units (12/1/1989): 80
Total Units (12/1/1989): 80
Distribution: US-80;Can-0;Overseas-0
North America: . . . . .1 State
Concentration: . . . . 80 in CA
Registered: . . . . CA
. . . .
Average # of Employees: . . . . 1-6 FT, 1-3 PT
Prior Industry Experience: . . . . . . Helpful

FINANCIAL:
Cash Investment: $7-12K
Total Investment: $7-12K
Fees: Franchise - $3-7K
Royalty: 75/Mo., Advert: 0%
Contract Periods (Yrs.): 5/5
Area Development Agreement: . .No
Sub-Franchise Contract: . . . . .No
Expand in Territory: . . . . . . Yes
Passive Ownership: . . . Discouraged
Encourage Conversions: . . . . .No
Franchisee Purchase(s) Required: .No

FRANCHISOR TRAINING/SUPPORT:
Financial Assistance Provided: . . .Yes(D)
Site Selection Assistance: . . . . . . .NA
Lease Negotiation Assistance: . . . . .NA
Co-operative Advertising: . . . . . . .NA
Training: . . . . . .3 Days Sacramento, CA
. . . .
On-Going Support: . . . . b,C,D,H,I
Full-Time Franchisor Support Staff: . . .7
EXPANSION PLANS:
US: . . . . .All US
Canada - No, ...Overseas - No

ULTRA WASH

2335 Naomi St.
Houston, TX 77054
TEL: (713) 796-2431
FAX:
Mr. Brian Peskin, President

State-of-the-art mobile pressure washing franchise, specializing in commercial fleet washing at the customer's location. $150,000 initially. Profitable accounts included. 1,000,000 population, exclusive areas. Proprietary equipment and detergents.

HISTORY: . . . .
Established in 1981; . . 1st Franchised in 1984
Company-Owned Units (As of 12/1/1989): . .0
Franchised Units (12/1/1989): 36
Total Units (12/1/1989): 36
Distribution: US-36;Can-0;Overseas-0
North America: . . . . 8 States
Concentration: . . 10 in TX, 8 in CA, 3 in MO
Registered: . . . . All States
. . . .
Average # of Employees: . . . . . . 3 FT, 2 PT
Prior Industry Experience: . . . . . . Helpful

FINANCIAL:
Cash Investment: $4550K
Total Investment: $90K
Fees: Franchise - $37.5K
Royalty: 8-6%, Advert: 0%
Contract Periods (Yrs.): 8/8
Area Development Agreement: . .No
Sub-Franchise Contract: . . . . .No
Expand in Territory: . . . . . . Yes
Passive Ownership: . . . Discouraged
Encourage Conversions: . . . . .No
Franchisee Purchase(s) Required: .No

FRANCHISOR TRAINING/SUPPORT:
Financial Assistance Provided: . . . Yes(I)
Site Selection Assistance: . . . . . . .Yes
Lease Negotiation Assistance: . . . . .NA
Co-operative Advertising: . . . . . . .NA
Training: . . . . 2 Wks. Headquarters
. . . .
On-Going Support: . . . .B,C,D,E,F,G,H,I
Full-Time Franchisor Support Staff: . . .6
EXPANSION PLANS:
US: . . . . .All US
Canada - No, ... Overseas - Yes

UNICLEAN SYSTEMS

642 W. 29th St.
North Vancouver, BC V7N2K2 CAN
TEL: (604) 986-4750 C
FAX:
Mr. Jack Karpowicz, President

Professional office cleaning franchise. Franchisees provide cleaning services to office and other commercial buildings on a long-term contract basis. UNICLEAN will provide training, equipment and help secure initial contract in franchisee home town. Also, Master Franchises are available in select metropolitan areas or states/provinces. Minimum investment $18,500.

HISTORY: . . . . IFA/CFA
Established in 1976; . . 1st Franchised in 1981
Company-Owned Units (As of 12/1/1989): . .1
Franchised Units (12/1/1989): 128
Total Units (12/1/1989): 129
Distribution: US-21;Can-108;Overseas-0
North America: . . . . . 4 States, 5 Provinces
Concentration: . 24 in BC, 16 in ON, 11 in NB
Registered: . . . . .FL,OR
. . . .
Average # of Employees: . . . . . . 2 FT, 1 PT
Prior Industry Experience: . . . . . . Helpful

FINANCIAL:
Cash Investment: $7.5-12K
Total Investment: $7.5-12K
Fees: Franchise - $6.5-11K
Royalty: 5-8%, Advert: 0-2%
Contract Periods (Yrs.): 6/6
Area Development Agreement: Yes/12
Sub-Franchise Contract: . . . . . Yes
Expand in Territory: . . . . . . Yes
Passive Ownership: . . . Discouraged
Encourage Conversions: . . . . Yes
Franchisee Purchase(s) Required: .No

FRANCHISOR TRAINING/SUPPORT:
Financial Assistance Provided: . . .Yes(D)
Site Selection Assistance: . . . . . . .Yes
Lease Negotiation Assistance: . . . . .NA
Co-operative Advertising: . . . . No
Training: . . . . . . 1 Wk. Franchisee Area
. . . .
On-Going Support: . . . . A,B,C,D,G,H,I
Full-Time Franchisor Support Staff: . . . 6
EXPANSION PLANS:
US: . . . . All US
Canada - Yes, ...Overseas - No

UNIMAX BUILDING SERVICES OF AMERICA

P. O. Box 70251, Riverfront Station
Louisville, KY 40270
TEL: (812) 944-0360 C
FAX:
Mr. Lloyd Pate, President

UNIMAX will finance 55% of total package on local franchise. 70% on Master Franchise with approved credit through UNIMAX Financial Service. UNIMAX is a complete carpet and janitorial cleaning service.

HISTORY: . . . .
Established in 1986; . . 1st Franchised in 1986
Company-Owned Units (As of 12/1/1989): . .2
Franchised Units (12/1/1989): 4
Total Units (12/1/1989): 6
Distribution: US-6;Can-0;Overseas-0
North America: . . . . 4 States
Concentration: . . . 2 in KY, 1 in FL, 1 in NC
Registered: . . . . FL,HI,IL,IN,MD,OR,RI,SD
. . . . VA
Average # of Employees: . . . . .1 FT
Prior Industry Experience: . . . . Helpful

FINANCIAL:
Cash Investment: $2-4K
Total Investment: $14.5K
Fees: Franchise - . . . .$
Royalty: 2%, Advert: 3%
Contract Periods (Yrs.): 3/3
Area Development Agreement: .No
Sub-Franchise Contract: . . . . . Yes
Expand in Territory: . . . . . . Yes
Passive Ownership: . . . . . .Allowed
Encourage Conversions: . . . . .No
Franchisee Purchase(s) Required: Yes

FRANCHISOR TRAINING/SUPPORT:
Financial Assistance Provided: . . .Yes(D)
Site Selection Assistance: . . . . . . .Yes
Lease Negotiation Assistance: . . . . .No
Co-operative Advertising: . . . . . . .Yes
Training: . . . . 5 Days Headquarters,
. . . . .5 Days On-site, On-going
On-Going Support: . . A,B,C,D,E,F,G,H,I
Full-Time Franchisor Support Staff: . . 20
EXPANSION PLANS:
US: . . . . .Southeast, KY,TN,NC,SC,FL
Canada - No, ...Overseas - No

WINCO WINDOW CLEANING & MAINTENANCE SERVICES

710 S. Gholson
Knoxville, IA 50138
TEL: (515) 828-8836 C
FAX:
Mr. David Wolett, Fran. Dir.

WINCO offers a nationally-registered service mark, copyrighted manuals and workshop. Thorough and complete training, covering 20 profit centers providing: window cleaning, pest control and janitorial services. With on-going consultation and support. WINCO provides future businessman uncompromised information and instruction essential for a successful business.

HISTORY: . . . .
Established in 1977; . . 1st Franchised in 1987
Company-Owned Units (As of 12/1/1989): . .4
Franchised Units (12/1/1989): 3
Total Units (12/1/1989): 7
Distribution: US-7;Can-0;Overseas-0
North America: . . . . 3 States
Concentration: . . . . 4 in IA, 1 in TX, 1 in OR
Registered: . . . .
. . . .
Average # of Employees: . . . . .1 FT
Prior Industry Experience: . . . . Helpful

FINANCIAL:
Cash Investment: $3.9K
Total Investment: $3.9K
Fees: Franchise - $3.9K
Royalty: 0%, Advert: 0%
Contract Periods (Yrs.): . . . .Varies
Area Development Agreement: Yes/Var
Sub-Franchise Contract: . . . . . Yes
Expand in Territory: . . . . . . .No
Passive Ownership: . . . . . .Allowed
Encourage Conversions: . . . . NA
Franchisee Purchase(s) Required: .No

FRANCHISOR TRAINING/SUPPORT:
Financial Assistance Provided: . . .Yes(D)
Site Selection Assistance: . . . . . . .Yes
Lease Negotiation Assistance: . . . . .No
Co-operative Advertising: . . . . . . .Yes
Training: . . . . . .3-10 Days in Franchisee
. . . . Area
On-Going Support: . . . . . . C,D,E,F,G,i
Full-Time Franchisor Support Staff: . . . 6
EXPANSION PLANS:
US: . . . . All US
Canada - Yes, ...Overseas - Yes

SUPPLEMENTAL LISTING OF FRANCHISORS

ABBEY CARPET CLEANING SERVICE . . . . .5740 Yonge St., # 201, Willowdale ON M2M3T4 CAN
ACCU-WASH CORP. .83 Bigwin Rd., # 11, Hamilton ON L0R1P0 CAN
ACTION CLEAN AIR SERVICES . . . . 460 Woody Rd., # 5, Oakville ON L6K3T6 CAN
AEROWEST . . . . 25100 S. Normandie Ave., Harbor City CA 90710
AL-VIN . . . . .P. O. Box 534, Port Colbourne ON L3K5X7 CAN
AMERICLEAN MOBILE POWER WASH/RESTOR. . . . . . .943 Taft-Vineland Rd., Orlando FL 32824
AMERISEAL . . . . .3060 Leon Rd., Jacksonville FL 32216
ARTIS SYSTEMS . . . . 704 S. Bunn St., Bloomington IL 61702
BEE-CLEAN . . . . 4128A 97th St., # 226, Edmonton AB T6E5Y6 CAN
BLACKMON MOORING . . . . 1601 109th St., Grand Prairie TX 75050
BLUE DIAMOND . . . . .2399 Windsor Dr., Mississauga ON L5J1K9 CAN
BLUE DIAMOND WINDOW CLEANING . . . . .100 Union Park St., Boston MA 02118
BUCK-A-STALL PARKING LOT PAINTING . . . . P.O. Box 1156, Madison TN 37115
BUILDING SERVICE & MAINTENANCE . . . . 575 Airport Blvd., Gallatin TN 37066
CANADIAN RESTORATION SERVICES . . . . .1680 Woodward Dr., # 201, Ottawa ON K2C9R8 CAN
CARPET COLOR TINT . . . . 20438 NE 15th, Miami FL 33179
CARPET WORKS . . . . 600 W. Diversey, # 916, Chicago IL 60614
CEILING SAVERS, THE . . . . .P. O. Box 371, Thornhill ON L3T4AZ CAN
CHEMBROOM INTERNATIONAL . . . . .674 Enterprise Dr., Westerville OH 43081
CLEAN UP SYSTEMS/CLEAN CEILINGS . . . . P. O. Box 86310, North Vancouver BC V7L4K6 CAN
CLEANING IDEAS . . . . P.O. Box 7269, San Antonio TX 78207
CLEANMARK . . . . .185 Greens Farm Rd., Westport CT 06880
COLOR YOUR CARPET . . . . 2465 Ridgecrest Ave., Orange Park FL 32065
CONCORD CARPET CARE . . . . .2721 Benedict Rd., Kelowna BC V1Z1V1 CAN
CRITTER CONTROL . . . . .32932 Warren, # B, Westland MI 48185
DYNO-ROD . . . . 112 Brookhollow Dr., Santa Ana CA 92705
ELDON DRAPERY CLEANERS . . . . 9291 Arleta Ave., Arleta CA 91331
ENVIRONMENTAL AIR TREATMENTS . . . . .N. 2602 Sullivan Rd., Spokane WA 99216
FLY CLEAN INTERNATIONAL . . . . .9009 N. Loop E., # 155, Houston TX 77029
FOREST HILL ENTERPRISES . . . . Rte. 9, Box 1A, Charlottesville VA 22901
H.O.M.E.S. GUILD . . . . 31255 Cedar Valley Dr., # 203, Westlake Village CA 91362
HANDYMAN HOUSE CALLS . . . . .640 Northland Rd., # 33, Forest Park OH 45240
HEAVEN'S BEST CARPET/UPHOLST. CLEANING . . . . P. O. Box 607, Rexburg ID 83440
HIGHLAND'S MAINTENANCE SYSTEMS . . . . 1525 Chelten Way, S. Pasadena CA 91030
INTERCLEAN SERVICE SYSTEM . . . . 1325 10th Ave., Greeley CO 80631
JANI-KING CANADA . . . . 121 Ilsley Ave., # Y, Dartmouth NS CAN B3B1S4 CAN
JANUZ MAINTENANCE SYSTEMS . . . . 356 N. Marshall Ave., # B, El Cajon CA 92020
LET THE SUNSHINE IN WINDOW CLEANING . . . . 35 High St., Belfast ME 04915
LIEN CHEMICAL COMPANY . . . . 501 W. Lake St., Elmhurst IL 60126
MASTERWORKS INTERNATIONAL . . . . 121 Interstate Blvd., Greenville SC 29615
MODERNISTIC CARPET CLEANING . . . . .1271 Rankin, Troy MI 48084
MR. HANDYMAN . . . . 34 Grenfell Cres., Ottawa ON K2G0G2 CAN
ON-SITE DRAPERY DRY CLEANING . . . . 16400 Ventura Blvd., # 312, Encino CA 91436
PLUMBER-ROOTER . . . . .167 Chestnut Ln., Mt. Carmel CT 06518
PROTOUCH . . . . 100 E. 20th St., Kansas City MO 64108
QUALITY MARKETING . . . . .6278 N. Federal Hwy., # 284, Ft. Lauderdale FL 33308
RAINBOW INTERNATIONAL . . . . .1010 University Parks Dr., Waco TX 76707
READY ROOFING . . . . 8248 Waterford Ave., Tamarac FL 33321
REDI-NATIONAL PEST ELIMINATORS . . . . .6983 Brockton Ave., Riverside CA 92506
REPELE INTERNATIONAL . . . . .219 Newbury St., Boston MA 02116
RESCUE INDUSTRIES .P.O. Box 85095, San Diego CA 92138
SATISFIED SYSTEMS . . . . 704 S. Bunn St., Bloomington IL 61702
SERMAC INDUSTRIES . . . . .2612 18th St., Altoona PA 16601

SERVICEMASTER (CANADA) . . . . .6315 Shawson Dr., Mississauga ON L5T1J2   CAN
SERVICEMASTER RESIDENTIAL/COMMERCIAL . . . . . . 888 Ridge Lake Blvd., Memphis TN 38119
SERVICEWORLD MAINTENANCE . . . . .5405 Eglinton Ave. W., # 209, Etobicoke ON M9C5K6   CAN
SHADE SHOWER . . . . 7820 E Evans Rd., # 200, Scottsdale AZ 85260
STEAMATIC . . . . 1601 109th St., Grand Prairie TX 75050
STEAMATIC FRANCHISES . . . . 31 Durward Pl., Waterloo ON N2L4E5   CAN
THEE CHIMNEY SWEEP . . . . Rte. # 8, Box 36 N.E., Rome GA 30161
TOTAL GUARD . . . . 20438 NE 15th, Miami FL 33179
UNIVERSAL SWEEPING SERVICES . . . . P.O. Box 5993, San Jose CA 95150
VALU INNS . . . . 520 Pike St., # 1200, Seattle WA 98101
VALUE LINE MAINTENANCE SYSTEMS . . . . 3801 River Dr. N., Great Falls MT 59401
WESTAIR WASHROOM SANITATION . . . . 25100 S. Normandie Ave., Harbor City CA 90710
WORTH HYDROCHEM . . . . .413 E. Magnolia, Ft. Worth TX 76104
WRIGHT-WAY CLEANING SRVICES . . . . P.O. Box 8058, Tyler TX 75711

CHAPTER 29

MOTELS / HOTELS / CAMPGROUNDS

AMERICINN INTERNATIONAL

1501 Northway Dr., P.O. Box 1595
St. Cloud, MN 56302
TEL: (612) 252-6034
FAX:
Mr. Rod Lindquist, Sr. VP

AMERICINN MOTELS provide the finest quality and friendliest service in lodging today. Our primary market is towns of population under 25,000. AMERICINN MOTELS are in their own niche within this market, that being "luxury budget." Our company motto is "Absolutely nobody will equal our quality, service or performance - and that's a promise!"

HISTORY: . . . .
Established in 1979; . . 1st Franchised in 1987
Company-Owned Units (As of 12/1/1989): . .0
Franchised Units (12/1/1989): 23
Total Units (12/1/1989): 23
Distribution: US-23;Can-0;Overseas-0
  North America: . . . . 5 States
  Concentration: . . . 12 in MN, 4 in WI, 2 in IL
Registered: . . . . All States
. . . .
Average # of Employees: . . . . . . 4 FT, 7 PT
Prior Industry Experience: . . . . Helpful

FINANCIAL:
Cash Investment: $250K
Total Investment: $1.0MM
Fees: Franchise - $10K
  Royalty: 3.5%, Advert: 0%
Contract Periods (Yrs.): 25/25
Area Development Agreement: . Yes
Sub-Franchise Contract: . . . . . .No
Expand in Territory: . . . . Yes
Passive Ownership: . . . . . .Allowed
Encourage Conversions: . . . . . .No
Franchisee Purchase(s) Required: Yes

FRANCHISOR TRAINING/SUPPORT:
Financial Assistance Provided: . . . Yes(I)
Site Selection Assistance: . . . . .Yes
Lease Negotiation Assistance: . . . . .Yes
Co-operative Advertising: . . . . .Yes
Training: . . . . 1 Day HQ, 2 Days On-site,
  . . . . 7 Days Direct Supervision
On-Going Support: . . . a,B,C,D,E,F,G,H
Full-Time Franchisor Support Staff: . . . 8
EXPANSION PLANS:
  US: . . . . . . Upper Midwest, IL and AZ
  Canada - Yes, ... Overseas - No

HOTELS, MOTELS AND CAMPGROUNDS

	1988	1989	1990	Percentage Change 1988–1989	Percentage Change 1989–1990
Number of Establishments:					
Company–Owned	1,208	1,235	1,284	2.2%	4.0%
Franchisee–Owned	8,103	8,903	9,819	9.9%	10.3%
Total	9,311	10,138	11,103	8.9%	9.5%
% of Total Establishments:					
Company–Owned	13.0%	12.2%	11.6%		
Franchisee–Owned	87.0%	87.8%	88.4%		
Total	100.0%	100.0%	100.0%		
Annual Sales ($000):					
Company–Owned	$5,981,751	$6,228,920	$6,817,882	4.1%	9.5%
Franchisee–Owned	13,767,428	15,075,333	17,046,349	9.5%	13.1%
Total	19,749,179	21,304,253	23,864,231	7.9%	12.0%
% of Total Sales:					
Company–Owned	30.3%	29.2%	28.6%		
Franchisee–Owned	69.7%	70.8%	71.4%		
Total	100.0%	100.0%	100.0%		
Average Sales Per Unit ($000):					
Company–Owned	$4,952	$5,044	$5,310	1.9%	5.3%
Franchisee–Owned	1,699	1,693	1,736	–0.3%	2.5%
Total	2,121	2,101	2,149	–0.9%	2.3%
Sales Ratio	291.4%	297.9%	305.9%		

	1st Quartile	Median	4th Quartile
Average 1988 Total Investment:			
Company–Owned	N. A.	$1,500,000	$4,500,000
Franchisee–Owned	425,000	1,350,000	4,125,000
Single Unit Franchise Fee	$13,125	$20,000	$30,000
Multiple Unit Franchise Fee	N. A.	17,500	
Franchisee Start–up Cost	200,000	425,000	575,000

	1988	Employees/Unit	Sales/Employee
Employment:			
Company–Owned	N. A.	N. A.	N. A.
Franchisee–Owned	N. A.	N. A.	N. A.
Total	N. A.	N. A.	N. A.
Employee Performance Ratios		N. A.	N. A.

Source: Franchising In The Economy, 1988 – 1990, IFA Education Foundation & Horwath International, Published January, 1990.

1) 1989 and 1990 data were estimated by respondents.

BUDGET HOST INNS

2601 Jacksboro Hwy., # 202
Ft. Worth, TX 76114
TEL: (817) 626-7064
FAX:
Mr. Ray Sawyer, President

Referral chain of affiliated independent inns (a la Best Western) that meet AAA or Mobil Travel Guide, or equivalent, standards and provide moderate room rates for respective market area. BUDGET HOST provides full-service program for advertising, promotion and national account savings on supplies, equipment and services.

HISTORY: . . . .
Established in 1975; . . 1st Franchised in 1976
Company-Owned Units (As of 12/1/1989): . .0
Franchised Units (12/1/1989): 220
Total Units (12/1/1989): 220
Distribution: US-214;Can-6;Overseas-0
North America: . . . . . 39 States, 1 Province
Concentration: . 22 in KS, 18 in MO, 18 in CO
Registered: . . . .
. . . .
Average # of Employees: . . . .
Prior Industry Experience: . . . . Helpful

FINANCIAL:
Cash Investment: . . . . $2+K
Total Investment: . . . . $2+K
Fees: Franchise - $950
  Royalty: Var., Advert: . . . . Var.
Contract Periods (Yrs.): 1/1
Area Development Agreement: . .No
Sub-Franchise Contract: . . . . . .No
Expand in Territory: . . . . Yes
Passive Ownership: . . . . .Allowed
Encourage Conversions: . . . . .No
Franchisee Purchase(s) Required: .No

FRANCHISOR TRAINING/SUPPORT:
Financial Assistance Provided: . . . . .No
Site Selection Assistance: . . . . .No
Lease Negotiation Assistance: . . . . .No
Co-operative Advertising: . . . . . . .Yes
Training: . . . .
. . . .
On-Going Support: . . . . B,C,G,H
Full-Time Franchisor Support Staff: . . . 3
EXPANSION PLANS:
US: . . . . .All US
Canada - Yes, ...Overseas - No

COMPRI HOTEL SYSTEMS

410 N. 44th St., # 700
Phoenix, AZ 85008
TEL: (800 4-COMPRI (602) 220-6783
FAX: (602) 244-0125
Mr. Kevin Holt, VP Development

A four-star, quality, limited-service hotel concept which competes in the upper mid-price hotel market. Features an airline-style club room rather than a traditional restaurant and lounge. Complimentary cocktails and cooked-to-order breakfast are served in the Club.

HISTORY: . . . . IFA
Established in 1984; . . 1st Franchised in 1986
Company-Owned Units (As of 12/1/1989): . .6
Franchised Units (12/1/1989): 17
Total Units (12/1/1989): 23
Distribution: US-22;Can-1;Overseas-0
North America: . . . . . 13 States, 1 Province
Concentration: . . . 6 in CA, 3 in NC, 2 in PA
Registered: . . . . All Except AB
. . . .
Average # of Employees: . . . . .46 FT, 8 PT
Prior Industry Experience: . . . . Helpful

FINANCIAL:
Cash Investment: $2-4MM
Total Investment: $10-20MM
Fees: Franchise - $30K
  Royalty: 3%, Advert: 3%
Contract Periods (Yrs.): 20/0
Area Development Agreement: . .No
Sub-Franchise Contract: . . . . . .No
Expand in Territory: . . . . Yes
Passive Ownership: . . . . . .Allowed
Encourage Conversions: . . . . Yes
Franchisee Purchase(s) Required: .No

FRANCHISOR TRAINING/SUPPORT:
Financial Assistance Provided: . . . . .No
Site Selection Assistance: . . . . .Yes
Lease Negotiation Assistance: . . . . .No
Co-operative Advertising: . . . . . . .Yes
Training: . . . . .1 Wk. Headquarters,
. . . . 2 Wks. Pre-Opening at Hotel
On-Going Support: . . . . . . b,C,D,E,h
Full-Time Franchisor Support Staff: . . 99
EXPANSION PLANS:
US: . . . . .All US
Canada - Yes, . . . Overseas - Yes

HAMPTON INN / HAMPTON INNS

6799 Great Oaks Rd., # 100
Memphis, TN 38138
TEL: (901) 756-2811
FAX:
Mr. Donald H. Dempsey, VP Devel.

Hotels designed for travelers seeking quality rooms with great service and select extras at affordable rates. Guests get free continental breakfast, free telephone calls, free in-room movie channel, availability of no-smoking rooms. Hotels are growing in popularity and bring good return on investment.

HISTORY: . . . . IFA
Established in 1983; . . 1st Franchised in 1984
Company-Owned Units (As of 12/1/1989): . 28
Franchised Units (12/1/1989): 182
Total Units (12/1/1989): 210
Distribution: US-210;Can-0;Overseas-0
North America: . . . . 36 States
Concentration: . .18 in TX, 17 in NC, 15 in FL
Registered: . . . . All States
. . . .
Average # of Employees: . . . . 25 FT
Prior Industry Experience: . . . . . .Necessary

FINANCIAL: NYSE-HOL
Cash Investment: . . . . . $.6-1.5MM
Total Investment: $3-6MM
Fees: Franchise - $35K
  Royalty: 4%, Advert: 3%
Contract Periods (Yrs.): 20
Area Development Agreement: . .No
Sub-Franchise Contract: . . . . . .No
Expand in Territory: . . . . .No
Passive Ownership: . . . Discouraged
Encourage Conversions: . . . . . .No
Franchisee Purchase(s) Required: .No

FRANCHISOR TRAINING/SUPPORT:
Financial Assistance Provided: . . . Yes(I)
Site Selection Assistance: . . . . .No
Lease Negotiation Assistance: . . . . .No
Co-operative Advertising: . . . . .Yes
Training: . . . . . . Training Programs Are
. . . . At Extra Cost
On-Going Support: . . . . . . A,b,C,d,G,h
Full-Time Franchisor Support Staff: . . 50
EXPANSION PLANS:
US: . . . . .All US
Canada - Yes, ...Overseas - No

HAWTHORN SUITES HOTELS

131 State St., # 820
Boston, MA 02109
TEL: (800) 527-1133 (617) 367-5880
FAX:
Mr. Joseph McInerney, President

HAWTHORN SUITES is an all-suite, limited-service hotel chain designed to meet the needs of the upper mid-scale, extended-stay customer. The building style will be high-rise, mid-rise, as well as garden-style, featuring one and two bedroom suites with separate living room, full kitchen, swimming pool and health/fitness center, full complimentary breakfast and complimentary cocktail hour.

HISTORY: . . . . IFA
Established in 1986; . . 1st Franchised in 1986
Company-Owned Units (As of 12/1/1989): . .1
Franchised Units (12/1/1989): 8
Total Units (12/1/1989): 9
Distribution: US-9;Can-0;Overseas-0
 North America: . . . . 5 States
 Concentration: . . . . 5 in TX
Registered: . . . . All States
. . . .
Average # of Employees: . . . . 32 FT
Prior Industry Experience: . . . . Helpful

FINANCIAL:
Cash Investment: \$20-30%
Total Investment: . . . . .\$65K+/Unit
Fees: Franchise - . . . . \$Varies
 Royalty: 4%, Advert: 2.5%
Contract Periods (Yrs.): 15/10
Area Development Agreement: Yes/3-5
Sub-Franchise Contract: . . . . . .No
Expand in Territory: . . . . Yes
Passive Ownership: . . . . . .Allowed
Encourage Conversions: . . . . . Yes
Franchisee Purchase(s) Required: .No

FRANCHISOR TRAINING/SUPPORT:
Financial Assistance Provided: . . . Yes(I)
Site Selection Assistance: . . . . .Yes
Lease Negotiation Assistance: . . . . . No
Co-operative Advertising: . . . . .Yes
Training: . . . . . Seminars of 3-5 Days on
 . . . Each Phase Are Held in Var. Locat.
On-Going Support: . . . . . b,C,D,E,f,g,h
Full-Time Franchisor Support Staff: . . . 8
EXPANSION PLANS:
 US: . . . . .All US
 Canada - Yes, . . . Overseas - Yes

HILTON INNS

9336 Civic Center Dr.
Beverly Hills, CA 90210
TEL: (213) 278-4321
FAX: (213) 278-9218
Mr. Donald L. Harrill, EVP

In 1965, HILTON INNS was established to meet the need for a first-class hotel franchise program. HILTON franchises enjoy strong name recognition, system-wide marketing programs, central reservation service, central purchasing and development, operations and training support from HILTON regional and corporate offices.

HISTORY: . . . . IFA
Established in 1948; . . 1st Franchised in 1965
Company-Owned Units (As of 12/1/1989): . 51
Franchised Units (12/1/1989): 215
Total Units (12/1/1989): 266
Distribution: . . . US-263;Can-0;Overseas-3
 North America: . . . . 43 States
 Concentration: . . . .
Registered: . . . . All States
. . . .
Average # of Employees: . . . . 100 FT, 25 PT
Prior Industry Experience: . . . . Helpful

FINANCIAL: NYSE-HLT
Cash Investment: . . . .\$20% of Cost
Total Investment: . . . . . . \$10MM+
Fees: Franchise - . . . . \$25K+
 Royalty: 5%, Advert: 0%
Contract Periods (Yrs.): . . . 10-20/5
Area Development Agreement: . .No
Sub-Franchise Contract: . . . . . .No
Expand in Territory: . . . . .No
Passive Ownership: . . . . . .Allowed
Encourage Conversions: . . . . . .No
Franchisee Purchase(s) Required: Yes

FRANCHISOR TRAINING/SUPPORT:
Financial Assistance Provided: . . . Yes(I)
Site Selection Assistance: . . . . .Yes
Lease Negotiation Assistance: . . . . . No
Co-operative Advertising: . . . . .Yes
Training: . . . . . . 1 Wk. Regional Offices
. . . .
On-Going Support: . . . . . . .B,C,D,G,H
Full-Time Franchisor Support Staff: . . 90
EXPANSION PLANS:
 US: . . . . .All US
 Canada - No, ...Overseas - No

KAMPGROUNDS OF AMERICA / KOA

550 N. 31st, 4th Fl.
Billings, MT 59101
TEL: (800) 548-7239 (406) 248-7444
FAX: (406) 248-7414
Mr. David W. Johnson, VP Fran. Sales

KAMPGROUNDS OF AMERICA is America's largest system of campgrounds for recreational vehicles. The average campground contains 100 sites equipped with water and electrical hookups; many sites have sewer hookups. Each campground features clean restrooms with hot showers, a convenience store, laundry equipment and playground equipment. Most have swimming pools.

HISTORY: . . . . IFA
Established in 1961; . . 1st Franchised in 1962
Company-Owned Units (As of 12/1/1989): . 14
Franchised Units (12/1/1989): 632
Total Units (12/1/1989): 646
Distribution: US-593;Can-53;Overseas-0
 North America: . . . . 46 States,10 Provinces
 Concentration: . .38 in CA, 35 in FL, 30 in CO
Registered: . . . . All States Except HI
. . . .
Average # of Employees: . . . . . . 2 FT, 1 PT
Prior Industry Experience: . . . . Helpful

FINANCIAL:
Cash Investment: . . . . \$85K+
Total Investment: . . . .\$250K+
Fees: Franchise - \$20K
 Royalty: 8%, Advert: 2%
Contract Periods (Yrs.): 5/5
Area Development Agreement: . .No
Sub-Franchise Contract: . . . . .No
Expand in Territory: . . . . Yes
Passive Ownership: . . . Discouraged
Encourage Conversions: . . . . . Yes
Franchisee Purchase(s) Required: Yes

FRANCHISOR TRAINING/SUPPORT:
Financial Assistance Provided: . . . . . No
Site Selection Assistance: . . . . .Yes
Lease Negotiation Assistance: . . . . .NA
Co-operative Advertising: . . . . .No
Training: . . . . 3 Days Headquarters
. . . .
On-Going Support: . . . . . B,C,D,E,G,h,I
Full-Time Franchisor Support Staff: . . 56
EXPANSION PLANS:
 US: . . . . .All US Except Hawaii
 Canada - Yes, ...Overseas - No

MASTER HOST INNS/RED CARPET INNS/SCOTTISH INNS

1152 Spring St., # A
Atlanta, GA 30309
TEL: (800) 247-4677 (404) 873-5926
FAX: (404) 872-6358
Mr. Bill Fowler, Fran. Dev. Coord.

A major franchise for budget, limited service, and full-service properties, at a fraction of the cost of other major chains. Bed and Breakfast Program will be starting to accept franchises in mid-1990.

HISTORY: . . . . .IFA/CFA
Established in 1978; . . 1st Franchised in 1978
Company-Owned Units (As of 12/1/1989): . .0
Franchised Units (12/1/1989): 325
Total Units (12/1/1989): 325
Distribution: US-322;Can-3;Overseas-0
North America: . . . . 39 States, 2 Provinces
Concentration: . .57 in FL, 51 in GA, 29 in TN
Registered: . . . . All Except HI and WA
. . . .
Average # of Employees: . . . . 30 FT
Prior Industry Experience: . . . . Helpful

FINANCIAL:
Cash Investment: $100-400K
Total Investment: $1.2-4.8MM
Fees: Franchise - $5-15K
Royalty: 2-3%, Advert: 05%
Contract Periods (Yrs.): 20/5
Area Development Agreement: . .No
Sub-Franchise Contract: . . . . . .No
Expand in Territory: . . . . Yes
Passive Ownership: . . . . .Allowed
Encourage Conversions: . . . . . Yes
Franchisee Purchase(s) Required: .No

FRANCHISOR TRAINING/SUPPORT:
Financial Assistance Provided: . . . Yes(I)
Site Selection Assistance: . . . . .Yes
Lease Negotiation Assistance: . . . . .Yes
Co-operative Advertising: . . . . .Yes
Training: . . . . 1 Wk. Headquarters
On-Going Support: . . . . . B,C,D,E,G,h,I
Full-Time Franchisor Support Staff: . . 32
EXPANSION PLANS:
US: . . . . All US
Canada - Yes, . . . Overseas - Yes

NATIONAL BED N' BREAKFAST

Belmont
Colchester County, NS B0M1C0 CAN
TEL: (902) 662-3733
FAX:
Ms. Carol Robertson, President

Turn your extra room into extra income! Because of overwhelming curiosity by the public, please send $20 with your franchise inquiry. We will send you a detailed prospectus that tells you if B & B is right for you.

HISTORY: . . . .
Established in 1985; . . 1st Franchised in 1987
Company-Owned Units (As of 12/1/1989): . .1
Franchised Units (12/1/1989): 9
Total Units (12/1/1989): 10
Distribution: US-0;Can-10;Overseas-0
North America: . . . . .1 Province
Concentration: . . . . .10 in NS
Registered: . . . .
. . . .
Average # of Employees: . . . . . . 1 FT, 1 PT
Prior Industry Experience: . . . . Helpful

FINANCIAL:
Cash Investment: $600
Total Investment: $600
Fees: Franchise - $600
Royalty: 4%, Advert: 1%
Contract Periods (Yrs.): 10/10
Area Development Agreement: Yes/10
Sub-Franchise Contract: . . . . Yes
Expand in Territory: . . . . . . Yes
Passive Ownership: . . . . . .Allowed
Encourage Conversions: . . . . . Yes
Franchisee Purchase(s) Required: .No

FRANCHISOR TRAINING/SUPPORT:
Financial Assistance Provided: . . . Yes(I)
Site Selection Assistance: . . . . .Yes
Lease Negotiation Assistance: . . . . .NA
Co-operative Advertising: . . . . .Yes
Training: . . . . . . 3 Wks. Study Course, 1
. . . . Day Video, 1 Wk. Headquarters
On-Going Support: . . . . C,D,G,H,i
Full-Time Franchisor Support Staff: . . . 2
EXPANSION PLANS:
US: . . . . Seeking Sub-franchisors
Canada - Yes, ...Overseas - No

NEW WORLD BED & BREAKFAST

150 5th Ave., # 711
New York, NY 10011
TEL: (800) 443-3800 (212) 675-5600
FAX:
Ms. Laura Tilden, President

Selected as ONE OF THE BEST franchise buys! Combine the Old World charm of bed and breakfast with a new world business opportunity. Reservation services in major cities provide an attractive alternative to hotels. Minimal working capital requirements, low start-up costs, no cold-calling environment and a 9-5 lifestyle with NO WEEK-ENDS.

HISTORY: . . . . .WIF
Established in 1984; . . 1st Franchised in 1989
Company-Owned Units (As of 12/1/1989): . .0
Franchised Units (12/1/1989): 1
Total Units (12/1/1989): 1
Distribution: US-1;Can-0;Overseas-0
North America: . . . . .1 State
Concentration: . . . . 1 in NY
Registered: . . . . FL,IL,NY,WA
. . . .
Average # of Employees: . . . . . . 1 FT, 1 PT
Prior Industry Experience: . . . . Helpful

FINANCIAL:
Cash Investment: $25-60K
Total Investment: $25-60K
Fees: Franchise - $10-30K
Royalty: 9%, Advert: 1%
Contract Periods (Yrs.): 5/5/5
Area Development Agreement: . .No
Sub-Franchise Contract: . . . . . .No
Expand in Territory: . . . . . . .No
Passive Ownership: . . . Not Allowed
Encourage Conversions: . . . . . Yes
Franchisee Purchase(s) Required: .No

FRANCHISOR TRAINING/SUPPORT:
Financial Assistance Provided: . . . Yes(I)
Site Selection Assistance: . . . . .Yes
Lease Negotiation Assistance: . . . . .No
Co-operative Advertising: . . . . .Yes
Training: . . . . . . 1-2 Wks. Headquarters
On-Going Support: . . . . . .C,D,E,G,H,I
Full-Time Franchisor Support Staff: . . . 1
EXPANSION PLANS:
US: . . . . All US
Canada - No, ...Overseas - No

RODEWAY INN

P.O. Box 52005, 3838 E. Van Buren
Phoenix, AZ 85072
TEL: (602) 273-4550
FAX:
Mr. Luis Acosta, SVP

Franchise motor inns to the economy segment of the middle-market traveler, i.e. business, family, senior citizen, group tour.

HISTORY: . . . . IFA	FINANCIAL: NYSE-RAM	FRANCHISOR TRAINING/SUPPORT:
Established in 1962; . . 1st Franchised in 1962	Cash Investment: . . . . . $60-100K+	Financial Assistance Provided: . . . Yes(I)
Company-Owned Units (As of 12/1/1989): . .1	Total Investment: $2.0-4.0MM	Site Selection Assistance: . . . . .Yes
Franchised Units (12/1/1989): 179	Fees: Franchise - . . . . $20K+	Lease Negotiation Assistance: . . . . .Yes
Total Units (12/1/1989): 180	Royalty: 3%, Advert: 3.5%	Co-operative Advertising: . . . . .Yes
Distribution: US-178;Can-2;Overseas-0	Contract Periods (Yrs.): . . . 20/10	Training: . . . . Varies
North America: . . . . . 35 States, 1 Province	Area Development Agreement: . Yes	. . . .
Concentration:	Sub-Franchise Contract: . . . . . .No	On-Going Support: . . . . . .b,C,D,E,G,h
Registered: . . . . .All	Expand in Territory: . . . . Yes	Full-Time Franchisor Support Staff: . . 95
. . . .	Passive Ownership: . . . . .Allowed	EXPANSION PLANS:
Average # of Employees: . . . . Varies	Encourage Conversions: . . . . . Yes	US: . . . . .All US
Prior Industry Experience: . . . . . . Helpful	Franchisee Purchase(s) Required: .No	Canada - Yes, . . . Overseas - Yes

SLEEP INNS, COMFORT INNS, QUALITY INNS, CLARION HOTELS

10750 Columbia Pike
Silver Spring, MD 20901
TEL: (301) 236-5093
FAX:
Mr. Frederick W. Mosser, Sr. VP

Hotel/motel franchisor.

HISTORY: . . . . IFA	FINANCIAL: OTC-MNR	FRANCHISOR TRAINING/SUPPORT:
Established in 1939; . . 1st Franchised in 1963	Cash Investment: . . . . . $.2-2.0MM	Financial Assistance Provided: . . . . . No
Company-Owned Units (As of 12/1/1989): . 10	Total Investment: $2-15MM	Site Selection Assistance: . . . . .Yes
Franchised Units (12/1/1989): 1310	Fees: Franchise - . . . . $30K+	Lease Negotiation Assistance: . . . . . No
Total Units (12/1/1989): 1320	Royalty: 3-4%, Advert: 1.1%	Co-operative Advertising: . . . . No
Distribution: . . US-1155;Can-57;Overseas-108	Contract Periods (Yrs.): . . . 20/Var	Training: . . . . . 1 Day at Property, 1 Day
North America: . . . . 50 States, 5 Provinces	Area Development Agreement: . .No	. . . . at Headquarters, Periodic Sessions
Concentration:	Sub-Franchise Contract: . . . . . .No	On-Going Support: . . . . . . .b,C,D,G,H
Registered: . . . . .All	Expand in Territory: . . . . Yes	Full-Time Franchisor Support Staff: . . 32
. . . .	Passive Ownership: . . . . . .Allowed	EXPANSION PLANS:
Average # of Employees: . . . . . .24 FT, 6 PT	Encourage Conversions: . . . . . Yes	US: . . . . .All US
Prior Industry Experience: . . . . Helpful	Franchisee Purchase(s) Required: .No	Canada - Yes, . . . Overseas - Yes

SUPER 8 MOTELS

P. O. Box 4090
Aberdeen, SD 57402
TEL: (800) 843-1960 (605) 225-2272
FAX: (605) 225-5060
Ms. Joan Ganje-Fischer, VP Mktg.

SUPER 8 MOTELS is the nation's largest economy motel chain. Four affiliate companies, Super 8 Builders, Midwest Motel Supply, HOTEC and Super 8 Management can design, build, equip and operate your motel. Our franchise fees are documented to be the lowest of the major economy motel competitors.

HISTORY: . . . . IFA	FINANCIAL:	FRANCHISOR TRAINING/SUPPORT:
Established in 1973; . . 1st Franchised in 1976	Cash Investment: $100-250K	Financial Assistance Provided: . . . . . No
Company-Owned Units (As of 12/1/1989): . 40	Total Investment: . . . . .$.7-3.0MM	Site Selection Assistance: . . . .
Franchised Units (12/1/1989): 619	Fees: Franchise - $20K	Lease Negotiation Assistance: . . . . . No
Total Units (12/1/1989): 659	Royalty: 4%, Advert: 2%	Co-operative Advertising: . . . . No
Distribution: US-655;Can-4;Overseas-0	Contract Periods (Yrs.): . . 20/Varies	Training: . . . . 3 Wks. Headquarters
North America: . . . . 46 States, 4 Provinces	Area Development Agreement: . Yes	. . . . . As Needed On-site/Other Motels
Concentration: . 42 in MN, 38 in IL, 37 in NY	Sub-Franchise Contract: . . . . Yes	On-Going Support: . . . . a,B,C,D,e,G,H,I
Registered: . . . . .All	Expand in Territory: . . . . Yes	Full-Time Franchisor Support Staff: . .300
. . . .	Passive Ownership: . . . . . .Allowed	EXPANSION PLANS:
Average # of Employees: . . . . 12-20 FT	Encourage Conversions: . . . . . Yes	US: . . . . .All US
Prior Industry Experience: . . . . Helpful	Franchisee Purchase(s) Required: .No	Canada - Yes, . . . Overseas - Yes

TRAVELODGE / THRIFTLODGE
1973 Friendship Dr.
El Cajon, CA 92020
TEL: (800) 255-3050 (619) 448-1884
FAX:
Mr. Jere M. Hooper, EVP Franchising

Under Trusthouse Forte PLC, we are a worldwide network and reservation system generating international referrals between over 800 hotels and 32 sales offices in 18 countries. In North America, Forte Hotels now franchises full-service TRAVELODGE HOTELS, HOTEL SUITES, limited service TRAVELODGES and TRAVELODGE SUITES, as well as our new budget-brand THRIFTLODGE, a limited-service motel.

HISTORY: . . . .
Established in 1946; . . 1st Franchised in 1966
Company-Owned Units (As of 12/1/1989): 214
Franchised Units (12/1/1989): 234
Total Units (12/1/1989): 448
Distribution: . . . US-415;Can-333;Overseas-0
North America: . . . . 46 States, 5 Provinces
Concentration: . 200 in CA,32 in FL, 24 in TX
Registered: . . . . .All
. . . .
Average # of Employees: . . . .
Prior Industry Experience: . . . . Helpful

FINANCIAL:
Cash Investment: $500K
Total Investment: $1.0MM
Fees: Franchise - $15-25K
   Royalty: 3%, Advert: 4%
Contract Periods (Yrs.): 10/10
Area Development Agreement: . .No
Sub-Franchise Contract: . . . . . .No
Expand in Territory: . . . . Yes
Passive Ownership: . . . . . .Allowed
Encourage Conversions: . . . . Yes
Franchisee Purchase(s) Required: .No

FRANCHISOR TRAINING/SUPPORT:
Financial Assistance Provided: . . . . .No
Site Selection Assistance: . . . . .Yes
Lease Negotiation Assistance: . . . . .No
Co-operative Advertising: . . . . .Yes
Training: . . . . . . 4 Days Los Angeles, 4
. . . . Days New York
On-Going Support: . . . . . . .B,C,D,G,H
Full-Time Franchisor Support Staff: . . 10
EXPANSION PLANS:
US: . . . . .All US
Canada - Yes, ...Overseas - No

YOGI BEAR JELLYSTONE PARK CAMP/RESORTS
6201 Kellogg Ave.
Cincinnati, OH 45230
TEL: (800) 358-9165 (513) 232-6800
FAX: (513) 232-1191
Mr. Rob Schutter, Fran. Dir.

A unique recreation camp-resort for the entire family. Yogi and friends offer daily activities with a full amenity package, clean restrooms and Yogi souvenirs. Each camp-resort is independently owned and operated and maintains system standards.

HISTORY: . . . . .IFA
Established in 1969; . . 1st Franchised in 1969
Company-Owned Units (As of 12/1/1989): . .0
Franchised Units (12/1/1989): 79
Total Units (12/1/1989): 79
Distribution: US-75;Can-4;Overseas-0
North America: . . . . 25 States, 2 Provinces
Concentration: . . . . 8 in WI, 8 in VA, 7 in IN
Registered: . . . FL,IL,IN,MD,MI,MN,VA,WI
. . . .
Average # of Employees: . . . . .3 FT, 25 PT
Prior Industry Experience: . . . . Helpful

FINANCIAL: NASD-GACC
Cash Investment: $6-25K
Total Investment: $23-250K
Fees: Franchise - $15-23K
   Royalty: 6%, Advert: 1%
Contract Periods (Yrs.): . . 5-20/5-10
Area Development Agreement: . .No
Sub-Franchise Contract: . . . . . .No
Expand in Territory: . . . . .No
Passive Ownership: . . . Discouraged
Encourage Conversions: . . . . . Yes
Franchisee Purchase(s) Required: Yes

FRANCHISOR TRAINING/SUPPORT:
Financial Assistance Provided: . . .Yes(D)
Site Selection Assistance: . . . . . . .Yes
Lease Negotiation Assistance: . . . . .Yes
Co-operative Advertising: . . . . .Yes
Training: . . . . . .2-3 Days Site, 3-4 Days
. . . . . Headquarters, 1-3 Days/Yr. Site
On-Going Support: . . . . .B,C,D,E,G,H,I
Full-Time Franchisor Support Staff: . . .6
EXPANSION PLANS:
US: . . . . .All US
Canada - Yes, ... Overseas - No

SUPPLEMENTAL LISTING OF FRANCHISORS

ARBORGATE INN . . . . P. O. Box 32999, Columbus OH 43232
AUBERGE DES GOUVERNEURS . . . . 6550 Cote de Liesse, Montreal PQ H4T1S7   CAN
BEST INNS OF AMERICA . . . . RR #3. P. O. Box 1719, Marion IL 62959
BEST WESTERN INTERNATIONAL (CANADA) . . . . 5915 Airport Rd., # 320, Mississauga ON L4V1T1   CAN
BUDGETEL INNS . . . . 212 W. Wisconsin Ave., Milwaukee WI 53203
CARLSON HOSPITALITY GROUP . . . . .12755 State Hwy. 55, Minneapolis MN 55441
CLUBHOUSE INNS OF AMERICA . . . . 7101 College Blvd., # 1310, Overland Park KS 66210
COMFORT INN . . . . 10750 Columbia Pike, Silver Springs MD 20901
COUNTRY HOSPITALITY INNS . . . . 7800 Metro Pkwy., Minneapolis MN 55425
DAYS INN/DAYS LODGE . . . . 2751 Buford Hwy., NE, Atlanta GA 30324
DOWNTOWNER MOTOR INNS . . . . 454 Moss Trail, Goodlettsville TN 37072
ECONO LODGES OF AMERICA . . . . .6135 Park Rd., # 200, Charlotte NC 28210
EMBASSY SUITES . . . . Xerox Ctr.,# 1700, 222 Los Colina, Irving TX 75039

FAMILY INNS OF AMERICA	P.O. Box 1345, Pigeon Forge TN 37863	
FRIENDSHIP INNS	2627 Patterson Plank Rd., North Bergen NJ 07047	
HOLIDAY INNS	3796 Lamar Ave., Memphis TN 38195	
HOMEWOOD SUITES	3742 Lamar Ave., Memphis TN 38195	
HOSPITALITY INTERNATIONAL	1152 Spring St., # A, Atlanta GA 30309	
HOWARD JOHNSON FRANCHISE SYSTEMS	P.O. Box 2700, Fairfield NJ 07007	
HOWARD JOHNSON'S	96 Skyway Ave., Rexdale ON M9W4Y9	CAN
KAMPGROUNDS OF AMERICA (CANADA)	6A Tilbury Ct., # 4, Brampton ON L6T3T4	CAN
KNIGHTS INN/KNIGHTSTOP/KNIGHTS COURT	P. O. Box 32901, Columbus OH 43232	
MICROTEL	One Airport Way, # 200, Rochester NY 14624	
NENDEL'S INNS	520 Pike St., # 1200, Seattle WA 98101	
ORANGE ROOF	96 Skyway Ave., Rexdale ON M9W4Y9	CAN
PARK INN INTERNATIONAL	4425 W. Airport Fwy., Box 152083, Irving TX 75062	
PARK PLAZA	4425 W. Airport Fwy., Box 152083, Irving TX 75062	
PASSPORT INNS	454 Moss Trail, Goodlettsville TN 37072	
QUALITY INNS INTERNATIONAL (CANADA)	4174 Dundas St. W., #301, Toronto ON M8X1X3	CAN
RADISSON HOTELS INTERNATIONAL	Carlson Pkwy., P.O. Box 59159, Minneapolis MN 55441	
RAMADA INNS	P.O. Box 29004, Phoenix AZ 85038	
RAMADA INNS OF CANADA	2300 Yonge St., # 1700, Toronto ON M4P1E4	CAN
RESIDENCE INN BY MARRIOTT	One Marriott Dr., Washington DC 20058	
ROUSSILLON, RESEAU HOTELIER	4333 Sainte-Catherine ouest, #250, Westmount PQ H3Z1P9	CAN
SHERATON INNS	60 State St., Boston MA 02109	
SLUMBER LODGE MOTEL	1827 W. 5th Ave., 2nd Fl., Vancouver BC V6J1P5	CAN
STANLAKE LUXURY BUDGET MOTELS	6200 S. Syracuse Way, # 125, Englewood CO 80111	
SUMMIT HOTELS INTERNATIONAL	P.O. Box 52005, Phoenix AZ 85072	
TREADWAY INNS CORPORATION	50 Kenny Place, P.O. Box 1912, Saddle Brook NJ 07662	
VENTURE INNS	925 Dixon Rd., Rexdale ON M9W1J8	CAN
WANDLYN INNS	88 Prospect St., P.O. Box 430, Fredericton NB E3B4X4	CAN

**For a full explanation of the data provided in
the Franchisor Format, please refer to Chapter 2,
*"How To Use The Data."***

CHAPTER 30

OPTICAL / DENTAL / MEDICAL

AMIGO MOBILITY CENTER

6693 Dixie Hwy.
Bridgeport, MI 48722
TEL: (800) 821-2710 (517) 777-0910 C
FAX: (517) 777-8184
Mr. Jay V. Redlin, Franchise Dir.

AMIGO MOBILITY CENTERS specialize in the sales and service of mobility aids for the walking impaired. Supported by the Amigo factory with quality three wheeled scooters for the growing health care industry. Perfect family-oriented type business for both the young and old alike.

HISTORY: . . . . IFA
Established in 1968; . . 1st Franchised in 1984
Company-Owned Units (As of 12/1/1989): . .2
Franchised Units (12/1/1989): 10
Total Units (12/1/1989): 12
Distribution: US-12;Can-0;Overseas-0
 North America: . . . . 7 States
 Concentration: . . . . 3 in MI, 3 in FL, 2 in AZ
Registered: . . . . CA,IL,MI
. . . .
Average # of Employees: . . . . . . 3 FT, 1 PT
Prior Industry Experience: . . . . Helpful

FINANCIAL:
Cash Investment: $50-100K
Total Investment: $50-100K
Fees: Franchise - $15K
 Royalty: 5-3%, Advert: 1%
Contract Periods (Yrs.): 10/5
Area Development Agreement: . .No
Sub-Franchise Contract: . . . . .No
Expand in Territory: . . . . . . Yes
Passive Ownership: . . . Discouraged
Encourage Conversions: . . . . . Yes
Franchisee Purchase(s) Required: .No

FRANCHISOR TRAINING/SUPPORT:
Financial Assistance Provided: . . .Yes(D)
Site Selection Assistance: . . . . .Yes
Lease Negotiation Assistance: . . . . .Yes
Co-operative Advertising: . . . . .Yes
Training: . . . . . 1 - 2 Wks. SOP Training
. . . .
On-Going Support: . . . . .B,C,D,E,G,H,I
Full-Time Franchisor Support Staff: . . . 3
EXPANSION PLANS:
 US: . . . . NOrtheast and Southeast
 Canada - No, ... Overseas - No

CLAFLIN HOME HEALTH CENTERS

486 Silver Spring St.
Providence, RI 02904
TEL: (401) 331-0154
FAX:
Mr. Richard Westlake, President

CLAFLIN HOME HEALTH CENTERS is a chain of owner-operated, full-service, health care equipment and supply centers. Equipment is both rented and sold. A broad variety of supplies are also offered, making CLAFLIN a one-stop shopping concept. Billing and collection service is available.

HISTORY: . . . .
Established in 1900; . . 1st Franchised in 1982
Company-Owned Units (As of 12/1/1989): . .0
Franchised Units (12/1/1989): 5
Total Units (12/1/1989): 5
Distribution: US-5;Can-0;Overseas-0
North America: . . . . 2 States
Concentration: . . . . 4 in MA, 1 in RI
Registered: . . . . .NY,RI
. . . .
Average # of Employees: . . . . .2 FT
Prior Industry Experience: . . . . Helpful

FINANCIAL:
Cash Investment: $50-100K
Total Investment: $175K
Fees: Franchise - $25K
Royalty: 5%, Advert: 1%
Contract Periods (Yrs.): 10/5
Area Development Agreement: Yes/Var
Sub-Franchise Contract: . . . . .No
Expand in Territory: . . . . Yes
Passive Ownership: . . . Not Allowed
Encourage Conversions: . . . . . Yes
Franchisee Purchase(s) Required: .No

FRANCHISOR TRAINING/SUPPORT:
Financial Assistance Provided: . . . Yes(I)
Site Selection Assistance: . . . . .Yes
Lease Negotiation Assistance: . . . . .Yes
Co-operative Advertising: . . . . .Yes
Training: . . . . . 1 Wk. Classroom, 2 Wks.
. . . . Company Store, 1 Wk.+ Site
On-Going Support: . . . a,B,C,D,E,f,G,H,I
Full-Time Franchisor Support Staff: . . . 6
EXPANSION PLANS:
US: . . . . .All US
Canada - No, ...Overseas - No

FIRST OPTOMETRY EYECARE CENTERS

32600 Gratiot
Roseville, MI 48066
TEL: (313) 296-7800
FAX: (313) 294-2623
Mr. D. M. Borsand, CEO

Sale of visioncare services and optical products - eyeglasses, contact lenses and sunglasses.

HISTORY: . . . .
Established in 1980; . . 1st Franchised in 1981
Company-Owned Units (As of 12/1/1989): . 11
Franchised Units (12/1/1989): 20
Total Units (12/1/1989): 31
Distribution: US-31;Can-0;Overseas-0
North America: . . . .
Concentration: . . . .
Registered: . . . .
. . . .
Average # of Employees: . . . . . . 3 FT, 1 PT
Prior Industry Experience: . . . . Helpful

FINANCIAL:
Cash Investment: $25-35K
Total Investment: $75-100K
Fees: Franchise - $6.5K
Royalty: 7%, Advert: 5%
Contract Periods (Yrs.): 10/10
Area Development Agreement: Yes/10
Sub-Franchise Contract: . . . . . Yes
Expand in Territory: . . . . Yes
Passive Ownership: . . . Discouraged
Encourage Conversions: . . . . . Yes
Franchisee Purchase(s) Required: .No

FRANCHISOR TRAINING/SUPPORT:
Financial Assistance Provided: . . . Yes(I)
Site Selection Assistance: . . . . .Yes
Lease Negotiation Assistance: . . . . . .Yes
Co-operative Advertising: . . . . .Yes
Training: . . . . . . 40 Hours Headquarters
. . . .
On-Going Support: . . . . B,C,D,E,F,G,H
Full-Time Franchisor Support Staff: . . 10
EXPANSION PLANS:
US: . . . . Midwest Only
Canada - No, ...Overseas - No

HEALTHCALL

728 N. 7th St.
Milwaukee, WI 53233
TEL: (800) 558-7130 *558-7144 (WI)
FAX:
President

HEALTHCALL CORPORATION is the only national home health care company to offer franchises in both home intravenous therapy and durable medical equipment/consumable supplies. HEALTHCALL provides a complete system for survival and success to the independent dealer, including operations manuals, advertising and identification package, on-going training and consultation.

HISTORY: . . . .
Established in 1965; . . 1st Franchised in 1987
Company-Owned Units (As of 12/1/1989): . .1
Franchised Units (12/1/1989): 25
Total Units (12/1/1989): 26
Distribution: US-26;Can-0;Overseas-0
North America: . . . . 11 States
Concentration: . . . . 4 in WI, 3 in FL, 3 in PA
Registered: . . . . All States
. . . .
Average # of Employees: . . . . . . 5 FT, 1 PT
Prior Industry Experience: . . . . Helpful

FINANCIAL:
Cash Investment: . . . .$
Total Investment: $28-142K
Fees: Franchise - $3-16K
Royalty: 4-9%, Advert: 1%
Contract Periods (Yrs.): 5/5
Area Development Agreement: .No
Sub-Franchise Contract: . . . . .No
Expand in Territory: . . . . Yes
Passive Ownership: . . . Not Allowed
Encourage Conversions: . . . . . Yes
Franchisee Purchase(s) Required: .No

FRANCHISOR TRAINING/SUPPORT:
Financial Assistance Provided: . . . Yes(I)
Site Selection Assistance: . . . . .NA
Lease Negotiation Assistance: . . . .NA
Co-operative Advertising: . . . . .Yes
Training: . . . . 1 Wk. Headquarters
. . . .
On-Going Support: . . . .B,C,D,E,F,G,H,I
Full-Time Franchisor Support Staff: . . . .
EXPANSION PLANS:
US: . . . . .All US
Canada - No, ...Overseas - No

HEMORRHOID CLINIC, THE

25 Weebetook Ln.
Cincinnati, OH 45212
TEL: (800) NO-HEMIS (513) 871-7336
FAX:
Dr. Roy D. "Bob" Anning, President

Highly efficient and automated out-patient clinics for hemorrhoid and related rectal procedures. Proprietary laser techniques developed by Dr. Anning ensure painless, 20-minute procedure and minimal recuperative discomfort. Lucrative business that takes advantage of the fact that 1 in 8 adults requires rectal surgery. 12 week training at headquarters clinic. All procedures on video. Excellent opportunity to work with the best!

HISTORY: . . . . IFA
Established in 1987; . . 1st Franchised in 1988
Company-Owned Units (As of 12/1/1989): . .6
Franchised Units (12/1/1989): 8
Total Units (12/1/1989): 14
Distribution: US-12;Can-2;Overseas-0
North America: . . . . . 5 States, 2 Provinces
Concentration: . . . 3 in OH, 2 in KY, 2 in MS
Registered: . . . . CA,FL,IL,WA,AB
. . . .
Average # of Employees: . . . . . . 3 FT, 4 PT
Prior Industry Experience: . . . . . . Required

FINANCIAL:
Cash Investment: $80-125K
Total Investment: $140-225K
Fees: Franchise - $25K
Royalty: 6%, Advert: 1%
Contract Periods (Yrs.): 10/10
Area Development Agreement: Yes/10
Sub-Franchise Contract: . . . . . Yes
Expand in Territory: . . . . Yes
Passive Ownership: . . . Not Allowed
Encourage Conversions: . . . . . Yes
Franchisee Purchase(s) Required: Yes

FRANCHISOR TRAINING/SUPPORT:
Financial Assistance Provided: . . . Yes(I)
Site Selection Assistance: . . . . .Yes
Lease Negotiation Assistance: . . . . .Yes
Co-operative Advertising: . . . . .Yes
Training: . . . . . . 12 Wks. Anning Clinic,
. . . . . 3 Wks. On-site, On-going Video
On-Going Support: . . . . . .C,D,E,G,H,I
Full-Time Franchisor Support Staff: . . 12
EXPANSION PLANS:
US: . . . . .All US
Canada - Yes, ...Overseas - No

MIRACLE-EAR CENTER

600 S. County Rd. 169, # 701
St. Louis Park, MN 55426
TEL: (800) 433-6761 (612) 546-1118
FAX: (612) 542-1890
Mr. Dale R. Erickson, Dir. Fran.

Dahlberg, Inc. is a full-line retail hearing aid business. National advertising has made us the #1 name in the industry, and provides leads to franchisees. Complete training and marketing programs are offered.

HISTORY: . . . .
Established in 1948; . . 1st Franchised in 1984
Company-Owned Units (As of 12/1/1989): . 42
Franchised Units (12/1/1989): 446
Total Units (12/1/1989): 488
Distribution: US-488;Can-0;Overseas-0
North America: . . . . 50 States
Concentration: . 47 in CA, 31 in FL, 29 in NY
Registered: . . . . .All
. . . .
Average # of Employees: . . . . 40 FT
Prior Industry Experience: . . . . . . Helpful

FINANCIAL: OTC-DAHL
Cash Investment: $20-45K
Total Investment: $35-65K
Fees: Franchise - . . . . $15K+
Royalty: 10%, Advert: 0%
Contract Periods (Yrs.): . . . 10/10
Area Development Agreement: Yes/3-5
Sub-Franchise Contract: . . . . .No
Expand in Territory: . . . . . . Yes
Passive Ownership: . . . Discouraged
Encourage Conversions: . . . . .No
Franchisee Purchase(s) Required: Yes

FRANCHISOR TRAINING/SUPPORT:
Financial Assistance Provided: . . . . .Yes
Site Selection Assistance: . . . . .Yes
Lease Negotiation Assistance: . . . . . No
Co-operative Advertising: . . . . No
Training: . . . .5 Days HQ, 4 Days On Site
. . . . . (2 Sales Training, 2 Technical)
On-Going Support: . . . .A,B,C,D,E,g,H,I
Full-Time Franchisor Support Staff: . . . 8
EXPANSION PLANS:
US: . . . . .All US
Canada - No, ...Overseas - No

O2 EMERGENCY MEDICAL CARE SERVICE

5829 W. Maple Rd., # 123
W. Bloomfield, MI 48322
TEL: (800) 777-4535 (313) 737-2180 C
FAX:
Mr. Donald M. Stern, President

A sales/marketing franchise that provides an emergency medical program, including emergency oxygen equipment, first aid kits, first aid training and equipment maintenance to all businesses, organizations, facilities and government offices.

HISTORY: . . . .
Established in 1986; . . 1st Franchised in 1989
Company-Owned Units (As of 12/1/1989): . .1
Franchised Units (12/1/1989): 6
Total Units (12/1/1989): 7
Distribution: US-7;Can-0;Overseas-0
North America: . . . . 3 States
Concentration: . . . . 3 in MI, 2 in FL, 2 in PA
Registered: . . . .FL,HI,IN,MI,OR,RI,WA,WI
. . . .
Average # of Employees: . . . . .1 PT
Prior Industry Experience: . . . . . . Helpful

FINANCIAL:
Cash Investment: $27-30K
Total Investment: $33-54K
Fees: Franchise - $12.5K
Royalty: Varies, Advert: . . . 3%
Contract Periods (Yrs.): . . 12/12/12
Area Development Agreement: Yes/10
Sub-Franchise Contract: . . . . .No
Expand in Territory: . . . . . . Yes
Passive Ownership: . . . Discouraged
Encourage Conversions: . . . . . Yes
Franchisee Purchase(s) Required: Yes

FRANCHISOR TRAINING/SUPPORT:
Financial Assistance Provided: . . .Yes(D)
Site Selection Assistance: . . . . . . .NA
Lease Negotiation Assistance: . . . .NA
Co-operative Advertising: . . . . .NA
Training: . . . . . .Minimum 5 Days Head-
. . . . quarters
On-Going Support: . . . . . .B,C,D,G,H,I
Full-Time Franchisor Support Staff: . . .5
EXPANSION PLANS:
US: . . . . .All US
Canada - Yes, . . . Overseas - Yes

OPTOMETRIC EYE CARE CENTER

2325 Sunset Ave., P. O. Box 7185
Rocky Mount, NC 27804
TEL: (800) 334-3937 (919) 937-6650
FAX: (919) 937-7080
Mr. Blair Harrold, President

A leader in retail eye care, from professional exams and services to optical eyeware. OECC's achieve success through innovative marketing, experienced management and one-hour super store development.

HISTORY: . . . .
Established in 1976; . . . 1st Franchised in 19
Company-Owned Units (As of 12/1/1989): . 13
Franchised Units (12/1/1989): 27
Total Units (12/1/1989): 40
Distribution: US-40;Can-0;Overseas-0
North America: . . . . .1 State
Concentration: . . . . 40 in NC
Registered: . . . .
. . . .
Average # of Employees: . . . . . . 3 FT, 2 PT
Prior Industry Experience: . . . . . .Necessary

FINANCIAL:
Cash Investment: $10-35K
Total Investment: $100-350K
Fees: Franchise - . . . .$K
Royalty: 1-3%, Advert: 1-2%
Contract Periods (Yrs.): 5/5
Area Development Agreement: Yes/5
Sub-Franchise Contract: . . . . . Yes
Expand in Territory: . . . . Yes
Passive Ownership: . . . Discouraged
Encourage Conversions: . . . . . Yes
Franchisee Purchase(s) Required: .No

FRANCHISOR TRAINING/SUPPORT:
Financial Assistance Provided: . . . Yes(I)
Site Selection Assistance: . . . . .Yes
Lease Negotiation Assistance: . . . . .Yes
Co-operative Advertising: . . . . .Yes
Training: . . . . .1 Wk. Headquarters,
. . . . .3 Wks. On-site, On-going
On-Going Support: . . . . a,C,D,E,f,G,H,I
Full-Time Franchisor Support Staff: . . 12
EXPANSION PLANS:
US: . . . . . . N. & S. Carolina, Virginia
Canada - No, ...Overseas - No

PROCARE VISION CENTERS

926 N. 21st St.
Newark, OH 43055
TEL: (614) 366-7341
FAX: (614) 366-5453
Dr. Frank Bickle, President

PROCARE provides vision care services and products through franchises owned and operated by licensed vision care professionals.

HISTORY: . . . . IFA
Established in 1981; . . 1st Franchised in 1985
Company-Owned Units (As of 12/1/1989): . .1
Franchised Units (12/1/1989): 14
Total Units (12/1/1989): 15
Distribution: US-15;Can-0;Overseas-0
North America: . . . . .1 State
Concentration: . . . . 15 in OH
Registered: . . . .
. . . .
Average # of Employees: . . . . . . 3 FT, 2 PT
Prior Industry Experience: . . . . . .Necessary

FINANCIAL:
Cash Investment: $0-30K
Total Investment: $30-200K
Fees: Franchise - $4.5K
Royalty: 5%, Advert: 1%
Contract Periods (Yrs.): . . . 10/10
Area Development Agreement: .No
Sub-Franchise Contract: . . . . .No
Expand in Territory: . . . . Yes
Passive Ownership: . . . Not Allowed
Encourage Conversions: . . . . . Yes
Franchisee Purchase(s) Required: .No

FRANCHISOR TRAINING/SUPPORT:
Financial Assistance Provided: . . . Yes(I)
Site Selection Assistance: . . . . .Yes
Lease Negotiation Assistance: . . . . .Yes
Co-operative Advertising: . . . . .Yes
Training: . . . . .1 Wk. Headquarters,
. . . . 3 Days Franchisee Site
On-Going Support: . . . .B,C,D,E,F,G,H,i
Full-Time Franchisor Support Staff: . . .6
EXPANSION PLANS:
US: . . . . . . Ohio & Surrounding States
Canada - No, ...Overseas - No

STERLING OPTICAL

357 Crossways Park Dr.
Woodbury, NY 11797
TEL: (516) 364-2600
FAX:
Mr. Keith R. Albright, VP - Fran.

STERLING OPTICAL offers retail optical franchises to qualified optometrists, opticians and other eye care professionals. The franchise may involve the conversion of an existing company-owned store to a franchised unit, the opening of a new location as a franchised unit or the conversion of a private retail optical operation to a franchised STERLING OPTICAL CENTER.

HISTORY: . . . . IFA
Established in 1912; . . 1st Franchised in 1987
Company-Owned Units (As of 12/1/1989): 200
Franchised Units (12/1/1989): 50
Total Units (12/1/1989): 250
Distribution: US-240;Can-10;Overseas-0
North America: . . . . 21 States, 1 Province
Concentration: . .70 in NY, 16 in WI, 13 in FL
Registered: . . . . .IL,IN,MD,VA
. . . .
Average # of Employees: . . . . 2-3 FT, 1-3 PT
Prior Industry Experience: . . . . . .Necessary

FINANCIAL: NYSE-IHS
Cash Investment: $20-40K
Total Investment: $200-400K
Fees: Franchise - $15K
Royalty: 8%, Advert: 6%
Contract Periods (Yrs.): . . . 10/10
Area Development Agreement: .No
Sub-Franchise Contract: . . . . .No
Expand in Territory: . . . . . . .No
Passive Ownership: . . . Not Allowed
Encourage Conversions: . . . . . Yes
Franchisee Purchase(s) Required: .No

FRANCHISOR TRAINING/SUPPORT:
Financial Assistance Provided: . . .Yes(D)
Site Selection Assistance: . . . . .Yes
Lease Negotiation Assistance: . . . . .Yes
Co-operative Advertising: . . . . .Yes
Training: . . . . 5-10 Days On-site
. . . .
On-Going Support: . . . . .B,C,D,E,F,G,h
Full-Time Franchisor Support Staff: . . .6
EXPANSION PLANS:
US: . . . . NE, SE and Midwest
Canada - No, ... Overseas - No

SUPPLEMENTAL LISTING OF FRANCHISORS

AMERICAN PHYSICAL REHABILITATION NETWK . . . . 4050 Talmadge Rd., Toledo OH 43623
BIO PED FOOT CARE CENTERS . . . . 1170 Burnhamthorpe Rd. W, # 16, Mississauga ON L5C4E6 CAN
C.P.Q. HEALTH SERVICES . . . . 1777 S. Harrison, # 1006, Denver CO 80210
CHART REHABILITATION . . . . Two Annabel Ln., # 105, San Ramon CA 94583
CHS DENTAL LABORATORIES . . . . .955 Dairy Ashford, # 222, Houston TX 77070
DENTALWORKS . . . . 831 - 845 Hamilton Mall, Allentown PA 18101
DOCTORS TO YOUR DOOR . . . . P. O. Box 23354, Lexington KY 40523
DR. SCOTT'S OPTICAL OUTLET . . . . 1323 Jackson St., Omaha NE 68102
EAR LABS . . . . 18662 MacArthur Blvd., # 103, Irvine CA 92715
EATON MEDICAL SYSTEMS . . . . .3116 E. Shea Blvd., # 219, Phoenix AZ 85028
JONATHON DENTAL . . . . 5909 Baker Rd., # 575, Minnetonka MN 55345
MEDIPOWER . . . . .P.O. Box 310310, New Braunfels TX 78130
NORTH AMERICAN MEDICAL . . . . .3116 E. Shea Blvd., # 219, Phoenix AZ 85028
NUVISION OPTICAL . . . . 2284 S. Ballenger Hwy.,P.O. Box 2, Flint MI 48501
OPTICAL FACTORY .1120 Caledonia Rd., Toronto ON M6A2W5 CAN
OXYGEN THERAPY INSTITUTE . . . . 1835 Moriah Woods Blvd., # 1, Memphis TN 38117
PEARLE VISION CENTERS . . . . 2534 Royal Ln., Dallas TX 75229
REFLECTIONS BREAST HEALTH CENTER . . . . .9735 Valley View Rd., Macedonia OH 44056
SINGER DISCOUNT VISION CENTER . . . . .1909 Chestnut St., Philadelphia PA 19103
SITE FOR SORE EYES . . . . 100 Hegenberger Rd., # 110, Oakland CA 94621
SPECS DISCOUNT VISION CENTER . . . . .1909 Chestnut St., Philadelphia PA 19103
TEXAS STATE OPTICAL . . . . 2534 Royal Ln., Dallas TX 75229
UNITED CHIROPRACTIC . . . . .3900 N. Causeway Blvd., # 1295, Metairie LA 70002
WESTERN MEDICAL SERVICES . . . . .301 Lennon Ln., Walnut Creek CA 94598

CHAPTER 31

PET PRODUCTS AND SERVICES

CRITTER CARE

1825 Darren Dr.
Baton Rouge, LA 70816
TEL: (800) 443-4808 (504) 273-3356
FAX: (504) 293-2901
Ms. Pamela Runnels, President

CRITTER CARE is a new concept in the care of pets, home and plants. We make calls to your home to meet your individual needs while you are away. We have developed a profitable and professional, personalized pet and home care service. We have the best logo and performance standard in this evolving industry. Entrepreneur recognized us as one of the top 25 low-investment franchises in the US.

HISTORY: . . . .
Established in 1980; . . 1st Franchised in 1984
Company-Owned Units (As of 12/1/1989): . .1
Franchised Units (12/1/1989): 12
Total Units (12/1/1989): 13
Distribution: US-13;Can-0;Overseas-0
North America: . . . . 7 States
Concentration: . . . 3 in LA, 3 in TX, 3 in PA
Registered: . . . . .CA,FL,IL,NY

. . . .
Average # of Employees: . . . . . . 2 FT, 2 PT
Prior Industry Experience: . . . . Helpful

FINANCIAL:
Cash Investment: $2.5-5K
Total Investment: $4-9K
Fees: Franchise - $2.5-9K
 Royalty: 5%, Advert: 2%
Contract Periods (Yrs.): 10/5
Area Development Agreement: Yes/Var
Sub-Franchise Contract: . . . . . .No
Expand in Territory: . . . . Yes
Passive Ownership: . . . Discouraged
Encourage Conversions: . . . . . Yes
Franchisee Purchase(s) Required: Yes

FRANCHISOR TRAINING/SUPPORT:
Financial Assistance Provided: . . .Yes(D)
Site Selection Assistance: . . . . . . .Yes
Lease Negotiation Assistance: . . . . .No
Co-operative Advertising: . . . . . . .Yes
Training: . . . . . . 4 15-Hour Days at HQ,
 . . . . .2 Days On-site
On-Going Support: . . . . . .a,b,C,D,E,h,I
Full-Time Franchisor Support Staff: . . . 3
EXPANSION PLANS:
US: . . . . .All US
Canada - Yes, ...Overseas - Yes

DOCKTOR PET CENTER

355 Middlesex Ave.
Wilmington, MA 01887
TEL: (800) 325-6011
FAX:
Mr. Tim Hochuli, Dir. Fran. Sales

The largest chain of franchised department stores for pets. Located in major regional shopping centers throughout the US. We are growing at a rate of about 25-30 new stores per year. Over 60% of our franchisees are multiple store owners.

HISTORY: . . . . IFA	FINANCIAL:	FRANCHISOR TRAINING/SUPPORT:
Established in 1927; . . 1st Franchised in 1967	Cash Investment: $50-60K	Financial Assistance Provided: . . . . . No
Company-Owned Units (As of 12/1/1989): . .0	Total Investment: $149-199K	Site Selection Assistance: . . . . .Yes
Franchised Units (12/1/1989): 270	Fees: Franchise - $15K	Lease Negotiation Assistance: . . . . .Yes
Total Units (12/1/1989): 270	Royalty: 4.5%, Advert: 1%	Co-operative Advertising: . . . .
Distribution: US-270;Can-0;Overseas-0	Contract Periods (Yrs.): 20/10	Training: . . . . 3 Wks. Headquarters,
North America: . . . . 37 States	Area Development Agreement: . .No	. . . . .2 Wks. Site, On-going
Concentration: . 26 in CA, 23 in TX, 21 in OH	Sub-Franchise Contract: . . . . .No	On-Going Support: . . . . . . B,C,D,E,H,I
Registered: . . . . All States	Expand in Territory: . . . . Yes	Full-Time Franchisor Support Staff: . . 85
. . . .	Passive Ownership: . . . Not Allowed	EXPANSION PLANS:
Average # of Employees: . . . . . . 6 FT, 6 PT	Encourage Conversions: . . . . . Yes	US: . . . . .All US
Prior Industry Experience: . . . . Helpful	Franchisee Purchase(s) Required: .No	Canada - No, ... Overseas - Yes

DOG WASH

5724 SW Green Oaks Blvd.
Arlington, TX 76017
TEL: (817) 572-5106 C
FAX:
Ms. Jeannie Powell, VP Fran. Dev.

Do-it-yourself pet bathing, dipping, grooming and veterinary care. The DOG WASH and DOGGIE DRUGSTORE promote "responsible pet ownership and humane treatment for pets at an affordable cost to pet owners." Low overhead, non-labor intensive - highly profitable.

HISTORY:	FINANCIAL:	FRANCHISOR TRAINING/SUPPORT:
Established in 1972; . . 1st Franchised in 1988	Cash Investment: $10-20K	Financial Assistance Provided: . . . . . No
Company-Owned Units (As of 12/1/1989): . .3	Total Investment: $30-50K	Site Selection Assistance: . . . . .Yes
Franchised Units (12/1/1989): 0	Fees: Franchise - $7.5K	Lease Negotiation Assistance: . . . . .Yes
Total Units (12/1/1989): 3	Royalty: 5.5%, Advert: 2%	Co-operative Advertising: . . . . . .Yes
Distribution: US-3;Can-0;Overseas-0	Contract Periods (Yrs.): 10/10	Training: . . . . .1 Wk. Headquarters,
North America: . . . . .1 State	Area Development Agreement: . .No	. . . . 1 Wk. On-site
Concentration: . . . . 3 in TX	Sub-Franchise Contract: . . . . . Yes	On-Going Support: . . A,B,C,D,E,F,G,H,I
Registered: . . . . .FL	Expand in Territory: . . . . Yes	Full-Time Franchisor Support Staff: . . 15
. . . .	Passive Ownership: . . . Discouraged	EXPANSION PLANS:
Average # of Employees: . . . . . . 1 FT, 1 PT	Encourage Conversions: . . . . . .No	US: . . . . .All US
Prior Industry Experience: . . . . Helpful	Franchisee Purchase(s) Required: Yes	Canada - Yes, . . . Overseas - Yes

HOUSESITTERS, THE

530 Queen St. E.
Toronto, ON M5A1V2 CAN
TEL: (800) 387-1377 (416) 947-1295
FAX: (416) 947-0075
Mr. Cameron Dalsto, VP

Home security and child/senior care for travellers provided by bonded and insured sitters on a live-in basis. Also, hourly babysitting, weekday dog walking and residential cleaning (maid service). Minimum population base of 100,000.

HISTORY:	FINANCIAL:	FRANCHISOR TRAINING/SUPPORT:
Established in 1981; . . 1st Franchised in 1987	Cash Investment: $10-150K	Financial Assistance Provided: . . . . . No
Company-Owned Units (As of 12/1/1989): . .2	Total Investment: $15-200K	Site Selection Assistance: . . . . .NA
Franchised Units (12/1/1989): 16	Fees: Franchise - $10-150K	Lease Negotiation Assistance: . . . . .NA
Total Units (12/1/1989): 18	Royalty: 8%, Advert: 0%	Co-operative Advertising: . . . . .NA
Distribution: US-0;Can-18;Overseas-0	Contract Periods (Yrs.): 3/5	Training: . . . . . . 1-2 Wks. Headquarters
North America: . . . . 5 Provinces	Area Development Agreement: Yes/Var	. . . .
Concentration: . . . . ON, NS	Sub-Franchise Contract: . . . . . Yes	On-Going Support: . . . . B,G
Registered:	Expand in Territory: . . . . .No	Full-Time Franchisor Support Staff: . . . 8
. . . .	Passive Ownership: . . . Not Allowed	EXPANSION PLANS:
Average # of Employees: . . . . . . 1 FT, 30 PT	Encourage Conversions: . . . . . NA	US: . . . . .All US
Prior Industry Experience: . . . . Helpful	Franchisee Purchase(s) Required: .No	Canada - Yes, . . . Overseas - Yes

PET NANNY

1000 Long Blvd., # 9
Lansing, MI 48911
TEL: (517) 694-4400
FAX:
Ms. Rebecca Brevitz, President

The PET NANNY franchised business provides professional pet care at the pet's home while the owners are away. The business can be operated from franchisee's own home. Franchisee is provided with a complete system of forms and operational aids, together with an extensive video-taped training program for its representatives.

HISTORY: . . . .
Established in 1983; . . 1st Franchised in 1986
Company-Owned Units (As of 12/1/1989): . . 1
Franchised Units (12/1/1989): 16
Total Units (12/1/1989): 17
Distribution: US-17;Can-0;Overseas-0
North America: . . . . 7 States
Concentration: . . . 8 in MI, 3 in OH, 2 in NM
Registered: . . . . IL,MI
. . . .
Average # of Employees: . . . . 2 FT
Prior Industry Experience: . . . . Helpful

FINANCIAL:
Cash Investment: $7.1-11.4K
Total Investment: $7.1-11.4K
Fees: Franchise - $7.1K
  Royalty: 5%, Advert: 2%
Contract Periods (Yrs.): 5/5
Area Development Agreement: Yes/10
Sub-Franchise Contract: . . . . . Yes
Expand in Territory: . . . . . . .No
Passive Ownership: . . . . . .Allowed
Encourage Conversions: . . . . .No
Franchisee Purchase(s) Required: .No

FRANCHISOR TRAINING/SUPPORT:
Financial Assistance Provided: . . .Yes(D)
Site Selection Assistance: . . . . .NA
Lease Negotiation Assistance: . . . . .NA
Co-operative Advertising: . . . . .Yes
Training: . . . . 5 Days Headquarters
. . . .
On-Going Support: . . . . D,E,G,H,I
Full-Time Franchisor Support Staff: . . . 6
EXPANSION PLANS:
  US: . . . . All US
  Canada - Yes, ...Overseas - No

PET VALU

720 Tapscott Rd.
Scarborough, ON M1X1C6 CAN
TEL: (416) 291-9157
FAX: (416) 291-1729
Mr. Colin R. Freel, VP Fran. Devel.

PET VALU is a chain of specialty stores that feature exclusively pet foods, supplies and accessories. We concentrate on customer service, provide a wide selection of brands and product sizes, and offer everyday low, low pricing on all products.

HISTORY: . . . .
Established in 1976; . . 1st Franchised in 1987
Company-Owned Units (As of 12/1/1989): . 54
Franchised Units (12/1/1989): 47
Total Units (12/1/1989): 101
Distribution: US-0;Can-101;Overseas-0
North America: . . . . .1 Province
Concentration: . . . . .101 in ON
Registered: . . . .
. . . .
Average # of Employees: . . . . . . 2 FT, 3 PT
Prior Industry Experience: . . . . Helpful

FINANCIAL:
Cash Investment: $60K
Total Investment: $135K
Fees: Franchise - $20K
  Royalty: 6%, Advert: 0%
Contract Periods (Yrs.): 10/5
Area Development Agreement: . .No
Sub-Franchise Contract: . . . . .No
Expand in Territory: . . . . . . .No
Passive Ownership: . . . Not Allowed
Encourage Conversions: . . . . Yes
Franchisee Purchase(s) Required: Yes

FRANCHISOR TRAINING/SUPPORT:
Financial Assistance Provided: . . . . . No
Site Selection Assistance: . . . . .Yes
Lease Negotiation Assistance: . . . . .Yes
Co-operative Advertising: . . . . .Yes
Training: . . . . 3 Wks. Headquarters
. . . .
On-Going Support: . . . . B,C,E,F,H
Full-Time Franchisor Support Staff: . .175
EXPANSION PLANS:
  US: . . . . .No
  Canada - Yes, ...Overseas - No

PETLAND

195 N. Hickory St., P.O. Box 1606
Chillicothe, OH 45601
TEL: (800) 221-5935 *221-3479 (OH)
FAX:
Mr. L.H. Heuring, VP Mktg.

PETLAND is a franchisor of full-service, family pet centers across the US and Canada. With over 20 years' experience, PETLAND provides you with the systems and on-going support to operate your own independent business.

HISTORY: . . . . IFA
Established in 1967; . . 1st Franchised in 1972
Company-Owned Units (As of 12/1/1989): . .5
Franchised Units (12/1/1989): 170
Total Units (12/1/1989): 175
Distribution: US-166;Can-8;Overseas-1
North America: . . . . 32 States, 2 Provinces
Concentration: . . 30 in OH,22 in FL,16 in TX
Registered: . . . . All States
. . . .
Average # of Employees: . . . .
Prior Industry Experience: . . . . Helpful

FINANCIAL:
Cash Investment: $40-100K
Total Investment: $165-350K
Fees: Franchise - $0
  Royalty: 4%, Advert: 5%
Contract Periods (Yrs.): 20/10
Area Development Agreement: . .No
Sub-Franchise Contract: . . . . .No
Expand in Territory: . . . . . . Yes
Passive Ownership: . . . Discouraged
Encourage Conversions: . . . . Yes
Franchisee Purchase(s) Required: .No

FRANCHISOR TRAINING/SUPPORT:
Financial Assistance Provided: . . . Yes(I)
Site Selection Assistance: . . . . .Yes
Lease Negotiation Assistance: . . . . .Yes
Co-operative Advertising: . . . . .No
Training: . . . . . . 6 Days Headquarters, 6
. . . . . . Days Classroom, 10 Days Site
On-Going Support: . . . . .C,D,E,F,G,H,I
Full-Time Franchisor Support Staff: . .100
EXPANSION PLANS:
  US: . . . . All US
  Canada - Yes, . . . Overseas - Yes

PETMART

7390 Trade St.
San Diego, CA 92121
TEL: (800)621-0852(CA) (619)693-3639
FAX:
Ms. Julie Miller, Asst. to Pres.

PETMART retail stores offer the customer a vast selection of high-quality pet food and accessories at reasonable prices. The franchisee receives a turn-key, modern, efficient, professionally-merchandised retail store. PETMART carries pet supplies only - no livestock.

HISTORY: . . . . IFA	FINANCIAL:	FRANCHISOR TRAINING/SUPPORT:
Established in 1973; . . 1st Franchised in 1984	Cash Investment: . . . .$	Financial Assistance Provided: . . . . . No
Company-Owned Units (As of 12/1/1989): . 12	Total Investment: $62-79K	Site Selection Assistance: . . . . .Yes
Franchised Units (12/1/1989): 13	Fees: Franchise - $15K	Lease Negotiation Assistance: . . . . .Yes
Total Units (12/1/1989): 25	Royalty: 6%, Advert: 2%	Co-operative Advertising: . . . . . . .Yes
Distribution: US-25;Can-0;Overseas-0	Contract Periods (Yrs.): 10/5	Training: . . . . 2 Wks. Headquarters
North America: . . . . .1 State	Area Development Agreement: . Yes	. . . .
Concentration: . . . . 24 in CA	Sub-Franchise Contract: . . . . .No	On-Going Support: . . A,B,C,D,E,F,G,H,I
Registered:	Expand in Territory: . . . . Yes	Full-Time Franchisor Support Staff: . . 12
. . . .	Passive Ownership: . . . Discouraged	EXPANSION PLANS:
Average # of Employees: . . . . . . 2 FT, 2 PT	Encourage Conversions: . . . . .No	US: . . . . . . All US Beginning Early 90
Prior Industry Experience: . . . . Helpful	Franchisee Purchase(s) Required: Yes	Canada - No, ...Overseas - No

PETS ARE INN

27 N. Fourth St., # 500
Minneapolis, MN 55401
TEL: (800) 248-PETS (612) 339-6255
FAX:
Mr. Harry Sanders-Greenberg, Pres.

PETS ARE INN has turned the kennel industry into a cottage industry. We board companion animals and household pets in private homes, eradicating disease, stress and isolation that often occur with kennel boarding. Our computer program analyzes pet characteristics to find the most compatible home. A thorough knowledge of demographic variables enables us to carefully target our markets to 25 million pet owners throughout the US.

HISTORY: . . . . .WIF	FINANCIAL:	FRANCHISOR TRAINING/SUPPORT:
Established in 1982; . . 1st Franchised in 1986	Cash Investment: $2.1-8.5K	Financial Assistance Provided: . . . . .No
Company-Owned Units (As of 12/1/1989): . .0	Total Investment: $5-20K	Site Selection Assistance: . . . . .NA
Franchised Units (12/1/1989): 22	Fees: Franchise - $2.1-8.5K	Lease Negotiation Assistance: . . . . .NA
Total Units (12/1/1989): 22	Royalty: 4.5%, Advert: 1%	Co-operative Advertising: . . . . . . .Yes
Distribution: US-22;Can-0;Overseas-0	Contract Periods (Yrs.): 5/5	Training: . . . . 4 Days Headquarters
North America: . . . . 12 States	Area Development Agreement: . .No	. . . .
Concentration: . . . 3 in MN, 3 in CA, 2 in TX	Sub-Franchise Contract: . . . . .No	On-Going Support: . . . . . . B,C,d,G,H,I
Registered: . . . . CA,FL.IL,IN	Expand in Territory: . . . . Yes	Full-Time Franchisor Support Staff: . . . 3
. . . .	Passive Ownership: . . . Not Allowed	EXPANSION PLANS:
Average # of Employees: . . . . . . 1 FT, 2 PT	Encourage Conversions: . . . . . Yes	US: . . . . .All US
Prior Industry Experience: . . . . Helpful	Franchisee Purchase(s) Required: .No	Canada - No, ... Overseas - No

SUPPLEMENTAL LISTING OF FRANCHISORS

CHAPTER 32

PUBLICATIONS

BINGO SCENE MAGAZINE

9330 Johnnycake Ridge
Mentor, OH 44060
TEL: (216) 639-0057
FAX:
Mr. P. J. Janes, President

"Hit the Jackpot," become independent and financially secure. Own your own Bingo publication - a FREE, local Bingo player's guide. Low investment, training, on-going assistance, exclusive territory - a proven success, coast-to-coast.

HISTORY: . . . .
Established in 1982; . . 1st Franchised in 1983
Company-Owned Units (As of 12/1/1989): . .1
Franchised Units (12/1/1989): 9
Total Units (12/1/1989): 10
Distribution: US-10;Can-0;Overseas-0
 North America: . . . . 4 States
 Concentration: . . . 5 in OH, 2 in CA, 2 in FL
Registered: . . . . CA,FL,IL

. . . .
Average # of Employees: . . . . .1 FT
Prior Industry Experience: . . . . Helpful

FINANCIAL:
Cash Investment: $9.5-18K
Total Investment: $9.5-18K
Fees: Franchise - . . . .$
 Royalty: 5%, Advert: 0%
Contract Periods (Yrs.): 10
Area Development Agreement: . .No
Sub-Franchise Contract: . . . . . Yes
Expand in Territory: . . . . . . .No
Passive Ownership: . . . Discouraged
Encourage Conversions: . . . . .No
Franchisee Purchase(s) Required: .No

FRANCHISOR TRAINING/SUPPORT:
Financial Assistance Provided: . . . . .No
Site Selection Assistance: . . . . . . .Yes
Lease Negotiation Assistance: . . . . .NA
Co-operative Advertising: . . . . .NA
Training: . . . . 7 Days Site
. . . .
On-Going Support: . . . . .b,D,I
Full-Time Franchisor Support Staff: . . . 6
EXPANSION PLANS:
 US: . . . . .All US
 Canada - No, ... Overseas - No

BUSINESS DIGEST MAGAZINE

650 Main St.
South Portland, ME 04106
TEL: (207) 772-1971 C
FAX:
Mr. Mark Girr, Fran. Dir.

A BUSINESS DIGEST MAGAZINE offers its owner incredible prestige in the business community it serves, the benefit of a high income potential and a significant number of perks. With your high visibility and release of your first issue, you become recognized as a local business leader, someone to know.

HISTORY: . . . . IFA
Established in 1978; . . 1st Franchised in 1981
Company-Owned Units (As of 12/1/1989): . . 1
Franchised Units (12/1/1989): 17
Total Units (12/1/1989): 18
Distribution: US-18;Can-0;Overseas-0
  North America: . . . . 9 States
  Concentration: . . . 4 in MA, 4 in CT, 2 in NC
Registered: . . . . FL,IN,MI,RI,WI
. . . .
Average # of Employees: . . . . . . 8 FT, 1 PT
Prior Industry Experience: . . . . Helpful

FINANCIAL:
Cash Investment: $100-125K
Total Investment: . . . .$
Fees: Franchise - $20K
  Royalty: 4%, Advert: 0%
Contract Periods (Yrs.): 10/10
Area Development Agreement: . Yes
Sub-Franchise Contract: . . . . . Yes
Expand in Territory: . . . . . . .No
Passive Ownership: . . . Discouraged
Encourage Conversions: . . . . Yes
Franchisee Purchase(s) Required: .No

FRANCHISOR TRAINING/SUPPORT:
Financial Assistance Provided: . . . . . No
Site Selection Assistance: . . . . . . .Yes
Lease Negotiation Assistance: . . . . .Yes
Co-operative Advertising: . . . . . . .NA
Training: . . . . 3 Days Headquarters
. . . .
On-Going Support: . . . . .c,d,G,h,I
Full-Time Franchisor Support Staff: . . 15
EXPANSION PLANS:
US: . . . . .All US
Canada - Yes, ...Overseas - No

BUSINESS PEOPLE MAGAZINE

18818 Teller Ave., # 130
Irvine, CA 92715
TEL: (714) 250-4101
FAX: (714) 756-0475
Ms. Victoria I. Conte, EVP

BUSINESS PEOPLE MAGAZINE is a national network of local magazines. Each issue focuses on local business personalities and their successes in the business community for which the magazine is published. And, . . . it's a franchise operation.

HISTORY: . . . . IFA
Established in 1978; . . 1st Franchised in 1981
Company-Owned Units (As of 12/1/1989): . . 1
Franchised Units (12/1/1989): 20
Total Units (12/1/1989): 21
Distribution: US-21;Can-0;Overseas-0
  North America: . . . . 9 States
  Concentration: . . . .4 in MA, 3 in CT, 2 in IN
Registered: . . . . .All
. . . .
Average # of Employees: . . . . .8 FT
Prior Industry Experience: . . . . Helpful

FINANCIAL:
Cash Investment: $115-165K
Total Investment: $115-165K
Fees: Franchise - $40K
  Royalty: 5%, Advert: 0%
Contract Periods (Yrs.): 10/10
Area Development Agreement: . .No
Sub-Franchise Contract: . . . . . .No
Expand in Territory: . . . . . . .No
Passive Ownership: . . . Discouraged
Encourage Conversions: . . . . Yes
Franchisee Purchase(s) Required: .No

FRANCHISOR TRAINING/SUPPORT:
Financial Assistance Provided: . . . . . No
Site Selection Assistance: . . . . No
Lease Negotiation Assistance: . . . . . No
Co-operative Advertising: . . . . No
Training: . . . . 2 Wks. Headquarters
On-Going Support: . . . . . . C,D,E,G,H,I
Full-Time Franchisor Support Staff: . . 15
EXPANSION PLANS:
US: . . . . .All US
Canada - Yes, . . . Overseas - Yes

BUYING & DINING GUIDE

80 Eighth Ave.
New York, NY 10011
TEL: (212) 243-6800
FAX:
Mr. Allan Horwitz, President

A unique money-maker for both the local advertiser and the franchisee/publisher. BUYING & DINING GUIDE is a free publication offering total market coverage of the active "buyers" and "diners" throughout the area. Publishing and distribution costs are minimal, and the advertiser receives 14 days of effective advertising - and for the price of just a single ad!

HISTORY: . . . .
Established in 1973; . . 1st Franchised in 1987
Company-Owned Units (As of 12/1/1989): . .0
Franchised Units (12/1/1989): 5
Total Units (12/1/1989): 5
Distribution: US-5;Can-0;Overseas-0
  North America: . . . . 2 States
  Concentration: . . . . 3 in NY
Registered: . . . CA,FL,IL,IN,MD,MI,MN,NY
. . . . OR,RI,VA,WA,WI
Average # of Employees: . . . . . .2-4 FT,2 PT
Prior Industry Experience: . . . . Helpful

FINANCIAL:
Cash Investment: $5K
Total Investment: $25K
Fees: Franchise - $25K
  Royalty: 4%, Advert: 0%
Contract Periods (Yrs.): 20/20
Area Development Agreement: . .No
Sub-Franchise Contract: . . . . . .No
Expand in Territory: . . . . . . Yes
Passive Ownership: . . . Discouraged
Encourage Conversions: . . . . Yes
Franchisee Purchase(s) Required: .No

FRANCHISOR TRAINING/SUPPORT:
Financial Assistance Provided: . . .Yes(D)
Site Selection Assistance: . . . . . . .Yes
Lease Negotiation Assistance: . . . . .NA
Co-operative Advertising: . . . . . . .Yes
Training: . . . . .1 Wk. HQ,
. . . . 3 Days Site
On-Going Support: . . . . . . B,C,D,E,H,I
Full-Time Franchisor Support Staff: . . .8
EXPANSION PLANS:
US: . . . . .All US
Canada - No, ...Overseas - No

CHANNEL CHOICES WEEKLY
T.V. NEWSMAGAZINE
36 C Stoffel Dr.
Rexdale, ON M9W1A8 CAN
TEL: (800) 284-2987 (416) 248-5556
FAX: (416) 248-5558
Mr. Thom Tyson, Publisher

CHANNEL CHOICES is a locally-owned shopper's guide and TV magazine. Ads are sold to small (and large) businesses for prices ranging from $10/week to $375/week. Local involvement is stressed and community affairs are featured. Distribution is free. The training and management programs make success attainable by people without prior experience.

HISTORY: . . . . IFA
Established in 1982; . . 1st Franchised in 1983
Company-Owned Units (As of 12/1/1989): . .3
Franchised Units (12/1/1989): 24
Total Units (12/1/1989): 27
Distribution: US-1;Can-26;Overseas-0
North America: . . . . . .1 State, 2 Provinces
Concentration: . . . 25 in ON, 1 in NB, 1 in FL
Registered: . . . .
. . . .
Average # of Employees: . . . . .2 FT
Prior Industry Experience: . . . . Helpful

FINANCIAL:
Cash Investment: $7.5-19.5K
Total Investment: $7.5-19.5K
Fees: Franchise - $7.5-19.5K
  Royalty: $50/Wk., Advert: . . . 0%
Contract Periods (Yrs.): 10/10
Area Development Agreement: Yes/10
Sub-Franchise Contract: . . . . . Yes
Expand in Territory: . . . . Yes
Passive Ownership: . . . Discouraged
Encourage Conversions: . . . . . Yes
Franchisee Purchase(s) Required: Yes

FRANCHISOR TRAINING/SUPPORT:
Financial Assistance Provided: . . .Yes(D)
Site Selection Assistance: . . . . .NA
Lease Negotiation Assistance: . . . . .NA
Co-operative Advertising: . . . . .Yes
Training: . . . . 4 Days Headquarters,
  . . . 2 Days or More On-site As Required
On-Going Support: . . . . . b,C,D,E,G,H,I
Full-Time Franchisor Support Staff: . . 12
EXPANSION PLANS:
  US: . . . . .All US
Canada - Yes, ...Overseas - No

CREATE-A-BOOK

6380 Euclid Rd.
Cincinnati, OH 45236
TEL: (513) 793-5151 C
FAX:
Mr. Robert Young, Director

CREATE-A-BOOK is a company that prints and sells personalized childrens' books. Any child can have his/her name printed throughout colorful storybooks along with friends, relatives, pets, age, hometown, etc. It takes just 4 minutes from start to finish to print, bind and place a book in a hard cover. Excellent home business - either part or full time.

HISTORY: . . . .
Established in 1980; . . 1st Franchised in 1982
Company-Owned Units (As of 12/1/1989): . .2
Franchised Units (12/1/1989): 350
Total Units (12/1/1989): 352
Distribution: US-346;Can-6;Overseas-0
North America: . . . .
Concentration: . . . .
Registered: . . . . .All
. . . .
Average # of Employees: . . . . .1 PT
Prior Industry Experience: . . . . . . Helpful

FINANCIAL:
Cash Investment: $3K
Total Investment: $4K
Fees: Franchise - $3K
  Royalty: 0%, Advert: 0%
Contract Periods (Yrs.): . . . .
Area Development Agreement: . .No
Sub-Franchise Contract: . . . . .No
Expand in Territory: . . . . Yes
Passive Ownership: . . . . . .Allowed
Encourage Conversions: . . . . .No
Franchisee Purchase(s) Required: .No

FRANCHISOR TRAINING/SUPPORT:
Financial Assistance Provided: . . . . .No
Site Selection Assistance: . . . . . . .Yes
Lease Negotiation Assistance: . . . . .Yes
Co-operative Advertising: . . . . .No
Training: . . . . .1 Day Headquarters,
  . . . . .Also Video Training
On-Going Support: . . . . .b,G,H,I
Full-Time Franchisor Support Staff: . . . 8
EXPANSION PLANS:
  US: . . . . .All US
Canada - Yes, ...Overseas - No

EXECUTIVE, THE

10 Inverness Ctr., # 350
Birmingham, AL 35242
TEL: (205) 991-2970
FAX:
Mr. Kevin A. Foote

THE EXECUTIVE is a coupon-oriented business magazine that is distributed to employees of companies, businesses and residences. The business sells advertising to merchants and professionals wanting to reach an exclusive market of managers, secretaries, workers and others.

HISTORY: . . . .
Established in 1987; . . 1st Franchised in 1989
Company-Owned Units (As of 12/1/1989): . .1
Franchised Units (12/1/1989): 2
Total Units (12/1/1989): 3
Distribution: US-3;Can-0;Overseas-0
North America: . . . . .1 State
Concentration: . . . . 3 in AL
Registered: . . . .
. . . .
Average # of Employees: . . . . . . 1 FT, 1 PT
Prior Industry Experience: . . . . Helpful

FINANCIAL:
Cash Investment: $15K
Total Investment: $15K
Fees: Franchise - $10-15K
  Royalty: 5%, Advert: 0%
Contract Periods (Yrs.): 5/5
Area Development Agreement: . Yes
Sub-Franchise Contract: . . . . . Yes
Expand in Territory: . . . . Yes
Passive Ownership: . . . Discouraged
Encourage Conversions: . . . . . Yes
Franchisee Purchase(s) Required: .No

FRANCHISOR TRAINING/SUPPORT:
Financial Assistance Provided: . . . . .NA
Site Selection Assistance: . . . . . . .NA
Lease Negotiation Assistance: . . . . .NA
Co-operative Advertising: . . . . .No
Training: . . . . 3 Days Headquarters
. . . .
On-Going Support: . . . . D,E,H
Full-Time Franchisor Support Staff: . . . 1
EXPANSION PLANS:
  US: . . . . South
Canada - No, ...Overseas - No

FINDERBINDER/SOURCE BOOK DIRECTORIES
4679 Vista St.
San Diego, CA 92116
TEL: (619) 284-1145
FAX:
Mr. Gary Beals, President

The FINDERBINDER News Media Directory and the SOURCE BOOK Directory of Clubs and Associations are locally-produced reference books created by existing communications firms, such as an advertising agency or public relations consultant. It is an added profit center that builds public awareness for the local company.

HISTORY: . . . .
Established in 1973; . . 1st Franchised in 1978
Company-Owned Units (As of 12/1/1989): . .2
Franchised Units (12/1/1989): 18
Total Units (12/1/1989): 20
Distribution: US-20;Can-0;Overseas-0
North America: . . . . 13 States
Concentration: . . . .4 in CA,2 in MO,2 in TX
Registered: . . . . CA
. . . .
Average # of Employees: . . . . . . 2 FT, 2 PT
Prior Industry Experience: . . . . Helpful

FINANCIAL:
Cash Investment: $6-12K
Total Investment: $10-15K
Fees: Franchise - . . . .$
Royalty: 5+%, Advert: 0%
Contract Periods (Yrs.): . . . . Inf.
Area Development Agreement: . .No
Sub-Franchise Contract: . . . . .No
Expand in Territory: . . . . . . Yes
Passive Ownership: . . . . Discouraged
Encourage Conversions: . . . . .No
Franchisee Purchase(s) Required: .No

FRANCHISOR TRAINING/SUPPORT:
Financial Assistance Provided: . . . . .No
Site Selection Assistance: . . . . .NA
Lease Negotiation Assistance: . . . . .NA
Co-operative Advertising: . . . . .Yes
Training: . . . . 1 Day Site
. . . .
On-Going Support: . . . . . . b,C,D,G,H,I
Full-Time Franchisor Support Staff: . . . 4
EXPANSION PLANS:
US: . . . . All US
Canada - Yes, . . . Overseas - Yes

NATIONAL BRIDAL PUBLICATIONS

303 E. Livingston Ave.
Columbus, OH 43215
TEL: (614) 224-1992
FAX:
Mr. Marvin Brown, President

NATIONAL BRIDAL magazines are highly-localized versions of immensely successful national magazines. Contents include articles, photographs, information of import and interest to engaged couples and self-contained wedding planning guide. Franchisor furnishes major portion of basic articles, photographs. Semi-annual publishing schedule permits part-time operation of franchise.

HISTORY: . . . .
Established in 1984; . . 1st Franchised in 1986
Company-Owned Units (As of 12/1/1989): . .1
Franchised Units (12/1/1989): 4
Total Units (12/1/1989): 5
Distribution: US-5;Can-0;Overseas-0
North America: . . . . 3 States
Concentration: . . . .3 in OH, 1 in MI, 1 in PA
Registered: . . . .
. . . .
Average # of Employees: . . . . .2 PT
Prior Industry Experience: . . . . Helpful

FINANCIAL:
Cash Investment: $5-25K
Total Investment: $25-90K
Fees: Franchise - $15-70K
Royalty: 3%, Advert: 0%
Contract Periods (Yrs.): 1/1
Area Development Agreement: . .No
Sub-Franchise Contract: . . . . .No
Expand in Territory: . . . . . . Yes
Passive Ownership: . . . Discouraged
Encourage Conversions: . . . . NA
Franchisee Purchase(s) Required: .No

FRANCHISOR TRAINING/SUPPORT:
Financial Assistance Provided: . . .Yes(D)
Site Selection Assistance: . . . . . . .NA
Lease Negotiation Assistance: . . . .NA
Co-operative Advertising: . . . . .NA
Training: . . . . Unlimited at Headquarters
. . . .
On-Going Support: . . . . b,c,d,G,H
Full-Time Franchisor Support Staff: . . . 5
EXPANSION PLANS:
US: . . . . All US
Canada - No, ...Overseas - No

PENNYSAVER

80 Eighth Ave.
New York, NY 10011
TEL: (212) 243-6800
FAX:
Mr. Allan Horwitz, President

Recognized as the #1 local shopping guide throughout the US, PENNYSAVER is a free publication offering advertisers total market coverage of all the households and businesses throughout the community. Many PENNYSAVERS started out in basements and garages, and have grown into multi-million dollar publishing empires.

HISTORY: . . . .
Established in 1973; . . 1st Franchised in 1976
Company-Owned Units (As of 12/1/1989): . .0
Franchised Units (12/1/1989): 240
Total Units (12/1/1989): 240
Distribution: US-240;Can-0;Overseas-0
North America: . . . . 40 States
Concentration: . . . .
Registered: . . . CA,FL,IL,IN,MD,MI,MN,NY
. . . . OR,RI,VA,WA,WI
Average # of Employees: . . . . . 4 FT, 2 PT
Prior Industry Experience: . . . . Helpful

FINANCIAL:
Cash Investment: $5k
Total Investment: $24.9k
Fees: Franchise - $24.9k
Royalty: 4%, Advert: 0%
Contract Periods (Yrs.): 20/20
Area Development Agreement: . .No
Sub-Franchise Contract: . . . . .No
Expand in Territory: . . . . . . Yes
Passive Ownership: . . . Discouraged
Encourage Conversions: . . . . . Yes
Franchisee Purchase(s) Required: .No

FRANCHISOR TRAINING/SUPPORT:
Financial Assistance Provided: . . .Yes(D)
Site Selection Assistance: . . . . . . .Yes
Lease Negotiation Assistance: . . . . .NA
Co-operative Advertising: . . . . . . .Yes
Training: . . . . .1 Wk. Headquarters,
. . . . 3 Days Site
On-Going Support: . . . . . . B,C,D,E,H,I
Full-Time Franchisor Support Staff: . . 18
EXPANSION PLANS:
US: . . . . All US
Canada - No, ...Overseas - No

TV NEWS MAGAZINE

80 Eighth Ave.
New York, NY 10011
TEL: (212) 243-6800
FAX:
Mr. Allan Horwitz, President

TV NEWS is an award-winning, free community publication combining the 7-day readership of a TV Guide with the total market coverage of a "shopper" and the efficiencies of scale of a major national publication. TV NEWS attracts readers, has low ad rates and excellent response that attracts and holds advertisers.

HISTORY:	FINANCIAL:	FRANCHISOR TRAINING/SUPPORT:
Established in 1973; . . 1st Franchised in 1976	Cash Investment: $5-24.9K	Financial Assistance Provided: . . .Yes(D)
Company-Owned Units (As of 12/1/1989): . .1	Total Investment: $5-24.9K	Site Selection Assistance: . . . . . . .Yes
Franchised Units (12/1/1989): 9	Fees: Franchise - $24.9K	Lease Negotiation Assistance: . . . . .NA
Total Units (12/1/1989): 10	Royalty: 4%, Advert: 0%	Co-operative Advertising: . . . . . . .Yes
Distribution: US-10;Can-0;Overseas-0	Contract Periods (Yrs.): 20/20	Training: . . . . .1 Wk. Headquarters,
North America: . . . . 3 States	Area Development Agreement: . .No	. . . . 3 Days Site
Concentration: . . . .6 in NY, 3 in FL, 1 in SC	Sub-Franchise Contract: . . . . . .No	On-Going Support: . . . . . . B,C,D,E,H,I
Registered: . . . CA,FL,IL,IN,MD,MI,MN,NY	Expand in Territory: . . . . Yes	Full-Time Franchisor Support Staff: . . . 8
. . . . OR,RI,VA,WA,WI	Passive Ownership: . . . Discouraged	EXPANSION PLANS:
Average # of Employees: . . . . . 2-4 FT, 2 PT	Encourage Conversions: . . . . . Yes	US: . . . . .All US
Prior Industry Experience: . . . . . . Helpful	Franchisee Purchase(s) Required: .No	Canada - No, ...Overseas - No

TV TIMES

Box 2487
Chapel Hill, NC 27515
TEL: (919) 967-5657
FAX:
Mr. Benjamin F. Saxon, President

Franchisee will be the associate publisher of a weekly TV magazine distributed in his area by local supermarkets and businesses. Magazine is free and is supported by local advertising. Free expert training included. $10,500 - no other fees.

HISTORY:	FINANCIAL:	FRANCHISOR TRAINING/SUPPORT:
Established in 1976; . . 1st Franchised in 1983	Cash Investment: $13.5K	Financial Assistance Provided: . . .Yes(D)
Company-Owned Units (As of 12/1/1989): . .1	Total Investment: $13.5K	Site Selection Assistance: . . . . . . .Yes
Franchised Units (12/1/1989): 2	Fees: Franchise - $10.5K	Lease Negotiation Assistance: . . . . .NA
Total Units (12/1/1989): 3	Royalty: 0%, Advert: 0%	Co-operative Advertising: . . . . . . .NA
Distribution: US-3;Can-0;Overseas-0	Contract Periods (Yrs.): 10/10	Training: . . . . .1 Wk. On-site,
North America: . . . . 3 States	Area Development Agreement: . .No	. . . . Ongoing at Headquarters
Concentration: . . . . 2 in NC, 1 in FL	Sub-Franchise Contract: . . . . . Yes	On-Going Support: . . . . B,C,D,H
Registered: . . . . .FL	Expand in Territory: . . . . Yes	Full-Time Franchisor Support Staff: . . . 2
. . . .	Passive Ownership: . . . Not Allowed	EXPANSION PLANS:
Average # of Employees: . . . . .1 FT	Encourage Conversions: . . . . . NA	US: . . . . .Northeast, Southeast
Prior Industry Experience: . . . . . . Helpful	Franchisee Purchase(s) Required: .No	Canada - No, ...Overseas - No

TV TRAVEL MAGAZINE

2482 Lorrie Dr., P. O. Box 669051
Marietta, GA 30066
TEL: (404) 977-1468
FAX:
Mr. W. Ken Acree, VP

Dining, entertainment, shopping guide for travelers. Income derived from sale of advertising in magazine. Bi-weekly publication reduces overhead, maximizes profits. 4-color cover, 4 color advertising. Break-even point approximately $700/week ad revenue. Great opportunity for independence and wealth. Furnished free to hotels, who place magazines in guest rooms.

HISTORY:	FINANCIAL:	FRANCHISOR TRAINING/SUPPORT:
Established in 1983; . . 1st Franchised in 1987	Cash Investment: $15.5K	Financial Assistance Provided: . . . . .No
Company-Owned Units (As of 12/1/1989): . .1	Total Investment: $20-25K	Site Selection Assistance: . . . . . . .NA
Franchised Units (12/1/1989): 0	Fees: Franchise - $15.5K	Lease Negotiation Assistance: . . . . .NA
Total Units (12/1/1989): 1	Royalty: 0%, Advert: 0%	Co-operative Advertising: . . . . . . .NA
Distribution: US-1;Can-0;Overseas-0	Contract Periods (Yrs.): 5/5	Training: . . . . 3 Days Headquarters,
North America: . . . . .1 State	Area Development Agreement: . .No	. . . . .Field As Needed
Concentration: . . . . 1 in GA	Sub-Franchise Contract: . . . . . .No	On-Going Support: . . . . C,d,G
Registered:	Expand in Territory: . . . . . . .No	Full-Time Franchisor Support Staff: . . . 2
. . . .	Passive Ownership: . . . Not Allowed	EXPANSION PLANS:
Average # of Employees: . . . . . . 1 FT, 1 PT	Encourage Conversions: . . . . . .No	US: . . . . Southeast, Southwest
Prior Industry Experience: . . . . . . Helpful	Franchisee Purchase(s) Required: .No	Canada - No, ...Overseas - No

TV, VIDEO, ENTERTAINMENT MAGAZINE
P. O. Box 420-215
Atlanta, GA 30342
TEL: (404) 843-2383 C
FAX:
Mr. Usman Mirza, President

Local magazine publishing and distribution. Sell advertising to local businesses. Complete support and training is provided - customized. Requires hard work, understanding of marketing, advertising, selling and management. New magazine name, new services. New advertising and promotions for 1990.

HISTORY:	FINANCIAL:	FRANCHISOR TRAINING/SUPPORT:
Established in 1974; . . 1st Franchised in 1974	Cash Investment: $30-100K	Financial Assistance Provided: . . . Yes(I)
Company-Owned Units (As of 12/1/1989): . .1	Total Investment: $75-150K	Site Selection Assistance: . . . . . . .NA
Franchised Units (12/1/1989): 116	Fees: Franchise - $10-40K	Lease Negotiation Assistance: . . . . .NA
Total Units (12/1/1989): 120	Royalty: 3-10%, Advert: . . . 2-5%	Co-operative Advertising: . . . . .Yes
Distribution: US-120;Can-0;Overseas-0	Contract Periods (Yrs.): 1-10	Training: . . . . . .2-6 Wks. Headquarters,
North America: . . . . 18 States	Area Development Agreement: . .No	. . . .2-4 Wks. Regional, 1-4 Wks. Local
Concentration: . . 18 in GA, 10 in TX, 7 in FL	Sub-Franchise Contract: . . . . . .No	On-Going Support: . . . . . . a,b,C,d,g,h,I
Registered:	Expand in Territory: . . . . Yes	Full-Time Franchisor Support Staff: . . . 4
. . . .	Passive Ownership: . . . . .Allowed	EXPANSION PLANS:
Average # of Employees: . . . . . . 2 FT, 2 PT	Encourage Conversions: . . . NA	US: . . . . .All US
Prior Industry Experience: . . . . Helpful	Franchisee Purchase(s) Required: .No	Canada - Yes, . . . Overseas - Yes

WEDDING PAGES, THE

11128 John Galt Blvd.
Omaha, NE 68137
TEL: (800) 843-4983 (402) 331-7755
FAX:
Mr. Kenneth Nanfito, EVP

THE WEDDING PAGES represents one of the most dynamic direct marketing tools ever developed to help retailers reach the $28 billion bridal market. The program is centered around a 250-page wedding planner called THE WEDDING PAGES and the corresponding list of brides-to-be generated through its distribution. Involves sales of advertising in a protected territory.

HISTORY:	FINANCIAL: OTC-WINN	FRANCHISOR TRAINING/SUPPORT:
Established in 1982; . . 1st Franchised in 1984	Cash Investment: $15K	Financial Assistance Provided: . . . . . No
Company-Owned Units (As of 12/1/1989): . .0	Total Investment: $25-65K	Site Selection Assistance: . . . . .NA
Franchised Units (12/1/1989): 76	Fees: Franchise - $15K	Lease Negotiation Assistance: . . . . .NA
Total Units (12/1/1989): 76	Royalty: 10%, Advert: 0%	Co-operative Advertising: . . . . .NA
Distribution: US-75;Can-1;Overseas-0	Contract Periods (Yrs.): 5/5	Training: . . . . 2 Days Headquarters,
North America: . . . . 37 States	Area Development Agreement: . .No	. . . . 1 Wk. Field
Concentration: . . . .8 in CA, 5 in TX, 4 in FL	Sub-Franchise Contract: . . . . . .No	On-Going Support: . . . . . . A,D,E,G,H,I
Registered: . . . .FL,HI,IL,MN,NY,RI,VA,WI	Expand in Territory: . . . . Yes	Full-Time Franchisor Support Staff: . . 30
. . . .	Passive Ownership: . . . . . .Allowed	EXPANSION PLANS:
Average # of Employees: . . . . .1 FT	Encourage Conversions: . . . . .No	US: . . . . .All US
Prior Industry Experience: . . . . . . Helpful	Franchisee Purchase(s) Required: Yes	Canada - No, ...Overseas - No

WHAT! A MAGAZINE

401 - 115 Bannatyne Ave.
Winnipeg, MB R3B0R3 CAN
TEL: (800) 665-9428 (204) 942-2214
FAX: (204) 957-1467
Mr. Richard A. Lavergne, Dir. Ops.

WHAT! A MAGAZINE is a publishing system that allows the franchisee to economically publish a glossy, high-quality regional magazine targeted to the high school market. Our operations manual guides you from editorial collection and advertising sales to the technical process of publishing.

HISTORY:	FINANCIAL:	FRANCHISOR TRAINING/SUPPORT:
Established in 1987; . . 1st Franchised in 1989	Cash Investment: $25-50K	Financial Assistance Provided: . . . . . No
Company-Owned Units (As of 12/1/1989): . .3	Total Investment: $35-65K	Site Selection Assistance: . . . . .NA
Franchised Units (12/1/1989): 1	Fees: Franchise - $25-40K	Lease Negotiation Assistance: . . . . .NA
Total Units (12/1/1989): 4	Royalty: 0-5%, Advert: . . . . NA	Co-operative Advertising: . . . . .NA
Distribution: US-0;Can-4;Overseas-0	Contract Periods (Yrs.): 5/5	Training: . . . . . . 3 Days at Agreed Upon
North America: . . . . 4 Provinces	Area Development Agreement: . .No	. . . . .Location
Concentration: . . . 1 in ON, 1 in AB, 1 in BC	Sub-Franchise Contract: . . . . . .No	On-Going Support: . . . . . . A,b,C,D,G,I
Registered: . . . . AB	Expand in Territory: . . . . Yes	Full-Time Franchisor Support Staff: . . . 4
. . . .	Passive Ownership: . . . Discouraged	EXPANSION PLANS:
Average # of Employees: . . . . .1 FT	Encourage Conversions: . . . . NA	US: . . . . .All US
Prior Industry Experience: . . . . . . Helpful	Franchisee Purchase(s) Required: Yes	Canada - Yes, ... Overseas - No

SUPPLEMENTAL LISTING OF FRANCHISORS

AMATEUR SPORT JOURNAL . . . . P. O. Box 6996, Hollywood FL 33081
BINGO BUGLE NEWSPAPER . . . . .7522 20th N.E., Seattle WA 98115
COUNTRY PRESS LTD. . . . . .P. O. Box 56, Dartmouth NS   CAN
FOCUS ON BINGO MAGAZINE . . . . One Anderson Ave., P.O. Box 133, Fairview NJ 07022
HOMES & LAND MAGAZINE . . . . .2365 Centerville Rd., Tallahassee FL 32308
K & O PUBLISHING . . . . .7522 20th N.E., Seattle WA 98115
MYWAY HOMEFINDER MAGAZINE . . . . .2749 Glendale, # B, Toledo OH 43614
OFFICIAL SPORTS BOOK . . . . .2 Lansing Sq., # 1002, Willowdale ON M2J4P8   CAN
PRIMESOURCE . . . . 95 Thorncliffe Park Dr., # 3201, Toronto ON M4H1L7   CAN
SMALL BUSINESS DIGEST . . . . 1858-C Independence Sq., Dunwoody GA 30338
TV FACTS . . . . Liberty Square, Danvers MA 01923
TV FOCUS . . . . .P.O. Box 133, One Anderson Ave., Fairview NJ 07022
TV TOPICS VIDEO GUIDE . . . . 566 S. Oliver, P. O. Box 20230, Wichita KS 67208
VENDOR-SELL PUBLICATIONS . . . . R. R. # 1, Newtonville ON L0A1J0   CAN
YOUR CITY'S OFFICIAL WEDDING GUIDE . . . . .P.O. Box 73042, Metairie LA 70033

CHAPTER 33

REAL ESTATE

AMBIC BUILDING INSPECTION CONSULTANTS
1200 Rt. 130
Robbinsville, NJ 08691
TEL: (800) 88-AMBIC (609) 426-1212
FAX: (609) 426-1230
Mr. David Goldstein, President

AMBIC BUILDING INSPECTION CONSULTANTS offers complete training in the home inspection field and related services. Computer training and software is included, as well as computer updates. On-going technical, sales, marketing and administrative support are provided. AMBIC offers over 15 years of experience by a licensed building inspector trained in home inspections.

HISTORY: . . . .
Established in 1987; . . 1st Franchised in 1988
Company-Owned Units (As of 12/1/1989): . .0
Franchised Units (12/1/1989): 8
Total Units (12/1/1989): 8
Distribution: US-8;Can-0;Overseas-0
North America: . . . . 2 States
Concentration: . . . . .6 in NJ, 2 in PA
Registered: . . . . MD,NY

. . . .
Average # of Employees: . . . . .2 FT
Prior Industry Experience: . . . . Helpful

FINANCIAL:
Cash Investment: $22K
Total Investment: $26.6-27.5K
Fees: Franchise - $16.5K
  Royalty: 6%, Advert: 0%
Contract Periods (Yrs.): 10/10
Area Development Agreement: . .No
Sub-Franchise Contract: . . . . .No
Expand in Territory: . . . . . . Yes
Passive Ownership: . . . Discouraged
Encourage Conversions: . . . . Yes
Franchisee Purchase(s) Required: Yes

FRANCHISOR TRAINING/SUPPORT:
Financial Assistance Provided: . . . . . No
Site Selection Assistance: . . . . .NA
Lease Negotiation Assistance: . . . . .NA
Co-operative Advertising: . . . . .NA
Training: . . . . 4 Wks. Headquarters
. . . .
On-Going Support: . . . .a,B,C,D,F,G,H,I
Full-Time Franchisor Support Staff: . . . 5
EXPANSION PLANS:
  US: . . . . .All US
  Canada - No, ... Overseas - No

REAL ESTATE

	1988	1989	1990	Percentage Change 1988-1989	Percentage Change 1989-1990
Number of Establishments:					
Company-Owned	142	118	118	-16.9%	0.0%
Franchisee-Owned	15,152	15,830	16,837	4.5%	6.4%
Total	15,294	15,948	16,955	4.3%	6.3%
% of Total Establishments:					
Company-Owned	0.9%	0.7%	0.7%		
Franchisee-Owned	99.1%	99.3%	99.3%		
Total	100.0%	100.0%	100.0%		
Annual Sales ($000):					
Company-Owned	$66,664	$68,515	$73,640	2.8%	7.5%
Franchisee-Owned	5,856,613	6,176,129	6,676,785	5.5%	8.1%
Total	5,923,277	6,244,644	6,750,425	5.4%	8.1%
% of Total Sales:					
Company-Owned	1.1%	1.1%	1.1%		
Franchisee-Owned	98.9%	98.9%	98.9%		
Total	100.0%	100.0%	100.0%		
Average Sales Per Unit ($000):					
Company-Owned	$469	$581	$624	23.7%	7.5%
Franchisee-Owned	387	390	397	0.9%	1.6%
Total	387	392	398	1.1%	1.7%
Sales Ratio	121.5%	148.8%	157.4%		

	1st Quartile	Median	4th Quartile
Average 1988 Total Investment:			
Company-Owned	N. A.	$37,500	N. A.
Franchisee-Owned	20,000	25,000	50,000
Single Unit Franchise Fee	$7,500	$10,000	$15,000
Multiple Unit Franchise Fee	N. A.	N. A.	N. A.
Franchisee Start-up Cost	9,000	15,000	20,000

	1988	Employees/Unit	Sales/Employee
Employment:			
Company-Owned	2,582	18.2	$25,819
Franchisee-Owned	194,883	12.9	30,052
Total	197,465	12.9	29,997
Employee Performance Ratios		141.4%	85.9%

Source: Franchising In The Economy, 1988 - 1990, IFA Education Foundation & Horwath International, Published January, 1990.

1) 1989 and 1990 data were estimated by respondents.

2) Sales are reported as Gross Commissions.

AMERISPEC HOME INSPECTION SERVICE
1507 W. Yale Ave.
Orange, CA 92667
TEL: (800) 426-2270 (714) 998-2442
FAX: (714) 998-2366
Ms. Sheilah Hyman, VP Sales

High profit potential. Low overhead. No inventory. Much-needed service business. These are just 4 reasons why you should join the fastest-growing home inspection company and one of the fastest-growing franchise opportunities in America. We offer qualified candidates an exclusive territory, professional training and on-going support.

HISTORY: . . . . IFA
Established in 1987; . . 1st Franchised in 1988
Company-Owned Units (As of 12/1/1989): . .0
Franchised Units (12/1/1989): 74
Total Units (12/1/1989): 74
Distribution: US-74;Can-0;Overseas-0
  North America: . . . . 20 States
  Concentration: . . . 13 in CA, 6 in IL, 5 in VA
Registered: . . . CA,FL,HI,IL,IN,MD,MI,MN
  . . . . NY,OR,VA,WA,WI
Average # of Employees: . . . . . . 3 FT, 1 PT
Prior Industry Experience: . . . . . . Helpful

FINANCIAL:
Cash Investment: $26-44K
Total Investment: $26-44K
Fees: Franchise - $13-19K
  Royalty: 7%, Advert: 3%
Contract Periods (Yrs.): 10/10
Area Development Agreement: . .No
Sub-Franchise Contract: . . . . .No
Expand in Territory: . . . . Yes
Passive Ownership: . . . Discouraged
Encourage Conversions: . . . . .No
Franchisee Purchase(s) Required: Yes

FRANCHISOR TRAINING/SUPPORT:
Financial Assistance Provided: . . . . . No
Site Selection Assistance: . . . . . . .Yes
Lease Negotiation Assistance: . . . . .NA
Co-operative Advertising: . . . . . . .Yes
Training: . . . . 2 Wks. Headquarters
. . . .
On-Going Support: . . . .B,C,D,E,F,G,H,I
Full-Time Franchisor Support Staff: . . 10
EXPANSION PLANS:
US: . . . . All US
Canada - Yes, ...Overseas - No

APARTMENT SELECTOR

P.O. Box 8355
Dallas, TX 75205
TEL: (800) 444-5484 (214) 361-4420 C
FAX:
Mr. Kendall A. Laughlin, Chairman

APARTMENT SELECTOR is the nation's oldest and largest FREE apartment and home rental service. Our fee is paid by apartment owners. Extensive training systems for agents and management. Referral network called Official Relocation Network.

HISTORY: . . . .
Established in 1959; . . 1st Franchised in 1982
Company-Owned Units (As of 12/1/1989): . .0
Franchised Units (12/1/1989): 22
Total Units (12/1/1989): 22
Distribution: US-22;Can-0;Overseas-0
  North America: . . . . 3 States
  Concentration: . . .16 in TX, 4 in GA, 2 in CO
Registered: . . . .
. . . .
Average # of Employees: . . . . Varies
Prior Industry Experience: . . . . Helpful

FINANCIAL:
Cash Investment: $20K
Total Investment: $25K
Fees: Franchise - $7-10K
  Royalty: 5%, Advert: 1%
Contract Periods (Yrs.): 3/3
Area Development Agreement: . .No
Sub-Franchise Contract: . . . . .No
Expand in Territory: . . . . Yes
Passive Ownership: . . . Not Allowed
Encourage Conversions: . . . . Yes
Franchisee Purchase(s) Required: Yes

FRANCHISOR TRAINING/SUPPORT:
Financial Assistance Provided: . . . . . No
Site Selection Assistance: . . . . No
Lease Negotiation Assistance: . . . . No
Co-operative Advertising: . . . . No
Training: . . . . 1 Wk. Headquarters
. . . .
On-Going Support: . . . . . .B,c,d,e,G,h,I
Full-Time Franchisor Support Staff: . . .2
EXPANSION PLANS:
US: . . . . All US
Canada - No, ...Overseas - No

BETTER HOMES & GARDENS REAL ESTATE SERVICE
2000 Grand Ave.
Des Moines, IA 50312
TEL: (800) 274-7653 (515) 284-3252
FAX:
Mr. Craig King, Natl. Mktg. Dir.

BETTER HOMES AND GARDENS is an exclusive-territory franchise that shares equal logo identity with its independently-owned and operated members. Through its Home Marketing System, BETTER HOMES provides comprehensive tools to facilitate the growth of real estate companies. Major emphasis on management training.

HISTORY: . . . . IFA
Established in 1902; . . 1st Franchised in 1978
Company-Owned Units (As of 12/1/1989): . .2
Franchised Units (12/1/1989): 1416
Total Units (12/1/1989): 1418
Distribution: . . . US-1,418;Can-0;Overseas-0
  North America: . . . . 50 States
  Concentration: . .193 in CA,85 in FL,84 in PA
Registered: . . . . All States
. . . .
Average # of Employees: 350
Prior Industry Experience: . . . . Helpful

FINANCIAL: NY-MERDTH
Cash Investment: . . . .$
Total Investment: . . . .$
Fees: Franchise - $11-40K
  Royalty: Var., Advert: . . . Var.
Contract Periods (Yrs.): 3/4
Area Development Agreement: . .No
Sub-Franchise Contract: . . . . .No
Expand in Territory: . . . . Yes
Passive Ownership: . . . Discouraged
Encourage Conversions: . . . . Yes
Franchisee Purchase(s) Required: .No

FRANCHISOR TRAINING/SUPPORT:
Financial Assistance Provided: . . . Yes(I)
Site Selection Assistance: . . . . .NA
Lease Negotiation Assistance: . . . . .Yes
Co-operative Advertising: . . . . . . .Yes
Training: . . . . 4 Days Headquarters,
. . . . Varies at Site
On-Going Support: . . . . A,B,C,D,G,H,I
Full-Time Franchisor Support Staff: . . . .
EXPANSION PLANS:
US: . . . . All US
Canada - Yes, ...Overseas - No

BRITETECH INTERNATIONAL

6350 McDonough Dr., # G
Norcross, GA 30093
TEL: (800) 237-3119 (404) 449-8244
FAX: (404) 729-0567
Mr. Terry P. Robson, President

Indoor environmental assessment and remediation. BRITETECH evaluates commercial buildings for deficiencies in air quality, possible toxins and pollutants and provides the remediation services associated with correcting problems.

HISTORY: . . . . IFA	FINANCIAL:	FRANCHISOR TRAINING/SUPPORT:
Established in 1988; . . 1st Franchised in 1989	Cash Investment: $30-35K	Financial Assistance Provided: . . . . . No
Company-Owned Units (As of 12/1/1989): . . 0	Total Investment: $40-50K	Site Selection Assistance: . . . . NA
Franchised Units (12/1/1989): 17	Fees: Franchise - $30-35K	Lease Negotiation Assistance: . . . . NA
Total Units (12/1/1989): 17	Royalty: 4%, Advert: 0%	Co-operative Advertising: . . . . NA
Distribution: US-17;Can-0;Overseas-0	Contract Periods (Yrs.): 10/10	Training: . . . . 1 Wk. Atlanta, GA
North America: . . . . 12 States	Area Development Agreement: . .No	. . . .
Concentration: . . . 2 in NC, 2 in FL, 2 in GA	Sub-Franchise Contract: . . . . . No	On-Going Support: . . . . A,B,C,D,G,H,I
Registered: . . . . All Except AB	Expand in Territory: . . . . No	Full-Time Franchisor Support Staff: . . . 9
. . . .	Passive Ownership: . . . . . .Allowed	EXPANSION PLANS:
Average # of Employees: . . . . . . 3 FT, 2 PT	Encourage Conversions: . . . . . Yes	US: . . . . All US
Prior Industry Experience: . . . . . . Helpful	Franchisee Purchase(s) Required: Yes	Canada - Yes, ...Overseas - No

BUILDING INSPECTOR OF AMERICA

684 Main St.
Wakefield, MA 01880
TEL: (800) 321-4677 (617) 246-4215
FAX:
Mr. Larry Finklestone, Dir. Sales

Pre-purchase home inspections, conducted to help buyer make informed buying decisions. Franchisee gets extensive marketing, business and technical training for 2 weeks at corporate headquarters. On-going help provided to franchisees. 800 Hotline # available.

HISTORY: . . . . IFA	FINANCIAL:	FRANCHISOR TRAINING/SUPPORT:
Established in 1985; . . 1st Franchised in 1985	Cash Investment: $15-50K	Financial Assistance Provided: . . . . . No
Company-Owned Units (As of 12/1/1989): . . 0	Total Investment: $21-56K	Site Selection Assistance: . . . . NA
Franchised Units (12/1/1989): 57	Fees: Franchise - $15-50K	Lease Negotiation Assistance: . . . . NA
Total Units (12/1/1989): 57	Royalty: 6%, Advert: 3%	Co-operative Advertising: . . . . NA
Distribution: US-57;Can-0;Overseas-0	Contract Periods (Yrs.): 10/10	Training: . . . . 2 Wks. Headquarters
North America: . . . . 21 States	Area Development Agreement: . .No	. . . .
Concentration: . . . 9 in NJ, 6 in MD, 5 in PA	Sub-Franchise Contract: . . . . . No	On-Going Support: . . . . C,D,G,H,I
Registered: . . . . CA,FL,IL,IN,MD,MI,NY,RI	Expand in Territory: . . . . No	Full-Time Franchisor Support Staff: . . . 7
. . . . VA	Passive Ownership: . . . Discouraged	EXPANSION PLANS:
Average # of Employees: . . . . . . 1 FT, 1 PT	Encourage Conversions: . . . . . No	US: . . . . All US
Prior Industry Experience: . . . . . . Helpful	Franchisee Purchase(s) Required: .No	Canada - Yes, . . . Overseas - Yes

BY OWNER REALITY NETWORK

N 8884 Government Way, # A
Hayden Lake, ID 83835
TEL: (208) 772-4094
FAX:
Jerry or Ann Wall, Pres./VP Mktg.

Real estate marketing centers of "BY OWNER" properties in retail locations, featuring professional pictorial property displays. Local and network exposure. No percentage commissions! Our federally registered "BY OWNER" logo and concept in high-traffic retail locations naturally attract sellers and buyers.

HISTORY:	FINANCIAL:	FRANCHISOR TRAINING/SUPPORT:
Established in 1985; . . 1st Franchised in 1986	Cash Investment: $14.8K	Financial Assistance Provided: . . . Yes(I)
Company-Owned Units (As of 12/1/1989): . .0	Total Investment: $31.4K	Site Selection Assistance: . . . . .Yes
Franchised Units (12/1/1989): 12	Fees: Franchise - $16.5K	Lease Negotiation Assistance: . . . . .Yes
Total Units (12/1/1989): 12	Royalty: 12%, Advert: 0%	Co-operative Advertising: . . . . .Yes
Distribution: US-10;Can-2;Overseas-0	Contract Periods (Yrs.): 5/5	Training: . . . . . 2 1/2 Days Headquarters,
North America: . . . . . 3 States, 2 Provinces	Area Development Agreement: . .No	. . . 2 Days Site, 2 Days Grand Opening
Concentration: . . . 4 in MT, 3 in ID, 2 in WA	Sub-Franchise Contract: . . . . Yes	On-Going Support: . . . . . . C,D,E,G,H,I
Registered: . . . . WA,AB	Expand in Territory: . . . . No	Full-Time Franchisor Support Staff: . . . 3
. . . .	Passive Ownership: . . . Discouraged	EXPANSION PLANS:
Average # of Employees: . . . . . 1 FT, 1-2 PT	Encourage Conversions: . . . . . No	US: . . . . . Northwest. Master Fran. US
Prior Industry Experience: . . . . . . Helpful	Franchisee Purchase(s) Required: .No	Canada - Yes, . . . Overseas - Yes

CENTURY 21

2601 S. E. Main St.
Irvine, CA 92713
TEL: (714) 553-2100
FAX: (714) 553-2133
Mr. Robert V. Muir, Dir. Fran. Sales

World's largest real estate franchising organization. Established to provide support system to independently-owned and operated offices. Offers advertising, referral system, sales and management training, corporate real estate and relocation services, client follow-up, etc. Insurance, mortgage and securities services also available.

HISTORY: . . . . IFA
Established in 1972; . . 1st Franchised in 1972
Company-Owned Units (As of 12/1/1989): . .0
Franchised Units (12/1/1989): 7168
Total Units (12/1/1989): 7168
Distribution: . US-6046;Can-471;Overseas-651
 North America: . . . . 50 States,10 Provinces
 Concentration: 1000 in CA, 800 in NY,400 TX
Registered: . . . . .All
 . . . .
Average # of Employees: . . . . 15 FT
Prior Industry Experience: . . . . . .Necessary

FINANCIAL:
Cash Investment: $15-30K
Total Investment: $25-100K
Fees: Franchise - $13.5-25K
 Royalty: 6%, Advert: 2%
Contract Periods (Yrs.): 5/5
Area Development Agreement: . .No
Sub-Franchise Contract: . . . . . Yes
Expand in Territory: . . . . . . .No
Passive Ownership: . . . Not Allowed
Encourage Conversions: . . . . Yes
Franchisee Purchase(s) Required: Yes

FRANCHISOR TRAINING/SUPPORT:
Financial Assistance Provided: . . .Yes(D)
Site Selection Assistance: . . . . .No
Lease Negotiation Assistance: . . . . .No
Co-operative Advertising: . . . . .Yes
Training: . . . . 5 Days Headquarters
 . . . .
On-Going Support: . . . . .A,C,D,E,G,H,I
Full-Time Franchisor Support Staff: . .500
EXPANSION PLANS:
 US: . . . . .All US
 Canada - Yes, . . . Overseas - Yes

COLDWELL BANKER RESIDENTIAL AFFILIATES

5000 Birch St., # 8000
Newport Beach, CA 92660
TEL: (800) 854-6800 (714) 851-7600
FAX: (714) 833-8148
Mr. James P. Cherry, VP, Dir. Mktg.

COLDWELL BANKER RESIDENTIAL AFFILIATES is in the business of offering and selling franchises for the operation of real estate brokerage businesses (franchises) to qualifying real estate brokers throughout the US and Canada. The franchise consists of a license permitting franchisees to offer designated real estate brokerage services to customers under the COLDWELL BANKER trademark.

HISTORY: . . . . IFA
Established in 1981; . . 1st Franchised in 1981
Company-Owned Units (As of 12/1/1989): 600
Franchised Units (12/1/1989): 1250
Total Units (12/1/1989): 1850
Distribution: . . . US-1820;Can-30;Overseas-0
North America: . . . . 50 States, 1 Province
Concentration: . . . .
Registered: . . . . All Except AB
 . . . .
Average # of Employees: . . . .
Prior Industry Experience: . . . . . .Necessary

FINANCIAL:
Cash Investment: $80-100K
Total Investment: $125-200K
Fees: Franchise - $20K
 Royalty: 6%, Advert: 2.5%
Contract Periods (Yrs.): 5/5
Area Development Agreement: . .No
Sub-Franchise Contract: . . . . .No
Expand in Territory: . . . . . . .Yes
Passive Ownership: . . . Discouraged
Encourage Conversions: . . . . . Yes
Franchisee Purchase(s) Required: .No

FRANCHISOR TRAINING/SUPPORT:
Financial Assistance Provided: . . .Yes(D)
Site Selection Assistance: . . . . .No
Lease Negotiation Assistance: . . . . .No
Co-operative Advertising: . . . . . . .Yes
Training: . . . . 4 Days Headquarters,
 . . . 2 Days On-site, 4-6 Visits Annually
On-Going Support: . . . . . . B,C,D,G,h,I
Full-Time Franchisor Support Staff: . .190
EXPANSION PLANS:
 US: . . . . .All US
 Canada - Yes, ...Overseas - No

COUNTRYWIDE REAL ESTATE GROUP

54 Village Centre Pl.
Mississauga, ON L4Z1V9 CAN
TEL: (800) 387-5946 (416) 566-5500
FAX: (416) 566-5505
Mr. Bill Croft, Chairman

Real estate franchise system with high-quality sales aids, marketing program, broker assistance, start-up planning, administrative systems, office design, recruiting program and one of the best success ratios in franchising - no failures in 4 years.

HISTORY: . . . . .CFA
Established in 1985; . . 1st Franchised in 1986
Company-Owned Units (As of 12/1/1989): . .0
Franchised Units (12/1/1989): 58
Total Units (12/1/1989): 58
Distribution: US-0;Can-58;Overseas-0
 North America: . . . . 2 Provinces
 Concentration: . . . . 54 in ON, 4 in AB
Registered: . . . . AB
 . . . .
Average # of Employees: . . . . 25-40 FT
Prior Industry Experience: . . . . . .Necessary

FINANCIAL:
Cash Investment: $50-150K
Total Investment: $50-250K
Fees: Franchise - $4.5-14.5K
 Royalty: $85/PP/M, Advert:$30/PP/M
Contract Periods (Yrs.): 5/5
Area Development Agreement: . .No
Sub-Franchise Contract: . . . . Yes
Expand in Territory: . . . . . . Yes
Passive Ownership: . . . Not Allowed
Encourage Conversions: . . . . NA
Franchisee Purchase(s) Required: .No

FRANCHISOR TRAINING/SUPPORT:
Financial Assistance Provided: . . . . .NA
Site Selection Assistance: . . . . .NA
Lease Negotiation Assistance: . . . . .NA
Co-operative Advertising: . . . . .NA
Training: . . . . . . 2 Days Regional Office
 . . . .
On-Going Support: . . . . . B,C,d,E,G,h,I
Full-Time Franchisor Support Staff: . . 16
EXPANSION PLANS:
 US: . . . . No
 Canada - Yes, ...Overseas - No

ELECTRONIC REALTY ASSOCIATES / ERA
4900 College Blvd.
Overland Park, KS 66211
TEL: (800) 728-0999 (913) 491-1000
FAX: (913) 491-1000
Mr. David Taylor, Natl. Sales Admin.

Real estate services that include home protection plans, guaranteed sales/equity advance program, relocation services, various training programs and real estate-related financial services.

HISTORY: . . . . IFA
Established in 1971; . . 1st Franchised in 1972
Company-Owned Units (As of 12/1/1989): . . .0
Franchised Units (12/1/1989): 2954
Total Units (12/1/1989): 2954
Distribution: . . US-2304;Can-0;Overseas-650
North America: . . . . 50 States
Concentration: . 282 in FL, 255 in CA, 166 NY
Registered: . . . . .All Exc. AB
. . . .
Average # of Employees: . . . . 11 FT
Prior Industry Experience: . . . . . .Necessary

FINANCIAL:
Cash Investment: $10-25K
Total Investment: $27-44K
Fees: Franchise - $16.9-18.9K
Royalty: Flat, Advert: . . . . . Flat
Contract Periods (Yrs.): 5/5
Area Development Agreement: . .No
Sub-Franchise Contract: . . . . . .No
Expand in Territory: . . . . . . Yes
Passive Ownership: . . . . . .Allowed
Encourage Conversions: . . . . Yes
Franchisee Purchase(s) Required: .No

FRANCHISOR TRAINING/SUPPORT:
Financial Assistance Provided: . . .Yes(D)
Site Selection Assistance: . . . . No
Lease Negotiation Assistance: . . . . . No
Co-operative Advertising: . . . . No
Training: . . . . . 5 Days Kansas City, MO
. . . .
On-Going Support: . . . . b,C,d,E,f,G,h,I
Full-Time Franchisor Support Staff: . .342
EXPANSION PLANS:
US: . . . . .All US
Canada - No, ... Overseas - Yes

FACTUAL DATA
736 Whalers Way. Bldg. F, # 436
Ft. Collins, CO 80522
TEL: (800) 759-3400 (303) 226-3600
FAX:
Mr. Jerry Donnan, President

FACTUAL DATA offers a unique professional opportunity for providing the mortgage lender a FACTUAL DATA mortgage credit report. Your clients will be banks, savings and loans - your employees will be highly-motivated, customer service-oriented office professionals. Bottom line - $100,000 plus.

HISTORY: . . . .
Established in 1984; . . 1st Franchised in 1987
Company-Owned Units (As of 12/1/1989): . .1
Franchised Units (12/1/1989): 8
Total Units (12/1/1989): 9
Distribution: US-9;Can-0;Overseas-0
North America: . . . . 5 States
Concentration: . . . 3 in CO, 3 in CA, 1 in WA
Registered: . . . . CA,WA
. . . .
Average # of Employees: . . . . .4-6 FT
Prior Industry Experience: . . . . . . Helpful

FINANCIAL:
Cash Investment: $150K
Total Investment: $150K
Fees: Franchise - $120K
Royalty: 7-11%, Advert: 0%
Contract Periods (Yrs.): 10/10
Area Development Agreement: Yes/10
Sub-Franchise Contract: . . . . . Yes
Expand in Territory: . . . . Yes
Passive Ownership: . . . . . .Allowed
Encourage Conversions: . . . . .No
Franchisee Purchase(s) Required: Yes

FRANCHISOR TRAINING/SUPPORT:
Financial Assistance Provided: . . . Yes(I)
Site Selection Assistance: . . . . . . .Yes
Lease Negotiation Assistance: . . . .Yes
Co-operative Advertising: . . . . . . .Yes
Training: . . . . 4 Wks. Headquarters,
. . . . .4 Wks. On-site
On-Going Support: . . A,B,C,D,E,F,G,H,I
Full-Time Franchisor Support Staff: . . .8
EXPANSION PLANS:
US: . . . . .All Except Colorado
Canada - No, ...Overseas - No

FSBO DEVELOPMENT CORP.
12995 S. Cleveland Ave., # 230
Ft. Myers, FL 33907
TEL: (813) 936-1152
FAX:
Ms. Cheryl Harry, VP Fran. Devel.

FSBO DEVELOPMENT CORP. - not just another real estate company. Expanded to 4 locations in its first year, FSBO's finely-tuned, computerized real estate marketing service is setting the standard of excellence in the marketing industry. Looking for success? Want to get in on the ground floor? Become a part of our team and watch us grow!

HISTORY: . . . . IFA
Established in 1986; . . 1st Franchised in 1988
Company-Owned Units (As of 12/1/1989): . .4
Franchised Units (12/1/1989): 2
Total Units (12/1/1989): 6
Distribution: US-5;Can-0;Overseas-1
North America: . . . . 2 States
Concentration: . . . . 4 in FL, 1 in NH
Registered: . . . . .FL
. . . .
Average # of Employees: . . . . . . 2 FT, 1 PT
Prior Industry Experience: . . . . . . Helpful

FINANCIAL:
Cash Investment: $10-25K
Total Investment: $20-50K
Fees: Franchise - $10-25K
Royalty: 4%, Advert: 2%
Contract Periods (Yrs.): 10/10
Area Development Agreement: Yes/10
Sub-Franchise Contract: . . . . .No
Expand in Territory: . . . . . . Yes
Passive Ownership: . . . Not Allowed
Encourage Conversions: . . . . . .No
Franchisee Purchase(s) Required: .No

FRANCHISOR TRAINING/SUPPORT:
Financial Assistance Provided: . . .Yes(D)
Site Selection Assistance: . . . . . . .Yes
Lease Negotiation Assistance: . . . . .Yes
Co-operative Advertising: . . . . . . .Yes
Training: . . . . . . 2 Wks. Headquarters, 1
. . . . .Wk. On-site, Continuous Support
On-Going Support: . . . . . a,B,C,D,E,H,I
Full-Time Franchisor Support Staff: . . 14
EXPANSION PLANS:
US: . . . . .All US
Canada - Yes, . . . Overseas - Yes

GALLERY OF HOMES

201 S. Orange Ave., P.O. Box 2900
Orlando, FL 32802
TEL: (800) 241-8320 (407) 841-6540
FAX: (407) 841-6543
Mr. Gil De Hamer, VP Natl. Sales

GALLERY OF HOMES is the first real estate franchisor in the US. GALLERY offers its members a full line of products and services to more effectively market residential real estate, including corporate referrals, homefinding, classroom and video-based training, featuring Tom Hopkins, national advertising, business planning, computer services, warranty, E & O insurance, agent insurance and recruiting manuals.

HISTORY: . . . .
Established in 1950; . . 1st Franchised in 1950
Company-Owned Units (As of 12/1/1989): . .0
Franchised Units (12/1/1989): 300
Total Units (12/1/1989): 300
Distribution: US-250;Can-50;Overseas-0
North America: . . . . 4 States
Concentration: . 45 in FL, 25 in MA, 20 in NY
Registered: . . . . All States Except SD
. . . .
Average # of Employees: . . . . 10 FT
Prior Industry Experience: . . . . . .Necessary

FINANCIAL:
Cash Investment: . . . . $3K+
Total Investment: $15-30K
Fees: Franchise - $10-16.9K
  Royalty: 4%, Advert: 2%
Contract Periods (Yrs.): 5/5
Area Development Agreement: . .No
Sub-Franchise Contract: . . . . . Yes
Expand in Territory: . . . . .No
Passive Ownership: . . . Discouraged
Encourage Conversions: . . . . .No
Franchisee Purchase(s) Required: .No

FRANCHISOR TRAINING/SUPPORT:
Financial Assistance Provided: . . .Yes(D)
Site Selection Assistance: . . . . .Yes
Lease Negotiation Assistance: . . . . .No
Co-operative Advertising: . . . . .Yes
Training: . . . . .3-4 Days HQ Orientation,
  . . Video Training + Classroom Training
On-Going Support: . . . . . . b,C,d,G,H,I
Full-Time Franchisor Support Staff: . . 12
EXPANSION PLANS:
US: . . . . All US
Canada - No, ...Overseas - No

HELP-U-SELL

57 W. 200 S.
Salt Lake City, UT 84101
TEL: (800) 366-1177 (801) 355-1177
FAX: (801) 521-6018
Mr. Carter Knapp, VP

Set-fee, full-service real estate counseling. No cold calling, canvassing or holding open houses. Marketing system generates buyer and seller leads.

HISTORY: . . . . IFA
Established in 1976; . . 1st Franchised in 1978
Company-Owned Units (As of 12/1/1989): . .3
Franchised Units (12/1/1989): 522
Total Units (12/1/1989): 525
Distribution: US-501;Can-24;Overseas-0
North America: . . . . 40 States, 4 Provinces
Concentration: . . 252 in CA, 48 in FL, 27 MA
Registered: . . . . .All
. . . .
Average # of Employees: . . . . .6 FT
Prior Industry Experience: . . . . . .Necessary

FINANCIAL:
Cash Investment: . . . . $Varies
Total Investment: . . . . $25K+
Fees: Franchise - $5.5-35K
  Royalty: 7%, Advert: 7%
Contract Periods (Yrs.): 5/5
Area Development Agreement: Yes/Var
Sub-Franchise Contract: . . . . . Yes
Expand in Territory: . . . . Yes
Passive Ownership: . . . Discouraged
Encourage Conversions: . . . . . Yes
Franchisee Purchase(s) Required: Yes

FRANCHISOR TRAINING/SUPPORT:
Financial Assistance Provided: . . .Yes(D)
Site Selection Assistance: . . . . . .Yes
Lease Negotiation Assistance: . . . . . No
Co-operative Advertising: . . . . . . .Yes
Training: . . . . 5 Days Headquarters,
  . . . . 1 Hr. Bi-weekly via Satellite
On-Going Support: . . . . . b,C,D,e,G,H,I
Full-Time Franchisor Support Staff: . . 57
EXPANSION PLANS:
US: . . . . All US
Canada - Yes, . . . Overseas - Yes

HOME CONNECTION

125 Pheasant Run, Continental Center
Newtown, PA 18940
TEL: (215) 860-7060
FAX:
Mr. Bernie Farrell, Fran. Dir.

Complete multi-listing service, specifically designed for owners who sell their own homes.

HISTORY: . . . .
Established in 1987; . . 1st Franchised in 1988
Company-Owned Units (As of 12/1/1989): . .1
Franchised Units (12/1/1989): 1
Total Units (12/1/1989): 2
Distribution: US-2;Can-0;Overseas-0
North America: . . . . .1 State
Concentration: . . . . 1 in PA
Registered: . . . .
. . . .
Average # of Employees: . . . . . 2 FT, 1 PT
Prior Industry Experience: . . . . . .Necessary

FINANCIAL:
Cash Investment: $40-60K
Total Investment: $50-75K
Fees: Franchise - $12-15K
  Royalty: 8%, Advert: 4%
Contract Periods (Yrs.): 10
Area Development Agreement: . .No
Sub-Franchise Contract: . . . . .No
Expand in Territory: . . . . .No
Passive Ownership: . . . Discouraged
Encourage Conversions: . . . . . Yes
Franchisee Purchase(s) Required: .No

FRANCHISOR TRAINING/SUPPORT:
Financial Assistance Provided: . . . . .No
Site Selection Assistance: . . . . .Yes
Lease Negotiation Assistance: . . . . .Yes
Co-operative Advertising: . . . . . . .Yes
Training: . . . . 1 Wk. Headquarters
. . . .
On-Going Support: . . . . b,C,d,e,h,I
Full-Time Franchisor Support Staff: . . .4
EXPANSION PLANS:
US: . . . . All US
Canada - Yes, . . . Overseas - Yes

HOMETREND

P. O. Box 6974
Denver, CO 80206
TEL: (303) 796-8700 C
FAX:
Ms. Amy Trowbridge, Dir. Broker Serv

Real estate management consulting network - complete broker package - including sales and management training, computer with complete software, international/national relocation, home warranties and more.

HISTORY: . . . .
Established in 1981; . . 1st Franchised in 1981
Company-Owned Units (As of 12/1/1989): . .0
Franchised Units (12/1/1989): 54
Total Units (12/1/1989): 54
Distribution: US-54;Can-0;Overseas-0
North America: . . . . 12 States
Concentration: . .13 in CA, 12 in MO , 7 in FL
Registered: . . . . .CA,FL,HI,IN,ND
. . . .
Average # of Employees: . . . . .3 FT
Prior Industry Experience: . . . . Helpful

FINANCIAL: OTC-HOMET
Cash Investment: $1-5K
Total Investment: $9-51K
Fees: Franchise - $7-50K
Royalty: 5%, Advert: 5%
Contract Periods (Yrs.): 3-15
Area Development Agreement: Yes/15
Sub-Franchise Contract: . . . . . Yes
Expand in Territory: . . . . Yes
Passive Ownership: . . . . . .Allowed
Encourage Conversions: . . . . Yes
Franchisee Purchase(s) Required: Yes

FRANCHISOR TRAINING/SUPPORT:
Financial Assistance Provided: . . .Yes(D)
Site Selection Assistance: . . . . . . .Yes
Lease Negotiation Assistance: . . . . .NA
Co-operative Advertising: . . . . .Yes
Training: . . . . 3 Days Headquarters,
. . . . .On-going in District
On-Going Support: . . . A,B,C,D,E,F,G,h
Full-Time Franchisor Support Staff: . . . 3
EXPANSION PLANS:
US: . . . . All US
Canada - Yes, . . . Overseas - Yes

HOUSEMASTER OF AMERICA

421 W. Union Ave.
Bound Brook, NJ 08805
TEL: (800) 526-3939
FAX:
Mr. Robert Hardy, President

A home inspection service catering primarily to home buyers. Appealing to men and women alike who are business or marketing minded. Engineers are readily available to perform the inspections, which are backed by an optional warranty. This is a much-needed service and HOUSEMASTER has a proven format for developing and conducting the business.

HISTORY: . . . . IFA
Established in 1976; . . 1st Franchised in 1979
Company-Owned Units (As of 12/1/1989): . .0
Franchised Units (12/1/1989): 116
Total Units (12/1/1989): 116
Distribution: US-116;Can-0;Overseas-0
North America: . . . . 35 States
Concentration: . . .15 in NJ, 11 in FL, 8 in NY
Registered: . . . . . CA,IL,IN,MD,MN,NY,RI
. . . . .SD,VA,WA,WI
Average # of Employees: . . . . . . 5 FT, 2 PT
Prior Industry Experience: . . . . Helpful

FINANCIAL:
Cash Investment: $20-38K
Total Investment: $27-50K
Fees: Franchise - $17-35K
Royalty: 6%, Advert: 4%
Contract Periods (Yrs.): 10/10
Area Development Agreement: . .No
Sub-Franchise Contract: . . . . .No
Expand in Territory: . . . . . . .No
Passive Ownership: . . . Not Allowed
Encourage Conversions: . . . . . Yes
Franchisee Purchase(s) Required: .No

FRANCHISOR TRAINING/SUPPORT:
Financial Assistance Provided: . . . Yes(I)
Site Selection Assistance: . . . . . . .NA
Lease Negotiation Assistance: . . . . .NA
Co-operative Advertising: . . . . .No
Training: . . . . 1 Wk. Tech., 4 Days Sales
. . . . 1 Day Ops. - Headquarters
On-Going Support: . . . . b,C,G,H,I
Full-Time Franchisor Support Staff: . . 17
EXPANSION PLANS:
US: . . . . All US
Canada - Yes, . . . Overseas - Yes

I LIKE SELLING MY HOUSE SYSTEM

#201 - 1252 Burrard St.
Vancouver, BC V6Z1Z1 CAN
TEL: (604) 687-2900
FAX:
Mr. Donald Burdeny, President

U-sell real estate kits - save seller the real estate commission. Investment of $14,900.

HISTORY: . . . .
Established in 1972; . . 1st Franchised in 1972
Company-Owned Units (As of 12/1/1989): . .1
Franchised Units (12/1/1989): 0
Total Units (12/1/1989): 1
Distribution: US-0;Can-1;Overseas-0
North America: . . . . .1 Province
Concentration: . . . . 1 in BC
Registered: . . . .
. . . .
Average # of Employees: . . . . .5 FT
Prior Industry Experience: . . . . Helpful

FINANCIAL:
Cash Investment: $20K
Total Investment: $25K
Fees: Franchise - $14.9K
Royalty: 0%, Advert: 5%
Contract Periods (Yrs.): 3/3
Area Development Agreement: . Yes
Sub-Franchise Contract: . . . . . Yes
Expand in Territory: . . . . Yes
Passive Ownership: . . . Not Allowed
Encourage Conversions: . . . . . .No
Franchisee Purchase(s) Required: Yes

FRANCHISOR TRAINING/SUPPORT:
Financial Assistance Provided: . . . . .NA
Site Selection Assistance: . . . . . . .NA
Lease Negotiation Assistance: . . . . .NA
Co-operative Advertising: . . . . . . .NA
Training: . . . . 3 Wks. Headquarters
. . . .
On-Going Support: . . . a,B,c,d,E,F,G,H,I
Full-Time Franchisor Support Staff: . . .2
EXPANSION PLANS:
US: . . . . All US
Canada - Yes, ...Overseas - No

KEY ASSOCIATES

P.O. Box 495
Rockport, IN 47635
TEL: (812) 649-9716 C
FAX:
Mr. Don Schulte, President

Program offers low cost, low control system which is adaptable to large or small real estate firms.

HISTORY: . . . .
Established in 1977; . . 1st Franchised in 1978
Company-Owned Units (As of 12/1/1989): . .0
Franchised Units (12/1/1989): 66
Total Units (12/1/1989): 66
Distribution: US-66;Can-0;Overseas-0
North America: . . . . 2 States
Concentration: . . . . 45 in IN, 21 in KY
Registered: . . . . IN
. . . .
Average # of Employees: . . . . . . 1 FT, 1 PT
Prior Industry Experience: . . . . Helpful

FINANCIAL:
Cash Investment: $15K
Total Investment: $15K
Fees: Franchise - $5K
Royalty: Flat Fee, Advert: . . . 1%
Contract Periods (Yrs.): . . . Infinite
Area Development Agreement: Yes/10
Sub-Franchise Contract: . . . . . .No
Expand in Territory: . . . . Yes
Passive Ownership: . . . Discouraged
Encourage Conversions: . . . . . NA
Franchisee Purchase(s) Required: .No

FRANCHISOR TRAINING/SUPPORT:
Financial Assistance Provided: . . .Yes(D)
Site Selection Assistance: . . . . No
Lease Negotiation Assistance: . . . . . No
Co-operative Advertising: . . . . No
Training: . . . . .3 Days Field
. . . .
On-Going Support: . . . . . . b,C,d,G,H,I
Full-Time Franchisor Support Staff: . . .2
EXPANSION PLANS:
US: . . . . Midwest
Canada - No, ...Overseas - No

MORTGAGE SERVICE ASSOCIATES

21 Brock St.
North Haven, CT 06473
TEL: (800) 637-5459 (800) 544-8167
FAX: (203) 787-0114
Mr. Joseph D. Raffone, President

A unique approach to the property preservation, servicing and inspection side of mortgage servicing. Our custom software and intensive marketing effort have resulted in a position of industry leadership and requires local market control through additional franchises. On-going support is guaranteed as clients are common to all franchises. Immediate cash flow.

HISTORY: . . . . .IFA
Established in 1946; . . 1st Franchised in 1986
Company-Owned Units (As of 12/1/1989): . .1
Franchised Units (12/1/1989): 11
Total Units (12/1/1989): 12
Distribution: US-12;Can-0;Overseas-0
North America: . . . . 8 States
Concentration: . . . 3 in TX, 1 in CA, 1 in CO
Registered: . . . . . CA,FL,HI,IL,MI,MN,VA
. . . .
Average # of Employees: . . . . . . 1 FT, 1 PT
Prior Industry Experience: . . . . Helpful

FINANCIAL:
Cash Investment: $26-38K
Total Investment: $26-38K
Fees: Franchise - $26K
Royalty: 5-15%, Advert: . . . Flat
Contract Periods (Yrs.): 5/5
Area Development Agreement: Yes/Var
Sub-Franchise Contract: . . . . .No
Expand in Territory: . . . . .No
Passive Ownership: . . . Discouraged
Encourage Conversions: . . . . . Yes
Franchisee Purchase(s) Required: .No

FRANCHISOR TRAINING/SUPPORT:
Financial Assistance Provided: . . . Yes(I)
Site Selection Assistance: . . . . .Yes
Lease Negotiation Assistance: . . . . .Yes
Co-operative Advertising: . . . . .Yes
Training: . . . . . . 1 Wk. Headquarters, 15
. . . . Hrs. Site, 15 Hrs. Site
On-Going Support: . . . A,B,C,D,E,G,H,I
Full-Time Franchisor Support Staff: . . .8
EXPANSION PLANS:
US: . . . . .All US
Canada - No, ...Overseas - No

NATIONAL BROKERS REGISTRY / NBR

560 Brant St.
Burlington, ON L7R2G8 CAN
TEL: (416) 333-1122 C
FAX: (416) 333-4550
Ms. Lynda D. Prouse, Dir. Mktg.

An NBR Master Franchisee is entitled to contract with other real estate brokers and confer upon them the rights to membership into NBR. The brokers can form their own companies within the Master Franchisee's office or one of their own within the Master Franchisee's territory. The fees charged to them are determined by and paid to the Master Franchisee.

HISTORY: . . . .
Established in 1984; . . 1st Franchised in 1986
Company-Owned Units (As of 12/1/1989): . .0
Franchised Units (12/1/1989): 18
Total Units (12/1/1989): 18
Distribution: US-0;Can-18;Overseas-0
North America: . . . . .1 Province
Concentration: . . . . 18 in ON
Registered: . . . .
. . . .
Average # of Employees: . . . . NA
Prior Industry Experience: . . . . .Necessary

FINANCIAL:
Cash Investment: . . . .$NA
Total Investment: . . . .$NA
Fees: Franchise - $12K
Royalty: $1200/Mo, Advert: Varies
Contract Periods (Yrs.): 5/5
Area Development Agreement: . .No
Sub-Franchise Contract: . . . . . Yes
Expand in Territory: . . . . Yes
Passive Ownership: . . . . . .Allowed
Encourage Conversions: . . . . . Yes
Franchisee Purchase(s) Required: .No

FRANCHISOR TRAINING/SUPPORT:
Financial Assistance Provided: . . . . .No
Site Selection Assistance: . . . . .NA
Lease Negotiation Assistance: . . . . .NA
Co-operative Advertising: . . . . .Yes
Training: . . . . On-going
. . . .
On-Going Support: . . . . B,G,H,I
Full-Time Franchisor Support Staff: . . .1
EXPANSION PLANS:
US: . . . . .No
Canada - Yes, ...Overseas - No

NATIONAL HOUSING INSPECTIONS

1817 North Hills Blvd.
Knoxville, TN 37917
TEL: (615) 525-5017 C
FAX:
Mr. Brad Raney, VP Marketing

NHI is a proven, copyrighted program that allows the franchisee all the benefits of entrepreneurship without the financial risks. With over 350 dealers nationwide, NHI offers protected territories, complete training and set-up, and 20 years of documented success stories. Make or save money with NHI!

HISTORY: . . . .
Established in 1970; . . 1st Franchised in 1970
Company-Owned Units (As of 12/1/1989): . .0
Franchised Units (12/1/1989): 350
Total Units (12/1/1989): 350
Distribution: US-350;Can-0;Overseas-0
North America: . . . . 47 States
Concentration: . 40 in NY, 37 in CA, 27 in OH
Registered: . . . . All Except AB
. . . .
Average # of Employees: . . . . . . 2 FT, 2 PT
Prior Industry Experience: . . . . Helpful

FINANCIAL:
Cash Investment: $100
Total Investment: . . . . $100 + Time
Fees: Franchise - $100
 Royalty: 20%, Advert: 0%
Contract Periods (Yrs.): . .90 Days +
Area Development Agreement: . .No
Sub-Franchise Contract: . . . . .No
Expand in Territory: . . . . Yes
Passive Ownership: . . . Discouraged
Encourage Conversions: . . . . . NA
Franchisee Purchase(s) Required: Yes

FRANCHISOR TRAINING/SUPPORT:
Financial Assistance Provided: . . . . .No
Site Selection Assistance: . . . . .No
Lease Negotiation Assistance: . . . . .No
Co-operative Advertising: . . . . .Yes
Training: . . . .
. . . .
On-Going Support: . . . . D,F,G,I
Full-Time Franchisor Support Staff: . . 10
EXPANSION PLANS:
US: . . . . Various Locations
Canada - No, ...Overseas - No

NATIONAL PROPERTY INSPECTIONS

236 S. 108th Ave., # 3
Omaha, NE 68154
TEL: (800) 333-9807 (402) 333-9807
FAX:
Mr. Roland Bates, President

Home inspection is one of the fastest-growing industries in the country. Few opportunities offer such a large potential for such a small investment ($14,000). No franchisor anywhere will give you more support. Can operate full or part-time. We help you every step of the way.

HISTORY: . . . .
Established in 1987; . . 1st Franchised in 1987
Company-Owned Units (As of 12/1/1989): . .0
Franchised Units (12/1/1989): 37
Total Units (12/1/1989): 37
Distribution: US-37;Can-0;Overseas-0
North America: . . . . 21 States
Concentration: . . . 5 in WI, 4 in CA, 4 in NY
Registered: . . . . All States
. . . .
Average # of Employees: . . . . .1-2 FT
Prior Industry Experience: . . . . Helpful

FINANCIAL:
Cash Investment: $10K
Total Investment: $14K
Fees: Franchise - $10K
 Royalty: 8%, Advert: 0%
Contract Periods (Yrs.): 10/10
Area Development Agreement: . .No
Sub-Franchise Contract: . . . . .No
Expand in Territory: . . . . Yes
Passive Ownership: . . . Discouraged
Encourage Conversions: . . . . . Yes
Franchisee Purchase(s) Required: .No

FRANCHISOR TRAINING/SUPPORT:
Financial Assistance Provided: . . .Yes(D)
Site Selection Assistance: . . . . .NA
Lease Negotiation Assistance: . . . . .NA
Co-operative Advertising: . . . . .NA
Training: . . . . .1 Wk. Headquarters,
. . . .
On-Going Support: . . . . A,B,C,D,G,H,I
Full-Time Franchisor Support Staff: . . .4
EXPANSION PLANS:
US: . . . . .All US
Canada - Yes, ...Overseas - No

RE/MAX INTERNATIONAL

P.O. Box 3907
Englewood, CO 80155
TEL: (800) 525-7452 (303) 770-5531 C
FAX: (303) 220-9534
Mr. Daryl Jesperson, Sr. VP

RE/MAX is an international real estate franchise network. The franchise offered is set up to allow Sales Associates who join a RE/MAX franchise to keep 100% of their commissions. RE/MAX offers to its franchisees training programs, awards banquets, corporate relocation, a referral network, advertising research, company publications, educational seminars and bi-annual conventions.

HISTORY: . . . . IFA
Established in 1973; . . 1st Franchised in 1976
Company-Owned Units (As of 12/1/1989): . .0
Franchised Units (12/1/1989): 1624
Total Units (12/1/1989): 1624
Distribution: . . US-1203;Can-419;Overseas-2
North America: . . . . 49 States,11 Provinces
Concentration: . 203 in ON, 136 in CA, 108 IL
Registered: . . . . .All
. . . .
Average # of Employees: . . . . . . 2 FT, 1 PT
Prior Industry Experience: . . . . Helpful

FINANCIAL:
Cash Investment: $15-25K
Total Investment: $25-100K
Fees: Franchise - $15-25K
 Royalty: Var., Advert: . . . . Var.
Contract Periods (Yrs.): 5/5
Area Development Agreement: Yes/20
Sub-Franchise Contract: . . . . . Yes
Expand in Territory: . . . . Yes
Passive Ownership: . . . Discouraged
Encourage Conversions: . . . . . Yes
Franchisee Purchase(s) Required: .No

FRANCHISOR TRAINING/SUPPORT:
Financial Assistance Provided: . . . Yes(I)
Site Selection Assistance: . . . . . . .Yes
Lease Negotiation Assistance: . . . . .Yes
Co-operative Advertising: . . . . . . .Yes
Training: . . . . . . 40+ Hrs. Headquarters,
. . . . Varies at Site
On-Going Support: . . . . .C,D,E,F,G,H,I
Full-Time Franchisor Support Staff: . . 95
EXPANSION PLANS:
US: . . . . .All US
Canada - Yes, . . . Overseas - Yes

REALTY EXECUTIVES / EXECU*SYSTEMS
4427 N. 36th St.
Phoenix, AZ 85018
TEL: (800) 528-0365 (602) 957-0444 C
FAX: (602) 955-8768
Mr. William Powers, Natl. Mktg. Dir.

REALTY EXECUTIVES is the originator of the "100% commission concept" in real estate, which attracts the top-producing agents in the industry and ends the "revolving door syndrome" that is so common with traditional brokerages.

HISTORY: . . . .
Established in 1965; . . 1st Franchised in 1973
Company-Owned Units (As of 12/1/1989): . . 22
Franchised Units (12/1/1989): 63
Total Units (12/1/1989): 85
Distribution: US-83;Can-2;Overseas-0
 North America: . . . . 22 States, 2 Provinces
 Concentration: . . .38 in AZ, 9 in CA, 6 in TX
Registered: . . . . All Except ND and SD
. . . .
Average # of Employees: . . . . . . 2 FT, 1 PT
Prior Industry Experience: . . . . Helpful

FINANCIAL:
Cash Investment: $15-20K
Total Investment: $15-75K
Fees: Franchise - $15K
 Royalty: Flat, Advert: 0%
Contract Periods (Yrs.): 5/5
Area Development Agreement: . .No
Sub-Franchise Contract: . . . . .No
Expand in Territory: . . . . Yes
Passive Ownership: . . . . . .Allowed
Encourage Conversions: . . . . . Yes
Franchisee Purchase(s) Required: .No

FRANCHISOR TRAINING/SUPPORT:
Financial Assistance Provided: . . .Yes(D)
Site Selection Assistance: . . . . . . .Yes
Lease Negotiation Assistance: . . . .Yes
Co-operative Advertising: . . . . No
Training: . . . . 2 Days Headquarters
. . . .
On-Going Support: . . . . A,B,c,d,e,G,h,I
Full-Time Franchisor Support Staff: . . 6
EXPANSION PLANS:
 US: . . . . .All US
 Canada - Yes, ...Overseas - No

RED CARPET REAL ESTATE SERVICES
4180 Ruffin Rd.
San Diego, CA 92123
TEL: (800) 654-7653 (619) 571-7181
FAX: (619) 277-5352
Mr. J. T. Morgan, EVP

RED CARPET is a full-service real estate franchise, with heavy focus on franchise management systems integrated to computer software for the recruitment and development of sales associates, with complete support through a totally-integrated success system. Master franchising available in some geographic areas.

HISTORY: . . . .
Established in 1966; . . 1st Franchised in 1966
Company-Owned Units (As of 12/1/1989): . .0
Franchised Units (12/1/1989): 450
Total Units (12/1/1989): 450
Distribution: US-430;Can-20;Overseas-0
 North America: . . . . 22 States, 1 Province
 Concentration: . . 165 in CA, 100 in MI, 44 IL
Registered: . . . .CA,FL,HI,IL,IN,MD,MI,NY
. . . . .OR,VA
Average # of Employees: . . . . 50 FT
Prior Industry Experience: . . . . . .Necessary

FINANCIAL: NASD-CHOL
Cash Investment: $10-25K
Total Investment: $15-30K
Fees: Franchise - $9.5K
 Royalty: 8%, Advert: 0%
Contract Periods (Yrs.): 5/5
Area Development Agreement: . .No
Sub-Franchise Contract: . . . . .No
Expand in Territory: . . . . Yes
Passive Ownership: . . . Not Allowed
Encourage Conversions: . . . . . Yes
Franchisee Purchase(s) Required: .No

FRANCHISOR TRAINING/SUPPORT:
Financial Assistance Provided: . . .Yes(D)
Site Selection Assistance: . . . . . . .Yes
Lease Negotiation Assistance: . . . . .No
Co-operative Advertising: . . . . . . .Yes
Training: . . . . 4 Days Headquarters,
. . . . On-going Region
On-Going Support: . . . . .b,C,G,h,I
Full-Time Franchisor Support Staff: . . 20
EXPANSION PLANS:
 US: . . . . .All US
 Canada - Yes, ...Overseas - No

RENET FINANCIAL

2400 E. Katella, # 930
Anaheim, CA 92806
TEL: (714) 385-1244
FAX:
Mr. Tom Van Wagoner, Mktg. Dir.

As franchisor, we provide an extensive loan data network of multiple lenders, both local and national, with a fully-computerized regional loan processing center, including pre-qualification software and TRW access. A 1-week initial training program with continuous support and financing of initial franchise fee.

HISTORY: . . . .
Established in 1988; . . 1st Franchised in 1988
Company-Owned Units (As of 12/1/1989): . .0
Franchised Units (12/1/1989): 22
Total Units (12/1/1989): 22
Distribution: US-22;Can-0;Overseas-0
 North America: . . . . .1 State
 Concentration: . . . . 22 in CA
Registered: . . . . CA
. . . .
Average # of Employees: . . . . .1 FT
Prior Industry Experience: . . . . Helpful

FINANCIAL:
Cash Investment: $5.9-6.5K
Total Investment: $6.4-11.5K
Fees: Franchise - $5.9-6.4K
 Royalty: 15%, Advert: 0%
Contract Periods (Yrs.): 7/7
Area Development Agreement: Yes/7
Sub-Franchise Contract: . . . . .No
Expand in Territory: . . . . Yes
Passive Ownership: . . . . . .Allowed
Encourage Conversions: . . . . . Yes
Franchisee Purchase(s) Required: .No

FRANCHISOR TRAINING/SUPPORT:
Financial Assistance Provided: . . .Yes(D)
Site Selection Assistance: . . . . . . .No
Lease Negotiation Assistance: . . . . .No
Co-operative Advertising: . . . . . . .No
Training: . . . . . . 1 Wk. Regional Office
. . . .
On-Going Support: . . . . .a,H
Full-Time Franchisor Support Staff: . . . 8
EXPANSION PLANS:
 US: . . . . . CA, Northwest & Southwest
 Canada - No, ...Overseas - No

RENTMASTER PROPERTY MANAGEMENT
170 N. Holmes Ave.
Idaho Falls, ID 83401
TEL: (208) 523-0039
FAX:
Mr. Brent J. Hart, Natl. Sales Mgr.

RENTMASTER is a real estate franchise, specializing in full-service property management. In addition, RENTMASTER offers a computerized rental catalogue and a rental agency service.

HISTORY: . . . .
Established in 1985; . . 1st Franchised in 1988
Company-Owned Units (As of 12/1/1989): . . 1
Franchised Units (12/1/1989): 6
Total Units (12/1/1989): 7
Distribution: US-7;Can-0;Overseas-0
North America: . . . . 4 States
Concentration: . . . . 3 in ID, 2 in UT, 1 in NV
Registered: . . . . CA,FL,OR,SD
. . . .
Average # of Employees: . . . . . . 2 FT, 1 PT
Prior Industry Experience: . . . . Helpful

FINANCIAL:
Cash Investment: $30-35K
Total Investment: $30-35K
Fees: Franchise - $20K
Royalty: 5%, Advert: 2%
Contract Periods (Yrs.): 5/5
Area Development Agreement: . .No
Sub-Franchise Contract: . . . . .No
Expand in Territory: . . . . . . .No
Passive Ownership: . . . . .Allowed
Encourage Conversions: . . . . Yes
Franchisee Purchase(s) Required: .No

FRANCHISOR TRAINING/SUPPORT:
Financial Assistance Provided: . . . . .No
Site Selection Assistance: . . . . . . .Yes
Lease Negotiation Assistance: . . . . .Yes
Co-operative Advertising: . . . . No
Training: . . . . . . 3 Days Headquarters

On-Going Support: . . . . . . C,D,E,G,h,i
Full-Time Franchisor Support Staff: . . . 4
EXPANSION PLANS:
US: . . . . All US
Canada - No, ...Overseas - No

ROOM-MATE REFERRAL SERVICE CENTERS
P. O. Box 760328
Oklahoma City, OK 73176
TEL: (405) 636-0625 C
FAX:
Ms. Florence S. Cook, CEO

A service company that handles the placement of persons as roommates for economic and a variety of other needs.

HISTORY: . . . ; . . . .
Established in 1979; . . 1st Franchised in 1985
Company-Owned Units (As of 12/1/1989): . . 1
Franchised Units (12/1/1989): 17
Total Units (12/1/1989): 18
Distribution: US-18;Can-0;Overseas-0
North America: . . . . 6 States
Concentration: . . . 4 in PA, 4 in GA, 4 in TX
Registered: . . . .
. . . .
Average # of Employees: . . . . .1 PT
Prior Industry Experience: . . . . Helpful

FINANCIAL:
Cash Investment: $3-15K
Total Investment: $10-25K
Fees: Franchise - $7.5-15K
Royalty: 5%, Advert: 1%
Contract Periods (Yrs.): . . . 10/10
Area Development Agreement: . .No
Sub-Franchise Contract: . . . . Yes
Expand in Territory: . . . . . . Yes
Passive Ownership: . . . Discouraged
Encourage Conversions: . . . . Yes
Franchisee Purchase(s) Required: .No

FRANCHISOR TRAINING/SUPPORT:
Financial Assistance Provided: . . .Yes(D)
Site Selection Assistance: . . . . . . .Yes
Lease Negotiation Assistance: . . . .Yes
Co-operative Advertising: . . . . . . .Yes
Training: . . . . .3-5 Days Franchisee Area
. . . .
On-Going Support: . . . . . . D,e,G,H,i
Full-Time Franchisor Support Staff: . . . .
EXPANSION PLANS:
US: . . . . All US
Canada - Yes, . . . Overseas - Yes

WATERMASTER AMERICA

1255 N. High St.
Columbus, OH 43201
TEL: (800) 444-WATER (614) 291-3141
FAX:
Mr. Jack Bernstein, Fran. Dir.

WATERMASTER AMERICA provides sub-metering services for owners of apartments, shopping centers, mobile home parks, offices and condos. The service includes installation, reading and billing of individual sub-meters, resulting in the elimination of the property owner's water/service expenses.

HISTORY: . . . .
Established in 1987; . . 1st Franchised in 1987
Company-Owned Units (As of 12/1/1989): . . 1
Franchised Units (12/1/1989): 2
Total Units (12/1/1989): 3
Distribution: US-3;Can-0;Overseas-0
North America: . . . . .1 State
Concentration: . . . . 3 in OH
Registered: . . . .
. . . .
Average # of Employees: . . . . .1 FT
Prior Industry Experience: . . . . Helpful

FINANCIAL:
Cash Investment: . . . .$None
Total Investment: . . . .$None
Fees: Franchise - . . . .$None
Royalty: 5%, Advert: 1%
Contract Periods (Yrs.): 10/10
Area Development Agreement: . .No
Sub-Franchise Contract: . . . . .No
Expand in Territory: . . . . . . Yes
Passive Ownership: . . . Discouraged
Encourage Conversions: . . . . . NA
Franchisee Purchase(s) Required: Yes

FRANCHISOR TRAINING/SUPPORT:
Financial Assistance Provided: . . . . .NA
Site Selection Assistance: . . . . . . .NA
Lease Negotiation Assistance: . . . .NA
Co-operative Advertising: . . . . . . .NA
Training: . . . . 1 Wk. Headquarters
. . . .
On-Going Support: . . . . . .A,C,D,G,H,I
Full-Time Franchisor Support Staff: . . 3
EXPANSION PLANS:
US: . . . . All US
Canada - No, ... Overseas - No

SUPPLEMENTAL LISTING OF FRANCHISORS

ALTUS MORTGAGE USA .1110 Montlimar Dr., # 300, Mobile AL 36609
ANCHOR HOME MARKETING CONSULTANTS . . . . .1881 Yonge St., Toronto ON M4S1Y6 CAN
BETTER HOMES REALTY/BETHOM . . . . .1556 Parkside Dr., P. O. Box 8181, Walnut Creek CA 94596
BUSINESS BROKERS/HAWAII . . . . 2395 S. Kihei Rd., # 206, Kihei HI 96753
BUYER'S MARKET REALTY . . . . 10 Kerr St., Mississauga ON L5M1T8 CAN
CENTURY 21 REAL ESTATE CANADA . . . . . . 10551 Shellbridge Way, #135, Richmond BC V6X2W9 CAN
CHERRYHILL HOMEMARKETING CONSULTANTS . . . . .27 Bennett Ave., Guelph ON N1E2C6 CAN
COMPUFUND NATIONAL MORTGAGE NETWORK . . 3860 Blackhawk Rd., # 160, Danville CA 94506
COMPUSEARCH . . . . 330 Front St. W., # 1100, Toronto ON M5V3B7 CAN
COMREAL . . . . .8725 NW 18th Terrace, # 200, Miami FL 33172
CONDOTELS . . . . 2703 Hwy. 17 S., N. Myrtle Beach SC 29582
DISCOUNT REALTY INTERNATIONAL . . . . .P.O. Box 7836, Thousand Oaks CA 91360
EARL KEIM REALTY . . . . .1740 W. Big Beaver, # 200, Troy MI 48084
EGAL-AMERICA'S HOME INSPECTION SERVICE . . . . .12345 W. 95th St., # 203, Lenaxa KS 66215
EXTENDED SERVICE OF AMERICA . . . . .P.O. Box 566396, Atlanta GA 30356
FINANCIAL PARTNERS INTERNATIONAL . . . . 625 Broadway, # 1111, San Diego CA 92101
HEIMER INSPECTIONS . . . . 1923 New York Ave., Huntington Station NY 11746
HELP-U-SELL . . . . 57 W. 200 South, Salt Lake City UT 84101
HELP-U-SELL CANADA . . . . 4230, boul. St-Jean, # 104, Dollard des Ormeaux PQ H9H3X4 CAN
HMS FRANCHISEES .17350 W. 10 Mile Rd., # 103, Southfield MI 48075
HOMEOWNERS CONCEPT . . . . 3508 W. Galbraith Rd., Cincinnati OH 45239
HOMETREND . . . . .3600 S. Beeler St., # 300, Denver CO 80237
INCOME SYSTEMS INTERNATIONAL . . . . .1500 E. Chevy Chase Dr., # 201, Glendale CA 91206
NATIONAL NETWORK OF DISCOUNT BROKERS 1865 Lakeshore Rd. W, #202, Mississauga ON L5J1J6 CAN
NATIONAL TENANT NETWORK . . . . .P.O. Box 1664, Lake Grove OR 97035
PEACHTREE HOE MARKETING CONSULTANTS . . . . . . .200 Bond St W., # 5, Oshawa ON L1J2L7 CAN
PROPERTY INSPECTION SERVICE . . . . 1741 Saratoga Ave., # 106, San Jose CA 95129
PROPERTY TAX USA . . . . P.O. Box 15448, Baton Rouge LA 70895
RADON DETECTION SERVICES . . . . P.O. Box 419, Route 179, Ringoes NJ 08551
REAL ESTATE ONE . . . . .725 S. Garfield Ave., Traverse City MI 49684
REALTY 500 . . . . 1539 Vassar St., # 101, Reno NV 89502
REALTY WORLD . . . . 12500 Fair Lakes Circle, # 300, Fairfax VA 22033
REALTY WORLD CANADA . . . . 430 - 6450 Roberts St., Burnaby BC V5G4E1 CAN
RENTAL SOLUTIONS . . . . 273 W. 500 South, # 21, Bountiful UT 84010
RESIDENTIAL BUILDING INSPECTORS . . . . .701 Fairway Dr., Clayton NC 27520
SHOWN BY OWNER . . . . .10398 E. 21st St., Tulsa OK 74129
STATE WIDE REAL ESTATE SERVICES . . . . .P.O. Box 297, Escanaba MI 49829
SUPER MANAGEMENT SERVICES . . . . 1935 Friendship Dr., El Cajon CA 92020

CHAPTER 34

RECREATION AND ENTERTAINMENT

AMERICAN POOLPLAYERS ASSOCIATION
1000 Lake St. Louis Blvd., # 325
Lake St. Louis, MO 63367
TEL: (314) 625-8611
FAX:
Mr. Phil Martin, Dir. Mktg.

AMERICAN POOLPLAYERS ASSOCIATION franchisees own and operate a nationwide network of amateur billiard leagues. The year-round format, handicap system and higher level tournament structure have broad appeal to players of all abilities. The APA is recognized as the "World's Largest Pool League" in the USA.

HISTORY: . . . .
Established in 1980; . . 1st Franchised in 1982
Company-Owned Units (As of 12/1/1989): . .0
Franchised Units (12/1/1989): 167
Total Units (12/1/1989): 167
Distribution: US-153;Can-14;Overseas-0
  North America: . . . . 42 States, 5 Provinces
  Concentration: . 15 in OH, 14 in IL, 10 in MO
Registered: . . . . All States

. . . .
Average # of Employees: . . . . . . 1 FT, 1 PT
Prior Industry Experience: . . . . Helpful

FINANCIAL:
Cash Investment: $7.5K
Total Investment: $7.5K
Fees: Franchise - $0
  Royalty: 25%, Advert: 0%
Contract Periods (Yrs.): 5/5
Area Development Agreement: Yes/5
Sub-Franchise Contract: . . . . . .No
Expand in Territory: . . . . . . Yes
Passive Ownership: . . . Discouraged
Encourage Conversions: . . . . .No
Franchisee Purchase(s) Required: .No

FRANCHISOR TRAINING/SUPPORT:
Financial Assistance Provided: . . . . . No
Site Selection Assistance: . . . . .NA
Lease Negotiation Assistance: . . . . .NA
Co-operative Advertising: . . . . .NA
Training: . . . . 3 Days Headquarters
. . . .
On-Going Support: . . . . C,D,G,H,I
Full-Time Franchisor Support Staff: . . 22
EXPANSION PLANS:
US: . . . . All US
  Canada - Yes, ... Overseas - No

RECREATION, ENTERTAINMENT & TRAVEL

	1988	1989	1990	Percentage Change 1988-1989	Percentage Change 1989-1990
Number of Establishments:					
Company–Owned	395	407	438	3.0%	7.6%
Franchisee–Owned	8,381	9,139	9,906	9.0%	8.4%
Total	8,776	9,546	10,344	8.8%	8.4%
% of Total Establishments:					
Company–Owned	4.5%	4.3%	4.2%		
Franchisee–Owned	95.5%	95.7%	95.8%		
Total	100.0%	100.0%	100.0%		
Annual Sales ($000):					
Company–Owned	$671,536	$714,258	$761,276	6.4%	6.6%
Franchisee–Owned	2,871,485	3,356,123	3,959,834	16.9%	18.0%
Total	3,543,021	4,070,381	4,721,110	14.9%	16.0%
% of Total Sales:					
Company–Owned	19.0%	17.5%	16.1%		
Franchisee–Owned	81.0%	82.5%	83.9%		
Total	100.0%	100.0%	100.0%		
Average Sales Per Unit ($000):					
Company–Owned	$1,700	$1,755	$1,738	3.2%	–1.0%
Franchisee–Owned	343	367	400	7.2%	8.9%
Total	404	426	456	5.6%	7.0%
Sales Ratio	496.2%	477.9%	434.8%		

	1st Quartile	Median	4th Quartile
Average 1988 Total Investment:			
Company–Owned	$60,000	$100,000	$200,000
Franchisee–Owned	70,000	100,000	125,000
Single Unit Franchise Fee	$10,000	$22,500	$27,500
Multiple Unit Franchise Fee	N. A.	N. A.	N. A.
Franchisee Start–up Cost	30,000	49,500	57,500

	1988	Employees/Unit	Sales/Employee
Employment:			
Company–Owned	2,927	7.4	$229,428
Franchisee–Owned	29,834	3.6	96,249
Total	32,761	3.7	108,148
Employee Performance Ratios		208.2%	238.4%

Source: Franchising In The Economy, 1988 – 1990, IFA Education Foundation & Horwath International, Published January, 1990.

1) 1989 and 1990 data were estimated by respondents.

ATEC GRAND SLAM U.S.A.

115 Post St., P.O. Box 1317
Santa Cruz, CA 95061
TEL: (800) 547-6273 (408) 425-1484 C
FAX:
Mr. Dave Shepard, Franchise Coord.

ATEC GRAND SLAM U.S.A. is the only known franchisor of baseball and softball automated batting ranges and training academies. Our state-of-the-art training equipment can be used indoors or outdoors and ATEC's Casey. Hummer Pitching Machines are used by all 26 Major League Baseball teams.

HISTORY: . . . . IFA
Established in 1976; . . 1st Franchised in 1982
Company-Owned Units (As of 12/1/1989): . . 0
Franchised Units (12/1/1989): 79
Total Units (12/1/1989): 79
Distribution: US-78;Can-1;Overseas-0
North America: . . . . 30 States, 1 Province
Concentration: . . . 9 in CA, 8 in PA, 8 in NY
Registered: . . . CA,HI,IL,IN,MD,MI,MN,NY
. . . . .RI,VA,WA,,WI,AB
Average # of Employees: . . . . . . 3 FT, 2 PT
Prior Industry Experience: . . . . Helpful

FINANCIAL:
Cash Investment: . . . .$
Total Investment: $60-150K
Fees: Franchise - $3-12K
 Royalty: 6%, Advert: 8%
Contract Periods (Yrs.): 10/10
Area Development Agreement: Yes/Var
Sub-Franchise Contract: . . . . . Yes
Expand in Territory: . . . . . . .No
Passive Ownership: . . . Discouraged
Encourage Conversions: . . . . . Yes
Franchisee Purchase(s) Required: .No

FRANCHISOR TRAINING/SUPPORT:
Financial Assistance Provided: . . . . .No
Site Selection Assistance: . . . . . . .Yes
Lease Negotiation Assistance: . . . . .Yes
Co-operative Advertising: . . . . . . .Yes
Training: . . . . . .3 Days Clackamas, OR,
. . . . . On-going at Site & Headquarters
On-Going Support: . . . . . b,C,D,E,G,h,I
Full-Time Franchisor Support Staff: . . 65
EXPANSION PLANS:
US: . . . . .All US
Canada - Yes, . . . Overseas - Yes

CHAMPIONSHIP MINIATURE GOLF

1506 W. College Ave.
State College, PA 16801
TEL: (814) 238-4653
FAX:
Mr. Kevin M. Ream, President

Designers, builders, developers and franchisors of elaborate miniature golf facilities. Courses are designed incorporating beautiful landscaping, realistic holes, spectacular water features (fountains, water falls, streams). Services include feasibility study, site evaluation, all aspects of design (building, course, parking), construction, training and complete on-going and operational assistance.

HISTORY: . . . .
Established in 1984; . . 1st Franchised in 1987
Company-Owned Units (As of 12/1/1989): . .2
Franchised Units (12/1/1989): 3
Total Units (12/1/1989): 5
Distribution: US-5;Can-0;Overseas-0
North America: . . . . 2 States
Concentration: . . . . 2 in PA, 3 in MD
Registered: . . . . FL,HI,MD,OR,VA
. . . .
Average # of Employees: . . . . . . 2 FT, 4 PT
Prior Industry Experience: . . . . . . Helpful

FINANCIAL:
Cash Investment: $20-35K
Total Investment: $115-250K
Fees: Franchise - $10K
 Royalty: 4%, Advert: 2%
Contract Periods (Yrs.): 10/5
Area Development Agreement: Yes/Var
Sub-Franchise Contract: . . . . .No
Expand in Territory: . . . . . . Yes
Passive Ownership: . . . Discouraged
Encourage Conversions: . . . . . Yes
Franchisee Purchase(s) Required: Yes

FRANCHISOR TRAINING/SUPPORT:
Financial Assistance Provided: . . . Yes(I)
Site Selection Assistance: . . . . . . .Yes
Lease Negotiation Assistance: . . . . .Yes
Co-operative Advertising: . . . . . . .Yes
Training: . . . . 1 Wk. Site
. . . .
On-Going Support: . . A,B,C,D,E,F,G,H,I
Full-Time Franchisor Support Staff: . . . 4
EXPANSION PLANS:
US: . . . . Northeast
Canada - No, ...Overseas - No

CINEMA 'N' DRAFTHOUSE

2204 N. Druid Hills Rd.
Atlanta, GA 30329
TEL: (404) 633-8988
FAX:
Mr. John Duffy, VP

CINEMA 'N' DRAFTHOUSE is a multi-media movie theatre/restaurant entertainment center . . .offering current movie releases while in an art deco atmosphere, offering light menu items . . .along with ideal setting for conference/meeting setting for daytime use.

HISTORY: . . . . IFA
Established in 1975; . . 1st Franchised in 1982
Company-Owned Units (As of 12/1/1989): . .7
Franchised Units (12/1/1989): 31
Total Units (12/1/1989): 38
Distribution: US-38;Can-0;Overseas-0
North America: . . . . 8 States
Concentration: . . . 8 in FL, 5 in GA, 3 in CA
Registered: . . .CA,FL,IN,MD,MI,MN,VA,WI
. . . .
Average # of Employees: . . . . . . 1 FT, 10 PT
Prior Industry Experience: . . . . Helpful

FINANCIAL:
Cash Investment: $200K
Total Investment: $400K
Fees: Franchise - $25K
 Royalty: 3%, Advert: 1%
Contract Periods (Yrs.): 10/10
Area Development Agreement: Yes/10
Sub-Franchise Contract: . . . . . Yes
Expand in Territory: . . . . . . Yes
Passive Ownership: . . . . . .Allowed
Encourage Conversions: . . . . . Yes
Franchisee Purchase(s) Required: Yes

FRANCHISOR TRAINING/SUPPORT:
Financial Assistance Provided: . . . . .No
Site Selection Assistance: . . . . . . .Yes
Lease Negotiation Assistance: . . . . .Yes
Co-operative Advertising: . . . . . . .NA
Training: . . . . 1-2 Wks. Atlanta,
. . . . 1-2 Wks. Dallas
On-Going Support: . . . . . C,d,E,F,G,h,i
Full-Time Franchisor Support Staff: . . 10
EXPANSION PLANS:
US: . . . . . . All Metro areas over 500K
Canada - No, ...Overseas - No

CLUB NAUTICO

5450 NW 33rd Ave., # 106
Ft. Lauderdale, FL 33309
TEL: (800)628-8426 (800)262-8736(FL)
FAX: (305) 739-9892
Mr. Nino Martini, President

Powerboat rental operation and boating club. Franchisee maintains fleet of boats and sells memberships. Members receive preferential rates at all CLUB NAUTICO locations.

HISTORY: . . . .
Established in 1986; . . 1st Franchised in 1986
Company-Owned Units (As of 12/1/1989): . 13
Franchised Units (12/1/1989): 49
Total Units (12/1/1989): 62
Distribution: US-62;Can-0;Overseas-0
North America: . . . . 13 States
Concentration: . . . 38 in FL, 5 in CA, 4 in TX
Registered: . . . . All States
. . . .
Average # of Employees: . . . . . . 3 FT, 1 PT
Prior Industry Experience: . . . . Helpful

FINANCIAL:
Cash Investment: $65-98K
Total Investment: $65-98K
Fees: Franchise - $25K
  Royalty: 10%, Advert: 2%
Contract Periods (Yrs.): 5/5
Area Development Agreement: . .No
Sub-Franchise Contract: . . . . .No
Expand in Territory: . . . . Yes
Passive Ownership: . . . Not Allowed
Encourage Conversions: . . . . . Yes
Franchisee Purchase(s) Required: Yes

FRANCHISOR TRAINING/SUPPORT:
Financial Assistance Provided: . . . Yes(I)
Site Selection Assistance: . . . . . . (.Yes
Lease Negotiation Assistance: . . . . .Yes
Co-operative Advertising: . . . . .Yes
Training: . . . . .1 Wk. Headquarters,
  . . . . 1 Wk. Site
On-Going Support: . . . A,B,C,D,E,G,H,I
Full-Time Franchisor Support Staff: . . 21
EXPANSION PLANS:
US: . . . . .All US
Canada - No, ...Overseas - No

CLUB NAUTIQUE

1150 Ballena Blvd., # 161
Alameda, CA 94501
TEL: (800) 343-SAIL (415) 865-4700
FAX:
Mr. Don Durant, President

CLUB NAUTIQUE is uniquely positioned to capitalize on the growing sailboat rental and sailing school business. Clubs sell memberships, lessons, charters and boats and enjoys a broad profit base.

HISTORY: . . . .
Established in 1980; . . 1st Franchised in 1986
Company-Owned Units (As of 12/1/1989): . .2
Franchised Units (12/1/1989): 0
Total Units (12/1/1989): 2
Distribution: US-2;Can-0;Overseas-0
North America: . . . . .1 State
Concentration: . . . . 2 in CA
Registered: . . . .
. . . .
Average # of Employees: . . . . . 3 FT, 3-6 PT
Prior Industry Experience: . . . . Helpful

FINANCIAL:
Cash Investment: $30-60K
Total Investment: $50-100K
Fees: Franchise - $25K
  Royalty: 8%, Advert: 2%
Contract Periods (Yrs.): 10/10
Area Development Agreement: . .No
Sub-Franchise Contract: . . . . .No
Expand in Territory: . . . . Yes
Passive Ownership: . . . Discouraged
Encourage Conversions: . . . . . Yes
Franchisee Purchase(s) Required: .No

FRANCHISOR TRAINING/SUPPORT:
Financial Assistance Provided: . . . . .No
Site Selection Assistance: . . . . . . .Yes
Lease Negotiation Assistance: . . . .Yes
Co-operative Advertising: . . . . . . .Yes
Training: . . . . . . 3-6 Wks. Headquarters
. . . .
On-Going Support: . . . . . B,C,d,E,G,H,I
Full-Time Franchisor Support Staff: . . 12
EXPANSION PLANS:
US: . . . . West Coast
Canada - No, ...Overseas - No

COMPLETE MUSIC

8317 Cass
Omaha, NE 68114
TEL: (800) 843-3866 (402) 391-4847
FAX:
Mr. Gerald Maas, President

COMPLETE MUSIC is the country's largest D. J. entertainment franchise. Owners need not be entertainers, but should show a strong aptitude in sales and management. To those who qualify, we offer an exciting opportunity to be part of a fun and entertaining franchise.

HISTORY: . . . . .WIF
Established in 1976; . . 1st Franchised in 1981
Company-Owned Units (As of 12/1/1989): . .2
Franchised Units (12/1/1989): 55
Total Units (12/1/1989): 57
Distribution: US-57;Can-0;Overseas-0
North America: . . . .
Concentration: . . . 9 in NE, 7 in KS, 4 in OH
Registered: . . .CA,FL,IL,IN,MD,MN,MI,MN
. . . . .SD
Average # of Employees: . . . . .1 PT
Prior Industry Experience: . . . . Helpful

FINANCIAL:
Cash Investment: $15-25K
Total Investment: $15-25K
Fees: Franchise - $13.5K
  Royalty: 8%, Advert: 2%
Contract Periods (Yrs.): . . . . Lease
Area Development Agreement: . .No
Sub-Franchise Contract: . . . . .No
Expand in Territory: . . . . Yes
Passive Ownership: . . . Not Allowed
Encourage Conversions: . . . . .No
Franchisee Purchase(s) Required: .No

FRANCHISOR TRAINING/SUPPORT:
Financial Assistance Provided: . . .Yes(D)
Site Selection Assistance: . . . . .NA
Lease Negotiation Assistance: . . . . .NA
Co-operative Advertising: . . . . .Yes
Training: . . . . . . 10 Days Headquarters,
. . . . 4 Days Franchisee City
On-Going Support: . . . A,B,c,D,E,F,G,h
Full-Time Franchisor Support Staff: . . .5
EXPANSION PLANS:
US: . . . . Northwest
Canada - No, ...Overseas - No

GOLFUN

31531 1st Ave. S.
Federal Way, WA 98003
TEL: (206) 941-8933 C
FAX:
Mr. Jim Contini, VP

GOLFUN, a new family recreation, is played like a conventional golf game, but uses a "Big Ball" (approximately the size of a grapefruit) on a beautiful, fully-landscaped course constructed on only 6 1/2 acres.

HISTORY: . . . .
Established in 1985; . . 1st Franchised in 1988
Company-Owned Units (As of 12/1/1989): . . 1
Franchised Units (12/1/1989): 2
Total Units (12/1/1989): 3
Distribution: US-3;Can-0;Overseas-0
  North America: . . . . 3 States
  Concentration: . . . 1 in WA, 1 in TX, 1 in FL
Registered: . . . .
. . . .
Average # of Employees: . . . . . . 2 FT, 2 PT
Prior Industry Experience: . . . . Helpful

FINANCIAL:
Cash Investment: . . . . $300K+Land
Total Investment: . . . . . $.3-1.5MM
Fees: Franchise - $38.5K
  Royalty: 7%, Advert: 1%
Contract Periods (Yrs.): . . . 20/20
Area Development Agreement: Yes/20
Sub-Franchise Contract: . . . . .No
Expand in Territory: . . . . Yes
Passive Ownership: . . . . . .Allowed
Encourage Conversions: . . . . . Yes
Franchisee Purchase(s) Required: Yes

FRANCHISOR TRAINING/SUPPORT:
Financial Assistance Provided: . . . . . No
Site Selection Assistance: . . . . .Yes
Lease Negotiation Assistance: . . . . .Yes
Co-operative Advertising: . . . . No
Training: . . . . 5 Days Seattle, WA
. . . .
On-Going Support: . . . a,b,C,D,E,F,G,h,I
Full-Time Franchisor Support Staff: . . . 3
EXPANSION PLANS:
US: . . . . .All US
Canada - Yes, . . . Overseas - Yes

MINI-PUTT INTERNATIONAL

6135 Metropolitan Blvd. E.,
St-Leonard, PQ H1P1X7 CAN
TEL: (514) 323-9864
FAX: (514) 323-9938
Mr. Raymond Longtin, VP Sales

MINI-PUTT INTERNATIONAL offers 20 years' experience in evaluating, constructing and managing miniature golf operations. Our leadership is known throughout Quebec and Canada. Our expertise will give you what you are looking for - protected area, training programs, promotional support, competition activities and recognition.

HISTORY: . . . . .CFA
Established in 1971; . . 1st Franchised in 1971
Company-Owned Units (As of 12/1/1989): . .0
Franchised Units (12/1/1989): 35
Total Units (12/1/1989): 35
Distribution: US-0;Can-35;Overseas-0
  North America: . . . . .1 Province
  Concentration: . . . . .35 in PQ
Registered: . . . .
. . . .
Average # of Employees: . . . . .3 FT
Prior Industry Experience: . . . . Helpful

FINANCIAL:
Cash Investment: $30K
Total Investment: $150K
Fees: Franchise - $30K
  Royalty: 5,000/Yr, Advert: 3,000/Yr
Contract Periods (Yrs.): 5/5
Area Development Agreement: . .No
Sub-Franchise Contract: . . . . .No
Expand in Territory: . . . . Yes
Passive Ownership: . . . Discouraged
Encourage Conversions: . . . . . Yes
Franchisee Purchase(s) Required: Yes

FRANCHISOR TRAINING/SUPPORT:
Financial Assistance Provided: . . . Yes(I)
Site Selection Assistance: . . . . .Yes
Lease Negotiation Assistance: . . . . . No
Co-operative Advertising: . . . . .Yes
Training: . . . . 7 Days Headquarters
. . . .
On-Going Support: . . . . . B,C,D,E,G,H
Full-Time Franchisor Support Staff: . . . 7
EXPANSION PLANS:
US: . . . . .All US
Canada - Yes, ...Overseas - No

PAY 'N PLAY RAQUETBALL OF AMERICA

23165 Vista Way
El Toro, CA 92630
TEL: (714) 951-3991
FAX: (714) 451-3991
Mr. Bill McClintock, Fran. Devel.

PAY 'N PLAY RACQUETBALL OF AMERICA develops and franchises automated racquetball centers. Computerized court controller units dispense court time to the public. No memberships, monthly dues or reservations. Franchise owner spends approximately 5 hours per week at center. No employees needed, all cash business. Great second business.

HISTORY: . . . .
Established in 1979; . . 1st Franchised in 1986
Company-Owned Units (As of 12/1/1989): . .4
Franchised Units (12/1/1989): 15
Total Units (12/1/1989): 19
Distribution: US-19;Can-0;Overseas-0
  North America: . . . . 3 States
  Concentration: . . 14 in CA, 4 in OR, 1 in WA
Registered: . . . . .CA,OR,WA
. . . .
Average # of Employees: . . . . . . 0 FT, 0 PT
Prior Industry Experience: . . . . Helpful

FINANCIAL:
Cash Investment: $38-68K
Total Investment: $38-68K
Fees: Franchise - $30-60K
  Royalty: 10%, Advert: . . . 2.5%
Contract Periods (Yrs.): 10/5/5
Area Development Agreement: . .No
Sub-Franchise Contract: . . . . .No
Expand in Territory: . . . . Yes
Passive Ownership: . . . Discouraged
Encourage Conversions: . . . . . Yes
Franchisee Purchase(s) Required: .No

FRANCHISOR TRAINING/SUPPORT:
Financial Assistance Provided: . . . Yes(I)
Site Selection Assistance: . . . . .Yes
Lease Negotiation Assistance: . . . . .NA
Co-operative Advertising: . . . . .Yes
Training: . . . . 3 Days Headquarters
. . . .
On-Going Support: . . . . . A,C,D,e,G,H,I
Full-Time Franchisor Support Staff: . . . 2
EXPANSION PLANS:
US: . . . . West
Canada - No, ...Overseas - No

SELECTRA-DATE

2175 Lemoine Ave
Fort Lee, NJ 07024
TEL: (201) 461-8401
FAX:
Mr. Robert Friedman, President

SELECTRA-DATE is a computerized social introduction service that has been going strong for over 20 years. No direct experience is required, as all processing is done by the home office. There is almost no franchisee turn-over and some regions are still open.

HISTORY: . . . .
Established in 1966; . . 1st Franchised in 1967
Company-Owned Units (As of 12/1/1989): . .3
Franchised Units (12/1/1989): 7
Total Units (12/1/1989): 10
Distribution: US-10;Can-0;Overseas-0
  North America: . . . . 6 States
  Concentration: . . . 2 in CA, 2 in TX, 2 in PA
Registered: . . . .
. . . .
Average # of Employees: . . . . . . 1 FT, 1 PT
Prior Industry Experience: . . . . . . Helpful

FINANCIAL:
Cash Investment: $5-8K
Total Investment: $8-15K
Fees: Franchise - $5K
  Royalty: 10%, Advert: 0%
Contract Periods (Yrs.): . . . . . Inf.
Area Development Agreement: . .No
Sub-Franchise Contract: . . . . .No
Expand in Territory: . . . . . . .No
Passive Ownership: . . . Discouraged
Encourage Conversions: . . . . .No
Franchisee Purchase(s) Required: .No

FRANCHISOR TRAINING/SUPPORT:
Financial Assistance Provided: . . .Yes(D)
Site Selection Assistance: . . . . . . .Yes
Lease Negotiation Assistance: . . . . .Yes
Co-operative Advertising: . . . . .No
Training: . . . . .1 Wk. Site
. . . .
On-Going Support: . . . . . .A,B,C,D,E,I
Full-Time Franchisor Support Staff: . . .3
EXPANSION PLANS:
US: . . . . Large Cities
Canada - No, ...Overseas - No

SPORTSMAN'S CLUB INTERNATIONAL

30 W. Stauffer Ln.
Murray, UT 84107
TEL: (801) 262-2911
FAX:
Mr. Stephen Putnam, Owner

You will operate a SPORTSMAN'S CLUB, sell memberships, lease/own resorts/hunting properties, be a tour guide, set up world hunting and fishing tours. Own your own club, small override. Potential to retire in less than 10 years. Called Sportsman's Club of America in USA. Other countries - i.e. Sportsman's Club of Japan. Ground- floor opportunity.

HISTORY: . . . .
Established in 1969; . . 1st Franchised in 1987
Company-Owned Units (As of 12/1/1989): . .2
Franchised Units (12/1/1989): 3
Total Units (12/1/1989): 5
Distribution: US-5;Can-0;Overseas-0
  North America: . . . . 3 States
  Concentration: . . . .
Registered: . . . .
. . . .
Average # of Employees: . . . . .1-2 FT, 5+ PT
Prior Industry Experience: . . . . Helpful

FINANCIAL:
Cash Investment: $5-15K
Total Investment: $5-15K
Fees: Franchise - . . . .$
  Royalty: , Advert: . . . .
Contract Periods (Yrs.): 3/3
Area Development Agreement: . .No
Sub-Franchise Contract: . . . . . Yes
Expand in Territory: . . . . . . Yes
Passive Ownership: . . . Not Allowed
Encourage Conversions: . . . . . Yes
Franchisee Purchase(s) Required: .No

FRANCHISOR TRAINING/SUPPORT:
Financial Assistance Provided: . . . Yes(I)
Site Selection Assistance: . . . . . . .Yes
Lease Negotiation Assistance: . . . . .Yes
Co-operative Advertising: . . . . .No
Training: . . . . 3 Wks. Site
. . . .
On-Going Support: . . . . .C,D,g,h,i
Full-Time Franchisor Support Staff: . . . .
EXPANSION PLANS:
US: . . . . .All US
Canada - Yes, . . . Overseas - Yes

TOTE-A-SHOWER

112 SE Logan, Box 325
Emden, IL 62635
TEL: (217) 376-3391
FAX:
Mr. Ron Black, Sales Dir.

A TOTE-A-SHOWER franchise provides a flexible, home-based career. And, since TOTE-A-SHOWER is the first franchised party service offering total party packages and tote cards in the US, franchisees offer their customers a service they can find nowhere else.

HISTORY: . . . .
Established in 1984; . . 1st Franchised in 1985
Company-Owned Units (As of 12/1/1989): . .1
Franchised Units (12/1/1989): 12
Total Units (12/1/1989): 13
Distribution: US-13;Can-0;Overseas-0
  North America: . . . . 2 States
  Concentration: . . . . .11 in IL, 2 in IN
Registered: . . . . IL,IN
. . . .
Average # of Employees: . . . . .1 FT
Prior Industry Experience: . . . . . . Helpful

FINANCIAL:
Cash Investment: $1.5-2K
Total Investment: $2-4K
Fees: Franchise - $500
  Royalty: 6-10%, Advert: 0%
Contract Periods (Yrs.): 1/1
Area Development Agreement: . .No
Sub-Franchise Contract: . . . . .No
Expand in Territory: . . . . . . Yes
Passive Ownership: . . . Not Allowed
Encourage Conversions: . . . . . NA
Franchisee Purchase(s) Required: Yes

FRANCHISOR TRAINING/SUPPORT:
Financial Assistance Provided: . . . . .No
Site Selection Assistance: . . . . . . .NA
Lease Negotiation Assistance: . . . . .NA
Co-operative Advertising: . . . . .NA
Training: . . . . .1 Day Headquarters
. . . .
On-Going Support: . . . . . . .b,C,D,G,I
Full-Time Franchisor Support Staff: . . .1
EXPANSION PLANS:
US: . . . . .Midwest
Canada - No, ...Overseas - No

WOODY'S WOOD SHOPS

P. O. Box 12488
Oakland, CA 94604
TEL: (415) 547-1590
FAX: (415) 835-3779
Mr. Chris "Cooter" Hondo, President

WOODY'S WOOD SHOPS offer instruction and use of virtually all shop tools in a fully-outfitted wood shop. After detailed instruction and testing, members have full use of shop and related facilities. Open 15 hours/day, 7 days/week. Also sell small tools and all power equipment at cost plus 5%. Members pay front-end fees plus dues.

HISTORY: . . . .
Established in 1978; . . 1st Franchised in 1980
Company-Owned Units (As of 12/1/1989): . 13
Franchised Units (12/1/1989): 26
Total Units (12/1/1989): 39
Distribution: US-34;Can-5;Overseas-0
  North America: . . . . . 7 States, 2 Provinces
  Concentration: . . . 8 in CA, 4 in OR, 3 in WA
Registered: . . . . . CA,IL,FL,OR,WA,WI,AB
. . . .
Average # of Employees: . . . . . . 1 FT, 4 PT
Prior Industry Experience: . . . . Helpful

FINANCIAL:
Cash Investment: $72K
Total Investment: $85-185K
Fees: Franchise - $22K
  Royalty: 6%, Advert: 2%
Contract Periods (Yrs.): 15/15
Area Development Agreement: Yes/15
Sub-Franchise Contract: . . . . . Yes
Expand in Territory: . . . . . . .No
Passive Ownership: . . . Discouraged
Encourage Conversions: . . . . . Yes
Franchisee Purchase(s) Required: .No

FRANCHISOR TRAINING/SUPPORT:
Financial Assistance Provided: . . .Yes(D)
Site Selection Assistance: . . . . .Yes
Lease Negotiation Assistance: . . . . .Yes
Co-operative Advertising: . . . . .Yes
Training: . . . . 3 Wks. Headquarters,
  . . . . 2 Wks. Site, Opening
On-Going Support: . . . . . A,C,D,g,H,i
Full-Time Franchisor Support Staff: . . 21
EXPANSION PLANS:
  US: . . . . .All US
  Canada - Yes, ... Overseas - No

SUPPLEMENTAL LISTING OF FRANCHISORS

ARTHUR MURRAY INTERNATIONAL	1077 Ponce De Leon Blvd., Coral Gables FL 33134	
BETWEEN FRIENDS	747 Farmington Ave., New Britain CT 06053	
CELEBRATIONS, THE CLASS ACT	4329 Merriweather Rd., Toledo OH 43623	
COMPATIBILITY TODAY	2498 Yonge St., # 845, Toronto ON M4P2H2	CAN
DOC & EDDY'S	P.O. Box 20878, Billings MT 59104	
DUFFERIN GAMES ROOM STORE	98 Advance Rd., Toronto ON M8Z2T7	CAN
EMPIRE PUBS	273 Richmond St. W., Toronto ON M5V1X1	CAN
FUTURE GOLF	4418 Buhl Rd., Crystal Lake IL 60014	
GARRY ROBERTSON MUSIC SERVICES	160 - 208 Provencher Blvd., Winnipeg MB R2H3B4	CAN
GREAT EXPECTATIONS	11040 Santa Monica Blvd., # 300, Los Angeles CA 90025	
HAUNTED HAYRIDES	3520 W. Genesee St., Syracuse NY 13219	
MATCHMAKER INTERNATIONAL	5103 Kingston Pike, Box 10963, Knoxville TN 37939	
MISS TORONTO YACHT CHARTERS	679 Queens Quay W., Toronto ON M5V3A9	CAN
MR. MALE AMERICA PAGEANT	Rd. # 3, Box 6, Throckmorton St., Freehold NJ 07728	
PITCHING MACHINE MFG. CO.	P.O. Box 5445, Akron OH 44313	
PRO D.J.'S	1252 1/2 Remington Rd., Schaumburg IL 60173	
PROFESSIONAL BOAT CARE	3732 W. Century Blvd., # 6, Inglewood CA 90303	
PUTT-PUTT GOLF COURSES OF AMERICA	P.O. Box 35237, Fayetteville NC 28303	
PUTT-R-GOLF	P.O. Box 5445, Akron OH 44313	
RECORDS ON WHEELS	255 Shields Ct., # C, Markham ON L3R8V2	CAN
SOUNDS EXCITING STUDIOS	1777 S. Harrison St., # 610, Denver CO 80210	
SPEEDS BILLIARDS AND GAMES	2203 Obenchain St., Dallas TX 75208	
SUN CREATIVE SYSTEM/WOOZ	190 S. Orchard St., # B230, Vacaville CA 95688	
TOGETHER DATING SERVICE	171 Main St., # 102, Ashland MA 01721	
TRUNKS IN DISGUISE	34 Grenfell Cres., Ottawa ON K2G0G2	CAN
WHEELS ENTERTAINMENT	255 Shields Ct., # C, Markham ON L3R8V2	CAN
WOOZ	190 S. Orchard St., # B230, Vacaville CA 95688	
WORLD CLASS ARM WRESTLING	P.O. Box 882, Ames IA 50010	

CHAPTER 35

RENTAL SERVICES

COLORTYME

P. O. Box 1781
Athens, TX 75751
TEL: (214) 675-9291
FAX: (214) 675-8085
Mr. Ken Dolen, VP Franchising

COLORTYME is the largest franchised rent-to-own company specializing in the rental of TV's, VCR's, furniture, appliances and audio products in the US. The COLORTYME franchised dealers are supported by a staff that has in excess of 100 years' experience in the rent-to-own industry.

HISTORY: . . . . IFA
Established in 1979;   . . 1st Franchised in 1982
Company-Owned Units (As of 12/1/1989):   . 62
Franchised Units (12/1/1989):   438
Total Units (12/1/1989):   500
Distribution: US-500;Can-0;Overseas-0
 North America: . . . . 40 States
 Concentration: . 83 in TX, 31 in CA, 28 in OH
Registered: . . . . All Exc. WI and AB
 . . . .
Average # of Employees: . . . . .4 FT
Prior Industry Experience: . . . . . . Helpful

FINANCIAL:
Cash Investment: $61-123K
Total Investment: $83-163K
Fees: Franchise - $10K
 Royalty: 3%, Advert: 2%
Contract Periods (Yrs.): 5/5
Area Development Agreement: . .No
Sub-Franchise Contract: . . . . .No
Expand in Territory: . . . . Yes
Passive Ownership: . . . Not Allowed
Encourage Conversions: . . . . . Yes
Franchisee Purchase(s) Required: .No

FRANCHISOR TRAINING/SUPPORT:
Financial Assistance Provided: . . .Yes(D)
Site Selection Assistance: . . . . . . .Yes
Lease Negotiation Assistance: . . . . .Yes
Co-operative Advertising: . . . . .No
Training: . . . . 2 Wks. Headquarters,
 . . . . 1 Wk. In Field
On-Going Support: . . . . .B,C,D,E,F,G,h
Full-Time Franchisor Support Staff: . . 32
EXPANSION PLANS:
 US: . . . . .All US
 Canada - No, ... Overseas - No

EQUIPMENT RENTAL SERVICES

	1988	1989	1990	Percentage Change 1988-1989	Percentage Change 1989-1990
Number of Establishments:					
Company-Owned	736	816	896	10.9%	9.8%
Franchisee-Owned	2,282	2,167	2,462	−5.0%	13.6%
Total	3,018	2,983	3,358	−1.2%	12.6%
% of Total Establishments:					
Company-Owned	24.4%	27.4%	26.7%		
Franchisee-Owned	75.6%	72.6%	73.3%		
Total	100.0%	100.0%	100.0%		
Annual Sales ($000):					
Company-Owned	$203,333	$230,740	$264,950	13.5%	14.8%
Franchisee-Owned	474,314	464,225	546,095	−2.1%	17.6%
Total	677,647	694,965	811,045	2.6%	16.7%
% of Total Sales:					
Company-Owned	30.0%	33.2%	32.7%		
Franchisee-Owned	70.0%	66.8%	67.3%		
Total	100.0%	100.0%	100.0%		
Average Sales Per Unit ($000):					
Company-Owned	$276	$283	$296	2.4%	4.6%
Franchisee-Owned	208	214	222	3.1%	3.5%
Total	225	233	242	3.8%	3.7%
Sales Ratio	132.9%	132.0%	133.3%		

	1st Quartile	Median	4th Quartile
Average 1988 Total Investment:			
Company-Owned	$60,000	$105,000	$147,500
Franchisee-Owned	100,000	130,000	200,000
Single Unit Franchise Fee	$12,750	$15,000	$20,000
Multiple Unit Franchise Fee	N. A.	N. A.	N. A.
Franchisee Start-up Cost	30,000	40,000	75,000

	1988	Employees/Unit	Sales/Employee
Employment:			
Company-Owned	4,197	5.7	$48,447
Franchisee-Owned	10,919	4.8	43,439
Total	15,116	5.0	44,830
Employee Performance Ratios		119.2%	111.5%

Source: Franchising In The Economy, 1988 – 1990, IFA Education Foundation & Horwath International, Published January, 1990.

1) 1989 and 1990 data were estimated by respondents.

FORMALS ETC.

4600 Shreveport Hwy.
Pineville, LA 71360
TEL: (318) 640-3766
FAX:
Mr. Sam Brimer, President

Rental of ladies' formalwear, including prom, party, pageant, bridesmaid and bridal gowns. FORMALS ETC. also designs and manufactures one-piece gowns, with emphasis on quality and style. FORMALS ETC. would like to re-define the ladies' formalwear industry. With our experience and commitment to customer service, quality, selection and style, we feel we are in a good position to participate in the growth phase of a new industry!

HISTORY: . . . .
Established in 1984; . . 1st Franchised in 1990
Company-Owned Units (As of 12/1/1989): . .3
Franchised Units (12/1/1989): 1
Total Units (12/1/1989): 4
Distribution: US-4;Can-0;Overseas-0
North America: . . . . 2 States
Concentration: . . . . 3 in LA, 1 in TN
Registered: . . . .
. . . .
Average # of Employees: . . . . . . 2 FT, 1 PT
Prior Industry Experience: . . . . Helpful

FINANCIAL:
Cash Investment: $55-80K
Total Investment: $64-96K
Fees: Franchise - $15K
  Royalty: 6%, Advert: 1%
Contract Periods (Yrs.): 10/10
Area Development Agreement: . .No
Sub-Franchise Contract: . . . . .No
Expand in Territory: . . . . Yes
Passive Ownership: . . . Discouraged
Encourage Conversions: . . . . . Yes
Franchisee Purchase(s) Required: .No

FRANCHISOR TRAINING/SUPPORT:
Financial Assistance Provided: . . . . . No
Site Selection Assistance: . . . . .Yes
Lease Negotiation Assistance: . . . . .Yes
Co-operative Advertising: . . . . .Yes
Training: . . . . . . 1 Wk. Training Center,
. . . . 1 Wk. Franchisee's Store
On-Going Support: . . . . B,C,D,E,F,G,h,I
Full-Time Franchisor Support Staff: . . .3
EXPANSION PLANS:
US: . . . . Southeast
Canada - No, ...Overseas - No

GINGISS FORMALWEAR

180 N. LaSalle St.
Chicago, IL 60601
TEL: (800) 621-7125 (312) 236-2333
FAX:
Mr. John Heiser, VP Dir. Fran.

GINGISS FORMALWEAR specializes in the rental and sales of men's formal-wear and related accessories. Primarily shopping center locations. Extensive outside PR and sales promotion is necessary.

HISTORY: . . . . IFA
Established in 1936; . . 1st Franchised in 1968
Company-Owned Units (As of 12/1/1989): . 28
Franchised Units (12/1/1989): 208
Total Units (12/1/1989): 236
Distribution: US-236;Can-0;Overseas-0
North America: 37
Concentration: . . 40 in CA, 37 in TX, 30 in IL
Registered: . . .CA,IL,IN,MD,MI,MN,NY,OR
. . . . RI,VA,WA,WI
Average # of Employees: . . . . . 1 FT, 3-6 PT
Prior Industry Experience: . . . . . . Helpful

FINANCIAL:
Cash Investment: $50-100K
Total Investment: $120-170K
Fees: Franchise - $15K
  Royalty: 6-10%, Advert: 3%
Contract Periods (Yrs.): . . . 10/10
Area Development Agreement: . .No
Sub-Franchise Contract: . . . . .No
Expand in Territory: . . . . Yes
Passive Ownership: . . . Not Allowed
Encourage Conversions: . . . . . Yes
Franchisee Purchase(s) Required: .No

FRANCHISOR TRAINING/SUPPORT:
Financial Assistance Provided: . . . Yes(I)
Site Selection Assistance: . . . . .Yes
Lease Negotiation Assistance: . . . . .Yes
Co-operative Advertising: . . . . .Yes
Training: . . . . 2 Wks. Headquarters,
. . . . 1 Wk. Site
On-Going Support: . . . . .b,C,D,E,F,G,H
Full-Time Franchisor Support Staff: . . 35
EXPANSION PLANS:
US: . . . . All US
Canada - No, ...Overseas - No

NATION-WIDE GENERAL RENTAL CENTERS

1805 Nembree Rd.
Alpharetta, GA 30201
TEL: (800) 227-1643 (404) 644-7765
FAX: (404) 664-0052
Mr. Ike Goodvin, President

A full-line rental center which includes items for the contractor and do-it-yourself homeowner, such as baby equipment, camping supplies, contractors' equipment and tools, invalid needs, lawn and yard tools, party and banquet needs, etc. Building required is 1,800 - 3,000 SF with good traffic flow and parking for 6 - 10 cars.

HISTORY: . . . .
Established in 1976; . . 1st Franchised in 1976
Company-Owned Units (As of 12/1/1989): . .0
Franchised Units (12/1/1989): 189
Total Units (12/1/1989): 189
Distribution: US-189;Can-0;Overseas-0
North America: . . . . 36 States
Concentration: . . . .
Registered: . . . .
. . . .
Average # of Employees: . . . . . . 3 FT, 1 PT
Prior Industry Experience: . . . . Helpful

FINANCIAL:
Cash Investment: $30-40K
Total Investment: $75-140K
Fees: Franchise - $0
  Royalty: 0%, Advert: 0%
Contract Periods (Yrs.): 3/1
Area Development Agreement: . .No
Sub-Franchise Contract: . . . . .No
Expand in Territory: . . . . .No
Passive Ownership: . . . Discouraged
Encourage Conversions: . . . . . Yes
Franchisee Purchase(s) Required: .No

FRANCHISOR TRAINING/SUPPORT:
Financial Assistance Provided: . . .Yes(D)
Site Selection Assistance: . . . . .Yes
Lease Negotiation Assistance: . . . . .Yes
Co-operative Advertising: . . . . .No
Training: . . . . 1 Wk. Columbia, SC
. . . .
On-Going Support: . . . . . B,C,D,E,F,G,I
Full-Time Franchisor Support Staff: . . . .
EXPANSION PLANS:
US: . . . . .All Except Illinois
Canada - Yes, . . . Overseas - Yes

NATION-WIDE MEDICAL EQUIPMENT

1805 Hembree Rd., # C
Alpharetta, GA 30201
TEL: (800) 662-5008
FAX:
Mr. Ohlen Hippler, President

A complete "turn-key" package with training, exclusive area, accounting, site assistance, proven equipment, display features, buy-back agreement, group insurance and many other services.

HISTORY: . . . .
Established in 1988; . . 1st Franchised in 1988
Company-Owned Units (As of 12/1/1989): . . 1
Franchised Units (12/1/1989): 7
Total Units (12/1/1989): 8
Distribution: US-8;Can-0;Overseas-0
North America: . . . . 6 States
Concentration: . . . .
Registered: . . . .
. . . .
Average # of Employees: . . . . .3 FT
Prior Industry Experience: . . . . . . Helpful

FINANCIAL:
Cash Investment: $60-100K
Total Investment: $135K
Fees: Franchise - $0
Royalty: 0%, Advert: 0%
Contract Periods (Yrs.): . . . . 3/Inf.
Area Development Agreement: Yes/Var
Sub-Franchise Contract: . . . . .No
Expand in Territory: . . . . . . .No
Passive Ownership: . . . . . .Allowed
Encourage Conversions: . . . . . Yes
Franchisee Purchase(s) Required: .No

FRANCHISOR TRAINING/SUPPORT:
Financial Assistance Provided: . . . Yes(I)
Site Selection Assistance: . . . . . . .Yes
Lease Negotiation Assistance: . . . . .Yes
Co-operative Advertising: . . . . .Yes
Training: . . . . 2 Wks. Headquarters,
. . . . .Min. 3 Wks. On-site
On-Going Support: . . . . . B,C,D,E,F,G,I
Full-Time Franchisor Support Staff: . . . 8
EXPANSION PLANS:
US: . . . . .All US
Canada - No, ... Overseas - Yes

PARTY FASHIONS

2551 A Pacific Coast Hwy.
Torrance, CA 90505
TEL: (800) 762-8300 (213) 325-6300
FAX: (213) 547-9543
Mr. Satish C. Mehta, President

PARTY FASHIONS offers a unique concept of rental and sales of ladies' formalwear and accessories. Formalwear covers all styles from prom, graduation, cruises, pageants, mother-of-the-bride to black tie. Appeals to women from 14 - 70 years of age. Major emphasis on service.

HISTORY: . . . .
Established in 1989; . . 1st Franchised in 1989
Company-Owned Units (As of 12/1/1989): . . 1
Franchised Units (12/1/1989): 0
Total Units (12/1/1989): 1
Distribution: US-1;Can-0;Overseas-0
North America: . . . . .1 State
Concentration: . . . . 1 in CA
Registered: . . . . CA
. . . .
Average # of Employees: . . . . . . 1 FT, 2 PT
Prior Industry Experience: . . . . . . Helpful

FINANCIAL:
Cash Investment: $133-159K
Total Investment: $133-159K
Fees: Franchise - $20K
Royalty: 5%, Advert: 2%
Contract Periods (Yrs.): 10/5
Area Development Agreement: . .No
Sub-Franchise Contract: . . . . .No
Expand in Territory: . . . . Yes
Passive Ownership: . . . Not Allowed
Encourage Conversions: . . . . . Yes
Franchisee Purchase(s) Required: .No

FRANCHISOR TRAINING/SUPPORT:
Financial Assistance Provided: . . . . .No
Site Selection Assistance: . . . . . . .Yes
Lease Negotiation Assistance: . . . . .Yes
Co-operative Advertising: . . . . .Yes
Training: . . . . . . 1-2 Wks. Headquarters
. . . .
On-Going Support: . . . . D,E,F,H,I
Full-Time Franchisor Support Staff: . . . 2
EXPANSION PLANS:
US: . . . . .All US
Canada - No, ...Overseas - No

PCR-PERSONAL COMPUTER RENTALS

2557 Rte. 130
Cranbury, NJ 08512
TEL: (800) 727-7079
FAX:
Mr. Scott Burgess, Fran. Sales Mgr.

PCR RENTAL CENTERS perform short-term rentals of personal computers and peripherals to the business community.

HISTORY: . . . .
Established in 1983; . . 1st Franchised in 1985
Company-Owned Units (As of 12/1/1989): . .0
Franchised Units (12/1/1989): 60
Total Units (12/1/1989): 60
Distribution: US-60;Can-0;Overseas-0
North America: . . . . 19 States
Concentration: . . . .5 in FL, 5 in CA, 3 in TX
Registered: . . . CA,FL,IL,IN,MD,MI,NY,OR
. . . . VA,WI
Average # of Employees: . . . . .3 FT
Prior Industry Experience: . . . . . . Helpful

FINANCIAL: OTC-PCR
Cash Investment: $80-120K
Total Investment: . . . .$
Fees: Franchise - $29.5K
Royalty: 7%, Advert: 1%
Contract Periods (Yrs.): 10/10
Area Development Agreement: . .No
Sub-Franchise Contract: . . . . .No
Expand in Territory: . . . . Yes
Passive Ownership: . . . Discouraged
Encourage Conversions: . . . . . Yes
Franchisee Purchase(s) Required: .No

FRANCHISOR TRAINING/SUPPORT:
Financial Assistance Provided: . . . Yes(I)
Site Selection Assistance: . . . . . . .Yes
Lease Negotiation Assistance: . . . . .Yes
Co-operative Advertising: . . . . .Yes
Training: . . . . .1 Wk. Headquarters,
. . . . .1 Wk. Franchise Location
On-Going Support: . . . . C,D,E,H,I
Full-Time Franchisor Support Staff: . . 11
EXPANSION PLANS:
US: . . . . .All US
Canada - Yes, ...Overseas - No

RENAPPLI OF AMERICA

1600 S. Grand Ave., # E
Springfield, IL 62703
TEL: (217) 544-4177
FAX: (217) 544-3699
Mr. Lou R. Messervy, President

Rent-to-own appliances, TV's, stereos, microwaves, vacuum cleaners and full line of furniture. Full and complete training program. Computerized buying power through RENAPPLI. No investment required. Obtain ownership anytime within 10 years.

HISTORY: . . . .
Established in 1972; . . 1st Franchised in 1984
Company-Owned Units (As of 12/1/1989): . .5
Franchised Units (12/1/1989): 12
Total Units (12/1/1989): 17
Distribution: US-17;Can-0;Overseas-0
North America: . . . . 3 States
Concentration: . . . . 14 in IL, 2 in IA, 1 in IN
Registered: . . . .
. . . .
Average # of Employees: . . . . . . 2 FT, 1 PT
Prior Industry Experience: . . . . . . Helpful

FINANCIAL:
Cash Investment: $0
Total Investment: $0
Fees: Franchise - $0
Royalty: 0%, Advert: 0%
Contract Periods (Yrs.): . . .10/Open
Area Development Agreement: Yes/Var
Sub-Franchise Contract: . . . . . .No
Expand in Territory: . . . . Yes
Passive Ownership: . . . Discouraged
Encourage Conversions: . . . . . Yes
Franchisee Purchase(s) Required: Yes

FRANCHISOR TRAINING/SUPPORT:
Financial Assistance Provided: . . .Yes(D)
Site Selection Assistance: . . . . . . .Yes
Lease Negotiation Assistance: . . . . .Yes
Co-operative Advertising: . . . . . . .NA
Training: . . . . 2 Wks. Headquarters
. . . .
On-Going Support: . . .A,B,C,D,E,F,G,h,I
Full-Time Franchisor Support Staff: . . 12
EXPANSION PLANS:
US: . . . . . . Illinois, Iowa, Indiana, MO
Canada - No, ...Overseas - No

TAYLOR RENTAL

1000 Stanley Dr.
New Britain, CT 06050
TEL: (203) 229-9100
FAX:
Mr. Dick Dandurand, President

TAYLOR RENTAL is the largest general rental chain in the rental industry. We offer a full range of support services, including building design and layout, inventory analysis, advertising support, professional field support, computer systems, etc.

HISTORY: . . . .
Established in 1946; . . 1st Franchised in 1963
Company-Owned Units (As of 12/1/1989): 106
Franchised Units (12/1/1989): 251
Total Units (12/1/1989): 357
Distribution: US-357;Can-0;Overseas-0
North America: . . . . 44 States
Concentration: . 40 in MA, 27 in FL, 24 in PA
Registered: . . . . All States
. . . .
Average # of Employees: . . . . . . 3 FT, 1 PT
Prior Industry Experience: . . . . . . Helpful

FINANCIAL: NYSE-SWK
Cash Investment: $90K
Total Investment: $235-275K
Fees: Franchise - $20K
Royalty: 2.75%, Advert: 0%
Contract Periods (Yrs.): 10/5
Area Development Agreement: Yes/10
Sub-Franchise Contract: . . . . . .No
Expand in Territory: . . . . .No
Passive Ownership: . . . Discouraged
Encourage Conversions: . . . . . .No
Franchisee Purchase(s) Required: .No

FRANCHISOR TRAINING/SUPPORT:
Financial Assistance Provided: . . . . . No
Site Selection Assistance: . . . . .Yes
Lease Negotiation Assistance: . . . . . No
Co-operative Advertising: . . . . No
Training: . . . . 2 Wks. Headquarters
. . . .
On-Going Support: . . . . B,C,D,E,f,G,h,I
Full-Time Franchisor Support Staff: . . 70
EXPANSION PLANS:
US: . . . . .All US
Canada - No, ...Overseas - No

YARD CARDS

2940 West Main St.
Belleville, IL 62223
TEL: (618) 233-0491
FAX:
Mr. Michael Hoepfinger, President

Rental of 8' greeting cards for any and all occassions, including storks to announce new babies, graduation, Valentine's Day, birthday, retirement, Mother's Day, Father's Day and anniversary cards. Can be operated as a home-based business or added on to an existing business.

HISTORY: . . . . .IFA
Established in 1983; . . 1st Franchised in 1986
Company-Owned Units (As of 12/1/1989): . .1
Franchised Units (12/1/1989): 20
Total Units (12/1/1989): 21
Distribution: US-21;Can-0;Overseas-0
North America: . . . . 9 States
Concentration: . . . .10 in IL, 3 in CA, 1 in IN
Registered: . . . . CA,FL,IL,IN,MI,VA
. . . .
Average # of Employees: . . . . .1-2 FT
Prior Industry Experience: . . . . . . Helpful

FINANCIAL:
Cash Investment: $5-15K
Total Investment: $5-23K
Fees: Franchise - . . . . $1K+
Royalty: 5%, Advert: 2%
Contract Periods (Yrs.): 20/5/5
Area Development Agreement: Yes/Var
Sub-Franchise Contract: . . . . . .No
Expand in Territory: . . . . Yes
Passive Ownership: . . . Discouraged
Encourage Conversions: . . . .
Franchisee Purchase(s) Required: Yes

FRANCHISOR TRAINING/SUPPORT:
Financial Assistance Provided: . . . . . No
Site Selection Assistance: . . . . . . .NA
Lease Negotiation Assistance: . . . . .NA
Co-operative Advertising: . . . . .NA
Training: . . . . . Maximum 3 Days Head-
. . . . quarters
On-Going Support: . . . . B,C,G,h
Full-Time Franchisor Support Staff: . . .3
EXPANSION PLANS:
US: . . . . .All US
Canada - No, ... Overseas - No

SUPPLEMENTAL LISTING OF FRANCHISORS

AL'S FORMAL WEAR . . . . 2021 Airport Fwy., Euless TX 76039
FAIRY GODMOTHERS . . . . .1045 E. Sorenson, Mesa AZ 85203
FORMAL WEAR SERVICE . . . . 639 V.F.W. Parkway, Chestnut Hill MA 02167
MUMS THE WORD . . . . .RR 1, P.O. Box 109, Crawfordsville IN 47933
PARTY FASHIONS . . . . .2551 Pacific Coast Hwy., Torrance CA 90505
PRESIDENT TUXEDO . . . . .32185 Hollingsworth, Warren MI 48092
UNITED RENT-ALL . . . . 6269 Variel Ave., # A, Woodland Hills CA 91367

CHAPTER 36

RETAIL: ART, ART SUPPLIES AND FRAMING

20TH CENTURY CRAFTS

79 Parkingway, P. O. Box 7169
Quincy, MA 02169
TEL: (617) 773-0530
FAX:
Mr. Leo Meady, President

Moderate-sized arts and crafts retail store. Designed for approximately 1,500 S.F. in malls, shopping centers or downtown areas. Can be operated by 2 persons with 5 - 6 part-timers. Excellent variety of crafts. 100% mark-up on most items.

HISTORY: . . . .
Established in 1989; . . 1st Franchised in 1990
Company-Owned Units (As of 12/1/1989): . . 1
Franchised Units (12/1/1989): 0
Total Units (12/1/1989): 1
Distribution: US-1;Can-0;Overseas-0
 North America: . . . . .1 State
 Concentration: . . . . .1 in MA
Registered: . . . .

. . . .
Average # of Employees: . . . . . . 2 FT, 5 PT
Prior Industry Experience: . . . . Helpful

FINANCIAL:
Cash Investment: $65-75K
Total Investment: $65-75K
Fees: Franchise - $10K
 Royalty: 6%, Advert: 0%
Contract Periods (Yrs.): 10/10
Area Development Agreement: . .No
Sub-Franchise Contract: . . . . .No
Expand in Territory: . . . . . . .No
Passive Ownership: . . . . . .Allowed
Encourage Conversions: . . . . . NA
Franchisee Purchase(s) Required: .No

FRANCHISOR TRAINING/SUPPORT:
Financial Assistance Provided: . . . . .No
Site Selection Assistance: . . . . . . .Yes
Lease Negotiation Assistance: . . . . .Yes
Co-operative Advertising: . . . . . . .Yes
Training: . . . . 3 Days Home Office,
 . . . . .3 Days Franchisee's Store
On-Going Support: . . . . . . B,C,D,E,H,I
Full-Time Franchisor Support Staff: . . . 1
EXPANSION PLANS:
 US: . . . . .All US
 Canada - Yes, ... Overseas - No

RETAILING – NON-FOOD

	1988	1989	1990	Percentage Change 1988–1989	Percentage Change 1989–1990
Number of Establishments:					
Company–Owned	11,880	12,504	13,139	5.3%	5.1%
Franchisee–Owned	34,292	36,669	40,923	6.9%	11.6%
Total	46,172	49,173	54,062	6.5%	9.9%
% of Total Establishments:					
Company–Owned	25.7%	25.4%	24.3%		
Franchisee–Owned	74.3%	74.6%	75.7%		
Total	100.0%	100.0%	100.0%		
Annual Sales ($000):					
Company–Owned	$7,111,480	$8,029,041	$8,662,994	12.9%	7.9%
Franchisee–Owned	16,232,351	17,971,890	19,979,594	10.7%	11.2%
Total	23,343,831	26,000,931	28,642,588	11.4%	10.2%
% of Total Sales:					
Company–Owned	30.5%	30.9%	30.2%		
Franchisee–Owned	69.5%	69.1%	69.8%		
Total	100.0%	100.0%	100.0%		
Average Sales Per Unit ($000):					
Company–Owned	$599	$642	$659	7.3%	2.7%
Franchisee–Owned	473	490	488	3.5%	–0.4%
Total	506	529	530	4.6%	0.2%
Sales Ratio	126.5%	131.0%	135.0%		

	1st Quartile	Median	4th Quartile
Average 1988 Total Investment:			
Company–Owned	$75,000	$130,000	$200,000
Franchisee–Owned	84,250	120,000	180,000
Single Unit Franchise Fee	$15,000	$20,000	$25,000
Multiple Unit Franchise Fee	9,500	15,000	25,000
Franchisee Start–up Cost	40,000	50,000	75,000

	1988	Employees/Unit	Sales/Employee
Employment:			
Company–Owned	93,535	7.9	$76,030
Franchisee–Owned	180,267	5.3	90,046
Total	273,802	5.9	85,258
Employee Performance Ratios		149.8%	84.4%

Source: Franchising In The Economy, 1988 – 1990, IFA Education Foundation & Horwath International, Published January, 1990.

1) 1989 and 1990 data were estimated by respondents.

FASTFRAME

30495 Canwood St.
Agoura, CA 91301
TEL: (800) 521-3726 (818) 707-1166 C
FAX: (818) 707-0164
Mr. Mike Minihane, VP Fran. Sales

Offers instant custom framing and related services to the highest standards of quality. Each retail store includes a fully-equipped and inventoried workshop. Service spans both retail and commercial sector and enjoys the highest gross margins in the industry.

HISTORY: . . . . IFA/CFA
Established in 1983; . . 1st Franchised in 1986
Company-Owned Units (As of 12/1/1989): . .7
Franchised Units (12/1/1989): 181
Total Units (12/1/1989): 188
Distribution: US-89;Can-0;Overseas-99
North America: . . . . 15 States
Concentration: . . . 31 in CA, 6 in VA, 5 in IL
Registered: . . . . All States
. . . .
Average # of Employees: . . . . .2 FT
Prior Industry Experience: . . . . Helpful

FINANCIAL:
Cash Investment: $45K
Total Investment: $115K
Fees: Franchise - $25K
Royalty: 7.5%, Advert: 5%
Contract Periods (Yrs.): . . . 10/10
Area Development Agreement: Yes/5
Sub-Franchise Contract: . . . . .No
Expand in Territory: . . . . Yes
Passive Ownership: . . . . . .Allowed
Encourage Conversions: . . . . . NA
Franchisee Purchase(s) Required: .No

FRANCHISOR TRAINING/SUPPORT:
Financial Assistance Provided: . . . Yes(I)
Site Selection Assistance: . . . . . . .Yes
Lease Negotiation Assistance: . . . . .Yes
Co-operative Advertising: . . . . .Yes
Training: . . . . 2 Wks. Headquarters,
. . . . .1 Wk. In Store, Regular Regional
On-Going Support: . . .a,B,C,D,E,F,G,H,I
Full-Time Franchisor Support Staff: . . 57
EXPANSION PLANS:
US: . . . . .All US
Canada - No, ...Overseas - No

FRAMING EXPERIENCE

1175 Appleby Lane
Burlington, ON L7L5H9 CAN
TEL: (416) 332-6116
FAX:
Mr. David Gale, President

Quality custom and do-it-yourself framing stores across Canada, supplied from our own warehouses and select suppliers; management, sales training and marketing programs provided along with the detailed start-up training.

HISTORY: . . . . IFA
Established in 1974; . . 1st Franchised in 1977
Company-Owned Units (As of 12/1/1989): . .1
Franchised Units (12/1/1989): 30
Total Units (12/1/1989): 31
Distribution: US-1;Can-30;Overseas-0
North America: . . . . .1 State, 4 Provinces
Concentration: . . .23 in ON, 4 in BC, 1 in AB
Registered: . . . . AB
. . . .
Average # of Employees: . . . . .3 FT
Prior Industry Experience: . . . . Helpful

FINANCIAL:
Cash Investment: $35-50K
Total Investment: $60-90K
Fees: Franchise - $16K
Royalty: 5%, Advert: 0%
Contract Periods (Yrs.): 5/5
Area Development Agreement: Yes/3
Sub-Franchise Contract: . . . . .No
Expand in Territory: . . . . Yes
Passive Ownership: . . . Not Allowed
Encourage Conversions: . . . . . Yes
Franchisee Purchase(s) Required: .No

FRANCHISOR TRAINING/SUPPORT:
Financial Assistance Provided: . . . Yes(I)
Site Selection Assistance: . . . . . . .Yes
Lease Negotiation Assistance: . . . . .Yes
Co-operative Advertising: . . . . .Yes
Training: . . . . . . 4-6 Wks. Headquarters
. . . .
On-Going Support: . . . A,B,C,d,E,F,G,h,i
Full-Time Franchisor Support Staff: . . 18
EXPANSION PLANS:
US: . . . . .No
Canada - Yes, ...Overseas - No

GRAPHICS GALLERY

219 Marine Ave., P. O. Box JJ
Balboa Island, CA 92662
TEL: (714) 673-4125
FAX: (714) 673-3675
Mr. Rob Shively, Fran. Devel.

GRAPHICS GALLERY carries a large selection of framed and unframed fine art posters, original art work and full custom picture framing. The prompt service, frame shop organization, competitive prices and visual appeal make GRAPHICS GALLERY unique in the retail art and picture framing business.

HISTORY: . . . .
Established in 1982; . . 1st Franchised in 1987
Company-Owned Units (As of 12/1/1989): . .2
Franchised Units (12/1/1989): 15
Total Units (12/1/1989): 17
Distribution: US-16;Can-0;Overseas-1
North America: . . . . .1 State
Concentration: . . . . 16 in CA
Registered: . . . . CA,OR
. . . .
Average # of Employees: . . . . . . 2 FT, 1 PT
Prior Industry Experience: . . . . Helpful

FINANCIAL:
Cash Investment: $25-35K
Total Investment: $77.5-107K
Fees: Franchise - $20K
Royalty: 6%, Advert: 2%
Contract Periods (Yrs.): 10/5
Area Development Agreement: Yes/10
Sub-Franchise Contract: . . . . .No
Expand in Territory: . . . . Yes
Passive Ownership: . . . Discouraged
Encourage Conversions: . . . . . Yes
Franchisee Purchase(s) Required: .No

FRANCHISOR TRAINING/SUPPORT:
Financial Assistance Provided: . . . Yes(I)
Site Selection Assistance: . . . . . . .Yes
Lease Negotiation Assistance: . . . . .Yes
Co-operative Advertising: . . . . .Yes
Training: . . . . .1 Wk. Headquarters,
. . . . 10 Days Corp. Store, 10 Days Site
On-Going Support: . . A,B,C,E,E,F,G,H,I
Full-Time Franchisor Support Staff: . . .5
EXPANSION PLANS:
US: . . . . Northwest and Southwest
Canada - Yes, . . . Overseas - Yes

GREAT FRAME UP

9335 Belmont Ave.
Franklin Park, IL 60131
TEL: (800) 55-FRAME (312) 671-2530
FAX:
Ms. Arlene Kozemzak, Dir. Fran.

We are the high-volume, top-quality, low-priced leaders in the do-it-yourself and custom picture framing industry. We aggressively pursue markets in major cities and suburbs.

HISTORY: . . . . .IFA/WIF
Established in 1971; . . 1st Franchised in 1975
Company-Owned Units (As of 12/1/1989): . .1
Franchised Units (12/1/1989): 119
Total Units (12/1/1989): 120
Distribution: . . . US-120;Can-0;Overseas-0
North America: . . . . 25 States
Concentration: . . .26 in IL, 20 in CA, 8 in CO
Registered: . . . . All States
. . . .
Average # of Employees: . . . . .2 FT
Prior Industry Experience: . . . . Helpful

FINANCIAL:
Cash Investment: $26K
Total Investment: . . . .$~104K
Fees: Franchise - $19.5K
  Royalty: 6%, Advert: 2%
Contract Periods (Yrs.): . . . . NA
Area Development Agreement: . .No
Sub-Franchise Contract: . . . . .No
Expand in Territory: . . . . . . Yes
Passive Ownership: . . . Discouraged
Encourage Conversions: . . . . Yes
Franchisee Purchase(s) Required: .No

FRANCHISOR TRAINING/SUPPORT:
Financial Assistance Provided: . . . . .Yes
Site Selection Assistance: . . . . .Yes
Lease Negotiation Assistance: . . . . .Yes
Co-operative Advertising: . . . . .Yes
Training: . . . . 5 Wks. Headquarters
. . . .
On-Going Support: . . A,B,C,D,E,F,G,H,I
Full-Time Franchisor Support Staff: . . . .
EXPANSION PLANS:
US: . . . . .All US
Canada - No, ... Overseas - Yes

POSTERS PLUS

12 Levendale Rd.
Richmond Hill, ON L4C4H2 CAN
TEL: (416) 770-4234
FAX:
Mr. Barye Kadis, President

Custom picture framing and deep discount fine art prints and posters. We are able to offer prints that retail for up to $45.00 and more for only $6.00 each, unframed - a great loss leader that doesn't lose money!

HISTORY: . . . .
Established in 1984; . . 1st Franchised in 1984
Company-Owned Units (As of 12/1/1989): . .1
Franchised Units (12/1/1989): 8
Total Units (12/1/1989): 9
Distribution: US-0;Can-9;Overseas-0
North America: . . . . 3 Provinces
Concentration: . . . . ON, BC, MB
Registered: . . . .
. . . .
Average # of Employees: . . . . . 1 FT, 2-4 PT
Prior Industry Experience: . . . . . . Helpful

FINANCIAL: COATS-PPMC
Cash Investment: . . . . . . $25K+
Total Investment: $115K
Fees: Franchise - $25K
  Royalty: 6%, Advert - 4%
Contract Periods (Yrs.): 5/5/5
Area Development Agreement: . .No
Sub-Franchise Contract: . . . . .No
Expand in Territory: . . . . . . Yes
Passive Ownership: . . . Not Allowed
Encourage Conversions: . . . . Yes
Franchisee Purchase(s) Required: .No

FRANCHISOR TRAINING/SUPPORT:
Financial Assistance Provided: . . . Yes(I)
Site Selection Assistance: . . . . . . .Yes
Lease Negotiation Assistance: . . . . .Yes
Co-operative Advertising: . . . . . . .Yes
Training: . . . . 3 Days Headquarters
. . . .
On-Going Support: . . . . B,C,D,E,F,G,h,I
Full-Time Franchisor Support Staff: . . .2
EXPANSION PLANS:
US: . . . . .No
Canada - Yes, ... Overseas - No

SUPPLEMENTAL LISTING OF FRANCHISORS

ATHENA INTERNATIONAL . . . . .1351 Matheson Blvd., # 1, Mississauga ON L4W2A1		CAN
CONSIGNMENT GALLERIES . . . . .27 Signal Rd., Stamford CT 06902		
CREATIVE WORLD MANAGEMENT SERVICE . . . . 13450 Farmington Rd., Livonia MI 48150		
DECK THE WALLS . . . . 12450 Greenspoint, Houston TX 77060		
DELPHI STAINED GLASS CENTERS . . . . 2116 E. Michigan Ave., Lansing MI 48912		
FLARE-U FRAME IT . . . . 300 - 321 McDermott Ave., Winnipeg MB R3A0A3		CAN
FRAME FACTORY/FRAMIN' PLACE . . . . 9605 Dalecrest, Houston TX 77080		
FRAME LAND . . . . 1760 Avenue Rd., Toronto ON M5M3Y9		CAN
FRAME N' ART FRANCHISE SYSTEMS . . . . . . .P.O. Box 2016, 1016 S. Main St., Cheshire CT 06410		
GALLERY 1 AFFORDABLE ART . . . . 6601 Northwest 14th St., Ft. Lauderdale FL 33313		
INSTAFRAME GALLERIES . . . . 187 BarkerBlvd., Winnipeg MB R3R2E3		CAN
IT'S A WRAP . . . . 1210 Howard St., Omaha NE 68102		
KOENIG ART EMPORIUM . . . . .1777 Boston Post Rd45 Woodmont Rd, Milford CT 06460		

LEEWARD'S CRAFT BAZAAR . . . . 1200 St. Charles St., Elgin IL 60120
MILLION DOLLAR BOX . . . . 1210 Howard St., Omaha NE 68102
POSTER GALLERY . . . . 4200 S. Freeway, # P13, Fort Worth TX 76115

CHAPTER 37

RETAIL: ATHLETIC WEAR AND SPORTING GOODS

ATHLETE'S FOOT, THE

57 King St., W.
Kitchener, ON N2G1A1 CAN
TEL: (519) 576-9300
FAX: (519) 576-7229
Mr. Doug Marr, President

Be a part of one of Canada's most respected athletic footwear and apparel retail chains.

HISTORY: . . . .
Established in 1974;   . . 1st Franchised in 1974
Company-Owned Units (As of 12/1/1989):   . 14
Franchised Units (12/1/1989):   16
Total Units (12/1/1989):   30
Distribution: US-0;Can-30;Overseas-0
  North America: . . . . 3 Provinces
  Concentration: . . . 25 in ON, 3 in PQ, 2 in NS
Registered: . . . .
. . . .
Average # of Employees: . . . . . . 2 FT, 3 PT
Prior Industry Experience: . . . . Helpful

FINANCIAL:
Cash Investment: . . . .$NA
Total Investment: . . . .$NA
Fees: Franchise -   . . . .$NA
  Royalty: 3%, Advert: 1%
Contract Periods (Yrs.): 10/5
Area Development Agreement: . Yes
Sub-Franchise Contract: . . . . .No
Expand in Territory: . . . . Yes
Passive Ownership: . . . Discouraged
Encourage Conversions: . . . . . NA
Franchisee Purchase(s) Required: .No

FRANCHISOR TRAINING/SUPPORT:
Financial Assistance Provided: . . . . .No
Site Selection Assistance: . . . . . . .Yes
Lease Negotiation Assistance: . . . . .Yes
Co-operative Advertising: . . . . . . .Yes
Training: . . . . Varies
. . . .
On-Going Support: . . . . .d,e,H,I
Full-Time Franchisor Support Staff: . . 35
EXPANSION PLANS:
  US: .No
  Canada - Yes, ... Overseas - No

CYCLEPATH, THE

6465 Millcreek Ave., # 205
Mississauga, ON L5N5R3 CAN
TEL: (800) 387-8335 (416) 567-4180
FAX: (416) 567-5355
Mr. George Kostopoulos, Fran. Dev.

THE CYCLEPATH is Canada's foremost retail specialty bicycle franchise, with a successful chain of corporately-owned and franchised stores. We carry an extensive selection of brand name and private label bicycles, parts and accessories, catering to the needs of all cyclists, from the racing enthusiast to the recreational cyclist.

HISTORY: . . . .
Established in 1981; . . 1st Franchised in 1988
Company-Owned Units (As of 12/1/1989): . .2
Franchised Units (12/1/1989): 9
Total Units (12/1/1989): 11
Distribution: US-0;Can-11;Overseas-0
 North America: . . . . .1 Province
 Concentration: . . . . 11 in ON
Registered: . . . .
. . . .
Average # of Employees: . . . . 1-3 FT, 1-4 PT
Prior Industry Experience: . . . . Helpful

FINANCIAL:
Cash Investment: $50-100K
Total Investment: $195-250K
Fees: Franchise - $40K
 Royalty: 0%, Advert: 3%
Contract Periods (Yrs.): 10/10
Area Development Agreement: . .No
Sub-Franchise Contract: . . . . .No
Expand in Territory: . . . . . . .No
Passive Ownership: . . . Not Allowed
Encourage Conversions: . . . . . Yes
Franchisee Purchase(s) Required: Yes

FRANCHISOR TRAINING/SUPPORT:
Financial Assistance Provided: . . . Yes(I)
Site Selection Assistance: . . . . .Yes
Lease Negotiation Assistance: . . . . .Yes
Co-operative Advertising: . . . . .Yes
Training: . . . . . 2-3 Wks. Headquarters -
 . . . .Classroom Training, 1 Wk. On-site
On-Going Support: . . . . . .B,C,D,E,F,H
Full-Time Franchisor Support Staff: . . . .
EXPANSION PLANS:
 US: . . . . Not Currently
Canada - Yes, ...Overseas - No

FLEET FEET SPORTS

1555 River Park Dr., # 102
Sacramento, CA 95815
TEL: (800) 444-3713 (916) 646-1122
FAX: (916) 646-1270
Ms. Maria Bobenrieth, Dir. Marketing

Retail sports franchise that is committed to developing and selling athletic footwear, apparel and accessories in a highly-promotional way. We seek individuals who follow a fitness lifestyle and love to participate in sports. We sponsor community-oriented events, sell name-brand products in a retail store.

HISTORY: . . . .
Established in 1976; . . 1st Franchised in 1979
Company-Owned Units (As of 12/1/1989): . .3
Franchised Units (12/1/1989): 33
Total Units (12/1/1989): 36
Distribution: US-36;Can-0;Overseas-0
 North America: . . . . 12 States
 Concentration: . . . 17 in CA, 3 in FL, 3 in TX
Registered: . . . .CA,FL,MD,NY,OR,VA,WA
. . . .
Average # of Employees: . . . . . . 1 FT, 3 PT
Prior Industry Experience: . . . . Helpful

FINANCIAL:
Cash Investment: $20K
Total Investment: $90-110K
Fees: Franchise - $17.5K
 Royalty: 4-2%, Advert: 0%
Contract Periods (Yrs.): 20/20
Area Development Agreement: . .No
Sub-Franchise Contract: . . . . .No
Expand in Territory: . . . . . . Yes
Passive Ownership: . . . Not Allowed
Encourage Conversions: . . . . .No
Franchisee Purchase(s) Required: Yes

FRANCHISOR TRAINING/SUPPORT:
Financial Assistance Provided: . . . Yes(I)
Site Selection Assistance: . . . . .Yes
Lease Negotiation Assistance: . . . . .Yes
Co-operative Advertising: . . . . .Yes
Training: . . . . .10 Days Headquarters
. . . .
On-Going Support: . . . . . C,D,E,F,G,h,I
Full-Time Franchisor Support Staff: . . .7
EXPANSION PLANS:
 US: . . . . .All US
Canada - Yes, . . . Overseas - Yes

ISLAND WATER SPORTS

Ten Fairway Dr., # 302
Deerfield Beach, FL 33441
TEL: (800) 873-3133 (305) 698-9700
FAX:
Mr. Rick Englert, President

Retail surf apparel store, selling water sporting equipment goods according to area. Outlets also sell skateboards.

HISTORY: . . . . .IFA
Established in 1978; . . 1st Franchised in 1989
Company-Owned Units (As of 12/1/1989): . .2
Franchised Units (12/1/1989): 24
Total Units (12/1/1989): 26
Distribution: US-25;Can-1;Overseas-0
 North America: . . . . . .5 States, 1 Province
 Concentration: . . . 12 in FL, 2 in CO, 2 in SC
Registered: . . . .
. . . .
Average # of Employees: . . . . . . 2 FT, 3 PT
Prior Industry Experience: . . . . Helpful

FINANCIAL:
Cash Investment: . . . .$
Total Investment: . . . .$
Fees: Franchise - $25K
 Royalty: 6%, Advert: 2%
Contract Periods (Yrs.): 10/10
Area Development Agreement: Yes/10
Sub-Franchise Contract: . . . . . Yes
Expand in Territory: . . . . Yes
Passive Ownership: . . . Discouraged
Encourage Conversions: . . . . . Yes
Franchisee Purchase(s) Required: .No

FRANCHISOR TRAINING/SUPPORT:
Financial Assistance Provided: . . . Yes(I)
Site Selection Assistance: . . . . .Yes
Lease Negotiation Assistance: . . . . .Yes
Co-operative Advertising: . . . . .Yes
Training: . . . . .1 Full Week Headquarters
. . . .
On-Going Support: . . . . . C,D,E,f,G,h,I
Full-Time Franchisor Support Staff: . . .5
EXPANSION PLANS:
 US: . . . . .SW, SE, NE, NW & Midwest
Canada - Yes, . . . Overseas - Yes

LAS VEGAS DISCOUNT GOLF & TENNIS / ST. ANDREWS GOLF CORP.
5325 S. Valley View Blvd., # 10
Las Vegas, NV 89118
TEL: (702) 798-7777
FAX: (702) 798-6847
Mr. Larry Jordan, President

LAS VEGAS DISCOUNT GOLF & TENNIS has franchised retail outlets throughout the US, Canada, Spain, France and Japan. It has been in business since 1974 and is a well-known and respected name among golf enthusiasts. The franchisee is buying a proven and successful method of doing business, which includes ways to merchandise product, product knowledge, product sources, sales training, opeations training, store layout and much more.

HISTORY: . . . . IFA
Established in 1974; . . 1st Franchised in 1984
Company-Owned Units (As of 12/1/1989): . .0
Franchised Units (12/1/1989): 50
Total Units (12/1/1989): 50
Distribution: US-44;Can-2;Overseas-4
 North America: . . . . 25 States, 2 Provinces
 Concentration: . . . 6 in CA, 5 in NY, 3 in FL
Registered: . . . . All States Except SD
. . . .
Average # of Employees: . . . . . . 2 FT, 2 PT
Prior Industry Experience: . . . . Helpful

FINANCIAL: OTC-LVDG
Cash Investment: $100-175K
Total Investment: $225-350K
Fees: Franchise - $40K
 Royalty: 3%, Advert: . . . . . Flat
Contract Periods (Yrs.): 15/5
Area Development Agreement: . .No
Sub-Franchise Contract: . . . . .No
Expand in Territory: . . . . Yes
Passive Ownership: . . . Discouraged
Encourage Conversions: . . . . .No
Franchisee Purchase(s) Required: Yes

FRANCHISOR TRAINING/SUPPORT:
Financial Assistance Provided: . . . . .No
Site Selection Assistance: . . . . . . .Yes
Lease Negotiation Assistance: . . . . .Yes
Co-operative Advertising: . . . . .No
Training: . . . . 2 Wks. Headquarters
. . . .
On-Going Support: . . . . B,C,D,E,F,G,H
Full-Time Franchisor Support Staff: . . 15
EXPANSION PLANS:
 US: . . . . .All US
Canada - Yes, . . . Overseas - Yes

MERLE HARMON'S FAN FAIR

12425 Knoll Rd.
Elm Grove, WI 53122
TEL: (414) 784-8884 C
FAX:
Mr. Keith Harmon, VP Marketing

Sports fan's gift shop, featuring apparel and accessories bearing logos of pro teams and college teams. Stores are approximately 1,000 SF and located in regional shopping malls. FAN FAIR offers total supervisory services on a fee basis for passive investors.

HISTORY: . . . . IFA
Established in 1977; . . 1st Franchised in 1982
Company-Owned Units (As of 12/1/1989): . .0
Franchised Units (12/1/1989): 125
Total Units (12/1/1989): 125
Distribution: . . . US-125;Can-0;Overseas-0
 North America: . . . . 25 States
 Concentration: . . 17 in TX, 12 in IL, 12 in OH
Registered: . . . . . All States Except HI,OR
. . . .
Average # of Employees: . . . . . . 2 FT, 2 PT
Prior Industry Experience: . . . . Helpful

FINANCIAL:
Cash Investment: . . . .$
Total Investment: $90-140K
Fees: Franchise - $15-20K
 Royalty: 5%, Advert: 1%
Contract Periods (Yrs.): 15/10
Area Development Agreement: . .No
Sub-Franchise Contract: . . . . .No
Expand in Territory: . . . . Yes
Passive Ownership: . . . . . .Allowed
Encourage Conversions: . . . . . Yes
Franchisee Purchase(s) Required: Yes

FRANCHISOR TRAINING/SUPPORT:
Financial Assistance Provided: . . . . .No
Site Selection Assistance: . . . . . . .Yes
Lease Negotiation Assistance: . . . . .Yes
Co-operative Advertising: . . . . .Yes
Training: . . . . .1 Wk. Headquarters,
. . . . .1 Wk. In Store
On-Going Support: . . . a,b,C,D,E,f,G,H,I
Full-Time Franchisor Support Staff: . . 30
EXPANSION PLANS:
 US: . . . . .All US
Canada - Yes, . . . Overseas - Yes

NEVADA BOB'S PRO SHOPS

3333 E. Flamingo Rd.
Las Vegas, NV 89121
TEL: (702) 451-3333
FAX: (702) 451-9378
Mr. Bob Hulley, Fran. Dir.

Selling discount golf equipment in an attractive atmosphere, specializing in top-of-the-line golf clubs, golf bags and accessories from McGregor, Spalding, Prima, Mizuno, Dunlop. etc. Also, professional advice on all golf equipment given by our professional staff.

HISTORY: . . . .
Established in 1974; . . 1st Franchised in 1978
Company-Owned Units (As of 12/1/1989): . .4
Franchised Units (12/1/1989): 254
Total Units (12/1/1989): 258
Distribution: . . . US-222;Can-22;Overseas-14
 North America: . . . . 42 States, 2 Provinces
 Concentration: . .29 in CA, 20 in TX, 17 in FL
Registered: . . . . .All
. . . .
Average # of Employees: . . . . . . 4 FT, 3 PT
Prior Industry Experience: . . . . Helpful

FINANCIAL:
Cash Investment: $125K
Total Investment: $250K
Fees: Franchise - $57.5K
 Royalty: 3%, Advert: 0%
Contract Periods (Yrs.): 10/10
Area Development Agreement: . .No
Sub-Franchise Contract: . . . . .No
Expand in Territory: . . . . Yes
Passive Ownership: . . . Not Allowed
Encourage Conversions: . . . . . NA
Franchisee Purchase(s) Required: .No

FRANCHISOR TRAINING/SUPPORT:
Financial Assistance Provided: . . . . .NA
Site Selection Assistance: . . . . . . .Yes
Lease Negotiation Assistance: . . . . .Yes
Co-operative Advertising: . . . . .NA
Training: . . . . 1 Wk. Headquarters
. . . .
On-Going Support: . . . .B,C,D,E,F,G,H,I
Full-Time Franchisor Support Staff: . . 80
EXPANSION PLANS:
 US: . . . . .All US
Canada - Yes, . . . Overseas - Yes

PLAY IT AGAIN SPORTS

1550 Utica Ave. S.
Minneapolis, MN 55416
TEL: (800) 433-2540 (612) 593-0683
FAX: (612) 593-0730
Ms. Martha Morris, President

PLAY IT AGAIN SPORTS fills a unique niche by selling used and new sports equipment. We buy, sell, trade and consign used equipment. We sell new goods through liquidations, close-outs and special purchases.

HISTORY: . . . .
Established in 1983; . . 1st Franchised in 1988
Company-Owned Units (As of 12/1/1989): . .9
Franchised Units (12/1/1989): 21
Total Units (12/1/1989): 30
Distribution: US-30;Can-0;Overseas-0
North America: . . . . 8 States
Concentration: . . . 11 in MN, 3 in WI, 3 in IL
Registered: . . . . .IL,MI,MN,OR,SD,WA,WI
. . . .
Average # of Employees: . . . . . . 1 FT, 1 PT
Prior Industry Experience: . . . . Helpful

FINANCIAL:
Cash Investment: $50-127K
Total Investment: $50-127K
Fees: Franchise - $15K
Royalty: 3%, Advert: 5%
Contract Periods (Yrs.): 10/5
Area Development Agreement: Yes/10
Sub-Franchise Contract: . . . . . .No
Expand in Territory: . . . . Yes
Passive Ownership: . . . Discouraged
Encourage Conversions: . . . . . Yes
Franchisee Purchase(s) Required: .No

FRANCHISOR TRAINING/SUPPORT:
Financial Assistance Provided: . . . . . No
Site Selection Assistance: . . . . .Yes
Lease Negotiation Assistance: . . . . .Yes
Co-operative Advertising: . . . . No
Training: . . . . 1 Wk. Headquarters
. . . .
On-Going Support: . . . .B,C,D,E,F,G,H,I
Full-Time Franchisor Support Staff: . . . 7
EXPANSION PLANS:
US: . . . . .All US
Canada - No, ...Overseas - No

PRO GOLF DISCOUNT

31884 Northwestern Hwy.
Farmington Hills, MI 48018
TEL: (313) 737-0553
FAX: (313) 737-9077
Mr. Lee Vlisides, Corp. Devel.

PRO GOLF OF AMERICA is the oldest and largest chain of golf-only retail stores. PRO GOLF has been operating since 1964 and franchising since 1972. PRO GOLF retail stores offer a complete line of golf equipment and accessories from every major manufacturer in the golf industry. PRO GOLF offers the most complete line of exclusive merchandise from many manufacturers.

HISTORY: . . . .
Established in 1964; . . 1st Franchised in 1972
Company-Owned Units (As of 12/1/1989): . .3
Franchised Units (12/1/1989): 125
Total Units (12/1/1989): 128
Distribution: US-115;Can-7;Overseas-3
North America: . . . . 30 States, 2 Provinces
Concentration: . .16 in MI, 13 in FL, 10 in CA
Registered: . . . . .All
. . . .
Average # of Employees: . . . . . . 4 FT, 2 PT
Prior Industry Experience: . . . . Helpful

FINANCIAL:
Cash Investment: $85-110K
Total Investment: $175-225K
Fees: Franchise - $45K
Royalty: 2%, Advert: 0%
Contract Periods (Yrs.): 30/30
Area Development Agreement: Yes/30
Sub-Franchise Contract: . . . . . .No
Expand in Territory: . . . . Yes
Passive Ownership: . . . . . .Allowed
Encourage Conversions: . . . . . Yes
Franchisee Purchase(s) Required: .No

FRANCHISOR TRAINING/SUPPORT:
Financial Assistance Provided: . . . . . No
Site Selection Assistance: . . . . .Yes
Lease Negotiation Assistance: . . . . .Yes
Co-operative Advertising: . . . . .Yes
Training: . . . . .Up To 2 Wks. HQ
. . . .
On-Going Support: . . . . B,C,D,E,f,G,H,I
Full-Time Franchisor Support Staff: . . 15
EXPANSION PLANS:
US: . . . . .All US
Canada - Yes, . . . Overseas - Yes

WORLD CLASS ATHLETE

1814 Franklin St., # 700
Oakland, CA 94612
TEL: (800) SURF-RAT (415) 547-1596
FAX: (415) 835-3779
Mr. Jeff McKee, President

WORLD CLASS ATHLETE offers a unique, specialty sporting goods concept. Product mix concentrates on athletic footwear, running, tennis and swimwear. Emphasis on race sponsorship, training programs and custom fitting. All major lines of footwear, accessories, warm-up suits and bags. Custom re-soling at Company-owned distribution centers.

HISTORY: . . . . .IFA
Established in 1976; . . 1st Franchised in 1977
Company-Owned Units (As of 12/1/1989): . 15
Franchised Units (12/1/1989): 66
Total Units (12/1/1989): 81
Distribution: US-74;Can-7;Overseas-0
North America: . . . . 15 States, 2 Provinces
Concentration: . . 25 in CA, 8 in WA, 5 in KY
Registered: . . . CA,FL,HI,IL,MN,MI,NY,OR
. . . . WA,WI,AB
Average # of Employees: . . . . . . 2 FT, 4 PT
Prior Industry Experience: . . . . Helpful

FINANCIAL: OTC-WCA
Cash Investment: $75K
Total Investment: $120-225K
Fees: Franchise - $18K
Royalty: 6%, Advert: 2%
Contract Periods (Yrs.): 15/15
Area Development Agreement: Yes/15
Sub-Franchise Contract: . . . . . Yes
Expand in Territory: . . . . .No
Passive Ownership: . . . Not Allowed
Encourage Conversions: . . . . . Yes
Franchisee Purchase(s) Required: Yes

FRANCHISOR TRAINING/SUPPORT:
Financial Assistance Provided: . . .Yes(D)
Site Selection Assistance: . . . . .Yes
Lease Negotiation Assistance: . . . . .Yes
Co-operative Advertising: . . . . .Yes
Training: . . . . 3 Wks. Headquarters,
. . . . .2 Wks. Site, On-going
On-Going Support: . . . a,B,C,D,E,f,G,H,I
Full-Time Franchisor Support Staff: . . 24
EXPANSION PLANS:
US: . . . . .All US
Canada - Yes, ... Overseas - No

SUPPLEMENTAL LISTING OF FRANCHISORS

ATHLETE'S FOOT, THE . . . . 3735 Atlanta Industrial Pkwy., Atlanta GA 30331
ATHLETIC ATTIC . . . . P.O. Box 14503, Gainesville FL 32604
ATHLETIC LADY . . . . P.O. Box 14503, Gainesville FL 32604
COMPLETE ATHLETE . . . . .1850 Delmar Dr., Folcroft PA 19032
FITNESS INDUSTRIES . . . . 19201 Orbit Dr., Gaithersburg MD 20879
ISLAND WATER SPORTS . . . . .10 Fairway Dr., # 302, Deerfield Beach FL 33441
JERSEY CITY . . . . 135 16 Ave. NW, Calgary AB T2M0H3   CAN
JUST FOR FEET . . . . .3460 Galleria Cir., Birmingham AL 35226
MARK-IT STORES, THE . . . . .316 Yale St., P.O. Box 187, St. Joseph MO 64504
N. B. SPORTS . . . . .2050 Dundas St. E., Mississauga ON L4X1L9   CAN
PRO GOLF OF CANADA . . . . 2550 Goldenridge Rd., # 44, Mississauga ON L4X2S3   CAN
RYAN'S SOCCER INTERNATIONAL . . . . 330 Enfield Rd., Centerville OH 45459
SECOND SOLE . . . . .3524 Charlotte St., Pittsburgh PA 15201
SHOWCASE . . . . .1850 Delmar Dr., Folcroft PA 19032
SPORT CONNECTION . . . . 1500 Fisher St., # 115, North Bay ON P1B2H3   CAN
SPORT SHACK . . . . .450 Oak Grove Pkwy., # 106, St. Paul MN 55127
SPORTS ARENA . . . . 414 N. Orleans, # 608, Chicago IL 60610
SPORTS FANTASY . . . . P.O. Box 1847, Columbus GA 31902
TOUCHDOWN SPORTSWEAR . . . . 3515 Rupp Parkway, Decatur IL 62526
WALK & JOG . . . . P.O. Box 51273, Jacksonville Beach FL 32240

CHAPTER 38

RETAIL: CLOTHING AND SHOES

AGNEW/AGGIES/ASHTON SHOES

298 Park Road N.
Brantford, ON N3T5T9 CAN
TEL: (519) 752-7854
FAX: (519) 752-9419
Mr. E. F. Mayne, VP Franchising

AGNEW, AGGIES and ASHTON SHOES Retail Footwear franchises offer a proven business opportunity. Choose your existing profitable location from over 345 stores across Canada.

HISTORY: . . . . .CFA
Established in 1900; . . 1st Franchised in 1988
Company-Owned Units (As of 12/1/1989):   300
Franchised Units (12/1/1989): 48
Total Units (12/1/1989): 348
Distribution: US-0;Can-348;Overseas-0
 North America: . . . . 10 Provinces
 Concentration: . 149 in ON, 42 in AB,37 in BC
Registered: . . . . AB
 . . . .
Average # of Employees: . . . . . . 3 FT, 3 PT
Prior Industry Experience: . . . . Helpful

FINANCIAL:
Cash Investment: $60-120K
Total Investment: $180-350K
Fees: Franchise - $30K
 Royalty: 6%, Advert: 2%
Contract Periods (Yrs.): 20/5
Area Development Agreement: . .No
Sub-Franchise Contract: . . . . . .No
Expand in Territory: . . . . Yes
Passive Ownership: . . . Discouraged
Encourage Conversions: . . . . . NA
Franchisee Purchase(s) Required: Yes

FRANCHISOR TRAINING/SUPPORT:
Financial Assistance Provided: . . . Yes(I)
Site Selection Assistance: . . . . .NA
Lease Negotiation Assistance: . . . . .Yes
Co-operative Advertising: . . . . .Yes
Training: . . . . 2 Wks. Headquarters
 . . . .
On-Going Support: . . . A,B,C,D,E,F,G,H
Full-Time Franchisor Support Staff: . 1800
EXPANSION PLANS:
 US: .No
 Canada - Yes, ... Overseas - No

BLUE JUNCTION /
FASHION WAVES
590 Gordon Baker Rd.
Willowdale, ON M2H3B4 CAN
TEL: (416) 490-1719
FAX:
Mr. R. E. Tanna, General Manager

FASHION WAVES offers a great casual wear concept for the market at mid-range prices.

HISTORY: . . . .
Established in 1974; . . 1st Franchised in 1977
Company-Owned Units (As of 12/1/1989): . .2
Franchised Units (12/1/1989): 16
Total Units (12/1/1989): 18
Distribution: US-0;Can-18;Overseas-0
North America: . . . . .1 Province
Concentration: . . . . 18 in ON
Registered: . . . .
. . . .
Average # of Employees: . . . . . . 1 FT, 5 PT
Prior Industry Experience: . . . . Helpful

FINANCIAL:
Cash Investment: $50K
Total Investment: $100K
Fees: Franchise - $20-25K
Royalty: 4%, Advert: 1%
Contract Periods (Yrs.): 5/5
Area Development Agreement: . .No
Sub-Franchise Contract: . . . . .No
Expand in Territory: . . . . Yes
Passive Ownership: . . . Not Allowed
Encourage Conversions: . . . . . Yes
Franchisee Purchase(s) Required: Yes

FRANCHISOR TRAINING/SUPPORT:
Financial Assistance Provided: . . . . .No
Site Selection Assistance: . . . . . . .Yes
Lease Negotiation Assistance: . . . . .Yes
Co-operative Advertising: . . . . . . .Yes
Training: . . . . . 2 Wks. Training at Store,
. . . . .3 Wks. Own Store
On-Going Support: . . . a,B,C,D,E,f,G,h,i
Full-Time Franchisor Support Staff: . . 10
EXPANSION PLANS:
US: . . . . .No
Canada - Yes, ...Overseas - No

CENTMIL CHEMISES, LE /
THE MATCH
5650 Cypihot
Ville St-Laurent, PQ H4S1V7 CAN
TEL: (514) 334-8203
FAX: (514) 4656
Mr. Jean Guy LeBlanc, President

Men's accessories retail outlets, selling shirts, ties, bow ties, socks, belts, sweaters, underwear, scarves, gloves and other accessories.

HISTORY: . . . . .CFA
Established in 1987; . . 1st Franchised in 1987
Company-Owned Units (As of 12/1/1989): . .2
Franchised Units (12/1/1989): 8
Total Units (12/1/1989): 10
Distribution: US-0;Can-10;Overseas-0
North America: . . . . .1 Province
Concentration: . . . . .10 in PQ
Registered: . . . .
. . . .
Average # of Employees: . . . . . . 1 FT, 2 PT
Prior Industry Experience: . . . . Helpful

FINANCIAL:
Cash Investment: $40-70K
Total Investment: $65-90K
Fees: Franchise - $10-15K
Royalty: 6%, Advert: 1%
Contract Periods (Yrs.): . . . .5+/5
Area Development Agreement: Yes/10
Sub-Franchise Contract: . . . . .No
Expand in Territory: . . . . Yes
Passive Ownership: . . . . . .Allowed
Encourage Conversions: . . . . .No
Franchisee Purchase(s) Required: Yes

FRANCHISOR TRAINING/SUPPORT:
Financial Assistance Provided: . . . Yes(I)
Site Selection Assistance: . . . . . . .Yes
Lease Negotiation Assistance: . . . .Yes
Co-operative Advertising: . . . . . . .Yes
Training: . . . . . . 2-4 Days Retail Outlet,
. . . . .2-4 Days Office (Administrative)
On-Going Support: . . . . b,c,d,e,g,h
Full-Time Franchisor Support Staff: . . 14
EXPANSION PLANS:
US: . . . . .No
Canada - Yes, ...Overseas - No

FASHION CROSSROADS

2130 N. Hollywood Way
Burbank, CA 91505
TEL: (800) 227-4632 (818) 843-4340
FAX: (818) 567-2442
Ms. Pat Trowbridge, Dir. Fran.

Franchisor of women's retail clothing stores.

HISTORY: . . . .
Established in 1937; . . 1st Franchised in 1937
Company-Owned Units (As of 12/1/1989): . 44
Franchised Units (12/1/1989): 265
Total Units (12/1/1989): 309
Distribution: US-309;Can-0;Overseas-0
North America: . . . . .27 States
Concentration: . 43 in CA, 23 in OR, 23 in WA
Registered: . . .CA,IL,IN,MN,ND,SD,WA,WI
. . . .
Average # of Employees: . . . . . . 1 FT, 2 PT
Prior Industry Experience: . . . . Helpful

FINANCIAL:
Cash Investment: $10-20K
Total Investment: $24-68K
Fees: Franchise - $3K
Royalty: 7.5%, Advert: 0%
Contract Periods (Yrs.): 5/5
Area Development Agreement: . .No
Sub-Franchise Contract: . . . . .No
Expand in Territory: . . . . Yes
Passive Ownership: . . . Discouraged
Encourage Conversions: . . . . . Yes
Franchisee Purchase(s) Required: Yes

FRANCHISOR TRAINING/SUPPORT:
Financial Assistance Provided: . . . . .No
Site Selection Assistance: . . . . . . .Yes
Lease Negotiation Assistance: . . . .Yes
Co-operative Advertising: . . . . . . .Yes
Training: . . . . . 2 Wks. Headquarters Not
. . . . .Included in Franchise Fee
On-Going Support: . . . A,B,C,D,E,f,G,h,I
Full-Time Franchisor Support Staff: . . . .
EXPANSION PLANS:
US: . . . . . Where Currently Have Units
Canada - No, ...Overseas - No

FASHION IS

2901 Steeles Ave. W.
Downsview, ON CAN
TEL: (416) 661-1212
FAX: (416) 661-1217
Mr. Mike Mehta

Ladies' accessories, handbags, costume jewelry.

HISTORY: . . . .
Established in 1983; . . 1st Franchised in 1986
Company-Owned Units (As of 12/1/1989): . .7
Franchised Units (12/1/1989): 9
Total Units (12/1/1989): 16
Distribution: US-0;Can-16;Overseas-0
  North America: . . . . .1 Province
  Concentration: . . . . 16 in ON
Registered: . . . .
. . . .
Average # of Employees: . . . . . . 1 FT, 2 PT
Prior Industry Experience: . . . . Helpful

FINANCIAL:
Cash Investment: $50K
Total Investment: $100K
Fees: Franchise - $25K
  Royalty: 5%, Advert: 1%
Contract Periods (Yrs.): 5/5
Area Development Agreement: . .No
Sub-Franchise Contract: . . . . . Yes
Expand in Territory: . . . . . . Yes
Passive Ownership: . . . Not Allowed
Encourage Conversions: . . . . .No
Franchisee Purchase(s) Required: .No

FRANCHISOR TRAINING/SUPPORT:
Financial Assistance Provided: . . . Yes(I)
Site Selection Assistance: . . . . . . .Yes
Lease Negotiation Assistance: . . . . .Yes
Co-operative Advertising: . . . . . . .Yes
Training: . . . .
. . . .
On-Going Support: . . .A,B,C,D,E,F,G,h,i
Full-Time Franchisor Support Staff: . . 25
EXPANSION PLANS:
US: . . . . . Northeast, Midwest, South
Canada - Yes, . . . Overseas - Yes

FINE THREADS

2660 NE University Village Mall
Seattle, WA 98015
TEL: (206) 525-5888
FAX:
Mr. Garry Davidson, President

Boy's and young men's traditional clothing and sportswear. One-stop shopping, sizes 8-20 and 36-43, depth of selection, quality service. Private label merchandise, except for Polo (Ralph Lauren) and Levi (boys - carry regular, husky and slim sizes). Young men's regular, short and long, for slimmer man as well.

HISTORY: . . . .
Established in 1982; . . 1st Franchised in 1988
Company-Owned Units (As of 12/1/1989): . .1
Franchised Units (12/1/1989): 0
Total Units (12/1/1989): 1
Distribution: US-1;Can-0;Overseas-0
  North America: . . . . .1 State
  Concentration: . . . . .1 in WA
Registered: . . . . .CA,NY,WA
. . . .
Average # of Employees: . . . . . . 1 FT, 2 PT
Prior Industry Experience: . . . . Helpful

FINANCIAL:
Cash Investment: $40-60K
Total Investment: $170-290K
Fees: Franchise - $20K
  Royalty: 6%, Advert: 2%
Contract Periods (Yrs.): 8/8
Area Development Agreement: . .No
Sub-Franchise Contract: . . . . .No
Expand in Territory: . . . . . . Yes
Passive Ownership: . . . . . .Allowed
Encourage Conversions: . . . . .No
Franchisee Purchase(s) Required: .No

FRANCHISOR TRAINING/SUPPORT:
Financial Assistance Provided: . . . . .No
Site Selection Assistance: . . . . . . .Yes
Lease Negotiation Assistance: . . . . .No
Co-operative Advertising: . . . . . . .Yes
Training: . . . . . Training at Headquarters
. . . .
On-Going Support: . . . .B,C,D,E,F,G,H,I
Full-Time Franchisor Support Staff: . . .3
EXPANSION PLANS:
US: . . . . .CA, NY, NJ and CT
Canada - No, ...Overseas - No

FRAT HOUSE, THE

57 King St. W.
Kitchener, ON N2G1A1
TEL: (519) 576-9300
FAX: (519) 576-7229
Mr. Doug Marr, President

THE FRAT HOUSE . . . for those classic basics in every man's wardrobe.

HISTORY: . . . .
Established in 1983; . . 1st Franchised in 1983
Company-Owned Units (As of 12/1/1989): . 16
Franchised Units (12/1/1989): 9
Total Units (12/1/1989): 25
Distribution: US-0;Can-25;Overseas-0
  North America: . . . . 4 Provinces
  Concentration: . . .23 in ON, 1 in BC, 1 in AB
Registered: . . . . AB
. . . .
Average # of Employees: . . . . . . 2 FT, 3 PT
Prior Industry Experience: . . . . Helpful

FINANCIAL:
Cash Investment: . . . .$
Total Investment: . . . .$
Fees: Franchise - . . . .$
  Royalty: 3%, Advert: 1%
Contract Periods (Yrs.): 10/5
Area Development Agreement: . . Yes
Sub-Franchise Contract: . . . . . .No
Expand in Territory: . . . . . . Yes
Passive Ownership: . . . Discouraged
Encourage Conversions: . . . . . NA
Franchisee Purchase(s) Required: .No

FRANCHISOR TRAINING/SUPPORT:
Financial Assistance Provided: . . . . . No
Site Selection Assistance: . . . . . . .Yes
Lease Negotiation Assistance: . . . . .Yes
Co-operative Advertising: . . . . . . .Yes
Training: . . . . Varies
. . . .
On-Going Support: . . . . .d,e,H,I
Full-Time Franchisor Support Staff: . . 20
EXPANSION PLANS:
US: .No
Canada - Yes, ...Overseas - No

JUST PANTS

1034 Bonaventure Dr.
Elk Grove Village, IL 60007
TEL: (312) 894-7500 C
FAX:
Mr. Robert Tischler, Dir. Fran. Dev.

America's largest chain of franchised stores specializing in jeans and casual tops for young men and women.

HISTORY: . . . .
Established in 1969; . . 1st Franchised in 1969
Company-Owned Units (As of 12/1/1989): . .0
Franchised Units (12/1/1989): 96
Total Units (12/1/1989): 96
Distribution: US-96;Can-0;Overseas-0
North America: . . . . 17 States
Concentration: . . . .
Registered: . . . . All States

. . . .
Average # of Employees: . . . . . 4 FT, 4-6 PT
Prior Industry Experience: . . . . . . Helpful

FINANCIAL:
Cash Investment: $70-100K
Total Investment: $108-225K
Fees: Franchise - $15K
  Royalty: 5%, Advert: 3%
Contract Periods (Yrs.): . . . . Lease
Area Development Agreement: . Yes
Sub-Franchise Contract: . . . . . .No
Expand in Territory: . . . . . . Yes
Passive Ownership: . . . Discouraged
Encourage Conversions: . . . . . .No
Franchisee Purchase(s) Required: .No

FRANCHISOR TRAINING/SUPPORT:
Financial Assistance Provided: . . . . . No
Site Selection Assistance: . . . . .Yes
Lease Negotiation Assistance: . . . . .Yes
Co-operative Advertising: . . . . .NA
Training: . . . . 1 Wk. Field,
. . . . 4-7 Days Headquarters
On-Going Support: . . . . C,D,E,F,h
Full-Time Franchisor Support Staff: . . 12
EXPANSION PLANS:
US: . . . . .All US
Canada - No, ...Overseas - No

KETTLE CREEK CANVAS COMPANY

194 Main St.
Port Stanley, ON N0L2A0 CAN
TEL: (519) 782-3318
FAX: (519) 782-4617
Mr. Stephen Moore, Controller

KETTLE CREEK sells an exclusive line of casual clothes for men and women. Our products offer unique designs and styles, all made from 100% natural materials.

HISTORY: . . . .
Established in 1979; . . 1st Franchised in 1990
Company-Owned Units (As of 12/1/1989): . 10
Franchised Units (12/1/1989): 45
Total Units (12/1/1989): 55
Distribution: US-0;Can-55;Overseas-0
North America: . . . . 8 Provinces
Concentration: . . .35 in ON, 8 in BC, 3 in AB
Registered: . . . . AB

. . . .
Average # of Employees: . . . . . . 3 FT, 3 PT
Prior Industry Experience: . . . . Helpful

FINANCIAL:
Cash Investment: $50-75K
Total Investment: $140-180K
Fees: Franchise - $25K
  Royalty: 2%, Advert: 2%
Contract Periods (Yrs.): 5/5
Area Development Agreement: . .No
Sub-Franchise Contract: . . . . . .No
Expand in Territory: . . . . Yes
Passive Ownership: . . . Not Allowed
Encourage Conversions: . . . . . .No
Franchisee Purchase(s) Required: Yes

FRANCHISOR TRAINING/SUPPORT:
Financial Assistance Provided: . . . Yes(I)
Site Selection Assistance: . . . . .Yes
Lease Negotiation Assistance: . . . . .Yes
Co-operative Advertising: . . . . .Yes
Training: . . . . . . Varies With Franchisee
. . . .
On-Going Support: . . . .B,C,D,E,F,G,H,I
Full-Time Franchisor Support Staff: . .300
EXPANSION PLANS:
US: . . . . .No
Canada - Yes, ...Overseas - No

KIDDIE KOBBLER

68 Robertson Rd., # 106
Nepean, ON K2H8P5 CAN
TEL: (613) 820-0505
FAX:
Mr. Errol Bingley, Mktg. Mgr.

Children's shoe stores, featuring a unique store design, located in major shopping malls. The extensive marketing program is designed to develop new and repeat business through intensive customer service. The product mix includes brand name children's footwear, dancewear, athletic and prescription footwear and accessories.

HISTORY: . . . .
Established in 1951; . . 1st Franchised in 1968
Company-Owned Units (As of 12/1/1989): . .3
Franchised Units (12/1/1989): 57
Total Units (12/1/1989): 59
Distribution: US-3;Can-56;Overseas-0
North America: . . . . 2 States, 7 Provinces
Concentration: . . .37 in ON, 7 in BC, 6 in PQ
Registered: . . . . NY,AB

. . . .
Average # of Employees: . . . . . . 2 FT, 3 PT
Prior Industry Experience: . . . . Helpful

FINANCIAL:
Cash Investment: $50-70K
Total Investment: $100-150K
Fees: Franchise - $25K
  Royalty: 4%, Advert: 1%
Contract Periods (Yrs.): 10/5
Area Development Agreement: . .No
Sub-Franchise Contract: . . . . . .No
Expand in Territory: . . . . .No
Passive Ownership: . . . Discouraged
Encourage Conversions: . . . . . Yes
Franchisee Purchase(s) Required: .No

FRANCHISOR TRAINING/SUPPORT:
Financial Assistance Provided: . . . Yes(I)
Site Selection Assistance: . . . . .Yes
Lease Negotiation Assistance: . . . . .Yes
Co-operative Advertising: . . . . .Yes
Training: . . . . . .3 Months Nearest Exist-
. . . . ing Unit
On-Going Support: . . . a,b,C,D,E,F,G,H,I
Full-Time Franchisor Support Staff: . . 10
EXPANSION PLANS:
US: . . . . Northeast
Canada - Yes, ...Overseas - No

LADY'S A CHAMP, THE

57 King St. W.
Kitchener, ON N2G1A1 CAN
TEL: (519) 576-9300
FAX: (519) 576-7229
Mr. Doug Marr, President

Offering you the latest in women's activewear and accessories.

HISTORY:	FINANCIAL:	FRANCHISOR TRAINING/SUPPORT:
Established in 1980; . . 1st Franchised in 1981	Cash Investment: . . . .$NA	Financial Assistance Provided: . . . . . No
Company-Owned Units (As of 12/1/1989): . 16	Total Investment: . . . .$NA	Site Selection Assistance: . . . . . . .Yes
Franchised Units (12/1/1989): 13	Fees: Franchise - . . . .$NA	Lease Negotiation Assistance: . . . . .Yes
Total Units (12/1/1989): 29	Royalty: 3%, Advert: 1%	Co-operative Advertising: . . . . . . .Yes
Distribution: US-0;Can-29;Overseas-0	Contract Periods (Yrs.): 10/5	Training: . . . . Varies
North America: . . . . 4 Provinces	Area Development Agreement: . Yes	. . . .
Concentration: . . .27 in ON, 1 in AB, 1 in BC	Sub-Franchise Contract: . . . . .No	On-Going Support: . . . . .d,e,,H,I
Registered: . . . . AB	Expand in Territory: . . . . . . Yes	Full-Time Franchisor Support Staff: . . 35
. . . .	Passive Ownership: . . . Discouraged	EXPANSION PLANS:
Average # of Employees: . . . . . . 2 FT, 3 PT	Encourage Conversions: . . . . . NA	US: . . . . No
Prior Industry Experience: . . . . Helpful	Franchisee Purchase(s) Required: .No	Canada - Yes, ...Overseas - No

LE BATEAU BLANC

5500 Bl. des Gradins
Quebec City, PQ G2J1A1 CAN
TEL: (418) 627-1846
FAX: (418) 627-4125
Mr. Pierre Yelle, President

LE BATEAU BLANC offers consumers children's fashion of superior workmanship in the latest styles.

HISTORY: . . . . .CFA	FINANCIAL:	FRANCHISOR TRAINING/SUPPORT:
Established in 1975; . . 1st Franchised in 1984	Cash Investment: $25-25K	Financial Assistance Provided: . . . Yes(I)
Company-Owned Units (As of 12/1/1989): . .1	Total Investment: $125K	Site Selection Assistance: . . . . . . .Yes
Franchised Units (12/1/1989): 16	Fees: Franchise - $20K	Lease Negotiation Assistance: . . . . .Yes
Total Units (12/1/1989): 17	Royalty: 5%, Advert: 2%	Co-operative Advertising: . . . . . . .Yes
Distribution: US-0;Can-17;Overseas-0	Contract Periods (Yrs.): 5/5	Training: . . . . 1 Wk. Franchise Site
North America: . . . . 2 Provinces	Area Development Agreement: . .No	. . . .
Concentration: . . . . . . .15 in PQ, 2 in ON	Sub-Franchise Contract: . . . . .No	On-Going Support: . . . . B,C,d,E,H
Registered:	Expand in Territory: . . . . . . Yes	Full-Time Franchisor Support Staff: . . . 5
. . . .	Passive Ownership: . . . Not Allowed	EXPANSION PLANS:
Average # of Employees: . . . . . . 2 FT, 2 PT	Encourage Conversions: . . . . . Yes	US: . . . . No
Prior Industry Experience: . . . . Helpful	Franchisee Purchase(s) Required: Yes	Canada - Yes, ...Overseas - No

MARK'S WORK WEARHOUSE

1035 64th Ave. SE, # 30
Calgary, AB T2H2J7 CAN
TEL: (800) 661-1360 (403) 255-9220
FAX: (403) 255-6005
Mr. Kirk Marleau, VP Franchising

MARK'S WORK WEARHOUSE sells name-brand, private and captive label products competitively priced and supported by active sales promotion. Our stores are easily accessible, one-stop retail outlets, offering a complete range of workwear, casual wear and related apparel in a comfortable environment.

HISTORY:	FINANCIAL: TSE-MWW	FRANCHISOR TRAINING/SUPPORT:
Established in 1977; . . 1st Franchised in 1985	Cash Investment: $100-125K	Financial Assistance Provided: . . . . . No
Company-Owned Units (As of 12/1/1989): 115	Total Investment: $320-345K	Site Selection Assistance: . . . . . . .Yes
Franchised Units (12/1/1989): 40	Fees: Franchise - $50K	Lease Negotiation Assistance: . . . . .Yes
Total Units (12/1/1989): 155	Royalty: 6-8%, Advert: 0%	Co-operative Advertising: . . . . No
Distribution: . . . US-0;Can-155;Overseas-0	Contract Periods (Yrs.): . . . Infinite	Training: . . . . . . 6 Wks. Corporate Store
North America: . . . . 9 Provinces	Area Development Agreement: . .No	. . . .
Concentration: . 46 in ON, 30 in AB, 23 in BC	Sub-Franchise Contract: . . . . .No	On-Going Support: . . A,B,C,D,E,F,G,H,I
Registered: . . . . AB	Expand in Territory: . . . . . . Yes	Full-Time Franchisor Support Staff: . .100
. . . .	Passive Ownership: . . . Discouraged	EXPANSION PLANS:
Average # of Employees: . . . . . . 2 FT, 3 PT	Encourage Conversions: . . . . . Yes	US: . . . . No
Prior Industry Experience: . . . . Helpful	Franchisee Purchase(s) Required: .No	Canada - Yes, ...Overseas - No

MS. EMMA DESIGNS

275 Queen St. W.
Toronto, ON M5V1Z9 CAN
TEL: (416) 598-2471
FAX:
Ms. Sofia Verna, Owner

MS. EMMA offers high-quality designer clothing, handcrafted in natural fibres. The owner-operated, cozy, comfortable atmosphere appeals to the professional woman who appreciates quality and service.

HISTORY: . . . .
Established in 1972; . . 1st Franchised in 1988
Company-Owned Units (As of 12/1/1989): . .2
Franchised Units (12/1/1989): 2
Total Units (12/1/1989): 4
Distribution: US-0;Can-4;Overseas-0
North America: . . . .
Concentration: . . . .
Registered: . . . .
. . . .
Average # of Employees: . . . . . . 1 FT, 1 PT
Prior Industry Experience: . . . . . . Helpful

FINANCIAL:
Cash Investment: $35K
Total Investment: $42K
Fees: Franchise - $7K
  Royalty: 4%, Advert: 3-5%
Contract Periods (Yrs.): 5/5
Area Development Agreement: . . .
Sub-Franchise Contract: . . . . .No
Expand in Territory: . . . . . . .No
Passive Ownership: . . . Not Allowed
Encourage Conversions: . . . . . NA
Franchisee Purchase(s) Required: Yes

FRANCHISOR TRAINING/SUPPORT:
Financial Assistance Provided: . . . Yes(I)
Site Selection Assistance: . . . . . . .Yes
Lease Negotiation Assistance: . . . .Yes
Co-operative Advertising: . . . . . . .Yes
Training: . . . . . . 4-6 Wks. Headquarters

On-Going Support: . . . . B,E,F
Full-Time Franchisor Support Staff: . . 10
EXPANSION PLANS:
  US: . . . . .No
Canada - Yes, ...Overseas - No

LISA'S LEATHER AND LACE

P.O. Box 12488
Oakland, CA 94604
TEL: (415) BIG-BOYS
FAX: (415) 835-3779
Ms. Lisa D. Curotto, President

Nationally-renowned lingerie designer Lisa Curotto has established a high-margin chain of retail outlets, featuring the finest in quality and design in women's and men's undergarments. The unique product mix includes leather, lace, spandex, etc. - all at reasonable prices and of unparalleled quality Preview shows for otherwise shy male buyers. This $500 million /year industry is skyrocketing, so the potential is unlimited. LISA'S LEATHER AND LACE is destined for great growth.

HISTORY: . . . .
Established in 1985; . . 1st Franchised in 1986
Company-Owned Units (As of 12/1/1989): . .3
Franchised Units (12/1/1989): 3
Total Units (12/1/1989): 6
Distribution: US-6;Can-0;Overseas-0
North America: . . . . 2 States
Concentration: . . . . 4 in CA, 2 in NV
Registered: . . . . CA
. . . .
Average # of Employees: . . . . . . 1 FT, 3 PT
Prior Industry Experience: . . . . . . Helpful

FINANCIAL:
Cash Investment: $100K
Total Investment: $120K
Fees: Franchise - $20K
  Royalty: 5%, Advert: 1%
Contract Periods (Yrs.): 5/5
Area Development Agreement: Yes/1
Sub-Franchise Contract: . . . . . Yes
Expand in Territory: . . . . Yes
Passive Ownership: . . . . . .Allowed
Encourage Conversions: . . . . . Yes
Franchisee Purchase(s) Required: .No

FRANCHISOR TRAINING/SUPPORT:
Financial Assistance Provided: . . . . . No
Site Selection Assistance: . . . . . . .Yes
Lease Negotiation Assistance: . . . .Yes
Co-operative Advertising: . . . . No
Training: . . . . 2 Wks. Headquarters,
. . . . 1-2 Wks. Site
On-Going Support: . . . A,B,C,D,E,f,g,h,i
Full-Time Franchisor Support Staff: . . 13
EXPANSION PLANS:
  US: . . . . .All US
Canada - Yes, ...Overseas - Yes

SUPPLEMENTAL LISTING OF FRANCHISORS

A'GACI . . . . 3201 Cherry Ridge, # 210, San Antonio TX 78230
ACA JOE . . . . .148 Townsend St., San Francisco CA 91407
AIKO INTERNATIONAL . . . . 2441 Beta Ave., Burnaby BC V5C5N1   CAN
ALAIN MANOUKIAN . . . . .4200 boul. St-Laurent, Montreal PQ H2W2R2   CAN
ALBERT ANDREWS .111 Speen St., # 510, Framingham MA 01701
ALLISON'S PLACE . . . . 3161 E. Washington Blvd., Los Angeles CA 90023
AMARRAS . . . . .3617 A Silverside Rd., Wilmington DE 19810
ANGELO RETAIL CORP. . . . . 6155 Tomken Rd., # 16, Mississauga ON L5T1K3   CAN
APPARELMASTER . . . . P. O. Box 41687, Cincinnati OH 45241
BENCONE OUTLET CENTERS .121 Carver Ave., Westwood NJ 07675
BRAS 'N THINGS . . . . 1300 West McNab Rd., Ft. Lauderdale FL 33309
CANTERBURY OF NEW ZEALAND . . . . .21339 Cabot Blvd., Hayward CA 94545
CHEROKEE FRANCHISING CORP. . . . . .9545 Wentworth St., Sunland CA 91040

CYCLOTH . . . . 6517 Liggett Dr., Oakland CA 94611
DAINES WESTERN SHOPS . . . . Box 6, # 2, RR # 1, Penhuld AB T0N1R0   CAN
DREAM SHOPPE LINGERIE . . . . 1299 Hilton Ln., Oakville ON L6M2V3   CAN
ENTR. CHAUSSURES PANDA . . . . 132, boul. Labelle, # 160, Rosemere PQ J7A2H1   CAN
ESPIRIT . . . . .900 Minnesota St., San Francisco CA 94107
FASHIONS UNDER $10 .1036 E. Sibley Blvd., Dolton IL 60419
FRANCHISES VAG . . . . .323 ouest, boul. Henri Bourassa, Montreal PQ H3L1N8   CAN
HELEN'S HANDBAGS . . . . .7799 Leesburg Pike, # 900, Falls Church VA 22043
JEUNIQUE BOUTIQUE . . . . 19501 E. Walnut Dr., City of Industry CA 91748
JILENE . . . . P.O. Box 3038, Santa Barbara CA 93130
KRUG'S BIG & TALL . . . . 16 N. Washington Ave., Bergenfield NJ 07621
LANZ FRANCHISING . . . . 8680 Hayden Place, Culver City CA 90232
MAGNIFEET . . . . 425 Elm St., # 002, Cincinnati OH 45202
MARCO POLO ASSOCIATES . . . . 1540 Market St., # 425, San Francisco CA 94102
MARILYN BROOKS . . . . 700 King St. W., # 606, Toronto ON M5V2Y6   CAN
NORMA PETERSON FASHIONS . . . . 20 Steeplechase Rd. W., # 3, Markham ON L4S1B2   CAN
NORTH BY NORTHWEST . . . . 30 Pacific Ct., # 4, London ON N5V3K4   CAN
ROBIN KAY CLOTHING COMPAMY . . . . .201 Dufferin St., 3rd Fl., Toronto ON M6K1Y9   CAN
SIGNOR ANGELO & MADAME ANGELO . . . . . .1100 Finch Ave. W., # 622, Downsview ON M3J2T2   CAN
TOP-10 . . . . .1278 St. Clair Ave. W., Toronto ON M6S1B5   CAN
TRAIL N TOE . . . . 34 Grenfell Cres., Ottawa ON K2G0G2   CAN
WILD TOPS . . . . .600 Worcester Rd., Framingham MA 01701
WORK WORLD .1325 Eglinton Ave. E., Mississauga ON L4W4L9   CAN

CHAPTER 39

RETAIL: COMPUTER SALES AND SERVICE

COMPUTER MAINTENANCE SERVICE
P.O. Box 335
San Marcos, TX 78667
TEL: (512) 353-5333
FAX:
Mr. F. MacKenzie, Mgr. Sales/Mktg.

Repair and maintenance of computer peripherals and PC computers.

HISTORY: . . . .
Established in 1986; . . 1st Franchised in 1987
Company-Owned Units (As of 12/1/1989): . . 1
Franchised Units (12/1/1989): 0
Total Units (12/1/1989): 1
Distribution: US-1;Can-0;Overseas-0
  North America: . . . . .1 State
  Concentration: . . . . 1 in TX
Registered: . . . .
. . . .
Average # of Employees: . . . . .3 FT
Prior Industry Experience: . . . . . .Necessary

FINANCIAL:
Cash Investment: $10K
Total Investment: $10-20K
Fees: Franchise - . . . .$
  Royalty: 3%, Advert: 1%
Contract Periods (Yrs.): 5/5
Area Development Agreement: . .No
Sub-Franchise Contract: . . . . . .No
Expand in Territory: . . . . .No
Passive Ownership: . . . Discouraged
Encourage Conversions: . . . . . .No
Franchisee Purchase(s) Required: .No

FRANCHISOR TRAINING/SUPPORT:
Financial Assistance Provided: . . . . . No
Site Selection Assistance: . . . . .NA
Lease Negotiation Assistance: . . . . .NA
Co-operative Advertising: . . . . .NA
Training: . . . . . Continuous Headquarters
  . . . . and Site
On-Going Support: . . . .A,B,C,D,F,G,h,I
Full-Time Franchisor Support Staff: . . .3
EXPANSION PLANS:
  US: . . . . .All US
  Canada - Yes, ... Overseas - No

COMPUTERLAND CORPORATION

P.O. Box 9012
Pleasanton, CA 94566
TEL: (415) 734-4000
FAX:
Mr. Martin L. Strayer, VP Field Ops.

COMPUTERLAND CORPORATION is the oldest and largest computer retail franchise in the world, with over 700 stores in 26 countries. The COMPUTER-LAND name is synonymous with success and leadership in the computer retail industry.

HISTORY: . . . . IFA
Established in 1976; . . 1st Franchised in 1977
Company-Owned Units (As of 12/1/1989): . . .0
Franchised Units (12/1/1989): 725
Total Units (12/1/1989): 725
Distribution: . . US-461;Can-65;Overseas-199
 North America: . . . . 50 States, 9 Provinces
 Concentration: . . 65 in CA, 32 in IL, 18 in TX
Registered: . . . . .All
. . . .
Average # of Employees: . . . . 15 FT
Prior Industry Experience: . . . . . . Helpful

FINANCIAL:
Cash Investment: $250-900K
Total Investment: $200-1000K
Fees: Franchise - $7.5-35K
 Royalty: 5%, Advert: 1%
Contract Periods (Yrs.): 10/10
Area Development Agreement: . .No
Sub-Franchise Contract: . . . . . .No
Expand in Territory: . . . . Yes
Passive Ownership: . . . Not Allowed
Encourage Conversions: . . . . . Yes
Franchisee Purchase(s) Required: Yes

FRANCHISOR TRAINING/SUPPORT:
Financial Assistance Provided: . . . . . No
Site Selection Assistance: . . . . .Yes
Lease Negotiation Assistance: . . . . .Yes
Co-operative Advertising: . . . . .Yes
Training: . . . . 3 Days Headquarters
. . . .
On-Going Support: . . . . . A,B,C,E,G,h,I
Full-Time Franchisor Support Staff: . .150
EXPANSION PLANS:
 US: . . . . .All US
 Canada - No, ... Overseas - Yes

CX COMPUTER EXCHANGE

2800 Lafayette Rd.
Portsmouth, NH 03801
TEL: (603) 427-0221
FAX: (603) 433-3014
Mr. Robert M. Tortoriello, Fran.Dir.

Up-scale retail sales and service centers, specializing in used, late-model computers and accessories. Also sell new systems and some software. No experience necessary. Full training in all areas. Excellent margins with substantial on-going support from franchisor in inventory locator and procurement service.

HISTORY: . . . . IFA
Established in 1984; . . 1st Franchised in 1989
Company-Owned Units (As of 12/1/1989): . .2
Franchised Units (12/1/1989): 6
Total Units (12/1/1989): 8
Distribution: US-8;Can-0;Overseas-0
 North America: . . . . 3 States
 Concentration: . . . 4 in MA, 2 in NH, 2 in CT
Registered: . . . . FL,RI
. . . .
Average # of Employees: . . . . 2 Ft, 1 PT
Prior Industry Experience: . . . . Helpful

FINANCIAL:
Cash Investment: $20-25K
Total Investment: $75-90K
Fees: Franchise - $25K
 Royalty: 5%, Advert: 2%
Contract Periods (Yrs.): 15/5
Area Development Agreement: Yes/Var
Sub-Franchise Contract: . . . . . Yes
Expand in Territory: . . . . Yes
Passive Ownership: . . . . . .Allowed
Encourage Conversions: . . . . . NA
Franchisee Purchase(s) Required: .No

FRANCHISOR TRAINING/SUPPORT:
Financial Assistance Provided: . . . Yes(I)
Site Selection Assistance: . . . . .Yes
Lease Negotiation Assistance: . . . . .Yes
Co-operative Advertising: . . . . .Yes
Training: . . . . .1 Wk. Headquarters.
 . . 1 Wk. On-site, 3 Days Grand Opening
On-Going Support: . . . .A,B,C,D,E,F,H,I
Full-Time Franchisor Support Staff: . . 11
EXPANSION PLANS:
 US: . . . . . .All US, Franchisees East C.
 Canada - Yes, . . . Overseas - Yes

INACOMP COMPUTER CENTERS

1800 W. Maple Rd.
Troy, MI 48084
TEL: (313) 649-5580
FAX:
Mr. Richard Stopa, VP Corp. Fran.

INACOMP COMPUTER CENTERS sell the leading microcomputers, software, peripherals and supplies to businesses, institutions and the general public. IN-ACOMP has regional bases located in Detroit, Chicago, Atlanta, Orlando, Minneaplois, Cincinnati, Charlotte and Los Angeles. They provide fast order turn-around time, reducing the inventory needed to operate and provide franchise support services.

HISTORY: . . . . IFA
Established in 1976; . . 1st Franchised in 1981
Company-Owned Units (As of 12/1/1989): . 50
Franchised Units (12/1/1989): 60
Total Units (12/1/1989): 110
Distribution: US-110;Can-0;Overseas-0
 North America: . . . . 16 States
 Concentration: . 28 in MI, 18 in GA, 17 in CA
Registered: . . . CA,FL,HI,IL,IN,MD,MI,MN
. . . . RI,WI
Average # of Employees: . . . . . .10 FT, 8 PT
Prior Industry Experience: . . . . . .Necessary

FINANCIAL: OTC-INAC
Cash Investment: $100-150K
Total Investment: $200-400K
Fees: Franchise - $14-50K
 Royalty: 3-5%, Advert: 0%
Contract Periods (Yrs.): 10/10
Area Development Agreement: . .No
Sub-Franchise Contract: . . . . . .No
Expand in Territory: . . . . Yes
Passive Ownership: . . . Not Allowed
Encourage Conversions: . . . . . Yes
Franchisee Purchase(s) Required: Yes

FRANCHISOR TRAINING/SUPPORT:
Financial Assistance Provided: . . . Yes(I)
Site Selection Assistance: . . . . .Yes
Lease Negotiation Assistance: . . . . .Yes
Co-operative Advertising: . . . . .Yes
Training: . . . . .1 Wk. Headquarters,
. . . . 1 Wk. Regionally
On-Going Support: . . . . b,C,D,E,f,G,H,I
Full-Time Franchisor Support Staff: . .100
EXPANSION PLANS:
 US: . . . . .All US
 Canada - No, ...Overseas - No

RICHARD YOUNG

508 S. Military Trail
Deerfield Beach, Fl 33442
TEL: (800) 828-9949 (305) 426-8100
FAX: (305) 421-4654
Mr. Crawford G. Paton, VP

RICHARD YOUNG is establishing a network of franchise distributors selling major brand-name computer supplies and accessories to businesses and end-users. The four-color "Richard Young Journal of Computer Supplies" is provided as a sales tool to complement an active, well-trained sales force in maximizing profitability and market share.

HISTORY: . . . .
Established in 1979; . . 1st Franchised in 1985
Company-Owned Units (As of 12/1/1989): . . 2
Franchised Units (12/1/1989): 21
Total Units (12/1/1989): 23
Distribution: US-23;Can-0;Overseas-0
North America: . . . . 16 States
Concentration: . . . . 4 in CA, 3 in FL, 2 in PA
Registered: . . . . All States
. . . .
Average # of Employees: . . . . . . 5 FT, 1 PT
Prior Industry Experience: . . . . . . Necessary

FINANCIAL:
Cash Investment: $150K
Total Investment: $300K
Fees: Franchise - $27-85K
Royalty: 5.5%, Advert: 2%
Contract Periods (Yrs.): 10/10
Area Development Agreement: . .No
Sub-Franchise Contract: . . . . .No
Expand in Territory: . . . . Yes
Passive Ownership: . . . Not Allowed
Encourage Conversions: . . . . . Yes
Franchisee Purchase(s) Required: .No

FRANCHISOR TRAINING/SUPPORT:
Financial Assistance Provided: . . .Yes(D)
Site Selection Assistance: . . . . . . .Yes
Lease Negotiation Assistance: . . . . .Yes
Co-operative Advertising: . . . . .Yes
Training: . . . . .1 Wk. Headquarters,
. . . . . 1 Wk. Franchisee Site, On-going
On-Going Support: . . .A,B,C,D,E,F,G,h,I
Full-Time Franchisor Support Staff: . . 96
EXPANSION PLANS:
US: . . . . .All US
Canada - No, ...Overseas - No

SOFTWARE CITY

111 Galway Pl.
Teaneck, NJ 07666
TEL: (800) 222-0918 (201) 833-8510
FAX:
Mr. S. Altshuler, President

Leading chain of computer software specialty stores, offering hardware, software, peripherals and accessories to the home market, corporate accounts and educational institutions.

HISTORY: . . . .
Established in 1980; . . 1st Franchised in 1982
Company-Owned Units (As of 12/1/1989): . . 0
Franchised Units (12/1/1989): 90
Total Units (12/1/1989): 90
Distribution: US-89;Can-1;Overseas-0
North America: . . . .
Concentration: . . . .
Registered: . . . . All States
. . . .
Average # of Employees: . . . . . . 4 FT, 1 PT
Prior Industry Experience: . . . . Helpful

FINANCIAL:
Cash Investment: $104-140K
Total Investment: $104-140K
Fees: Franchise - $15K
Royalty: 5%, Advert: 1.5%
Contract Periods (Yrs.): 5/5
Area Development Agreement: . .No
Sub-Franchise Contract: . . . . .No
Expand in Territory: . . . . . . .No
Passive Ownership: . . . Discouraged
Encourage Conversions: . . . . . Yes
Franchisee Purchase(s) Required: .No

FRANCHISOR TRAINING/SUPPORT:
Financial Assistance Provided: . . . . .No
Site Selection Assistance: . . . . . . .Yes
Lease Negotiation Assistance: . . . . .No
Co-operative Advertising: . . . . . . .Yes
Training: . . . . .1 Wk.Headquarters,
. . . . .1 Wk. Franchisee Site
On-Going Support: . . . . B,C,D,E,f,G,h,I
Full-Time Franchisor Support Staff: . . 25
EXPANSION PLANS:
US: . . . . .All US
Canada - Yes, ...Overseas - Yes

SUPPLEMENTAL LISTING OF FRANCHISORS

COMPUCENTRE . . . . .9001 Louis H. LaFontaine, Ville Danjou PQ H1J2C5   CAN
COMPUTER MANIA . . . . 1021 Blossom Hill Rd., San Jose CA 95123
COMPUTER RENAISSANCE . . . . .400 Penn Center, # 900, Pittsburgh PA 15235
CONNECTING POINT OF AMERICA . . . . 7979 E. Tufts Ave. Pky., # 700, Denver CO 80237
ENTRE' COMPUTER CENTER . . . . .411 Eagle View Blvd., Exton PA 19335
INFOBRIDGE SOFTWARE BROKERS . . . . # 410 - 1801 Hamilton St., Regina SK S4P4B4   CAN
INTELLIGENT ELECTRONICS . . . . .411 Eagleview Blvd., Exton PA 19341
LASERQUIPT . . . . .7615 Washington Ave. S., Edina MN 55435
MICRO AGE COMPUTER STORES . . . . .2308 S. 55th St., Tempe AZ 85281
MICRO AGE COMPUTER STORES . . . . 9001 Louis H. LaFontaine, Ville Danjou PQ H1J2C5   CAN
OFFICELAND . . . . 44 Nashua Rd., Londonderry NH 03053
SOFTWARE PIPELINE . . . . .19265 SW Martinazzi Ave., Tualatin OR 97062
T & P VIDEO GAMES AND COMPUTERS . . . .# 1778, 8770 - 170 St., Edmonton AB T5T4J2   CAN

TODAYS COMPUTERS BUSINESS CENTERS . . . . .411 Eagleview Blvd., Exton PA 19335
TYPING TIGERS . . . . .P.O. Box 310310, New Braunfels TX 78130
UPGRADE! SOFTWAIRE CENTER . . . . 210 Porter Dr., # 220, San Ramon CA 94583

CHAPTER 40

RETAIL: FLOWERS AND PLANTS

CELEBRITY FLORIST

Florist shop franchise. Florist training, recognized trademark in BC.

206 - 1111 West Georgia St.
Vancouver, BC V6E3G7 CAN
TEL: (604) 684-3314
FAX: (604) 684-2542
Mr. Jerry Kroll, Franchise Manager

HISTORY: . . . . .CFA
Established in 1983; . . 1st Franchised in 1986
Company-Owned Units (As of 12/1/1989): . . .0
Franchised Units (12/1/1989): 8
Total Units (12/1/1989): 8
Distribution: US-0;Can-8;Overseas-0
  North America: . . . . .1 Province
  Concentration: . . . . 8 in BC
Registered: . . . .
. . . .
Average # of Employees: . . . . .1-3 FT
Prior Industry Experience: . . . . Helpful

FINANCIAL:
Cash Investment: $15-50K
Total Investment: $15-50K
Fees: Franchise - $5K
  Royalty: 0%, Advert: 0%
Contract Periods (Yrs.): 5/5
Area Development Agreement: Yes/5+
Sub-Franchise Contract: . . . . . .No
Expand in Territory: . . . . Yes
Passive Ownership: . . . . . .Allowed
Encourage Conversions: . . . . . Yes
Franchisee Purchase(s) Required: .No

FRANCHISOR TRAINING/SUPPORT:
Financial Assistance Provided: . . . Yes(I)
Site Selection Assistance: . . . . .Yes
Lease Negotiation Assistance: . . . . .Yes
Co-operative Advertising: . . . . .No
Training: . . . . .4 Weeks Vancouver
. . . .
On-Going Support: . . . . C,E,H,I
Full-Time Franchisor Support Staff: . . .1
EXPANSION PLANS:
US: .No
Canada - Yes, ... Overseas - No

CONROY'S FLOWERS

6621 E. Pacific Coast Hwy.
Long Beach, CA 90803
TEL: (213) 594-4484 C
FAX:
Mr. Christopher Barr, COO

The nation's largest flower shop franchise in total sales and in sales per unit. This opportunity combines a retail concept proven for nearly 30 years with the most advanced techniques in flower processing, merchandising and customer retention.

HISTORY: . . . . IFA	FINANCIAL:	FRANCHISOR TRAINING/SUPPORT:
Established in 1960; . . 1st Franchised in 1974	Cash Investment: $100-300K	Financial Assistance Provided: . . . . . No
Company-Owned Units (As of 12/1/1989): . .3	Total Investment: $100-300K	Site Selection Assistance: . . . . . . .Yes
Franchised Units (12/1/1989): 74	Fees: Franchise - $75K	Lease Negotiation Assistance: . . . .Yes
Total Units (12/1/1989): 77	Royalty: 7.75%, Advert: 3%	Co-operative Advertising: . . . . . . .Yes
Distribution: US-77;Can-0;Overseas-0	Contract Periods (Yrs.): 20	Training: . . . . 5 Wks. Southern CA
North America: . . . . 2 States	Area Development Agreement: . .No	. . . .
Concentration: . . . . .74 in CA, 3 in TX	Sub-Franchise Contract: . . . . .No	On-Going Support: . . . . . A,C,D,E,G,H
Registered: . . . . CA	Expand in Territory: . . . . Yes	Full-Time Franchisor Support Staff: . . 34
. . . .	Passive Ownership: . . . Discouraged	EXPANSION PLANS:
Average # of Employees: . . . . 4-5 FT, 2-6 PT	Encourage Conversions:	US: . . . . Pacific Coast & Arizona
Prior Industry Experience: . . . . . . Helpful	Franchisee Purchase(s) Required: .No	Canada - No, ...Overseas - No

CUMMINGS EUROPEAN FLOWERS

701 E. Ball Rd., # 103
Anaheim, CA 92805
TEL: (714) 772-5395
FAX:
Mr. Jim Cummings, President

CUMMINGS EUROPEAN was founded by Jim Cummings, former president and CEO of Century 21 Real Estate. 2 franchise opportunities are offered - retail only and wholesale only. The franchisee is trained to operate the business through extensive training and support systems. We play hard to win!

HISTORY:	FINANCIAL:	FRANCHISOR TRAINING/SUPPORT:
Established in 1985; . . 1st Franchised in 1986	Cash Investment: $20-50K	Financial Assistance Provided: . . . Yes(I)
Company-Owned Units (As of 12/1/1989): . .0	Total Investment: $50K	Site Selection Assistance: . . . . . . .Yes
Franchised Units (12/1/1989): 25	Fees: Franchise - $10K	Lease Negotiation Assistance: . . . . . No
Total Units (12/1/1989): 25	Royalty: Flat, Advert: 2%	Co-operative Advertising: . . . . . . .Yes
Distribution: US-25;Can-0;Overseas-0	Contract Periods (Yrs.): 10/10	Training: . . . 30 Days Orange County, CA
North America: . . . . .1 State	Area Development Agreement: Yes/20	. . . .
Concentration: . . . . 25 in CA	Sub-Franchise Contract: . . . . .No	On-Going Support: . . . .b,C,D,E,F,G,H,I
Registered: . . . . CA	Expand in Territory: . . . . Yes	Full-Time Franchisor Support Staff: . . .7
. . . .	Passive Ownership: . . . . . .Allowed	EXPANSION PLANS:
Average # of Employees: . . . . . . 2 FT, 4 PT	Encourage Conversions: . . . . .No	US: . . . . All Exc. Registration
Prior Industry Experience: . . . . . . Helpful	Franchisee Purchase(s) Required: .No	Canada - No, ...Overseas - No

FLOWERAMA

3165 W. Airline Hwy.
Waterloo, IA 50702
TEL: (800) 553-1774
FAX:
Mr. Charles Nygren, VP Fran.

FLOWERAMA offers franchise opportunities in the regional mall and free-standing locations. FLOWERAMA's mass merchandising, cash and carry concept offers its customers quality floral products at affordable prices. Comprehensive training in all areas of shop operations is provided along with continued support to franchise owners.

HISTORY: . . . . IFA	FINANCIAL:	FRANCHISOR TRAINING/SUPPORT:
Established in 1967; . . 1st Franchised in 1972	Cash Investment: $25-100K	Financial Assistance Provided: . . . Yes(I)
Company-Owned Units (As of 12/1/1989): . 14	Total Investment: $40-500K	Site Selection Assistance: . . . . . . .Yes
Franchised Units (12/1/1989): 75	Fees: Franchise - $17-30K	Lease Negotiation Assistance: . . . . .Yes
Total Units (12/1/1989): 89	Royalty: 5%, Advert: 0%	Co-operative Advertising: . . . . No
Distribution: US-89;Can-0;Overseas-0	Contract Periods (Yrs.): . . . . . Inf.	Training: . . . . . . .10 Days Headquarters
North America: . . . . 24 States	Area Development Agreement: . .No	. . . .
Concentration:	Sub-Franchise Contract: . . . . .No	On-Going Support: . . . . C,D,E,G,I
Registered: . . . . FL,IL,IN,SD,WI	Expand in Territory: . . . . Yes	Full-Time Franchisor Support Staff: . . 90
. . . .	Passive Ownership: . . . . . .Allowed	EXPANSION PLANS:
Average # of Employees: . . . . . . 2 FT, 4 PT	Encourage Conversions: . . . . . Yes	US: . . . . S, SE, NE and Midwest
Prior Industry Experience: . . . . . . Helpful	Franchisee Purchase(s) Required: .No	Canada - No, ...Overseas - No

FOLIAGE DESIGN SYSTEMS

1553 SE Fort King
Ocala, FL 32671
TEL: (904) 629-7351 (904) 732-8212
FAX:
Mr. John Hagood, President

FOLIAGE DESIGN SYSTEMS is the 3rd largest interior plant maintenance company in the US, according to Nursery Business Magazine. Foliage Design franchisees learn the business from the ground up in an intensive training program at headquarters, followed by 2 different training sessions in the field. Franchisees are taught design, sales and maintenance of interior foliage plants.

HISTORY: . . . .
Established in 1971; . . 1st Franchised in 1980
Company-Owned Units (As of 12/1/1989): . .3
Franchised Units (12/1/1989): 38
Total Units (12/1/1989): 41
Distribution: US-41;Can-0;Overseas-0
North America: . . . . 15 States
Concentration: . . . . 11 in FL,3 in SC,2 in TN
Registered: . . . . .FL,IL,MD
. . . .
Average # of Employees: . . . . . . 4 FT, 2 PT
Prior Industry Experience: . . . . . . Helpful

FINANCIAL:
Cash Investment: $18-30K
Total Investment: $30-50K
Fees: Franchise - $16-40K
  Royalty: 4%, Advert: 0%
Contract Periods (Yrs.): 20/5
Area Development Agreement: . .No
Sub-Franchise Contract: . . . . .No
Expand in Territory: . . . . Yes
Passive Ownership: . . . Discouraged
Encourage Conversions: . . . . .No
Franchisee Purchase(s) Required: .No

FRANCHISOR TRAINING/SUPPORT:
Financial Assistance Provided: . . . . . No
Site Selection Assistance: . . . . .Yes
Lease Negotiation Assistance: . . . . .Yes
Co-operative Advertising: . . . . .Yes
Training: . . . . . . 2 Wks. Headquarters, 3
. . . . Days Field, 4-5 Days Field
On-Going Support: . . . .B,C,D,E,F,G,H,I
Full-Time Franchisor Support Staff: . . . 6
EXPANSION PLANS:
US: . . . . .All US Except FL
Canada - Yes, . . . Overseas - Yes

PARKER INTERIOR PLANTSCAPE

1325 Terrill Rd.
Scotch Plains, NJ 07076
TEL: (800) 526-3672 (201) 322-5552
FAX: (201) 322-4818
Mr. Richard Parker, President

PARKER is the largest, privately-owned, top award-winning, interiorscape company in the US. We offer an excellent opportunity to learn from the best and to help you start a successful business with an enjoyable product everyone loves and that actually helps your client's health.

HISTORY: . . . .
Established in 1948; . . 1st Franchised in 1985
Company-Owned Units (As of 12/1/1989): . .4
Franchised Units (12/1/1989): 1
Total Units (12/1/1989): 5
Distribution: US-5;Can-0;Overseas-0
North America: . . . . 5 States
Concentration: . . . .1 in NJ, 1 in NY, 1 in PA
Registered: . . . . MD,NY
. . . .
Average # of Employees: . . . . . 10 FT, 2 PT
Prior Industry Experience: . . . . . . Helpful

FINANCIAL:
Cash Investment: $25K
Total Investment: $25K
Fees: Franchise - $25K
  Royalty: 0%, Advert: 0%
Contract Periods (Yrs.): 1/1
Area Development Agreement: Yes/1
Sub-Franchise Contract: . . . . . Yes
Expand in Territory: . . . . .No
Passive Ownership: . . . . . .Allowed
Encourage Conversions: . . . . .No
Franchisee Purchase(s) Required: .No

FRANCHISOR TRAINING/SUPPORT:
Financial Assistance Provided: . . . . . No
Site Selection Assistance: . . . . .Yes
Lease Negotiation Assistance: . . . . .Yes
Co-operative Advertising: . . . . .Yes
Training: . . . . 4 Wks. Headquarters
. . . .
On-Going Support: . . . . a,b,c,D,E,f,g,h,I
Full-Time Franchisor Support Staff: . .225
EXPANSION PLANS:
US: . . . . All US Except Northeast
Canada - Yes, . . . Overseas - Yes

SILK PLANTS, ETC.

1755 Butterfield Rd.
Libertyville, IL 60048
TEL: (800) 843-7455 (708) 362-8210 C
FAX: (708) 362-8260
Mr. Steven E. Santos, Dir. Fran.

SILK PLANTS, ETC. is the largest franchised retailer of silk plants, flowers, natural wood trees and accessories in the US. Direct importation of products, manufacturing, commercial application and retail distribution make SILK PLANTS, ETC. America's silk plant specialists. We are the largest in a $6 billion industry.

HISTORY: . . . . .IFA
Established in 1984; . . 1st Franchised in 1985
Company-Owned Units (As of 12/1/1989): . 83
Franchised Units (12/1/1989): 69
Total Units (12/1/1989): 152
Distribution: . . . US-151;Can-1;Overseas-0
North America: . . . . 27 States, 1 Province
Concentration: . . . 29 in IL, 14 in MI, 9 in IN
Registered: . . . . .All
. . . .
Average # of Employees: . . . . 1-2 FT, 1-3 PT
Prior Industry Experience: . . . . . . Helpful

FINANCIAL: NASD-FOLI
Cash Investment: $75-80K
Total Investment: $75-80K
Fees: Franchise - $25K
  Royalty: 6%, Advert: 1%
Contract Periods (Yrs.): 10/5
Area Development Agreement: Yes/3
Sub-Franchise Contract: . . . . .No
Expand in Territory: . . . . Yes
Passive Ownership: . . . Not Allowed
Encourage Conversions: . . . . . Yes
Franchisee Purchase(s) Required: .No

FRANCHISOR TRAINING/SUPPORT:
Financial Assistance Provided: . . . Yes(I)
Site Selection Assistance: . . . . .Yes
Lease Negotiation Assistance: . . . . .Yes
Co-operative Advertising: . . . . .Yes
Training: . . . . 1 Wk. Headquarters, 1 Wk.
. . Pre-Opening Site,3-5 Days Post-Open
On-Going Support: . . . .B,C,D,E,F,G,H,I
Full-Time Franchisor Support Staff: . . 15
EXPANSION PLANS:
US: . . . . .All US
Canada - Yes, . . . Overseas - Yes

WESLEY BERRY FLOWERS

15305 Schoolcraft
Detroit, MI 48227
TEL: (800) 356-5690 (313) 273-8590
FAX: (313) 273-1503
Mr. Bryan Crosby, Devel. Dir.

Full-service flower shop franchise. Product line will include fresh-cut flowers, blooming plants, green plants, floral arrangements, fine gifts, cards, balloons and other associated gift items. Site selection, pre-opening assistance, training, store lay-out, advertising and buying strength. Largest in the Mid-west.

HISTORY: . . . . IFA
Established in 1946; . . 1st Franchised in 1985
Company-Owned Units (As of 12/1/1989): . .2
Franchised Units (12/1/1989): 18
Total Units (12/1/1989): 20
Distribution: US-20;Can-0;Overseas-0
 North America: . . . . 4 States
 Concentration: . . . 17 in MI, 1 in IL, 1 in GA
Registered: . . . FL,IL,MD,MI,OR,RI,VA,WA
. . . .
Average # of Employees: . . . . . . 2 FT, 1 PT
Prior Industry Experience: . . . . Helpful

FINANCIAL:
Cash Investment: $64-88K
Total Investment: $64-88K
Fees: Franchise - $22K
 Royalty: 5%, Advert: 3%
Contract Periods (Yrs.): 20/20
Area Development Agreement: Yes/Var
Sub-Franchise Contract: . . . . . Yes
Expand in Territory: . . . . Yes
Passive Ownership: . . . Not Allowed
Encourage Conversions: . . . . . .No
Franchisee Purchase(s) Required: .No

FRANCHISOR TRAINING/SUPPORT:
Financial Assistance Provided: . . . Yes(I)
Site Selection Assistance: . . . . .Yes
Lease Negotiation Assistance: . . . . .Yes
Co-operative Advertising: . . . . .Yes
Training: . . . . 2 Wks. Headquarters
. . . .
On-Going Support: . . . .b,C,D,E,F,G,H,I
Full-Time Franchisor Support Staff: . . 10
EXPANSION PLANS:
 US: . . . . .All US
 Canada - Yes, ...Overseas - Yes

SUPPLEMENTAL LISTING OF FRANCHISORS

AFFORDABLE LOVE . . . . 7103 Cresswyck Ct., Wexford PA 15090
AMLINGS FLOWERS & GIFTS . . . . 540 W. Ogden Ave., Hinsdale IL 60521
BLOOMFIELDS AND DESJARDINS . . . . . . 5100 Erin Mills Pkwy., Box 42, Mississauga ON L5M4Z5   CAN
BOTANICAL ENVIRONMENTS SYSTEMS . . . . 9201 Livingston Rd., Ft. Washington MD 20744
FLOWER POT, THE . . . . 1000 de la Montagne, Montreal PQ H3G1Y7   CAN
LE POT DE FLEUR . . . . 1000 de la Montagne, Montreal PQ H3G1Y7   CAN
NEW FLOWER MARKET, THE . . . . 13 Mac Dade Blvd., Collingdale PA 19023
SHE'S FLOWERS . . . . .740 S. Olive St., Los Angeles CA 90014

CHAPTER 41

RETAIL: HOME FURNISHINGS

ARISE FUTON MATTRESS CO.

272 N. Bedford Rd.
Mt. Kisco, NY 10549
TEL: (914) 666-2770
FAX:
Ms. Terri Rae Kuhajda, VP

ARISE FUTON offers a unique specialty furniture concept. Join the fastest-growing aspect of the blossoming lifestyle market. We emphasize a complete line of exclusive, high-quality futons, futon frames and accessories. Fun, popular, high-volume business. Ground floor opportunity.

HISTORY: . . . .
Established in 1980;   . . 1st Franchised in 1987
Company-Owned Units (As of 12/1/1989):   . . .6
Franchised Units (12/1/1989): 11
Total Units (12/1/1989): 17
Distribution: US-17;Can-0;Overseas-0
  North America: . . . . 4 States
  Concentration: . . . 10 in NY, 5 in IL, 1 in MA
Registered: . . . . FL,IL,NY
. . . .
Average # of Employees: . . . . . . 1 FT, 2 PT
Prior Industry Experience: . . . . Helpful

FINANCIAL:
Cash Investment: $57-85K
Total Investment: $57-85K
Fees: Franchise - $15K
  Royalty: 3-2%, Advert: 1%
Contract Periods (Yrs.): 25
Area Development Agreement: . .No
Sub-Franchise Contract: . . . . . .No
Expand in Territory: . . . . Yes
Passive Ownership: . . . Discouraged
Encourage Conversions: . . . .
Franchisee Purchase(s) Required: Yes

FRANCHISOR TRAINING/SUPPORT:
Financial Assistance Provided: . . . . .No
Site Selection Assistance: . . . . . . .Yes
Lease Negotiation Assistance: . . . . .No
Co-operative Advertising: . . . . . . .Yes
Training: . . . . 1 Wk. in Either New York
  . . . . .or Chicago
On-Going Support: . . . . . B,C,D,E,f,G,h
Full-Time Franchisor Support Staff: . . . 6
EXPANSION PLANS:
  US: . . . . .All US
  Canada - No, ... Overseas - No

BOCA RATTAN PREMIUM RATTAN FURNITURE
127 Mohawk Ave.
Scotia, NY 12302
TEL: (800) 678-2622 (518) 393-2200
FAX: (518) 393-2338
Mr. Paul Rutherford, President

BOCA RATTAN is a full business format franchise that packages privately-labeled, premium rattan furniture and accessories into a specialty retail concept that is unique in the marketplace. Features up-scale, gallery-style presentations, more than 1,000 furniture styles, over one dozen finishes, combined with a comprehensive business system, training and on-going support.

HISTORY: . . . . IFA
Established in 1988; . . 1st Franchised in 1989
Company-Owned Units (As of 12/1/1989): . .2
Franchised Units (12/1/1989): 1
Total Units (12/1/1989): 3
Distribution: US-3;Can-0;Overseas-0
North America: . . . . 2 States
Concentration: . . . . 2 in NY, 1 in FL
Registered: . . . . . All States Exc. ND & WA
. . . .
Average # of Employees: . . . . . . 2 FT, 2 PT
Prior Industry Experience: . . . . Helpful

FINANCIAL:
Cash Investment: $75-125K
Total Investment: $135-215K
Fees: Franchise - $28.5K
Royalty: 5%, Advert: 1%
Contract Periods (Yrs.): 10/10
Area Development Agreement: Yes/10
Sub-Franchise Contract: . . . . .No
Expand in Territory: . . . . . . .No
Passive Ownership: . . . . . .Allowed
Encourage Conversions: . . . . Yes
Franchisee Purchase(s) Required: .No

FRANCHISOR TRAINING/SUPPORT:
Financial Assistance Provided: . . . . .No
Site Selection Assistance: . . . . . . .Yes
Lease Negotiation Assistance: . . . . .Yes
Co-operative Advertising: . . . . . . .Yes
Training: . . . 8 Working Days New York,
. . . . 4 Working Days On-site
On-Going Support: . . . . B,C,D,E,F,G,h,I
Full-Time Franchisor Support Staff: . . . 3
EXPANSION PLANS:
US: . . . . .All US
Canada - Yes, . . . Overseas - Yes

CARPETERIA

28159 Stanford Ave.
Valencia, CA 91355
TEL: (805) 295-1000
FAX:
Franchise Division

Buy one store or a whole market under our unique franchising program. Join our successful franchise family in the retail floor covering business and take advantage of over 25 years of growth, trademarks and experienced operation.

HISTORY: . . . .
Established in 1960; . . 1st Franchised in 1972
Company-Owned Units (As of 12/1/1989): . 23
Franchised Units (12/1/1989): 51
Total Units (12/1/1989): 74
Distribution: US-74;Can-0;Overseas-0
North America: . . . . 6 States
Concentration: . . .64 in CA, 3 in OR, 3 in NV
Registered: . . . . .CA,OR,WA
. . . .
Average # of Employees: . . . . .6-9 FT
Prior Industry Experience: . . . . Helpful

FINANCIAL:
Cash Investment: $100K
Total Investment: $250K
Fees: Franchise - . . . . $50+K
Royalty: 3-4%, Advert: 1/4%
Contract Periods (Yrs.): 35/35
Area Development Agreement: Yes/10
Sub-Franchise Contract: . . . . Yes
Expand in Territory: . . . . . . Yes
Passive Ownership: . . . Not Allowed
Encourage Conversions: . . . . . Yes
Franchisee Purchase(s) Required: .No

FRANCHISOR TRAINING/SUPPORT:
Financial Assistance Provided: . . .Yes(D)
Site Selection Assistance: . . . . . . .Yes
Lease Negotiation Assistance: . . . .Yes
Co-operative Advertising: . . . . . . .Yes
Training: . . . . 2 Wks. Headquarters,
. . . . 2-3 Wks. Site
On-Going Support: . . . B,C,D,E,F,G,H
Full-Time Franchisor Support Staff: . . 75
EXPANSION PLANS:
US: . . . . Sunbelt States
Canada - No, ...Overseas - No

CLASSY CLOSETS ETC.

1403 W. 10th Place, # B-111
Tempe, AZ 85281
TEL: (612) 263-1225
FAX:
Mr. Kenneth Hollowell, Mktg. Dir.

THE CLASSY CLOSETS ETC. outlet is a business establishment which will design, manufacture and install custom storage systems for individuals and businesses.

HISTORY: . . . .
Established in 1984; . . 1st Franchised in 1988
Company-Owned Units (As of 12/1/1989): . .1
Franchised Units (12/1/1989): 1
Total Units (12/1/1989): 2
Distribution: US-2;Can-0;Overseas-0
North America: . . . . 2 States
Concentration: . . . . 1 in AZ, 1 in NV
Registered: . . . .
. . . .
Average # of Employees: . . . . .4 FT
Prior Industry Experience: . . . . Helpful

FINANCIAL:
Cash Investment: $15-25K
Total Investment: $90-165K
Fees: Franchise - $25K
Royalty: 6%, Advert: 2%
Contract Periods (Yrs.): 10/10
Area Development Agreement: . .No
Sub-Franchise Contract: . . . . . .No
Expand in Territory: . . . . Yes
Passive Ownership: . . . Not Allowed
Encourage Conversions: . . . . . .No
Franchisee Purchase(s) Required: .No

FRANCHISOR TRAINING/SUPPORT:
Financial Assistance Provided: . . . . .No
Site Selection Assistance: . . . . . . .Yes
Lease Negotiation Assistance: . . . .Yes
Co-operative Advertising: . . . . . . .Yes
Training: . . . . 5 Days Headquarters

On-Going Support: . . . . . .C,D,,E,G,h,I
Full-Time Franchisor Support Staff: . . .7
EXPANSION PLANS:
US: . . . . Southwest
Canada - No, ...Overseas - No

CLOSET FACTORY, THE

12800 S. Broadway
Los Angeles, CA 90061
TEL: (800)692-5673(CA) (213)516-7000
FAX: (213) 538-2676
Ms. Nancy Seyfert, Fran. Dir.

Design, manufacturing and installation of custom closet systems. Fully adjustable and interchangable systems with wide selection of materials and finishes and numerous options and accessories.

HISTORY: . . . . IFA	FINANCIAL:	FRANCHISOR TRAINING/SUPPORT:
Established in 1983; . . 1st Franchised in 1986	Cash Investment: $62.5-95.5K	Financial Assistance Provided: . . . Yes(I)
Company-Owned Units (As of 12/1/1989): . . 1	Total Investment: $104-144.5K	Site Selection Assistance: . . . . Yes
Franchised Units (12/1/1989): 5	Fees: Franchise - $28.5K	Lease Negotiation Assistance: . . . . . Yes
Total Units (12/1/1989): 6	Royalty: 5.75%, Advert: . . . . NA	Co-operative Advertising: . . . . Yes
Distribution: US-6;Can-0;Overseas-0	Contract Periods (Yrs.): 5/5/5	Training: . . . . . 7-10 Days Headquarters,
North America: . . . . 3 States	Area Development Agreement: . .No	. . . . .2 Wks. On-site
Concentration: . . . .2 in CA, 2 in NY, 1 in NJ	Sub-Franchise Contract: . . . . .No	On-Going Support: . . . . . .B,C,D,E,F,H
Registered: . . . . .CA,FL,IL,MI,NY,OR	Expand in Territory: . . . . Yes	Full-Time Franchisor Support Staff: . . 65
. . . .	Passive Ownership: . . . Discouraged	EXPANSION PLANS:
Average # of Employees: . . . . .7 FT	Encourage Conversions: . . . . Yes	US: . . . . All US
Prior Industry Experience: . . . . Helpful	Franchisee Purchase(s) Required: .No	Canada - No, ...Overseas - No

CLOSET SYSTEMS OF . . . .

99 - 899 Iwaena St.
Aiea, HI 96701
TEL: (800) 367-8047 (808) 488-0811
FAX: (808) 487-6407
Mr. Jerry Olinski, President

CLOSET SYSTEMS OF . . . . offers the state-of-the-art product line in closet remodeling. Over the past 8 years, we have refined our systems, while incorporating the 32 mm European design. Simplified construction, along with our years of experience, are our greatest assets.

HISTORY:	FINANCIAL:	FRANCHISOR TRAINING/SUPPORT:
Established in 1982; . . 1st Franchised in 1987	Cash Investment: $17K	Financial Assistance Provided: . . . . .No
Company-Owned Units (As of 12/1/1989): . . 1	Total Investment: $32K	Site Selection Assistance: . . . . Yes
Franchised Units (12/1/1989): 3	Fees: Franchise - $10K	Lease Negotiation Assistance: . . . . . Yes
Total Units (12/1/1989): 4	Royalty: 5%, Advert: 0%	Co-operative Advertising: . . . . No
Distribution: US-4;Can-0;Overseas-0	Contract Periods (Yrs.): 10/5	Training: . . . . 2 Wks. Honolulu
North America: . . . . .1 State	Area Development Agreement: . .No	
Concentration: . . . . .4 in HI	Sub-Franchise Contract: . . . . Yes	On-Going Support: . . . . . B,D,E,F,G,I
Registered:	Expand in Territory: . . . . Yes	Full-Time Franchisor Support Staff: . . . 6
. . . .	Passive Ownership: . . . Discouraged	EXPANSION PLANS:
Average # of Employees: . . . . . . 6 FT, 2 PT	Encourage Conversions: . . . . . NA	US: . . . . . All US Without Registration
Prior Industry Experience: . . . . Helpful	Franchisee Purchase(s) Required: .No	Canada - No, ...Overseas - No

CLOSETS TO GO

9540 SW Tigard St.
Tigard, OR 97223
TEL: (503) 639-5089
FAX:
Mr. Jeff Turner, Franchise Director

CLOSETS TO GO (portable custom closet and storage systems) offers an innovative way to conquer the storage dilemma. Through pre-manufactured parts, each outlet can assemble any configuration in a matter of minutes. The simplicity of no manufacturing and instant service puts CLOSETS TO GO light-years ahead of the competition.

HISTORY:	FINANCIAL:	FRANCHISOR TRAINING/SUPPORT:
Established in 1985; . . 1st Franchised in 1987	Cash Investment: $70K	Financial Assistance Provided: . . . . .No
Company-Owned Units (As of 12/1/1989): . . 1	Total Investment: $80K	Site Selection Assistance: . . . . Yes
Franchised Units (12/1/1989): 2	Fees: Franchise - $3.3-9.9K	Lease Negotiation Assistance: . . . . . Yes
Total Units (12/1/1989): 3	Royalty: 5%, Advert: 2%	Co-operative Advertising: . . . . .NA
Distribution: US-3;Can-0;Overseas-0	Contract Periods (Yrs.): 10/5	Training: . . . . 2 Wks. Headquarters,
North America: . . . . 3 States	Area Development Agreement: . .No	. . . 2 Wks. Franchisee Site, On-going
Concentration: . . . 1 in WA, 1 in OR, 1 in CA	Sub-Franchise Contract: . . . . .No	On-Going Support: . . . . . B,C,D,E,F,I
Registered: . . . . CA,FL,OR	Expand in Territory: . . . . .No	Full-Time Franchisor Support Staff: . . .2
. . . .	Passive Ownership: . . . Not Allowed	EXPANSION PLANS:
Average # of Employees: . . . . . . 4 FT, 1 PT	Encourage Conversions: . . . . Yes	US: . . . . . .All US, Concentrating West
Prior Industry Experience: . . . . Helpful	Franchisee Purchase(s) Required: .No	Canada - Yes, ...Overseas - No

DECORATING DEN SYSTEMS

4630 Montgomery Ave.
Bethesda, MD 20814
TEL: (800) DEC-DENS (301) 652-6393
FAX: (301) 652-9017
Michael A. Riddiough, VP Fran. Dev.

America's first shop-at-home, affordable decorating service. A professionally-trained decorator brings over 5,000 samples to the customer's home or business in a specially-equipped ColorVan.

HISTORY: . . . . IFA
Established in 1970; . . 1st Franchised in 1970
Company-Owned Units (As of 12/1/1989): . . 0
Franchised Units (12/1/1989): 1000
Total Units (12/1/1989): 1000
Distribution: US-932;Can-63;Overseas-5
North America: . . . . 50 States, 4 Provinces
Concentration: . . 128 in CA, 91 in TX, 69 FL
Registered: . . . . All Except AB
. . . .
Average # of Employees: . . . . . . 1 FT, 1 PT
Prior Industry Experience: . . . . . . Helpful

FINANCIAL:
Cash Investment: $7-19K
Total Investment: $15-30K
Fees: Franchise - $7-19K
  Royalty: 6-15%, Advert: . . . 0-2%
Contract Periods (Yrs.): 10/10
Area Development Agreement: . .No
Sub-Franchise Contract: . . . . . Yes
Expand in Territory: . . . . Yes
Passive Ownership: . . . Discouraged
Encourage Conversions: . . . . . .No
Franchisee Purchase(s) Required: .No

FRANCHISOR TRAINING/SUPPORT:
Financial Assistance Provided: . . . . . No
Site Selection Assistance: . . . . .NA
Lease Negotiation Assistance: . . . . .NA
Co-operative Advertising: . . . . .Yes
Training: . . . . 1 Wk. Headquarters
. . . .
On-Going Support: . . . . . . C,D,E,G,H,i
Full-Time Franchisor Support Staff: . . 45
EXPANSION PLANS:
US: . . . . All US
Canada - Yes, . . . Overseas - Yes

DRAPERY FACTORY, THE

80 Tanforan Ave., # 10
So. San Francisco, CA 94080
TEL: (415) 583-1300
FAX:
Mr. Le Roy Stark, Dir. Fran. Mktg.

Your association with THE DRAPERY FACTORY connects you to professionals who have operated successful custom drape sales teams themselves - who are motivated to establish you in a well-supported, professionally-operated DRAPERY FACTORY sales business.

HISTORY: . . . . IFA
Established in 1980; . . 1st Franchised in 1988
Company-Owned Units (As of 12/1/1989): . . 1
Franchised Units (12/1/1989): 13
Total Units (12/1/1989): 14
Distribution: US-14;Can-0;Overseas-0
North America: . . . . .1 State
Concentration: . . . . 14 in CA
Registered: . . . . CA
. . . .
Average # of Employees: . . . . . . 2 FT, 1 PT
Prior Industry Experience: . . . . . . Helpful

FINANCIAL:
Cash Investment: $35-40K
Total Investment: $50-55K
Fees: Franchise - $25K
  Royalty: 5%, Advert: 2%
Contract Periods (Yrs.): 7/7
Area Development Agreement: . .No
Sub-Franchise Contract: . . . . . .No
Expand in Territory: . . . . .No
Passive Ownership: . . . Discouraged
Encourage Conversions: . . . . . Yes
Franchisee Purchase(s) Required: .No

FRANCHISOR TRAINING/SUPPORT:
Financial Assistance Provided: . . . Yes(I)
Site Selection Assistance: . . . . .Yes
Lease Negotiation Assistance: . . . . .Yes
Co-operative Advertising: . . . . No
Training: . . . . 2 Wks. Headquarters
. . . .
On-Going Support: . . . . . . C,D,E,G,H,I
Full-Time Franchisor Support Staff: . . . 8
EXPANSION PLANS:
US: . . . . All US
Canada - Yes, ...Overseas - No

DWOSKIN'S

5903 Peachtree Industrial Blvd.
Norcross, GA 30092
TEL: (404) 449-5180 C
FAX:
Mr. Myron Dwoskin, President

Specialty retailer selling wallcoverings and blinds at discount prices.

HISTORY: . . . .
Established in 1973; . . 1st Franchised in 1988
Company-Owned Units (As of 12/1/1989): . . 9
Franchised Units (12/1/1989): 7
Total Units (12/1/1989): 16
Distribution: US-16;Can-0;Overseas-0
North America: . . . . .1 States
Concentration: . . . . 16 in GA
Registered: . . . .
. . . .
Average # of Employees: . . . . . . 3 FT, 1 PT
Prior Industry Experience: . . . . . . Helpful

FINANCIAL:
Cash Investment: $25-35K
Total Investment: $120-140K
Fees: Franchise - $15K
  Royalty: 3-5%, Advert: 5%
Contract Periods (Yrs.): 10/10
Area Development Agreement: . Yes
Sub-Franchise Contract: . . . . . .No
Expand in Territory: . . . . . . Yes
Passive Ownership: . . . Not Allowed
Encourage Conversions: . . . . . Yes
Franchisee Purchase(s) Required: .No

FRANCHISOR TRAINING/SUPPORT:
Financial Assistance Provided: . . . . . No
Site Selection Assistance: . . . . .Yes
Lease Negotiation Assistance: . . . . .Yes
Co-operative Advertising: . . . . .Yes
Training: . . . . 4 Wks. Atlanta, GA
. . . .
On-Going Support: . . . . .B,C,D,E,F,G,h
Full-Time Franchisor Support Staff: . . 85
EXPANSION PLANS:
US: . . . . Southeast
Canada - No, ...Overseas - No

FINE DESIGNS SOFA GALLERY

Rts. 18 & 20 By-pass
Norwalk, OH 44857
TEL: (800) 837-2565
FAX:
Mr. Bill Gerken, President

Custom-order upholstered furniture in 35 days. 1,000 fabrics, 400 styles, lifetime product warranty. We assist in site selection, training for sales and service, advertising, design of store and operations.

HISTORY: . . . . IFA	FINANCIAL:	FRANCHISOR TRAINING/SUPPORT:
Established in 1986; . . 1st Franchised in 1987	Cash Investment: $80-100K	Financial Assistance Provided: . . . . .No
Company-Owned Units (As of 12/1/1989): . .2	Total Investment: $150-200K	Site Selection Assistance: . . . . . . .Yes
Franchised Units (12/1/1989): 17	Fees: Franchise - $15K	Lease Negotiation Assistance: . . . . .Yes
Total Units (12/1/1989): 19	Royalty: 1.5%, Advert: 0%	Co-operative Advertising: . . . . .Yes
Distribution: US-19;Can-0;Overseas-0	Contract Periods (Yrs.): 5/5	Training: . . . . 1 Wk. Norwalk, OH, 1 Wk.
North America: . . . . 10 States	Area Development Agreement: Yes/5	. . . . Atlanta, GA, 1 Wk. On-site
Concentration: . . . . 2 in GA	Sub-Franchise Contract: . . . . . .No	On-Going Support: . . .B,C,D,E,F,G,H,I
Registered: . . . . All Except HI	Expand in Territory: . . . . Yes	Full-Time Franchisor Support Staff: . . 10
. . . .	Passive Ownership: . . . Not Allowed	EXPANSION PLANS:
Average # of Employees: . . . . . . 1 FT, 5 PT	Encourage Conversions: . . . . . Yes	US: . . . . East of Rockies
Prior Industry Experience: . . . . . . Helpful	Franchisee Purchase(s) Required: Yes	Canada - No, ...Overseas - No

FLOOR TO CEILING STORE

4909 N. Highway 52
Rochester, MN 55901
TEL: (507) 285-1918
FAX:
Franchise Administrator

Our retail home improvement product stores sell quality decorative products for the interior of the home that require some installation. Our product line includes floor coverings, wall coverings, window treatments and kitchen and bath products.

HISTORY: . . . . IFA	FINANCIAL:	FRANCHISOR TRAINING/SUPPORT:
Established in 1981; . . 1st Franchised in 1981	Cash Investment: $10-30K	Financial Assistance Provided: . . . Yes(I)
Company-Owned Units (As of 12/1/1989): . .2	Total Investment: $125-185K	Site Selection Assistance: . . . . . . .Yes
Franchised Units (12/1/1989): 46	Fees: Franchise - $25K	Lease Negotiation Assistance: . . . . .Yes
Total Units (12/1/1989): 48	Royalty: 5%, Advert: 1-4%	Co-operative Advertising: . . . . .Yes
Distribution: US-48;Can-0;Overseas-0	Contract Periods (Yrs.): . . . 10/10	Training: . . . . . 3-4 Wks. On-site "Hands
North America: . . . . 8 States	Area Development Agreement: Yes/3	. . . . .On," 1-2 Wks. Classroom
Concentration: . . . 18 in MN, 8 in IL, 7 in IA	Sub-Franchise Contract: . . . . . .No	On-Going Support: . . a,B,C,D,E,f,G,H,I
Registered: . . . CA,IL,IN,MI,MN,ND,SD,WI	Expand in Territory: . . . . Yes	Full-Time Franchisor Support Staff: . . 30
. . . .	Passive Ownership: . . . Discouraged	EXPANSION PLANS:
Average # of Employees: . . . . . . 3 FT, 2 PT	Encourage Conversions: . . . . . Yes	US: . . . . Midwest
Prior Industry Experience: . . . . . . Helpful	Franchisee Purchase(s) Required: .No	Canada - No, ...Overseas - No

JUNORS, THE KITCHEN COLLECTION

16 Goodrich Rd.
Toronto, ON M8Z4Z8 CAN
TEL: (416) 259-7861
FAX: (416) 259-7592
Mr. Randy T. Cork, President

At retail, sale of quality, basic and unique kitchenware and tabletop products. Kitchen accessories, such as food preparation, gadgets, kitchen linens, bakeware, ovenware, ceramics and knives. Tabletop merchandise, such as serving, glassware, glass tumblers, stemware and woodenware. Stores are located in major regional shopping centres across Canada to take advantage of high consumer traffic.

HISTORY: . . . . .CFA	FINANCIAL: TSE-FIL	FRANCHISOR TRAINING/SUPPORT:
Established in 1941; . . 1st Franchised in 1985	Cash Investment: $65-80K	Financial Assistance Provided: . . . Yes(I)
Company-Owned Units (As of 12/1/1989): . 30	Total Investment: $190-230K	Site Selection Assistance: . . . . . . .Yes
Franchised Units (12/1/1989): 4	Fees: Franchise - $25K	Lease Negotiation Assistance: . . . . .Yes
Total Units (12/1/1989): 34	Royalty: 6%, Advert: 1%	Co-operative Advertising: . . . . .Yes
Distribution: US-0;Can-34;Overseas-0	Contract Periods (Yrs.): . . . Lease	Training: . . . . 1 Wk. + Headquarters
North America: . . . . 4 Provinces	Area Development Agreement: .No	. . . .
Concentration: . . .18 in ON, 9 in AB, 2 in SK	Sub-Franchise Contract: . . . . . .No	On-Going Support: . . . . . . B,C,D,E,h
Registered: . . . . AB	Expand in Territory: . . . . Yes	Full-Time Franchisor Support Staff: . . 50
. . . .	Passive Ownership: . . . Not Allowed	EXPANSION PLANS:
Average # of Employees: . . . . . . 3 FT, 4 PT	Encourage Conversions: . . . . . NA	US: . . . . .No
Prior Industry Experience: . . . . . . Helpful	Franchisee Purchase(s) Required: Yes	Canada - Yes, ...Overseas - No

KING KOIL BEDQUARTERS

770 Transfer Rd., # 13
St. Paul, MN 55113
TEL: (800) 888-6070 (612) 646-6882
FAX:
Mr. Paul Sullivan, Natl. Sales Mgr.

Specialty retailing of sleep products. The BEDQUARTERS program provides the complete formula necessary for the successful sleep specialist. This includes display, marketing, merchandising and advertising direction, in addition to providing the actual merchandise.

HISTORY:	FINANCIAL:	FRANCHISOR TRAINING/SUPPORT:
Established in 19; . . . 1st Franchised in 1982	Cash Investment: . . . .$	Financial Assistance Provided: . . . . . No
Company-Owned Units (As of 12/1/1989): . .0	Total Investment: $60-85K	Site Selection Assistance: . . . . .NA
Franchised Units (12/1/1989): 200	Fees: Franchise - $5K	Lease Negotiation Assistance: . . . . . No
Total Units (12/1/1989): 200	Royalty: 0%, Advert: 0%	Co-operative Advertising: . . . . .Yes
Distribution: US-180;Can-20;Overseas-0	Contract Periods (Yrs.): . . . .Varies	Training: . . . . On-going On-site
North America:	Area Development Agreement: . .No	
Concentration:	Sub-Franchise Contract: . . . . .No	On-Going Support: . . . . . . C,D,F,G,H,I
Registered:	Expand in Territory: . . . . Yes	Full-Time Franchisor Support Staff: . . . .
. . . .	Passive Ownership: . . . . . .Allowed	EXPANSION PLANS:
Average # of Employees: . . . . . 2-3 FT, 1 PT	Encourage Conversions: . . . . .No	US: . . . . .All US
Prior Industry Experience: . . . . Helpful	Franchisee Purchase(s) Required: Yes	Canada - Yes, . . . Overseas - Yes

LAURA'S DRAPERIES & BEDSPREADS SHOWROOM

2200 Post Oak Blvd., # 515
Houston, TX 77056
TEL: (800) 654-7922 (713) 626-5610
FAX:
Mr. Harold Nedell, Chairman

Ready-made, made-to-measure and custom draperies, bedspreads and accessories combine to provide LAURA'S licensed decorators with a full range of home fashion decor. Location, training, marketing, resourcing and continuing support are provided. Established over 30 years.

HISTORY: . . . . .IFA	FINANCIAL:	FRANCHISOR TRAINING/SUPPORT:
Established in 1937; . . 1st Franchised in 1987	Cash Investment: $75K	Financial Assistance Provided: . . . . . No
Company-Owned Units (As of 12/1/1989): . .0	Total Investment: $75K	Site Selection Assistance: . . . . .Yes
Franchised Units (12/1/1989): 22	Fees: Franchise - $20K	Lease Negotiation Assistance: . . . . .Yes
Total Units (12/1/1989): 22	Royalty: 6%, Advert: 7%	Co-operative Advertising: . . . . No
Distribution: US-22;Can-0;Overseas-0	Contract Periods (Yrs.): 20/20	Training: . . . . . . 3 Wks. Headquarters, 2
North America: . . . . 5 States	Area Development Agreement: . .No	. . Wks. Grand Opening, 1/4ly Meetings
Concentration: . . . 6 in AZ, 5 in NY, 3 in TX	Sub-Franchise Contract: . . . . .No	On-Going Support: . . . . . C,D,E,G,H,I
Registered: . . . . .CA,IL,MI,NY	Expand in Territory: . . . . Yes	Full-Time Franchisor Support Staff: . . . 8
. . . .	Passive Ownership: . . . Not Allowed	EXPANSION PLANS:
Average # of Employees: . . . . .1+ FT	Encourage Conversions: . . . . Yes	US: . . . . .Northwest, Southwest
Prior Industry Experience: . . . . . . Helpful	Franchisee Purchase(s) Required: .No	Canada - No, ...Overseas - No

LIGHTING UNLIMITED

131 Cartwright Ave.
Toronto, ON M6A1V4 CAN
TEL: (416) 781-5691 C
FAX: (416) 781-9429
Mr. Ray Denis, Dir. Corp. Devel.

LIGHTING UNLIMITED is considered the most aggressive and dynamic retail lighting chain in Canada. The concept of innovation, quality and style have made our chain the most visually enticing in the North American retail marketing field. If you have a desire to become your own boss, then LIGHTING UNLIMITED could be your answer.

HISTORY: . . . . .CFA	FINANCIAL: TSE-MOL	FRANCHISOR TRAINING/SUPPORT:
Established in 1953; . . 1st Franchised in 1969	Cash Investment: $80-120K	Financial Assistance Provided: . . . Yes(I)
Company-Owned Units (As of 12/1/1989): . 18	Total Investment: $250-300K	Site Selection Assistance: . . . . .Yes
Franchised Units (12/1/1989): 40	Fees: Franchise - $25K	Lease Negotiation Assistance: . . . . .Yes
Total Units (12/1/1989): 58	Royalty: 5%, Advert: 3%	Co-operative Advertising: . . . . .Yes
Distribution: US-3;Can-55;Overseas-0	Contract Periods (Yrs.): 10/10	Training: . . . . 1 Wk. Headquarters, 1 Wk.
North America: . . . . . .1 State, 6 Provinces	Area Development Agreement: . .No	. . . . Field, 2 Wks. On-site
Concentration: . . .36 in ON, 7 in AB, 6 in BC	Sub-Franchise Contract: . . . . Yes	On-Going Support: . .C,D,E,F,G,H
Registered: . . . . AB	Expand in Territory: . . . . Yes	Full-Time Franchisor Support Staff: . .130
. . . .	Passive Ownership: . . . Not Allowed	EXPANSION PLANS:
Average # of Employees: . . . . . . 3 FT, 2 PT	Encourage Conversions: . . . . Yes	US: . . . . .No
Prior Industry Experience: . . . . Helpful	Franchisee Purchase(s) Required: .No	Canada - Yes, ...Overseas - No

LIVING LIGHTING

39 Orfus Rd.
Toronto, ON M6A1L7 CAN
TEL: (416) 789-3251
FAX:
Mr. Girts Steinhards, Fran. Sales

We are North America's largest retail lighting franchise. Our product mix consists of lighting fixtures, accessories, fans, lamps, prints, shades, chandeliers and mirrors. Our hands-on head office support assures franchisee's success. Our sites are premium, our training program in-depth and our profit margins are high. Consider our proven track record, year after year!

HISTORY: . . . . .CFA	FINANCIAL:	FRANCHISOR TRAINING/SUPPORT:
Established in 1968; . . 1st Franchised in 1968	Cash Investment: $80-120K	Financial Assistance Provided: . . . Yes(I)
Company-Owned Units (As of 12/1/1989): . .2	Total Investment: . . . .$250K+	Site Selection Assistance: . . . . . . .Yes
Franchised Units (12/1/1989): 57	Fees: Franchise - $30K	Lease Negotiation Assistance: . . . . .Yes
Total Units (12/1/1989): 59	Royalty: 7%, Advert: 5%	Co-operative Advertising: . . . . . . .Yes
Distribution: US-0;Can-59;Overseas-0	Contract Periods (Yrs.): 10/10	Training: . . . . . 4 Wks. Headquarters and
North America: . . . . 2 Provinces	Area Development Agreement: . .No	. . . . Stores
Concentration: . . . . 54 in ON, 5 in BC	Sub-Franchise Contract: . . . .No	On-Going Support: . . . . . . C,D,E,F,G,h
Registered: . . . . AB	Expand in Territory: . . . . Yes	Full-Time Franchisor Support Staff: . . 52
. . . .	Passive Ownership: . . . Not Allowed	EXPANSION PLANS:
Average # of Employees: . . . . . . 3 FT, 3 PT	Encourage Conversions: . . . . . Yes	US: . . . . .No
Prior Industry Experience: . . . . Helpful	Franchisee Purchase(s) Required: .No	Canada - Yes, ...Overseas - No

NAKED FURNITURE, SOFAS & MORE

1099 Jay St., Bldg. 3, Watertwr.Pk.
Rochester, NY 14611
TEL: (800) 333-2402 (716) 436-4060
FAX:
Mr. Peter Judd, Dir. Fran. Dev.

NAKED FURNITURE is the nation's largest retailer of better quality, solid wood, ready-to-finish and custom finished furniture. Also offered is a complete line of custom-tailored upholstery, all done in a fully-decorated, accessorized showroom.

HISTORY: . . . . .IFA	FINANCIAL:	FRANCHISOR TRAINING/SUPPORT:
Established in 1972; . . 1st Franchised in 1979	Cash Investment: . . . . . . $50K+	Financial Assistance Provided: . . . Yes(I)
Company-Owned Units (As of 12/1/1989): . .2	Total Investment: $130-185K	Site Selection Assistance: . . . . . . .Yes
Franchised Units (12/1/1989): 57	Fees: Franchise - $16.5K	Lease Negotiation Assistance: . . . .Yes
Total Units (12/1/1989): 59	Royalty: 4%, Advert: 2%	Co-operative Advertising: . . . . . . .Yes
Distribution: US-59;Can-0;Overseas-0	Contract Periods (Yrs.): 10/10	Training: . . . . 7 Days Headquarters
North America: . . . . 16 States	Area Development Agreement: . .No	. . . .
Concentration: . . .12 in MI, 10 in IL, 6 in OH	Sub-Franchise Contract: . . . .No	On-Going Support: . . . .B,C,D,E,F,G,H,I
Registered: . . . . All States	Expand in Territory: . . . . Yes	Full-Time Franchisor Support Staff: . . 15
. . . .	Passive Ownership: . . . Discouraged	EXPANSION PLANS:
Average # of Employees: . . . . . . 3 FT, 2 PT	Encourage Conversions: . . . . . Yes	US: . . . . Northeast & Southeast
Prior Industry Experience: . . . . Helpful	Franchisee Purchase(s) Required: . .	Canada - No, ...Overseas - No

SLUMBERLAND INTERNATIONAL

3060 Centerville Rd.
Little Canada, MN 55117
TEL: (612) 482-7500
FAX: (612) 482-0157
Mr. Ken Larson, President

SLUMBERLAND is a home furnishing specialty retailer, featuring name-brand mattresses, sleep sofas, reclining chairs, sofas and chairs, daybeds and related bedroom furniture. SLUMBERLAND is a market-share driven retailer that outpaces national averages in sales/SF and gross margins.

HISTORY:	FINANCIAL:	FRANCHISOR TRAINING/SUPPORT:
Established in 1967; . . 1st Franchised in 1978	Cash Investment: $50-100K	Financial Assistance Provided: . . . . .No
Company-Owned Units (As of 12/1/1989): . .9	Total Investment: $100-200K	Site Selection Assistance: . . . . . . .Yes
Franchised Units (12/1/1989): 17	Fees: Franchise - $10K	Lease Negotiation Assistance: . . . .Yes
Total Units (12/1/1989): 26	Royalty: 3%, Advert: 0%	Co-operative Advertising: . . . . .No
Distribution: US-26;Can-0;Overseas-0	Contract Periods (Yrs.): 10/10	Training: . . . . . . 3-4 Wks. St. Paul, MN
North America: . . . . 5 States	Area Development Agreement: . .No	. . . .
Concentration: . . . 13 in MN, 6 in IA, 3 in WI	Sub-Franchise Contract: . . . . .No	On-Going Support: . . . . . b,C,d,E,G,H,I
Registered: . . . . IL,MN,ND,SD,WI	Expand in Territory: . . . . Yes	Full-Time Franchisor Support Staff: . . . .
. . . .	Passive Ownership: . . . Discouraged	EXPANSION PLANS:
Average # of Employees: . . . . . . 5 FT, 2 PT	Encourage Conversions: . . . . . Yes	US: . . . . Midwest
Prior Industry Experience: . . . . Helpful	Franchisee Purchase(s) Required: .No	Canada - No, ...Overseas - No

TOP DRAWER CUSTOM CLOSETS

699 Clay St.
Winter Park, FL 32789
TEL: (407) 644-9665 C
FAX:
Ms. Tania Torruella, President

Our goal is to provide ambitious franchise owners with high income opportunities in the growing home improvement industry. The broad T.D.C.C. product line goes beyond closets to create sales in every room of the home! We'll have your store opened in less than 45 days!

HISTORY: . . . .
Established in 1985; . . 1st Franchised in 1988
Company-Owned Units (As of 12/1/1989): . . 1
Franchised Units (12/1/1989): 4
Total Units (12/1/1989): 5
Distribution: US-5; Can-0; Overseas-0
North America: . . . . 2 States
Concentration: . . . . 4 in FL, 1 in MI
Registered: . . . .
. . . .
Average # of Employees: . . . . .3-4 FT
Prior Industry Experience: . . . . . . Helpful

FINANCIAL:
Cash Investment: $35K
Total Investment: $60K
Fees: Franchise - $13.7K
Royalty: 5%, Advert: 5%
Contract Periods (Yrs.): 10/10
Area Development Agreement: . .No
Sub-Franchise Contract: . . . . .No
Expand in Territory: . . . . . . Yes
Passive Ownership: . . . Not Allowed
Encourage Conversions: . . . . . NA
Franchisee Purchase(s) Required: .No

FRANCHISOR TRAINING/SUPPORT:
Financial Assistance Provided: . . . . . No
Site Selection Assistance: . . . . No
Lease Negotiation Assistance: . . . . .Yes
Co-operative Advertising: . . . . .Yes
Training: . . . . . . 5-6 Days Orlando, FL,
. . . . 5-6 Days On-site
On-Going Support: . . . . C,D,E,G,I
Full-Time Franchisor Support Staff: . . . 4
EXPANSION PLANS:
US: . . . . .All US
Canada - No, ...Overseas - No

WINDOW WORKS INTERNATIONAL

2101 NW 33rd St., # 300A
Pompano Beach, FL 33069
TEL: (800) 326-2659
FAX: (305) 977-4754
Mr. Jeffrey W. Greene, Dir. Fran.

Join America's leading franchisor of custom window treatment stores, specializing in vertical blinds, mini-blinds, draperies and shutters. This recession-proof franchise operates with no receivables and no inventory. This $6 billion industry has high average sales and high gross margins and has led WINDOW WORKS to a successful 12-year track record.

HISTORY: . . . . .IFA/WIF
Established in 1978; . . 1st Franchised in 1978
Company-Owned Units (As of 12/1/1989): . .0
Franchised Units (12/1/1989): 102
Total Units (12/1/1989): 102
Distribution: . . . US-102; Can-0; Overseas-0
North America: . . . . 22 States
Concentration: . .28 in FL, 27 in NJ, 10 in MA
Registered: . . . . All Except AB
. . . .
Average # of Employees: . . . . .3 FT
Prior Industry Experience: . . . . . . Helpful

FINANCIAL: OTC-APOGEN
Cash Investment: $75-80K
Total Investment: $75-80K
Fees: Franchise - $25.5K
Royalty: 4%, Advert: 1.5%
Contract Periods (Yrs.): 5/5
Area Development Agreement: . .No
Sub-Franchise Contract: . . . . .No
Expand in Territory: . . . . . . Yes
Passive Ownership: . . . Discouraged
Encourage Conversions: . . . . . Yes
Franchisee Purchase(s) Required: .No

FRANCHISOR TRAINING/SUPPORT:
Financial Assistance Provided: . . . . . No
Site Selection Assistance: . . . . .Yes
Lease Negotiation Assistance: . . . . .Yes
Co-operative Advertising: . . . . .Yes
Training: . . . . 2 Wks. Home Study,
. . . . 2-3 Wks. Headquarters
On-Going Support: . . . . B,C,D,E,f,G,H,I
Full-Time Franchisor Support Staff: . . 12
EXPANSION PLANS:
US: . . . . .All US
Canada - No, ...Overseas - No

WORLD BAZAAR

4849 Massachusetts Blvd.
College Park, GA 30337
TEL: (404) 994-7979 C
FAX: (404) 994-7950
Mr. Paul J. Modzelewski, VP Sales

We are a retail import specialty store, very similar to Pier 1. We specialize in wicker and rattan furniture, silk flowers, brassware, baskets and assorted gift and home decor items. Stores are situated in malls, shopping centers and free-standing locations.

HISTORY: . . . . .IFA
Established in 1965; . . 1st Franchised in 1968
Company-Owned Units (As of 12/1/1989): . 13
Franchised Units (12/1/1989): 121
Total Units (12/1/1989): 134
Distribution: US-134; Can-0; Overseas-0
North America: . . . . 23 States
Concentration: . . 38 in FL, 13 in GA, 7 in TX
Registered: . . . . . FL,IL,IN,MD,MI,MN,NY
. . . .
Average # of Employees: . . . . . . 3 FT, 4 PT
Prior Industry Experience: . . . . Helpful

FINANCIAL:
Cash Investment: $135-230k
Total Investment: . . . .$
Fees: Franchise - $15-50K
Royalty: 8%, Advert: 0%
Contract Periods (Yrs.): . . . . Lease
Area Development Agreement: . .No
Sub-Franchise Contract: . . . . .No
Expand in Territory: . . . . . . Yes
Passive Ownership: . . . Discouraged
Encourage Conversions: . . . . . Yes
Franchisee Purchase(s) Required: .No

FRANCHISOR TRAINING/SUPPORT:
Financial Assistance Provided: . . .Yes(D)
Site Selection Assistance: . . . . . . .Yes
Lease Negotiation Assistance: . . . . .Yes
Co-operative Advertising: . . . . .No
Training: . . . . 5 Days Headquarters,
. . . . 10 Days Franchise Store
On-Going Support: . . . . B,C,D,E,F,G,H
Full-Time Franchisor Support Staff: . . 25
EXPANSION PLANS:
US: . . . . .All US
Canada - No, ... Overseas - No

SUPPLEMENTAL LISTING OF FRANCHISORS

BABY'S ROOM, THE . . . . .115 Drumlin Cr., # 1, Concord ON L4K2X7   CAN
BOCA RATTAN . . . . 127 Mohawk Ave., Scotia NY 12302
CALIFORNIA CEILINGS . . . . 7370 Woodbine Ave., # 2, Markham ON L3R1A5   CAN
CALIFORNIA CLOSET COMPANY . . . . 21300 Victory Blvd., # 1150, Woodland Hills CA 91367
CLOSET-TIER . . . . 5822 Forward Ave., Pittsburgh PA 15217
CLOSETTEC . . . . .123 East St., Dedham MA 02026
COMFORTABLES, THE LIVING ROOM STORE . . . . 500 W. Wayne St., Celina OH 45822
COMPLEAT ENGRAVER, THE . . . . .5850 Lakehurst Dr., # 150-2, Orlando FL 32819
CUSTOM MATTRESS FACTORY OUTLET CTRS. . . . . 3401 Lake Ave., Fort Wayne IN 46805
DESCAMPS . . . . 454 Columbus Ave., New York NY 10024
EXPRESSIONS CUSTOM FURNITURE . . . . 3212 W. Esplanade, Metairie LA 70002
FCS DISTRIBUTORS . . . . 4909 N. Highway 52, Rochester MN 55901
FLOOR COVERINGS INTERNATIONAL . . . . .5182 B Old Dixie Hwy., Forest Park GA 30050
FUTON SHOP, THE . . . . 206 Picadilly St., London ON N6A1S1   CAN
GIVNER CARPET . . . . 1101 Finch Ave., W., Downsview ON M3J2C9   CAN
HILLSIDE BEDDING . . . . 700 Havemeyer Ave., Bronx NY 10473
JUST BASKETS . . . . 111 Kane Concourse, # 511, Bay Harbor Island FL 33154
JUST CLOSETS . . . . .25 Pelican Way, San Rafael CA 94901
PEPPERMINT FUDGE . . . . P.O. Box 77243, Oklahoma City OK 73177
PER VITA . . . . 420 Mendocino Ave., # 100, Santa Rosa CA 95401
SCANDIA DOWN SHOP . . . . P.O. Box 88819, Seattle WA 98138
SIESTA SLEEP SHOPS . . . . 386 Lindelof Ave., Stoughton MA 02072
SPACE OPTIONS . . . . .2506 N. Clark St., Chicago IL 60414
SPRING CREST DRAPERY CENTERS . . . . 505 W. Lambert Rd., Brea CA 92621
STOREHOUSE . . . . 2403 Johnson Ferry Rd., # D, Atlanta GA 30341
STOW-IT! . . . . 9 S. Washington Ave., Bergenfield NJ 07621
TMF SYSTEMS . . . . 127 Mohawk Ave., Scotia NY 12302
UNIQUE AND UNFINISHED FURNITURE . . . . 1425 Dundas St. E., Mississauga ON L4X2W4   CAN
VAN DE VEN IMPORTS . . . . 34 Grenfell Cres., Ottawa ON K2G0G2   CAN
WEEKEND FURNITURE . . . . .21 W. Main St., Malone NY 12953

CHAPTER 42

RETAIL: HOME IMPROVEMENT
AND HARDWARE

ALMOST HEAVEN HOT TUBS

Rt. 5-FS
Renick, WV 24966
TEL: (304) 497-3163 C
FAX: (304) 497-2698
Ms. Danette Brandy, VP Fran. Sales

ALMOST HEAVEN is the world's largest manufacturer of hot water health and leisure products. Their line includes hot tubs, spas, steamrooms, saunas and whirlpool baths.

HISTORY: . . . . IFA
Established in 1971; . . 1st Franchised in 1975
Company-Owned Units (As of 12/1/1989): . .0
Franchised Units (12/1/1989): 1473
Total Units (12/1/1989): 1473
Distribution: . . US-1095;Can-51;Overseas-327
 North America: . . . .
 Concentration: .60 in MA, 45 in NY, 38 in MD
Registered: . . . . .All
. . . .
Average # of Employees: . . . . . . 3 FT, 2 PT
Prior Industry Experience: . . . . Helpful

FINANCIAL:
Cash Investment: $5-10K
Total Investment: $10-20K
Fees: Franchise - $0
 Royalty: 0%, Advert: 0%
Contract Periods (Yrs.): 5/5
Area Development Agreement: Yes/5
Sub-Franchise Contract: . . . . . Yes
Expand in Territory: . . . . Yes
Passive Ownership: . . . . . .Allowed
Encourage Conversions: . . . . . Yes
Franchisee Purchase(s) Required: Yes

FRANCHISOR TRAINING/SUPPORT:
Financial Assistance Provided: . . . Yes(I)
Site Selection Assistance: . . . . .Yes
Lease Negotiation Assistance: . . . . .Yes
Co-operative Advertising: . . . . .Yes
Training: . . . . 2 Wks. Factory
. . . . 2 Wks. Site
On-Going Support: . . .A,B,C,D,E,F,G,h,I
Full-Time Franchisor Support Staff: . .102
EXPANSION PLANS:
 US: . . . . .All US
 Canada - Yes, ...Overseas - Yes

GARAGEMAN

80975 Indio Blvd., # B-15
Indio, CA 92201
TEL: (800) 433-7164 (619) 342-1696
FAX: (619) 347-9529
Mr. Robert Phillips, Sr., Director

GARAGEMAN offers a line of fabicated, modular, garage storage cabinets by and through a unique marketing concept. GARAGEMAN showrooms are designer-replicated. Residential garage models are located in up-scale retail locations.

HISTORY: . . . . IFA
Established in 1986; . . 1st Franchised in 1989
Company-Owned Units (As of 12/1/1989): . .1
Franchised Units (12/1/1989): 5
Total Units (12/1/1989): 6
Distribution: US-6;Can-0;Overseas-0
North America: . . . . .1 State
Concentration: . . . . 6 in CA
Registered: . . . . CA
. . . .
Average # of Employees: . . . . . . 3 FT, 1 PT
Prior Industry Experience: . . . . . . Helpful

FINANCIAL:
Cash Investment: $50-65K
Total Investment: $69-125K
Fees: Franchise - $17.5K
Royalty: 7.5%, Advert: 1%
Contract Periods (Yrs.): 10/10
Area Development Agreement: . .No
Sub-Franchise Contract: . . . . . .No
Expand in Territory: . . . . Yes
Passive Ownership: . . . . . .Allowed
Encourage Conversions: . . . . .No
Franchisee Purchase(s) Required: Yes

FRANCHISOR TRAINING/SUPPORT:
Financial Assistance Provided: . . .Yes(D)
Site Selection Assistance: . . . . . . .Yes
Lease Negotiation Assistance: . . . .Yes
Co-operative Advertising: . . . . . . .Yes
Training: . . . . 2 Wks. Headquarters,
. . . . . . .2 Wks. Franchisee's Location
On-Going Support: . . A,B,C,D,E,F,G,H,I
Full-Time Franchisor Support Staff: . . 21
EXPANSION PLANS:
US: . . . . Western US
Canada - No, ...Overseas - No

MR. BUILD PLUS

628 Hebron Ave., # 110
Glastonbury, CT 06033
TEL: (800) 242-8453 (203) 657-3607
FAX: (203) 657-3719
Mr. Ronald F. Buckley, Dir. Ops.

MR. BUILD PLUS is a home improvement showroom where consumers choose materials, get project designs and cost estimates and arrange installation. The showrooms feature kitchen and bathroom layouts, as well as ideas and concepts for other remodeling, renovation and additions. They also provide interior decorating.

HISTORY: . . . .
Established in 1987; . . 1st Franchised in 1988
Company-Owned Units (As of 12/1/1989): . .0
Franchised Units (12/1/1989): 6
Total Units (12/1/1989): 6
Distribution: US-4;Can-2;Overseas-0
North America: . . . . . 4 States, 2 Provinces
Concentration: . . . .
Registered: . . . . CA,FL,IL,IN
. . . .
Average # of Employees: . . . . . . 6 FT, 2 PT
Prior Industry Experience: . . . . . . Helpful

FINANCIAL:
Cash Investment: $90-221K
Total Investment: $90-221K
Fees: Franchise - $35K
Royalty: 4%, Advert: 4%
Contract Periods (Yrs.): 6/6
Area Development Agreement: Yes/25
Sub-Franchise Contract: . . . . . .No
Expand in Territory: . . . . Yes
Passive Ownership: . . . Not Allowed
Encourage Conversions: . . . . . Yes
Franchisee Purchase(s) Required: Yes

FRANCHISOR TRAINING/SUPPORT:
Financial Assistance Provided: . . . Yes(I)
Site Selection Assistance: . . . . . . .Yes
Lease Negotiation Assistance: . . . .Yes
Co-operative Advertising: . . . . . . .Yes
Training: . . . . .2 Wks. Hartford, CT
. . . .
On-Going Support: . . . a,B,C,D,E,F,G,h,i
Full-Time Franchisor Support Staff: . . . 8
EXPANSION PLANS:
US: - . . . . .All US
Canada - Yes, . . . Overseas - Yes

PLUMBING MART

285 Midwest Rd.
Scarborough, ON M1P3A6 CAN
TEL: (416) 752-4550 C
FAX:
Mr. William Gibson, President

PLUMBING MART stores concentrate and specialize on marketing everything for the bathroom, from retail parts and fixtures to complete renovations. We are the only chain that goes "all out" to service the "do-it-yourselfer," providing expert information and "know-how" on the retail floor, with an excellent selection of bathroom products at competitive prices.

HISTORY: . . . .
Established in 1959; . . 1st Franchised in 1975
Company-Owned Units (As of 12/1/1989): . .0
Franchised Units (12/1/1989): 10
Total Units (12/1/1989): 10
Distribution: US-0;Can-10;Overseas-0
North America: . . . . .1 Province
Concentration: . . . . 10 in ON
Registered: . . . .
. . . .
Average # of Employees: . . . . . . 3 FT, 1 PT
Prior Industry Experience: . . . . . . Helpful

FINANCIAL: ONT-PLUM
Cash Investment: $150K
Total Investment: $150
Fees: Franchise - $25K
Royalty: 5%, Advert: 5%
Contract Periods (Yrs.): 5/5
Area Development Agreement: . .No
Sub-Franchise Contract: . . . . . .No
Expand in Territory: . . . . Yes
Passive Ownership: . . . Not Allowed
Encourage Conversions: . . . . . Yes
Franchisee Purchase(s) Required: .No

FRANCHISOR TRAINING/SUPPORT:
Financial Assistance Provided: . . . Yes(I)
Site Selection Assistance: . . . . . . .Yes
Lease Negotiation Assistance: . . . .Yes
Co-operative Advertising: . . . . . . .Yes
Training: . . . . .2 Months Site,
. . . . 1 Month Classroom
On-Going Support: . . . . C,d,E,f,H
Full-Time Franchisor Support Staff: . . . 7
EXPANSION PLANS:
US: . . . . .No
Canada - Yes, ...Overseas - No

STAINED GLASS OVERLAY

2392 Morse Ave.
Irvine, CA 92714
TEL: (800) 654-7666 (714) 852-0424
FAX: (714) 755-4211
Mr. William Slippy, VP Fran Ops.

STAINED GLASS OVERLAY is a rapidly-growing international franchise organization. The foundation of the STAINED GLASS OVERLAY business is the patented process used to manufacture solid, seamless, one-piece stained glass in any design or pattern. Exclusive territories, turn-key package.

HISTORY: . . . . IFA	FINANCIAL:	FRANCHISOR TRAINING/SUPPORT:
Established in 1974; . . 1st Franchised in 1981	Cash Investment: $45K	Financial Assistance Provided: . . . . . No
Company-Owned Units (As of 12/1/1989): . .0	Total Investment: $60K	Site Selection Assistance: . . . . .Yes
Franchised Units (12/1/1989): 400	Fees: Franchise - $45K	Lease Negotiation Assistance: . . . . .NA
Total Units (12/1/1989): 400	Royalty: 5%, Advert: 2%	Co-operative Advertising: . . . . . . .Yes
Distribution: . . . US-258;Can-15;Overseas-27	Contract Periods (Yrs.): 5/5	Training: . . . . 6 Days Headquarters
North America: . . . . 43 States,12 Provinces	Area Development Agreement: . .No	. . . .
Concentration: . .51 in CA, 22 in TX, 20 in FL	Sub-Franchise Contract: . . . . .No	On-Going Support: . . . . B,G,H,I
Registered: . . . . .All	Expand in Territory: . . . . . . Yes	Full-Time Franchisor Support Staff: . . 17
. . . .	Passive Ownership: . . . Not Allowed	EXPANSION PLANS:
Average # of Employees: . . . . .1-2 FT	Encourage Conversions: . . . . . NA	US: . . . . .Midwest
Prior Industry Experience: . . . . . . Helpful	Franchisee Purchase(s) Required: Yes	Canada - Yes, . . . Overseas - Yes

WINDOW VISIONS

4983 Hulen St.
Fort Worth, TX 76132
TEL: (800) 999-7331 (817) 370-0450
FAX: (817) 370-1272
Mr. David Jennings, VP Fran.

We are an established leader in the window treatment industry, specializing in a full-line of ready-made and custom window treatment products. We have the ability to custom fit a ready-made product to exact window dimensions while a customer waits, in several colors, thus producing a custom ready-made product on a cash and carry basis. We are one of the largest distributors in the country of Levelor ready-made products, along with many customs.

HISTORY:	FINANCIAL:	FRANCHISOR TRAINING/SUPPORT:
Established in 1982; . . 1st Franchised in 1989	Cash Investment: $20-30K	Financial Assistance Provided: . . .Yes(D)
Company-Owned Units (As of 12/1/1989): . .1	Total Investment: $60-80K	Site Selection Assistance: . . . . .Yes
Franchised Units (12/1/1989): 9	Fees: Franchise - $20K	Lease Negotiation Assistance: . . . . .Yes
Total Units (12/1/1989): 10	Royalty: 3%, Advert: 1%	Co-operative Advertising: . . . . . . .Yes
Distribution: US-10;Can-0;Overseas-0	Contract Periods (Yrs.): 7/5	Training: . . . . .1 Wk. Headquarters,
North America: . . . . 5 States	Area Development Agreement: . .No	. . . . 3 Days On-site, On-going
Concentration: . . . 5 in TX, 2 in AR, 1 in TN	Sub-Franchise Contract: . . . . .No	On-Going Support: . . . .B,C,D,E,F,G,H,I
Registered: . . . . FL,ND	Expand in Territory: . . . . . . Yes	Full-Time Franchisor Support Staff: . . 20
. . . .	Passive Ownership: . . . . . .Allowed	EXPANSION PLANS:
Average # of Employees: . . . . .2 FT	Encourage Conversions: . . . . . Yes	US: . . . . Midwest and Southeast
Prior Industry Experience: . . . . . . Helpful	Franchisee Purchase(s) Required: Yes	Canada - Yes, ... Overseas - No

SUPPLEMENTAL LISTING OF FRANCHISORS

ACE HARDWARE . . . . .2200 Kensington Court, Oakbrook IL 60521	
ARMSTRONG WORLD INDUSTRIES . . . . P.O. Box 3001, Lancaster PA 17604	
BEAVER LUMBER COMPANY . . . . 7303 Warden Ave., Markham ON L3R5Y6	CAN
BUY THE YARD DECORATING . . . . .4457 Chesswood Rd., Downsview ON M3J2C1	CAN
CLOVERDALE PAINT . . . . 6950 King George Hwy., Surrey BC V3W4Z1	CAN
COAST TO COAST TOTAL HARDWARE STORES . . . . .501 S. Cherry St., Denver CO 80222	
COLOR YOUR WORLD . . . . 10 Carson St., Toronto ON M8W3R5	CAN
DO-IT CENTER STORES OF CANADA . . . . 635 Southdale Rd., London ON N6A4G8	CAN
EASTERN BUILDING CENTRES . . . . 1320 Rocky Lake Dr., P.O. Box 10, Waverly NS B0N2S0	CAN
INTILE DESIGNS . . . . .9716 Old Katy Rd., # 110, Houston TX 77055	
J. PASCAL . . . . .901 Bleury, # 360, Montreal PQ H2Z1M5	CAN
MR. MINIBLIND . . . . 17985-F Skypark Cir., Irvine CA 92714	
P.S. PAINT SHOP/P.S. ATLANTIC . . . . P. O. Box 546, Mount Pearl NF A1N2W4	

PAPER THE WALL . . . . 121 Interpark Blvd, #1204, San Antonio TX 78216
PRODUITS MKS . . . . 1755, rue Cunard, Laval PQ H7S2B4   CAN
RODICK MOULDING CENTERS . . . . 215 N. Marengo Ave., # 115, Pasadena CA 91101
ST. CLAIR PAINT & WALLPAPER . . . . 2600 Steeles Ave., W., Concord ON L4K3C8   CAN
STUDIO BECKERMANN . . . . 2000 Powell St., # 1650, Emeryville CA 94608
WALLPAPERS GALORE . . . . .11155 Bluegrass Pkwy., Louisville KY 40299
WALLPAPERS TO GO . . . . 12450 Greenspoint, Houston TX 77060
WINDSOR PLYWOOD . . . . Box 560, 10382 - 176th St., Surrey BC V3T5M5   CAN

For a full explanation of the data provided in

the Franchisor Format, please refer to Chapter 2,

"*How To Use The Data.*"

CHAPTER 43

RETAIL: PHOTOGRAPHY PRODUCTS AND SERVICES

AMERICAN FAST PHOTO
& CAMERA
157 S. Pine St.
Spartanburg, SC 29302
TEL: (800) 336-1467 (803) 585-3686 C
FAX:
Ms. Diane Worman, Development Dir.

AMERICAN FAST PHOTO & CAMERA is "America's Only Total Photo Center." All services, including color processing, enlargements, black and white, slides, portraiture and retail camera sales, are performed in-house. This allows store owners to retain profits on services otherwise sent out, and quicker turn-around times for the customer.

HISTORY: . . . . IFA/WIF
Established in 1984; . . 1st Franchised in 1984
Company-Owned Units (As of 12/1/1989): . . .0
Franchised Units (12/1/1989): 18
Total Units (12/1/1989): 18
Distribution: US-18;Can-0;Overseas-0
North America: . . . . 4 States
Concentration: . . . .2 in MI, 5 in SC, 3 in GA
Registered: . . . . .FL,MI
. . . .
Average # of Employees: . . . . . . 3 FT, 2 PT
Prior Industry Experience: . . . . Helpful

FINANCIAL:
Cash Investment: $40-60K
Total Investment: $115-165K
Fees: Franchise - $27.5K
  Royalty: 4-6%, Advert: 2%
Contract Periods (Yrs.): 20/20
Area Development Agreement: Yes/20
Sub-Franchise Contract: . . . . . Yes
Expand in Territory: . . . . Yes
Passive Ownership: . . . Discouraged
Encourage Conversions: . . . . . Yes
Franchisee Purchase(s) Required: .No

FRANCHISOR TRAINING/SUPPORT:
Financial Assistance Provided: . . . . .Yes
Site Selection Assistance: . . . . . . .Yes
Lease Negotiation Assistance: . . . . .Yes
Co-operative Advertising: . . . . .Yes
Training: . . . . 1 Wk. HQ, 2 Wks. On-site,
  . . . . 2 Wks. Texas/Minnesota
On-Going Support: . . . . .C,D,E,F,G,H,I
Full-Time Franchisor Support Staff: . . . 6
EXPANSION PLANS:
US: . . . . .All US
Canada - Yes, ... Overseas - No

GLITTER PHOTOGRAPHY

1655 Mesa Verde Ave., # 230
Ventura, CA 93003
TEL: (800) 545-4887 (805) 650-8406
FAX: (805) 650-9319
Ms. Peggy Hatfield, VP Admin.

The first and only franchise of its kind! GLITTER PHOTOGRAPHY brings a high-fashion glamour experience to today's woman. The salons offer a complete make-over, hair enhancement, furs, boas and jewelry, along with a 20-pose selection in 2-3 clothing changes.

HISTORY: . . . . IFA	FINANCIAL:	FRANCHISOR TRAINING/SUPPORT:
Established in 1988; . . 1st Franchised in 1989	Cash Investment: $75-150K	Financial Assistance Provided: . . . Yes(I)
Company-Owned Units (As of 12/1/1989): . .1	Total Investment: $100-190K	Site Selection Assistance: . . . . . . .Yes
Franchised Units (12/1/1989): 1	Fees: Franchise - $21K	Lease Negotiation Assistance: . . . . .Yes
Total Units (12/1/1989): 2	Royalty: 5%, Advert: 3%	Co-operative Advertising: . . . . . . .Yes
Distribution: US-2;Can-0;Overseas-0	Contract Periods (Yrs.): . . . 10/10	Training: . . . . 2 Wk.s Headquarters,
North America: . . . . .1 State	Area Development Agreement: . .No	. . . . .1 Wk. Franchisee's Salon
Concentration: . . . . 2 in CA	Sub-Franchise Contract: . . . . .No	On-Going Support: . . . . . . A,C,D,E,I
Registered: . . . . CA	Expand in Territory: . . . . Yes	Full-Time Franchisor Support Staff: . . .2
	Passive Ownership: . . . Discouraged	EXPANSION PLANS:
Average # of Employees: . . . . . 3-4 FT, 3 PT	Encourage Conversions: . . . . . NA	US: . . . . CA and Western States
Prior Industry Experience: . . . . Helpful	Franchisee Purchase(s) Required: .No	Canada - No, ... Overseas - Yes

JAPAN CAMERA CENTRE 1 HOUR PHOTO

150 Lesmill Rd.
Don Mills, ON M3B2T5 CAN
TEL: (800) 268-7740 (416) 445-1481
FAX: (416) 445-0519
Mr. Roy Townshend, Fran. Div.

JAPAN CAMERA 1 HOUR PHOTO offers a full-line camera store and 1-hour film processing, all under one roof for shopping convenience. This is a unique and exciting business that offers excellent opportunities. Put yourself in the picture!

HISTORY:	FINANCIAL:	FRANCHISOR TRAINING/SUPPORT:
Established in 1951; . . 1st Franchised in 1981	Cash Investment: $75K	Financial Assistance Provided: . . . Yes(I)
Company-Owned Units (As of 12/1/1989): . 40	Total Investment: $200-250K	Site Selection Assistance: . . . . . . .Yes
Franchised Units (12/1/1989): 150	Fees: Franchise - $40K	Lease Negotiation Assistance: . . . . .Yes
Total Units (12/1/1989): 190	Royalty: 8%, Advert: 3.5%	Co-operative Advertising: . . . . . . .Yes
Distribution: US-0;Can-190;Overseas-0	Contract Periods (Yrs.): . . . 10/10	Training: . . . . . 10 Days Headquarters, 5
North America:	Area Development Agreement: . .No	. . . . . . Days Site, 10 Days 1/4ly Site
Concentration: . 55 in ON, 30 in PQ, 25 in BC	Sub-Franchise Contract: . . . . .No	On-Going Support: . . . .B,C,D,E,F,G,H,I
Registered: . . . . AB	Expand in Territory: . . . . Yes	Full-Time Franchisor Support Staff: . .100
	Passive Ownership: . . . Not Allowed	EXPANSION PLANS:
Average # of Employees: . . . . . . 4 FT, 4 PT	Encourage Conversions: . . . . Yes	US: . . . . .No
Prior Industry Experience: . . . . . .Necessary	Franchisee Purchase(s) Required: Yes	Canada - Yes, ...Overseas - No

KITS CAMERAS

6051 S. 194th St.
Kent, WA 98032
TEL: (206) 872-3688 C
FAX: (206) 872-8419
Mr. Mike Greenen, Fran. Div. Mgr.

KITS CAMERAS is the largest specialty camera and photo-finishing retailer on the West Coast, catering to both the novice and advanced amateur photographer. Stores carry major lines of cameras, camcorders and photo accessories, along with KITS private label products and photo-finishing.

HISTORY:	FINANCIAL:	FRANCHISOR TRAINING/SUPPORT:
Established in 1975; . . 1st Franchised in 1978	Cash Investment: . . . . $50K+	Financial Assistance Provided: . . . Yes(I)
Company-Owned Units (As of 12/1/1989): . 54	Total Investment: $110-140K	Site Selection Assistance: . . . . . . .Yes
Franchised Units (12/1/1989): 32	Fees: Franchise - $19.5K	Lease Negotiation Assistance: . . . . .Yes
Total Units (12/1/1989): 86	Royalty: 6%, Advert: 1.5%	Co-operative Advertising: . . . . . . .Yes
Distribution: US-86;Can-0;Overseas-0	Contract Periods (Yrs.): . . . 10/10	Training: . . . . .8 Days Head Office,
North America: . . . . 6 States	Area Development Agreement: . .No	. . . . 16 Days Training Store
Concentration: . .37 in CA, 32 in WA, 7 in AZ	Sub-Franchise Contract: . . . . .No	On-Going Support: . . . A,B,C,D,E,F,G,H
Registered: . . . . .CA,OR,WA	Expand in Territory: . . . . Yes	Full-Time Franchisor Support Staff: . . 60
	Passive Ownership: . . . Not Allowed	EXPANSION PLANS:
Average # of Employees: . . . . . . 3 FT, 2 PT	Encourage Conversions: . . . . Yes	US: . . . . West Coast
Prior Industry Experience: . . . . Helpful	Franchisee Purchase(s) Required: .No	Canada - No, ...Overseas - No

ONE HOUR MOTO PHOTO

4444 Lake Center Dr.
Dayton, OH 45426
TEL: (800) 333-6686 (513) 854-6686
FAX:
Mr. Paul Pieschel, VP Fran. Devel.

World's largest one-hour film processor, featuring related add-on imaging services, such as portrait studios, video transfer systems, etc. A company with over 40 years in the industry, now positioned in the exploding growth market of on-site processing stores.

HISTORY: . . . . IFA
Established in 1981; . . 1st Franchised in 1982
Company-Owned Units (As of 12/1/1989): . 80
Franchised Units (12/1/1989): 255
Total Units (12/1/1989): 335
Distribution: . . . US-293;Can-17;Overseas-25
North America: . . . . . 27 States, 1 Province
Concentration: . 29 in NY, 25 in GA, 25 in OK
Registered: . . . . . .All States Exc. ND & SD
. . . .
Average # of Employees: . . . . 3-4 FT, 3-4 PT
Prior Industry Experience: . . . . . . Helpful

FINANCIAL: OTC-MOTO
Cash Investment: $45-60K
Total Investment: $170-220K
Fees: Franchise - $35K
 Royalty: 6%, Advert: 1/2%
Contract Periods (Yrs.): 10/10
Area Development Agreement: Yes/5
Sub-Franchise Contract: . . . . . .No
Expand in Territory: . . . . Yes
Passive Ownership: . . . Discouraged
Encourage Conversions: . . . . . Yes
Franchisee Purchase(s) Required: Yes

FRANCHISOR TRAINING/SUPPORT:
Financial Assistance Provided: . . . Yes(I)
Site Selection Assistance: . . . . . . .Yes
Lease Negotiation Assistance: . . . . .Yes
Co-operative Advertising: . . . . . . .Yes
Training: . . . . . .1 Wk. Regional Store, 2
 . . . . Wks. Headquarters, 1 Wk. On-site
On-Going Support: . . .a,B,C,D,E,f,G,H,I
Full-Time Franchisor Support Staff: . . 85
EXPANSION PLANS:
 US: . . . . .All US
 Canada - Yes, . . . Overseas - Yes

PORTRAIT AMERICA

22511 Telegraph Rd.
Southfield, MI 48034
TEL: (800) 669-0911 (313) 356-5030
FAX:
Mr. Edward R. Schlager, VP Devel.

Full-service, professional photography business, specializing in weddings, family, children, school and special events. Unique programs geared to penetrate high profit markets.

HISTORY: . . . .
Established in 1987; . . 1st Franchised in 1987
Company-Owned Units (As of 12/1/1989): . .1
Franchised Units (12/1/1989): 29
Total Units (12/1/1989): 30
Distribution: US-30;Can-0;Overseas-0
North America: . . . . 2 States
Concentration: . . . . . . .29 in MI, 1 in OH
Registered: . . . . .MI
. . . .
Average # of Employees: . . . . . . 2 FT, 1 PT
Prior Industry Experience: . . . . . . Helpful

FINANCIAL:
Cash Investment: $10-20K
Total Investment: $20-30K
Fees: Franchise - $12.6K
 Royalty: 6%, Advert: 2%
Contract Periods (Yrs.): . . . 10/10
Area Development Agreement: Yes/10
Sub-Franchise Contract: . . . . .No
Expand in Territory: . . . . . . Yes
Passive Ownership: . . . Discouraged
Encourage Conversions: . . . . Yes
Franchisee Purchase(s) Required: .No

FRANCHISOR TRAINING/SUPPORT:
Financial Assistance Provided: . . .Yes(D)
Site Selection Assistance: . . . . . . .Yes
Lease Negotiation Assistance: . . . .Yes
Co-operative Advertising: . . . . . . .Yes
Training: . . . . .1 Wk. Headquarters,
. . . .
On-Going Support: . . A,B,C,D,E,F,G,H,I
Full-Time Franchisor Support Staff: . . .5
EXPANSION PLANS:
 US: . . . . .All US
 Canada - No, ...Overseas - No

SOOTER'S

88 Sherbrook St.
Winnipeg, MB R3C2B3 CAN
TEL: (204) 775-8188
FAX:
Mr. Peter Holfener, Fran. Dir.

SOOTER's is a professional portrait studio and photo finishing outlet. We offer good quality photo finishing and portraits at very reasonable prices. Many of our franchisees recover their total investment in less than one year.

HISTORY: . . . .
Established in 1962; . . 1st Franchised in 1965
Company-Owned Units (As of 12/1/1989): 142
Franchised Units (12/1/1989): 196
Total Units (12/1/1989): 338
Distribution: . . . US-2;Can-336;Overseas-0
North America: . . . . 1 State, 10 Provinces
Concentration: .158 in ON, 44 in BC, 30 in MB
Registered: IL
. . . .
Average # of Employees: . . . . . . 1 FT, 2 PT
Prior Industry Experience: . . . . . . Helpful

FINANCIAL:
Cash Investment: $50K
Total Investment: $50K
Fees: Franchise - $30K
 Royalty: 5%, Advert: 10%
Contract Periods (Yrs.): . . . 10/10
Area Development Agreement: Yes/10
Sub-Franchise Contract: . . . . . Yes
Expand in Territory: . . . . Yes
Passive Ownership: . . . Discouraged
Encourage Conversions: . . . . . Yes
Franchisee Purchase(s) Required: Yes

FRANCHISOR TRAINING/SUPPORT:
Financial Assistance Provided: . . . Yes(I)
Site Selection Assistance: . . . . . . .Yes
Lease Negotiation Assistance: . . . . .Yes
Co-operative Advertising: . . . . . . .Yes
Training: . . . . .1 Wk. Headquarters,
. . . . Up to 2 Wks. Site
On-Going Support: . . . . B,C,D,E,F,G,H
Full-Time Franchisor Support Staff: . .175
EXPANSION PLANS:
 US: . . . . .No
 Canada - Yes, ...Overseas - No

SPORTS SECTION, THE

3120 Medlock Bridge Rd.
Norcross, GA 30091
TEL: (800) 321-9127 (404) 416-6604
FAX:
Mr. Daniel Burgner, President

Entrepreneur will become a business-minded sales and marketing expert while TSS trains him/her in photography. Rated in top 500 national franchises. Great profits. No royalty fees. 3 franchise levels to choose from, starting at $9,500. Operate from home. Send for free pack of information and photos.

HISTORY: . . . . IFA
Established in 1983; . . 1st Franchised in 1984
Company-Owned Units (As of 12/1/1989): . 12
Franchised Units (12/1/1989): 43
Total Units (12/1/1989): 55
Distribution: US-55;Can-0;Overseas-0
  North America: . . . . 21 States
  Concentration: . . . 5 in TX, 5 in GA, 4 in TN
Registered: . . . . .FL,AB
. . . .
Average # of Employees: . . . . .2 FT
Prior Industry Experience: . . . . . . Helpful

FINANCIAL:
Cash Investment: $9.5-25K
Total Investment: $9.5-25K
Fees: Franchise - $9.5-25K
  Royalty: 0%, Advert: 0%
Contract Periods (Yrs.): 5/5
Area Development Agreement: Yes/Var
Sub-Franchise Contract: . . . . . .No
Expand in Territory: . . . . Yes
Passive Ownership: . . . . . .Allowed
Encourage Conversions: . . . . . Yes
Franchisee Purchase(s) Required: Yes

FRANCHISOR TRAINING/SUPPORT:
Financial Assistance Provided: . . .Yes(D)
Site Selection Assistance: . . . . .NA
Lease Negotiation Assistance: . . . . .NA
Co-operative Advertising: . . . . .NA
Training: . . . . . . 1-5 Days Site for Sales/
  . . . Mktg., 1-5 Days Site - Photography
On-Going Support: . . . . D,G,H,I
Full-Time Franchisor Support Staff: . . 16
EXPANSION PLANS:
  US: . . . . .All US
  Canada - Yes, ...Overseas - Yes

SUPPLEMENTAL LISTING OF FRANCHISORS

CAMERAAMERICA ONE HOUR PHOTO . . . . P. O. Box 12786, Overland Park KS 66212
CHROMA COPY FRANCHISING OF AMERICA . . . . .423 W. 55th St., New York NY 10019
CUT-UPS INTERNATIONAL . . . . 12113 Roxie Dr., Austin TX 78729
JET PHOTO INTERNATIONAL . . . . .P.O. Box 1609, Minot ND 58702
ONE HOUR MOTO PHOTO . . . . 85 Ellesmere Rd., # 209, Scarborough ON M1R4B9   CAN
ONE HOUR PHOTO . . . . 8440 Market St., Youngstown OH 44512
PHOTO PET INTERNATIONAL . . . . .365 Evans Ave., # L-8, Toronto ON M8Z1K2   CAN
SCULPTURE ME STUDIOS . . . . 24 Martin Ross Ave., Downsview ON M3J2K9   CAN
SOOTER STUDIOS/SOOTER FOTO . . . . 1559 N. Mannheim Rd., Stone Park IL 60016
VIDEO PRINTS WORKLAB . . . . .2121 W. Oakland Park Blvd., Ft. Lauderdale FL 33311

CHAPTER 44

RETAIL: SPECIALTY SHOPS

14 KARAT PLUM, THE

46-022 Alaloa, # 205
Kaneohe, HI 96744
TEL: (808) 247-1127 C
FAX:
Ms. Sansy Gottesman, VP/Dir. Fran.

14 KARAT PLUM offers quality 14 karat gold jewelry, merchandised at affordable prices, appealing to youth and fashion markets. Inventory risks are minimized by eliminating expensive items, creating inventory turns far exceeding those of traditional jewelry stores. High volume per square foot facilitates acquisition of desirable mall locations.

HISTORY: . . . . IFA
Established in 1989; . . 1st Franchised in 1989
Company-Owned Units (As of 12/1/1989): . . 1
Franchised Units (12/1/1989): 4
Total Units (12/1/1989): 5
Distribution: US-5;Can-0;Overseas-0
 North America: . . . . .1 State
 Concentration: . . . . .5 in IH
Registered: . . . . .HI
 . . . .
Average # of Employees: . . . . . . 3 FT, 2 PT
Prior Industry Experience: . . . . Helpful

FINANCIAL:
Cash Investment: $160-225K
Total Investment: $160-225K
Fees: Franchise - $25K
 Royalty: 7%, Advert: 1%
Contract Periods (Yrs.): . . . .Varies
Area Development Agreement: . .No
Sub-Franchise Contract: . . . . . .No
Expand in Territory: . . . . Yes
Passive Ownership: . . . Not Allowed
Encourage Conversions: . . . . . .No
Franchisee Purchase(s) Required: .No

FRANCHISOR TRAINING/SUPPORT:
Financial Assistance Provided: . . . Yes(I)
Site Selection Assistance: . . . . .Yes
Lease Negotiation Assistance: . . . . .Yes
Co-operative Advertising: . . . . No
Training: . . . . 10 Days-2 Wks. HQ,
 . . . . 7 Days-2 Wks. On-site
On-Going Support: . . . . . C,D,E,F,G,h,I
Full-Time Franchisor Support Staff: . . . 3
EXPANSION PLANS:
 US: . . . . Northwest
 Canada - No, ... Overseas - No

ALL-IN-ONE CENTER
DRY CLEAN-POSTAL-PHOTO
13013 Lee Jackson Hwy., # 1400
Fairfax, VA 22033
TEL: (703) 385-3533
FAX: (703) 281-6855
Mr. C. C. Martucci, Chairman

The ALL-IN-ONE CENTER offers a unique "three profit centers under one roof" concept. The three major services - dry cleaning, postal and 1-hour photo are complemented by shoe repairing, tailoring, mail boxes, copying, faxing, picture frames and three chances to be successful instead of one!

HISTORY: . . . .
Established in 1987; . . 1st Franchised in 1987
Company-Owned Units (As of 12/1/1989): . .1
Franchised Units (12/1/1989): 45
Total Units (12/1/1989): 46
Distribution: US-46;Can-0;Overseas-0
North America: . . . . 16 States
Concentration: . . . 14 in CA, 8 in PA, 6 in FL
Registered: . . . . . CA,FL,MD,NY,VA,WA

. . . .
Average # of Employees: . . . . .5 FT
Prior Industry Experience: . . . . Helpful

FINANCIAL:
Cash Investment: $50-60K
Total Investment: $230-280K
Fees: Franchise - $20-25K
Royalty: 5%, Advert: 2%
Contract Periods (Yrs.): 10/10
Area Development Agreement: Yes/10
Sub-Franchise Contract: . . . . . Yes
Expand in Territory: . . . . . . Yes
Passive Ownership: . . . . . .Allowed
Encourage Conversions: . . . . NA
Franchisee Purchase(s) Required: .No

FRANCHISOR TRAINING/SUPPORT:
Financial Assistance Provided: . . . Yes(I)
Site Selection Assistance: . . . . . . .Yes
Lease Negotiation Assistance: . . . .Yes
Co-operative Advertising: . . . . . . .Yes
Training: . . . . . 4 Wks. Dry Clean Store,
. . 1 Wk. Postal, 2 Wks. Photo Manufact
On-Going Support: . . . . B,C,D,E,F,G,H
Full-Time Franchisor Support Staff: . . .4
EXPANSION PLANS:
US: .All US
Canada - Yes, . . . Overseas - Yes

BALLOON BOUQUETS

500 23rd St. NW
Washington, DC 20037
TEL: (800) 424-2323 (202) 785-1131
FAX:
Mr. Joseph Del Vecchio, VP

Nationwide balloon delivery and decorating service. Network of franchisees, licensees and subscribers nationwide. BALLOON BOUQUETS Nationwide Delivery Service toll-free telephone number advertised in over 120 telephone books. Customer referrals made to franchisee for exclusive territory.

HISTORY: . . . .
Established in 1976; . . 1st Franchised in 1979
Company-Owned Units (As of 12/1/1989): . .0
Franchised Units (12/1/1989): 16
Total Units (12/1/1989): 16
Distribution: US-16;Can-0;Overseas-0
North America: . . . .
Concentration: . . . .
Registered: . . . . CA,NY,RI,VA

. . . .
Average # of Employees: . . . . . . .6FT, 6 PT
Prior Industry Experience: . . . . Helpful

FINANCIAL:
Cash Investment: $10-15K
Total Investment: $15-20K
Fees: Franchise - . . . . . . $Varies
Royalty: 5%, Advert: 3%
Contract Periods (Yrs.): 5/5
Area Development Agreement: .No
Sub-Franchise Contract: . . . . .No
Expand in Territory: . . . . . . Yes
Passive Ownership: . . . Not Allowed
Encourage Conversions: . . . . Yes
Franchisee Purchase(s) Required: .No

FRANCHISOR TRAINING/SUPPORT:
Financial Assistance Provided: . . . . . No
Site Selection Assistance: . . . . No
Lease Negotiation Assistance: . . . . . No
Co-operative Advertising: . . . . . . .Yes
Training: . . . . .2-3 Days Wash., DC
. . . .
On-Going Support: . . . . B,C,D,G,I
Full-Time Franchisor Support Staff: . . .6
EXPANSION PLANS:
US: .All US
Canada - No, ...Overseas - No

BATH & A-HALF

999 Elmhurst Rd.
Mt. Prospect, IL 60056
TEL: (312) 259-8979 C
FAX:
Mr. John Lehrer, VP

BATH & A-HALF stores combine great fashion bath merchandise and personal care products, full service, outstanding selection. Franchisees receive full training, powerful advertising, operating systems, established vendor relations and support of experts. Stores located in regional malls.

HISTORY: . . . . IFA
Established in 1985; . . 1st Franchised in 1985
Company-Owned Units (As of 12/1/1989): . .7
Franchised Units (12/1/1989): 11
Total Units (12/1/1989): 18
Distribution: US-18;Can-0;Overseas-0
North America: . . . . 6 States
Concentration: . . . .10 in IL,2 in MN,2 in WI
Registered: . . . . .FL,IL,MN,WI

. . . .
Average # of Employees: . . . . . . 2 FT, 2 PT
Prior Industry Experience: . . . . Helpful

FINANCIAL:
Cash Investment: $40-60K
Total Investment: $80-125K
Fees: Franchise - $9-18K
Royalty: 4-5%, Advert: 1%
Contract Periods (Yrs.): 10/5/5
Area Development Agreement: .No
Sub-Franchise Contract: . . . . .No
Expand in Territory: . . . . . . Yes
Passive Ownership: . . . Discouraged
Encourage Conversions: . . . . .No
Franchisee Purchase(s) Required: .No

FRANCHISOR TRAINING/SUPPORT:
Financial Assistance Provided: . . . Yes(I)
Site Selection Assistance: . . . . . . .Yes
Lease Negotiation Assistance: . . . .Yes
Co-operative Advertising: . . . . . . .Yes
Training: . . . . . . 3-5 Days Headquarters,
. . . . 3-5 Days Site
On-Going Support: . . A,B,C,D,E,F,G,H,I
Full-Time Franchisor Support Staff: . . .5
EXPANSION PLANS:
US: .All US
Canada - No, ... Overseas - Yes

BATHTIQUE

247 N. Goodman St.
Rochester, NY 14607
TEL: (716) 442-9190 C
FAX:
Mr. Don Seipel, President

A unique gift and bath shop, located in malls and shopping centers. This specialty shop capitalizes on 2 current trends - increased emphasis on the home and the fact that the average person gives 12 gifts/year. Complete services from lease negotiation to on-going advertising co-op.

HISTORY: . . . . IFA	FINANCIAL:	FRANCHISOR TRAINING/SUPPORT:
Established in 1969; . . 1st Franchised in 1969	Cash Investment: $25-40K	Financial Assistance Provided: . . . . . No
Company-Owned Units (As of 12/1/1989): . 26	Total Investment: $80-120K	Site Selection Assistance: . . . . .Yes
Franchised Units (12/1/1989): 55	Fees: Franchise - $30K	Lease Negotiation Assistance: . . . . .Yes
Total Units (12/1/1989): 81	Royalty: 5%, Advert: 0%	Co-operative Advertising: . . . . . . .Yes
Distribution: US-80;Can-0;Overseas-1	Contract Periods (Yrs.): 10/10	Training: . . . . 6 Days HQ, 2 Wks.
North America: . . . . 35 States	Area Development Agreement: Yes/10	. . . . Site, 3 Days Follow-up
Concentration: . . . 8 in CA, 8 in FL, 7 in NY	Sub-Franchise Contract: . . . . .No	On-Going Support: . . A,B,C,D,E,F,G,H,I
Registered: . . . . CA,FL,IN,MD,MI,NY,WA	Expand in Territory: . . . . Yes	Full-Time Franchisor Support Staff: . . 40
. . . .	Passive Ownership: . . . . .Allowed	EXPANSION PLANS:
Average # of Employees: . . . . . . 1 FT, 4 PT	Encourage Conversions: . . . . . Yes	US: . . . . .All US
Prior Industry Experience: . . . . . . Helpful	Franchisee Purchase(s) Required: .No	Canada - Yes, . . . Overseas - Yes

BUTTERFIELDS, ETC.

1250 Capitol of TX Hwy. S, #2, #100
Austin, TX 78746
TEL: (512) 328-6960
FAX:
Mr. Stan Butterfield, President

BUTTERFIELDS is a gourmet retail store with gadgets, cookware, table settings, "everything to get you cooking." Locations are in regional shopping centers.

HISTORY: . . . . IFA	FINANCIAL:	FRANCHISOR TRAINING/SUPPORT:
Established in 1985; . . 1st Franchised in 1986	Cash Investment: $150K	Financial Assistance Provided: . . . . . No
Company-Owned Units (As of 12/1/1989): . .0	Total Investment: $150K	Site Selection Assistance: . . . . . . .Yes
Franchised Units (12/1/1989): 21	Fees: Franchise - $20K	Lease Negotiation Assistance: . . . .Yes
Total Units (12/1/1989): 21	Royalty: 5%, Advert: 1%	Co-operative Advertising: . . . . . . .Yes
Distribution: US-21;Can-0;Overseas-0	Contract Periods (Yrs.): 10/10	Training: . . . . 1 Wk. HQ
North America: . . . . 9 States	Area Development Agreement: Yes/10	. . . . 1 Wk. Site
Concentration:	Sub-Franchise Contract: . . . . .No	On-Going Support: . . . . .C,D,E,F,G,H,I
Registered: . . . . FL,IN	Expand in Territory: . . . . Yes	Full-Time Franchisor Support Staff: . . . 4
. . . .	Passive Ownership: . . . Discouraged	EXPANSION PLANS:
Average # of Employees: . . . . . .2 FT,3-5 PT	Encourage Conversions: . . . . . .No	US: . . . . .All US
Prior Industry Experience: . . . . Helpful	Franchisee Purchase(s) Required: .No	Canada - No, ...Overseas - No

CREATIVE MIND

11010 Metcalf
Overland Park, KS 66210
TEL: (913) 451-2789 C
FAX:
Ms. Nancy Sullivan, Owner/Manager

Retail store selling self-improvement books, tapes, videos, technology and seminars.

HISTORY:	FINANCIAL:	FRANCHISOR TRAINING/SUPPORT:
Established in 1986; . . 1st Franchised in 1989	Cash Investment: $150K	Financial Assistance Provided: . . . Yes(I)
Company-Owned Units (As of 12/1/1989): . .1	Total Investment: $175K	Site Selection Assistance: . . . . . . .Yes
Franchised Units (12/1/1989): 2	Fees: Franchise - $19.5K	Lease Negotiation Assistance: . . . .Yes
Total Units (12/1/1989): 3	Royalty: 4%, Advert: 1%	Co-operative Advertising: . . . . . . .Yes
Distribution: US-3;Can-0;Overseas-0	Contract Periods (Yrs.): 10/10	Training: . . . . 9 Days Headquarters
North America: . . . . 3 States	Area Development Agreement: . .No	. . . .
Concentration:	Sub-Franchise Contract: . . . . .No	On-Going Support: . . . .B,C,D,E,F,G,H,I
Registered:	Expand in Territory: . . . . Yes	Full-Time Franchisor Support Staff: . . . 4
. . . .	Passive Ownership: . . . Discouraged	EXPANSION PLANS:
Average # of Employees: . . . . . . 2 FT, 2 PT	Encourage Conversions: . . . . . NA	US: . . . . .All US
Prior Industry Experience: . . . . Helpful	Franchisee Purchase(s) Required: Yes	Canada - Yes, . . . Overseas - Yes

CUTLERY WORLD

2841 Hickory Valley Rd.
Chattanooga, TN 37421
TEL: (800) 537-2962 (615) 855-4200
FAX: (615) 855-4268
Mr. Robert Scudder, Dir. Franchising

The largest chain of cutlery specialty stores in the US. Exclusively a regional mall concept. State-of-the-art store design. We carry the top brands of kitchen, hunting, fishing and pocket knives, as well as scissors, manicure implements and shaving accessories. Many high-quality, high-profit private label goods.

HISTORY: . . . . IFA
Established in 1970; . . 1st Franchised in 1977
Company-Owned Units (As of 12/1/1989): 162
Franchised Units (12/1/1989): 20
Total Units (12/1/1989): 182
Distribution: . . . US-182;Can-0;Overseas-0
 North America: . . . . 35 States
 Concentration: . .22 in TX, 20 in FL, 20 in CA
Registered: . . . .
 . . . .
Average # of Employees: . . . . 2-3 FT, 1-3 PT
Prior Industry Experience: . . . . Helpful

FINANCIAL:
Cash Investment: $40-70K
Total Investment: $125-175K
Fees: Franchise - $20K
 Royalty: 5.8-6.5%, Advert: 1% Max.
Contract Periods (Yrs.): . . . . Lease
Area Development Agreement: . .No
Sub-Franchise Contract: . . . . .No
Expand in Territory: . . . . . . .No
Passive Ownership: . . . Discouraged
Encourage Conversions: . . . . . NA
Franchisee Purchase(s) Required: Yes

FRANCHISOR TRAINING/SUPPORT:
Financial Assistance Provided: . . . . . No
Site Selection Assistance: . . . . .Yes
Lease Negotiation Assistance: . . . . .Yes
Co-operative Advertising: . . . . .Yes
Training: . . . . . . 2 Wks. Company Store,
 . . . . .5 Days Franchisee's Store
On-Going Support: . . . . C,D,E,G,I
Full-Time Franchisor Support Staff: . . . 2
EXPANSION PLANS:
 US: . . . . All US
 Canada - No, ...Overseas - No

EXQUISITE CRAFTS

108 Gleneida Ave.
Carmel, NY 10512
TEL: (914) 225-2606
FAX:
Ms. Marianne Montagna, President

EXQUISITE CRAFTS is a special craft supply store that offers over 30 different departments, as well as workshops and quality-finished crafts and designs. Customer service is a strong point in selling needlecrafts, candy, art supplies, stenciling, flowers, baskets, ribbons, children's crafts, fabrics, paints, wood and dollhouse miniatures in only 1,200 SF of space.

HISTORY: . . . .
Established in 1973; . . 1st Franchised in 1988
Company-Owned Units (As of 12/1/1989): . .1
Franchised Units (12/1/1989): 1
Total Units (12/1/1989): 2
Distribution: US-2;Can-0;Overseas-0
 North America: . . . . 2 States
 Concentration: . . . . 1 in NY, 1 in VT
Registered: . . . . NY
 . . . .
Average # of Employees: . . . . . . 1 FT, 2 PT
Prior Industry Experience: . . . . Helpful

FINANCIAL:
Cash Investment: $45-55K
Total Investment: $45-55K
Fees: Franchise - $10K
 Royalty: 4%, Advert: 5%
Contract Periods (Yrs.): 10/10
Area Development Agreement: . .No
Sub-Franchise Contract: . . . . .No
Expand in Territory: . . . . . . .No
Passive Ownership: . . . Not Allowed
Encourage Conversions: . . . . . Yes
Franchisee Purchase(s) Required: .No

FRANCHISOR TRAINING/SUPPORT:
Financial Assistance Provided: . . . . . No
Site Selection Assistance: . . . . .Yes
Lease Negotiation Assistance: . . . . .Yes
Co-operative Advertising: . . . . .Yes
Training: . . . . . . 10 Days Headquarters
 . . . .
On-Going Support: . . . . a,C,D,E,F,G,H,I
Full-Time Franchisor Support Staff: . . . 2
EXPANSION PLANS:
 US: . . . . .Northeast, Southeast
 Canada - No, ...Overseas - No

FLAG SHOP, THE

1755 West 4th Ave.
Vancouver, BC V6J1M2 CAN
TEL: (800) 663-8681 (CAN)
FAX: (604) 736-6439
Ms. Doreen Braverman, President

Every kind of flag imaginable. If we don't stock it, we'll sew it or print it. Flag accessories - poles, brackets, stands, pins, crests, books, charts - anything flag related. Custom designs and guaranteed workmanship.

HISTORY: . . . .
Established in 1975; . . 1st Franchised in 1987
Company-Owned Units (As of 12/1/1989): . .2
Franchised Units (12/1/1989): 2
Total Units (12/1/1989): 4
Distribution: US-0;Can-4;Overseas-0
 North America: . . . . 3 Provinces
 Concentration: . . . 2 in BC, 1 in AB, 1 in ON
Registered: . . . . AB
 . . . .
Average # of Employees: . . . . . . 2 FT, 1 PT
Prior Industry Experience: . . . . Helpful

FINANCIAL:
Cash Investment: $20-50K
Total Investment: $20-80K
Fees: Franchise - $2.5-20K
 Royalty: 5%, Advert: 3%
Contract Periods (Yrs.): . . . 5-10/10
Area Development Agreement: . .No
Sub-Franchise Contract: . . . . Yes
Expand in Territory: . . . . . . Yes
Passive Ownership: . . . Not Allowed
Encourage Conversions: . . . . NA
Franchisee Purchase(s) Required: Yes

FRANCHISOR TRAINING/SUPPORT:
Financial Assistance Provided: . . . . . No
Site Selection Assistance: . . . . .Yes
Lease Negotiation Assistance: . . . . .Yes
Co-operative Advertising: . . . . .Yes
Training: . . . . . . 1-2 Wks. Headquarters,
 . . . . 1-3 Days Site Location
On-Going Support: . . .A,B,C,D,E,F,G,h,I
Full-Time Franchisor Support Staff: . . 19
EXPANSION PLANS:
 US: . . . . .All US
 Canada - Yes, . . . Overseas - Yes

HAPPI-NAMES

1225 Park Place Mall
Memphis, TN 38119
TEL: (901) 767-6067
FAX:
Mr. J. Richard Holley, President

Personalized gifts and gifts that can be personalized through the medium of paint, imprinting and engraving. Our demonstrating artist is always ready to personalize.

HISTORY: . . . .
Established in 1975; . . 1st Franchised in 1983
Company-Owned Units (As of 12/1/1989): . . 1
Franchised Units (12/1/1989): 14
Total Units (12/1/1989): 15
Distribution: US-15;Can-0;Overseas-0
North America: . . . . 7 States
Concentration: . . . 6 in TN, 5 in MS, 1 in GA
Registered: . . . . .FL
. . . .
Average # of Employees: . . . . . . 2 FT, 4 PT
Prior Industry Experience: . . . . . . Helpful

FINANCIAL:
Cash Investment: $15-25K
Total Investment: $75-125K
Fees: Franchise - $25K
 Royalty: 6-4%, Advert: 0%
Contract Periods (Yrs.): . . . 20/10
Area Development Agreement: . .No
Sub-Franchise Contract: . . . . .No
Expand in Territory: . . . . . . .No
Passive Ownership: . . . Discouraged
Encourage Conversions: . . . . .No
Franchisee Purchase(s) Required: .No

FRANCHISOR TRAINING/SUPPORT:
Financial Assistance Provided: . . . . .No
Site Selection Assistance: . . . . . . .Yes
Lease Negotiation Assistance: . . . . .Yes
Co-operative Advertising: . . . . . . .Yes
Training: . . . . .1 Wk. Headquarters,
 . . . . . .2 Wks. over 12 Months On-site
On-Going Support: . . . A,C,D,E,F,G,H,I
Full-Time Franchisor Support Staff: . . .5
EXPANSION PLANS:
 US: . . . . .All US
Canada - Yes, ...Overseas - No

HOBBYTOWN USA

220 N. 66th St., East Park Mall
Lincoln, NE 68505
TEL: (402) 464-2896
FAX:
Mr. Jim Hogg, Fran. Ops. Manager

HOBBYTOWN allows you the rare opportunity to play and work at the same time. Compared to other businesses, HOBBYTOWN offers low investment and high returns. We carry radio-controlled cars, planes, boats; also adventure games, trains, models, rockets, computers, computer games, stamps and coins.

HISTORY: . . . .
Established in 1969; . . 1st Franchised in 1986
Company-Owned Units (As of 12/1/1989): . .1
Franchised Units (12/1/1989): 17
Total Units (12/1/1989): 18
Distribution: US-18;Can-0;Overseas-0
North America: . . . . 7 States
Concentration: . . . 8 in NE, 3 in CO, 2 in CA
Registered: . . . . All States
. . . .
Average # of Employees: . . . . 1-3 FT, 1-3 PT
Prior Industry Experience: . . . . . . Helpful

FINANCIAL:
Cash Investment: $25K
Total Investment: $75-90K
Fees: Franchise - $15K
 Royalty: 3%, Advert: 2%
Contract Periods (Yrs.): . . . 10/10
Area Development Agreement: Yes/3
Sub-Franchise Contract: . . . . . Yes
Expand in Territory: . . . . Yes
Passive Ownership: . . . . . .Allowed
Encourage Conversions: . . . . . Yes
Franchisee Purchase(s) Required: .No

FRANCHISOR TRAINING/SUPPORT:
Financial Assistance Provided: . . . Yes(I)
Site Selection Assistance: . . . . . . .Yes
Lease Negotiation Assistance: . . . . .Yes
Co-operative Advertising: . . . . . . .Yes
Training: . . . . 2-4 Wks. On-site
. . . .
On-Going Support: . . A,B,C,D,E,F,G,H,I
Full-Time Franchisor Support Staff: . . . 6
EXPANSION PLANS:
 US: . . . . .All US
Canada - Yes, . . . Overseas - Yes

LATEX CITY

1814 Franklin St., # 700
Oakland, CA 94612
TEL: (800) LOVE-AID (415) 428-1899
FAX: (415) 835-3779
Mr. Bob Merkin Kantor, President

Unique ground-floor specialty retailing opportunity in booming latex novelty aid business. Complete line of proprietary products. Turn-key package includes lease negotiation, fully-stocked inventory, in-store merchandising/display. On-going support. LATEX CITY is ideal for aggressive couples. This is not smut - but a highly profitable, high-margin, fully legal business.

HISTORY: . . . .
Established in 1972; . . 1st Franchised in 1986
Company-Owned Units (As of 12/1/1989): . .4
Franchised Units (12/1/1989): 7
Total Units (12/1/1989): 11
Distribution: US-8;Can-2;Overseas-1
North America: . . . . . .3 States, 1 Province
Concentration: . . . 3 in CA, 3 in NY, 2 in OR
Registered: . . . . CA,NY,OR,WA,AB
. . . .
Average # of Employees: . . . . .2 FT
Prior Industry Experience: . . . . . . Helpful

FINANCIAL: OTC-MERK
Cash Investment: $65K
Total Investment: $85-235K
Fees: Franchise - $15K
 Royalty: 6%, Advert: 2%
Contract Periods (Yrs.): . . . 10/10
Area Development Agreement: Yes/5
Sub-Franchise Contract: . . . . .No
Expand in Territory: . . . . . . .No
Passive Ownership: . . . Discouraged
Encourage Conversions: . . . . . Yes
Franchisee Purchase(s) Required: Yes

FRANCHISOR TRAINING/SUPPORT:
Financial Assistance Provided: . . .Yes(D)
Site Selection Assistance: . . . . . . .Yes
Lease Negotiation Assistance: . . . . .Yes
Co-operative Advertising: . . . . . . .Yes
Training: . . . . . . 3 Wks. Headquarters, 1
 . . . . Wk. Plant, 2 Wks. Site
On-Going Support: . . . . . A,B,C,D,G,H
Full-Time Franchisor Support Staff: . . . 6
EXPANSION PLANS:
 US: . . . . .All US
Canada - Yes, . . . Overseas - Yes

LEMSTONE BOOK BRANCH

1123 Wheaton Oaks Ct.
Wheaton, IL 60187
TEL: (708) 682-1400
FAX:
Mr. Lynn Wheaton, Sales Manager

Christian bookstores in regional shopping centers.

HISTORY:	FINANCIAL:	FRANCHISOR TRAINING/SUPPORT:
Established in 1981; . . 1st Franchised in 1982	Cash Investment: $30-50K	Financial Assistance Provided: . . . . . No
Company-Owned Units (As of 12/1/1989): . . 1	Total Investment: $100-150K	Site Selection Assistance: . . . . .Yes
Franchised Units (12/1/1989): 35	Fees: Franchise - $25K	Lease Negotiation Assistance: . . . . .Yes
Total Units (12/1/1989): 36	Royalty: 4%, Advert.): 1%	Co-operative Advertising: . . . . .Yes
Distribution: US-36;Can-0;Overseas-0	Contract Periods (Yrs.): 10/5	Training: . . . . 5 Days Headquarters,
North America: . . . . 14 States	Area Development Agreement: . .No	. . . . .5 Days On-site
Concentration:	Sub-Franchise Contract: . . . . .No	On-Going Support: . . . . . .C,D,E,F,G,H
Registered: . . . . FL,IL,IN,MI,NY,WI	Expand in Territory: . . . . Yes	Full-Time Franchisor Support Staff: . . . 7
. . . .	Passive Ownership: . . . Discouraged	EXPANSION PLANS:
Average # of Employees: . . . . . 1 FT, 2-3 PT	Encourage Conversions: . . . . . Yes	US: . . . . .Midwest, Mid-Atlantic, S, SE
Prior Industry Experience: . . . . Helpful	Franchisee Purchase(s) Required: .No	Canada - No, ...Overseas - No

LITTLE PROFESSOR BOOK CENTER

110 N. Fourth Ave.
Ann Arbor, MI 48104
TEL: (800) 899-6232 (313) 994-1212 C
FAX:
Ms. Carla Garbin, Sr. VP

LITTLE PROFESSOR BOOK CENTERS are full-line, full-service retail book stores. Each store carries a complete selection of books, magazine and book-related sidelines. Franchisor provides complete assistance and counsel needed to open and operate a book store from site selection to store opening through the life of the agreement.

HISTORY: . . . . IFA	FINANCIAL:	FRANCHISOR TRAINING/SUPPORT:
Established in 1961; . . 1st Franchised in 1969	Cash Investment: $40-60K	Financial Assistance Provided: . . . Yes(I)
Company-Owned Units (As of 12/1/1989): . . 1	Total Investment: $140-235K	Site Selection Assistance: . . . . .Yes
Franchised Units (12/1/1989): 129	Fees: Franchise - $21K	Lease Negotiation Assistance: . . . . .Yes
Total Units (12/1/1989): 130	Royalty: 2.75%, Advert: 5%	Co-operative Advertising: . . . . .Yes
Distribution: . . . US-130;Can-0;Overseas-0	Contract Periods (Yrs.): 15/10	Training: . . . . . 10 Days Headquarters, 5
North America: . . . . 35 States	Area Development Agreement: . .No	. . . Days On-site, 2 Days Follow-up Site
Concentration: . 19 in OH, 15 in FL, 12 in CA	Sub-Franchise Contract: . . . . .No	On-Going Support: . . . a,b,C,D,E,F,G,h,I
Registered: . . . CA,FL,IL,IN,MD,MI,MN,ND	Expand in Territory: . . . . Yes	Full-Time Franchisor Support Staff: . . 22
. . . . OR,RI,VA,WA,WI	Passive Ownership: . . . Discouraged	EXPANSION PLANS:
Average # of Employees: . . . . . . 1 FT, 2 PT	Encourage Conversions: . . . . . Yes	US: . . . . .All US
Prior Industry Experience: . . . . Helpful	Franchisee Purchase(s) Required: .No	Canada - No, ...Overseas - No

MONOGRAMS PLUS

3630 IH-35 S.
Waco, TX 76706
TEL: (800) 228-6333 (817) 662-5050
FAX: (817) 662-3223
Mr. David Byrd, Sr. VP Development

High-tech, computerized monogramming and embroidery. Create unique, personalized gifts in seconds from wide selection of high-profit, brand-name fashion items and accessories. Custom-designed kiosks in select regional mall locations. High profit margin with minimal space requirements. Complete assistance, including start-up, financing, training and on-going support from in-house market research and field management teams.

HISTORY: . . . . IFA	FINANCIAL:	FRANCHISOR TRAINING/SUPPORT:
Established in 1988; . . 1st Franchised in 1988	Cash Investment: $30-50K	Financial Assistance Provided: . . . Yes(I)
Company-Owned Units (As of 12/1/1989): . .0	Total Investment: $45-80K	Site Selection Assistance: . . . . .Yes
Franchised Units (12/1/1989): 84	Fees: Franchise - . . . . $25K+	Lease Negotiation Assistance: . . . . .Yes
Total Units (12/1/1989): 84	Royalty: 6%, Advert: 1%	Co-operative Advertising: . . . . .Yes
Distribution: US-84;Can-0;Overseas-0	Contract Periods (Yrs.): 10/5	Training: . . . . 9 Days Headquarters,
North America:	Area Development Agreement: Yes/15	. . . . .3 Days On-site
Concentration:	Sub-Franchise Contract: . . . . .No	On-Going Support: . . . . .B,C,D,E,G,H,I
Registered: . . . . .All	Expand in Territory: . . . . . . .No	Full-Time Franchisor Support Staff: . . 52
. . . .	Passive Ownership: . . . Discouraged	EXPANSION PLANS:
Average # of Employees: . . . . 1-2 FT, 2-3 PT	Encourage Conversions: . . . . . Yes	US: . . . . .All US
Prior Industry Experience: . . . . Helpful	Franchisee Purchase(s) Required: Yes	Canada - Yes, . . . Overseas - Yes

ONE STOP PARTY SHOP

2615 Calder, # 420
Beaumont, TX 77702
TEL: (409) 833-2551
FAX: (409) 833-4751
Mr. Marvin C. Newman, President

Specialty party store facilities for the retail sale of a wide assortment of high-quality party decorations, party goods, party favors, balloons, costumes, gift wrapping and related merchandise and accessories. Providing decorating services for commercial customers and private parties.

HISTORY: . . . . IFA
Established in 1988; . . 1st Franchised in 1988
Company-Owned Units (As of 12/1/1989): . .2
Franchised Units (12/1/1989): 0
Total Units (12/1/1989): 2
Distribution: US-2;Can-0;Overseas-0
North America: . . . . .1 State
Concentration: . . . . 2 in TX
Registered: . . . . . .All Except IL, NY & AB

. . . .
Average # of Employees: . . . . . . 3 FT, 2 PT
Prior Industry Experience: . . . . Helpful

FINANCIAL:
Cash Investment: $30-50K
Total Investment: $150-200K
Fees: Franchise - $18.5-28.5K
  Royalty: 5%, Advert: 1%
Contract Periods (Yrs.): . . . Lease/10
Area Development Agreement: . Yes
Sub-Franchise Contract: . . . . . Yes
Expand in Territory: . . . . Yes
Passive Ownership: . . . . . .Allowed
Encourage Conversions: . . . . . Yes
Franchisee Purchase(s) Required: .No

FRANCHISOR TRAINING/SUPPORT:
Financial Assistance Provided: . . . Yes(I)
Site Selection Assistance: . . . . .Yes
Lease Negotiation Assistance: . . . . .Yes
Co-operative Advertising: . . . . .Yes
Training: . . . . .12-14 Days Headquarters,
. . . . 12-14 Days Nederland, TX
On-Going Support: . . . . .C,D,E,F,G,H,I
Full-Time Franchisor Support Staff: . . 10
EXPANSION PLANS:
US: . . . . .Southwest, All US Master Fr.
Canada - Yes, . . . Overseas - Yes

PAPER OUTLET, THE

445 Hanover Ave.
Allentown, PA 18103
TEL: (215) 439-4030
FAX:
Mr. David Mulligan, President

THE PAPER OUTLET - own a fun, profitable business in a growing industry. Customers shop here for the variety and depth of selections in party, school and office products. Owning your own PAPER OUTLET is"Where the Fun Starts."

HISTORY: . . . .
Established in 1981; . . 1st Franchised in 1986
Company-Owned Units (As of 12/1/1989): . .6
Franchised Units (12/1/1989): 2
Total Units (12/1/1989): 8
Distribution: US-8;Can-0;Overseas-0
North America: . . . . .1 State
Concentration: . . . . 8 in PA
Registered: . . . .

. . . .
Average # of Employees: . . . . . . 1 FT, 2 PT
Prior Industry Experience: . . . . Helpful

FINANCIAL:
Cash Investment: $100-150K
Total Investment: $100-150K
Fees: Franchise - $20K
  Royalty: 2.5%, Advert: 0%
Contract Periods (Yrs.): . . . 20/20
Area Development Agreement: . .No
Sub-Franchise Contract: . . . . .No
Expand in Territory: . . . . Yes
Passive Ownership: . . . Not Allowed
Encourage Conversions: . . . . . NA
Franchisee Purchase(s) Required: .No

FRANCHISOR TRAINING/SUPPORT:
Financial Assistance Provided: . . . Yes(I)
Site Selection Assistance: . . . . .Yes
Lease Negotiation Assistance: . . . . .Yes
Co-operative Advertising: . . . . .Yes
Training: . . . . 2 Wks. Headquarters
. . . .
On-Going Support: . . . . . .a,b,C,D,E,f,I
Full-Time Franchisor Support Staff: . . 39
EXPANSION PLANS:
US: . . . .PA,NJ,DE,NY,MD,VA,OH,CT
Canada - No, ...Overseas - No

PAPYRUS

1349 Powell St.
Emeryville, CA 94608
TEL: (800) 872-7978 (415) 428-0166
FAX: (415) 428-0615
Ms. Sandra Lipkowitz, Dir. Fran.

PAPYRUS is . . . an up-scale, unique and award-winning gallery approach to the alternative greeting card business. Specializing in the finest quality greeting cards, gift wrap, paper products and related gift items. Offering a wide selection of vendors, while showcasing the Marcel Schurman line of greeting cards and paper products. Emphasizing the highly-profitable area of personalized stationery.

HISTORY: . . . . IFA
Established in 1988; . . 1st Franchised in 1988
Company-Owned Units (As of 12/1/1989): . .9
Franchised Units (12/1/1989): 11
Total Units (12/1/1989): 20
Distribution: US-20;Can-0;Overseas-0
North America: . . . . .1 State
Concentration: . . . . 20 in CA
Registered: . . . . . .CA,FL,HI,MD,OR,WA

. . . .
Average # of Employees: . . . . . . 2 FT, 2 PT
Prior Industry Experience: . . . . Helpful

FINANCIAL:
Cash Investment: $132k
Total Investment: $205k
Fees: Franchise - $29.5K
  Royalty: 6%, Advert: 1%
Contract Periods (Yrs.): 10/5
Area Development Agreement: Yes/2
Sub-Franchise Contract: . . . . .No
Expand in Territory: . . . . . . .Yes
Passive Ownership: . . . Not Allowed
Encourage Conversions: . . . . Yes
Franchisee Purchase(s) Required: .No

FRANCHISOR TRAINING/SUPPORT:
Financial Assistance Provided: . . . . . No
Site Selection Assistance: . . . . .Yes
Lease Negotiation Assistance: . . . . .Yes
Co-operative Advertising: . . . . .NA
Training: . . . . . . 12 Days San Francisco
. . . . .Bay Area
On-Going Support: . . . . .C,D,E,F,G,H,I
Full-Time Franchisor Support Staff: . . 10
EXPANSION PLANS:
US: . . . . Western US
Canada - No, ...Overseas - No

PARTY WORLD

10701 Vanowen St.
North Hollywood, CA 91605
TEL: (818) 762-7717
FAX: (818) 509-8676
Mr. Stanley Tauber, President

We specialize in the sale of party supplies, utilizing a marketing strategy unique in the industry. By offering a large variety of selections, depth of stock and heavily discounted prices, we "bring the customer to us." The buying public seeks us out and we become the destination shop.

HISTORY:	IFA
Established in 1979; 1st Franchised in 1987	
Company-Owned Units (As of 12/1/1989):	10
Franchised Units (12/1/1989):	4
Total Units (12/1/1989):	14
Distribution:	US-14;Can-0;Overseas-0
North America:	1 State
Concentration:	14 in CA
Registered:	CA
Average # of Employees:	6 FT
Prior Industry Experience:	Helpful

FINANCIAL:	
Cash Investment:	$100K
Total Investment:	$250K
Fees: Franchise -	$20K
Royalty: 4%, Advert:	2%
Contract Periods (Yrs.):	10/10
Area Development Agreement:	No
Sub-Franchise Contract:	No
Expand in Territory:	No
Passive Ownership:	Not Allowed
Encourage Conversions:	No
Franchisee Purchase(s) Required:	No

FRANCHISOR TRAINING/SUPPORT:	
Financial Assistance Provided:	Yes(I)
Site Selection Assistance:	Yes
Lease Negotiation Assistance:	Yes
Co-operative Advertising:	Yes
Training:	3 Wks. Northridge, CA
On-Going Support:	B,C,D,E,F,H
Full-Time Franchisor Support Staff:	8
EXPANSION PLANS:	
US:	Only California
Canada - No,	Overseas - No

PRO IMAGE

563 West 500 South, # 330
Bountiful, UT 84010
TEL: (801) 292-8777
FAX: (801) 292-4603
Mr. Mark Gilliland, Natl. Fran. Dir.

Largest and fastest-growing franchisor of "Sport Fan Gift Shops." The stores are located in regional shopping malls and retail licensed, authentic and replica logo'd products from all the professional and college teams. This is the fastest-growing segment of the sporting retail industry. Complete turn-key operation with custom computerized store system and company warehouse.

HISTORY:	IFA
Established in 1985; 1st Franchised in 1985	
Company-Owned Units (As of 12/1/1989):	1
Franchised Units (12/1/1989):	150
Total Units (12/1/1989):	151
Distribution:	US-136;Can-14;Overseas-1
North America:	33 States
Concentration:	28 in CA, 11 in AZ, 10 in UT
Registered:	All States
Average # of Employees:	2 FT, 4 PT
Prior Industry Experience:	Helpful

FINANCIAL:	
Cash Investment:	$
Total Investment:	$125K
Fees: Franchise -	$16.5K
Royalty: 4%, Advert:	3%
Contract Periods (Yrs.):	10/10
Area Development Agreement:	No
Sub-Franchise Contract:	No
Expand in Territory:	No
Passive Ownership:	Allowed
Encourage Conversions:	Yes
Franchisee Purchase(s) Required:	No

FRANCHISOR TRAINING/SUPPORT:	
Financial Assistance Provided:	No
Site Selection Assistance:	Yes
Lease Negotiation Assistance:	Yes
Co-operative Advertising:	NA
Training:	4 Days Headquarters, 2 Days Site
On-Going Support:	B,C,D,E,F,G,H
Full-Time Franchisor Support Staff:	20
EXPANSION PLANS:	
US:	All US
Canada - Yes,	Overseas - Yes

RAFTERS STORES/PANHANDLER SHOPS/ABINGTONS

4699 Keele St., # 3
Downsview, ON M3J2N8 CAN
TEL: (416) 661-9916 C
FAX:
Mr. Michael Mayerson, Fran. Dir.

From kitchen gadgets to limited edition collectables of fine porcelain, The Liv Group, with over 80 stores, is Canada's largest gift chain. Every major city in Canada now has either a PANHANDLER SHOPPE or a RAFTERS STORE. Hundreds of unique gift ideas make this a shopper's paradise.

HISTORY:	IFA
Established in 1973; 1st Franchised in 1974	
Company-Owned Units (As of 12/1/1989):	11
Franchised Units (12/1/1989):	79
Total Units (12/1/1989):	90
Distribution:	US-0;Can-90;Overseas-0
North America:	9 Provinces
Concentration:	30 in ON, 13 in AB, 5 in BC
Registered:	AB
Average # of Employees:	1 FT, 3 PT
Prior Industry Experience:	Helpful

FINANCIAL:	
Cash Investment:	$50-60K
Total Investment:	$150-200K
Fees: Franchise -	$25K
Royalty: 6%, Advert:	1%
Contract Periods (Yrs.):	Lease
Area Development Agreement:	No
Sub-Franchise Contract:	No
Expand in Territory:	Yes
Passive Ownership:	Discouraged
Encourage Conversions:	Yes
Franchisee Purchase(s) Required:	No

FRANCHISOR TRAINING/SUPPORT:	
Financial Assistance Provided:	Yes(D)
Site Selection Assistance:	Yes
Lease Negotiation Assistance:	Yes
Co-operative Advertising:	Yes
Training:	Varies at Dealer's Store
On-Going Support:	C,D,E,F,G,H,I
Full-Time Franchisor Support Staff:	28
EXPANSION PLANS:	
US:	No
Canada - Yes,	Overseas - No

RECOGNITION EXPRESS INTERNATIONAL

31726 Rancho Viejo Rd., # 115
San Juan Capistrano, CA 92675
TEL: (714) 493-3666
FAX:
Mr. Jeff Tino, VP Fran. Dev.

RECOGNITION EXPRESS is the pioneer and leader in the recognition industry, the most exciting and positive new industry in the world today. RECOGNITION products include name badges, corporate awards, trophies, plaques, ad specialties, etc. Become part of this rapidly-expanding recognition products business with RECOGNITION EXPRESS.

HISTORY: . . . . IFA	FINANCIAL:	FRANCHISOR TRAINING/SUPPORT:
Established in 1972; . . 1st Franchised in 1974	Cash Investment: $30K	Financial Assistance Provided: . . . Yes(I)
Company-Owned Units (As of 12/1/1989): . .0	Total Investment: $70-126K	Site Selection Assistance: . . . . .Yes
Franchised Units (12/1/1989): 105	Fees: Franchise - $30K	Lease Negotiation Assistance: . . . . .Yes
Total Units (12/1/1989): 105	Royalty: 6%, Advert: 2%	Co-operative Advertising: . . . . .Yes
Distribution: US-65;Can-16;Overseas-24	Contract Periods (Yrs.): 10/10	Training: . . . . . . 1-2 Wks. Headquarters
North America: . . . . 31 States, 7 Provinces	Area Development Agreement: Yes/20	. . . .
Concentration:	Sub-Franchise Contract: . . . . . .No	On-Going Support: . . . . .B,C,D,E,G,H,I
Registered: . . .CA,FL,HI,IL,MD,MN,NY,OR	Expand in Territory: . . . . Yes	Full-Time Franchisor Support Staff: . . . 5
. . . . .VA,WA,WI,AB	Passive Ownership: . . . Discouraged	EXPANSION PLANS:
Average # of Employees: . . . . Varies	Encourage Conversions: . . . . . Yes	US: . . . . .All US
Prior Industry Experience: . . . . . . Helpful	Franchisee Purchase(s) Required: .No	Canada - Yes, . . . Overseas - Yes

SCREEN PRINTING USA

534 W. Shawnee Ave.
Plymouth, PA 18651
TEL: (717) 779-5175
FAX:
Mr. Russell Owens, President

Unique, computer-aided silk screen printing operation. Printing on t-shirts, hats, jackets, decals, signs, wood, metal, glass and 100 more items.

HISTORY:	FINANCIAL:	FRANCHISOR TRAINING/SUPPORT:
Established in 1988; . . 1st Franchised in 1988	Cash Investment: $25K	Financial Assistance Provided: . . . Yes(I)
Company-Owned Units (As of 12/1/1989): . .1	Total Investment: $60K	Site Selection Assistance: . . . . .Yes
Franchised Units (12/1/1989): 4	Fees: Franchise - $22.5K	Lease Negotiation Assistance: . . . .Yes
Total Units (12/1/1989): 5	Royalty: 6%, Advert: 2%	Co-operative Advertising: . . . . .Yes
Distribution: US-5;Can-0;Overseas-0	Contract Periods (Yrs.): 10/5	Training: . . . . 2 Wks. Headquarters
North America: . . . . 2 States	Area Development Agreement: Yes/10	. . . .
Concentration: . . . . 4 in PA, 1 in WI	Sub-Franchise Contract: . . . . . Yes	On-Going Support: . . . . .B,C,D,E,G,H,I
Registered:	Expand in Territory: . . . . Yes	Full-Time Franchisor Support Staff: . . . 2
. . . .	Passive Ownership: . . . . . .Allowed	EXPANSION PLANS:
Average # of Employees: . . . . .1 FT	Encourage Conversions: . . . . . .No	US: . . . . .All US
Prior Industry Experience: . . . . Helpful	Franchisee Purchase(s) Required: Yes	Canada - Yes, ...Overseas - No

SHEFIELD & SONS

2265 W. Railway St., Box 490
Abbotsford, BC V2S5Z5 CAN
TEL: (604) 859-1014
FAX: (604) 859-1711
Mr. Wolfgang Lehmann, Secty.

SHEFIELD & SONS is a specialty store, featuring the exclusive "SHEFIELD & SONS" tobaccos, smoker's accessories, tobacco-related products, gift items, souvenirs, confectionary items, newspapers and magazines, books and, in many instances, lottery tickets. Stores are turn-key operations, fully-stocked, fixtured and ready for business.

HISTORY:	FINANCIAL:	FRANCHISOR TRAINING/SUPPORT:
Established in 1976; . . 1st Franchised in 1978	Cash Investment: $35-50K	Financial Assistance Provided: . . . . .No
Company-Owned Units (As of 12/1/1989): . .2	Total Investment: $75-105K	Site Selection Assistance: . . . . . . .Yes
Franchised Units (12/1/1989): 66	Fees: Franchise - $10K	Lease Negotiation Assistance: . . . .Yes
Total Units (12/1/1989): 68	Royalty: 2%, Advert: 2%	Co-operative Advertising: . . . . .No
Distribution: US-0;Can-68;Overseas-0	Contract Periods (Yrs.): . . . .Varies	Training: . . . . 1 Wk. Site
North America: . . . . 7 Provinces	Area Development Agreement: .No	. . . .
Concentration: . 31 in BC, 16 in AB, 15 in ON	Sub-Franchise Contract: . . . . . .No	On-Going Support: . . . . . . C,D,E,F,G,I
Registered: . . . . AB	Expand in Territory: . . . . Yes	Full-Time Franchisor Support Staff: . . . 9
. . . .	Passive Ownership: . . . Discouraged	EXPANSION PLANS:
Average # of Employees: . . . . . . 4 FT, 4 PT	Encourage Conversions: . . . . . .No	US: . . . . .No
Prior Industry Experience: . . . . Helpful	Franchisee Purchase(s) Required: .No	Canada - Yes, ...Overseas - No

SOX APPEAL

401 N. Third St., # 4900
Minneapolis, MN 55401
TEL: (612) 333-5415
FAX:
Mr. Bill Travis, Dir. Fran.

SOX APPEAL offers the best selection of socks and hosiery for men, women and kids. As a new and exciting specialty store, SOX APPEAL gives the customer a fun and fashionable place to shop. As a business, SOX APPEAL has given its owners a fun and profitable opportunity.

HISTORY: . . . .
Established in 1984; . . 1st Franchised in 1986
Company-Owned Units (As of 12/1/1989): . .2
Franchised Units (12/1/1989): 15
Total Units (12/1/1989): 17
Distribution: US-17;Can-0;Overseas-0
North America: . . . . 5 States
Concentration: . . . 6 in MN, 3 in CO, 2 in MI
Registered: . . . CA,FL,IL,IN,MD,MI,MN,ND
. . . . OR,RI,SD,WA,WI
Average # of Employees: . . . . . . 2 FT, 4 PT
Prior Industry Experience: . . . . Helpful

FINANCIAL:
Cash Investment: $120-170K
Total Investment: $120-170K
Fees: Franchise - $20K
Royalty: 5%, Advert: 0%
Contract Periods (Yrs.): 10/10
Area Development Agreement: Yes/Var
Sub-Franchise Contract: . . . . . .No
Expand in Territory: . . . . Yes
Passive Ownership: . . . Discouraged
Encourage Conversions: . . . . . .No
Franchisee Purchase(s) Required: Yes

FRANCHISOR TRAINING/SUPPORT:
Financial Assistance Provided: . . . . . No
Site Selection Assistance: . . . . .Yes
Lease Negotiation Assistance: . . . . .Yes
Co-operative Advertising: . . . . .NA
Training: . . . . 1 Wk. Headquarters
. . . .
On-Going Support: . . . . C,D,E,G,I
Full-Time Franchisor Support Staff: . . . 8
EXPANSION PLANS:
US: . . . . .All US
Canada - No, ...Overseas - No

SOX CLINIC, THE

9 Maryvale Cres.
Richmond Hill, ON L4C6P6
TEL: (416) 886-3537
FAX: (416) 886-2934
Mr. Raj Nathwani, President

THE SOX CLINIC offers a unique hosiery concept. Product mix concentrates on fashion and basic hosiery for men, women and children. Excellent operating system ensures growth and profitability.

HISTORY: . . . .
Established in 1984; . . 1st Franchised in 1986
Company-Owned Units (As of 12/1/1989): . .2
Franchised Units (12/1/1989): 8
Total Units (12/1/1989): 10
Distribution: US-0;Can-10;Overseas-0
North America: . . . . 4 Provinces
Concentration: . . . . 5 in ON, 2 in BC
Registered: . . . .
. . . .
Average # of Employees: . . . . . . 2 FT, 2 PT
Prior Industry Experience: . . . . Helpful

FINANCIAL:
Cash Investment: $30-50K
Total Investment: $100-130K
Fees: Franchise - $25K
Royalty: 6%, Advert: 2%
Contract Periods (Yrs.): 10/10
Area Development Agreement: . .No
Sub-Franchise Contract: . . . . . .No
Expand in Territory: . . . . Yes
Passive Ownership: . . . Not Allowed
Encourage Conversions: . . . . . Yes
Franchisee Purchase(s) Required: Yes

FRANCHISOR TRAINING/SUPPORT:
Financial Assistance Provided: . . . Yes(I)
Site Selection Assistance: . . . . .Yes
Lease Negotiation Assistance: . . . . .Yes
Co-operative Advertising: . . . . .Yes
Training: . . . . .2 Wks. On-site
. . . .
On-Going Support: . . . . . . C,D,E,F,G,h
Full-Time Franchisor Support Staff: . . 21
EXPANSION PLANS:
US: . . . . No
Canada - Yes, . . . Overseas - Yes

T-SHIRTS PLUS

3630 IH-35 S.
Waco, TX 76706
TEL: (800) 992-7255 (817) 662-5050
FAX: (817) 662-3223
Mr. David Byrd, Sr. VP Devel.

Ranked #1 in its category by Entrepreneur Magazine. Continuing as the industry trendsetter with successful 14-year track record. In-store custom decorating on private label garments. Select regional mall locations available with extensively-researched, contemporary store design. Complete start-up, training, financing assistance and on-going support provided.

HISTORY: . . . . IFA
Established in 1975; . . 1st Franchised in 1976
Company-Owned Units (As of 12/1/1989): . .1
Franchised Units (12/1/1989): 188
Total Units (12/1/1989): 189
Distribution: US-189;Can-0;Overseas-0
North America: . . . . 47 States
Concentration: . . . . CA, TX AND FL
Registered: . . . . All States
. . . .
Average # of Employees: . . . . 1-2 FT, 2-3 PT
Prior Industry Experience: . . . . Helpful

FINANCIAL:
Cash Investment: $40-45K
Total Investment: $120-150K
Fees: Franchise - $30K
Royalty: 7%, Advert: 1%
Contract Periods (Yrs.): 15/5/5
Area Development Agreement: Yes/15
Sub-Franchise Contract: . . . . . .No
Expand in Territory: . . . . .No
Passive Ownership: . . . Discouraged
Encourage Conversions: . . . . . Yes
Franchisee Purchase(s) Required: Yes

FRANCHISOR TRAINING/SUPPORT:
Financial Assistance Provided: . . . Yes(I)
Site Selection Assistance: . . . . .Yes
Lease Negotiation Assistance: . . . . .Yes
Co-operative Advertising: . . . . .Yes
Training: . . . . . . 5 Days Home Office, 3
. . . . Days Home Office, 3 Days On-site
On-Going Support: . . . . .B,C,D,E,G,H,I
Full-Time Franchisor Support Staff: . . 52
EXPANSION PLANS:
US: . . . . .All US
Canada - Yes, . . . Overseas - Yes

TALE OF THE ELEPHANT'S TRUNK

4 North St.
Waldwick, NJ 07463
TEL: (800) 776-4343 (201) 670-4343
FAX: (201) 670-4511
Mr. Barnett Tessler, VP Operations

Pesonalized gifts - professional artist on premises. Birthday parties in "Elephant Party Room." Birthday party favors and supplies. Trendy impulse items. Unique pre-packaged gift assortments and much more!

HISTORY: . . . . IFA	FINANCIAL:	FRANCHISOR TRAINING/SUPPORT:
Established in 1986; . . 1st Franchised in 1987	Cash Investment: $81K	Financial Assistance Provided: . . . Yes(I)
Company-Owned Units (As of 12/1/1989): . .0	Total Investment: $100K	Site Selection Assistance: . . . . . . .Yes
Franchised Units (12/1/1989): 32	Fees: Franchise - $18K	Lease Negotiation Assistance: . . . . .Yes
Total Units (12/1/1989): 32	Royalty: 6%, Advert: 0%	Co-operative Advertising: . . . . . . .Yes
Distribution: US-32;Can-0;Overseas-0	Contract Periods (Yrs.): 15/15	Training: . . . . . 4 Days Midland Park, NJ,
North America: . . . . 11 States	Area Development Agreement: . .No	. . . . 1 Day Headquarters
Concentration: . . . 11 in NJ, 7 in NY, 3 in FL	Sub-Franchise Contract: . . . . .No	On-Going Support: . . . . .B,C,D,E,G,H,I
Registered: . . . . All Except HI and AB	Expand in Territory: . . . . Yes	Full-Time Franchisor Support Staff: . . 10
. . . .	Passive Ownership: . . . Discouraged	EXPANSION PLANS:
Average # of Employees: . . . . . . 2 FT, 2 PT	Encourage Conversions: . . . . . NA	US: . . . . .All US
Prior Industry Experience: . . . . . . Helpful	Franchisee Purchase(s) Required: .No	Canada - Yes, ...Overseas - No

TINDER BOX INTERNATIONAL

19060 S. Dominguez Hills Dr.
Compton, CA 90220
TEL: (800) 322-4824 (213) 632-7171
FAX: (213) 639-0803
Mr. Wayne Best, Dir. Fran. Dev.

Specialty retail chain, with product mix consisting of premium-quality tobaccos and pipes, with unique gifts from a wide range of categories.

HISTORY:	FINANCIAL:	FRANCHISOR TRAINING/SUPPORT:
Established in 1928; . . 1st Franchised in 1965	Cash Investment: $20-75K	Financial Assistance Provided: . . . Yes(D)
Company-Owned Units (As of 12/1/1989): . 24	Total Investment: $116-305K	Site Selection Assistance: . . . . . . .Yes
Franchised Units (12/1/1989): 149	Fees: Franchise - $10-50K	Lease Negotiation Assistance: . . . . .Yes
Total Units (12/1/1989): 177	Royalty: 4%, Advert: 3%	Co-operative Advertising: . . . . . . .Yes
Distribution: US-177;Can-0;Overseas-0	Contract Periods (Yrs.): 10/5	Training: . . . . .10 Days LA,
North America: . . . . 37 States	Area Development Agreement: Yes/5	. . . . .5-10 Days Site
Concentration: . . . . 42 in CA	Sub-Franchise Contract: . . . . .No	On-Going Support: . . .B,C,D,E,F,G,H,I
Registered: . . . . All States	Expand in Territory: . . . . Yes	Full-Time Franchisor Support Staff: . .143
. . . .	Passive Ownership: . . . Discouraged	EXPANSION PLANS:
Average # of Employees: . . . . . . 2 FT, 3 PT	Encourage Conversions: . . . . . Yes	US: . . . . .All US
Prior Industry Experience: . . . . Helpful	Franchisee Purchase(s) Required: Yes	Canada - No, ...Overseas - No

UNITED SURGICAL CENTERS

380 Warwick Ave.
Warwick, RI 02888
TEL: (800) 556-7641 (401) 781-2166
FAX:
Mr. David Datz, Operations Mgr.

Retail home medical equipment (HME) outlet - specializing in the sales and rentals of equipment for home use. Turn-key operation - training by our staff at our headquarters and at franchise location.

HISTORY:	FINANCIAL:	FRANCHISOR TRAINING/SUPPORT:
Established in 1973; . . 1st Franchised in 1979	Cash Investment: $75K	Financial Assistance Provided: . . . . . No
Company-Owned Units (As of 12/1/1989): . .2	Total Investment: $100-125K	Site Selection Assistance: . . . . . . .Yes
Franchised Units (12/1/1989): 3	Fees: Franchise - $20K	Lease Negotiation Assistance: . . . . .Yes
Total Units (12/1/1989): 5	Royalty: 5%, Advert: 0%	Co-operative Advertising: . . . . . . .Yes
Distribution: US-5;Can-0;Overseas-0	Contract Periods (Yrs.): 7/7	Training: . . . . . Training at Both Head-
North America: . . . . 3 States	Area Development Agreement: . .No	. . . . quarters and Franchise Site
Concentration: . . . 2 in MA, 2 in RI, 1 in NH	Sub-Franchise Contract: . . . . .No	On-Going Support: . . . . .B,C,D,E,F,H,I
Registered:	Expand in Territory: . . . . Yes	Full-Time Franchisor Support Staff: . . 21
. . . .	Passive Ownership: . . . Discouraged	EXPANSION PLANS:
Average # of Employees: . . . . . . 2 FT, 1 PT	Encourage Conversions: . . . . .No	US: . . . . New England Only
Prior Industry Experience: . . . . Helpful	Franchisee Purchase(s) Required: .No	Canada - No, ...Overseas - No

WILD BIRDS UNLIMITED

1716 Broad Ripple Ave.
Indianapolis, IN 46220
TEL: (317) 257-8884
FAX:
Mr. Paul E. Pickett, Fran. Asst.

WILD BIRDS UNLIMITED offers unique retail shops that specialize in supplying birdseed, feeders and gift items for the popular hobby of backyard bird feeding. This is the perfect occupation for nature enthusiasts.

HISTORY: . . . .
Established in 1981; . . 1st Franchised in 1983
Company-Owned Units (As of 12/1/1989): . . 0
Franchised Units (12/1/1989): 43
Total Units (12/1/1989): 43
Distribution: US-42;Can-1;Overseas-0
North America: . . . . . 15 States, 1 Province
Concentration: . . . . 9 in MI, 7 in IN, 7 in OH
Registered: . . . CA,FL,IL,IN,MD,MI,NY,OR
. . . . VA,WA,WI
Average # of Employees: . . . . 1 FT
Prior Industry Experience: . . . . Helpful

FINANCIAL:
Cash Investment: $30-40K
Total Investment: $30-40K
Fees: Franchise - $7-8K
  Royalty: 3%, Advert: 0%
Contract Periods (Yrs.): 10/5
Area Development Agreement: Yes/Var
Sub-Franchise Contract: . . . . . No
Expand in Territory: . . . . Yes
Passive Ownership: . . . Not Allowed
Encourage Conversions: . . . . . No
Franchisee Purchase(s) Required: . No

FRANCHISOR TRAINING/SUPPORT:
Financial Assistance Provided: . . . . . No
Site Selection Assistance: . . . . Yes
Lease Negotiation Assistance: . . . . Yes
Co-operative Advertising: . . . . No
Training: . . . . 3 Days Headquarters,
. . . . 1-2 Days Store Site
On-Going Support: . . . A,C,D,E,F,G,H,I
Full-Time Franchisor Support Staff: . . . 4
EXPANSION PLANS:
US: . . . . All US
Canada - Yes, ...Overseas - Yes

SUPPLEMENTAL LISTING OF FRANCHISORS

800-BUBBLES . . . . 2347 S. Queen St., Arlington VA 22202
ABC BOOKS & VIDEO/ABC CULTURAL . . . . .11 Princess St., Kingston ON K7L5C7   CAN
ANNIE'S BOOK STORE . . . . 15 Lackey St., Westborough MA 01581
BALLOON EXPRESS COMPANY . . . . .224 Adelaide St., W, Toronto ON M5H1W4   CAN
BALLOON-AGE . . . . .340 Millburn Ave., Millburn NJ 07041
BANDITS FASHION ACCENT BOUTIQUES . . . . 6535 Millcreek Dr., # 57, Mississauga ON L5N2M2   CAN
BARGAIN BOOK . . . . .476 Main St., Middlefield CT 06455
BASQUETTES . . . . 430 Woodruff Rd., # 325, Greenville SC 29607
BASS RIVER CHAIRS . . . . 50 Thornhill Ave., # 6, Dartmouth NS B3B1S1   CAN
BATH N' BEDTIME . . . . 1911 Dundas St. E., Mississauga ON L4X1M1   CAN
BIGHORN SHEEPSKIN COMPANY . . . . 11600 Manchaca Road, Austin TX 78748
BLACKBERRY COTTAGE . . . . 3107 Eubank NE, # 5, Albuquerque NM 87111
BLIND DESIGNS . . . . 703 State Road 584 West, # 170, Oldsmar FL 34667
BOOK BANK . . . . 5 Roberta Cres., Nepean ON K2J1G5   CAN
CARDWARE STORE, THE . . . . 4025 W. 183rd St., Country Club Hills IL 60478
CLOCK GALLERY, THE . . . . 3400 Pharmacy Ave., # 5, Agincourt ON M1W3J8   CAN
COMIC COLLECTIONS . . . . 11600 Manchaca Road, Austin TX 78748
ELEPHANT'S TRUNK, THE . . . . .4 North St., Waldwick NJ 07463
FABRIC SOLUTION . . . . 1555 Finch Ave. E., # 1103, Willowdale ON M2J4X9   CAN
FRIEDMANS MICROWAVE OVENS . . . . .2301 Broadway, Oakland CA 94612
GOLD 'N LINKS . . . . 2 CMI Center, # 625, Salt Lake City UT 84101
HAPPI-COOK . . . . 1225 Park Place Mall, Memphis TN 38119
HATS IN THE BELFRY . . . . .1410 Forest Dr., # 33, Annapolis MD 21403
HOBBY BOX MARKETING . . . . 140 N. Westmonte Dr., # 101, Altamonte Springs FL 32714
HONORE JEWELRY . . . . One Civic Center Plaza, Hartford CT 06103
HOUR GLASS CLOCKSHOP . . . . .600 Broadway, # 580, Kansas City MO 64105
IMPOSTERS COPY JEWELS . . . . .651 Gateway Blvd., # 900, South San Francisco CA 94080
JEWELRY REPAIRS BY US . . . . .Summerton Plaza, 339 Rte. 9, Manalapan NJ 07726
JOHN SIMMONS GIFTS . . . . 1503 Union Ave., # 216, Memphis TN 38104
KIDS CORP. . . . . .300 Eagleson Rd., Kanata ON K2M1C9   CAN
LE GROUPE MULTI LUMINAIRE . . . . 4 Place Laval, # 200, Laval PQ H7N5Y3   CAN
LEGS BEAUTIFUL . . . . 1875 Leslie St., # 20, Don Mills ON M3B2M5   CAN
LES SALLE DE BAINS FALRO . . . . 7900 ouest boul. Henri Bourassa, Ville St-Laurent PQ H4S1V4   CAN
LIV GROUP, THE . . . . .4699 Keele St., # 3, Downsview ON M3J2N8   CAN

LOGOS AND LABELS . . . . 1732 C West Park Center Dr., St. Louis MO 63026
LOVE SHOP, THE . . . . P.O. Box 200, Station A, Vancouver BC V6C2W2   CAN
M.G.M. LIQUOR WAREHOUSE . . . . .1124 Larpenteur Ave. W., St. Paul MN 55113
MICRO COOKING CENTRES . . . . 30 Pacific Ct., # 2, London ON N5V3K4   CAN
MISS BOJANGLES . . . . .9711 Cortana Pl., Baton Rouge LA 70815
MONOGRAMS TO GO . . . . 14200 E. Alameda Ave., Aurora CO 80112
MUPPET STUFF . . . . 371 Bradwick Dr., # 8, Concord ON L4K2P4   CAN
NAMES 'N THINGS . . . . 2021 N. Highland, Old Hickory Mal, Jackson TN 38305
ONLY SEXY THINGS . . . . 14983 S. Dixie Hwy., Miami FL 33176
PAPER WAREHOUSE . . . . .7120 Shady Oak Rd., Eden Prairie MN 55344
PARTY FAIR . . . . Pond Rd. Ctr., Rte. # 9, Freehold NJ 07728
PARTY HARTY   . . . . 520 Fellowship Rd., Mt. Laurel NJ 08054
PARTY LAND . . . . .842 Redlion Rd., Philadelphia PA 19115
PERFUMERY, THE . . . . 724 W. 21st St., Houston TX 77008
PINCH A PENNY . . . . 14480 62nd St. N, Clearwater FL 34620
PRESS BOX NEWS-DRIVE-THRU NEWSSTAND . . . . .2600 Columbia Ave., Lancaster PA 17603
RODAN JEWELERS . . . . .7011 Kingsway, Burnaby BC V5E1E5   CAN
ROLLING PIN . . . . 4264 Winters Chapel Rd., Atlanta GA 30360
SAN FRANCISCO MUSIC BOX COMPANY . . . . .6121 Hollis St., Emeryville CA 94608
SCIENCE & THINGS. . . . . 2025 Marie, Westland MI 48185
SEAT COVERS UNLIMITED . . . . 5377 Kings Hwy., Brooklyn NY 11203
SIMPLY CHARMING . . . . .7011 Kingsway, Burnaby BC V5E1E5   CAN
SUN SHADE OPTIQUE . . . . .884 North Point, San Francisco CA 94109
TANDY LEATHER CONPANY . . . . .120 Brock St., Box 13000, Barrie ON L4M4W4   CAN
TENDER SENDER . . . . P. O. Box 427, West Linn OR 97068
THREADS 'N MORE! . . . . .79 Parkingway, P. O. Box 7169, Quincy MA 02169
TOYCITY/TOYVILLE . . . . 62 Belfield Rd., Rexdale ON M9W1G2   CAN
TRINKETS FINE JEWELRY . . . . 1299 Hilton Ln., Oakville ON L6M2V3   CAN
VERTECH BACK AND BED STORES . . . . 2 Market Place, Bates Bldg., Baltimore MD 21222
VIVAH JEWELRY . . . . .3715 Chesswod Dr., Toronto ON M3J2P6   CAN
WEDDING EXPRESSIONS . . . . 2100 N. Amidon, # 530, Wichita KS 67204
WICKS 'N' STICKS . . . . 12450 Greenspoint, Houston TX 77060
WIDE WORLD OF MAPS . . . . 2626 W. Indian School Rd., Phoenix AZ 85017
WILLSON STATIONERS . . . . .6625 Millcreek Dr., Mississagua ON L5N4G4   CAN
YU FASHION JEWELRY & ACCESSORIES . . . . 550 Champagne Dr., Downsview ON M3J2T9   CAN

CHAPTER 45

RETAIL: VIDEO / AUDIO / ELECTRONICS

APPLAUSE VIDEO

2622 S. 156th Circle
Omaha, NE 68130
TEL: (800) 323-9999 (402) 330-1000
FAX:
Mr. Bruce Shackman, President

APPLAUSE VIDEO, with its aggressive marketing and retailing expertise, provides a unique retail environment in which to rent and sell pre-recorded video cassettes and related video accessories. An extensive inventory providing the proper selection, as well as depth, is part of what makes APPLAUSE VIDEO so successful.

HISTORY: . . . . IFA
Established in 1983;   . . 1st Franchised in 1985
Company-Owned Units (As of 12/1/1989):   . 21
Franchised Units (12/1/1989):   36
Total Units (12/1/1989):   57
Distribution: US-57;Can-0;Overseas-0
  North America: . . . . 7 States
  Concentration: . . 20 in NE, 19 in MO, 3 in KS
Registered: . . . .

. . . .
Average # of Employees: . . . . . . 3 FT, 4 PT
Prior Industry Experience: . . . . Helpful

FINANCIAL:
Cash Investment: $400K
Total Investment: $400K
Fees: Franchise - $15K
  Royalty: 5%, Advert: 1%
Contract Periods (Yrs.): 5/5
Area Development Agreement: Yes/5
Sub-Franchise Contract: . . . . . Yes
Expand in Territory: . . . . . . Yes
Passive Ownership: . . . Discouraged
Encourage Conversions: . . . . . Yes
Franchisee Purchase(s) Required: .No

FRANCHISOR TRAINING/SUPPORT:
Financial Assistance Provided: . . . . . No
Site Selection Assistance: . . . . . . .Yes
Lease Negotiation Assistance: . . . .Yes
Co-operative Advertising: . . . . . . .Yes
Training: . . . . 2 Wks. Headquarters,
  . . . . 1 Wk. Site
On-Going Support: . . .A,B,C,D,E,F,G,h,I
Full-Time Franchisor Support Staff: . . 65
EXPANSION PLANS:
  US: . . . . All US
  Canada - Yes, ... Overseas - No

DR. VIDEO

1131 Bay Ave.
Point Pleasant, NJ 08742
TEL: (800) 533-5362
FAX:
Mr. Joseph F. DeGraw, Chairman

DR. VIDEO offers an exciting opportunity in the booming field of VCR repair. No electronic background necessary. We provide all training and complete turn-key package. There are 60 million potential customers. We also service Nintendo game machines and cartridges.

HISTORY: . . . . IFA
Established in 1988; . . 1st Franchised in 1988
Company-Owned Units (As of 12/1/1989): . .1
Franchised Units (12/1/1989): 7
Total Units (12/1/1989): 8
Distribution: US-8;Can-0;Overseas-0
North America: . . . . 5 States
Concentration: . . . . .3 in NJ, 2 in CA
Registered: . . . . CA,MD
. . . .
Average # of Employees: . . . . . . 1 FT, 1 PT
Prior Industry Experience: . . . . Helpful

FINANCIAL:
Cash Investment: $25K
Total Investment: $25K
Fees: Franchise - $17.5K
  Royalty: 5%, Advert: 2%
Contract Periods (Yrs.): 5/5
Area Development Agreement: . .No
Sub-Franchise Contract: . . . . .No
Expand in Territory: . . . . . . Yes
Passive Ownership: . . . . . .Allowed
Encourage Conversions: . . . . .No
Franchisee Purchase(s) Required: .No

FRANCHISOR TRAINING/SUPPORT:
Financial Assistance Provided: . . . . .No
Site Selection Assistance: . . . . . . .NA
Lease Negotiation Assistance: . . . . .NA
Co-operative Advertising: . . . . . . .NA
Training: . . . . 3 Wks. Headquarters
. . . .
On-Going Support: . . . . .C,d,G,h,I
Full-Time Franchisor Support Staff: . . . 5
EXPANSION PLANS:
US: . . . . All US
Canada - Yes, ...Overseas - No

JUMBO VIDEO

1075 N. Service Rd. W., # 202
Oakville, ON L6M2G2 CAN
TEL: (416) 847-7212
FAX: (416) 847-7276
Mr. Graham A. Ashdown, VP/GM

Our commitment is to provide the very best in home entertainment for the whole family in an enjoyable, exciting, fun-filled environment. For our franchisees, we will provide the most knowledgeable direction, guidance, support and expertise available in the home entertainment industry.

HISTORY: . . . . .CFA
Established in 1987; . . 1st Franchised in 1987
Company-Owned Units (As of 12/1/1989): . 15
Franchised Units (12/1/1989): 35
Total Units (12/1/1989): 50
Distribution: US-0;Can-50;Overseas-0
North America: . . . . 7 Provinces
Concentration: . . 35 in ON, 7 in AB, 3 in MB
Registered: . . . . AB
. . . .
Average # of Employees: . . . . . .5 FT, 20 PT
Prior Industry Experience: . . . . Helpful

FINANCIAL:
Cash Investment: $350-400K
Total Investment: $625-650K
Fees: Franchise - $75K
  Royalty: 5%, Advert: 2%
Contract Periods (Yrs.): 15/15
Area Development Agreement: . .No
Sub-Franchise Contract: . . . . .No
Expand in Territory: . . . . . . Yes
Passive Ownership: . . . Discouraged
Encourage Conversions: . . . . .No
Franchisee Purchase(s) Required: .No

FRANCHISOR TRAINING/SUPPORT:
Financial Assistance Provided: . . . Yes(I)
Site Selection Assistance: . . . . . . .Yes
Lease Negotiation Assistance: . . . . .Yes
Co-operative Advertising: . . . . . . .Yes
Training: . . . . . 1 Wk. Headquarters, 3-5
. . . Wks. Selected Store, 2 Wks. On-site
On-Going Support: . . . . . . b,C,d,E,G,H
Full-Time Franchisor Support Staff: . . 30
EXPANSION PLANS:
US: . . . . .No
Canada - Yes, ...Overseas - No

LE CLUB INTERNATIONAL VIDEO FILM

350 Elaine
Fabreville (Laval), PQ H7P2R1 CAN
TEL: (800) 361-9156 (514) 628-1910
FAX: (514) 628-1034
Mr. Manon Belisle,, Mktg. Director

The support that we are offering, the involvement of all our members and our commitment to professionalism are certainly the facts that have made us the best video franchisor in Canada.

HISTORY: . . . .
Established in 1981; . . 1st Franchised in 1982
Company-Owned Units (As of 12/1/1989): . .1
Franchised Units (12/1/1989): 53
Total Units (12/1/1989): 54
Distribution: US-0;Can-54;Overseas-0
North America: . . . . .1 Province
Concentration: . . . . .54 in PQ
Registered: . . . .
. . . .
Average # of Employees: . . . . . . 3 FT, 4 PT
Prior Industry Experience: . . . . Helpful

FINANCIAL:
Cash Investment: $100K
Total Investment: $200K
Fees: Franchise - $25K
  Royalty: 5%, Advert: 3%
Contract Periods (Yrs.): 10/10
Area Development Agreement: . .No
Sub-Franchise Contract: . . . . .No
Expand in Territory: . . . . . . Yes
Passive Ownership: . . . Discouraged
Encourage Conversions: . . . . Yes
Franchisee Purchase(s) Required: .No

FRANCHISOR TRAINING/SUPPORT:
Financial Assistance Provided: . . . Yes(I)
Site Selection Assistance: . . . . . . .Yes
Lease Negotiation Assistance: . . . . .Yes
Co-operative Advertising: . . . . . . .Yes
Training: . . . . . 1 Wk. Chomedey, Laval,
. . . . .2 Wks. On-site
On-Going Support: . . . . B,C,D,E,F,G,H
Full-Time Franchisor Support Staff: . . 17
EXPANSION PLANS:
US: . . . . .No
Canada - Yes, ...Overseas - No

MOVIE WAREHOUSE

1575 Winchester Rd., # 100
Lexington, KY 40505
TEL: (800) 726-3182 (606) 293-6223
FAX: (606) 293-6352
Ms. Angela J. Forsee, Fran. Sales

MOVIE WAREHOUSE offers a video superstore concept that has developed high revenues in retailing and sell-through, with a unique wholesale and leasing program. We maintain the lowest super store start-up cost in the industry and our company has the knowledge, foresight and the personnel to supply necessary support. Ranked in the top 3 fastest-growing video chains by Video Store Magazine (1989).

HISTORY: . . . .
Established in 1986; . . 1st Franchised in 1987
Company-Owned Units (As of 12/1/1989): . .4
Franchised Units (12/1/1989): 31
Total Units (12/1/1989): 35
Distribution: US-35;Can-0;Overseas-0
North America: . . . . 2 States
Concentration: . . . . 33 in KY, 2 in IN
Registered: . . . . FL,IN
. . . .
Average # of Employees: . . . . . . 3 FT, 3 PT
Prior Industry Experience: . . . . Helpful

FINANCIAL:
Cash Investment: $180-240K
Total Investment: $180-240K
Fees: Franchise - $20K
  Royalty: 5%, Advert: 2%
Contract Periods (Yrs.): 20/5
Area Development Agreement: Yes/3
Sub-Franchise Contract: . . . . . .No
Expand in Territory: . . . . . . Yes
Passive Ownership: . . . Discouraged
Encourage Conversions: . . . . . Yes
Franchisee Purchase(s) Required: .No

FRANCHISOR TRAINING/SUPPORT:
Financial Assistance Provided: . . . . . No
Site Selection Assistance: . . . . .Yes
Lease Negotiation Assistance: . . . . .Yes
Co-operative Advertising: . . . . .Yes
Training: . . . . 3-4 Days Ft. Thomas, KY,
. . . . 2-5 Days Lexington, KY
On-Going Support: . . . . .B,C,D,E,G,H,I
Full-Time Franchisor Support Staff: . . 20
EXPANSION PLANS:
US: . . . . .All US
Canada - No, ...Overseas - No

MOVIELAND USA

4120 Rogers Ave., # K
Ft. Smith, AR 72903
TEL: (501) 783-4737
FAX:
Mr. Kelly Rubottom, Franchise VP

Because MOVIELAND USA has been in the retail video industry for so many years, we have seen many changes occur and can better predict what changes will affect the video industry and you, the franchisee, in the immediate and distant future. Our methods are proven winners!

HISTORY: . . . .
Established in 1984; . . 1st Franchised in 1984
Company-Owned Units (As of 12/1/1989): . .9
Franchised Units (12/1/1989): 20
Total Units (12/1/1989): 29
Distribution: US-29;Can-0;Overseas-0
North America: . . . . 6 States
Concentration: . . .17 in AR, 7 in OK, 2 in TN
Registered: . . . .
. . . .
Average # of Employees: . . . . 2-3 FT, 3-6 PT
Prior Industry Experience: . . . . Helpful

FINANCIAL:
Cash Investment: $100-125K
Total Investment: $200-250K
Fees: Franchise - $10K
  Royalty: 4%, Advert: 1%
Contract Periods (Yrs.): 5/5
Area Development Agreement: . .No
Sub-Franchise Contract: . . . . . Yes
Expand in Territory: . . . . . . .No
Passive Ownership: . . . Discouraged
Encourage Conversions: . . . . . Yes
Franchisee Purchase(s) Required: .No

FRANCHISOR TRAINING/SUPPORT:
Financial Assistance Provided: . . . . .No
Site Selection Assistance: . . . . .Yes
Lease Negotiation Assistance: . . . . .No
Co-operative Advertising: . . . . .Yes
Training: . . . . .7 Working Days Store #1,
. . . . .7 Working Days Store #2
On-Going Support: . . . . .b,c,d,E,F
Full-Time Franchisor Support Staff: . . .1
EXPANSION PLANS:
US: . . . . . States Surrounding Arkansas
Canada - No, ...Overseas - No

MOVIES & MORE

1429 Warwick Ave.
Warwick, RI 02888
TEL: (800) 825-0035 (401) 463-8130
FAX:
Mr. Arnold Kornstein, President

MOVIES & MORE will set you up as the owner of a state-of-the-art video superstore to rent movies and to sell movies and related products and services. Sale of VCRs, camcorders and TVs is optional. Assistance provided to secure bank financing, floor plan financing and leasing of computer equipment and fixtures.

HISTORY: . . . .
Established in 1981; . . 1st Franchised in 1982
Company-Owned Units (As of 12/1/1989): . .0
Franchised Units (12/1/1989): 44
Total Units (12/1/1989): 44
Distribution: US-44;Can-0;Overseas-0
North America: . . . . 5 States
Concentration: . . . 20 in MA,12 in CT,7 in RI
Registered: . . . . .RI
. . . .
Average # of Employees: . . . . . . 4 FT, 4 PT
Prior Industry Experience: . . . . Helpful

FINANCIAL:
Cash Investment: $60-175K
Total Investment: $60-175K
Fees: Franchise - $20K
  Royalty: 4%, Advert: 0%
Contract Periods (Yrs.): 10/10
Area Development Agreement: Yes/10
Sub-Franchise Contract: . . . . . Yes
Expand in Territory: . . . . . . Yes
Passive Ownership: . . . . . .Allowed
Encourage Conversions: . . . .
Franchisee Purchase(s) Required: .No

FRANCHISOR TRAINING/SUPPORT:
Financial Assistance Provided: . . . Yes(I)
Site Selection Assistance: . . . . . . .Yes
Lease Negotiation Assistance: . . . . .Yes
Co-operative Advertising: . . . . . . .Yes
Training: . . . . . . 1-2 Wks. Headquarters,
. . . . 1-2 Wks. Site, On-going
On-Going Support: . . a,B,C,D,E,f,G,H,I
Full-Time Franchisor Support Staff: . . .5
EXPANSION PLANS:
US: . . . . .Eastern US
Canada - No, ...Overseas - No

NEEDLE IN A HAYSTACK

3999 Parkway Ln.
Hilliard, OH 43026
TEL: (614) 876-8014
FAX:
Mr. Jim Bowser, Fran. Sales

NEEDLE IN A HAYSTACK is a franchisor of retail products and services in the expanding aftermarket of home electronics. The store is an audio/video service center addressing the needs of home electronics owners through hard-to-find products, quality repair and retail attitude.

HISTORY: . . . .
Established in 1974; . . 1st Franchised in 1986
Company-Owned Units (As of 12/1/1989): . .0
Franchised Units (12/1/1989): 9
Total Units (12/1/1989): 9
Distribution: US-9;Can-0;Overseas-0
North America: . . . . 4 States
Concentration: . . . 4 in OH, 2 in MD, 2 in VA
Registered: . . . CA,FL,IL,IN,MD,MI,NY,VA
. . . . .WI
Average # of Employees: . . . . . . 2 FT, 1 PT
Prior Industry Experience: . . . . . . Helpful

FINANCIAL:
Cash Investment: $21-51K
Total Investment: $87-117K
Fees: Franchise - $20K
Royalty: 5%, Advert: 3%
Contract Periods (Yrs.): 10/10
Area Development Agreement: Yes/10
Sub-Franchise Contract: . . . . . .No
Expand in Territory: . . . . Yes
Passive Ownership: . . . . . .Allowed
Encourage Conversions: . . . . .No
Franchisee Purchase(s) Required: .No

FRANCHISOR TRAINING/SUPPORT:
Financial Assistance Provided: . . . Yes(I)
Site Selection Assistance: . . . . . . .Yes
Lease Negotiation Assistance: . . . . .Yes
Co-operative Advertising: . . . . . . .Yes
Training: . . . . 5 Days Headquarters,
. . . . 4 Days Site
On-Going Support: . . A,B,C,D,E,F,G,H,I
Full-Time Franchisor Support Staff: . . .6
EXPANSION PLANS:
US: . . . . .NE and SE
Canada - No, ...Overseas - No

PALMER VIDEO SUPERSTORES

1767 Morris Ave.
Union, NJ 07083
TEL: (800) 288-3456 (201) 686-3030
FAX:
Mr. Harry Dossick, Dir. Fran. Dev.

PALMER VIDEO offers an opportunity in attractive, well-inventoried video superstores based on a professional franchise system. Emphasis on sound operating principles and aggressive marketing concepts to obtain a disproportionate market share. Our top management's on-going support is dedicated to driving customers to our franchised video superstores.

HISTORY: . . . . IFA
Established in 1981; . . 1st Franchised in 1982
Company-Owned Units (As of 12/1/1989): . 29
Franchised Units (12/1/1989): 133
Total Units (12/1/1989): 162
Distribution: US-162;Can-0;Overseas-0
North America: . . . . 13 States
Concentration: . . . 76 in NJ, 26 in CO, 8 in IL
Registered: . . . CA,FL,IL,IN,MD,MI,MN,NY
. . . . OR,RI,VA,WA,WI
Average # of Employees: . . . . . . 2 Ft, 6 PT
Prior Industry Experience: . . . . . . Helpful

FINANCIAL:
Cash Investment: $50-100K
Total Investment: $200-400K
Fees: Franchise - $29K
Royalty: 5%, Advert: . . . . . Var.
Contract Periods (Yrs.): 10/10
Area Development Agreement: Yes/Var
Sub-Franchise Contract: . . . . . .No
Expand in Territory: . . . . Yes
Passive Ownership: . . . . . .Allowed
Encourage Conversions: . . . . . Yes
Franchisee Purchase(s) Required: .No

FRANCHISOR TRAINING/SUPPORT:
Financial Assistance Provided: . . . Yes(I)
Site Selection Assistance: . . . . . . .Yes
Lease Negotiation Assistance: . . . . .Yes
Co-operative Advertising: . . . . . . .Yes
Training: . . . . 5 Days Headquarters,
. . . . .2 Days Field
On-Going Support: . . . .A,B,C,D,E,g,H,I
Full-Time Franchisor Support Staff: . . 49
EXPANSION PLANS:
US: . . . . All US
Canada - Yes, ...Overseas - No

VIDEO BIZ

2981 West S/R 434, # 100
Longwood, FL 32779
TEL: (800) 582-7347 (407) 774-5000 C
FAX:
Mr. Ed Fainelli, Fran. Sales

Video movie rental and sales. Locations normally in strip centers anchored by supermarkets. Prices encourage 2 and 3-day rentals coinciding with normal consumer food shopping patterns. Average ticket is $8 - 10, involving 3 - 4 movies each time with higher profitability.

HISTORY: . . . . IFA
Established in 1981; . . 1st Franchised in 1983
Company-Owned Units (As of 12/1/1989): . .2
Franchised Units (12/1/1989): 158
Total Units (12/1/1989): 160
Distribution: US-160;Can-0;Overseas-0
North America: . . . . 38 States
Concentration: . . 39 in FL, 19 in CA, 12 in NJ
Registered: . . . . All States
. . . .
Average # of Employees: . . . . . . 1 FT, 2 PT
Prior Industry Experience: . . . . . . Helpful

FINANCIAL:
Cash Investment: . . . .$100K+
Total Investment: . . . . . .$100K+
Fees: Franchise - $20K
Royalty: 2.5%, Advert: 2.5%
Contract Periods (Yrs.): 10/5/5
Area Development Agreement: Yes/35
Sub-Franchise Contract: . . . . . Yes
Expand in Territory: . . . . Yes
Passive Ownership: . . . . . .Allowed
Encourage Conversions: . . . . . Yes
Franchisee Purchase(s) Required: .No

FRANCHISOR TRAINING/SUPPORT:
Financial Assistance Provided: . . . . .No
Site Selection Assistance: . . . . . . .Yes
Lease Negotiation Assistance: . . . . .Yes
Co-operative Advertising: . . . . . . .Yes
Training: . . . . 4 Days Site
. . . .
On-Going Support: . . . . D,E,F,G,I
Full-Time Franchisor Support Staff: . . 11
EXPANSION PLANS:
US: . . . . All US
Canada - No, ...Overseas - No

VIDEO DATA SERVICES

24 Grove St.
Pittsford, NY 14534
TEL: (716) 385-4773
FAX:
Mr. Stuart Dizak, President

Provide a unique video photography service to business and consumers. Complete package includes all equipment, training, marketing and field assistance. Can be started part-time. Ideal as a family or retirement business. VIDEO DATA SERVICES is the largest video taping service in North America. Also provide film-to-tape transfer.

HISTORY: . . . . IFA	FINANCIAL:	FRANCHISOR TRAINING/SUPPORT:
Established in 1981; . . 1st Franchised in 1984	Cash Investment: $18K	Financial Assistance Provided: . . . . . No
Company-Owned Units (As of 12/1/1989): . . 1	Total Investment: $18K	Site Selection Assistance: . . . . NA
Franchised Units (12/1/1989): 240	Fees: Franchise - $8K	Lease Negotiation Assistance: . . . . . NA
Total Units (12/1/1989): 241	Royalty: Flat, Advert: 0%	Co-operative Advertising: . . . . Yes
Distribution: US-239;Can-2;Overseas-0	Contract Periods (Yrs.): . . . 10/10	Training: . . . . 4 Days Field,
North America: . . . . 38 States, 2 Provinces	Area Development Agreement: . .No	. . . . 6 Wks. Training at Home
Concentration: . . . 12 in CA, 8 in FL, 7 in LA	Sub-Franchise Contract: . . . . . No	On-Going Support: . . . . B,C,E,F,G,H,I
Registered: . . . CA,FL,IL,IN,MD,MI,MN,NY	Expand in Territory: . . . . . . Yes	Full-Time Franchisor Support Staff: . . . 6
. . . . RI,VA,WA,WI	Passive Ownership: . . . Not Allowed	EXPANSION PLANS:
Average # of Employees: . . . . .2 PT	Encourage Conversions: . . . . .No	US: . . . . All US
Prior Industry Experience: . . . . Helpful	Franchisee Purchase(s) Required: .No	Canada - Yes, ...Overseas - No

VIDEO EDITOR

5975 Roswell Rd.
Atlanta, GA 30328
TEL: (404) 256-4108
FAX:
Mr. Tom Lang, VP Franchising

State-of-the-art, do-it-yourself, full-service video post-production facility. Services offered are video editing in all formats, video duplications and film-to-video tape transfers.

HISTORY:	FINANCIAL:	FRANCHISOR TRAINING/SUPPORT:
Established in 1985; . . 1st Franchised in 1989	Cash Investment: $50-75K	Financial Assistance Provided: . . . . .NA
Company-Owned Units (As of 12/1/1989): . .2	Total Investment: $126-165K	Site Selection Assistance: . . . . . . .Yes
Franchised Units (12/1/1989): 1	Fees: Franchise - . . . .$	Lease Negotiation Assistance: . . . .Yes
Total Units (12/1/1989): 3	Royalty: 9%, Advert: 0%	Co-operative Advertising: . . . . . . .Yes
Distribution: US-3;Can-0;Overseas-0	Contract Periods (Yrs.): 7/7	Training: . . . . 2 Wks. Headquarters
North America: . . . . 3 States	Area Development Agreement: . .No	. . . .
Concentration: . . . .1 in GA, 1 in TX, 1 in FL	Sub-Franchise Contract: . . . . .No	On-Going Support: . . . . B,C,D,E,F,H,I
Registered: . . . . FL,IN,MD,MI,MN	Expand in Territory: . . . . . . Yes	Full-Time Franchisor Support Staff: . . . 4
. . . .	Passive Ownership: . . . Discouraged	EXPANSION PLANS:
Average # of Employees: . . . . . . 2 FT, 1 PT	Encourage Conversions: . . . . .No	US: . . .SE,SW,NE,Midwest,MidAtlantic
Prior Industry Experience: . . . . . . Helpful	Franchisee Purchase(s) Required: .No	Canada - Yes, ...Overseas - No

VIDEO GALAXY

101 West Rd.
Vernon, CT 06066
TEL: (203) 871-7831
FAX:
Mr. William Corbin, Dir. Fran.

Video rental and sales, including accessories, VCRs, TVs and other related equipment.

HISTORY:	FINANCIAL:	FRANCHISOR TRAINING/SUPPORT:
Established in 1981; . . 1st Franchised in 1986	Cash Investment: $50-100K	Financial Assistance Provided: . . . . . No
Company-Owned Units (As of 12/1/1989): . .0	Total Investment: $125-200K	Site Selection Assistance: . . . . . . .Yes
Franchised Units (12/1/1989): 38	Fees: Franchise - $20K	Lease Negotiation Assistance: . . . .Yes
Total Units (12/1/1989): 38	Royalty: 5%, Advert: . . . . . Flat	Co-operative Advertising: . . . . . . .Yes
Distribution: US-38;Can-0;Overseas-0	Contract Periods (Yrs.): . . . 10/10	Training: . . . . 1 Wk. Headquarters
North America: . . . . .1 State	Area Development Agreement: Yes/1	. . . .
Concentration: . . . . .38 in CT	Sub-Franchise Contract: . . . . .No	On-Going Support: . . . . B,C,D,E,F,G,H
Registered:	Expand in Territory: . . . . . . .No	Full-Time Franchisor Support Staff: . . . .
. . . .	Passive Ownership: . . . . . .Allowed	EXPANSION PLANS:
Average # of Employees: . . . . . . 2 FT, 3 PT	Encourage Conversions: . . . . . Yes	US: . . . . Northeast
Prior Industry Experience: . . . . . . Helpful	Franchisee Purchase(s) Required: .No	Canada - No, ...Overseas - No

VIDEO LEASE, THE

409 Horton St.
London, ON N6B1L9 CAN
TEL: (519) 432-5196
FAX:
Mr. James Mathe, President

THE VIDEO LEASE offers a unique video concept where all stores are open 24 hours, 7 days a week. Each store carries over 10,000 movies. We are well known as the home of the $.01 movie. Each store has over 20 different movie categories, from new releases to drama to educational.

HISTORY: . . . . .CFA
Established in 1982; . . 1st Franchised in 1983
Company-Owned Units (As of 12/1/1989): . .5
Franchised Units (12/1/1989): 7
Total Units (12/1/1989): 12
Distribution: US-0;Can-12;Overseas-0
North America: . . . . .1 Province
Concentration: . . . . 12 in ON
Registered: . . . .
. . . .
Average # of Employees: . . . . . .5 FT, 10 PT
Prior Industry Experience: . . . . Helpful

FINANCIAL:
Cash Investment: . . . .$250K+
Total Investment: . . . .$500K+
Fees: Franchise - $35K
  Royalty: 5%, Advert: 4%
Contract Periods (Yrs.): . . . 20/20
Area Development Agreement: Yes/25
Sub-Franchise Contract: . . . . .No
Expand in Territory: . . . . Yes
Passive Ownership: . . . Discouraged
Encourage Conversions: . . . . Yes
Franchisee Purchase(s) Required: .No

FRANCHISOR TRAINING/SUPPORT:
Financial Assistance Provided: . . . Yes(I)
Site Selection Assistance: . . . . .Yes
Lease Negotiation Assistance: . . . . .Yes
Co-operative Advertising: . . . . .Yes
Training: . . . . 2 Wks. Headquarters
. . . .
On-Going Support: . . . . .B,C,D,E,F,G,h
Full-Time Franchisor Support Staff: . . 35
EXPANSION PLANS:
US: . . . . All US
Canada - Yes, ...Overseas - No

VIDEO UPDATE

287 East 6th St.
St Paul, MN 55101
TEL: (800) 433-1195 (612) 222-0006
FAX: (612) 297-6629
Mr. John Bedard, President

VIDEO UPDATE has developed the highest-quality retail rental/sales stores in the world. Our merchandising and marketing skills are unsurpassed. We attribute our achievement to our uncompromising commitment to franchisee support.

HISTORY: . . . . IFA
Established in 1982; . . 1st Franchised in 1983
Company-Owned Units (As of 12/1/1989): . .2
Franchised Units (12/1/1989): 61
Total Units (12/1/1989): 63
Distribution: US-61;Can-0;Overseas-2
North America: . . . . 13 States
Concentration: . . . . MN, VA, OH
Registered: . . . . MN
. . . .
Average # of Employees: . . . . . . 1 FT, 4 PT
Prior Industry Experience: . . . . . . Helpful

FINANCIAL:
Cash Investment: $20-50K
Total Investment: $90-160K
Fees: Franchise - $19.5K
  Royalty: 5%, Advert: 1%
Contract Periods (Yrs.): . . . 10/Var
Area Development Agreement: . .No
Sub-Franchise Contract: . . . . .No
Expand in Territory: . . . . Yes
Passive Ownership: . . . . . .Allowed
Encourage Conversions: . . . . NA
Franchisee Purchase(s) Required: .No

FRANCHISOR TRAINING/SUPPORT:
Financial Assistance Provided: . . .Yes(D)
Site Selection Assistance: . . . . .Yes
Lease Negotiation Assistance: . . . . .Yes
Co-operative Advertising: . . . . .Yes
Training: . . . . .5 Days Owner's Store
. . . .
On-Going Support: . . A,B,C,D,E,F,G,H,I
Full-Time Franchisor Support Staff: . . . .
EXPANSION PLANS:
US: . . . . All US
Canada - Yes, . . . Overseas - Yes

VIDEO VALUE

350 Keewatin St., # 5
Winnipeg, MB R2X2R9 CAN
TEL: (204) 694-2930
FAX:
Mr. I. D. Oiring, President

Setting up video movie departments in established businesses. Providing fully-serviced products and marketing information. Master Franchisor inquiries from USA invited.

HISTORY: . . . .
Established in 1983; . . 1st Franchised in 1983
Company-Owned Units (As of 12/1/1989): . .0
Franchised Units (12/1/1989): 26
Total Units (12/1/1989): 26
Distribution: US-0;Can-26;Overseas-0
North America: . . . . 3 Provinces
Concentration: . . 13 in MB, 6 in ON, 5 in SK
Registered: . . . .
. . . .
Average # of Employees: . . . . . . 1 FT, 1 PT
Prior Industry Experience: . . . . Helpful

FINANCIAL:
Cash Investment: $7-75K
Total Investment: $7-75K
Fees: Franchise - $7K
  Royalty: 4%, Advert: 0%
Contract Periods (Yrs.): 5/5
Area Development Agreement: Yes/5
Sub-Franchise Contract: . . . . . Yes
Expand in Territory: . . . . Yes
Passive Ownership: . . . . . .Allowed
Encourage Conversions: . . . . Yes
Franchisee Purchase(s) Required: Yes

FRANCHISOR TRAINING/SUPPORT:
Financial Assistance Provided: . . . . .No
Site Selection Assistance: . . . . No
Lease Negotiation Assistance: . . . . .No
Co-operative Advertising: . . . . No
Training: . . . .
. . . .
On-Going Support: . . . . .A,B,F,G
Full-Time Franchisor Support Staff: . . . 4
EXPANSION PLANS:
US: . . . . All US
Canada - Yes, ...Overseas - No

VIDEO VAN

254A N. Broadway
Salem, NH 03079
TEL: (800) 635-3720 (603) 898-1193 C
FAX: (603) 898-2082
Mr. Frank J. Jordan, President

Pick-up and delivery service of movies to the customer's home, utilizing a sophisticated computer system, a lock box and monthly movie updates.

HISTORY:	FINANCIAL:	FRANCHISOR TRAINING/SUPPORT:
Established in 1987; . . 1st Franchised in 1989	Cash Investment: $108-175K	Financial Assistance Provided: . . . . . No
Company-Owned Units (As of 12/1/1989): . .2	Total Investment: $108-175K	Site Selection Assistance: . . . . . . .NA
Franchised Units (12/1/1989): 10	Fees: Franchise - $22.5K	Lease Negotiation Assistance: . . . . .NA
Total Units (12/1/1989): 12	Royalty: 5%, Advert: 4%	Co-operative Advertising: . . . . .Yes
Distribution: US-11;Can-1;Overseas-0	Contract Periods (Yrs.): 10/10	Training: . . . . 3 Days Headquarters,
North America: . . . . . .5 States, 1 Province	Area Development Agreement: Yes/10	. . . . .2 Days On-site
Concentration: . . . 5 in MA, 2 in OH, 1 in NJ	Sub-Franchise Contract: . . . . . Yes	On-Going Support: . . . .b,C,D,E,F,G,H,I
Registered: . . . . FL,MI,RI	Expand in Territory: . . . . . . .No	Full-Time Franchisor Support Staff: . . 14
. . . .	Passive Ownership: . . . Discouraged	EXPANSION PLANS:
Average # of Employees: . . . . . 2 FT, 4-5 PT	Encourage Conversions: . . . . . .No	US: . . . . All US
Prior Industry Experience: . . . . Helpful	Franchisee Purchase(s) Required: Yes	Canada - Yes, . . . Overseas - Yes

VIDEOMATIC INTERNATIONAL

1060 W. Covina Pkwy.
West Covina, CA 91790
TEL: (818) 960-5454
FAX: (818) 338-7004
Mr. Harold Brown

Fully-automated video store. No employees. Keep present position. An investment, not a job. On-line, computerized credit card system, no cash. Rent only top hits. Locate in high-visibility, high-traffic shopping centers, using 3 parking spaces.

HISTORY: . . . . IFA	FINANCIAL:	FRANCHISOR TRAINING/SUPPORT:
Established in 1988; . . 1st Franchised in 1989	Cash Investment: $40K	Financial Assistance Provided: . . . Yes(I)
Company-Owned Units (As of 12/1/1989): . .1	Total Investment: $150K	Site Selection Assistance: . . . . . . .Yes
Franchised Units (12/1/1989): 27	Fees: Franchise - $25K	Lease Negotiation Assistance: . . . . .Yes
Total Units (12/1/1989): 28	Royalty: 5%, Advert: 2.5%	Co-operative Advertising: . . . . .No
Distribution: US-28;Can-0;Overseas-0	Contract Periods (Yrs.): 10/10	Training: . . . . 2-5 Days On-site
North America: . . . . .1 State	Area Development Agreement: Yes/20	. . . .
Concentration: . . . . 28 in CA	Sub-Franchise Contract: . . . . . Yes	On-Going Support: . . . . . . .C,D,E,F,G
Registered: . . . .CA,FL,HI,IL,IN,MD,MI,NY	Expand in Territory: . . . . . . .No	Full-Time Franchisor Support Staff: . . . 8
. . . . OR,RI,VA,WA,WI	Passive Ownership: . . . . . .Allowed	EXPANSION PLANS:
Average # of Employees: . . . . .1 PT	Encourage Conversions: . . . . . .No	US: . . . . All US
Prior Industry Experience: . . . . Helpful	Franchisee Purchase(s) Required: Yes	Canada - Yes, ...Overseas - No

WEST COAST VIDEO

9990 Global Rd.
Philadelphia, PA 19115
TEL: (800) 433-5171 (215) 677-1000+4
FAX:
Mr. John Barry, VP Sales

Join the "World's Largest Video Chain" in a $10 billion a year industry! Top 1% of America's fastest-growing companies according to Inc. Magazine (12/88). Top 100 Franchisor according to Venture Magazine (12/88).

HISTORY: . . . . IFA	FINANCIAL:	FRANCHISOR TRAINING/SUPPORT:
Established in 1983; . . 1st Franchised in 1985	Cash Investment: $240-350K	Financial Assistance Provided: . . . Yes(I)
Company-Owned Units (As of 12/1/1989): . 70	Total Investment: $240-350K	Site Selection Assistance: . . . . . . .Yes
Franchised Units (12/1/1989): 700	Fees: Franchise - $40K	Lease Negotiation Assistance: . . . . .Yes
Total Units (12/1/1989): 770	Royalty: 5%, Advert: 2%	Co-operative Advertising: . . . . .Yes
Distribution: US-749;Can-15;Overseas-6	Contract Periods (Yrs.): 10/10	Training: . . . . . 1 Wk. Headquarters, On-
North America: . . . . 50 States,10 Provinces	Area Development Agreement: Yes/1-3	. . . . .going at Franchise Location
Concentration: . . .45 in PA, 27 in NJ, 6 in BC	Sub-Franchise Contract: . . . . . Yes	On-Going Support: . . A,B,C,D,E,F,G,H,I
Registered: . . . . .All	Expand in Territory: . . . . . . Yes	Full-Time Franchisor Support Staff: . . . .
. . . .	Passive Ownership: . . . . . .Allowed	EXPANSION PLANS:
Average # of Employees: . . . . . . 2 FT, 8 PT	Encourage Conversions: . . . . . Yes	US: . . . . All US
Prior Industry Experience: . . . . Helpful	Franchisee Purchase(s) Required: .No	Canada - Yes, ...Overseas - Yes

SUPPLEMENTAL LISTING OF FRANCHISORS

21ST CENTURY ELECTRONICS	240 Columbia St., Bogalusa LA 70427	
ACTION VIDEO & CASSETTE DUPING	#310 3 Clienango St., Buffalo NY 14213	
BANDITO VIDEO	2423 Princess St., # A, Kingston ON K7M3P1	CAN
BLOCKBUSTER VIDEOS	901 E. Las Olas Blvd., Ft. Lauderdale FL 33301	
BOUTIQUE MICRO ELECTRONIQUE	1299 Hilton Ln., Oakville ON L6M2V3	CAN
BUDGET TAPES & RECORDS	2773 S. Parket Rd., # 152, Aurora CO 80014	
C & M VIDEO	P. O. Box 1226, Effingham IL 62401	
COMPACT DISK WAREHOUSE	14300 Beach Blvd., Westminster CA 92683	
CURTIS MATHES	P. O. Box 2160, Athens TX 75751	
FUTURE TRONICS	347 N. Oak St., Inglewood CA 90301	
GO-VIDEO	4141 N. Scottsdale Rd.,#204, Scottsdale AZ 85251	
LASER LAND CANADA	2200 Dundas St. E., Mississauga ON L4X2V3	CAN
LASERLAND	15700 E. 1st Ave., Aurora CO 80011	
MEGAVIDEO	25th and Butler, Easton PA 18042	
MOVIE KING	Liberty Plaza at Possum Park, Newark DE 19711	
MOVIE WAREHOUSE	50 Weybright Ct., # 44, Toronto ON M1S4E4	CAN
MR. MOVIES	6566 Edenvale Blvd., Eden Prairie MN 55346	
NATIONAL VIDEO	2830 NE Hogan Rd., # G, Gresham OR 97030	
NATIONAL VIDEO YEARBOOK	275 Southland Dr., # 202, Lexington KY 40503	
NETWORK VIDEO	5562 Quail Run, N. Olmsted OH 44070	
RADIO SHACK (CANADA)	P.O. Box 34000, Barrie ON L4M4W5	CAN
RADIO SHACK DIVISION	1600 One Tandy Center, Fort Worth TX 76102	
RENT-A-DISC	210 Spring Valley Rd., Kitchener ON N2H4X6	CAN
SOUND TRACKS RECORDING STUDIO	424 Parkway, Sevierville TN 37862	
STARLITE VIDEO	2321 W. Royal Palm Rd., # 107, Phoenix AZ 85021	
STEREO DEN	2300 Lawrence Ave. E., # 10, Scarborough ON M1P2R2	CAN
TOP FORTY	10333 174th St., Edmonton AB T5S1H1	CAN
VIDEO 5000	211 E. 43rd St., New York NY 10017	
VIDEO CUBE	700 Boul. Cremazie Ouest, # 10, Montreal PQ H3N1A1	CAN
VIDEO EXCHANGE, THE	7862 W. Jewell, Lakewood CO 80226	
VIDEO INFO	#511 - 1505 Baseline Rd., Ottawa ON K2C3L4	CAN
VIDEO INTERNAT'L. VENDING	1060 W. Covina Pkwy., West Covina CA 91790	
VIDEO KING	Liberty Plaza at Possum Park, Newark DE 19711	
VIDEO YEARBOOKS	25 Century Blvd., # 507, Nashville TN 37214	
VIDEO'S 1ST	11 N. Pearl St., 4th Fl., Albany NY 12207	
VIDEOLA STORE, THE	7111 Ohms Ln., Minneapolis MN 55435	
VIDEOMATIC	1060 W. Covina Pkwy., West Covina CA 91790	
VIDEOMATIC / VIDEOFLEX	1800 Le Corbusier, # 136, Laval PQ H7S2K1	CAN
VIDEOVILLE USA	Box 585, Plymouth MI 48170	
VIDTRON DRIVE THRU MOVIE RENTALS	2616 S. Loop, W., # 610, Houston TX 77054	
ZM VIDEO RENTAL	3501 Chateau Blvd., # E-2B, Kenner LA 70065	

CHAPTER 46

RETAIL: MISCELLANEOUS

BEN FRANKLIN STORES

500 E. North Ave.
Carol Stream, IL 60188
TEL: (708) 462-6100
FAX: (708) 690-1356
Mr. Wayne Pyrant, Natl. Dir. Sales

BEN FRANKLIN STORES feature one of the most complete and outstanding opportunities to operate your own franchised BEN FRANKLIN CRAFT STORE or BEN FRANKLIN VARIETY STORE.

HISTORY: . . . . IFA
Established in 1924; . . 1st Franchised in 1927
Company-Owned Units (As of 12/1/1989): . .0
Franchised Units (12/1/1989): 1300
Total Units (12/1/1989): 1300
Distribution: US-1299;Can-0;Overseas-1
 North America: . . . . 49 States
 Concentration: . 106 in MN,104 in WI,95 in IL
Registered: . . . . All States
. . . .
Average # of Employees: . . . .
Prior Industry Experience: . . . . Helpful

FINANCIAL: NYSE-NII
Cash Investment: $150K
Total Investment: $350-900K
Fees: Franchise - $24K
 Royalty: Flat/Mo., Advert: . 0-1/2%
Contract Periods (Yrs.): . . . 5-1-/10
Area Development Agreement: Yes/Var
Sub-Franchise Contract: . . . . . .No
Expand in Territory: . . . . . . Yes
Passive Ownership: . . . . . .Allowed
Encourage Conversions: . . . . Yes
Franchisee Purchase(s) Required: Yes

FRANCHISOR TRAINING/SUPPORT:
Financial Assistance Provided: . . . Yes(I)
Site Selection Assistance: . . . . .Yes
Lease Negotiation Assistance: . . . . .Yes
Co-operative Advertising: . . . . .Yes
Training: . . . . . . 1-2 Wks. Headquarters,
 . . . . .2 Wks. Training Store
On-Going Support: . . .a,B,C,D,E,F,G,H,I
Full-Time Franchisor Support Staff: . .908
EXPANSION PLANS:
 US: . . . . .All US
 Canada - No, ... Overseas - No

DOLLAR DISCOUNT STORES

7 Boulden Creek
New Castle, DE 19720
TEL: (800) 227-5314 (302) 322-6820 C
FAX: (302) 322-6840
Mr. Paul Cohen, President

DOLLAR DISCOUNT STORES feature a wide variety of discount close-out merchandise at rock-bottom prices. Product categories include toys, candy, seasonal products, health and beauty aids, party and paper goods, pet supplies and other new and unusual products.

HISTORY:	. . . . IFA
Established in 1982;	. . 1st Franchised in 1987
Company-Owned Units (As of 12/1/1989):	. .0
Franchised Units (12/1/1989):	 40
Total Units (12/1/1989):	 40
Distribution:	. . . . . US-40;Can-0;Overseas-0
North America:	. . . . 4 States
Concentration:	. . . . .MD, NJ, PA
Registered:	. . . . FL,MD,NY,RI,VA
Average # of Employees:	. . . . . . 3 FT, 3 PT
Prior Industry Experience:	. . . . Helpful

FINANCIAL:	
Cash Investment:	. . . . . $20-40K
Total Investment:	. . . . . $80-90K
Fees: Franchise -	. . . . $15K
Royalty: 3%, Advert:	. . . . . . 1%
Contract Periods (Yrs.):	10
Area Development Agreement:	. Yes
Sub-Franchise Contract:	. . . . .No
Expand in Territory:	. . . . . . .No
Passive Ownership:	. . . Discouraged
Encourage Conversions:	. . . . Yes
Franchisee Purchase(s) Required:	.No

FRANCHISOR TRAINING/SUPPORT:	
Financial Assistance Provided:	. . . Yes(I)
Site Selection Assistance:	. . . . . . .Yes
Lease Negotiation Assistance:	. . . .Yes
Co-operative Advertising:	. . . . . . .Yes
Training:	. . . . . . 2 Wks. Headquarters
On-Going Support:	. . A,B,C,D,E,F,G,H,I
Full-Time Franchisor Support Staff:	. . 35
EXPANSION PLANS:	
US:	. . . . Mid-Atlantic Region
Canada - No,	. . . . .Overseas - No

HEEL QUIK / SEW QUIK

1720 Cumberland Pt. Dr., # 15
Marietta, GA 30067
TEL: (800) 888-4335 (404) 951-9440
FAX: (404) 933-8268
Ed, Jim or Dennis, Sales Reps.

Instant shoe repair, clothing alterations and monogramming. No failures to date. 670% growth in last 3 years. Ranked #1 in our industry by Entrepreneur Magazine. Listed in top 100 franchises for women by Woman's Enterprise.

HISTORY:	. . . . IFA
Established in 1984;	. . 1st Franchised in 1985
Company-Owned Units (As of 12/1/1989):	. .5
Franchised Units (12/1/1989):	 86
Total Units (12/1/1989):	 91
Distribution:	. . . . . US-85;Can-1;Overseas-5
North America:	. . . . . 26 States, 1 Province
Concentration:	. . 15 in GA, 14 in FL, 5 in OH
Registered:	. . . . CA,FL,IL,IN,MI,NY,RI,VA
Average # of Employees:	. . . . . 3 FT, 1 PT
Prior Industry Experience:	. . . . Helpful

FINANCIAL:	
Cash Investment:	. . . . . . $10-30K
Total Investment:	. . . . . $40-120K
Fees: Franchise -	. . . $10.5-12.5K
Royalty: 4%, Advert:	. . . . . . 2%
Contract Periods (Yrs.):	. . . 15/10
Area Development Agreement:	Yes/10
Sub-Franchise Contract:	. . . . . .No
Expand in Territory:	. . . . . . Yes
Passive Ownership:	. . . . . .Allowed
Encourage Conversions:	. . . . Yes
Franchisee Purchase(s) Required:	.No

FRANCHISOR TRAINING/SUPPORT:	
Financial Assistance Provided:	. . . Yes(I)
Site Selection Assistance:	. . . . . . .Yes
Lease Negotiation Assistance:	. . . .Yes
Co-operative Advertising:	. . . . . . .Yes
Training:	. . . . . . 2-3 Wks. Headquarters
On-Going Support:	. . . . .C,D,E,F,G,H,I
Full-Time Franchisor Support Staff:	. . 21
EXPANSION PLANS:	
US:	. . . . .All US
Canada - Yes,	. . . Overseas - Yes

LAROSSA INSTANT SHOE REPAIR

199 State St.
Boston, MA 02109
TEL: (617) 227-8499
FAX:
Mr. William LaRossa, President

While-you-wait instant shoe repair centers with equal emphasis on quick turnover and craftsmanship. Very successful format in Boston area has produced a proven track record.

HISTORY:	. . . .
Established in 1984;	. . 1st Franchised in 1984
Company-Owned Units (As of 12/1/1989):	. .4
Franchised Units (12/1/1989):	8
Total Units (12/1/1989):	 12
Distribution:	. . . . . US-12;Can-0;Overseas-0
North America:	. . . . 2 States
Concentration:	. . . . 10 in MA, 2 in NH
Registered:	. . . .
Average # of Employees:	. . . . . 2 FT, 3 PT
Prior Industry Experience:	. . . . Helpful

FINANCIAL:	
Cash Investment:	. . . .$100K
Total Investment:	. . . . .$85-125K
Fees: Franchise -	. . . . $25K
Royalty: 7%, Advert:	. . . . . 0%
Contract Periods (Yrs.):	3
Area Development Agreement:	. Yes
Sub-Franchise Contract:	. . . . .No
Expand in Territory:	. . . . . . Yes
Passive Ownership:	. . . . .Allowed
Encourage Conversions:	. . . . .No
Franchisee Purchase(s) Required:	Yes

FRANCHISOR TRAINING/SUPPORT:	
Financial Assistance Provided:	. . . Yes(I)
Site Selection Assistance:	. . . . . . .Yes
Lease Negotiation Assistance:	. . . .Yes
Co-operative Advertising:	. . . . . . .Yes
Training:	. . . . 3 Months Weymouth, MA,
	. . . . .3 Months Boston, MA
On-Going Support:	. . A,B,C,D,E,F,G,H,I
Full-Time Franchisor Support Staff:	. . .5
EXPANSION PLANS:	
US:	. . . . .All US
Canada - No,	. . . . .Overseas - No

LES CONSULTANTS CHEV'HAIR

221 St. Georges
St-Barnabe Nord, PQ G0X2K0 CAN
TEL: (819) 264-2116
FAX:
Mr. Gaston Gelinas, President

Manufacturer of hairpieces and products for hair and scalp care and treatments.

HISTORY: . . . .
Established in 1968; . . 1st Franchised in 1985
Company-Owned Units (As of 12/1/1989): . .2
Franchised Units (12/1/1989): 4
Total Units (12/1/1989): 6
Distribution: US-2;Can-4;Overseas-0
North America: . . . . . .2 States, 1 Province
Concentration: . . . . 4 in PQ, 1 in TN, 1 in FL
Registered: . . . . .FL
. . . .
Average # of Employees: . . . . .2 FT
Prior Industry Experience: . . . . . . Helpful

FINANCIAL:
Cash Investment: $32K
Total Investment: $69K
Fees: Franchise - $19K
Royalty: 6%, Advert: 0%
Contract Periods (Yrs.): 10/5
Area Development Agreement: Yes/2
Sub-Franchise Contract: . . . . . Yes
Expand in Territory: . . . . . . Yes
Passive Ownership: . . . Discouraged
Encourage Conversions: . . . . . Yes
Franchisee Purchase(s) Required: Yes

FRANCHISOR TRAINING/SUPPORT:
Financial Assistance Provided: . . . . .No
Site Selection Assistance: . . . . . . .Yes
Lease Negotiation Assistance: . . . . .Yes
Co-operative Advertising: . . . . . . .Yes
Training: . . . . 1 Wk. Carabeans,
. . . . 1 Wk. Quebec
On-Going Support: . . . A,B,C,D,E,F,G,H
Full-Time Franchisor Support Staff: . . . 2
EXPANSION PLANS:
US: . . . . .All US
Canada - Yes, ...Overseas - No

MONEYSWORTH & BEST QUALITY SHOE REPAIR

80 Galaxy Blvd., # 10
Toronto, ON M9W4Y8 CAN
TEL: (800)387-4807 (800)668-7969-CAN
FAX: (416) 674-8945
Ms. Carole Rowsell, VP Fran. Dev.

Complete shoe repair, while-you-wait, plus full line of MONEYSWORTH and BEST branded shoe care merchandise. Guaranteed customer satisfaction. Locations in major shopping malls. Distinctive turn-of-the-century designed stores, reminiscent of The Good Old Days. Full training at M & B's College; no experience required.

HISTORY: . . . . IFA
Established in 1984; . . 1st Franchised in 1987
Company-Owned Units (As of 12/1/1989): . 20
Franchised Units (12/1/1989): 80
Total Units (12/1/1989): 100
Distribution: US-25;Can-75;Overseas-0
North America: . . . . . 8 States, 7 Provinces
Concentration: . . 35 in ON, 9 in AB, 6 in WA
Registered: . . . . CA,FL,MD,OR,RI,VA,WA
. . . .
Average # of Employees: . . . . 2-3 FT, 1-2 PT
Prior Industry Experience: . . . . Helpful

FINANCIAL:
Cash Investment: $25K
Total Investment: $130-150K
Fees: Franchise - $10K
Royalty: 8%, Advert: 4%
Contract Periods (Yrs.): . . . 10/10
Area Development Agreement: . .No
Sub-Franchise Contract: . . . . .No
Expand in Territory: . . . . . . Yes
Passive Ownership: . . . Not Allowed
Encourage Conversions: . . . . . NA
Franchisee Purchase(s) Required: Yes

FRANCHISOR TRAINING/SUPPORT:
Financial Assistance Provided: . . .Yes(D)
Site Selection Assistance: . . . . . . .Yes
Lease Negotiation Assistance: . . . . .Yes
Co-operative Advertising: . . . . . . .Yes
Training: . . . . . . 5 Wks. M & B College
. . . .
On-Going Support: . . A,B,C,D,E,F,G,H,I
Full-Time Franchisor Support Staff: . . 35
EXPANSION PLANS:
US: . . . . NW, SW, NE AND SE
Canada - Yes, . . . Overseas - UK

PAPER FIRST

517 N. Polk St.
Pineville, NC 28134
TEL: (704) 889-5965
FAX: (704) 889-5965
Mr. Mel Frank, President

Wholesale and retail distribution and sale of paper products, janitorial supplies, catering and party supplies and related items to business and walk-in customers from a store-front, warehouse-type location.

HISTORY: . . . .
Established in 1982; . . 1st Franchised in 1988
Company-Owned Units (As of 12/1/1989): . .4
Franchised Units (12/1/1989): 6
Total Units (12/1/1989): 10
Distribution: US-10;Can-0;Overseas-0
North America: . . . . 3 States
Concentration: . . . 6 in NC, 3 in VA, 1 in SC
Registered: . . . . FL,MD,VA
. . . .
Average # of Employees: . . . . . . 3 FT, 3 PT
Prior Industry Experience: . . . . Helpful

FINANCIAL:
Cash Investment: $66-95K
Total Investment: $75-100K
Fees: Franchise - $10K
Royalty: 2.5-.5%, Advert: . . .5%
Contract Periods (Yrs.): 20/20
Area Development Agreement: . .No
Sub-Franchise Contract: . . . . .No
Expand in Territory: . . . . . . Yes
Passive Ownership: . . . Not Allowed
Encourage Conversions: . . . . . Yes
Franchisee Purchase(s) Required: .No

FRANCHISOR TRAINING/SUPPORT:
Financial Assistance Provided: . . . Yes(I)
Site Selection Assistance: . . . . . . .Yes
Lease Negotiation Assistance: . . . .Yes
Co-operative Advertising: . . . . . . .Yes
Training: . . . . . . Total 140 Hrs. at 3 NC
. . . Locations, 80 Hrs. Franchisee Site
On-Going Support: . . . . .B,C,D,E,F,G,H,I
Full-Time Franchisor Support Staff: . . . 3
EXPANSION PLANS:
US: . . . . . .SE, Midwest, South Central
Canada - Yes, ...Overseas - No

SHOE FIXERS

1884 Breton Rd. SE, # 201
Grand Rapids, MI 49506
TEL: (800) 333-5874 (616) 453-4754
FAX:
Mr. Sal Pirrotta, President

The franchised business offers instant shoe repair services, together with the sale of shoe care products and key duplication services. Franchisee will benefit from centralized purchasing of all supply items and on-going technical support from experienced personnel.

HISTORY: . . . . IFA
Established in 1987; . . 1st Franchised in 1987
Company-Owned Units (As of 12/1/1989): . .0
Franchised Units (12/1/1989): 37
Total Units (12/1/1989): 37
Distribution: US-37;Can-0;Overseas-0
  North America: . . . . 13 States
  Concentration: . . . 10 in MI, 4 in IA, 3 in VA
Registered: . . . . . .CA,IL,IN,MI,MN,RI,VA
. . . .
Average # of Employees: . . . . . . 1 FT, 1 PT
Prior Industry Experience: . . . . Helpful

FINANCIAL:
Cash Investment: $25-35K
Total Investment: $53-120K
Fees: Franchise - $15-20K
  Royalty: 5%, Advert: 2%
Contract Periods (Yrs.): . . . 10/10
Area Development Agreement: Yes/5
Sub-Franchise Contract: . . . . . .No
Expand in Territory: . . . . . . Yes
Passive Ownership: . . . . . .Allowed
Encourage Conversions: . . . . . Yes
Franchisee Purchase(s) Required: Yes

FRANCHISOR TRAINING/SUPPORT:
Financial Assistance Provided: . . . Yes(I)
Site Selection Assistance: . . . . . . .Yes
Lease Negotiation Assistance: . . . .Yes
Co-operative Advertising: . . . . . . .Yes
Training: . . . . . . 14 Days Headquarters,
. . . . .5 Days On-site
On-Going Support: . . . . B,C,d,E,F,G,H,I
Full-Time Franchisor Support Staff: . . .7
EXPANSION PLANS:
US: . . . . All US
Canada - Yes, . . . Overseas - Yes

STEDMANS

7622 Keele St.
Concord, ON L4K2R5 CAN
TEL: (416) 669-1810
FAX: (416) 669-9822
Mr. Ivan Steele, Fran. Dir.

Junior general merchandise retailers, serving small towns in Canada.

HISTORY: . . . . .CFA
Established in 1907; . . 1st Franchised in 1949
Company-Owned Units (As of 12/1/1989): . .9
Franchised Units (12/1/1989): 234
Total Units (12/1/1989): 243
Distribution: . . . US-0;Can-243;Overseas-0
  North America: . . . . 10 Provinces
  Concentration: . 126 in ON, 28 in NS,26 in AB
Registered: . . . . AB
. . . .
Average # of Employees: . . . . . . 1 FT, 2 PT
Prior Industry Experience: . . . . Helpful

FINANCIAL:
Cash Investment: $40-70K
Total Investment: $120-221K
Fees: Franchise - $0
  Royalty: 0%, Advert: 0%
Contract Periods (Yrs.): 3/3
Area Development Agreement: . .No
Sub-Franchise Contract: . . . . . .No
Expand in Territory: . . . . . . Yes
Passive Ownership: . . . Discouraged
Encourage Conversions: . . . . . Yes
Franchisee Purchase(s) Required: .No

FRANCHISOR TRAINING/SUPPORT:
Financial Assistance Provided: . . .Yes(D)
Site Selection Assistance: . . . . . . .Yes
Lease Negotiation Assistance: . . . .Yes
Co-operative Advertising: . . . . . . .Yes
Training: . . . . .2-3 Wks. Field
. . . .
On-Going Support: . . . . B,C,D,E,F,G,H
Full-Time Franchisor Support Staff: . .210
EXPANSION PLANS:
US: . . . . No
Canada - Yes, ...Overseas - No

TOOL SHACK

5236 Colony Dr.
Agoura, CA 91301
TEL: (818) 991-0755
FAX:
Mr. Ross Manarchy, VP New Fran. Dev.

Sales of name-brand tools to the professional trades. Specialized advertising attracts builders, contractors, auto repair, plumbers, electricians, etc.

HISTORY: . . . .
Established in 1978; . . 1st Franchised in 1981
Company-Owned Units (As of 12/1/1989): . .1
Franchised Units (12/1/1989): 30
Total Units (12/1/1989): 31
Distribution: US-31;Can-0;Overseas-0
  North America: . . . . 10 States
  Concentration: . . . 25 in CA, 3 in AZ, 2 in FL
Registered: . . . . .CA,FL,MD,VA
. . . .
Average # of Employees: . . . . .3 FT
Prior Industry Experience: . . . . Helpful

FINANCIAL:
Cash Investment: $100K
Total Investment: $125K
Fees: Franchise - $24.5K
  Royalty: 3%, Advert: 3%
Contract Periods (Yrs.): . . . 10/10
Area Development Agreement: Yes/10
Sub-Franchise Contract: . . . . . Yes
Expand in Territory: . . . . . . Yes
Passive Ownership: . . . Discouraged
Encourage Conversions: . . . . . .No
Franchisee Purchase(s) Required: .No

FRANCHISOR TRAINING/SUPPORT:
Financial Assistance Provided: . . . Yes(I)
Site Selection Assistance: . . . . . . .Yes
Lease Negotiation Assistance: . . . .Yes
Co-operative Advertising: . . . . . . .Yes
Training: . . . . . 15 Days Company Store,
. . . . .15 Days HQ Man in Store
On-Going Support: . . . .B,C,D,E,F,G,H,I
Full-Time Franchisor Support Staff: . . .6
EXPANSION PLANS:
US: . . . . . . Southwest and Southeast
Canada - No, ... Overseas - No

SUPPLEMENTAL LISTING OF FRANCHISORS

COMPUTERIZED COBBLER	4911-B Clairemont Dr., San Diego CA 92117	
CONSUMER DISTRIBUTING	62 Belfield Rd., Rexdale ON M9W1G2	CAN
HERBRAND TOOLS CORPORATION	340 Dufferin St., Toronto ON M6K1Z9	CAN
M.M.O.S.	20 Champlain Blvd., Downsview ON M3H2Z1	CAN
MARINE MAIL ORDER SUPPLY	20 Champlain Blvd., Downsview ON M3H2Z1	CAN
SHINES 'N MORE	94 Country Place, Cordova TN 38018	
SHOE STOP INSTANT SHOE REPAIR	13625 NE 126th Pl., Kirkland WA 98013	
SHOESMITH, THE	15 Engle St., # 304, Englewood NJ 07631	
US FACTORY OUTLETS	Box 1001, Kendall Park NJ 08824	

CHAPTER 47

SECURITY AND SAFETY SYSTEMS

ALLIANCE SECURITY SYSTEMS

5 - 140 McGovern Dr.
Cambridge, ON N3H4R7 CAN
TEL: (519) 650-5353
FAX: (519) 650-1704
Mr. Brien Welwood, Mktg. Dir.

Security alarm dealership. Complete with training, products and support services.

HISTORY: . . . .
Established in 1969;   . . 1st Franchised in 1971
Company-Owned Units (As of 12/1/1989):   . .1
Franchised Units (12/1/1989):   77
Total Units (12/1/1989):   78
Distribution: US-0;Can-78;Overseas-0
  North America: . . . . 4 Provinces
  Concentration: . . .66 in ON, 4 in NF, 3 in AB
Registered: . . . . AB
. . . .
Average # of Employees: . . . . . 2 FT, 1-2 PT
Prior Industry Experience: . . . . Helpful

FINANCIAL:
Cash Investment: . . . .$
Total Investment: $10K
Fees: Franchise - $10K
  Royalty: 1.2/Yr., Advert: 0%
Contract Periods (Yrs.): 3/1
Area Development Agreement: . .No
Sub-Franchise Contract: . . . . .No
Expand in Territory: . . . . Yes
Passive Ownership: . . . Not Allowed
Encourage Conversions: . . . . . Yes
Franchisee Purchase(s) Required: Yes

FRANCHISOR TRAINING/SUPPORT:
Financial Assistance Provided: . . . Yes(I)
Site Selection Assistance: . . . . .NA
Lease Negotiation Assistance: . . . . .NA
Co-operative Advertising: . . . . .No
Training: . . . . .5 Days HQ
. . . .
On-Going Support: . . . . . . B,D,F,G,H,I
Full-Time Franchisor Support Staff: . . .7
EXPANSION PLANS:
  US: . . . . No
  Canada - Yes, ... Overseas - No

DICTOGRAPH SECURITY SYSTEMS

21 Northfield Ave.
Edison, NJ 08818
TEL: (800) 526-0672 (201) 225-4433
FAX:
Mr. Myles Goldberg, Sr. VP

Residential specialists - over 1 million installations nationwide. Company name established in 1902 - recently joined forces with Holmes Group, which has been in business since 1858. Proven training and marketing skills.

HISTORY:	FINANCIAL: London	FRANCHISOR TRAINING/SUPPORT:
Established in 1902; . . 1st Franchised in 1948	Cash Investment: $50K	Financial Assistance Provided: . . . . . No
Company-Owned Units (As of 12/1/1989): . .3	Total Investment: $100K	Site Selection Assistance: . . . . Yes
Franchised Units (12/1/1989): 53	Fees: Franchise - $7.5-25K	Lease Negotiation Assistance: . . . . No
Total Units (12/1/1989): 56	Royalty: 6%, Advert: 0%	Co-operative Advertising: . . . . . . .Yes
Distribution: US-53;Can-0;Overseas-3	Contract Periods (Yrs.): 5/5	Training: . . . . . . 10 Days Headquarters,
North America: . . . . 3 States	Area Development Agreement: . .No	. . . . On-going in Territory
Concentration: . . . . Eastern Region	Sub-Franchise Contract: . . . . .No	On-Going Support: . . . . .B,C,D,F,G,H,I
Registered: . . . . Several in Registration	Expand in Territory: . . . . Yes	Full-Time Franchisor Support Staff: . . 16
. . . . Process	Passive Ownership: . . . Discouraged	EXPANSION PLANS:
Average # of Employees: . . . . Varies	Encourage Conversions: . . . . . Yes	US: . . . . .All US
Prior Industry Experience: . . . . . . Helpful	Franchisee Purchase(s) Required: Yes	Canada - No, ...Overseas - No

FIRE DEFENSE CENTERS

3919 Morton St.
Jacksonville, FL 32217
TEL: (904) 731-0244 C
FAX:
Mr. I.A. LaRusso, Mktg. Dir.

Sales and service of fire extinguishers, automatic restaurant hood systems, municipal supplies and first aid kits. Everything we sell, we service.

HISTORY:	FINANCIAL:	FRANCHISOR TRAINING/SUPPORT:
Established in 1973; . . 1st Franchised in 1986	Cash Investment: $22-29K	Financial Assistance Provided: . . . . .Yes
Company-Owned Units (As of 12/1/1989): . .2	Total Investment: $22-29K	Site Selection Assistance: . . . . Yes
Franchised Units (12/1/1989): 18	Fees: Franchise - $13.5K	Lease Negotiation Assistance: . . . . Yes
Total Units (12/1/1989): 20	Royalty: 7%, Advert: 2%	Co-operative Advertising: . . . . . . .Yes
Distribution: US-20;Can-0;Overseas-0	Contract Periods (Yrs.): 10/5	Training: . . . . . . 2 Wks. Headquarters
North America: . . . . .1 State	Area Development Agreement: . .No	. . . .
Concentration: . . . . .20 in FL	Sub-Franchise Contract: . . . . .No	On-Going Support: . . A,B,C,D,E,F,G,H,I
Registered: . . . . IL,FL,NY	Expand in Territory: . . . . Yes	Full-Time Franchisor Support Staff: . . 12
. . . .	Passive Ownership: . . . Not Allowed	EXPANSION PLANS:
Average # of Employees: . . . . .2 FT	Encourage Conversions: . . . . . .No	US: . . . . .All US
Prior Industry Experience: . . . . . . Helpful	Franchisee Purchase(s) Required: .No	Canada - Yes, . . . Overseas - Yes

HOMEWATCH

2865 S. Colorado Blvd.
Denver, CO 80222
TEL: (800) 777-9770 (303) 758-7290
FAX: (303) 692-9524
Mr. Paul Sauer, President

HOMEWATCH SERVICES - since 1973. In-home services are a "ballooning" business. Start your cash business part-time from your home. Offers good returns, with a diversity of affordable, repeatable services. Services for pets, homes and the elderly. Minimum cash outlay, fun and easy to operate and has public demand. Training and support provided for profitability.

HISTORY:	FINANCIAL:	FRANCHISOR TRAINING/SUPPORT:
Established in 1973; . . 1st Franchised in 1984	Cash Investment: $10-15K	Financial Assistance Provided: . . . . . No
Company-Owned Units (As of 12/1/1989): . .5	Total Investment: $12-16K	Site Selection Assistance: . . . . No
Franchised Units (12/1/1989): 23	Fees: Franchise - $6K	Lease Negotiation Assistance: . . . . . No
Total Units (12/1/1989): 28	Royalty: 0%, Advert: 0%	Co-operative Advertising: . . . . . . .NA
Distribution: US-27;Can-1;Overseas-0	Contract Periods (Yrs.): 10/5	Training: . . . . 5 Days Headquarters
North America: . . . . . .9 States, 1 Province	Area Development Agreement: Yes/3	. . . .
Concentration: . . . 4 in CO, 3 in AZ, 2 in OH	Sub-Franchise Contract: . . . . .No	On-Going Support: . . . . A,c,g,h,i
Registered: . . . . CA,FL,MN	Expand in Territory: . . . . Yes	Full-Time Franchisor Support Staff: . . . 4
. . . .	Passive Ownership: . . . Discouraged	EXPANSION PLANS:
Average # of Employees: . . . . .2-3 FT	Encourage Conversions: . . . . . Yes	US: . . . . .All US
Prior Industry Experience: . . . . . . Helpful	Franchisee Purchase(s) Required: .No	Canada - Yes, ...Overseas - No

MY ALARM SECURITY RENTAL CENTER

3701 Hwy. 151 East
Marion, IA 52302
TEL: (800) 835-5378 (319) 377-6343
FAX: (319) 377-3327
Mr. William Ginalski, VP Fran. Dev.

Company provides residential alarm security. Company designs, manufactures, markets and monitors proprietary intrusion, fire and environmental security systems. Operates professional Command Center, providing 24-hour, 2-way audio monitoring of installed systems. The MY ALARM system is reliable, easy to install, affordable and uniquely packaged as a modern, conventional telephone.

HISTORY: . . . . IFA
Established in 1988; . . 1st Franchised in 1989
Company-Owned Units (As of 12/1/1989): . . 3
Franchised Units (12/1/1989): 5
Total Units (12/1/1989): 8
Distribution: US-8;Can-0;Overseas-0
North America: . . . . 7 States
Concentration: . . . . 2 in OH
Registered: . . .CA,FL,IL,MD,MI,MN,NY,OR
. . . . RI
Average # of Employees: . . . . . . 4 FT, 1 PT
Prior Industry Experience: . . . . Helpful

FINANCIAL:
Cash Investment: . . . . $20K+
Total Investment: . . . . $75K+
Fees: Franchise - . . . . $Min. 18.5K
Royalty: 6%, Advert: 1%
Contract Periods (Yrs.): 5/5
Area Development Agreement: Yes/5
Sub-Franchise Contract: . . . . . .No
Expand in Territory: . . . . Yes
Passive Ownership: . . . Discouraged
Encourage Conversions: . . . . . .No
Franchisee Purchase(s) Required: Yes

FRANCHISOR TRAINING/SUPPORT:
Financial Assistance Provided: . . . . .No
Site Selection Assistance: . . . . . . .Yes
Lease Negotiation Assistance: . . . . .No
Co-operative Advertising: . . . . .Yes
Training: . . . . .1 Wk. Headquarters,
. . 1 Wk. Franchisee Location, On-going
On-Going Support: . . . . . .C,D,E,G,H,I
Full-Time Franchisor Support Staff: . . 25
EXPANSION PLANS:
US: . . . . .Central and East
Canada - No, ...Overseas - No

PROFILES - Personal Security Assessments

P. O. Box 880461
San Diego, CA 92108
TEL: (619) 280-3486
FAX:
Mr. Phil Sprague, President

Assess an applicant's or employee's past and their potential capabilities - attitudes, security risk, alcohol/drug abuse, psychological adjustment, voice analysis for theft detection. From laborers to executives. Asset or Liability? Employers need to know. Make money by providing these valuable answers!

HISTORY: . . . .
Established in 1980; . . 1st Franchised in 1982
Company-Owned Units (As of 12/1/1989): . .1
Franchised Units (12/1/1989): 6
Total Units (12/1/1989): 7
Distribution: US-7;Can-0;Overseas-0
North America: . . . . 3 States
Concentration: . . . .4 in CA, 1 in AZ, 1 in NJ
Registered: . . . . CA
. . . .
Average # of Employees: . . . . . . 1 FT, 2 PT
Prior Industry Experience: . . . . Helpful

FINANCIAL:
Cash Investment: $2-15K
Total Investment: $6-18K
Fees: Franchise - . . . .$NA
Royalty: 5%, Advert: 0%
Contract Periods (Yrs.): 5/5
Area Development Agreement: Yes/5
Sub-Franchise Contract: . . . . . .No
Expand in Territory: . . . . Yes
Passive Ownership: . . . Discouraged
Encourage Conversions: . . . . . .No
Franchisee Purchase(s) Required: Yes

FRANCHISOR TRAINING/SUPPORT:
Financial Assistance Provided: . . . . .NA
Site Selection Assistance: . . . . . . .NA
Lease Negotiation Assistance: . . . . .NA
Co-operative Advertising: . . . . .NA
Training: . . . . 7 Days Headquarters
. . . .
On-Going Support: . . . . .D,G,I
Full-Time Franchisor Support Staff: . . . 2
EXPANSION PLANS:
US: . . . . .All US
Canada - Yes, ...Overseas - No

SLAYMAKER SECURITY STORE

419 12th St.
Huntington, WV 25701
TEL: (304) 525-3537
FAX: (304) 523-4830
Mr. Robert Wickline, CEO

Innovative new retail security store that offers a selection of over 600 security and safety products conveniently assembled under one roof. Included are home security systems, smoke detectors, personal safety products, auto safety kits, safes, phone scramblers, first-aid kits and many other items.

HISTORY: . . . . IFA
Established in 1986; . . 1st Franchised in 1988
Company-Owned Units (As of 12/1/1989): . .1
Franchised Units (12/1/1989): 5
Total Units (12/1/1989): 6
Distribution: US-6;Can-0;Overseas-0
North America: . . . . 5 States
Concentration: . . . 2 in WV, 1 in FL, 1 in PA
Registered: . . . . FL,IL
. . . .
Average # of Employees: . . . . . . 3 FT, 2 PT
Prior Industry Experience: . . . . Helpful

FINANCIAL:
Cash Investment: . . . . $Varies
Total Investment: $111-232K
Fees: Franchise - $20K
Royalty: 5%, Advert: 5%
Contract Periods (Yrs.): 10/5/5
Area Development Agreement: Yes/5
Sub-Franchise Contract: . . . . . .No
Expand in Territory: . . . . Yes
Passive Ownership: . . . Discouraged
Encourage Conversions: . . . . . Yes
Franchisee Purchase(s) Required: .No

FRANCHISOR TRAINING/SUPPORT:
Financial Assistance Provided: . . . . .No
Site Selection Assistance: . . . . . . .Yes
Lease Negotiation Assistance: . . . . .Yes
Co-operative Advertising: . . . . .Yes
Training: . . . . .1 Wk. Headquarters,
. . . . 1 Wk. On-site
On-Going Support: . . . A,B,C,D,E,F,G,h
Full-Time Franchisor Support Staff: . . 10
EXPANSION PLANS:
US: . . . . .All US
Canada - Yes, ...Overseas - No

SONITROL

424 N. Washington St.
Alexandria, VA 22314
TEL: (703) 549-3900
FAX: (703) 549-2053
Mr. William G. Bell, Mkt. Dev. Mgr.

Franchised dealer is granted an area of primary responsibility where he is responsible for sales, installation, monitoring and service of SONITROL security systems for business and residential customers.

HISTORY: . . . .
Established in 1960; . . 1st Franchised in 1965
Company-Owned Units (As of 12/1/1989): . 17
Franchised Units (12/1/1989): 158
Total Units (12/1/1989): 175
Distribution: US-170;Can-3;Overseas-2
North America: . . . . . 38 States, 1 Province
Concentration: . . 22 in CA, 13 in FL, 12 in IN
Registered: . . . . . .All States Exc. ND & SD
. . . .
Average # of Employees: . . . . 15 FT
Prior Industry Experience: . . . . . . Helpful

FINANCIAL:
Cash Investment: $70-500K
Total Investment: $200-900K
Fees: Franchise - $20-50K
Royalty: 2.5%, Advert: . . . .
Contract Periods (Yrs.): 10/10
Area Development Agreement: . .No
Sub-Franchise Contract: . . . . . .No
Expand in Territory: . . . . Yes
Passive Ownership: . . . Discouraged
Encourage Conversions: . . . . . Yes
Franchisee Purchase(s) Required: Yes

FRANCHISOR TRAINING/SUPPORT:
Financial Assistance Provided: . . . Yes(I)
Site Selection Assistance: . . . . . . .Yes
Lease Negotiation Assistance: . . . . . No
Co-operative Advertising: . . . . No
Training: . . . . 2 Wks. Headquarters,
. . . . 1 Wk. On-site
On-Going Support: . . . . .B,C,D,E,G,H,I
Full-Time Franchisor Support Staff: . . . .
EXPANSION PLANS:
US: . . . . .All US
Canada - Yes, . . . Overseas - Yes

SPY HEADQUARTERS

1235 E. Northern
Phoenix, AZ 85020
TEL: (602) 263-1225
FAX:
Mr. Kenneth Hollowell, Mktg. Dir.

THE SPY HEADQUARTERS outlet is a business establishment which offers, on a retail basis, various items for personal security, protection, surveillance and counter-surveillance.

HISTORY: . . . .
Established in 1988; . . 1st Franchised in 1988
Company-Owned Units (As of 12/1/1989): . .1
Franchised Units (12/1/1989): 1
Total Units (12/1/1989): 2
Distribution: US-2;Can-0;Overseas-0
North America: . . . . 2 States
Concentration: . . . . 1 in AZ, 1 in OH
Registered: . . . .
. . . .
Average # of Employees: . . . . . 2 FT, 1 PT
Prior Industry Experience: . . . . . . Helpful

FINANCIAL:
Cash Investment: $10-20K
Total Investment: $158-215K
Fees: Franchise - $15K
Royalty: 5%, Advert: 2%
Contract Periods (Yrs.): 10/10
Area Development Agreement: . .No
Sub-Franchise Contract: . . . . . .No
Expand in Territory: . . . . Yes
Passive Ownership: . . . Not Allowed
Encourage Conversions: . . . . . .No
Franchisee Purchase(s) Required: Yes

FRANCHISOR TRAINING/SUPPORT:
Financial Assistance Provided: . . . . .No
Site Selection Assistance: . . . . . . .Yes
Lease Negotiation Assistance: . . . . .Yes
Co-operative Advertising: . . . . . . .Yes
Training: . . . . 5 Days Headquarters
. . . .
On-Going Support: . . . . C,D,E,G,h,I
Full-Time Franchisor Support Staff: . . . 5
EXPANSION PLANS:
US: . . . . Southwest
Canada - Yes, ... Overseas - No

SUPPLEMENTAL LISTING OF FRANCHISORS

ALARM DATA ASSOCIATES . . . . 8716 Production Ave., San Diego CA 92121
ALARMEFORCE INDUSTRIES . . . . 1370 Don Mills Rd., # 205, Don Mills ON M3B3N7 CAN
CHAMBERS SECURITY SYSTEMS . . . . .1103 Fredericksburg Rd., San Antonio TX 78201
DYNAMARK SECURITY CENTERS . . . . P.O. Box 2068, Hagerstown MD 21742
EMPLOYMENT SCREENING SYSTEMS . . . . 2340 Industrial Blvd., Norman OK 73069
FIRST RESPONSE HOME SECURITY SYSTEMS . . . . 20 Amber St., # 4, Markham ON L3R5P4 CAN
IDENT-A-KID OF CANADA . . . . 150 Clark Blvd., # 238, Brampton ON L6T4Y8 CAN
JUST SECURITY . . . . 4480 Treat Blvd., # 224, Concord CA 94521
OUT OF HARM'S WAY . . . . .1530 Eagleview Dr., Pickering ON L1V5H4 CAN
SECURITY TECH/SECURITY TIME . . . . 1025 Gessner, Houston TX 77055
SHURLOCK HOMES SECURITY . . . . .P. O. Box 8034, # 41, London ON N6G3M7 CAN

CHAPTER 48

SIGNS

BANACOM INSTANT SIGNS

One Civic Plaza, # 265
Newport Beach, CA 92660
TEL: (800) 633-5580
FAX:
Mr. Sheldon Fidler, Dir. New Bus.

World's largest network of instant sign centers - full-service stores offering promotional paper signage, vinyl banners and signs produced with the latest computer-driven sign-making equipment - including scanners, lasers, etc. Software developers to sign industry since 1982.

HISTORY: . . . . IFA
Established in 1987; . . 1st Franchised in 1988
Company-Owned Units (As of 12/1/1989): . .0
Franchised Units (12/1/1989): 35
Total Units (12/1/1989): 35
Distribution: US-35;Can-0;Overseas-0
  North America: . . . . 22 States
  Concentration: . . . Primarily NJ, GA and PA
Registered: . . . . All States
. . . .
Average # of Employees: . . . . . . 4 FT, 2 PT
Prior Industry Experience: . . . . Helpful

FINANCIAL:
Cash Investment: $50-60K
Total Investment: $70-90K
Fees: Franchise - $10K
  Royalty: Flat, Advert: 0%
Contract Periods (Yrs.): 10/10
Area Development Agreement: Yes/20
Sub-Franchise Contract: . . . . . .No
Expand in Territory: . . . . .No
Passive Ownership: . . . . . .Allowed
Encourage Conversions: . . . . . Yes
Franchisee Purchase(s) Required: .No

FRANCHISOR TRAINING/SUPPORT:
Financial Assistance Provided: . . . Yes(I)
Site Selection Assistance: . . . . . . .Yes
Lease Negotiation Assistance: . . . . . No
Co-operative Advertising: . . . . No
Training: . . . . 2 Wks. Headquarters
. . . .
On-Going Support: . . . . . . A,B,e,G,H,I
Full-Time Franchisor Support Staff: . . 12
EXPANSION PLANS:
  US: . . . . .All US
  Canada - Yes, ...Overseas - Yes

MR. SIGN

159 Keyland Ct.
Bohemia, NY 11716
TEL: (800) 222-7075 (516) 567-3132 C
FAX: (516) 567-3356
Mr. Harold Kestenbaum, President

MR. SIGN offers a unique concept in signmaking. Computerized vinyl signmaking services for the business and residential community. We provide substantial on-going technical support, 3-week training program and proprietary, copyrighted software programs.

HISTORY: . . . . IFA	FINANCIAL: NASD-FICO	FRANCHISOR TRAINING/SUPPORT:
Established in 1984; . . 1st Franchised in 1985	Cash Investment: $50-65K	Financial Assistance Provided: . . . Yes(I)
Company-Owned Units (As of 12/1/1989): . . .0	Total Investment: $80-110K	Site Selection Assistance: . . . . . . .Yes
Franchised Units (12/1/1989): 93	Fees: Franchise - $25K	Lease Negotiation Assistance: . . . .Yes
Total Units (12/1/1989): 93	Royalty: 5%, Advert: 2%	Co-operative Advertising: . . . . No
Distribution: US-93;Can-0;Overseas-0	Contract Periods (Yrs.): 20/5	Training: . . . . 3 Wks. Headquarters
North America: . . . . 20 States	Area Development Agreement: Yes/20	. . . .
Concentration: . . 18 in NY, 11 in NJ, 7 in MA	Sub-Franchise Contract: . . . . Yes	On-Going Support: . . . . .B,C,D,E,G,H,I
Registered: . . . CA,FL,IL,IN,MD,MI,MN,NY	Expand in Territory: . . . . . . Yes	Full-Time Franchisor Support Staff: . . 15
. . . . OR,RI,VA,WI	Passive Ownership: . . . . . .Allowed	EXPANSION PLANS:
Average # of Employees: . . . . . . 2 FT, 1 PT	Encourage Conversions: . . . . .No	US: . . . . .All US
Prior Industry Experience: . . . . Helpful	Franchisee Purchase(s) Required: Yes	Canada - Yes, ...Overseas - No

OUTDOOR FUN SIGNS

138 River Corner Rd.
Conestoga, PA 17516
TEL: (717) 872-6916
FAX:
Ms. Dianne Shiffer, Owner

OUTDOOR FUN SIGNS is a unique, all-occasion lawn sign rental opportunity. Hand-crafted and designed for maximum visibility and designed as a total package, including all supplies needed to start business. Also, the largest selection of signs available in the US.

HISTORY:	FINANCIAL:	FRANCHISOR TRAINING/SUPPORT:
Established in 1986; . . 1st Franchised in 1989	Cash Investment: $15K	Financial Assistance Provided: . . . . .No
Company-Owned Units (As of 12/1/1989): . .1	Total Investment: $15K	Site Selection Assistance: . . . . .NA
Franchised Units (12/1/1989): 0	Fees: Franchise - $15K	Lease Negotiation Assistance: . . . .NA
Total Units (12/1/1989): 1	Royalty: $500, Advert: 0%	Co-operative Advertising: . . . . .No
Distribution: US-1;Can-0;Overseas-0	Contract Periods (Yrs.): 5/5/5	Training: . . . . . . Over Phone and Mail
North America: . . . . 1 State, 1 in PA	Area Development Agreement: .No	. . . .
Concentration:	Sub-Franchise Contract: . . . . .No	On-Going Support: . . . . .G
Registered:	Expand in Territory: . . . . . . Yes	Full-Time Franchisor Support Staff: . . . 1
. . . .	Passive Ownership: . . . Discouraged	EXPANSION PLANS:
Average # of Employees: . . . . .1 FT	Encourage Conversions: . . . . NA	US: . . . . .All US
Prior Industry Experience: . . . . . . Helpful	Franchisee Purchase(s) Required: Yes	Canada - Yes, ...Overseas - No

SIGN EXPRESS

6 Clarke Circle, P.O. Box 309
Bethel, CT 06801
TEL: (800) 525-7446 (203) 791-0004
FAX: (203) 743-7028
Mr. Gary A. Gass, VP Fran. Devel.

SIGN EXPRESS is a multi-service, computerized signmaking and graphics business. Customers include corporations, retail stores, real estate, professionals, etc. It is not labor intensive, does not require expensive retail space and it's creative work with graphics and design. SIGN EXPRESS does not require prior experience and is ideal for women, men and families.

HISTORY: . . . . IFA	FINANCIAL:	FRANCHISOR TRAINING/SUPPORT:
Established in 1986; . . 1st Franchised in 1988	Cash Investment: $30-52K	Financial Assistance Provided: . . . Yes(I)
Company-Owned Units (As of 12/1/1989): . .0	Total Investment: $30-52K	Site Selection Assistance: . . . . . . .Yes
Franchised Units (12/1/1989): 17	Fees: Franchise - $20K	Lease Negotiation Assistance: . . . .Yes
Total Units (12/1/1989): 17	Royalty: 5%, Advert: 0%	Co-operative Advertising: . . . . .No
Distribution: US-17;Can-0;Overseas-0	Contract Periods (Yrs.): 10/10	Training: . . . . 6 Days Headquarters,
North America: . . . . 8 States	Area Development Agreement: Yes/Var	. . . . .5 Days On-site
Concentration: . . . 4 in CT, 3 in NY, 3 in MA	Sub-Franchise Contract: . . . . .No	On-Going Support: . . A,B,C,D,E,F,G,H,I
Registered: . . . CA,FL,IL,IN,MD,MI,NY,OR	Expand in Territory: . . . . . . Yes	Full-Time Franchisor Support Staff: . . 10
. . . . RI,VA,WA,WI	Passive Ownership: . . . Discouraged	EXPANSION PLANS:
Average # of Employees: . . . . .3 FT	Encourage Conversions: . . . . .No	US: . . . . .All US
Prior Industry Experience: . . . . . . Helpful	Franchisee Purchase(s) Required: .No	Canada - Yes, . . . Overseas - Yes

SIGN STOP

256 Post Rd. E.
Westport, CT 06880
TEL: (800) 822-5945 (203) 454-1313 C
FAX: (203) 454-8792
Mr. John Oudheusden, President

Strong customer demand and new technology creates the opportunity to market high-quality custom signs to small businesses. Operating from a store location and using computer-generated vinyl lettering, SIGN STOP fabricates custom signs, trade exhibits, graphs and charts, backlit awnings and lettering for vans, trucks and boats.

HISTORY: . . . . IFA
Established in 1985; . . 1st Franchised in 1986
Company-Owned Units (As of 12/1/1989): . .1
Franchised Units (12/1/1989): 16
Total Units (12/1/1989): 17
Distribution: US-17;Can-0;Overseas-0
North America: . . . . 5 States
Concentration: . . . 6 in MA, 5 in CT, 3 in NJ
Registered: . . . . FL,MD,NY,RI,VA
. . . .
Average # of Employees: . . . . Varies
Prior Industry Experience: . . . . . . Helpful

FINANCIAL:
Cash Investment: $37.3-73.2K
Total Investment: $59.3-95.2K
Fees: Franchise - $17.5K
 Royalty: 5%, Advert: 1%
Contract Periods (Yrs.): 15/5
Area Development Agreement: Yes/Var
Sub-Franchise Contract: . . . . .No
Expand in Territory: . . . . . . Yes
Passive Ownership: . . . . . .Allowed
Encourage Conversions: . . . . NA
Franchisee Purchase(s) Required: .No

FRANCHISOR TRAINING/SUPPORT:
Financial Assistance Provided: . . . Yes(I)
Site Selection Assistance: . . . . . . .Yes
Lease Negotiation Assistance: . . . . .Yes
Co-operative Advertising: . . . . . . .Yes
Training: . . . . . . 7+ Days Headquarters,
. . . . .2+ Days On-site
On-Going Support: . . . . .B,C,D,E,G,H,I
Full-Time Franchisor Support Staff: . . . 9
EXPANSION PLANS:
US: . . . . .All US
Canada - Yes, . . . Overseas - Yes

SIGNERY, THE

614 W. 5th Ave.
Naperville, IL 60563
TEL: (708) 357-2252 C
FAX:
Mr. James C. Gurke, VP

THE SIGNERY shops are fully-formatted, computerized businesses serving primarily business customers of all sizes. THE SIGNERY specializes in wide variety, high quality and prompt service and delivery of its products. We offer extenive training and support services to our franchisees.

HISTORY: . . . . IFA
Established in 1986; . . 1st Franchised in 1986
Company-Owned Units (As of 12/1/1989): . .1
Franchised Units (12/1/1989): 24
Total Units (12/1/1989): 25
Distribution: US-25;Can-0;Overseas-0
North America: . . . . 5 States
Concentration: . . . .21 in IL, 1 in WI, 1 in IA
Registered: . . . CA,FL,IL,IN,MI,MN,OR,VA
. . . . .WI
Average # of Employees: . . . . . . 3 FT, 1 PT
Prior Industry Experience: . . . . . . Helpful

FINANCIAL:
Cash Investment: $40-50K
Total Investment: $75-85K
Fees: Franchise - $18.9K
 Royalty: 6%, Advert: 2%
Contract Periods (Yrs.): . . . 20/20
Area Development Agreement: Yes/Var
Sub-Franchise Contract: . . . . . Yes
Expand in Territory: . . . . . . Yes
Passive Ownership: . . . Discouraged
Encourage Conversions: . . . . Yes
Franchisee Purchase(s) Required: .No

FRANCHISOR TRAINING/SUPPORT:
Financial Assistance Provided: . . . Yes(I)
Site Selection Assistance: . . . . . . .Yes
Lease Negotiation Assistance: . . . .Yes
Co-operative Advertising: . . . . No
Training: . . . . 3 Wks. Headquarters,
. . . . .1 Wk. Franchisee Location
On-Going Support: . . . . . . C,D,E,G,H,I
Full-Time Franchisor Support Staff: . . 12
EXPANSION PLANS:
US: . . . . .All US
Canada - Yes, . . . Overseas - Yes

SIGNS NOW

660 Azalea Rd., # 121-B
Mobile, AL 36609
TEL: (800) 356-3373 (205) 660-0895
FAX: (205) 661-4275
Mr. John Carpenter, Dir. Fran. Sales

Computerized sign shop with 24-hour turn-around; produces vinyl signs and lettering, including banners, real estate signs, vehicle lettering and graphics, building signs, window lettering, etc. Vinyl products guaranteed for 5 years against fading. Classroom and in-store training for franchisee and one key employee, assistance with site location, building, set-up, opening, advertising and complete on-going support.

HISTORY: . . . . IFA
Established in 1986; . . 1st Franchised in 1987
Company-Owned Units (As of 12/1/1989): . .3
Franchised Units (12/1/1989): 50
Total Units (12/1/1989): 53
Distribution: US-53;Can-0;Overseas-0
North America: . . . . 22 States
Concentration: . . . . .FL, CO, OR
Registered: . . . . .All States Except VA
. . . .
Average # of Employees: . . . . .2 FT
Prior Industry Experience: . . . . . . Helpful

FINANCIAL:
Cash Investment: $38.1-87.7K
Total Investment: $38.1-87.7K
Fees: Franchise - $12K
 Royalty: 7%, Advert: 4%
Contract Periods (Yrs.): 5/5/5
Area Development Agreement: Yes/Var
Sub-Franchise Contract: . . . . . Yes
Expand in Territory: . . . . . . Yes
Passive Ownership: . . . Discouraged
Encourage Conversions: . . . . .No
Franchisee Purchase(s) Required: .No

FRANCHISOR TRAINING/SUPPORT:
Financial Assistance Provided: . . . Yes(I)
Site Selection Assistance: . . . . . . .Yes
Lease Negotiation Assistance: . . . .Yes
Co-operative Advertising: . . . . . . .Yes
Training: . . . . 2 Wks. Headquarters,
. . . . .1 Wk. In-Store
On-Going Support: . . . .B,C,D,E,F,G,H,I
Full-Time Franchisor Support Staff: . . 26
EXPANSION PLANS:
US: . . . . .All US
Canada - Yes, ...Overseas - No

SIGNS TO GO

200 Honeysuckle Rd., # I
Dothan, AL 36301
TEL: (205) 793-8223 C
FAX:
Mr. Charles Stephenson, VP

Instant computerized custom sign center. Major difference with SIGNS TO GO is the 15 years of sign industry experience that is taught in training class, giving franchisee in-depth understanding of the sign industry, which allows product and market diversification. Successfully tested marketing program, with national account contacts established.

HISTORY: . . . . IFA
Established in 1988; . . 1st Franchised in 1989
Company-Owned Units (As of 12/1/1989): . .3
Franchised Units (12/1/1989): 2
Total Units (12/1/1989): 5
Distribution: US-5;Can-0;Overseas-0
North America: . . . . 2 States
Concentration: . . . . .4 in AL, 1 in FL
Registered: . . . . .FL
. . . .
Average # of Employees: . . . . . . 3 FT, 2 PT
Prior Industry Experience: . . . . . . Helpful

FINANCIAL:
Cash Investment: $40-50K
Total Investment: $60-100K
Fees: Franchise - $20K
Royalty: 4.5%, Advert: 1.5%
Contract Periods (Yrs.): 10/10
Area Development Agreement: Yes/10
Sub-Franchise Contract: . . . . . .No
Expand in Territory: . . . . Yes
Passive Ownership: . . . . . .Allowed
Encourage Conversions: . . . . . Yes
Franchisee Purchase(s) Required: .No

FRANCHISOR TRAINING/SUPPORT:
Financial Assistance Provided: . . . Yes(I)
Site Selection Assistance: . . . . . . .Yes
Lease Negotiation Assistance: . . . . .Yes
Co-operative Advertising: . . . . .Yes
Training: . . . . 2 Wks. Headquarters,
. .1 Wk. Location, 1 Wk. Grand Opening
On-Going Support: . . . . .C,D,E,F,G,H,I
Full-Time Franchisor Support Staff: . . .5
EXPANSION PLANS:
US: . . . . .All US
Canada - No, ...Overseas - No

SPEEDI-SIGN

P. O. Box 2882, 9 N. Fahm St.
Savannah, GA 31402
TEL: (800) 666-8007 (912) 651-8887
FAX: (912) 651-8007
Ms. Karen Melton, Mktg. Dir.

Full-service, computerized sign shop, serving the vast and growing sign, banner and lettering market. Sells to businesses, institutions, governments, individuals, etc. Modern retail business requiring no previous experience. Vinyl and paper signmaking systems supplemented with a starter kit of materials, tools, manuals and training. Great opportunity for men and women seeking independence and super profit potential.

HISTORY: . . . .
Established in 1987; . . 1st Franchised in 1989
Company-Owned Units (As of 12/1/1989): . .4
Franchised Units (12/1/1989): 5
Total Units (12/1/1989): 9
Distribution: US-8;Can-0;Overseas-1
North America: . . . . 4 States
Concentration: . . . .4 in GA, 2 in FL, 1 in SA
Registered: . . . .
. . . .
Average # of Employees: . . . . .2 FT
Prior Industry Experience: . . . . Helpful

FINANCIAL:
Cash Investment: $29-75K
Total Investment: $29-75K
Fees: Franchise - $13.5K
Royalty: 0%, Advert: 0%
Contract Periods (Yrs.): 10/10
Area Development Agreement: Yes/10
Sub-Franchise Contract: . . . . . .No
Expand in Territory: . . . . .No
Passive Ownership: . . . Discouraged
Encourage Conversions: . . . . . NA
Franchisee Purchase(s) Required: Yes

FRANCHISOR TRAINING/SUPPORT:
Financial Assistance Provided: . . . Yes(I)
Site Selection Assistance: . . . . . . .Yes
Lease Negotiation Assistance: . . . . . No
Co-operative Advertising: . . . . .NA
Training: . . . . .1 Wk. Headquarters,
. . . . 1-5 Days On-site
On-Going Support: . . . . B,C,D,g,h,i
Full-Time Franchisor Support Staff: . . .8
EXPANSION PLANS:
US: . . . . . .All US, Primarily Southeast
Canada - Yes, . . . Overseas - Yes

SPEEDY SIGN A RAMA, U.S.A.

1640 New Highway
Farmingdale, NY 11735
TEL: (800) 645-9840 (516) 420-5627 C
FAX:
Mr. Robert Emmett, VP

A full-service sign business in a retail format that combines 3M technology with available financing, computerized, copyrighted software and machinery and MINUTEMAN PRESS's (Parent) proven marketing program.

HISTORY: . . . .
Established in 1986; . . 1st Franchised in 1987
Company-Owned Units (As of 12/1/1989): . .2
Franchised Units (12/1/1989): 67
Total Units (12/1/1989): 69
Distribution: US-69;Can-0;Overseas-0
North America: . . . . 12 States
Concentration: . . 19 in CA, 15 in NY, 7 in NJ
Registered: . . . CA,FL,IL,MD,MI,MN,NY,RI
. . . . VA,WA,WI
Average # of Employees: . . . . .2 FT
Prior Industry Experience: . . . . Helpful

FINANCIAL:
Cash Investment: $33-47K
Total Investment: $92-107K
Fees: Franchise - $27.5K
Royalty: 6%, Advert: 0%
Contract Periods (Yrs.): 35/35
Area Development Agreement: .No
Sub-Franchise Contract: . . . . .No
Expand in Territory: . . . . Yes
Passive Ownership: . . . Not Allowed
Encourage Conversions: . . . . .No
Franchisee Purchase(s) Required: .No

FRANCHISOR TRAINING/SUPPORT:
Financial Assistance Provided: . . . Yes(I)
Site Selection Assistance: . . . . . . .Yes
Lease Negotiation Assistance: . . . . .Yes
Co-operative Advertising: . . . . .NA
Training: . . . . 2 Wks. Headquarters,
. . . . 40 Hrs. Franchisee Location
On-Going Support: . . . . . . b,C,D,E,h,I
Full-Time Franchisor Support Staff: . . 40
EXPANSION PLANS:
US: . . . . .All US
Canada - No, ... Overseas - No

SUPPLEMENTAL LISTING OF FRANCHISORS

60 MINUTE SIGNS . . . . 35 Alexandra Blvd., Toronto ON M4R1L8   CAN
AMERICAN SIGN SHOPS . . . . 1460-A Diggs Rd., Raleigh NC 27603
ASI SIGN SYSTEMS . . . . 548 W. 28th Street, New York City NY 10001
BUDGET SIGNS . . . . .4109 Brown Trail, # 100, Colleyville TX 76034
FASTSIGNS/AMERICAN FASTSIGNS . . . . 4951 Airport Pkwy., # 530, Dallas TX 75248
KWIK SIGNS . . . . P.O. Box 370, 2211 Meriden-Waterb, Marion CT 06444
NEXT DAY SIGNS . . . . 5442 W. 86th, Indianapolis IN 46268
QUIKSIGNS . . . . .1 First Canadian Pl., # 5900, Toronto ON M5X1K2   CAN
SAME DAY SIGNS . . . . 34 Grenfell Cres., Ottawa ON K2G0G2   CAN
SIGN UP OF AMERICA . . . . 6707 Maynardville Hwy., Tice Pl., Knoxville TN 37918
SIGN WORLD CANADA . . . .#8 - 12342 - 82A Ave., Surrey BC V3W0L6   CAN
SIGNS BY TOMORROW . . . . .10744 Baltimore Ave., Beltsville MD 20705
VINYLGRAPHICS . . . . 1733 Keele St., Toronto ON M6M3W7   CAN

CHAPTER 49

TRAVEL

ALGONQUIN TRAVEL

657 Bronson Ave.
Ottawa, ON K1S4E7 CAN
TEL: (613) 233-7713
FAX:
Mr. Ron Greenwood, VP

We are in the travel agency market development and market domination business. Our travel agencies average sales that are more than double the industry average. We offer full training to new franchisees. Our average commission revenue per transaction is substantially higher than the industry average. Our franchisees are our best supporters.

HISTORY: . . . .
Established in 1964; . . 1st Franchised in 1978
Company-Owned Units (As of 12/1/1989): . .2
Franchised Units (12/1/1989): 53
Total Units (12/1/1989): 55
Distribution: US-0;Can-55;Overseas-0
  North America: . . . . 3 Provinces
  Concentration: . . 50 in ON, 3 in MB, 2 in PQ
Registered: . . . . AB
. . . .
Average # of Employees: . . . . . . 5 FT, 1 PT
Prior Industry Experience: . . . . Helpful

FINANCIAL:
Cash Investment: $80-150K
Total Investment: $135-400K
Fees: Franchise - $40-50K
  Royalty: 6-10%, Advert: . . . 1-5%
Contract Periods (Yrs.): 5/5
Area Development Agreement: . .No
Sub-Franchise Contract: . . . . . .No
Expand in Territory: . . . . Yes
Passive Ownership: . . . Not Allowed
Encourage Conversions: . . . . . Yes
Franchisee Purchase(s) Required: .No

FRANCHISOR TRAINING/SUPPORT:
Financial Assistance Provided: . . . Yes(I)
Site Selection Assistance: . . . . .Yes
Lease Negotiation Assistance: . . . . .Yes
Co-operative Advertising: . . . . .Yes
Training: . . . . 4 Wks. Headquarters
. . . .
On-Going Support: . . . . .B,C,D,E,G,H,I
Full-Time Franchisor Support Staff: . . 10
EXPANSION PLANS:
  US: . . . . .No
  Canada - Yes, ... Overseas - No

CRUISE HOLIDAYS

4740 Murphy Canyon Rd., Box 23559
San Diego, CA 92123
TEL: (800) 345-7245 (619) 279-4780
FAX: (619) 279-4788
Mr. David Pava, VP Fran. Mktg.

North America's largest franchisor of cruise-only travel agencies. Complete training, including cruise, start-up assistance, use of proprietary software, national advertising and marketing support. Franchisor negotiates volume discounts on cruises. A perfect owner-operator business in the most profitable segment of the travel industry.

HISTORY: . . . . IFA
Established in 1984; . . 1st Franchised in 1985
Company-Owned Units (As of 12/1/1989): . . 2
Franchised Units (12/1/1989): 86
Total Units (12/1/1989): 88
Distribution: US-75;Can-13;Overseas-0
North America: . . . . 21 States, 2 Provinces
Concentration: . . . 35 in CA, 7 in NJ, 3 in ON
Registered: . . .CA,FL,IL,IN,MD,NY,OR,WA
. . . . .WI
Average # of Employees: . . . . .3 FT
Prior Industry Experience: . . . . . . Helpful

FINANCIAL:
Cash Investment: $69-95K
Total Investment: $69-95K
Fees: Franchise - $25K
  Royalty: 1%, Advert: 3/4%
Contract Periods (Yrs.): 5/5
Area Development Agreement: . .No
Sub-Franchise Contract: . . . . .No
Expand in Territory: . . . . Yes
Passive Ownership: . . . Discouraged
Encourage Conversions: . . . . . Yes
Franchisee Purchase(s) Required: .No

FRANCHISOR TRAINING/SUPPORT:
Financial Assistance Provided: . . . . .No
Site Selection Assistance: . . . . . . .Yes
Lease Negotiation Assistance: . . . .Yes
Co-operative Advertising: . . . . . . .Yes
Training: . . . . 2 Wks., Miami, FL,
. . . . .Including Cruise
On-Going Support: . . . .B,C,D,E,F,G,h,I
Full-Time Franchisor Support Staff: . . 24
EXPANSION PLANS:
US: . . . . All US
Canada - Yes, ...Overseas - No

GOLIGER'S TRAVEL

201 - 40 St. Clair Ave. W.
Toronto, ON M4V1M2 CAN
TEL: (416) 926-0814 C
FAX: (416) 926-9120
Franchise Department

Full-service travel agencies, serving the Canadian corporate and vacation traveller for over 35 years. We offer a unique system of fixed royalty fees and comprehensive training. An exciting "lifestyle" franchise in the world's largest single industry.

HISTORY: . . . . IFA
Established in 1955; . . 1st Franchised in 1979
Company-Owned Units (As of 12/1/1989): . .1
Franchised Units (12/1/1989): 90
Total Units (12/1/1989): 91
Distribution: US-0;Can-91;Overseas-0
North America: . . . . 9 Provinces
Concentration: . . .78 in ON, 6 in BC, 4 in AB
Registered: . . . . AB
. . . .
Average # of Employees: . . . . . . 2 FT, 1 PT
Prior Industry Experience: . . . . . . Helpful

FINANCIAL:
Cash Investment: $75K
Total Investment: $125K
Fees: Franchise - $48K
  Royalty: Flat, Advert: . . . . Flat
Contract Periods (Yrs.): 10/5
Area Development Agreement: . .No
Sub-Franchise Contract: . . . . Yes
Expand in Territory: . . . . . . Yes
Passive Ownership: . . . Discouraged
Encourage Conversions: . . . . Yes
Franchisee Purchase(s) Required: .No

FRANCHISOR TRAINING/SUPPORT:
Financial Assistance Provided: . . . . .Yes
Site Selection Assistance: . . . . . . .Yes
Lease Negotiation Assistance: . . . .Yes
Co-operative Advertising: . . . . . . .Yes
Training: . . . . 2 Wks. Headquarters,
. . . . 1 Wk. Headquarters
On-Going Support: . . . . . . C,D,E,G,h,I
Full-Time Franchisor Support Staff: . . 15
EXPANSION PLANS:
US: . . . . .No
Canada - Yes, ...Overseas - No

TRAVEL AGENTS INTERNATIONAL

111 Second Ave., 15th Fl., Box 31005
St. Petersburg, FL 33731
TEL: (800) 678-8241 (813) 894-1537
FAX: (813) 894-6318
Mr. James Sahley, Sr. VP

TRAVEL AGENTS INTERNATIONAL is the leading US-based franchisor of retail travel agencies. The franchise package establishes a professional look, uniform and integrated system and quality-control program. It translates to a strong support system for franchise owners and professional-level travel services for the public.

HISTORY: . . . . IFA
Established in 1980; . . 1st Franchised in 1982
Company-Owned Units (As of 12/1/1989): . .3
Franchised Units (12/1/1989): 380
Total Units (12/1/1989): 383
Distribution: US-340;Can-43;Overseas-0
North America: . . . . 39 States, 7 Provinces
Concentration: . .25 in CA, 25 in FL, 29in ON
Registered: . . . . All Except ND and SD
. . . .
Average # of Employees: . . . . . 3 FT, 1 PT
Prior Industry Experience: . . . . . . Helpful

FINANCIAL:
Cash Investment: $80-110K
Total Investment: $80-110K
Fees: Franchise - $44.5K
  Royalty: $485/Mo., Advert: $75/Mo.
Contract Periods (Yrs.): 10/5
Area Development Agreement: Yes/10
Sub-Franchise Contract: . . . . .No
Expand in Territory: . . . . . . Yes
Passive Ownership: . . . . . .Allowed
Encourage Conversions: . . . . .No
Franchisee Purchase(s) Required: .No

FRANCHISOR TRAINING/SUPPORT:
Financial Assistance Provided: . . . Yes(I)
Site Selection Assistance: . . . . . . .Yes
Lease Negotiation Assistance: . . . .Yes
Co-operative Advertising: . . . . . . .Yes
Training: . . . . 2 Wks. Headquarters,
. . . . 1 Wk. Houston Computer Training
On-Going Support: . . . A,B,C,D,E,G,H,I
Full-Time Franchisor Support Staff: . . 92
EXPANSION PLANS:
US: . . . . All US
Canada - Yes, . . . Overseas - Yes

TRAVEL AGENTS INTERNATIONAL (CANADA)

175 - 5945 Airport Rd.
Mississauga, ON L4V1R9 CAN
TEL: (800) 678-8241 (416) 671-4114
FAX: (416) 673-3329
Mr. Ash Mukherjee, President/CEO

We have every tool you need to compete effectively in your market place. If you have faith in yourself, you will fall in the 97% of our franchisees who succeed. Call our franchisees. Call their's before you decide.

HISTORY: . . . . IFA	FINANCIAL:	FRANCHISOR TRAINING/SUPPORT:
Established in 1980; . . 1st Franchised in 1980	Cash Investment: $44.5K	Financial Assistance Provided: . . .Yes(D)
Company-Owned Units (As of 12/1/1989): . .1	Total Investment: $85K	Site Selection Assistance: . . . . . . .Yes
Franchised Units (12/1/1989): 54	Fees: Franchise - $44.5K	Lease Negotiation Assistance: . . . . .Yes
Total Units (12/1/1989): 55	Royalty: $385/Mo., Advert:$175/Mo.	Co-operative Advertising: . . . . .Yes
Distribution: US-0;Can-55;Overseas-0	Contract Periods (Yrs.): 10/10	Training: . . . . . 2 Wks. St. Petersburg, FL
North America: . . . . 8 Provinces	Area Development Agreement: . .No	. . . . 1 Wk. Toronto, ON
Concentration: . . .34 in ON, 9 in BC, 6 in AB	Sub-Franchise Contract: . . . . .No	On-Going Support: . . A,B,C,D,E,F,G,H,I
Registered: . . . . AB	Expand in Territory: . . . . Yes	Full-Time Franchisor Support Staff: . . . 9
. . . .	Passive Ownership: . . . Discouraged	EXPANSION PLANS:
Average # of Employees: . . . . .3 FT	Encourage Conversions: . . . . . Yes	US: . . . . .No
Prior Industry Experience: . . . . Helpful	Franchisee Purchase(s) Required: Yes	Canada - Yes, . . . Overseas - Yes

TRAVEL NETWORK, LTD.

560 Sylvan Ave.
Englewood Cliffs, NJ 07632
TEL: (800) TRAV-NET (201) 567-8500 C
FAX: (201) 567-4405
Mr. Michael Y. Brent, EVP

International travel agency franchise chain, offering full-service programs to leisure, corporate and group accounts. All offices are computerized and use state-of-the-art IBM automation. On-line access to corporate locations, brand-name advertising, merchandising and sales promotions. Full 3-week training and on-going support provided.

HISTORY: . . . . IFA	FINANCIAL:	FRANCHISOR TRAINING/SUPPORT:
Established in 1982; . . 1st Franchised in 1982	Cash Investment: $80-100K	Financial Assistance Provided: . . . Yes(I)
Company-Owned Units (As of 12/1/1989): . .2	Total Investment: $80-100K	Site Selection Assistance: . . . . . . .Yes
Franchised Units (12/1/1989): 94	Fees: Franchise - $29.9K	Lease Negotiation Assistance: . . . . .Yes
Total Units (12/1/1989): 96	Royalty: $350+/Mo, Advert.$400/Mo.	Co-operative Advertising: . . . . .Yes
Distribution: US-96;Can-0;Overseas-0	Contract Periods (Yrs.): 10/10	Training: . . . . 1 Wk. Headquarters, 1 Wk.
North America: . . . . 17 States	Area Development Agreement: Yes/20	. . . . .Orlando, FL, 1 Wk. Houston, TX
Concentration: . . 23 in NJ, 20 in NY, 19in CA	Sub-Franchise Contract: . . . . . Yes	On-Going Support: . . . a,B,C,D,E,f,G,H,I
Registered: . . .CA,FL,IL,MD,MI,MN,NY,OR	Expand in Territory: . . . . Yes	Full-Time Franchisor Support Staff: . . 14
. . . . VA	Passive Ownership: . . . . . .Allowed	EXPANSION PLANS:
Average # of Employees: . . . . . . 3 FT, 6 PT	Encourage Conversions: . . . . . Yes	US: . . . . .All US
Prior Industry Experience: . . . . Helpful	Franchisee Purchase(s) Required: .No	Canada - Yes, . . . Overseas - Yes

TRAVEL PROFESSIONALS INTERNATIONAL

10172 Linn Station Rd., # 360
Louisville, KY 40223
TEL: (800)626-2469 (800)292-2741(KY)
FAX: (502) 423-9914
Mr. John Boyce, Dir. Fran. Sales

A network of full-service travel agencies, founded by agency owners and operators. We provide marketing and sales support and assistance in day-to-day operations. Training is continuous. We have programs designed to allow our agencies to increase their commission potential, and decrease their costs of operations.

HISTORY:	FINANCIAL:	FRANCHISOR TRAINING/SUPPORT:
Established in 1982; . . 1st Franchised in 1983	Cash Investment: $77.7K	Financial Assistance Provided: . . . . .No
Company-Owned Units (As of 12/1/1989): . .1	Total Investment: $77.7K	Site Selection Assistance: . . . . . . .Yes
Franchised Units (12/1/1989): 34	Fees: Franchise - $10.5-27.5K	Lease Negotiation Assistance: . . . . .Yes
Total Units (12/1/1989): 35	Royalty: 5-1%, Advert: . . $150/Qtr	Co-operative Advertising: . . . . .No
Distribution: US-35;Can-0;Overseas-0	Contract Periods (Yrs.): 10/10	Training: . . . . 2 Wks. Headquarters,
North America: . . . . 15 States	Area Development Agreement: . .No	. . . .2 Wks. Headquarters, 2 Wks. Field
Concentration: . . . 12 in KY, 4 in FL, 4 in AL	Sub-Franchise Contract: . . . . . .No	On-Going Support: . . . . .B,C,D,E,G,H,i
Registered: . . . . .CA,FL,MD,VA	Expand in Territory: . . . . Yes	Full-Time Franchisor Support Staff: . . 18
. . . .	Passive Ownership: . . . Discouraged	EXPANSION PLANS:
Average # of Employees: . . . . . . 2 FT, 2 PT	Encourage Conversions: . . . . . Yes	US: . . . . .All US
Prior Industry Experience: . . . . Helpful	Franchisee Purchase(s) Required: .No	Canada - Yes, . . . Overseas - Yes

TRAVEL PROS

3001 N. Rocky Pt. Rd. NE, # 160
Tampa, FL 33607
TEL: (813) 281-5670
FAX: (813) 281-2304
Mr. Bernhard Benet, President

TRAVEL PROS specializes in setting up persons with no prior travel experience in the highly lucrative field of international air and tours. No license or bond or qualified manager needed. Extremely high commissions.

HISTORY: . . . .
Established in 1986; . . 1st Franchised in 1989
Company-Owned Units (As of 12/1/1989): . . 1
Franchised Units (12/1/1989): 40
Total Units (12/1/1989): 41
Distribution: US-38;Can-0;Overseas-3
North America . . . . 15 States
Concentration: . . . 6 in CA, 3 in FL, 2 in IL
Registered: . . . . All States
. . . .
Average # of Employees: . . . . . . 1 FT, 1 PT
Prior Industry Experience: . . . . Helpful

FINANCIAL:
Cash Investment: $6-25K
Total Investment: $10-60K
Fees: Franchise - $6-12K
Royalty: $175/Mo., Advert: . . NA
Contract Periods (Yrs.): 5/5
Area Development Agreement: . .No
Sub-Franchise Contract: . . . . .No
Expand in Territory: . . . . Yes
Passive Ownership: . . . . . .Allowed
Encourage Conversions: . . . . Yes
Franchisee Purchase(s) Required: Yes

FRANCHISOR TRAINING/SUPPORT:
Financial Assistance Provided: . . . . . No
Site Selection Assistance: . . . . No
Lease Negotiation Assistance: . . . . . No
Co-operative Advertising: . . . . No
Training: . . . . 2 Days On-site,
. . . . .1 Wk. Kansas City
On-Going Support: . . . . .A,B,C,D,e,g,H
Full-Time Franchisor Support Staff: . . . 4
EXPANSION PLANS:
US: . . . . .All US
Canada - Yes, . . . Overseas - Yes

UNIGLOBE TRAVEL (INTERNATIONAL)

3001 Bethel Rd., # 118
Columbus, OH 43220
TEL: (614) 459-6690
FAX:
Mr. Willian L. Hart, Sr. VP Sales

UNIGLOBE TRAVEL is the largest and #1 franchisor of travel agencies in North America. UNIGLOBE TRAVEL is designed to build the profitability of new and existing independent travel agencies. UNIGLOBE agencies benefit from a common image, professional training, business development counseling, owners and managers meeting, etc. Growing at the rate of 1 office every business day.

HISTORY: . . . . IFA/WIF
Established in 1979; . . 1st Franchised in 1980
Company-Owned Units (As of 12/1/1989): . .0
Franchised Units (12/1/1989): 775
Total Units (12/1/1989): 775
Distribution: . . . US-643;Can-131;Overseas-1
North America . . . . 45 States,10 Provinces
Concentration: . .116 in CA, 62 in OH, 51 ON
Registered: . . . . .All
. . . .
Average # of Employees: . . . . .6 FT
Prior Industry Experience: . . . . Helpful

FINANCIAL:
Cash Investment: $15-55K
Total Investment: $15-150K
Fees: Franchise - $6-45K
Royalty: .1-.05%, Advert: . . Flat
Contract Periods (Yrs.): 10/5
Area Development Agreement: Yes/25
Sub-Franchise Contract: . . . . . Yes
Expand in Territory: . . . . Yes
Passive Ownership: . . . Discouraged
Encourage Conversions: . . . . Yes
Franchisee Purchase(s) Required: .No

FRANCHISOR TRAINING/SUPPORT:
Financial Assistance Provided: . . . Yes(I)
Site Selection Assistance: . . . . . . .Yes
Lease Negotiation Assistance: . . . .Yes
Co-operative Advertising: . . . . . . .Yes
Training: . . . . .4 Days Headquarters, On-
. . . . .going Weekly Training at Region
On-Going Support: . . . . .B,C,D,E,G,H,I
Full-Time Franchisor Support Staff: . .265
EXPANSION PLANS:
US: . . . . .All US
Canada - Yes, ...Overseas - Yes

SUPPLEMENTAL LISTING OF FRANCHISORS

AIR & STEAMSHIP TRAVEL OF FLORIDA . . . . .260 Sunny Isles Blvd., North Miami Beach FL 33160
ASK MR. FOSTER TRAVEL SERVICE . . . . .12755 State Hwy. 55, Minneapolis MN 55441
BAY CRUISE CENTERS . . . . 1608 Bonnie St., # 101, Metairie LA 70001
COMPUTRAVEL . . . . .1851 Alexander Bell Dr., 4th Fl., Reston VA 22091
CRUISE OF A LIFETIME USA . . . . .237 Park Ave., 21st Fl., New York NY 10017
CRUISECRAFTERS . . . . .201 Barclay Pavillion W., Cherry Hill NJ 08034
CRUISESHOPPES AMERICA . . . . 115 Metairie Rd., # E, Metairie LA 70005
EMPRESS TRAVEL . . . . 450 Harmon Meadow, P.O. Box 1568, Secaucus NJ 07096
GALAXSEA CRUISES . . . . 3247 Electric Rd., SW #1-A, Roanoke VA 24018
INTERNATIONAL TOURS . . . . .2840 E. 51st, 2nd Fl., Tulsa OK 74105
JEFFLEASE .1206 Currie Ave., P.O. Box 978, Minneapolis MN 55440
MUHAMMED ALI TRAVEL PROS . . . . 3001 N. Rocky Point Rd., # 160, Tampa FL 33607
PROMINENT TRAVEL . . . . .3455 Fairview St., Burlington ON L7N2R4 CAN

TRANSERV . . . . 20700 Boening, Southfield MI 48075
TRAVEL TRAVEL . . . . 4350 La Jolla Village Dr., # 300, San Diego CA 92122
TRAVEL TRUST INTERNATIONAL . . . . 180 Attwell Dr., # 501, Rexdale ON M9W6A9   CAN
TRAVEL WITH US . . . . .6991 E. Camelback Rd., # C-152, Scottsdale AZ 85251
TRAVELHOST AGENCY . . . . 8080 N. Central Expy., Dallas TX 75234
UNIGLOBE TRAVEL (INTERNATIONAL) . . . . . . .1199 W. Pender St., # 900, Vancouver BC V6E2R1   CAN
WINGTIPS . . . . 640 Cowpath Rd., 5 Point Plaza, Lansdale PA 19446

CHAPTER 50

MISCELLANEOUS

AIR BROOK LIMOUSINE

Box 123
Rochelle Park, NJ 07662
TEL: (201) 368-3974
FAX: (201) 587-8385
Mr. Mark Milmar, Franchise Director

Fully-certified (state (48) and federal), including federal registration insurance. Transportation service for business/personal with a fleet of sedans, station-wagons, vans and stretch limousines. All airports, etc. Complete "business format" franchise. Everything provided: reservations, dispatching, billing, collecting (including all customers). Pre-paid income, etc.

HISTORY: . . . .
Established in 1969; . . 1st Franchised in 1971
Company-Owned Units (As of 12/1/1989): . .0
Franchised Units (12/1/1989): 135
Total Units (12/1/1989): 135
Distribution: US-135;Can-0;Overseas-0
 North America: . . . . .1 State
 Concentration: . . . . 135 in NJ
Registered: . . . .
. . . .
Average # of Employees: . . . . . . 1 FT, 1 PT
Prior Industry Experience: . . . . Helpful

FINANCIAL:
Cash Investment: $9.5-12.5K
Total Investment: $11-14.5K
Fees: Franchise - $7-11K
 Royalty: NA, Advert: . . . . . . NA
Contract Periods (Yrs.): 10/10
Area Development Agreement: . .No
Sub-Franchise Contract: . . . . . .No
Expand in Territory: . . . . Yes
Passive Ownership: . . . Discouraged
Encourage Conversions: . . . . . Yes
Franchisee Purchase(s) Required: .No

FRANCHISOR TRAINING/SUPPORT:
Financial Assistance Provided: . . .Yes(D)
Site Selection Assistance: . . . . .NA
Lease Negotiation Assistance: . . . . .NA
Co-operative Advertising: . . . . .NA
Training: . . . . . 3 Days Office, On-going
. . . .
On-Going Support: . . . A,B,C,D,E,G,H,I
Full-Time Franchisor Support Staff: . .150
EXPANSION PLANS:
 US: . . . . .NJ Only or License Use
 Canada - Yes, ...Overseas - Yes

ARMOLOY CORPORATION

1325 Sycamore Rd.
DeKalb, IL 60115
TEL: (815) 758-6657 C
FAX: (815) 758-0268
Mr. Jerome Bejbl, President

Unique, proprietary chromium alloy metal surface finishing process that extends wear-life, corrosion resistance and improves friction reducing characteristics to all ferrous and non-ferrous finished machine and equipment parts.

HISTORY: . . . .
Established in 1957; . . 1st Franchised in 1969
Company-Owned Units (As of 12/1/1989): . .2
Franchised Units (12/1/1989): 9
Total Units (12/1/1989): 11
Distribution: US-7;Can-0;Overseas-4
North America: . . . . 7 States
Concentration: . . . .
Registered: . . . . .All
. . . .
Average # of Employees: . . . . . . 3 FT, 2 PT
Prior Industry Experience: . . . . Helpful

FINANCIAL:
Cash Investment: $50-100K
Total Investment: $250-350K
Fees: Franchise - . . . . $50K+
Royalty: 7%, Advert: 1%
Contract Periods (Yrs.): 15/5
Area Development Agreement: . .No
Sub-Franchise Contract: . . . . .No
Expand in Territory: . . . . Yes
Passive Ownership: . . . Discouraged
Encourage Conversions: . . . . .No
Franchisee Purchase(s) Required: Yes

FRANCHISOR TRAINING/SUPPORT:
Financial Assistance Provided: . . . . .No
Site Selection Assistance: . . . . . . .Yes
Lease Negotiation Assistance: . . . .Yes
Co-operative Advertising: . . . . . . .Yes
Training: . . . . . 4-6 Wks. Headquarters +
. . . . .As Required on Plant Site
On-Going Support: . . . . . . C,D,E,F,H,I
Full-Time Franchisor Support Staff: . . .6
EXPANSION PLANS:
US: . . . . .All US
Canada - Yes, . . . Overseas - Yes

BADGE MAKER, THE

2806 W. King Edward Ave.
Vancouver, BC V6L1T9 CAN
TEL: (604) 733-4323
FAX:
Mr. Paul McCrea, President

Manufacturing and marketing of name badges, buttons and other personalized identification pieces. Specialize in corporate logo identification. Largest company in Canada, with over 20 offices nationwide. U.S. parent is Recognition Express.

HISTORY: . . . . IFA
Established in 1978; . . 1st Franchised in 1979
Company-Owned Units (As of 12/1/1989): . .0
Franchised Units (12/1/1989): 21
Total Units (12/1/1989): 21
Distribution: US-0;Can-21;Overseas-0
North America: . . . . 9 Provinces
Concentration: . . . .
Registered: . . . . AB
. . . .
Average # of Employees: . . . . .2 FT
Prior Industry Experience: . . . . . . Helpful

FINANCIAL:
Cash Investment: $18.5K
Total Investment: $20K
Fees: Franchise - $5K
Royalty: 6%, Advert: 2%
Contract Periods (Yrs.): 5/5
Area Development Agreement: . .No
Sub-Franchise Contract: . . . . . .No
Expand in Territory: . . . . .No
Passive Ownership: . . . Not Allowed
Encourage Conversions: . . . . .No
Franchisee Purchase(s) Required: .No

FRANCHISOR TRAINING/SUPPORT:
Financial Assistance Provided: . . . Yes(I)
Site Selection Assistance: . . . . . . .NA
Lease Negotiation Assistance: . . . .NA
Co-operative Advertising: . . . . . . .Yes
Training: . . . . .1 Wk. Headquarters
. . . .
On-Going Support: . . . . . .B,C,D,G,H
Full-Time Franchisor Support Staff: . . .2
EXPANSION PLANS:
US: . . . . .No
Canada - Yes, ...Overseas - No

BYOB WATER STORE

29047 Road 29 S.
Stratton, CO 80836
TEL: (719) 962-3432
FAX:
Mr. Richard L. Cure, President

BYOB WATER STORE manufactures its main product, water, then retails that high-quality water to the consumer in his own bottle. Since the first BYOB WATER STORE was installed in 1984, ten stores have been licensed. January, 1990 marks the beginning of our franchise program.

HISTORY: . . . .
Established in 1987; . . 1st Franchised in 1989
Company-Owned Units (As of 12/1/1989): . .0
Franchised Units (12/1/1989): 0
Total Units (12/1/1989): 0
Distribution: US-0;Can-0;Overseas-0
North America: . . . . Starting
Concentration: . . . . Starting
Registered: . . . . .FL
. . . .
Average # of Employees: . . . . . . 1 FT, 1 PT
Prior Industry Experience: . . . . Helpful

FINANCIAL:
Cash Investment: $48-58K
Total Investment: $48-5*K
Fees: Franchise - $10K
Royalty: 6%, Advert: 3%
Contract Periods (Yrs.): 7/7
Area Development Agreement: . .No
Sub-Franchise Contract: . . . . Yes
Expand in Territory: . . . . .No
Passive Ownership: . . . Discouraged
Encourage Conversions: . . . . Yes
Franchisee Purchase(s) Required: Yes

FRANCHISOR TRAINING/SUPPORT:
Financial Assistance Provided: . . . Yes(I)
Site Selection Assistance: . . . . . . .Yes
Lease Negotiation Assistance: . . . .Yes
Co-operative Advertising: . . . . No
Training: . . . . . 10 Days Designated Area
. . . . .Store, 1-5 Days Franchise Store
On-Going Support: . . . . .a,B,C,D,E,F,G
Full-Time Franchisor Support Staff: . . .1
EXPANSION PLANS:
US: . . . . .Southern US
Canada - Yes, ...Overseas - No

CROWN TROPHY

1034 Yonkers Ave.
Yonkers, NY 10704
TEL: (800) 227-1557 (914) 237-9500 C
FAX: (914) 237-9598
Mr. Chuck Weisenfeld, President

CROWN TROPHY. We provide you with the buying and marketing power of a large corporation and, most of all, the experience of successful leaders in the trophy industry. All work is done on premises with state-of-the-art computer engraving equipment.

HISTORY: . . . . IFA
Established in 1978; . . 1st Franchised in 1986
Company-Owned Units (As of 12/1/1989): . .2
Franchised Units (12/1/1989): 11
Total Units (12/1/1989): 13
Distribution: US-13;Can-0;Overseas-0
North America: . . . . 4 States
Concentration: . . . .8 in NY, 2 in NJ, 1 in PA
Registered: . . . . IL,MD,NY,VA
. . . .
Average # of Employees: . . . . . . 1 FT, 2 PT
Prior Industry Experience: . . . . . . Helpful

FINANCIAL:
Cash Investment: $36-48K
Total Investment: $46-56K
Fees: Franchise - . . . .$
  Royalty: 4%, Advert: . . . . . Var.
Contract Periods (Yrs.): 10/10
Area Development Agreement: . .No
Sub-Franchise Contract: . . . . .No
Expand in Territory: . . . . Yes
Passive Ownership: . . . Discouraged
Encourage Conversions: . . . . .No
Franchisee Purchase(s) Required: .No

FRANCHISOR TRAINING/SUPPORT:
Financial Assistance Provided: . . . Yes(I)
Site Selection Assistance: . . . . . . .Yes
Lease Negotiation Assistance: . . . . .Yes
Co-operative Advertising: . . . . . . .Yes
Training: . . . . 1 Wk. Headquarters
. . . .
On-Going Support: . . . .B,C,D,E,F,G,H,I
Full-Time Franchisor Support Staff: . . .5
EXPANSION PLANS:
US: . . . . East Coast
Canada - No, ...Overseas - No

CULLIGAN, USA

One Culligan Pkwy.
Northbrook, IL 60062
TEL: (708) 205-6000
FAX: (708) 498-6765
Ms. Kathleen DiBacco, Fran. Admin.

CULLIGAN, a leader in the water treatment industry for over 50 years, offers non-exclusive franchises specializing in water treatment services and water treatment products, using CULLIGAN'S methods and products. Franchise may be granted for any or all of CULLIGAN's eight product lines and services.

HISTORY: . . . . IFA
Established in 1936; . . 1st Franchised in 1939
Company-Owned Units (As of 12/1/1989): . 23
Franchised Units (12/1/1989): 758
Total Units (12/1/1989): 781
Distribution: . . . US-781;Can-0;Overseas-0
North America: . . . .
Concentration: . 57 in MN, 53 in CA, 41 in IN
Registered: . . . . All Exc. HI
. . . .
Average # of Employees: . . . . .6-7 FT
Prior Industry Experience: . . . . Helpful

FINANCIAL:
Cash Investment: . . . .$
Total Investment: $75-160K
Fees: Franchise - $0
  Royalty: .5-5%, Advert: . 2.0-4.1%
Contract Periods (Yrs.): 5/5
Area Development Agreement: .No
Sub-Franchise Contract: . . . . .No
Expand in Territory: . . . . Yes
Passive Ownership: . . . Not Allowed
Encourage Conversions: . . . . . Yes
Franchisee Purchase(s) Required: Yes

FRANCHISOR TRAINING/SUPPORT:
Financial Assistance Provided: . . . . No
Site Selection Assistance: . . . . No
Lease Negotiation Assistance: . . . . No
Co-operative Advertising: . . . . . . .Yes
Training: . . . . 1 Wk. Headquarters
. . . .
On-Going Support: . . . . . . C,d,G,H,I
Full-Time Franchisor Support Staff: . .625
EXPANSION PLANS:
US: . . . . .All US
Canada - No, ...Overseas - No

DEKRA-LITE

17945 Sky Park Circle
Irvine, CA 92714
TEL: (800) 888-8319 (714) 852-9977
FAX: (714) 852-9539
Mr. Arnold Mahler, President

Guaranteed to turn you on! Exciting new franchise featured on CNN, USA, Entrepreneur, etc. Operate year-round or part-time. Design, installation, removal of exterior Christmas lighting for residential and commercial properties. Decorative pole mounts for commercial customers. Low-voltage landscape lighting. Window frosting with DEKRA-FROST.

HISTORY: . . . .
Established in 1986; . . 1st Franchised in 1988
Company-Owned Units (As of 12/1/1989): . .1
Franchised Units (12/1/1989): 29
Total Units (12/1/1989): 30
Distribution: US-28;Can-2;Overseas-0
North America: . . . . 18 States, 1 Province
Concentration: . . . .6 in CA, 2 in AZ, 2 in FL
Registered: . . . . CA,FL,HI,IL,IN,MD,OR,RI
. . . . SD,VA,WA
Average # of Employees: . . . . . . 2 FT, 8 PT
Prior Industry Experience: . . . . . . Helpful

FINANCIAL:
Cash Investment: $25K
Total Investment: $11-35K
Fees: Franchise - $8.5K
  Royalty: 5%, Advert: 2%
Contract Periods (Yrs.): 5/5
Area Development Agreement: . .No
Sub-Franchise Contract: . . . . .No
Expand in Territory: . . . . Yes
Passive Ownership: . . . Discouraged
Encourage Conversions: . . . . . Yes
Franchisee Purchase(s) Required: Yes

FRANCHISOR TRAINING/SUPPORT:
Financial Assistance Provided: . . . . .NA
Site Selection Assistance: . . . . . . .NA
Lease Negotiation Assistance: . . . . .NA
Co-operative Advertising: . . . . . . .Yes
Training: . . . . 4 Days
. . . .
On-Going Support: . . . A,B,C,D,F,G,H,I
Full-Time Franchisor Support Staff: . . .6
EXPANSION PLANS:
US: . . . . .All US
Canada - Yes, . . . Overseas - Yes

DIAL-A-GIFT

2265 E. 4800 S.
Salt Lake City, UT 84117
TEL: (800) 453-0428 (801) 278-0413
FAX: (801) 278-0449
Mr. Clarence Jolley, President

DIAL-A-GIFT is an international gift wire service that operates much like the flower-by-phone or wire services. Local and international delivery of fruit baskets, gourmet foods, cheeses, wines, candies, meats, cakes, balloons, etc. through a network of 4,000 franchisees and dealers.

HISTORY: . . . .
Established in 1980; . . 1st Franchised in 1984
Company-Owned Units (As of 12/1/1989): . .2
Franchised Units (12/1/1989): 88
Total Units (12/1/1989): 90
Distribution: US-89;Can-1;Overseas-0
  North America: . . . . 50 States, 9 Provinces
  Concentration: . . . .
Registered: . . . . CA,FL,IL,IN,NY,OR,RI,VA
. . . .
Average # of Employees: . . . . . 2 FT, 1-8 PT
Prior Industry Experience: . . . . Helpful

FINANCIAL: OTC
Cash Investment: $20-50K
Total Investment: $20-50K
Fees: Franchise - $10K
  Royalty: 4%, Advert: . . $100/Mo.
Contract Periods (Yrs.): . . . . . Inf.
Area Development Agreement: . .No
Sub-Franchise Contract: . . . . .No
Expand in Territory: . . . . . . Yes
Passive Ownership: . . . Discouraged
Encourage Conversions: . . . . . Yes
Franchisee Purchase(s) Required: .No

FRANCHISOR TRAINING/SUPPORT:
Financial Assistance Provided: . . . Yes(I)
Site Selection Assistance: . . . . .Yes
Lease Negotiation Assistance: . . . . . No
Co-operative Advertising: . . . . No
Training: . . . . 3 Days Headquarters
. . . . 1-2 Wks. Franchisee Store
On-Going Support: . . . . . . A,B,G,H,I
Full-Time Franchisor Support Staff: . . 15
EXPANSION PLANS:
US: . . . . .All US
Canada - Yes, . . . Overseas - Yes

GOODWILL CANDLE

300 E. Milwaukee
Detroit, MI 48202
TEL: (313) 875-2700 C
FAX:
Mr. Chester Flam, President

The only franchise specializing in the distribution of religious-occult merchandise to ethnic groups.

HISTORY: . . . .
Established in 1970; . . 1st Franchised in 1971
Company-Owned Units (As of 12/1/1989): . .0
Franchised Units (12/1/1989): 1
Total Units (12/1/1989): 1
Distribution: US-1;Can-0;Overseas-0
  North America: . . . . .1 State
  Concentration: . . . . 1 in GA
Registered: . . . . .MI
. . . .
Average # of Employees: . . . . .2 FT
Prior Industry Experience: . . . . Helpful

FINANCIAL:
Cash Investment: $15.5K
Total Investment: $13.5-25K
Fees: Franchise - $13.5K
  Royalty: 5%, Advert: 0%
Contract Periods (Yrs.): . . . 20/20
Area Development Agreement: . .No
Sub-Franchise Contract: . . . . .No
Expand in Territory: . . . . . . .No
Passive Ownership: . . . Discouraged
Encourage Conversions: . . . . .No
Franchisee Purchase(s) Required: Yes

FRANCHISOR TRAINING/SUPPORT:
Financial Assistance Provided: . . . . .No
Site Selection Assistance: . . . . . . .Yes
Lease Negotiation Assistance: . . . .Yes
Co-operative Advertising: . . . . No
Training: . . . . .1 Wk. Headquarters,
. . . . 1 Wk. Franchisee Location
On-Going Support: . . . . E,I
Full-Time Franchisor Support Staff: . . .1
EXPANSION PLANS:
US: . . . . . . Cities With Ethnic Populat.
Canada - No, ...Overseas - No

KELLY'S LIQUIDATORS

1310 NW 21st St.
Ft. Lauderdale, FL 33311
TEL: (305) 763-4841
FAX:
Mr. Edward Kelly, President

Clearing house service agency, bringing buyers and sellers of used, second-hand personal property together - household goods, antiques, etc. Selling piece-meal, package deal or one day public sale. NOT auctions. Franchisees charge 25% commission on gross sales on a contractual basis. They sell other people's goods on their premises.

HISTORY: . . . .
Established in 1954; . . 1st Franchised in 1979
Company-Owned Units (As of 12/1/1989): . .1
Franchised Units (12/1/1989): 5
Total Units (12/1/1989): 6
Distribution: US-6;Can-0;Overseas-0
  North America: . . . . .1 State
  Concentration: . . . . 6 in FL
Registered: . . . . .FL
. . . .
Average # of Employees: . . . . . 1 FT, 4-9 PT
Prior Industry Experience: . . . . Helpful

FINANCIAL:
Cash Investment: $2K
Total Investment: $2.2K
Fees: Franchise - $2K
  Royalty: 0%, Advert: 0%
Contract Periods (Yrs.): 3/5
Area Development Agreement: Yes/3-5
Sub-Franchise Contract: . . . . .No
Expand in Territory: . . . . . . .No
Passive Ownership: . . . Not Allowed
Encourage Conversions: . . . . .No
Franchisee Purchase(s) Required: .No

FRANCHISOR TRAINING/SUPPORT:
Financial Assistance Provided: . . . . .No
Site Selection Assistance: . . . . No
Lease Negotiation Assistance: . . . . .NA
Co-operative Advertising: . . . . No
Training: . . . . 5 Days Headquarters
. . . .
On-Going Support: . . . .
Full-Time Franchisor Support Staff: . . .1
EXPANSION PLANS:
US: . . . . .Florida Only
Canada - No, ...Overseas - No

LEROS POINT TO POINT

861 Franklin Ave.
Thornwood, NY 10594
TEL: (800) 82-LEROS (914) 747-2300 C
FAX: (201) 387-8990
Ms. Lonnie Lehrer, President

LEROS POINT TO POINT is an executive transport and limousine franchise that offers complete training and computerization. Franchise owners manage regional limousine business that dispatches and manages 5- 50 vehicles.

HISTORY: . . . . IFA
Established in 1980; . . 1st Franchised in 1986
Company-Owned Units (As of 12/1/1989): . .1
Franchised Units (12/1/1989): 6
Total Units (12/1/1989): 7
Distribution: US-7;Can-0;Overseas-0
North America: . . . . 4 States
Concentration: . . . 3 in NY, 2 in NJ, 1 in MA
Registered: . . . . .FL,MD,NY,VA
. . . .
Average # of Employees: . . . . . . 2 FT, 1 PT
Prior Industry Experience: . . . . Helpful

FINANCIAL:
Cash Investment: $30K
Total Investment: $60-96K
Fees: Franchise - $15-21K
Royalty: 5%, Advert: . . . .
Contract Periods (Yrs.): 10
Area Development Agreement: . .No
Sub-Franchise Contract: . . . . .No
Expand in Territory: . . . . Yes
Passive Ownership: . . . Discouraged
Encourage Conversions: . . . . . Yes
Franchisee Purchase(s) Required: .No

FRANCHISOR TRAINING/SUPPORT:
Financial Assistance Provided: . . . Yes(I)
Site Selection Assistance: . . . . . . .Yes
Lease Negotiation Assistance: . . . . .Yes
Co-operative Advertising: . . . . . . .Yes
Training: . . . . 2 Wks. Headquarters
. . . .
On-Going Support: . . A,B,C,D,E,F,G,H,I
Full-Time Franchisor Support Staff: . . 20
EXPANSION PLANS:
US: . . . . .All US
Canada - No, ... Overseas - Yes

PRO-AUTOFINDERS

132 2nd St. E., #304, P.O. Box 1916
Cornwall, ON K6H6N6 CAN
TEL: (613) 932-1007
FAX:
Mr. R. Chenier, President

Fact: $42 billion of used car transactions take place per year between private individuals, not car dealers! Why? Dealers offer them wholesale! Answer: We sell automobiles like a real estate company sells homes! Test marketed since 1985, profits average over $800 per car! Available to the emerging auto salesperson by consultant or franchise agreement.

HISTORY: . . . .
Established in 1985; . . 1st Franchised in 1986
Company-Owned Units (As of 12/1/1989): . .0
Franchised Units (12/1/1989): 2
Total Units (12/1/1989): 2
Distribution: US-0;Can-2;Overseas-0
North America: . . . . .1 Province
Concentration: . . . . 2 in ON
Registered: . . . .
. . . .
Average # of Employees: . . . . . . 2 FT, 1 PT
Prior Industry Experience: . . . . Helpful

FINANCIAL:
Cash Investment: $10-30K
Total Investment: $10-30K
Fees: Franchise - $10K
Royalty: 1%, Advert: 25%
Contract Periods (Yrs.): 5/5
Area Development Agreement: Yes/5
Sub-Franchise Contract: . . . . .No
Expand in Territory: . . . . Yes
Passive Ownership: . . . Discouraged
Encourage Conversions: . . . . . Yes
Franchisee Purchase(s) Required: .No

FRANCHISOR TRAINING/SUPPORT:
Financial Assistance Provided: . . . . .No
Site Selection Assistance: . . . . . . .Yes
Lease Negotiation Assistance: . . . . .Yes
Co-operative Advertising: . . . . . . .Yes
Training: . . . . 2 Days On-site,
. . . . 2 Days Headquarters
On-Going Support: . . A,B,C,D,E,F,G,H,I
Full-Time Franchisor Support Staff: . . .3
EXPANSION PLANS:
US: . . . . .No
Canada - Yes, ...Overseas - No

PROFESSIONAL MARINE RESTORATION

3732 W. Century Blvd., #6
Inglewood, CA 90303
TEL: (800) 444-8827 (213) 671-4995
FAX: (213) 671-1146
Mr. Richard Crites, President

You can enter the yacht and boat restoration industry now. We will train you on over 2 dozen services that all boat owners need and want. Pull out of your rut and, with one step, enter the profitable and prestige-filled marine industry.

HISTORY: . . . .
Established in 1987; . . 1st Franchised in 1987
Company-Owned Units (As of 12/1/1989): . .1
Franchised Units (12/1/1989): 9
Total Units (12/1/1989): 10
Distribution: US-1;Can-0;Overseas-9
North America: . . . . .1 State
Concentration: . . . . 1 in CA
Registered: . . . . CA
. . . .
Average # of Employees: . . . . .3 FT
Prior Industry Experience: . . . . Helpful

FINANCIAL: NA
Cash Investment: $45K
Total Investment: $40-50K
Fees: Franchise - $30K
Royalty: 10%, Advert: 3%
Contract Periods (Yrs.): 5/5
Area Development Agreement: . .No
Sub-Franchise Contract: . . . . Yes
Expand in Territory: . . . . .No
Passive Ownership: . . . Discouraged
Encourage Conversions: . . . . . Yes
Franchisee Purchase(s) Required: .No

FRANCHISOR TRAINING/SUPPORT:
Financial Assistance Provided: . . . . .No
Site Selection Assistance: . . . . . . .Yes
Lease Negotiation Assistance: . . . . .Yes
Co-operative Advertising: . . . . . . .No
Training: . . . . . . 2-4 Wks. Headquarters,
. . . . 2-3 Wks. On-site
On-Going Support: . . . . . . C,d,E,G,h,I
Full-Time Franchisor Support Staff: . . .4
EXPANSION PLANS:
US: . . . . .All US
Canada - Yes, . . . Overseas - Yes

SAVE-T-STRIP INDUSTRIES

202 - 31822 Village Center Rd.
Westlake Village, CA 91361
TEL: (805) 498-0767 (818) 991-4334
FAX: (805) 498-0293
Mr. Timothy Mahoney, President

A new system of paint removal for the automotive, equipment and parts industries which utilizes plastic pellets in a blasting booth, representing the most cost-effective means of paint removal available to date, and in an environmentally-safe manner.

HISTORY: . . . .
Established in 1988; . . 1st Franchised in 1989
Company-Owned Units (As of 12/1/1989): . .2
Franchised Units (12/1/1989): 0
Total Units (12/1/1989): 2
Distribution: US-0;Can-2;Overseas-0
  North America: . . . . .1 Province
  Concentration: . . . . 2 in BC
Registered: . . . .
. . . .
Average # of Employees: . . . . .5 FT
Prior Industry Experience: . . . . Helpful

FINANCIAL:
Cash Investment: $80-120K
Total Investment: $240-280K
Fees: Franchise - $15K
  Royalty: 5%, Advert: 2%
Contract Periods (Yrs.): 10/10
Area Development Agreement: Yes/10
Sub-Franchise Contract: . . . . . Yes
Expand in Territory: . . . . . . Yes
Passive Ownership: . . . Discouraged
Encourage Conversions: . . . . .No
Franchisee Purchase(s) Required: Yes

FRANCHISOR TRAINING/SUPPORT:
Financial Assistance Provided: . . . Yes(I)
Site Selection Assistance: . . . . No
Lease Negotiation Assistance: . . . . . No
Co-operative Advertising: . . . . .Yes
Training: . . . . . .5 Days Vancouver, BC,
. . . . 5 Days Los Angeles, CA
On-Going Support: . . . . B,C,D,I
Full-Time Franchisor Support Staff: . . . 8
EXPANSION PLANS:
US: . . . . .All US
Canada - Yes, . . . Overseas - Yes

TEMPACO

1701 Alden Rd.
Orlando, FL 32803
TEL: (800) 868-7226 (407) 898-3456
FAX:
Mr. Charles Clark, President

Wholesale parts and controls for heating, air conditioning, refrigeration, steam and process hot water, controls systems.

HISTORY: . . . .
Established in 1946; . . 1st Franchised in 1972
Company-Owned Units (As of 12/1/1989): . .5
Franchised Units (12/1/1989): 14
Total Units (12/1/1989): 19
Distribution: US-19;Can-0;Overseas-0
  North America: . . . . 5 States
  Concentration: . . . 14 in FL, 2 in AL, 1 in NC
Registered: . . . . .FL
. . . .
Average # of Employees: . . . . .2 FT
Prior Industry Experience: . . . . . .Necessary

FINANCIAL:
Cash Investment: $20-75K
Total Investment: $20-75K
Fees: Franchise - $20-50K
  Royalty: 4%, Advert: 0%
Contract Periods (Yrs.): 5/5/5
Area Development Agreement: Yes/2-4
Sub-Franchise Contract: . . . . . .No
Expand in Territory: . . . . Yes
Passive Ownership: . . . Not Allowed
Encourage Conversions: . . . . . Yes
Franchisee Purchase(s) Required: .No

FRANCHISOR TRAINING/SUPPORT:
Financial Assistance Provided: . . . . .Yes
Site Selection Assistance: . . . . . . .Yes
Lease Negotiation Assistance: . . . . .Yes
Co-operative Advertising: . . . . . . .Yes
Training: . . . . 2 Wks. Headquarters
. . . .
On-Going Support: . . A,B,C,D,E,F,G,H,I
Full-Time Franchisor Support Staff: . . 44
EXPANSION PLANS:
US: . . . . Southeast
Canada - No, ...Overseas - No

UNITED CONSUMERS CLUB

8450 Broadway
Merrillville, IN 46410
TEL: (800) 827-6400 (219) 736-1100
FAX:
Mr. Scott Powell, Dir. Fran. Devel.

UNITED CONSUMERS CLUB provides its members with the ability to purchase from over 500 manufacturers at the wholesale price. Franchisees are in the business of selling and servicing these memberships.

HISTORY: . . . . IFA
Established in 1971; . . 1st Franchised in 1971
Company-Owned Units (As of 12/1/1989): . .4
Franchised Units (12/1/1989): 71
Total Units (12/1/1989): 75
Distribution: US-75;Can-0;Overseas-0
  North America: . . . . 23 States
  Concentration: . . . . 9 in OH, 8 in TX, 7 in IL
Registered: . . . CA,FL,IL,IN,MD,MI,NY,OR
. . . . RI,VA,WA
Average # of Employees: . . . . . 10 FT, 2 PT
Prior Industry Experience: . . . . Helpful

FINANCIAL:
Cash Investment: $60-75K
Total Investment: $100-115K
Fees: Franchise - $55K
  Royalty: 22%, Advert: 0%
Contract Periods (Yrs.): 12/12
Area Development Agreement: . .No
Sub-Franchise Contract: . . . . . .No
Expand in Territory: . . . . Yes
Passive Ownership: . . . Not Allowed
Encourage Conversions: . . . . . Yes
Franchisee Purchase(s) Required: .No

FRANCHISOR TRAINING/SUPPORT:
Financial Assistance Provided: . . .Yes(D)
Site Selection Assistance: . . . . . . .No
Lease Negotiation Assistance: . . . . .No
Co-operative Advertising: . . . . . . .NA
Training: . . . . 4 Wks. Headquarters
. . . .
On-Going Support: . . . . . A,B,C,D,G,H
Full-Time Franchisor Support Staff: . .100
EXPANSION PLANS:
US: . . . . .All US
Canada - No, ...Overseas - No

UNITED SNACK GROUP

2025 Centre Point Blvd., # 250
Mendota Heights, MN 55120
TEL: (800) 535-9977 (612) 683-0883
FAX:
Mr. Edwin Klein, President

UNITED SNACK GROUP offers you a unique and dynamic concept for sales of packaged snack foods to over 95% of the nation's businesses. $12 million in sales at 29 locations in 1989. All initial and expansion sales done for you. Tremendous cash flow - no vending!

HISTORY: . . . .
Established in 1984; . . 1st Franchised in 1988
Company-Owned Units (As of 12/1/1989): . . 1
Franchised Units (12/1/1989): 11
Total Units (12/1/1989): 12
Distribution: US-12;Can-0;Overseas-0
North America: . . . . 8 States
Concentration: . . . . 2 in CT, 2 in AZ
Registered: . . . . CA,FL,MI,MN,OR
. . . .
Average # of Employees: . . . . .6 FT
Prior Industry Experience: . . . . . . Helpful

FINANCIAL:
Cash Investment: $70-110K
Total Investment: $70-110K
Fees: Franchise - $20K
Royalty: 2-5%, Advert: 0%
Contract Periods (Yrs.): 10/5
Area Development Agreement: Yes/2
Sub-Franchise Contract: . . . . . .No
Expand in Territory: . . . . Yes
Passive Ownership: . . . . . .Allowed
Encourage Conversions: . . . . . Yes
Franchisee Purchase(s) Required: .No

FRANCHISOR TRAINING/SUPPORT:
Financial Assistance Provided: . . . . .No
Site Selection Assistance: . . . . .Yes
Lease Negotiation Assistance: . . . . .Yes
Co-operative Advertising: . . . . .NA
Training: . . . . 7 Days Headquarters,
. . . . 5 Days Franchisee Site
On-Going Support: . . . .B,C,D,E,F,G,H,I
Full-Time Franchisor Support Staff: . . 10
EXPANSION PLANS:
US: . . . . .All US
Canada - Yes, . . . Overseas - Yes

VALET PARK INTERNATIONAL

2052 Hwy. 35, # 104
Wall Township, NJ 07719
TEL: (800) 727-5123 (201) 974-0677
FAX:
Mr. Barry Auchenbach, VP Fran. Sales

International valet parking franchise network. Complete insurance package. Guaranteed accounts. Clients include hotels, hospitals, malls, country clubs, office complexes, condominiums, night clubs, restaurants, catering halls and private parties.

HISTORY: . . . .
Established in 1983; . . 1st Franchised in 1987
Company-Owned Units (As of 12/1/1989): . .0
Franchised Units (12/1/1989): 20
Total Units (12/1/1989): 20
Distribution: US-19;Can-1;Overseas-0
North America: . . . . . .4 States, 1 Province
Concentration: . . . . NJ, FL, CA
Registered: . . . . .CA,FL
. . . .
Average # of Employees: . . . . Varies
Prior Industry Experience: . . . . Helpful

FINANCIAL:
Cash Investment: $24-30K
Total Investment: $24-30K
Fees: Franchise - $19.5K
Royalty: 7%, Advert: . . . . . NA
Contract Periods (Yrs.): . . . 10/10
Area Development Agreement: Yes/10
Sub-Franchise Contract: . . . . . .No
Expand in Territory: . . . . Yes
Passive Ownership: . . . Discouraged
Encourage Conversions: . . . . NA
Franchisee Purchase(s) Required: .No

FRANCHISOR TRAINING/SUPPORT:
Financial Assistance Provided: . . . . .No
Site Selection Assistance: . . . . .NA
Lease Negotiation Assistance: . . . . .NA
Co-operative Advertising: . . . . .NA
Training: . . . . . . .10 Days Headquarters
. . . .
On-Going Support: . . . . . .A,B,C,D,G,I
Full-Time Franchisor Support Staff: . . .7
EXPANSION PLANS:
US: . . . . .All US
Canada - Yes, ...Overseas - Yes

SUPPLEMENTAL LISTING OF FRANCHISORS

ADVANTAGE REFRESHMENT SYSTEMS/ARS . . . 1925 Century Park E., # 940, Los Angeles CA 90067
AG-MART . . . . P. O. Box 370, Hwy. 377 S., Brownwood TX 76804
AGWAY . . . . .P. O. Box 4746, Syracuse NY 13221
ARMOR SHIELD . . . . .7685 Fields Ertel Rd., Cincinnati OH 45241
ASSOCIATED BROKERS & CONSULTANTS . . . . . . 663 D Park Meadow Rd., Westerville OH 43081
BIZOU INTERNATIONAL . . . . 1915 2nd Ave., Notre Dame des Pins PQ G0M1K0   CAN
CENTRE DU RASOIR FINE LAME . . . . 752 chemin du Golf, Ile Souers, Verdun PQ H3E1A8   CAN
COPS & CONVICTION SERVICE . . . . 1310 Dundas St. E., # 210, Mississauga ON L4Y2C1   CAN
CULLIGAN OF CANADA LTD. . . . . .2213 N. Sheridan Way, Mississauga ON L5K1A5   CAN
GROUP CANTREX . . . . 4445 Garand, Ville St-Laurent PQ H4R2H9   CAN
GROUPE JEAN COUTU . . . . .530, rue Beriault, Longueuil PQ J4G1S8   CAN
GROUPE LYRAS . . . . 8, rue Ste-Agathe, Ste-Agathe-des-Mont PQ J8C2J4   CAN
HALL OF NAMES CANADA . . . . 55 Savage Dr., Box 664, Cambridge ON N1R5W6   CAN

HOLLY THE PHONE IN SUPERMARKET	945 Middlefield Rd., # 14, Scarborough ON M1V5E1	CAN
IDENT-A-KID PROGRAM, THE	8430 Sixth St. N., St. Petersberg FL 33702	
INTERNATIONAL HOME SHOPPER	42 Worthington Access Dr., St. Louis MO 63043	
INTERNATIONAL LE COTONNIER CONCEPT	8501 boul. Ray Lawson, Ville d'Anjou PQ H1J1K6	CAN
IT'S THE THOUGHT	27 Applegate Cres., North York ON M2H2R5	CAN
JOE LOUE TOUT	28, rue Vanier, Chateauguay PQ J6J3W8	CAN
LEISURE INCOME	6380 Euclid Rd., Cincinnati OH 45236	
LIVING GREEN HYDROPONIC GROWING	321 S. Main St., # 555, Sebastopal CA 95472	
MCMAHON-ESSAIM	10301, rue Colbert, Ville d'Anjou PQ H1J2G5	CAN
MEAN GREEN	#108-1861 Welch St., N. Vancouver BC V7P1B7	CAN
MOWERS PLUS	P.O. Box 5293, Wilmington DE 19808	
MR. LOCKSMITHY CONVENIENCE CENTER	1828 Tribute Rd., # M, Sacramento CA 95815	
MULTIPLICANT	550 boul. des Gradins, Quebec City PQ G2J1A1	CAN
MUZAK	300 N. 34th St., Seattle WA 98103	
ON OCCASION	145 Curtis Cres., King City CAN L0G1K0	CAN
PARK-N-SELL	3535 State St., Santa Barbara CA 93105	
PERMASEAL	2124 Jody Rd., Florence SC 29501	
PINGOUIN	300, boul. Laurentien, # 100, St-Laurent PQ H4M2L4	CAN
PIPER STUDIO'S WEDDING CENTRE	431 Wilson Ave., Downsview ON M3H1T5	CAN
PISCINES TREVI	510, boul. Labelle, Laval PQ H7P2P4	CAN
PISCINES UNIES	54 rue Roy, Ormstown PQ J0S1K0	CAN
PROBE	4806 Shelly Dr., Wilmington NC 28405	
PROMAFIL CANADA	300, boul. Laurentien, # 100, St-Laurent PQ H4M2L4	CAN
RAINSOFT WATER CONDITIONING COMPANY	2080 Lunt Ave., Elk Grove Village IL 60007	
RECEPTIONS PLUS	1970 Jerome Ave., Bronx NY 10453	
RESEAU C.L.I.C.	20, rue Bryant, Sherbrooke PQ J1J3E4	CAN
SCIENCE SHOP, THE	140-B Archer St., San Jose CA 95112	
SOLUTIONS	2739 Pasadena Blvd., Pasadena TX 77502	
SONMARK	130 Quigley Blvd., New Castle DE 19720	
STELLARVISION	5812 E. Burnside, Portland OR 97215	
STREAKERS TELECONVENIENCE STORE	115 Collier St., Barrie ON L4M1H2	CAN
UNITED WORTH HYDROCHEM CORPORATION	P.O. Box 366, Fort Worth TX 76101	
VACUUM FRANCHISE, THE	40 Wynford Dr., # 315, Don Mills ON M3C1J5	CAN
WALLPAPER WAGON SYSTEMS	482 Elizabeth St., Burlington ON L7R2G7	CAN
WATERCARE CORPORATION	1520 N. 24th St., Manitowoc WI 54221	
WATERMARK CORP.	1505 Bridgeway Blvd., Sausalito CA 94965	
WEDDING BELL BRIDAL BOUTIQUES	27 W. Judson Ave., Youngstown OH 44507	
WORLD LASER CORP.	9600 Cameron St., # 240, Burnaby BC V3J7N3	CAN
YELLOW PHONE	870 Market St., # 428, San Francisco CA 94102	

SOURCE BOOK OF FRANCHISE OPPORTUNITIES
1990 FRANCHISOR QUESTIONNAIRE

1. Name of Franchise:

_____

              Are you a ☐ Franchisor   ☐ Distributor   ☐ Consultant

2. Parent Company Name (if different): _____

3. Address:_____City_____
   State/Prov._____ Zip_____(To ensure accuracy, please include a business card/letterhead)

4. Telephone: (800) _____or (   ) _____ Collect? ☐ Yes ☐ No
         Fax Number: (   ) _____

5. Contact: _____Position:_____

6. From Sample Page, note the <u>single category</u> # that best describes your firm's products/services: _____

7. Description of Business: (Use this space to set yourself apart from other franchising opportunities, i.e. sell the potential franchisee. Text of 45 words or less will be printed verbatim. Text over 45 words may be edited).

_____

_____

_____

_____

_____

8. Are you a member of IFA?   ☐ Yes ☐ No; If Yes, since 19____ : ☐ Assoc. Member ☐ Full Member
   Are you a member of CFA?   ☐ Yes ☐ No; If Yes, since 19____ : ☐ Assoc. Member ☐ Regular Member

9. Company founded in 19_____ .

10. First year as franchisor was 19_____ .

                                  Actual

11. Number of Company-Owned Units   _____

12. Number of Franchised Units   _____
         Total Units   _____

13. Of above Total Units,   _____ were in the U.S.
                           _____ were in Canada.
                           _____ were Overseas.

14. Combining both Company-Owned and Franchised Units, A) in how many States/Provinces did you have operating units and B) what 3 States/Provinces had the largest number of operating units)

A) Have Operating Units in	B) Top 3 States/Provinces	# Units in Each
_____ States	1. _____	_____
_____ Provinces	2. _____	_____
	3. _____	_____

15. The following States/Province require a separate registration (or disclosure*) document. In which are you currently registered to franchise?

☐ All Below or   ☐ IN   ☐ ND   ☐ WA
☐ CA   ☐ MD   ☐ OR*   ☐ WI
☐ FL*   ☐ MI   ☐ RI   ☐ Alberta
☐ HI   ☐ MN   ☐ SD
☐ IL   ☐ NY   ☐ VA

16. How many <u>full-time, paid personnel</u> are currently on your staff? _____

17. Is prior industry experience by the franchisee ☐ Necessary ☐ Unnecessary, But Helpful

18. Even though the cash investment may vary substantially by individual unit, what is the <u>range of cash investment</u> required? $_____

19. What is the <u>range of total investment</u> required? $_____

20. How much is the initial franchise fee? Please indicate all front-end fees paid to the franchisor that would generally be considered a franchise fee. (Give range if necessary). $_____

21. How much is the on-going royalty fee?   _____%

22. How much is the on-going advertising fee?   _____%

23. What is the term of the original franchise agreement?   _____ Years

24. What is the term of the renewal period?   _____ Years

25. Do you have Area Development Agreements? ☐ Yes ☐ No
     If Yes, what is the period of agreement?   _____ Years

26. Do you have Sub-Franchisor Contracts covering specified territories? ☐ Yes ☐ No

27. Can the franchisee establish additional outlets within his area? ☐ Yes ☐ No

28. Is passive ownership of the initial unit ☐ Allowed ☐ Allowed, But Discouraged ☐ Not Allowed

29. Do you encourage conversions? ☐ Yes ☐ No ☐ N.A

30. If stock of Parent is publicly traded, please list the Stock Exchange _____ and Stock Symbol _____.

31. Is financial assistance available? ☐ Yes ☐ No ☐ N.A.
     If Yes, is assistance ☐ Direct or ☐ Indirect

32. Do you assist the franchisee in site selection?   ☐ Yes ☐ No ☐ N.A.

33. Do you assist in lease negotiations?   ☐ Yes ☐ No ☐ N.A.

34. Do you participate in co-operative advertising?   ☐ Yes ☐ No ☐ N.A.

35. What is the location and duration of initial training sessions included in the franchise fee?

	Location	Duration
A.	_____	_____
B.	_____	_____
C.	_____	_____

36. Which of the following on-going services do you provide to the franchisee?

Service	Included in Fees	At Additional Cost	N.A.
Central Data Processing	A. ☐	a. ☐	☐
Central Purchasing	B. ☐	b. ☐	☐
Field Operations Evaluation	C. ☐	c. ☐	☐
Field Training	D. ☐	d. ☐	☐
Initial Store Opening	E. ☐	e. ☐	☐
Inventory Control	F. ☐	f. ☐	☐
Newsletter	G. ☐	g. ☐	☐
Regional Or National Meetings	H. ☐	h. ☐	☐
Telephone Hotline	I. ☐	i. ☐	☐

37. Including the owner/operator, how many employees are recommended to properly staff the _average_ franchised unit?_____ Full-Time _____ Part-Time

38. Do you have "Proprietary Products?"   ☐ Yes ☐ No
    If Yes, must the franchisee buy directly from you?   ☐ Yes ☐ No

39. In which specific regions of the U.S. are you actively seeking new franchisees? For example: All U.S. or NW & SW or NJ Only._____

40. Are you actively seeking franchisees in Canada?   ☐ Yes ☐ No

41. Are you actively seeking franchisees Overseas?   ☐ Yes ☐ No

_____

Name of Respondent _____ Telephone No: ( ) _____

Thanks very much for taking the time and trouble to answer the questionnaire. Hopefully the information will result in numerous leads and many happy franchisees.

While we rarely give recommendations, we do, however, suggest that potential franchisees contact specific franchisors with whom we are familiar. So that we might be better informed about your operation, please send your most recent promotional package. We will keep the information on file.

RENT OUR CUSTOM FRANCHISOR MAILING LIST

- **GUARANTEED ACCURACY - $.50 REBATE FOR ANY INCORRECT ADDRESS**

- CONTINUOUSLY UPDATED FOR ADDRESS CHANGES / NEW ADDITIONS

- SORTED BY ZIP / POSTAL CODE / BUSINESS CATEGORY / MARKET AREAS

- ALSO **CUSTOM SORTING** AND CUSTOM LABELS

- **QUICK TURN-AROUND TIME**

	U.S. ONLY	CANADIAN ONLY	COMBINED LISTING
APPROXIMATE LISTINGS:	~1,800	~750	~2,550

STANDARD PRICING SCHEDULE:

Standard Size:	$135	$60	$175
3 7/8" x 2 7/8" with Return Address:	$185	$100	$240

Director of Franchising
World Class Athlete
1814 Franklin Street, # 700
Oakland, CA 94612

Director of Franchising
Cottman Transmission Services
240 New York Drive, # 2014
Fort Washington, NY 19034

Standard Pressure Sensitive Label

OR

RETURN TO:
Your Company Name
Return Address
Your City, State, Zip

President
World Class Athlete
1814 Franklin Street # 700
Oakland, CA 94612

Larger 3 7/8" by 2 7/8" Presddure Sensitive Label

FOR INFORMATION, PLEASE CONTACT: **SOURCE BOOK**
P.O. BOX 12488
OAKLAND, CA 94604
415/547-3245

ALPHABETICAL LISTING
OF FRANCHISORS

C

D

E

I

J

K

L

M

O

P

Q

R

T

Y

Z